SCIENTIFIC INVESTIGATION
OF COPIES, FAKES AND FORGERIES

T0399669

SCIENTIFIC INVESTIGATION
OF COPIES, FAKES AND FORGERIES

Paul Craddock

Routledge
Taylor & Francis Group

LONDON AND NEW YORK

First published 2009 by Butterworth-Heinemann

2 Park Square, Milton Park, Abingdon, Oxfordshire OX14 4RN
52 Vanderbilt Avenue, New York, NY 10017

Routledge is an imprint of Taylor & Francis Group, an informa business

First issued in paperback 2020

British Library Cataloguing in Publication Data
Scientific investigation of copies, fakes and forgeries 1. Art – Forgeries 2. Forgery of antiquities
   3. Criminal investigation 4. Forensic sciences
   I. Craddock, P.T. (Paul T.)
   702.8′74

Library of Congress Cataloguing in Publication Data
Library of Congress Control Number: 2008934414

ISBN 13: 978-0-7506-4205-7 (hbk)
ISBN 13: 978-0-367-60627-5 (pbk)

Contents

Foreword

The craving for authenticity is widespread.

Lowenthal (1999)

Introduction

This book is intended as a comprehensive guide to the technical and scientific study of the authenticity of a wide range of antiquities and artistic creations. Most works on authenticity approach the subject from a stylistic and art historical perspective. This work seeks to bridge the perceived gap between the art historian and scientist to create a more co-ordinated approach.

The research for this volume has been carried out by the author over many years in libraries, laboratories, museums and galleries and has benefited from a lifetime's experience of antique shops, auction rooms and street markets, as well as the many authenticity studies carried out whilst a member of the erstwhile British Museum Research Laboratory.

This book is intended primarily for those who need to understand the available approaches to and methods of scientific and technical authentication. This includes both those wishing to instigate such a study and those called upon to carry it out. In the first category come collectors and curators who will not normally be expected to have a scientific background, and whose training will not usually have included authenticity studies.

In the author's experience, most curatorial departments in museums do not even possess a decent binocular microscope, much less an ultra-violet lamp. Thus, an attempt has been made to lead the non-specialist into these topics by giving a brief description of the principles of the various methods of investigation, backed up by a comprehensive bibliography. The expectation is not that the curators/collectors will carry out these investigations for themselves, but rather that they will understand more of the large and steadily growing array of available approaches, together with their potentials and pitfalls. With this knowledge, illustrated where possible by case histories, they will hopefully be better placed to put together, with the scientist, a programme of investigation and be better able independently to interpret the results.

There are relatively few laboratories in the world specialising in authentication work, and perforce many investigations will be carried out by scientists not routinely familiar with the examination of antiquities. This book attempts to bring together some of the problems in their study, not least the extraordinary things that can happen to an object during its existence first as an artefact, then as buried archaeology and, finally, as an antiquity. Over the centuries materials will often have undergone physical and chemical changes that lie well outside those described in the standard scientific literature.

Museum-based scientists and conservators will already have experience in both art historical and scientific approaches, and, for them, this book will hopefully extend their knowledge of the range of faking and forgery and the methods now employed to investigate them. The final chapter is of special relevance to conservators dealing with the contentious issue of restoration.

Acknowledgements

This work necessarily has a very wide remit, including ancient technology, material science, conservation science and archaeometry over an enormous range of materials through almost every culture the world has known, or, at least, those thought worth faking. This has been a huge undertaking and could only have been contemplated from within an organisation such as the Department of Conservation and Scientific Research in the British Museum.

The author has been greatly assisted by detailed discussions with Janet Ambers, Spike Bucklow, Caroline Cartwright, Mike Cowell, Vincent Daniels, Ian Freestone, Marc Ghysels, Duncan Hook, Louise Joyner, Susan La Niece, Nigel Meeks, Andrew Middleton, Thilo Rehren, Rebecca Stacey and Mike Wayman. These colleagues have read chapters for the author, and Professor Wayman, of the University of Alberta in Edmonton, additionally undertook the onerous but very necessary task of reading the whole volume. These indispensible contributions from colleagues revealed much to the author, not least a fuller appreciation of the true nature of individual methods, materials and case histories. Despite this, many errors of approach and omissions must still be present; these are the fault of the author's understanding, rather than that of those trying to advise him in fields in which he was previously unfamiliar.

Key to acronyms

AAS	Atomic Absorption Spectrometry
AMS RC	Accelerator Mass Spectrometry Radio Carbon
CL	Cathodoluminescence
CR	Cation Ratio
CT	Computed Tomography
EDX (or EDAX)	Energy-Dispersive X-ray Analysis
EPMA	Electron Microprobe Analysis
EMR	Electron Emission Radiography
ES	Emission Spectrography
ESR	Electron Spin Resonance. Also known as Electron Paramagnetic Resonance (EPR)
FTIR	Fourier-Transform Infra-Red
FTRM	Fourier-Transform Raman Microscopy
FTRS	Fourier–Transform Raman Spectroscopy
GC MS	Gas Chromatography Mass Spectrometry
GLC MS	Gas–Liquid Chromatography Mass Spectrometry
HPLC	High-Performance Liquid Chromatography
ICP AES	Inductively Coupled Plasma Atomic Emission Spectroscopy
ICP MS	Inductively Coupled Plasma Mass Spectrometry
IRS	Infra-Red Spectrometry
LA ICP MS	Laser-ablated Inductively Coupled Plasma Mass Spectrometry
MagS	Magnetic Susceptibility
MS	Mass Spectrometry
NAA	Neutron Activation Analysis
NMR	Nuclear Magnetic Resonance
PIGE	Particle (or Proton)-Induced Gamma-ray Emission
PIXE	Particle (or Proton)-Induced X-ray Emission
Pyr GC	Pyrolysis Gas Chromatography
RBS	Rutherford BackScatter
RC	Radio Carbon
RI	Refractive index
RM	Raman Microscopy
RS	Raman Spectroscopy
SEM	Scanning Electron Microscopy
SERS	Surface-Enhanced Raman Scattering
SERRS	Surface-Enhanced Resonance Raman Scattering
SIA	Stable Isotope Analysis
TEM	Transmission Electron Microscopy
TIMS	Thermal Ionisation Mass Spectrometry
TL	Thermoluminescence

XRD	X-ray Diffraction
XRF	X-ray Fluorescence
UV	Ultraviolet
VRT	Volume Rendering Technique
WD XRF	Wavelength-Dispersive X-ray Fluorescence

1

Introduction: Sources, motives, approaches and disclosures

. . .falsifications that mislead the public, corrupt aesthetic standards, distort history and waste money.

Pope (1939)

A (very) brief history of faking and forgery

The deceptive simulation of fanything of value goes back into antiquity, and ancient accounts abound with descriptions of adulterated gold (Ramage and Craddock, 2000, pp. 27–53) and imitation gemstones (Taniguchi *et al.*, 2002); moreover, the earliest known coin hoard contains counterfeits. Once antiques began to be appreciated they were copied, although the Roman copies of Greek originals do not seem to have been made with deceptive intent. Chinese Song period imitations of Han and earlier bronzes, made a thousand years ago, are more equivocal. They often do not seem to us to be deliberate forgeries, but they do have fake patinas and there are contemporary writings warning of the prevalence of forgeries and how to make them, the first on record (see Chapter 14, p. 356; Figure 14.7). From Late Antiquity in the West, the cult of relics flourished and, with that, the production of fakes and forgeries, exemplified by what is now perhaps the most famous of them all, the Shroud of Turin (see Chapter 5, p. 102). These began to be scientifically investigated by the Vatican in the late nineteenth century, probably the earliest dedicated authentication unit anywhere. Another prolific area of Medieval forgery was that of documents, particularly of supposedly old land grant charters, which could be used in cases of disputed ownership.

The interest in antiquities of all types that characterised the Renaissance led to the establishment of more formal collections and ultimately to the establishment of museums. The faking and forging of antiquities began at much the same time and has flourished ever since. Most of the early productions are not very convincing either stylistically or technically; this was due to a general lack of detailed stylistic information and an almost total ignorance

of the appropriate materials and technology. The former began to be seriously addressed by art historians, notably Frederick Winckelmann, in the eighteenth century, and informed both collectors and forgers. This problem of information dissemination or restriction generated a debate that continues to this day (see p. 17).

In the nineteenth century there developed an interest in collecting archaeological, palaeontological, geological and ethnographic material, closely followed by their forgery (see Chapter 17, p. 429 and Chapter 19). For example, forgeries of pre-Hispanic antiquities were already being made in Mexico in the 1820s for sale to tourists and collectors and were major trade items in some localities by the late nineteenth century (Holmes *et al.*, 1886).

In Europe, interest in antique styles spread to the middle classes and brought about growth in the production of often quite passable copies of a wide range of decorative arts of all periods on an industrial scale. This process was very much aided by new replication techniques such as electroforming (see Chapter 4, p. 78) and color printing (see Chapter 13, p. 332). The combination of increasing art historical knowledge of past styles, coupled with often superb craftsmanship, enabled convincing fakes and forgeries of ceramics, glass, metalwork and jewellery, etc. to be produced. Fortunately, a combination of the Victorian attitude of knowing better than their predecessors, and a lack of technical knowledge of the past, means that there are often glaring anachronisms of materials and technique, which has, more recently, enabled some of their fakes and forgeries to be unmasked after scientific examination.

Through the twentieth century the availability of traditional craft skills may have declined, in Europe at least, but the ever-increasing prices realised by antiquities and *objet d'art* of all kinds have ensured

1

that fraudulent production continues. Furthermore, craft skills at low cost are still widely available outside Europe, and there is a growing influx of passable copies of just about every class of antique and collectable item from fake-patinated Shang jade to Clarice Cliff pots, coming from the Far East. These 'shamtiques', available in every market, high street and shopping mall, are instantly recognisable for what they are and not usually sold as the genuine item even though they often have some rudimentary ageing and patination treatments. However, many of the traditional techniques used, from cloisonné enamelling to lost wax casting are fundamentally correct, and with a little more application convincing forgeries could, and probably are, being made in quantity in the same workshops.

At the same time new techniques of copying, exemplified by the ink-jet printer, and new materials, exemplified by epoxy resins, have made it much easier to produce copies that are visually convincing.

The combination of the above factors and the markets created by the ever-expanding middle classes across the world with too much ready cash and too little discrimination has resulted in a wider range and greater extent of fraudulent copying than ever before.

Fortunately, there has been a continuing improvement in the scientific methods of materials examination which has helped to counter this. There is also now a greatly expanded knowledge of the materials and technologies used in the past together with a more fundamental understanding of the physical and chemical processes of natural ageing and corrosion.

This book, being aimed at both the curator/collector and the scientist, encounters the broader problem of the relationship between the arts and the sciences in the study of antiquities and works of art. So often the art historian/curator does not appreciate the capabilities or understand the limitations of modern scientific investigation, and equally the scientist often seems not to understand the real nature of the questions asked, or sufficiently appreciate the problems and opportunities presented by the materials.

Arts *versus* science?

The impression is sometimes given of the hapless and subjective art historian being brushed aside by the objective scientist who carries out a series of tests that rapidly and conclusively demonstrate the true age of the suspect piece, and everything else

about it. Statements such as 'The scientist with cold, calculated clinical methods today can expose the forgery which will appear in any field . . .' (Mills, 1972, p. 60), are fairly typical. Von Bothmer (1964), writing of the application of ultraviolet (UV) examination to rehabilitate an antiquity, noted with satisfaction that 'The introduction of technical considerations somewhat spoils the sport of attacking works of art since intuition and stylistic appreciation now have to be coordinated with laborious scientific investigation'. Indictor (1998), discussing the examination of the Buyid silks (see Chapter 18, p. 462), made the contentious claim that 'objective dating [AMS dating in this instance] should routinely precede stylistic or other technical studies in order to avoid the embarrassment of misattribution' (but see Spier, 1990 for a counterview).

In reality, the two approaches are very similar and must work together. The elements of the information they contain are complementary, information from one discipline often being essential to the study of the other, and the scientific data should be seen as extending the range of existing information, certainly not replacing it. The supposed Roman lamp in the form of a gladiator's helmet is a high-profile example of a case where, apparently science conclusively overturned the previous art historical opinion. The helmet had graced the cover of the British Museum's popular guide to Classical pottery lamps (Figure 1.1) (Bailey, 1972) before being shown to be a forgery by TL (Bailey, 1988, p. 433, Q3401). The reality was that Don Bailey, the curator responsible for the Museum's collection of Classical lamps, had become worried about the authenticity of the lamp during the compilation of his magisterial catalogue of the collection, and requested that it be tested to confirm his suspicions.

Many of the authors of books on fakes and forgeries seem to take the view that scientific tests are fundamentally different in approach from those of the art historian and are somehow more reliable. In fact, the art historical/stylistic criteria are based on ordinary physical properties of color, texture, weight, dimensions, etc. that the art historian is mentally quantifying and comparing to a canon of genuine pieces. This is exactly the process carried out by the scientist, except that the information is often obtained using a piece of apparatus that produces the data as a number.

Part of the problem is that these numerical results are perceived by the non-scientist as being somehow sacrosanct and unchallengeable. The non-specialist usually lacks the knowledge to assess how

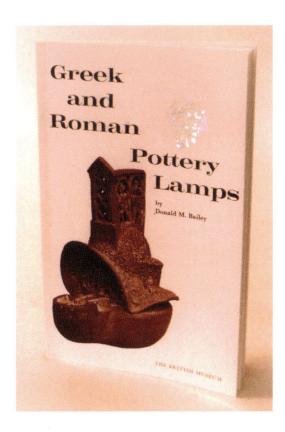

Figure 1.1 A fall from grace: The cover of the British Museum's popular guide to Greek and Roman Pottery Lamps featuring a Roman lamp in the form of a gladiator's helmet, subsequently exposed as a modern forgery by TL testing. (Courtesy J. Heffron/British Museum)

meaningful the figures are, and also, very often, the qualifying data on accuracy, precision and detection limits (see Chapter 3, p. 41) which is necessary for this to be done is not provided. Even so it is not the numerical value itself of whatever parameter which condemns or authenticates the suspect piece, but rather the value judgement put upon it, based upon comparison with other pieces, which is exactly the same approach as that adopted by the art historian.

An example is given by Drake's Plate of brass (see Chapter 7, p. 150). This was supposedly left by the great voyager near present-day San Francisco, and is condemned partly because of the very high zinc content of 34.2%, which is above the 33.3% maximum believed to be the limit attainable in the sixteenth century. However, it would be very incautious to condemn the piece on that 0.9% of zinc alone. What is the reliability (the *accuracy*) of the figure, and the significance of the 0.9% (the *precision*)? Also, how certain is the upper limit of 33.3%? Certainly the zinc content is unusually high for the sixteenth century, but is it impossible to have been achieved? This is where value judgements based on a more general experience must be made, very much as an art historian would do.

Even some of the most famous and extensively investigated authenticity cases are not fully resolved, or at least not universally accepted. Forgeries, such as the infamous ceramics from Glozel, which archaeologists, notably O.G.S. Crawford and Glyn Daniels in Britain and A. Vayson de Pradenne in France, could not resist repeatedly and almost gleefully attacking, were latterly shown to be almost certainly ancient after all (see Chapter 6, p. 119). Some, such as the Vinland Map, are still tenaciously defended (see Chapter 13, p. 340), while others produce scientific data that is presently irresolvable and thus remain undecided, such as the real age of King Arthur's Round Table at Winchester Castle (see Chapter 6, p. 133). If nothing else, these cases help to dispel belief in the inflexible objective certainty of conclusions based on scientific examination and perhaps may encourage a more thoughtful and informed use of the data generated by the scientists and the conclusions drawn from them.

Attempts have already been made to bridge the supposed gap between the two approaches by trying to make the art historical data more quantifiable and thus capable of undergoing the same statistical treatments as the scientific data. An early attempt, known as pictology, was devised by M.M. van Dantzig (1953a) for the study of pictures. His system listed several hundred characteristics of a particular artist, use of color, sense of perspective, brush technique, etc. In the examination of a suspect painting each of these features would be given a plus or a minus depending on whether the particular feature on the picture was typical of the artist. The picture could be then be rated numerically by the percentage of pluses it received. This was clearly a very crude system with little means of weighing the importance of individual characteristics, or how close the characteristic features were reproduced on the picture. Modern digital image analysis now offers a much more sophisticated approach to this problem (see Chapter 12, p. 272). It can allow the 'objective' quantification of traditional 'subjective' features such as an artist's brush technique (Berezhnoy *et al.*, 2005), although the latter's compartmentalisation of the scientist's 'objectivity' and the connoisseur's 'subjectivity' seems too simplistic.

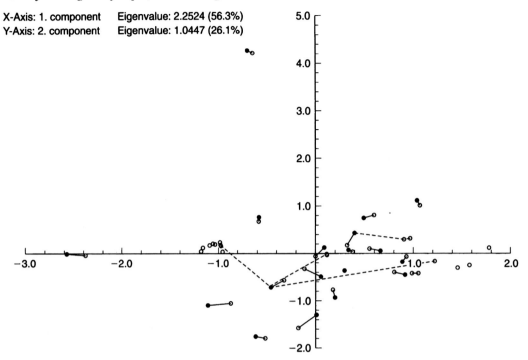

X-Axis: 1. component   Eigenvalue: 2.2524 (56.3%)
Y-Axis: 2. component   Eigenvalue: 1.0447 (26.1%)

Figure 1.2   Principal components plot of a group of 27 Roman fibulae of dubious authenticity. The solid lines measure the similarity between original (black dots) and copy (open circles). The dotted lines measure links between different copies. (Courtesy Teegen, 2002)

Principal components analysis offers a more rigorous statistical method of assessing a variety of parameters. Teegen (2002) adopted the method to distinguish between genuine and reproduction Roman fibulae (Figure 1.2; Table 1.1). In 1863 a hoard of about 300 fibulae was found at Pyrmont in Germany. Almost from their discovery good copies were made for sale to visitors but soon became confused with the originals, such that the 1869 publication on the fibulae almost certainly included copies. Further copies were made at least until the early twentieth century, and, being unmarked, have proven difficult to differentiate from the originals. Teegen used measurable parameters such as the dimensions, weight, composition, degree of corrosion, wear patterns, evidence of manufacture, repairs and documentary evidence.

Although this represents a considerable advance in quantifying disparate information there remained the problem of weighing particular parameters. For example, the composition was found not to be particularly helpful in most instances, both originals and copies being of brass, but in a small number of cases the zinc content was so high as to in itself rule out the possibility of the fibulae being Roman (see Chapter 7, p. 147).

Table 1.1   Degree of certainty of the authenticity of the 27 selected dubious fibulae. This ranges from: O, which is almost certainly original; O > R where the probability of being original is significantly greater than reproduction; O ≥ R where the probability of originality is greater than or equal to that of reproduction; O = R and R = O where the probabilities are the same; R ≥ O where the probability of reproduction is greater than or equal to originality; R > O where the probability of reproduction is significantly greater than originality; and R, almost certainly a reproduction. On this basis 8 (O + O > R + O ≥ R) were judged original, 14 were judged replicas (R + R > O + R ≥ O) and 5 remained uncertain (O = R + R = O).

O	O > R	O ≥ R	O = R	R = O	R ≥ O	R > O	R
3	5	–	1	4	1	4	9

Source: Teegen, 2002

The integration of purely numerical data with other factors in statistical treatments is the subject of Bayesian statistics. This is a very well established technique, and its application to archaeological data and radiocarbon (RC) dating is now becoming routine (Litton and Buck 1995; Buck *et al.*, 1996; and see Chapter 5, p. 93 for an example of its application). The system specifically allows prior knowledge and experience, the very stuff of the art historical and stylistic approach, to be built into the statistical equations.

Range of enquiry

It is clearly imperative that the scientist carrying out the investigation fully understands the problems involved. The questions posed in authentication studies are rarely as simple as 'Is it genuine?'. More usually one is trying to establish the history of the artefact: why, how and of what it was originally made and what has happened to it thereafter. This can include establishing what alterations, if any, have been made (Figure 1.3) together with restoration and conservation treatments. Questions such as provenance, the likelihood that the object could have come from where it was claimed to have been discovered, etc. can also be addressed. It is obviously imperative that the art historical problems concerning the piece are carefully formulated at the outset in close conjunction with the curator. The various scientific techniques now available

are impressive; they are 'big guns' but they must be carefully targeted.

A good example is provided by a Medieval European bronze *aquamanile* (a vessel for sprinkling water onto the hands of guests at a feast) in the form of a unicorn that was once offered to the British Museum. If it had come straight to the laboratory with no information, just the question 'Is it genuine?', we would naturally have directed our attention to inconspicuous areas such as the underside of the hooves where such sampling and surface preparation as was necessary could have been done with the minimum of visible damage. This would have shown the composition to be appropriate for the Medieval period, and such patina as it possessed to be natural and thus likely to have been of some age. On that basis alone we could have pronounced the piece genuine, although hopefully we would have carried out a more general examination of the whole piece. In fact the value of the piece arose because it was apparently a rare depiction of a unicorn – horses are much more common – and this was naturally reflected in the asking price. Thus the interest centred on the creature's horn, to which we were directed. X-ray fluorescence (XRF) analysis of the surface showed that it had a different composition from the rest of the beast, and radiography

Figure 1.3 From Chalice to Coffee Pot. The inverted silver coffee pot on the right would purport to have been made in London in 1571, almost a century before coffee drinking was introduced into England. The explanation is that the body of the pot, which carries the hallmarks, is from an Elizabethan chalice (left) to which an unmarked spout and lid have been added. This probably represents an unusual and risible adaptation with no intention to deceive (although as the lid and spout have not been submitted to assay, the piece is technically illegal). (Courtesy Goldsmiths' Company)

revealed that it was an addition. X-ray diffraction (XRD) analysis of the corrosion around the join showed it was a modern make-up placed there to hide the junction. Approximately 90% of the value of the piece lay in about 1% of its mass.

Close collaboration between the curator and the scientist through the investigation can sometimes lead to conclusions markedly different from the original art historical or scientific indications.

A recent authenticity examination of an unusual Etruscan statuette is a case in point. The style was very unconvincing, and the alloy was found to contain several per cent of zinc, which is almost never found in Etruscan copper alloys (see Chapter 7, p. 147), and thus apparently style and science combined to condemn the piece. However, the patina was naturally formed and of considerable age. The consensus now is that the piece is likely to be a rare but not unparalleled example of a Roman piece made in an Etruscan style.

Authenticity studies as an academic discipline

The problems that fakes and forgeries bring to collecting and curatorship are well understood but the subject of authenticity does not seem to be seriously studied or taught to prospective art historians/curators, much less to materials scientists or even to archaeometrists (an honourable exception being the centre for the study of forgery, with its own museum at the University of Salerno).

This deficiency becomes even more glaring when looking at the comparable subject of forensic science in which there are apparently 488 higher education courses in Britain alone (reported in New Scientist, 16 June 2007, p. 60), including first degrees in the subject and with a dedicated periodical *The Journal of Forensic Science*. Although there is no journal dedicated to authentication studies it is noticeable that the scientific literature generally does contain an appreciable and growing number of authenticity reports. In the author's experience of researching this book between about 5 and 10% of the papers on archaeometry are concerned with authenticity.

Legal aspects

Sources: Easby and Colin (1968); Karlen (1986); Merryman and Elsen (1987); Malaro (1998, pp. 393–405); Spencer (2004).

There is currently no professional regulatory body to set standards of practice and to offer individual practitioners advice or legal protection, such as exists for valuers and assessors, for example the Appraisers Association of America (Okil, 2004) although independent bodies such as IFAR (International Foundation for Art Research) in the US do go some way to providing this service (see the IFAR Journal). This is an area of potential concern for any individual or organisation contemplating offering a commercial authentication service. Authentication work can generate considerable contention resulting in lawsuits that could prove ruinously expensive for the unwary scientist in time, money and reputation.

Prudence is essential in answering queries, and judicious and carefully worded reports are an absolute necessity. These should never come to conclusions over and above that which can be proved, even if it means that the all-important questions concerning authenticity are left without a categorical answer. Reports should be both circumspect and clearly stated to be confidential. These considerations are especially true now that freedom of information acts are in place in many countries, allowing the public general access to all information held by institutions, and this could include authenticity reports held by museums.

A good safeguard is to have a prepared release form for the prospective client to sign before any work commences, specifically that no legal redress will be sought, even if the findings are subsequently found to be in error. However, this will not in itself automatically protect the investigator from all claims (Malaro, 1998, pp. 393–405). Those undertaking commercial authentication should consider taking out insurance to cover the contingency of having to defend reports and statements.

Some disputes can turn decidedly nasty, resulting in litigation that could see the investigator with the unenviable prospect of trying to explain scientific techniques and results to a court of law. This again could prove ruinously expensive and time-consuming, no matter who actually won. The potential danger areas can be dealt with under three categories (and are given here in American terminology).

1. **Misrepresentation** That is, stating that an artefact is or is not authentic and then having that opinion disputed. This could arise if it was claimed either that a forgery was not detected, or alternatively that a genuine piece had been wrongly condemned. In either case this could

result in serious financial loss to the owner, who might well seek redress.

2. **Disparagement** That is, divulging the results of the investigation of an artefact to a third party without the owner's permission. Freedom of information legislation could have serious repercussions on confidentiality where work has been carried out for, or even communicated to, a public institution. If a piece is publicly condemned by the investigator or a third party made privy to the results, the owner can reasonably claim that the value of the piece has been diminished thereby. Here the clearly stated confidentiality of the report is all-important, but the investigator must make every reasonable effort to ensure that only the owner who commissioned the investigation receives the results. If the investigation is carried out for a third party such as a potential purchaser or for a dealer or auction house charged with selling the artefact, the investigator should make sure that the owner is aware of this and has given permission for the work to go ahead and it be made clear beforehand who is to be made privy to the results of the investigation.

3. **Defamation** This is a difficult area arising where it is stated or implied that the judgement or probity of another person or organisation is called into question. This could be another investigator, art expert, dealer or the auction house concerned. A more direct case could arise where the authenticator has been asked to comment or report on the validity, etc. of an existing report of another expert. If the comments were unfavourable and became public, under freedom of information legislation for example, there certainly could be a case for defamation.

Literature

There is an enormous literature on all aspects of fakes and forgery (Reisner, 1950; Koobatian, 1997), but much of it is popular and anecdotal, containing little serious information and even less instruction. Even the more serious works which have some information on the methods of the forger/faker, contain little on the methods of detection. Almost all are written from an art historical perspective and the judgements of whether genuine or spurious are usually based on unquantified stylistic considerations. One can sometimes sense an author's frustration at not being able to put over the

criteria. George Ortiz (1990) in his condemnation of a number of antiquities on aesthetic grounds attempted to quantify his reasons: 'It is a personal reaction . . . it is like falling in love, I cannot give you a formula for falling in love'. Mills (1972, p. 55) wrote of 'the look of true old silver having some strange indefinable quality that cannot be aptly described other than to state it is something that one grows to understand and recognise'. Some, such as Eisenberg (1992) have attempted to set out the mental analytical methods by which the determination of stylistic authenticity can be attempted generally, and others such as von Bothmer (1998) have attempted the same for specific groups of antiquities. As Pope (1939) stated when making his plea for more objective or 'scientific' art criticism, 'The essence [of] scientific method is the formulation of all of its processes in universal terms such as can be communicated to others and by them independently tested. Evidence that is incommunicable lacks scientific character and can have no claim to acceptance'. Of course prolonged study of the genuine article is imperative to curation, but unfortunately this is difficult to impart in a book, no matter how well illustrated. Tietze (1948) used large-scale photogravure plates of genuine works and forgeries to enable stylistic comparisons to be made, but with only limited success; Rawlins' *From the National Gallery Laboratory* (1940) was much more successful comparing pictures viewed by light with images created by IR and X-rays.

Rather surprisingly some of the more popular books can offer quite practical advice, especially those written (not surprisingly) by dealers. Among those that the author found especially useful were *Is it Genuine?* edited by John Bly (1986, 2002) and *The Antiques Roadshow How to Spot a Fake* edited by Lars Tharp (1999), both backed up by excellent illustrations. *Art Detective* by Madeleine Marsh (1993) gives a practical guide to how the amateur collector should set about authenticity studies, with good sections on the relevant societies, literature and accessible comparative collections, (although scientific examination is conspicuous by its absence). Alice Beckett's *Fakes: Forgery and the Art World* (1995) gives an interesting account of the often equivocal attitude to authenticity by those who evaluate, buy and sell art.

There are also a few works manuals of forgery and faking, notably Eric Hebborn's *The Art Forger's Handbook* (see Chapter 12, p. 302 and p. 19) for fine art and Charles M. Larson's *Numismatic Forgery* for coins (see Chapter 8, p. 182 and p. 19).

Among the works on authentication are the following:

General: Schüller (1960); Mills and Mansfield (1979); Jones (ed) (1992); Magnusson (2006). Art and Antiquities fraud: Kurz (1948); Arnau (1961); Jeppson (1971); Savage (1976); Bly (ed) (1986); Marsh (1993); Hoving (1996); Radnóti (1999); Tharp (ed) (1999); Muscarella (2000). Archaeological fraud: Munro (1905); Vayson de Pradenne (1932); Cole (1955); Rieth (1967).

Several authors have attempted to insert a little science into their books, most notably and knowledgeably in *Forgeries*, by George Savage (1976). Museum-based scientists, usually conservators, have sometimes included authenticity examinations in their publications. For example, the first substantive work on museum conservation in English includes a short section on fakes (Scott, 1926, pp. 56–58) and now some of the general works on archaeometry are including chapters on authentication (see Chapter 2, p. 22).

Previously the only major work devoted to scientific authentication was Stuart Fleming's *Authenticity in Art* (1975). Fleming, a physicist, carried out many thermoluminescence (TL) authenticity studies on ceramics; indeed he helped to establish TL as a routine authentication method (e.g. Fleming 1976, 1979c; and see Chapter 6). *Authenticity in Art* describes the application of a wide range of scientific techniques to authentication, especially of paintings, ceramics and metals. Its main drawback is its brevity but it was an excellent taster for the subject and still, thirty years on, contains many useful ideas. More recently there have been the *Fakebusters* volumes (McCrone and Weiss (eds), 1999; Weiss and Chartier (eds), 2004).

A series of major exhibitions took place in the twentieth century, the catalogues of which form a major component of the literature on the subject. They include those at the Kunsthistorische Museum, Vienna (Kunsthistorische Museum, 1923); the Burlington Fine Arts Club, London (Burlington, 1924); the Corning Museum of Glass (van Dantzig, 1953b); the British Museum in 1961 (British Museum, 1961; Cole, 1961) and 1990 (Jones (ed), 1990); the Museum Folkwang, Essen (Ertz, 1976/77); the Minneapolis Institute of Art (Johnson, 1973 [excellent bibliography]); the Bibliothèque Nationale, Paris (Hillmann, 1988); the Eretz Israel Museum, Tel Aviv (Eretz, 1989); the Kunstmuseum, Aarhus (Aarhus Kunst, 1989) and the Nelson-Atkins Museum of Art, Kansas City (Cohon, 1996).

Approaches to authenticity

Authenticity is a fluid concept (Lowenthal, 1988, 1999), different groups having different concepts of authenticity. For archaeologists and art historians, the object has to be materially original, but for many other groups it is the much more fluid concept of links with the original or the appearance that has to be preserved, or the concept. Thus many 'restored' warplanes contain few original parts, but are regarded as authentic because those few original bits have been rebuilt to original specifications; as Holtorf and Schadla-Hall (1999) put it, 'What makes the replica aircraft authentic is the fact that it is a faithful reproduction of the original concept'. As Lowenthal (1999) noted, if a holy relic produced cures it was authentic, no matter how dubious its origins!

This fluidity is also temporal, one era's fake being another's interesting discovery, for just as there is no constancy in art values so the perspectives by which artefacts are judged are continually reassessed. Examples of this change of attitude are provided by some vessels of semi-precious stones in a Renaissance style. One is an inlaid cup and cover of agate and chalcedony which was purchased by the Victoria and Albert Museum (V & A 442-1882) in 1882. It was condemned as a spurious Renaissance piece shortly afterwards, and banished to a store room, only to re-emerge almost a century later as an important example of the revival of interest in Renaissance decorative arts in the late eighteenth century (Wainwright, 1971; Jones (ed), 1990, pp. 44–45; Cat. 19). Moreover, it was shown to have been designed by William Beckford, who is now regarded as one of the most important connoisseurs and leaders of style in Georgian Britain. The cup was intended for his ill-fated creation, Fonthill Abbey in Wiltshire, and reflecting this newly appreciated connection, it is now known as the Beckford Cup.

A similar fate befell a superb ewer now in the Metropolitan Museum of Art, New York (1982.60.138) (Stone, 1997). This was initially believed to have been made by the Renaissance craftsman, Benvenuto Cellini, but was soon rejected as a forgery. It is now believed that the quartz bowl is of late seventeenth century Bohemian work and that the bejewelled golden mounts were designed, partly at least, by Beckford himself. Thus the object has passed from being a fake Cellini to a genuine Beckford and, as such, is now known as the Fonthill Ewer. Stone considered it 'a *good* fake' (his italics).

Another, but very different, example is afforded by the many fakes and forgeries of barbarian jewellery and regalia that proliferated in the first part of the twentieth century throughout much of Europe, exemplified by the notorious Adler fibula, given to Hitler as a genuine piece (Rieth, 1970, p. 136; and see Chapter 15, p. 371) and the Lombard Treasure, condemned as a forgery shortly after going on exhibition in London in 1932 (Jones (ed), 1990, pp. 173–176, Cats 179–183; Kidd, 1990; and see Chapter 15, p. 382). These, and other pieces are now regarded as interesting pieces, documenting not Early Medieval Europe but instead the rise of fascism in Europe, as collectors sought to obtain artefacts of the Aryan barbarians who had populated their various countries during the Dark Ages.

In the Far East there is a very different attitude to the preservation of the past, i.e. preservation by replication. This is especially true of religious and ritual items, statuary, etc. Exact copies of the old item, what we would term the original, are made, not just of the form of the piece, but using the same materials and technology, sometimes even specifying that they must be made in the same workshop, thereby regenerating the piece, which becomes the original and therefore authentic.

Motives

Before the history of a piece can be reconstructed from the physical data of its present form, it is important to have some idea of the possible motives for doing this in the first place. The production of legitimate copies of antiquities and works of art has a long history, these being made either as decorative items in a particular pleasing antique style or as more rigorously accurate copies for serious collectors, museum display and general instruction. Some of the methods used in the creating three-dimensional copies are the subject of Chapter 4, and two-dimensional copies are discussed in Chapter 13.

The same methods are used on occasion to produce both legitimate and clandestine copies. Thus, for example, moulding techniques were used, quite legitimately, by firms such as J. Chiurazzi and Sons, Sabatino de Angelis and Sons (Tarbell, 1909) and G. Sommer and Son, of Naples, and by others elsewhere, to produce excellent copies of the classical antiquities found at Pompeii and Herculaneum in the nineteenth and early twentieth centuries (Jones (ed), 1990, pp. 46–47). These techniques were much the same as those used by the forger, and indeed examples

of their work are sometimes passed off as genuine antiquities. The casting techniques were, however, rather different from those used in classical antiquity, when art bronzes tended to be cast by the lost wax process. The nineteenth-century commercial copies tended to be cast in two-piece moulds with details cast separately and soldered into place (Bailey, 1996, pp. 123–124). Similarly, copies of antique ceramics were made by a number of specialist firms in the nineteenth century (Savage, 1976, pp. 140–6; and see Chapter 9, p. 196). Other firms used electroforms to create convincing copies of antiquities (see Chapter 4, p. 78). Most major international museums have the old catalogues of these firms to show to members of the public when they bring in examples of these copies, hopeful that they have a real antiquity.

Sommer and Son usually marked their pieces, whereas other firms did not. Even so it is all too easy to disguise or remove these markings. On metal artefacts stamped marks can be filled in with metal of similar composition and raised stamps can be ground away. (Note that the mark can sometimes be recovered by etching with acid, the base of the removed mark reacting differently from the surrounding metal. This method is used by forensic scientists to recover serial numbers that have been filed off firearms.) Similar problems occur with other legitimate copies. For example, a recent copy of a Guarneri violin was marked internally and even branded to thwart attempts to pass it off as an early eighteenth-century original, but nevertheless it appeared at auction with the identification marks removed (Harvey, 1995). The Parisian enameller Theophile Soyer always signed his excellent copies of sixteenth-century Limoges enamels, but his signature was frequently scratched off by dishonest dealers (Speel, 1998, p. 55). (See Chapter 9, p. 208, for the problems associated with the removal of marks from legitimate copies of ceramics and Chapter 12, p. 288 for the problems of producing permanent identification marks on legitimate copies of paintings of the Great Masters.)

Copies of Prehistoric and Dark Age European metal antiquities are currently produced by several firms. Some are made employing the same materials and methods as used in the manufacture of the originals and these could in the future be mistaken for genuine antiquities, thereby presenting serious difficulties in distinguishing them as copies, especially if they have become corroded. For coin copies see Chapter 8, p. 178.

Copies of ancient Chinese bronze vessels were produced for sale in the 1970s and 1980s by the

Palace Museum in Taiwan (Liu Wann-Hong, 1976; for details of the patination processes see Chapter 14, p. 363). The originals would have been made by piece moulding (see Chapter 8, p. 160), but the copies were made by lost wax casting, partly because this gave a more faithful reproduction of the original, but also one suspects, because lost wax casting is now a more familiar technique. Similar museum replicas were made in Beijing under British supervision (Lowenthal, 1987; Beckett, 1995, pp. 123–124).

Kenoyer (1996), an archaeologist much concerned with prehistoric sites in South Asia, encouraged the production of convincing copies of ancient stone beads in order to provide an alternative supply for collectors and thereby protect ancient sites from despoliation. In practice if this had achieved any success, it was more likely to have been the case that the modern copies caused a lack of confidence in the authenticity of the beads offered for sale, thereby precipitating a fall in prices.

Copies have been made with the aim of protecting the original and highly vulnerable or valuable originals. Thus, jewellery set with very expensive stones often came with an identical piece set with simulants to be worn at balls, etc., whilst the originals remained in the bank or, in some cases, the pawnbrokers (see Chapter 16, p. 403). Similarly, the spate of street robberies of jewellery and expensive watches has led to a market in so-called replica Rolexes. Royal Replica Watches (www.onlinereplicastore.com) advertise their '. . . genuine Rolex fakes', commenting on the difference between 'Swiss high quality replicas to the lesser Chinese replicas'.

The convincing coral simulant, known as 'created coral', was developed by Pierre Gilson to save the coral reefs from destruction, inspired by the diver and environmentalist, Jacques-Yves Cousteau (Elwell, 1979, pp. 149–150).

Copies have served a more clandestine purpose, disguising the fact that the originals had gone missing. This has happened at the Museo del Oro Peru, in Lima, where the collection of the Manuel Murjíca Gallo foundation was systematically stripped of an estimated 80% of its holdings of Inca gold artefacts in the 1980s and 1990s, and replaced with copies (Atwood, 2001, p. 80; *The Times*, 18 August 2001). This also occurred at the Ligong Palace in Hebei province of China where the curator substituted no fewer than 259 items, selling the originals (*The Times*, 19 August 2004).

Genuine pieces have been given false wear or evidence of age for a variety of motives. Wear has been added to antiques in perfect condition so that they

would appear even more genuine (see Chapter 10, p. 234), and spurious patinas have been applied to antique bronzes to conform with the expectations of collectors (see Chapter 14, p. 353).

Sometimes antiquities have been accused of being forgeries as part of unrelated disputes. A good example is provided by the so-called Avar Treasure, offered for sale in 1981 (Sotheby's, 1981). The treasure included a series of Avar gold and silver belt fittings stylistically dateable to about AD 700 together with some Byzantine silver vessels. The sale was not a success, with the majority of the lots being bought in. Subsequently the dealer Michel van Rijn claimed that it had been commissioned by him in order to get even with Sotheby's (van Rijn, 1993, pp. 168–186; Beckett, 1995, pp. 52–63). Sotheby's rigorously denied this, pointing out that van Rijn's claimed grievance actually took place *after* the Avar material had been entered for sale (Page, 1992). More prosaically, the examination carried out at the British Museum on the material prior to its abortive auction in 1981 suggest that van Rijn's claim is most unlikely to be true.

An even more devious case concerned the dealer Jonathan Tokerley-Parry, who acquired genuine but looted antiquities in Egypt. In some instances the originals had been replaced by copies so that their theft from the Government antiquities stores would not be immediately noted. The originals were then given rather garish fake patinas, etc. in order to deceive customs officials and ensure easy export from Egypt as rather poor copies. Once out of Egypt the fake treatments were removed, revealing the genuine articles. These were then further treated to make it appear that they had been in long-established European collections and could thus be legitimately offered for sale (*The Times*, 15 February 2002).

Scientific approaches to authenticity

These approaches can be categorised as follows:

1. Visual examination, aided by light microscopy, and where appropriate and available, UV, IR, electron microscopy and radiography. This seeks evidence for technique, evidence of repair or alteration and usage, and the sequence of manufacture, wear damage and repair (see Chapter 2, p. 36).
2. Analysis of the materials to establish:
   a) The composition of the original materials, together with that of later additions. With synthetic materials this seeks to establish

whether they are similar to those used in the period ascribed to the object. With natural materials the emphasis is more on characterising the source, and whether that source is commensurate with the period assigned on the basis of other criteria.

  b) Physical/chemical changes to the materials indicative of age or treatment.

3. Determination of age by means of the various physical dating techniques, notably radio carbon (RC) (see Chapter 5), TL and dendrochronology (see Chapter 6), to establish, if not always a real date expressed in calendar years, then at least an indication of whether the piece is likely to be of the age ascribed to it stylistically or historically.

Copies or alterations made with fraudulent intent fall into four main categories.

1. A forgery, that is, a whole new work in imitation of something else.
2. A fake, that is, an object that has been altered such that it appears to be something else, usually more valuable.
3. A pastiche, that is, something made up of unrelated pieces.
4. A genuine object that has been deceptively restored, such that serious damage is hidden or disguised.

In addition, it is often necessary to test other aspects of the artefact's story that may be contributing to its interest and thereby to its value. These can include provenance, association and identity.

Evidence of provenance

Antiquities can be given false provenances for a variety of reasons, including increasing their value or interest, and enabling illegally obtained material to be disposed of more easily.

For example, an ancient Italian bronze or ceramic found buried in an ancient context in Britain would be very rare and consequently of much greater value than the equivalent piece found in Italy. Back in the mid-nineteenth century the antiquarian A. W. Franks (1858) noted that:

> the numerous local antiquaries who have sprung up since archaeology has become more carefully studied are anxious to obtain antiquities from some particular locality. Spurious localities are therefore invented, and Greek, Etruscan, Egyptian and Italian antiquities are palmed off on the unwary as having been found in his native soil.

Thus, considerable controversy surrounds the Italian *bronzetti* such as the Blandford Forum Group and others which are apparently of early Italian origin, but claimed to have been found in Britain (Rigby *et al.*, 1995). Many such pieces were made in Italy in the nineteenth century for sale to tourists, either as curios or intentional forgeries, and most are of brass (Atzeni *et al.*, 2004, pp. 183–185). Even where scientific examination shows that they genuinely are ancient and that they really were dug up in Britain, there is often no proof that they were deposited in antiquity. It is more likely that they were acquired by some much later tourist as a souvenir and subsequently lost.

Peacock and Williams (1997) examined a genuine Etruscan ceramic cup, said to have been dug up in Cheshire, England. Although the majority of the encrustation had been removed, a very small quantity survived beneath the rim, sufficient to enable identification of minute flakes of minerals typical of central Italy but not of Cheshire. This strongly suggested that the cup had lain buried in the soil of Etruria, and had come to England in the fairly recent past.

Another example is the classical bronzes from the collection of the nineteenth-century antiquarian Joshua Brooke (Robinson, 2003). These are mainly small votive figurines for which he paid inflated prices because they were said to have been found near the prehistoric ritual monuments at Avebury in Wiltshire. As such the bronzes could be taken to provide evidence for some continuing ritual activity. It now seems much more likely that these minor antiquities were acquired in the eighteenth and nineteenth centuries in Italy.

Only finding pieces in stratified deposits can provide certain proof of ancient loss or deposition, and can sometimes thereby authenticate similar pieces if they are distinctive. For example, two small bronze figurines found on the foreshore at Aust Ferry in Gloucestershire, England, in the early twentieth century had long been regarded as either local Iron Age productions or as Iberian Iron Age imports (Figure 1.4a). One was acquired by the British Museum fairly soon after its discovery but the Museum only had the chance to acquire the second figure in the 1980s. This occasioned some rethinking; they were typologically difficult to parallel, and were just chance finds with no real context. Were they Iberian and if so had they come to Britain in antiquity or more recently, or, possibly, were they nineteenth-century forgeries? Analysis of the metal and examination of the patina suggested they were

Figure 1.4a Two small bronze figurines found at Aust Ferry. That on the right was acquired by the British Museum shortly after their discovery (BM Reg. PRB 1900, 10-12, 1). That on the left was acquired much later (BM Reg. PRB 1986, 11-6, 1).

Figure 1.4b A third figurine, now in the North Somerset Museum at Weston-super-Mare, which is clearly typologically related to the other two, found during the excavation of a nearby Roman Temple. (Courtesy T. Milton/British Museum)

likely to be of some age but nothing could be done to resolve the question of their origins. However, excavations at the Roman temples at Henley Wood in Somerset a few kilometres to the south, produced a third very similar figure (Figure 1.4b) from a sealed archaeological context, thereby establishing the antiquity and local origin of the Aust figurines (Henig in Watts and Leach, 1995, pp. 131–133).

False objects can be salted onto a legitimate excavation in order to legitimise subsequent forgeries, as certainly happened with the Pevensey tile fragments (see Chapter 19, p. 479) and was probably the intention behind the Clazomenae coin hoard (see p. 17).

Another consideration is that of legality. Most reputable museums and even some dealers would not now acquire an antiquity that was likely to have been illegally exported and thus require some form of provenance or documentation demonstrating that it had been out of the country of origin for many years, before the current legislation came into force (see, for example, the case of the bronze

Nataraja statue, Chapter 20, p. 501). The seemingly accepted practice of regularly concealing, or, even worse, of giving a false provenance, is rightly lambasted by Muscarella (2000).

Thus there are motives to claim that artefacts have been found where it is most profitable to find and legally sell them. For example, antiquities found in Ireland are the property of the state, which rewards the finder. It is sometimes perceived that a better price could be obtained in Britain, but it is illegal to take the antiquities out of Ireland. Thus, many small Celtic artefacts of Irish manufacture are coming onto the market in Britain that are claimed to have been found in Britain, and are therefore saleable to British institutions and collectors, but the true origins of some of the pieces are suspect.

Checking the provenance of an artefact's burial can be difficult, but is not impossible if it has not been too carefully cleaned. There are a wide range of forensic tests that can establish if any adhering soil is likely to originate from the claimed find spot. It is also possible that distinctive patinations may provide some clues as to where the object has lain.

For example, an unprovenanced Roman bronze statuette of Minerva (BM GR Reg. 1873,8-20,45) stylistically dating from the first century AD was examined (Freestone *et al.*, 1984). The corrosion was found to be an unusually rich mixture of copper and lead carbonates, chlorides and sulphates. It also contained minute grains of the mineral salite, which is associated with volcanic rocks with inclusions of lava. Salite minerals are typical of Italian volcanic rocks and a high chloride content is a feature of the Vesuvian lavas. Thus, it seems that the statuette lay for long periods in such lavas, and most realistically is likely to have come from Pompeii or nearby.

Evidence of association

The stone whereby Goliath died,
Which cures the headache, well applied.
A whetstone, worn exceeding small,
Time used to whet his scythe withal.
The pigeon stuff'd, which Noah sent
To tell him when the waters went.
A ring I've got of Samson's hair
The same which Delilah did wear,
St Dunstan's tongs, which story shows
Did pinch the devil by the nose.
The very shaft, as you may see
That Cupid shot at Anthony.
(Sir Charles Hanbury Williams,
a friend of Sir Hans Sloane)

The prime examples of association are the relics associated with spiritual and religious events and personages. Even today an object associated with a famous person or event, does have an enormously increased value. This is exemplified by the discovery of an ossuary claimed to be that of James, the brother of Jesus Christ (Keall, 2003; Silberman and Goren, 2003; Ayalon *et al.*, 2004).

The ossuary, carved from a block of limestone, quite typical of those used in Palestine in the first century AD, has been the centre of controversy since it was examined by the French palaeographer, André Lemaire, in 2002. The Aramaic inscription on its side proclaims it to have belonged to Joseph, brother of Jesus (Shanks and Witherington 3rd, 2003). If genuine, this would make it by far and away the most important artefact related to

Jesus Christ to have been found since Saint Helen and the age of relics in the fourth century AD. The authenticity was initially questioned quite simply because the find was felt to be too good to be true, but also, more seriously, because the ossuary lacked any credible archaeological provenance. It was in the remarkable private collection of Oded Golan, and was claimed to have been found in the 1960s. Golan's collection contains many other unprovenanced pieces, some with startling inscriptions such as an ivory pomegranate (Shanks, 2003a) including the Yehoash Tablet. The inscription on this purports to record the collection of funds for the repair of the First Temple in the ninth century BC, but has been condemned as a fake on palaeographic grounds (Shanks, 2003a), although not before a team from the Geological Survey of Israel (GSI) had apparently authenticated it (Ilani *et al.*, 2003) only to be challenged by Yuval Goren (www.bibleinterp .com/articles/alternative_interpretation.htm).

The examination of the Joseph ossuary has proved no less contradictory and acrimonious. The first scientific report from the GSI (reproduced in *Biblical Archaeological Review* 26, 2; p. 29) found that the ossuary itself was likely to be genuine and no one has seriously disputed that subsequently. More crucially, although the letters of the inscription had been recently mechanically cleaned, enough of the patina remained to establish that it was of the 'cauliflower' variety, likely to have formed naturally in an underground damp and calcareous environment (see Chapter 11, p. 256).

In the autumn of 2003 the ossuary was sent to the Royal Ontario Museum in Toronto. It was poorly packed, and on arrival in Canada it was found that the cracks which already existed had spread, the ossuary thereby effectively being in five pieces. This calamity did at least allow detailed scientific examination while it was being restored by the museum's conservators (Keall, 2003). This led them to concur with the GSI that the patina in the inscription was likely to be ancient, although it had been largely removed from all but the right hand end of the inscription. They also reported that the harder veins in the limestone stood slightly proud of the surface, which they attributed to differential weathering of the surfaces of the stone and, moreover, that this could be observed both on the sides of the stone and in the cut grooves. They believed the surfaces would originally have been completely flat after polishing and took this slight irregularity to be evidence that the carving of the ossuary and the inscription were contemporary. In fact, polishing of a surface containing hard and soft areas will leave the hard areas standing proud.

Meanwhile, the Israel Antiquities Authority appointed a team of archaeologists, epigraphers and scientists to examine both the ossuary and the Yehoash inscription and their report unanimously pronounced both inscriptions to be faked (Shanks, 2003b). Although this was generally accepted (Silberman and Goren, 2003), the individual statements of the various experts were somewhat contradictory (Shanks, 2003b). It was variously claimed that the inscription cut through the existing patina, that it had been cut *or cleaned* (Shanks' italics), or that the uncleaned end was authentic. On that last claim, it seems inherently unlikely that the original inscription would have just occupied one end of the ossuary, but if there was more then it must have lain where the grooves of the present re-cut or cleaned inscription now lies, and unless there had been gross alteration the original presumably read much the same as at present. A rather more serious claim was that the 'patinisation' of both the ossuary and the Yehoash inscription was very similar, which in itself is puzzling as they are different stones from supposedly different environments.

An accelerator mass spectrometry (AMS) RC date was obtained on a minute sample of some of the carbonates of the patina collected from several locations and reported as lying between 390 and 200 BC (taken from an abstract of the report of the Materials Committee). The RC dating expert of the Committee, Elisabetta Boaretto, dismissed this date because carbon of the right age could have been added and because 'the objects [the ossuary], since their discovery, have passed through many different places without any documentation'. These points are true although the carbon was apparently in the form of carbonates, not charcoal or other forms of elemental carbon which is usually the case where carbon of the appropriate age has been added to a fake patina. The main problem is that the samples of carbon in carbonates forming a patina underground are very prone to contamination from the surrounding carbonates of geological age and are very unreliable dating materials (see Chapter 11, p. 266). However, if the date was going to be rejected as unreliable it raises the question of why the dating exercise was done at all.

Stable isotope analysis (SIA) of the oxygen in the ossuary patina was also undertaken, and some more reliable information has now been separately reported by Ayalon *et al.* (2004), at last in a peer-reviewed journal. As the calcite of the patina is believed to have formed by the precipitation of carbonates from solution in the ground water of the surroundings, the oxygen isotope ratios should reflect the values in the ground water at the time. The ratios on the patina from the surfaces of the ossuary were similar to those taken from the surfaces of control ossuaries but ratios from the majority of the samples taken from within the inscription were very different. In addition, the presence of marine cocoliths strongly suggests the patina did not precipitate from a solution as genuine patina would have done, but was applied as a paste. Furthermore, as the oxygen isotope ratio is a function of the temperature of the local ground water (Figure 1.5) it could be established that the patina could only have formed naturally at temperatures in the region of 40 to 50°C. This is far above the ambient ground temperature pertaining in Jerusalem over the last few thousand years, and furthermore the oxygen isotope ratios are very different from those of the ground waters in the Jerusalem region. Ayalon *et al.* (2004) speculated that the patina could have been applied as a slurry of chalk that had been in boiling water, thereby inferring that in some way this could change the isotopic ratios, which seems unlikely. In an extraordinary new twist the James ossuary has now been linked to the 'Jesus Family Tomb' group of ossuaries excavated in 1980 (Jacobovici and Pellegrino, 2007; Kingsley, 2007). They claim the James ossuary to be genuine, the missing ossuary from that group and that somehow Golan had obtained it. As this book goes to press Golan is standing trial for forgery.

Evidence of identity

Many famous (and thus expensive) antiquities and art objects have been studied, authenticated, exhibited and published on over many years. They are offered for sale, and change owners, sometimes disappearing for lengthy periods before reappearing for sale. This creates the potential for substitution, and part of an authentication investigation must be to check that the original artefact, and not a copy thereof, is being offered for sale.

In the nineteenth century there were cases of fraudulent substitution by restorers, most blatantly by Salomon Weininger (Destrée, 1927; Kurz, 1948, pp. 177–178, 218–219; Hayward, 1974).

Salomon Weininger's speciality lay in taking in important antiquities for restoration, and making copies thereof which were duly substituted for the originals. He subsequently sold the latter as the genuine

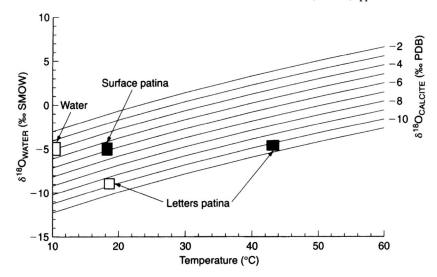

Figure 1.5 The calculated relationship between the calcite ($\delta^{18}O$) possible contribution of water $\delta^{18}O$ and temperature. The specific example here is the patina in the letters of the 'James, brother of Christ' ossuary. The open squares show the values that would have been expected if the patina had formed naturally, and the closed squares show the actual value for which an impossibly high ambient temperature would have been necessary. (Courtesy Ayalon *et al.*, 2004)

antiquities that they were. This was obviously very risky, especially when high-profile antiquities from public institutions were involved and eventually led to his downfall when some of the originals were spotted in another collection. When the restored original and Weininger's copy are seen together, the lack of attention to detail is at once apparent; sometimes there is a noticeable difference in the actual dimensions and weight. Weininger could get away with these substitutions because the legitimate restorations were themselves somewhat drastic, and thus the curators expected the artefact to look different. In addition, record photography was still rare and most of the collections that were targeted lacked adequate record drawings or even records of the dimensions and weight of their pieces.

Perhaps the Geistliche Schatzkammer (the Spiritual Treasury of the Holy Roman Empire) in Vienna suffered the greatest losses when it sent some of its treasures to Weininger for restoration in 1860. At least five major Medieval pieces were substituted, and the originals sold. The substitutions were very successful and still largely unsuspected when the collection was taken over 60 years later by the Austrian government in 1922.

The most famous of these is the enamelled Reliquary of the Holy Thorn. Long after the substitute had been sent to the Geistliche Schatzkammer,

the original was innocently purchased by Baron Anselm von Rothschild in the 1870s, then sold on to Ferdinand Rothschild, who in turn bequeathed it together with his other collections to the British Museum in 1898 as part of the Waddesdon Bequest (Tait, 1981, 1986 and 1988). The substitution was first revealed by Destrée (1927), and briefly acknowledged in the second edition of the British Museum Guide Catalogue of the Bequest (Dalton, 1927, p. 15).

The conditions of the Waddesdon Bequest to the British Museum were that the collection was not to be split up, but always displayed as a unit. Unfortunately, some of the more spectacular pieces of silver were deceptive restorations of badly damaged pieces, often of different original form. Others were outright forgeries, nineteenth-century electroforms of fifteenth- and seventeenth-century Baroque plate (see Chapter 4, p. 84). Thus the reliquary, a genuine object but fraudulently substituted, is surrounded by deceptive restoration and forgery, not quite the aspects of Victorian collecting that Rothschild had anticipated would be perpetuated by his munificence.

Sometimes an antiquity may be original, but can have grown over the years since its last appearance. This is exemplified by the so-called Raab Treasure, which was offered for sale in 1891 with

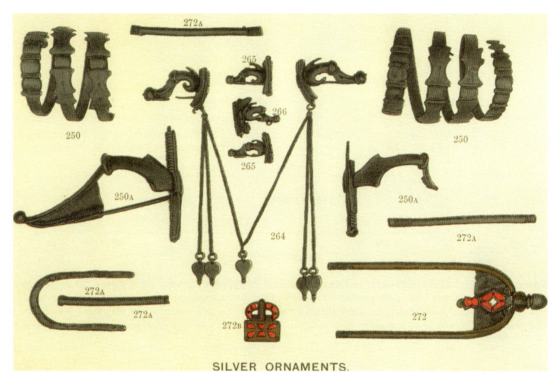

Figure 1.6 The 1891 sale catalogue entry for the Raab Treasure. This was found near Komarón in Hungary and was deposited in the fifth or sixth century AD. It shows a total of four silver binding strips, spread through the other items, and the chape from the sword sheath. (Courtesy J. Heffron/British Museum)

a well-illustrated catalogue (Figure 1.6). The sword chape was then accompanied by four silver binding strips belonging to the sheath. When, almost a century later it was offered for purchase to the British Museum it was found to have extra strips (Jones (ed), 1990, p. 254). Even more suspicious was the fact that four of the strips were apparently identical (Figure 1.7). Cursory inspection revealed the rosy hue of copper showing through on the three of them that were silver-plated copper electroforms of the fourth original silver strip. Thus, in reality there were two fewer original strips than in 1891, not one more. Currently the reconstructed sheath is on display in the British Museum with no indication that three of the strips are electroforms.

Establishing a context

Creating a context is important for the credibility of the fake or forgery and thus investigating the

Figure 1.7 Fragments of the Raab sword sheath (BM MME Reg. 1987, 3-8, 1 & 2). By the 1980s the number of strips had risen to five. The three binding strips on the right are electroforms of the original strip to the immediate left of the chape. Note the small area of damage replicated in each instance. (Courtesy T. Milton/British Museum)

background to a suspect piece can be as important as investigating the artefact itself. The created context can take many forms, often dictated by the different types of artefact. Thus, for example, in fine art, the catalogue raisonné of an artist might be altered to include the new forgery or an old art book be updated to include a reproduction of the forgery (see Chapter 12, p. 271). A more familiar example includes the addition of spurious items to country house auctions, thereby giving the impression that they had been in the house for generations.

Dealers in false antiquities have often gone to considerable lengths to give their creations convincing archaeological backgrounds. Thus, the coin-forger Wilhelm Becker sent his creations to Turkey so that they could subsequently appear on the market with a plausible provenance (Jones (ed), 1990, p. 144; and see Chapter 8, p. 180). Wakeling (1912, pp. 18–19; and see Chapter 20, p. 503) recorded the complex methods adopted by forgers in Egypt at the beginning of the twentieth century. One Cairo goldsmith arranged for his forgeries to be buried out in the countryside ready to be 'discovered' by a fellah, who could then, in all honesty, swear that he had dug them up from the place indicated.

Sometimes forgeries have been introduced onto excavations, and in the most spectacular case of all, the Piltdown fraud, the excavation was created for the remains which otherwise would surely never have been accepted (see Chapter 19, p. 475).

A more recent case concerned the small hoard of electrum staters found in a pot excavated at the Ionian city of Clazomenae, now in western Anatolia, Turkey (Işik, 1992), and discussed in reviews by Hurter (1993) and Spier (1994). Detailed study of the coins, which are of a unique type, suggested that they are all forgeries. Spier speculated that they were introduced onto the excavation in order to provide an archaeological provenance for this unusual type of coin that had already been on the market but rejected as being forgeries, in which aim they failed. An alternative explanation was that they were planted in order to discredit the excavator, in which aim they were more successful.

Forgeries are often accompanied by false documentation which usually seeks to demonstrate that the artefact in question was in a legitimate collection decades previously, thus establishing its authenticity and that it was not an illegal export (p. 12 and Chapter 11, p. 262).

The noted collector and authority on Waterford Glass, and, as it was latterly revealed, forger,

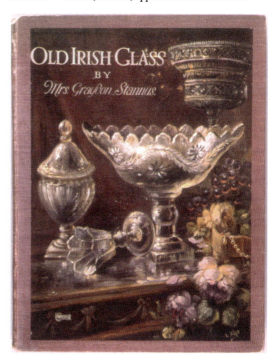

Figure 1.8   Front cover of *Old Irish Glass*, which contains many illustrations of pieces in the author's collection that were subsequently shown to be forgeries. (Courtesy T. Springett)

Mrs Graydon Stannus, created an ideal context for her work (McConnell, 2004). Photographs of pieces, 'from the author's collection', were included in her authoritative book on Waterford Glass *Old Irish Glass* (1931) (Figure 1.8). Periodically these pieces would appear on the market, with their authenticity guaranteed and price enhanced because they had appeared in the volume, but many were forgeries (see Chapter 15, p. 373 for a similar case).

Questions of disclosure

Do you risk educating forgers or having generations of ignorant museum curators?

Jack Ogden, reported in Beckett (1995), p. 116

In dealing with fraud and deceit how much information, if any, should be disclosed? More specifically, should this book have been written at all? Will it be of more use to the fakers than to the investigators?

There are four main areas of potentially useful information. These are as follows:

1. Disclosing the correct materials and techniques by which the genuine artefact should have been made.
2. Disclosing the scientific and other methods by which fakes and forgeries may be unmasked.
3. Disclosing the evidence of natural ageing.
4. Disclosing the methods by which artefacts may be produced and made to appear old or genuine.

Perhaps the overriding factor is that forgery and authentication are not isolated from the rest of the world. Archaeologists, those studying the technologies of the past and those studying artists' techniques, regularly publish details of new research on early processes. New scientific techniques often have obvious application to authentication studies. The appearance and nature of the ageing processes of materials is the business of conservation studies. Producing the appearance of age has long been part of the legitimate craftsman's training and the methods appear in books on surface treatments. It is perhaps significant that there appears no parallel concern with the publication of methodology in forensic science.

The first area concerns the publication of technical detail that could be of use to the forger. For example, at the Conference on Far Eastern Fakes and Forgeries held in Singapore in November 2000 (Harrison-Hall, 2001, p. 571), one delegate called for the suppression of technical information from catalogues, archaeological reports, etc. to stop forgers gaining access to the information. These calls also provide a rather interesting insight into the art historian's unconscious evaluation of the relative potency of style and science. There is apparently no concern about publishing stylistic information; it is only technique and materials that must be suppressed as dangerous!

Emma Bunker (1994) found that shortly after giving details at conferences in 1992 of the unusual and distinctive methods by which some Central Asian belt plaques were cast, forgeries started to appear on the market made by the same method. As Bunker put it 'Technology has simultaneously promoted the skills of forgery and of its detection'.

The British Museum's Head of a Tetrarch (GR Reg. 1974, 12-13, 1) was pronounced a forgery mainly on the evidence of the incorrect technique used to carve the very hard porphyry (Cook, B., 1984; and see Chapter 11, p. 248). The details of the technical mistakes that had exposed the fraud

were deliberately withheld on the grounds that this information would assist future forgers (it was however made clear that *bona fide* enquiries would be dealt with at the Museum).

The adoption of the correct technique by the forger once it has been published is as widespread as it is inevitable. For example, following the publication in the 1970s of the methods by which gold and silver wire was made in antiquity (see Chapter 15, p. 376) most forgers adopted the correct ancient method, or at least imitated the spiral grooves on the wires (Figures 15.5–15.11), such that the presence of strip twisted or swaged wire is no longer taken as a significant indicator of antiquity unless the piece is known to pre-date the 1970s.

Similarly the fuller understanding of how the Greeks fired their red and black figure ceramics to achieve oxidised and reduced zones in one firing has led to copies and forgeries that are much more technically correct (see Chapter 9, p. 195).

This problem should be seen as part of the broader result of disseminating information on artefacts generally, both stylistic and technical. In the nineteenth century the new techniques of good color printing, together with electroforming and plaster casting, enabled accurate copies of fine art, sculpture, decorative items and antiquities to become very widely available (see Chapter 4). This, together with studies on art history generally, certainly enabled curators and collectors alike to be more discriminating, such that earlier forgeries were easily detected. However, it inevitably meant that forgers were also better informed, leading to big improvements in their productions.

The technology and materials that form an object are an integral part of it and as such the technical description cannot realistically be withheld. It is also difficult to see how in practice such information could be made accessible to authenticators but to no one else. All sorts of problems can be envisaged; the results of examinations would be reduced to stating that the artefact in question was or was not genuine for reasons that could not be given. There would also surely be legal problems with such secrecy and failure to divulge information.

The second area concerns disclosure of the methods of investigation. It might be argued that if the forgers had a good idea of the tests to which their productions were going to be subjected then, like van Meegeren in the 1930s, they could take steps to counter them, forewarned is forearmed. However, the methods used in scientific authentication are in practice the standard methods for the scientific examination of materials generally. There are no methods that are used specifically for authenticity testing; even the physical dating methods described in Chapters 5 and 6 are much more widely used for archaeological and geological dating. Thus, the forgers have only to read the scientific literature to gain an awareness of the techniques appropriate to the investigation of the materials that they intend to use.

The continual advances in new approaches and improvements in established techniques soon nullify attempts to create the undetectable forgery. Van Meegeren must have thought that preparing his own pigments from what he believed were the appropriate materials in exactly the same way as they would have been prepared in the seventeenth century would render them indistinguishable from genuine old paints. He could not have known of the ^{210}Pb isotope, for example, and the significance of its elevated content in his lead white which conclusively showed that the lead from which his pigments had been prepared was still in the ground as ore long after Vermeer was dead (see Chapter 12, p. 295).

The third area, concerning chemical and physical ageing, is necessarily dealt with in considerable detail by conservation texts. Before natural corrosion or other decay can be arrested it is necessary to understand how it occurred and be able to recognise its form. Another potentially more serious aspect is that, in testing new materials and treatments, objects are routinely subjected to accelerated ageing. Full practical details of these ageing procedures are routinely published for a wide range of materials throughout the conservation literature. These more chemically correct treatments are far more pernicious than the cosmetic surface treatments usually applied which by and large only have the appearance of age. Kawanoba *et al.* (1996) seem to be almost alone in recognising this danger.

Finally, there are publications that deal specifically with deceptive ageing or, even more bluntly, how to create a forgery. Most surface-treatment manuals, especially those dealing with wood and metals, give quite open and innocent instruction on how to create an antique appearance (see Chapters 17 and 14 respectively). Similarly, the standard works on restoration of antiques generally include instructions on how to make the new work blend in with the old, effectively offering a guide to deceptive restoration (see Chapter 20).

Larson's *Numismatic Forgery* and Hebborn's *The Art Forger's Handbook* deliberately set out to be rogues, although both authors justify their works on the grounds that knowledge of the techniques used is the best defence against them. Crawley (1971), after many years converting and deceptively restoring antique furniture, wrote an excellent account of what to look out for and included a chapter, entitled appropriately enough *The Birth of an Antique*, giving a blow-by-blow account of how a Victorian chest of drawers was to be transformed into a Georgian piece.

The dichotomy in attitude to these works is neatly summed up by the comment on Larson's book, 'This book is dangerous', opined by H. Robert Campbell, the past president of the august American Numismatic Society, quoted in an article on the book, entitled 'Coin Dealers Braced for a Forgery Orgy' in the London *Times* of 22 July 2004. By contrast, in the introduction to the book itself, the self-same Campbell related how he was suspicious of a particular modern rarity valued at over US$25 000, but could not see how it could have been forged until he had read Larson's book.

The book describes no more than standard metalworking procedures applied to coins, which any coin forger would have to be familiar with anyway. What it does do very effectively is alert collectors and curators to the probable extent of forgeries in circulation as well as revealing how the fakes and forgeries have been achieved.

The Art Forger's Handbook purports to give a detailed account of how to fake and forge easel art, which the Art and Antiques Squad of the London Metropolitan Police considered 'could cause serious problems for the market which is already concerned about how much fake material they have accepted as genuine'. It is instructive to follow through the four categories listed above to see how much real new information was given away in a work that was trying hard to do just that.

The techniques and materials aspects are covered adequately but give no information that has not already been published in the standard works listed in Chapter 12 of this volume. Significantly, the three works Hebborn himself considered 'the basic instruments' (Hebborn, 1997, p. 193) for the art forger are art historical, not technical. Scientific examination is not dealt with to any great extent, and there is far more on scientific investigation in the standard works on art techniques. The general ethos of the book seems to be that if the forgery was prepared using the correct technique and the appropriate materials, with a little largely cosmetic ageing the finished work should pass as genuine.

There is no attempt to describe how specific scientific tests, such as those outlined here in Chapter 12, can be circumvented. Instead, common-sense solutions to problems are given, such as when the use of a modern material is unavoidable, employ such material to restore a damaged area. The actual decay processes are not very well covered and instructions for the ageing of paintings and drawings mainly repeat recipes and tricks of the trade that have been published elsewhere.

The National Gallery in London has published an excellent series on the methods by which paintings of the Renaissance, Dutch and other periods were created in great technical detail from the stretcher to the varnish (see Chapter 12, p. 271). The motives for producing these books had nothing to do with forgery, but nevertheless as the latter are far more instructive to forgers than is Hebborn's manual, should the National Gallery have been dissuaded from publishing them?

The question to be considered is, even if it were feasible or enforceable, would an overall advantage be gained by suppression? On balance the increased range of knowledge on technology is probably more useful in detecting forgeries than facilitating better ones. One does not fight fraud with ignorance.

The role of authentication in the trade in looted and illegally exported antiquities

From the discussion above it is clear that forgery techniques evolve to respond to advances in our knowledge of the materials and techniques used in the past, and to a lesser degree to advances in modern investigative techniques. Thus, putative antiquities with documentation to prove their existence before the date at which a particular early technology or material was first published will be likely to be genuine if they contain evidence that the particular technique or material in question was used. But what of the great flood of antiquities on the market which usually have no documentation at all beyond the adhering soil that sometimes betrays their very recent excavation?

These considerations lead inevitably to the unsavoury subject of the clandestine trade in looted and illegally exported antiquities and the very real support potentially offered to it by scientific authentication and conservation. The enormous and ongoing trade in illicit antiquities looted from the ground or even stolen from museums has been widely debated for many years now (Meyer, 1973; Tubb, (ed), 1995; O'Keefe, 1997; Renfrew, 2000). Herscher (1998, p. 67) quotes Ricardo Elia who claimed that 'virtually every archaeological object acquired from abroad by collectors and museums in the U.S. in the last 30 years is the product of clandestine looting and smuggling'. As if to reinforce this statement, rather sadly, by the side of this quote is an advert for an on-line auction of geological samples, fossils and dinosaur remains, many of which were almost certain to have been smuggled out of their country of origin.

The various conventions and international agreements, notably the 1970 UNESCO *Convention on the Means of Prohibiting and Preventing the Illicit Import, Export and Transfer of Ownership of Cultural Property* (quoted in Meyer, 1973, Appendix F), have been powerless to even slow down the growth in the international traffic in looted antiquities, much less stop it. Ultimately, the prices collectors and museums around the world have been prepared to pay are just too tempting.

The one threat which has been shown to curb the demand is not fear of legal action, much less of conscience, but fear of forgery. In an area where, for obvious reasons, the objects are not expected to have any verifiable documented provenance, forgery can and does flourish. It was noted that when a large number of suspicious Cycladic marble figurines appeared on the market towards the end of the 1960s there was a significant reduction in the despoilation of the archaeological sites from which the genuine figurines were stolen, either because the market was sated or because of suspicion over their authenticity (Gill and Chippindale, 1993). The fear of forgery in these unsavoury dealings was well exemplified by the Haçilar ceramic figurines (see Chapter 9, p. 193), where once it was established that a substantial proportion of the figurines that had been acquired by major museums were forgeries, the market in them collapsed. If curators from the British Museum and the Ashmolean in Oxford could be so easily fooled what chance had the ordinary collector? The only defence was scientific authentication, in this instance TL.

Terracotta figurines from Mali (see Chapter 6, p. 117) were being looted and offered for sale on the market through the 1970s and 80s. It was known that there were many fakes and forgeries and TL tests were vital for the acceptance of genuine items. Thus, the rather extraordinary situation arose where the activities of the forgers were actually curbing the illicit trade but their efforts were bring undermined by the university-based authenticators. Effectively the authentication laboratories were supporting an illegal trade that was despoiling the cultural heritage of West Africa.

Thus, one response to the argument that the technical details of antiquities should not be published could be that only those antiquities with no documented history, which are by and large the illegal pieces, would be made more difficult to authenticate. Museums and legitimate collectors should only be acquiring material with reliable documentation to prove that it had left its presumed country of origin before the local legislation there was enacted prohibiting its export. In most countries this was approximately in the mid-twentieth century, or, at the latest, from the time of the UNESCO convention of 1970. In the case of documented antiquities that it is legitimate to acquire, the publication of technical detail in the subsequent years is of positive benefit in their authentication.

Responsible laboratories therefore should not, as a general rule, undertake the authentication of the undocumented antiquities except possibly to remind the collecting world of the prevalence of fakes and forgeries and thus keep the market depressed. Unfortunately, the likelihood that a piece has been stolen or looted does not seem to deter purchasers; the possibility that it is forged does.

2

Physical examination I: Observation

Scientists should use the instrument(s) best suited for their immediate problem. Instead, we all use the instrument we have and that is usually the most expensive, biggest and most automated instrument we can talk our supervisor or NSF to buy for us. We like those instruments into which you insert the sample and, in a few seconds, get a hard-copy print-out of the 'answer'.

Walter McCrone (1987/88a)

This chapter surveys the principal observational techniques used in the examination of antiquities, followed by a discussion of the evidence of wear. The following chapter deals with analytical techniques. Some techniques, notably scanning electron microscopy, combine both observational and analytical facilities and are dealt with in this chapter.

Sources for scientific examination and analysis

The works in this selection cover both observational and analytical scientific methods applied to antiquities and art objects. For works on authenticity in general, see Chapter 1, p. 7.

Michael Tite's excellent 1972 *Methods of Physical Examination in Archaeology* is now out of date in many areas. It has been replaced by works such as *Modern Analytical Techniques in Art and Archaeology* (Ciliberto and Spoto (eds), 2000), which concentrates on the scientific examination and analysis of objects and materials. Ferretti's (1993) *Scientific Investigations of Works of Art*, gives a succinct description of a variety of physical and chemical techniques. Pollard and Heron's (1996) *Archaeological Chemistry* has a very good chapter on analytical techniques. In many books on more general scientific archaeology, such as those of Goffer (1980), Hours (ed) (1980), Bowman (ed) (1991), Lambert (1997), and Henderson (2000), much of the work is taken up with artefact-orientated case studies. Some of Joseph Lambert's examples are authenticity studies and the books of Zvi Goffer and Sheridan Bowman both include whole sections devoted to scientific authenticity. Stuart Fleming's *Authenticity in Art* (1975) is the one work devoted to scientific authentication (see Chapter 1, p. 8).

There are many articles available dealing with scientific authentication, exemplified by Riederer (1977), Fleming (1979a, 1993), Beale (1990), Craddock and Bowman (1991), Newman (1992a), Craddock (1997), and Roy (2006).

There are also several series of conference proceedings on archaeometry, generally that contain many articles on the scientific examination of objects, including some specifically on authenticity. Examples of these include: the *Application of Science in Examination of Works of Art* series, published by the Research Laboratory of the Museum of Fine Arts, Boston; the *Material Issues in Art and Archaeology* series published by the Materials Research Society of America; the various *Proceedings* of the Archaeometry conferences; the *Archaeological Chemistry* series published by the American Chemical Society and the preprints of the International Institute for Conservation (IIC) conferences.

Relevant articles are to be found in a very wide range of specialised periodicals, but a cursory glance at the Bibliography shows the especial importance of *Studies in Conservation* and *Archaeometry*.

The Art and Antiquities Technical Abstracts (AATA) published by the IIC are an invaluable source, and these are now published electronically. Web sites generally are assuming ever greater importance as sources of information and some have been included in this work.

Examination

It is well known that one sees with the brain rather than with the eye, and thus the brain tends to 'see' the familiar and expected. This can be both positive and negative in authenticity investigations. It can be positive because the diagnostic features of a particular style or type, or the typical ageing or patination phenomena become ingrained and appear strongly, or conversely, they are conspicuously absent or are jarringly wrong. This familiarity can be negative when there is an unconscious tendency to try to push the visual evidence into a preconceived scenario.

It is best to carry out the first examination without knowing too much about the background of the piece, and thus what one is expected to find. This first visual examination should be carried out unhurriedly after a preliminary discussion on the object's general background, but omitting leading detail. One should always use some form of magnification, a hand lens at least, or preferably a binocular microscope. The purpose of this general examination is simply to get to know the object. At this stage one is not directed to the specific areas or questions upon which the authenticity will depend, but rather to gather evidence on how the piece was made and what evidence there is for use, alteration, repair and the sequence of events, etc.; the relationships between wear and tool marks are particularly important (see p. 36). The individual elements of evidence and observations should be sketched and written down and can initially result in dozens of separate observations that are often contradictory. One must then return to the microscope and check the observations, now consciously trying to build scenario(s) that encompass all the observations. It should be noted that small amounts of wax or other modelling materials are frequently observed in depressions on the surface of many artefacts, both ancient and modern. There is nothing particularly significant in this; it is just where an impression has been made for record purposes.

The digitisation of images is having a continuing impact on all visual techniques (MacDonald (ed), 2006). The digital image is often more accurate than the photograph analogue and can be manipulated in ways that are inconceivable by conventional imagery (see Chapter 12, p. 272).

Light microscopy

The most versatile and powerful tool for the examination of antiquities for authentication, as for more general studies, remains the human eye with an informed brain at one end and a good stereo-binocular reflected light microscope at the other.

A single hand-lens can only give a relatively low magnification over a rather small area or depth of field without serious distortion, and is thus most useful for gemmology studies or patinas, or for examining maker's marks, hall marks, registration marks, etc. For higher magnification the compound lens is essential (Bradbury and Bracegirdle, 1998; Tite, 1972).

Illumination can be effected either by transmission, that is from beneath, through the specimen, or by reflectance off the specimen from above or to the side. Transmitted light is directed through a thin slice of the material mounted on a glass microscope slide, or through the unmounted specimen if it is sufficiently transparent, as is the case with most gemstones (see Chapter 16, p. 395 for more on gemmological microscopy).

For reflectance microscopy a good light source is essential. To provide uniform and shadowless illumination a high-intensity ring light attached to the end of the microscope tube is necessary. To provide raking light at suitable angles to pick up any slight surface irregularities by their shadows, a pair of fibre-optic tubes that can be set to any angle is useful.

The stereo-binocular reflected light microscope should have a good depth of field and zoom facilities to vary the magnification continuously between about ×5 to ×50. At a more practical level, it is important that objects can be freely manoeuvred beneath the objective lens during examination without becoming entangled in clamps or adjusting screws etc., and that the microscope is stable without being affected by vibration. It is imperative that the microscope has good facilities for photographic recording of the images. The images from digital cameras with direct PC operation can be displayed on a monitor, enabling several people to view them simultaneously and to directly discuss significant points.

A top-range instrument with a variety of attachments can be obtained for well under £5000, although the digital camera setup will cost in the region of £8000 and should top the list of essential apparatus for any institution involved with the examination of antiquities or works of art.

A petrological microscope is a compound microscope with facilities to transmit and analyse polarised light (McCrone *et al.*, 1999). The purpose of its use is to study the effect on the orientation of light as it passes through various materials, and it is especially useful for the identification of mineral species seen in polished thin sections in the study of ceramics, glass and stone (see Figure 11.1).

The petrological thin sections have to be cut from the artefact and this does real damage. Thus in authenticity studies it is rarely possible to take such samples except perhaps from large objects such as stone statuary. More often a tentative identification of the stone has to be done on the surface with the aid of a hand lens or binocular microscope. CT scans can non-destructively provide some petrological information (see p. 32 and Figure 2.11).

Metallography reveals the structure of a metal (Scott, 1991a) which is determined by composition and the forming processes (see Chapter 8 and Figure 14.3). It is also invaluable for establishing whether a corrosion layer is likely to have developed naturally or is artificial (see Figure 14.3).

The samples are ideally obtained by making 'v' cuts into the artefact. This exposes a section through the metal from the surface to the interior. However, such sections, which could be up to a centimetre in length, would create very real damage even when reinserted, and as such their use is not usually feasible in authenticity investigations. It may be permissible to polish the necessary optical flat upon an edge of the object. This is known as a taper section. Although this does not involve removing much material from the object it nevertheless does damage the surface, and the bright shiny metal exposed can be very conspicuous especially on corroded objects. This can be toned down afterwards with a patinating agent such as potassium sulphide solution.

The problem with taper sections is that they necessarily present only the surface of the object. This may be useful for studying the penetration of corrosion into the metal beneath, but if one is seeking to characterise the bulk composition and microstructure, one has to assume that the surface layers are representative of the metal as a whole. Unfortunately, very often this is unlikely to be the case (see Chapters 7, 8 and 15).

The polished sections are viewed by reflected light in the metallurgical microscope. Typical magnifications are in the range of between ×40 to ×1000, but some systems allow much higher magnifications. The most widely used metallurgical microscopes have an inverted stage geometry. The object, or mount, is placed with the polished section face down on the stage.

The section is usually viewed first in an unetched state to observe inclusions, especially their color. The section is then etched, common etchants being ferric chloride in hydrochloric acid for non-ferrous metals and nital (2% nitric acid in alcohol) for iron and steel to reveal the structure of the metal.

Electron microscopy

Sources: José-Yacamán and Ascencio (2000, pp. 405–444); Pollard and Heron (1996).

In optical microscopy a light beam is manipulated and focused with lenses, and the ultimate factor limiting the resolution of a magnified image is the wavelength of the light. In electron microscopy, light is replaced by a beam of electrons, which have a much smaller wavelength than light and, being charged, can be focused and otherwise controlled by electromagnets, which are analogous to the lenses found in a light microscope (Figure 2.1).

Through the second half of the twentieth century a number of extremely powerful and versatile electron microscopy techniques developed, enabling both the inner structure and surface topography of materials to be examined at very high magnification. These are usually coupled with a variety of microanalytical facilities. This has especial relevance for conservation and authenticity studies where the processes of ageing and degradation can be viewed, especially at the surfaces.

There are two principal forms of electron microscopy, transmission electron microscopy (TEM) and scanning electron microscopy (SEM).

TEM

In TEM the electron beam passes through a thin section of the material (José-Yacamán and Ascencio, 2000, pp. 414–429). Thus, TEM is mainly used for the study of the internal structure of materials at very high magnification, up to several hundred thousand times (Figure 13.26). As there is some diffraction of the transmitted electrons as they pass through the sample, the phases present can often be identified as well as observed. TEM has been relatively little used in the study of antiquities and art objects compared with the scanning version.

SEM

The scanning electron microscope with its magnification ranging from ×10 to many thousands at high resolution, together with microanalytical facilities (see p. 26), is one of the most versatile tools for the examination of antiquities (Olsen, (ed), 1988; José-Yacamán and Ascencio 2000, pp. 407–413). The electron beam is rapidly scanned in a stepwise manner (*rastered*) over the surface of the sample, which can be a flat polished section or the actual surfaces of the whole artefact if small enough to fit in the chamber. The electron interactions with the sample produce a variety of effects that are

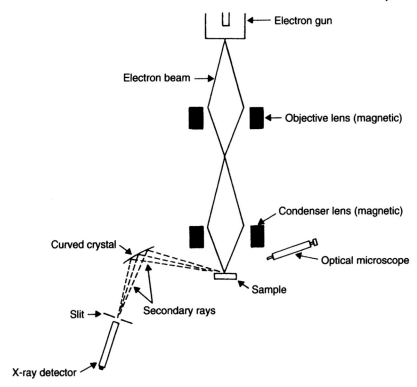

Electron gun

Electron beam

Objective lens (magnetic)

Condenser lens (magnetic)

Curved crystal

Optical microscope

Sample

Slit

Secondary rays

X-ray detector

Figure 2.1 Principles of SEM microscopy, with WDX crystal analytical attachment, for detecting the secondary X-rays emitted by the sample. (Courtesy Pollard and Heron, 1996)

detected and used for imaging and analysis. These are principally:

1. Low-energy secondary electrons that are used for conventional imaging.
2. High-energy primary beam back-scattered electrons that are useful for imaging phases in polished samples or for topographical studies.
3. X-rays generated with energies characteristic of the elements present in the sample, which provide analytical information.

For the examination of fractures or original surfaces a back-scattered electron image detector is positioned just off-axis and can produce excellent topographic images (see Figures. 8.29, 13.22 and 15.11). This is particularly useful for highlighting scratches from wear and polishing. The lines should be at right-angles to the detector, and it is necessary to ensure that none is missed by rotating and tilting the sample (Meeks, 1988a).

If the sample is a plane surface from a cut or taper section, the back-scattered electrons will record an image in the plane of the surface, based on variation in the composition (see Figure 4.21). This is because the number of back-scattered electrons generated depends on the electron density

in the surface which, in turn, depends on the elements present, the heavier the element the greater the number of back-scattered electrons. Thus, the image is in reality a compositional map of the main elements present and this can be very useful in cases where there are not many different elements present in the section.

Sample preparation and precautions
In a high-vacuum system it is necessary to allow the electrons to dissipate quickly from the surface, otherwise charging and heating problems will occur. If the sample is metal, this is usually not a problem (although areas of non-conducting corrosion can create difficulties). With high-vacuum SEM, for the majority of non-conducting materials it is necessary to coat the sample with a conductor, usually carbon, although gold is sometimes used. Clearly it would not be permissible to carbon-coat, much less gild, the surface of a valuable antiquity. This problem does not arise with more recent variable-pressure instruments. It can also be circumvented by examining an impression of the original, usually of silicone rubber, which picks up all the detail with remarkable accuracy (see Figure 2.13b), although with no analytical information (Meeks,

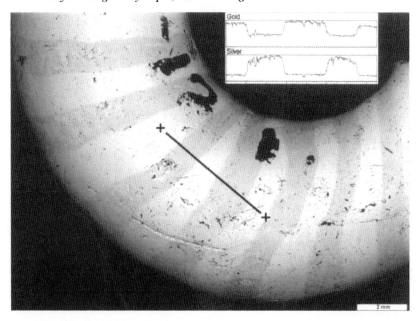

Figure 2.2 Superimposition of a line scan over the corresponding back-scattered compositional image. This has been taken across the surface of a Bronze Age gold tress ring that has been inlaid with silver-rich gold. (Courtesy Meeks *et al.*, in preparation)

1987, 1988a; Sax *et al.*, 2004). It is often possible to get much better topographical images with the impression than from the original. This is because the thin silicone skin is much more manoeuvrable within the microscope chamber. This is especially true for the investigation of deeply folded surfaces and other inaccessible regions such as drill holes.

Microanalysis in the SEM

The electron beam bombarding the sample generates fluorescent X-rays and their energy is characteristic of the elements that produced them.

As the beam size can be controlled, this enables very precisely defined areas to be analysed. For metals these can be as small as $1\,\mu m^3$, but somewhat larger for glass or ceramics. The most common method of detecting the characteristic X-rays is the use of energy dispersive X-ray analysis (EDX).

Alternatively, the fluorescent X-rays can be resolved into their various wavelengths, using a crystal spectrometer, that is wavelength dispersive X-ray microanalysis (WDX) (see Figure 2.1). EDX systems are quicker and more versatile, but WDX systems have traditionally had greater sensitivity and precision. This is the same as with conventional XRF (see Chapter 3, p. 47), but the differentiation is more important here because some of the higher energy transitions produced by a primary X-ray beam in XRF are not available in the electron microscope. Thus, the constituents of some ancient materials are currently only capable of detection or

meaningful quantification using the electron probe microanalyser (see p. 27).

Modern instruments employ detectors which allow very low energy X-rays from light elements to be detected, although variable-pressure scanning electron microscopes operating with air in the chamber have problems with elements lighter than oxygen unless flushed with helium.

The fluorescent X-rays can be used in a variety of ways. To provide an analysis of a defined and observed area, a line scan can be made across a sample and superimposed on the image (Figure. 2.2). Alternatively, a compositional map can be built up over a specified area, and where several elements are being measured their respective constituents can be represented in false color (Figure 2.3).

Assessment   The great depth of field at high magnification is an advantage of SEM over light microscopy (Figure 2.4). The ability to characterise features of the topography of naturally weathered and worn surfaces is clearly of great importance in authenticity studies as these are difficult to replicate artificially on the sub-millimetre scale. The ability to characterise the marks made by a variety of tools is also important.

One important drawback with electron microscopy is that it is, of course, impossible to see the natural colors of a material.

There is a small possibility of the electron beam damaging some materials, including glass (see Chapter 10, p. 222) and gems (see Chapter 16, p. 397).

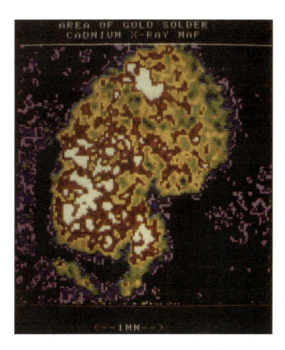

Figure 2.3 False-color digital EDX analytical map scanned across a blob of gold solder on a gold brooch from the supposed 'Lombard Treasure' (see Chapter 15, p. 381, Figure 15.16b). The map outlines the concentration of cadmium across the blob, showing that this is a cadmium gold solder of the type prevalent from about 1850 to 1950. (Courtesy Jones (ed), 1990)

Most scanning electron microscopes are now produced as variable-pressure devices, sometimes known as environmental SEMs, capable of working from high vacuum to about 1 torr pressure (Schnarr 1998; José-Yacamán and Ascencio 2000, pp. 436–444). The higher pressure circumvents both the vacuum problems in older SEM instruments and the need to coat non-conducting samples, and this is very useful for examining delicate and non-conducting antiquities.

Electron microprobe analysis (EPMA)
The electron beam is used for the production of fluorescent X-rays from the sample for WDX analysis. Because the apparatus is dedicated to analysis alone, it generally provides sensitivity and accuracy superior to that of the comparable WDX on a scanning electron microscope (Pollard and Heron 1996, p. 52; Northover 1998).

Modern EPMA apparatus always has EDX as well as WDX. It also has back scattered electron detectors in order to create the SEM-type image necessary to locate and identify the area analysed.

Figure 2.4 Comparison of depth of field, for light and secondary electrons at same magnification, of the radiolarian *Trochodissus longispinns*. The electron-image is much sharper. (Courtesy Goldstein *et al.*, 2002)

An unetched flat surface perpendicular to the electron beam is required for optimum analytical performance, and thus a sample is normally required, although small items such as coins can be analysed directly with a taper section polished to reveal a clean representative surface.

Assessment The analysis normally involves the use of a very small volume, which can be very useful when directed at minor inclusions, microscopic phases, compositional changes, etc. In order to obtain a representative analysis of the matrix a number of small area or spot analyses must be

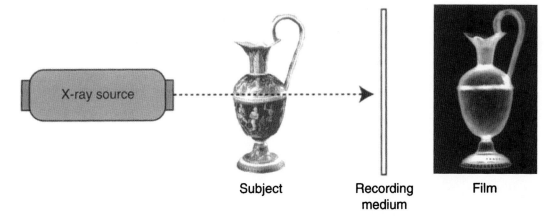

Subject   Recording   Film
medium

Figure 2.5   How an X-radiograph is generated. Note that the radiographic image is essentially two-dimensional. (Courtesy Lang and Middleton (eds), 2005)

averaged to counter problems relating to micro-heterogeneity. The very small spot size can create problems where the sample is very heterogeneous, for example in leaded copper alloys where the lead is very often distributed as microscopic globules in the copper, and one could have a scenario where one analysis was almost 100% lead and the immediately adjacent analysis was almost 100% copper.

Radiography

Sources: Meyers (1978); Gilardoni *et al.*, (1994); Borel (1995) Lang and Middleton (eds) (2005).

Several forms of radiation, e.g. neutrons, gamma-rays $\lambda(\gamma)$, electrons and X-rays, are to a greater or lesser extent absorbed as they pass through matter. In general, the heavier the atoms and the thicker the material through which they are directed, the more radiation is absorbed (Figure 2.5).

The potential of X-radiography for authentication studies, looking not *at* objects but *through* them, was realised within months of Röntgen's discovery (Bridgman, 1964). Damning details carefully hidden from investigation by reflected light are exposed by X-rays transmitted through the object and any disguises, as the following examples show.

The technique is quick and, in the main, non-destructive. As it finds such wide use for examining paintings, paper and gemstones, specialist radiography applications are dealt with in the appropriate chapters throughout this book.

The stone statuette (Figure 2.6a) purports to be an intact Egyptian antiquity. It is part of the

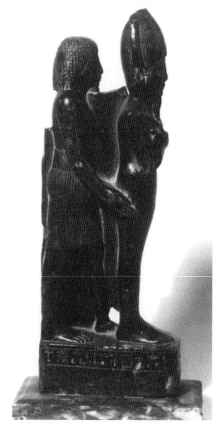

Figure 2.6a   Figure of a donor holding a figure of Osiris, an iconographically unusual arrangement, LDFRD 3132. (Courtesy of Freud Museum)

Figure 2.7a   Small Islamic glazed ceramic jug (BM OA Reg. 1952, 2-14, 1). (Courtesy Jones (ed), 1990)

Figure 2.6b   Radiograph showing large areas of plaster make-up (near-transparent) on the feet, etc., and stone elements such as the head of Osiris (moderately opaque) secured by metal dowels (very opaque), and probably not belonging at all. (© Freud Museum)

extensive collection of antiquities formed by the eminent psychologist Sigmund Freud (Jones (ed), 1990, p. 270). X-radiography (Figure 2.6b) revealed various fragments of probably genuine, but unassociated sculpture, which have been brought together and held with metal dowels with the rest made up with plaster.

The rather sweet, and apparently intact, little Islamic jug, BM OA Reg. 1952, 2-14, 1 (Figure 2.7a) was shown by radiography to be made up from a collection of sherds which comprised the majority of the original pot but with some areas, such as the handle and most of the rim, missing and restored with plaster (Figure 2.7b). As Susan La Niece (2005) remarked of this piece, 'A complete and undamaged example of a fragile ceramic is a

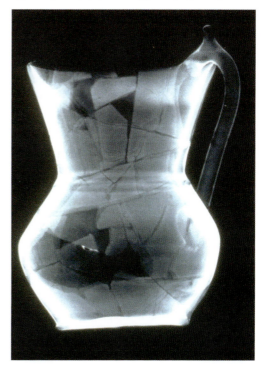

Figure 2.7b   Radiograph showing the jug has been completely remade from sherds, with some missing. Note the handle and much of the rim are of a more transparent plaster make-up.

collector's item, but only an archaeologist is interested in a bag of sherds'. She might also have noted that fakers can also very often appreciate the financial potential of a bag of sherds.

Neutron radiography is potentially useful as it is complementary to X-radiography in that neutrons are strongly absorbed by light elements such as carbon, rather than the heavy elements, and thus the technique has been used to detect cloth or skin linings inside metal artefacts (Deschler-Erb *et al.*, 2004). However, it is a complex procedure requiring access to a nuclear reactor or a linear accelerator to generate the neutrons. There is also a danger of short-term radioactivity being induced in the piece under examination.

Gamma-rays are more energetic than X-rays and thus have better penetrating power (Middleton and Lang 2005, pp. 4–5). Consequentially they have, on occasion, been used for the examination of heavy castings, as exemplified by the Greek bronze horse in the Metropolitan Museum, New York (see Chapter 8, p. 166). Gamma-rays are generated by the decay of radioactive atoms, and are much cheaper to produce than X-rays. The setup is also much more portable, although there are health and safety constraints with radioactive sources. A major drawback is that the sources lose their activity over a few years and it is not possible to modulate a source in any way, and the gamma-radiographs produced tend to be of poorer quality than corresponding X-radiographs. Thus, overall, gamma-radiography is inferior to X-radiography except when very high penetrating power or portability is required.

Electrons can produce radiographs but they only have very limited penetration, and thus are of little use for examining most artefacts, important exceptions being paintings and paper (see Chapters 12 and 13).

X-rays remain by far the most widely used form of irradiation. In most arrangements a linear beam of X-rays is directed at the object under investigation and the emerging X-rays are recorded either on film or electronically.

The degree of absorption is strongly dependent on the atomic weight of the material; thus, for example, copper (atomic weight 63.5) requires an 18 times longer exposure time than the same thickness of aluminium (atomic weight 26.98). Artefacts of gold (atomic weight 197) or lead (atomic weight 207) can thus present real problems.

The emerging beam produces an image that is approximately the same size as the object, although it is possible to produce an enlarged sharp image, without scatter, of selected areas with a special high-definition microfocus tube up to a maximum of about ×20.

A typical tube for industrial use produces X-rays with energies in the range 50 to 320 Kv, which enables a wide range of objects, from prints to statues, to be satisfactorily examined. For some very thin items, lower energies may be more useful or an alternative electron-based technique may be preferable (see Chapter 13, pp. 320). For larger items such as bronze statues (Born, (ed), 1985), more powerful specialist X-ray sets may be needed. Medical X-ray sets have a maximum energy of around 70 Kv, which is quite adequate for a wide range of purposes, but they are designed to operate only for very short durations and thus are only really useful for the examination of organic material of a thickness or density not much greater than that of the human body for which they were designed.

Digital radiography

Traditionally, radiographic images have been recorded photographically; however, X-rays are now routinely recorded electronically, and the resultant images are intensified (Lang *et al.*, 2005, pp. 25–31). These images are formed almost instantaneously and continuously, opening the way to several very important and interesting developments.

This procedure enables the correct beam energy to be quickly optimised, no small advantage over 'blind' film recording when the nature of the object is not known.

Another advantage is that the object can be set on a turntable and moved by remote control, which obviously greatly facilitates examination. The image on the screen is moving and, at a stroke, this overcomes one of the major problems associated with film radiography, namely that one is recording three-dimensional objects in two dimensions. With a static film the superimposition of the two sides of a vessel or of a hollow casting, for example, can be difficult to disentangle but, once the image is moving, the eye and brain resolve the components into a three-dimensional image. The moving image can be video recorded, making it possible to record a 3-D trip through an object. It should be noted that such prolonged exposure to X-rays could, potentially, be damaging for some objects and compromise TL authenticity testing (see p. 32). The digitised image can be enhanced, enabling more detail to be revealed than with film recording. This is an area wherein a great deal of development is taking place (Lang *et al.*, 2005, pp. 31–35; O'Connor *et al.*, 2002).

Ideally, radiography is carried out in a purpose-built room, lined with lead to prevent the escape of X-rays. Some systems confine the X-rays to a lined cabinet but there are constraints on the energy of the beam as well as on the size of object that can be accommodated and manoeuvred.

Xeroradiography

As well as recording the image on film or electronically, it can also be recorded electrostatically in a method akin to photocopying but which is sensitive to X-rays instead of light (Lang *et al.*, 2005). As with photocopies the resulting image has a very high contrast, and therefore sharp boundary changes, such as the outline of inclusions or voids (Figure 2.8; see also Figure 20.13), or the structure

Figure 2.8 Xeroradiograph of a seventeenth-century Bellamine jar from the Museum of London. Here the voids and filler particles are clearly revealed, and their oblique orientation is characteristic of pottery made on a fast wheel. (Courtesy Lang and Middleton, 2005)

of bone or of wood, are emphasised. The method also has a wide exposure range, which can be very useful when recording a composite object made up of materials of differing density. It is impervious to scatter, which is one of the problems with traditional film radiography (see below).

Xeroradiography is, or rather was, on the whole complementary to standard radiography. Regrettably, the past tense must be used because the method to all intents and purposes is no more. Xeroradiography sets have not been manufactured for some years and it is now impossible to obtain spares or servicing and the number of operational sets has dwindled almost to zero, one set still being currently operational at the laboratories of the Freer Gallery in Washington. Some of the major advantages of Xeroradiography such as edge enhancement have been obtained by digital image processing of conventional radiographs (O'Connor *et al.*, 2002).

Problems in radiography

One of the main problems with the radiography of art objects and antiquities is their very wide range of shape, condition and material, sometimes totally unexpected. This is much more so than in most industrial radiography applications, where the materials tend to be known and fairly standard. Also, the nature of the problem is often not clear at the outset; to a degree everything is a one-off. The apocryphal 'Made in Birmingham' stamped on an object in an inconspicuous place and disguised, could be as unexpected as it would be damning, but may well only be revealed with the object set at a certain angle and then only within a very close range of energy and exposure times. Image intensification is of considerable help here for preliminary survey, allowing real-time viewing while altering the position of the object and the energy settings, etc.

Scatter

Some X-rays are scattered from the tube or from the film cassette or are reflected from the walls of the chamber and pass randomly through the cassette, fogging the film and reducing the sharpness of the image (Figure 2.9). This problem can be alleviated by careful shielding of the cassette and by filtering out the softer X-rays, which are more prone to scatter.

Masking

This is a problem with composite objects where denser material masks the presence of lighter

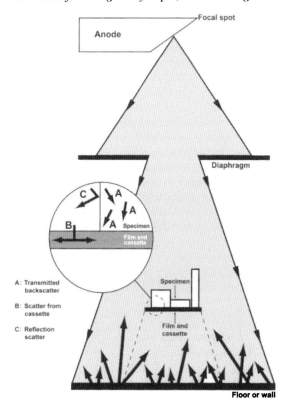

Figure 2.9 Origin of scattering. (Courtesy Middleton and Lang, 2005)

material. A good example is armour with cloth or fur linings. If available, CT scanning (see below) or neutron radiography could be applied (see p. 30), but often the only real option is to try to position the object so that the denser material is not in the way. It may be more advantageous to place small pieces of film in or around the object itself such that the denser materials are not in the path of the X-rays.

Superimposition

Film radiographs record, in two dimensions, information that is often three dimensional. For some items such as vessels or statuary that are well and truly three dimensional, image intensification can be a great help. On linear objects, such as sword blades that are inscribed and/or pattern-welded, stereo radiography provides a good solution. Two radiographs are taken of the same aspect, moving the source a few centimetres between exposures and viewed through ordinary stereo viewers. Alternatively, red–green stereo pairs can be made. The two images are scanned and superimposed, one in red and one in green, as a single image. When viewed through red–green

glasses of the sort issued in cinemas showing experimental 3-D films, a stereo image is seen.

TL enhancement

There is a danger that X-rays, and, even more so, gamma rays, absorbed by ceramic materials will generate TL, contaminating such natural TL that the ceramic already possesses (see Chapter 6, pp. 112–113). Rye (1977) and Braun D.P. (1982) suggested that exposure to X-rays would compromise subsequent TL dating but did not provide conclusive evidence.

The best known example of this problem occurred during authentication studies on the ancient Greek bronze horse at the Metropolitan Museum in New York (see Chapter 8, p. 166).

This is clearly of some significance in authenticity testing where both radiography and TL testing are important parts of the examinational procedure. Ghysels (2003) carried out experiments on a series of ceramic and terracotta samples which were TL tested then exposed to CT scans with X-rays and again TL tested with no apparent difference. Unpublished work by Debenham at the British Museum (quoted in La Niece, 2005, pp. 176–177) showed that when a piece of Roman tile was subjected to an X-ray dose sufficient for an ordinary film radiograph there was no significant increase in the TL.

However, as La Niece pointed out, if the ceramic was subjected to prolonged real-time examination by image intensification there could be a risk of building up a significant TL contribution. Also, in a court of law it would be difficult if not impossible to prove that the TL of a suspect piece had not been affected if radiography had been carried out beforehand. Thus, it is recommended that if it is intended to carry out TL testing as well as radiography, the TL sample should be taken beforehand (Rowlett, 1975; Carr and Riddick, 1990, pp. 61–62).

X-ray computed tomography (CT) scanning

Sources: Bonadies (1994); Illerhaus *et al.* (1994); Ghysels (2003); Goebbels (2003); Mees *et al.* (eds) (2003).

CT provides a radiographic 'slice' or succession of slices through an object and can thus reveal the internal structure of an artefact, avoiding the 'masking' of less dense regions common in conventional radiography. CT was developed for the internal examination of living people, but a natural extension was the examination of Egyptian mummies. The images of the internal organs of the still-wrapped bodies were quite stunning, and in turn prompted

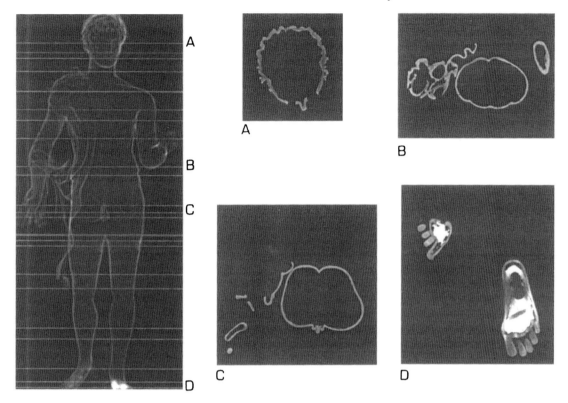

Figure 2.10   Selection of CT scans through a bronze statue of Hercules, showing the thickness of the bronze at various levels on the casting, as indicated on a conventional radiograph of the statue. (Courtesy Goebbels, 2003)

the application of the technique to art objects and antiquities generally (marc.ghysels@skynet.be).

CT is useful for revealing wall thicknesses and the inner surfaces of hollow metal or ceramic objects (Ghysels, 2003; Goebbels, 2003) (Figure 2.10). It can also reveal changes in the interior density of the materials, be they of metal, stone, ceramic or wood (Ghysels 2003). This is especially useful for determining whether an item has been extensively restored (Figure 2.11) or is made up of series of separate pieces (Figure 2.12). Because of the excellent resolution of the method it is able to detect very thin changes of density, voids or cracks in a variety of materials that would be invisible to the naked eye or to conventional radiography. A special and currently very prevalent variant on this theme consists the detection of forgeries of terracottas made up of carefully carved fragments of old bricks etc., skilfully disguised at the surface, to circumvent TL tests (see Chapter 6, p. 115, Figures 6.4 and 6.5).

CT has also been applied to dendrochronology, obviating the need to prepare an edge or take a sample (see Chapter 6, p. 128).

Other non-destructive examination techniques

Endoscopy

Endoscopy is particularly useful for inspecting the insides of hollow castings and vessels with constricted necks. Endoscopes are now available with a range of recording devices. Some have a tiny TV camera mounted on the end of the probe (Accardo *et al.*, 1988).

Infra-red (IR) and Ultraviolet (UV)

The necessary equipment is relatively cheap and portable. The examinations are quick, non-destructive and cover the whole object simultaneously. They are very useful for exposing repairs and restorations.

IR

Sources: van Asperen de Boer (1985); Kodak (1987).

Infra-red has a longer wavelength than light and thus is less liable to be scattered by small particles and is able to penetrate deeper into materials. Also, many materials, pigments, varnishes, etc. that are visually

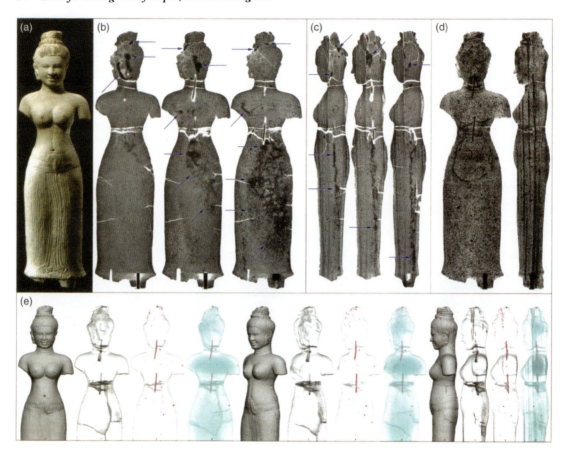

Figure 2.11 (a) CT scans. Khmer Banteay Srei style sandstone goddess of the tenth century AD from Cambodia. (Courtesy R. Asselberghs); (b) Three 1 mm thick coronal multiplanar reconstruction (MPR) revealed major breaks at the neck and waist held with metal dowels. The dark patches (indicated by arrows) are due to resin injected into the cracks. Were all the fragments original? (c) Three 1 mm thick sagittal MPRs; (d) anteroposterior and lateral maximum intensity projection. Together these show the differences in internal density of the stone, particularly the long lines of iron oxide inclusions in the sandstone in the lateral view which continue through the various breaks and demonstrate beyond question the fragments of the statuette are from one piece of stone; and (e) CT:Volume Rendering Technique (VRT) snapshots performed with 3D medical imaging dedicated software. They allow both the processing of high volume data sets and the simultaneous production of videos displayng 3D images in motion. These videos permit smooth 360° object rotation with the assignment of distinct colors and translucency in order to differentiate and enhance the various structural materials. (Courtesy Ghysels, 2003)

similar have very different IR reflectance or absorption properties. IR is much used in the examination of paintings (see Chapter 12, p. 287), and documents and cloth are also regularly examined by IR to look for alterations and restorations etc. (Chapter 13, pp. 324, 338 and Chapter 18, p. 461 respectively).

UV
Sources: Rorimer (1931); Moss (1954).

The use of UV in the investigation of antiquities was pioneered by James J. Rorimer, who would seem to have risen to the Directorship of the Metropolitan Museum of Art, New York, largely on the strength of this, according to his successor, Thomas Hoving (1996, p. 116).

The technique has been much used for many years by professional dealers, auction houses and museum curators as exemplified by Savage (1976, pp. 294–304; Hoving 1996, pp. 115–118, 146–148), as well as in forensic examinations. Exposure to UV radiation causes fluorescence in many materials. The characteristic colors and intensity of the fluorescence of a variety of materials can distinguish simulants from authentic materials, or reveal that a

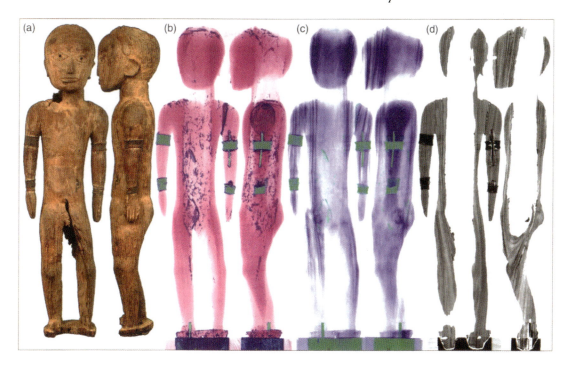

Figure 2.12 (a) Grave marker of wood with iron arm bands of the nineteenth century AD belonging to the Bongo people of the Sudan. (Courtesy M. Ghysels); (b) Volume rendering technique (VRT) imaging showing the interface between air voids and the wood. Most of the interior of the trunk of the statuette has been eaten by termites. The denser purple areas are restoration, and the green areas are metal. Note the proper left arm appears joined by a metal dowel in the region of the upper bracelet and to be held in place by an adhesive at the shoulder; (c) VRT imaging showing the denser ligneous wood fibres in the surviving wood in the head, shoulders and arms. Note the grain on the proper left arm does not match that of the adjacent body, showing it is a separate piece of wood, very probably a restoration. In contrast, the grain of the wood of the arm itself above and below the doweled join masked by the bracelet, is continuous showing that the arm itself, although probably broken, is at least one piece of wood. (d) Coronal and sagittal MPR reveals the grain of the wood particularly well, and also show that the proper left arm is of a different piece of wood to the rest. (Courtesy Ghysels, 2003)

surface has been freshly exposed and is not ancient, or that it has been recently treated or cleaned. The usual approach is to compare the suspect object with a genuine example. It is thus very good at quickly exposing deceptive restoration and additions (Chapter 11, p. 258; Figure 11.5).

The UV lamp was a favourite tool of Harold Plenderleith, who was for many years in charge of the British Museum Research Laboratory. He relates (1952) that:

It is an amusing experience to walk around the galleries of the British Museum at dead of night carrying portable ultra-violet equipment. The eyes become sensitive to the various fluorescences of different kinds of marble, occasionally an 'invisible' mend stands out as a livid scintillating streak cleaving the neck or limb of a statue, and equally conspicuous are such features as mastic [that is, gum or resin, nowadays epoxy resins]

stoppings and plaster fillings. The ability to differentiate freshly exposed surfaces makes it possible at times to tell with the lamp whether the inscriptions cut in the stones are ancient or modern.

As well as revealing the authenticity or otherwise of the Museum's marbles, this also clears up another mystery. The ghostly figure with strange fluorescent lights said to haunt the British Museum at night was not an insomniac Egyptian Mummy; it was an equally insomniac Dr Plenderleith.

Specific applications of UV in gem-testing are dealt with in Chapter 16 (pp. 396, 409), and applications in the examination of ceramics, sculpture, paintings, prints, the patina on metals, organic materials and cloth, are dealt with in Chapters 9 (p. 189), 11 (p. 258, Figure 11.5), 12 (p. 287), 13 (pp. 324–325), 14 (p. 367, Figure 14.13), 17 (pp. 426, 429 & 438) and 18 (p. 461) respectively.

It is necessary to allow a few minutes for the lamp to warm up and for the eyes to become accustomed to the darkened conditions. Note that UV safety goggles must be worn while the UV source is switched on. In common with all quick techniques that examine the surface only, there is the danger of contamination from materials used in restoration and cleaning. Modern detergents contain powerful fluorescing agents. There is also the possibility of treatments by forgers quite specifically to give newly carved surfaces a convincing UV spectra and Rorimer's UV lamp let him down on more than one occasion (Hoving 1996, pp. 144–146, p. 118).

Ultrasonics
Source: Gilmore (1999).

This technique is very widely used in industry to check for cracks etc. in the internal structure of materials, and should in theory be able to allow differentiation between a cast, worked or electroformed structure. However, it does require a good contact between the ultrasonic transducer and the test piece and unfortunately most antiquities have some degree of surface alteration which would have to be removed. In practice, radiography gives more reliable information and ultrasonics has been little used in the examination of antiquities.

The related technique of scanning acoustic microscopy has been applied to worn metal artefacts in an attempt to recover obliterated hall marks etc. (Benson and Gilmore, 2003). The degree of strain or working in the metal affects the ultrasonic waves travelling through the metal and these can be focused to create an image either from the surface for near-surface deformation, or on thin artefacts by direct reflection through the artefact giving information on the deeper structure.

Other techniques for the non-destructive determination of metallic structures include Laue diffractometry and neutron diffraction (Chapter 4, p. 86 and Chapter 8, pp. 157, 183).

Tool mark recognition

The investigation of tool marks has two very different approaches, the recognition of the type of tool used, and in a more forensic sense, recognition of the same tool used on several artefacts.

Tool mark studies in authenticity usually concentrate on showing that the tool marks were made by a tool inappropriate for the particular period suggested by the style and are described in the relevant chapters for particular materials (metals, Chapter 8, p. 173; jewellery and jade, Chapter 16, pp. 412, 418; and woodwork, Chapter 17, p. 444).

Recognising a particular tool from the marks that it leaves on different artefacts, thereby linking them to the same workshop, is another approach. This would seem an obvious approach where suddenly there are too many of a particular type of artefact on the market, which, although similar, were unlikely to have been made in the same workshop if genuine. Frinta's (1978, 1982) study of the punchmarks on supposedly genuine early panel paintings and frames, demonstrated that the same tools had been used on works that could not have been created in the same workshop if genuine. This approach has also been applied to the study of genuine antiquities, usually of precious metals, in order to try to establish that specific pieces were made in the same workshop (exemplified by Treister, 2001 on Greek and Roman jewellery; Coles and Taylor, 1971 on Early Bronze Age British gold; and Mortimer and Stoney, 1997 on Anglo-Saxon punch marks).

SEM with its combination of high magnification and excellent depth of field is especially suitable for examination either of the object directly (Fiegenbaum, 1996) or of a silicone rubber impression. Meeks (1988a, 1990) investigated the relationship of the two Celtic flagons from Basse-Yutz (Megaw and Megaw, 1990). The highly ornate and complex flagons have cast handles in the form of animals that were drilled to form the settings for inlays and the eyes of the creatures (Figures 2.13a and 2.13b). In addition cast bronze ducks are attached to the tops of the flagons and they also have drilled eyes. Inspection by binocular microscope showed that they were of similar profile, raising the possibility that the same tool could have been used to drill them. Silicone rubber impressions were taken and measured in the SEM and this confirmed that the principal dimensions of the eyes were identical and that they had been drilled with the same tool.

Wear

Evidence of wear is an important aspect of the history of an artefact, but is different for each material and thus is covered mainly in the individual chapters. Clearly, wear should be subsequent to the manufacture. However, where a plain but genuine item has been given an inscription or decoration more recently to enhance its value this sequence can be reversed, and the additions cut through or overlie the wear.

Figure 2.13a Bronze handle in the form of a springing animal from one of the Basse-Yutz flagons (BM PRB Regs. 1929, 5-11, 1 & 2). (© British Museum)

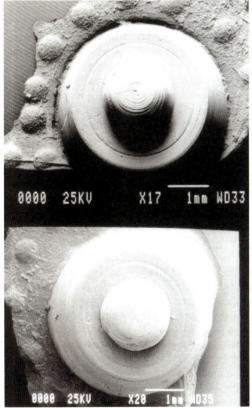

Figure 2.13b SEM back-scattered topographical image of silicone impressions taken from the Basse-Yutz flagons. The images show the eyes of the springing animal were made with a drill bit of complex profile. The depth and diameter of the two cones and angles of their sides are almost identical, showing the same tool was used and thus the flagons are likely to have been made in the same workshop. (Courtesy Meeks, 1988a)

The wear on an object falls into three principal categories, brought about by contact, cleaning and usage. All three leave distinctive marks concentrated in different regions and can be difficult to replicate convincingly.

Contact wear

This is the wear brought about by day-to-day contact with the world. Thus, the bowl of a wine glass might be expected to collect a little fine dust which could scratch the glass when cleaning it out with a dry cloth before use, and the foot of the glass could be expected to carry wear marks in an annulus on the underside of the base but strictly confined to the parts that would have been in contact with the surface beneath. The wear should be in the form of small, faint multi-directional scratches, superimposed randomly over each other, caused by rubbing against fine but hard dust particles caught between the base of the glass and the table or shelf and clearly they should not extend beyond the contact surface. Applied wear will often extend too far. Genuine contact wear can be expected to be concentrated at exposed extremities. The scratches on exposed extremities such as a spout or lip tend to be random and fine. Scratches on the handles can be more orientated as usually there is a preferred way to grasp the handle. One would expect wear on the front corners of a dresser top projecting into the room, but much less on the back corners which should have been standing against the wall. Contact wear can occur where one material has been fitted into another – for example the wear on a stone tool where it has been hafted (see Chapter 11, p. 269).

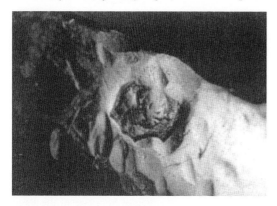

Figure 2.14 Wear pattern around the hallmark on the shank of a lady's ring. Such rough marks would be unlikely unless the lady concerned wore the ring while working on a chain gang. (Courtesy Duroc-Danner, 2000)

As with most simulated wear, faked contact wear is usually too coarse. For example, Duroc-Danner (2000) published details of a zirconia diamond simulant which he believed had been fraudulently passed off as a genuine diamond by being set in a worn ladies' ring. The wear (Figure 2.14) has been simulated by quite rough hammering and is most unconvincing. The typical abrasion of gold alloys during everyday wear has attracted some study (Heidsiek and Clasing 1983). Mechanical distressing by scratching with fine emery paper, sandblasting or rolling with pebbles have been used to imitate the appropriate degree of age and wear.

Damage can also be revealing, the forger having often clearly been torn between giving his creation some realistic damage but baulking at spoiling the piece. Thus damage is often confined to the rear side or in protected and thus unlikely places, leaving the more exposed but decorated areas intact. A good example is the famed Tiara of Saitaphernes (Vayson de Pradenne 1932, pp. 519–573; Jones, (ed), 1990, p. 33, Cat 4; Hoving, 1996, pp. 180–188). Such damage as it had suffered always seemed to avoid the areas of exquisite decoration or high relief, where wear and damage could have been expected. This, right from the start, was one of the features which raised doubts.

Polishing wear

Long years of polishing will produce pronounced and very characteristic wear on many materials. This can be distinctive both in its position and extent and in the wear patterns and texture of the polished surfaces. Thus, for example, on an Indian

brass statuette fixed to its back plate or *mandala*, it is possible that the front will bear the marks of heavy polishing, the back, protected by the *mandala*, less so, and the underside of the base should not have been polished at all. The build-up of polishing wear, possibly over generations of repeated hand-rubbing with cloths or brushes impregnated with generally mild abrasives is very difficult to replicate quickly. The scratches will tend to be rather random in their orientation, spacing and cross-section, although with a certain degree of common direction often dictated by the shape of the object.

The pattern of hand-polishing with a rag or with a brush over an uneven surface can be quite distinctive, the exposed surfaces being well worn but the recesses barely touched. This is, of course, common to all wear and polishing, but the regions in between can be revealing, leading to a distinctive borderland where the overall wear and polishing marks gradually diminish and cease. This region will tend to be very regular around, say for example, a cabriole or a baluster leg on furniture, when built up by regular but gentle polishing. When produced by a single operation even using successively more gentle tools and abrasives, the gradation of wear away from the exposed areas will be more abrupt. The wear induced by rubbing with an abrasive as a single episode to simulate prolonged wear and polishing will tend to be more oriented and regular than innocent polishing scratches (Burkart 1960). They are often relatively deep compared to either natural wear or polishing scratches and form small groups sometimes zig-zagging in formation, resulting from individual pulls of the abrasive.

However, wear or its absence is not conclusive, Cescinsky (1931, p. 14) in his work on fake furniture opining that 'Wear alone is a very unsafe criterion'. He then went on to give the example of some reproduction chairs that after a very few years of use in a London Gentlemen's club had acquired excellent patina and wear, and, as the converse, a set of chairs that had entered a house at the time of its construction in the eighteenth century had never been used and consequently looked new.

Evidence of now missing handles, locks, castors, etc., can be significant in exhibiting the history of an artefact and their former presence can sometimes be revealed by discrepancies in the wear patterns around where they originally fitted. Alternatively, an addition may have no corresponding polish wear pattern around it.

Although the evidence of wear is often more obvious on softer materials such as wood and most other organic materials, wear will form in some degree on all materials, even diamond. In general, faked scratches will tend to be too deep, and many will run in the same parallel patterns, simply because they have been made at the same time with the same abrasive (Savage 1976, pp. 234–235).

True wear is random in direction and gentle, and attempting to replicate this by hand is a very time consuming process; therefore there is a tendency to resort to power tools and to much coarser abrasives than would have been encountered in the formation of real-life wear. The latter tend to produce scratches that are of similar cross-section, regularly spaced and strictly parallel. The scratches produced by a power tool, either hand-held or a fixed buffing wheel, will tend to be unidirectional, or, even more revealingly, curved in longitudinal section.

In the same way that one should be suspicious of a piece in a condition that is too pristine, one should also be concerned about an ostentatiously over-worn piece, especially if the wear is uniform all over. Conversely, the over-zealous cleaning of real antiquities can give them the appearance of more recent artefacts (see Chapter 20, p. 503) and genuine antiques can be given spurious wear to make them appear more authentic (see Chapter 10, p. 234).

Use wear

This relates to the function of the object. For example, the clasp on a brooch could be expected to be worn through contact with the pin, which itself should carry reciprocal wear, unless it is a replacement (Leigh, 1985). The wear can be restricted to very specific areas of contact when resulting from real use, as exemplified by the wear on one of the links on the 'half-and-half' necklace (see Chapter 15, p. 384; Figure 2.15).

Wear on ancient stone tools has been extensively studied (see Chapter 11, p. 269). Faking wear can be difficult, although André Meiffert, the noted

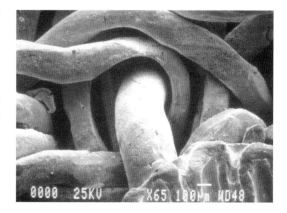

Figure 2.15 Typical genuine wear pattern on a gold link of the 'half-and-half' necklace caused by gentle rubbing of one link against another over long periods of time but with the necklace always at the same angle around the wearer's neck. Wear produced artificially by tumbling the necklace would be much more random. (Courtesy N. Meeks/British Museum)

French furniture forger, claimed to have employed workers simply to open and shut the drawers on his forged antiques in order to build up the appropriate wear (see Chapter 17, p. 444).

Moving components such as metal drop handles on a drawer may have made an impression against the adjacent wood after years of minor impacts and even though the handles may have been removed, the depressions remain. The canny faker may have realised that new handles freshly fitted should have made an impression in the wood indicative of long usage, and impacted these handles onto it, thereby creating indentations that might, however, prove to be quite unlike those caused by innumerable gentle contacts made over the course of many years. Only comparison with the genuine article will enable artificial distressing to be discerned.

3

Physical examination II: Determining composition

Basically if you don't know what it's made of you don't know much about it at all. (traditional)

Unless one happens to be lucky enough to be blessed with some kind of metallurgical divining skill it is impossible to judge the composition of an alloy by sight and feel alone. If it served no other purpose, scientific investigation at least stopped me making a fool of myself, and saved others from reading a lot of irrelevant nonsense based on a false premise.

Pinn (1999, p. 59)

This chapter surveys the principal physical analytical techniques used in the examination of antiquities. As with the previous chapter the emphasis will be on the informed interpretation of the data through an understanding of the principles behind them. In addition, the particular strengths and weaknesses of the various methods will be evaluated, together with their sampling requirements, as applied to authenticity studies.

Analytical techniques have been steadily improving over the last 100 years or so. Current areas of interest to archaeometry and authenticity work include sensitivity, versatility and accessibility. The ever-improving sensitivity of a variety of techniques is of potential interest for the sourcing and comparison of materials. An increasing number of methods now offer the potential not just to give a point analysis but much more versatile information in the form of a depth profile or a compositional map (see Figure 2.3), which can be of great value in the investigation of surface treatments. Apparatus is becoming more compact and thus the standard techniques are increasingly available in portable forms, enabling them to be brought to the object.

In authenticity studies there are two main approaches to the use of composition. For synthetic materials, the constituent elements or compounds can be analysed to ascertain if a material has the appropriate composition for the period to which it is supposed to belong. For both synthetic and natural materials, the respective trace elemental and isotopic composition can give information on their provenance (Wilson and Pollard, 2001). Even if the actual source cannot be determined it may still be possible to ascertain if the trace element and isotopic patterns are similar to those found in genuine objects of the same type.

The problem with the investigation of antiquities compared with other classes of material is their variety – in composition, construction, form and condition. Many of the materials encountered are unknown to most material scientists, who are familiar only with a relatively narrow range of modern materials, and completely unfamiliar with the potential changes wrought by prolonged burial and subsequent conservation and restoration treatments. These problems for metals, ceramics, glass and stone are discussed in the relevant chapters (Chapter 7, p. 137; Chapter 9, p. 191; Chapter 10, p. 222).

Sampling

As the sensitivity and precision of the analytical methods get ever better, when samples need to be taken, the amount required becomes ever smaller. This in itself is good news, but it does mean that there is an ever-increasing concern to ensure that the sample is representative and not contaminated.

When the composition of an object is requested by the curator/collector, there is rarely any formulated question beyond the obvious – what is it made of? Yet in order to be of maximum value it is essential that there are carefully formulated questions for analysis to answer. These will influence the method selected, the elements, molecules or minerals sought and the place(s) on the artefact selected for analysis. Sampling strategy should always be determined by the art historian/curator and analyst together.

There is also the vexed question of destructive sampling. In order to obtain information, of either the composition or the structure of the material it is usually necessary to examine the body of the material, which involves penetrating beneath the surface. Some techniques such as specific gravity measurements or radiography are truly non-destructive but for most techniques it will be necessary to cut or drill a sample or to expose a surface to obtain a truly representative sample. Some techniques sample by sputtering the artefact with a high-energy laser beam (see p. 46) or protons (see p. 50). Holes are created thereby, which to all intents and purposes are invisible, although the process may prove harmful for the object as a whole. Sometimes recent scratches expose the material beneath the immediate surface for analysis by microanalytical techniques on SEM systems (Andrasko *et al.*, 1979).

More usually for a quantitative analysis representative of the artefact as a whole, the choice lies between grinding away the surface to expose the interior or taking a drilling. In general, for analytical purposes, a drilling, although it may involve removing more material, is actually visually less damaging (Figure 3.1). To some degree the choice also depends on the material (see Chapter 7, p. 137 for metals), and for some such as glass it is very difficult to sample or prepare a surface that does not result in visual damage (see Chapter 10, p. 222).

Polished areas can be toned down afterwards either with paint or with patinating chemicals and holes can be filled. As a general rule it is preferable to do as little masking as possible. After all, the

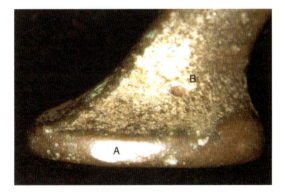

Figure 3.1 Comparison of the damage to the visual appearance of a metal artefact by a) polishing the surface for 'non-destructive' XRF analysis; b) drilling with a size 60 (1 mm diameter) bit to remove a sample for destructive analysis. (Courtesy S. La Niece)

sampling is part of the object's history and disguising it can add yet another element of deception to an object that may already contain much evidence of fakery or deceptive restoration. If the sampling position is undisguised it is clear to future investigators that work has already been done, and where. It is also important for the scientist to establish beyond doubt, and preferably in writing, the degree of destructive sampling and preparation that is permissible before work starts.

Finally, there is the question of the authenticity of the sample. Ideally, the analyst should conduct the sampling, but this is often not feasible, in which case the report must make this clear and that the analyst cannot vouch that the sample has come from the piece in question.

Accuracy, precision, error estimates and detection limits

Sources: Moroney (1956); Miller and Miller (1993).

It is necessary to know the accuracy, precision and detection limits of the figures in respect of all physical measurements. In authenticity investigations these relate especially to the figures produced by analysis or dating studies. The main physical dating techniques methods of radio carbon (RC), thermoluminescence (TL) and dendrochronology have very different theoretical backgrounds, practical applications, potentials and pitfalls, and their specific statistical treatments will be considered in the appropriate chapters.

Before any physical data can be used, be it a line measured with a ruler or an analysis made by MS, it is necessary to establish the reliability or confidence with which it may be used. For example, imagine a situation where, if a suspect silver artefact contains more than 0.1% of gold it is genuine, and if below that figure it is a forgery, and that analysis shows it to contain 0.12% of gold. By itself that figure is rather meaningless. If the precision is such that there is a high probability that the figure lies somewhere between, say, 0.11% and 0.13%, the analysis supports the authenticity of the piece. But if the analytical method is such that one can only say with confidence that the composition lies between 0.05% and 0.15%, the analysis is useless for the purpose required. Alternatively, we might have a situation in which gold was reported as not present, but where the detection limit was, say, 0.2% gold in silver. The analysis here is not just useless for the purpose required; if the detection limit has not been stated then it is potentially extremely misleading. In general, analyses given without the precision, the detection limits and an indication of which elements were specifically sought, are of limited use.

Accuracy and precision

Accuracy and precision are two very different concepts fundamental to all physical measurements. Accuracy is the measure of how close the result is to the true value, and precision is the measure of the confidence in the range over which results are spread (Figure 3.2a). Accuracy is self-evident, although difficult to estimate. Precision, also known as error, is a more difficult concept to grasp, at least to the non-experimental scientist, but is easier to calculate. For example an RC date which was quoted as having a 95% chance of lying between 950 and 1050 years ago would have a much greater precision than one having a 95% chance of lying between, say, 900 and 1100 years ago, even though they both centre around an age of 1000 years old. Estimates of accuracy are provided by running standard samples of known age or composition, whatever is appropriate, alongside the unknown test samples. Inter-laboratory tests run on standard samples are also undertaken to ensure an acceptable degree of comparability between laboratories. RC dating is perhaps the best example of a technique with a well-regulated and internationally standardised procedure.

Precision or error can be calculated in two quite different ways. Either one can take a number of replicate readings of the same event or process (always a sobering experience) and produce a statistical estimate of precision from the data produced, or one can assess the likely sources of experimental error, background noise from electronic instrumentation, ability to make up solutions accurately, etc.

A very simple and revealing experiment sometimes assigned to budding experimental scientists is to measure the length of a short bar of metal, say 20 centimetres in length, with Vernier callipers, and make say, ten repeat measurements. Of course there is variation, and the precision or error can be estimated statistically from the degree of variation between the ten readings, producing a Gaussian or normal distribution (see Figure 3.2a), expressed as the upper or lower limit, together with an estimate of the confidence that the true value lies within these limits (Figure 3.2b). This is usually expressed either as 1σ, which is 68.3%, or 2σ, which is 95.4%, or, very rarely, 3σ, 99.7%, confidence that the measured result (but not necessarily the true

value) lies within these limits. Most results are still expressed at 1σ although 2σ is becoming more standard, as scientists have at last realised the often woeful non-comprehension and misinterpretation of published physical data by the rest of the academic community.

To return to the metal bar, the statistical treatment of the measurements may have been such as to produce the result 19.9 ± 0.1 cm at 1σ. This should be interpreted to mean that there is a 68.3% chance that the measurements made lie between a lower limit of 19.8 cm and an upper limit of 20.0 cm, 19.9 ± 0.3 cm at 2σ; that is, there is a 95.3% probability that the length of the bar lies somewhere between 19.6 cm and 20.2 cm. Note this is an estimate only of the precision; a catastrophic error might have been made such as to read the Vernier off against the feet and inches scale instead of the metric, and here the results would still have the same precision, albeit wildly inaccurate.

The publication of the analyses must also provide an estimate of the detection limit, i.e. the lower limit of the concentration of an element, molecule or mineral in a given sample below which it cannot be detected. It is also imperative to state which elements or compounds have actually been sought. 'Not present' is analytically an almost meaningless statement, whereas 'not detected below 0.1%', for example, *is* meaningful, and allows the results to be compared with others, even if obtained by methods of different sensitivities.

An example of the problems caused by the omission of information on the detection limits was the report by Milazzo and Cicardi (1998) on the analysis of the various components of the *Corona Ferrea*. One of the objectives was to establish which pieces dated from Late Antiquity and which ones were more recent restorations. The central band of the crown was described as being of 'pure silver' but without any qualification or estimate of the detection limits. If the silver really was pure and had a gold content below about 0.05% then this would suggest that the band was modern. However, in their first analytical table, the silver band has an undefined '-' in the gold and copper columns, but the silver only totalled 99%. There was apparently a missing 1% which could easily accommodate the gold, copper and lead (the latter element rather mysteriously was not included in the analysis), but without an estimate of the detection limits it is impossible to know what, if anything, might be missing and thus no conclusion can be drawn as to authenticity.

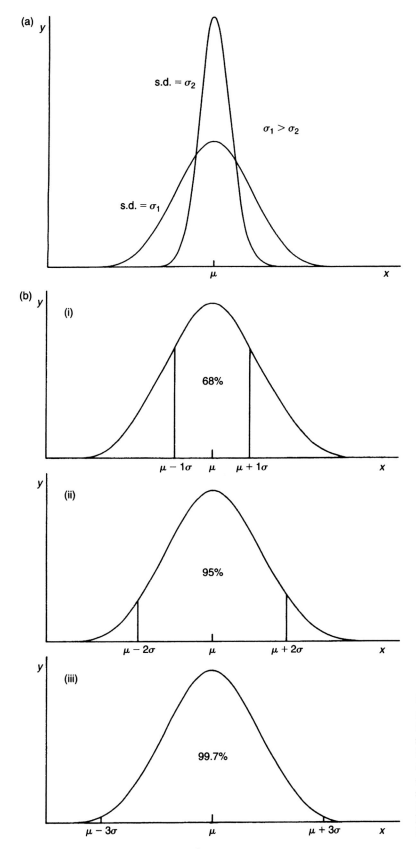

Figure 3.2 Gaussian or normal distributions of data. (a) Two sets of data with the same mean value but one set having a much wider standard deviation or error than the other. (b) The graphical expression of confidence at the 68% (1σ), 95% (2σ) and 99.7% (3σ) levels. (Courtesy Miller and Miller, 1993)

Analytical comparability

Analytical error

Another topic which has to be broached is the possibility of actual mistakes in the analysis. An inter-laboratory comparison carried out between 21 laboratories from around the world that were regularly engaged in the analysis of antiquities using a variety of techniques revealed some startling differences and should make sobering reading for those basing their conclusions on minor differences in composition (Chase, 1974).

Another inter-comparison, this time of the analysis of eight Roman brass coins by seven laboratories, all regularly engaged in the analysis of antiquities, found somewhat better agreement (Carter *et al.*, 1983). Even so, the differences between the results were still well outside the quoted precision of the individual measurements. Similar experiences were found in the inter-comparison organised by Cowell and Ponting (2000). The differences in the latter tests stemmed mainly from the different sampling strategies used; some methods required dissolution of portions of the coins, whereas others only analysed surfaces.

Perhaps a comparison of two of the case studies in this book which involved multiple analyses is more revealing. These are the Jüngling from Magdalensberg (see Chapter 8, p. 167) and four bronze statuettes now in the Ashmolean Museum (see Chapter 7, p. 143). In the first case study, portions of the same sample drillings were sent off to the various laboratories that had agreed to participate, two laboratories using ICP AES and two using atomic absorption spectrometry (AAS). It can be seen from Table 8.1 that there is good agreement between the analyses and that this should be fairly typical of replicate analysis of the same sample by the same method.

In the second case history (see Table 7.1), two different methods of analysis were employed – electron microprobe analysis (EPMA) and wavelength-dispersive X-ray fluorescence (XRF) – and different samples were used; indeed, the samples were not necessarily taken from the same part of the main casting of each piece. Brownsword's XRF method was used to analyse drillings mounted between Mylar film and Scotch Tape (Brownsword and Pitt, 1983). The EPMA analyses done for Fleming by Peter Northover, although not specified, are likely to have been done on cut metallographic sections taken from the body metal, with each reported analysis usually based on an average of three spot analyses taken on tiny areas over the face of the sample

(now considerably increased, see Northover, 1998). Comparison of the two sets of analyses shows considerable variation between the main alloying elements, namely the zinc, tin and lead, which almost certainly results from the various segregation phenomena in the castings, outlined in Chapter 7 (see p. 138). The trace elements, by and large, are in better agreement, especially as regards the nickel and silver. These elements are easy to quantify at the levels normally encountered in early copper alloys, leading to relatively precise results. The precision of the analyses was not stated but one suspects that for the arsenic and antimony at least, the detection limit was being approached by both methods and thus the precision will have been poor. Therefore, neither set of analyses was in overall error, but they do show that metals, in common with other materials, do not have a single overall composition.

Physical analytical techniques

The examination and analysis of antiquities is now dominated by instrumental techniques, but simple spot tests with the appropriate chemicals still have a role. They are inexpensive, require little or no infrastructure and, above all, are eminently transportable. They lack the sensitivity of some of the instrumental methods, and thus the detection of trace elements is not usually possible. There is also the ever-present danger of damage both to the objects and to the operatives that has to be carefully considered; Odegaard *et al.* (2000) describe some of the techniques used.

The basic principle behind most physical analytical techniques is to expose the sample to some form of energy and to record the response characteristic of the individual isotope, element, compound or mineral, etc. Very often the energy is in the form of electromagnetic radiation, which includes a wide range of familiar radiation, from radio frequencies through IR, light and UV to X- and γ-rays. The latter caused the electrons in the constituent atoms to move to higher-energy orbitals, from which they fall back releasing energy characteristic of the atom. The materials are often identified by the energies of the radiation they emit or modify, which are inversely proportional to their wavelength, λ; that is, the more energetic the ray, the shorter its wavelength.

Some methods automatically seek for a wide range of elements or molecules etc., whilst in others the specific elements etc. have to be individually sought sequentially. This is an important distinction, especially in authenticity studies where the unexpected can be of crucial importance. Often the analyst has little prior knowledge of which elements might be present and should be quantified, and in sequential methods usually a standard suite of elements is routinely sought for each of the main types of material – ceramic, glass, copper alloys, etc. – and thus the out-of-the-ordinary is also likely to remain the unanalysed. This could be circumvented by a preliminary qualitative survey by techniques such as emission spectrography (ES) or XRF.

It is important to be aware that some of the analytical methods that have become popular are insensitive to the lighter elements, such that for practical purposes it is currently difficult to detect, say, minor quantities of aluminium in a bronze and impossible to detect boron in a glass, both being elements whose presence would condemn their respective host materials as modern. This applies especially to XRF, EPMA and particle-induced X-ray emission (PIXE) (see pp. 47 & 50). The suite of elements regularly sought in the analysis of ancient materials often ignores those that feature in small quantities in modern materials, such as aluminium, silicon, phosphorus and manganese in copper alloys, and whose presence above trace levels would immediately show that the material was of recent origin.

The description given below of each of the analytical techniques will include an outline of the method, the sample required and an assessment of the particular advantages and disadvantages.

Emission spectrography (ES)

Sources: Britton and Richards (1969).

The sample is mounted on a graphite electrode and subjected to a powerful DC electrical or spark discharge. This excites the electrons in the atoms momentarily into higher-energy orbitals before falling back and giving off radiation of characteristic wavelength. The radiation is resolved into its various wavelengths by means of a prism or diffraction grating; it was recorded in the past on a photographic plate, and, now more usually, is registered electronically (Figure 3.3).

Emission spectrography was the first physical method to gain widespread usage and it was extensively employed to analyse antiquities up to the 1970s, and rather later in Eastern Europe and the former USSR, with some variants still being in use at the end of the twentieth century (Gegus, 1998). ES has now largely been superseded by techniques such as AAS and ICP but will remain important in the analytical study of antiquities quite simply

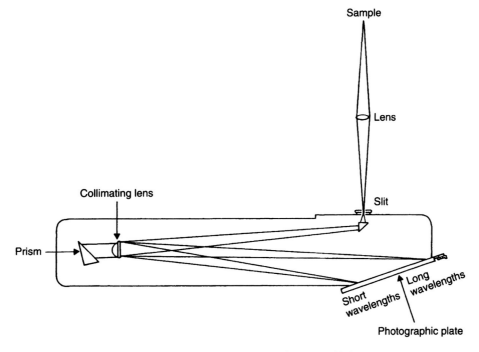

Figure 3.3 ES with photographic recording. (Courtesy Pollard and Heron, 1996)

because the method was used in so many important projects, some involving the analysis of thousands of samples.

Samples: For qualitative analysis a tiny solid sample from the artefact can be analysed directly. For quantitative work a sample, normally in the range 1 to 5 mg, is required. This is dissolved, followed by absorption of the resultant solution onto graphite powder, or onto the electrode. Some work has been done with laser excitation where the object is sampled and ionised directly by the laser, without a sample as such being removed (Gegus, 1998).

Assessment: The technique is sensitive over a wide range of elements; approximately 40 can be realistically quantified, including the light elements such as boron. The method excites and records the elements present automatically without their having to be specifically sought.

The photographic plates used in the past provided permanent records, which were very useful when dealing fleetingly with objects that thereafter would no longer be accessible, and this was the only opportunity for an analysis. The author frequently consults the old spectrographic plates made in the 1960s and 1970s to check the original identifications and to look for traces of elements, the significance of which may have been missed at the time.

The main disadvantages of the method are the inherent instability in the discharge and lack of reproducibility in the excitation conditions, resulting in rather imprecise analyses. This may be acceptable for trace elements, but means that the method is little better than semi-quantitative for the main elements.

Inductively coupled plasma atomic emission spectroscopy (ICP AES)

Sources: Potts (1987); Hook (1998); Young and Pollard (2000, pp. 32–40).

ICP AES can be regarded as a descendant of ES, the unstable excitation by electrical discharge having been replaced by a high-temperature plasma (Figure 3.4). The sample is usually introduced into the plasma as a solution. The elements present are excited and give off characteristic radiation which can be resolved according to wavelength and recorded electronically. ICP AES enables the elements present to be quantified over several orders of magnitude of concentration from minor traces to major component levels. A wide range of elements can be simultaneously determined on most instruments.

Inductively coupled plasma mass spectrometry (ICP MS)

Sources: Potts (1987); Tykot and Young (1996); Young *et al.* (1997); Williams (1998).

In another adaptation the ICP source is linked with a mass spectrometer. The ions formed in the plasma being analysed are passed into the mass spectrometer. This combination creates a method of extraordinary sensitivity for many elements. To date, archaeometric provenancing work has concentrated on gold (see Chapter 15, p. 371). Other materials such as stone have also been investigated (see Chapter 11, p. 251).

ICP MS instruments are now also capable of carrying out isotope analysis on heavy elements such as lead with sufficient precision to enable them to be used in archaeological provenancing studies (Gebel and Schmidt 2000; Young and Pollard 2000; and see Chapter 7, p. 139).

Sample: A sample must be taken and dissolved. A typical sample for a copper alloy would be between about 5 and 20 mg, and about 50 mg for ceramic material. Alternatively, the sample can be removed directly from the artefact by laser ablation (LA ICP MS), provided the object is small enough (c. 4–5 cm diameter) to fit into the sample chamber. The hole left by the laser is about 0.1 mm in diameter, too small to be seen with the naked eye. Clearly, only a tiny volume of material is analysed such that if the artefact is at all heterogeneous in composition this could lead to misleading results.

Assessment: The methods are very sensitive for a wide range of elements over an extensive concentration range. Owing to the great sensitivity compared to those of the methodologies it has replaced, ICP-AES has enabled elements at very low concentrations to be quantified for the first time and the potential of this for provenance studies is currently being investigated. A significant advantage for the analysis of metals is the ability to quantify non-metals such as sulphur and phosphorus down to trace levels. Hook (1998) for example suggested that the ability to detect the phosphorus in modern phosphor bronzes (only added since the mid-nineteenth century) may help in the detection of recent copies and fakes.

Atomic absorption spectrometry (AAS)

Sources: Hughes *et al.* (1976); Hughes (1998); Young and Pollard (2000, pp. 27–31).

In this technique, light beamed through a flame containing atoms from the sample solution is

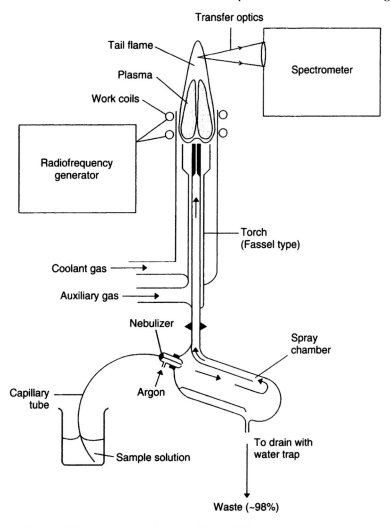

Figure 3.4 The torch of an ICP spectrometer. (Courtesy Hook, 1998)

selectively absorbed, the absorbance being proportional to the concentration of the element present. The source of the radiation is a hollow cathode lamp with the cathode formed from the element to be quantified, and the methodology is therefore sequential (Figure 3.5).

Sample: The sample once taken is dissolved. A typical sample weight for a copper alloy would be 5 to 20 mg, and for a ceramic about 50 mg.

Assessment: The method is versatile, and has a good sensitivity over a wide range of elements for the standard flame excitation method, much enhanced with the heated graphite attachment (Figure 3.6). Approximately 40 elements can realistically be quantified down to trace levels.

X-ray fluorescence (XRF)

Sources: Lutz and Pernicka (1996); Pollard and Heron (1996, pp. 41–49); Milazzo and Cicardi (1997); Cowell (1998); Moens *et al.* (2000, pp. 55–80); Glinsman (2006).

The technique was famously described as 'the curator's dream instrument' by Hanson (1973), offering instant non-destructive analysis.

The micro-components of the sample or object are excited by a beam of X-rays. The excited atoms in the sample give off secondary fluorescent X-rays, with energy characteristic of the particular element. There are two basic systems of separating and quantifying the secondary X-rays, energy-dispersive

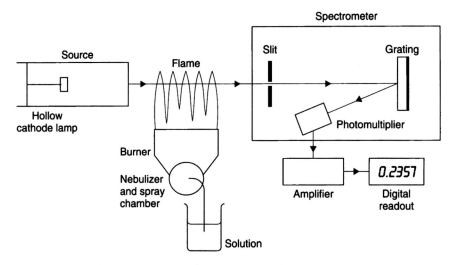

Figure 3.5 The operation of AAS. (Courtesy Hughes, 1998)

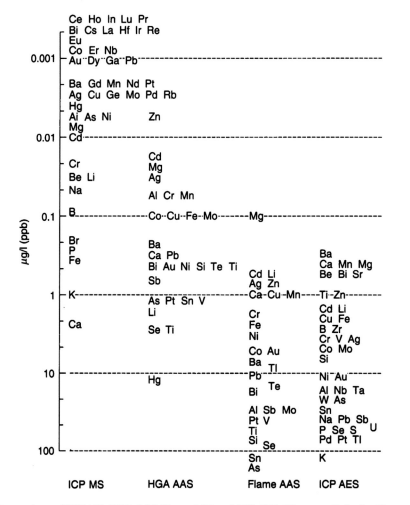

Figure 3.6 Comparison of ICP MS, HGA AAS, Flame AAS, and ICP AES. (Courtesy Pollard e Heron, 1996)

XRF (ED XRF) and wavelength-dispersive XRF (WD XRF).

In ED XRF the secondary X-rays are treated as energetic particles and their energies are analysed by a solid-state detector (Figure 3.7) (Cowell, 1998). All energies are detected and quantified simultaneously. The sensitivity of the method is rather varied, with the lighter elements difficult to detect.

In WD XRF the secondary X-rays are resolved with a crystal into their various wavelengths (Carter, 1998). The analysis is usually sequential. WD XRF has been perceived as being more sensitive than ED XRF with better precision for some elements, but over most of the range the two methods are comparable. Potts *et al.* (1985) compared ED and WD XRF for silicate rocks, and Verità *et al.* (1994) carried out a similar comparison for glasses and both found that, overall, the two methods were comparable in detection limits and precision. ED XRF is generally quicker.

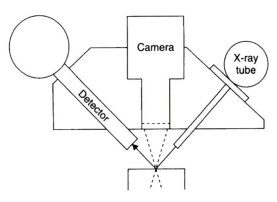

Figure 3.7 ED XRF. Note the video camera, and image below, for viewing of the area to be analysed, which allows very precise positioning of the artefact.

Sample: Both methods require a solid sample, but ED XRF has the potential to analyse the object directly, whereas WD XRF normally needs a solid sample that has been pressed or cast to give a flat surface. Most ED XRF instruments incorporate a chamber from which the air can be evacuated and can accommodate small objects, such as a coin.

Some instruments are set within a large cabinet to protect the operator from inadvertent exposure, and the chamber can thus be dispensed with. The artefact can be positioned directly in the path of the beam without sampling (Figure 3.8). Although this is very convenient and non-destructive there are some attendant problems. An air-path analysis will apply, with some of the X-rays being absorbed, unless the cabinet is flushed with helium. A surface analysis entails all the problems of relating this to the composition of the body material as a whole (see p. 40). Conversely the ability to analyse selective features on the surface can be invaluable.

Scott (2001) described the application of scanning XRF to the study of antiquities and art objects to build up compositional pictures in a similar fashion to those produced by the EDX systems in an SEM, but operating with higher energy X-rays.

Heterogeneity within solid samples can be resolved by taking drillings and analysing them either contained within gelatine capsules (Cowell, 1998) or evenly spread upon adhesive tape (Brownsword and Pitt, 1983). In either case, numbers of turnings or powder from different parts of the drilling will contribute to the analysis. The alternative is to polish a flat surface on the object, although this is usually far more damaging than a drilling (Figure 3.1).

Portable XRF systems are now available (Ferretti and Moioli 1998; Gigante *et al.*, 2003).

Assessment: In general, XRF is not as sensitive as some of the other methods described in this chapter, but, nevertheless, it is still adequate to quantify most elements occurring in above trace quantities currently with atomic weights above that of sodium. The ability to carry out non-destructive analysis directly on the object and to obtain the results almost instantaneously is particularly advantageous. ED XRF can be an extremely valuable adjunct to a stereo-binocular microscope in the rapid, routine authenticity examination of objects made from a wide range of inorganic materials. Thus, zinc can be easily detected in copper alloys, manganese in iron (see Chapter 7, pp. 147, 154) and lead or chromium in glass (see Chapter 10, pp. 224, 225), these often being important chronological indicators.

Figure 3.8   Bronze statuette positioned in the X-ray beam of an open-architecture ED XRF enabling instant and non-destructive analysis to appear on the screen to the right. (Courtesy A. Milton/British Museum)

It is worth repeating that light elements may not be detected especially if the X-rays have to pass through the air, as the following case history illustrates. Preparatory to the major changes in the British copper-base coinage made in 1860 there were a number of trial issues of different designs and alloys (Cowell, 1988). Some of these coins were analysed by ED XRF and initially reported to be of pure copper. However, the distinctive golden surface suggested that something else was also present and a combination of specific gravity measurements and EDX analysis in the SEM showed the coins to contain about 6.5% of aluminium, thus revealing them to be important early examples of the use of aluminium as a component of copper alloys. Cowell estimated the detection limit for aluminium in copper by air-path ED XRF to then be about 10% and, thus, it had not been detected using this method.

Proton (or particle)-induced X-ray emission (PIXE) and particle-induced gamma-ray emission (PIGE)

Sources: Pollard and Heron (1996, pp. 53–54); Kallithrakas-Kontos and Katsanos (1998); Andersen

and Rehn (eds) (2000); Demortier (2000); Demortier and Adriaens (eds) (2000); Dran *et al.* (2000, pp. 135–166).

This powerful technique uses a beam generated by a particle accelerator. The particle beam excites the sample atoms, causing them to give off X-rays or gamma rays, which can be identified and quantified by solid-state detectors in a similar manner to ED XRF.

Sample: A sample or a small object can be analysed in a vacuum chamber. Alternatively, the beam can be directed onto the artefact and analysed without sampling. This will take place in air and some of the shorter-wavelength X-rays generated will be absorbed.

In the related technique of Rutherford back-scatter, the energy of the protons that are scattered back from the surface is analysed. The change in energy is characteristic of both the depth of penetration and of the protons encountered.

By the controlled use of high-energy protons to sputter the surface it is possible to achieve deep depth-profiling through, for example, the corrosion layers on metals such as bronzes and surface-enriched gold alloys, through the various layers of a painting, etc. (Griesser and Denker, 2000; Neelmeijer *et al.*, 2000b), in one example even the analysis of gold plating beneath several millimetres of glass being possible (Denker and Maier, 2000a, b).

Assessment: A wide range of elements are automatically sought, and the sensitivity is generally very good, much better than for EDX in the SEM or EPMA. The detection of light elements such as carbon, sodium and silicon is relatively poor although better than for other techniques such as XRF.

The major practical disadvantage of PIXE is the very high cost of the apparatus (in the order of millions of pounds) and the large amount of space that is taken up. That having been acknowledged, the method has been applied to a wide range of archaeological materials and Pappalardo *et al.* (2003) have described the use of a portable PIXE system using a radioactive source to enable examination of antiquities.

Neutron activation analysis (NAA)

Sources: Hughes *et al.* (eds) (1991); Pollard and Heron (1996, pp. 54–61); Gilmore (1998); Neff (2000).

The sample or object is irradiated with neutrons in a nuclear reactor thereby rendering some of the atoms radioactive. Most of the isotopes thus created have a relatively short half-life and decay by emitting α and β particles, and γ rays. Often only the γ radiation is measured, or 'counted', and from the characteristic decay patterns the elements can be identified and quantified. Different elements have different half-lives and this can necessitate several such countings. There are usually two counts, one immediately on receipt, followed by another after several days or weeks have passed by which time most of the short half-life radiation will have decayed (Hughes *et al.*, 1991). NAA normally quantifies about 40 elements, including some, such as the lanthanides and actinides, which are difficult to quantify by other methods.

Sample: Strictly speaking, the method is non-destructive since the atoms return to their original state relatively soon after irradiation and the structure of the material is not changed. Thus, it might be thought to be a viable method of achieving whole-object analysis on small artefacts such as coins, but in practice this is not so because the outer parts of the material shield the interior from irradiation and thus the interior can be under-represented. Another problem is that the level of irradiation necessary for an accurate analysis down

to trace level could leave the object dangerously radioactive for decades, if not longer.

Postma *et al.* (2004) used the related technique of neutron resonance capture analysis on some genuine and forged Etruscan copper alloy statuettes. The method they employed enabled the whole object to be analysed without any sampling, although lead was difficult to determine. The procedure requires access to a powerful accelerator and, as Postma *et al.* stated, 'Only a very limited number of such facilities are available worldwide'.

Gordus (1972) developed a streak method for the analysis of coins, a roughened quartz rod being rubbed against a cleaned edge of the coin. Unfortunately the technique suffers all the problems of surface analysis such as those encountered by Walker (1976, 1977 & 1978) in his ED XRF analysis of silver coins (see Chapter 7, p. 138), although this situation was apparently investigated by Gordus and Gordus (1974) and found not to be serious. Karras (1988) compared whole-coin neutron activation analysis (NAA) with neutron activation streak analysis for a group of Bohemian silver pennies alloyed with copper, and predictably found that the streak analyses were much higher in silver. Rather more worrying, microchemical analysis of the streaks showed marked differences from the NAA results, with the silver content determined by NAA usually being higher. Mancini (1984) used transmission NAA to carry out whole-coin analyses of Roman silver *denarii* that were of very variable composition, and overcame the problem of surface enrichment. In common with most techniques, the most satisfactory method of obtaining a representative body sample is by drilling. Gilmore (1998) recommended samples of about 15 mg from metals (see Chapter 9, p. 190 for ceramic samples).

Assessment: The method is very sensitive over a wide range of elements although it is not as effective with certain common elements, such as silicon, calcium and magnesium, and a major problem, especially with glass and metals, is that lead cannot be detected. Even so, distinct analytical fingerprints can be established, which have proved very useful in establishing compositional grouping and in provenance studies for a variety of materials such as stone and, in particular, ceramics. The technique requires access to a nuclear reactor pile not too far from the counting facilities and, as many reactors have shut down in Britain and elsewhere, it has become increasingly difficult to have the samples irradiated, although Glascock and Neff (2003) commented that despite the number of reactors

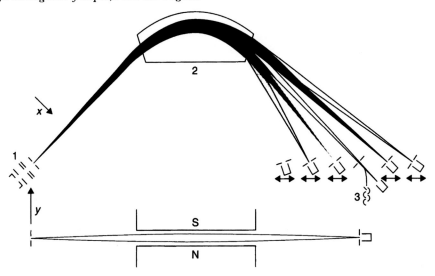

Figure 3.9   A 60° sector MS. (Courtesy Stos Gale, 1998)

having decreased, improvements in the counting technology meant that 'NAA was still readily available'. However, newer methods such as inductively coupled plasma mass spectrometry (ICP MS) (see Chapter 9, p. 190) have comparable sensitivity over a broadly similar range of elements, with the advantage that lead content can be analysed.

Mass spectrometry (MS)

Source: Pollard and Heron (1996, pp. 61–66)

In this technique the sample is ionised, either by ionisation of a gas for lighter elements, or by evaporation off a wire at high temperature, known as thermal ionisation (TIMS) for heavier elements. Each of the ions so created carries a small uniform positive charge, having lost one or more electrons. A beam of the ions passes through a powerful magnetic or electrostatic field that causes them to experience a uniform pull towards the negative pole (Figure 3.9). The heavier the ion the less will be its deflection, owing to its greater momentum. In practice the field energy is varied to produce a uniform deflection and the deflected beam is picked up and quantified by detectors, and thus the ions are separated by their mass/charge ratio. The standard instruments scan automatically and quickly through a range of elements. The great advantage of this method is that, as the separation is purely on the basis of mass, the various isotopes of individual elements are separated, and, indeed, isotope analysis is perhaps the most important application of mass spectrometry.

Sample: A sample has to be taken. The weight required is usually very small, such that in practice the amount removed is governed by the need to obtain a representative sample.

Assessment: The method is very sensitive and automatically covers a wide range of elements. Apart from isotope determinations, mass spectrometry tends not to be much used for elemental analysis but is used in conjunction with techniques such as inductively coupled plasma mass spectrometry (ICP MS), gas chromatography (GC) and high-performance liquid chromatography (HPLC). The determination of the isotopic composition of some elements, notably carbon, oxygen and lead, can be of great importance establishing provenance, and, thereby, authenticity (see Chapter 7, p. 139; Chapter 10, p. 222; Chapter 11, p. 252; and Chapter 12, p. 295 for metals, glass, stone and paintings respectively).

The radiogenic isotopes of strontium $^{86}Sr/^{87}Sr$ are increasingly important in the provenancing of a variety of materials, including glass (see Chapter 10, p. 223) and stone (see Chapter 11, p. 253), and in more biogenically focused studies such as the sourcing and authentication of vintage wines (Horn *et al.*, 1993, 1998; Barbaste *et al.*, 2002). Wines and spirits can also be characterised by the isotope ratios of their hydrogen and carbon, and RC dated (see Chapter 5, p. 96). Carbon from various sources can have very different $^{13}C/^{12}C$ ratios (Figure 3.10) and these differences can be very useful in authenticity studies, in particular showing that various carbonaceous materials are modern synthetic oil-based rather than

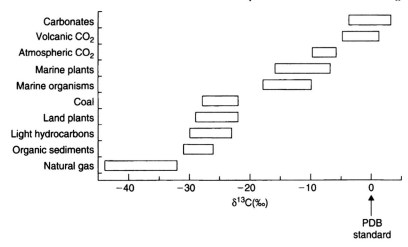

Figure 3.10 $^{13}C/^{12}C$ ratios for carbon from various sources. The ratio is expressed as the deviation δ of the isotope ratio from the Cretaceous-era Peedee formation in South Carolina. (Courtesy Fleming, 1975)

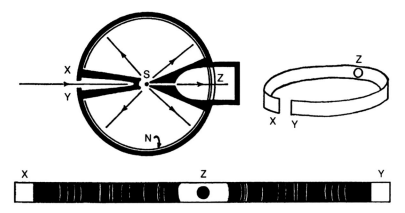

Figure 3.11 XRD camera. The X-rays are focused on the sample mounted at 'S' in the centre and diffracted on to the photographic film 'N' (and right). Below: Typical diffraction pattern. The position of the lines identifies the mineral. (Courtesy Hodges, 1964)

the natural plant-based materials they should be if old. The ratios can also be useful determining if wines and spirits have been adulterated, for example showing that the alcohol from an adulterated brandy owed more to an oil refinery than a grape.

Thus far the techniques described have been for the identification and quantification of elements. In many materials the elements are present as minerals or as complex molecules and it is important to be able to identify and to quantify these.

The disequilibrium which occurs during the smelting of metals between Radium ^{226}Ra and Uranium ^{238}U offers a possibility of distinguishing old from recently smelted metal (Ioannis, 2006), in much the same way as Lead-^{210}Pb disequilibrium is already applied (Chapter 12, p. 295).

X-ray diffraction (XRD) analysis

Sources: Lahanier (1986); Mantler *et al.* (2000).

XRD is used to identify crystalline materials. Whereas chemical analysis will give the amounts of the various elements present, XRD can identify the molecules. The atoms in a crystal are in a regular array with a uniform inter-atomic spacing and can diffract X-rays.

The diffraction pattern can be recorded photographically with an X-ray camera (Figure 3.11) or electronically using a diffractometer. The minerals present are identified by comparing the patterns against standard reference patterns. This is done either manually, or more usually, electronically and inevitably there are many instances where the spacings of different minerals are close together or overlap and it is a great help to carry out a quick XRF or other qualitative analysis to determine which elements are present and thereby narrow down the mineralogical possibilities.

Sample: In the standard powder methods an extremely small solid sample is required. Technically speaking the sampling is destructive, but in reality it is so small-scale that usually no perceptible damage is done. New completely non-destructive methods on unprepared surfaces are now available that can accommodate artefacts of up to 60 cm in diameter, and have been successfully used to identify the minerals in artefacts as diverse as a jade axe, a corroded bronze, a gemstone and the pigments on a manuscript (Chiari *et al.*, 1996).

Assessment: XRD is invaluable for identifying minerals across a wide range of inorganic materials including ceramics, the crystalline phases within glasses and glazes, and stone (including gemstones, see Chapter 16, p. 396 and pigments, see Chapter 12, p. 299). Although Raman spectroscopy (RS) is of increasing importance, XRD is currently the main method used to identify corrosion and patination products, especially on metals (see Chapter 14, p. 365). The appearance of the XRD pattern can also provide information on the crystal lattice itself, giving important clues as to its formation. For example, a natural patination on a metal will have built up slowly over the years and developed a regular crystalline lattice which, in turn, will produce clear and sharply defined XRD patterns, whereas rapidly developed patinas of the same mineral will tend to give much more diffuse patterns. XRD is also of considerable use for the identification of a wide range of natural and synthetic organic fibres (French and Gardner, 1980).

The determination of metallographic structure by XRD
As metals are crystalline, XRD can be used in certain cases to determine physical properties such as grain size and residual stress. This information can give some indication of the methods by which the artefact was formed – wrought, cast or electroformed. An advantage is that this technique is essentially non-invasive, unlike most metallographic techniques.

The most familiar method is Laue back-reflectance diffractometry, in which X-rays are beamed onto the surface of the metal. The form of the resulting pattern is very much dependent on the grain size at the surface of the metal (Figure 3.12). Large grains, associated with castings, give a pattern made up of a number of discrete dots, whereas

small grains typical of hammered or struck metal produce large numbers of smaller dots that join to form continuous rings, and the very fine grains of electroforms give another distinctive pattern (see Chapter 4, p. 86). The grains in rolled metalwork are highly orientated and produce a distinctive pattern made up of a few large dots. Striegel (1998) reviewed the methodology specifically for coins and medals (see Chapter 8, pp. 157, 183).

Although the use of Laue diffractometry has been suggested for the testing of antique metalwork since the 1950s the method has not been widely applied.

Two other related XRD techniques, diffraction profiling (Andrasko *et al.*, 1979) and residual stress analysis (Striegel, 1998), also provide information on grain size and crystalline structure of metals, and these again can be related to the original methods of forming the artefact, differentiating between cast structures, hot and cold deformation, etc.

A serious problem with these reflectance methods is that they are all interacting with the immediate surface of the artefact, and thus any surface tooling, heavy wear or polishing together with surface treatments or patination will interfere with the pattern generated by the underlying structure of the object as a whole. If the artefact is sufficiently thin and a source of high-energy X-rays is available to penetrate the metal, transmission X-ray analysis can be used to examine the whole structure. Stephenson *et al.* (2001) used high-energy X-rays generated by a synchrotron to differentiate between cast, hammered and rolled components of two brass astrolabes (Figure 3.12).

Raman spectroscopy (RS) and Raman microscopy (RM)

Sources: Coupry and Brissaud (1996); Turrell and Corset (1996); Cariati and Bruni (2000, pp. 255–278); Edwards (2001); Lewis and Edwards (eds) (2001); Smith and Clark (2001) (good bibliography); Clark (2002); Kiefer, (ed) (2004); Edwards and Chalmers (eds) (2005); Vandenabeele and Edwards (2005).

On exposing some materials to a monochromatic source of light, most light is either transmitted or reflected, but a small proportion is scattered; that is, it is momentarily absorbed by the molecules before being re-emitted as scattered radiation at the same frequency. A very tiny amount of the re-emitted light will be at a slightly different frequency, and this is known as Raman scattered light. The frequency change for a given monochromatic source is

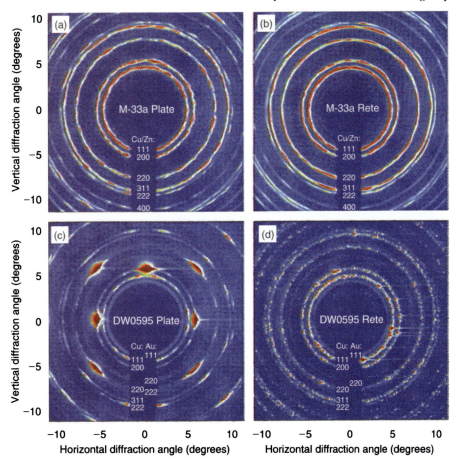

Figure 3.12 X-ray transmission Laueogram using high-energy X-rays revealing different structures in two astrolabes (see Chapter 8, p. 157). a) and b) both have the continuous ring pattern typical of the small grains in hammered or struck metalwork, c) has the distinctive pattern generated by the highly orientated grains of rolled metals and d) has the numerous points generated by the grains of cast metal. (Courtesy Stephenson *et al.*, 2001)

characteristic of the molecule. A very wide range of both inorganic and organic molecules have characteristic Raman scattered frequencies, and this forms the basis for the analytical technique (Figure 3.13).

RS is an extremely versatile technique that can be used in the analysis of a wide range of organic and inorganic materials, both crystalline and amorphous. As such, the technique is finding application for a wide range of materials. It can be non-destructive and materials can be analysed *in situ* and in some circumstances even when still behind their protective glass. Hänni *et al.* (1997) for example, described the analysis of the diamonds on the hands of a watch still behind the watch glass, and Derbyshire and Withnall (1999) were able to identify the pigments in a miniature through the surrounding glass.

The addition of a microscope to the RS systems has greatly increased the usefulness of the method, enabling the analyst to focus on very small specific areas, such as a single painted line on a watercolor or an individual crystal and analyse these to the exclusion of the surroundings (Figure 3.14).

The Raman effect extends to the IR region and can be analysed by interferometry and Fourier transform treatments applied in a very similar manner to FTIR described below (see p. 58), with similar gains in sensitivity. Another advantage of using IR is the avoidance of many of the problems of fluorescence associated with the interaction of light with many organic materials (Edwards, 2001).

Surface-enhanced Raman scattering (SERS) and surface-enhanced resonance Raman scattering

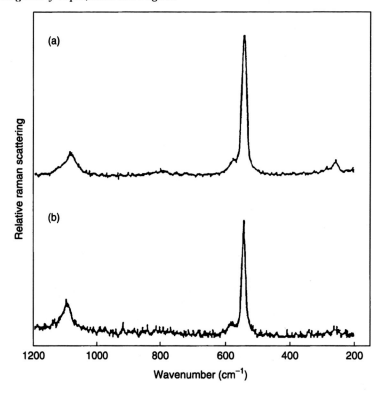

Figure 3.13 Typical Raman trace of wave number *vs* reflectance. The upper trace is from a blue pigment on a twelfth-century manuscript, the lower is a reference spectrum for ultramarine prepared from lapis lazuli. (Courtesy Coupry and Brissaud, 1996)

(SERRS) are very sensitive variant techniques especially useful for the detection and estimation of chromophones (Withnall *et al.*, 2005). These techniques are proving especially useful for characterising specific dye and ink samples etc. in forensic studies and the extension to authenticity work is obvious. The spectra obtained are complex and are not always easy to translate into real compounds. However, just by being complex it can be shown that the spectra of the original and the suspected alterations are the same or different.

Sample: A small sample of a few micrograms may be necessary, but RM is non-destructive.

Assessment: Probably the greatest advantage is the ability to focus on specific areas and identify these quickly and non-destructively. Portable RM systems are also available utilising fibre optics (Reiche *et al.*, 2004).

The presence of materials that fluoresce has been a major problem. Thus the method has not been much used on paintings in oil media, although some work has been reported (Mathieson and Nugent, 1996).

RS and related techniques are used on a very wide range of materials, both inorganic and organic. As the methodology can be used to analyse both organic and inorganic materials simultaneously, it finds use in the study of their interactions, in oil paint and on parchment for example (Edwards and Pull Perez, 2004), which could potentially be very useful for recognition of the characteristic natural long-term ageing of such mixed materials (Chapter 12, p. 298).

Comparison of XRD, infra-red spectrometry (IRS) and RS

The methodology has affinities with IRS where the latter technique uses the absorbance of the radiation rather than the scattering, and the two techniques are often complementary, materials that are not easy to identify by one technique being more tractable when investigated using the other. As the technique is concerned with the identification of molecules and compounds there is also an overlap with XRD if the material is crystalline. As XRD is

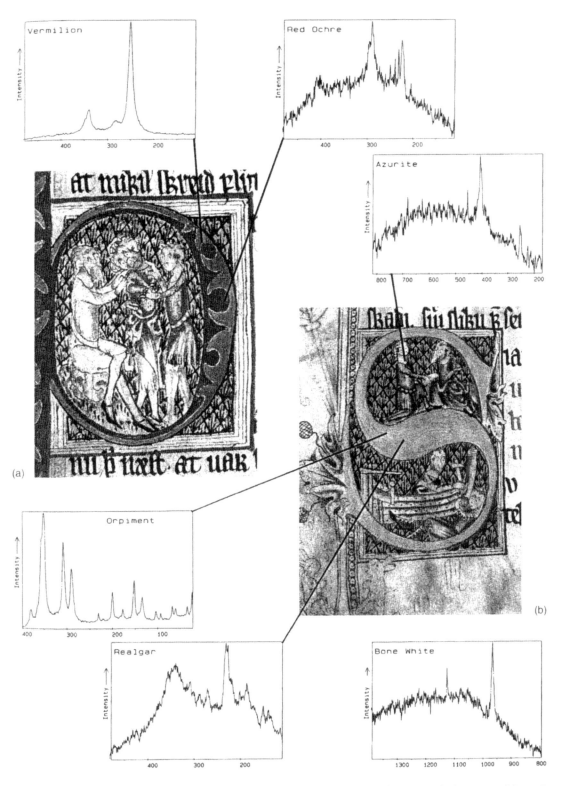

Figure 3.14 The examination of an illuminated Medieval Icelandic manuscript by RM with the traces of the various pigments identified in areas of different color. (Courtesy Best *et al.*, 1995)

a much longer-established method it currently has a much more comprehensive library of identified materials, but the comparable reference material for RS is growing at a very fast rate.

Analysis of organic materials

The analysis of organics concerns the identification and quantification of molecules often of great complexity, rather than of elements. There are two basic approaches, spectroscopy, the reaction of the material on exposure to a variety of electromagnetic radiation, UV, light, IR etc., and a separation of the molecular components using chromatography.

Spectroscopy enables specific molecular bondings to be identified in the molecule.

Chromatography at one level is just a separation technique, although the time taken for a given constituent to pass through the medium can be characteristic. Usually the suspected composition of a sample is checked by comparison to a known standard. When linked to MS, chromatography can be a very powerful technique, enabling many of the separated constituents to be identified.

However, there are many complex molecular mixtures, especially among natural polymerised materials such as amber, that give characteristic spectra, chromatograms, etc., of which the actual structure is still unknown.

Infra-red spectrometry (IRS) and Fourier-transform infra-red (FTIR)

Sources: Mills and White (1994, pp. 18–30); Bacci (2000, pp. 321–362); Doménech Carbó *et al.* (1996); Bertani and Consolandi (2006).

IR radiation interacts with the electrons in the molecules of the irradiated sample causing them to absorb some of the IR at frequencies characteristic of the molecular groups. The remainder of the radiation is either transmitted through the sample or reflected back. The radiation is recorded as a plot of the wave number (the reciprocal of the frequency) against the percentage transmitted, the interest being in the regions where the radiation has been absorbed by the material. Thus a typical plot consists of a series of troughs at the wave numbers where the IR has been absorbed.

Complex organic molecules are made up of simpler, more familiar molecules that can be easily and unambiguously identified. However, as organic materials are often made up of a number of different compounds that are themselves complex, identification

can be well-nigh impossible. Instead a 'fingerprint' method is adopted where the spectrum of a sample of the unknown is compared with spectra in a database library of previously measured standard materials. This approach can be taken further and differences noted between the two and degrees of degradation or adulteration of the sample determined by comparison with standards, although there exists the problem that degraded materials in general tend to produce diffuse spectra that can be difficult to interpret.

The application of Fourier transform (FT) to the transmitted spectra increases the sensitivity by several orders of magnitude such that it is now possible to carry out analyses on samples of the order of micrograms.

In standard transmission IRS the radiation passes through the material, which normally necessitates a sample being taken; in reflectance IRS the radiation is beamed at the surface of the object without sampling (Shearer, 1987). The IR radiation penetrates the surface to different depths depending on the material and on the frequency, and thus a composite surface such as a painting on analysis could produce spectra simultaneously from different layers, creating confusion. Conversely, by manipulating the frequency, etc. different layers can be analysed separately. Reflectance IRS has been applied to paintings using fibre-optics (Bacci *et al.*, 1992; Bacci, 2000). For the examination of small, precisely defined regions FTIR microscopy enables very small areas to be observed and analysed (Scott Williams, 1997).

Sample: In some cases it is feasible to analyse the whole object, such as a thin sheet of paper or cloth, transmitting the radiation straight through it, and in the reflectance mode the method is non-destructive. However, usually a tiny sample of the order of micrograms is required.

Assessment: FTIR provides quick identification of a very wide range of functional groups, enabling the type of organic material to be ascertained. By comparison with spectra of known materials more complex materials can be identified.

Since the 1970s FTIR has been widely applied to works of art (see Chapter 12, p. 289) and to other organic (see Chapters 17 and 18) and inorganic materials (see Chapter 10, p. 225, Chapter 14, p. 365 and Chapter 16, pp. 396, 419).

Chromatography

Sources: Mills and White (1994, pp. 14–17); Pollard and Heron (1996, pp. 66–72); Evershed (2000, pp. 177–240).

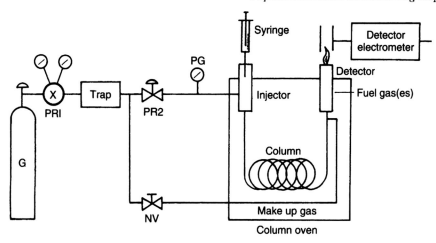

Figure 3.15 GC system. (Courtesy Pollard and Heron, 1996)

The main chromatography methods are techniques for separating complex mixtures of organic compounds, which can then be identified by other techniques such as FTIR or MS. When a solution moves on or in an inert stationary medium the various molecules dissolved in the solution move at different rates thereby effecting a separation. For example, when orange juice is spilt onto newspaper it is often noted that after a few seconds at the edge of the spreading spill the color is yellow, but behind there is a pinkish region. Two components of the orange juice have separated themselves in a very simple example of paper chromatography. Rather more sophisticated versions of paper chromatography are still in use, but the main methods used for the microanalysis of works of art and antiquities are gas chromatography (GC) (Figure 3.15) and liquid chromatography, usually in the form of the variant known as high-performance liquid chromatography (HPLC) (Figure 3.16).

In GC the material to be analysed is vaporised to form a gas. This is then mixed with an inert carrier gas and fed into the separation column. The components can be identified by the length of time it takes them to get through the system, judged against known standards.

A major problem is that many compounds decompose when vaporised. This can be overcome in certain cases by the pyrolysis (Pyr) of the solid sample to break it up into molecules that are more stable, but which are still characteristic of the material (Shedrinsky *et al.*, 1989; and see Chapter 12, p. 290, for examples of the use of Pyr-GC on painting media and Chapter 17, p. 439, for amber). Pyr-GC is also

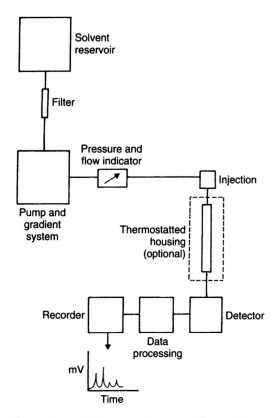

Figure 3.16 HPLC system. (Courtesy Pollard and Heron, 1996)

useful for organic materials of high molecular weight such as polymers that are involatile and insoluble.

However, the inability of many compounds to form stable vapours remains the most serious drawback to GC, and this is where HPLC is becoming increasingly important. The sample is dissolved, if possible, in an appropriate solvent and fed under high pressure into the column.

When linked with MS the material emerging from the columns is fed directly into the ionisation chamber of the spectrometer (Evershed, 2000). This enables much more precise identifications to be made, and, if required, the isotopes of the various elements, particularly carbon, can be differentiated.

Sample: The techniques are destructive but only require tiny samples. Even where inorganic materials are also present the sample need only be of the order of 1–2 mm^2.

4

Making a three-dimensional copy

But part of the point of art is that it has to be a one-off. We need what the philosopher Walter Benjamin famously describes as 'the aura of the original'.

Rachel Campbell Johnston in *The Times*, Wednesday 26 May 2004

Introduction

In order to be able to differentiate copies from the original it is necessary to understand something of the processes by which they were made. The copying processes considered here include original technology, the making of casts, pointing, digital scanning and electroforming. Two-dimensional copying processes are considered in Chapter 13 and simulated and synthetic gemstones in Chapter 16.

Editions

Before describing how copies are made it is necessary to establish what constitutes an original (Hughes and Ranfft (eds), 1997). Many 'original' works are issued in limited editions and as such are copies made using reproduction processes. Prints are familiar examples of the concept of the issue of an original as an edition, but editions in other less obvious materials such as bronze and stone can also be produced from master carvings which might be in a different material altogether. In addition, moulds can be taken of any three-dimensional object and castings made, sometimes as after-casts from an existing casting (Kurz 1948, pp. 177–181). The degree to which works such as these constitute originals is a matter of some debate (Van Mensch, 1985).

The concept of works of art as editions of more or less exact copies seems only to have begun in the Late Medieval–Renaissance period in Europe, most obviously with the print (see Chapter 13, p. 325 for a parallel discussion of the problems with editions of two-dimensional work). In classical antiquity, copies of sculpture were certainly made both by moulding and by a simple form of pointing (see p. 73), but seemingly not as identical editions (Bieber, 1977). Mattusch (1990, 1999) has suggested the possibility of mass production of bronze statuettes by the Romans but the results seem to have been fairly free copies to judge from surviving examples. Some multiple copies, such as those of Donnatello's *Madonna*, were made in the early fifteenth century, but these too are not exact copies and do not seem to constitute an edition as such (Radcliffe, 1992a,b).

Some posited contemporary 'original' copies have turned out to be modern after-casts taken from the finished original. This is exemplified by the apparent sixteenth-century edition of seven castings of the bust of Pope Paul III Farnese, by Guglilmo della Porta in the 1540s, which have been shown to be relatively modern after-casts of the original because of the crudity of their finish, and more specifically by their composition (Barbour and Glinsman, 1993). Surface analysis by X-ray fluorescence (XRF) showed the zinc content of the seven busts to vary between 23% and 36% with about 2% of lead and a percent of tin. They also have very similar trace elements. This similarity are suggested that the busts were cast at the same time and as two of them have zinc contents that unlikely to have been not be attained by the technology available in the sixteenth century (see Chapter 7, p. 147) this suggests they are all relatively modern.

Contemporary after-casts were sometimes made of famous sculptures, either in plaster or terracotta, such as the surviving terracotta after-cast of Pollajuolo's *Combat of nude men*, a lost bronze frieze of the fifteenth century. The after-cast, now in the Victoria and Albert Museum, London, was long regarded as a nineteenth-century production, until rehabilitated by TL dating (Fleming, 1979b).

Only from the late seventeenth century does the concept of an original work as an edition emerge, as exemplified by a surviving contract of the 1780s

Case study: Remington's Broncos

An entire exhibition which addressed the subject of what constitutes an original was made based on the work of the well-known American sculptor Frederic Remington (Shapiro, 1981a, b). Some of his more famous works, such as *The Bronco Buster, Cheyenne*, and *The Mountain Man*, were enormously popular in the nineteenth and twentieth centuries and exist in a variety of editions, forms and materials. Some clarification can be made by technical examination as exemplified by the study of *The Bronco Buster* (Johnson 1973, Cats 167–169). The statues of the original edition were sand cast with a fired finish at the Henry-Bonnard Bronze Company in New York from 1895 until the foundry burnt down in 1898. Casting from the original models, after some reworking by Remington himself, recommenced at the Roman Bronze Works in New York where the lost wax process was used. Production continued there under Remington's supervision until his death in 1909 and these bronzes were numbered and registered. The lost wax technique allowed much better rendition of detail and so the bronzes of this edition are more faithful reproductions than those of the first, sand-cast edition. Remington's widow continued a very lucrative production but the moulds from which the wax impressions were taken were getting decidedly well-used. First the tail of the horse no longer hung freely but had to be melded into the general casting of the body, and then the ears became damaged and the replacements resembled *burros* rather than *broncos*. After Mrs Remington's death the moulds were supposed to have been destroyed, but in fact further, unnumbered casts were taken from the original moulds until at least 1922. Thereafter after-casts have been taken from existing bronzes, and constitute forgeries if sold as being from the original editions. A study of two Remington bronzes, now in the Metropolitan Museum of Art, New York, showed them to be such unauthorised after-casts probably taken from original models (Hickmann, 1989).

It should also be noted that castings made from moulds taken from existing works will almost inevitably be slightly smaller than the original (see p. 72).

with the French sculptor Houdon for a bronze and 30 plaster copies to be made. The plaster cast, originally an intermediary stage in the indirect lost wax casting process (see Chapter 8, p. 160), became an end product as an edition in its own right (Baker, 1992). By the late eighteenth to early nineteenth centuries, even stone sculptures were regularly produced as editions, as exemplified by the sculpture workshop of Canova in Rome (Figure 4.15). The concepts of authenticity become even more complex with extra copies and pirated editions, made from the surviving moulds, often made long after the sculptor's death, or with after-casts (also known as *surmoulages*) taken from the original members of the edition (Beckett, 1995, pp. 40–42; and see Beale, 1975, for a fuller discussion on nineteenth-century sculpture copies in a variety of techniques and materials). There are legal implications as well. Whilst an original wax, terracotta or plaster model exists the present owner can quite legitimately make further castings from them, unless they are covered by a copyright agreement, although the new copies are often inferior in size and finish (Hochfield, 1989).

An interesting debate continues over the sculptures in wax and clay by Degas concerning whether these are to be considered as the finished work or should be regarded as the models for editions in bronze that were not realised in his life time. This debate has centred on the status of the bronze castings taken from *The Little Dancer* and other pieces, made and sold for huge sums of money long after the death of the artist (Failing, 1988; Beckett, 1995, pp. 41–42; Czestochowski and Pingeot, 2002).

Making a copy

Historical

Taking casts of small antiquities such as coins and medals (see Chapter 8, p. 181) or carved gemstones in plaster or glass paste (see Chapter 16, p. 416) grew in popularity through the Renaissance and beyond and informed both the collector and the forger on the appearance of real antiquities. The development of sophisticated techniques for making reproductions, exemplified by photogravure (see Chapter 13, p. 332) and electroforming (see p. 78), which were at least visually convincing, was most pronounced in the nineteenth century.

Casts and electroforms of famous works of art were made for museums, many of which had cast rooms as an integral part of their displays. After long neglect through most of the twentieth century they are now once more being appreciated, exemplified by the reinstatement of the cast gallery at the Victoria & Albert Museum, and the redisplay of the nineteenth-century Elkington electroforms (see p. 78) in the same museum.

At a more domestic level quality reproductions of works of art were extremely popular, as exemplified by the casts of Romano-British sculpture, available from the Society for the Promotion of Roman Studies in the early years of the twentieth century, the chromolithographs (Chapter 13, p. 339) and other more three-dimensional productions of the Arundel Society in the 19th century (Button, 1997 and see Chaptet 17, p. 425), and the photogravures of the Art Union. Sometimes forgeries followed on from the legitimate moulding of a genuine piece. This is exemplified by the shrine of St Gertrude at Nivelles in Belgium, where following the production of a cast of the shrine in 1897, clandestine copies of its statuettes began to be offered as genuine pieces (Didier, 1996).

In the twentieth century, demand for rigorously accurate reproduction declined, and most of the skilled and labour-intensive copying processes also declined or ceased. Traditional materials were replaced by epoxy resins and other synthetic moulding materials, from the 1950s (see p. 67), and copying techniques by digital scanning (see p. 77).

Methods of producing a copy

Original Technology (Figure 4.1)

With the ever-increasing publication of research describing the materials and technologies of the ancients, forgeries have the potential to become more authentic, if that is the correct term in this context! For example, only the most ill-informed forger would now use drawn gold wire on a piece purporting to be an antiquity (see Chapter 15, p. 376). Similarly, the discovery of the technique developed by the ancient Greek potters to produce the black and red figure painted ceramics enables convincing copies to be made (see Chapter 9, p. 195).

General features of modern replications

The problems faced by forgers opting to use the appropriate contemporary technology are two-fold. First and most obviously the item has to be stylistically and artistically convincing, with all the problems of creating original work outside the forger's own period and experience. These artistic problems are well known, but the technical problems are equally serious. The original artisans worked in the most obvious and natural way, the way they

Figure 4.1 Wall poster at Xian. It claims that the modern copies are 'Same quality, same materials...'. (Courtesy P. Craddock)

had been taught as apprentices and which probably was the only way they knew to tackle a given task. By contrast, modern copyists would be working in an alien manner from that in which they had been trained, the tools, methods and materials all being more or less different. The unnaturalness and awkwardness this engenders is never quite absent. Also, there is the temptation to take short-cuts, especially if the authentic method is slow and boring. One may learn a particular obsolete technique but cannot quite lose the knowledge that it *is* obsolete. A craftsman may work assiduously on a piece with a bow drill mounted with a spoon bit, or with a smoothing pebble for hours if there is no other way, but this is not necessarily the case if the craftsman has been brought up in the world of power tools! Furthermore, the forger in the modern Western World does not have access to the child-labour apprentices of the past or some parts of the present Third World to perform repetitive tasks such as hand polishing for a pittance.

Making a cast

Sources: Spon (1936, pp. 169–177); Wager (1938); Nimmo and Prescott (1968); Barkman (1969); Larsen (1981); Sharpe (1997).

Historical

Taking an impression from a mould is the most obvious method of replicating a shape. Ceramics have been moulded (see Chapter 9, p. 187) and metals cast from moulds (see Chapter 8, p. 160) almost from the inception of use of these materials the world over. Here, casts of plaster of Paris and of epoxy resins will be considered.

The technique has been widely used by forgers as exemplified by a series of neo-Babylonian inscribed clay tablets which, many years after the Oriental Institute of Chicago purchased them, roused suspicion by coming apart, quite literally at the seams (Leichty, 1970). Inspection revealed that they had been cast in two halves in moulds taken from genuine tablets now in the British Museum. It transpired that both the British Museum's originals and the casts had come from the same London dealer in the 1880s. It is most likely that moulds had been taken of the originals before they were sold to the Museum and new casts produced.

The copying of original Greek works by moulding was apparently already common in Roman times. Lucan (*Zeus Rants* II 33–4, Harmon, 1925, pp. 139–141) stated that in second-century AD Athens the famous *Hermes Agoraios* statue was always being covered in pitch (*pitta*), presumably applied as a releasing agent by artists wishing to take casts, and thereby creating a public nuisance. Pliny, in the *Natural History* (N.H. 35.153, Rackham 1952, pp. 373–375), referred to the making of casts. The best surviving evidence for this is the Roman plaster casts found at Baiae, which had probably been taken from original Greek statuary (Richter, 1970a; Landwehr, 1985).

The moulding of an antiquity can present special difficulties owing to the porosity of the material and flaking surfaces and any protective coatings must be removable. This precept was not always followed, Nimmo and Prescott (1968), for example, recommending filling in worm holes in old wood with araldite or other non-reversible epoxy resins. This would certainly stop penetration by the moulding material, but it would be impossible to remove afterwards and thus create a permanent change in the original artefact.

Mould materials

Traditionally, clay or plaster has been popular, as was gutta-percha until the arrival of synthetic materials in the mid-twentieth century (Percy, 1965). Although clay and plaster are both cheap and take a good impression they are inordinately heavy and rather fragile, and completely inflexible and thus of no use where there are undercuts on the original. In these cases a strong but flexible moulding material such as the gelatine-based 'jelly' moulds was necessary; however gelatine, being a natural material, has a tendency to go off unless kept cold. Gutta-percha was a favoured material in the nineteenth and twentieth centuries before the arrival of the synthetics. It is a latex-like material tapped from the tropical *Palaquium Gutta* or *Palaquium oblongifolia* trees of the *Sapotaceae* family. The juice rapidly solidifies and the gutta was prepared by boiling in water. It can be rendered extremely soft and malleable at temperatures of about 65°C, rapidly hardening at room temperature, but without becoming brittle. Therefore it could be used to a certain extent where there were undercuts. Also, unlike jelly moulds, it does not swell in water and was thus an ideal moulding material for electroforms (see p. 80).

Modern alternatives are vinyl (Tiranti, 1998), polyester resin (Tiranti, 1997) and silicone rubber (Tiranti, 1999). The latter was introduced in the

1960s and has replaced most other materials, being strong but very flexible and it sets without the need for heat. It has the general formula:

$$O-\underset{\underset{R}{|}}{\overset{\overset{R}{|}}{Si}}\left[O-\underset{\underset{R}{|}}{\overset{\overset{R}{|}}{Si}}\right]_n O-\underset{\underset{R}{|}}{\overset{\overset{R}{|}}{Si}}-O$$

where R is usually an alkyl group such as methyl, CH_3. The length of the polymer chain, $[-O-Si-O]^n$, determines properties such as the fluidity whilst liquid and the strength and flexibility when set. Thus, a range of silicone rubbers is available, each being appropriate to particular moulding problems. The liquid rubber monomer takes some hours to polymerise and set after being mixed with the catalyst and thus it is mixed just before moulding commences.

Typically an object to be moulded will be painted, or preferably sprayed, with a fluid silicone rubber of low molecular weight to avoid the formation of entrapped air bubbles, which is then allowed to set. A rubber of higher molecular weight will then be poured around this to a depth of around 5 mm. If the object is more than about 15 cm in its maximum dimensions then the mould must be backed with a stiff material such as plaster of Paris, polyurethane foam or an epoxy resin, to give it rigidity. Without this there is the danger of distortion when the casts come to be made (Figure 4.2).

Usually the object to be copied will be three-dimensional and will have to be moulded in the round, that is in sections, at the very least in two halves. To do this the original is divided up by fences built up on the surface such that each section can be moulded and the solidified mould pulled away from the surface without damage (Wager, 1938, p. 5 & pp. 16–19; Sharpe, 1997) (Figure 4.3) This is one area where those making after-casts encounter problems not met by those using the original models. If the original model, which was made to be moulded, had overhanging components creating difficult undercuts then these could quite simply be detached and separately moulded. If a finished original is being copied, the copyist does not normally have the option to cut off awkward overhangs, and hence may have to modify the copy.

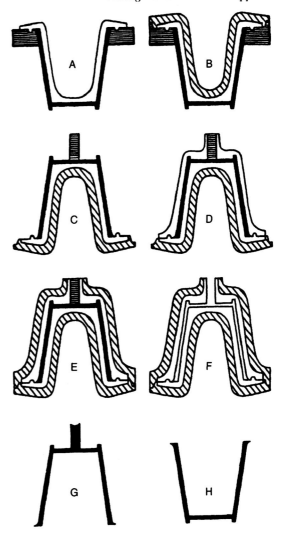

Figure 4.2 Stages in making a casting of a simple vessel using a two-piece mould of silicone rubber (A) supported by epoxy resin (B) for the inside. This is repeated (C–E) for the outside after coating the exposed surface of the rubber with a releasing agent and the addition of a pouring channel (C). The original is then removed (F), the casting made (G) and pouring channel, etc. removed (H) (Courtesy Larsen, 1981).

Plaster casts

Traditionally, plaster of Paris has been the main material for making both the moulds and the casts. Dry plaster was carefully mixed to a creamy consistency and applied to the surface to be moulded. To protect the surface of the original a releasing agent of grease or of oil had to be applied (recalling the comments of Lucan, p. 64). These could stain

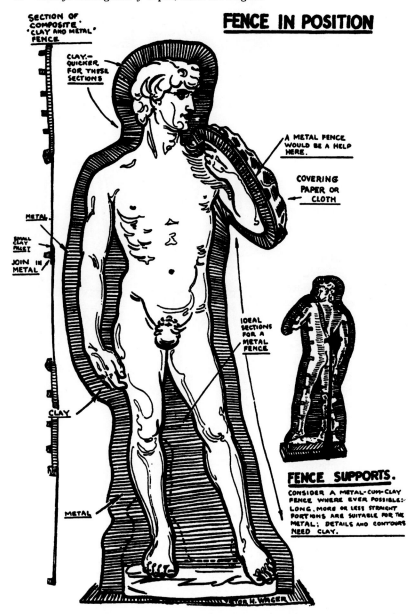

Figure 4.3   Fence in place, which will keep the two halves of the plaster mould separate whilst setting. (Courtesy Wager, 1938)

white marble, and for stones such as this an alternative releasing agent such as soft curd soap was preferred. After the first layers of plaster had been brushed on, strips of loose weave clothe soaked in plaster (known as *scrim*), could be applied to give the forming mould greater strength. If the mould was of any size, lengths of wood could be set in the plaster to give further reinforcement.

After the plaster had set it was removed from the original, but before use it had to be rendered impervious by the application of several coats of French polish (shellac dissolved in methylated spirits), followed by a light greasing or oiling to act as a releasing agent.

The cast

The production of a plaster cast is similar to the production of the mould. After casting, the surface treatment of the plaster casts typically began by the application of several coats of shellac to render the surface impervious and to strengthen it. This was followed by brush application of the appropriate pigments in a stiff solution of shellac. When fully dry the surface was polished to the required texture. If it was required to imitate the irregular variegated surface of a corroded bronze, then, after the application of the pigments, a further application was made of a paste made up of the pigments in a stiff aqueous solution of animal glue. This was applied by brush with a stippling action as appropriate to match the original. When dry, the surface could be lightly waxed and polished as required. It should be fairly easy to detect such an applied corrosion layer, using solvents which should dissolve the shellac binder, and UV radiation, under which the glue should fluoresce. Wakeling (1912, p. 24, Plate II) related how he nearly bought two supposedly ancient Egyptian necklaces of carnelian and gold bottle beads. Only on close microscopic examination was a thin seam noticed on one of the beads, revealing that the purportedly solid gold was in fact gold foil carefully wrapped over plaster of Paris. As the beads were but a component of a much larger item the difference in density between gold and plaster of Paris would not have been apparent. In the nineteenth century plaster of Paris copies were also electroplated to imitate metal, although more usually they were bronzed (Spon, 1895, p. 268; Spiro, 1968, p. 9; and see Chapter 14, p. 359).

Plaster of Paris copies are easy to detect. They are of relatively low density, transparent to X-rays (see Figure 2.6b) and physically very weak such that they can be penetrated with a hand-held mounted needle.

Since the 1950s when polyester and epoxy resins became available, a whole new technology has arisen known as cold-casting (Percy, 1965, pp. 1–64) (Figure 4.4) Depending on the viscosity of the resulting mixture and the mould shape, the casting material will be poured, pasted or injected into the mould. Reser (1981), for example, described the use of silicon rubber moulds and epoxy resins to make precision castings of small fossils. Epoxys are much harder and stronger than plaster and give altogether more satisfactory copies (Barkman, 1969; Larsen, 1981). As they are colorless and transparent they are also widely used as simulants for glass, enamel and gemstones (Kühnemann, 1969).

Another big advantage of polyester and epoxy resins is that the color, opacity and density can all be adjusted by the addition of suitable materials to match those of the original being copied. Additions

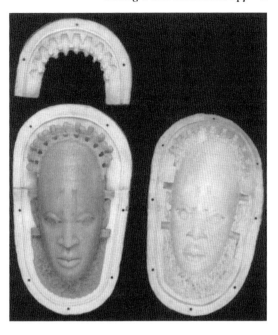

Figure 4.4 Cold casting. A resin copy sat in a plaster piece mould from which two of the five sections have been removed. The copy is of an ivory pectoral of the Oba of Benin (BM ETH 1910, 5-13, 1). (Courtesy Jones (ed), 1990)

of powders of the same material as the original may be made, for example powdered flint to a copy of a flint tool, or metal powder to a copy of a bronze (Figure 4.5a, b) This could lead to misleading interpretations of a surface analysis. Jacob (1962) described the production of casts of bronze artefacts, stating that the mould was spun while the resin containing the bronze powder was still liquid so that the denser metal particles could move to the surface where they formed a more or less continuous layer. This was then chemically patinated and polished almost as if it was an ordinary metal surface. Jacob commented 'on the great authenticity when compared to the originals'. Alternatively, the appropriate metal powder may be applied to the mould surface to be picked up by the resin.

Variation in the concentrations of the additives can be used to give a streaking effect, simulating for example, the graining of stone. For local surface coloring, the appropriate pigments can be carefully applied to the mould surface with a little liquid resin so as to become incorporated in the surface of the cast. The surfaces can be touched up once the cast has been removed, but painting as such should

Figure 4.5a   Cold casting of an Egyptian bronze cat. (Courtesy British Museum)

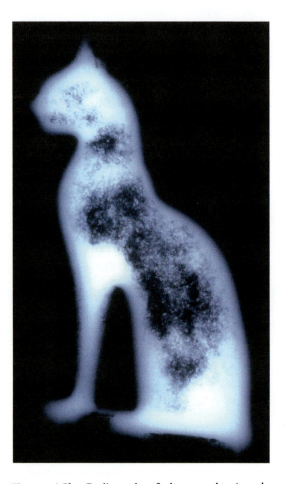

Figure 4.5b   Radiograph of the cat, showing the bronze powder in the resin mix. (Courtesy J. Heffron/ British Museum)

be kept to strict minimum as it lacks realism and is prone to chipping and flaking.

When carefully done, polyester and epoxy resin copies can be quite realistic, as exemplified by a series of plaques taken from original marble carvings by artists such as the nineteenth-century sculptor and medallist E.W. Wyon, which circulated in Britain in the 1990s (Figure 4.6) They were regularly entered at auction as originals, leading the *Antiques Trade Journal* (16 October 1996) to issue a warning. Several years later, people were still being taken in (*The Times*, 1 June 1999), although by now the plaques are being produced in enormous numbers for sale in shamtique shops and market stalls.

Recognition

Examination of the surface by the methods outlined in Chapter 14 (p. 365), could reveal evidence of treatment. A polyester or an epoxy resin can be recognised as organic by a simple flame test in which the sample would burn on ignition and would be consumed (although any inorganic fillers present would remain). Radiography should reveal the presence of inorganic fillers (see Figure 4.5b). Application of a paint stripper such as Nitromors, containing methylene chloride, should significantly soften the surface of an epoxy resin. Positive identification of a polyester or epoxy resin would require techniques such as IRS or RS (see Chapter 3, p. 58).

If, as is often the case, the chosen material for the final copy is a metal then an intermediary stage must be made to create a heat-resistant mould. This is best exemplified by the indirect lost wax process as described in Chapter 8, p. 161, but the special case of making a bronze copy of an ancient work is given below.

Recognition of metal casts

Minor casting faults are good indicators that a piece is a casting. Where a cast has been taken, all of the surface detail including worked areas, damage, or corrosion will be cast. Thus, the copier has the dilemma that an exact copy would reveal all of the original worked details as casts, but any work done by the copier to remove the evidence that the piece is a cast changes it such that it is no longer an exact copy. Careful microscopic examination can reveal evidence of minor casting blemishes running over features which should be the tool marks of apparent post-casting work or damage of a putative original.

A good example of this is the copy of a sword, now in the collections of the Tower Armouries (CX2 357) (Figure 4.7a), which has been known since the first part of the nineteenth century. It is apparently a cast Bronze Age sword that has had its hilt reattached rather crudely by casting on a replacement. Such repairs were quite common in antiquity, but the sides have rough file marks that were seemingly made with a steel file, suggesting that this had been done after the sword was first

Figure 4.6 Epoxy cast of a marble plaque depicting Oberon with Titania, by E.W. Wyon. (Courtesy A. Milton)

Case study: A Hellenistic statue of a youth

Source: Rinne and Frel (1975).

Shortly after the J. Paul Getty Museum had purchased the head and foot of a youth from a life-size Hellenistic statue it was realised that they belonged with a torso and leg which were already in the Burdur Museum in Turkey. It was agreed that whilst the originals should remain in their respective institutions, it would be very valuable if a bronze copy could be made for each museum, incorporating all the extant components.

Moulds were taken from the surviving components. First, small holes and cracks in the surface were temporarily plugged with wax. The torso was then sectioned into two halves with masking tape, thereby creating a front and back, each to be moulded separately. The whole surface was lightly waxed to ensure that the mould pulled away cleanly from the somewhat corroded and porous bronze surface. The moulding material was an aqueous emulsion of natural latex rubber, and was applied horizontally in a total of 14 thick coats, allowing six hours drying time between coats. This mould was flexible, enabling it to be pulled away from the undercuts in the original without any damage, but being flexible it would distort unless supported and therefore before it was removed from the original the latex was backed with polyurethane foam to a depth of about 10 cm.

The latex moulds from Turkey and America were then brought together for the production of the bronze copy. First, a plaster cast was made (this was because of the further work necessary on the components to ensure that they fitted together satisfactorily prior to the production of the final mould). The casts were made by carefully painting liquid plaster of Paris into the surface details of the latex mould, then scrim. Once the plaster had reached a sufficient thickness, splints of wood were added with additional plaster. The moulds were then removed, and the plaster sections brought together and joined, adding extra plaster where the joins no longer met. The next stage was the creation of the final mould. First, the positive plaster cast was carefully painted with shellac to render it impervious, and then hot liquid gelatine was applied all over the cast creating a layer 3 centimetres thick. After this had set it was cut so that it could be pulled away easily and cleanly from the plaster cast. Before this was done the flexible gelatine negative was backed with plaster of Paris to give the mould rigidity. This performed the same function as the polyurethane had done but was much heavier and more fragile. In this instance this did not matter as the mould was not going to be moved.

The gelatine moulds were then removed from the plaster cast and assembled as a hollow negative mould. Next, hot wax was poured in and carefully run all over the mould surfaces to build up a continuous layer approximately 6 mm thick. Once the wax had set, a slurry of plaster with sand, brick dust and organic fillers was poured in and allowed to set to form the porous refractory core. The gelatine mould was then pulled away, revealing the wax positive around its core. The pouring and feeder channels and the vents (*risers*) were then added as a series of wax tubes (see Figure 8.7). Iron nails were driven through the wax and into the core to act as *chaplets*, supporting it once the wax was removed.

The whole assembly was now ready for the application of the mould material. The first layer, lying directly against the wax which had to pick up all the detail was of fine clay mixed with organic material including chopped straw and horse dung, the latter still fermenting and producing gas holes in the body of the mould. This was said to be done in order to absorb some of the gasses generated when the hot metal was poured in. However, the holes could fill with metal during the casting, thereby spoiling the surface, and most manuals of casting recommend a slip of fine clay alone for the first coat, carefully applied by brush. After the first coat had dried against the wax a second, coarser, coat of clay was applied, strengthened with iron wire netting until a thickness of about 12 to 18 cm had been attained. Over this an outer coat of plaster, 6 cm thick, was applied. The mould was baked, ensuring that all the wax was melted or burnt out, an operation usually taking many hours. The hot mould was then lifted into a casting pit and loosely buried in soil to provide an enveloping support. With only the heads of the pouring channels and risers protruding; the bronze was poured into the mould, which was then allowed to cool for 24 hours.

The composition of the 'bronze' was not specified, but 'the major components, presented in order of greatest percentage were copper, zinc, tin and lead' – in other words a leaded gunmetal typical of the modern statuary 'bronzes' but certainly not of ancient statuary (see Chapter 7, p. 147).

After cooling the mould was broken away and the core removed, the feeder and riser channels being cut away and filed flush with the surface of the bronze. The metal surface was very variegated where the molten metal had reacted with the mould. This would normally have been polished away, but here the decision was taken 'to preserve many of the colors and areas of green oxidation [?] on our statue to give it an appearance more nearly resembling an ancient one that had been excavated from the ground'. Such damaged areas in the casting as had formed and the holes left by the removal of the chaplets, were repaired by pouring in more bronze.

It is instructive to consider how this statue, copied in precise detail from a genuine antiquity by traditional technology, could be established as a modern copy.

First, the alloy contains zinc; the founders should have known that this was wrong, but modern bronze founders are very reluctant to use copper alloys that do not contain a good deoxidant, zinc or phosphorus being preferred. It is surprising how many forgeries are given away by the presence of zinc in the alloy (see Chapter 7, p. 145).

Some of the core material almost certainly survives, sufficient to perform a TL test which would show that the core had been very hot in the recent past. Given the rather complex mixture it is possible that the core might contain modern synthetic materials, such as the nylon fibres found in the core of the head formerly in the Getty collection (see p. 72 and Chapter 8, p. 163 for more on core materials).

The statue was cast in one from the assembled moulds, rather than assembled from the separately cast constituent parts which was usual in classical antiquity (Steinberg, 1973), although shortly after this exercise the Getty Museum obtained another Hellenistic life-size statue of a youth, which is claimed to have been cast in one piece (Frel, 1982). The repairs were effected by pouring in additional metal. Once again, although this practice can be paralleled, it is unusual. The normal practice in Classical Antiquity was to cut out affected areas and insert rectangular patches of metal, held mechanically. There exists the problem, already discussed, that if the object is intended as an exact copy then the amount of work that can be done on the casting with scraper, etc. is limited. Examination of silicone rubber impressions of the surface by scanning electron microscopy could be instructive for differentiating between fresh tool marks and casts of tool marks (see Chapter 1, p. 25).

The formation in the space of 24 hours of the 'areas of green oxidation' referred to is rather difficult to envisage in the dry, hot and reducing environment of the mould. Black or brown copper oxides would have been expected and the unidentified green minerals must be very different morphologically and probably mineralogically from a natural patina slowly formed in a damp and oxidising environment.

Figure 4.7a Detail of the hilt of a Late Bronze Age sword that has been crudely repaired and filed. (Courtesy T. Springett/British Museum)

found. However, examination by binocular microscope (Figure 4.7b) revealed small globules of metal all over the surface including on the filed surfaces thus revealing the piece to be a cast, probably made from a genuine piece that had been roughly repaired after its discovery (the composition of the sword is also somewhat suspect; see Chapter 7, p. 42).

The problem of cast damage is exemplified by a statuette of Herakles with a ram skin, now in the Institute of Fine Arts, New York (Johnson, 1973, cat. 16). The lower limbs are missing, which is not uncommon. However, examination of the piece showed that the breaks on the legs are on the casting, and not subsequent. Presumably the piece is a cast taken from a genuine ancient bronze that really had lost its lower limbs.

Figure 4.7b The presence of small globules of bronze sat on the file marks shows clearly that this is not an original but a cast of a repaired piece (width 1.2 cm). (Courtesy S. La Niece/British Museum)

Figure 4.8 Large copper alloy head, apparently Hellenistic, but see Figure 4.9. (Formerly in the Paul Getty Collection)

Figure 4.9 Roman marble head of a young man, now in the Naples Museum. A cast of this was made to produce the copper alloy cast shown in Figure 4.8. Note the crack running down the proper left cheek and the hair style on both pieces. (© Naples Museum)

Where there is a major defect in the original, the forger has two options, either to remove it by infilling, etc. on the wax or clay positive, or to try to make the defect look like a first-generation casting fault, or post-casting damage caused by working on the cast copy. A good example of this approach can be seen on the bronze head, formerly in the J. Paul Getty Collection (Figure 4.8) After it had entered Getty's collection it was noted that a marble head in the Naples Museum bore a very strong resemblance (Figure 4.9). This head had a crack in the stone running down through the proper left cheek and forehead and this was made to resemble a casting crack in the copper alloy cast made from it. Subsequent scientific examination revealed that the bronze head was in fact of brass, an alloy never

encountered in ancient Classical statuary; there was no evidence that the piece had ever been corroded and remains of the core material inside the head contained strands of nylon.

Cast copies are almost invariably smaller than the original (Allison and Pond, 1983; and see Chapter 8, p. 181 and Chapter 9, p. 199). This is because although the original may be perfectly invested to create an exact negative mould, the casting made from this mould will be smaller by between 2.5 and 3.2% (for bronze) and up to 10% (for ceramics), owing to the shrinkage of the solidifying material in the mould. This is of major importance in differentiating casts of coins from the originals, when the dimensions are precisely known. There tends to be a much lesser degree of shrinkage in the synthetic organic materials used in cold casting.

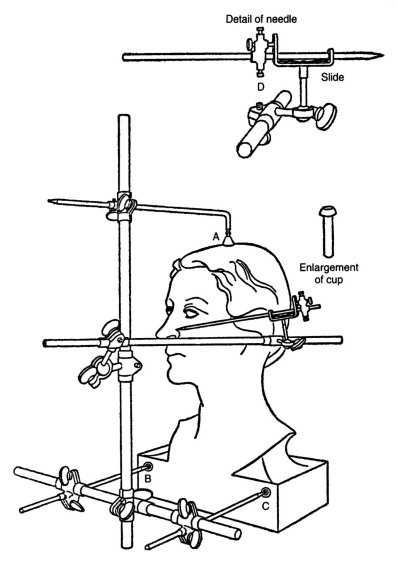

Detail of needle

Slide

D

A

Enlargement
of cup

B

C

Figure 4.10 Pointing frame.
(Courtesy Wager, 1938)

Pointing: Copying onto stone

Principal sources: Maryon (1933, pp. 44–47, 210);
AP (1944); Garbe in Miller (1948, pp. 82–89);
Rockwell (1993, pp. 121–122).

Pointing is a technique which enables three-
dimensional shapes to be accurately copied onto
a solid material, normally stone. This is done by
determining the position of a large number of
points on the original and establishing them as
holes drilled into the piece of stone to be sculpted
(Figure 4.10). When a sufficient number of points
have been established the drilled stone is chiselled
away leaving the three-dimensional shape to be

finished by fine chiselling and polishing. Pointing
was much used in the sculpture workshops of
Europe from at least the eighteenth century until
the early twentieth century to translate carving
from a clay or wax original to stone or to make
copies of existing sculpture. Many copies could be
made from the original and consequently many
stone statues were issued as editions.

History

The history of the technique is rather uncertain
and there is a wide divergence of published opinion. Ridgway (1969), for example, believed that

a primitive system of pointing was used from the fifth century BC, and Bieber (1977, p. 222) believed that pointing was 'probably used' by the Hellenistic Greeks. Conversely, Bartman (1992, p. 70), Rich (1947) and Touchette (2000) concluded that the pointing machine was invented in the eighteenth century. There is no doubt that sculpture in the round was regularly copied in the Ancient World, especially by the Romans. As Bartman (1992, p. 69) put it, 'That the Romans but not their Hellenistic predecessors employed the pointing machine is a *leitmotif* of modern discussion of the copying process'. Traditionally, it was believed that the process was developed in the Hellenistic period and very extensively used by the Romans (Strong and Claridge, 1976). Gardiner (1890) believed the process was developed in the first century BC, and Richter (1951, pp. 42–43; 1955, pp. 105–111; 1962; 1970b), following Furtwängler (1893), believed the process found first use somewhat earlier, and that 'the thousands of Roman copies of Greek works that we have today were doubtless produced in this way' (that is, by pointing). The evidence for these assertions was rather shaky but seemed in part to rest on the perception that the adventurous and innovative Greeks would create the sculpture directly in the stone, whereas the more conservative and cautious Romans would wish to perfect the sculpture in clay beforehand or, more likely, be content just to accurately copy existing works.

All the necessary technical and psychological conditions for the development of the copying of sculpture onto stone using the drill were already in place. The Greeks seem to have developed the concept of sculptural copying as exemplified by the technique of indirect lost wax casting. The question of how the concept, which worked so well for bronze, could be applied to stone, must have exercised the minds of both sculptors and patrons. The Greeks also seem to have developed the use of the drill as a tool for carving (Adam, 1966, pp. 40–73; and see Chapter 11, p. 247) and thereafter the way was clear for a copying method based on drilling. Finally, there was a large demand for sculpture, especially as the works of individual Greek sculptors rose to fame all around the Hellenistic world. This trend received a huge impetus from the Romans, both for copies of the famous Greek statuary, and latterly to disseminate copies of statuary to the far ends of the Empire, for artistic appreciation and official commemoration.

From the Greek period the evidence for pointing is sparse. The oft-quoted passage in Pliny (NH 35.153; Rackham 1952, Vol 9, pp. 373–375) which states that the Hellenistic sculptor, Lysistratos 'discovered how to take casts from statues, a practice which was extended to such a degree that no figure or statue was made without a clay model' was taken by many, including Richter (1970b, p. 119) as evidence for pointing. They reasoned that as the Greeks already used clay models prior to Lysistratos, Pliny must have meant something more momentous, that is the discovery of how to completely translate a sculpture from a cast to stone. In fact stone is not even mentioned in the passage; it could equally well refer to the stages in the production of bronze statuary by the indirect lost wax process. However, the passage does carry the suggestion that working from models, rather than directly onto the stone, was already developing in Hellenistic Greece.

Some engraved intaglio gemstones show sculptors at work, taking measurements from statues with a plumb-bob (Bluemel 1969, pp. 44–45). Presumably these measurements would have been translated into the stone to produce a rough outline. As these measured points must have been transferred to the inside of the block of stone, it would have been necessary to drill them, which, as the Greeks already used the stone drill, would have presented no problem.

Several incomplete statues survive which appear to have been produced using just a plumb-bob and line for measurement purposes (Pfanner, 1989) (Figure 4.11) The measurements may well just have been taken from the front and back to create the

Figure 4.11 Details of the incomplete terminal bust from Knidus, dated to the first to second centuries AD (BM GR Reg. 1859, 12-26, 728), showing holes drilled to act as guides to the carving. They were laid out with plumb-bob and line, enabling a whole series of almost identical terminals to have been produced for architectural purposes, etc. (Courtesy T. Springett/British Museum)

outline seen face-on (Hollinshead, 2002). An early example of this is shown in Figure 4.12 where there are many parallel holes defining the outline seen from the front, but comparatively few defining the actual contours of the body surfaces. In the next stage the drill holes covered the entire surface, front and back, but they are all at right-angles to the face of the squared block of stone and parallel to each other (Figure 4.13) Here the profile of the original work as viewed from the front or back was defined by a series of drilled holes.

It seems likely that there was an intermediate stage between the plumb-bob and line and the development of a pointing machine. This was to mark out a few key points from front and back, probably again measured just using the plumb-bob

and line. These points would have been drilled into the block, stopping well short of the intended surface. The stone was then carved away around the holes almost to the intended surface, thus leaving the bottom of the drill holes standing proud (Figure 4.14). These *puntelli*, when indented, could act as bases for compasses to translate details of the topography from the original to the stone. They survive on a number of ancient statues

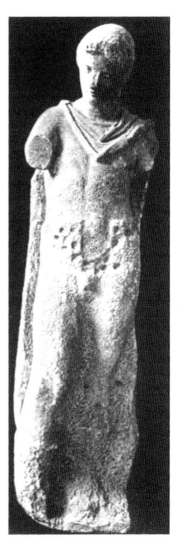

Figure 4.12 Unfinished figure of Hermes, dated to 550 BC. The drill holes clearly define the profile as seen from the front. The measurements were almost certainly taken from the original with a plumb-bob and line. (Courtesy Chittenden and Seltman, 1947)

Figure 4.13 Unfinished figure of a youth from Rhenia in the Aegean, dated to the first century BC. Note the drill holes are all in the plane at right angles to the plane of the front of the statue, suggesting that the measurements were taken from the original using only a plumb-bob and line. (Courtesy Bluemel, 1969)

(Furtwängler, 1893; Richter, 1970b, p. 119, fn 37; Strong and Claridge, 1976). The statue of a barbarian, now in the Vatican, has more than 30 *puntelli* (Pfanner, 1989, pp. 188–190, Figure 14a–c), but as Rockwell (1993, p. 122) has pointed out, an equivalent modern pointed copy would have had about 150 points.

There is at present no evidence for more sophisticated pointing techniques in antiquity. There are no known examples of incomplete statuary bearing the ends of a series of multi-directional holes which could only have been positioned with the aid of some special pointing frame, or fragments of discarded marble pierced with many drill holes. The general absence of screw-held clamps and screw adjustors would have been a big drawback in designing such a machine that had accurately to define and rigidly hold a position in three dimensions, especially whilst the hole was being drilled using it as the guide. Thus it is likely that whilst the principles of pointing were known and used there was no special apparatus comparable to the Post-Medieval pointing machine for taking multi-directional points.

From the Renaissance onwards copies of classical sculpture began to be produced in quantity, for collections and also for architectural features and furnishings. There was therefore a very considerable demand for work that was competent but not necessarily very original. To meet this requirement modern pointing seems to have developed in Italy, both for original works taken from clay models or copied directly from antique statuary, attaining mechanical perfection in the workshops of Cavaceppi and Canova at the end of the eighteenth century (see Chapter 20, p. 516).

The process

The description of the process given below follows Garbe in Miller (1948, pp. 82–89).

The copy was made by accurately determining the position of a number of points in three dimensions on the surface of the original and transferring them into the block of stone by drilling. The original was fixed to a base, and small cups were attached to its surface into which the pointing apparatus was fixed by being screwed firmly into the cups (Figure 4.15) The pointing operation commenced by determining the most prominent place and taking measurements with the point, the tip of the nose, for example, in the sculpture illustrated in Figure 4.10. The pointing apparatus was then taken

Figure 4.14 Unfinished marble statue of a barbarian from a Roman workshop on the Campus Martius in Rome. It shows four *puntelli*, raised cups on the stone to position the point of compass. (Courtesy Strong and Claridge, 1976)

off the original and hung on the block of stone and adjusted so that the most prominent points were all inside the points as determined by the pointing needle, and cups fixed to the stone to hold the frame. The pointing apparatus was taken off the stone and re-fixed in the cups on the original, the needle brought to the surface and the frame rigidly screwed. A mark was made in pencil on the surface and the length the needle projected precisely noted. The needle was then carefully withdrawn and the pointing apparatus fixed into the cups on the stone. A hole was then drilled into the stone through the slide frame at exactly the same angle that the pointing needle had been until the hole was about 5 mm short of the needle length. The drilling was then continued with a hand-rotated spoon bit drill until there was only about 1 or 2 mm left, at which point the procedure was halted and the bottom of the hole was marked with a soft pencil.

Figure 4.15 Canova's bust of the poetess Corrinna, with cups for locating the pointing frame. (Reproduced with permission of Country Life, 13 March 2003)

This process was repeated systematically over the surface of the original until sufficient points had been taken and transferred as holes to the stone, which, by the end of the operation, could resemble a sponge. The number of points depended on the confidence of the operator and the degree of accuracy required for the stone; spacing between the points of between 10 and 40 mm were typical. For large pieces the work sometimes proceeded in stages. For example AP (1944) recommended for a life-size statue an initial pointing every six inches (15 cm), stopping well short of the final surface, followed by a second and even a third pointing operation, getting closer to the final form each time. After the pointing operations the stone was chiselled away down to the pencil-marks at the bottom of the holes. Thus one had a slightly larger copy of the original and the final carving and polishing could proceed from there.

In the nineteenth century the principle of the pantograph was adapted to the pointing machine, enabling originals to be copied at different scales. The Parisian sculptor, Achille Collas, developed this with great success in producing large numbers of reduced versions of famous originals (Hughes and Rowe, 1982, p. 17).

Recognition

The carving operation would normally be expected to remove all evidence of the pointing process, but sometimes the bottoms of the holes do survive in some inaccessible areas, such as behind the ears. Budde and Nicholls (1964, p. 123) included in their catalogue a fine early nineteenth-century head of Carrara marble (Cat 205), on the surface of which a pattern of drillings could still be faintly discerned, confirming that it had not been carved in antiquity.

Digital scanning

The modern equivalent of pointing is the various methods of three-dimensional digital scanning. Most methods in effect 'paint' the surface to be recorded or copied with a laser beam. The laser spots are recorded with one or more cameras linked to a computer system. The developing image can usually be simultaneously viewed on the computer screen. The digital data so produced is ideal for feeding to a computer numerical controlled (CNC) milling machine to carve out the three-dimensional shape in whatever solid medium is selected. The milled surface is usually recognisable as such, but after more conventional polishing and surface treatments it could be very difficult to recognise that the laser scan–CNC milling method had been used.

Electroforming

(The process was formerly known as galvanoplastic in English, the name it retains in French and German. In English the process has also been known as electrotyping from its inception.)

General sources: Langbein (1891); Spiro (1968); Westphal (1985). Forgeries: Mundt (1980).

In essence the process involves the creation of an exact positive of an object by the electrodeposition of the metal onto the surface of a mould taken from it.

History

Sources: Langbein (1891, pp. 1–23); Krämer (1959); Wardle (1963, pp. 41–48); Anon (1973); Raub (1993); Doktor *et al.* (2001); Scott (2002, pp. 22–26).

The development of electroforming was closely linked to the related process of electroplating (see Chapter 8, p. 176) and sprang directly from the developments with electrical cells, or batteries, in the 1830s and 1840s and from the discovery that a satisfactory plated layer of copper, gold or silver could be deposited from a solution of the cyanide salt of the metal.

The first announcement of the reproduction of surface detail by electrodeposition was made in the spring of 1838 in Riga by Moritz von Jacobi (Krämer, 1959), reported in Britain in a paper entitled 'Galvanic Engraving', stating that Prof. Jacobi:

> had made a discovery which promises to be of little less importance to the arts than the discovery of M. Daguerre and Mr. Fox Talbot [see Chapter 13, p. 335]. He has found a method – if we understand our informant correctly – of converting any line, however fine, engraved on copper, into a relief by the galvanic process. Athenaeum, 8 May 1839

This prompted C.J. Jordan of London and Thomas Spencer of Liverpool to separately (and acrimoniously) publish their own claims to have discovered the process.

Thus far the electroforms had all been formed on the surfaces of metal artefacts which acted as the cathode, but in 1840 Murray made the crucial innovation of rendering the surface of non-metals conducting by dusting with graphite. This meant that a cast could be taken of any surface, made to be conducting, and exact positive electroforms made therefrom.

The process attracted the attention of the Elkington brothers, proprietors of the famous firm of silver manufacturers in Birmingham. With the help of some technical improvements relating to moulding materials made by their principal chemist, Alexander Parkes (see Chapter 18, p. 447, for his pioneering work on plastics), and by buying up the patents of related processes, notably John Woolrich's 1842 patent on a dynamo to replace the voltaic cell as the source of electrical power (Figure 4.16) they soon had controlling rights on both the electroforming and electroplating processes. They sold licences to operate the process, and very rapidly a major industry sprang up all over Europe and

North America. Elkingtons were to remain a major producer of electroforms themselves well into the twentieth century (Anon, 1973). They copied many famous pieces as well as commissioning a wide range of original work from famous contemporary artists, which they then copied and sold in limited editions, often stamped on the base with their dates of 'publication', in the manner of contemporary prints.

Ornate pieces of ancient, Medieval and more recent metalwork were copied both for academic museum display and for commercial sale in the nineteenth and early twentieth centuries. Electroforms of some of the more famous and elaborate examples of the goldsmith's art over the centuries were in demand for the mock baronial halls as well as the more humble villas of the middle classes all over Europe. For example, the superb early Roman treasure of silver vessels, found at Hildersheim in 1868, caught the public imagination, and the French firm of Christofle brought out electroforms of many of the pieces (Boetzkes and Stein, 1997, p. 205). The Würtembergerische Metallwarenfabrik of Geislingen in Germany and Brucciani and Co. of London produced excellent electroform copies of many of Schliemann's discoveries at Mycenae and Troy, and continued to produce very high quality electroforms well into the twentieth century.

Pieces of top-quality Elizabethan and Jacobean silver are rare in Britain, having almost all been melted down during the English Civil War and its aftermath in the mid-seventeenth century. However, superb collections which had been presented by Elizabethan and Jacobean ambassadors to the Russians, survive in Moscow and St Petersburg. Elkingtons sent workmen to Russia to mould some of the more spectacular pieces (Miles 1884, p. 10). Some of the resulting electroforms were purchased by the Victoria and Albert Museum where they now form an important part of the silver display.

The ease with which the technique picked up and replicated minute detail suited the Victorian taste for the ornate and complex. The technique was applied to a wide range of materials, and even had some effect on design in the Victorian era. Thus, G.R. Elkington wrote in the 1840s that:

> The recent discovery of the Electrotype process has already worked important changes in many branches of the arts and results hitherto unobtainable have in most astonishing perfection been accomplished. This is one of those instances where Science in her most

Figure 4.16 Plating shop at Elkington's Newhall Street Works, Birmingham, showing the new dynamo. (Reproduced with permission of Cassell's Illustrated Exhibitor 1, 1852, Guide to the Great Exhibition)

exalted shape stoops to the aid of her Sisters Art and Manufacture, and familiarizes to them an agent which we have been accustomed to contemplate in the Whirlwind and the Thunderstorm.

Elkington Records 8, quoted in
Wardle 1963, p. 47

Among the other leading producers contemporary with the Elkingtons in Britain were von Jacobi in Russia, Christofle in France and Kres in Germany.

Rapid developments in the dynamos used in commercial electroforming led to the generation of much more powerful currents. This meant that much thicker deposits of copper could be made, and truly enormous electroforms could be contemplated. Many of the large 'bronze' statues erected in Germany in the second half of the nineteenth century are electroforms (Haber and Heimler, 1994). Elkingtons produced many life-size and over-life-size statues (Figures 4.17a, 4.17b) (Aitken, 1866), and Christofle produced one statue standing 29' 6'' tall (9 m), which weighed three and a half tons, the electrodeposition having taking 10 weeks!

From an early date Jacobi specialised in the electroforming of enormous monuments as an alternative to the more conventional casting methods. Huge statuary groups and bas reliefs were made to adorn public buildings, such as those on the Bolshoi

Theatre in Moscow and St Isaac's Cathedral and the Winter Palace in St Petersburg (Pavlova, 1963; Raub, 1993).

These large productions made a considerable impression on the technically minded of the day, and thus W.C. Aitken (1866) was moved to write:

Though at first received with suspicion at the gates of industry, [electroforming] once fairly within her portals, with a tub for a kitchen, and an earthenware tube for a parlour, fed on cakes of zinc, buttered with quicksilver, and with acid to drink (i.e. The voltaic cell), it first showed a specimen of its working powers in the copy of a little coin, but so thin, so very thin! With further encouragement it produced a basso relievo- a little thicker:- then it produced a statuette. "Give me more elbow-room," it cried; "Increase the number of my chambers! Give me more cakes, more drink! Lengthen my arms of copper wire! Make my workshop bigger, I care not how far distant I will work from eve to morn, from morn to dewy eve; I want no day of rest! Give me what I ask, and leave me alone to work!" And its kindly masters (G.R. and Henry Elkington),- now alas! No more,-gave it all it asked and left it. Weeks and weeks afterwards, in the plaster mould left in its workshop-bath of coppery blue water, was found the metal statue of a man, not a mere film in thickness, but strong and stout.

Figure 4.17a   Electroform copper statue over 2 m tall, personifying Fine Art. One of four figures standing on the Holborn Viaduct, London. Made by Farmer and Brindley and electroformed by Elkingtons in the late 1860s

Figure 4.17b   Detail. (Courtesy P. Craddock)

Electroforming was used extensively in the printing trade for copying pages of type, and electroform copies were made of original engraved plates and woodcut blocks thereby hugely increasing the number of copies that could be made (see Chapter 13, p. 330).

The process

Commercial processes: Napier (1852); Langbein (1891, pp. 273–316); Spon (1895, pp. 316–371, repeated almost verbatim in the 1932 edition, pp. 129–138); Watt and Philip (1911, pp. 79–147); Spiro (1968). Craft methods: Untracht (1968, pp. 379–92); Spencer (1973). Museum reproductions: Moss (1956); Larsen (1984).

A mould was taken of the original, in the nineteenth century common moulding materials being plaster of Paris, beeswax, stearic acid 'styrene', low-melting-point 'fusible alloys' based on bismuth, lead and tin, and the most popular material for the first hundred years or more, gutta-percha (see p. 64). Whilst still warm, gutta-percha has some flexibility, but if the object to be moulded had many undercuts then the moulding often had to be done in sections, the evidence of which can identify the piece as an electroform (Figures 4.18a, 4.18b). An alternative was to use a more flexible moulding material such as the traditional 'jelly' gelatine; however, it tended to swell in the solutions (Watt and Philip, 1911, p. 105).

Graphite powder was dusted onto the faces of the mould to be copied to make them conducting. Conversely, if the mould was of metal, and thus conducting, the areas not to be copied would be varnished.

Suitably coated, the moulds had wires affixed which would carry the current. Unfortunately, graphite is not a good conductor of electricity, and if the piece was large or complex then thin layers of silver or even of gold might be precipitated from their salts onto the graphite surface to ensure a uniform distribution of the current. More usually the problem was overcome by judicious soldering of a whole series of wires so placed that the current was supplied more or less evenly over the whole surface. The assembly, which formed the cathode, could then be placed in the electrolyte, which was usually formulated around either acidic copper sulphate solutions or basic solutions of copper and potassium cyanide and carbonates.

Figure 4.18a An early twentieth-century electroform of an ancient Persian silver dish with high relief decoration; the original was made as a single piece by the repousse technique.

The principle of the electroplating reaction is shown in Figure 4.19. When the current was applied the copper began to deposit on the mould which formed the negative electrode, the cathode. The positive electrode, the anode, was of copper, which was slowly dissolved, replenishing the electrolyte.

It was essential for the copper to be deposited slowly if the forming layer was to be homogeneous and thus of acceptable strength, building up in columnar grains (Figures 4.20 and 4.21) Thus, many hours were required before the layer could be fully deposited. The deposited layers were typically between one thirty-second and one quarter of an inch (0.8 mm and 6.4 mm respectively) thick, depending on the size of the object. After deposition the sections were removed from the moulds, washed and the surplus copper trimmed from the edges. They were then assembled and soldered together. The interior surfaces were also usually coated with soft solder, which acted both as a backing to strengthen the electroform and also gave the appropriate weight to the piece. The surface was plated or patinated (see Chapter 14), as necessary, to resemble the original.

Figure 4.18b The gutta percha mould had to be taken in four sections and the join line can clearly be seen running up the centre where the mould was assembled prior to electroforming. (Courtesy A. Milton/British Museum)

For large items such as statues rather different methods were devised because of the problems of distributing the current evenly through the graphite. One was the indirect electroforming process, using positive plaster casts rather than negative moulds in the first instance (Watt and Philip, 1911, p. 148). The cast was rendered impervious, etc. and the process carried forward resulting in a negative electroform. This was then cut up, the plaster removed and the inner face carefully cleaned as it was now itself to form the mould surface. Before being placed in the tanks the mould sections were exposed to hydrogen sulphide to create a thin layer of copper sulphide in order that the electro-deposited metal should not adhere too firmly to the copper of the mould. The deposits were typically between one eighth of an

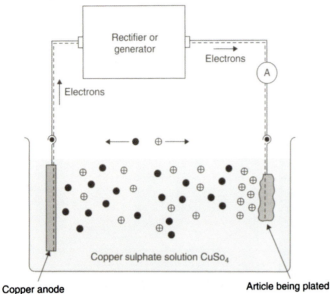

Figure 4.19 Principles of electrodeposition. The current is flowing from left to right. The positively charged cations are attracted to the right where they are deposited, while the negatively charged sulphate anions are attracted to the left where they will dissolve more copper from the anode. 'A' denotes the ammeter (Courtesy B. Craddock).

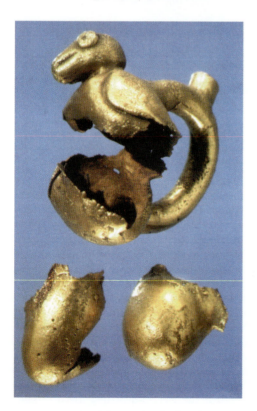

Figure 4.20 Electroform of a bird sitting on eggs, purporting to belong to the South American Chimu culture (BM Reg. Ethno 1947 Am21.1.abc). (Courtesy A. Milton/British Museum)

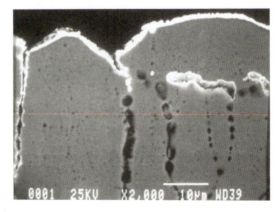

Figure 4.21 SEM micrograph of a section through Figure 4.20 showing the very distinctive columnar structure of the copper grains typical of electroforming. Note the depressed edges at the surface where the grains meet, which gives the distinctive slightly puckered appearance to many electroforms. The thin bright layer at the surface is the very thin layer of gold plating that gives the appearance of a gold antiquity. (Courtesy S. La Niece/ British Museum)

inch (3.2 mm) and one third of an inch (8 mm) thick for a life-size human statue.

Another approach was to first make gutta-percha moulds, which were assembled to form a hollow negative (Langbein, 1891, pp. 309–310; Watt and Philip, 1911, p. 148). The anode was formed from a complex network of platinum wires which ran just inside the figure, following all the principal contours. The hollow mould was then filled with copper sulphate electrolyte, and the process was commenced, forming the positive electroform directly on the graphite-treated gutta-percha mould. Note that the electroform made in this process was complete, standing in three dimensions and had no joins at all. If the surface had subsequently been extensively worked and treated as is the usual practice with major statuary, and there was no access to the inside of the piece to enable examination to take place, then it could be very difficult to detect that it was indeed an electroform, without recourse to sampling and analysis.

In the twentieth century the traditional moulding materials, gutta-percha and gelatine, etc., were replaced by silicone rubber (see p. 64), which is both impervious and very flexible, but otherwise there have been few major changes.

The process has continued to be used to make high-quality replicas of small antiquities for museums (Larsen, 1984). The mould surface is made conducting by being brushed either with graphite, or more usually, silver or bronze powder.

The electrolyte is usually an acidic aqueous solution of copper sulphate (although Untracht 1968, pp. 379–383, also used cyanide solutions). To this is added small amounts of urea, which promotes the formation of a fine, even grain structure, and of a wetting agent, usually ethanol, to discourage the retention of bubbles of hydrogen which form at the growing electroform face.

A low DC current is applied and, at the current densities used, a deposition thickness of 1 mm takes about 75 hours to form. Small items are typically between 0.2 mm and 0.5 mm in thickness, and larger electroforms can be up to 1 mm in thickness, a far cry from the thicknesses of 5 mm and more of some of the massive Victorian productions.

Throughout the operation the electrolyte is kept agitated and held at a constant temperature of about 25°C to avoid streaking on the surface of the electroform (see p. 85 and Figure 4.22).

The rate of deposition depends on the distance of the electroform surface from the anode. The optimum distance is 15 to 20 cm apart. With a non-uniform shape it is important that the anode is very approximately the same shape so that the electrode distances remain comparable over the entire electroform surface. There is a tendency for more

Figure 4.22 Underside of an electroform of one of the silver dishes from the Sutton Hoo burial, showing streaking. (Courtesy A. Milton/British Museum)

copper to be deposited at the edges, at the expense of flat central areas. This can be partially compensated for by placing in the electrolyte baffles of a non-conducting material before the edge which the copper ions must negotiate before deposition. Alternatively, a conducting ring of copper wire may be placed near the edges to compete locally for the copper ions.

The copper used in the solutions and for the anode must be of high purity – traces of elements such as arsenic and antimony can cause grain coarsening of the electroform. It is advisable to place the anode in a permeable bag of nylon net to retain particles of copper oxide, etc. which form during the process. These could cause disfigurement and weakening if they were to be deposited.

After a sufficient deposit has built up the mould is removed from the tank and washed. Despite the precautions mentioned above there is still usually a build-up of copper around the edge. This can be cut free from the remainder of the electroform whilst still in the mould, which acts as a support. The trimmed sections are then backed with soft solder and joined, either with more solder or an adhesive such as araldite. The edges can now be given a final trim with burins and files preparatory to coloring or plating as required.

Diagnostic features of electroforms

Various features of such a distinctive process should render electroforms easy to detect, but some of these can be overcome or disguised. Thus, electroforms have been found in major museum collections around the world after having been accepted and published on as genuine antiquities for generations (see Chapter 1, p. 15).

The presence of a join, usually soft-soldered, along the edges of what should have been a single sheet is indicative of electroforming. Inevitably, two sheets soldered together are going to be thicker than many of the originals, as exemplified by Figures. 4.23a and 4.23b. The maker had tried to make this less noticeable at the edges by rather obvious filing. Also, a soldered double sheet will not possess the distinctive 'ring' of a single sheet.

The process produces a near-perfect reproduction of just the side against the mould face. The other, growing electrolyte face, will usually show many distinctive features of electro-deposition, specifically a very granular surface. However, these faces are not usually visible in the finished electroform. Sometimes the electrolytic side can be

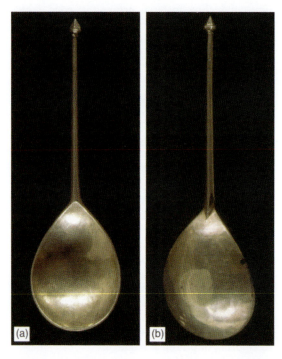

Figure 4.23a and b Front (a) and back (b) of an electroform of a medieval silver spoon. Note the underside has a distinctive dent, which is not visible on the inside of the bowl, showing it is of two separate sections. The bowl has a thick edge, only partially remedied by filing, and gives a dull ring when struck. All-in-all, a more convincing copy of the bowl could have been made from a single electroform, soldered to the shank. (Courtesy A. Milton/British Museum)

easily exposed, for example, on the agate standing cup with silver mounts, from the Waddesdon Bequest, now in the British Museum (Tait, 1991a, p. 171, Figure. 187), purporting to date to the sixteenth century. The silver calyx supporting the agate bowl is a single electroform, with the electrolyte side against the bowl, clearly visible and identifiable as an electroform once the cup was taken apart.

Where the original is of thin sheet metal with little variation in surface topography on one side, a single electroform could be made and the electrolyte face worked or polished to make it appear like ordinary sheet metal. For example, the two hemispheres which formed the main part of a silver gilt globe in the form of a goblet, now in the National Maritime Museum, Greenwich (Reg. GL 00177) were each formed of a single silver electroform. The outer surface with much engraving was the untouched electroform face but the inner face had been trimmed and carefully lathe-polished to give it the appearance of worked metal.

When first made the joins would have been disguised beneath plating, but, as is often the case on electroforms, after a few years the joins begin to show through (Figures 4.24a and 4.24b).

On other occasions complex pieces were moulded in one when in fact the detail should have been done separately if the piece had been meant to be a convincing copy (Figures 4.25a and 4.25b).

Although the actual contact surface is claimed to be a perfect rendition of the original, it usually carries marks characteristic of the process, as shown in the magnified photographs of a poor-quality electroform of the Early Bronze Age gold cup from Rillaton, in Devon. This electroform was rejected because the features of electro-deposition were too obvious, but they appear to some degree on most electroforms. There is a distinctive overall fine matt texture to the surface and a tendency for slight hollows to develop along the columnar grain boundaries, resulting in a slight puckering of the surface (Figure 4.26a, cf. Figure 4.21). Rendition of details such as engraved lines can often appear diffuse and discontinuous when magnified.

The electroform is only as good as the mould, and any defects thereon will be faithfully copied (Figure 4.26b and see Figure 8.26). The most common of these are small air bubbles trapped in the surface of the mould material, which appear as small bubbles of metal *on* the electroform surface, unless the graphite or silver conducting powder fills or covers them. The exact opposite fault, small

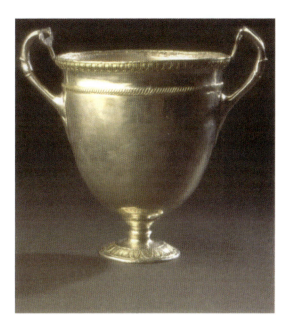

Figure 4.24a Copy of a Roman silver cup found at Welwyn, England (BM PRB Reg. 1911, 12-8, 28). The body is of wrought silver to which an electroform of the decorated band has been attached.

Figure 4.24b Detail of the strip bent around the rim where the join is now clearly visible. (Courtesy A. Milton/British Museum)

Figure 4.25a Electroform of a damaged Roman gold bracelet on which the original separately attached beaded wire borders were becoming detached.

Figure 4.25b On the electroform they are all part of the moulded surface, clearly showing that this is an impression of the damaged face. (Courtesy A. Milton/British Museum)

holes *in* the electroform surface, results from small gas bubbles forming in the electrolyte against the surface and becoming incorporated in the forming metal. These defects can be polished out if the surface is plain, and so they are best observed in recesses or in areas of high relief.

Where the deposition has been locally heavy the adjacent solution becomes depleted in metal ions, rending the solution lighter. It tends to rise, creating a shadow or streaking effect on the electroform surface where the solution was locally depleted (Figures 4.22 and 4.26b). Streaking can also occur if the temperature of the electrolyte was too low.

Another distinctive feature is the composition. Copper, nickel, silver and gold form good coherent deposits, whereas other metals are much less satisfactory. Far and away the most common metal used has been copper, although electroforms of gold and silver are known (Desthomas, 1983). Thus, on most electroforms the distinctive pink copper surface has to be plated or patinated to resemble the original, and analysis of a worn area, or of a small inconspicuous area from which the immediate surface can be removed, will often reveal the true nature of a suspect piece. For example, cursory inspection of the electroform copies of side strips on the sword chape from the Raab Treasure (see Chapter 1, p. 15, Figure 1.7) revealed the rosy hue of copper showing through the silver electroplate.

Figures 4.26a and b   Details from an electroform of the Rillaton gold cup. The electroform is a single sheet of copper that has been electroplated, thereby exhibiting characteristic features from both faces. (Courtesy S. La Niece/ British Museum) (a) Contact face of the outside of the cup. In the depths of the grooves that remain unpolished the surface is very matted and there is evidence of puckering in the centre (see Figure 4.21 showing how the columnar grains develop) (5 cm across). (b) Front face forming the inside of the electroform. Note the overall roughness of the surface and the several bubbles of metal where there were small air bubbles in the mould material. The pronounced streaking is due to localised deficiencies in copper ions in the plating solution. This is an exaggerated example of common faults found on electroforms. If the whole piece had not been rejected the developing face would have been polished, which would have removed many of these diagnostic features. (4 cm across).

Electroforms can be used to embellish antiquities as exemplified by a genuine but plain Hellenistic bronze mirror, now in the Getty Museum, which has a fine relief on the back that turned out on close inspection to be an electroform (Scott, 2002, pp. 22–24).

The very distinctive fine grain structure of electroforms should be easily detected by Laue back reflectance (see Chapter 3, pp. 54, Figure 3.12).

An interesting example of a forgery that was half-way between electroform and electroplating was some gold plated vessels that appeared for sale in Panama in the 1930s (Gettens and Mooradian, 1937). Examination showed that genuine ancient ceramic pots had been made conducting, a heavy layer of copper having been deposited and superficially gilded. Metallographic examination by S.K. Lothrop showed the characteristic long columnar grains of copper.

5

Physical dating techniques I: Radiocarbon dating

In this chapter and that which follows it, the principles of the three main techniques, i.e. radiocarbon (RC) dating, followed by thermoluminescence (TL) and dendrochronology, are described, emphasising their particular potentials and problems for authenticity studies.

The interpretation of seemingly objective scientific tests should be straightforward. However, it is noticeable that the most high-profile authenticity case studies utilising the three techniques have become deeply enmeshed in continuing controversy.

As Martin Aitken (1985, pp. 37–38) of the Oxford Laboratory for Archaeology and the History of Art, ruefully remarked:

> ... it shows the quagmire of embittered controversy in which a physical scientist is likely to have to wade once he involves himself with material of doubtful origin. Readers having it in mind to involve themselves in authenticity testing take warning.

These remarks concluded his account of the Glozel affair (see Chapter 6, pp. 119), but perhaps he had another, even more contentious, authenticity test at the back of his mind when he wrote those words, namely the Shroud of Turin (see p. 102) with which the Oxford Laboratory was heavily and acrimoniously involved at the time.

There is a fundamental difference in approach between archaeological dating and authentication. The former seeks to establish an absolute date whereas, by and large, authenticity studies need only establish whether the material dated is old. A suspect antiquity is usually already sufficiently typologically familiar to be placed within an existing chronological framework; what is at issue is whether it is ancient at all. Ethnographic material can form an exception, where traditional materials and techniques are still be in use, and physical dating methods may be the only method of establishing the true age.

A further exception is provided by some dendrochronological studies where very precise dates are capable of resolving questions over the involvement of specific artists or craftsmen (see Chapter 6, p. 134).

Radiocarbon dating

Principal sources: Aitken (1990, pp. 56–114); Bowman (1990; 1991a, pp. 117–140; 1994); Taylor (1997, 2001); Hedges (2000).

Although RC dating is perhaps the most familiar physical dating technique, the results as conventionally presented have been widely misunderstood and misinterpreted. It is necessary to stress two important practical considerations at the outset that curtail the applicability of carbon dating to authenticity studies.

1. The method dates the time when the raw material stopped growing, not when the artefact was made or used. The heartwood from a long-lived tree used in a piece of furniture could predate it by centuries.
2. The dates are usually expressed in RC years and translating these into calendar years can be difficult; in the case of materials that were growing between the seventeenth century AD and the 1950s this can prove almost impossible without other evidence.

The method was developed by Willard Libby in the late 1940s (Taylor 1987, pp. 147–170) and the details of the first dates were published in the early 1950s. The very first dating of real archaeological material was performed on a piece of acacia wood from an Egyptian tomb, dated typologically to the third millennium BC, and the RC date was in close agreement. This was just as well because for the next test the scientists requested a piece of wood of the Hellenistic period to be dated. The counts from this caused dismay as they were indistinguishable from those for modern wood. As J.R. Arnold, one of Libby's collaborators later recollected, 'My Christmas was ruined that year' (reported in

Table 5.1   A comparative guide to the sample sizes required for conventional, small counter and AMS dating methods. Since 1990 the amounts of sample required for AMS dating have become significantly smaller still.

Material	Conventional (g)	Mini-counting (g)	AMS (mg)
Wood (whole)	10–25	0.1–0.5	50–100
(cellulose)	50–100	0.5–1.0	200–500
Charcoal (& other charred materials)	10–20	0.1–0.5	10–100
Peat	50–100	0.5–1.0	100–200
Textiles	20–50	0.05–0.10	20–50
Bone	100–400	2.0–5.0	500–1000
Shell	50–100	0.5–1.0	50–100
Sediment, soils	100–500	2.0–10.0	500–25 000

Source: Bowman, 1990, p. 34

Marlowe, 1980). Fearing their new method was somehow fatally flawed, the innocent scientists investigated every possibility except the obvious one – the piece they had been given was not Hellenistic at all but a modern forgery (Libby, 1967, p. 17).

For the next 30 years or so RC dating required many grams of sample and it was only with the introduction of the accelerator mass spectrometry (AMS) direct counting on tiny samples (Gove, 1999, and see below), that RC dating has become of significance to authenticity studies (Table 5.1). RC dating is potentially applicable to a wide range of organic materials that were alive during the last 40 000 years, including wood, paper, bone, ivory, leather, horn, antler, eggshell, textile and even some gemstones such as coral or pearl (but not amber as it is too old). The carbon of some synthetic materials as diverse as bone glue and charcoal-smelted iron may also be dated.

Principles of RC dating

The Earth's atmosphere contains small amounts of carbon dioxide. The carbon atoms themselves exist in three forms, known as *isotopes*. Ninety-nine per cent have an atomic weight of 12 (written ^{12}C), that is, each atom has six *protons* and six *neutrons*. One per cent have an atomic weight of 13 (^{13}C), each atom having an extra neutron, that is six *protons* and seven *neutrons*, and there is a tiny amount (one part in a million million) of carbon with an atomic weight of 14 (^{14}C), the atoms each having two extra neutrons, that is six *protons* and eight

neutrons. The ^{14}C is produced in the upper atmosphere by neutrons generated by cosmic radiation interacting with nitrogen atoms, which have an atomic weight of 14, made up of seven *protons* and seven *neutrons*. One of the protons in the nitrogen atom is replaced with a neutron, thereby converting nitrogen atoms into carbon atoms:

$$^{14}N + n \rightarrow {}^{14}C + P$$

The heavy carbon is fundamentally unstable, that is, it is radioactive, and will ultimately decay.

The newly created carbon reacts with oxygen to form carbon dioxide, which in turn can be absorbed into growing plants by photosynthesis (Figure 5.1). At this time the ^{14}C content of the plant reflects that of the atmosphere; after it has ceased growing the ^{14}C will continue to decay, but no new radioactive atoms will replenish those lost. As there are steadily fewer ^{14}C atoms left with the potential to decay the emissions from a given sample decline with time. This imposes a time limit, and after about 40 000 years have elapsed the number of decays coming from the remaining ^{14}C atoms is so small that it is difficult to measure them against the background radiation and instrument 'noise'.

The half-life

In order to translate this decline into years it is essential to have a knowledge of how long it takes for the ^{14}C to decay away. Although the decays are constant and immutable it is impossible to predict

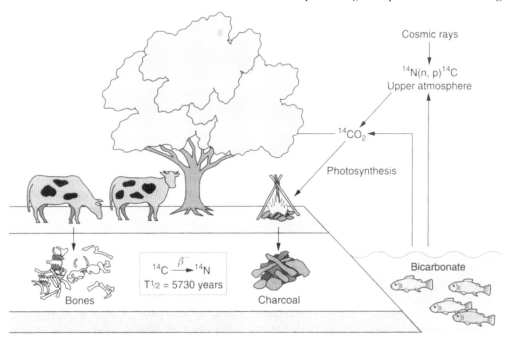

Figure 5.1   Life, death and RC. A simplified version of the production of ^{14}C: its incorporation into living matter, together with its ultimate fate. (Courtesy N.D. Meeks and T. Simpson)

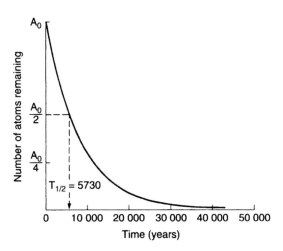

Figure 5.2   Exponential decay of ^{14}C. It can be seen that the full life of the ^{14}C stretches away towards infinity, and is certainly unmeasurable, but the time taken for half of the radioactive atoms to decay can be determined.

when any individual ^{14}C atom will decay. The numbers of decays from a given sample will just decline into an indefinite and immeasurable future. Thus the concept of the full radioactive life of any radioactive element is theoretically meaningless and practically

unmeasurable. Instead the time taken for the activity to halve is used (Figure 5.2). This is known as the half-life, and can be measured with some precision.

Measurement

^{14}C atoms are not very different from ordinary carbon atoms except for their brief moment of glory and extinction as carbon when they decay back to nitrogen and give off a beta particle. Thus, one obvious way to estimate the quantity of ^{14}C present is to measure the number of these decays per unit mass; the fewer decays per unit mass of carbon the less ^{14}C was present and the older the sample, as outlined above.

This was the basis for the traditional counting methods. The problem is that not only is the proportion of ^{14}C atoms very small, but the chance of any one of them doing something interesting, such as decaying, is also very small (there is a 50:50 chance of this for any one atom in 5730 years). In other words there is not much activity, so quite a large sample is required even when the sample is counted for several weeks (see Table 5.1). The amounts required for destructive testing have effectively precluded the use of the method for most art objects or antiquities.

Even though there is only a tiny amount of ^{14}C relative to ordinary carbon in the earth's atmosphere, this still amounts to a large number of radioactive atoms in quite a small sample. Large enough for measurements to be statistically viable and reproducible, one milligram of carbon absorbed from the atmosphere will contain about 50 000 atoms of ^{14}C.

The obvious solution is to measure these ^{14}C atoms directly using mass spectrometry, which differentiates between atoms by their atomic weight (see Chapter 3, p. 52). However, in the 1950s no instrument could estimate such tiny quantities of a light element especially in the all-pervading atmosphere of ordinary ^{14}N, which has the same atomic weight. By the 1970s the problem was resolved by the application of a very high voltage to accelerate the atoms through high velocities when it became possible to isolate and estimate very low quantities of ^{14}C directly (Donahue and Jull, 1999; Gove, 1999). Using accelerator mass spectrometry (AMS) dating there has been a dramatic and continuing fall in sample size, typically a thousand-fold (see Table 5.1). Suddenly RC dating became a viable authentication technique applicable, in theory at least, to any organic materials that had been alive during the last 40 000 years.

RC and calendar years

One would have thought that with a technique apparently so objective and 'scientific' there would be no difficulties in interpretation. One problem has been that many art historians, collectors and dealers, as with archaeologists before them, have tended to regard the stated RC age as an absolute figure and, even worse, to directly equate RC years with calendar years. Unfortunately life, especially RC life, is not that simple (see for example the changing RC data for the piltdown material through the last 50 years, Chapter 19, p. 492).

Very fortunately and with great prescience, the founders of RC dating, realising that they were making assumptions about such matters as the constancy or otherwise of the amount of ^{14}C in the atmosphere, its half-life, and the ability of plants to discriminate between the various isotopes of carbon, in order to arrive at their date, gave the dates as an 'RC age' not a true age. They also realised that they had a new technique that was likely to come into widespread use rapidly and this was their one chance to impose discipline. Thus, every date published would be calculated always using the same set of criteria, and so it has remained. It would be for the individual user in the future to apply whatever calibration was then current to the RC age, but the date as published would have been calculated under the same set of parameters no matter where and when produced. This is perhaps the appropriate place to discuss these assumptions and how the growing understanding of the true situation has altered the relationship not just between RC years and calendar years but the significance and application of RC dating generally.

1. Libby used the then best available figure of 5680 years for the half-life of carbon. Soon afterwards it was determined that 5730 years was a more accurate figure, but for the calculation of the RC age the original figure, now known as the Libby half-life, is still used.
   RC dates are often quoted as before present BP (Before Present); since in the world of RC age even the present is fixed, it will always be 1950 AD (if only they had chosen AD 2000, it would have made translating between BC and BP much simpler!).

2. Isotopic fractionation is the propensity of plants to discriminate between the various isotopes of carbon in their uptake of CO_2 from their surroundings in the atmosphere or water. Thus, the proportion of ^{14}C may very well not be the same in the living organism as in the surrounding environment. The phenomenon was known in the 1950s but the extent of different degrees of fractionation between plants using different photosynthetic pathways was not fully appreciated. Also, the consistent differences between different materials, bone and marine plants, for example, were not anticipated and so a single correction was applied across the board to all materials. All dates, no matter what the origin of the samples, are automatically corrected as if they were once wood, charcoal having being perceived as the likely main source of samples, and the fractionation is expressed as a δ ^{13}C figure.
   In reality, many factors influence the extent of fractionation and fortunately this can be estimated for each sample quite easily. The much more abundant ^{13}C is also subject to isotopic fractionation by living organisms and thus is a good indicator of the likely discrimination that took place against the ^{14}C. ^{13}C is stable and thus the amount present is the same as when the organism was living, and being relatively abundant is easily detected by ordinary mass spectrometry (MS), and of course is measured alongside the ^{14}C in the accelerator mass

spectrometry (AMS) process. The proportion of ^{13}C present, known as the $\delta\,^{13}C$ figure, is usually given so that a correction can be made. In the early days of RC dating, $\delta\,^{13}C$ determinations were not usually carried out individually on the specific sample but instead the published figures of the $\delta\,^{13}C$ for the species being dated were used, with an attendant increase in the error factor thereby making the date more imprecise.

3. The most complex and serious problem for RC dating was the assumption that the quantities of ^{14}C in the Earth's atmosphere over the past 40 or so millennia was likely to have remained constant. That this was incorrect began to emerge as early as the 1950s judging from the RC dates obtained on some ancient wooden Egyptian artefacts which had known precise historical dates. Moreover, discrepancies were found in the RC dates obtained on wood from tree trunks that had been directly dated by dendrochronology. Both sets of RC results gave dates that were several centuries too young. This was not immediately publicized, probably because the first RC dates on archaeological material were regarded by many archaeologists as being too old, and thus the possibility that they would have to become even older was regarded as too challenging a prospect if RC was to be accepted at all.

The problem was eventually addressed by carrying out a major research programme of RC dating of samples taken from bristle cone pines (*Pinus aristata*) that had been precisely dated by dendrochronology (Suess, 1970; and see Chapter 6, p. 126). These trees, growing in the arid mountains of the southwest USA, can live for thousands of years putting down very thin (0.25 mm typically) growth rings each year. Thus, it was possible to establish a direct correlation between the RC age and calendar years on a sample drilled from a living tree dating back for several thousand years by counting the rings and carrying out RC dating at regular intervals. The range was further extended back to 8000 years by matching the pattern of rings in the centre of the living trees with the pattern on the outer rings of trees that had been dead for hundreds, if not thousands, of years, but which survived because of their high resin content and the arid conditions. From this programme it was immediately clear that there was a significant difference between the RC age and calendar years as determined by dendrochronology.

When plotted against each other the RC age oscillated around the calendar years through a period of about 9000 years. Thus, in the Medieval period the RC age is about 100 years too old, and by the first millennium BC the two are more or less in agreement, but after that the RC age become progressively too young to a maximum of about 900 years in the early fourth millennium BC, thereafter the difference decreases again. At first this caused great consternation, not least among astronomers for the clear implications it carried for considerable long-term cyclic variation in the sun's output of cosmic radiation. However, it is now known that the underlying cause is the periodic variation in the earth's magnetic field – when this is high the charged cosmic radiation is deflected more than when the field is low.

The plot of RC years against calendar years contained an even more unexpected feature, which became known as wiggles. Although the curve was generally sinusoidal it was certainly not smooth. Some put this down to experimental error, background noise, etc., but worryingly some of the more prominent wiggles showed up repeatedly in dates from laboratories around the world, dating different materials. Perhaps there were short-term variations to contend with as well. The original programme on the bristle cone pine had been done on groups of rings taken together. For the new project, much smaller groups of thicker rings were taken from faster-growing trees such as ancient oaks that had survived in a variety of waterlogged environments, from locations around the world and dated at different centres. This was done to obviate any single laboratory bias and to show that this was a genuine world-wide phenomenon dependent solely on the amount of ^{14}C in the Earth's atmosphere.

The results, published in the 1980s (Pearson and Stuiver 1986; Stuiver and Pearson, 1986), showed conclusively that the amount of ^{14}C had varied significantly over quite short periods of time varying from 200 years to only decades (Figure 5.3). These short-term variations have very serious repercussions for RC dating, which are both good and bad. The good news is that the RC age can be translated into calendar years. The bad news is that for some periods of the past the short-term fluctuations are such as to make translation from RC age to calendar date quite complex (Figure 5.4).

Thus the RC age is still presented as it always has been under the old unchanging parameters that governed the very first published dates, together now with a calibrated date. Sometimes the dates are presented graphically, which can give a much more accurate representation of the true age (Figure 5.5). The translation from RC date into calendar years is relatively straightforward. Most laboratories reporting an RC age give a calibrated date in addition,

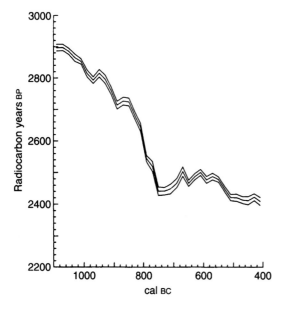

Figure 5.3 Section of Pearson and Stuiver's (1986) calibration curve for the period 1100 to 400 BC. Two RC dates, one of 2600 BP and one of 2500 BP, both with errors of ± 50 at 1σ, would have dramatically different calibrations. The former intercepts a steep part of the curve, but the latter, passing through several wiggles in the curve, covers many centuries between 800 and 400 BC. Although this wide spread may be useless for archaeological dating purposes, it could still be of use for authenticity studies (Courtesy Bowman, 1990).

as in the example given here. However, where this has not been done it can be achieved by consulting the on-line Oxcal calibration facility put out by the Research Laboratory for Art and Archaeology, Oxford University.

Here is a typical, real RC date performed by AMS dating at the Dating Laboratory of the University of Arizona at Tucson for the author, on a sample drilled from the wooden handle of a stone mining hammer from the copper mines at Chuquicamata, Chile, and reported by them in the conventional form:

Sample: AA 18886, T 4362, Wood fragments from hammer handle

$$\delta\ ^{13}C =\ -23.05 \pm 0.01\ \text{permil}$$
Radiocarbon age = 1804 ± 48 B.P.

Calibrated calendar age range:

one sigma AD145–AD320
two sigma AD120–AD375

As is conventional the radiocarbon and calendar ages have been normalized to $\delta\ ^{13}C =\ -25.0$ permil. The wood fragments were treated with HCL to remove inorganic carbonates, and with NaOH to remove organic humic acids, then with HCL again.

First, the laboratory's identifying code is given, in this case A for the University of Arizona, the second A denoting that this is an AMS determination. The number that follows is the unique identification of this specific sample. All dates should have this accompanying information; a date without an accompanying identification which enables it to be confirmed and checked should be treated with suspicion.

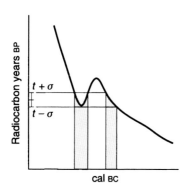
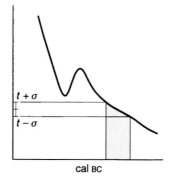
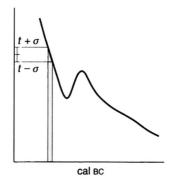

Figure 5.4 Graphical representation of calibration. In the first instance the RC years intercept encounters a wiggle and cuts the calibration curve twice and thus two calendar dates are possible. In the second the RC years intercept encounters a gentle slope on the curve, which means that the calendar date range will be wider than that for the RC years. In the third case the RC years intercept encounters the calibration curve where it is steep and the calendar date will have a narrower date range.

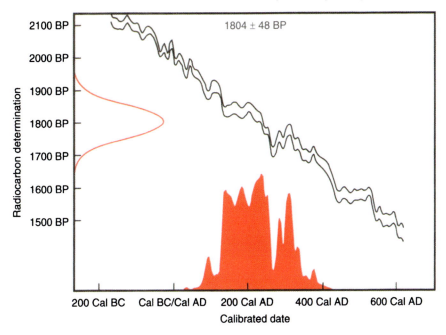

Figure 5.5   Graphical representation of the calibrated RC date of a stone mining hammer (AA 18886. T 4362). (Courtesy J. Ambers and T. Simpson)

Then follows the determination of the isotopic fractionation of the ^{13}C based on the AMS measurements on the sample, the estimates of the error in that determination and the date in RC years together with the estimate of the precision of that determination based on the sample, number of counts made, etc. Note that this is expressed at a one sigma (σ) confidence level, meaning that there is a 68.3% chance that the age in RC years lies between 1756 and 1852 years BP (Before Present and the RC Present will always be 1950).

The RC date is then calibrated, using first one σ confidence level, that is a 68.3% chance that the calendar age lies in the given range, and secondly calculated at the two σ confidence level, that is a 95.3% chance that the calendar age lies within the extended date range. Two σ is normally used nowadays.

There then follows a statement that the RC age has been normalised to δ ^{13}C equaling -25.0 permil, that is, slightly different from the measured figure. This corrects for the natural biochemical fractionation processes in the plants (see p. 90).

Finally, there is a note concerning the pretreatment of the sample prior to dating. First, possible inorganic carbonates were removed with hydrochloric acid. Then sodium hydroxide was added to remove any recent humic acid contaminants from the wood, followed by more acid being added to neutralise the sample, followed by prolonged washing in distilled water. The possible contamination by modern organic materials can be quite significant (see p. 102 and Chapter 13, p. 344).

Problems and potentials with the RC dating of recent materials

The main problem, as noted above, lies in the non-linear regions of the curve – those wiggles. For certain periods, sometimes extending over several centuries, due ultimately to fundamental fluctuations in the cosmic radiation dose, and thus beyond any correction or remedy, the 'curve' is extremely erratic and a whole range of calibrated dates are equally possible. This is most serious from the point of view of authentication for the last few hundred years (Figure 5.6), sometimes referred to as the Stradivarius Gap, after the violin-maker whose products fall neatly into this period. The fluctuations together with the effects of atmospheric pollution after the mid-eighteenth century make carbon dating of organic materials that are likely to have been growing after the seventeenth century meaningless in most circumstances without additional dating

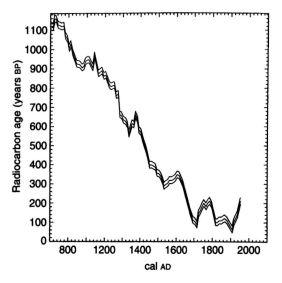

Figure 5.6 Section of Stuiver and Pearson's (1986) calibration curve for the Post-Medieval period. It can be seen that a series of wiggles from the seventeenth to twentieth centuries preclude any meaningful estimate of true age to be given in the absence of other factors, the so-called Stradivarius Gap. This should be borne in mind when considering RC dates for post-medieval material. (Courtesy Jull and Donahue, 1990)

evidence (Taylor 1997, p. 68). An RC date of, say 220 ± 60 BP, when translated into calendar years at 2σ, would have a 95% chance of lying between 1642 and 1679, between 1743 and 1802, or between 1938 and 1955. If the piece in question had no history at all then the RC date would be useless. If, however, it was known with certainty to have been in existence in the early twentieth century, the RC date would show that the material from which the piece was made, be it bone, cloth, paper or wood, had been growing in the seventeenth or eighteenth centuries, which could be useful information.

On occasion, some of the possible dates can be excluded through examination of other evidence. This is exemplified by the study made by Van Strydonck *et al.* (1998) on the canvases of two paintings.

One was a depiction of the *Calvary* painted on canvas that had been mounted onto a panel, apparently but not certainly, soon after the painting was made. The second was a picture of *The Fall of Icarus*, attributed to Breughel the Elder, and this had subsequently been relined twice (see Chapter 12, p. 291). The dates are reproduced in Table 5.2. It can be seen that even though the RC ages have very low error ranges (known as high-precision dates) when calibrated, a whole range of calendar years are possible, especially at 2σ. For example, in the absence of any other information, nothing at all could have

Table 5.2 AMS dating results from two post-medieval paintings on canvas: one, an anonymous *Calvary*, the other *The Fall of Icarus* attributed to Jan Breughel the Elder.

Sample from:	Lab. ref.	Conventional date (BP)	Calibrated age [9, 10]*	
			68.2% confidence (1σ)	95.4% confidence (2σ)
Calvary canvas	UtC-5397	395 ± 25	1450(0.81)1510 1600(0.19)1620	1440(0.73)1520 1570(0.27)1630
The Fall of Icarus canvas	UtC-5396	380 ± 30	1460(0.64)1520 1590(0.36)1630	1440(0.55)1530 1550(0.45)1640
first lining	UtC-5398	200 ± 25	1660(0.21)1680 1760(0.54)1810 1930(0.25)...	1650(0.21)1690 1740(0.57)1810 1930(0.22)...
second lining	UtC-5124	210 ± 25	1660(0.25)1680 1770(0.49)1810 1940(0.25)...	1650(0.25)1690 1740(0.53)1810 1930(0.22)...

Source: Van Strydonck *et al.*, 1998

*Figures in brackets refer to the relative area under the probability distribution.

been said about the relining of *The Fall of Icarus*, the RC age of 200 years BP being completely meaningless. However, in both cases something *can* be said about the painting on the canvas.

Dendrochronology on the oak panel to which the *Calvary* had been stuck, showed that the tree was still growing in 1523 (it may well have been growing considerably later, but with the outer sapwood rings missing that is all that can be safely deduced; see Chapter 6, p. 129). Thus *if* the canvas really had been stuck to the panel very soon after the painting was finished then it cannot have been painted before 1523, and the range 1440 to 1520 can be excluded. It is important to note that by removing one of the possibilities, and the application of Bayesian statistics (see Chapter 1, p. 4), the probability and range of the others change slightly, and the age of the canvas now moves to between 1560 to 1675 at 2σ (Figure 5.7a).

Turning now to *The Fall of Icarus*, Breughel's date of birth is unknown, but his career began around 1550. Thus once again the earlier date range can be excluded and the recalibrated date range for the remaining period becomes 1555 to 1635 (Figure 5.7b).

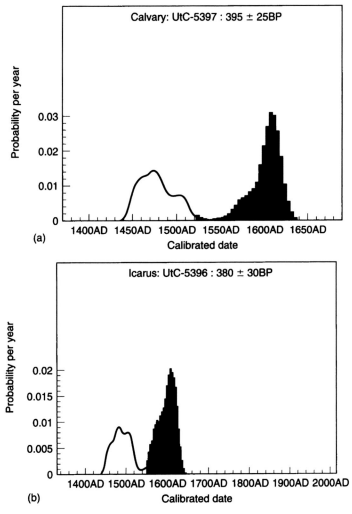

(a)

(b)

Figure 5.7 The incorporation of other non-RC dating evidence by the application of Bayesian statistics can sometimes provide more meaningful dates, as exemplified by the treatment of the calibrated AMS dates of the two paintings considered here. (Courtesy Van Strydonck *et al.*, 1998) (a) *Calvary*. The dendrochronological evidence rules out the earlier, unshaded part of the graph. (b) *The Fall of Icarus*. Historical evidence rules out the earlier, unshaded part of the graph.

Breughel died in 1569, thus making the attribution of the picture to him a little unlikely, but not the 'almost impossible' claimed by Van Strydonck *et al.*

Fossil fuel and bomb carbon

A well as the natural variations outlined above, the amount of ^{14}C in the Earth's atmosphere has been changed over the past two centuries by man's industrial and military activities. Fossil fuel was laid down many millions of years ago and thus its constituent carbon has long since lost all its ^{14}C. It was very soon realised from ^{14}C determinations on many samples from the eighteenth century onwards that the global burning of fossil fuel, primarily coal, was adding a significant amount of 'dead' carbon to the Earth's atmosphere, thereby diluting the ^{14}C.

The opposite effect was caused by the testing of nuclear weapons in the atmosphere in the 1950s and early 1960s. This created vast quantities of ^{14}C, roughly doubling the amount previously present by 1965 (Figure 5.8). With the cessation of atmospheric testing after 1963 the amount of ^{14}C in the air began to fall away quite quickly as it became absorbed in the oceans, etc. The amount of bomb carbon has not been uniform in the atmosphere all over the earth, and detailed measurements on recent tree rings from around the world have allowed the resultant dates to be calibrated with some accuracy (Hua and Barbetti, 2004). Bomb carbon does provide a reliable method of identifying organic materials which were growing in the second half of the twentieth century. They will have an RC content above the 1950 baseline, normally designated 'post bomb' by RC scientists. The figure is usually expressed as a figure over the 1950 atmospheric ^{14}C levels. Thus, a figure of 110 pMC (percent modern carbon) would be 110% of the 1950 figure.

Plants have a very rapid response to the changes in the atmospheric ^{14}C levels. This has already found application for the authentication of single malt whiskies (Figure 5.9), and a very similar curve has been produced for vintage wines where in both instances the barley or grapes of a single year are used (Baxter and Walton, 1971). Isotope studies on the water which constitutes 80–90% of most wines has enabled them to be provenanced quite precisely, which taken together with the dating evidence is of considerable use in authenticating rare vintages (Breas *et al.*, 1994).

Keisch and Miller (1972) showed that linseed oil and paper produced from materials that were growing over a period from 1936 to 1970 showed a marked increase in ^{14}C content from the mid-1950s (Figure 5.10). They suggested this could have useful applications in the authenticity testing of paintings (see Chapter 12, p. 290).

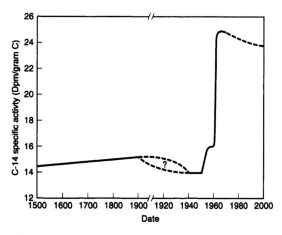

Figure 5.8 A century of contamination of the Earth's atmosphere. From 1890 to 1950 the percentage of ^{14}C in the atmosphere slowly declined as levels of carbon dioxide, derived from 'dead' carbon, built up, caused by the burning of coal and mineral oil. This effect was dramatically reversed by atmospheric nuclear testing with the attendant release of ^{14}C. Once testing ceased, the amounts of ^{14}C equally quickly began to decline, but plants growing through this period will have absorbed carbon at this enhanced level and their carbon remains will have very distinctive high ^{14}C for some centuries to come, providing a very useful chronological indicator for authenticity studies (Courtesy Keisich, 1973).

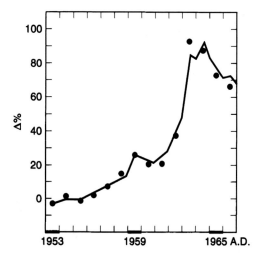

Figure 5.9 Close correlation between ^{14}C in atmospheric CO_2 (line) and in single-year malt whiskies (dots), during the rapid increase in ^{14}C caused by atmospheric testing. It would also reveal the presence of post-1950s whisky in a supposedly earlier vintage (Courtesy Fleming, 1976).

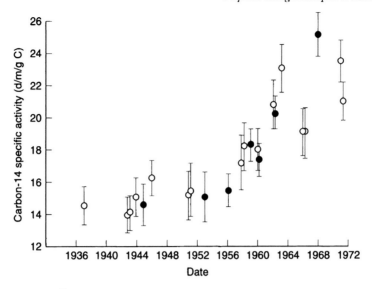

Figure 5.10   The rise in the ^{14}C concentration in linseed oil ○, and paper ●, in the mid-twentieth century, due to atmospheric nuclear testing.

For animals there is a still greater potential as their different parts contain different amounts of ^{14}C. Soft tissue, for example, will tend to have more carbon that was recently absorbed than will bone in the same living creature, and thus in a post-bomb world where the amount of ^{14}C is declining quite quickly the soft tissue will be measurably less radioactive than the bone, other factors being equal. Thus, by dating several body parts it is sometimes possible to get very accurate dates for creatures that have lived and died post-1950s.

Case study: The Persian Mummy. Authentication meets forensic investigation

Sources: Romey and Rose (2001); Kretschner *et al.* (2004).

In October 2000 a spectacular mummy of a young woman was seized at the city of Quetta in Pakistan. The damaged outer coffin of wood revealed an inner stone coffin that contained the mummy wrapped in linen bandages and lying on a mat of bast fibre. Although apparently very much in the Egyptian tradition, this was no ordinary mummy. The mummy had a golden crown and a gold plate that proclaimed her to be Ruduuna, daughter of Xerxes, king of the Persians, who had died almost 2500 years ago.

Although the mummy had been seized in Quetta no one was sure where it was actually dug up. The Pakistan authorities asserted that it was from Kharan, but the Iranian government insisted it had really been found in Iran and demanded it back. Not wishing to be left out of a scrap, the Taleban claimed it had come from Afghanistan.

However, doubts were soon raised over the authenticity of the mummy; no other Persian mummies are known, and there were technical problems with the coffins, as well as with the calligraphy of the inscription. Pieces from the mat and from the linen were taken for RC determinations, which showed that the plant material for both items belonged to the post-bomb era with figures around 113 pMC. This prompted further studies on the bone and muscle tissue of the body itself. Collagen from the bone gave a figure of 115.1 pMC and the muscle tissue a figure of 111.0 pMC.

From these figures it now appears that the body is that of a young woman who died in 1995. The body must have been taken from the morgue, dug up from a grave, or perhaps something even more sinister.

Further problems in the interpretation and use of RC dates for specific materials

Wood

Trees grow by laying down annual growth rings (see Chapter 6, p. 126) and, once they are laid down, there is little addition or exchange of other carboniferous matter. Thus, the wood in the centre of a living tree trunk has its carbon derived from that absorbed from the atmosphere when the tree was young, probably very many years earlier. Unless there is some indication that the particular piece of wood being dated was near to the surface (the presence of sapwood or, better still, of the bark) there is an unknown factor which, in the case of the heartwood of hardwoods, could run to centuries.

If a wooden artefact purports to be thousands of years old then ^{14}C dating may be useful, but if supposedly of a Post-Medieval date, for example, then there are many problems of interpretation that arise, quite separate from those of calibration. If the sample yielded a date in the sixteenth century, this could be for wood cut down and fashioned in the sixteenth century, but could equally well be for the heartwood of a tree growing in the sixteenth century that was only cut down and fashioned centuries later, or be for wood cut down at some intermediate date for another purpose and subsequently reused (sometimes with fraudulent intent; see Chapter 17, p. 443). RC dating by itself could not distinguish between these scenarios.

Marine-derived materials

Another problem concerns artefacts made of organic materials that have their ultimate origin in the sea. The oceans of the world contain the main reservoir of carbon dioxide dissolved from the atmosphere, where it can remain in the deep waters for millennia before being absorbed by living organisms. The near-surface waters contain predominantly freshly dissolved atmospheric carbon dioxide together with some much older dissolved carbon dioxide brought up from the deep waters. Also, some carbon will derive from dissolved calcium carbonate of geological origin and thus be of 'dead' carbon. The effect is to dilute the fresh ^{14}C content, and organisms deriving their carbon from this water will appear older than they really are. Overall, the contribution adds up to between about 400 years in most waters but as much as 1200 years in arctic waters (Stuiver and Polach, 1977). The

'reservoir' effect depends on many factors, such as where the particular organisms were growing, either at the surface, or on the sea bed, etc. and seems to vary with time, the discrepancy increasing with age, although this only becomes significant for material that is many thousands of years old (Sikes *et al.*, 2000). Thus, the contribution cannot be easily established for any particular marine material, thereby adding to the overall error factor. Therefore, whilst RC can authenticate a piece it cannot provide a very precise date, because the reservoir effect cannot be calculated for each individual piece but must be taken as an average figure for marine organic materials generally.

Products from the various sea mammals that live predominantly on fish provide good examples (Tauber, 1979). In some northern lands the teeth or tusks of sea mammals such as the walrus have been widely used since antiquity (see Chapter 17, p. 423). Whalebone will also be affected. For example, a whalebone plaque (Figure 5.11), carved in the Spanish Romanesque style of about AD 1000, gave an AMS date of 1480 ± 80 BP (OxA-1164), calibrated to between AD 410 and 690 at 2σ. After the apparent marine ageing effect is taken into account, this shows that the age of the whalebone is in accord with the art historical dating of the piece.

Because of the uncertainty surrounding the specific marine ageing factor to be applied for any particular piece, the precision is reduced, thereby increasing the error bands which, in turn, rather precludes the use of RC as a dating or even as an authentication tool for most Post-Medieval marine-derived material. Thus, it would be impossible to arrive at any meaningful date for a piece of scrimshaw carved on whalebone, for example, even if the whale had been living in the post-bomb era (see Chapter 17, p. 424).

Shells will have absorbed carbonate material of indeterminate age from their surroundings during their formation, and also have a propensity to exchange carbonate material with their environment after they have formed, and as such are not suitable for RC dating.

Bone

Bone consists of both inorganic and organic components. The inorganic are hydroxyapatite with some calcium carbonate, and the organic is collagen. The hydroxyapatite, which is mainly calcium phosphate, attracts calcium carbonate from ground waters, etc. during burial and thus is not suitable for dating. Fortunately, it can be easily separated from

Figure 5.11 Spanish Romanesque whalebone carving of two seated figures (BM MLA Reg. 1987, 10-5, 1). The piece is dated stylistically to about AD 1000 AD, but the whalebone gave an RC date several centuries older because of the so-called reservoir effect. (Courtesy A. Milton/British Museum)

the collagen by dissolution in dilute acid. The collagen is made up of proteins and is suitable for dating.

Iron

Sources: Cresswell (1991, 1992); Cook *et al.* (2001, 2003); Craddock *et al.* (2002).

Iron was traditionally smelted with charcoal and during this process the forming iron absorbed small quantities of carbon coming from the charcoal. The latter is assumed to have been made from trees growing approximately contemporary with the smelting.

Wrought iron or mild steel typically contains of the order of 0.02 to 0.2% carbon, steel 0.2 to 1.0% and cast iron 2.0 to 4.0% percent. With AMS dating only a few milligrams of iron are required.

Fossil fuel – coal and coke – was probably first used around the 7th century AD for the smelting process in China, but only considerably later elsewhere, the eighteenth century in Europe, for example. The proponents of the RC dating of iron argue that iron smelted with charcoal is potentially dateable and that the presence of carbon derived from fossil fuel will be immediately apparent because of the geological age obtained; however, reality is much more complicated (Eylon, 2002; Craddock *et al.*, 2002).

Even assuming that the carbon in the iron all comes from the charcoal, there is no way of ascertaining the age of the wood that formed the charcoal. In Post-Medieval Europe, charcoal was usually obtained from trees pollarded at 10- to 20-year intervals to promote the quick growth of poles suitable for the charcoal burners. In these instances the date of the charcoal should be quite close to the date of the smelting, but more generally timber of any age could have been used. Eylon (2002) for example, documented the selection of oaks that were hundreds of years old for the production of charcoal for iron smelting in Lebanon in the recent past.

Carbon from other sources could enter the iron during smelting. The iron ore itself often included siderite – iron carbonate – although it was usual practice to calcine the ore before smelting, driving off the carbonates. The usual flux in the blast furnace process was limestone, calcium carbonate, which was not calcined before being charged. Some of the flux would calcine in the upper or outer regions of the furnace but some carbonate material would almost inevitably enter the very reducing conditions of the reaction zone and produce carbon monoxide. This carbon monoxide would join that produced from the fuel to reduce the iron oxides and carburise the forming metal, thereby introducing dead carbon into the iron, even in a charcoal-fuelled process.

Cresswell (1992) recognised the problem and suggested that where the slag inclusions in the iron were found to be calcium-rich the metal might not be suitable for dating. Unfortunately cast iron, or the wrought iron often made from it, does not retain any slag inclusions, calcareous or otherwise, from the initial smelting process; they will all have been separated from the iron while it was molten. Moreover, it is almost impossible to distinquish

Case study: Martin Frobisher's *Osmonds*

The most extensive application of the RC dating of iron published so far has been on rough blooms of unrefined iron excavated at Kodlunarn Island, off Baffin Island in the Canadian Arctic. These are apparently associated with Martin Frobisher's ill-starred attempts to find either the North West Passage or gold (Harbottle *et al.*, 1993). The blooms were a mystery, and remain so even after the dating exercise.

In the well-documented lists of supplies carried by Frobisher's ships there is no record of iron blooms, and it would have made no sense to have sent out raw iron that required large quantities of fuel to use to forge it into useable iron. A totally different explanation was suggested by one of the expedition accounts which mentioned the discovery of 'divers osmondes of iron'. Osmond was often used to denote unrefined iron, so perhaps the blooms of iron had been smelted centuries before by the Vikings.

It was suggested that perhaps an RC date could resolve the mystery. On cutting the blooms, one, KeDe-1:87, revealed a small inclusion of charcoal entrapped in the iron. This gave an RC age of 970 ± 60 BP, calibrated at 1 σ to between AD 1006 and 1150. However, the carbon dissolved in the iron near the surface of the bloom gave an RC age of 1340 ± 70 BP, calibrated at 1 σ to between AD 640 and 760. This discrepancy at first suggested to Cresswell (1992) that there could be contamination from the limestone flux, and subsequently two further determinations were performed from deeper in the bloom. They gave RC ages of 550 ± 60 BP, calibrated at 1 σ to between AD 1307 and 1355; and 500 ± 60 BP, calibrated again at 1 σ to between AD 1400 and 1442.

The various RC dates from one bloom are disquieting to say the least, with the apparent age of the outer part of the bloom being almost twice as old as the interior, and with neither of the regions matching the date of the charcoal that should have been the source of the carbon in the iron. It is known that the Frobisher expedition had about 30 tons of coal with it, and coal was found in the smithy area where the bloom was found. A possible explanation is that the blooms really are of Viking age (although the youngest dates from the interior of the bloom are rather young for that hypothesis). The Frobisher expedition could have stumbled upon them and taken them back to their smithy and heated them strongly in a coal fire, causing carburisation at the surface with geological age carbon, even to the extent of depositing some carbon on the charcoal inclusions.

between wrought iron derived from the bloomery or blast furnace processes (see Chapter 7, p. 153).

Another potential problem lies in the contamination by corrosion, either through the formation of carbonates with young ^{14}C from the atmosphere, or if the iron is buried, ingress of water contaminated with carbonates of geological age. There are also problems if the corroded iron has been impregnated with organic materials as part of a conservation treatment; Scharf *et al.* (2004) experienced great difficulty in removing all of the organic matter from iron corrosion, despite using a variety of organic solvents and Soxhlet extraction.

Another major problem is the possibility of the iron containing carbon derived from both charcoal and fossil fuel. This can come about in two quite separate ways.

1. From multi-stage processes, some of which use charcoal and some fossil fuel. For example, in the eighteenth and early nineteenth centuries wrought iron was made by heating coke-smelted cast iron with charcoal. Similarly, in the European crucible steel processes, from the mid-nineteenth century the feedstock was often coke-smelted iron that was carburised with charcoal.

2. A more serious, and more prevalent problem is the indiscriminate mixing of charcoal- and coke-smelted scrap iron. In China, for example, the smelting of iron with coal and coke continued alongside charcoal for over 1000 years until the twentieth century, very often for the same class of goods such as coins or statuary (Craddock *et al.*, 2003). Thus for over a thousand years Chinese iron could be made from scrap iron

Table 5.3 AMS dates of some armour from the Metropolitan Museum, New York, purporting to be medieval.

Sample (V)	Identification	%C Yield	14C BP ©	Presumed manufacture	Donor
N-5	Italian armor	0.2	1640 ± 50	c 1400 AD	Metropolitan Museum of Art, New York
N-7	Italian armor	0.66	570 ± 50	late 15th century	Metropolitan Museum of Art, New York
N-8	Italian sword	0.11	4250 ± 50	c 16th century	Metropolitan Museum of Art, New York
N-9	Italian armor plate	0.35	510 ± 40	c 1480 AD	Metropolitan Museum of Art, New York
N-6	German armor	0.04	2790 ± 50	c 1550 AD	Metropolitan Museum of Art, New York
N-ll	German armor	0.9	2580 ± 40	mid 16th century	Metropolitan Museum of Art, New York

Source: Cook *et al.* 2003

containing both charcoal- and coke-smelted iron in any proportions, which could give almost any RC date on testing, irrespective of its real age.

Similarly in the West, although coke-smelted iron rapidly took over as the usual smelting fuel, in some countries such as Brazil, charcoal is still used as a primary smelting fuel. In North America, and even in European countries such as Sweden, the use of charcoal to smelt iron continued well into the twentieth century. It has been suggested that fossil fuel-smelted iron can be recognised by its enhanced sulphur content. This may be true of old Chinese iron, and European iron before the mid-eighteenth century, but in more recent iron the sulphur levels are as low as those found in charcoal-smelted iron.

This problem of potential mixing is exemplified by the AMS dates obtained on some armour from the Metropolitan Museum, New York by Cook *et al.* (2003) (Table 5.3). The armour purported to be Italian and German of the fifteenth to seventeenth centuries AD. Of the six pieces dated, only one date fell within the period assigned stylistically, the others covering a range of several thousand years. As Cook *et al.* pointed out, this means that a substantial proportion of the carbon must be derived from fossil fuel, which in turn can only have entered the iron in such quantity during the smelting. On the basis of the RC dates they suggest that the use of fossil fuel to smelt iron must have started several centuries earlier than previously believed. The suggestion that coal and coke were being regularly used in Central Europe and in Italy to smelt iron is just

not tenable. However, a more mundane explanation that does not require the rewriting of the history of metallurgy is that these suits of armour are of a later date than their style would suggest. They are, in fact, nineteenth-century reproductions, made of iron containing carbon from mixed sources.

The use of carbon dating for iron is clearly a problematic area, and it is, of course, possible that a deliberate mix of iron containing charcoal- and fossil fuel-derived carbon could be made in anticipation of AMS dating to produce the desired date for a forgery of an iron antiquity.

There have been instances where AMS has produced unequivocal early dates. Two Luristan iron swords produced calibrated AMS dates centring on 1044 BC and 1160 BC (Rehder, 1991). Both swords had been known to scholars for decades and the chances of a random mix of modern charcoal- and fossil fuel-derived charcoal twice arriving at the likely stylistic date are minimal; clearly, in this instance, the swords have been not only authenticated but dated by AMS.

The RC dating of corrosion products

Many of the corrosion products forming on the surfaces of metal antiquities are carbonates (see Chapter 14, p. 350), which should have reached a stable state relatively soon after deposition and thus it should be possible to date the burial. The problem is that although the carbon in a carbonate corrosion should come from carbonic acid derived from the atmosphere or humic acids, there is exchange with carbonates of geological age in the ground water, which renders the method unreliable. However, there is a possibility that a ^{14}C determination could be useful in authenticity tests if it was suspected that the carbonate corrosion had been induced by exposure to organic salts such as carboxylic acids (see Chapter 14, pp. 361, 363). If the acid was of recent organic origin, malt vinegar for example, or inorganic, industrial acetic acid made from oil-based chemicals, then the RC data obtained should be distinctive and diagnostic, bomb-carbon for the former and geological-age carbon for the latter. There is also the possibility of patination with chemicals of mixed origin, as well as of innocent conservation treatment with chemicals such as sodium sesquicarbonate, or of the application of waxes, etc. to an authentic patina, all of which could be fatally confusing.

Attempts to date the formation of oxalate patinas on stone have also encountered difficulties (see Chapter 11, p. 287).

Problems of contamination and precautions in packaging

Antiquities and art objects of organic materials that are potential material for RC dating are at risk from a variety of contaminants. These include both the detergents and other chemicals used to clean materials as well as the adhesives and consolidants impregnated into the original organic material to strengthen it.

Many antique or ancient textiles or documents will have been washed using organic-based soaps and detergents, followed by treatment with more organic materials to reduce their brittleness and then with consolidants. The continuing presence of these chemicals can be the source of contamination in RC dating, especially if unsuspected. The standard RC washing pretreatments should remove them but clearly, in some cases, they do not. This is best exemplified by the Dead Sea Scrolls (Jull *et al.*, 1995), where a variety of treatments have been used since the 1940s (Caldararo, 1995). Bonani *et al.* (1992) showed that of one of 14 dated scrolls was of the order of several centuries too early, and that this was very likely because some of the oil-based detergents containing carbon of geological age that had been used to clean the parchment after their discovery, had not been fully removed. Conversely, Rasmussen *et al.* (2001) have suggested that the natural castor oil used to make the scrolls more supple had also not been fully removed in the cleaning processes, modern

carbon thereby being retained in the samples, and producing dates that were too young.

Sometimes the information gained by dating the fraction washed out of the sample during pretreatment can itself provide invaluable information, as exemplified by the Vinland Map (see Chapter 13, p. 344). Presumably, a conscientious forger could make up organic consolidants and sizing agents from materials of the appropriate age (old parchment, etc.) in order that the recent treatments would pass undetected.

The impregnation of organic material with consolidants is described in the standard conservation books. Irreversible consolidants such as epoxy resins should never be used, but even the apparently reversible and recommended chemicals such as polyethylene glycol and polyvinyl acetate can prove very difficult to remove completely after a few years have elapsed. These are made from materials ultimately derived from mineral oil or natural gas and thus are of 'dead' carbon, and if included in the RC sample would have an apparent ageing effect. If a sample is being submitted to a dating laboratory, one should advise on any suspected contaminants of this nature. Where irreversible setting organics have been incorporated into the material then meaningful RC dating is probably impossible.

Samples sent for RC dating should ideally be sealed in two polythene bags with the label in the outer bag out of direct contact with the sample itself. Paper or other organic materials that are prone to disintegrate should not be in direct contact with the sample. If the sample is damp, it should be air-dried first to avoid the dangers of mould growth once sealed, but fungicides should not be applied, as these will contain 'dead' carbon.

Dating the Turin Shroud: An object lesson in authenticity studies

I think analytical chemistry is in trouble. If the Shroud is an indication of how modern Hi-Tech instruments can mislead analytical chemists, then how many not-so-visible problems in everyday research and technology are mishandled?

McCrone (1987/1988a)

Sources: Vignon (1902); Walsh (1964); Schwalbe and Rogers (1982); Meacham (1983); Jumper *et al.* (1984); Sox (1988); Gove (1996; 1999, pp. 146–169); Hedges (1997); Caldararo (1997); Wilson (1998).

See also the journal *Approfondimento Sindon* devoted to serious Shroud studies.

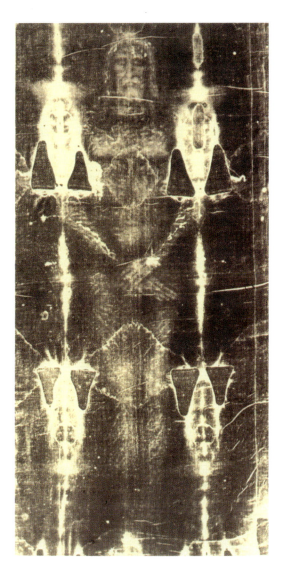

Figure 5.12 Detail from the photographic negative of the Shroud of Turin, taken by Guiseppe Enrie at the 1931 exposition of the Shroud. (Courtesy Barnes, 1934)

The scientific studies on the Shroud are, at one and the same time, among the most conclusive and most unsatisfactory. A scrupulously conducted RC dating exercise seems to have established that the flax from which the linen of the Shroud was made was growing at about the same time as the Shroud made its first well-documented appearance in the fourteenth century (Damon *et al.*, 1989; Hall, 1989). In total contrast, the less-than-ideal scientific examinations seem to have reached no consensus at all

on how the image on the Shroud was formed. The often contradictory results, and, at times, very acrimonious atmosphere existing between the various scientific groups studying the Shroud, should come as an eye-opener to those believing in the supposed objective and disinterested scientific approach. Gove (1989, 1996) and Wilson (1998) give good accounts of the often poisonous relations existing between not only the various groups but sometimes even the individual scientists within the groups.

The Shroud and its history

The Shroud is a length of twill-woven linen cloth, approximately 4.3 m long by 1.3 m wide. It carries the life-size impressions of the front and back of a man with his arms crossed before him. The cloth also carries red 'blood' stains apparently emanating from various wounds depicted on the image (Figure 5.12).

The Shroud was first mentioned in the fourteeth century as belonging to the de Charney family, who built and endowed a church and college of six canons to house it at the small village of Lirey in south-eastern France, where it was displayed at intervals from 1357 (Walsh, 1964, pp. 39–43). Some forty years later it was condemned by the local bishop, Pierre d'Acris, who claimed that the forger was known and had stated that he had painted the image around 1352 in a confession to the bishop's predecessor (see Sox, 1981, pp. 148–152 for a translation of the bishop's statement). The Shroud passed to the Dukes of Savoy in 1453 and was housed at Chambéry, where it was regularly displayed, and furthermore does seem to have been generally accepted as genuine by the Church. The Shroud had a narrow escape in 1532 when the family chapel burnt down, although the folded corners were burnt and the rest of the Shroud suffered water-staining. At the time of its restoration by the Poor Clares a very detailed description was made which shows that the image was much clearer in the sixteenth century than it is now, suggesting it may not have been very old at that time. The image continued to be regularly displayed through the centuries, being transferred to the Ducal Chapel at Turin in 1578.

The Shroud gained international fame when it was photographed by Secundo Pia during its exposition in 1898. The by now very faded image was revealed with quite astonishing clarity on the photographic negatives, which had the additional effect of displaying the image with the more natural contrasts of light and shadow. Almost immediately a French historian, Ulysee Chevalier (1899), condemned the Shroud as a painted fake, citing bishop d'Acris, but a scientific commission set to work to try to establish how the image had been made (Delage, 1902; Vignon, 1902), thereby inaugurating an acrimonious debate that continues to this day. Further photography in 1931 by Guiseppe Enrie and others through the twentieth century has revealed the image with ever greater clarity. Medical experts such as the French surgeon Barbet (1950, 1953) studied Enrie's photographs and became convinced of the authenticity of the image because of the reality of the anatomical detail. The more it became obvious that the image was not a simple painting the more the question began to be posed: could this really be the shroud in which Christ had been wrapped after the crucifixion?

RC dating of the linen was the obvious way of differentiating between the two main contending dates, first century AD or fourteenth century AD, and the advent of AMS meant that only a few threads of the Shroud would need to be sacrificed. The proposed and the actual procedures for the sampling and dating took many years and much acrimony to set up (Gove, 1989, 1996) but finally replicate samples together with ancient and Medieval linen control samples were dated by the three official AMS laboratories (and unofficially by the IsoTrace AMS Laboratory at Toronto; Gove, 1996, p. 306). Fortunately, all four dates were in close agreement and the calibrated date of the three official laboratories was given as lying between 1260 and 1390 at 95% confidence (Damon *et al.*, 1989). Nothing could apparently be more conclusive, and, as Gove (1989) put it: 'The final result is a triumph for AMS if not for the "true believers"'.

The other aspect of any authenticity investigation is: how was the image produced? Caldararo's 1997 survey of the examinational work already carried out revealed many shortcomings in terms of poor research design, absence of comparative material and lack of objective reporting, and concluded much more could be done.

Bishop Pierre d'Acris, who had the great advantage of being near-contemporaneous with the creation of the Shroud, if the carbon dates are to be taken at face value, was in no doubt that the image had been 'cunningly painted' (Walsh, 1964, pp. 41–42). The French scientists reporting in 1902 were equally clear that the image had *not* been painted. Instead, they believed it had been projected from some three-dimensional image, possibly from an actual body (Delage, 1902; Vignon, 1902). It must be stressed that Vignon, as well as Chevalier, were

working from the photographs, and neither side had actually seen the Shroud in the flesh, so to speak. They proposed a chemical reaction between urea from a sweating body reacting with the cloth treated with oil of aloes to create the image. The active interest and espousal of the Shroud by Vignon and Delage, two of the most eminent men in their respective fields, seemed to raise hostility in the French scientific community and suspicion in the Church authorities in Turin, such that their very promising investigations were stopped (Walsh, 1964, pp. 45–84; Sox, 1981, pp. 19–21). This set an unhappy precedent for other scientific investigations of the Shroud through the rest of the century. Thus, no systematic analysis of the cloth was, or indeed, has ever been properly carried out to ascertain the nature of the chemicals that may still be present.

Hoare (1994) and Mills (1995) also put forward theories based on a live, warm body. Mills postulated that a severely stressed body produces charged oxygen radicals. These travelled by convection currents generated by the warm body to the surface of the cloth where they catalysed the local disintegration of the cloth fibres.

Another scientific study which initially gained some standing was carried out by the Swiss criminologist Dr Max Frei. He applied sticky tape to the Shroud and then studied the adherent pollen grains. He claimed that these were from plants which grew in the Eastern Mediterranean only (Wilson, 1998, p. 100). However, it was subsequently pointed out that the pollen only allowed identification down to plant genus, not to the species that Frei claimed, and that in fact the plants he had identified grew all over the Mediterranean and beyond. It was also pointed out that Frei had no experience in the specialist discipline of pollen analysis. Subsequently Dr Frei took on the role of handwriting expert and pronounced the Hitler Diaries genuine (Harris, 1986, p. 180).

In the 1970s a group of American scientists, known as the Shroud of Turin Research Project (STURP), came together to study the Shroud (Bortin 1980; Weaver 1980; Pellicori and Evans 1981; Schwalbe and Rogers 1982; Heller 1983; Jumper *et al.*, 1984; Doyle *et al.*, 1986). Though the group claimed to be disinterested, Harry Gove, one of the leading AMS dating specialists suspected that there was already a degree of belief within the group that this was indeed the Shroud of Christ (Gove, 1996, pp. 6, 8, 36, etc.). Following its researches that led it to believe that the Shroud was not a simple painted forgery but was produced by some unknown process, about which it carefully refrained from speculation, STURP became ever more convinced and partisan in its support for the Shroud's authenticity. Though the team had many members it is surprising that it did not include experts in the examination of either textiles or of paintings. It remains true that relatively little has been published on the textile itself, but see Tyrer (1981) and Gervasio (1986), who could only work from STURP's photographs, and, more recently, Flury-Lemberg (2003), who conserved and restored the Shroud. STURP's methods, partially dictated by the various proscriptions on adequate sampling, consisted in examining the surface of the Shroud by light microscopy, IR and UV. Detailed X-radiography and optical microscopy were performed, backed up by image enhancement to bring out details (Doyle *et al.*, 1986). X-ray fluorescence analysis of the surface of the cloth was allowed but is unlikely to have been sufficiently sensitive to have detected significant traces, and seems to have picked up little of importance (Morris *et al.*, 1980).

Sampling was limited to the somewhat odd and wholly inadequate method of attaching sticky tape to likely areas of the Shroud and seeing what came off. This was roundly condemned by experts in the examination of paintings (Joyce Plesters in Wilson, 1998, p. 83). Sampling should have been done directly with scalpel or needle point from the cloth, observed through a microscope by the person who was going to carry out the investigation. It is also surprising that electron microscopy and microanalysis was apparently not performed on the samples that were taken. A very few fibres were allowed to be removed for analysis and these did reveal more useful information, particularly on what was not present.

Overall, STURP reported that the linen fibres in the image area contained nothing that was not in the fibres of the non-image areas, although no organic analysis was attempted, the only difference being that the former were more discolored and 'aged'. It was as if the linen in these areas had in some way been treated with chemicals which left no other trace, or had been scorched (the similarity with the fibres taken from the undoubted scorched fibres from the 1532 fire was remarked upon). There was certainly no evidence of the application of putative chemicals or of any binder, neither was there any indication of solutions such the tidemarks left on the Shroud by the water used to extinguish the 1532 fire. The 'blood' marks are in striking and total contrast – they do come from a liquid that had actually soaked through the cloth to the other side. Dried remains of this liquid abound in and around

the flax fibres, and it was identified by STURP and others as being blood (Heller and Adler, 1981). Interestingly, the image effect is not present on the fibres within the blood flow areas, suggesting that the blood had already soaked into these areas before the image-forming process commenced.

Lest it be thought that it was unambiguously established that the image was not painted, the counterview of the microscopist Walter McCrone must be given here (McCrone and Skirius, 1980; McCrone, 1981, 1986, 1987/8a, 1997). McCrone was part of the original STURP team but was expelled for independently seeking a sample for RC dating. However, that was not before the sticky tapes had been delivered to him for examination. He was quite properly unhappy with this form of sampling but his detailed examination led him to unequivocal conclusions totally at variance with the remaining team members. He found large numbers of minute iron oxide particles which he suspected had been applied to the cloth in an aqueous medium containing proteins, probably of collagen tempera, prepared, McCrone suggested, by boiling up old scraps of parchment. The particles were concentrated on the stained areas, suggesting to him that they had been deliberately applied. McCrone did not consider the possibility that they could be the result of later retouching of the image, which through the course of centuries is eminently possible. He also found particles of other inorganic pigment minerals, notably vermilion, which together with the iron oxides explained – for him – why the 'blood' was still red. As he intransigently replied to reports of blood still being present on the Shroud, 'All this is a fiction – there is *no* blood in the Shroud image', arguing (1987/8a, p. 56, plate II), that the 'blood' stains were unlike real blood stains in their color and spread on the linen.

According to McCrone the STURP team failed to pick up the pigment particles optically because they were only using a ×50 binocular microscope. His comments on other STURP reports and members include descriptives such as 'asinine' and 'drivel', and comments such as 'he is an ass, you may quote me' (Wilson, 1998, p. 82). To level up the score on the insults front, E.T. Hall of the dating consortium expressed himself as 'totally unimpressed by McCrone as a scientist' (Wilson, 1998, p. 198), even though they supposedly held similar opinions on the authenticity of the Shroud.

Despite all the limitations on the sampling and examinations carried out and the contradiction and acrimony among the various experts, it *does* seem that the present image was not directly painted or even applied as a liquid, in contrast to the 'blood'. Significantly, the image layer, for want of a better term, does not permeate the fabric but is restricted to the top 150 microns of the surface.

The various methods postulated by which the image may have been created are summarised in Wilson (1998) and Caldararo (1997) and can be outlined here.

STURP, whilst rejecting painting, seemed unwilling to accept that the image resulted from contact with a three-dimensional body shape, pointing out quite properly that the image is present even in areas that cannot have been in direct contact. They maintained that the image has the appearance of a projection, thereby echoing the conclusions of the original Vignon and Delage investigation and experimental replication of which the STURP team apparently seem unaware. Craig and Bresee (1994) suggested that a freshly executed painting was laid against the cloth and burnished from behind, transferring the image, but with no obvious brush strokes. Note that the image need not have been painted with pigments but with some staining solution which need leave no trace of itself beyond the stain, especially after washing.

Most postulated schemes require a template in three dimensions, perhaps a real body, divine or otherwise. One suggestion is that the image marks are scorches, produced by wrapping the Shroud around a hot metal statue (Ashe, 1966). A variation on this method could be to make the template of wood that had been soaked in a solution of some astringent chemicals, and, after allowing the template to drain, to wrap the linen around it to absorb the vapours.

There are, however, major problems with scenarios that require a direct transfer of the image from a three-dimensional image, be it of metal, wood or a human. First, if the body is lying horizontally upon the shroud then there should be evidence of pressure points where the weight of the body was transmitted into the cloth beneath, and surely if the body had been at all soft then the image should be somewhat flattened against the linen at these points.

Also, the lack of distortion of the image on the now flat Shroud is a major problem. When removed and flattened out, the image would inevitably have been distorted. It really does seem that the image was formed on the cloth when it was flat, and the most convincing reproductions have been done on flat linen.

Some, notably Delage and Vignon, suggested that an ammoniacal vapour was given off by the body and transferred to the cloth lying flat – Vignon's 'vaporgraph'. However, the image seems too precise to have been formed in this way. A problem with the body vapour theories is that the long hair and beard are prominently represented, yet it is difficult to see how the hairs could have given off warm vapours.

It does seem to have been established that the image was created on the flat linen by exposure to chemicals or, possibly, heat, which caused local oxidation/dehydration, leading to the darkening of the linen at points of contact. The chemicals penetrated only a very short distance into the cloth, thereby ruling out an application by soaking or brushing on a liquid. By contrast the blood (or whatever) does seem to have soaked into the cloth at selected points of contact. The image itself could have been created on the linen by application of some acidic or caustic chemical that would oxidise the linen and so discolor it.

There are other, less scientific but more practical considerations with the Shroud that lead one to doubt its authenticity. If the image on the Shroud was a fortuitous creation of the contact of the body on cloth then it is quite extraordinary that every part of both sides of the body is equally and completely recorded.

Similarly, the flagellation wounds cover almost every part of the body in a very even, regular pattern, having all the appearance of having been carefully set out by an artist rather than inflicted during a real beating.

The other aspect of completeness is even more puzzling – the blood stains from the Shroud seem to record at one moment all the events of the Passion. The Shroud has soaked up, and thereby preserved, the blood as it started to flow from fresh open wounds. Yet the events producing these *stigmata*, the flagellation, the crown of thorns, the crucifixion and the spear thrust to the side, would have occurred over a minimum period of about 12 hours. It seems inconceivable that all these wounds could be open simultaneously and have just started to bleed free-flowing blood without even a smear. However, it should be borne in mind that in fourteenth-century Europe there was a strong cult of the Passion, and the instruments of the Passion, the whip, crown of thorns, crucifix, nails and spear are always depicted together. In the same way images of the crucified Christ bear evidence of all stages of the passion, and so would the Shroud as the ultimate icon of the Resurrection.

Alternatively, if one allows the premise that the Shroud is part of a pre-ordained Resurrection then a whole range of causal explanations become valid. The completeness of the image and its catalogue of all the injuries suffered by Christ could be regarded as evidence that the Shroud was divinely intended as a record for the inspiration of mankind. As Rinaldi (1972, p. 45) put it:

> *When we think of the unusual process that has caused the images on the Shroud and consider all the circumstances that were necessary for their production, we cannot but admire the Providence of God who was pleased to leave to the Church and to the world the material document of the Passion and Death of Christ.*

It is now necessary to return to the RC dating and the reaction to the publication of the date. Most of the world accepted the date (Sox, 1988), although some were cautious; STURP, for example, cast doubt on the result (Adler, 1996), and other groups suggested possible ways of explaining the result (Wilson, 1998; Hoare, 1994) or that more comparative studies were still necessary (Caldararo and Kahle, 1989). Predictably there were a few, small in number but vociferous in action, who sought to show that the date had been deliberately falsified. One group, led by Bruno Bonnet-Eymard in special issues of their journal *The Catholic Counter-Reformation in the XXth Century* (issue 223, September–October 1989, pp. 238 & 239, April 1991), declared the whole exercise was a fraudulent collusion between, of all unlikely collaborators in crime, the British Museum and the Vatican, with the coordinator of the samples, Dr Michael Tite of the British Museum, switching the samples so that the three laboratories got samples of thirteenth century cloth instead of samples from the Shroud (Kersten and Gruber, 1994). The convoluted reasoning behind this was the Vatican's fear that if the Shroud was shown to be genuine then it would imply that Jesus had survived the crucifixion and had been alive in the tomb, and thus the central tenet of Christianity, the Resurrection, would be shown to be false, and the Church would be out of business. Kersten and Gruber seemed less concerned to explain what the British Museum was supposed to have got out of it. As Wilson (1998, p. 11) put it, theses based on fraudulent actions by any of the participants in the dating exercise are as unworthy as they are risible. In fact the whole ridiculous hypothesis can be discredited easily, as attempts to preserve the anonymity of the Shroud samples had signally failed. This was because the distinctive twill weave of the Shroud could not be matched in either the ancient or the Medieval control samples, and thus the dating laboratories knew which was the Shroud sample, and it most certainly had not been switched.

During the conservation of the Shroud in 2002, Flury-Lemberg (2003) noted very considerable quantities of soot lodged in pockets between the Shroud and the backing cloth and patches stitched on after the fire. She claimed that this could have affected the RC result, but it is difficult to see how this could be so, as any soot adhering to the fibres would have been noted and mechanically removed during the pretreatment. Also, presumably the bulk of the soot must have come from the burning Shroud and thus should have given the same RC date.

Kouznetsov *et al.* (1996a, b; and see also Gove, 1996, pp. 307–308 and Wilson, 1998, pp. 219–223) reported some experiments which allegedly showed that the ^{14}C content of the linen could have been affected by heat, thereby repeating a claim made earlier by William Meacham (1983; and see also Gove, 1996, pp. 100, 113, 283–285; 1999, pp. 163–168). Kouznetsov *et al.* reported experiments to replicate the conditions to which the Shroud was briefly exposed during the fire of 1532. They claimed to have heated a piece of 2000-year-old linen to about 200°C for about 90 minutes, after which ^{14}C had somehow been absorbed from the atmosphere and the subsequent AMS dating indicated an age of only about 800 years.

The detailed and complex mechanisms to explain this extremely unlikely event were ultimately found to be in error. Also, experiments carried out on linen by the AMS dating scientists in response to these claims, failed to show any change in the ^{14}C at all (Jull *et al.*, 1996a, b) or in cotton heated to about 200°C (Long, 1998; Hedges *et al.*, 1998). Further work was promised by Kouznetsov, but since then other papers based on fraudulent data have been published in peer-reviewed journals (Meacham, 2007). This sad little story is best seen as a warning to those outside the scientific community not to accept all scientific work too uncritically, even when published in a supposedly quality and peer-reviewed journal.

A more serious and sustainable challenge was made by Dr L.A. Garza-Valdès (1990). His study of a suspect Mayan stone figurine showed it had originally been blood-stained but over this a shiny fungal bioplastic varnish had built up over the centuries. The coating gave an AMS date which, whilst old, was some six centuries younger than the stylistic date for the piece. He investigated further and found evidence of this coating on other Mayan artefacts, and this led him to speculate that the linen of the Shroud could be similarly affected. By a combination of luck, charm, and, one suspects, foot-in-the-door persistence, he managed not only to examine the Shroud but to obtain a sample. In his own words, 'As soon as I looked at a segment in the microscope, I knew it was heavily contaminated. I knew that what had been RC dated was a mixture of linen and bacteria and fungi and bioplastic coating that had grown on the fibres for centuries' (reported in Wilson, 1998, p. 224; and see also Gove *et al.*, 1997; Gove, 1999, pp. 164–166). Garza-Valdès was able sufficiently to impress Gove for him to acknowledge the validity of his claim that the bioplastic coating was indeed present on the linen fibres of the Shroud (see letter from Gove, quoted in Wilson, 1998, p. 261).

It might be claimed that the standard pretreatment to clean the sample should have removed such material (details of the pretreatment for the Shroud samples are given in Damon *et al.*, 1989 and in Gove, 1996, p. 259). Garza-Valdès found that, using these and much stronger treatments, the bioplastic coating was unaffected. However, an AMS date on a linen covering from one of the Dead Sea Scrolls, which should form a good comparator for the linen of the Shroud was apparently unaffected by this problem and gave a date in close agreement with the parchment AMS and historical dates (Jull *et al.*, 1995). It must also be pointed out here that each of the laboratories followed different pretreatment routines, but all gave the same date for the Shroud samples, and the correct date for the historically dated control samples.

These developments came to the attention of Dr Rosalie David, an Egyptologist of Manchester University who had instigated the RC dating of an Egyptian mummy. This had apparently shown that the linen bandages were from a time a thousand years later than the body they bound. This seemed inherently unlikely but the dating of neither the bones nor the linen could be faulted on conventional grounds. Therefore, David became interested in any theories that could explain the thousand-year discrepancy. After meeting with Garza-Valdès, a collaborative experiment was set up with David and Gove in which samples were taken from the bones and linen bindings of an ancient Egyptian mummified ibex for AMS dating, following the pretreatment procedures used by the laboratories that had dated the Shroud samples. Having been excluded from the main Shroud dating exercise after being instrumental in setting it up, Gove probably did not need too much persuading to take part in an experiment that could show the date the other laboratories had obtained for the Shroud was wrong.

First, detailed microscopic examination of the ibex mummy linen fibres showed about the same build-up of bioplastic as was visible on the Shroud sample examined by Garza-Valdès and Gove. The AMS dates suggested that the linen was apparently about half a millennium younger than the bones of the ibex it contained, and it is extremely unlikely that this was in fact the case. It has been suggested that if the ibex had been fed on a marine diet, there could be an apparent ageing effect of about 400 years (the reservoir effect, described above, p. 98). However, if that had been the case then the $\delta\,^{13}C$ factor should have been about zero as is usual for marine-derived samples (p. 90), but in fact it was about -21.

The experiments of Kouznetsov *et al.* and the microorganisms of Garza-Valdès may possibly be rationalised. If Kouznetsov and colleagues' 2000-year-old piece of linen also had the bioplastic coating, the experimental heating could have rendered the coating impervious to the subsequent cleaning treatment. Similarly, the cleaning pretreatments that removed the ordinary contaminants could be less successful in removing the coating from the Shroud that had been in a fire, although it is unlikely that the bulk of the carefully folded textile could have become seriously heated during the fire.

Even if the bioplastic, raw or cooked, is a reality and had survived the pretreatment, the correction still would not bring the date of the Shroud back to the first century AD, but the episode does demonstrate that scientific 'certainties' are there to be challenged and that there are alternative explanations to be given.

There are those who seek more esoteric explanations. Shortly after the 1989 publication of the AMS date, it was suggested in no less a journal than *Nature* that the body as it resurrected may have radiated strong pulses of light, heat and neutrons, with the latter generating sufficient new ^{14}C in the Shroud to make a 2000-year-old piece of linen appear to be only about 650 years old (Phillips, 1989). The premise of the argument was dismissed by Hedges (1989), one of the Oxford AMS team, on the grounds that 'if a supernatural explanation is proposed it seems pointless to make any scientific measurements at all'. Hedges seemed not to have considered the significance of what he had written: if a body can be physically dead and buried for three days and then come to life again, as is the central belief of the Christian religion, it is no more far-fetched that it may also have emitted radiation.

Carter (1984) had already suggested something similar, with the putative body generating intense pulses of light, ion discharge or X-rays to transfer the image to the Shroud. Interestingly, back in 1902 Vignon had toyed with the idea of some electrical discharge associated with a Resurrection, but chose to reject all supernatural phenomena, which was surely a rather confused position to defend if, as he believed, the linen could be the real Shroud of Christ.

In reality, the position of the scientists as expressed by Hedges is fundamentally illogical. If one believes in the Resurrection then one has to accept, like it or not, that Hedge's 'supernatural' events did happen. If one does not believe in the Resurrection then presumably the Shroud cannot be genuine anyway. Ultimately it comes down to faith, which, as yet, we cannot test with a spectrometer.

6

Physical dating techniques II: Thermoluminescence and dendrochronology

Thermoluminescence dating

This is probably the best known of the luminescence dating methods, the term being used to cover both thermoluminescence (TL) induced by radiogenic materials within and around the sample and its immediate surroundings, and optically stimulated luminescence, induced by sunlight and now much used for dating archaeological and geological sediments.

Principal sources: Fleming (1973b; 1975, pp. 73–97; 1976, pp. 110–132; 1979a, c); Aitken (1985; 1989; 1990, pp. 141–186; 1997); Bowman (1991a, pp. 130–137); Handberry (1997); Troja and Roberts (2000, pp. 585–644); Grün (2001).

Aitken (1985, p. 32) has remarked:

> It is in the field of authenticity testing that thermo-luminescence has had a revolutionary impact comparable with that of radiocarbon dating in archaeology.

All natural materials contain a few parts per million of radioactive isotopes of the elements thorium, uranium and potassium. These decay at a slow but steady rate over the millennia, producing α, β and γ rays. These are so energetic that when they interact with an atom they remove an electron. The footloose electron is the cause of TL – in most instances it soon meets with an oppositely charged ion and is neutralised. But in some crystalline materials, notably quartz and feldspars, which are common in ceramics, the crystal lattice contains defects, known as deep traps, which can hold the electron for millennia at ambient temperatures, and therein lies the basis of the dating technique. The entrapped electrons retain some of the original energy of the ionising collision and their number steadily increase as more and more such collisions take place and more of the deep traps become filled. On heating, the electrons are freed and lose their energy as light, hence the term, *thermo–luminescence* (heat–light). The amount of light emitted is proportional to the number of electrons released, which in turn is proportional to the time that has elapsed since the last time the material was heated. In the case of ceramics this is usually when it was manufactured (Figure 6.1).

Ceramic materials of all kinds have proved to be the most fruitful area for TL dating, such that TL authentication of many expensive ceramics before auction or sale is now considered routine (Franklin, 1990; Stoneham, 1990a).

In order to produce a date, one needs to know to how much radiation the material had been exposed, the susceptibility of the piece to radiation (that is, the amount of TL produced per unit of radiation) and the amount of light, the TL, stored in the sample. The age will then be the product of:

$$\frac{TL}{\text{susceptibility} \times \text{annual dose}}$$

Practical determination of TL in ceramics

A sample is required, typically between about 30 and 100 mg of powder drilled with an ordinary steel drill bit from the base or other inconspicuous part of the object. This leaves a hole between 2 to 4 mm in diameter and several millimetres deep (Figure 6.2). For porcelain or other hard ceramics this method would generate too much heat, thereby risking the premature release of the TL and for these a core is taken using a water-cooled trepanning drill (Fleming, 1971; Stoneham, 1983). Michael *et al.* (1997) have developed methods that require much smaller quantities of sample.

Ceramics usually comprise clay with a variety of minerals, quartz and feldspars for example, and the TL is usually measured on a particular mineral or size of particle, the choice of method depending on the particular ceramic body (pp. 112, 113). The

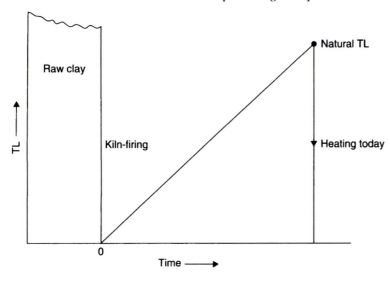

Figure 6.1 Life cycle of TL in a ceramic. TL stored in the clay minerals over geological time is removed when the ceramic is fired. Thereafter it slowly but steadily builds up until the next time the ceramic is heated. The amount of TL stored is directly proportional to the time that has elapsed since the last heating. (Courtesy Fleming, 1976)

Figure 6.2 Sampling drill and pot showing the typical position and size of a sample drilling for TL dating. Note just one drilling will normally suffice. (Courtesy A. Milton/British Museum)

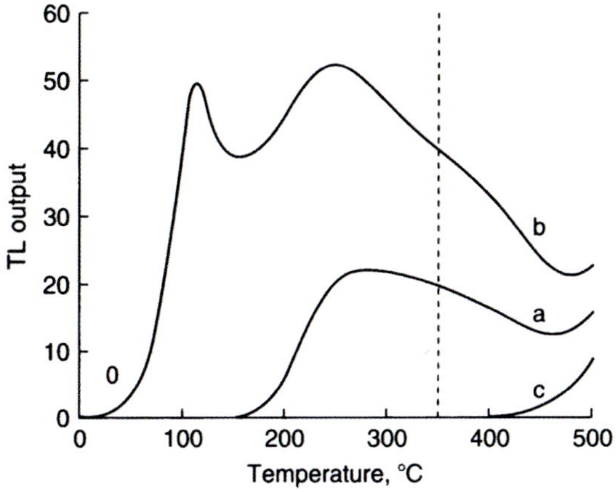

Figure 6.3 Typical TL glow curve: 'a' is the natural TL glow curve from a fine-grain pottery sample; 'b' is the glow curve from the natural TL plus the laboratory TL dose from a known amount of irradiation; 'c' is the incandescence above about 400°C as the pot sample begins to glow.

sample is gently crushed and the individual grains are separated. The grain of the size required can be collected by sieving or by suspending the crushed sample in liquid and decanting the required fraction.

The TL is determined in the sample by rapid but controlled heating of the sample from room temperature to about 500°C in a few seconds and recording the resultant TL. The plot of temperature against light emitted is known as the glow curve (Figure 6.3), which is made up of several components. TL is emitted at about 110°C, but the emission is not stable, which means that the TL does not persist and thus is of no direct use for dating;

the more stable TL emission occurs at between 300 to 500°C, which however, also includes a growing component from the incandescence of the sample heated above 400°C.

To determine the susceptibility of the ceramic, another portion of the sample is exposed to a radioactive source of known strength for several days and the TL determined. This is done on the dry sample, with little or no knowledge of the moisture content through most of its existence. A problem arises here because water absorbs α radiation – thus the moisture content of the piece through its life is a crucial factor in determining how much TL will have built up.

Finally, it remains to establish the radiation dose to which the ceramic will have been exposed. As noted above, the radiation will have come from radioactive isotopes with half-lives extending over millions of years, such that for the lifespan of ceramics their radioactivity may be taken as constant. The activity emanating from within the ceramic can be determined easily; the problem is that some of the radiation will have come from the environment, either, if the item had been buried, from the soil, which is weakly radioactive, or, for material that has been above ground for a substantial part of its life, from cosmic radiation resulting in bleaching. The requirements for authenticity testing, where all that is necessary is a determination of whether the object is at least centuries old or not, mean that some of these parameters which are difficult to estimate are of no real importance (Fleming *et al.*, 1970). For example, Wang and Zhou (1983) and Leung *et al.* (1995) have proposed a simplified authentication technique for Chinese ceramics whereby a standard annual dose rate is assumed, based on measurements they made on a selection of pots from all over China. However, this does not get around the problems of unknown environmental conditions.

In the absence of knowledge of the environment in which the piece has existed, the dose can only be determined on the material within the ceramic body itself, although fortunately this will usually have been the major source. The α activity attributable to the thorium and uranium can be measured directly by sticking the sample to scotch tape containing a phosphor which fluoresces when irradiated, and measuring the light generated by placing it against a light detector for several days. The potassium can be determined spectrochemically and the β activity calculated.

Two further caveats must be mentioned here. First, the TL build-up in some ceramic bodies is unstable, suffering from what is known as anomalous fading. This phenomenon was first noted on volcanic lavas, and ceramic bodies that include volcanic material, notably feldspars, seem to be especially prone to this problem; thus, TL age estimation on ceramics containing these minerals, such as some Italian maiolica (Bowman, 1988, 1991b), presents problems that may require more specialised techniques (see p. 113).

Secondly it must be borne in mind that the TL method yields an estimate of the time that has elapsed since the last occasion on which the piece was very hot, and this need not be the time of its production. For example, at the onset of World War II the Liverpool Museum's collection of West African bronze was moved from the Walker Gallery in the city centre to various places supposedly of greater safety. Sadly, one of these stores was nevertheless set alight in an air raid and the bronzes were badly damaged by fire. TL measurements of the core material would date, if anything, the air raid rather than the casting of the bronzes. Similarly, some of the 319 Tanagra terracotta figures (see Chapter 9, p. 200) tested by Goedicke (1994) from German museums were found to have been affected by burning during the war.

More prosaically it is sometimes claimed that heat treatments may have been applied to ceramics purporting to be antiquities as part of conservation or restoration treatments (exemplified by the Haçilar figurines, Chapter 9, p. 193). Total removal of the ancient accumulated TL is only feasible if high temperatures of over 500°C had penetrated the entirety of the ceramic. Under even the most rigorous drying operations some portions of the higher-temperature TL should be preserved to appear in the glow curve and application of the pre-dose method (described below) should establish whether secondary heating had indeed taken place (Fleming and Stoneham, 1971). Even so, ceramics should not be heated if their authenticity is likely to be questioned.

A very few published restoration treatments do involve the application of quite strong heat. Adreeva and Tcheremkhin (1988) for example, suggest setting fragments of broken ceramics in a plaster of bentonite clay and firing to between 550 and 930°C. The authors claim the results are aesthetically pleasing; this may be so but the treatment is clearly disastrous for any future technical study, including the determination of the TL.

X- and γ-radiography can affect the TL (see Chapter 3, p. 32). To prevent future uncertainty if TL testing is anticipated, the sample should be taken before radiography, and then, after radiography, it should be replaced within the matrix. Routine security X-rays at airports, etc. however, should not have a discernible effect on the TL.

Varieties of process

If the ceramic is relatively coarse with large quartz grains, the *quartz inclusion method* may be used

(Fleming, 1979c, pp. 40–57; Aitken 1985, pp. 17–23). Quartz is usually very pure, containing little or no radioactive elements. Thus, all the ionising radiation in a quartz inclusion will have come from outside. The α particles, which are rather difficult to estimate, are only of very short range, and thus by taking grains of *c.* 100 microns diameter, and stripping off their surface with hydrofluoric acid, the α contribution can be entirely removed, leaving the β and γ radiation as the only contributors to the TL.

Another advantage is that the TL in the quartz is not subject to anomalous fading. This was disputed in a court case over some alleged faked ceramics where it was claimed that the TL had somehow faded from the quartz, and thus the TL age was too young. The suggestion was vigorously rebutted by Doreen Stoneham, who had carried out the TL tests, but nevertheless the defendant was acquitted (Crane, 1994).

The technique usually applied to fineware ceramics is the *fine grain method* (Zimmerman, 1971; Fleming, 1979c, pp. 58–80; Aitken, 1985, pp. 24–28). It utilises particle sizes in the range from about 2.5 to 9 microns diameter. In this range the α, β and γ particles all contribute to the TL. The method was used to test certain Chinese pottery figurines against supposedly genuine examples of the Warring States period (405–205 BC), known as Hui Hsien wares (Fleming and Sampson, 1972; Fleming, 1979c, p. 160). Their authenticity had long been controversial; indeed a whole issue of the *Far Eastern Ceramic Bulletin* (Vol. VI. 1, March 1954) was devoted to the question. The TL tests simplified things considerably by showing that all the pieces, both dubious and controls, were recent.

The *zircon-inclusion* technique utilises the TL signal generated by the highly radioactive zircon inclusions occurring in some ceramics (Sutton and Zimmerman, 1976; Zimmerman 1978; Fleming, 1979c, p. 115; Aitken 1985, pp. 172–175; Stoneham and Winter, 1988). Inside these inclusions the TL originates almost entirely from α particles released from the decay of the radioactive uranium and thorium contained within the inclusion.

The method is especially useful in authenticity studies where the application of outside radiation is suspected, by comparing the TL in the zircons with that in the remainder of the body. If the TL has developed naturally then there is a concentration in the zircons; if induced from outside, the TL is uniform. This could be either a deliberate attempt to build up a spurious TL in the ceramic by exposing it to γ radiation, or, more innocently, the result of exposure to X-rays during radiography (see p. 112). An example of the latter contingency was establishing that the famous Greek bronze horse in the Metropolitan Museum was indeed ancient (see Chapter 8, p. 166).

The pre-dose technique and the TL dating of porcelain and later ceramics

There are problems inherent in authenticating ceramics that are only a few centuries old (Fleming, 1973a; 1975, pp. 87–95; 1979a; 1979c, pp. 81–99; Aitken, 1985, pp. 153–157). Less time will have elapsed for the build up of TL, but the accuracy and precision need to be greater in order to differentiate between originals and later copies with any confidence. The *pre-dose technique* was developed by Stuart Fleming in part to overcome these problems (Fleming and Stoneham, 1973). It has also been successfully used to date porcelain where most of the TL traps are shallow and release the electrons at lower temperatures than in other ceramics (Stoneham, 1983). The method utilises the TL emitted at 110°C by the quartz fraction of the ceramic. This, as previously noted, is of no direct use in dating, since at ambient temperatures the traps are unstable and the electrons, and thus the TL, will not build up over time. However, in some way not fully understood, a cumulative memory of these events *is* preserved and may be unlocked by heating to above 500°C whereupon the 110°C region becomes sensitised, the degree of sensitisation being related to the previous cumulative radiation dose.

The enhancement of the susceptibility is not endless – in practice the effect tails off with most samples after about 1200 years but for many later ceramics the method has proved invaluable. This still leaves the question of just what levels of precision and accuracy are attainable. As a rule of thumb it is usually possible to differentiate between 17th and 19th century ceramics using the pre-dose technique, but for example, would it be possible to differentiate between a modern (2000) forgery of a Bernard Leach pot made in the 1920s? The question to some degree is specific to each pot but in practice few pieces that should date from the recent past seem to have been subjected to TL tests. Saltron *et al.* (1992) addressed these problems when they sought to distinguish genuine terracottas by the French sculptors, Marin and P. Michel Clodion, in the late eighteenth century, from copies made in the nineteenth and twentieth centuries. They used fine grain and pre-dose techniques. All the pieces were too young to be dated in the conventional sense but by comparing the glow curves produced by the pieces under question with those produced by a number of genuine pieces it was possible to differentiate originals from copies.

TL on the clay cores of hollow metal castings

Sources: Fleming (1979c, pp. 162–178); Stoneham (1990b, 1995a).

Because many metal castings still retain vestiges of their clay casting cores, they can be candidates for TL testing (Martini *et al.*, 1995; and see Chapter 8, pp. 165, 169, Chapter 14, p. 366 and Chapter 20, p. 503 for examples). However, there are problems: often the cores are insufficiently fired to remove the existing TL dose. There can also be problems if a casting has been subsequently reheated, most plausibly during repairs which involved pouring in additional metal (see Chapter 8, p. 163 and Chapter 7, p. 144). Martini and Sibilia (2003) attempted to date the famous ancient *Lupa Capitolina* bronze group in Rome by TL on the core, but all the dates centred on the fifteenth and sixteenth centuries AD, and probably relate to restoration of the group ordered by Pope Sextus IV in the late fifteenth century. They also dated core material from the equally famous statue of the enthroned Saint Peter, now in the Vatican Museum, to resolve whether the statue was of the early Christian or Late Medieval period. The fourteenth-century date obtained was said to show the piece belonged to the Late Medieval period. For some reason the possibility that it too could have been repaired was not considered.

The dating of the cores from a series of West African copper alloy heads now in the British Museum and other institutions (Willett and Fleming, 1976) was an early demonstration of the method. However, the apparent success of this procedure was somewhat tempered by the subsequent inability to obtain satisfactory TL from similar cores taken from other West African heads (Bowman, 1985).

In order for modern forgeries to appear old, the core can be removed and replaced by a paste made up of mud and finely ground pottery of the required age. This has been reported on some Nigerian forgeries of Benin bronzes.

TL on stone

Sources: Theocaris *et al.* (1997); Liritzis and Galloway (2000); Polikreti *et al.* (2000); Polikreti (2007).

The possibility of dating carved marble or limestone by TL has recently been explored. Sunlight bleaches the natural TL stored in calcite minerals; at the very surface and for the first millimetre of depth the bleaching is apparent after a matter of hours; thereafter the bleaching penetrates more slowly but is still measurably penetrating into the marble even after centuries of exposure. Thus, the depth of penetration of bleaching is directly proportional to the age. Polikreti *et al.* (2000) obtained an age of 204 years on a sample from a marble cross dated to 1698, which was presumed to have always been exposed to sunlight. Another sample, a loose piece of marble with ancient tool marks from a quarry on the Pentelikon Mountain, in Greece, was shown to be over 500 years old. A problem that arose was that the piece was only 7 cm thick and the penetration of bleaching had reached the centre of the piece, indicating one limitation on the material's dateability should the method become general: it is also necessary of course to cut a section from the stone. It is also possible that exposure to X- or γ-rays could simulate long exposure to sunlight.

If the stone has been buried after exposure then the TL is built up again at the surface principally from the γ radioactivity of the surrounding soil and the α and β radiation from within the stone. Polikreti *et al.* obtained a piece of marble freshly dug up from the excavations at Vergina, in the north of Greece, for dating. The piece was believed to be of the 3rd century BC and an age of 2554 ± 499 years was deduced from the TL content. Liritzis and Galloway (2000), using their optical TL method, obtained a date of 420 ± 300 BC on a marble block from the Temple of Apollo at Delphi that should date to around 550 BC. The date was obtained on a surface that had been carved and exposed to the sun, thereby bleaching it. The stone had then been set in place, removing the surface from exposure and allowing the TL to slowly build up through the centuries. In order for a date to be calculated it was necessary to know the environmental conditions and to be able to determine the ambient radioactivity. It is also vital that the marble is not exposed to light after it has been dug up.

For authenticity studies of ancient sculptures most pieces are likely to have been exposed to sunlight, then buried, and finally re-exposed to sunlight after excavation. As Poliketri *et al.* pointed out, the stone will have to be more than 3 cm thick because of the rapid bleaching. It is possible that remains of deep bleaching in thick samples could still show that a piece being analysed had undergone long exposure at some time and thus be of some age.

Greilich *et al.* (2005) have used the related technique of optically stimulated luminescence to date the burial of granite surfaces.

TL has also been used to date burnt flint and Rowlett *et al.* (1974) used TL to authenticate a fine Upper Palaeolithic pressure-flaked laurel leaf point, because it had been heat-treated immediately prior to the flaking. However, surviving evidence of heat-treatment on flints is very rare.

Presentation of TL results

This is based on the already established practice for RC results (Aitken and Alldred 1972; Aitken 1976; Aitken 1985, pp. 30–32). The following real example is quoted by Aitken:

1070 BC (± 100, ± 220, Ox TL 143e)

The date is followed by two error estimates, the first *a*, based on the statistical treatment of the results of a number of repeat samples, the second *p*, based on the estimates of error. As most authenticity determinations are only made on single objects, the first estimate does not usually apply, and in the absence of knowledge of the burial environment the second will be large. Aitken estimated a figure of around ± 7–10% of the age, typically for ceramics where the burial environment is known, rising to ± 20% where it is not. Finally, there is the identification code for the laboratory, in this case Oxford, followed by the specific object number.

Falsification of TL

It is feasible that TL could be induced in a ceramic by exposure to X-rays or to a radioactive source. Meyer (1973, p. 113) stated that a forger known to him claimed to be able to irradiate a ceramic such that it would pass a simple TL test. Von Bothmer (1998) believed that some forgeries of ancient Greek ceramics had been exposed to 'a friendly dentist's X-ray machine sometimes producing sufficient radiation to mislead laboratory technicians'. Fleming (1979c, p. 146) noted:

The principal threat to TL analysis comes from the forger who can master artificial irradiation of a spurious piece using, for example a ^{60}Co γ facility of the kind routinely employed by radiotherapists. Even using a rough rule that an ancient ceramic absorbs about 0.5 rad y^{-1} must allow an approach quite close to (say within a factor of 2) the dose the pottery should carry to appear of the correct antiquity.

In practice it would also be necessary to have access to all the facilities of a TL laboratory in order to determine the susceptibility and radioactivity of the ceramic body forming the copy, and to check that the artificially produced TL glow curve appeared convincing. Only then could the correct dosage be applied with confidence for the supposed age of the piece. Setting up a TL facility should present no great problem in infrastructure requirements and the TL measuring equipment itself is not very expensive, especially when compared with the prices realised by some oriental ceramics.

Fleming pointed out that γ-ray exposure would not replicate the pattern of natural radiation exposure through the various components of a ceramic. Becker and Moreno (1974) described a technique to distinguish between the glow curves produced by natural TL and those from recently irradiated samples. If the clay of a ceramic fired in antiquity contained inclusions of quartz, with almost no radioactivity, and zircon with a great deal, then the natural build-up of TL in these two minerals would be very different over time. If, however, the ceramic had been recently fired and then subjected to an outside γ source, this would have resulted in the irradiation of both types of inclusion equally, creating a similar TL pattern in each. Even in the absence of zircons the presence of TL through the quartz inclusions would reveal the irradiation. However, routine authenticity testing usually determines the TL on the fine grain fraction, and the size of sample required for such detailed testing would be unacceptable for most art ceramics. This having been said, very few suspect pieces have ever been found where it was suspected that the TL had been induced in this manner, but the possibility always remains, especially with very expensive pieces.

There are simpler and far safer methods available with which to cheat TL tests. The simplest is merely to fake the TL certificate. For example the terracottas offered for sale to Michel Brent (2001) at Bamako in Mali all had TL authentication certificates, and he had every reason to believe that terracottas and certificates were both false. The point was also made that it is often impractical for the artefact to come to the laboratory for sampling; very often a sample is taken locally and dispatched, opening up a potential for fraud.

Another method consists in taking contemporary local ceramics such as bricks, and to cut and carve

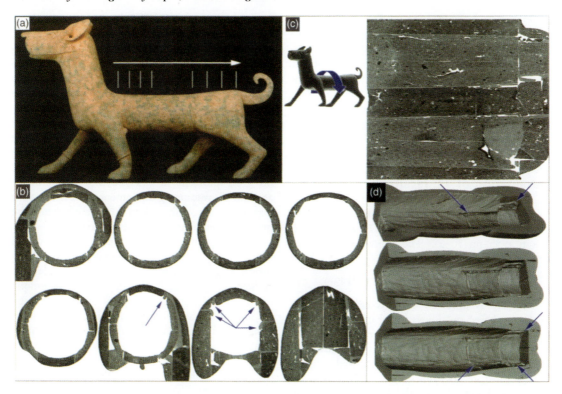

Figure 6.4   (a) A terracotta dog in the style of the Han period, giving an appropriate TL signal for approximately 2000 years old. The white lines indicate where the computed tomography scans were made; the arrow shows their sequence. (b) Scans through the body as indicated in 6.4a, showing it is made up of sections of differing density and thickness. The arrows indicate the bulges and drips of the low-density cement used to hold the fragments together. (c) CT of the body of the dog flattened following the movements of the arrow, showing clearly that the dog has been assembled from carefully cut sections. (d) CT inclined 3-D views of the inner wall of the dog's body. This shows that the assembled terracotta fragments had been scraped out to reduce weight. For this a section had to be removed to allow access before being cemented back in place; the arrows indicate the runs of cement. (Courtesy Ghysels, 2003)

them gently (to avoid heating) into pieces that can be assembled into the required figurine. Stoneham (1995b, 1998) reported an increasing number of Far Eastern ceramics that are skilful and complex montages of fragments, necessitating multiple sampling, although in many instances there is little or no modern ceramic present. Radiography could reveal that the piece was an assemblage, although in some instances more advanced techniques such as CT may be necessary (see Chapter 2, p. 32) (Figure 6.4).

Another example is provided by the terracotta scarified head in the style of the Ife culture of the twelfth to fourteenth centuries AD in southern Nigeria (Figure 6.5). There, genuine old terracotta fragments had been set in a cement made up of ground-up terracotta in a cold-setting liquid polymer. Six TL determinations were made on samples drilled through the cement into old terracotta, which showed it to be approximately 900 years old. Interestingly, the quartz grains within the cement gave TL dates comparable to those for the intact terracotta fragments, and may very well have been their source, and this shows that the fakers were taking the precaution of ensuring that even the modern cement would pass the quartz inclusion measurements.

Yet another method is to take ceramic sherds of the correct age, gently grind them, and then reconstitute them with an inorganic cement into the desired form, without using any heat and thus

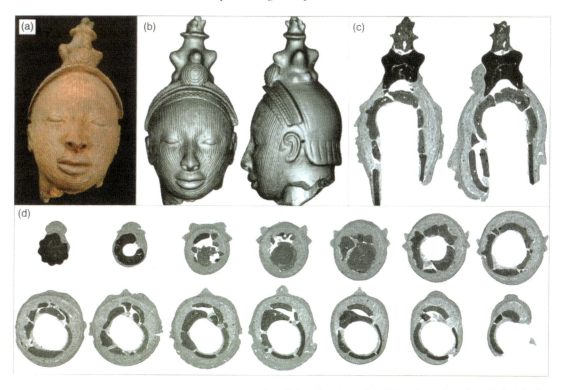

Figure 6.5 (a) Photo. Terracotta head purporting to be of the Ife culture. (b) CT: orthongal surface shaded display views. Note the small (black) hole behi nd the ear from where the TL sample was drilled into the old ceramic behind. (c) CT: Coronal and sagittal lateral sections. Ceramic fragments of varying thickness and density have been set in a much less dense cement. The dark dots in the latter are quartz grains. (d) CT: Thin axial slices through the head confirm that it has been built up from fragments of terracotta set in a much less dense cement. (Courtesy Marc Ghysels)

preserving the TL, especially in the quartz grains. Hall (1975) suggested that this was the explanation for the apparent TL in the Glozel ceramics (see p. 123). However, quite apart from problems of spurious TL from the cement and the absence of an archaeomagnetic moment from the ceramic (see Chapter 9, p. 189), it is very difficult to make a cement that closely resembles a ceramic body.

Forgeries of ancient ceramics from West Africa apparently regularly have inserts of plugs of real ancient terracotta fitted into the recently fired ceramic or cement in the places where TL sampling is likely (Brent, 2001). Examination of ceramics by UV might be of assistance in revealing such pastiches; radiography and CT are the only certain methods to detect restoration but are often precluded because of possible effects on the TL itself. Allen (2001, pp. 43–44) reported, with photographs, ancient fired clay being inserted into the core material of Chinese bronze forgeries. The position of these inserts are made known to dishonest TL

practitioners so that they can produce an ancient date for the pieces.

This raises the question of whether TL testing should be made available for unprovenanced antiquities (see Chapter 1, p. 20 for more on this contentious issue). For example, ceramic artefacts made recently as legitimate copies, fakes and outright forgeries, make up a fair percentage of African art that is offered for sale (Cole *et al.*, 1975). Up until the early 1990s, scientific authenticity studies, mainly TL, were playing no small part in facilitating the despoliation of Africa's archaeological heritage, especially in Mali, by authenticating unprovenanced pieces offered for sale on the international market that had been clandestinely excavated and illegally exported. Following an outcry against the trade in such looted material from Africa (Dembélé and van der Waals, 1991), the Oxford Laboratory For Archaeology and the History of Art set up protocols for vetting samples and refusing those from such unprovenanced material (Inskeep, 1992).

Case studies

Zapotec ceramics: Forged or looted determined by market forces

Forgeries of antiquities in Mexico began to be made as early as 1820 and were already recognised as a problem by collectors and museums in the late nineteenth century (Holmes, 1886).

Distinctive and handsome moulded ceramic vessels purporting to belong to the Zapotec culture from Oaxaca State in southern Mexico (Figure 6.6), often in dramatic and elaborate anthropomorphic or zoomorphic forms, began to come onto the market in the late nineteenth century in considerable quantity and were sought by collectors and by museums around the world (Ekholm, 1964; Shaplin, 1978). Many years later after archaeological excavations, mainly at the Zapotec capital at Mont Alban, just outside the city of Oaxaca, it soon became clear that many of the pieces previously obtained from dealers could not be paralleled and were thus suspect. In the 1970s TL authenticity studies were undertaken by R.D. Shaplin and D. Zimmerman (Shaplin, 1978) on the putative Zapotec ceramics acquired by the St Louis Museum, mainly in the 1960s and early 1970s. Shortly afterwards studies were undertaken on material acquired much earlier, in the late nineteenth and early twentieth centuries, by the British Museum (Craddock and Bowman, 1991) and by the Völkerunde Museums in Vienna and Berlin, etc. (Feest *et al.*, 1984; Mongne 1988, 1992, 2000). Shaplin set out the criteria that raised suspicions about some of the St Louis ceramics, summarised as follows:

1. The use of unusual materials, surface treatments, techniques and iconographic motifs.
2. Pieces that were similar to other pieces that were already suspected of being forgeries.

Figure 6.6   Forged Zapotec ceramic figure of a deity (BM ETH 1946 Am. 16-1), its true age revealed by TL testing. (© British Museum)

3. Sometimes suspicion fell on a piece because it seemed to be beautiful by today's criteria rather than those of the Zapotec; some pieces were described as being simply just too 'cute'!

The intercomparison between stylistic criteria and TL was illuminating, if unexpected. Of the 101 St Louis pieces believed to be genuine, only five were found to be forgeries, but 14 of 16 suspect pieces also proved to be genuine. This suggested to Shaplin 'that the criteria we established for suspecting some of the urns need re-examining'.

The discovery that so many of the suspect pieces at the St Louis Museum were apparently ancient engendered some concern that some of the pieces could have been artificially irradiated to create a spurious TL. Zimmerman carried out zircon inclusion dating on three of the suspect pieces to check this. In each case the zircon inclusions had received β doses about 10 times higher than for the ceramic as a whole, thereby showing beyond doubt that the irradiation had come from within the zircons, not from an outside source, and was thus natural.

What did become evident from the study was that the real authenticity-determining factor was the date when a piece appeared on the antiquities market. Up to the 1960s few sites were known, but international demand was strong and so forgery was rife (Boos, 1966, p. 15). From the second half of the twentieth century rapid development in Mexico revealed many ancient sites and their illicit excavation now provides the market with huge quantities of genuine ceramics and puts the forgers out of business.

Thus, six suspect pieces tested by Shaplin and Zimmerman from the Peabody Museum of Harvard University, acquired between 1900 and 1930, much earlier than the St Louis pieces, were all found to be forgeries. The British Museum's collection of Zapotec material was formed at the end of the nineteenth and the beginning of the twentieth century, and TL tests performed on suspect pieces showed that a high percentage were forgeries as was the case with the Viennese collection.

L'Affaire Glozel

Sources: Crawford (1927a, b); Reinach (1927, 1928); Vayson de Pradenne (1927, 1930); Morlet (1929, 1932); Rieth (1967, pp. 92–107); McKerrell *et al.* (1974, 1975); McKerrell and Mejdahl (1978); Fleming (1979c, pp. 160–162); Aitken (1985, pp. 35–38); Jones (ed) (1990, pp. 301–303); Magnusson (2006, pp. 137–160).

Glozel is the prime example of where the art historical/antiquarian and the scientific evidence are seemingly at variance. If the Glozel ceramics are indeed modern but give respectable glow curves suggestive of antiquity then this has serious implications for TL generally. As the TL scientist, S.J. Fleming (1979c, p. 162) admitted some years ago, 'a calm seems to have settled over the Glozel affair once more, but it is a singularly uneasy one'.

In 1924 a young farmer Emile Fradin at the village of Glozel near Vichy in central France uncovered a mass of brick and other material. On digging deeper he soon came down to an oval paved area with heavily vitrified brick walls that were almost certainly the remains of a Medieval glass-making furnace. The local archaeological society took an interest and delegated one of its members, M. Clément, to help with the investigation. He believed the remains could be part of an ancient burial, and also stirred the Fradins' latent cupidity by showing them a lump of schist found locally, on which were roughly scratched marks resembling an arrow and the letters S, T and X, and intimated that this was important. Sure enough, a few weeks later Fradin junior produced a schist pebble bearing the S, T and X marks. Clément asked the local society for funds to continue the excavation, but was refused, whereupon Fradin discovered that one of the bricks he had previously dug up was also covered in signs. Although Clément had already seen this brick and not noticed any signs then, his suspicions were not raised, neither were they aroused by the fact that they closely resembled the symbols illustrated in a book Clément had lent to Fradin [NB McKerrell and Mejdahl (1978) claim that the inscribed bricks had been excavated and recognised even before Clément arrived

Figure 6.7   But what does it say? Inscribed clay tablet
from Glozel. (From Vayson de Pradenne, 1927)

on the scene]. At this stage a young local doctor, M. Morlet, took an interest, and soon effectively
took over the project, as well as the field, renaming it Le Champs des Morts. As Vayson de Pradenne
(1930) unkindly put it, 'by his incompetence, rashness and lack of judgement [he] gave the impetus
to a hoax that otherwise would have miscarried at the outset'. Morlet was certainly injudicious in
his dealings with the Fradins, telling them that the site should be wired off and admission charged,
which it duly was. Secondly, he gave money for the excavations and intimated that more would be
forthcoming if more interesting finds were made, which of course they were, and in quantity. There
were stones carved, or more correctly, scratched, with a variety of crude designs and a variety of
animals, including reindeer, and a series of exceedingly crude clay pots and figures and many tablets,
'dog biscuits' as the British archaeologist O.G.S. Crawford was pleased to call them (1927a, b), bearing roughly incised symbols or letters (Figure 6.7).

The site was brought to the attention of the noted archaeologist Salomon Reinach, Keeper of
the Museum of National Antiquities at St Germain-en-Laye, near Paris. He believed that the Upper
Pleistocene cultures and even the reindeer had survived in France much longer than generally
thought. He had also written a book, *Le Mirage Occidental*, claiming that, contrary to the commonly
held opinion that civilisation had begun in the Middle East and spread north-west to Europe, in
fact it was the other way round. Morlet sent a copy of his latest pamphlet to Reinach, inscribed 'To
the father of the Mirage Oriental, an unrecognised child'. Here in the reindeer scratches and the
inscribed tablets was the evidence for which Reinach had been searching for years. As Vayson de
Pradenne (1930), clearly no admirer of Reinach, related:

*Salomon Reinach set out for Glozel. He was lost before he started, for to counterbalance so great a temp-
tation he would have required a highly disciplined critical faculty. Now this great man of learning, whose
brain is essentially receptive, has always conspicuously lacked this faculty. He has moreover, always looked at*

archaeological facts only through a veil of literary form, and he has neglected the study of things and of technical matters; so that it is not hard to perceive why he has so often been the victim of forgers. [For his mistake over the tiara of Saitaphernes (Chapter 2), though the most famous, is but one of a long series.]

On his visit, Reinach, with child-like innocence, told Morlet what he would like to see unearthed. This was related to Fradin, who indicated the most likely spot for Morlet to dig and find the items before Reinach's delighted gaze (Crawford, 1927a, b). Thereafter Reinach was a staunch and active supporter of the antiquity and importance of Glozel: 'I think that any expression of scepticism is now out of date, and need not even be discussed' (Reinach, 1927).

Others were more sceptical, including the French prehistorian A. Vayson de Pradenne (1927, 1930), and the English archaeologist and editor of *Antiquity*, O.G.S. Crawford (1927a, b), who, after independent visits, roundly condemned the finds as forgeries and Fradin and Morlet as villains and fools. Indeed, their extremely disparaging and often quite gratuitously insulting remarks at such an early stage in the affair have done much to color attitudes to Glozel ever since, as exemplified by the intemperate remarks made over the years in *Antiquity* by Crawford's successor as editor, Glyn Daniel (1974, 1977, and many other editorials in *Antiquity* at around this period). For more friendly, if no less biased, accounts of the initial discoveries, see Reinach (1927, 1928) and Morlet (1932, reissued many times, most recently in 1970). At Glozel, Vayson de Pradenne was allowed to do a little digging, first in the company of Fradin, when a tablet was found, but de Pradenne felt certain that the ground in which it had been found had been disturbed and the tablet planted. When he returned and dug by himself in undisturbed ground, he found nothing.

The site and the controversy it was raising were drawing considerable international attention, somewhat to the embarrassment of the French authorities, with accusations and insults flying freely. But, if authentic, the site was producing evidence of a hitherto unsuspected literate society, developing in France at some time between the Upper Palaeolithic and Neolithic Ages, which would revolutionise the whole archaeology of Europe and the Middle East.

Accordingly, the International Anthropological Congress meeting in Amsterdam in 1927, together with the French Ministry of Culture brought together an international investigation team. They visited the site, studied the artefacts and carried out limited excavation (Garrod, 1968). Their report was unanimous and damning (*La Commission Internationale*, issued in Paris, 1928). The artefacts were all false, and the tombs of recent construction, and the team found evidence that their excavations had been tampered with. Returning to the site on the second morning they found that the turf where they intended to dig was disturbed and had been replaced over freshly dug soil, at the bottom of which lay the sole significant find of the excavation, an inscribed tablet. Regrettably, this important evidence was not photographed.

This was not the only investigation; Champion, the technical assistant at St-Germain-en-Laye, who was sent to make a full inventory of all the finds, stated unequivocally that all the stone working had been done with steel drills, gravers, rasps and files.

Dr Morlet was not one to let these reports go unchallenged, so he appointed his own committee of twelve experts, naturally including Reinach, as well as some police forensic experts, who were present 'at excavations made by workmen in the clay' where yet further artefacts were uncovered (Figure 6.8). They announced themselves 'formally convinced that the finds clearly belonged to the beginning of the Neolithic period without admixture of later objects'.

Finally, the Societé Préhistorique prosecuted the Fradins. The proceedings were initiated and a police raid on the Fradins' premises led to the discovery of the debris of artefact production and trays of apparently newly made and inscribed tablets awaiting firing. The forensic report on the tablets concluded that the tablets were unfired and thus could not possibly have survived many years buried in the ground, dissolving as they did when placed in water (but see p. 124). Furthermore, they were found to contain cotton threads colored with aniline dyes, and pieces of grass and moss that were still green.

This report, coming on top of that of the Anthropology Commission, effectively ended belief in Glozel and largely killed media and public interest.

Figure 6.8   Scientific excavation: Dr Morlet's Committee of Investigation at Glozel in 1928. Such chaotic conditions seem typical of all the early excavations. (Courtesy Roger Violett, Paris; printed in Daniel, 1974)

Amidst all the polemic, Crawford and Vayson de Pradenne did make some valuable observations on the discovery of the finds. Vayson de Pradenne (1930) noted that:

1. different classes of object appeared in succession, not together;
2. the techniques of manufacture and the sophistication of the symbols improved with time (in fact they finally became Phoenician);
3. the artefacts corresponded to those in the various books, etc. provided by Morlet to Fradin;
4. succeeding finds were clearly influenced by the comments and criticisms made regarding the previous finds;

and that

> *the hoax evolved itself gradually; it was unconsciously directed by the dupes themselves, and its course was directed by the criticisms of its opponents. It was the offspring of collaboration.*

More prophetically than he can ever have imagined, Vayson de Pradenne finished his comments thus:

> *As for Dr. Morlet, he has attained Nirvana, where no event has power to disturb his serenity; and he passes through life with his eyes fixed on the Glozelian paradise! Science rejects the Truth he offered it, so he appealed to the great heart of the People; but the People has failed him. He appeals now to future generations; and then surely, at last there will come a day...*

As late as 1970, the English edition of Rieth's book on archaeological fakes stated that 'Morlet remained a believer till he died, proof of the rule that a forgery will only drop out of sight when all the protagonists are dead'.

This apparently final comment on Glozel was about to change dramatically.

The Oxford Research Laboratory for Archaeology and the History of Art established conferences on archaeometry, at which venues arcane matters of the application of physical science to the study of the past are discussed. They are not normally the setting for sensation but this is what happened at the 1974 meeting. Vagn Mejdahl from the Danish Atomic Energy Commission gave a paper co-authored with Hugh McKerrell of the Laboratory of the National Museum of Antiquities of Scotland, with Henri François and Guy Portal of the Centre Étude Nuclaire, entitled, innocently enough, 'The TL of the Ceramics from Glozel'. This would presumably show that the inscribed ceramic tablets, etc. were of no great age, scientifically dotting the 'i's and crossing the 't's of what everyone already knew from the forensic studies of the material and the circumstances of its discovery. So it was with some consternation that the audience heard Dr Mejdahl report that all the pieces tested were ancient. The good doctor's English was excellent, but surely he had meant to say that the pieces were *not* ancient? No, the three established and respected TL laboratories had taken a selection of the ceramic tablets, vessels, clay phalli, etc. and subjected them to the standard TL dating procedures. All of the pieces, tested at each of the laboratories, gave glow curves which suggested that they had been fired in antiquity (McKerrell *et al.* 1974, 1975; McKerrell and Mejdahl, 1978). To establish an actual age was more difficult because the burial contexts were not known, and the pieces had been out of the ground for half a century. A rough estimate of the environmental radiation was made and from this a 'provisional' (but apparently never corrected) date range of from 700 BC to AD 100 was suggested.

The paper caused consternation, ranging from outright disbelief of the data presented through to hypotheses to explain away the results, and as Aitken and Huxtable (1975) prudently put it:

> The Glozel tablets must have a message for either archaeologists or for the thermoluminescence dating specialists, and, having been in business for only seven years it behoves the latter to peer anxiously in case the message is for them.

And peer they did, adopting three main approaches:

1. The very poorly fired nature of the ceramic was somehow interfering with the TL.
2. The samples examined in the 1970s were either not those produced in the 1920s *or* they had been subsequently irradiated – much was made of a nearby uranium mine.
3. Hall (1975) made the more prosaic suggestion that perhaps the tablets, etc. were made up from crushed Roman pottery, reconstituted into whatever form took the forger's fancy and cemented together. In view of the modern foreign matter reported in the ceramics, threads, moss, etc., this was a quite plausible explanation.

The very obvious, very poor condition of much of the material suggested low firing temperatures, which in turn meant that there was a possibility that some of the original geological-age TL might have survived in the clay, sufficient to give an apparent archaeological age. But this should have been apparent on the glow curves, with the lower-temperature region of the curve removed, leaving only the high-temperature portion of the glow curve. This was not the case on any of the published glow curves. Also, thermogravimetric analysis carried out on 14 of the ceramics showed they had been heated to well over 400°C, sufficient to wipe out the geological-age TL from the clay.

A study of the remanent magnetism of the ceramics was made by Barbetti (1976) – that is, measuring the magnetic intensity that the ceramic body picked up during its firing and which will have 'set' on cooling. As the intensity of the Earth's geomagnetic field varies both geographically and with time, there is considerable dating potential here, as well as information on the firing process itself (see Chapter 9, p. 189). The six samples tested by Barbetti cleared up a number of points. First, the artefacts *had* magnetic moments – they were real ceramics, not just reconstituted ceramic powder moulded to shape. Secondly, the magnetic moment confirmed that five of the six pieces had been heated strongly enough to remove all of the geological TL. The final conclusion was more important, and apparently damning. The two inscribed tablets tested showed that they had been fired and cooled in a geomagnetic field that was of similar intensity to that presently existing in central France. Moreover, this field was apparently totally unlike that which had pertained in central France over a period of 3000 years from about 1500 BC to AD 1500. The result received a mixed reception – relief, because at last a scientific method had got the expected answer, but unease because that really did suggest there was something wrong with TL itself. However, very soon after-wards studies showed that in the Gallo-Roman period there was a temporary, but pronounced change, when the intensity of the geomagnetism was similar to that of the present day (Shaw, 1979). Thus, the archaeomagnetism of the Glozel tablets was in agreement with the TL age.

Further work on the ceramic material using Mossbäuer spectrometry (Bakas *et al.*, 1980) on one tablet suggested firing temperatures in the range 400 to 600°C, and Mejdahl (1980) reported firing temperatures estimated by differential thermal analysis which showed that 10 out of the 14 samples had been fired above 400°C, but that four others were poorly fired.

The possibility that the ceramics had been artificially irradiated was also investigated both by the quartz grain method (Aitken and Huxtable, 1975) and by the zircon inclusion method (McKerrell *et al.*, 1975; McKerrell and Mejdahl, 1978). These methods showed conclusively that there had been no significant external γ radiation, and that the TL dose was predominantly the result of ionising radiation originating inside the ceramics themselves.

In their 1974 paper, McKerrell *et al.* also gave a very preliminary report on the dating and scien-tific examination of the organic material from Glozel. This included an RC date quoted as SRR–434, 50 AD ±80, obtained on some ox teeth apparently found within one of the crude vessels. This is in conflict with the unsubstantiated report, originating from Glyn Daniel, and quoted in McKerrell *et al.* (1975) of an RC date on an unidentified bone plaque that indicated a modern date. McKerrell *et al.* (1975) and McKerrell and Mejdahl (1978) also reported on nitrogen, fluorine and amino acid studies then in progress on the bone (see Chapter 17, p. 429). These, in common with all the Glozel studies, have never been adequately published, but the preliminary results did show a substantial decrease in the nitrogen content of much of the bone. The fluorine contents were similar to the levels found in modern bone.

It must be said that the condition and survival or otherwise of the bone material from Glozel in general is contradictory and unsatisfactory. On the one hand the absence of human remains from the claimed burial chambers was explained by the total destruction of the putative bones in the acid clays, yet the engraved bone items survived with their polished and decorated surfaces in pristine condition. Some of the ceramics may be ancient, but much of the other material presented with them is deeply suspect.

Colin Renfrew (1975), who was present at the original 1974 and subsequent meetings, succinctly stated the very real archaeological, and, to a large degree, common-sense objections to the Glozel phenomena. These are:

1. Almost all of the material supposedly found at Glozel is unparalleled elsewhere, either locally or beyond; it is a collection of unique material. The assemblage contains no ordinary material; everything is unusual. Excavations before and since in Central France, (or anywhere else for that matter) have singularly failed to match any of the finds, the only possible exception being some tablets found in Spain, and roundly condemned, as much as anything because they were like those from Glozel (Cuardo-Ruiz and Vayson de Pradenne, 1931).
2. The collection is made up of material that, although apparently found as an archaeological entity, has stylistic echoes as diverse as the Upper Palaeolithic, the Neolithic and the Phoenicians.

Colin Renfrew also drew attention to the fact that no Iron Age or Roman specialist had ever become involved in the discussion.

This leads to considerations of the other aspect of the archaeological problem, namely the site itself. Apart from what are now taken to be the remains of a Medieval glass furnace the site is fea-tureless. There were apparently just three layers, the topsoil, a layer of yellow clay which was said to contain the finds, and a harder, sterile clay beneath. Hundreds of artefacts were found but no features, no walls, pits, ditches, or ... anything. Yet the only way that these extremely fragile ceramics could have survived is if they had been buried in some form of pit.

Thus the contradictory situation exists in which TL on the ceramics suggests that many of them are probably in the region of about 2000 years old, but the site from which they are said to have come in the Champs des Morts does not archaeologically exist, as confirmed by archaeological excavations that finally took place at the site in the 1990s. This leads inexorably to the conclusion that the bulk of the material came from somewhere else. The close similarity between the clay in the field and that in the ceramics (Peacock, 1976), suggests the 'somewhere else' is not far away. The obvious suggestion is that the ceramics come from a site, maybe on a neighbouring farm, that did not belong to the Fradin family. The tablets found in trays in outhouses of the Fradin farm, could be finds in storage prior to their 'discovery' in the Champs des Morts. They clearly were in a very soft state and the apparent contradiction of finding aniline-dyed threads and fresh moss and grains buried in 2000-year-old ceramics could be resolved if they had been incorporated during storage and during excessive cleaning and home-made conservation treatments carried out on the very soft clay.

The 1990's reassessment of the site involved further TL which although showing many of the ceramics were recent, confirmed that some of them had been fired approximately 2000 years ago.

The stones with Upper Palaeolithic-style engravings made with steel tools are almost certainly a modern addition, but the bone material is more problematic. As discussed above, the condition of the bones suggests that they almost certainly did not come from the site, and the Upper Palaeolithic style of many of the depictions on them make it unlikely that they were originally deposited together with the ceramic material about 2000 years ago, if indeed they are of any age at all. The promised RC dates on the bone never materialised. The teeth that were supplied for RC dating in the 1970s are not necessarily from the 1920s material. To obtain a couple of ox teeth of the appropriate age would be no problem at all – Romano-Gaulish archaeological sites produce such material by the kilogram.

This leaves just the ceramics. Perhaps the signs themselves may not be so inexplicable – the Phoenician element has always been recognised, and way back in 1927 Camille Julian suggested that they could be associated with a sorcerer (Vayson de Pradenne 1930, p. 211). Over 133 symbols have been recognised, far too many for a real alphabetic writing system such as Phoenician, Greek or Latin. But could they be the creation of an illiterate Iron Age shaman who was vaguely aware of the inscriptions and writings to be found in the temples of the Phoenician and Greek settlements springing up on the shores of the western Mediterranean?

The promised archaeological excavations never got beyond a preliminary magnetic survey, and similarly, properly documented publication of the dating evidence and studies on the organic materials from the site has never appeared, making the title of McKerrell and colleagues' 1975 paper 'A plea for patience', seem, 30 years on, more than a little wry. The remainder of the TL scientists, satisfied that there was nothing wrong with their TL measurements, withdrew, albeit uncertainly, from the subject (see the comments of Aitken and Huxtable and of Fleming, quoted above, p. 123 and 119 respectively).

Some archaeologists, notably Daniel, took the opposite view, and in his concluding editorial on the subject in 1977 stated that it was the TL methodology that was wrong, opining that 'thermoluminescence dates give us less and less assurance that they are a primary and reliable chronological document'.

More recently, Renfrew and Bahn (1999) castigated the TL specialists, and were quoted with approval by Magnusson (2006, p. 158):

> It is surely incumbent upon those who set out to investigate material which had been declared fraudulent nearly 50 years earlier, and who used their scientific techniques to declare it genuine, to explain . . . what went wrong.

In his 1986 autobiography (p. 354) Daniel went further and magisterially summed up:

> The whole affair has been a great lesson in the credulity and creditability of scientists.

Thus science is to be blamed for archaeology's shortcomings.

Dendrochronology

Sources: Fleming (1976, pp. 31–55); Baillie (1982, 1984, 1995); Klein (1982, 1999); Eckstein (1984); Aitken (1990, pp. 36–55); Lavier and Lambert (1996); Dean (1997); Kuniholm (2001).

The application of dendrochronology in authenticity studies is limited to substantial pieces of temperate-zone timber. However, in the areas where it can be applied, dendrochronology can provide accurate and precise dates of great significance (Fletcher and Tapper, 1984). These include musical instruments (see p. 134), furniture (Pousset, 2000; and see Chapter 17, p. 145), exemplified by St Peter's Chair in the Vatican (Weaver, 1982), the leather-bound wooden panels of manuscript covers (Neyses, 1996), and, above all, panel paintings (Chapter 12, p. 290 and p. 131).

Dendrochronology was developed by the American astronomer A.E. Douglass, who came to realise that it had archaeological applications (Douglass, 1921). However, the method only rose to international significance almost 50 years later with the realisation that this was the only method with which to check, correct and ultimately calibrate the RC timescale (see Chapter 5, p. 91).

Trees grow upward and outward, the trunk and branches increasing their girth by the addition of an annual increment in the *cambium*, the zone between the wood and the bark (Figure 6.9). In the cold and temperate zones growth is very seasonal; after the winter dormancy the cambium produces new cells in the summer growing season. The changes in size and thickness of the cells through the growing season create quite discernable ring boundaries. In the tropics growth is more or less continuous, and it is difficult, although not impossible, to distinguish material laid down during individual years. Thus, dendrochronology is far less developed for tropical timbers than for those growing in colder climes (Grant, 1992) and is not applicable at present on tropical timbers such as mahogany or the various varieties of rosewood.

The thickness of the rings primarily depends on the weather during the growing season, and so just as there are good and bad seasons, so there are broad and narrow rings. Clearly, it is imperative to establish the area over which a given seasonal weather pattern can be said to extend before comparisons with standard tree chronologies can be made. This enormous and ongoing task has necessitated the study of the ring patterns on trees from known locations across much of the temperate zone of the northern hemisphere and through many thousands

Figure 6.9   Section through an oak log showing the tree rings. (Courtesy P. Craddock)

of years. These have been built up from living trees for several centuries, and then continued back into the past through the recognisable overlap of the inner rings on the living tree with the outer rings on major structural timbers on old buildings etc., and then on back through a succession of major timbers from archaeological sites and bogs, through thousands of years (Figure 6.10). A number of reference chronologies exist of which the International Tree-Ring Data Base (ITRDB) at the National Oceanic and Atmospheric Administration Palaeoclimatology Program, at Boulder, Colorado in the USA is one of the more complete. Fortunately, specific climatic regions do distinguish themselves in the tree-ring sequences and the extent that these regions cover is such that one can speak, for example, of North Sea or East Baltic zones, each covering tens of thousands of square kilometres. Many of the European climatic zones have now been established from which the timber for many wooden artefacts will have come. By contrast, dendrochronology may not yet be possible on timber which grew in the southern hemisphere, even that from temperate or cold climates with a distinctive and potentially recognisable ring sequence.

The growth of each individual tree is dependent on its micro-climate, its health, infestation, etc., and very local factors such as forest fires. Therefore, no individual tree ring sequence will exactly match with an established tree ring chronology, and so in order to make a match, between 50 and 100 rings are necessary on the sample sequence. Even so, it can still be an uncertain match, with sometimes quite widely separated possibilities having similar probabilities, as exemplified below by the case of the Messiah violin (see p. 134). Sometimes, the

Figure 6.10 Construction of a tree ring chronology by the overlap of rings in timbers from a variety of ever-older sources. (Courtesy Baillie, 1985)

approximate position in a chronology can be established or confirmed by RC dating, as exemplified by case studies such as the Courtrai Chest (see Chapter 17, p. 445).

Just occasionally two sequences of tree rings on separate pieces of wood are found to be almost identical and this can be taken as evidence that the pieces are from the same tree. This can have great significance in authenticity studies and in the association of panel paintings (see p. 130).

Most work has been done on oak, but also some on beech, spruce, lime, larch, fir and pine. Dendrochronology can be applied to other temperate and cold climate species, but as yet with less confidence. There are exceptions: poplar, which was widely used in Renaissance Italy for panel paintings, is a fast-growing tree with correspondingly wide rings, and thus the panels used for painting usually have no more than about 40 rings (Klein and Baulch, 1990). The rings themselves are rather indistinct, and overall there is not much variation in their widths (Fleming, 1975, p. 61). Also, the poplar panels were often cut tangentially from the logs, which means that even fewer rings are represented (Figure 6.11). Maple and sycamore, which were used for the sides and backs of stringed instruments of the violin family, are also unsuitable for dendrochronological dating owing to erratic growth patterns (Klein and Pollens, 1998).

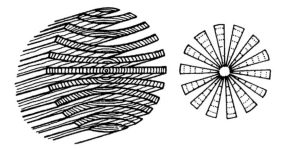

Figure 6.11 Methods of splitting or cutting a log into panels or planks. (Left) Shows the cut across the log, tangential to the growth rings. (Right) Shows the cut radial to the log, at right angles to the growth rings. Most oak panels of good quality were cut radially as this minimised warping. (Courtesy Bomford *et al.*, 1989)

Practical dating

For most dendrochronological work a sawn or drilled sample is necessary. This is clearly inappropriate for art objects or antiquities, but rings may be revealed on the bases of statues or posts, or on the ends of planks or panels. Planks are now normally sawn as slices through the trunk of the log tangential to the rings, and on those from the outer regions the rings will be more tangential, and

Figure 6.12 Quarter-sawing a log to obtain wood suitable for panels or, as in this instance, for a violin front, exposing long runs of tree rings. Note the bark and a normally indeterminate number of the outer rings of sapwood will have been removed. (Courtesy Topham and McCormick, 2000)

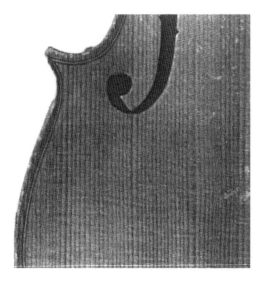

Figure 6.13 Part of the front of a nineteenth-century French violin, made of spruce with the growth rings clearly visible. (Courtesy Topham and McCormick, 2000)

maybe too few to be meaningfully measured (see Figure 6.11). However, panels intended for painting, and for making the bodies of musical instruments, were usually split or quarter-sawn radially from the log in order to minimise warping and thus are at right-angles to the rings (Figure 6.12). The rings of musical instruments of the violin family may be read directly from the front (Figure 6.13), but for other panels, perhaps covered with paint, etc., it will still be necessary to expose the rings by careful cleaning of the surface with a sharp blade or razor, followed by light sanding, and thus this should not be attempted on a visible edge.

The measurements can be made using a magnifying glass with a scale, and this may be the only feasible way with a piece of furniture or a large panel painting. It is better, if possible, to measure the sample beneath a specially adapted binocular microscope, fitted with a Vernier scale for direct reading.

Experiments have been carried out to measure the thickness of the rings by computed tomography, thereby doing away with the need for any sampling or surface preparation, or indeed manual counting; instead the data is fed directly as a digital image into a PC (Reimers *et al.*, 1989). Ordinary radiography often reveals the rings very clearly (see Figure 12.5).

The actual dating procedure consists in comparing the sample tree ring sequence to that of the tree ring chronology of the region from where it is believed the wood grew. This can be done by eye or more usually and effectively by the appropriate computer program. As there is never an exact correspondence between an individual sequence and the appropriate chronology, various statistical treatments have to be applied. Clearly, the more rings that are present the greater the chances of a match, but there are occasions where no meaningful match can be established.

As with RC, the event being dated is the growth of the tree, but the information required is the date of the use of the timber. Before that can be attempted factors such as the seasoning and the amount of outer soft sapwood that is likely to have been removed in the preparation of the timber must be estimated.

Seasoning

In general it seems that construction timbers were often used almost immediately after felling (Eckstein, 1984). Fleming (1976, pp. 44–45, Figure 2.6) illustrates a nice example of a timber-framed house in north Wales where the date of felling the timbers can be assessed precisely to 1615 and the house bears an inscription dated 1616; so much for prolonged seasoning! Similarly, the study of violins made in Cremona during its 'Golden Age' by masters including the great Antonio Stradivari, indicates that seasoning of the spruce and larch could not have been prolonged. Harvey (1995) suggested 5 to 6 years of seasoning were typical but John Topham, an experienced violin-maker, believed 2 or 3 years was more likely (Topham and McCormick, 1998). The dendrochronological study of the famous statues on the retable at Issenheim dated to 1490 showed that the lime wood from which they were carved was still growing as late as 1487 (Lavier and Lambert, 1996). The timber intended for the cabinet-maker and panel-maker may have been seasoned for rather longer, typically for many months, but still well under 5 years. Thus, overall, seasoning should not be a significant factor in determining the age of an artefact by dendrochronology (but see the report on the timbers of King Arthur's Table, p. 133). Conversely there is always the possibility of the reuse of timber; thus, for example Mayer (nd, p. 300) writing on the subject of panel painting, noted that 'in England well-aged boards from old panelling or furniture were often used. Modern painters should seek such well-aged panels'.

Preparation

The outer rings of a tree carrying the moisture and nutrients up to the branches constitute the sapwood, which is soft and weak and so is usually removed when the tree is cut up into usable timber; beech is an exception where only the bark need be removed (Klein and Baulch, 1983). Herein lies the major drawback in the application of dendrochronology to wooden artefacts, i.e. the unknown gap in time between the latest ring and the felling of the tree. Where some of the inner sapwood rings survive and can be identified as such, above all on oak, an estimate can be made. Sapwood can be identified on some other species by staining with safranin-astrablue, although this is clearly not permissible on an antiquity or work of art.

The wood may be in one of four cases, represented in Figure 6.14. In the first (top), the sapwood survives to the bark, and here the date of felling of the tree is potentially realisable to the year. Except in rare instances, piles for bridges for example, the bark and sapwood are usually missing. Where only a little of the sapwood has been removed (centre) the date of felling can still be estimated with some precision.

In many more artefacts a very little of the sapwood survives (bottom left). Here the last surviving ring cannot have been too far away from the felling. The problem is trying to estimate how far. The number of sapwood rings on an oak for example is highly variable from tree to tree, and thus complex statistical estimates are rather meaningless when applied to an individual tree. That having been said, various estimates have been made on the number of rings that can be expected on a mature oak tree, varying from 15 to 50 (Eckstein, 1984, pp. 21–25). Hughes *et al.* (1981) suggested a mean of 30 with a 95% confidence that the number lay between 19 and 50, based on their study of oaks growing in the west of England.

In the fourth category (bottom right of Figure 6.14) where no sapwood is present, realistically, no date of felling can be given, but dendrochronology can still be useful in providing a *terminus post quem*. Thus, in the case of a painting, it would be possible to establish the maximum age of the panel, if not the age of the painting on it and this can be of decisive value. For example, if the tree was still growing after the subject was dead, then the painting cannot be contemporary, as shown by the following example.

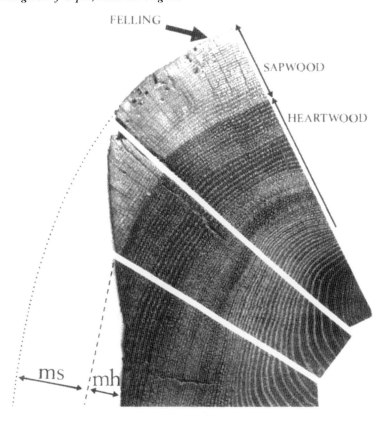

Figure 6.14   An oak trunk split into three timbers. The top has complete survival of the bark, and its date of felling can be ascertained to the year. The middle piece has most of the sapwood surviving and an accurate estimate of the date of felling can still be made. At the top of the third timber a tiny amount of sapwood survives and so an estimate can be made as to the date of felling. At the bottom no sapwood survives and it is impossible even to estimate the date of felling. The last rings do, however, give a *terminus post quem*. (Courtesy Eckstein, 1984)

Case study: A life-portrait of Edward IV?

Studies were made on the series of Tudor portraits of the earlier kings of England, stretching back to William the Norman, now held by the Society of Antiquaries of London (Fletcher *et al.*, 1974; Fleming 1975, pp. 61–65; Fletcher, 1976, 1980). No one seriously believed the portraits of the Norman kings to be contemporary studies from life, but there was a possibility that some of the fifteenth-century portraits of the Lancastrian and Yorkist kings, the immediate precursors of the Tudors, could be contemporary (Tudor-Craig, 1973, Figure 6.15). However, dendrochronology studies showed that the oak trees from which the panels were cut were still growing in the early sixteenth century, decades after the subjects of the portraits were dead and buried. In addition, the patterns of the rings for the panels carrying the portraits of Edward IV (1461–83) (Figure 6.15) and Richard III (1483–85), both now in the Society of Antiquaries of London, are so close that these panels were almost certainly cut from the same tree (Hall *et al.*, 1978).

Figure 6.15   Portrait of Edward IV (1422–83) painted on an oak panel (p. 45 in Tudor-Craig, 1973). He is depicted resting his hands on the lower frame, as was the usual contemporary convention. In a Tudor portrait he might be expected to have been fingering a ring. However, dendrochronology established that the last remaining ring grew in 1498 and thus this cannot have been a life portrait. (Reproduced with permission of the Society of Antiquaries)

The difficulties in estimating the extent of the missing sapwood has lain behind some of the most debated controversies in dendrochronology concerned with the dating of panel paintings, and, hence, often at one remove, the artist.

Case study: Problems with panels

Sources: Bauch and Eckstein (1970, 1978, 1981); Baillie *et al.* (1985, 1995); Bauch (1978); Fletcher (1974, 1976, 1978, 1980, 1982); Klein (1989; 1998a, b; 1999).

At the start of this work there were problems experienced with the actual sequence. Both Bauch and Eckstein and Fletcher worked in the 1960s and 1970s dating oak panels painted in the sixteenth and seventeenth centuries in the Low Countries or in England, and assumed that the oak was local to the North Sea region. As more data became available it became obvious that the majority of the oaks were not local, but almost certainly came from the eastern Baltic, itself an important

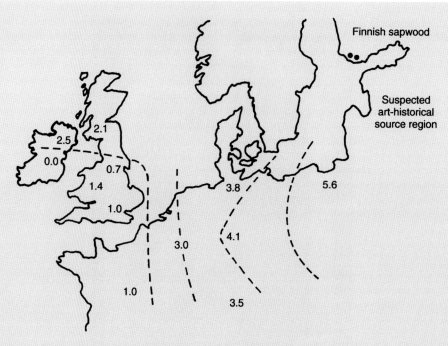

Figure 6.16 The correction factor in years that should be applied to 'English oak' tree ring dates, obtained from panel paintings that have been in England since their execution. The discrepancy gets progressively larger, up to 5.6 years as one moves east. This is significant, as much of the oak used for panels in the sixteenth and seventeenth centuries in the countries bordering the North Sea has been shown to come from the east Baltic region.

discovery (Bonde *et al.*, 1997). An effect of this misattribution was a small, but consistent over-estimate of age of about 5 years by both Bauch and Eckstein, and Fletcher (Figure 6.16). This was published by Baillie (1984), Baillie *et al.* (1985) and Hillam and Tyers (1995), and was fully accepted by both Bauch and Eckstein (Eckstein *et al.*, 1986) and Fletcher (1986).

Fletcher's rather inconsistent approach to the problem of the missing sapwood was to prove more serious. He seems to have assumed a somewhat arbitrary estimate of between 20 to 30 rings would have been removed, that is the tree was felled some 20 to 30 years after the latest, outermost surviving ring. Unfortunately, Fletcher seems to have varied his estimates of the number of rings removed for each painting, unconsciously bringing in art-historical considerations, which of course were the very criteria dendrochronology was supposed to be independently checking.

Clearly, where one is dealing with the problem of differentiating between the works of artists who were near contemporaries there are great difficulties. Thus, for example, Baillie (1995, p. 49) quoted the example of a painting, *E Cosi Desio me Mena*, supposedly by Holbein, painted on a panel of which the last ring was laid down in 1491 (subsequently revised to 1495–96). Fletcher (1982) applied his correction for the years of missing sapwood, and with the supposed association of the panel in question with two others used on undoubted Holbeins, came up with a date of 1526 for the painting of the picture by Holbein. This is clearly taking the tree-ring evidence by itself much too far, although it is still generally supportive; the tree was growing some 30 or so years before the most favoured art-historical date for the work.

A more serious instance was revealed by Starkey (1985, also discussed by Baillie 1995, p. 56) in his analysis of the conclusions reached by Fletcher on another suspect Holbein. This painting was condemned on the dendrochronological grounds that it was painted 7 years after the painter's demise in 1543 – a seemingly unassailable argument, but one based on the evidence of the last tree ring of 1530, which, with the addition of the 20 to 30 years of missing sapwood, gave a felling date in the 1550s. If, for some reason, the amount of missing sapwood was somewhat less than Fletcher's estimate, the panel could well have been available to Holbein.

Sometimes RC and dendrochronology can be at odds, as exemplified by the following example. The detailed study that was supposed to promote certainty ended up by creating an ever-increasing divide between the two methods.

Case study: King Arthur's Round Table

For over 500 years a great painted round table top made up of oak planks has dominated the hall of Winchester Castle, in southern England (Figure 6.17) (Biddle (ed), 2000). It is truly enormous, being 18 feet in diameter and weighing one and a quarter tons. The table was painted apparently no earlier than the early sixteenth century, indicating the names and places of the 24 knights of the Round Table. Thus it was already ascribed by tradition to King Arthur as *the* Round Table, but there is no extant record of how or when it came to be at Winchester, the earliest record being of 1464, when it was already in the Castle. The comprehensive study initiated by Martin Biddle included a detailed scientific study with an examination of the joinery techniques, a comprehensive X-ray survey, IR reflectography of the paint and exhaustive RC and dendrochronology dating programmes. However, the serious discrepancies between the latter two techniques mean that the real origin of the Table remains uncertain.

There are a number of possible occasions when the Table could have been made. Biddle believed it could have been built for a great Arthurian tournament held in Winchester in 1290 by

Figure 6.17   King Arthur's Round Table. The mighty table has been at Winchester Castle since at least the late fifteenth century; its exact origins remain uncertain (by permission of Hampshire County Council).

King Edward I. Alternatively, it could be associated with Edward III, who in 1344 instigated the Order of the Round Table and commissioned the building of a special chamber at Windsor Castle to house the order. This was never completed, and, although there is no mention of a table, one was surely intended, if not constructed.

The table top is made of 49 radially split oak planks that seem to have come from about seven or eight trees, although the majority are likely to have come from no more than three trees. Although it was easy enough to determine the time when the individual rings of the planks were laid down, it was much less easy to give a date for felling as only a few planks retained any sapwood. After making estimates of the gap between the latest surviving ring and the felling of the tree for a number of the planks, it seemed that the latest felling dates were likely to have been in the 1250s or 1260s, which, after allowing for seasoning, etc., would give a probable date of construction of the Table between 1260 and 1280. A truly surprising discovery was that the trees had apparently been felled over a period of between 30 and 50 years. None of the timbers showed any signs of reuse and the conclusion was that top-quality wood was being stored for decades against a prestige project that would require such timbers. It has to be stressed that there is no other evidence for such a practice – it is yet another mystery surrounding the Table.

In contrast, the RC dates on the same timbers favoured latest felling dates in the early fourteenth century. On one tree the difference between the estimated felling dates by the two methods was of the order of 60 to 70 years, and 'shows no semblance of agreement' (Biddle, (ed), 2000). The RC dating programme did however support the dendrochronological conclusion that the timbers were likely to have been felled over a considerable period of time.

Thus, there are two possibilities which can fit either of the two proposed historical scenarios: dendrochronological dating would fit the Table being constructed for Edward I's 1290 tournament, but the RC dates would support it being constructed for Edward III's Order of the Round Table.

The principal dating work was done in the 1970s, but despite much later checking and reappraisal, discussed at great length in Biddle (ed), 2000, the cause of the discrepancy remains unknown. It is salutary to note that if only one method had been used the dates would have been in no doubt as the results of both methods were internally consistent.

Dating instruments of the violin family

Sources: Corona (1980, 1990); Klein (1985, 1987, 1994, 1999); Lavier and Lambert (1996).

The fronts of musical instruments of the violin family are made of radially cut panels of spruce or larch (Figures 6.12 and 6.13). Thus, there are often sufficient rings to determine a *Terminus poste quem* for an instrument. Studies have naturally concentrated on Italian-made instruments, and, to a lesser extent, on German instruments (Klein *et al.*, 1984, 1986); a study of British stringed instruments has been published by Topham and McCormick (1998).

In related scientific studies Korte and Staat (1993) made IR studies of the varnishes used to coat early violins. Von Bohlen and Meyer (1996, also reported in Moens *et al.*, 2000, pp. 75–77) performed XRF analysis of traces of the heavy metals present in the varnishes to date them.

The 'Messie' or Messiah violin

Sources: Hill (1891); Inglis (1998); Klein and Pollens (1998); Pollens (1999); Topham and McCormick (2000); Grissino-Mayer *et al.* (2004).

Copies and forgeries of early stringed instruments of the violin family by famous makers, particularly Italian and German, are common from the nineteenth century onwards (Harvey, 1992, 1995). Antonio Stradivari is perhaps the most famous of the Cremona violin makers and forgeries and copies of his instruments abound. Pollens, quoted in *The Times* of 27 October 2000, estimated that 90% of the instruments labelled as being by Stradavari are false. The copies made by the Voller brothers and sold as genuine in the early twentieth century are among the most notorious instances (Harvey, 1992). The furore they caused seemed for a while likely to be eclipsed by the controversy that raged

Figure 6.18 The 'Messiah' violin, perhaps Anton Stradavaris' best-preserved instrument. (© Ashmolean Museum)

over Stradavari's most perfect, and certainly most valuable violin, the Messiah, now displayed in the Ashmolean Museum, Oxford (Figure 6.18).

This violin remained in Stradavari's possession until his death in 1737. Thereafter, it passed through a number of well-documented collections before being acquired by the Parisian violin-maker Jean-Baptiste Vuillaume in 1855. It was subsequently acquired by the London dealers W.E. Hill, who researched and published the violin (1891), and ultimately presented it to the Ashmolean. Although the violin is apparently well documented, few people actually saw it, much less studied or played it, prior to its display by Vuillaume

(it acquired its sobriquet because, as with the Messiah, people waited but it never appeared) and it was rumoured that the present Messiah had been made by Vuillaume himself (Inglis, 1998).

The arguments were based on a number of factors, the superb condition of the instrument, some stylistic peculiarities and the inconsistencies between certain early recorded features of the violin and the present instrument (Pollens, 1999). Even when taken together these objections were very inconclusive, and thus the Stradivari expert, Stewart Pollens, resolved to try dendrochronology. To this end he sent a set of life-size photographs of the front of the Messiah, but without revealing its identity, to the well-known dendrochronology expert Peter Klein, who had examined literally thousands of panel paintings and other items, including many musical instruments (see Bibliography and Chapter 12, p. 290). The best fit of the pattern dated the youngest ring to 1738. That is, the tree was apparently still growing a year after Stradavari's death, and thus not only was the violin not the Messiah, but it was not by Stradavari at all. Klein, however, stressed that his dating was provisional (he had, after all, not seen the original), but his dating was confirmed independently by another dendrochronologist, presumably using the same chronology.

However, John Topham included the Messiah in his survey of 33 Cremonese instruments of the late seventeenth to mid-eighteenth century (Topham and McCormick, 2000). Based on their data Topham and McCormick created their own Italian Instrument Master Chronology and tied it in with the existing North Alpine spruce and larch chronologies. Using the new chronology, the best fit indicated that the youngest ring was laid down in 1682, some 34 years before the recorded date of the manufacture of the real Messiah in 1716, and thus was entirely appropriate. Furthermore, the patterns on the Messiah very closely matched those on two other Stradavaris of undoubted authenticity (Figure 6.19).

Pollen's reaction was to insist that the Messiah was a forgery, and to accuse Topham of being an amateur. Klein, who had been unwittingly brought into the controversy, then back-tracked and tried to extricate himself from the mess, saying in an interview with *The Times* of 27 October 2000, that although he did not agree with Topham and McCormick's date, now, having seen the Messiah, 'I cannot date this violin'.

A year on, the matter was resolved after a team assembled by the Violin Society of America and led

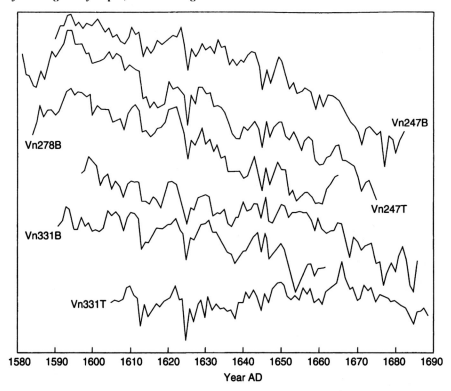

Figure 6.19   Sequences of tree rings, all from the spruce fronts of Stradavari violins (see Figures 6.12 and 6.13). The fronts are made up of two panels joined together (hence the B and T suffixes denoting bow or treble side on the same violin). Some years, such as the mid-1620s and again in the 1640s, are clearly defined; in other regions the patterns are not so clear. Violin fronts traditionally have been made of matched pieces, although here the variation between the bow and treble sides is so great as to suggest that the wood came from different trees. Overall, the similarity between woods used for the Messiah, Vn 247B & T, and the two other Stradavari instruments suggests the Messiah is genuine. (Courtesy Topham and McCormick, 1998)

by Henri Grissino-Mayer, inspected the unstrung violin in Oxford and concurred with Topham and McCormick. Subsequently, a study of the violin and other Stradivari instruments of undoubted authenticity showed that although the wood of the Messiah could not be exactly matched to the Alpine master chronology, it was very likely to have been growing between about 1577 and 1687 and was thus entirely appropriate for the date suggested for the violin (Grissino-Mayer *et al.*, 2004).

The differences between the two initial datings would seem to have stemmed from the use of different chronologies. It does show the difficulties that can arise even with a method as apparently straightforward as dendrochronology.

7

Metals I: Composition

This chapter concentrates on the composition of copper alloys, pewter and iron as related to authenticity (see Chapter 8 for fabrication, Chapter 14 for copper patination and Chapter 15 for gold and silver).

Analysis

Factors effecting surface composition

Metals can have compositions at the surface different from those in their interior, and this is an especially relevant point in authenticity studies where, so often, sampling is not permissible (see also Chapter 3, p. 40, 51). The differences can be due to segregation effects that took place even as the artefact was being produced, to deliberate surface treatment, to changes that have occurred during burial, or to changes resulting from subsequent conservation and restoration.

In cast alloys there are a number of segregation effects (Bailey, A.R., 1960, pp. 389–391, and p. 138). One such effect, to which bronze alloys are especially prone, is known as inverse segregation, or, more graphically, as *sweating*. As the metal cools it shrinks, causing the remnant liquid in the solidifying metal to be squeezed to the surface. In a bronze this will be a tin-rich phase, as tin has a much lower melting point than copper. Thus, the surface of a bronze casting can often be quite grey owing to the concentration of tin, so concentrated in fact that it can be difficult to differentiate between sweating and deliberate plating (Meeks, 1993). Similar problems occur in arsenical copper where the arsenic will preferentially concentrate at the surface, and this was sometimes deliberately induced (La Niece and Carradice, 1989). Lead does not dissolve in copper alloys and thus, in addition to sweating, it is often very heterogeneously distributed both microscopically and macroscopically through the alloy (Hughes *et al.*, 1982), and this can be a serious problem with techniques such as electron microprobe analysis (EPMA) which are used to analyse very small areas (see Chapter 2, p. 27).

Once an alloy is buried there is a tendency for the more active or electronegative elements to preferentially corrode from the alloy surface, resulting in the depletion of the more electronegative and corresponding enhancement of the less electronegative. Thus, silver will tend to be depleted at the surface of a gold–silver alloy, and in its turn copper will be depleted at the surface of a silver–copper alloy (unless there is the not-infrequent occurrence of a silver artefact being covered in copper corrosion coming from corroding copper-alloy artefacts with which it was buried).

Conversely, the corrosion of copper alloys tends to be enriched in the more electronegative elements, although this is very dependent on the burial environment. This is very well exemplified by the published X-ray fluorescence (XRF) analyses on the untreated dirty and corroded surfaces of some Etruscan mirrors (Follo *et al.*, 1981). The mirrors were reported as containing up to 53% of tin, and up to 10% of iron, whereas Etruscan mirrors usually contain between about 8 and 16% of tin and only traces of iron.

All metal objects potentially may have been deliberately plated with a variety of metals by a variety of methods, which will interfere with the analysis of the body metal. Past conservation or embellishment treatments are another potential source of analytical confusion and error on unprepared surfaces, well exemplified by the following case history. The copper-alloy artefacts from the famous Etruscan tomb at Poledrara, near Vulci, which have been one of the treasures of the British Museum since it was acquired in the 1840s, were being analysed by the author. A (too) quick qualitative surface analysis of the superb footed basin, BM GR Reg. 1850, 2–27, 19, showed that it contained substantial quantities of zinc. As the tomb dates from the sixth century BC, about half a millennium before zinc began to be incorporated into copper alloys (see p. 146), this was seemingly a strong indication that the piece was not genuine. This was communicated to the Department of Greek and Roman Antiquities, who understandably readily gave their permission for sample drillings to be taken. To the chagrin of the analyst and the immense relief of the Department the drillings were found to be of bronze with no detectable zinc.

The explanation was that the bowl must have been extensively covered in corrosion products when dug up, and at some time these were partially removed by electrochemical stripping, which was once a common procedure, especially in the first half of the twentieth century (see Chapter 20, p. 498). This would have involved wrapping the bowl in zinc wool or sheet in a solution of dilute acid and applying a current (Plenderleith and Werner, 1971, pp. 194–197; Gilberg 1988). Some of the zinc salts generated had permeated the remaining layer of corrosion products and remained, so confusing the analyst. It might be thought that such treatments were a thing of the past but Sharma *et al.* (1995) have recommended treating freshly excavated bronzes with zinc dust to form stable zinc salts on the surface as a protection against the chloride-induced bronze disease, and thus the contamination of surfaces is still advocated and may even be practised.

Another less drastic, but still potentially confusing conservation treatment was the control of outbreaks of bronze disease by spotting the affected surface with silver oxide, forming stable silver chloride (Organ, 1961; Plenderleith and Werner, 1971, p. 253). This silver in the corroded surface could be interpreted as evidence for silver plating.

Thus it can be seen there are real problems in trying to obtain a meaningful overall or body composition from the analysis of unprepared surfaces. Even if cleaning and some minimal polishing is permitted, the composition just beneath the surface may well still be significantly different from that of the original body metal. A major series of surface analyses by XRF of hundreds of Roman silver coins (Walker, 1976, 1977, 1978) ran into problems even though some surface preparation was carried out because of the depth to which the copper had been depleted, leading to a serious overestimate of the purity of the coins (Schmitt-Korte and Cowell, 1989; Butcher and Ponting, 1998). Studies by Cowell and Ponting (2000) and Klockenkämper *et al.* (1999) on Roman silver coins, and by Karras (1988) on Medieval silver coins all showed regular and considerable enhancement of the silver at the surface, calling into question the validity of other surface analytical techniques such as streak neutron activation analysis (NAA) (see Chapter 3, p. 51).

Studies on copper-base Roman coins carried out by Condamin and Picon (1972) suggested the problem is most serious for silver in copper alloys, quite serious for the depletion of lead in leaded copper alloys, and less serious for the depletion of tin in bronzes, and that there was little depletion away from the immediate surface for the zinc in brasses. However, the latter depends on the burial circumstances as there is sometimes severe depletion of zinc from the immediate surface (Scott, 2002, p. 27), and analyses of Roman *oreichalkos* coins performed by Calliari *et al.*, (1998) showed a massive depletion of zinc at the surface.

Body metal heterogeneity

It is important to understand what is meant by an overall or bulk composition of an artefact, and in some instances whether it is a meaningful concept or even attainable. Castings of alloys will rarely have a uniform composition throughout unless they are very small or the metal freezes extremely quickly. Usually there is time for the constituent metals to begin to segregate. Normal segregation is where the last metal to freeze contains the material with lowest melting point. For example, in a bronze, the metal from the centre of the casting up and into the pouring cup will normally have been the last to set and may be significantly higher in tin. Gravity segregation is where the heaviest phase of the alloy sinks whilst the metal is still molten in the mould. In practice this only seriously affects the distribution of the lead in copper alloys, but this can be quite dramatic as evidenced by the recent study of some Egyptian statuettes (Taylor *et al.*, 1998). The composition at the extremities of a casting may not represent the overall composition.

Thus, in general it can be seen that if a reliable analysis that gives an accurate estimate of the composition of the body metal is required then a drilling into the body is to be preferred, and this was the conclusion of Lutz and Pernicka (1996) in their study of the analysis of copper alloys by XRF. In practice a drilling does less real damage than surface grinding or polishing (see Figure 3.1). For metals a sample of the order of 5 to 20 mg, which can be obtained using a bit 0.7 to 1.0 mm in diameter, is usually adequate for most analytical techniques. The corrosion and immediate surface layers are discarded and the clean metal turnings then collected for analysis. This usually involves acid dissolution, but when a solid sample is required for XRF analysis, homogeneity can still be achieved by placing the drillings in a gelatine capsule or attaching them to a sticky Mylar film (Chapter 3, p. 49).

Composition

There are some technical manuals giving tables of alloys, together with their trade names and composition ranges, that are invaluable for identifying unusual compositions as deliberate alloys. For example, *Metals and Alloys*, published by the Louis Cassier Co. in 1949, lists thousands of alloys for every conceivable function from solders to denture fillings.

Trace elements

The trace elements occurring in some metals have been determined both as indicators of age and to establish provenance or cultural links.

The common perception is that modern metals will be much purer than those used in previous ages, but this assumption is not borne out by such analyses as have been carried out on modern metals used for works of art or craft work (e.g. Riederer, 1999b). There are exceptions; modern silver really does have much less gold than the silver used in previous ages, and metals that have been electro-refined are much purer than those treated by the traditional fire refining. The purity of copper generally improved through the nineteenth century through more rigorous fire-refining. Electrolytic refining of copper was first introduced in the 1860s, and the rapidly expanding electrical industry demanded high-purity copper, and thus much twentieth-century copper has been electrolytically refined (CDA Publication 1964a, b). Note that native copper is also often of very high purity (Craddock, 1995, pp. 95–97).

The metals from some specific cultures, places or periods can have distinctive trace element patterns, but in general the trace element levels in the copper alloy of a twentieth-century statue, for example, would not be out on place in that of its Roman counterpart. Conversely, there are elements that have only been added to metals in small amounts in recent times as exemplified by phosphorus or aluminium in some copper alloys and manganese in iron (see p. 154). Since the mid-nineteenth century, small additions of phosphorus (typically about 0.1 to 1.0%) have been added to some high-quality copper alloys (phosphor bronze). However, phosphorus was not routinely included in the elements sought during analysis before the introduction of inductively coupled plasma (ICP) techniques, and

therefore there is little information on its prevalence (Brownsword and Pitt, 1996), although the Department of Conservation and Scientific Research in the British Museum has regularly determined phosphorus since 1991 (D.R. Hook, personal communication).

Perhaps the most widespread objective of the analysis of ancient metals has been attempts to provenance copper and its alloys by the trace element content (Meyers, 1990; Pernicka, 1999; Wilson and Pollard, 2001). The trace elements have been joined latterly by the isotope ratios of the small amounts of lead contained within the copper (see below). This approach requires that a range of concentration of an element, or more normally of a suite of elements, be assigned to the metalwork of a particular region, period or type. Such an analytical fingerprint is invaluable for authenticity studies.

The programmes have been mostly concentrated on the copper alloys of the European Copper or Bronze Age cultures. Fewer programmes of analysis have been carried out for other regions or later periods, but such analyses as do exist have been used in authenticity studies as exemplified by the suspect Roman bronze statue known as the *Jüngling* (see Chapter 8, p. 167).

Great caution has to be exercised in using the analytical data. Usually it cannot be said that a particular trace element composition is impossible for the culture or at the date concerned, merely that it has not previously been encountered.

Studies are now taking place using more advanced analytical techniques, such as LA ICP–MS (see Chapter 3, p. 46) to study much wider patterns of elements occurring in the metal at much lower concentrations, in the parts per billion range. Thus far these have been largely confined to prehistoric gold (see Chapter 15, p. 371).

Lead isotope analysis

Sources: Pollard and Heron (1996, pp. 302–340); Stos-Gale (1998); Gale and Stos-Gale (2000, pp. 503–584).

The method has been applied to three metals, lead itself and silver and copper because of the traces of lead the latter contain. The application of this technique for metal provenancing has expanded rapidly in recent years using thermal ionisation MS (Gale and Stos-Gale, 2000). Further expansion can be expected as ICP-MS is also applied (see Chapter 3, p. 46) such that lead isotope data will be routinely determined along with elemental data.

Lead occurs in the earth as four major isotopes. There is the intrinsic primordial ^{204}Pb, and three others ^{206}Pb, ^{207}Pb and ^{208}Pb, which are the product of the radioactive decay of the uranium and thorium associated with the primordial lead over millions of years. Once the lead forms galena – lead sulphide – the uranium and thorium usually become separated and thus contribute no further lead. As a consequence the amount of the three higher-mass isotopes depends on the quantities of uranium and thorium originally present in the primordial lead and on the age of the deposit. Thus, the lead isotope data can provide not only a fingerprint but an indication of the likely age of the deposit from which the lead came, which in itself can be useful in ruling out certain deposits on geological grounds. (For details of the related ^{210}Pb method which can distinguish relatively recently smelted metal, see Chapter 12, p. 295.)

When first announced, lead isotope analysis was hailed as a major advance in provenance studies because it appeared to avoid two of the major problems which beset standard chemical trace element analysis. Because the isotopes of an element have almost identical physical and chemical properties it was believed that the lead from any one deposit would have the same isotopic fingerprint and that the processing of the ore to produce the metal (or glaze or pigment) would not affect the isotopic ratio. The problem of mixing of lead from different sources remained, both geographic and analytical (Attanasio *et al.*, 2001), but it was believed that lead isotope analysis could be used with much more confidence than the generally discredited trace element provenancing.

This is probably true, but as with all new approaches great caution is necessary, especially as the number of analyses of artefacts is very much greater than the number of analyses carried out on potential ore sources. Hence there are metal artefacts grouped by their lead isotope ratios without real understanding of how these groups came about. The exemplary work of Brenda Rohl (Rohl and Needham, 1998) on some of the potential copper and lead deposits worked in antiquity in the British Isles has shown some of the problems that exist.

Problems can occur in copper deposits which are still radiogenic, leading to very varied isotope ratios throughout the deposits (Pernicka, 1993). This phenomenon seems to have caused little concern as yet, even though it is now becoming increasingly clear that it is quite common in many of the deposits exploited in antiquity. Fortunately, the radiogenically enhanced lead isotopes are themselves distinctive, all having relatively high proportions of ^{206}Pb. Thus, it should be possible to recognise that the lead had come from a radiogenic deposit, even though it would be impossible to tell from which one. However, it has to be said that relatively few ancient metals seem to contain lead from radiogenic sources.

The major problem with the application of lead isotope measurements to authenticity studies lies in the assumption that the isotopes have undergone no mixing or change during processing (Gale and Stos-Gale, 1996; Budd *et al.*, 1995). The problems are somewhat different for the two principal metals concerned, copper and silver, and therefore they will be discussed separately.

Copper

It seems likely that during the smelting of copper the small amount of lead which the ore would normally contain will come through to the metal with the isotope ratio unchanged, although additional lead may be introduced with the flux. However, when the copper is alloyed, small quantities of lead can be introduced with the other metals. Over the last 2000 years much copper was converted into brass by mixing it with zinc ore, which almost invariably contains small but variable amounts of lead. This will lead to an irresolvable mixture of lead from two different sources, and thus the lead isotope ratios are meaningless in any provenance study on brasses. Recent studies suggest it may be possible to differentiate zinc sources based on the stable zinc isotope ratios (John *et al.*, 2007).

Many copper ores contain significant quantities of silver, which was traditionally removed by liquation, that is, mixing the molten copper with large quantities of lead to absorb the silver (Craddock, 1995, pp. 232–233). The lead remaining in the copper after liquation will be predominantly from the added lead, not the original lead in the copper ore. Liquation was practised in Classical Antiquity and most Japanese copper and much European copper from the Medieval and Post-Medieval periods was treated in this way. Isotopic grouping may be possible but it will be based on the lead used to remove the silver rather than lead from the copper ore itself, and this is potentially dangerous especially if lead from a variety of sources was used.

Silver

The problems relating the lead isotope ratios in silver artefacts to the intrinsic lead accompanying the silver ores are varied and fundamental, and thus potentially more serious than those for copper.

First, the assumption that the traces of lead in the silver metal will have been associated with the silver in the ground is often incorrect. This may be true for argentiferous galena ores, such as those from Laurion near Athens, but there are also major deposits of silver that contain very little lead, such as the jarosites which formed the main silver deposits at the famous mine of Rio Tinto in the south of Spain (Craddock *et al.*, 1985; and see Chapter 15, p. 387). To smelt these so-called dry ores, lead had to be added to the ore. Thus, the traces of lead remaining in the silver will have come from the lead added not from that in the ore. At Rio Tinto, Roman ingots of lead marked 'Cartagena' have been found that had clearly been brought in from some hundreds of kilometres distant to be used in the silver-smelting process. Cartagena also produced some silver from its own argentiferous lead and thus considerable quantities of Rio Tinto silver could carry the lead isotope signature of the Cartagena silver. Presumably Rio Tinto obtained supplies of lead from all over the western Mediterranean, making it impossible to identify silver from Rio Tinto and other similar dry ore sources by lead isotope ratios. Programmes of analysis on silver sources around the Roman Empire such as that undertaken by Gebel and Schmidt (2000) seem not to appreciate this, and also other problems originating in metallurgy processing.

Most silver will have been subjected to cupellation at some stage in its production. During the process considerable quantities of the lead will have evaporated with a strong possibility of fractionation. That is, the lighter isotopes will have been more likely to evaporate, leading to an enhancement of the heavier isotopes in the lead remaining in the silver itself. This possibility has been investigated by Budd *et al.* (1995) and by Gale and Stos-Gale (1996), who suggested that fractionation is not a significant problem. In the latter paper, lead isotope figures from ores of the Laurion lead–silver mines were compared with the lead isotope ratios of some of the Athenian coins whose silver undoubtedly came from those mines. It was claimed that there is no significant fractionation between ores and coins, both lying inside the hand-drawn ellipse that defines the field. However, simple inspection of the figures shows that there is in fact a significant shift of the lead isotopes of the coins towards the heavier isotopes, presumably brought about by preferential loss of the lighter isotopes by evaporation during cupellation. The shift can actually be quantified and according to this author's calculations equates to a loss of about 20% of the lead, which equates remarkably well with Pliny's estimate that about two ninths of the lead was lost during cupellation (Natural History 34.159, Rackham 1952, pp. 240–243).

The need in authenticity studies is to characterise or finger-print the metal rather than to provenance it. Thus, meaningful lead isotope groupings have been established for many typologically defined groups of metal objects, notably Chinese bronzes (Barnes *et al.*, 1988), where as yet little or nothing is known of the sources of the metal or of the smelting technology. It is still a little unsettling to be using data where one is unsure of the factors that could have influenced it.

Copper and its alloys

Sources: General: Many thousands of metal analyses have been reported throughout the literature and some are referred to, as appropriate, elsewhere in this book. There are currently very few works that give a worldwide perspective, including Craddock (1985a, microfiche) and Josef Riederer's many papers reporting analyses of copper alloys from around the globe. The latter are mainly published in the *Berlin Beiträge*. For the specific use of composition for authenticity see Otto (1957), Riederer (1977) and Werner (1980).

Trace elements

Of all the metals used in the past, copper tends to have the widest range of minor and trace elements. Typically these can include lead, silver, arsenic, antimony, bismuth, nickel and cobalt, and their combined total can sometimes amount to several per cent by weight in the metal as exemplified by much of the Medieval and Post-Medieval copper from Central European and Alpine sources.

A substantial quantity of arsenic, sometimes amounting to several per cent, with minor amounts of antimony and nickel, is often found in very early copper artefacts. Similar compositions occur in Medieval (Brownsword and Pitt, 1983) and Post-Medieval European metalwork. Right up to the end of the nineteenth century, European copper could be surprisingly impure, as evidenced by the composition of the copper manillas, made in their millions in Birmingham for the West African market in the nineteenth and first half of the twentieth century (Craddock, 1985b). Arsenic is also found in some of the more recent Japanese *irogane* patinated alloys (La Niece, 1991). Note that arsenic tends to become concentrated at the surface of copper alloys, and also that arsenic salts were common components of many nineteenth- and twentieth-century 'bronzing' patination treatments (see Chapter 14, p. 360). Thus, a high arsenic content in the surface of a copper alloy does not necessarily mean that the metal as a whole has the same arsenic content; and even if it does, this may not be an indicator of great age.

Antimony also occurs as a substantial trace element in many early copper alloys, and is especially prevalent in Medieval and Post-Medieval European copper alloys, only dying out with the decline of the Central European copper sources from the mid-eighteenth century (Chapter 8, p. 164). It is often taken as an indication of Medieval or Post-Medieval date (Bangs and Northover, 1999).

By contrast, bismuth is relatively rare in early copper alloys in quantities above minor trace amounts, usually below 0.01% (Craddock 1985a, microfiche). However, much eighteenth- and nineteenth-century copper can contain quite substantial traces of bismuth and this is apparently to be associated with the copper sources of south-west Britain (Edwards and Charles, 1982), which provided much of the copper entering international trade at that time. Thus, an elevated bismuth content could provide a useful indication of date (Craddock and Hook, 1990; Wayman *et al.*, 1992, pp. 7–15, Tables 2 and 5; and the copies of Bronze Age swords [see Chapter 4, p. 71] and the 'Coptic' lamps from Ghana [see p. 149]). Bismuth is much more prevalent in cast metalwork, which is to be expected as even traces of bismuth seriously embrittle copper making it almost impossible to work (Hook and Craddock, 1988, 1990).

Quite substantial quantities of nickel, sometimes amounting to several per cent, can occasionally be found in ancient copper (Cheng and Schwitter, 1957). Nickel is particularly prevalent in ancient artefacts from Mesopotamia, where the copper is believed to have come from mines around the Gulf. Scott and Podany (1990) suggested that deliberate cupro-nickel alloys were used in the ancient Near East, but this is difficult to substantiate before the Hellenistic period.

Nickel also occurs as a substantial trace in Medieval and Post-Medieval copper. Werner (1978, 1980), followed by Riederer (1981, 1987/88, 1999a), postulated that the nickel content rose from below 0.1% before the thirteenth century AD to 0.5% and more in the sixteenth and seventeenth centuries, declining from the early eighteenth century as new sources of copper became dominant. This would seem to offer the possibility of dating copper alloys by composition. However, given the

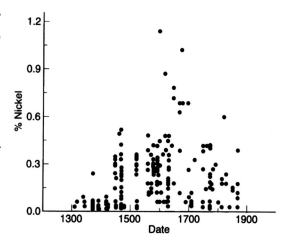

Figure 7.1 Nickel content of European brass jettons plotted against time. There is an average increase but wide individual variation. (Courtesy Pollard and Heron, 1996)

large number of mines in operation in Medieval Europe and the variation in composition within a deposit, such statements on the nickel can be no more than a generalisation and in practice the relation between the nickel content and date can fall down badly. For example the 20 'melon' ingots of Central European copper from the *St. Anthony*, wrecked in 1527, consist of between 0.05 and 0.08% nickel, which should place them all in the thirteenth century or earlier (Craddock and Hook, 1997). Pollard and Heron (1996, p. 215) have published the nickel content of some European brass jettons dating from the fourteenth to the eighteenth century (Figure 7.1). Whilst these do show an *average* rise in nickel content many of the individual later jettons have a low nickel content – too many jettons with figures too low for this to be a reliable dating criterion. Riederer (1995) has published analyses of the bronze plates from the doors of Augsburg Cathedral, some of the eleventh century and others of sixteenth-century date, expressing amazement that there was no difference in the overall trace-element pattern of the copper in the plates, separated by half a millennium, the nickel content being generally low, under 0.1%.

However, this has not stopped some analysts from using the nickel content to date individual bronzes, as exemplified by the four bronze figures now in the Ashmolean Museum, Oxford, and which are now discussed below.

Case study: The Ashmolean Four

Sources: Mitchell (1921); Fleming (1981); Brownsword and Blackwell (1984); Brownsword and MacGregor (1986).

These bronzes were the subject of scientific study first by Fleming (1981) and then by Brownsword and Blackwell (1984), between them bringing to bear TL dating, optical and metallurgical microscopy, SEM examination, lead isotope determination, and elemental analysis by both EPMA and wavelength-dispersive (WD) XRF (see Table 7.1).

The studies are interesting not only for the comparison of the two sets of analytical data, the significance of which is dealt with in Chapter 3, p. 44, but for the difference in interpretation, reflecting the different specialisations of the two groups. Fleming concentrated on the TL aspects, Brownsword and his colleagues on the composition.

The first record of the four small bronze figures representing Noah, King David, Moses and an unidentified prophet, occurs shortly after they were transferred from the Bodleian Library, Oxford, to the Ashmolean in 1887. In 1921 Mitchell suggested that two of them, the figures of Moses and of the prophet, were the work of one of the greatest of the Medieval sculptors, Nicholas of Verdun, and went on to suggest that they had originally stood on an altar at the Abbey at Klosterneuberg, near Vienna, on which Nicholas is known to have worked in the 1180s. The other two figures, representing Noah and King David, were regarded as inferior fourteenth-century replacements for figures lost in a fire.

Mitchell noted that Noah was similar to Moses and that David was apparently based on the prophet, and that the two later figures were very slightly smaller. This suggested that moulds had been taken from the putatively earlier figures, as the castings made from these moulds would be expected to be a little smaller than the originals owing to the shrinkage of metal cooling and setting in the mould (see Chapter 4, p. 72).

The attribution of Moses and the figure of the prophet to Nicholas of Verdun was generally accepted, but the association of the other two figures to the fourteenth century was more tenuous, and some scholars preferred to attribute them stylistically to the sixteenth century. Thus it was that Fleming came to date them by TL (see Chapter 6, p. 114) on material drilled from their clay cores (Fleming 1979c, pp. 206–207; 1981). This suggested that Noah belonged to the early eighteenth century [AD 1725 ± 25, OxTL 81p98 (fig)]. Fleming then ran TL tests on the clay core from Moses to confirm the twelfth-century date, only to find that the figure apparently belonged to the seventeenth century [AD 1650 ± 30, OxTL 81p100 (fig)].

Hence, not only were the Moses and prophet figures not by Nicholas of Verdun, none of the figures was even Medieval, seeming in the words of Brownsword and MacGregor (1986) 'to have dealt a devastating blow to the authenticity of the figures'.

However, the conclusions of this study were challenged by Brownsword and Blackwell (1984) and Brownsword and MacGregor (1986). They carried out their own quantitative analyses, using WD XRF on samples drilled from the statuettes, but not necessarily from the same location as for the samples taken for the previous analyses. The results of the two analytical surveys are given together in Table 7.1. As can be seen, there are serious discrepancies between the two sets of analyses particularly for antimony, and less so for the arsenic content (discussed in Chapter 3, p. 44). Fortunately the arguments put forward by Brownsword and his colleagues for the dating of the bronzes on analytical grounds can be made from either set of analyses, being largely based on the nickel content.

They noted that the trace element content of Moses and the prophet fit the compositional criteria for the thirteenth century or earlier, established in part by Brownsword's own analyses, in which the nickel content was below 0.15%, the antimony below 0.35% and the arsenic content below 0.2%. Incorporating this data with that of Werner (1978, 1980, given above), this was revised to nickel and cobalt contents of below 0.1% for the eleventh to thirteenth centuries.

Table 7.1   Comparative analyses of the Ashmolean Four by (above) WD XRF and by (beneath) EPMA.

Sample	Cu	Sn	Pb	Zn	As	Ag	Sb	Ni	Fe
Noah: Brownsword	88.4	4.87	2.2	3.3	0.22	0.06	0.29	0.06	0.44
Noah: Fleming	90.7	2.72	1.8	3.3	0.23	≤0.08	0.30	0.34	0.16
David: Brownsword	83.9	6.62	4.8	2.9	0.36	0.08	1.05	0.25	0.10
David: Fleming	91.7	2.69	1.9	1.8	0.22	≤0.08	0.34	0.32	0.11
Moses: Brownsword	87.8	2.04	1.8	7.4	0.02	0.06	0.29	0.06	0.44
Moses Insert: Brownsword	89.7	2.99	0.9	5.8	0.05	0.09	0.14	0.05	0.29
Moses: Fleming	89.8	1.05	2.3	6.9	≤0.04	0.09	0.13	0.08	0.38
Prophet: Brownsword	88.9	4.61	1.3	4.6	0.04	0.06	0.21	0.04	0.28
Prophet: Fleming	92.1	2.19	2.3	4.2	0.07	≤0.08	0.15	0.07	0.36

Sources: WD XRF: Brownsword and Blackwell, 1984; EPMA: Fleming, 1981

On this basis Brownsword and colleagues claimed that the dating of Noah and David to the early eighteenth century by TL was supported by their containing 0.26% and 0.25% nickel respectively (Brownsword's figures), but that the 0.08% and 0.06% nickel found respectively in Moses and the prophet was indicative of a much earlier date, commensurate with Nicholas of Verdun.

Moreover, the copper-alloy components of the well-known Siegburg shrine, which is definitely by Nicholas of Verdun, have compositions which are very similar to those of Moses and the prophet (Brownsword and MacGregor, 1986).

Developing their argument that the latter figures are indeed by Nicholas of Verdun, Brownsword and his colleagues attempted to explain the TL date which placed them in the eighteenth century. They ruled out the reuse of earlier metal, but suggested that the two figures are originals with additional components cast on in the eighteenth century and that the heat generated by this operation would have erased the existing TL. Inspection of the back of Moses showed that there was indeed an additional cast component. Unfortunately for the argument that this was cast on centuries later, it has an almost identical trace element composition to that of the original main casting, suggesting contemporaneity. However, the lead isotope ratios are different, which Brownsword and his colleagues believed demonstrated that the additional metal, whilst being early, was in fact not the same as that used for the main casting, and thus could be much later.

The two very different conclusions are based on what is essentially the same data. To some extent both groups favoured their preferred evidence, be it TL or composition, beyond what is strictly permissible, and at the end of the day the four statuettes remain as enigmatic as ever.

Fleming's dating seems too precise, especially as the environmental conditions in which the statuettes were kept through most of their existence are totally unknown. Also, Fleming failed to consider the possibility that the statuettes might have been reheated, when even a cursory glance of the rear of Moses would have revealed evidence of alteration.

Brownsword and his colleagues put too much emphasis on the immutable increase in the trace element content of copper, and especially of the nickel, through the Medieval period. The association of the composition of Noah and David with the eighteenth century could have been strengthened if the bismuth content had also been determined (p. 142).

The suggestion that the main casting of Moses differs from the cast-on components must also be re-examined. The apparent contradiction between the trace element content and lead isotope can be resolved quite easily. The trace elements will have come largely with the copper, which quite clearly are the same in both the main casting and addition. The different lead isotope figures can be explained if different sources of lead had been employed for the minor amounts added to the alloy.

This leads on to the final part of the argument, the putative reheating of the core resetting the TL clock. To eradicate the accumulated TL from the quite substantial clay core would require sustained heating at above 500°C. This seems unlikely to have occurred during a minor repair, and would certainly have damaged the much-praised pristine surface of the bronze.

Thus, on balance, it seems likely that the casting of the figures is Post-Medieval, but perhaps not dated with the precision suggested by Fleming.

Copper alloys

As a broad generalisation early copper alloys, especially those used for art metalwork, from all over the world tend to be of bronze, the alloy of copper and tin (Craddock, 1985a). More recent metalwork, including both forgeries and innocent reproductions, tend to be of brass, the alloy of copper and zinc, or at least to include zinc in the alloy along with other alloying metals.

The presence of zinc in a copper alloy in quantities above trace amounts is such a widely used and potent indicator of recent date that the origin and significance of the zinc content in copper alloys will be discussed here in some detail.

Zinc (*spelter*)

Metallic zinc is very volatile (BP 917°C) and on smelting zinc ores the metal is produced as a vapour rather than as a liquid. Moreover, the zinc vapour is extremely reactive, liable to reoxidise and must be condensed out of contact with air, necessitating some form of distillation/condensation system. The commercial production of metallic zinc probably began in India about 1000 years ago, in China about 500 years ago and in Europe within the last 250 years (Craddock, (ed), 1998). Thus, metallic zinc is not to be expected from antiquity but in the last century and a half, small decorative castings in zinc have been produced by the million and many of these are in an antique style even if not directly copying a specific antiquity. It is perhaps inevitable that some of these, especially those discarded on rubbish heaps where they will have acquired a patina of sorts, have been put forward as antiquities.

Can all of the few postulated examples of ancient zinc be dismissed? The argument that zinc is too reactive a metal to survive burial is proved wrong by the numerous examples of zinc coins that have survived burial for centuries in reasonable condition, in India for instance. The absence of the appropriate technology for smelting the metal is also not the automatic barrier it first appears. Small amounts of metallic zinc can occur as a byproduct in the flues of silver/lead smelting furnaces, as exemplified by the discovery of a small lump of metallic zinc at the Roman lead mines at Charterhouse on Mendip, Somerset, England, in archaeological levels dated to the first century AD (Todd, 1996). The well-known small rolled sheet of zinc metal recovered from excavated Hellenistic levels in the Athenian Agora is almost certainly ancient (Farnsworth *et al.*, 1949), but is still the only piece of worked zinc to come from controlled excavation of a site of classical antiquity.

Caley (1964, pp. 104–115) and Craddock (1998) discuss, and largely dismiss, other possible antiquities of zinc. More recently Brownsword (1988) suggested that ornate fragments, possibly part of the foot ring of a major liturgical vessel in the Romanesque style but cast in zinc, could be ancient. The piece was found in a ditch at Pipe Aston in Shropshire, in 1955. A sample of the zinc was analysed by WD XRF and found to comprise 0.7% of lead as the only major impurity, a composition typical of zinc made using the more recent retort processes. The fragments are quite corroded but in the absence of any stratigraphical evidence at the find spot, they are likely to be the remains of a piece of ecclesiastical metalwork by one of a number of specialist firms in the nineteenth century. [210]Pb isotope analysis (see Chapter 12, p. 295) could possibly establish whether the metal was smelted in the Romanesque period or in the nineteenth century.

A supposed Romano–Celtic plaque bearing an inscription has attracted more serious attention (Rehren, 1996). This is a corroded zinc plaque found with the aid of a metal detector, supposedly from the site of a Romano–Celtic sanctuary at the Engel Peninsular near Berne in Switzerland, but, it must be stressed, lacking any real archaeological context. The front face carries a punched inscription which reads DOBNORAERO GOBANO BRENADOR NANTAROR, which has been interpreted as being in a Latinised version of a Celtic language. XRD showed the corrosion to contain zinc hydroxycarbonate. Atomic absorption spectrometry (AAS) found the zinc to contain lead (1.06%), iron (0.287%), cadmium (1040 ppm), copper (1090 ppm) and tin (690 ppm). These figures are quite typical of modern low-quality zinc, except that for iron. Detailed examination showed that the iron content is very heterogeneous, rising to several per cent in places on the inscribed front face. The metallographic section showed that the plaque had been cast, and the suggestion was made that it had been cast in an open mould made of iron.

Iron moulds are unattested from classical antiquity and if the iron of the putative mould really was dissolving in the molten zinc then the mould would have become firmly welded to the plaque and impossible to separate. There is, however, another and more mundane explanation for the origin of the iron in the metal. The ubiquitous modern plating process known as galvanising consists in dipping the iron workpieces into a tank of molten zinc. Small amounts of iron dissolve into the zinc, and iron content figures of several thousand ppm are typical for the zinc in present-day galvanising baths. The plaque has certainly been cast in a one-piece mould, and the first metal to freeze against the side of the mould would be rich in the high melting iron.

Presently the plaque languishes in the 'not proven' limbo. RC dating of the hydroxycarbonates of the corrosion products was suggested but abandoned because of the likelihood of the exchange of carbon with ancient carbonates in the soil. ^{210}Pb isotope analysis is a possible method of determining whether the zinc was smelted recently or in antiquity.

The most recent supposed example of ancient zinc was a fragmentary zinc sheet found in a tomb designated 978 in the cemetery lying to the east of the famous Khirbet Qumran settlement in Israel and dated to the last century BC (Eshel *et al.*, 2002). The sheet is badly corroded and it was suggested that it had originally formed the lid of a coffin.

As the sheet was only of the order of one millimetre in thickness it must have been formed by hammering, or more likely by rolling, processes not believed to have been applied to zinc before the early nineteenth century. The context was more worrying. It had been recovered from what was described as a relatively recently robbed tomb, but old aerial photographs showed that in fact the tomb was part of group of tombs excavated in the 1960s.

It is difficult to envisage how a large sheet of metal could have been missed by the archaeologists if it was present in the tomb at that time. These considerations, together with its large size and modern fabrication technology, suggest it is a modern intrusion rather than an antiquity.

The earliest zinc artefacts, coins apart, would appear to be some gem-encrusted vessels of early sixteenth century date, now preserved in the Topkapi Palace Museum, Istanbul, but believed to be from eastern Iran or Afghanistan (Atil *et al.*, 1985, pp. 28–29; Craddock *et al.*, 1998, p. 76; Plates 1 and 2, p. 113).

Brass

To appreciate the chronological significance of the presence of zinc in a copper alloy it is necessary to have some understanding of the routes by which the zinc could have got into the copper in the first place, prior to the production of metallic zinc.

Zinc is a not an uncommon component of copper ores and thus zinc in a copper alloy could be regarded as the unconscious result of smelting a mixed copper–zinc ore. However, as described above, in the furnace the zinc would be in the form of a highly reactive vapour at the usual smelting temperature of copper ores (at least 1100°C), and thus under most conditions would be expected to escape with the waste gases rather than enter the copper.

Some very early brasses from prehistoric Europe, the Mediterranean and the Middle East, etc. have been reported (Caley, 1964, pp. 3–12; Craddock 1978) that were not from controlled excavation, and when they have been scientifically examined they have usually been found to be recent. For example, two cheek pieces in the Ashmolean Museum were published as being in the style of Luristan metalwork of the early first millennium BC (Figure 7.2). Their zinc content of 17% and 18% had raised doubts over their authenticity. Scientific study at the suggestion of Roger Moorey, confirmed the composition and found that the patina was of synthetic copper nitrate that had been painted onto the bright uncorroded metal beneath (Craddock, 1980 and see Chapter 14, p. 367).

There are also early excavated artefacts published as being of brass but which reanalysis has shown are not brass at all (Craddock, 1980). That having been stated, there are a very few brasses that have been found on archaeological excavations from well-recorded contexts from China through Iran to Mesopotamia which date from the third

Figure 7.2 Brass cheekpiece in the form of a winged sphinx standing on hares (Ashmolean Museum, inv.1951.195) (Courtesy Craddock, 1980)

millennium BC and which must surely be the result of co-smelting a mixed copper–zinc ore at relatively low temperatures which allowed the zinc to be retained (Thornton *et al.*, 2002).

It must be stressed that these very early brasses are all very small items and extremely rare. Thus, the presence of more than trace amounts of zinc in a copper alloy purporting to be more than about 2000 years old should normally be regarded as highly suspicious and the higher the zinc content the more unlikely the authenticity of the metal.

Brass first began to be made on an industrial scale in the closing centuries of the first millennium BC, somewhere in the Hellenistic world, although copper alloys containing more than traces of zinc are very rare in both Greek (Craddock, 1976, 1977) and Etruscan artefacts (Craddock, 1986). Only from the first century BC was brass adopted for some copper-base coins, most famously the *dupondii* and *sestertii* of the reformed Roman coinage system after 23 BC (Craddock *et al.*, 1980; Burnett *et al.*, 1982) as well as for fibulae.

The coins were minted by the million and thereafter brass was common in the Roman world (Craddock, 1978, 1985a), and probably also in the East, at least as far as northern India. In the Roman period there was some degree of alloy selection. Thus, whilst some classes of Roman art metalwork, such as large statuary (Craddock, 1985a, b; Craddock *et al.*, 1987/88) and mirrors (Meeks, 1993) continued to be made of bronze, much small jewellery, such as fibulae and brooches (Bayley and Butcher, 2004), and most military copper-alloy items, were usually made of brass (Craddock, 1978; Jackson and Craddock, 1995).

Brass became established as the prevalent copper alloy through the first millennium AD (Hook and Craddock, 1996) in the Late Roman Empire and in the succeeding Byzantine (Schweizer, 1994a) and Islamic world (Craddock *et al.*, 1998; Ponting, 2003).

The adoption of brass did not proceed uniformly even within the Roman Empire (Cowell *et al.*, 2000) and its successors (Schweizer and Bujard, 1994). In other regions, such as Avar and Slavic Eastern Europe or the Celtic West, the adoption of brass was much slower with bronze continuing as the preferred alloy until the end of the first millennium AD (Craddock, 2001). Right through the Medieval and Post-Medieval periods bronze continued in selective use for statuary and other major castings as exemplified by the Lion of Venice (Sentimneti *et al.*, 1990) and the Arezzo Chimera (Nicosia and Ferretti (eds), 1992).

Riederer (1980, 1982a & b, etc.) found that in Renaissance and Baroque periods in southern Germany there were distinct regional tendencies. Thus for example the art metal foundries of Nuremberg favoured brass, whereas the contemporary foundries in Munich and Augsburg favoured bronze. Thus, it is essential in authenticity studies to compare the composition of a suspect piece with other metalwork, not only of the same date but of the same type and cultural affiliation.

The zinc content of brass as chronological indicator

Before the regular production of zinc metal, brass was prepared by reacting the zinc ore with copper metal (Craddock and Eckstein, 2003). In the Ancient and Medieval world this was done by adding the calcined zinc ore to molten copper in the presence of charcoal in a closed crucible. At the temperature of molten copper (1083°C), the charcoal reduced the zinc oxide to zinc, which dissolved in the copper. The maximum zinc content of the resulting alloy is controlled by the vapour pressure of the zinc in the molten copper, which is determined by the temperature.

Various experiments to recreate the early direct processes to make brass have produced different maximum zinc contents with figures up to almost 40% (Welter, 2003), although they seem unable to reach these high figures consistently. The experiments of Haedeke (Werner, 1970) suggested the equilibrium figure for zinc absorbance by pure copper was a maximum of about 28%. Furthermore, the analysis of very many ancient and Medieval brasses, and the statements of some Post-Medieval writers and brassmakers combine to suggest the 28% figure has some reality and that very few copper alloys have been reported with more than 30% of zinc prior to about AD 1500 (Craddock and Eckstein, 2003). This is of some significance as many modern brasses have rather high zinc contents, typically in the range of 30 to 40%. Thus, a brass purporting to be ancient that contains more than about 28% of zinc should be regarded with suspicion. This is especially so if the alloy also contains more than trace amounts of tin or lead, both of which inhibit the absorption of zinc, although a few per cent of lead is quite common in all brasses, originating in the zinc ore. The metal can also have a rather high iron content, again introduced from the zinc ore. Overall, zinc contents tend to rise through the Medieval–Post-Medieval period (Werner, 1980; Brownsword, 2004), but once again this is too general to be reliably applied to a specific artefact. Unfortunately, this has not stopped some from applying Werner's various rules in order to date brasses (Martinot *et al.*, 2000, for example).

Copper alloys in Europe

It is somewhat surprising that there seems to be a much more comprehensive coverage of the composition of very early metalwork than for later periods. Thus, we have a much better idea of the composition of metals from the European Bronze Age than we do in general for the Medieval and Post-Medieval periods. The principal exceptions are:

Medieval Germany: Werner (1977, 1981, 1982)
Post-Medieval Germany: Riederer (1980, 1982a, b, 1983, 1988, 2000) One of the main stated aims of Werner's (1980, 1982) and Riederer's (1977) work was to be able to differentiate between genuine Medieval copper alloys and nineteenth-century copies
Medieval and Post-Medieval Britain: Caple (1995) and Brownsword (2004)
European nineteenth- and twentieth-century copper-alloy art metalwork generally: Riederer (1999b).

In Post-Medieval Europe a true cementation process evolved for the production of brass. The forming zinc vapour dissolved in finely divided solid copper in the crucible at lower temperatures than previously, probably rather below 1000°C (Craddock and Eckstein, 2003). This lowered the vapour pressure of the zinc in the forming brass and thereby enabled more to be absorbed. The earliest description is that of Biringuccio (Smith and Gnudi, 1942, pp. 70–76), made in the 1540s. The process was slower but the maximum zinc content rose to about 33%. This remained the maximum attainable to the end of the process (Percy, 1861, p. 616). Thus, from the sixteenth century in Europe, some brasses are found containing up to 33% of zinc. The high zinc brasses have been found in items such as memorial brasses (Cameron, 1974; Craddock, 2000/01), scientific instruments (Mortimer, 1989), jettons (Pollard and Heron, 1996, pp. 205–238) (Figure 7.3) and pins (Caple, 1995).

Differentiating between brass made by mixing zinc and copper (known in English as *speltering*) and cementation brass where the zinc content is below 30% is very difficult. Some cementation brasses have quite appreciable iron contents, of the order of several per cent, derived from the zinc ore. However, this is by no means universal, and conversely some poorly refined copper can also have an appreciable iron content.

A very few sixteenth-century brasses, notably some jettons, have more than 33% of zinc and by the late seventeenth century the zinc content of the jettons regularly exceeded 33% (see Figure 7.3). The technical processes underlying these high zinc brasses are not certain but in the Post-Medieval period some brass was being made on a limited scale by mixing copper and the expensive zinc metals. Once zinc metal was available any composition was possible, although very few of the early speltered brasses exceed 30% of zinc. Some of the more famous speltered alloys, such as *pinchbeck* (Becker, 1988, pp. 34–38, 57–60) typically contain about 15% of zinc to give the metal a good golden color, and without the disfiguring ferruginous inclusions of the ordinary cementation brass. Items claimed to be of authentic eighteenth-century pinchbeck are now almost impossible to verify analytically, as they are, of course, identical to modern brass.

There were two available sources for the zinc metal before the start of production within Europe. From the early sixteenth century some was imported into Europe from India and China. From the seventeenth century some zinc was collected

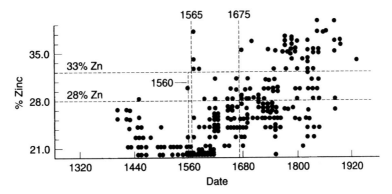

Figure 7.3 Zinc content of some European brass jettons with more than 20% of zinc. The very high zinc contents suggest some brass was made from copper and zinc metals from the late sixteenth century. (Courtesy Pollard and Heron, 1996)

from the flues of the silver smelters at mines such as Rammelsberg, near Goslar in southern Germany (Craddock, 1998) which was probably the source for the jettons. By the end of the eighteenth century zinc began to be smelted on a considerable scale across Europe, but only became common after about the 1820s.

Overall, Post-Medieval brasses containing more than 33% of zinc should be regarded with suspicion, and quite minor differences in the zinc content in the 25 to 35% range can be of critical importance in determining the processes by which the brass is likely to have been made, and thus its likely age, as the following case studies exemplify.

Case study: The chair that became a couch

The Museum für Vor- und Frühgeschichte in Frankfurt purchased the copper-alloy frame of what purported to be a Roman chair (Feucht *et al.*, 1999). However, analysis by XRF found that approximately two thirds of the copper-alloy components were of brass with in excess of 30% of zinc. When these were removed the authentic pieces that remained seemed more likely to have belonged to a couch.

Case study: The Ghanaian 'Coptic' lamps

Many years ago two cast copper-alloy lamps found in Ghana were suggested as being contemporary West African copies of Coptic lamps of the fifth to seventh centuries AD (Figure 7.4), and thus an important indication of links between Egypt and West Africa existing before the Islamic period (Arkell, 1950). The attribution was made entirely on stylistic grounds, and particularly on the chased decoration. Analysis carried out more recently on both pieces showed the metal to be of brass with 34% of zinc and traces of bismuth. One lamp had 0.065% of bismuth, which is far above the amount found in Coptic or early West African copper, but similar to the amounts found in

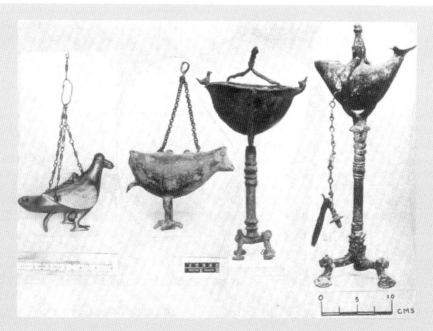

Figure 7.4   A group of copper alloy Coptic lamps in the form of birds, dated stylistically to the mid first millennium AD. The two on the outside are genuine pieces from Egypt; the centre two (BM Ethno. Reg. 1936, 10–22, 5 & 6) were obtained in Ghana. Analysis showed they are more compatible with the nineteenth century than with the fifth century AD. (Courtesy Arkell, 1950)

nineteenth-century copper from Britain (see p. 142). Thus, it is most unlikely that the lamps predate the Post-Medieval period (Shaw and Craddock, 1984).

Case study: Drake's Plate of Brass

In situations where the artefact purports to belong to an age when high zinc brasses were already in existence, condemning a piece on the grounds of composition becomes more problematic. The plate, which is about 20 cm long by 14 cm wide and about 3.4 mm thick, was found in Marin County in the San Francisco Bay area of California in 1936. The interest lies in the roughly carved inscription dated 1579, which claims the surrounding territories for Queen Elizabeth of England in the name of Francis Drake. This is apparently the very plate that Drake in *The World Encompassed*, his account of the epic voyage, claimed to have left behind on the west coast of America as a record of his visit.

Right from the start doubts were expressed about its authenticity, some believing it to be a hoax but following scientific study by Fink and Polushkin (1938) it was pronounced genuine. They based their conclusion on the metal's thickness, composition and patina, the very factors used subsequently by Michel and Asaro (1979) and Hedges (1979) to condemn it.

In the more recent study the dark surface layer was described as soft, and was suspected to be at last partially organic, but was not investigated further (a simple ignition test of a tiny particle on the end of a platinum wire would have demonstrated whether it was organic). Thickness measurements were carried out across the length and breadth of the plate and showed very little variation. The thickness was 3.38 ± 0.08 mm; the uniformity might suggest rolled metal and the thickness corresponds to a standard American 1930s wire gauge (8), although none of the other characteristic features of rolled sheet (see Chapter 8, p. 157) was described. Radiography could have established if the plate had been hammered (cf. Figure. 8.1, p. 157). However, as some undoubtedly genuine paintings of the early seventeenth century are on rolled copper sheet, the significance of hammered versus rolled may be of no great consequence anyway (see Chapter 12, p. 292).

The main evidence was the composition. Fink and Polushkin analysed samples by emission spectography (ES) to determine the trace elements. The zinc content was too great to be meaningfully quantified and instead it was estimated from a metallographic section taken from the plate which suggested the zinc content lay between about 34 and 39%. This was a good estimate in the light of Hedges's analyses of several drillings by XRF which gave an overall zinc content of 34.8 ± 0.4%. The trace-element content was uniformly low in both sets of analyses. Fink and Polushkin judged the zinc figure to be acceptable for the sixteenth century and the metal too impure for modern brass. But by comparison with other sixteenth-century brasses, analysed since the 1930s, the later investigators judged that metal was too pure to have been sixteenth-century copper and that the zinc content was too high to have arisen via the cementation process, and in general other commentators, such as Pollard and Heron (1996, pp. 113–114), have concurred.

However, the zinc content is uncomfortably close to the empirical upper limit of 33% mentioned above and several of the sixteenth-century jettons analysed by Pollard and colleagues exceed 33% of zinc (Figure 7.3). Even so, 34.8% is a very high zinc content for a cementation brass and, on balance, it is more likely that the plate was made by the mixing of copper and zinc metals. This does not in itself necessarily condemn the plate; it should be borne in mind that zinc metal had been imported into Europe from India from the beginning of the sixteenth century, presumably mainly intended for brass making. An English memorial brass dating from 1530 was found to contain 33% of zinc and is considered to be of speltered brass (Craddock, 2000/01). Thus, there is no intrinsic reason why the plate should not have been made by speltering in the sixteenth century.

In summary, while none of the individual factors in itself conclusively condemns the piece, the absence of a proper burial context or of a recognisably natural patina, and the uniform thickness coupled with the purity of the copper and the high zinc content, combine to suggest that on balance this piece is unlikely to belong to the sixteenth century.

Copper alloys in India

Brass was probably made in north-west India by the direct process from the beginning of the first millennium AD, as evidenced by analyses of surviving artefacts. Although the contemporary and later statuettes and other items so far analysed are normally of brass, the zinc content is rarely more than 20% (Werner, 1972; Craddock, 1981b; Reedy, 1997, pp. 281–290). The earliest certain evidence for brass made by speltering is some sixteenth-century Islamic astrolabes made in Lahore, which have between 35 and 40% of zinc (Newbury *et al.*, 2003).

Elsewhere in South and South East Asia, generally the adoption of brass was less common (Bourgarit *et al.*, 2003). In the south of India, for example, the Chola cultures used copper and bronze to cast their magnificent statuary through the Medieval period, zinc only being added to the alloy on a regular, deliberate basis from the sixteenth to seventeenth centuries (Werner, 1972).

Copper alloys in China

In China bronze was the usual alloy (Barnard, 1961; Gettens, 1969; Werner, 1972). Brass was used only on a very limited scale up to about AD 1500 with the exception of some brass belt fittings associated with Buddhist monks (Zhou Weirong, 2001).

The distillation of metallic zinc began in the sixteenth century (Craddock and Zhou Weirong, 2003) and very quickly bronze was replaced by brass as the usual copper alloy, a changeover well documented by the *cash* copper-alloy coinage (Bowman *et al.*, 1989; Cowell *et al.*, 1993 Dai Zhiqiang and Zhou Weirong, 1992) and the later vessels and statuettes (Kerr, 1990; Cowell *et al.*, 2003). The zinc content of the Chinese brasses regularly exceeded 30% before the end of the sixteenth century, very different from the alloys used in India. In India the metal was usually highly polished and the color of the metal was of some significance, and thus lower zinc contents were favoured. In China, art metalwork was usually lacquered (see Chapter 14, p. 356) and thus the color of the casting was, in the main, of less importance, and higher zinc contents giving a rather greeny–grey brass could be tolerated.

Zhou Weirong and Fan Xiangxi (1994) and Cowell *et al.* (2003) sought to distinquish between cementation and speltered brass based on the zinc and cadmium contents. Zhou Weirong (2001) suggested that a cadmium content in excess of 10 ppm in the alloy is indicative of speltered brass in China, but the link between the use of metallic zinc and increased cadmium content is problematic. The very few early Chinese zinc ingots to be analysed (Craddock and Zhou Weirong, 2003) have highly variable cadmium contents.

Riederer's analytical surveys of seventeenth- and eighteenth-century European copper alloys typically reported cadmium contents at or below the detection limit of 0.001% (Riederer, 2000), but in the nineteenth- and twentieth-century brasses (Riederer, 1999b) the cadmium content was typically in the range 0.001–0.01%. However, there was greater variability, and it would be difficult to use the presence or absence of cadmium in a suspect brass as evidence of the process by which the alloy had been made.

Pewter

Sources: Massé (1911); Hedges (ed) (1960); North (1999); Trench (ed) (2000, pp. 363–364).

This metal, predominantly comprised of tin, was used on a relatively minor scale in antiquity, only occasionally becoming locally popular, for example in Roman Britain in the third and fourth centuries (Beagrie, 1989). Through the Medieval and Post-Medieval periods pewter became much more popular in Europe, but was generally perceived as a utilitarian, yeoman-class material, and, as such, pewter was not seriously collected until the end of the nineteenth century. Predictably, faking and forging began and flourished in the early twentieth century, with fakers such as Richard Neate

working in England (North, 1999, pp. 187–189). Massé, in his book on pewter collecting (1911, pp. 68–69), described the enormous amount of pewter copies or forgeries that were then being produced. He noted that:

> it is a curious thing that if a collector advertises for any unusual piece of pewter ..., the piece will be heard of in a remarkably short time.

and

> It is within the bounds of probability that an advertisement for specimens of spoons of the time of Alfred the Great, pepper pots of William Rufus, or a processional cross of the time of Lady Jane Grey would be promptly answered by the same enterprising manufacturer who has supplied other interesting objets d'art in pewter within the last few years.

Clearly, as with silver, there was a considerable body of skilled craftsmen able to produce hand made items at little cost. A century on, these technically competent forgeries, having acquired a genuine patina, will be almost impossible to detect.

The composition of the Roman pewter found in Britain tends to be very variable with from 45% to almost 100% of tin, the remainder being mostly of lead, even for vessels that were clearly intended for food (Beagrie, 1989). A minority also contain some copper.

From Late Medieval Britain and elsewhere there are a whole series of laws regulating the composition especially with regard to the lead content, and this is reflected in the contemporary compositions (Brownsword and Pitt, 1984; Carlson, 1977). Such pewter flatware that has been analysed tends to be of much better quality than the earlier pewter, being of almost pure tin with about 1 to 3% of copper to harden it. The lead contents are low, but there are exceptions with quite high lead contents of the order of 20%, even for flagons. A few pieces have significant antimony contents of the order of about 2%, which should be regarded as deliberate, and about 1% of bismuth, which may well have originated from the tin or lead ores. In the nineteenth century a more-specific alloy of tin with about 8% of antimony and 2% of copper or bismuth, known as Britannia Metal, was popular, especially when electroplated (often stamped EPBM). By contrast minor items such as spoons were of very irregular composition; for example, 24 spoons dating from the fourteenth to seventeenth centuries from the English Midlands contained between 16% and 87% of tin, the remainder being predominantly lead, with some copper (Muldroon and Brownsword, nd).

Pewter was normally cast in two piece moulds and decorated by engraving, with wriggled lines being particularly popular (see Chapter 8, p. 172). The forgeries are mainly castings, often taken directly from existing pieces. Thus, on these the worked details of the original metalwork such as the wriggled lines, the hammered gadrooning around the edges and even the quality and maker's punch marks are casts. As such, they should be relatively easy to detect with the aid of a binocular microscope.

Homer (1994) reported that pewter was never plated before the introduction of electroplating in the nineteenth century and wherever silver plating was encountered, even on pewter pre-dating the nineteenth century, it was invariably electroplate. Pewter is normally kept in a polished condition, but a corroded, weathered effect was achieved with limited success on forgeries by sprinkling the surface with acid (North, 1999, Cat 296, p. 189, illustrated an example of pewter with induced corrosion).

Relatively little work seems to have been done on the natural corrosion products of tin and its alloys (de Ryck *et al.*, 2004). The few pieces that have been examined by XRD often seem to contain in addition to the stannic oxide, cassiterite, SnO_2, the stannous oxide, SnO, romarchite (Plenderleith and Organ, 1953). SnO has been found on the tin sarcophagi of the *Kapuzinergruft*, the Imperial Crypt of the Hapsburgs, in Austria (Paulitsch and Wittmer, 1987). Organ and Mandarino (1971) found romarchite and also hydro-romarchite, $Sn_3O_2(OH)_2$, on some tin vessels from a river, and subsequent work identified the hydroxychloride, abhurite, $Sn_{21}Cl_{16}(OH)_{14}O_6$, on tin alloys recovered from saline conditions (Dunkle *et al.*, 2003).

Iron and Steel

Sources: Rostoker and Bronson (1990). Armour: Williams (2003).

Through most of its history iron ore was smelted at temperatures below the melting point of iron and thus the product was a mass of solid iron with some entrapped slag (known in English as the *bloom*). The bloom was hammered whilst still white-hot to consolidate it and to exclude as much of the slag as possible, but even so the *wrought* iron inevitably contains stringers of slag (Scott, 1991a, p. 102, Fig. 140, etc.) (Figure 7.5).

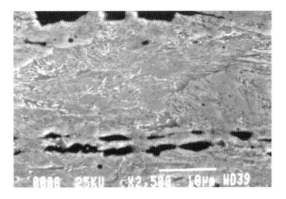

Figure 7.5 SEM micrograph of a section from the main spring of a seventeenth-century South German clock. The structure is of distorted pearlite and shows the black line of slag particles that have become elongated out into stringers during the forging of the iron. (Courtesy M.L. Wayman)

The successor to bloomery smelting was the blast furnace, which in essence is the method of smelting iron ore practised to this day. This produces liquid cast iron, containing about 3 to 5% of carbon. In order to convert this to wrought iron the carbon has to be burnt out. In Europe, from the Medieval period until about the mid-nineteenth century, this was done by remelting in an oxidising atmosphere, in a process known in English as *fining*. It might be thought that it would be easy to distinguish between wrought iron made by such different processes. However, during the fining process some of the molten iron oxidised and reacted with sand, lime or clay to produce a slag, some of which remained in the iron. Thus no matter how wrought iron was made, up until about the mid-nineteenth century it contained slag, usually dispersed as stringers through the metal (NB variants of the fining process such as puddling continued in production on a very limited scale well into the twentieth century). These stringers should be immediately apparent upon inspection of a section and their presence or absence can differentiate ancient from modern iron. For example, the cleanness and absence of slag inclusions in the polished section cut from a supposed medieval sallet helmet was one of the principal reasons for believing it to be modern (Ettmayer, 1984).

Iron castings began to be made in China from about the mid-first millennium BC, but cast iron was apparently never used in the rest of Asia, the Middle East or in Africa in the past. In Europe the first iron castings date from about the fourteenth century, but only became common from about the sixteenth century and were mainly for ordnance (Craddock, 2003).

Fuel as an indicator of age

Charcoal is a very pure fuel, imparting few elements to the iron apart from a little carbon. Thus charcoal-smelted iron tends to be relatively pure compared to that smelted with the fossil fuels coal, anthracite and coke, which can have a higher sulphur content. Bloomery iron was always smelted with charcoal as was early Chinese cast iron. The use of fossil fuels began in China in the second half of the first millennium AD, as documented by the high sulphur content, although charcoal-smelted iron continued to be produced up to the present day (Craddock *et al.*, 2002; Craddock, 2003). In Europe, fossil fuel began to be used in the eighteenth century and, by the nineteenth, it was the most commonly used fuel, although some charcoal-smelted iron continued to be made into the twentieth century, and very limited production continues in South America (see Chapter 5, p. 99, for the potentials and problems of the RC dating of carbon in iron).

Only the first early eighteenth-century coke-smelted European iron has a distinctively high sulphur content. From the mid-eighteenth century the sulphur level began to drop as increased furnace temperatures enabled the sulphur to be more effectively removed. Some modern irons are quite pure, and therefore the absence of sulphur is not necessarily an indication of charcoal smelting (NB see Charles Dawson's cast iron figurine, Chapter 19, p. 477).

Metallic additions as indicators of age

The only other metal regularly found in early iron is nickel; it can have a variety of origins. Meteoritic iron, which in some parts of the world was the first iron to be used, regularly contains between 5 and 10% of nickel, sometimes more but never less. Note that corroded meteoritic iron can have preferentially lost its nickel, thereby appearing as smelted iron, as exemplified by a Chinese halberd examined by Gettens *et al.* (1973). Meteoritic iron also has a very distinctive metallographic structure, which can still be recognised even after working in the solid state.

From the mid-nineteenth century, iron and steel began to be alloyed, and the presence of other metals can demonstrate that the iron is not ancient.

Much modern iron and steel contains recycled scrap, which inevitably contains some alloy steels and small amounts of other metals not found in ancient iron (NB corroding iron may well have picked up other metals, notably copper, if buried in their vicinity).

Perhaps manganese is the most useful element for determining that iron is of recent origin. Iron ores often contain small amounts of manganese oxides, which the early direct solid-state smelting processes were incapable of reducing to metal, and the manganese mineral went into the slag, some of which remained entrapped in the bloom. Thus, some slag inclusions in early iron can be rich in manganese oxides or silicates. However, because the volume of slag inclusions is small and there is no manganese in solution in the iron itself, the quantities overall will be much smaller than those found in modern iron. Cast iron made by the much hotter and more reducing blast furnace process can contain up to about 1% of manganese and some Medieval Asian crucible steels have similar amounts. When cast iron was fined to make wrought iron any manganese that it may have contained should have been retained.

In 1839 Joseph Heath patented his 'carburet of manganese' to nullify the deleterious effects of sulphur in iron, the result of using fossil fuel. The carburet, added to the molten iron, was a strange concoction in which the active ingredient was manganese metal. This removed the sulphur from the iron, forming manganese sulphide, which is much less harmful to the working properties of the iron. The carburet was an immediate success and, since the mid-nineteenth century, most ordinary iron and steel has contained between about 0.2 and 1% of manganese dissolved in the iron (Barraclough and Kerr, 1976; Wiltzen and Wayman, 1999). These quantities of manganese are quite easy to detect by non-destructive methods such as XRF, and hence a simple surface analysis can often reveal a modern iron.

Cast iron and crucible steel of any period may contain detectable amounts of manganese, but if found in wrought iron that is believed to have been made by the direct bloomery process then this should indicate a post-1840s date. Conversely, iron with no detectable manganese could be of any date.

From about the 1860s alloy steels came into use, alloyed with metals such as nickel, manganese, chromium, molybdenum, tungsten, etc. With the exception of nickel and manganese, these metals are never encountered above a few ppm in ancient iron, and thus their presence can be a useful indicator that the iron is recent although caution has to be exercised. For example, some years ago a steel chisel was found beneath the tumbled walls of Sigirya, an ancient capital of Sri Lanka. Although the context of the chisel should indicate that it was many centuries old, it was surprisingly uncorroded. Initial examination of the chisel showed it was of crucible steel, a commodity with a long history in Sri Lanka, but with few surviving early examples. Therefore the piece was of considerable interest, but EDX analysis revealed the presence of about 0.5% of chromium in solution in the steel, quite typical of some nineteenth- to twentieth-century tool steels. More recently Allan and Gilmour (2000, pp. 484–485) published a flint fire-striker, purporting to be Persian of the thirteenth century AD, which

was of crucible steel containing 1.2% chromium, 1.2% nickel, 0.3% manganese, 0.1% sulphur, 0.08% phosphorus, 0.05% vanadium and 0.03% silicon, which also seemed suspect. However, steel armour excavated from a late fourteenth- to early fifteenth-century AD context at Samarkand was found to contain about 0.8% chromium (Papachristou, 1996).

Ferrous fakes and forgeries

Arms and armour have always provided one of the main areas for faking and forgery in iron and steel (Watts, 1992; Segebade and Wessel, 1996). As well as forgeries, plain pieces of genuine iron often have inscriptions worked onto them claiming ownership by some famous leader or warrior.

Case study: A horrible helmet

The use of the manganese content as a quick and non-destructive demonstration that an iron object is recent is illustrated by the iron helmet found in the eroding bank of the River Tyne in Northumberland (Figure 7.6). The shape of the helmet and the decoration on it are vaguely Saxon,

Figure 7.6   Iron helmet from the River Tyne. The manganese content suggests that it is more likely to have been lost in a recent pageant than a Dark Age battle. (Courtesy A. Milton)

but it is a very rough piece in both design and execution, and was only superficially corroded. However, over the years a number of Saxon swords have been recovered in good condition from rivers in the north of England, and also to be considered is the remarkable Anglian iron and brass helmet dug up from York in pristine condition. Therefore, a scientific examination was felt necessary before the Northumberland helmet could be confidently rejected. XRF analysis of the uncorroded surfaces of the metal in a number of places showed the iron contained about 1% of manganese, confirming that it is most unlikely to be Saxon.

Iron castings

China and Korea were casting iron from the mid first millennium BC, and the iron was sometimes smelted with fossil fuel from the latter part of the first millennium AD. This is much earlier than in the West, creating a very different set of circumstances and criteria for authentication studies, especially with regard to potential problems and misinterpretations of RC dates (see Chapter 5, p. 100).

Case study: A Korean cast iron knight

Beukens *et al.* (1999) studied a cast iron statuette of a mounted warrior, similar in style to Korean examples in ceramic dating to about the mid first millennium AD. Doubts were expressed on its authenticity and a small sample of partially corroded metal was removed for examination. The carbon content was estimated to be approximately 3% and the structure was described as being a chilled grey cast iron. Usually grey cast iron has flakes of graphite visible in the microstructure, but these were not observed here, and it was assumed that the iron had cooled too quickly for these to form. The iron also contained 1.26% of silicon, which tends to occur when smelting iron with fossil fuel. Thus, it came as no surprise when an RC determination produced an apparent date of $32\,780 \pm 670$ BP, which showed that fossil fuel had indeed been used to smelt the iron. Note the date is slightly younger than the maximum age for an RC date of about 40 000 years, suggesting that there was likely to have been some contamination introduced from the corrosion products (see Chapter 5, p. 100).

The use of fossil fuels to smelt the iron in the mid first millennium AD did not unduly worry Beukens and colleagues, as they followed Needham (1958, p. 14), who stated that coal was in use for iron smelting from the fourth century AD at the latest. However, more recent opinion, based on half a century of excavation, would now suggest that the smelting of iron with coal began in China no earlier than the latter part of the first millennium AD (Craddock, 2003). Thus, whilst a date in the mid first millennium AD cannot be ruled out, it is rather unlikely. The sulphur content of the iron was below the stated detection limit of 0.1% over most of the areas analysed, which is low for early Oriental iron smelted with fossil fuels, and suggests a process more reminiscent of modern high-temperature smelting practice (see p. 154).

Neutron activation analysis showed the iron to consist of, among other things, about 0.3% of manganese, 0.2% of copper and varying trace amounts of chromium. Some early Chinese cast irons have been found to contain similar quantities of manganese. The copper and chromium contents are rather high for ancient iron. The copper could have been absorbed into the partially corroded iron if it was in contact with corroding copper alloys, but this does not explain the chromium. This might suggest that the iron was modern and made from scrap, which often contains small amounts of other metals.

8

Metals II: Metalwork and coins

This chapter considers changes through time in the methods of forming and decorating metal artefacts and concludes with a survey of authenticity in numismatics.

Metalworking techniques

Sources: Basic structure and metallography: Bailey, A.R. (1960). Ancient metals: Scott (1991a); Wayman (2004). Metalworking techniques: Maryon (1923); Untracht (1968); Born (1988); Craddock (1996).

Metallography can reveal the fabrication history of a metal artefact together with its likely authenticity if the piece is corroded (Chapters 14 and 15, pp. 365, 388). Unfortunately, metallography normally requires a section cut from the metal or polished on the surface, both of which can be very destructive.

Hammered or wrought metalwork

One of the principal differences between ancient and modern metalworking practice concerns the introduction of sheet metal made by rolling in Post-Medieval Europe (Pearce, 1982, gives a useful overview of the principal commercial methods of producing metal sheets from antiquity to the present). The earliest examples are the copper sheets used for several early seventeenth-century oil paintings, which are believed to have been hammered and then finished by rolling (see Chapter 12, p. 292). However, the production of rolled sheet did not really become prevalent until the nineteenth century even in Europe. Indeed, some items such as the pots and pans made in traditional brass working centres such as Stolberg and Bristol, continued to be hammered into shape until the early twentieth century, and craft products are still hammered. Thus, a vessel of hammered metal need not be of any great age.

Rolled sheet has a much more regular microstructure than that of hammered metal (Segebade and Wessel, 1996). The microstructure tends to be somewhat elongated in the direction of the rolling, and this can produce distinctive Laue diffractometry patterns, raising the possibility of non-destructive testing distinguishing between cast, hammered, rolled and electroformed sheet (see Chapter 3, p. 54, Figure 3.12). Stephenson et al. (2001) examined the discs of two astrolabes that purported to be Islamic and of the thirteenth century by transmission X-ray diffraction (XRD), using high-energy X-rays generated by a synchrotron. They were easily able to distinguish between the Laue patterns of the hammered plates on the one astrolabe from those of the other, which was already suspect on stylistic grounds, where the Laue patterns were typical of rolled metal. Rolled sheet tends to be of a much more regular thickness and may have series of thin parallel raised lines or indentations picked up from irregularities on the rolls (see Chapter 15, p. 374).

The distinctive pattern of hammer marks on hammered sheet is often revealed by radiography (Figure 8.1) although a forger may distress rolled sheet by hammering it before use. It is also common practice for traditional craftsmen in countries such as India to make their vessels out of ductile rolled sheet and then to work harden them by hammering

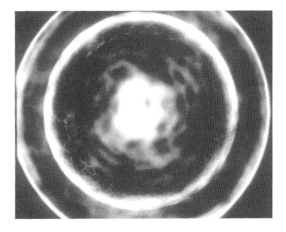

Figure 8.1 Radiograph of a Medieval Islamic dish, which has characteristic hammer marks of having been beaten to shape. (Courtesy S. La Niece/British Museum)

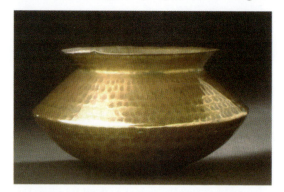

Figure 8.2a Traditional Indian brass vessel. Now made of sheet brass, hammered to give them the appearance of beaten wares. This vessel is made from two sheets; the soldered join is visible just below the sharp change in profile at the greatest width on Figure 8.2b below.

Figure 8.2b Detail of base showing the concentric pattern of hammer marks on the sheet hardening rather than forming it. (Courtesy T. Milton)

(Figures 8.2a and 8.2b). They are easy to differentiate from vessels made of hammered sheet because the hammer marks or dints are clearly on the sheet rather than forming it.

Shaping

The introduction of relatively inexpensive sheet metal produced by rolling had a profound effect on everyday metalworking practice from the eighteenth century onwards. Using rolled sheet the usual method of construction would be to cut and

bend pieces of sheet joined by solder or with rivets. Rolled sheet was also an ideal material for press-work from the eighteenth century on (see p. 159).

Craft and artistic productions are more difficult to differentiate. Thus, for example, up to the eighteenth century, a craftsman making a bowl or vase (*hollow ware*) would take a thin circular cast plate and either hammer the metal into a depression (*sinking*) to produce a concavity, or the exact reverse, hammering the metal against an anvil creating a convex shape by compression (*raising*) (Untracht 1968, pp. 240–263). The modern craft metal-smith would do exactly the same but the start material would be rolled sheet, and after creating the shape by sinking or raising, which both involve repeated cycles of hammering and annealing followed by planishing and polishing of the surface, it would be very difficult if not impossible to distinguish between the very different start materials.

Having roughly shaped the workpiece by hammering, the surface would be consolidated with finer hammers (known as *planishing*), and finished by filing, planing or scraping, before polishing, either by hand or if the object was circular, on a lathe to give a smooth surface. Visible hammer marks may well have been totally removed except in inaccessible areas such as on the inside of a vessel. Examining the surface by raking light can be revealing: hammered metalwork sometimes has concentric rings, whereas early rolled metal sometimes has a rather rippled effect.

The lathe has been used in the manufacture and finishing of hollow wares for a very long time, and unfortunately there is widespread confusion and incorrect terminology both in recognising the operation employed and in its correct description (Craddock and Lang, 1983; Jackson and Craddock, 1995). From about the first millennium BC the pole lathe, with its intermittent action, was introduced, and thereafter metal vessels and other circular shapes were regularly *polished* on the lathe. This is evidenced by the small depression or pip in the centre where the workpiece was secured to the spindle of the lathe as well as the concentric circular polishing lines on the metal surface. A cast circular piece or heavy hammered piece could be thinned and made more regular by *turning*. In this operation a chisel actually removes metal from the rotating workpiece. This operation was carried out in antiquity on an intermittent-action lathe as evidenced by some pieces of Roman silver plate that for some reason had never received their final polish (Figure 8.3). The workpiece often

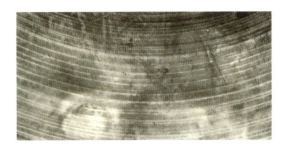

Figure 8.3 Details of the chatter marks on the base of the Achilles dish from the Kaiseraugst Roman silver treasure. The stepped pattern is indicative of the juddering action of the chisel on a low-powered lathe. (Courtesy J. Lang)

seems to have juddered around against the chisel, creating a distinctive pattern of chatter marks on the surface.

Note that it is only possible to carry out quite shallow carving with an intermittent-action lathe. There are a series of distinctive Roman bronze vessels with deeply grooved bases which Mutz (1972) claimed were lathe-carved, but the metallographic examination of a damaged piece in the British Museum has shown that they were cast (Craddock and Lang, 1983; Jackson and Craddock, 1995). Any deep-carved metalwork purportedly dating to before the invention of the continuous-action cranked lathe in the later first millennium AD should be regarded with suspicion.

Finally, there is the real lathe-shaping process known as *spinning* (Untracht 1968, pp. 301–310). A disc of metal is spun on the lathe and pushed with a flat tool against and around a wooden former. This technique requires a continuous-action high-powered lathe and appears to be no earlier than the Post-Medieval period (La Niece, 2003), not Medieval as claimed by Craddock and Lang (1983). The technique was widely used from the Post-Medieval period in Europe for producing everyday hollow wares. Up until the mid-twentieth century some of the better-quality copper or aluminium kitchen pots and pans were spun to shape, and the method still survives as a craft technique. The shapes usually have open profiles as it would ordinarily be difficult to release the wooden former if the metal vessel had enveloped it; in addition, the metal is usually rather thin. Otherwise it can be very difficult to recognise spun vessels. It is possible that XRD could produce characteristic Laue patterns.

The introduction of the metal-shaping press in eighteenth-century Europe had a profound effect on all aspects of metal-forming. Simple shapes could be pressed out and the more complex pieces assembled from several pressed components rather than fashioned from a single piece of metal (Hinman, 1941). Impressed decoration is easy to spot, being more rounded and diffuse that the equivalent done by repoussé or engraving. Presswork is a mass-production technique and requires considerable investment to create the steel dies and, thus, is not usually an appropriate method for producing a relatively small number of forgeries.

There are differences between early and more recent methods for such basic operations as cutting and drilling the sheet metal, all of which can leave distinctive marks on the metal.

In pre-Classical antiquity in the West, metals were cut either with a chisel or with a knife. The use of shears probably came about during the Hellenistic period. The principle of the shearing operation is that one blade cuts the metal whilst it is held against the other, and this latter blade very often leaves a line running parallel to and about a millimetre in from the cut edge. Saws for cutting metals seem to be Post-Medieval innovations, and usually leave a square-ended cut (see Chapter 15, p. 375 for more on the history of saws and snips).

The familiar twist drill with opposed edges cutting into the metal and removing the swarf up the lateral helical grooves in the shank of the drill is a Post-Medieval innovation. Prior to this, neatly piercing or drilling metal presented rather a problem. At its simplest, a hole could be just punched through relatively thin and soft metal, but otherwise drills mounted with spoon- or diamond-shaped bits would have been used to bore into the metal, abrading the metal in an action very similar to that of a modern broach. Born (1989) has surveyed the various piercing and drilling methods and of the characteristic features of the drill holes made in bronze using them. A punched hole may be of irregular circumference, and a hole drilled with a simple abrading bit may well produce a hole with sloping sides unless the drilling operation were to be continued until the bit had gone through the entire thickness of the workpiece. It should, however, be stressed that many early holes drilled in metal are extremely regular and neat and cannot easily be differentiated from the holes produced by modern twist drills.

Cast metalwork

Sources: Mills and Gillespie (1969); Bruni (1994); Thomas (1995); Lanteri (1911).

Casting technology developed quickly in antiquity and thus the overall chronological development is rather static. However, the use of particular techniques can show considerable geographic and cultural diversity.

Piece moulding

At its simplest, castings may be made by pouring the molten metal into any inert depression and covering while the metal sets. More complex three-dimensional shapes may be cast by taking negative impressions in clay from the two sides of the model. The impressions when joined form the mould, which can be baked and the metal positive cast. The technique developed early in the Bronze Age and has been popular ever since. The fins of metal that flowed into the space where the edges of the moulds met are the most obvious evidence for the employment of the process although these are often largely removed by filing the casting. In China the piece-moulding technique was developed to cast more complex shapes using multiple moulds, especially for vessels. The process began early in the Shang period in the second millennium BC and the tradition continues to this day (Barnard, 1961, 1996) (Figures 8.4, 8.5 and 8.6), joined by lost wax casting from about the beginning of our era (Kerr, 1990).

Lost wax casting

Lost wax casting seems to have been in use in the fourth millennium BC in the Near and Middle East (Hunt, 1980) as evidenced by the large number of sophisticated castings found in a cave at Nahal Mishmar in Israel (Bar-Adon, 1980), and by an intact clay but unused mould from Poliocohni, on Lemnos in the Aegean (Branigan, 1974, p. 82).

Hollow lost wax castings had already begun to be made in the third millennium BC in the Middle East, and their production developed through the second millennium BC; quite large thin-walled hollow statues began to be produced in Egypt in the early first millennium BC (Taylor *et al.*, 1998). From this background developed the superb hollow cast statuary of the Classical world. These were mainly direct lost wax castings in which the original wax model or maquette was invested with clay, heated and quite literally 'lost' as the wax melted and ran out.

At some stage the indirect process was introduced, wherein a plaster mould is taken of the orig-

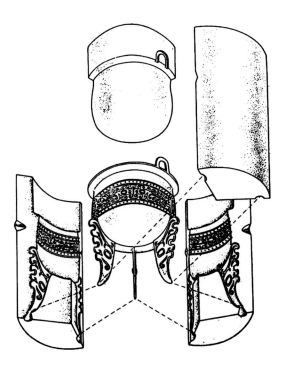

Figure 8.4 Typical Chinese piece mould in three sections and core for casting a *ding*, a vessel on legs (see Figure 8.6). Note the joins are run along the edges of the legs where they will be less noticeable.

inal, wax positives being taken from this (Mills and Gillespie, 1969; Cavanagh, 1990, and see Chapter 4, p. 69). Having, produced a mould there is no limit to the number of wax positives that can then be taken, and the 'original' can be issued and sold as an edition! The implications of this should be kept in mind very clearly. If the object one is dealing with has been made by an indirect lost wax casting process then there may well be other copies in existence; however, there is little or no evidence for series of exact copies of sculpture before the Renaissance (see Chapter 4, p. 61).

The indirect lost wax process seems to have been in use from Classical antiquity (Haynes, 1992; Taylor *et al.*, 1998), and was the usual practice from the Renaissance on (Bewer, 1995). It seems never to have spread outside Europe and the Eastern Mediterranean. Indian metal-smiths have always used the direct process (Reeves,1962; Reedy, 1997), in a very conservative tradition of casting sacred idols and other religious items where the actual casting process is part of the ritual and may not

Figure 8.6 Chinese bronze *ding* of the Shang period, cast in a piece mould with the join lines clearly visible (cf. Figure 8.5). (Courtesy British Museum)

Figure 8.5 Detail of a Chinese bronze *ding* of the Shang period, cast in a piece mould (see Figure 8.4). With the mould join running up the leg (cf. Figure 8.6). (Courtesy British Museum)

change or vary. The direct lost wax (or possibly lost latex) process was also prevalent in West Africa and in parts of the Americas (Bray, 1978; La Niece, 1998; Meeks, 1998a; and see Chapter 15, p. 79).

European bronze statuary from Classical antiquity onwards has been particularly well studied (Haynes, 1992; Bewer, 1995; Formigli (ed), 1999; Mattusch, 1999; Weisman and Reedy, 2002). Barbour and Glinsman (1993) carried out detailed studies of Renaissance casting technology specifically to more easily detect modern forgeries, although Weisman and Reedy (2002) found wide variation in casting practices on bronzes of the same period in the Kunsthistorisches Museum in Vienna. Even so, there are many technical details of casting procedure which have changed through the ages. For example, classical statuary tended to be built up from many

individual cast components, and by contrast, many Renaissance and Baroque statues were made as a single casting (Figure 8.7). The use of these diagnostic technical features in authentication and dating studies is well exemplified by the studies carried out on the bronze statue of the Jüngling (see p. 167).

Most modern casting techniques tend to have been developed for mass production rather than for individual work as they require quite complex jigs and dies. However, their products can still impinge on the world of the collector as exemplified by the small die-cast model vehicles, originally children's toys that are now so avidly collected by adults, and no less avidly copied.

Die-casting (Herb, 1936) began in the mid-nineteenth century, following on from the first type-casting machines and is used nowadays for making small precision castings by the million for the motor industry etc., usually in metals with low

(a)

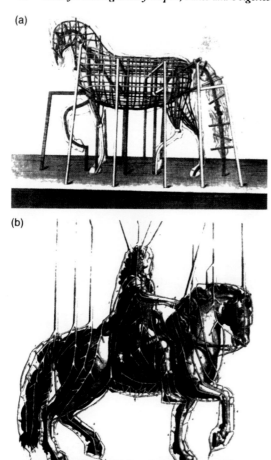

(b)

Figure 8.7 Armatures and moulds for an equestrian statue exemplifying Post-Medieval European bronze casting technique. a) arrangement of iron armatures inside the core. b) complete wax mould with risers attached ready to be cast in one piece. (From Germain Boffrand's *Description de ce qui a été pratiqué pour fondre en bronze d'un seul jet figure équestre de Louis XIV en Paris en 1699*, as used in Diderot's Encyclopédie [Gillespie (ed), 1959])

Figure 8.8 Small die-cast ring. The three stubs set at 120° around the underside of the ring are where the molten metal was forced under pressure into the mould and are indicative of die-casting. (Courtesy T. Springett)

melting points. In the nineteenth century the metals were restricted to tin and lead-based alloys, joined in the early twentieth century by zinc and aluminium alloys as well as brass. The technique gives good detail because the molten metal is injected into the mould under pressure. The best indicators of a die-casting are the circular stubs of the injection points and the impressions made in the hot metal by the push-out pins, which are normally visible on the inside or underside of the casting at a number of locations even on the smallest casting (Figure 8.8).

Sand-casting is more equivocal in both age and usage. At its very simplest the model or template of the object to be cast is embedded between two flat beds of compacted sand held in a frame (Untracht, 1968, pp. 325–330). The template is removed and the two halves are joined again, the metal then being poured in. As there are no permanent mould fragments, just sand, there is little surviving material evidence for the process in antiquity. Recent studies of Chinese coin production sites suggest the technique was introduced in China in the mid first millennium AD. La Niece (2003) has reviewed the Islamic evidence for the process and suggested that it was extensively used from at least the tenth century AD, but probably not before the sixteenth century in Europe. In particular, some cast brass candlesticks dated to the fourteenth and fifteenth centuries AD from India are early examples of sand-casting, and the traditional Indian *bidri* wares, dating from the seventeenth century on, seem to have always been cast in sand moulds (Untracht, 1968, pp. 136–149). However, the technique has generally been seen as more suitable for simple rough castings rather than for fine artistic work.

The cores

Hollow castings will have been poured around clay cores. The potential of TL dating of the core material has already been covered in Chapter 6, (see pp. 114), but the composition of the core can also be useful in authenticity studies as exemplified by the study of the Jüngling (see p. 169). The mineralogy of the clays and fillers can be traced to specific regions; thus, for example Freestone *et al.* (1984) were able to show that core material of a disputed statuette that was said to have come from Rome indeed contained clays that were likely to be from the Tiber. Schneider (Schneider and Zimmer, 1984; Schneider, 1989; Formigli and Schneider, 1993) carried out the first major petrological studies on core material, working on Classical statuary, including material from Phidias' workshop at Olympia and the Riace bronzes (see also Lombardi and Vidale, 1998). The integration of the petrological identification of the core material into the overall characterisation of the casting has been much advanced by Reedy (1991, 1997; Reedy and Meyers, 1987) on copper alloy statuettes from the North India–Himalayas region. The mixture of clays and fillers can sometimes be specific to particular cultures or times and this again can help in establishing the likely origin of a casting.

Holmes and Harbottle (1991) have carried out neutron activation analysis (NAA) of the core material surviving in the handles of some ancient Chinese bronze vessels in an attempt to characterise them.

There is a common misconception that removing the casting from the mould is the end of the process. In reality very few items are truly 'as cast', exceptions being where an exact reproduction of the surface detail of the original is required as a record, as exemplified by the Bronze Age sword from Aberdeen (see Chapter 4, p. 69) and the Risley Lanx (see Chapter 20, p. 508). More usually, work will typically include accentuating detail with the point and chisel as well as the general cleaning up of the surface with a scraper. Damaged areas will need to be repaired where the metal failed to flow or gas holes formed during the casting. Finally, the metal has to be smoothed and polished to the required finish. Two points of specific relevance to authenticity studies arise from this. First it can mean that large areas of a casting may not have any of the obvious superficial characteristics of a casting. It can also mean that successive castings made from moulds taken from a plaster cast may differ quite significantly from each other and all may differ from the original.

Repairs

Differences in the treatment of faults in the initial casting can be indicative of age. In Classical antiquity a rectangular area around the offending region was chiselled out and a patch mechanically inserted (Haynes, 1992, pp. 96–98). During the Renaissance it was the usual practice to chisel out the offending area, build a small mould round it and pour fresh metal in (sometimes known as a *burn in*). Small holes are now normally dealt with by drilling out the damaged area, tapping the side and then screwing in a plug of the same composition as the surrounding metal. When the screw is in place its surface and surroundings are carefully scraped and matted to disguise the insert. However, this will rarely be possible on the inside, and the presence of a perfectly circular insert would indicate at the very least a modern repair and probably a modern casting (Figure 8.12).

Cast surfaces can be recognised by their general lack of crispness and casting faults (e.g. see Figure 4.7b), and sometimes metallographic features of the cast metal are exposed (see Figures 8.9ab). For a discussion of the recognition of cast copies see Chapter 4 (p. 69), and for casts of coins see p. 181.

Designer damage

Imperfect castings have on occasion been passed off as damaged antiquities. Kurz (1948, p. 184) has related how a failed aftercast taken from Giovanni

Figure 8.9a Italian bronze helmet of the third century BC. It is likely to have been cast with a little forging (see Figure 8.9b).

Figure 8.9b Detail of Figure 8.9a, dendrites formed as the metal set, viewed under a binocular microscope, indicating a cast structure. They have been emphasised by selective corrosion of the surface. (Courtesy J. Lang/ British Museum)

da Bologna's well known *Mercury* was, with some additional deliberate and appropriate patination, passed off as ancient. It has also been claimed that by careful manipulation of the casting conditions,

damage has been built into the casting superficially giving the appearance of an antiquity. For example, George Ortiz (1990) suggested that the Etruscan head from a statuette of a youth now in the British Museum (BM GR Reg. 1898, 7–16, 2) constitutes such a forgery with the damage to the back of the head actually cast in. Analysis by the author showed it to contain 8% of tin, 0.3% of lead and the usual suite of trace elements associated with Etruscan bronzes. Examination of the patina suggested it was natural, showing that the head is authentic and in this instance the damage is real.

The following case studies offer interesting contrasts. All were detailed scientific and technical examinations of major pieces of considerable art historical significance. In the case of the bronze horse in the Metropolitan Museum, the scientists had the task of persuading the art historian that the work was genuine, whilst in the case of the Jüngling in the Kunsthistorische Museum, the scientists had to convince the art historians that the statue was not ancient.

Case study: Bronze head, purporting to be of a Hellenistic ruler, now in the Walker Gallery, Liverpool, Inv. 6534 (Figures 8.10–8.12)

The life-size bronze head was acquired by the collector Henry Blundell in Italy in the late eighteenth century, very possibly from Cavaceppi (see Chapter 20, p. 516), as a genuine antiquity of the Hellenistic period. More recent stylistic studies had cast doubts on the piece and scientific studies were performed to determine its authenticity. XRF analysis showed that the alloy contained about 4% of zinc, which is unparalleled in a major Greek bronze. In addition, the trace metal content was suspiciously high, with about 1% of antimony for example, which would be highly unusual in a Classical bronze, but quite acceptable in later copper alloys (see Chapter 7, p. 142). The patina was simply a coat of dark-green varnish, typical of eighteenth-century treatments (see Chapter 14, p. 357). There were small amounts of green mineral present, identified by XRD as consisting of the basic copper nitrate, gerhadite, which does not normally occur naturally (see Chapter 14, p. 352).

The main interest regarding the head, however, was in the casting itself. It is riven with large cracks and there are large droplets of metal embedded in the casting (see Figures 8.11 and 8.12). The cracks are almost certainly stress cracks brought about by cooling the metal too quickly in the mould. The droplets are likely to have been formed when the metal was poured into a mould that was slightly damp. The steam generated created a spray of metal droplets, some of which set on the mould face. Clearly, the metal was setting very quickly in a cold mould – just the right conditions for stress cracks to develop. Some of the damaged areas had been drilled out and replaced with the screw-threaded repairs (see Figure 8.12), but the main cracks were left, merely reinforced from behind by a coating of solder. It seems incredible that such a poor casting was not immediately returned to the melting crucible, or at least more effectively repaired. The likelihood must be that the damage was deliberately induced in the casting to give the appearance that the cracks were part of the ageing process of a genuine piece. If this is the case then the piece is of some considerable technical ingenuity.

Figure 8.10 Life-size bronze head of a youth now in the Walker Art Gallery, Liverpool, Inv. 6534. (Courtesy A. Milton/British Museum)

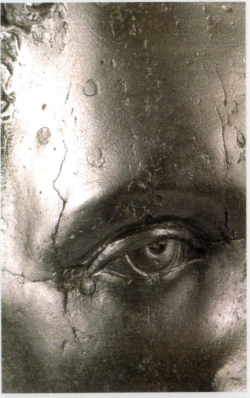

Figure 8.12 Detail of Figure 8.10 showing some of the embedded droplets above the eye and where small casting faults to the left of the eye and above have been drilled out, tapped and fitted with a screwed circular repair, typical of repair work from the eight-eenth century onwards. (Courtesy A. Milton/British Museum)

Figure 8.11 Detail of the face of Figure 8.10, showing stress cracks. (Courtesy A. Milton/British Museum)

Case study: The Metropolitan Horse

Sources: Noble (1968); Zimmerman *et al.* (1974); Lefferts *et al.* (1981); Hoving (1996, pp. 213–222).

The Metropolitan Museum of Art in New York since the 1920s had displayed a superb large bronze statuette of a horse, Ac. 2369, dating from the best period of Greek sculpture in the fifth century BC. (Figure 8.13) Or so everyone believed until the observation of Joseph Noble, after years of daily walking past the horse: 'One time in the summer of 1961 I saw something I had never seen before. I saw a line running from the tip of the nose up through his forelock, down the mane and back, up under the belly, and all the way round' (Noble, 1968). This line he interpreted as being the casting fin from a piece mould, and additionally, for reasons that were never quite explained, a sand mould. The discovery that the horse had a core held in place by iron chaplets further convinced Noble that the beast had been made by sand-casting. The final proof was provided for him and the luckless curator of Greek and Roman Art, Dietrich von Bothmer, when γ radiography showed that there was an iron armature present inside the horse embedded in the core. Seemingly plucking a date out of the air, Noble described sand-casting as a process that had been invented in AD 1400 (but see p. 162). Moreover, the presence of the armature apparently showed that the piece had been cast by a method known as the 'French Sand-casting Process', and was thus likely to have been cast in Paris.

Unfortunately there seems to have been no technical staff at the Metropolitan Museum to take Noble to one side and explain to him a little about casting processes, and to suggest some real scientific tests might be in order before he very publicly denounced the horse, ending his speech with the words '. . . it's famous but it's a fraud.'

Right from the moment of Noble's pronouncement on the presence of the core with its chaplets and armature, scholars from all over the world pointed out that all hollow castings had to have had a core originally. Furthermore, that core must have been held in place in the mould, and evidence of chaplets and iron armatures were well attested in Classical statuary.

Shortly afterwards a group of scientists, conservators and technicians from a variety of institutions outside the Metropolitan subjected the horse to detailed study (Lefferts *et al.*, 1981).

The metallographic studies showed the metal to be a casting with some evidence of intergranular corrosion.

The metal contained copper with 10% of tin in the body and 7.5% in the right foreleg, together with traces of lead and small traces of nickel and antimony, typical of Greek statuary (Craddock, 1977). A repair on the left rear leg was of bronze with about 18% of lead, which was suggested could represent a Roman repair. As it was cast on, the lead could have been a deliberate Greek addition in order to lower the melting point such that the molten metal flowed easily into the mould without melting the rest of the casting.

Lead isotope analysis was rather inconclusive, but suggested that sources in Italy or the Levant were possibilities (as indeed were sources over much of the rest of the world). A ^{210}Pb determination (see Chapter 12, p. 295) came up with the interesting result that ^{210}Po levels were lower than the ^{210}Pb levels, which could be interpreted as showing that the lead had not been smelted in antiquity. However, it was pointed out that the difference between the two levels was largely accounted for by the ^{210}Po apparently having a negative activity, which was clearly impossible; and thus the whole result could be set aside.

For some reason a specific gravity test was attempted that involved immersing the horse in water, and latterly it was noted that the core still contained about 20% of water which had seeped in during its recent baptism. There must have been a grave danger of an outbreak of corrosion on the inside of the bronze, especially as the core was salty, and this would have been nearly impossible to treat. To immerse the horse in water was highly irresponsible and revealed nothing.

The core material was of a sandy clay with no unusual features. It was suitable for TL dating, but before the samples had been taken the horse had been subjected to prolonged X- and γ-radiography, such that there was a very real chance that the natural TL had been contaminated by this heavy recent external dosage. To circumvent this problem Zimmerman *et al.* (1974) used the then recently developed zircon dating method (see Chapter 6, p. 113). The TL determination gave a date of 2250 ± 210 BP.

Examination of the surface, once the modern green varnish had been removed, revealed the presence of many rectangular patches and repairs, quite typical of classical practice (see p. 163). The surface also showed many signs of wear and scratches, the latter suggesting that the horse had been drastically mechanically cleaned. Some red and green corrosion products were found, which XRD analysis showed were cuprite and copper hydroxychloride, with both atacamite and para atacamite being identified. The tests were carried out at about the time that Lewin (1973) published his studies, which led him to suggest that the presence of atacamite and para atacamite together indicated that the patina was artificial (see Chapter 14, p. 351). The investigators had to carry out additional XRD analyses on material of undoubted authenticity to demonstrate that the two hydroxychloride minerals are regularly found together as the natural patina on genuine antiquities. Also, where the patina survived on the horse it was found to be hard and firmly adhering, strongly suggesting that it was natural.

The investigators concluded, on the basis of this evidence, that the horse was a genuine antiquity, made by the direct hollow lost wax process. And the line running along the nose of the creature that had been the cause of Noble's original disquiet? It turned out to be present only in the recent varnish that overlay the horse and was almost certainly the result of plaster casts having been taken of the horse in the 1930s for sale to the public, one of which belonged, so it transpired, to Noble himself.

Case study: The Jüngling

Sources: 'Jüngling' (1987/88); Pichler and Vendl (1987); Gschwantler and Bernhard-Walcher (eds) (1988).

The Jüngling from Magdalensberg has been Austria's most famous antiquity for the last four centuries (Figure 8.14). It is, or rather was, believed to be the only complete life-size bronze statue from Classical antiquity to have been found north of the Alps (Alföldy, 1974). It must also surely be the only authenticity study to form the subject of a play (*Phallacy* by Carl Djerassi).

But is it Roman? On the face of it the evidence in favour of it being authentic is incontrovertible. The statue (or more correctly, a statue) was dug up on the Magdalensberg in the mountainous province of Carinthia in Austria, in 1502. It almost immediately attracted great general and Imperial interest, soon entering the collection of the Bishop of Salzburg, there to be drawn by leading artists of the day including Dürer, and engraved by Apianus in 1534 (Figure 8.15). There can be no realistic doubt that a major statue very similar in appearance to the present statue was dug up in the sixteenth century. No one then would have known of the significance of the find spot at Magdalensberg. Excavations were not carried out until the nineteenth century at the site, which established the presence of a major temple complex dedicated to Mercury, and the Jüngling was almost certainly the cult statue. Furthermore, there is an original inscription carved into the right thigh, and clearly visible on the sixteenth-century woodcut, which states that the statue was donated by A. POBLICIUS ANTICOUS and T. BARBIUS TIBERI[A]NUS. Only in the nineteenth century were the families of the two donors, the Barbii and Poblicii, identified from the stamps on the bases of amphorae and other pottery vessels as the proprietors of major trading houses, who would have had the wealth and prestige to donate a major cult statue. Thus the authenticity of the statue seemed as unassailable as its central position in the Antikensammlung des Kunsthistorische Museum, in Vienna, where it had been on display since 1806.

Figure 8.13 Bronze Horse from the Metropolitan Museum. (© The Metropolitan Museum of Art)

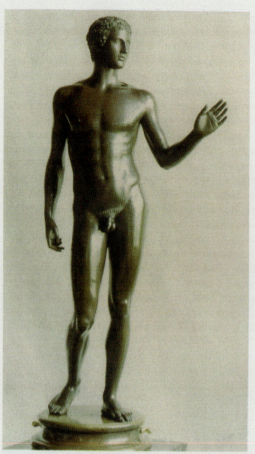

Figure 8.14 Roman or Renaissance? The *Jüngling*, now in the Kunsthistorische Museum, Vienna. (Frontispiece to Alföldy, 1974)

Doubts were raised over the statue's authenticity and so a detailed programme of scientific study was initiated. This evolved into two broadly parallel programmes of scientific study, each with different experts usually studying the same aspect of the statue, but nevertheless working quite independently. ('Jüngling' 1987/88; Gschwantler and Bernhard-Walcher (eds), 1988). Fortunately they agreed that the statue could not be Roman, but must be of a later period. The studies included the composition of the metal, and of the core, various aspects of the casting technology, the patina, and TL dating of the core.

Replicate sample drillings were taken of the bronze and analysed by several different laboratories (Craddock *et al.*, 1987/88; Vendl and Pichler, 1988). The results (Table 8.1) show a quite typical range of variation of replicate analyses carried out on the same sample drillings by various laboratories (compare these replicate analyses with those in Table 7.1 where both the analytical technique and the samples were different).

The analyses show that the metal is predominantly of bronze, with just two samples containing small amounts of zinc, which probably derive from repairs. The tin content is rather low for Roman statuary bronze, which also usually contains substantial quantities of lead (Craddock, 1985a), as exemplified by the other bronzes subsequently excavated at the Magdalensberg (Craddock *et al.*, 1987/88, p. 287, Table 11).

The trace and minor element levels of the metal are very high for Roman metal but quite typical of those found in the copper from the South German–Alpine sources used in Post-Medieval Europe (Riederer, 1982b). More specifically, the nickel content is significantly higher than in any Roman bronze

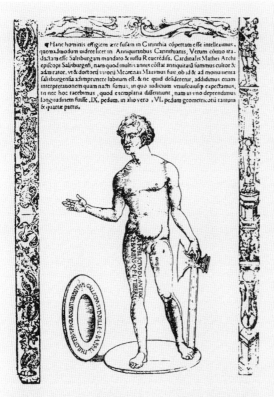

Figure 8.15 Woodcut of the *Jüngling*, made in 1534 by P. Apianus. It clearly shows the inscription on the right thigh, mentioning the Barbii and Poblicii families, names that no one in the sixteenth century could have known the significance of.

analysed to date (Figure 8.16).Note that the composition is not impossible for a Roman bronze – simply unparalleled – and many bronzes both before and after the Romans contained more nickel. If the equation of increasing nickel content with time for the Medieval–Post-Medieval period postulated by Werner (1978), and applied in this instance by Riederer (1987/88), has any validity, then the metal should be Post-Medieval. However, as already discussed in Chapter 7, p. 142, the increase in nickel content is only a general trend that cannot be rigorously applied in specific cases. It can, however, be said with confidence that the nickel content is far more typical of the copper alloys of Post-Medieval Europe than of those of Classical antiquity.

NAA was performed on the samples (Koeberl, 1987/1988a) and Begemann and Schmitt-Strecker (1987/88) carried out lead isotope analysis. Both studies produced data but unfortunately there was little relevant comparative material with which to assess its possible significance.

TL determinations on six samples of the core material were undertaken by Erlach (1987/88) and Vendl and Pichler (1988) using both fine-grain and pre-dose techniques. The results gave an aggregate age of 440 ± 45 years, which was translated as AD 1550 ± 45. The range of dates was quite close, with the oldest being 530 years and the youngest 380 years. It could be argued that the statue was Roman but that extensive repairs after its discovery including some cast-on repairs had affected the TL. However, the close range of the dates makes this explanation extremely unlikely.

The cores from the Jüngling and the Post-Medieval comparative piece were both composed of loam or marl mixed with copious quantities of coarse organic material (dung?), whereas the core material of the Roman comparator, in common with other Roman bronzes, was of sandy clay with fine organic material (Sauer *et al.*, 1987/88). Petrological examination of the Jüngling and the Post-Medieval comparison piece showed metamorphic rock fragments typical of Alpine sediments, but different from the Roman comparative piece. It is very likely that a genuine Roman life-size statue would have been cast in Rome itself, or possibly Aquileia, rather than locally. Koeberl (1987/88b) carried out NAA analyses on the Jüngling core material, but as with the NAA bronze analyses mentioned above, the programme lacked sufficient comparative material to make much constructive use of them.

The core was strengthened by a complex arrangement of iron bands and wire (Figure 8.17). Such an arrangement is unknown in classical statuary but was quite common in Renaissance and Baroque casting practice (Formigli, 1988).

Ettmayer and Simon (1987/88) carried out a metallographic investigation of the iron wire but concluded that the process by which the wire had been made was uncertain because of later heat treatments which had affected the grain structure. The surface topography of the wires, which should have been diagnostic, was not mentioned, but possibly the wires were too corroded.

Sperl (1988) however, in a separate study, believed that the wire had been drawn, and that iron wire was only produced by drawing from the fifteenth century. This dating is contentious, as drawn

Table 8.1 The analyses of 9 sample drillings taken from all over the Jungling statue. Replicate ICP-OES and AAS analyses by the four participating laboratories show good agreement. Labs W and G used ICP; labs B and L used AAS.

lab.	Nr.	Cu	Sn	Pb	Ag	Au	Ni	Zn	Fe	Sb	Bi	As	Mn	Cd	Co
J1	W	87.96	6.68	0.45	0.02	n.b.	0.11	4.38	0.053	0.11	<0.01	0.23	n.b.	n.b.	<0.005
	B	87.39	6.49	0.45	0.02	n.b.	0.10	4.36	0.93	0.08	<0.025	0.18	n.b.	n.b.	<0.001
	L	88.3	6.99	0.46	0.024	<0.004	0.11	4.10	0.058	0.13	<0.01	0.22	<0.001	0.001	<0.004
	G	87.51	7.52	0.51	0.022	n.b.	0.11	3.91	0.051	0.18	<0.01	0.17	n.b.	n.b.	0.002
J2	W	93.81	3.60	<0.025	0.02	n.b.	1.74	<0.001	0.022	0.30	<0.025	0.51	n.b.	n.b.	<0.005
	L	93.3	3.62	<0.01	0.020	<0.004	1.73	<0.003	0.021	0.31	<0.01	0.50	<0.001	<0.001	<0.004
J3	W	93.12	4.29	<0.025	0.014	n.b.	1.89	<0.001	0.029	0.29	<0.025	0.37	n.b.	n.b.	<0.005
	L	92.1	4.36	<0.01	0.015	<0.005	1.82	<0.003	0.037	0.26	<0.01	0.40	<0.001	<0.001	<0.005
	G	93.16	4.15	<0.1	0.006	n.b.	1.92	<0.05	0.022	0.32	<0.01	0.25	n.b.	n.b.	0.006
J4	W	91.39	6.01	<0.025	0.02	n.b.	1.61	<0.001	0.015	0.29	<0.025	0.67	n.b.	n.b.	<0.005
	B	92.19	5.45	<0.025	0.02	n.b.	1.54	<0.001	0.02	0.22	<0.025	0.56	n.b.	n.b.	<0.005
	L	87.8	8.17	0.02	0.022	<0.004	1.72	<0.003	0.014	0.59	<0.01	0.80	<0.001	<0.001	<0.004
	G	90.66	6.35	<0.1	0.013	n.b.	1.79	<0.05	0.015	0.50	<0.01	0.44	n.b.	n.b.	0.005
J6	W	93.56	4.01	<0.025	0.015	n.b.	1.77	<0.001	0.021	0.21	<0.025	0.41	n.b.	n.b.	<0.005
	B	93.86	3.85	<0.025	0.01	n.b.	1.75	<0.001	0.02	0.15	<0.025	0.36	n.b.	n.b.	<0.005
	L	92.7	4.79	<0.01	0.016	<0.005	1.83	0.023	0.028	0.38	<0.01	0.66	<0.001	<0.001	<0.005
	G	93.85	3.56	<0.1	0.009	n.b.	1.75	<0.05	0.067	0.31	<0.01	0.32	n.b.	n.b.	0.008
J8	W	92.44	5.07	<0.025	0.02	n.b.	1.72	<0.001	0.13	0.21	<0.025	0.41	n.b.	n.b.	<0.005
	B	91.74	5.83	<0.025	0.01	n.b.	1.70	<0.001	0.15	0.16	<0.025	0.41	n.b.	n.b.	<0.005
	L	92.4	4.99	0.01	0.013	<0.005	1.83	0.018	0.129	0.30	<0.01	0.47	<0.001	<0.001	<0.005
	G	92.30	4.75	<0.1	0.018	n.b.	1.78	<0.05	0.195	0.36	<0.01	0.39	n.b.	n.b.	0.005
J9	W	92.53	5.02	<0.025	0.015	n.b.	1.74	0.0019	0.11	0.18	<0.025	0.40	n.b.	n.b.	<0.005
	B	92.28	5.44	<0.025	0.01	n.b.	1.69	0.0016	0.02	0.15	<0.025	0.41	n.b.	n.b.	<0.005
	L	92.2	4.82	0.01	0.013	<0.004	1.83	<0.003	0.205	0.30	<0.01	0.41	<0.001	<0.001	<0.004
	G	92.47	4.76	<0.1	0.007	n.b.	1.83	<0.05	0.093	0.38	<0.01	0.28	n.b.	n.b.	0.005
J10	W	92.98	4.49	0.01	0.02	n.b.	1.78	0.003	0.05	0.24	<0.01	0.41	n.b.	n.b.	<0.005
	B	93.28	4.37	<0.025	0.02	n.b.	1.73	0.002	0.03	0.16	<0.025	0.41	n.b.	n.b.	<0.005
	L	91.5	4.48	0.01	0.018	<0.004	1.86	0.004	0.054	0.25	<0.01	0.46	<0.001	<0.001	<0.004
	G	92.81	4.41	<0.1	0.008	n.b.	1.82	<0.05	0.047	0.42	<0.01	0.25	n.b.	n.b.	0.079
J11	W	86.32	5.11	0.41	0.015	n.b.	1.43	6.05	0.15	0.15	<0.01	0.36	n.b.	n.b.	<0.005
	B	86.43	4.96	0.400	0.015	n.b.	1.40	6.13	0.189	0.138	<0.025	0.342	n.b.	n.b.	<0.005

Source: Craddock et al., 1987/88

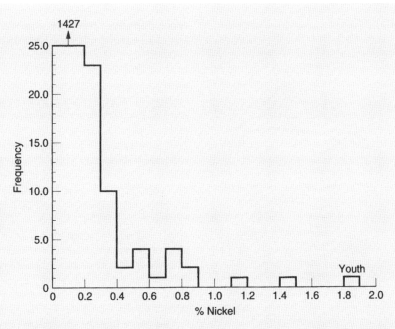

Figure 8.16 Histogram of nickel contents of approximately 1500 Roman copper alloys and of the *Jüngling*. It can be seen that the Ni content of the *Jüngling* is significantly higher than in any Roman bronze. (Courtesy Craddock *et al.*, 1987/88)

iron wire could be Roman (see Chapter 15, p. 376). Sperl also carried out metallographic work on the iron and concluded that the rather high phosphorus content indicated an Alpine rather than an Italian source. If the statue was Roman then, as already noted, it would almost certainly have been cast in Italy, and this suggested to Sperl that the statue was not ancient.

Both Sperl and Ettmayer and Simon (1987/88) believed that the number and morphology of the slag inclusions suggested that the iron was smelted by the *rennfeuer* process, which was only developed in the Late Medieval–Post-Medieval period.

Major Classical bronze statuary was usually cast in several main pieces joined with hard solder or by welding (Steinberg, 1973). But note that the Metropolitan Horse is apparently a single casting, apart from one leg (see p. 166). The painstaking examination carried out by Formigli (1988) showed that the Jüngling was cast in one piece, and that furthermore the metal was up to one centimetre in thickness, which is very thick indeed for a Roman statue.

The small casting faults on the Jüngling had been repaired by cutting out the damaged area and building up a small mould into which fresh metal was poured. This is definitely a Renaissance technique (Formigli, 1988).

The statue was supposedly buried for over a millennium, yet appears to have little or no chemical patina (Gschwantler, 1988). The present dark-green hue of the surface is due entirely to a thin coat of black lacquer over the unpatinated bronze surface (Freiberger *et al.*, 1988). This is once again typical of Post-Medieval practice. It was not unknown for the natural patina to be removed and replaced (see Chapter 14, p. 353). However, there should have been some evidence of residual mineral on the surface or of intergranular corrosion penetrating deep into the metal, yet there was none. Pichler and Erlach (1987/88) also examined metallographic sections and remarked on the absence of corrosion on the interior surfaces of the statue.

Of this comprehensive series of tests perhaps the TL dating and the nickel content of the alloy were individually the most decisive, but the other analyses and scientific examinations reinforce their

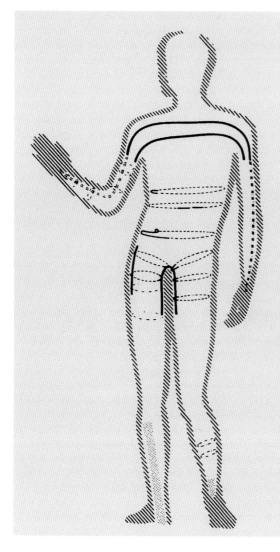

conclusion, and removed potential loopholes and caveats that could have been used to explain away the TL date and nickel content.

Thus, the scientific and technical examinations are apparently at variance with the known history of the discovery. How can the two apparently contradictory strands of evidence be reconciled?

Shortly after the discovery a copy was made and ostensibly sent to Spain. It now seems likely that the present *Jüngling* is the sixteenth-century copy. If this is so then there might be some evidence that the present piece is a casting taken from an original. Unfortunately, centuries of polishing and minor repairs would have obliterated most of the surface detail. Close inspection of the inscription, which has all the appearance of being carved into the metal, might be revealing. If it could be shown that it was a cast of a chiselled inscription this would support the theory that the present statue is a cast copy; if on the other hand it was shown to be original carving, there might have to be some serious rethinking!

Figure 8.17 Sketch of the *Jüngling* showing some of the bands and wires strengthening the core as revealed by radiography. Such arrangements are common in Renaissance statuary (cf. Figure 8.7a) but unknown in statuary from classical antiquity. (Courtesy Gschwantler, 1987/88)

Surface decoration and plating

Scribing, chasing and engraving

Once again it is the chronology of the techniques that is of significance for authenticity testing, but there is often confusion over the recognition of specific techniques and the correct terminology (Brittain *et al.*, 1958; Untracht, 1968; Lowery *et al.*, 1971; Ogden, 1982, p. 44). The subject of the identification of individual tool marks, and the recognition of where the same tool has been used on different artefacts, is discussed in Chapter 2 (see p. 36).

From the earliest days of metalworking, designs have been worked onto the surfaces of metals. This can be a simple procedure: to make a permanent groove on gold, for example, it is only necessary to draw firmly on the surface with a hard point, held like a pencil (Figure 8.18a). This is known as *scribing*, and the metal tool used is known as a *scriber*. The line tends to be shallow and continuous, and generally has a semicircular profile sometimes with striations along the groove and raised edges.

For most other metals two main techniques have been used through the ages, *chasing* and *engraving*. For all that the two techniques are very different in execution, the lines they produce can be very difficult to tell apart, especially when the metal is worn and corroded.

Engraving is done with a special chisel (the *graver*), usually with a diamond or 'v' profile, which is pushed along the surface and actually removes a sliver of metal (Figure 8.18b). The cut channel often has a 'v' profile with slightly raised edges, and may have some striations where the graver has cut through the metal. The most characteristic features are normally to be found at the end of the channel. Where the engraved line stops there will often be a quite sharp rough termination where the sliver has broken off (Figure 8.19). If the graver is not carefully held, it can skid across the surface giving a scribbled effect, and this is quite often done deliberately in a controlled fashion to matt or reserve areas. It is, for example, especially common on Post-Medieval pewter, but is also observed on Iron Age bronze mirrors from Britain (Lowery *et al.*, 1971), and is diagnostic of engraving.

Chasing is done by tapping a small flat chisel with a rounded tip (the *chaser*) into the metal and building up a continuous line from a series of individual indentations (Figure 8.18c). It might be thought that discontinuities would show, especially on a curve, but this is not always the case, except perhaps where the curve is tight (Figures 8.20 and 8.21). No metal is removed, so metal is pushed up and the edges of the line stand somewhat proud. However, as with engraved lines, wear and polishing will often have removed this. On thin metalwork, chased lines often leave a distinctive impression on the reverse side.

Whilst scorping and chasing could have been carried out from the inception of metalworking, engraving must be done with a tool of strong hard metal, nowadays always of steel, and thus it might be thought that engraving could not pre-date the Iron Age. In general it seems that chasing was the more common technique used throughout antiquity, but some Egyptian and Mycenaean goldwork of the second millennium BC have lines which bear all the characteristics of engraving (Williams and Ogden, 1994, p. 20; and see Chapter 15, pp. 374). For these a bronze graver would have been adequate, and indeed such a tool with the characteristic 'v' profile has been found in Egypt (Vernier, 1907, p. 121). The engraving of bronze only began around the mid first millennium BC when steel became available.

A separate problem arises with the possibility of the incised, chased or engraved line not being original; an added royal cypher, date or inscription can wonderfully add to the value of an otherwise mundane piece of metalwork. The problem is especially endemic with Chinese bronze vessels (Barnard, 1968; 1996, pp. 9–18, 365–382). Original inscriptions are likely to have been cast in but the spurious recent additions are chased on. Careful examination by binocular microscope may well reveal the relative freshness of the line, especially where the rest of the metal is corroded (Plenderleith, 1935). Barnard considered that many of the faked Chinese inscriptions had been acid-treated to disguise their freshness.

Sometimes the evidence is rather obvious, as in the example shown in Figure 8.22 of a genuine but plain Etruscan mirror which had a design engraved through the patina into the metal. Adding engraving to genuine but plain bronze surfaces is all too prevalent (de Grummond, 1982; de Puma, 2002), although sometimes scientific examination can retrieve an engraving denounced on stylistic grounds. For example, one of the numerous Etruscan *cista* condemned in the major survey of Bordenache Battaglia and Emiliozzi (1979 *et seq.*) was Townley's so-called *cista mystica*, now in the British Museum (BM GR Reg. 1814,7-4, 703). Analysis of the metal and of the corrosion showed the *cista* to be ancient, and binocular microscope examination showed the corrosion went over the engraved lines without a break (Bailey, 1986).

Similarly, Abraham (1999) studied suspect hieroglyph inscriptions chased into some Egyptian tools and weapons. He found that large, naturally formed crystals of the cuprite and malachite patination were continuous over the lines, and even where the corrosion had been cleaned off from the surface some usually survived in the interstices of the grooves, showing that the inscription pre-dated the corrosion.

Other approaches have to be adopted on uncorroded metal. Sometimes there are tiny particles of metal in a freshly engraved line that do not seem to survive use or burial. Another approach is to try to ascertain whether the myriad scratches of surface wear slip into the sides of the line or if the line cuts through surface wear. Both chased and engraved lines will have had slightly raised edges, and these subsequently will have been flattened. Where the line is original then subsequent wear patterns will run over these areas right up to the edge; where the line is a later addition, the original wear patterns will have been either distorted or obliterated if the raised edges had been removed by grinding.

Surface plating

Sources: Gilding: Drayman-Weisser (ed), (2000). Silver plating: Campbell (1933); La Niece (1993).

Thin coverings of silver or gold have been attached to base metals from very early times, and a variety

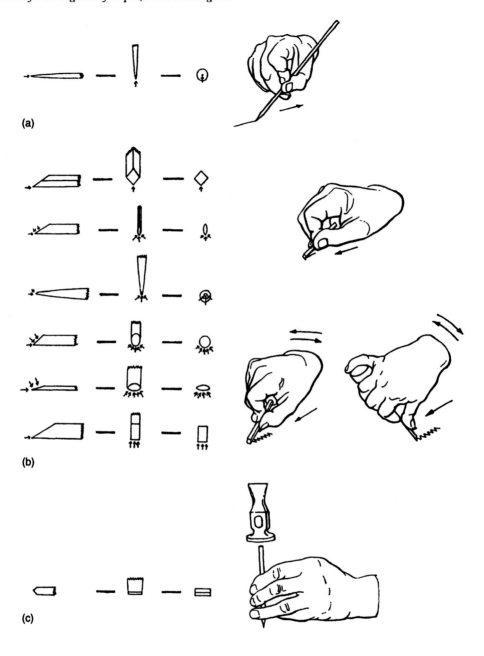

Figure 8.18   (a) Scribing; (b) Varieties of Engraving; (c) Chasing. (Courtesy Lowery *et al.*, 1971)

of techniques have evolved. Thin sheets or foils could be glued or tacked in place, and very thin foils of gold could be burnished onto the surface (*leaf gilding*). The technique of plating by the application of mercury-metal amalgams to base metal began in Hellenistic Greece (Craddock, 1977) and in the Warring States period in China (Bunker *et al.*, 1993). The amalgam was applied to the cleaned

Figure 8.19 Series of short engraved lines forming the background decoration on a high tin bronze Islamic *haft just* vessel. Note the abrupt ends where the sliver has broken off. (Courtesy S. La Niece/British Museum)

Figure 8.21 Chased lines on a fragment of a thirteenth-century brass incense burner. Note the ends of the straight line in the central curve, but they are much less obvious than on Figure 8.20. (Courtesy S. La Niece/British Museum)

Figure 8.20 Chased lines on a twentieth-century Moroccan brass plate. The curves are very obviously made up of straight segments (cf. Figure 8.21), unlike an engraved line, although the line could be smoothed with a scriber. (Courtesy S. La Niece/British Museum)

Figure 8.22 Detail of the engraving on the back of a plain bronze Etruscan mirror, BM GR Reg. 1840, 2–12, 11. The engraving cuts through the genuine patina, which it must therefore post-date. (Courtesy S. La Niece/ British Museum)

surface of the metal, which was then heated to drive off the mercury leaving a thin coat of the precious metal. The process is variously known as *mercury, fire* or *parcel* gilding. The usual evidence for mercury plating is the presence of traces of mercury in the surface, which can be very persistent. Note that the detection limit for mercury in gold or silver by XRF is currently only about 0.2%, which is rather high to exclude the possibility of mercury-plating. Unfortunately, the presence or absence of mercury is not in itself a watertight indicator of mercury gilding. It used to be common practice to treat the surface of the metal with mercury prior to electroplating (a process known

as *quicking* or *quickening*) (Field and Bonney, 1925, p. 114; Lins and Malenka, 2000). In addition, metals pick up mercury very easily and the presence of mercury could be no more than a recent contamination acquired in a rather dirty workshop. Fake patinas, especially from the Orient (see Chapter 14, p. 356), can include mercury salts, notably cinnabar and vermilion, and these could cause confusion where the surface is also plated (see p. 176).

Electroplating, mercury gilding and true leaf gilding are not possible on a mineralised surface. Thus, where it is clear that the plating is firmly attached to a heavily corroded surface, it is a strong indication of the antiquity of the plating.

Had the bronze been intended to be mercury gilt, it was very desirable that lead, and, to a lesser extent, tin, were excluded from the alloy. Thus, Roman statuary that is normally cast from a heavily leaded alloy with about 5 to 10% of tin, tends to be of copper with just 1 or 2% of tin if the metal is to be mercury gilt, as exemplified most famously by the Horses of San Marco, Venice (Oddy *et al.*, 1990). The alloy is viscous and is difficult to cast satisfactorily, and therefore the cast shapes were made very simple with few intricate or extended areas where the metal would not flow.

A good example of this is given by the Roman mercury gilt statuette of the Emperor Commodus posing as Hercules, now in the British Museum, PEE Reg. 1895, 4–8,1 (Figure 8.23) and which is said to have been found at Birdoswald, a fort on Hadrian's Wall in the north of England, (Coulston and Phillips, 1988, pp. 77–78).

The statuette, which stands over 50 cm tall, is solid cast of copper with about 2% of tin (Oddy *et al.*, 1990). The lionskin, which on most statuettes of Hercules stands free from the main casting and with the arms outstretched, is here tightly clamped against the body of the figure. The figure is so unusual that it has been branded as a forgery (Nikolaus-Havé, 1986). However, the low-tin bronze for metal intended to be gilt and the pattern and concentration of the trace elements are both entirely typical of Roman bronzes, and thus there can be no serious doubt over the statuette's authenticity.

Electroplating
Sources: Historical: Bury (1971). Technical: Langbein (1891); Watt and Philip (1911); Canning (1901 *et seq.*); Child (1993).

From the 1840s all of the traditional plating methods were rapidly displaced by the introduction of

Figure 8.23   Detail of the gilded bronze Hercules statuette from Birdoswald showing the lion skin, which is normally free-flowing, merely indicated against the proper left arm and thigh. (Courtesy J. Heffron/British Museum)

electroplating (see Figure 4.16). Thus, the presence of electroplating is an indication that the plating is post-1840, though not necessarily that the whole piece is modern.

Case study: The large Han bear

The investigation of gilded surfaces is illustrated by the large Han bear now in the British Museum (Figure 8.24a). Numerous small mercury-gilt figures of bears are known from the Han period and are typically around 5 to 8 cm in height, but this creature stands 17.2 cm tall. There are also other stylistic incongruities present, which led to a full scientific authenticity examination (Barker and Rawson, 1971–72). Further work was done in 1988 in advance of the 1990 Fake! exhibition (Jones (ed), 1990, p. 257).

The bear is a hollow casting with a separate soldered base plate. Analysis showed that the body is of copper with about 15% of lead and only about 1% of zinc and tin respectively. The base plate consists of about 19% lead and 5.6% tin, and about 1% zinc. The presence of zinc in a Han bronze is unusual, but 1% is too low to be significant and to condemn the piece. The pattern of trace elements in the body and the base are very similar, suggesting the two pieces were made at the same time.

There was little or no integranular corrosion, but the surface was partly covered with an applied patina comprised of ground-up mineral particles in wax. Cuprite was identified by XRD, and mercury, copper, tin, lead, zinc, silver, aluminium, silicon, calcium and barium were all detected qualitatively. Mercury was a traditional constituent of Chinese artificial patinas, providing a deep-red vermilion, and the calcium and barium could well be from an opaque white paint base. In among the mineral particles were particles of a deep-blue cobalt glass, the first time that this material had been recognised in an artificial patina.

The gilding is quite thick and covers most of the bear, and no trace of mercury could be detected by the very sensitive ES method. It does not have the appearance of leaf gilding – no straight edges or overlaps could be seen, and thus the bear is likely to have been electroplated. There are many small blisters on the surface (Figure 8.24b), which are found on electroplated metals where the surface has been inadequately cleaned, such that the gilding does not adhere properly.

It might be argued that this was just a re-gilding, the original mercury gilding having been scraped off. However, some mercury would be expected to have penetrated the copper, but none was detected. The presence of mercury salts in the artificial patina demonstrates the great care that has to be taken to guard against contamination or interference from adjacent areas.

The composition of the body metal is unusual but not impossible for the Han period, but there is no evidence either for an original mercury gilding or for a natural patina, both of which one would expect. Thus, overall, the bear is likely to be a modern production, although the evidence is negative and as is the way with such evidence, not completely conclusive.

Figure 8.24a The large gilded bronze Han Bear, BM OA 1947, 7–12, 382. (Courtesy Jones (ed), 1990)

Figure 8.24b Not only a forgery but dirty! Gilding blisters on Bear's shoulder. Blisters typically form during the electroplating of greasy or tarnished surfaces. (Courtesy Jones (ed), 1990)

Coins and medals

I probably need the scientist's help less than one per-cent of the time, and even then it's only to give an official back-up to what I already believe.
    John Kent in Mills and Mansfield (1979, p. 72.)

Sources: Junge (1992); Williams (ed) (1997).

Numismatists have a strong interest in the techni-cal and metallurgical aspects of coinage, exempli-fied by series such as the *Cahiers Ernest-Babelon*; Morrisson *et al.* (1999), Barrandon *et al.* (1994) etc., and the Royal Numismatic Society's Special Publications; Hall and Metcalf (eds), (1972), which inspired the series *Metallurgy in Numismatics* (here-after MIN) 1 (Metcalf and Oddy (eds), 1980); MIN 2 (Oddy (ed), 1988); MIN 3 (Archibald and Cowell (eds) 1993); MIN 4 (Oddy and Cowell (eds), 1998). Some of the Monographs of the American Numismatic Society are also very metallurgical in nature (e.g. Campbell, 1933; Caley, 1964). The main numismatic periodicals, such as *The Numismatic Chronicle* and *The British Numismatic Journal* carry many articles of a scientific nature, particularly with analytical data. The International Association of Professional Numismatists (IAPN) established the International Bureau for the Suppression of Counterfeit Coins (IBSCC) which, together with the Amateur Numismatic Association (ANA), pub-lishes the *Counterfeit Coin Bulletin*, successor to the *Bulletin of Counterfeits*, specifically to illustrate and draw attention to fakes and forgeries as they are identified. There is also *Counterfeit*, the journal of the Counterfeit Coin Club, which specialises in both counterfeit and fake coins and coining.

Two very different motivations exist for the fraud-ulent reproduction of coins. There are coins which are copies of current coins made with the inten-tion of passing them into circulation and obtaining no more than their face value, and there are copies of coins that are valued, usually far above their face value, and collected for their own sake, and prized for their beauty, historic interest or just plain rarity. For the purposes of this chapter alone the former will be designated as counterfeits and the latter as forgeries, although in the numismatic literature the two terms seem to be freely interchanged.

Copies, reproductions and forgeries

The problems of distinguishing between legitimate copies and forgeries have been discussed elsewhere

(see Chapter 1, p. 9). The specific problem of legiti-mate copies being subsequently passed off fraudu-lently as originals is especially acute in numismatics as coins exist in such large numbers compared with other collectibles, and the appearance of a few more examples does not automatically raise suspicion in the way that, for example, the appearance of a few more van Goghs certainly has done (see Chapter 12, p. 304). In a recent issue of the Coordinating Committee for Numismatics in Britain (CCNB) Newsletter, dedicated to this theme, the matter was discussed by both curators and producers of coins (Burnett, 1998). Carradice (1998) believed that good copies would inevitably appear at some stage on the market as genuine coins. He cited the excellent electroforms made for museums in the nineteenth century for comparison and display. Even where the original order is accounted for, there was always the possibility of further pieces being made on the side, sometimes many years later where the moulds survived. Marks identifying them as copies can be removed to deceive the collector. Reproductions, Carradice tersely concluded, 'are a mixed blessing'.

David Greenhalgh (1998), whose excellent Medieval coining demonstrations are well known at museums, coin meetings, schools, etc., defended the making of reproductions as being a good way of promoting interest in the subject, and in history generally, as well as providing new insights into the problems of coining. He mainly strikes in pewter, but has used copper, silver and even gold, open-ing up the very real danger that his productions could be mistaken for old coins. Note that it is not a question of genuine or forgery, as Greenhalgh (or *GRVNVAL*, the name he uses on his coins) does not produce direct copies – his coins are only in the style of Anglo-Saxon or Medieval coins. Where there is a danger of his coins being mistaken for real ancient coins he adds details such as the year in Arabic numerals. However, the clearly anachro-nistic date numerals could be filed off. As a further precaution against possible future misrepresentation of Greenhalgh's coins, he gives examples of all his coins to the British Museum.

Ultimately, publication and freely available sets of the productions of legitimate copies or forgeries is the best defence against their being too readily mistaken for the genuine article. Unfortunately, the problem does not cease the first time a good repro-duction is recognised, but potentially reappears each time the coin changes hands for as long as it exists.

In South-East Asia there is the rather different problem of the official re-issue of particular coin types over many hundreds of years. The coins of Medieval kings re-issued in the nineteenth century, etc. and the later issues can be difficult to differentiate from the originals (Mitchiner and Pollard, 1990).

Another problem concerns re-strikes, that is, old dies reused long after the original issue. Thus, for example, the dies used by Matthew Boulton to produce, among other things, the well-known cartwheel twopenny pieces in the late eighteenth century, were purchased by W.J. Taylor in the late nineteenth century and more coins struck (Peck 1964, pp. 219–229). The dies had become somewhat rusty and this is noticeable especially on the first of Taylor's re-strikes.

The collector of Russian coins has the *novodel* to contend with. From 1762 until 1890 anyone could order new copies of old coins to be restruck using the origin dies from the Russian Imperial mint. When worn, the die could be recut and the coins could be struck in any metal the collector chose; gold copies of silver coins were popular. It was also permitted to strike any combination of obverse and reverse dies, provided only that the original coins had been of the same size.

Some well-liked and well-recognised coins such as the silver Marie Theresa thaler continued in production for centuries after the Empress's demise. The Royal Mint in London continued to mint the gold sovereign with the head of George V and the date 1925 up until the 1950s. This led John Kent, of the Department of Coins and Medals at the British Museum, to muse whether the Mint had forged its own coin (Mills and Mansfield, 1979, p. 70). The Mint's justification was that in the Arab world, where many of these coins were destined, a sovereign with a king's head was actually more valuable than the same coin with the head of a queen.

Coin-making technology

Sources: Vermeule (1954); Sellwood (1976); Cooper (1988); Archibald and Cowell (eds) (1993).

Coining was mankind's introduction to mass production, where regularity was paramount. This was, after all, what a coin promised, guaranteed constant weight and purity. There are two main aspects to coin production, refining and testing the metal and making the coin. It seems likely that the techniques for purifying gold were only developed in response to the invention of coinage around the middle of the first millennium BC. The processes of refining silver and gold are outlined in Chapter 15,

p. 370. Assay was normally by touchstone, with techniques such as fire assay being applied more rarely, and specific gravity, although known in theory, only applied in the Post-Medieval period (Ramage and Craddock, 2000, pp. 245–250). The purified metals could then be mixed with the other metals to make alloys of the required fineness for the coins.

In the West, the majority of the coins were made by striking a blank or *flan* of metal between dies. The first stage was the production of blanks of regular weight in enormous numbers. In Celtic Europe many fragments of ceramic trays have been found, each containing many small indentations that clearly played a part in the production of the flans. Sellwood (1963) suggested that aliquots of the molten alloy were poured direct into the indentations. Experiments showed that it was possible to pour very regular quantities, probably as good as could be achieved by weighing with the balances available in the Celtic world.

In the Classical world it seems that the coin blanks were often cast in two-piece moulds, some of which survive, and sometimes the casting flash on the coin has survived the striking process.

In the Medieval period the process underwent quite fundamental changes. Cast bars were hammered into strip of the required thickness from which square blanks were cut and trimmed to produce a polygonal approximation of a circle. From the seventeenth century, rolled sheet began to be used, and by the nineteenth century circular blanks were stamped directly from the sheet prior to striking.

Little is known about the early striking processes. This is because, almost without exception in the official mints, the dies were destroyed as soon as they became worn. Those dies that have survived seem to have been used for making counterfeit coins and are often of a cast high-tin bronze. High-tin bronze dies would be quite easy to cast from a mould made from an existing genuine coin and would reproduce detail well, but they would be brittle with a rather short working life.

In Post-Medieval Europe it was usual practice to produce master dies of the obverse and reverse of the coin in negative (known as the *matrix*). This was carved and worked in soft annealed steel, which was then heat-treated to produce a stronger and harder metal. From the matrix a set of positives, known as *patrix* or punches, would be made, again in annealed steel (the process known as *hobbing*), and heat-treated to produce a strong hard steel from which the negative dies could be punched in soft annealed steel that, as before, would be heat-treated prior to use. A die could strike perhaps several thousand coins before it became worn, and a patrix could be used to strike hundreds of dies. Dozens of punches could be hobbed from the master dies, which then could ultimately have been the originators of millions of coins. Obviously the coiners would clean up and recut the worn dies as far as was possible to get the maximum life out of them, and these minor changes are detectable in the coins. Spotting the die links between coins is an important part of the study of numismatics, and of detecting forged coins.

Around AD 1500 in Europe, coin production underwent fundamental changes. Among these were the introduction of the screw press and the roller press (Cooper, 1988, pp. 39–122). In the former, the pressure was transmitted in a much more even fashion through a screw-operated press bed. In the latter, the coin design was repeated at intervals carved around the two steel cylinders of the rolls which simultaneously impressed the top and bottom of the strip of metal fed between the rollers to produce the obverse and reverse of the coins. The positive impressed strips were then cut up into shapes approximating to a circle. The first technologies were also introduced for striking a design around the rim of the coin to protect against clipping of the rough edges, a practice prevalent since the introduction of coinage.

From the end of the eighteenth century, steam power was applied to the production of coinage, further increasing the rate of production and the uniformity of the product (Cooper, 1988, pp. 123–222).

In ancient India coins were made of small squares of silver, cut from a hammered sheet onto which a number of small marks were struck with a punch.

In China, currency of a variety of shapes was usually cast from a variety of base metals, leaded bronze, cast iron or, latterly, brass. Elsewhere, casting was the method often adopted by the counterfeiter, and then by the coin forger.

The faking and forging of coins and medals

In Europe, coins and medals were among the earliest antiquities to be forged, being already prevalent in the sixteenth century (Burnett, 1992); indeed some of the first substantive works on numismatics such as the *Discorsi . . . sopra le medaglie antchi* by Enea Vico, published in 1555, had to deal with the problem. Many of these early copies or forgeries (it is unsure whether they were all originally intended

to deceive) are superb works of art in their own right, such as those made by Benvenuto Cellini's father, Giovanni dal Cavino of Padua. He specialised in copies of Roman *sestertii*, struck from dies he had sunk himself. Many years after his death the dies were used again and casts were taken from existing pieces and circulated in large numbers, becoming known as 'Paduans'.

Good die-struck imitations can be difficult to spot, and some of the forgeries of Carl Wilhelm Becker (1772–1830) and his assistant W. Zindel can only be detected because they tend to be better than the originals (Hill, 1924-25). The story goes that as an amateur collector, the young Becker purchased a rather expensive gold coin that was subsequently shown to be a forgery. On confronting the vendor, an aristocratic collector, he was turned away and told that the episode should be regarded as a lesson to teach him not to meddle in matters he did not understand. Infuriated and frustrated, the lesson Becker learnt was emulation. He quickly picked up the art of die-cutting and showed a quite remarkable aptitude for producing convincing copies, sometimes striking over old and worn but genuine coins. He had the satisfaction of seeing his productions sold to the collector who had originally duped him, and, as it was to turn out, to many other collectors and museums, right up to the present day.

Becker's is another interesting case in the recurring question of whether the products should be regarded as reproductions or forgeries. On one hand he was completely open, a well-known expert, who made excellent copies of coins from well-known collections. He even offered to sell his collection of dies to the Imperial Coin Cabinet in Vienna so that his copies could be more easily identified (this did not happen; instead they are in Berlin). On the other hand, he gave many of his coins a false appearance of wear and age, apparently by placing them in a box of iron filings, which was strung beneath his carriage and taken for a few trips along Vienna's bumpy streets. Patina was achieved by burying the coins for a few weeks and then soaking them in urine, being careful to select men's or women's urine as well as that of beer or wine drinkers for the desired patina. He also made arrangements with dealers in Turkey, etc. to secretly take his productions so that they appeared to have a convincing provenance.

The publication of well-illustrated catalogues and of casts, such as the famous *Description de médailles antiques grecques et romaines avec leur degré de rareté et leur estimation* by T.E. Mionnet from 1806, accompanied by no less than 20 000 sulphur casts, gave the collectors much needed information on the appearance of the authentic coins, but also informed the forgers. For example, in Britain the early nineteenth-century forgeries by James Edwards deceived no one after the publication of the first serious books on early English numismatics from the mid-nineteenth century. These works were also diligently studied by forgers such as Edward Emery, enabling them to produce much more convincing forgeries (Pagan, 1971). Emery frequently used common or worn contemporary coins as blanks overstruck with the dies that he had sunk of much rarer issues. He also had the successful forger's knack of providing what the market wanted. In particular he noted lacunae in the numismatic record, historically attested kings with whom no coins could be associated, and obligingly filled the gap.

Skilled die-struck productions continued into the twentieth century (Bendall, 1971), with the forgeries of classical coins struck by Constantine Christodoulos of Athens (Svoronos, 1922), for example. The age-old confusion between innocent copy and forgery also continues. Die-struck copies of ancient classical coins have been produced in very large numbers in Bulgaria, and are probably still in production (Dimitrov *et al.*, 1997; Marinescu, 1998). It is estimated that between 1990 and 1995 as many as 300 000 coins were struck. They were offered for sale in tourist outlets in the country as souvenir reproductions, but they are also seen sporting a false patina on sale as originals.

Yet another fraudulent activity is to alter a common coin into a much rarer, and consequently, more valuable item. This very often involves altering the date. Thus, for example, on British George V half-crowns the common 1928 is frequently altered to the much rarer 1923. Larson (2004) describes many methods of making subtle changes to recent coins by removal or addition of a stamp (Figure 8.25).

Faking and forging techniques

The easiest method of copying a coin or medal is to take a cast from a genuine piece. The vast majority of the copies sold as reproductions in the gift shops or hawked as genuine by small boys at ancient monuments through the Mediterranean and Middle East are simple castings, maybe acid-treated to give a semblance of age. Casts of struck coins should deceive no one. On even the best casting the rendition of the struck detail will lack crispness when

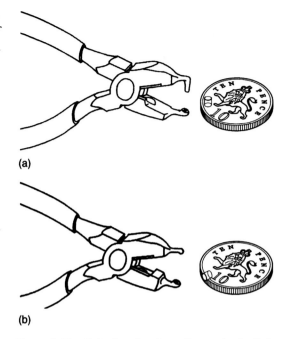

(a)

(b)

Figure 8.25 Coin alteration. A needle-nosed pair of pliers cut down and adapted to create a die and tressel for making a raised mint mark on to a genuine but otherwise common coin. (a) For thin coins the metal is pushed into the die from the other side, leaving a small depression that must be filled. (b) For thicker coins it is necessary to drill in from the side so that the die and tressel can be inserted from the edge. The hole in the edge will have to be filled and disguised.

viewed through a binocular microscope. Wear, scratches and minor damage on the original will be present but as cast detail, although these features can be difficult to detect if the piece is patinated. If such is the case then the patina itself can be investigated by XRD, etc. (see Chapter 14, p. 365).

One important feature common to all cast copies is that they are slightly smaller than the original owing to the shrinkage of the metal in the mould as it sets. For bronze the degree of shrinkage lies between about 2.5 and 3.2% (Allison and Pond, 1983). This is of especial significance for coins and medals where the dimensions of the original are accurately known. Note that organic casting materials such as epoxy resins are much less prone to shrinkage (see Chapter 4, p. 64).

Much better rendition of the surface detail can be achieved by electroforming (see Chapter 4, p. 78), and large numbers of such items were produced in the second half of the nineteenth century and the early twentieth century. Once again there is a lack of crispness when viewed under the binocular microscope and sometimes more obvious mistakes (Figure 8.26). The electroformed surfaces are very distinctive at the higher magnification of the scanning electron microscope.

The separate electroforms of the obverse and reverse faces are joined by solder, and careful inspection of the rim of a suspect piece may well reveal the line of the join (see Chapter 4, p. 84). Although the electroform could be of silver or gold or of their alloys, most electroforms were made of copper and then plated. The rosy hue of copper may well be apparent at the rim or some other prominent part of the coin.

Die-cutting or sinking is a highly skilled profession, and few forgers have the skill of the original craftsmen. Thus it was certain characteristic shortcomings on the coins of the Haslemere Hoard of Celtic gold coins that led to their unmasking (Van Arsdell, 1986). In particular, the forger seems to have had difficulties with curves – instead of a continuous line, the curves often proceeded in a series of steps.

The subject of coin forging, faking and ageing has recently been comprehensively described by Charles M. Larson (2004). Dealing mainly with modern rare coins, he describes how they may be produced by altering similar, more common issues or by creating new coins by making casts or striking from purpose-made dies. The making of these is described in great detail, either by casting, by

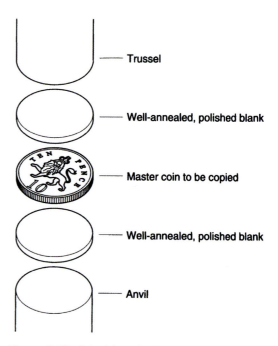

Figure 8.27 Principles of hubbing. After striking, the blanks will have picked up negative impressions of the coin. If they are struck several times they will begin to work-harden and can be used as dies for striking more coins.

creating an electroform (see Chapter 4, p. 80), or by hubbing, i.e. using an existing coin impressed into a plain disc to create the die impression (Figure 8.27) and he developed an ingenious method of carrying out his hubbing operations (Figure 8.28). The new appearance of Larson's creations or alterations is toned down by gentle heating to give them a superficial oxide layer. He claimed his die-struck forgeries are virtually identical to the real thing, having been made in the correct manner. As he deals mainly in coins selling for a few hundred dollars apiece the authentication checks are not likely to be too rigorous, but one suspects that trace element analysis of the alloy and inspection by SEM would reveal differences.

Larson's coins are aged in a simple rock tumbler. Patina for forgeries of ancient coins is produced by burying the coins in a pot in the ground for a few months with liberal applications of urine, following Becker's methods. Pitting is achieved by flicking acid onto the surface. Larson claims the patina is visually convincing, but it is likely to be rather flaky and to be easily detected by scientific examination, as described in Chapter 14 (see p. 365).

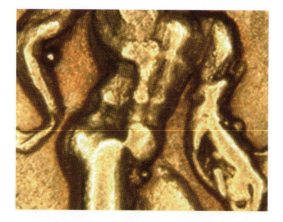

Figure 8.26 Details of the electroform of the reverse of a gold coin of the Emperor Probus, showing Hercules. A number of air bubbles in the surface of the mould have become plated and appear as balls on the surface of the electroform (note the ball in the armpit and the extra testicle). These are normally removed but some may be overlooked. (Courtesy S. La Niece/British Museum)

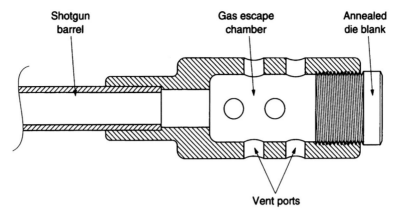

Figure 8.28 Explosive hubbing, only to be attempted with extreme caution! A cylinder of metal to which is attached a coin, is fired from an adapted shotgun into the chamber illustrated that holds the blank (on the right) and into which the coin will be propelled to form the die. This in turn will be used to strike a few forgeries.

Detection

Composition

The composition range of an increasing number of coin series, types and issues is being established and thus the analysis of suspect pieces is becoming an important feature of authenticity studies. Even where the issues have wide composition ranges, such as the Celtic gold coins, there may still be characteristic patterns. Thus the British coins are debased with a reasonably consistent alloy of two parts silver to one part copper, this combination best preserving the golden color of the metal (Cowell, 1992). Forgeries from the Haslemere Hoard had been debased with an alloy of three parts copper to one of silver (Van Arsdell 1986). Note the practice of some fakers to use old worn or common coins to overstrike.

For a meaningful quantitative analysis of the body metal, ideally a sample should be drilled or a section exposed. In practice, however, the method will usually have to be non-destructive using techniques such as XRF (Cowell, 1998) but leading to the problems of possible plating, and surface enrichment/depletion, especially for gold, silver and brass coins (see Chapter 15, p. 372, 388 and Chapter 7, p. 137). The only truly non-destructive method that overcomes these surface problems is that of specific gravity, and it is only applicable to gold coins (Oddy, 1998).

Structure

Castings and electroforms will have very different metallographic structures from the struck originals, even if of the correct metal composition (which in the case of the electroforms is extremely unlikely). As cutting or polishing a section is not usually feasible, micro-hardness testing and Laue diffractometry (Coins: Striegel, 1998; Andrasko *et al.*, 1979; medals: Wharton, 1984; Farrell, 1987; and see Chapter 3, p. 54) could provide a non-destructive means of differentiating the structure of the copy from the struck original, even if it had been annealed afterwards. Terry and de Laeter (1974) used Laue diffractometry to identify cast forgeries of seventeenth-century Spanish silver *reales* from the genuine struck coins by the difference in grain size.

The detail on die-struck coins is much sharper than on a cast or electroform copy as outlined above, but in addition there are distinctive surface features such as the surface striations known as die stress or flow marks. Some tend to radiate out across the coin. They originate from the metal being forced over the surface of the die during the actual moment of striking and also being scratched by the edges of the sunk detail resulting in striations (Figure 8.29). There are also stress marks that appear as series of densely packed sharp lines at the angles and edges of a struck coin (Birt and Wagner, 1974, 1975) (see Figure 8.30a).

Great care must be used in inferring anything from the presence or absence of these lines. As Newman (1974) noted, they are a feature of hand-striking; if sufficient pressure is applied then the lines will be flattened. Flow lines will only have formed in some places anyway and will often also have worn away except in areas of the coin protected against wear. It is possible that a good cast or electroform copy could pick these features up and, indeed, this resulted in a minor controversy

Figure 8.29 SEM micrograph of the surface of a struck gold Anglo-Saxon coin showing the characteristic flow lines running across the image and striations running down the image, caused as the metal is forced to flow over the cut edge of the die during the actual striking process. (Courtesy M. Cowell/British Museum)

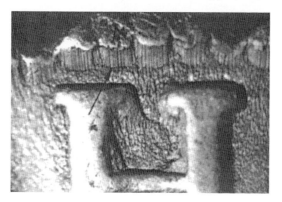

Figure 8.30a Die-stress or flow lines on the denticulated edge of a genuine struck silver 1747 pillar dollar from Mexico (see arrow). (×16).

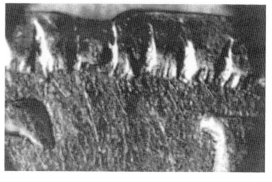

Figure 8.30b Detail of a cast copy of a 1754 struck silver pillar dollar, with no sharp rendition of the stress flow lines (×16). (Courtesy Birt and Wagner, 1975)

back in the 1970s. Birt and Wagner (1974) asserted that die stress lines were too fine to be replicated on a casting, and their presence constituted an infallible guide to the coin having been struck. Furthermore the marks, if present, should be easily visible through a ×16 hand lens. This brought down swift and robust rebuttals, with Newman (1974) and Hancock (1974) claiming that modern casting techniques *could* pick up the die stress lines. In addition Hancock also claimed that a ×16 hand lens was not sufficient to enable positive identification of a good casting. Birt and Wagner (1975)

defended their original article, illustrating struck and cast copies of the same coin (Figures 8.30a and 8.30b). Clearly, the truth or otherwise of the statement depends on the particular issue concerned. However, when viewed through the good binocular microscope recommended throughout this book, or better still by SEM, it would be observed that such lines are picked up not as sharply or as clearly defined as on the original.

Hoye (1983) suggested that the remanent magnetism could be a non-destructive indicator of whether a coin had been struck or was a casting.

Most ancient copper-alloy coins have remanent magnetism as, rather surprisingly, do silver and even gold coins. Only modern electrolytically refined metals and electroforms will have no remanent magnetism as they contain no iron impurities.

The Russian mint issued roubles of platinum from the Urals in the mid-nineteenth century when the technology for refining or even melting platinum was very much in its infancy. The coins were made by a sort of powder metallurgy, compressing and sintering the native grains (Bachmann and Renner, 1984). The impure platinum contained several per cent of iron and thus the coins of the original issue have quite pronounced ferromagnetism. By the end of the century, when the melting of platinum had been mastered, they were reissued as *novodel* (see p. 179), and more recently they have been forged. In appearance both the novodel and the forgeries are very similar to the original platinum coins except that the iron has been removed and they display no ferromagnetism.

9

Ceramics

Beauty is truth, truth beauty.

Keats, *Ode to a Grecian Urn*

Sources: General: Blakemore (1984); Freestone and Gaimster (eds) (1997); Cooper (2000); Trench (ed) (2000, pp. 73–80). Technical and Scientific examination: Rice (1987); Middleton (1991). Authenticity: Kurz (1948, pp. 228–257); Savage (1976, pp. 135–212); Lang (1986); Battie (1999).

Making pots

Sources: Hodges (1964, pp. 19–41); Wulff (1966, pp. 136–171); Rhodes (1969, 1977); Hamer (1975); Rye (1981); Peterson (1995).

Ceramics are fired clay. Clays are composed of small particles, with diameters rarely exceeding 0.01 mm, formed by the weathering of certain rocks (Trench (ed), 2000, pp. 88–90). The main constituent is often the aluminium silicate, kaolinite, but clays have a wide range of chemical composition; other metal silicates and oxides are frequently present in many mineral forms. Clays that are used for ceramics must be plastic when mixed with water, but as steam is evolved and the clays themselves undergo several volume changes during firing, a piece made of pure clay would probably collapse, and so rigid materials (known as *temper* or *fillers*) must be present in the clay to provide support during the firing. Primitive ceramics, fired in an open bonfire with little or no control, usually have large quantities of filler, typically 20 to 30%, and the individual particles can be several millimetres across, although usually smaller. Many clays already have sufficient sand or grit particles and need no added filler, but otherwise a variety of materials have been added including crushed rock, notably flint, shell, straw, or reused ceramic (known as *grog*).

The methods of shaping pottery are diverse. At its simplest, the clay could be rolled out into sheets and shaped rather like pastry. Many early pots were built up by coiling long sausages of clay to form the body (Varndell and Freestone, 1997). The coils could then be amalgamated and the walls of the vessel drawn up by hand or with a wooden bat and beater. Coil-building continues to be used in some pottery-making traditions and also for making some very large pots where hand-throwing is not viable (Wulff, 1966, pp. 152–153).

The pot is likely to have sat on a flat surface that could be turned as the coils were built up, and in time this evolved into a turntable. With this, a new technique, the drawing up of coil-built vessels as they turned relatively slowly, began in the fourth and third millennium BC in the Middle East and South Asia. From this evolved true wheel-thrown pottery with the lump of clay being drawn up by hand on a fast-turning wheel, around the end of the third millennium BC. The details of the introduction and spread of the fast-wheel technique are still very uncertain (Roux and Courty, 1998).

Differentiating between slab, coil-built, wheel-drawn and thrown vessels is not easy. Once the coils have been smoothed and drawn up to form the coherent wall of a vessel, it can be very difficult to differentiate coil-built pots from those made by any other method. Some of the surface features typical of wheel-thrown pots are described by Courty and Roux (1995) and Roux and Courty (1998). Informed visual inspection and radiography can often reveal how they were made (Rye, 1977) (Figures 9.1 and 9.2).

Pottery can also be formed by pressing the clay into a mould. This method was very widely used in pre-Hispanic America for example. Quite complex shapes were made up by joining together a number of individually moulded pieces with plastic clay (known as *luting*). A semi-industrial variant was

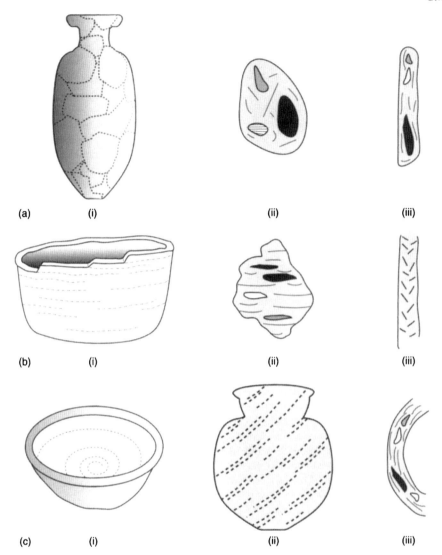

Figure 9.1 Diagram illustrating characteristic features of some techniques for making pots as they might appear by radiography. (Courtesy Lang and Middleton (eds), 2005) (a) Slab-building: (i) vessel built up from a series of slabs of clay; (ii) random orientation of particles in normal view; (iii) preferred orientation of particles parallel to vessel walls. (b) Coil-building (Figure 9.2): (i) vessel built up from coils of clay; (ii) preferred orientation of features and coils joins may be seen in normal view; (iii) random orientation of particles in cross-section. (c) Wheel-throwing: (i) spiral pattern of ridges and grooves on the surface; (ii) oblique arrangement of elongate voids and particles in normal view; (iii) preferred orientation of voids and particles parallel to the vessel wall.

developed in Europe to mass produce plates and open vessels by pressing the clay into a mould which was then spun and a template lowered onto it to remove the surplus clay and create the inner surface. This process is known as *jolleying* if the outside surface is moulded and *jigging* or *joggling* if the inner surface is moulded. Jolleying was used extensively by the Romans to make their Samian wares, etc. (see p. 196) and was revived in Post-Medieval Europe, but is now redundant as a commercial technique.

Ceramics can be cast. Liquid clay (known as a *slip*) is poured into a mould made of a material such as plaster of Paris or terracotta which absorbs much of the water, leaving the clay cast in the mould. This method has been popular in Europe since the eighteenth century for fashioning complex shapes

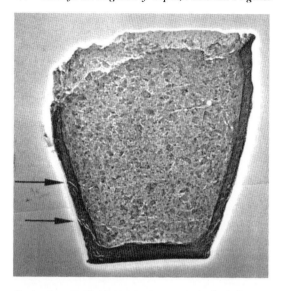

Figure 9.2   Xeroradiograph of a Late Bronze Age funerary vessel from Burton Fleming, Yorkshire. The arrows indicate the joins between coils. (Courtesy Lang and Middleton (eds), 2005)

fire the ceramic orange or red and reducing conditions fire ceramics black. The silica in the clay undergoes a reversible change at 573°C. Increasing the temperature further brings about sintering and then vitrification of the ceramic body, making it denser and impervious. The degree of sintering or vitrification also depends on the composition of the clay. The presence of metal ions such as iron and the alkalis, sodium and potassium, lower the vitrification temperature. Impure clays fire to a rather weak, porous, red or black ceramic up to about 900°C. These are sometimes termed terracottas, while purer clays fired at between 900° and 1000°C producing pale or white porous bodies are known as earthenwares (although terracottas are often classed as earthenwares; see Hamer, 1975 and Rice, 1987, pp. 5–6). Above about 1000°C impervious ceramics known as stonewares are produced, and porcelains (see p. 201) are normally fired at between 1300° and 1450°C. The vast majority of pottery produced in the past, prior to the Post-Medieval period in Europe and the Han period in China, would be now be classed as terracotta wares.

such as figurines and is very widely used in modern ceramics production.

The unfired surface can be decorated with incised or impressed designs. The surface may be embellished by burnishing or by painting with a slip of fine clay, or finely powdered minerals such as graphite or hematite can be rubbed in. The surface may be glazed (see p. 206), the glazing being applied either to the unfired clay or after the first (*biscuit*) firing.

Before firing, the ceramic body must be dried by gentle warming to remove as much of the free water as possible, leaving the clay in a condition known as *leather hard*. A wide variety of firing arrangements have been used in the past, from simple bonfires to complex kilns, themselves of a wide variety of shapes and sizes (Rhodes, 1969). Quite large vessels are still successfully fired in parts of Africa with fires that seem barely large enough to cover them, and thus a large complex pot need not necessarily be the product of a sophisticated kiln. However, if the pot is decorated by painting then a kiln of some sort would be necessary to protect the surface from contact with burning fuel and ash, and to establish some uniformity of the oxidising/reducing conditions across the surface of the pot, as this has a strong influence on the final color of traditional pottery. For the majority of clays containing some iron minerals, oxidising conditions

Scientific study

A number of approaches have been adopted in the scientific examination of ceramics. These include dating by age-related phenomena such as thermoluminescence (TL), thermal analysis and magnetic intensity; determination of how the ceramic artefact was made and possibly restored, as revealed by light microscopy, UV and radiography; and characterising and provenancing the ceramic body by thin-section petrology and chemical composition (Middleton, 1997).

Dating

TL

In many areas of ceramics collecting, TL is the most reliable method of authentication and is routinely applied to expensive pieces that lack a firm provenance (see Chapter 6).

Alpha recoil

Alpha recoil has been investigated as method of dating ceramics (Wagner 1998, pp. 212–217). The tiny amounts of uranium-238 and thorium-232 contained in all materials decay by emitting α particles. In certain materials the passage of these particles leaves discernible tracks. Thus far, the phenomenon has only been well studied for mica as a potential dating technique (Huang and Walker, 1967) although the methodology involved would seem to have potential for a range of stone or ceramic antiquities that contain mica and have been strongly heated at or near their creation. Muscovite-tempered pottery from some pre-Columbian cultures in what is now the southern United States and Mexico has been dated quite successfully thereby (Wolfman and Rolniak, 1979).

Thermal analysis
Flamini and de Lorenzo Flamini (1985) applied standard thermal analysis procedures to discriminate between genuine Etruscan pots that had been buried for millennia and modern forgeries. This was believed to be due to the very different water absorption properties of the ancient ceramics resulting from the leaching-out of calcareous minerals during prolonged burial, which created a more open structure in the ancient pieces than in the modern pieces made of the same clays. The method was quick, inexpensive and required no more than about 10 mg of sample taken from the pot.

Magnetic intensity
The Earth's magnetic field is constantly changing both in local direction and in intensity. Clays contain small amounts of iron oxides and these have a small magnetic moment, that is, put very simply, they tend to be more negative at the oxygen 'end' and more positive at the iron 'end'. During the firing of a pot these become slightly aligned to the Earth's field, a feature which is retained on cooling.

As the pots will have been moved, the orientation information is totally lost but the intensity can still be calculated, and it is sometimes possible to relate the remanent magnetic intensity to period, provided sufficient samples of known age and provenance have been taken from the location where it is believed the ceramic was fired, and studied. Thus far, the necessary studies of the local magnetic variations with time have only been carried out at a relatively few localities such as Greece through about the last 3000 years (Aitken *et al.*, 1989), and France through the last four millennia (Shaw, 1979). Measurements of the remanent magnetic intensity in some of the notorious clay tablets from Glozel in central France lent support to the controversial TL dates (see Chapter 6, p. 124).

Burnham and Tarling (1975) suggested that the sherds of a pottery vessel could be refitted or, at the least, their place on the reconstructed vessel accurately determined by measuring the angle of the ambient archaeomagnetic field of the sherds relative

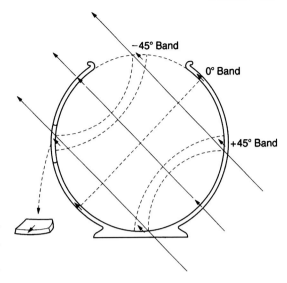

Figure 9.3 Directions of magnetic vectors through a stylised pot. Determining the angle of the magnetic vectors relative to the surface of a sherd, as illustrated, could reveal its place on the pot, or more significantly whether it belonged to the pot at all.

to their surface (see Figure 9.3). Such an approach could also be used to see if restored ceramics are indeed made up of sherds that belong together.

Scientific examination

UV
The technique is quick and non-destructive, and the apparatus is relatively cheap and portable (Rorimer 1931, pp. 31–34; Moss 1954, pp. 8–12; Savage 1976, pp. 296–298). As Savage (1976, p. 297) remarked, 'The acquisition of a UV lamp [is] worthwhile for every serious collector'. UV has two main functions in the authentication of ceramics: exposing restoration and characterising the glaze and body.

Microscopy
Both binocular light microscopy and scanning electron microscopy (SEM) can be invaluable for the detailed study of the surface topography of ceramics, being especially valuable for detecting evidence of how the piece was made, e.g. wheel-thrown or moulded.

Radiography and CT
These techniques can be very useful for revealing manufacturing techniques (Figures 9.1 and 9.2) (Rye, 1977; Carr and Riddick, 1990; Middleton,

2005). They may also indicate whether the pot was thrown on a fast wheel, by revealing the shape and orientation of large fillers (see Chapter 2, Figure 2.8). Radiography is also invaluable for revealing deceptive restoration (La Niece, 2005) (see Figure 2.7b). Note that it is best to take samples for TL before radiography, especially if extensive real-time viewing is anticipated (see Chapter 2, p. 32 and Chapter 6, pp. 112, 113). The technique of scanning CT enables a good three-dimensional image of the interior of the ceramic to be built up, allowing the filler particles to be clearly delineated where they are of a density different from that of the surrounding clay. It is also invaluable for detecting where pieces, usually terracottas, have been assembled from fragments to deceive TL testing (Ghysels, 2003; and see Chapter 2, p. 32 and Chapter 6, p. 115, Figures 6.4 and 6.5).

The structure of ceramic bodies and glazes can be investigated by using a number of techniques. The minerals can be determined by X-ray diffraction (XRD). XRD by itself can differentiate between the major porcelain types. A refinement of this was to include SEM examination and analysis of a small section cut through the glaze and into body ceramic beneath. This approach showed considerable potential for characterising ceramics of the same type but from different factories (Tite and Bimson, 1991; Tite, 1992; Freestone, 1999a, b).

Raman spectroscopy (RS) and Raman microscopy (RM) can also be used to determine ceramic composition and structure (Zoppi *et al.*, 2002; Kiefer (ed), 2004). These techniques require either a very small sample from the body (a few milligrams) or no sample at all, depending on the method and the individual piece. RM has been applied to the identification of Far Eastern and European antique porcelains (Colomban and Treppoz, 2001; Leslie 2003; Colomban, 2003, 2005). The method is essentially non-destructive; the problem is to find exposed areas of the ceramic body that are not covered by glaze.

Classification and provenancing

Traditionally, the scientific classification of ceramics was centred on the petrological examination of thin sections to identify minerals in the clay and fillers (Middleton, 1997; and see Chapter 2, p. 23), often being supplemented by SEM (Tite *et al.*, 1982b) and microanalysis (Freestone, 1982). This approach requires that a section be cut from the pot; however, in most instances with fine, largely intact ceramics, this is not feasible.

Composition

There are two main approaches to compositional studies, depending on the nature of the ceramic body: (1) the determination of the trace and minor elements to characterise the clay, and (2) the determination of the major components of ceramic bodies where significant amounts of other materials have been added to produce more specialised bodies, as exemplified by the European imitations of true Chinese 'hard paste' porcelain, etc.

Ceramics are sampled with abrasion drills. Details of standard procedures for neutron activation analysis (NAA) of ceramics have been published by Hughes *et al.* (eds) (1991) and some of the sources of uncertainty have been discussed by Gilmore (1991). Procedures for the ICP analysis of ceramics can be found in Potts (1987, pp. 153–187). For either method approximately 50 mg of sample is required, which is about the same quantity needed for TL, and if both techniques are to be used then the sample can be analysed after the TL determination has been made.

Many ceramics are slipped or glazed, necessitating the removal of a sample, but if areas of the body are exposed, such as on the foot ring for example, the surface can be analysed directly by techniques such as X-ray fluorescence (XRF). The sensitive and non-destructive techniques of particle (or proton)-induced X-ray emission (PIXE), particle (or proton)-induced γ-ray emission (PIGE) and Rutherford back-scatter (RBS) (see Chapter 3, p. 50) have also been applied to the analysis of ceramics (Demortier and Adriaens (eds), 2000).

Analysis of earthenwares

Sources: General: Hughes *et al.* (eds) (1991); Neff (ed) (1992); Neff (2000); Bishop and Blackman (2002). Ancient Greece: Jones (1986). Majolica: Olin *et al.* (1978).

For many years now, major analytical programmes have sought to characterise and provenance ceramics by trace element analysis such that a very considerable body of data now exists against which to test the composition of pieces of uncertain origin.

NAA has been the main analytical method employed (Perlman and Asaro, 1969) but some analysts such as Picon (1991a) have argued that it is not the most appropriate technique, and by the end of the twentieth century other methods, notably inductively coupled plasma (ICP)-related techniques, became more favoured. Other methods such as

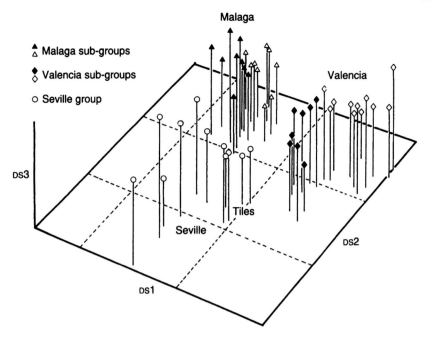

Figure 9.4 Discriminant analysis of trace element composition of Late Medieval to early Post-Medieval majolicas from Malaga, Valencia and Seville, as determined by NAA. Each symbol represents the analysis of an individual piece for about a dozen elements. This approach greatly clarifies the visual separation, and samples from suspect pieces can be analysed and checked to see if they fall within the field of the assigned pottery type or group. (Courtesy Hughes, 1991)

high-precision XRF have also been successfully applied (Adan-Bayewitz *et al.*, 1999).

The sea of figures generated by whatever technique for a whole range of trace elements is impossible to assimilate by eye. Therefore, statistical treatments are routinely applied to separate out the various compositional groups (Jones, 1986, pp. 56–83), the data often being arranged diagrammatically in two or three dimensions (Figure 9.4).

Ceramic bodies usually have added fillers and their presence will obviously affect the overall composition. However, they are usually of relatively pure silica and thus the only effect is one of dilution; this does not affect the ratios between the various elements. A potentially more serious problem for pottery that has been buried for long periods is the absorption of minerals from the burial environment, this situation being especially prevalent among porous ceramic bodies. The absorption of minerals such as phosphates, calcite, manganese and iron minerals in terrestrial environments (Lemoine and Picon, 1982) and magnesium in marine environments (Pradell *et al.*, 1996), has been extensively studied

and the overall conclusion is that this does not pose a major problem (Picon, 1976 [Mg]; Lemoine and Picon, 1982; Freestone *et al.*, 1985 [PO_4, Ca, Fe]; Jones 1986, pp. 33–38; Freestone, 2001). Indeed, the presence of such minerals permeating the ceramic body could be used as an indication of long burial. Conversely, the alkaline metals, sodium and potassium, and some alkaline earths, such as calcium, barium and strontium, may be leached from ceramics with calcareous bodies (Francaviglia *et al.*, 1975; Picon, 1991b; and see p. 206).

Analysis of porcelain and other fine wares

To determine the major elemental composition of the more composite synthetic ceramic bodies, a wider range of techniques has been applied including atomic absorption spectrometry (AAS) and ICP (Hughes *et al.*, 1976; Hatcher *et al.*, 1995).

An enormous amount of work has been taking place to characterise Chinese ceramics (Guo, 1987), employing a variety of techniques. Pollard and Hatcher (1986, 1994) used AAS to characterise porcelains from northern China, and specifically to chart major elemental changes in the porcelains from Jingdezhen through the centuries (Pollard and Wood 1986). Leung and Hongjie Luo (2000) and Leung *et al.* (2000) used XRF to analyse Chinese porcelain.

Trace element analysis has also been applied to characterise Oriental ceramics, often expensive finewares, usually with the specific objective of differentiating between ceramics of very similar appearance that have been in production over long periods of time, either as good copies or as forgeries. Li Hu Hou (1985) used NAA to characterise Longquan greenwares in this manner. Yap (1986a, d; 1987a) and Yap and Tang (1984, 1985a, b, c) used XRF to characterise Chinese porcelains, particularly of the later Imperial and Republican periods. The X-rays were directed at a reasonably flat and unglazed area such as the base ring. Yap and Tang (1985b) found relatively little variation in the major components of the ceramic, but much greater and consistent variation among the trace elements between the originals and later copies, reflecting different clay sources.

Yu and Miao (1996) also used XRF to differentiate between the blue and white porcelains produced at Jingdezhen, by differentiating between the trace elements associated with the cobalt minerals from different sources used at different periods. They were successful in characterising the more modern products copying the earlier wares. Yap (1988) made use of the arsenic/cobalt and manganese/cobalt ratios specifically to expose modern fakes of Qing porcelain. This approach has also been used in Europe to differentiate between Medieval and Post-Medieval cobalt–blue glasses (see Chapter 10, p. 227).

Being based in Singapore, Yap and his colleagues did some work on the Nonya or Straits Chinese porcelain (Yap 1986a, b; 1987b). This very distinctive ware was made in China at Jingdezhen specifically for the expatriate Chinese community living in Malaya and Singapore from the end of the eighteenth century until World War II. Legitimate production never recommenced but with the sharp rise in the prices paid for Oriental ceramics of all periods from the 1970s on, forgeries began to appear, and are now a serious problem. The small sample of known forgeries analysed by Yap had a much higher barium content than did the originals (Figure 9.5). Using this and other data it has proved possible to recognise traditional Jingdezhen porcelains through the Qing and Republican periods, as well as to spot

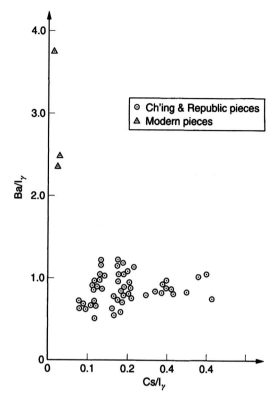

Figure 9.5 XRF analyses of nineteenth- to early twentieth-century Straits Chinese porcelain, made at Jingdezhen. Note the much higher Ba contents of the three modern forgeries.

the modern forgeries, which are probably no longer made at Jingdezhen.

Quang Liem *et al.* (2000) used RS to characterise Vietnamese proto-porcelains and celadons. Koh Choo (1995) analysed Korean celadon ceramics, using SEM/EDX (energy dispersive X-ray analysis) to determine body composition, and spectrophotometry, etc. to characterise the colors of the glazes. These analyses have proved useful for differentiating original works from later copies often from the same potteries.

Other techniques

It is interesting to compare pottery provenance studies with those for stone, and especially for marble, where the first serious provenancing attempts based on petrology and trace element analysis alone, were not very successful and over the years have been joined by a whole range of other physicochemical parameters (see Chapter 11, p. 248). In contrast, the determination of the trace element composition has by itself had a fair degree of success in provenancing ceramic bodies, such that only very recently have other analytical techniques been explored.

These include the determination of the cathodoluminescence (CL) (see Chapter 11, p. 254), the MagS, TL sensitivity and other magnetic properties (Verosub and Moskowitz, 1988; Rasmussen, 2001) which are related to the constituents of the clay and firing conditions. Picouet *et al.* (1999) examined the CL from the quartz and calcite grains in ceramics.

Forging pots

Earthenwares and terracottas

The earliest pottery tends to be rather utilitarian and is almost invariably in poor condition, commanding quite low prices. As a consequence relatively few forgeries have been made. There are exceptions however, such as the early Japanese Jomon wares and the Chinese Neolithic wares. Among the most notorious cases of the forging of early ceramics were the vessels and figurines from Haçilar.

Case study: The Haçilar ceramics

Sources: Mellaart (1970); Aitken *et al.* (1971); Jones (ed) (1990), pp. 286–288.

In the 1950s large quantities of sherds of painted pottery (Figure 9.6) began to be dug from an ancient tell at the small village of Haçilar in the Burdur region of south-west Turkey. These were extremely sophisticated, although the related material suggested that they belonged to the earliest phases of pottery production. Excavations of the settlement by James Mellaart (1970) revealed sherds from a range of hollow figurines and fine vessels, many painted with complex patterns and some in anthropomorphic forms, dating from the late seventh through the sixth millennium BC.

The excavators failed to locate the cemetery that they believed must have existed. However, they were soon aware that it had been found by the local peasants as fine ceramics in the Haçilar style

Figure 9.6 Forged or looted? The large double-headed vessel with obsidian inlaid eyes in the Haçilar style, acquired by the British Museum, was a legitimate export from Turkey but is a forgery. The small vessel on the right is genuine but looted. (Courtesy J. Heffron/British Museum)

began to appear on the market. The pieces were much more complete and in much better general condition, strongly suggesting that they had been buried intact in graves, rather than broken and trodden into the ground as was the case with the excavated pieces from the settlement. The alternative explanation was that they were forgeries. The anthropologist, Peter Ucko, who was studying early figurines, examined some of the pieces prior to their inclusion in a Sotheby's sale in London in 1962, suspecting that some were forgeries (Ucko in Aitken *et al.*, 1971). Over the next few years the international antiquities market became flooded with Haçilar-style vessels and figurines, which were eagerly purchased by both private collectors and major international collections.

Further investigation of the site was not helped when Mellaart was banned by the Turkish authorities from excavating because of his involvement with the mysterious Dorak Treasure (Pearson and Connor, 1967).

The generally better condition and wider range of forms of the ceramics on sale compared with those from the excavation could be explained in a number of ways, as Ucko set out:

1. The ceramics could be from a different part of the site, not excavated by Mellaart, probably from the putative cemetery.
2. There are many other tells in the general vicinity yielding Neolithic pottery; perhaps some of the more unusual pieces came from other sites that were now probably also being looted.
3. Some, or indeed all could be modern forgeries.

Because the quality and range of forms of the unprovenanced pieces was so far superior to the excavated pieces, ordinary typological studies were rendered all but impossible (Ucko and Hodges, 1963). For example, no evidence of the distinctive double figure vessels was found on the excavations, yet many were appearing on the market; were any of them genuine or were they a complete invention? Similar problems had arisen with some pre-Dynastic Egyptian figurines, where the unprovenanced pieces completely submerged the excavated material in quality and range of style (Ucko and Hodges, 1963; Ucko, 1968).

A major programme of scientific examination was initiated on the unprovenanced Haçilar-style material from the British, Ashmolean and Bristol Museums in Britain and the Metropolitan Museum, New York.

The scientific examination included quantitative emission spectography (ES) analysis on samples drilled from 42 pieces, mineralogy on thin sections taken from four pieces, estimation of the firing temperatures on seven pieces, examination of the surface encrustations on 35, and, most crucial, thermoluminescence (TL) tests on 68 pieces.

TL showed that a large proportion of the pieces had been fired very recently. It was suggested that perhaps the ceramics had been in a soft condition when dug up and had been re-fired to harden them. This was inherently unlikely, but even so the samples were examined by the then new pre-dose technique (see Chapter 6, p. 113), which established that the pieces had only been fired once; the recent firings did not mask much earlier original firings.

The ES analyses were performed at Oxford, where the first large-scale provenancing studies of pottery were already in progress (Jones, 1986). These studies were being carried out on Bronze Age pottery from Greece and Crete and thus the clays were likely to be not dissimilar to those from western Anatolia. The results were equivocal. The majority of the samples from excavated ceramics and the pieces pronounced genuine by TL formed one coherent compositional group. However, eleven of the pieces pronounced modern by TL, also fell into that group and the majority of the remainder of the forgeries fell into a second very distinctive compositional group. This suggested that there were two production centres, the first, probably local to Haçilar, and the other, not. In the prevailing burial conditions the absorption of phosphates could have been expected (see p. 191), but unfortunately phosphorus was not one of the elements sought, maybe because it would have required a separate colorimetric determination.

The mineralogical examination showed that all of the pieces contained calcite and three contained fragments of volcanic glass, including the one genuine piece. Henry Hodges, who conducted the examination, noted 'there is nothing to suggest a source other than Haçilar'.

The firing temperature determinations, carried out by Schweizer, suggested that all of the pieces, genuine and forgery alike, were fired at very low temperatures in the region of 650° to 750°C.

The study of the surface encrustations was more revealing. The genuine pieces had a hard grey encrustation that was difficult to physically remove or scratch, whilst the pieces shown by TL to be recent had a soft white encrustation that had only poor adhesion. Tests with nitric acid showed that the encrustation on the genuine ceramics had a high calcite content, but the soft white encrustation was in fact an applied white clay. Ceramics buried in the calcareous soils of the Haçilar area would be expected to form a calcite-based encrustation, whereas the clay coating on the forgeries would have required they be buried in a white clay deposit, which, as Hodges put it, 'seems fairly improbable' and even then calcite should also have been present. It also suggests that no technical or scientific examination had been carried out before purchase by any of the museums concerned. This seems extraordinary when a minute sample could have been quickly and positively identified by XRD, and thereby have cast considerable doubt on the authenticity of the pieces.

The revelation that a high proportion of the unprovenanced pieces on the market and purchased by leading museums were forgeries achieved what the Turkish antiquities authorities were unable or unwilling to enforce, that is the cessation of the clandestine excavation of the material. The market for the pieces had been killed stone dead.

This still leaves open the questions of the source of the genuine but unprovenanced ceramics and why so many reputable museums around the world were so eager to purchase material that their curators must have known were illegal exports and had been clandestinely dug up in circumstances which necessarily destroyed valuable information about the culture as a whole. As Mellaart stated in the introduction to the report on the excavations (1970, I, p. vi) the whole affair was 'one of the most tragic chapters in the history of archaeology'.

Classical earthenwares
Greek black and red figure wares
Sources: General: Boardman (2001). Technology: Noble (1988); Schreiber (1999). Scientific Examination: Bimson (1956); Tite *et al.* (1982a), Kingery (1991); Jones (1986); Maniatis *et al.* (1993). Authenticity: Kurz (1948, pp. 228–233); Cuomo de Caprio (1993); von Bothmer (1998).

Perhaps the most familiar and collectable classical ceramics are the Attic and Corinthian painted vessels produced in Greece in the centuries around the mid first millennium BC. These include the black figure wares, where the figures are depicted in black against a red background, followed in the fifth century BC by the red figure wares where the figures are red against a black background. The painted surfaces are often very shiny, but although some vitrification has been shown to have taken place, the surfaces are probably best described as glossed rather than glazed. They have often been emulated, either as innocent copies or as conscious forgeries. In the mid-nineteenth century the potters Vincenzo Fiorins and Antonio Scapini produced superb copies of Greek vases, which were meant to celebrate the revival of the Greek achievement and as such were usually signed by their creators.

Alongside these honest imitations, forgeries were being produced, especially in Italy, from at least the early nineteenth century. The white-slipped *lekythos* were very popular subjects for forgery, particularly as the surviving original vessels were prone to be in a very worn condition (Kurz, 1948, p. 229). A common expedient is to take a genuine but plain vessel and embellish it with a painting in a style that is at least approximately contemporary (von Bothmer, 1998). Sometimes this is done on broken vessels or even mere sherds that would otherwise be worthless.

The seemingly intractable technical problem with the black and red figure wares was how the lines were produced in both black and in red in a single firing, since the pigment for both black and red was iron oxide. If the painted pot had been fired under oxidising conditions it would all be red, and if under reducing conditions it would all be black. A combination of pigments could have been used, iron oxides for the red and manganese oxide for the black, with an oxidising firing for the pot. Manganese pigments had been used for millennia previously (Noll *et al.* 1973; Noll, 1979; Jones, 1986, pp. 762–763; and see p. 198), but for whatever reason the Greeks did not use this method. Forgeries using manganese black have a slightly purplish hue and would be easy to detect analytically. It should be noted here that manganese derived from the surrounding soil can be deposited on ceramics during burial by microbiological activity (Daniels, 1981 and see p. 191).

The Greeks used a paint containing the orange–red iron oxide, hematite, and possibly some hydrated iron oxide, goethite. The paint that was to be black had additions of a potash-rich illite clay where the silicate clays are in the form of tiny plates, whereas the red paint had no such additions. After painting, the pot was fired initially in oxidising conditions and all the painted areas would fire red, with the iron pigment in the form of hematite. The kiln was then banked down, making the conditions reducing, whereupon the painted surfaces all went black as the iron pigment changed to black magnetite and some soot was absorbed. At this stage the illite clays sintered across the surfaces painted with them. The conditions in the kiln were then restored to an oxidising regime and the iron oxides in the exposed areas once more changed to the red hematite form, but the illite-painted areas were sealed from the oxygen and thus remained black.

Legitimate copies using the correct technique are now made in the Mediterranean lands, often using clays that are very similar to the originals and thus technical examination and elemental analysis alone would not necessarily differentiate them (Figure 9.7). One could perhaps expect absorption of some minerals from the soil, notably phosphates

Figure 9.7 Copy of Greek vase painting. (Right) Copy of ancient lekythos, BM GR 1973.6–12.1, using same painting technique as that on the right. (Left) Genuine lekythos, BM GR 1864, 10–7, 180. (© British Museum)

during prolonged burial in the calcareous alkaline soils typical of the Mediterranean (p. 191). TL testing would be the most appropriate and certain scientific method of identifying modern pieces.

Roman Arretine and Samian wares
Sources: Johns (1971); Roberts (1997).

The Romans used the jolleying technique to produce the embossed Arretine and Samian wares (see p. 187). Such antiquities, being themselves replications, are especially easy to copy by use of the appropriate technology. Thus Georges Colas, of 'Les Saules' Coulange les Nevers, France, who made Samian copies, could state that his copies were 'réalisés à la main, par estampage, à partir des moules antiques'. These are legitimate copies, but forgeries do seem rare. The designs on the moulds were impressed into the soft clay of the unfired moulds with clay punches, also known as *punzen* (German) or *Poinçons* (French) and these, together with the moulds themselves, have been quite extensively forged either for the production of forged vessels or as antiquities in their own right as revealed by TL (Bailey and Bowman, 1981; Bémont and Gautier, 1985, 1987; Heilmeyer, 1989; Porten Palange, 1990). Examination showed that some of the more unusually elaborate scenes impressed into the moulds had been made up of several apparently genuine stamps glued together, their origin being betrayed by the join leaving a distinct line on the mould (Offmann *et al.*, 1995). Clay lamps, which had been normally wheel-thrown by the Greeks, were usually moulded by Roman times (Bailey, 1972), as are most forgeries of all periods (Bailey, D.M. 1960; and see Chapter 1, p. 3, Figure 1.1).

The Samian wares have a beautiful and distinctive red gloss paint, based on the same technology and clays that were already used by the Greeks for their red and black wares. Although much studied, the nature of the gloss has still not yet been fully understood or been convincingly or accurately copied. As Colas also noted in his 1982 catalogue, 'Le vernis rouge est une imitation, le recette antique n'étant pas redécouverte'.

Large moulded terracottas
Ceramics have also been used as a medium for large sculptures, usually in terracotta, in many parts of the world (Penny, 1993, pp. 201–214). They are much reproduced as innocent copies or as forgeries (Fleming, 1979c, pp. 154–159), as exemplified by the cult figures from West Africa (see Chapter 6, p. 115), Renaissance reliefs (Kurz, 1948, pp. 145–155), and, most spectacular of all, the great Etruscan terracotta figures.

Case study: The Etruscan terracottas

There is an absurd story going around that our t.c. dollies are modern and the work of Fioravanti . . . and I don't propose to pay any attention to it.
 Gisela Richter, curator of Classical Antiquities in the Metropolitan Museum of Art, quoted in von Bothmer and Noble (1961)

Sources: von Bothmer and Noble (1961); Parsons (1962); Jeppson (1971, pp. 157–190); Johnson (1973); Sox (1987).

A series of major Etruscan terracotta forgeries, all from Italy, but by different forgers, have succeeded in duping some of the major international museums from the 1860s on (Fleming *et al.*, 1971). The story starts with Pietro and Enrico Pirelli, who were both masons entrusted with restoring two badly damaged but genuine terracotta sarcophagi. The sarcophagi were very fragmentary and a good deal of imaginative restoration and even creation was needed to make them saleable, so much so that the brothers thought that they could produce their own from scratch. They did so with such success that their creation, an Etruscan sarcophagus, was purchased by the British Museum from the well-known dealers Domenico Fuschini and Alesandro Castellani, and for over 60 years the Castellani tomb, as it was known, was displayed as a major item of Etruscan art (Jones (ed), 1990, pp. 30–31).

Following on the initial success, Fuschini persuaded Pio Riccardi, patriarch of a family of artist–craftsmen, to set up shop in Orvieto, which in antiquity had been a centre for the production of major terracotta works of art, and thus a likely centre from which new works could be expected to appear.

And appear they did. In the early years of the twentieth century many terracotta architectural plaques came on the market, seemingly from a major, but unknown temple, somewhere in the vicinity of Orvieto. Most of these were acquired by the National Museum, Copenhagen and the Metropolitan Museum of Art, New York.

Pio's son Riccardo, and his lifelong companion Alfredo Fioravanti, together with Riccardo's cousins, Teodoro and Virgilio, decided on more ambitious pieces. They commenced with an above-life-size (2 m tall) statue of an Etruscan warrior (the Metropolitan Museum's *Old Warrior*). A large slab of clay forms the base, upon which the feet and lower limbs up to the knees were modelled in solid clay. The thighs and torso were modelled from tubes of clay. The *Old Warrior* and the other gigantic terracottas would have required enormous furnaces and very considerable skill to fire, neither of which the Riccardis possessed. However, they solved this problem quite simply. The completed figure was carefully painted, dried to leather hardness and then broken into many pieces which were then fired. Because of the high content of sand and grog fillers, there was very little distortion of the pieces on firing, such that they fitted back together again after firing and any pieces that manifestly did not join were simply knocked off as part of the convincing damage.

Years later in New York, when the ceramics expert Charles F. Binns examined the fragments of the *Old Warrior* he estimated that the figure had been fired at approximately 960°C and marvelled that there could not have been a difference of more than 20°C between the head and feet of the figure. Furthermore, he estimated that the Etruscans, after the maximum temperature had been attained, must have slowly cooled the piece over a period of months so that the vast ceramic did not crack. The alternative, more prosaic explanation, that it had neither been fired intact nor moulded by the Etruscans, seems never to have occurred to him. More recent forgeries of large terracotta Etruscan-style plaques dating from the 1960s have been fired in the same manner (Fleming *et al.*, 1971, p. 145).

In 1916 the fragments of the *Old Warrior* were at last being assembled in New York, at the Metropolitan Museum of Art before an excited curator of classical antiquities, the redoubtable Gisela Richter, who enthused 'How beautifully the painted patterns are preserved'. This was hardly surprising as they were in fact less than five years old at the time. Some of the fragments developed new cracks soon after arrival in New York, which again should have aroused suspicions in pieces purportedly fired over 2000 years previously.

Flushed with success (and money), the Riccardis decided on an even more impressive piece, a colossal terracotta head. The new head was 1.4 m tall when reassembled from the 178 fragments in which it was delivered to the Metropolitan Museum, which calculated that it must have come from a statue standing fully 23 feet (7 m) tall.

In 1919 an even bigger, better and more expensive piece appeared, an entire striding warrior standing some 2.7 m in height (latterly known as the *Big Warrior*).

The earlier pieces acquired by the Metropolitan still had not been published as the fruitless quest continued for the temple at which they had supposedly been found, and for more pieces. In both pursuits the Metropolitan's agents were destined to disappointment, for in 1919 while work on the *Big Warrior* was still in progress, Riccardo was killed in a riding accident. Bereft of his soul-mate, Fioravanti would create no more major works.

The three warriors were not publicly displayed until 1933, and Richter's monograph on them was delayed for a further 4 years until 1937. Only then could serious debate begin, and the major doubts held by many for years, especially in Italy, emerged in print. Unfortunately some of the early attacks used ill-informed technical evidence. In 1950, for example, M. Cagiano de Azevedo claimed that the cracks in the paint on the warriors were due to drying agents in the putative organic varnish. Unfortunately for this argument, there was no varnish – the cracks were due to differential shrinkage of the paint on the ceramic body. In 1955 the Italian art expert, Pico Cellini, claimed that ground glass from Peroni beer bottles had been added to the clay as filler. This was a stupid accusation to make with no evidence other than hearsay, and technical examination showed there was no ground glass present.

However, the rumours continued and doubts grew rather than diminished, such that a major art historical and technical study was undertaken by Richter's successor, Dietrich von Bothmer, together with John Veach Noble (1961), who had already carried out detailed studies of the techniques associated with Greek ceramics production (1988). Von Bothmer found stylistic faults aplenty, and Noble asserted that the *Big Warrior* and the others could never have been fired intact as they lacked vents, which were present on the other known genuine Etruscan major terracottas and necessary to allow the water vapour to escape during the drying and firing of intact pieces.

Noble also carried out spectrographic analysis of the pigments and discovered that they contained manganese, which he had not encountered on contemporary Greek painted pottery. In fact manganese-containing pigments *were* used by the Etruscans, as exemplified by the study of a terracotta head, now in the Le Musée d'art et d'histoire de Genève, Inv. no. 22009 (Schweizer and Rinuy, 1981, 1982). This head has been stylistically dated to the fifth century BC and its antiquity confirmed by TL. A combination of XRD and XRF identified both red iron oxide, hematite, and the mixed iron-manganese oxide, jacobsite, thus enabling red and black colors to be produced in one firing.

Meanwhile, back in Italy the American freelance art historian cum dealer, Harold W. Parsons, had been carrying out his own researches into the origins of the big terracottas, etc. (Parsons, 1962). In 1960 he confronted Fioravanti and obtained not only a full confession and the whole story of the production of the Warriors, but he got the missing thumb from the Old Warrior. Armed with a cast of the statue's thumbless hand, von Bothmer crossed the Atlantic and met up with Parsons and Fioravanti. The latter's detailed story was credible, but the perfect fit of the terracotta thumb into the plaster hand put the matter beyond all doubt. Parsons was also instrumental in the unmasking of yet another great terracotta sculpture, but this was not to be accomplished without a bitter dispute.

The investigation and eventual unmasking of the life-size terracotta figure the *Diana* (Figure 9.8) was above all else symptomatic of the uncertainty, suspicion and lack of communication between collectors, dealers, agents and even curators. The story is something of an eye-opener for those outside the world of antiquity dealers, and goes some way to showing why forgery can flourish, even when the forger is known. It also demonstrates why disclosure is the best policy and the sort of mess that otherwise can be envisaged should withholding of information in authenticity cases ever become general (see Chapter 1, p. 17). The terracotta, one of Alceo Dossena's most spectacular forgeries, purported to be ancient Greek work and was sold to the St Louis City Art Gallery as such in 1952, 15 years after Dossena's death, and 25 years after his exposure (see Chapter 11, p. 242, for more on the

Figure 9.8 The terracotta figure of Diana, photographed in many pieces roped together in the workshop of Alceo Dossena after having been deliberately broken to make it appear more genuine. (Courtesy Lusetti, 1955)

career of Alceo Dossena). Amidst the general critical praise for the figure there were other dissenting voices, such as Bieber's critical 1958 review of Herbig's 1956 supportive monograph. Parsons, with Cellini, decided on an unusual but quite devastating attack, the publication of a photographic record of Dossena's choice pieces, ostensibly in a biography by his son Walter Lusetti (1955). The 51 photographs were mostly taken of pieces in Dossena's workshop before they had appeared on the market and entered world-famous collections, including the *Diana* (Lusetti, 1955. Plates 7 and 8) (see Figure 9.8 and Chapter 11, p. 244, Figure 11.2). The impact of this little work, published in Rome, was initially slight in America, and even after Parson's 1962 article, which directly condemned the *Diana*, the St Louis Gallery continued to support the piece as genuine and very publicly attack Parsons. Finally, in 1968 the Museum had TL tests carried out on the terracotta (Fleming, 1975, pp. 90–91) (two actually, because they refused to believe the modern date given to the statue the first time round). And so 30 years after Alceo Dossena's death and 13 years after it was first publicly exposed, the St Louis Museum finally accepted, officially at least, that their *Diana* was not ancient. The Museum even allowed its inclusion in the major exhibition on fakes and forgeries in 1973, organised by the Minneapolis Institute of Arts, although with the proviso in the catalogue that 'there are still those who will tell you that the battle is not over' (Johnson, 1973, Cat. 21).

Authentication examination of della Robbia forgeries by Bouquillon and Gaborit (1998) included TL, PIXE and ICP analysis. The TL testing was able to distinguish between the Renaissance and nineteenth-century pieces but the compositional and technical analyses were much more equivocal.

Moulded and cast ceramics

Sources: Rich (1947, pp. 39–44); Penny (1993, pp. 165–190).

Moulded ceramics are perhaps the most attractive to forgers, be they Egyptian *shabti* figures, Chinese funerary figures, Greek Tanagra figurines, Pre-Hispanic Mesoamerican figures or eighteenth-century European slip-cast figurines where the clay

was poured into the mould. This is because it is easy to make a mould from an existing genuine piece and it is possible to make many figures from the mould. Furthermore, the technology is correct whereas in most authenticity studies, signs of moulding would be regarded as suspicious. One important problem for the forger taking moulds from existing figures is shrinkage, typically of about 10% on firing. Occasionally original genuine moulds have been found, in burial deposits, etc. and used either to make further copies directly or as an inspiration to the design and execution of new moulds, as exemplified by some Pre-Hispanic American anthropomorphic vessels (see p. 200) and some late nineteenth to early twentieth century copies of Chinese Tang terracottas (Fleming, 1974).

If the moulded pieces are made of the correct clays, and many of the forgeries are made from the same clays as used for the originals, and decorated and fired appropriately, it can be virtually impossible to distinguish new from old except by TL (but see Chapter 6, p. 115 for some of the methods used to circumvent the TL tests).

The technique of moulding goes back to the very inception of the use of ceramics. By the third millennium BC ceramic *shabti* figurines were being produced in Egypt from simple two-piece moulds, and latterly forged by the same method (Wakeling, 1912, p. 47, Plate VI.4; Jones, 1990, pp. 249–250; Eisenberg, 1998).

The Greeks produced terracottas of some sophistication from two-piece ceramic moulds (Higgins, 1976), as exemplified by the fine Hellenistic figurines originally found with burials at Tanagra, in Boeotia, Greece, which were extensively forged (Higgins, nd, pp. 63–78; Jones (ed), 1990, pp. 169–171, Cat. 176). TL testing of about 300 Tanagra figurines from various German collections, showed about 20% to be nineteenth-century forgeries (Goedicke, 1994). Etruscan moulded terracotta figurines are also regularly forged, and revealed for what they are by TL (Kohler, 1967; Gschwantler and Bernhard-Walcher, 1984).

Forgeries of Roman terracottas may be exemplified by a series of figures of Athena Parthenos now in a number of European museums. Prag (1972) originally believed them to be copies from the same mould and produced in the second century AD. Latterly (1983), TL testing of some of the figures showed that their clays still retained much of their natural TL and had not been heated above 500°C, thus effectively being unfired. It is very difficult to envisage how figures of unfired clay could survive burial for thousands of years and therefore it is likely that all the pieces are modern forgeries, although it is possible that the mould from which they were taken was ancient.

Moulded ceramics have a long tradition in China especially for use as tomb furniture, representing models of farmsteads right up to entire armies of life-size figures (Penny, 1993, pp. 168–173). The large glazed figures of horses, camels and attendants from tombs of the Tang period began to be seriously collected outside China in the early twentieth century (Fleming, 1975, pp. 79–81), and very rapidly were being forged on a considerable scale, sometimes original moulds being used (Karlbeck, 1957; Savage, 1976, p. 193). A Professor Yetts visited a factory just outside of Beijing in 1912 where he observed 'hundreds of newly-made figures. Comparison of these with the genuine originals which had served as patterns proved that certain modern replicas may defy detection' (quoted in Kurz, 1948, p. 240). Kurz noted that this trade was still flourishing, and that 'seeing that a large part of the original tomb figures were nothing but serial products, made from a limited number of moulds, there is no considerable difficulty in multiplying existing shapes by further moulding. The clays as well as the firing can be matched without much difficulty'. The ceramic copies of the soldiers of the Terracotta Army on sale in Xian and other places at the end of the twentieth century do but continue the tradition (Figures 9.9 and 9.10).

The various moulded ceramics of the indigenous cultures of the Americas have been very extensively copied and forged. The ceramic figurines of Mesoamerica, Peru (Jones (ed), 1990, pp. 229–230) and Ecuador (Baumann, 1980), together with moulded portrait pots – pre-Colombian South America's equivalent of Toby jugs – have all been copied since the mid-nineteenth century for sale

Figure 9.9 Modern terracotta figure of a seated deity sat in one half of a two-piece mould prior to removal and firing at Xian, China, 1994. (A. Giumlia Mair)

Figure 9.10 Modern reproductions of soldiers of the Terracotta Army and other figures for sale at Xian in 1994. (Courtesy P. Craddock)

to tourists and institutions. As in many other parts of South and Mesoamerica the commercial viability of forgery was and is dependent on the quantity of genuine pieces coming onto the market from clandestine excavations (see Chapter 6, p. 118). Sometimes the original moulds were buried along with their products in the tombs of potters, and the copies from these are virtually indistinguishable from the ancient vessels, especially as the same sources of clay were used. Since the appearance of TL testing, the antiquities market has had to adapt, and now genuine but simple or damaged pots are extensively altered and repainted (but not re-fired of course).

Porcelain and other fine ceramics

Sources: General: Sandon (1997). Chinese: Medley (1980); Kerr (1986); Vainker (1991); Harrison-Hall (1997); Carswell (2000). Japan: Jenyns (1974).

Islamic: Savage (1954); Tite (1989). European: Kingery (1986); Tite and Bimson (1991); Freestone (1999a, b); Gleeson (1998).

See also the *Transactions of the Oriental Ceramic Society* and the *Transactions of the English Ceramic Circle*.

Porcelain was the great ceramic technical achievement of the Chinese, first made in the mid first millennium AD. For the next 1000 years and more, potters, first in the Islamic lands of the Middle East and Central Asia, and latterly in Europe, attempted, more or less successfully, to imitate the appearance of the true Chinese porcelain (Carswell, 2000). In Post-Medieval Europe a range of ceramic bodies that were similar to those of the true porcelain were developed, such as soft paste (which is relatively low-fired) porcelain and bone China. Some of them are still in production, together with true hard paste (that is high-fired) porcelain, identical to the real Chinese porcelain (Freestone, 1999b).

True Chinese porcelain is a vitreous, translucent white ceramic body, which usually has a fine glazed surface. The ceramic body contains the minerals quartz, mica, kaolin and feldspar. These minerals occur naturally in the kaolin clays and the petuntse or porcelain stone, composed of feldspar, mica and quartz, which is found at Jingdezhen in southern China (Harrison-Hall, 1997; Tite *et al.*, 1984). This is the traditional centre of the Chinese porcelain industry and continues producing wares in traditional styles using much the same technology and the same raw materials.

The early European attempts to produce porcelain were dogged by a failure fully to understand the nature of the ceramic or to have access to the necessary kaolin clays. The first serious European attempt to produce a material that at least looked like porcelain was made at Florence in the later sixteenth century. The so-called Medici porcelain had a body rich in lime and quartz with a minimum of clay. This fired to a glassy-calcium silicate mass. The results were not good with a very high failure rate, such that the venture soon closed and few pieces survive.

More successful 'glassy' soft porcelains began to be made at St Cloud in France in the late seventeenth century, and by the 1740s other factories had become established at centres such as Chantilly, Mennecy and Vincennes, the latter moving to Sèvres under royal patronage in 1756. For these soft paste porcelains a glassy frit was made from ingredients such as soda, sand, gypsum and lime; this was ground and mixed with the clay. In Italy, silica-rich bodies were developed at factories such as Capodimonte.

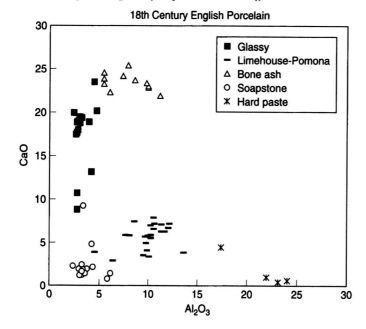

Figure 9.11 Plot of the calcium and aluminium contents of a range of English eighteenth-century porcelain types. Note the very high calcium content of the bone ash porcelains (see Table 9.1). (Courtesy Freestone, 1999b)

Table 9.1   Some eighteenth-century English soft paste and bone China, showing their characteristic main element compositions (see Figure 9.11).

	Typical English Porcelain Bodies				
Factory	*Chelsea*	*Worcester*	*Bow*	*Coalport*	*Limehouse*
Period	1745–49	c.1760	1755–60	1825	1745–48
Body	Glassy	Soapstone	Bone Ash	Bone China	Clay-rich
SiO_2	62.8	72.3	51.2	43.0	72.4
TiO_2	0.2	<0.2	0.3	<0.2	0.8
Al_2O_3	4.9	3.4	5.6	13.6	10.7
FeO	0.2	0.4	0.3	<0.2	0.5
MgO	0.3	11.0	0.6	0.5	0.7
CaO	20.1	1.9	23.2	17.4	7.1
Na_2O	0.8	1.4	0.6	1.6	2.8
K_2O	5.3	3.3	0.6	1.6	3.0
P_2O_5	0.3	0.3	15.3	21.2	<0.2
PbO	4.4	5.7	0.4	<0.3	1.0
SO_2	0.2	0.2	1.9	<0.2	<0.2

Weight per cent. Analyses by SEM-EDXA. Total iron as FeO. Errors typically c. 5% relative for oxides greater than 10%, c.10% relative for oxides greater than 2%.
Source: Freestone, 1999b

Soft paste porcelain was also made by some famous British producers such as Bow, Chelsea and Derby, with each factory developing a series of distinct soft paste bodies. Technical developments in porcelain production in Britain were quite complex during the eighteenth century and the changes in the composition of the ceramic bodies of many quite well known potteries are still not fully charted (Figure 9.11 and Table 9.1) (Freestone, 1999b). For about 100 years from the mid-eighteenth century, soapstone was used as a porcelain additive in Britain by potteries such as Vauxhall, early Worcester and Swansea. Soapstone, also known as steatite or talc, is a hydrated magnesium silicate and deposits occur in

Cornwall that are very pure with little or no iron. Soapstone was often use in conjunction with glass and silica for which clean iron-free sand or calcined flints was the usual source.

Another British approach to the problem of producing a white-firing body was the addition of calcined cow bones. Through the second half of the eighteenth century bone ash was added to the clay and ground glass soft paste bodies, by potteries such as Bow and Lowestoft, to give what is now called bone ash porcelain. After about 1800 the bone ash began to be added to the kaolin clays and feldspar-rich porcelain stones that had just begun to be exploited in Britain for true hard paste porcelain. Bow and Worcester were among the first to make what is now known as bone China, and production still continues.

The discovery of the true nature of the Oriental hard paste porcelain was made by Johann Friedrich Böttger, chemist and would-be alchemist, in the first decades of the eighteenth century whilst in the employ of the Elector of Saxony at Meissen (Kingery, 1986; Gleeson, 1998). The Elector was a keen collector of Chinese ceramics, and also of alchemists, as poor Böttger was to discover when he tried to leave. His first porcelain was made using the kaolin clays from the mines near Colditz mixed with a little gypsum, but this was then replaced by formulations based on kaolin with feldspar-rich stone (see Swann and Nelson, 2000, on PIXE analyses to differentiate genuine Böttger ceramics from copies and forgeries).

Thus for several decades in the early eighteenth century Meissen had a virtual European monopoly of the production of stonewares and porcelains that were technically very similar to those of the much-admired Chinese imports. Production of hard paste porcelain only slowly spread across Europe. Vienna was one of the few other major producers of hard paste porcelain in the eighteenth century.

In Britain the development of hard paste porcelain followed on the discovery of kaolin deposits in Cornwall. Factories were established, the first at Plymouth in the late 1760s, but production was soon moved to Bristol. Production also started at New Hall in Staffordshire in the 1780s, but here there was a change over to bone china in the early nineteenth century.

Within the broad categories of porcelain body there was considerable variation, and idiosyncrasies abound. The glassy porcelain produced in the early days of Longton Hall, for example, is rich in gypsum, often retaining crystals of calcium sulphate in the fired ceramic body, thus making it quite distinctive (Freestone, 1999a, b).

Over the past half-century the compositions of a wide range of ceramic bodies of prestige pottery and porcelain, both in the East and in the West, have been identified and their chronological ranges defined against which suspect pieces can be tested.

Fakes and forgeries of fine ceramic wares and porcelain

The formidable extent of the lurking, manifold and almost inescapable dangers waiting to ensnare the collector of Chinese ceramics is universally acknowledged.

So wrote Otto Kurz in 1948 (pp. 233–234) and half a century later, Jessica Harrison-Hall (2001, p. 571) could report that:

20 years later [from the 1980s] the technical advances in the production of fakes in mainland China, Taiwan and Japan are staggering.

Sources: China: Kurz (1948, pp. 233–247); Lang (1986, 151–168); Battie (1999, pp. 16–31); Allen (2000). Europe: Elliot (1939); Kurz (1948, pp. 248–257); Arnau (1961, pp. 170–177); Mills and Mansfield (1979, pp. 50–63); Lang (1986, pp. 169–192); Gaimster (1992); Sandon (1997); Battie (1999, pp. 32–51).

The Chinese have always imitated their earlier wares. The rest of the world copied the Chinese wares, especially the porcelains, to produce their own fine wares. Once these became collected they too were copied and forged. For example, the faking of early Iranian ceramics began in Iran almost immediately after they began to be collected from the mid-nineteenth century (Jones (ed), 1990, pp. 225–226). More recent ceramics are also collected and forged, as exemplified by the Russian porcelain dishes decorated in the Supremacist style in the early years after the 1917 Revolution (Lobanov-Rostovsky, 1990). It now seems likely that in addition to copying their own wares, the Chinese are now imitating European antique porcelains, and Sandon (1997) has estimated that approximately one sixth of the porcelain he saw offered for sale at country auctions in Britain were oriental forgeries.

Even pieces made as innocent copies could latterly be represented as being originals, sometimes with the genuine contemporary stamps and inscriptions removed and replaced with fallacious marks. In fact the alteration of fine ceramics, either to change their attribution or their decoration is another well-established area of faking (see p. 208).

The main producers of copies of fine Chinese ceramics have always been the Chinese themselves. Very often these copies have been made in the same factories as the originals using the same materials and technology. In the Ming and Qing dynasties excellent copies of Song period porcelain were produced quite openly and legitimately. Where they retain their contemporary stamps there is no problem. However, as stylistically it is often difficult to tell more recent copies from the original works, much of the present scientific study of Chinese ceramics is directed towards the objective differentiation between the original work and the later copies. Although the general recipes for the composition of the ceramic bodies may not have changed much through the centuries it is reasonable to expect some change in the proportions of the main components (see p. 191).

The serious collection of antique Post-Medieval European ceramics, notably majolicas, German stonewares and early porcelain, began in the mid-nineteenth century and rapidly became very popular (Jones 1990 (ed), p. 212). Inevitably, the onset of serious forgery was coincident with the onset of serious collecting.

The methods and scale of production of ceramics is perhaps wider than for almost any other antiquity or art object, ranging from the individual hand-moulded life-size terracottas to near-identical porcelain dishes that were produced by the thousand in factories by semi-industrial processes. Clearly this is going to affect the approach to the production of copies and even the viability of forgery. The production of innocent copies of some early ceramics in quantity might not now be viable by the original laborious hand technology, and the forging of some antique ceramics that were produced by semi-industrial processes requiring very considerable investment to replicate would also not be viable (see p. 186).

The German stonewares of the fifteenth to seventeenth centuries were hand thrown, and the decorative elements added as separate pieces (*sprigs*) that had been shaped by pressing the clay into a small mould. When the stonewares became fashionable again in the nineteenth century, legitimate copies began to be made (Gaimster, 1992, 1997, pp. 335–343; Jones (ed), 1990, pp. 204–206, 209–210). Some craft potters such as Peter Löwenich and Hubert Schiffer made their copies by hand throwing, but it was not feasible to make affordable copies of the often large and heavy vessels in quantity by the traditional methods, and instead firms such as C.W. Fleischmann made them by moulding. Some forgeries were hand thrown, sometimes

with the sprigged decoration using genuine sprig moulds picked up from the waste tips of the original potteries.

Where the pieces had been moulded, visual examination, possibly supported by radiography, should expose the nineteenth-century copies, but where the vessel had been thrown and the decoration applied from convincing sprigs there could be difficulties. Hook in Gaimster, 1997 (pp. 344–353) had some success distinguishing between the clay sources by NAA, but remarked that where the same clay source had been used it would be difficult to differentiate Renaissance originals from nineteenth-century copies. The use of TL is equivocal because the difference in age between the genuine pieces and the copies is not great, typically of the order of 300 years. However, despite the caution expressed in Gaimster (1997, p. 338), a stoneware tankard in the style of those made by the Frechen family in the sixteenth century, and with silver mounts hall marked for London 1576/7 (Jones (ed), 1990, Cat. 216a, pp. 20–46), was tested and gave a TL date of 1860 ± 40 (Gaimster, 1992, p. 110). The most likely explanation is that the stoneware is a replacement for a broken piece and only the mounts are original.

The problems posed by the copying of ceramics that had originally been made in quantity by semi-industrial processes can be exemplified by European eighteenth-century porcelains. Here a very considerable outlay in materials and equipment would be necessary. This might be a viable investment where production of a large number of copies was envisaged, but it would be a different story for the production of a relatively limited number of forgeries.

Mills and Mansfield (1979, p. 54) discussed this point in some detail after a visit to the Royal Worcester Porcelain works where they watched legitimate copies of some of the eighteenth-century wares being made. They commented on the large number of highly skilled operations and the considerable investment in apparatus necessary. At that time labour costs in Britain were high and the genuine pieces could be bought for a few hundred pounds, and hence forgery was not viable. But as Mills and Mansfield pointed out, in the nineteenth century when the necessary skills were readily available together with a large number of small pottery firms and labour costs were low, the forgery of complex and sophisticated pieces was very viable. They could not see into the future and predict the current tide of copies and forgeries of all manner of collectable ceramic wares, both Oriental and Occidental, imported from the Far East where the skills are available and labour costs low, in response to the enormous rise in prices for the originals.

The nineteenth century saw a great rise in the production of good copies of the arts and crafts of previous ages including ceramics and glass (Savage, 1976, pp. 146–153; Lang, 1986, pp. 169–191).

Ornate pieces such as the elaborately moulded and colored ceramics produced in Renaissance France by Bernard Palissy (1510–1590) were copied by French craftsmen such as Charles Avisseau, Renoleau, and many others, mainly based in Paris, the so-called Palissystes (Katz and Lehr, 1996). Another important centre for copies inspired by Palissy was in Portugal (Katz, 1999). The authentication of genuine pieces by TL and the analysis of the clays, is discussed by Amico (1996, Appendix IV, pp. 241–243).

Other examples of this type of copy include the excellent imitations of sixteenth-century Italian majolicas and Turkish Isnik wares produced in Italy by craft firms such as Cantogalli of Florence and Ferruccio Mengaroni of Pesaro (Jones, (ed), 1990, Cat. 210, pp. 198–200; Battie, 1999, pp. 32–33).

Samson et Cie

> *There are few collectors who, at some time or another, have not been deceived by some of Samson's work.*
>
> Savage (1954, p. 208)

Sources: Savage (1954, pp. 286–287; 1976, p. 158); Jones (ed) (1990, Cat. 230, pp. 214–215); Battie (1999, pp. 34–35, 44–45); Slitine (2002).

Some firms made copies in a whole range of styles, and produced their wares on a very considerable scale. Of these none is more famous than Samson et Cie of Paris. Samson copies are now collected in their own right and, inevitably, forged.

The firm began in 1845 when the potter, Edme Samson, was asked to make replacement pieces for an important porcelain dinner service. His replacements were so successful that other commissions came and soon he had established a business making replacements. From there it was a small step to making copies of a wide range of porcelains, both Oriental and Occidental as well as enamels (see Chapter 10, p. 239), and copies poured forth for over a century until the firm's closure in the 1970s.

The firm always had an uneasy relationship with dealers and collectors over the question of deceptive copies. Samson maintained that they produced innocent copies which were distinctively marked either with an SS, or with blue crossed lines, reminiscent of the Meissen crossed swords, or with a square red 'chop' mark on their copies of Oriental pieces. These were often positioned alongside imitations of the original marks. Battie (1999, p. 35) believed that in the final years of the company the SS marks were sometimes omitted, and Savage (1954, p. 117) made the point that although Samson generally marked their wares, the marks could be, and were, easily removed with acid or by grinding. Furthermore, Samson must have known this was going on, and that a proportion of their production was being disguised and sold as original. In their defence it must be stressed that they made no attempt to imitate the appropriate materials – all their work was in hard porcelain no matter what the original. Thus, some of their most successful imitations were of Chelsea soft paste porcelains which really should have deceived no one (Adams, 2001, pp. 190–195). However, imitations of Meissen hard paste porcelains, complete with crossed lines, or of Chinese porcelains, are another matter. Copies of cast figurines, etc. were made by moulding original figures and thus the figures cast from these moulds are somewhat smaller than the originals due to shrinkage.

The weathering and patination of ceramics

Sources: Weathering: Croyn (1990, pp. 103–106). Patination: Aronson and Kingery (1991). Wear: Bray (1982); Hally (1983).

By and large, ceramics do not undergo much chemical change during burial especially if non-porous. The most common form of weathering occurs in porous buried pots that have absorbed salts from aqueous solution. If these salts crystallise they can exert enormous internal pressures in the ceramic causing flaking and the lifting of glazes. This can be replicated by forgers: Savage (1976, p. 194) described how forged Tang glazed figures were deliberately broken and then buried in wet, salty ground and more salt added. After several months' immersion the glaze had an iridescence, albeit not very permanent, and there was flaking present.

Insoluble silicates, sulphates and carbonates can form hard, coherent and very tenacious encrustations on the surface. These are very difficult to replicate. The form of the encrustations is dependent on the burial environment and thus can indicate provenance and be very useful in authenticity work (as examplified by the HAC, KAR ceramics, p. 195).

Aronson and Kingery (1991) studied the distinctive patina found on some early Mexican figurines. Over long periods of burial in tombs, the genuine figures had developed a manganese-rich patina similar to the more familiar rock varnishes (see Chapter 11, p. 256). The structure of this naturally-forming patina of microbiological origin is very different from the artificial patinas applied to the modern copies. The ubiquity or otherwise of these patinas on ceramics seems not to have been well studied, although similar patinas have been observed on other ceramics (Daniels, 1981; O'Grady, 2006).

Many ancient earthenwares such as the Roman Samian wares (see p. 195) are quite calcareous, and in even quite moderately acidic burial conditions the calcareous salts are leached out leaving microscopic but quite characteristic voids once occupied by the lime or shell fillers (Francaviglia *et al.*, 1975; Picon, 1991b; Freestone, 2001).

Conversely, in alkaline environments calcium salts and phosphates can form permanent insoluble deposits inside porous ceramics (Freestone *et al.*, 1985; Freestone, 2001; and see p. 191). An enhanced phosphate content should indicate long burial and, thus, authenticity. Furthermore, the incoming elements have quite characteristic concentration profiles in from the surface (Figure 9.12). Waddell and Fountains (1984) suggested that the diffusion of material into earthenware ceramics could constitute a method of dating. This is unlikely, but it could be a good indication of long-term burial.

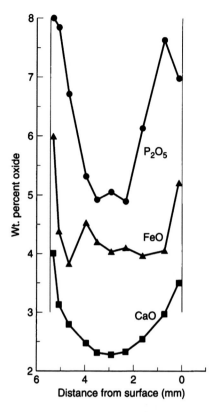

Figure 9.12 Compositional profiles for phosphates, calcium and iron oxides, through a typical Roman Samian pot, absorbed from their burial environment. (Courtesy Freestone *et al.*, 1985)

Glazes

Sources: Technical: Hodges (1964, pp. 42–53); Hamer (1975, pp. 144–148); Rhodes (1977); Vandiver (1990); Trench (ed) (2000, pp. 215–216). Scientific examination: Tite *et al.* (1998).

Glazes are the glassy coatings fired to the surfaces of ceramics. They render the ceramic impervious, protect the surface from crumbling and act as a medium for a wide range of polychrome decoration.

Making glazes

Glazes are formed by the reaction of the glaze *former*, which is usually silica, with a metal oxide *flux* which, on moderate heating, well below the vitrification temperature of the underlying ceramic, react to form a glass. The silica can be in the form of crushed quartz, calcined and crushed flint, as a silicate such as feldspar, or it can be the underlying clay body of the pot. The flux can be metal oxides such as those of lead, sodium and potassium. The

glass so formed tends to be rather unstable and so *stabilisers* such as lime or alumina are added, and in the past these were often present as impurities in the formers and fluxes. The lead was used in the form of the mineral, lead oxide, although very often the lead ore, galena – lead sulphide, was used directly without prior oxidation. The potassium formerly came from a variety of wood and plant ashes, and sodium came either from the mineral natron, found in the Middle East, from the ashes of salt-rich marine plants such as the aptly named glassmaker's wort, or from common salt. Sometimes all three components – former, flux and stabiliser – are combined in one material, notably as in the feldspar rock used by the Chinese for the high-firing glaze on much of their porcelain, with additions of silica or ash as required. A further wide variety of metal oxides were also used as opacifiers and colorants (discussed in Chapter 10, pp. 212, 225).

The clay can be glazed simply by applying the flux to the surface before firing. This was done in the past with some of the lead and ash glazes. The metal oxides in the clay body, mainly of iron, color the otherwise clear glaze. Quite often this was the desired effect, but it can also be a problem. Usually the clay body is fired to a ceramic (the *biscuit firing*) before the glaze is applied (the *glost firing*). In the case of very soluble fluxes such as those of the oxides of sodium and potassium, they are previously heated with silica to form a glass, known as (*fritting*) and then ground before application as a glass powder. Salt glazing is rather different: common salt is thrown into the kiln during the firing and the sodium oxide vapour attacks the silica in the surface of the forming ceramic to produce the glaze directly.

It is important that the glaze contracts to the same degree as the ceramic beneath (known as *fitting*); if it contracts to a lesser extent then the glaze will tend to flake or peel, whereas if the contraction is greater than desired, the glaze will craze or crackle. Crackling is sometimes deliberately induced as a decoration, but if too great it will ruin the surface. Forgers have sometimes deliberately used glazes that will scale, thereby giving an appearance of age; these are particularly prevalent on Tang terracotta forgeries (Fleming, 1975, pp. 79-83, but see Eggert, 2006). Things can go wrong: several glazed terracottas by Ferrante Zampini, the nineteenth-century forger of Renaissance pieces, showed an alarming propensity to scale several months after firing, which led to his unmasking (Mills and Mansfield, 1979, pp. 188–189).

The sequences of glazing that are possible are shown in Figure 9.13. If the ceramic is to be decorated, the painting may be done first in an *underglaze* painting scheme with the colorants in a hard glaze, fired and then covered by a transparent main glaze. Alternatively, the main glaze may be painted with a further *overglaze* or *enamel painting*. This would be a soft glaze containing the colorants, fixed by the *enamel firing*.

Glaze history

The earliest glazed materials were stones, quartz and steatite from Egypt and the Middle East in about the fourth millennium BC (Moorey, 1994, pp. 168–171; Tite *et al.*, 2002), followed by faience (see Chapter 10, p. 210). Pottery only began to be glazed from the mid second millennium BC, coincident with the first production of glass. The early glazes in the Near and Middle East are all alkali glazes, probably fritted, with the sodium coming either from mineral natron or from plant ash.

In China the story is very different, due in part to the availability of much more refractory clays. There, hard glazes of ground feldspar were being applied to stonewares from about 1500 BC.

Lead-glazed ceramics appear all over the Old World at the end of the first millennium BC. In the late first millennium AD, as one of the responses to Chinese porcelains, Islamic potters developed pottery with a fine white tin oxide-opacified lead glaze (Mason and Tite, 1997). These wares proved

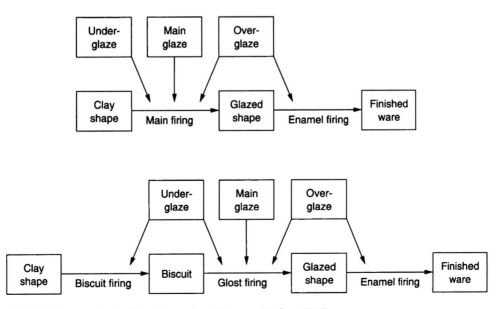

Figure 9.13 Various methods of applying a glaze (Courtesy Hodges, 1964).

extremely popular in the Islamic world as well as in Christian Europe, well exemplified by the Ottoman Isnik wares (Tite, 1989). Similar glazes were popular in Islamic Spain, and from there spread all over Europe, exemplified by the Italian maiolica, faience wares in France and Delft wares in Holland.

Salt glazes were developed for glazing stonewares in Europe from the Late Medieval period. Production has now almost totally ceased, in Europe at least, owing to environmental concerns over the emission of hydrochloric acid fumes into the atmosphere from the kilns.

Scientific examination

Scientific methodology has advanced very considerably since Bannister and Plenderleith (1936) carried out what was probably the first scientific authenticity study of a glazed artefact, which they were able to confirm was an ancient Egyptian scarab of glazed steatite, using UV.

Many porcelain glazes display very characteristic colors when exposed to UV, and thus comparison of suspect and genuine pieces can be very revealing. For example, Savage (1976, p. 297) noted that the glazes on many Samson imitations have a very distinctive mustard-yellow color under UV.

Yap (1986c) developed a rapid, non-destructive XRF technique for the trace element determination of ceramics, including the glazes on Qing, Republican and modern Chinese porcelains. With the problems of modern forgeries in mind, criteria were established to differentiate post World War II pieces from earlier porcelains.

As with glasses generally, the presence of elements only introduced in recent times can be a good indicator of a recent origin. Colorants such as chromium (green) and uranium (yellow) oxides have proved especially useful. For example, the Dougga people of southern Tunisia traditionally used copper salts to color their glazed wares but in more recent times they have instead changed to the use of glazes containing the mineral wollastonite, colored green by a small quantity of chromium (Colomban *et al.*, 2001a). Colomban *et al.* (2001a, b) have also characterised glazes on porcelain using RS.

Faking glazes

Perhaps the most contentious and difficult area in ceramic authentication lies in the detection of improvements or alterations of decorative glazes. These come in many forms and with as many motives in both East and West. Elliot, at the start of his classic 1939 paper on fakes of European porcelain, listed some of the varieties of alteration and these, together with others, can include:

1. the decoration of plain pieces
2. the addition of decoration to pieces with a simple or common design
3. the addition of a mark to an unmarked piece, or a piece from which the original mark has been removed
4. the removal of the existing enamelled design and its replacement with a rarer or more ambitious decorative scheme.

It was quite usual for plain white glazed pieces to leave the factory for decoration elsewhere and thus considerable stocks of such plain pieces often accumulated and they could sometimes come onto the market, notably when the factory ceased trading. For example large stocks of undecorated Vienna porcelain were sold off in 1864, each piece correctly marked in underglaze blue and some with date numerals. Similarly, stocks were sold off from the works of Samson et Cie in the 1960s. The Sèvres factory lost large quantities of undecorated stock in the early years of the Revolution and in 1848 the directors of the firm took it into their heads to sell off the undecorated seconds on a regular basis, thereby causing the markets to be flooded with genuine Sèvres porcelain with fake enamel painting. The seconds were later marked with a stamp impressed into the clay, but it was easy either to fill in the impression with a cement or to grind it out before decorating and reglazing.

The scientific detection of such pieces would depend on the examination of the pigments and enamel glaze materials, since the porcelain body is genuine.

Regarding points 2 and 3 in the above list, the additions are painted on followed by reglazing. The removal of existing marks can be easily achieved by grinding them out or by dissolution with hydrofluoric acid. The new mark can then be painted in and reglazed.

Once again scientific examination would have to concentrate on the nature of the pigments and enamel materials of the overglaze painting.

With regard to point 4, the existing genuine but mundane enamelled decoration is removed (known as *stripping* or *skinning*) by grinding or acid dissolution, and replaced with a more elaborate scheme (known as *clobbering*). Battie (1999, p. 37) gives an example of a mid eighteenth century Meissen dinner plate that was apparently worth about £20 before

Table 9.2 Ceramic paint materials recorded as having been used by Höroldt at Meissen (2nd column) and some of the elements detected by PIXE (3rd and 4th columns).

Color	Material*	Pigment**	Modification
Yellow	Naples yellow	$Pb(SbO_3)_2$ or $Pb_3(SbO_4)_2$	Lighter colors: addition of **SnO_2** or **ZnO**
Blue	Cobalt carbonate blue	$CoCO_3$ precipitation	
Green	Copper green	Incineration of brass (**Cu, Zn**) or **Cu**	Green of grass: copper green + yellow, bluish green: copper green + smalt (**Si, K, Co**)
Purple	Ducats + tin	Precipitation of **Au**- and **Sn** solution	
Red	Iron red	**Fe_2O_3** (+Al, Si) from iron ore	**Fe_2O_3** from natural rust or artificially gained from steel sheets + acid
Brown	English umber	**Fe_2O_3** (+**Mn** oxide) natural earth pigment	
Black	Brownstone + cobalt carbonate	**Mn** oxide, **$CoCO_3$**	

Source: Neelmeijer *et al.*, 2000a

*Mixed with colorless enamel (lead oxide + quartz), lead oxide: (i) minium **Pb_3O_4**, (ii) litharge **PbO**, (iii) carbonate of lead 2 **$PbCO_3$·$Pb(OH)_2$** + quartz **SiO_2**.

**PIXE/PIGE detected the chemical elements marked in bold.

being stripped and converted into a presentation plate; repainting with a much more ambitious scheme made the plate realise £19 000 at auction.

Scientific examination again would be limited to the materials of the paints and glaze. Neelmeijer *et al.* (2000a) for example used PIXE, PIGE and RBS to analyse eighteenth-century porcelain. They compared the composition of pigments found on the ceramics with that of those known from surviving documents to have been used by Meissen in the eighteenth century (Table 9.2). This has enabled spurious and misidentified pieces to be exposed.

It is often difficult to remove the interior glaze from a vase by grinding, and so it is allowed to remain. Thus there is a junction between the original interior glaze and the new exterior glaze that is often on the rim of the pot.

Otherwise, examination of the surface of the ceramic in strong raking light can be very informative, revealing traces of grinding activities or changes of use. Thus, for example, in the case of the cobbled plate described by Battie, examination revealed quite heavy wear, consistent with a dinner plate's frequent contact with knife and fork, but hardly with a presentation piece displayed in a cabinet. Evidence of heavy localised scratching can suggest that grinding has occurred. Where grinding and redecoration has taken place the scratches will pass beneath the new enamelled decoration, whereas ordinary wear and tear should pass over the decoration. Also, a fresh scratch on most glazes has a rather jagged edge, but the re-firing tends to partially re-melt the glaze smoothing out the edges.

In all of the cases where re-firing of the old piece is necessary, considerable problems can arise for the faker. Over the years the ceramic body will have absorbed moisture, which is trapped beneath the glaze. On re-firing, unless the piece is very slowly and carefully heated to dry it out there exists the possibility of water vapour bursting through the old glaze at a number of points giving a very recognisable speckled surface (also known as *spit back* or *peppery*). There is the additional danger that old glazes, having become partially devitrified, do not re-fire well but crack and spall, or become discolored.

10

Glass and enamels

This chapter deals with glass and enamels but commences with a section on their precursor, faience. Glass gem simulants are discussed in Chapter 16 (p. 405) and glazes on ceramics are discussed in Chapter 9 (p. 206).

Faience

Sources: General: Moorey (1994, pp. 166–186); Friedman (1998); Nicholson and Peltenberg (2000). Scientific Examination and Analysis: Vandiver (1982, 1983); Kaczmarczyk and Hedges (1983); Tite and Bimson (1986); Mao (2000).

First of all a potential confusion must be clarified; faience to the ceramicist, especially if French, is an earthenware ceramic with a tin-opacified lead glaze, but to the archaeologist faience artefacts are the small items made of sintered quartz with a colored glaze. The latter is one of mankind's earliest synthetic materials and continued to be made alongside glass in Egypt and the Middle East through Classical antiquity and survived in some remote parts until the recent past (Wulff *et al.*, 1968). The glazed faience can sometimes be difficult to differentiate from cast glass. For example, the fine moulded miniature head of Augustus Caesar that adorns the front cover of the catalogue of the prestigious *Glass of the Caesars* exhibition (Harden, 1987) was subsequently found to be of faience.

The manufacture of faience was quite sophisticated compared with contemporary ceramic techniques. The artefact was modelled from a paste made up of crushed quartz with small quantities of alkali such as the naturally occurring sodium bicarbonate, natron. This was carefully heated to a temperature that allowed the quartz to begin to fuse at the edges, but not to fully vitrify, the shape of the artefact thereby being retained, although the surface became glazed. This alkali glaze often contained small amounts of metal salts, especially copper or antimony to provide color. There seems to have been a variety of methods by which faience was made and glazed and these have been intensively investigated in recent years (see references above). As such it should be possible to check technology and composition against style for suspect pieces.

Analysis of faience artefacts, particularly from prehistoric European contexts, have been made to try to establish if they were imported from Egypt or were a local product (Stone and Thomas, 1956 etc.). While these studies were not particularly successful, they do suggest that it may be possible to analytically fingerprint faience from particular sources. Thermoluminescence (TL) dating has been applied (Fleming, 1979c, p.159).

Glass

Sources: General: Barrington Haynes (1959); Harden *et al.* (eds) (1968); Newman (1977); Blakemore (1984); Tait (ed) (1991); Lierkes (ed) (1997); Trench (ed) (2000, pp. 200–210); Davison (2003). Ancient Glass: Harden (1968, 1969, 1971, 1987); Grose (1989); Moorey (1994, pp.189–215); Stern and Schlick-Nolte (1994); Fleming (1999); Nicholson and Henderson (2000); Stern (2001); Whitehouse (2001a). Islamic: Liefkes (ed) (1997, pp. 26–35); Ward (ed) (1998); Carboni and Whitehouse (2001). Europe: Baumgartner and Krueger (1988); Tait (1991b); Venice: Tait (1979); Henderson (1998a).

See also the *Journal of Glass Studies* and the *Annales de L'Association Internationale pour l'Histoire du Verre*.

Technical history of glass

Sources: Composition: Brill (1999); Wedepohl (2003). Technical: Hodges (1964, pp. 54–63; 1970); Douglas and Frank (1972); Cummings (2002); Davison (2003, pp. 73–169). Islamic: Stern and Schlick-Nolte (1994, pp. 27–96); Gudenrath (2001).

Composition

Glass is a state of matter, not a composition, only the silicate glasses used for artefacts through the ages are considered here. Glass is defined as a supercooled liquid, that is the molecules are not arranged into any regular structure, but are disordered (Figures 10.1a and 10.1b). As a consequence, glasses do not have precise melting points but when heated the solid steadily softens, becoming more mobile as the temperature rises, although silicate glasses never become free flowing liquids that can be easily poured in the manner of molten metals (see p. 214).

The first synthetic glasses were the glazes produced on suitable stones or on faience bodies. Only from about the mid second millennium BC were they used independently of any support as the material now known as glass.

Glasses comprise a former, fluxes and stabilisers. The former usually makes up the bulk of the glass and is invariably silica, derived from a variety of sources. When heated with fluxes, which are usually oxides of the alkali metals or lead, the regular crystalline structure of the silica is broken up and the resulting irregular mixture of silica, metal oxides and silicates sets as a glass. A glass of silica and alkalis alone is not very stable owing to the solubility of the oxides (see p. 234). When natural materials were used the impurities present in the former or flux stabilised the glass. Otherwise, deliberate additions of alumina or lime have been added. Glasses were often whitened or colored with opacifiers and colorants.

The source of the silica glass former could either be crushed quartz, as already used in faience, or clean quartz sand, free of iron oxides; otherwise, the glass would be dark green or black. Crushed quartz was very pure and if this was used then separate additions of lime might have been necessary to stabilise the glass. In the Middle East and Egypt the sands used as glass formers usually contained small amounts of calcium and aluminium minerals which acted as stabilisers. In early times the fluxes were invariably alkalis, derived either from the ashes of some maritime or desert plants rich in sodium and potassium, as well as some calcium and magnesium, or alternatively, from natron, such as that obtained from the Wadi Natron in Egypt, which is almost pure bicarbonate of soda. The glasses can thus contain varied but characteristic amounts of sodium, potassium, calcium, aluminium and magnesium, depending on the sources of the materials used (Table 10.1).

It seems that up to early first millennium BC in the Mediterranean region, plant ashes were the usual source of the flux, but were then replaced by natron, which continued to be used through the Hellenistic, Roman and early Byzantine world. Desert and maritime plant ashes supplanted natron in the Early Islamic period in the production of a soda lime glass with a high magnesia content (Gratuze and Barrandon, 1990; Henderson, 2002). In temperate Medieval Europe ashes of trees, rich in potash, began to be used as fluxes, and potassium oxide was the key flux in the so-called forest glass.

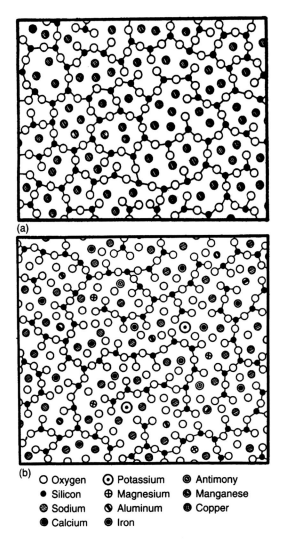

Figure 10.1 (a) Disordered arrangement of atoms of silica former and soda flux in a simple soda glass. The black atoms represent silicon, the white, oxygen, and the grey, sodium. (b) Disordered arrangement of various former, flux, stabilisers, opacifier and colorant atoms that could be expected in a typical Roman glass. (Courtesy Senmamat Chaudrai, 1985).

O Oxygen ☉ Potassium ◉ Antimony
● Silicon ⊕ Magnesium ◉ Manganese
◑ Sodium ◐ Aluminum ⊕ Copper
● Calcium ● Iron

Table 10.1   Typical composition of occidental glasses through four millennia.

	Egyptian 15th cen. BC	Roman 1st cen. AD	European 13th cen. AD	Syrian 14th cen. AD	Modern
Silica, SiO_2	65	68	53	70	73
Soda, Na_2O	20	16	3	12	16
Potash, K_2O	2	0.5	17	2	0.5
Lime, CaO	4	8	12	10	5
Magnesia, MgO	4	0.5	7	3	3
Batch Materials	plant ash quartz	natron sand	wood ash sand/quartz	plant ash sand/quartz	synthetic components
Glass Category	High Magnesia	Low Magnesia	Forest Glass	High Magnesia	

Source: Freestone, 1991, p. 40

This was used for window glass and poorer quality vessels. Fine quality glass, such as that produced in Venice, still relied on plant ash imported from the Eastern Mediterranean (Jacoby, 1993). In Post-Medieval Europe a variety of alkali-lime compositions were used (Mortimer, 1995; Wedepohl, 2003).

Everyday modern clear glass typically consists of approximately 75% silica, 15% sodium oxide and 10% calcium oxide; flint glass is comprised of between about 30 and 70% of silica, 15 to 65% of lead oxide and 5 to 20% of sodium and or potassium oxides.

The early Islamic world experimented with lead glasses – possibly learnt from the Chinese – and lead glazes had been produced by the Romans and Byzantines. Lead glasses were made in Europe (Wedepohl *et al.*, 1995), but did not become popular until the Post-Medieval period (Henderson, 1998a).

In early South and East Asia, glass was of less importance as a material than in the Middle East and Europe. The technical history of Chinese glass is very different from that in the West (Brill and Martin (eds), 1991). The earliest Chinese glasses, dated to the first millennium BC, are lead–barium and lead glasses, and there are some Han period glasses with mixed potash and barium oxide fluxes (Shi *et al.*, 1987). From the Tang and Song periods there are some lead glasses as well as potash–lime and soda–lime glasses that use nitre as the source of the alkali, together with lime and gypsum. Nitre, also known as saltpetre, is a mixture of sodium nitrate with other alkalis such as sodium carbonate and common salt.

Later Chinese glasses have a wide range of composition, reflecting local traditions and European contacts, using feldspar and quartz as the formers,

lead, potash and soda fluxes with fluorspar and arsenious oxide as opacifiers (Warren, 1977; Yang Boda, 1991). From the eighteenth century there was also a considerable import of European glass as a raw material (Redknap and Freestone, 1995). This should be kept in mind when considering the origins and authenticity of later Chinese glasses, glazes and enamels based on their composition alone. Genuine Chinese pieces of the eighteenth century could well have been made with imported European glass.

Glass has been made in India from the first millennium BC (Sen Mamata Chaudhuri, 1985; Bhardwaj (ed) 1987; Brill, 1987; Singh, 1989). In the past, vessel glass never seems to have been significant, but there has been an enormous production of glass beads and bangles (see p. 233). The glass formers are river sands, and the fluxes are mainly potash and soda obtained from the alkalis known as *reh,* which effervesce from the soils in Bihar and Uttar Pradesh, and are rich in silica, nitre and soda with some lime and alumina. Alternatively, the fluxes can be obtained from the sodium minerals recovered from the salt deposits of certain lakes such as Lake Sambhar in Rajasthan and Lake Lonar in Maharashtra.

Within this very broad outline there are very many more specific compositional groups (Brill, 1999; Wedepohl, 2003).

Glass can be either transparent or opaque (Turner and Rooksby, 1959, 1961). Opacity can be the result of many small air bubbles in the glass, as exemplified by the Post-Medieval European cotton-twist glasses (Barrington Haynes, 1959, pp. 254–261). The opacifier in ancient white glass was usually calcium antimonite; tin oxide seems not to

Table 10.2 Opacifiers used through the ages.

Period	Type of glass	Opacifying agent	Number of specimens
1450 BC to fourth century AD	Opaque white and blue	$Ca_2Sb_2O_7$ (occasionally $CaSb_2O_6$)	15
	Opaque yellow	Cubic $Pb_2Sb_2O_7$	10
	Opaque red	Cu_2O	
		$Cu_2O + Cu$ } or Cu	8
Fifth century AD to seventeenth century AD	Opaque white and blue	[SnO_2 usually	10
		[$3Ca_3(PO_4)_2.CaF_3$ occasionally	4
		Cubic Pb_5SnO_4	17
	Opaque yellow and green	Cu	
	Opaque red	Cu + Cu_2O rarely } Cu + SnO_2 sometimes	7
Eighteenth century AD to present day	Opaque white	$3Pb_2(AsO_4)_2.PbO$ (apatite-type structure)	4
		CaF or CaF_3 + NaF	Many
		$(Na_2Ca)_2Sb_2O_6F$	1

Source: Richter, 1994

have been generally introduced until the first millennium AD. Thereafter, it was the usual opacifier up to the nineteenth century. In the eighteenth century, lead arsenate opacifiers were used, notably at Venice, and arsenic continued to be added to glass. In the mid-nineteenth century, fluorides were introduced as opacifiers in Europe but were used earlier in China (Table 10.2).

In antiquity, colorants included cobalt and cupric copper ions for blues and greens, manganese for purple, and iron sulphide chromophore for yellow. Small amounts of iron oxides made the glass green; more iron could be deliberately added to make it appear black. Opaque glasses included the orange–red cuprite and yellow lead antimonate glasses. Reds were typically formed by minute particles of copper metal or of cuprous copper oxide in the glass. New metal ions were introduced as colorants in the nineteenth century, notably chromium, the presence of which is a good indication that the glass is not ancient (see p. 225). Conversely, both manganese and antimony oxides were added as decolorants, usually to counteract iron oxides present in the silica.

From the Post-Medieval period in Europe the composition of glass became more complex with the deliberate addition of a variety of other metal ions, such as zinc and, latterly, boron but with fewer minor and trace elements, since alkalis, etc. from the chemical works replaced natural materials.

Glass-shaping

Sources: Ancient: Schuler (1959a, b; 1962); Hodges (1964, pp. 54–63); Grose (1989, pp. 31–36); Gudenrath (1991, pp. 213–241). Recent: Cummings (2002).

Early glass was extensively worked by abrasion, grinding, wheel cutting and drilling for small items, especially seals, intaglios and cameos (see Chapter 16, p. 416). The Egyptians occasionally carved vessels out of solid blocks of glass, using the same technology as was used to make the contemporary stone vessels. The distinctive surface weathering and pitting of cold worked glass surfaces has been described by Pilosi and Wypyski (2002b; and see p. 231).

More ambitious overall abrasion or deep and intricate undercutting was practised by the Romans. The former technique is exemplified by the Roman cameo vessels, including the famous Portland Vase now in the British Museum (BM GR Reg. 1945, 9–27, 1) (Haynes, 1975; Harden, 1987, pp. 58–67).

Eisenberg (2003, 2004) suggested, on stylistic and iconographic grounds, that the Portland Vase should be dated to the Renaissance. This thesis was subsequently encouraged, after a fashion, by Lierke

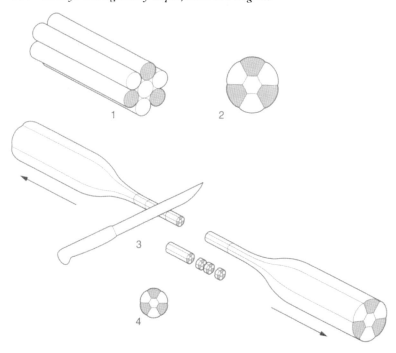

Figure 10.2 Making mille-fiore glass. (1) rods of differently colored glass brought together; (2) heated and fused; (3) stretched and cut; (4) The small pieces of mosaic glass ready for use in beads, vessels, etc. (Courtesy Davison, 2003).

(2004) on technical grounds. However, 20 years previously Bimson and Freestone (1983) and latterly Freestone (1991, Figures 3.4–3.6) had carried out a comparison of the compositions of Roman and Renaissance glass, including the Portland Vase. The composition of the Portland Vase is quite typical of Roman glass but different from that produced in the Renaissance in Italy. The small amount of lead detected in the white glass is only found in Roman opaque white glass up to the mid first century AD, to which time the Vase is ascribed stylistically (reiterated by Freestone, 2003 and Walker, 2004).

Lampwork or flamework

This very simple technique must have been practised from the dawn of glass-making, consisting simply in manipulating blobs of glass kept softened by a small heat source (the eponymous lamp) (Schuler, 1970). The glass could be pulled out into rods; one piece could be stuck to another, and glass trails wound around pieces. Attractive pieces could be made, especially if colored glasses were used. *Millefiore* glass probably developed from these simple doodles (Stern, 2001). Bundles of differently colored glass rods in whatever pattern is required are fused together in a furnace and pulled, creating miniature patterns (Figure 10.2). The 'thousand flowers' could then be sliced from the ends of the rod and used as beads (Figure 10.3) or inlays, or fused with other glass to decorate or even to form vessels.

Casting

The casting of glass has a long history (Schuler, 1959a; Grose, 1989, pp. 376–377). Because of the viscosity of molten glasses a variety of special methods evolved. The glass could be ground up into a fine, free-flowing powder that could be poured into the mould and melted (Figure 10.4). Alternatively, the glass could be ground to a fine powder, made into a paste with additional flux, pressed into a mould and melted. Another approach was to mix the glass powder with a little glue and mould it into a free standing shape that could be fired until the glass fused.

Cooney (1960) discussed ancient Egyptian glass castings, pointing out that many forgeries exist. The forgeries tend to be hollow cast, whereas the few genuine early pieces are solid. Some of the pieces questioned by Cooney on stylistic grounds were later analysed and found to contain appreciable quantities of lead oxide and alumina, but had a quite low soda content, very different from the prevalent soda glass used in New Kingdom Egypt at the time these pieces were supposed to have been

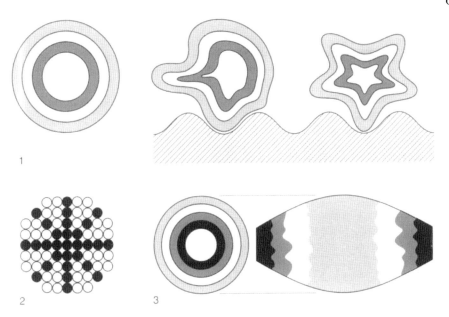

Figure 10.3 Stages in the production of a mosaic bead. (Courtesy Singh, 1989)

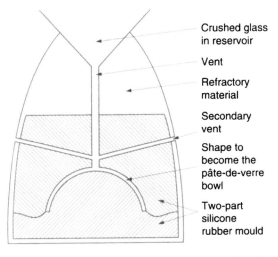

Figure 10.4 Casting glass in a mould by adding the glass as a finely crushed powder. (Courtesy Davison, 2003)

made (Brill, 1999). Cooney also questioned some ancient Egyptian cast glass canopic jars housed in the British Museum, glass being an unusual material for such vessels. Subsequent analysis showed the glass to contain 22% of lead oxide, which would be extraordinarily high for ancient Egyptian glass. It also contained about 1% of arsenic, which was not added to glass until the Post-Medieval period (Jones (ed), 1990, p. 282; Cat. 310) (cf. the Egyptian blue glass head from the Louvre; see p. 224).

Core-formed glass

Early glass vessels were usually shaped around a clay core (Schuler, 1962; Hodges, 1964, pp. 56–58; Grose, 1989, pp. 31–35; Cummings, 2002, pp. 46–55; Davison, 2003, pp. 88–90;) (Figure 10.5). The core could have been dipped in molten glass, but more probably a paste of ground glass and an adhesive was applied to the core and then heated to fuse it. Alternatively, a spiral of softened glass could have been wound around the core (Figure 10.6). The glass so formed around the core would then have been rolled while still soft on a flat surface to create a smooth flat surface (known as *marvering*). The core was usually removed to make a functional vessel, but often sufficient material adheres to the glass to enable thermoluminescence (TL) authenticity testing to be carried out.

The early blue-glass vessels were often decorated by winding trails of colored glass around the still soft body glass of the vessel, combing to produce a pattern if required, and then marvering to push the trail into the body glass (Figure 10.7). Having made the body of the vessel, the flared rim would usually be added separately together with handles, if required. These early cored vessels have been forged for many years (Eiland, 2003, 2005).

Moulding and pressing

Glass can also be shaped by pressing the heat-softened glass into or onto a mould. At its simplest a disc of glass could be pressed over a domed mould,

Labels in Figure 10.4: Crushed glass in reservoir; Vent; Refractory material; Secondary vent; Shape to become the pâte-de-verre bowl; Two-part silicone rubber mould

Figure 10.5 Typical Egyptian core-formed vessels. Those on the left and right have a trailed and marvered decoration. (Courtesy A. Milton/British Museum)

thereby forming the moulded inner surface of an open vessel, a process known as *slumping* or *sagging*. Alternatively, a vessel could be made by coil building with lengths of softened glass around the mould. The sophisticated *reticelli* glass was made with multicolored coils, either coiled directly against the template and heated to fuse and amalgamate them, or first made into a flat disc that was then moulded over the former. Sections of *millefiore* glass could be fused together either into a disc which was then moulded over a template, or created directly on the template and then heated. If the first technique is used, the outer *millefiore* pieces will tend to be stretched. These glasses were finished by very thorough grinding and polishing. Technically good imitations were made in the nineteenth century, notably by Venetian glassmakers (see p. 230).

Pressed glass

Sources: General: Trench (ed) (2000, pp. 392–393). Technique: Lattimore (1979); Cummings (2002, pp. 134–140).

Press moulding of glass was developed as a mass production technique from the beginning of the nineteenth century and is much used to imitate cut glass. The softened glass or glass powder is pressed into the mould with a plunger, forcing it into the mould details. The plunger can push right into the mould forming the interior of a vessel.

Although pressed glass is extremely common, moulded glasses of high quality manufactured by

sought-after makers, particularly in North America, have been forged. This is well exemplified by the study of moulded glasses originally believed to have been made by Mutzer in the USA in the late nineteenth century, but which are now believed to be more recent forgeries (Lanmon *et al.*, 1973). Sometimes the patterns used to make the moulds were reused long after original production had ceased. Thus, in the 1920s, nineteenth-century patterns were used to produce new moulds for innocent copies of glassware that are now sold as antique (Peterson, 1963; Hajdamach, 1986). Note that American glass producers have been required to add marks distinguishing reproductions as such since the 1970s, although these can be ground out.

Pressed glass can be detected where the glass was forced into the interstices of the mould by the lines of tiny air bubbles, together with the characteristic flow lines known as *striae*. Larger bubbles are often distorted in the direction of the glass flow.

Glass-blowing

Perhaps the single greatest innovation in glass-making was the invention of glass-blowing in the Eastern Mediterranean around the mid first century BC. It rapidly spread around the Roman Empire, transforming glass-making into a major industry (Schuler, 1959b). A gathering of molten glass was made on the end of a long iron pipe – the blowing iron – and blown to form a hollow bulb. Almost immediately two types of glass-blowing emerged, free-blowing and mould-blowing (Figure 10.8). With free glass-blowing

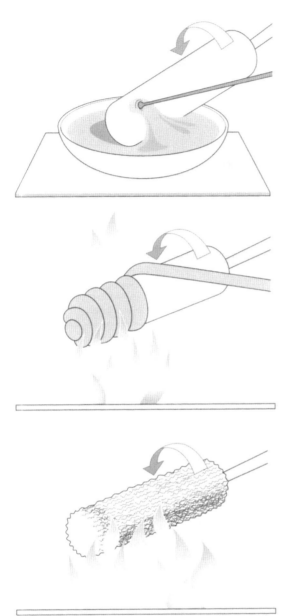

Figure 10.6 Ways of forming a glass vessel around a fired clay core. (Top) dipping; (Middle) winding; (Bottom) crushed glass. (Courtesy Cummings, 2002)

the bulb could be shaped by marvering. With mould-blowing the glass was shaped by blowing the bulb in a hot two-piece mould. Soon quite intricate shapes were being blown, including human heads, etc. Early blown glass tends to be very thin and usually contains many air bubbles. Imitation 'bubbly' glass is still made (Hajdamach, 1986) (Figures 10.9a and 10.9b).

The blown glass is thinnest adjacent to the blowing iron but it is usually desirable to have the thinner glass at the top or rim of the finished glass. Thus to make an open vessel or drinking glass the blown bulb was transferred from the blowing iron to a lump of soft glass on the end of a *punty* or *pontil* rod. The blowing rod was then removed, and the bulb opened up and smoothed to form the rim (Figure 10.10).

The cooled glass had to be broken from the pontil, leaving the distinctive broken-edged pontil mark (Figure 10.11). This is an obvious characteristic of free-blown glass and as such is widely perceived as a feature to differentiate Post-Medieval European glass from more modern mass-produced moulded glass (Hajdamach, 1986, p. 86). The pontil has been employed since the introduction of glass blowing, the distinctive marks having been found on bases of glass from Roman times onwards. However, while the marks are not uncommon on Medieval Islamic glass, they are very unusual on European glass before the Post-Medieval period.

Sometimes the pontil mark takes the form of a jagged ring, being especially common on vessels with a hollow base, and has been observed, for example, on some Anglo-Saxon glass vessels (Bimson, 1980). In Post-Medieval Europe, glassmakers, especially the Venetians, would sometimes impress the lump of glass on the end of the pontil with pincers to make four points stand proud, resulting in just four small points on the foot ring of the glass instead of the more obvious pontil marks. In the nineteenth century, improved pontils were developed, the foot of the glass being held in clamped iron jaws on the end of the pontil. The evidence for these can be seen on some wine glasses, a slight impression having been left on the upper side of the foot and a distinctive 'Y' or 'T' shape on the underside.

Moulded and mould blown glass does not carry a pontil mark, and the absence of the mark is an obvious indication that the glass may not have been free-blown. However, on engraved and cut glasses it was common to grind out the pontil marks with the grinding wheel, possibly leaving distinctive concentric striations on the base, unless these had been polished out.

Conversely, some makers of mould-blown reproductions in the style of free-blown glasses of the seventeenth and eighteenth centuries, would add a pontil mark to increase the 'antique' effect that their customers expected to see. The more legitimate firms impressed their own maker's mark into the glass while it was still soft.

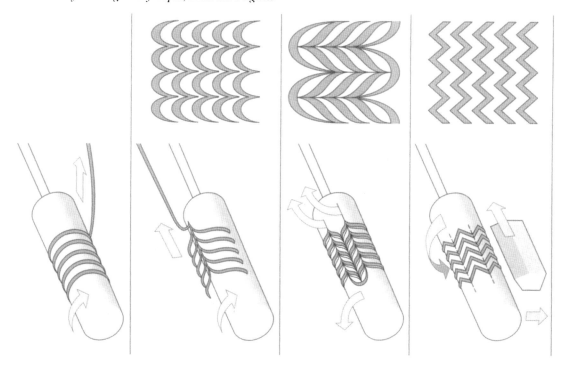

Figure 10.7   Trail decorating a glass vessel.

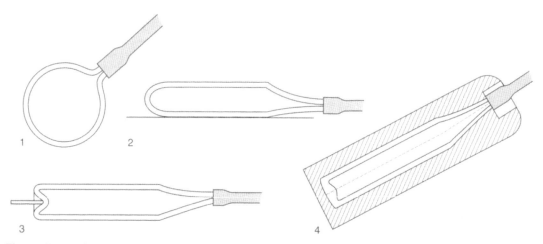

Figure 10.8   Glass-blowing: Free- and mould-blowing. (Courtesy Singh, 1989)

After shaping by whatever method, the glass will have many strains caused by unequal heating and will need to be annealed by careful reheating and controlled cooling. The surface can be polished mechanically or by a quick, but controlled re-firing, known as *fire polishing*.

Glass engraving, etching and cutting

Sources: General: Barrington   Haynes   (1959, pp. 116–125, engraved glass; pp. 131–134, cut glass); Trench (ed) (2000, pp. 108–109, cut glass; pp. 210–213 engraved glass). Islamic: Whitehouse

Figure 10.9a Reproduction teetering on forgery.

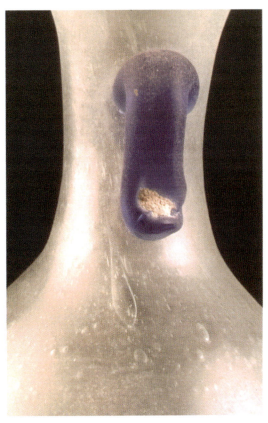

Figure 10.9b This modern reproduction of Roman glass displays many features of ancient buried glass: bubbly glass, etching of the surface, residual soil in the interstices of the handle. Purchased as a modern reproduction in Merida, Spain, 2001. (Courtesy T. Springett/ P. Craddock)

(2001b). Technique: Matcham and Dreiser (1982). Engraving: Seddon (1995); Davison (2003, pp. 96–103). Forgery: Hajdamach (1986, pp. 88–91, cut glass); Seddon (1995, pp. 230–246).

Engraving by point or wheel has been carried out since antiquity (Charleston, 1964, 1965), but is especially prevalent on Post-Medieval European glass.

Engraving or stippling could be performed with a hard mounted point held like a pen. Wheel engraving was widely used in antiquity and revived at the end of the Medieval period in Europe, replacing point engraving (Charleston, 1964, 1965). The cuts made with a wheel are quite distinct from those made with a point (see Chapter 16, p. 412).

Fake engravings usually refer to famous historical events, examples being found relating to the well-known Williamite or Jacobite glasses. They are often added to genuine but plain glasses (Seddon, 1995, pp. 230–246), as exemplified by the engraving carried out by Franz Tieze at the turn of the nineteenth century in Dublin on Irish glass of a century earlier (McConnell, 2004).

Cut glass

Glass has been deep cut since Roman times but from the seventeenth century some European glass was given adjacent deep cuts or facets, creating long prisms to bring out the brilliance and sparkle of the light refracted through them. This developed into a major decorative technique in its own right aided by the introduction of power-driven grinding wheels and the new lead glass which has a brilliant 'fire' when faceted. It became known as flint glass or lead crystal. This was because, initially, crushed flint was used as the former and despite the resemblance to natural rock crystal in clarity, it is not crystalline. Cut glass became very popular and firms such as Waterford (Warren, 1970) and Swarovski (Becker, 1995) are still producing it.

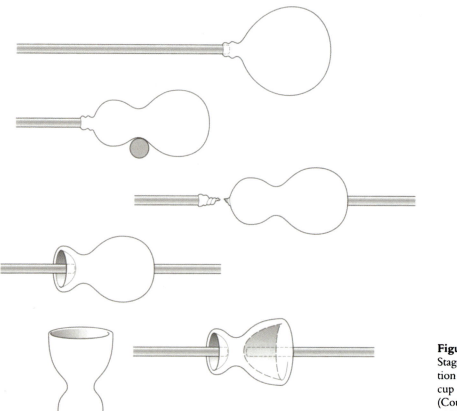

Figure   10.10
Stages in the production of a blown glass cup with a foot ring. (Courtesy Hodges, 1970)

Figure 10.11 Ring pontil mark on the base of an eighteenth-century free-blown bottle where it was broken off after the glass had cooled. (Courtesy T. Springett/ P. Craddock)

The technique of glass-cutting has barely changed since the eighteenth century; as Hajdamach (1986, p. 88) wrote, 'the recognition of cut glass must be one of the most difficult in all glass manufacture'.

There may be differences in the polished surfaces and in the composition that enable early glass to be differentiated from more modern. The early cuts were mechanically polished, but in the twentieth century this was replaced by acid polishing, which removes traces of the wheel marks or grains and gives an overall softer profile to the cuts. Although all are lead glasses, there are probably differences in composition. Certainly, the twentieth-century glass is clearer than earlier glass owing to the greater purity of the formers and fluxes.

It is possible that isotope measurements may be characteristic of the lead used by particular manufacturers (see Chapter 7, p. 139), although relatively little work has yet been done on European sources and determination of the strontium isotope ratios may also prove useful here. The determination of the ^{210}Pb content could determine when the lead was smelted (see Chapter 12, p. 295).

Cut glass lends itself to copying by pressing, but the edges of the pressed cuts are less sharp than those on the original mechanically abraded glasses. Note that in the nineteenth century the pressed designs were often sharpened with a wheel. If the work is well done the evidence of the original moulding in the cuts themselves may be very difficult to see, but the body of the glass may still reveal features such as striae associated with pressing (see below) and casting flashes.

All engraving and cutting, as well as scratches caused during use, creates some micro cracking in the surface of the glass. On buried glass these act as sites where weathering and corrosion pitting can develop such that the original lines are often totally obliterated. Pilosi and Wypyski (2002a, b) have studied the weathering of ancient cold worked glass surfaces and illustrate the characteristic surface pitting found in the incised and abraded lines (NB Lierke, 2002 has suggested that many of these lines are associated with the hot working of the glass). Whatever their origin, the pitting is aligned in the direction of the original lines. The pits by themselves could be artificially induced by acid attack, but not the orientation, as exemplified in the case studies given below (see p. 231). Another feature observed were series of short parallel lines of pitting that develop from the micro cracking associated with the chatter marks made by the wheel. The incipient micro cracking can also develop over long periods into more macroscopic cracks.

Scientific examination and analysis

Sources: Freestone (1991); Lilyquist and Brill (eds) (1993); Gratuze *et al.* (1997); Henderson (2001, 2002); Tite *et al.* (2002); Davison (2003, pp. 227–241); Wedepohl (2003).

Examination with a good binocular microscope is of prime importance. Reflected light microscopy can reveal evidence of the manufacturing process as well as of carving and polishing and whether the designs were cut or moulded. If the glass is transparent, additional information can be revealed by transmitted light. The present of air bubbles demonstrate that the material really is a glass and not a stone. Bimson (1974) was able to distinguish glass from semi-precious stones by microscopy alone in Tutankhamen's treasure. If the bubbles are round this suggests that the original glass was cast; if elongated, the glass is likely to have been worked hot, either lampwork, blown or pressed. Very often the *cords* (separate gatherings of molten glass that have remained distinct through the manipulation and annealing of the glass) and striae follow the line and elongation of the air bubbles, and their combined orientation can be useful in establishing how the

piece was shaped while hot. Abrupt changes can be evidence of repairs.

The surface of much once-transparent glass made opaque by weathering can be rendered transparent by wetting with liquids of approximately the same refractive index (RI). However, badly weathered glasses should not be immersed in any liquids.

Inclusions are also informative. High-magnification light microscopy can reveal the small particles that are to be found in some colorants and opacifiers. Polarising microscopes are useful for examining crystalline material in glass. Examination of the whole glass piece by transmitted cross-polarised light can reveal the presence of strain in the glass, as this causes interference, resulting in distinctive coloring (Figure 10.12). Abrupt changes may reveal repairs or alterations.

Measurement of the RI can be useful in characterising glass if no analytical facility is available. Birefringence of the refracted light is a good indication of strain in the glass and, possibly, of otherwise invisible repairs.

Radiography can be useful in revealing repairs to glass that have been disguised under heavy applied artificial weathering. Lead glasses show up very clearly; for example, nineteenth-century lead-fluxed enamel

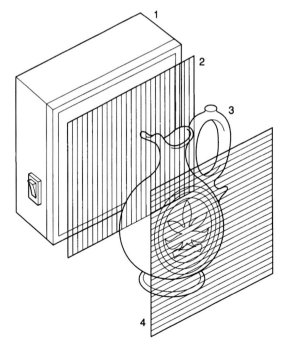

Figure 10.12 Examination of a piece of glass using a polariscope. 1 is the light box; 3 is the piece of glass under examination between the polarising sheets 2 & 4 set at right angles to each other. (Courtesy Hajdamach, 1986)

repairs made to Medieval or Renaissance enamels can be clearly revealed among the original lead-free work (see Chapter 20, p. 522).

UV, either reflected or transmitted, is especially useful for detecting repairs and restoration (Rorimer, 1931, pp. 42–45). Differences in the response to UV, such as the color or opacity of the fluorescence, can indicate different chemical compositions or different treatments. Lead glasses typically fluoresce blue, going to green with increasing lead content. As a general rule Medieval and Renaissance enamels do not fluoresce and Richter (1994; and see Chapter 20, p. 521) used UV as a quick but reliable method to identify areas restored with lead glass on the enamels he was examining. UV has been used successfully to distinguish between the paperweights produced in nineteenth-century France by makers such as Baccarat, Clichy and St Louis and their imitators (Newman, 1977).

Analysis

There are special difficulties in the sampling of glass antiquities and works of art. Even minor marks can be very prominent, especially on transparent glasses, and with a material as fragile as glass there is a very real risk of serious damage. However, samples are usually necessary as very often the surface has weathered to a considerable depth (Cox and Pollard, 1977), typically between 100 and 500 microns, with attendant local changes in composition (Freestone, 2001).

Emission spectrography (ES) has now been almost entirely superseded (Rising, 1999; and see Chapter 3, p. 45) but it is not without its good points for glass analysis. It requires only a minute sample, a full range of up to 40 elements is sought automatically and the method is extremely sensitive, especially in relation to the lighter elements such as boron (see p. 239).

The scanning electron microscope (SEM) (see Chapter 2, p. 24) is useful for examining the characteristic weathering topography and the structures of opacifiers and other minor constituents on fracture surfaces. Where the SEM system only has a vacuum chamber which may endanger the original piece, silicone moulds may be useful (Werner *et al.*, 1975; Meeks, 1987). Analyses can be performed by use of energy-dispersive and wavelength-dispersive X-ray analyses (EDX and WDX respectively) (Verità *et al.*, 1994). Electron microprobe analysis (EPMA) (see Chapter 2, p. 27) has been extensively used in glass analysis (Freestone, 1982; Henderson, 1988), as exemplified by Bronk *et al.* (1999) in their study of a suspect Limoges enamel.

In order to analyse some of the lighter elements by EDX or X-ray fluorescence (XRF) it is necessary to place the glass in a vacuum or in systems flushed with helium. However, many items are too large to fit into the vacuum chambers of older scanning electron microscopes, and badly weathered glass should not be subjected to vacuum conditions in the first instance as there is a danger of the surface bound water quickly evaporating, leading to irreversible crizzling or even macroscopic cracking. Glass inlays and enamels are also at risk of being forced out of their settings under vacuum.

Glasses are not simple structures and to fully study the range of materials present as separate opacifiers, colorants, etc., a small fragment from the unweathered interior must be examined. For EDX analysis it is necessary to remove a sample of about one square millimetre, which is mounted and polished flat. The sample can be cut with a diamond wheel or an edge scored with a stylus and broken off. Understandably for complete glass artefacts such sampling methods are unacceptable and an appropriate sampling technique has been developed using diamond-coated files to remove minute chips of glass, which are completely invisible to the naked eye but are still adequate for acceptable quantitative analysis and structural study by EDX (Bronk and Freestone, 2001).

For quick semiquantitative and non-destructive analyses on unprepared surfaces XRF is very convenient. Sometimes this can reveal damning elements such as chromium in the green coloring, which can be sufficient in itself to condemn a suspect antiquity.

Particle (or proton)-induced X-ray emission (PIXE) and particle (or proton)-induced gamma-ray emission (PIGE) techniques (see Chapter 3, p. 50) are much more sensitive than either EDX or XRF, especially for the lighter elements, and thus enable a wider range of trace elements to be analysed as well as elements occurring in more major concentrations. However, the particle beam can only penetrate for a very short distance into the glass (typically about 10 microns). Thus there are likely to be problems relating the surface analysis to that of the interior where the glass is corroded, and for good quantitative results the surface analysed should be polished flat. Weber *et al.* (2002) employed PIXE to study weathered glass surfaces as a possible dating method and as a means of determining authenticity. Biron *et al.* (1998) in their study of Medieval enamels, undertaken to rehabilitate pieces challenged stylistically by Neil Stratford of the British Museum (see Chapter 20, p. 524), rather pointedly noted that their PIXE apparatus could quantify trace elements that the British Museum laboratory could not even detect.

Atomic absorption spectrometry (AAS) and inductively coupled plasma (ICP) analytical techniques (see Chapter 3, p. 45) have been used to obtain quantitative analyses of a wide range of major, minor and trace elements in glasses. They enable a much more precise and sensitive analysis, especially of the light elements, to be made than with either EDX or XRF. Both methods require a sample of about 50 to 100 mg in solution.

For provenancing work both neutron activation analysis (NAA) (see Chapter 3, p. 51) and isotope analysis (see Chapter 7, p. 139) have been applied to glass. NAA can be used to analyse the whole object provided it is small enough to be placed in the container for irradiation, otherwise the removal of a sample is necessary (Olin and Sayre, 1974).

Radiogenic isotope measurements have concentrated on lead (Brill *et al.*, 1979, 1993). Freestone *et al.* (2003a) used strontium isotope ratios to differentiate between glasses from different sources, and as with stone provenancing studies (see Chapter 11, p. 253), this promises to be an important approach (Figure 10.13).

Brill (1970) and Brill *et al.* (1999) explored the possibilities of using the ^{16}O and ^{18}O stable oxygen isotopes. Their initial analyses suggested that modern glass has very different oxygen isotope ratios from those of ancient glass. In addition, the weathered surface layers of ancient glasses have very different ratios to those of the unchanged glass beneath and Brill and colleagues

argued that it should be possible to differentiate between the oxygen isotope ratios resulting from the very different natural and artificial processes of weathering and, in this way, expose forgeries. An alternative approach could be to demonstrate that there is a more abrupt change in the ratios between the weathered surface and unchanged glass beneath on artificially weathered glass than on naturally weathered glass (see also Bimson and Rose 183; p. 229).

Raman spectroscopy (RS) and Raman microscopy, (RM) of transparent glasses (see Chapter 3, p. 54) is likely to play an increasingly important role in glass analysis (Bertoluzza *et al.*, 1995; Kiefer (ed), 2004; Colomban, 2005). The technique, relying on light, has special potential for translucent glasses, offering the possibility of analysing the contents of gas bubbles, inclusions, etc. within the glass without the need to resort to sampling.

All glasses usually contain substantial amounts of the lighter elements, notably the alkali metals and oxygen, and modern glasses often contain boron, which can be difficult to detect and quantify by the standard physical analytical methods using either electron (SEM/EDX or EPMA) or X-ray (XRF) beams.

The use of composition as an indicator of authenticity

Glass compositions have changed over the millennia, and in different regions, as different sources of the main glass formers and fluxes have been used as well as different types of opacifier and colorant. Modern glasses can have a wide range of deliberate additions, but are all much purer than those made in the past which, translated into compositional terms, means a wider range of minor elements, but lower concentrations of trace elements. Modern glass generally has much lower levels of chlorine than ancient glasses, which typically contain between 0.5 and 1.0% (Pilosi and Wypyski, 2002a). The chlorides originate from the ash of maritime plants or from the natron used as fluxes, and weathered glass can pick up chlorides during burial (Freestone, 2001; Mao, 2000).

Copies or forgeries of early glasses of all periods and cultures were made in the nineteenth and early twentieth century and they are often technically and stylistically very convincing. Fortunately, they were made long before the composition of early glass had been properly studied and have nineteenth-century compositions, which can provide a very good guide to their true age. However, more recent replicas are now of the appropriate composition and could present problems in the future. For example,

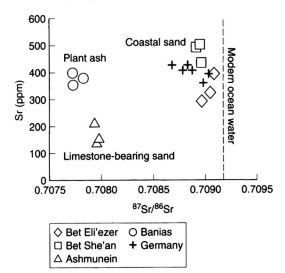

Figure 10.13 Isotope analysis provenancing applied to glass. Strontium contents and isotopic values for Roman period glasses from Egypt, Palestine and Germany. (Courtesy Freestone et al., 2003a)

a wide range of reproductions of Roman glasses are offered by Taylor and Hill (www.romanglass-makers. co.uk) that are specifically stated to be of the correct composition, and with the thin walls, small bubbles and striae typical of Roman glass. There has been no attempt made to artificially age them; instead they are offered in a fire-polished state as they would have appeared when new, and they are very lightly marked on their bases. However, the marks could easily be removed and the glass artificially aged.

Formers, fluxes and opacifiers

Ancient glasses are almost exclusively alkali silica glasses. Lead glasses are generally Post-Medieval, except for some colored glasses. The most important new flux has been borax – hydrated sodium borate (Douglas and Frank, 1972, pp. 85–86). This was first used in Europe in the eighteenth century for top-quality plate glass and for enamels. In the nineteenth century it began to be used for optical glasses as well as becoming a regular ingredient in enamels. Thus boron in a glass would normally be taken as an indication that the glass was modern; however, some ancient Greek glass from Aphrodisias was found to contain about 1% of boron (Brill, 1969). Boron is virtually invisible to many of the current analytical techniques (see p. 223) and consequently has not often featured in authenticity reports.

Case study

One of the finest of the nineteenth-century forgeries employing the wrong flux for the period is the blue-glass head of an Egyptian female, with a dark-blue wig, once attributed to the late eighteenth Dynasty of Egypt, and acquired as such by the Louvre in 1923 (inv. E 11658). Its authenticity was

Figure 10.14   Scarab of King Sheshonq II (c.825–773 BC), BM EA 64203. It purports to be ancient Egyptian but the glass is of the wrong composition, suggesting it is recent. (Courtesy A. Milton/British Museum)

questioned on stylistic grounds as long ago as 1960 by Cooney (who mistakenly described the wig as being of faience). The beautiful opaque sky-blue of the head was one of the features commented on, but analysis by PIXE and PIGE has now shown why it is so distinctive (Biron and Pierrat-Bonnefois, 2002). The glass is comprised of about 28% lead as one of the main glass formers, together with about 12% sodium (all expressed as oxides). There was also about 5% arsenic which, in combination with some of the lead, formed the lead arsenate opacifier. The blue colorant in both the head and the wig is cobalt. Genuine Egyptian glass of that period was a soda-lime glass with, at most, only traces of lead. The blue colorants would have been of copper or cobalt but the opacifier would have been a few per cent calcium antimonate, with no more than small traces of arsenic (Bimson and Freestone, 1988; Brill, 1999; and cf. the blue glass canopic jars in the British Museum, p. 215). Lead glasses with arsenic as opacifiers were common in Europe in the eighteenth and nineteenth centuries and it is to the latter that this head, beautiful though it is, must belong. Examination of the surface of the head showed it had been acid-treated, probably with hydrofluoric acid to give the appearance of age and also to modify the color.

The blue-glass cast scarab in the collections of the British Museum purports to be New Kingdom Egyptian (Figure 10.14). If genuine it should have been a soda-lime glass with a high sodium content (greater than 12% Na_2O) and only a little calcium, whereas in fact it contained little sodium (3% Na_2O) and no less than 15% of calcium oxide (Jones (ed), 1990, p. 282; Cat. 312).

Analytical programmes of more recent glasses can also be useful for authenticity. The technical secrets of Venetian glass were zealously guarded in the Late Medieval period, but inevitably workmen were tempted away, and passable copies made, the so-called *façon de Venise*. Much effort has been expended over many years in trying to differentiate these copies stylistically from the genuine Venetian glass, and there has now been some success in separating contemporary copies on the basis of composition. Bronk *et al.* (2000) and de Raedt *et al.* (2000), using a combination of techniques, were able to differentiate *façon de Venise* made in the Netherlands in the sixteenth century from the contemporary Venetian product. The Venetian glass-makers used chemically rather pure silica from quartz pebbles and specially prepared soda. The copies were much more impure and used a variety of fluxes including soda ash, potash, potash–chalk mixtures and even lead crystal. Even where soda had been used it was much more impure than that used in Venice. Presumably the databases that now exist could be used to detect more recent copies.

Jembrih-Simbürger *et al.* (2003) employed a battery of non-destructive techniques including EDX, FTIR and RS as well as PIXE and PIGE to characterise the composition of the Art Nouveau glasses made by Tiffany and Loetz in America in the late nineteenth century, and so to differentiate them from contemporary and recent copies.

The main change in opacifiers occurred when tin replaced antimony in the early centuries AD (see Table 10.2).

Colorants

One of the new colorants of the nineteenth century was chrome green. (Table 10.3) The main ore of chromium is chromite, $FeCr_2O_3$, but it is almost invariably found intermixed with iron oxides, which would render any glass to which it was added black rather than green, and natural chromite was actually used in the Medieval Islamic world as a black pigment for painting the outlines on glazed pots (Mason *et al.*, 2001). In 1802 Sèvres were using purified chromite to produce a chrome green in their glazes (Speel and Bronk, 2001). This seems to have been rather precocious but by the mid-nineteenth century it was in general use.

The Venetian glass-makers were using chrome green in their copies of antique mosaic glass vessels from about 1880 and more specifically it has been found in forgeries of ancient glass vessels (Carboni *et al.*, 1998; Page *et al.*, 2001) and forgeries of late antique gold glass (Henderson, 1992). Chromium green is also found in enamel forgeries such as the Botkin Byzantine enamels (see p. 239), forgeries of Limoges enamels (Biron *et al.*, 1996) and other forged Medieval French enamels (Netzer and England, 1989; Schweizer, 1994c).

Table 10.3 Some of the principal green and yellow translucent enamels of the last 500 years.

Date	Author	Green	Yellow
1576	Blaise de Vignère	1. Copper oxide (*cuivre bruslé*)	1. Silver stain (*jaune de l'argent*) 2. Iron oxide (*rouille de fer or limaille d'iceluy réduite en crocum*)
1583	Dominique Mouret	1. Copper oxide (*écaille d'cuivre*) with little iron oxide (*rouille de fer*)	No comment
1636	John Colladon	1. Iron or copper oxide? (pindust) 2. Copper oxide (verditer) with little iron or copper oxide? (see 1) 3. Copper oxide (bisgreene)	1. iron oxide (iron rust)
1721	Jacques-Philippes Ferrand	1. Copper oxide (*cendre verte calcinée*)	1. Iron oxide (*ochre jaune*) 2. Silver stain? (*couleur de stil de grain clair*)
1764	Robert Dossie	1. Copper oxide (precipitated copper) 2. Iron oxide (precipitated iron) with silver stain (calcinated silver) and cobalt oxide (zaffer)	1. Silver stain (with sulphur calcined silver) 2. Silver stain (calcinated silver) with iron oxide (precipitated iron) 3. Iron oxide (precipitated iron) 4. Iron oxide (scarlet ochre) 5. Sulphide of arsenic (orpiment)
1866	Claudius Popelin	1. Chromium oxide (*chromate de potasse*) with little iron oxide (*protoxyde de fer*) 2. Copper oxide (*nitrate de cuivre*)	1. Silver stain (*chlorure d'argent*)
1883	Thoires de Reboulleau	1. Chromium oxide (*oxyde de chrôme*) 2. Copper oxide (*deutoxyde de cuivre*)	1. Silver stain (*chlorure d'argent*)
1895	Alfred Meyer	1. Copper oxide (*oxyde des cuivre*) 2. Chromium oxide (*oxyde de chrôme*) with copper oxide (*oxyde de cuivre*)	1. Silver stain (*chlorure d'argent*) 2. Uranium oxide (*oxyde d'urane*)
1899	Henry Cunynghame	1. Chromium-iron oxide (chromate of iron) 2. Copper oxide (black oxide of copper) with chromium oxide (bichromate of potash) 3. Copper oxide (nitrate of copper)	1. Uranium oxide (uranate of soda) 2. Selenium oxide (metallic selenium)

Source: Davison, 2003, p. 10

Chromium is easy to detect by most analytical techniques and thus features regularly in glass and enamel authenticity studies. The usual quantities deliberately added as a colorant are in the range of several thousand ppm. However, caution must be exercised as traces of chromium can occur in earlier vitreous materials. For example, Olin and Sayre (1974) found in the region of 20 ppm chromium in some Medieval French colored window glass (one piece had no less than 649 ppm of chromium, but unlike the other pieces it was soda glass with a much higher sodium and a lower potassium content, and although not commented on by Olin and Sayre, this does raise the possibility that it was a replacement).

Traces of chromium were also found in the weathered white enamels on some early Greek gold

Table 10.4 Characteristic minor and trace elements associated with cobalt minerals from different sources used at different periods (see Figure 10.15).

Group	Chemical association	Chronological period	Ore provenance
1	Co, Co-Sb, Co-Cu, Co-Mn Co-Zn-Ni-Fe-Cr-As	From Protohistory until 12th century	Unknown: local, Near-East
2	Co-Zn-Pb-In-Fe	13th–15th century	Freiberg (Erzgebirge)
3	Co-Ni-Mo-Fe	15th–16th century	Erzgebirge
4	Co-As-Ni-Bi-Mo-U-Fe (W)	end 15th–18th century	Schneeberg (Erzgebirge)

Source: Gratuze et al., 2000

rosettes (see Chapter 15, p. 373). These had originally come under suspicion because they had appeared in large numbers on the market over a short space of time. The chromium was originally advanced as supporting evidence that they must be forgeries; however, the weathered nature of the enamel together with technical features on the gold, strongly support their authenticity. This seems to indicate that chromium can occur in small amounts of the order of a few tens of parts per million in ancient glasses.

Other notable new coloring metals in glasses include selenium oxide (pinky-yellows), nickel oxide (browns) (Richter, 1994) and antimony (ruby red) (Wypyski, 2002). All were used from the late nineteenth century and have been found in copies, restorations and forgeries of earlier glasses and enamels.

Uranium oxide was used from the mid-nineteenth century until the mid-twentieth century on a considerable scale to produce yellow and green colors in glass (Richter, 1994; Strahan 2001). In a frequently quoted paper, Manley (1912) reported 1.6% UO_2 in a Roman yellow glass mosaic tessera from a context at Posipilo apparently sealed by the eruption of Mt Vesuvius in 79 AD. However, the tessera was reported to have contained 20% potash, but no soda, which is totally at variance with Roman glass. Festag et al. (1976) studied this claimed occurrence in some detail, searching for radioactive mosaics with a Geiger counter all over the Bay of Naples without success and concluded that the original analysis was likely to have been at fault. Thus, glasses colored with uranium which purport to be pre-nineteenth century are unlikely to be genuine. The radioactivity of the uranium glasses is such that even nineteenth-century pieces can be precisely dated by their fission tracks (see p. 229).

Sometimes a colorant with a long history of usage can still be useful for authenticity work if new sources have been used more recently and if the mineral from the new source is associated with particular minor and trace elements not found in the earlier sources. Cobalt is a good example. The metal, or rather its oxide, has a very long history of use as a glass and glaze colorant, and a variety of different sources and minerals have been used at different times and places (Table 10.4).

Soulier et al. (1996) studied the trace elements associated with the cobalt in French glass from the Bronze Age to the Post-Medieval period. Gratuze et al. (1992, 1995, 1996, 2000) have characterised the cobalt from four different sources used in Medieval and Post-Medieval French glass (1992) and glazed ceramics (1996) (Figure 10.15) and extended this to other European glass. They found that the European cobalt sources, such as those at Schneeberg in Germany, which only began to be exploited in the sixteenth century AD, are characterised by relatively high nickel, arsenic and bismuth contents, compared to sources used earlier.

This distinction in the European cobalt sources has proved useful in distinguishing between early cobalt blue glasses and later reproductions, as exemplified by the *Bonus Eventus* plaque (see Chapter 16, p. 400). (For use of the same criteria in cobalt colorants in the dating and provenancing of other materials, see Chapter 9, p. 192 for glazes and Chapter 13, p. 322 for paper.)

Other cobalt sources have distinctive compositions; for example, the ancient Egyptians cobalt obtained from the Great Western Oases is chemically distinct from that from Iranian sources (Kaczmarczyk, 1986). This was of use in authenticating the Medieval Islamic glass vessel known as the Cavour Vase (Newby, 1998). The distinctive pattern of trace elements suggested a cobalt source that was known to have been exploited in the Medieval period (Henderson, 1998b).

Physical dating methods

The TL dating of glass has not been successful (Aitken, 1985, p. 202; Müller and Schvoerer, 1993; Schvoerer *et al.*, 1993). Other techniques such as hydration dating, glass layer counting and fission track dating have been applied with varying success.

Hydration dating

Sources: Lanford (1977, 1986); Ambrose (2001).

On exposure to water, most glasses hydrate. The depth of the hydration rind is directly proportional to time and, hence, this relation could form the basis of a dating method (Aitken, 1990, pp. 214–218; Wagner, 1998, pp. 304–321). This has been applied to obsidian artefacts; however, factors such as the composition and structure of the glass, the ambient temperature during burial, and other burial environment parameters all affect hydration

rates (Morgenstein *et al.*, 1999). It is potentially applicable as an authentication technique, capable of showing that a material is of some age, even if obtaining a precise date is not possible. Ericson *et al.* (2004) have suggested a similar method for dating rock crystal (see Chapter 16, p. 416).

As most synthetic glasses tend to be rather young compared to the prehistoric obsidian tools, the hydration layers are usually very thin. Lanford (1977, 1986) worked on recent glass, using a non-destructive nuclear resonance technique that enables hydration rinds as thin as 0.05 μm to be measured. He measured some nineteenth- and twentieth-century Steuben and other American glass and was able to demonstrate a linear relation between the thickness and time. This showed that it was possible to determine the age of the glass to within decades. For example, he was able to show that a decanter (Figure 10.16)

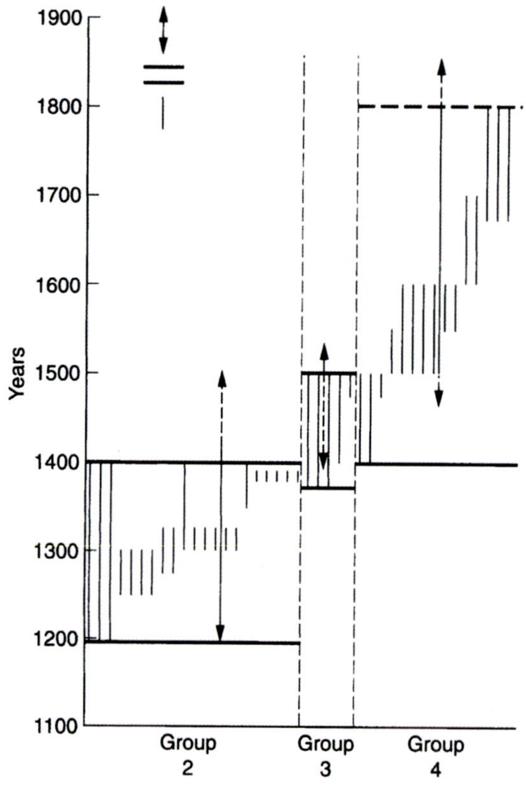

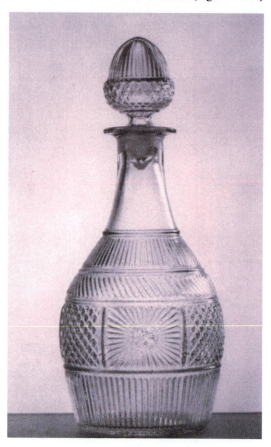

Figure 10.15 Periods of use of cobalt blue colorant from different sources in French glass and glazes. The cobalt in each group is characterised by composition (see Table 10.4). (Courtesy Gratuze *et al.*, 1996)

Figure 10.16 A blown glass decanter in the style of the 1820s, but the thinness of the hydration layer or rind suggested that it was only a few decades old when examined in 1975. (Courtesy Lanford, 1977)

in the style of the 1820s was actually only a few decades old. The environmental constraints should not be too serious for glass that has not been buried, and thus the hydration rate will be largely dependent on the chemistry of each piece of glass. However, Bates *et al.* (1982) suggested that a hydration layer identical to that observed on ancient glass could be induced quite rapidly by exposing the glass to water vapour at elevated temperature. Also, in synthetic glasses, the sharp boundary between the hydrated layer and unaffected glass beneath, observed on natural glasses such as obsidian, is rarely present.

Glass layer counting

Brill and Hood (1961) studied sections from a variety of glasses, ranging in age from about 150 to 1500 years old, and found many of the glasses had developed a weathering crust where the number of layers counted approximated to the age of the glass in years, in some way analogous to tree rings.

However, even the preliminary paper drew attention to what were to be fatal obstacles to the method becoming accepted. Many glasses in many environments produce no weathering crusts at all, many of the crusts that did develop were too soft for satisfactory polished sections to be prepared, and, most seriously, Brill and Hood were not able to explain the phenomenon. Suggestions that it was in some way related to changes in the seasons were quite literally sunk when the layers were observed on glass recovered from the bottom of the sea!

Newton (1971) studied the layering phenomena in more detail and sought to replicate them. Although he was able to confirm the build-up of the crusts through time by layers, they were in no way real annual phenomena and multi-layered structures could be developed by artificial ageing techniques over quite short time periods.

Fission track dating

The spontaneous fission of ^{238}U within glasses creates highly energetic particles which leave observable tracks. As the decay rate of the uranium is constant there is a direct linear relationship between the number of tracks and the age of the glass – the more tracks the older the glass (Brill *et al.*, 1964; Westgate *et al.*, 1997). The method works well for glasses of geological age (Wagner and Van Heute, 1992; Wagner, 1998).

Unfortunately, too few tracks will have developed in most synthetic glasses because of their relatively low uranium content and the short period of time that will have elapsed since the glass was made. A piece of Roman glass was studied as a test sample, and after 100 hours of repeated polishing and counting an area of $25\,cm^2$, the tracks from 29 spontaneous fissions were counted, for which a date of 150 AD $\pm$ 350 was obtained (Wagner 1998, p. 212). Although this was broadly correct, the huge amount of work necessary and the damage to the object would seem to rule this technique out even for authenticity studies.

An important exception is the glasses colored with uranium oxide (see p. 227). The many tracks generated by the fission of the added uranium enable quite precise dates to be obtained (Brill *et al.*, 1964).

Other methods

Bimson and Rose (1983) investigated the potential of the gases trapped within the glass to provide an indication of age. They initially hoped that there might be a very slow exchange between the gases in the glass and those in the atmosphere. Analyses of gases occluded in ancient Egyptian, Roman and eighteenth-century English glasses, all gave very much the same result. The gases were predominantly of nitrogen and carbon dioxide with no oxygen or water vapour, indicating that no exchange with the atmosphere had taken place.

However, the analyses did show that in almost every case the gases were an uncontaminated sample of the atmosphere of the furnace in which the glass had been made, and this could be indicative. Thus the atmosphere in a modern electric glass-making furnace should contain little carbon dioxide compared to ancient furnaces. It might also be possible to distinguish between the use of wood or charcoal and fossil fuel in earlier furnaces by measuring the $^{12}C/^{13}C$ ratios. However, although the isotope ratios are very different, there is a possibility of contamination from mineral carbonates in some of the components of the ancient glasses.

The methods used by Bimson and Rose were destructive, but RM offers the possibility of non-destructive determination of the occluded gases in transparent glass.

Glass copies and forgeries

Sources: General: Kurz (1948, pp. 258–267); Arnau (1961, pp. 156–161); Savage (1976, pp. 213–227); Hajdamach (1986, pp. 80–103). Ancient Glass: Cooney (1960); von Saldern (1972); Goldstein (1977); Grose (1989, pp. 375–384); Page *et al.* (2001); Whitehouse

(2001c). Post-Medieval: Strauss (1962); Tait (ed) (1991, pp. 17–19); Lanmon *et al.* (1973).

Von Saldern (1972), followed by Goldstein (1977), grouped glass forgeries into categories similar to those made for other materials, notably ceramics (see Chapter 9, p. 208). These included: 1. Innocent reproductions; 2. Historicising glasses; 3. Forgeries; 4. Conglomerates; and, finally, a catch-all 5th category to include glasses not originally intended to deceive, but which for a variety of reasons have acquired a false identity.

The first category was restricted to exact copies of individual pieces usually taken from well-known collections, whereas the second category more broadly covered all copies in the general appropriate style.

In the nineteenth century many firms, particularly in Germany, Austria, France and Italy, produced copies of ancient glass which, as is the case with so much nineteenth-century work, are technically of very high quality, although sometimes of a rather lifeless mechanical perfection. The better-known firms produced catalogues of their wares, which are now invaluable for the quick identification of their products. Although the reproductions were offered as legitimate, they were often given the appearance of age by acid treatments, the application of chemicals, smoking, and the sprinkling of sand onto the still-hot glass. Some of the more famous firms include, in Germany, the Rheinische Glashütten (producing copies of Roman, Venetian and Old German Glass, the so-called *Historismus* glasses); C.W. Fleischmann (Old German); and Ludwig Felmer (Roman). In Austria the firm of J. & L. Lobmeyr in collaboration with Meyr Neffe produced excellent free copies of Baroque Bohemian and German engraved and enamelled glass (Strauss, 1962). When originally produced, these pieces were almost invariably engraved with the company names but even so von Saldern (1972) opined that 'there is probably no large collection of engraved glass in existence that is without an undetected piece of Lobmeyr or Lobmeyr-style glass'.

In Italy a great deal of high-quality reproduction and historicising glass was produced from the nineteenth century on (Elbern, 1968). There are some problems with categorising the copies of earlier Venetian glass, as the more successful designs were kept in production sometimes for centuries as traditional styles. How does one differentiate between an old-fashioned design and one that is consciously historicising? Other enterprises such as the Venetian and Murano Cameo Glass Company were established specifically to reproduce ancient glass wares

(Hollister, 1983; Grose, 1989, pp. 380–381). Page *et al.* (2001) have studied how these nineteenth-century copies can be distinguished from the ancient originals. The techniques of manufacture are broadly similar, but with some differences in methods of attaching bases and handles, etc. The nineteenth-century Venetian mosaic glasses were made from crushed quartz pebbles and plant ash with some additional potash, resulting in much more variable compositions than the Roman glasses that were made from river or beach sand and natron (Figure 10.17). The clearest differences however, are in the colorants: the yellows were lead antimonate in the ancient glass but lead-tin antimonate in the nineteenth-century pieces, and in three out of four of the later pieces the greens were due to chromium oxides. The chloride content could also be expected to be higher in the ancient glasses (see p. 223).

The *Art Journal* noted in 1866 Salviati's comment that 'imitations of old Venetian glass are the most successful we have yet seen. Hence . . . it is difficult for any but the most expert judge to discriminate between the new and the old'. A century and a half of wear will have made the task even more onerous. *Riprodazoni Antica* glasses are still made in Murano for sale to tourists complete with the crizzle and chemically induced weathering, concerning

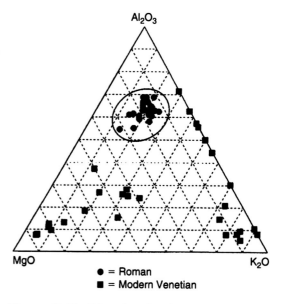

Figure 10.17 Triangular plot showing the ratios of the small quantities of alumina, manganese and potash in Roman and nineteenth-century Italian glass. (Page *et al.*, 2001)

which, Goldstein (1977) noted, 'once removed from context, these vessels have been misunderstood and offered for sale as Roman wares'.

Following important exhibitions in Paris and in London in the 1860s French and English glass-makers began to take an interest in the reproduction of the glass of earlier ages. In Paris, Philippe-Joseph Brocard produced excellent copies of Islamic enamelled glass (Whitehouse, 2001c, p. 298–299). In Britain, the donation of collections such as that of Felix Slade to the British Museum in 1868 (which inevitably contained a few forgeries; Tait, (ed), 1991), gave glass-makers the chance to study ancient glass of high quality at first hand. British glass-makers such as Jenkinson and Northwood as well as Latz in America began producing near fault-less copies of ancient glass (Hajdamach, 1986).

There seems to have been a big increase in the production of good-quality and technically convincing core-formed glass forgeries (Eiland, 2003, 2005) and also of moulded glass (Goldstein, 1977) in the Middle East through the twentieth century as the methods by which the ancients worked became more widely known. Goldstein believed that moulds were taken from pieces that were genuine but which had not yet been published on, and that forgeries were made from them by mould-blowing or press-moulding.

Damaged glasses can be fraudulently restored or newly created as conglomerates, by the addition of other antique fragments, new glass or even plastics such as epoxy resins (Tennent, 1979). Von Saldern (1972, pp. 316–317) cited the example of a conical-footed bowl where the foot was found to be of plastic and the bowl itself was likely originally to have been the neck of a large lamp or vessel.

Joins can sometimes be shown up by binocular microscopy, revealing trails of tiny air bubbles that form distinctive patterns, and by the use of a polarising screen, which can reveal abrupt changes in the striae patterns at the joins (see p. 221 and Figure 10.12) (Hajdamach, 1986, p. 103). Analysis can sometimes reveal differences in composition between the various components. Conglomerates are often given a coat of a weathering agent to disguise the joins and also to hinder examination by transmitted light or UV. Radiography is useful in detecting disguised joins.

Embellishments and fakes

Another activity is the addition of decoration to genuine but plain glasses. This is a relatively common practice on Late Antique glass by incision, gilding and enamelling (Carboni *et al.*, 1998). On later glasses the addition of designs relevant to popular historic themes is common (see p. 219).

A rather unusual case of embellishment was the irradiation of genuine but colorless Lalique glass to produce a much rarer and more expensive purple glass. These purple glasses began to appear on the market in the 1980s, but were declared fakes (court proceedings reported in the London *Evening Standard*, Monday, 14 December 1998). Glass that contains manganese (often added in small quantities as a decolorant) can be made purple by irradiation with X-rays. This arises because the Fe^{3+} and Mn^{2+} ions are changed to Fe^{2+} and Mn^{3+} ions by the irradiation, and the trivalent manganese is purple. Sunshine can produce a less-marked purpling effect known as solarisation. The court case centred around whether it would have been possible for the irradiation to have been done at the Lalique factories in the 1920s, or whether it was more likely to be much more recent. It was claimed that the necessary X-ray facilities were not available in the 1920s, and one of Lalique's old employees stated that such irradiated purple glasses were never made.

Case study: Two Roman engraved glasses

This study of two quite minor pieces of engraved Roman glass, now in the Metropolitan Museum, New York, may be taken as typical of glass authentication studies (Pilosi and Wypyski, 2002a, b). One is a small round bowl with an engraved looped pattern running around the rim and the head of Medusa in the centre of the underside, inside the foot-ring. The other is a fragment with an engraved inscription. Both were considered as nineteenth-century forgeries on stylistic and technical criteria (Caron, 1997).

Tiny fragments were removed from each piece for analysis by SEM/EDX and WDX (Table 10.5). This analysis showed that both were soda-lime-silica glass, with high silica contents, and low magnesia and potash, figures entirely consistent with genuine Roman glass. The glasses also have the relatively high alumina and chloride contents associated with early glass. The compositions were quite different from nineteenth-century glass in major, minor and trace elements, but at the time when these pieces entered the Metropolitan Museum the true composition of Roman glass was unknown.

Examination of the foot ring of the plate showed the surface to be weathered with much pitting. The engraving had been wheel cut, and, significantly, the pitting was not random but followed the lines of the engraving, showing that the engraving had been present before the weathering took place. Caron had previously suggested that the very evident weathering had been acid-induced and thus recent. However, acid-induced weathering produces randomly orientated pitting (Pilosi and Wypyski, 2002b). Despite this evidence of weathering, the surface iridescence layer is now very thin. Possibly the piece originally had a thicker layer that was largely removed after discovery, thereby giving the surface a rather artificial appearance.

The fragment with the engraved inscription also has a weathered surface, with some pitting in the light surface scratches. However, the wheel-cut lines of the inscription were found to go through the surface pitting with no pitting in the lines themselves. Moreover, the sides of the lines are quite clean and sharp-edged, although there is a little conchoidal fracturing along the edges of the lines, which Pilosi and Wypyski believed was probably the result of some deliberate attempt to age the lines by roughening them up. In some of the lines there was a shiny buff-colored material that had the superficial appearance of a corrosion product. However, it was not layered in the usual manner of corroded glass, but instead appeared dimpled, suggesting it had been applied as a liquid, a view reinforced by the discovery of a hair of a paint brush stuck in it! Thus, the inscription would seem to be a modern addition to an otherwise worthless but genuine fragment of Roman glass.

Table 10.5   Analyses of two Roman glasses. Cr, Co, Cu, Ni, Zn, As, Sn, Sb and Pb were sought but not detected.

	Glass Compositions (Weight Percentages)	
Component	Plate with Head of Medusa (81.10.238)	Fragment with Inscription (17.194.916)
Na_2O	16.2	16.0
MgO	0.6	0.6
Al_2O_3	2.4	3.2
SiO_2	70.5	66.7
P_2O_5	0.11	0.08
SO_3	0.15	0.16
Cl	1.2	1.1
K_2O	0.5	1.0
CaO	7.8	9.5
TiO_2	0.06	0.06
MnO	0.31	1.2
Fe_2O_3	0.34	0.46
BaO	0.02	0.04

Source: Pilosi and Wypyski, 2002a

Some special categories of glass

Beads

Sources: General: van der Sleen (1967); Dubin (1987); Becker (1988); Liu (1995); Lankton (2003). Technology: Küçükerman (1988); Sode (1996). Fakes: Liu (1980; 1995, pp. 220–227; 2001); Ogden (1982, pp. 151–172).

See also the periodicals: *Bead Study Trust Newsletter* and *Bead Journal* (now *Ornament Magazine*).

Glass beads are among the earliest glass products and almost certainly the most ubiquitous, often as gem simulants (see Chapter 16, p. 405). In India and China, glass production was largely concentrated on bead production until the fairly recent past, and this is now threatened by plastics (Sode and Kock, 2001).

Glass beads have been made by a wide variety of methods from antiquity, the only common feature being the necessity of making provision for a hole running through them. One of the earliest and still most widespread methods of the traditional making of beads is by winding the softened glass around a rod of ceramic or iron. Quite complex patterns can be built up by trailing or spotting glasses of different colors around the body cylinder of the glass and marvering in a manner analogous to the early methods of making vessels. The well-known Egyptian eye beads were made in this manner, and pieces of millefiore glass could be set in to the softened bead. More recently beads have been made by pulling out a blown cylinder into long tubes that could then be cut up into beads. Early blown-glass beads are not common, except in Japan, and evidence of this technique could provide grounds for suspicion.

Many legitimate copies and forgeries of traditional beads continue to be made in Europe, especially by Czech glass-makers, supplying ethnic communities around the world. They are often very convincing copies of the beads of local manufacture or of those imported from more traditional sources (Liu, 1974, 1987). Copies of glass beads are also made from a variety of plastics (Liu, 1995, pp. 270–227; 2001). Sometimes glass powders of various colors are carefully mixed in to an epoxy or similar resin. Liu (1995, p. 324) and Allen (1976b) both recommend rubbing the suspect bead against the incisor teeth; glass, stone and plastic apparently feel very different. Forgeries of complex multi-color beads are produced on a large scale around the world, often incorporating slices of millefiore. Face beads are particularly popular, although sometimes the face is merely painted onto the surface of the bead, which may itself be ancient.

Painted and enamelled window glass

Sources: General: Reyntiens (1977); Trench (ed) (2000, pp. 460–462); Davison (2003, pp. 61–67, 126–133). Weathering: Davison (2003, pp. 190–192, esp. pp. 159–160).

All colored window glass is popularly known as stained glass, but this is something of a misnomer as, strictly speaking, staining is a very specific coloring technique, not actually found to have been applied to many windows of colored glass. Making decorative windows of pieces of glass of various colors has been practised in Europe from the Post-Roman period to the present day. From about the eleventh century AD designs or pictures were painted on the glass surface with paints made up of pigments of iron or copper oxides in a frit of low-melting lead glass, mixed in an oil medium. After application this was fired to give black, dark purple or brown lines, depending on the pigment and firing conditions. The colored glass could be either a single sheet of glass, or where, as in the case of ruby glass it was judged too deep a color, a thin sheet of the red glass could be joined while hot (*flashed*) onto a piece of colorless glass.

One of the most important innovations was the introduction of true stained glass in the late thirteenth century in Western Europe (although Byzantine and Islamic glass-makers were already using silver oxide to decorate glass, probably in imitation of gold, several centuries earlier; Whitehouse *et al.*, 2000). In Medieval Europe silver sulphide or oxide was applied to one side of the glass which, after firing, became yellow. Initially it was just used on colorless glass to produce areas of yellow, but soon came the realisation that it could be used in combination with blue glass to produce areas of green for example, or some of the colored areas on flashed glass could be scraped away and the remaining colorless glass stained.

In Post-Medieval Europe there was a move away from composing pictures from separate pieces of colored glass. Instead, as translucent enamel glass became more available, simple rectangular panes or roundels of colorless glass were painted and enamelled. The Gothic revival in the nineteenth century saw the reintroduction of the Medieval techniques.

Interest in the 'Gothick' style had begun in the eighteenth century, and the Revolutionary Wars of the late eighteenth and early nineteenth centuries in Europe meant that there was an abundant supply of genuine Medieval and Post-Medieval glass from redundant religious establishments (Knowles, 1923,

1924, 1928). But from the mid-nineteenth century these sources began to dry up and both innocent and fraudulent copies began to appear on the market.

J. A. Knowles dealt systematically with the technical differences between Medieval, Post-Medieval and nineteenth-century painted and stained glass, and some of his observations can be noted here. The diamond glass cutter is a relatively recent invention and evidence of clean cut edges shows that the glass is not ancient. The rough edges found on the Medieval pieces could be imitated using pliers, but in the Medieval period the glass would have had the edge nibbled with a special tool known as a *grozing iron* (Figure 10.18), which leaves a very distinctive edge, rather different from that produced with pliers.

Early glass is generally much thinner than more recent glass, and window glass tends to be rather cockled and irregular on one surface. Medieval window glass was forest glass with a high potash content.

Schweizer (1985) was able to differentiate between Medieval and nineteenth-century painted glass using XRF, on the basis of the potassium to calcium ratio in the body of the glass and the calcium to iron ratio in the black paint.

The early painted and enamelled windows from European Medieval and Post-Medieval buildings, being of thin pieces or sheets of potash glass, are particularly vulnerable to weathering, especially in the acidic conditions of modern urban environments. Medieval window glass exposed to atmospheric moisture will weather by the formation first of hydroxides which, in turn, will form carbonates and finally in most environments, sulphates. This leads to the build-up of considerable thicknesses

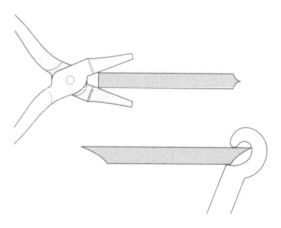

Figure 10.18 Use of modern pliers and of medieval grozing iron to trim the edges of glass. Note the characteristic chisel edge of the latter.

of gypsum, the calcium coming from the glass and the sulphur from the atmosphere. Glass that has been removed from buildings in remote rural locations, or anywhere before the onset of the Industrial Revolution, may well have weathering crusts composed mainly of calcite, calcium carbonate.

Old window glass is very often extensively pitted with depressions sometimes several millimetres across, in surfaces that are otherwise apparently undamaged.

Wear, corrosion, weathering and false patination

Sources: Newton (1985); Croyn (1990, pp. 128–134); Seddon (1995, pp. 230–246); Freestone (2001); Davison (2003).

Wear

Glass is a rather soft material and will scratch quite easily either in day-to-day use or during overly vigorous polishing (see Chapter 2, p. 37). Lanmon *et al.* (1973) in their study of some forged nineteenth-century American glass (see p. 216) found that some of the suspect pieces had little or no wear and others had heavy grind marks on the base made up of deep parallel scratches, totally unlike natural wear. Also, some of this wear was in areas that would not be expected to show signs of wear, a decanter with heavy zigzag scratching around the neck and sides, for example.

In addition, an old glass will usually have microcracking or pitting around the rim and around the edge of the base, especially if the latter is wider than the rim of the glass. This can be detected by running a fingernail around the rim or edge in question or examining with a hand lens.

Artificial wear can be found on genuine glass. Ivor Noël Hume (1974, p. 279) recounted the story of a collector at an antiques fair noticing a dealer busy abrading the foot of a glass with emery paper. Thinking he was going to expose a faker at work, he investigated only to discover the glass was genuine:

> 'What are you doing that for?' the amazed collector inquired, 'that's a perfectly good eighteenth-century glass.'
> 'I know,' replied the dealer, 'but Americans won't buy it unless they can spot a bit of wear on the bottom.'

Weathering or corrosion

The weathering or corrosion of glass is dependent on the environment to which the glass has been exposed and its composition.

Most ancient glass will have been buried (this section will only consider burial environments; for the weathering of painted and stained-glass windows see p. 234). If the conditions are very alkaline then the silica in the glass can be progressively dissolved, leaving a dulled and progressively eaten-away surface.

In the more normal neutral, slightly alkaline or acidic soil conditions, the usual form of corrosion is the progressive removal of the alkali metal ions, sodium and potassium, and some of the alkaline earth ions, notably calcium, from the glass. They are replaced by water and hydroxyl ions, OH^-, in the glass, a process sometimes erroneously referred to as devitrification. The surface can acquire other elements such as chlorine from the soil (Mao, 2000; Freestone, 2001). PIXE–PIGE has been used to study and characterise the surface degradation non-destructively, as exemplified by the recent work of Weber *et al.* (2002).

Although seriously weakened, the glass can still appear in good condition when first excavated from the damp ground. But on exposure to the air the moisture begins to evaporate from the glass leaving the weathered silica layers dulled and opaque with micro-cracking, often referred to as crizzling. The remaining silica seems to be in the form of plates, often in layers. These can either flake off or form more coherent layers sometimes several millimetres deep. They often have an onion-skin appearance that can appear iridescent owing to the interference patterns brought about by the diffraction of incident light (Lampropoulos *et al.*, 2002) (Figure 10.19). Attempts to imitate this or to accelerate its development are generally unsuccessful. Application of an acidic poultice, etc. generally only produces a thin and insubstantial layer that is soon rubbed off. The silica in genuine weathering crusts tends to be amorphous but acid-treated surfaces can be crystalline and the minerals present can be totally at variance with those normally produced under natural weathering conditions. For example, Werner and Bimson (1965) detected calcium fluorosilicate by XRD in the surface of glass that had been treated with hydrofluoric acid. The corrosion on ancient glass tends to be rather heterogeneous, the surfaces responding to their immediate surroundings, whereas the surfaces of artificially treated glasses are more uniform. This is especially clear when the glass surface is wetted, if that is possible. The earth on genuine excavated pieces almost invariably penetrates deep into the fissures within and beneath the corrosion, whereas the dirt on forgeries is usually added last and thus just sits on the corrosion.

Dyes can be applied to acid-roughened surfaces and then sprayed with lacquer to simulate iridescence. This can also be simulated by spraying on an alcoholic solution of stannic chloride and firing to produce a thin layer of tin oxide, in a variant of the method originally patented by Louis Tiffany (Kingery and Vandiver, 1985). Tin oxide by itself gives a silvery iridescence, but the addition of iron oxides can give a range of golden iridescence.

A simulated weathered surface can also be obtained by baking the glass in an iron box containing powdered mica. More usually, glass forgers will stick iridescent scaly material to the glass to give a semblance of age; even fish scales have been used in a manner reminiscent of some pearl simulants (see Chapter 16, p. 403).

The corrosion of glass is very dependent on its composition. In general, the higher the silica content the more stable the glass, and glasses with more than about two thirds weight per cent of silica will tend to be stable in most environments. The tendency to weathering also depends on the nature and amounts of other elements present in the glass from the fluxes and stabilisers.

As these change through the ages and with cultures, this means that to some degree characteristic weathering patterns can be established, which may be of some assistance in authenticity examinations. The earliest glasses used crushed quartz and plant ashes and the resultant glasses tend to have a rather low silica content, compensated in part by relatively high calcium and magnesium content, but these are still prone to weathering. In contrast, the Hellenistic and Roman natron-fluxed glasses are high in silica and alumina but relatively low in calcium and magnesium and are very resistant to weathering. Freestone (2001)

Figure 10.19 Naturally corroded glass, showing a weathered crust and some iridescence. Fragment from a fourteenth-century glass alembic excavated from the site of Selbourne Abbey, Hampshire. (© British Museum)

quoted the example of plant ash-fluxed Sasanian and natron-fluxed Roman glasses excavated from the same layers of certain sites in the Middle East, the former often having deep opaque weathering layers whereas the adjacent Roman glasses have just a light surface iridescence.

The Venetian glasses, made from purified plant ashes, also tend to be low in calcium oxide which would have stabilised the glass and they are thus unstable. The Medieval European Forest glasses have a rather low silica content and a high alkali content, particularly of potash, and they are consequently very prone to weathering as exemplified by colored window glass (see p. 233) and the Limoges enamels (see p. 238).

If the proportions of sodium and potassium are very high they can render the glass unstable without it ever having been buried. In extreme cases this can result in the glass surface becoming quite damp, known as *sweating* or *weeping*. The highly alkaline moisture promotes the mobility of the remaining alkalis within the glass, leading to progressive and deep seated decay with extensive crizzling and deep cracks developing in the glass. Some such glasses have been acquired by museums believing them to be antiquities, no doubt partially influenced by their deeply weathered appearances. Their true status often only became apparent somewhat later when, inevitably, they began to fall apart.

Case study: The Amiens Chalice and Slade Cup

Figure 10.20 The Slade Vase, Slade Col. 318. The instability of the glass brought about excessive crizzling and flaking, resulting in the collector, Felix Slade, believing it to be ancient. (© British Museum)

Sources: Werner (1959); Harden *et al.* (1968, pp. 182–183); Tait (2003).

The condition of the so-called Amiens Chalice (BM GR Reg. 1865, 1–3, 50) and the Slade Cup led many experts to believe that they must have been buried antiquities. The Chalice was supposed to have been dug up in the vicinity of Amiens, in northern France, and to be late Roman in date. The Slade Vase is very similar but has lost its handles (Figure 10.20). Both glasses suffer from advanced crizzling, with their surfaces permanently damp unless stored in dry conditions. Analysis showed they are of cobalt glass with a high potassium content and some sodium but only traces of calcium and, thus, are highly unstable. Such compositions are unparalleled in the Roman world, where the sodium content invariably exceeds that of the potassium and there is always some calcium.

Analysis of some other Post-Medieval glasses from France showed similar distinctive compositions with about 12% of potassium oxide, some sodium oxide and 1–3% of lead oxide, although these compositions were not so extreme as to cause the instability displayed by the Amiens and Slade glasses. Stylistically they are quite similar to some glazed earthenwares made at Nevers in the late seventeenth century, and this is the most likely origin of these glasses. Thus, they would seem to have been innocent productions that became mistaken for ancient glasses, not least on account of their weathered appearance. However, Tait (2003) in a reassessment of the Slade Vase, pointed out that when first shown to the Society of Antiquaries of London, it had gilt-metal mounts in the style of early Venetian glass, and suggested that they had been made in the early nineteenth century as forgeries.

Further evidence for Tait's hypothesis that some 'weeping glasses' could have been made deliberately to deceive is provided by yet another weeping glass. This is an amber-colored blown-glass bowl now in the Ashmolean Museum and said to have been purchased in Rome in 1882. The bowl was believed to be Hellenistic or Roman, but over the 100 years since its acquisition it had deteriorated so badly that, as Newton and Brill (1985) observed, 'It seemed inconceivable that such a deteriorating object could have existed intact for nearly two millennia'. By the 1980s it was in many pieces and was examined to discover the cause of its decay. It was analysed and found to contain 13.4% of potassium and 8% of sodium, but only 0.33% of calcium, and was thus inherently unstable. The barium, manganese, aluminium, magnesium and iron traces were all significantly lower than usually encountered in ancient glass, but were much more in line with the amounts found in nineteenth-century glasses. Thus, it would seem very likely that this vessel was made in a classical style, very probably only a short time before its purchase when it was already described as being in a poor condition. If this interpretation is correct then this and related vessels could be rare but important instances of the deliberate use of a glass composition to produce a convincing weathered appearance.

The characteristic weathering of lead glasses is less well defined. Most early lead glasses are red colored glasses or enamels (Freestone, 1987), and these can sometimes be extensively corroded.

In colored glasses, oxidation of the metal ions of the colorant can cause discoloration; for example copper red glasses can turn green. Iron salts can penetrate the weathered surfaces of colorless glasses, and this can be easily imitated by staining.

Glass can be given a superficial weathered/aged appearance by treatment with hydrofluoric acid (Figures 10.9a and 10.9b). The natural weathering crusts formed by the deposition of lime leached from the glass into the surface layers can be imitated by roughening the surface with acid, followed by the application of calcite. A sprinkling of sand, along with some acidic chemicals, is sometimes marvered into the hot glass in order to give it the superficial appearance of long-term burial.

Enamels on metal and glass

History and technique

Enamels are vitreous coatings, overlays or inlays applied to another solid, usually metal or glass.

Technically speaking glazes, vitreous coatings on ceramic, are also enamels, but the term enamel is only used in a ceramics context where a second vitreous application, usually decorative, is made to the existing glazed surface (see Chapter 9, p. 207).

Enamel on metals
Sources: General: Speel (1998). Technique: Maryon (1923, pp. 180–206) Bates (1951). Ancient: Butcher (1976); Ogden (1982, pp. 133–135). Byzantine: Wessel (1969). Far East: Garner (1962); Harris (1994, pp. 110–139). Europe: Biron *et al.* (1996); O'Neill (ed) (1996); Speel and Bronk (2001). Scientific Examination: Freestone (1987); Henderson (1991); Bronk *et al.* (1999). Fakes and Forgeries: Arnau (1961, pp. 146–147); Savage (1976, pp. 99–102); Buckton (1988); Henderson (1992); Richter (1994); Netzer and England (1989); Speel (1998, pp. 54–55); Tait and Freestone (2004).

The history of enamelled metalwork is very uncertain before the Romans (Ogden, 1982, pp. 133–135). There do seem to be true fused enamels on some Mycenaean gold, dated to the mid second millennium BC (Higgins, 1961, pp. 23–28). Enamels generally are very rare and uncertainly attested in the Middle East (Maxwell-Hyslop, 1971, pp. 214–215; Moorey, 1994, pp. 214–215) and in Egypt, although enamelling was quite widely used in Celtic Europe.

Enamelling was usually carried out on copper, copper alloy or gold; enamelled silver is much rarer, the earliest occurrence being in Byzantium from the twelfth century and in Europe from about the fourteenth century AD.

There are two principal methods of creating the cells in or on the metal surface (Speel, 1998, pp. 22–31). A network of cells can be created by soldering wires or thin strips of metal onto the surface (Figure 10.21a). This technique is known as *cloisonné* and was very popular in the Dark Ages in Europe, in the Ming and Qing Dynasties in China and in the Edo period in Japan (Garner, 1962; Henderson *et al.*, 1989). *Cloisonné* enamels in traditional styles are still produced in enormous quantity in China.

Early enamels are generally opaque, and translucent enamels only became available in Europe from the fourteenth century. This allowed a variation on the *cloisonné* technique known as *pique à jour* using a network of open wire cells set with translucent enamel (Figure 10.21c).

Alternatively, the cells could be carved into the surface of the metal (Figure 10.21b). This technique is known as *champlevé*, and is found on much Celtic,

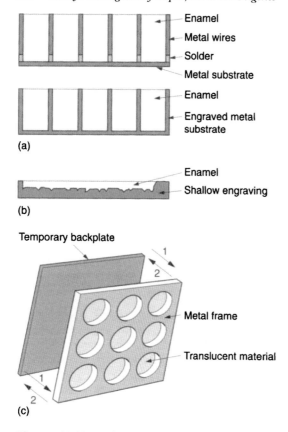

Figure 10.21 Techniques of enamelling on metal: a) Cloisonné, b) Champlevé, c) Plique à jour.

Roman and Byzantine work. The introduction of translucent enamels enabled the refinement of the *champlevé* technique known as *basse taille* (Richter, 1994; Wypyski and Richter, 1997). This consisted in carving the design, such as the folds of a cloak, deeply into the body of the cell, necessarily of a light-colored metal such as gold or silver. A deeply colored but translucent enamel, typically a ruby red or green, was used to impart a three-dimensional aspect to the enamel.

From the Late Medieval period the enamellers at Limoges began to completely cover the copper or silver plate with enamel, omitting the metal divisions separating the various colors making up the design. This method has been widely used ever since, not least by the Japanese Meiji enamellers at the end of the nineteenth and early twentieth century (Harris, 1994, pp. 110–139). In order to counteract the potential distortion of the metal by the cooling enamel after firing, both sides of the metal are often enamelled, the reverse side being known as the *contre email*. The Limoges enamels of the Renaissance period

sometimes carried maker's stamps (*poinçons*), and their creation or alteration has inevitably been an area of activity for forgers and fakers (Tait, 1999).

Another technique, known as *ronde boss*, was to coat the metal, usually gold, with white enamel. The technique was first used in Hellenistic Greece, and was reintroduced in Europe in the fourteenth century, becoming extensively used on jewellery of the Renaissance, and again on the nineteenth-century copies (Speel 1998, pp. 126–128).

Enamel on glass
Sources: General: Charleston (1972); Davison (2003, pp. 42–43, 111–113). Imitations and Forgeries: Savage (1976, pp. 221–223); Carboni *et al.* (1998); Tait (ed), (1991); Whitehouse (2001a, c).

The enamel is formed of a finely powdered frit of a glass with a melting point that is low, or containing additional flux to lower it, with the appropriately colored metal oxide, all mixed in an oily medium to create a paint ready for application to the surface of the glass to be decorated. The enamel is then fired in a muffle furnace, usually to between about 700° and 900°C. Enamels occasionally were applied to glass almost from the inception of glass-making. Enamelling was brought to a very high level by glass-makers in Medieval Syria and Egypt (Freestone and Stapleton, 1998; Ward (ed), 1998; Brill, 2001; Carboni and Whitehouse, 2001; Freestone, 2002). The technique was introduced to Europe in the thirteenth century and became popular from the Renaissance. Venice was the first major European centre for the production of enamelled glass (Freestone and Bimson, 1995). The enamelled armorial glasses of Venice seem to be the direct inspiration for the German enamelled glass such as the *Humpen* and *Stangenglas* drinking vessels (Barrington Haynes, 1959, pp. 102; Harden *et al.*, 1968, pp. 151–165).

Composition
The composition of enamels is often different from that of contemporary glass. It is clearly essential that the applied enamel has a melting point lower than that of the metal or glass to which it is applied (but see Freestone, 2002), and with enamel on metal the glaze should have approximately the same coefficient of expansion or contraction. Ancient enamels are generally soda-lime-silica glasses as were those in Early Medieval Europe up to the twelfth century; indeed it is possible that the Medieval European enamellers reused Roman glass tesserae. The translucent enamels used in Medieval and Post-Medieval Europe were both soda and potash-lime-silica glasses,

which are especially susceptible to corrosion (Smith *et al.*, 1987; Perez-y-Jorba *et al.*, 1993).

In antiquity lead oxide was only used in certain opaque colored enamels, notably lead antimonate yellows and copper 'sealing wax' reds (Freestone *et al.*, 2003b). Lead oxide began to be added in significant quantities as flux from the end of the sixteenth century, and by the nineteenth century lead had become an almost universal additive to enamels (e.g. Richter 1994; Biron *et al.*, 1996). Thus, Wypyski's (2002) study of the composition of Renaissance and Post-Medieval enamels on jewellery and their nineteenth-century copies found that whereas early pieces were all soda or mixed soda/potash glasses, the nineteenth-century copies were of lead/potash or lead/soda-silica glasses.

Borax was perhaps the major new constituent added to enamels in recent centuries as it significantly lowers the melting point and gives improved resistance to atmospheric corrosion. Thus, the presence of a few per cent of boron in an early enamel should be a cause for concern, but boron is difficult to detect by most of the presently preferred analytical techniques. Thus, for example, in Richter's 1994 study of some suspect enamels (see Chapter 20, p. 521), boron did not figure in the analysis not because it was potentially unimportant, but because the SEM/EDX and SEM/WDX systems were not able to detect it.

Enamel fakes and forgeries

Advances in methods of scientific examination and analysis have revolutionised the authenticity study of enamels, stylistic examinations now routinely being accompanied also by scientific examination. This is necessary because so many superb enamelled forgeries, along with very convincing fakes and major restorations, were made in the second half of the nineteenth century. Some workshops produced a large body of work of a very high standard. Fortunately, there are major differences in the composition of the enamels, which enables the nineteenth-century work to be unequivocally differentiated from the originals (Wypyski, 2002; Tait and Freestone, 2004; and see p. 225).

Mikhail Petrovitch Botkin

Sources: Kurz (1948, pp. 216–218); Buckton (1988); Stromberg (1988); Jones (ed) (1990, pp. 178–179).

Botkin was a noted St Petersburg collector of Early Medieval and Byzantine antiquities. From about 1892 he began to acquire Byzantine enamels on a considerable scale, such that he had built up a

collection of over 150 pieces by the time of his death in 1914 (Figure 10.22). None of these pieces had any provenance or history, but Botkin maintained in his 1911 catalogue of his collection that they were genuine because 'the difficulty of the cloisonné technique, or rather the lost skill, makes forgery almost impossible'. Most of them had a quite distinct and suspicious stylistic similarity, not least being that the figures all seem to have sharply down-turned mouths and to be looking warily to their left or right, as if expecting to be unmasked at any moment. This came about in the 1980s when the suspicions of scholars such as David Buckton (1988) were confirmed by chemical analysis which revealed chrome green and uranium yellow colorants in the enamels (Stromberg, 1988). It seems that the pieces were being made in St Petersburg, where there were several workshops – including those of Fabergé – employing craftsmen with the necessary skills.

Samson et Cie

The firm of Samson et Cie specialised in producing copies of porcelain of all periods and places, operating in Paris from about the mid-nineteenth to mid-twentieth century (see Chapter 9, p. 205). Samson also copied enamels (Speel, 1998, pp. 130–131; Slitine, 2002, pp. 19–47). Many types of European Medieval and Renaissance enamels were produced, but some of the most convincing pieces were copies of English eighteenth-century enamels, notably the little boxes and other trinkets produced at Bilston and Battersea (Benjamin, 1993, pp. 103–109).

Figure 10.22 Botkin enamel, BM MLA Reg. 1989, 7–8,1. (Courtesy A. Milton/British Museum)

Cunynghame (1906, pp. 156–157) in his authoritative book on European enamels stated:

> There is a factory now in Paris in which Battersea enamels are so perfectly imitated, broken chips and all, that it is impossible to distinguish them from the originals.
>
> The somewhat slovenly and rapid painting, the colors and the slender and refined states are copied to perfection.
>
> The practice of this and other firms engaged in similar work is to buy an original, imitate it a certain number of times, and then re-sell it. The retail dealers then chip the copies and dirty them according to taste.

Towards the end of the company's life the pieces were marked with an 'S', but this could be easily removed. There are some differences from the originals in the form of the hinges, and no doubt there are differences in the chemical composition of the enamels.

Samson stopped making enamels in the 1970s but the remaining stock of copper blanks was sold off, and so clandestine production probably continued.

Corrosion

The remains of corroded enamel of the appropriate composition can sometimes prove to be a crucial authenticating factor, especially when set in gold jewellery that might not otherwise display any features of age, as exemplified by the Minoan gold rosettes inlaid with white enamel (see Chapter 15, p. 373). Early enamels that have been buried are often very corroded and fragmentary, and require searching examination to locate the traces that could provide crucial authenticating evidence. This is exemplified by the Braganza Brooch.

Case study: The Braganza Brooch

Sources: Rowlett (1993); Stead and Meeks (1996).

The Braganza Brooch, also known as the Flannery or Warrior Fibula, first appeared on the (Figure 10.23) market in the 1950s with no previous history, and as Stead and Meeks (1996) stated:

> Concern about the authenticity of the Warrior Fibula is hardly surprising. It is a spectacular piece, and at first sight it seems to be too good to be true.

Indeed; and to address these concerns it was examined on a number of occasions over the next 40 years (Rowlett, 1993). Stylistically, the piece appears to combine disparate elements, which can be viewed either favourably as indicating an interesting example of the mixture of different cultural elements, or more negatively as indicating the production of a forger failing to achieve cultural consistency through ignorance.

An unusual feature of the fibula is the presence of a Platinum Group Element inclusion (see Chapter 15, p. 369) predominantly of platinum. PGE inclusions are rare in early Iberian goldwork (Nicolini 1990, p. 23). Platinoid inclusions are generally rare in gold artefacts, this in part is because platinoids, unlike most of the other PGE inclusions are soluble in molten gold. Platinoid grains do occur in some Spanish gold deposits (Ogden 1977) and some early Iberian goldwork has been found to contain traces of platinum in solution (Nicolini 1990, pp. 35–8).

The bow of the brooch has wire filigree that still contains the corroded traces of the original enamel. The traces are slight, but sufficient remained for it to be identified by binocular microscopy and SEM as a naturally weathered blue enamel (Rowlett, 1993) (Figure 10.24). XRF analysis on the weathered surfaces and

Figure 10.23 Detail of the Braganza Brooch. (Courtesy A. Milton/ British Museum)

Figure 10.24 SEM micrograph of the cracked and decayed blue enamel in the filigree decoration of the bow that was crucial in authenticating this enigmatic piece. (Courtesy N. Meeks/British Museum)

on the very few surviving areas of intact glass, showed it to be a soda-lime-silica glass, typical of classical antiquity. The opacifier is calcium antimonate and the blue colorant is cobalt. The presence of residual weathered enamel that is similar to other ancient weathered glasses and of the correct composition, is the strongest indication that the brooch is authentic.

11

Stone and sculpture

I must tell you that technical and scientific examination never amount to very much especially when it comes to ancient marbles.

Prof. F. Zeri, quoted in Hoving (1996, p. 295)

Sources: General: Richter (1970a); Mannoni and Mannoni (1989). Forgery: Kurz (1948, pp. 116–142); Arnau (1961, pp. 90–99); Ashmole (1961); Savage (1976, pp. 110–120); Mills and Mansfield (1979, pp. 181–198); Paul (1981); Türr (1984); Andrén (1986, esp. pp. 51–97); Penny (1993, pp. 1–122); Trench (ed) (2000, pp. 466–473); Polikreti (2007).

Historical

The copying of sculpture has a long history in Western art. Most of the works of the greatest Greek sculptors are known to us only through Roman copies (see Chapter 4, p. 64, for the copying techniques). To what extent, if any, these copies were passed off as genuine Greek antique works is uncertain; Hoving (1996, pp. 29–36) considered that most of the 'so-called Archaizing pieces are the products of deliberate chicanery', claiming that with suitable surface treatments, now lost, they would have been very difficult to tell apart from the Greek originals.

In the Renaissance period, classical sculpture was admired, collected and, naturally, faked and forged. Through the following centuries interest in antique sculpture continued to grow and whole workshops of sculptors became established in Italy to deal in, restore and fabricate antique art (see Chapter 20, p. 512). They served an ever-expanding market, as the nobility of Europe visited Italy on their Grand Tour, often with the acquisition of antique carvings as one of their prime objectives. This further developed in the nineteenth century with the establishment of public collections in museums all over the world, all eager to acquire ancient sculpture, and Italy remained the main source of reality, restored reality, pastiche, fake and outright forgery. There seems to have been any number of highly skilled modellers and stone carvers deeply steeped in the styles of ancient carving, which by the nineteenth century included that of the Renaissance period. This was coupled with long experience and knowledge of what collectors and curators wanted, the condition they would expect the stone to be in, and how to imitate this.

The combination produced some formidable fakes and forgeries, which, by the eighteenth and nineteenth centuries, encompassed just about all the decorative arts as well as sculpture and painting (Mazzoni (ed), 2004). As Meyer (1973, p. 120) remarked, 'Italy, without question has been the world's premier fake factory', exemplified by the sculptures of Alceo Dossena that duped some of the world's major museums.

Alceo Dossena 'The human anachronism'

Sources: Richter (1929); Schüller (1960, pp. 61–70); Arnau (1961, pp. 211–225); Ashmole (1961); Jeppson (1971, pp. 47–68); Sox (1987).

Alceo Dossena was born in Cremona in 1878 into a family that included various artists and craftsmen. Alceo seems to have developed great practical skills in a variety of media matched by an extraordinary ability to work in a variety of styles.

One fateful day in Christmas 1916 he offered one of his carvings, a marble relief of a Madonna and Child, for sale to the dealer Alfredo Fasoli, who recognised both the inherent quality of the carving, and also the possibilities of selling it as an antique piece. He purchased it and intimated that he would be interested in any other 'old pieces' that Dossena might have.

Fasoli cultivated Dossena, and in partnership with Roman Pales, set him up in a workshop in Rome to produce sculpture, specialising initially in Renaissance pieces, in which style Dossena soon became extremely proficient. At this stage some still claim that he was innocent, but his great skill in the production of false patinas was already apparent and it seems unlikely that he was not aware that his creations were being sold as genuine antiques.

Soon he was also creating ambitious works in a convincing classical style in both stone and in terracotta, his *Diana* being a well-known piece that, astonishingly, was purchased by the St Louis Museum as a genuine major Etruscan terracotta statue some 30 years after Dossena's activities had been revealed (see Chapter 9, p. 198).

One of the reasons for the success of Dossena's stone sculptures was their convincing patination, the details of which Dossena kept a close secret. The treatments seem to have involved repeated dipping in acids, presumably to create the right surface texture before the application of the surface finish. These treatments do seem to have been able to produce a convincing weathering crust on the marble (Newman, 1990).

An interesting and well-documented example is provided by the so-called Savelli Tomb. It was acquired by the Museum of Fine Arts, Boston and purports to be the tomb of Maria Caterina Savelli carved by Mino da Fiesole in the fifteenth century. Almost from its acquisition doubts were raised over its authenticity and thus the piece was one of the first to be scientifically examined (Hipkiss *et al.*, 1937; Jeppson, 1971, p. 65; Newman, 1990, esp. en 17). Photomicrographs of sections taken from various parts of the tomb were compared to sections through the surfaces of both ancient and modern marbles and on this basis the monument was judged to be basically authentic, although in fact the patina was Dossena's creation (Figures 11.1a–d).

The surface was impregnated with wax, as were many of Dossena's creations (Sox, 1987, p. 60). This had the effect of nullifying the UV test, which was the main method through much of the twentieth century of detecting freshly carved surfaces (see p. 258). Dossena's patinas were visually very effective, one art historian when commenting on the patination filling a crack in the aforementioned Savelli tomb, opining that 'the crack whispered softly of the passing centuries that had mellowed and stained the Cararra marble to a rich golden hue' (Sox, 1987, p. 54).

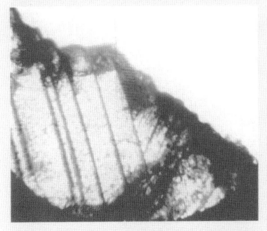 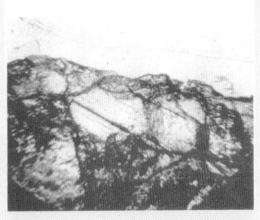

Figure 11.1a Photomicrographs (each 0.6 mm across) of cross-section of the altered surface on a genuine ancient sculpture with a dark channel between the grain and the surface. (Courtesy Young and Ashmole, 1968)

Figure 11.1b Cross-section through the surface of a modern forgery, with no darkening. (Courtesy Young and Ashmole, 1968)

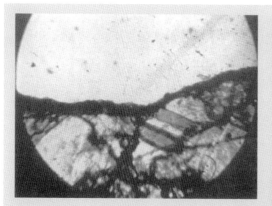

Figure 11.1c Cross-section through the altered surface of the Savelli tomb. Note the dark channels similar to those on the ancient sculpture. (Courtesy Hipkiss *et al.*, 1937)

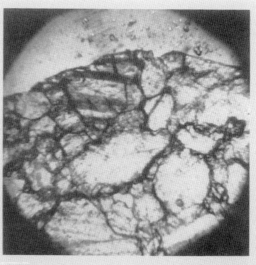

Figure 11.1d Cross-section through the surface layers on a reworked area on the inscription of the Savelli Tomb, similar to those on the modern forgery. (Courtesy Hipkiss *et al.*, 1937)

Figure 11.2 Detail of Dossena's Pallas Athene. The extensive but rather superficial damage to the face misses important features such as the eyes, and leaves the nose intact. This was unfortunate, as the slightly hooked nose was one of the statue's unusual features that was commented upon, although the statue was generally regarded as Dossena's most convincing forgery in the Archaic Greek style. (Courtesy Lusetti, 1955)

It was claimed by Schüller (1960, pp. 63–64) that as early as 1921 the Savelli tomb was shown to Miss Helen Clay Frick, the American heiress, with a view to purchase. When the story of its background was checked out, the ruined abbey where it was supposedly discovered was found not to exist and the sale fell through. Schüller went further (see p. 64) and claimed that Miss Frick's agents had actually discovered its real author, Dossena, who had freely admitted to having carved it. If so then this is extraordinary, for not only was the tomb sold as genuine three years later to Boston (Sox, 1987, pp. 60–62), but it would suggest that some in the art world had already made the connection between the appearance on the market of some spectacular and suspect sculptures and Fasoli and Dossena way back in 1921, years before the link became general knowledge in 1928. This occurred when Dossena sued Fasoli for extra payment for the pieces which he now revealed he had been making (Richter, 1929).

The reaction to the revelations in the art world that so many recently acquired major pieces were the product of one forger ranged from 'I-told-you-so' to outright disbelief. The New York dealer Jacob Hirsch, who had purchased several of Dossena's pieces, including a statue of *Pallas Athene*, which he had then sold to the Cleveland Museum of Art (Figure 11.2)

was one of those, understandably, who claimed that Dossena was merely bragging. He was only persuaded otherwise when, on visiting Dossena's workshop in Rome, Dossena was able to produce the missing hand from the statue that had been broken off to give it a little designer damage and which fitted perfectly.

After the very public revelations of Dossena's activities, the extent of his productions should have been rapidly established, but in the uncertain world of art dealing all manner of assertions and attributions were made for years afterwards, continuing long after Dossena's death in 1937. As already noted in Chapter 9, p. 198 prominent among those seeking out and exposing Dossena's forgeries were Harold Parsons and Pico Cellini, who produced the short illustrated biography of Dossena (Lusetti, 1955). Here at last was a photographic record, many of the photographs having been taken by Dossena himself of work in progress, including Boston's Savelli Tomb (Lusetti, plate 27) and three pictures of the Cleveland Museum's marble *Pallas Athene* (Lusetti, 1955, plates 5, 6 and 9).

Sculpture technique

Sources: General: Rich (1947); Miller (1948); Hodges (1964, pp. 105–111); Bessac (1988); Trench (ed) (2000, pp. 466–477). Egypt: Aston *et al.* (2000, pp. 63–77); Stocks (2003). Stone vessels: Stocks (1993; 2003, pp. 139–168); Aston (1994). Classical: Gardiner (1890); Casson (1933); Adam (1966); Bluemel (1969); Ridgway (1969); Stronge and Claridge (1976).

The sculptor, P. Rockwell (1990), complained that there had been very little work to characterise the marks made on stone that could identify specific tools and techniques. The systematic scanning electron microscopy (SEM) study of the characteristics of the surfaces produced by the various abrading processes would be of some value in authenticity studies of carvings of all periods, such as those being carried forward on gemstones and jade (see Chapter 16, pp. 412, 418).

Stone sculpture, in the round, seems to have commenced in the Neolithic period. For the developments in stone-shaping technology, the main divisions of the prehistoric period of Stone, Bronze and Iron Ages, are very relevant. Some real carving of stone with flint tools is possible, but it is likely that the main methods of shaping stone before metal tools were flaking, pounding and abrasion. In the succeeding Bronze Age, metal axes and punches could be used to rough out the sculpture preparatory to abrasion, and the advent of steel in the Iron Age introduced a material that could be much stronger than stone and permitted real carving with chisels. Greek sculptors possessed a range of hand tools not markedly different from those in use today (Figure 11.3). Note that Bluemel (1969, p. 18) stated that the Greeks did not have steel. This

is erroneous, as tools of heat-treated carbon steel, the equal of those used today, were available from at least the Geometric period, although bronze or copper tools were also used, then as now, when a softer edge was required.

Much sawing and drilling could be accomplished by abrasion either with another stone or a softer material fed with a sharp abrasive. No matter how they were initially shaped, most sculptures will have been finished by grinding and polishing. This will have largely removed the evidence of the earlier stages of the working, although some original tool marks may survive in deep depressions where it is difficult to introduce polishing tools. Gwinnett and Gorelick used SEM techniques developed for their lapidary studies to investigate the drilled holes on some ancient stone carvings (see Chapter 16, p. 413). They were able to recognise and characterise both the shape and abrasion patterns for holes made using a bow drill and the action of a hand-held drill. They also studied the characteristic abrasion patterns made by bits of flint, or of wood or copper rods impregnated with abrasives. For example, they were able to establish that the four holes drilled in a Cycladic marble figurine formed part of an ancient repair as they were likely to have been made with a hand-held drill mounted with a flint bit (Gwinnett and Gorelick, 1983). They also examined some strange stone carvings of birds and animals said to have come from eastern Anatolia (Gwinnett and Gorelick, 1982; Gorelick and Gwinnett, 1986). The style was unparalleled, and the carvings had no certain provenance, but the drilled impressions made for the creatures' eyes also seemed to have been made using hand-held flint drills, supporting their authenticity.

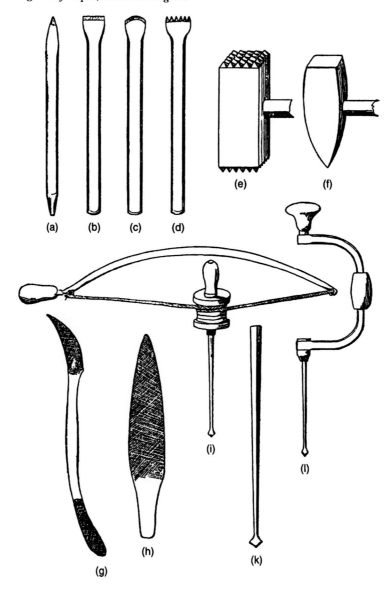

Figure 11.3   Sculptor's steel tools in use from the Iron Age, with the exception of l): a) point or punch; b) flat chisel; c) bull-nosed chisel; d) claw-chisel; e) doucharde; f) pointed or trimming hammer; g) and h) rasps; i) running drill; k) drill bit; l) brace and bit or augur, only introduced in the Renaissance. (Courtesy Bluemel, 1969)

Stross and Eisenlord (1965) suggested examining polished areas for particles of embedded abrasives, hoping to reveal particles of modern abrasives.

In the Bronze Age it is not clear how much actual chiselling of stone was achieved with bronze tools. It seems likely that most Bronze Age sculpture from the Eastern Mediterranean, Egypt and the Middle East, was done with stone pounders, followed by bronze punches held at right-angles to the surface, and with a limited amount of flat chisel work done in some cases to smooth the surface preparatory to grinding and polishing.

Case study: The Fitzwilliam Goddess

Sources: Casson (1927); Wace (1927); Budde and Nicholls (1964, pp. 114–116); Butcher and Gill (1993).

A whole series of forgeries of Minoan figures appeared in the 1920s, inspired by Sir Arthur Evans' Minoan discoveries at Knossos on Crete, and his own collecting activities. Many of these are figures of ivory (see Chapter 17, p. 422), but some are of marble, including the female figure in full flounced skirt, purchased by the Fitzwilliam Museum, Cambridge in January 1926. The statuette was purchased from the scholar–dealer Charles Seltman for the truly enormous sum of 2750 pounds sterling.

At the time of the acquisition of the statuette it was unique and was billed as the earliest piece of true Greek sculpture in marble, 'Great art before Pheidas'. The astronomic sum demanded for the piece seems almost to have made the statuette more desirable, Evans noting that 'very good things are priceless'. Winifred Lamb, the honorary curator of classical antiquities at the Fitzwilliam, was so desperate to acquire it that she even offered to put up more than half of the price herself, so that the statuette 'shall make my (deleted) our Dept. world famous' – all this, without Lamb actually having seen the piece, seemingly trusting to the price as an indication of its quality.

Wace (1927) stated in the definitive monograph that the piece was rumoured to have been found on Crete just east of Candia (now Heraklion). He surmised that 'it would seem that it had been found in the ruins of some building, perhaps a shrine which had been destroyed by fire'. As Butcher and Gill latterly pointed out, 'this was speculation bordering on complete fabrication about an object with no provenance'. Casson (1927) put it more bluntly: 'All the statements of all the peasants and dealers on Crete are worthless in comparison with one sound deduction from scientific excavation'.

It was also pointed out that – rather strangely for what purported to be a prestige piece – the statuette had not been carved from a single stone but from two pieces of nondescript marble, and furthermore it was not obvious how they could ever have been joined at the waist. Subsequently the two parts had been smashed into many pieces and possibly burnt.

Photographs circulated of other very similar, but generally inferior statuettes, in the same *marbre rouge clair*, or 'like corned beef' as someone rather unkindly but more prosaically described it.

The first and most consistent hostile claims that the piece was a local Cretan forgery came from Xanthoudides, curator of the Candia Museum, but his complaints were looked upon as sour grapes.

The statuette was condemned in reviews of Wace's monograph (Forsdyke, 1927). Casson (1927) also deplored that the figure was chosen as the frontispiece of the Plates Volume of the prestigious *Cambridge Ancient History* (edited by none other than Seltman), with the bald statement that it had been found in Crete, not far to the east of Candia – with no qualification that this was completely unsupported supposition.

Casson (1933, pp. 5–7) studied the figure and noted technical features that apparently condemned it outright. In particular he believed that the vertical grooves representing pleats on the figurine's skirt had been done with a steel gouge. He also speculated that the horizontal grooves on the skirt were done with abrasives or with a steel file. However, examination for Budde and Nicholls' catalogue (1964, p. 116) could not confirm the use of steel tools. Furthermore, no evidence of acid treatment or of blatantly obvious false patina could be found. Perhaps the figurine should be examined afresh using SEM, which might reveal characteristic tool or abrasion marks.

With the introduction of iron and, specifically, steel, sculpting tools could at last actually cut and carve the stone rather than just flake or crush it. Important new tool types introduced at this time include the claw or toothed chisel, the gouge or bull-nosed chisel with its curved profile, and the rasp. Overall, despite the introduction of these chisels it seems that punch work was used to a much greater extent through classical antiquity than in Renaissance and later sculpture (Rockwell, 1990). This is a good way of detecting forgeries on unfinished works (Bluemel, 1969, pp. 24–25). A noticeable feature is the increasing amount of drill work in classical carving. At some time in the Hellenistic period vertical drilling seems to have been joined by the running drill, which works obliquely with a milling action to produce deep grooves (Ashmole, 1961). These become very prominent on the rendering of the hair on Roman statuary, for example (Penny, 1993, pp. 81–92).

The use of the wrong drill technique eventually led to the unmasking of a group of porphyry heads of tetrarchs in the Late Antique style, but not before several museums had purchased them (Spier, 1990). These included the British Museum (BM GR Reg. 1974, 12–13, 1) (Cook, B., 1984; Jones, (ed), 1990, p. 242; and see Chapter 1, p. 18) and the Louvre (MNE 782) (Villard, 1977). They were almost certainly carved from fragments of ancient columns, as was the head of a Dacian that had been acquired by the Museum of Fine Arts, Boston back in 1913 (Reg. 13.2722), but which was soon revealed as a forgery (Johnson, 1973, no. 18).

Many of the technical developments since Hellenistic times concern methods of copying in sculpture, notably pointing, considered in Chapter 4 (p. 73).

The characterisation of marble and other stones

Sources: General: Herz and Waelkens (eds) (1988); True and Podany (eds) (1990b); Waelkens *et al.* (eds) (1992); Maniatis *et al.* (eds) (1995); Lambert (1997, pp. 1–32); Schvoerer (ed) (1999); Schilardi and Katsonopoulou (eds) (2000); Herz (2001); Herrmann *et al.* (eds) (2002); Polikreti (2007). Egypt: Klemm and Klemm (1993); Aston (1994); Aston *et al.* (2000). India: Newman (1984).

The scientific characterisation, or fingerprinting, of the various chemical and physical attributes of the stone has two principal applications in authenticity studies.

1. The long tradition of replacing missing extremities on ancient statuary or even of making up an entire statue from disparate fragments (see Chapter 20, p. 512). Analysis of the components of a sculpture can help to determine which pieces are likely to have belonged to the original or even whether there ever was an 'original' as such (Herz, 1990).
2. Characterisation to establish the likely provenance of the stone to a specific quarry. This can

be of great significance: for example, if a sculpture in the style of the Archaic Greek period was shown to be of marble from a quarry that was not used before the Roman period.

At the outset of this section it should be emphasised that despite the enormous advances that have been made in the determination of an ever-growing variety of chemical and physical parameters, the characterisation of a stone should always commence with its basic petrography and mineralogy.

Over the past 40 years there has been sustained research into methods for provenancing stone, resulting in tremendous advances in both the precision and variety of methods (Herz, 2001; Polikreti, 2007) (Table 11.1). In 1970 the Oxford classical archaeologist, Bernard Ashmole, clearly stung by Renfrew and Peacey's 1968 paper on marble analysis, could state that 'the chances of any scientific method, present or future, being able to determine *with certainty* [his italics] the source of any given specimen is nil'. In this context it is instructive to read Spier's rather dismissive 1990 article on scientific authentication. Many of the provenancing and authentication studies have focused on classical statuary and therefore work has tended to concentrate on Mediterranean marble sources. However, the methods are applicable to a wide range of stones worldwide once the appropriate databases have been established by sampling at the relevant quarries, something that is still in progress even for the relatively well known sources of classical marble.

The much-expanded databases of a variety of parameters from an ever-increasing number of ancient quarries have provided a clearer overall picture even if revealing, at the same time, the greater complexity of the actual situation. As the number of identified sources increases, the inevitable overlaps become ever more apparent, as noted many years ago by Germann *et al.* (1980). Lambert (1997, pp. 7–8) contrasted the original 1972 stable isotope plot (see p. 252) for just five major Greek marble quarries, each one well separated from its neighbour, with his 1997 plot of the isotope ratios for 14 Greek and Western Anatolian quarries, where overlap usually occurs and confusion is seemingly total.

It is still largely true that elemental analysis alone will rarely provenance a marble and that a sample of several hundred milligrams is usually required. However, a combination of parameters, particularly the trace element content together with stable isotope analysis (SIA) and the basic petrology,

Table 11.1 Evaluation of analytical methods for provenance determination.

Method[a]	Petrography	XRD	INAA	SEM, Probe	ICP	XRF, etc	SIA	CL	ESR	Mag	Fiss Track
Sample	thin section	powd	powd	ts or slice	powd	powd	powd	slice	powd	slice or entire piece	thin sec
Size[b]	large	small	small	medium	small	small	small	med	small	varies	med
Cost[b]	low	low	high	moderate	low	low	med-high	mod	low	low	high
Rock type[c]											
Obsidian	high	high	high	high	high	high	Sr, O	—	—	poten	poten
Basalt	high	high	high	high	high	high	Sr, O	—	—	poten	oldest rocks[d]
Granite	high	high	high	high	high	high	Sr, O	—	—	poten	—
Serpentine	high	high	high	high	high	high	Sr	—	—	—	—
Marble	high	high	high	high	high	high	C, Sr, O	high	high	—	—
Sandstone	high	high	high	high	high	high	poten Sr	—	—	—	—
Chert	high	high	high	high	high	high	O	poten	—	—	—
Carbonate	high	high	high	high	high	high	C, O, Sr	high	high	—	—

Source: Herz, 2001, Figure 16. 2

[a] The type of analysis for major and trace elements should be determined by: (a) what is the usual method used with this rock type; (b) what kinds of labs are available to the researcher; (c) how much funding is available.

[b] Cost—costs for any type of analysis will depend on factors such as the laboratory—is it non-profit university or commercial; the grant—many universities have a sliding scale, graduate student research vs. faculty Federal grant, etc.

[c] The types of analysis done with each rock type are evaluated as (a) high—highest priority, a commonly used system; (b) poten—a potentially useful method not commonly used or not used to date; and (c)—lowest priority, not useful or not proven to be useful.

[d] For fission track measurements to be meaningful, the rock should have a minimum content of U as well was a minimum age. Felsic rocks, such as obsidian generally meet the first requirement; mafic rocks such as basalt rarely do.

increasingly does allow a positive identification as to source (Moens *et al.* 1988a, b; 1992; 1995). Van der Merwe *et al.* (1995) suggested that SIA and X-ray diffraction (XRD), requiring no more than a few milligrams of sample, coupled with a simple surface identification of the mineralogy, would usually suffice to provenance the marble, especially when taken together with stylistic and documentary evidence. They supported their claim by reporting work on approximately 150 pieces from the Museum of Fine Arts, Boston and the Sackler collection at Harvard. Samples were simply scraped off from an inconspicuous surface using a Swiss Army knife (although one would have to be very careful to avoid the potential problems of weathering or of surface contamination). They further suggested that addition of isotopic determinations of heavy elements such as strontium and neodymium (for which databases are presently incomplete or in the case of neodymium non-existent) potentially could raise the success rate in provenancing marbles to over 90%, all on samples of a very few milligrams, and at very low cost.

The principal characterisation methods will now be outlined. As already noted, most have been developed for Mediterranean marble, but where they have been applied to other stones the specific examples will be mentioned.

Petrology

Source: Kempe and Harvey (eds) 1983.

A preliminary petrological examination using a hand lens to identify the stone is an essential precursor, ideally followed by a more detailed petrographical and mineralogical description made from a thin section. However, cutting a thin section from a sculpture is not usually permissible, especially on smaller pieces. Examination of broken surfaces can be revealing, estimating the maximum grain size, for example, can exclude many quarries. Recent advances in computed tomography (CT) have enabled considerable petrological information to be obtained non-destructively (Mees *et al.* (eds) 2003; and see Chapter 2, p. 32, Figure 2.11a–d).

Purely petrological descriptions of a selection of the most famous quarries of classical antiquity were made by Lepsius (1890) and Washington (1898), and for the next few decades until the work of Moltesen *et al.* (1992), remained virtually the only

Case study: The head of Pan (Herz et al., 1989)

This limestone head, now in the Cleveland Museum, was claimed to have been found on the Acropolis in Athens, near to where the monument erected by the Athenians to commemorate their victory over the Persians in 490 BC had stood. As the head would have been by far the most important fragment to have survived from the monument it was of considerable historical interest. However, petrography on the head and on a selection of fragments from the monument showed that whereas the fragments were all made of the Acropolis limestone, the head of Pan was of a totally different limestone. Neutron activation analysis (NAA) and SIA confirmed that the head was indeed different, but could not offer a source from among the known Greek quarries.

Schmid *et al.* (1999) applied quantitative fabric analysis to discriminate between quarries for white marble. In this approach, the most significant features of the grain boundaries as observed in thin section taken are quantified. These included the mean grain size, the axial difference (the major–minor axis), the perimeter/surface ratio and the PARIS-factor, which is a measure of the overall convexity/concavity within the analysed grain boundary network. These parameters were calculated for several hundred grains in each section, thereby allowing significant statistical treatment of what would otherwise have been unquantified observations. The method achieved some separation, but there were still overlaps for which a multi-disciplinary approach would still be necessary. Biricotti and Severi (2004) developed a scheme of recording various physical parameters of white marble, using a laser diode as the light source and a charged couple device camera with its lens and an interference filter. The method is fast, non-destructive and very portable, and could find application in quickly checking the homogeneity of a repaired group, for example.

The petrology of igneous rocks is more distinctive. However, chemical analysis is still necessary for more detailed characterisation of individual sources or on broader surveys covering a wider range of possible sources. Brown and Harrell (1995) characterised the main Egyptian granite sources used in the Roman period by a combination of petrography and composition. More specifically, Peacock *et al.* (1994) studied the granodiorite, the *granito del foro*, from Mons Claudianus, in the eastern desert of Egypt, used for columns, etc., by the Romans. Galetti *et al.* (1992) characterised Roman granite quarries in Sardinia and the other Italian islands, and in Turkey, using a combination of petrography and composition, although they were able to provenance many granite artefacts on the basis of their petrography alone.

geological data used for characterising the sources of classical marble sculpture.

Chemical analysis

Sources: *Marble*: Moens *et al.* (1988b, 1992, 1995); Moltesen *et al.* (1992); Matthews *et al.* (1995); Matthews (1997).

Limestone: Holmes *et al.* (1986, 1994); Harrell (1992); Holmes and Harbottle (1994, 2003).

Basalt: Williams-Thorpe (1988); Mallory-Greenough *et al.* (1999a, b; 2000).

Granite: Galetti *et al.* (1992); Brown and Harrell (1995); Williams-Thorpe *et al.* (1999, 2000a, b).

Sandstones and quartzite: Stross *et al.* (1988); Newman (1992b).

Steatite - soapstone: Allen *et al.* (1984); Truncer *et al.* (1998).

Schists: Newman (1988, 1992b).

NAA (see Chapter 3, p. 51) was the favoured method of trace element analysis (Matthews, 1997). More recently, inductively coupled plasma (ICP) techniques in conjunction with mass spectrometry (MS) (see Chapter 3, p. 46) have replaced NAA (Green *et al.*, 2002). Microprobe analysis has also been successfully used, combining analytical and microscopic capabilities allowing the composition of specific minerals or phases within the stone to be characterised, although the detection limits for most elements are poorer than with ICP–MS (Mallory-Greenough *et al.* 1999a, b; 2000; Newman, 1992b).

Although trace element analysis by itself rarely worked for marble, petrological and analytical studies on igneous rocks, such as basalts and granites, where the original magmatic materials are more distinctive in composition, have been able to characterise the sources and allow the artefacts to be provenanced. For example, a combination of petrography and microprobe analysis was used to determine the provenance of Egyptian basalts used variously for vessels (Mallory-Greenough *et al.*,

1999b) and temple paving (Mallory-Greenough *et al.*, 2000). Williams-Thorpe (1988) carried out a major provenance study of Roman basalt millstones using petrography and wavelength-dispersive X-ray fluorescence (WD XRF) to determine both major and trace elements (see Chapter 3, p. 47).

Williams-Thorpe *et al.* (1999) developed portable analytical systems for use in the field, including a non-destructive portable XRF system. They found that the weathered surfaces had compositions significantly different from those of the stone beneath. Such differences in the composition of weathered surfaces are also common in marbles, and, as with them, could be significant for authenticity studies (see p. 260). They also developed a non-destructive combination of portable XRF analysis with magnetic susceptibility (MagS) to provenance dolerite axes (Williams-Thorpe *et al.* 2003).

Williams-Thorpe *et al.* (2000b) have used gamma-ray spectrometry to quantify the radioactive isotopes of the elements potassium, uranium and thorium in some Roman granite columns, originally from Leptis Magna in North Africa, but now in Windsor Great Park, near London. This innovative analytical system is portable and non-destructive and enabled most of the columns to be provenanced.

Magnetic susceptibility (MagS)

Sources: Williams-Thorpe and Thorpe (1993); Williams-Thorpe *et al.* (1996).

The MagS of a material is the measure of the magnetism that can be induced by an applied magnetic field (Williams-Thorpe and Thorpe 1993). It depends very largely on the presence of ferro-magnetic materials, and the strongest ferromagnetic mineral is the iron oxide aptly named magnetite, the lodestone of yore. Many igneous rocks, such as granite or basalt, contain traces of magnetite, and these can be quantified by MagS. This forms a quick, cheap and non-destructive method for

Case study: The Colossi of Memnon

Heizer *et al.* (1973) determined the source of the ferruginous quartzite used in the Colossi of Memnon by a combination of petrography and composition. These famous statues of Amenhotep III were erected in the fourteenth century BC near Thebes in Upper Egypt, and repaired in the Roman period after an earthquake in 27 BC. They are truly colossal, each being carved from a single block of stone estimated at between 700 and 800 tons, such that they can only have been transported by water and thus Heizer and colleagues could reasonably discount any source that was not near to the Nile, thereby limiting the potential quarry sites to just three areas, two of them upstream, Aswan (200 km distant) and Edfu (100 km distant), and one downstream, the Gebel el Ahmar, near Cairo (650 km distant). NAA analysis on a total of 30 samples taken from the Colossi and adjacent structures, ruled out the first two areas and petrography confirmed that the Gebel el Ahmar quarry was the most likely source, although the extreme variability of the material at the quarries was stressed, and is a continuing problem.

The conclusion of Heizer and colleagues was challenged by Klemm *et al.* (1984), who, also on the basis of petrography and trace element composition, were adamant that the Colossi came from quarries at Aswan. Further work by Heizer's team (Bowman *et al.*, 1984) would seem to confirm their original conclusion. Additional support came from Stross *et al.* (1988), who analysed other Egyptian quartzite sources and statuary made from them and found that all the early Egyptian quartzite sculpture came from Gebel el Ahmar, and that the quarries in the south only began to be used in the Roman period. In fact the repairs to the northern Colossus constituted the earliest dated use of the Aswan quartzite. This episode does serve to show some of the difficulties encountered, especially when dealing with repaired statuary, not to mention the wide variation of composition within the quarries themselves.

provenancing granites in combination with mineralogy. The method can also be applied to the various strikingly colored and variegated porphyries (Delbrück, 1932) that together with a host of other colored stones, confusingly referred to as colored marble or *mamora Romana*, were so prized by the Romans (Gnoli, 1988; Penny, 1993, pp. 21–33, 93). Portable apparatus has been developed as many of the artefacts tend to be very large and heavy columns, etc. Ideally the measurements would be made against a flat surface, but most worked pieces are curved to a greater or lesser degree, and are also slightly weathered. As it is normally not permissible to grind clean flat surfaces on antiquities, corrections have to be made to the estimate of the MagS, based on measurements of the topography of the piece (Williams-Thorpe *et al.* 2000a). Mineralogy and MagS are not always sufficient, and as described above, a portable gamma-ray spectrometer has been devised to measure the traces of the radioactive isotopes of potassium, thorium and uranium found in the granites (Williams-Thorpe *et al.* 2000b).

Williams-Thorpe and her co-workers have concentrated on the sources used by the Classical World. Their MagS surveys have been carried out on

ancient quarries in Italy, Greece, western Anatolia and Egypt, together with no less than 285 Roman columns from Rome and its surroundings (Williams-Thorpe and Thorpe, 1993) and they were often able to assign the columns to a quarry on the basis of the appearance and MagS alone.

The method should be applicable to worked granite generally, and both Egypt and India, for example, have long traditions of using granite for sculpture and architecture, to which MagS could be usefully applied.

Stable isotope analysis (SIA)

Sources: Carbon and oxygen isotopes: Herz (1987, 1992); Moens *et al.* (1988a, 1992, 1995); Gorgoni *et al.* (2002).

Perhaps the most important advance made in limestone and marble provenance studies has been in the measurement of the isotopes of carbon ($^{13}C/^{12}C$) and oxygen ($^{18}O/^{16}O$) of the carbonates in the marble.

The methodology has been described by Herz (1987, 1992), and Matthews *et al.* (1995) describe some of the statistical treatments of the data. Particular advantages are that it requires only a few milligrams of sample and is relatively quick and inexpensive. SIA, in conjunction with petrography and trace element analysis, usually NAA, has been widely applied (Moens *et al.*, 1988b, 1992, 1995). Herz *et al.* (1985) published the first 'real' results, provenancing sculptures from the Cyrene Demeter Sanctuary, and see Herz (1992), Walker *et al.* (1993) and Chapter 20, p. 520, for work on Roman sarcophagi, etc. Forgeries have been exposed (Herz *et al.*, 1989), and restored or composite sculptures have been studied, establishing which components, if any, are likely to be original (Herz, 1990, Jones (ed), 1990, p. 283; and see Chapter 20, p. 512). Sometimes it has proved possible to demonstrate that two separate sculptures must have come from the same block of stone. For example, it was shown that the isotopic similarity between the *Nativity* by the seventeenth-century French sculptor, Michel Anguier, and a statue of *Pluto*, only recently ascribed to Anguier on stylistic grounds (Black and Nadeau, 1990), was so great that the two pieces must have come from the same block of marble, thereby confirming the attribution (Nadeau, 1992).

Herz and Doumas (1991) characterised marble from sources that were likely to have been used in the Cycladic and Early Bronze Ages in the Aegean. This information potentially is of use for authentication of Cycladic marble figurines, although, as pointed out by Gill and Chippindale (1993), many of the forgeries come from the Cyclades using the appropriate marble.

The combination of SIA with other techniques has proved useful, enabling particular parts of quarries to be characterised and their stone identified. This can be of great assistance with some of the major quarries, such as those on Paros that comprise a series of quarries each with their own specific periods of use (Herrmann *et al.* 2000). If the specific quarry can be characterised, this could enable some works to be much more precisely attributed and dated.

However, a word of caution must be expressed. So far the studies have tended to be rather regionalised, which may be permissible for remote antiquity, but falls down for the great Empires such as that of Rome. Lapuente and Turi (1995) have characterised many of the Iberian marble quarries used in antiquity, but noted that they had considerable overlap with some of the more famous quarries at the other end of the Mediterranean. This is of no great consequence until the Roman period when, along with other unexplored quarries along the North African coast, the Iberian quarries could have

been supplying stone all over the Empire. The very existence of these ancient Iberian quarries should give pause to all those whose marble provenance studies presently concentrate only on the quarries of Italy, Greece and western Anatolia.

Other isotopes

The use of carbon and oxygen isotope ratios has been supplemented by that of radiogenic strontium ($^{87}Sr/^{86}Sr$) isotope ratios (Herz, 1987, 1992). Castorina *et al.* (1997) carried out carbon, oxygen and strontium isotope measurements on samples from a selection of the most famous white marble quarries of antiquity, Naxos, Paros, Mt Penteli, Aphrodisias, Marmara and Carrara. The strontium isotope ratio by itself was not particularly diagnostic, and did require a much larger sample than for carbon and oxygen isotope determinations, typically of about 100 milligrams. However, the results taken in conjunction with the oxygen isotope ratios, enabled samples from Naxos, Paros, Penteli and Carrara to be clearly differentiated. Having analysed many more samples from Mediterranean quarries, Brilli *et al.* (2005) concluded that there is substantial overlap and that strontium isotope ratios by themselves are unlikely to be diagnostic.

Gale *et al.* (1988) used the isotopes of sulphur and strontium to source some of the gypsum used by the Mycenaeans.

Electron spin resonance (ESR)

Sources: Lloyd *et al.* (1985); Mandi *et al.* (1992): Armiento *et al.* (1997); Attanasio *et al.* (2002a); Polikreti and Maniatis (2002); Attanasio (2003).

The technique – also known as electron paramagnetic resonance (EPR) – is quite widely used in archaeometry studies on a range of ancient materials. Electrons in chemical bonds between atoms or in elemental orbits are usually paired, but sometimes single electrons exist, notably in some metals such as iron or manganese. As the electron is unpaired it gives the whole ion a magnetic moment, and the material is described as being paramagnetic. In a magnetic field the unpaired electrons will tend to align themselves with it. If a source of microwave energy is applied to the sample in the magnetic field, the aligned electrons will absorb some of the energy at specific wavelengths, characteristic of the particular metal ion and, to a lesser extent, its environment. The ESR can also be affected by previous heat treatments and Maniatis and Mandi (1992) used this to look for evidence of past frictional heating during the drilling, etc. of the marble.

The method is quick, cheap and, for marble, requires a sample of about 100 mg, which, as it is not destroyed during the ESR measurements, can then be used for other analyses. In marble studies the main paramagnetic ion is that of manganese, Mn^{2+}, which occurs in trace amounts in most marbles.

This approach to provenancing was tried on some American marble by Lloyd *et al.* (1985) and measurements began to be made on marble from ancient Mediterranean quarries from the 1980s. Armiento *et al.* (1997) studied samples from the quarries at Tharros on Sardinia. A number of the major Greek quarries have been sampled and the method seems to produce useful results, especially when used in conjunction with other techniques. Therefore, Attanasio *et al.* (2000) used a combination of petrography, ESR and SIA to differentiate the marble types from the three main quarries at Carrara. Maniatis and Polikreti (2000) and Polikreti and Maniatis (2002) used grain size measurements and ESR to differentiate between a number of Greek sources of white marble. Attanasio *et al.* (2002b) have suggested that close similarities in the ESR values may be of help in showing that marble fragments came from a single block of marble and thus are likely to belong to one sculpture.

Cathodoluminescence (CL)

Sources: General: Marshall (1988). Marble: Barbin *et al.* (1991, 1992).

When some minerals, calcite or dolomite in the case of marbles, are bombarded with electrons, light is emitted. The wavelength, or color, of the light is characteristic of the various impurities, particularly iron or manganese, in the crystal lattice. As such CL is well established as a method for characterising or provenancing many sedimentary rocks (Marshall, 1988).

The usual method is to place a thin section of the marble in the electron beam of a specially adapted electron microscope and then record the visual image. This methodology was tried for marble in the 1960s (Renfrew and Peacey, 1968) and with continuing advances in SEM microscopy it was applied again to marble in the 1980s with greater success (Barbin *et al.*, 1991, 1992). This project built up a database of over 1000 samples from quarries all around the Mediterranean, and was able to characterise the various sources, especially when used in conjunction with SIA (Barbin

et al. 1992) (Figure 11.4). Herrmann Jr and Barbin (1993) used a combination of CL and SIA to identify dolomitic marble from the quarries on Thasos in the northern Aegean.

If a petrographic section has been taken, this will suffice for CL excitation, otherwise either a core typically between 6 and 16 mm in diameter and from 1 to 5 cm in depth is trepanned. If the object is too small to be drilled, a small chip approximately 1 cm across is cut. The method is rapid, and the cores, etc. can be used afterwards for other analyses.

Borschneck *et al.* (2000) have quantified the visual images in terms of visual spectra, enabling comparative plots of the CL of marble from the various quarries to be produced in a similar fashion to those produced for SIA and statistical treatments applied.

Corazza *et al.* (2001) excited marble samples with an ion beam which gave much better definition of the CL, and trace element analysis could be performed at the same time.

The weathering of stone

The patina on stone antiquities is not so central to their value and authenticity as it is for bronzes, and consequently it is often removed (Newman, 1990). Hence it is important to be clear that many genuine ancient stones will have lost their patina, and also that restored stone sculptures will often have been colored or artificially patinated all over so that the replacements blend with the original. Some conservation treatments may also give the impression of being attempts to impart a weathered appearance to a forgery (see Chapter 20, p. 499).

The patina on stone may be considered in two main forms, the so-called rock or desert varnish that forms on many stones, largely formed of oxalates, and the carbonate-rich crusts that form on calcareous stones. The existence of the former, oxalate-based patinas on limestone and marbles, seems only fairly recently to have been generally realised (O'Grady, 2006), although Stross and Eisenlord (1965) in a little-known publication described the presence of 'desert varnish' and 'weathering crusts' on some disputed Egyptian limestone figures. Most famously, the patina on the Getty *kouros* (see p. 261) was initially described as calcite until re-testing revealed the presence of oxalates. It must be stressed that the patina which forms on stone, if any, is very much determined by the local environment, the nature of the stone, whether it is buried or not, etc. Even the presence of pigments can influence the

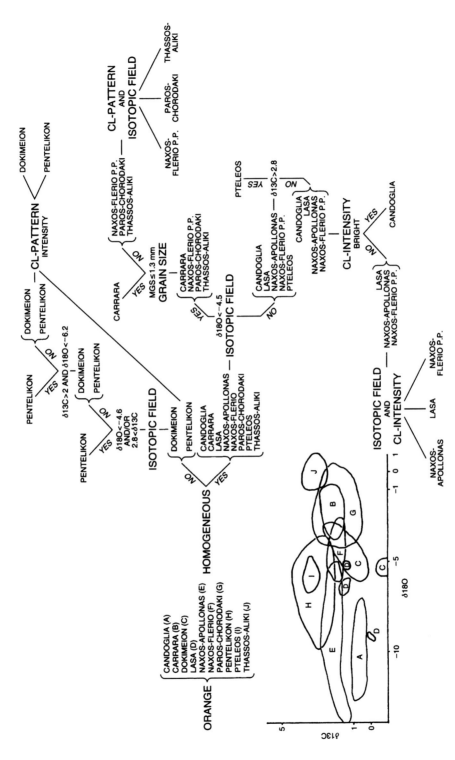

Figure 11.4 Process chart for establishing the source of a marble based on its CL and stable isotopes. (Courtesy Barbin et al., 1992)

microbiological activity (Lamprecht *et al.* (1997). In general, it seems that rock varnish is likely to form on exposed stone while calcitic crusts form on buried limestone or marble (Doehne *et al.* 1992) and many patinas contain both carbonates and oxalates.

The two forms will be considered separately.

Rock varnish

Sources: Alessandri (ed) (1989); Dorn (1991); Watchman (1991); Realini and Toniolo (eds) (1996); Lambert (1997, pp. 25–28); O'Grady (2006). For similar patinas on ceramics see Chapter 9, p. 206.

Lichens and other micro-organisms live and die on exposed surfaces, decaying to form deposits. On durable surfaces, notably of rocks, this can build up into coherent layers, often referred to as rock varnish (Lambert, 1997, pp. 25–28). The layers are a very variable mixture of clay and the material leached from the rock surface together with the organic remains of the micro-organisms, typically oxalates (Matteini and Moles, 1986). Iron or manganese derived from the rock can give the varnish a deep red or black coloration. The origins and age of rock varnish have been the subject of much contentious debate, especially where it happens to cover rock art (see p. 267).

Del Monte and Sabbioni (1987) and del Monte *et al.* (1987) postulated that the oxalates found on limestone and marble had a natural microbiological origin but Lazzarini and Salvadori (1989) suggested that the oxalates might in part be the final degradation product of the microbiological decay of the various organic materials applied to the surfaces during conservation and restoration treatments. This possibility has been studied further by Cariati *et al.* (2000).

Despite these uncertainties, the presence of a hard coherent layer containing oxalates should be an indication of age, and may be capable of yielding an absolute date (see p. 266). Heller and Herz (1995) have studied oxalate formation on dolomitic marbles and Prudêncio *et al.* (1995) that on granites.

Limestone and marble crusts

Sources: Young and Ashmole (1968); Margolis *et al.* (1988); Margolis and Showers (1988, 1990); Newman (1990).

The usual natural patination process for marble that has not been exposed to the sulphur dioxide-laden atmospheres of recent urban environments, consists in the deposition of carbonates to form a stable crust, which sits firmly on the surface of the marble. This is probably mainly formed by the activity of micro-organisms, as with the rock varnishes described in the previous section. Thus, the carbonic acid in the atmosphere or the groundwater, in combination with micro-organisms, will dissolve some of the carbonates on the surface, which is almost immediately re-deposited to form a crust on the surface. Under the microscope this can appear foliated, hence the description 'cauliflower' often given to it. Root marks are often left in the patina as it formed around the decaying plant remains (Young and Ashmole, 1968). In section the crusts often display layering, and can be several millimetres in thickness. This patination is composed largely of carbonates from the marble, and if the marble is buried then it can also contain a little carbonate material from the groundwater, together with some zeolites, clay, iron and manganese oxides and some calcium oxalates. The calcium carbonate is usually present as calcite but Margolis *et al.* (1988) also encountered some sulphates, in the form of gypsum, in their survey of natural patinas (*contra* Riederer 1976; and see p. 258). The clays and iron and manganese oxides can impart a yellow or reddish hue to the marble that was once white.

Most marbles are composed of calcite (calcium carbonate), but some are dolomitic – that is, they contain dolomite (calcium magnesium carbonate). Dolomitic marbles are found at some of the quarries of Thasos in the north Aegean, which seems to have been the source of some of the more controversial pieces of sculpture (see p. 261). As a consequence their usage, characterisation and weathering have been the subject of intensive study over recent years (Doehne *et al.* 1992). The characteristic degradation of dolomite is known as de-dolomitisation, which is the replacement of the magnesium carbonate by calcium carbonate in the form of calcite. However, de-dolomitisation often seems not to occur on exposed stones but only on buried marble.

Heller and Herz (1995) could find no evidence of de-dolomitisation-type formation of calcite on the exposed weathered marble at Thasos itself, only lichen-induced oxalate formation. Possibly the oxalates were protecting the stone from de-dolomitisation. The truth is that a variety of weathering processes are possible depending on the local environmental conditions. Thus, attempts to correlate the patina on weathered marble faces exposed at the ancient quarries with the patinas of sculptures made from the stone from those quarries, have not been very successful (Ulens *et al.* 1995).

Attack by atmospheric sulphur dioxide over the past two centuries has proved very destructive. Calcium sulphate is formed and tends to flake off, exposing fresh surfaces to attack, leading ultimately to the complete destruction of the carved surface. The ruination of the sculpture exposed on the outsides of the Medieval churches and cathedrals in cities across Europe is the all-too-familiar evidence of this.

A.P. Laurie, writing on 'Art Forgeries in Marble' in *The Times* of London (5 December 1928), and reported in Rorimer (1931, p.18) and Savage (1976, p. 300), noted the penetration of sulphates into limestone in the interior fabric of Lincoln Cathedral. The freshly quarried limestone contained virtually no sulphates but in the old limestone there was 4.3% $CaSO_4$ at a depth of 0.25 inch falling to 2.4% $CaSO_4$ at 1 inch, and Laurie suggested that this must represent a very slow reaction and possibly form the basis of a dating method. Unfortunately, it is largely an environmental problem brought about by the use of fossil fuels over the last two centuries, the phenomenon having more to do with the location of the stone, whether in an urban or rural or indoor or outdoor environment, than with age *per se*. Also, being a relatively recent phenomenon, the sulphates could not have been used to distinguish between Medieval carved stone and a nineteenth-century restoration.

That having been said, deep penetration of sulphates could be an indication that the stone was of some age as Laurie originally suggested. Many false patinas contain calcium sulphate (Riederer, 1976), and Skoulikidis and Beloyannis (1984) and Skoulikidis *et al.* (1995) proposed a method for converting the surface sulphates on marble back to carbonates, thus creating further possibilities for confusion when examining suspect and undocumented works.

Creation of a patina

Many of the popular general works on forgery suggest burying the forged marble sculpture for a period of up to a few months but it is difficult to see what that would achieve beyond making it dirty, and possibly impressing gullible prospective purchasers if it was re-excavated in their presence.

Heller and Herz (1995) managed to create a calcium oxalate deposit of whewellite on fresh clean surfaces of calcareous and dolomitic marble by immersion in an oxalate-rich mulch of potatoes for 4 months.

Elvidge and Moore (1980) rather innocently published details of a method to create an artificial 'desert varnish' on rock surfaces, complete with manganese and iron oxides, not as an aid for forgers, but to restore vandalised petroglyphs in the deserts of the American West.

The usual methods of patinating stone include chemically treating the freshly worked surface with acid to give it a weathered appearance and then applying a wet, slightly acid, salty clay poultice to induce rapid development of a crust. Solutions of salts such as ferrous sulphate, iodine, iron oxides and silver nitrate, can be added to the poultice to give the marble a more convincing antique color (Savage, 1976, p. 110). Newman (1990) concluded that the creation of a convincing artificial calcite patination on a limestone or marble surface is not easy, but the patina on the Savelli tomb (see p. 242 and Figure 11.1a–d), which is apparently the creation of Alceo Dossena, gave him pause. Very often, chemical patination is dispensed with and finely ground calcite or gypsum in a suitable binder is applied to the acid-weathered marble surface. Skoulikidis *et al.* (1993) describe some of the treatments applied to new marble replacements on ancient monuments in Greece. These included spraying on ferrous sulphate, or applying a lacquer containing iron oxides.

Johansen (1990) found that the weathering crust applied to a forged or massively restored marble portrait head was composed of ground calcite, marble and barytes with added coloring set in a modern synthetic binder. Modern stone sculptures from South-East Asia are given a weathered orange–brown surface by being packed in wet iron filings, some of which become embedded in the surface (Twilley, 1999). At an even simpler level, waxing or staining with coffee or tea can provide a superficial ageing.

Detection

Sources: Margolis (1989); Newman (1990); Herz *et al.* (1992); Ulens *et al.* (1995).

The rapidly developed artificial crusts tend to have poor adhesion, and the crystals are rather small compared to those on the natural crusts that have developed very slowly (Riederer, 1975), and thus the latter give a much clearer XRD pattern. The authenticity of many Cycladic figurines is highly contentious, as with many other aspects concerned with their collection (Elia, 1993; Gill and Chippindale, 1993; p. 253). Riederer (1976) found that, on the genuine pieces, the calcium carbonate of the crust was always in the form of calcite, whereas on the induced or applied patinas the calcium carbonate could be in the form of aragonite, or possibly the sulphate, gypsum. The broader survey of Margolis *et al.* (1988) on classical carved marble generally did encounter gypsum as a minor component in some natural patinas. Note that genuine ancient pieces now exposed to modern polluted atmospheres may be developing sulphates within their patinas in a similar manner to hydroxycarbonate patinas on copper alloys (see Chapter 14, p. 351).

UV examination

Sources: see Chapter 2, p. 34; Rorimer (1931, pp. 17–24); Savage (1976, pp. 300–301).

UV was the earliest scientific test, and the one that is still most widely applied, and, used, for example, by von Bothmer (1964) to note a detailed examination of a suspect marble. Freshly exposed surfaces of limestone or marble will give a vivid purple–red fluorescence, whereas an ancient surface will fluoresce white, yellow or orange. This can be conveniently and usefully employed to ascertain which parts of a sculpture are likely to have been reworked or replaced (Figures 11.5a and 11.5b) (Grossman and Maish, 2002). However, the fresh surfaces can be treated with wax, as Dossena did, such that they pass the UV test, even on occasion fooling Rorimer himself (Hoving, 1996, pp. 144–145), although in his book Rorimer stated that it is necessary to clean

the surface before testing. Heating the stone can also confuse the interpretation of the UV signal.

During the last 30 years many of the techniques developed to characterise and provenance marble have also been applied to the study of patinas.

Ulens *et al.* (1994a, 1995) applied trace element and isotopic profiles, cathodoluminescence (CL) and radiocarbon (RC), to the weathered surfaces of samples taken from marbles that had been worked but then abandoned and left exposed in several ancient quarries and to a variety of patinas on some ancient marble sculptures. Their general conclusion was that the various methods clearly authenticated the ancient weathered marbles from the quarries but worked less well on the sculpted pieces, which usually had much thinner patinas or crusts. They used laser-ablated inductively coupled plasma mass spectrometry (LA-ICP-MS) to obtain depth profiles of the trace elements through weathering crusts on the marble (Ulens *et al.*, 1994a, b) (Figure 11.6a–c). It was found that some elements, such as manganese and barium, tended to concentrate at the surface, and that others, notably the magnesium, were severely depleted in the immediate surface layers, confirming the findings of Margolis *et al.* (1988; and see p. 256) on dolomitic marble. They also applied CL to sections of some of the weathered quarry samples and were able to detect continuous change across the profile, based presumably on changes in the iron and manganese concentrations. This preliminary study did not knowingly

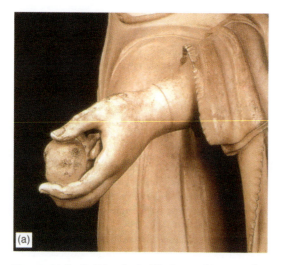 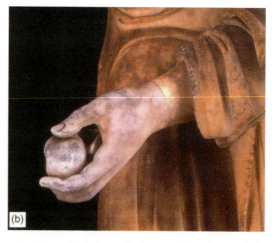

Figure 11.5   Left hand of a life-size marble statue, known as the Vénus Génitrix, in the Louvre. Viewed (a) by light, (b) by UV. Under UV the old marble surfaces appear amber or golden, and new surfaces appear purple. The purple fluorescence here strongly suggests that the hand is a replacement. (Courtesy Dubrana, 2001)

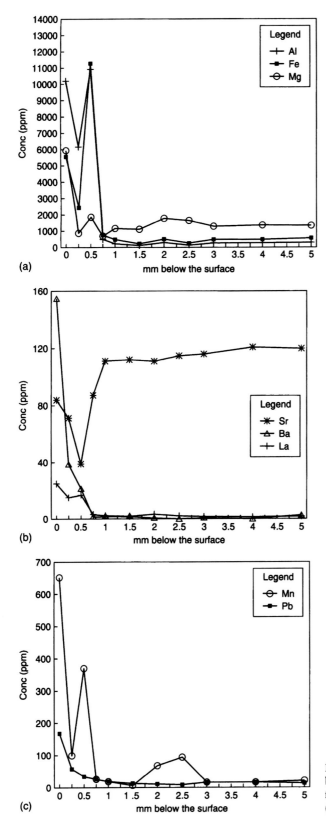

Figure 11.6 Depth profile of weathered marble from the ancient quarry of Afyon in Turkey, for (Top) Al, Fe and Mg; (Middle) Sr, Ba and La; (Bottom) Mn and Pb. (Courtesy Ulens *et al.*, 1995)

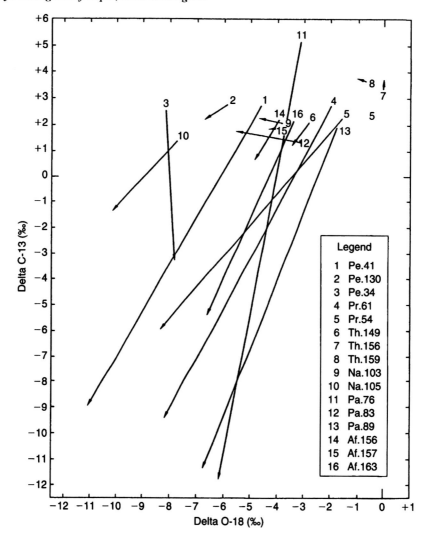

Figure 11.7 Influence of weathering on the isotopic composition of marble. In each case the arrows point from the unweathered marble through to the weathered surface. There is a shift in the isotopic composition of the weathered layer towards values of CO_2 in the atmosphere and in organic material in the soil, and H_2O in the atmosphere. (Na., Naxos; Pa., Paros; Pe., Pentelikon; Th., Thasos; Af., Afyon; Pr., Proconnesos). (Courtesy Ulens *et al.* 1995)

examine pieces with artificially induced weathering crusts, but it does seem a promising approach.

Ulens *et al.* (1995) carried out accelerator mass spectrometry radio carbon (AMS RC) dating. Once again the thick weathering crusts on the quarry stones gave a convincing profile from the geological age of the carbonates of the unchanged interior of the stone through to a date of just a few thousand years at the surface. The carbon for the dates in the crust was presumably from the carbonates and oxalates that were derived in part from the interior geological carbonates and in part from atmospheric carbon, getting younger as the surface was approached. These dates

were meaningless in terms of absolute age, but the profile was good for demonstrating that the crust was of considerable antiquity. By contrast the date profile on the very thin crusts of the sculptures showed no change until the very surface, where there is always the possibility of recent contamination rather than real age-related changes.

Profiles of the isotopes of carbon and oxygen through weathering crusts have also been studied (Margolis *et al.*, 1988; Herz *et al.*, 1992; Ulens *et al.*, 1994a, b; 1995; Heller and Herz, 1995). On crusts that had developed naturally the precipitated calcite was relatively depleted in ^{13}C and ^{18}O, the depletion increasing towards the surface, reflecting the contribution from atmospheric CO_2 (Figure 11.7). Ulens and colleagues found the effect much more pronounced on the thick weathering crusts on the quarry samples but it was still measurable on some of the carved pieces (see also the testing of the 'James, brother of Christ' ossuary, Chapter 1, p. 14)

Herz *et al.* (1992) studied the patina on a suspect marble antiquity and found a great difference in the $^{12}C/^{13}C$ ratio between the body of the marble and the crust, strongly suggesting that the carbonates in the crust did not have anything to do with the marble beneath. This need not in itself automatically condemn the piece, as it may have lain in calcareous soil that was the source of the deposited calcite. However, in this instance other tests showed that the crust was mainly of gypsum, and that it contained fibres that were suspected of being cotton, the carbon of which may have contributed to the $^{12}C/^{13}C$ ratio, and chlorine was detected on the surface of the marble beneath the crust. Together these items of evidence suggested that the fresh marble surface had been treated with hydrochloric acid before the application of an artificial crust of crushed gypsum with some binding threads.

More recently, Bassiakos and Doumas (1998) have studied the ESR properties of the weathering crusts on ancient and recently carved marbles. They claimed to be able to non-destructively distinguish between a natural and artificial patination, based mainly on the accumulation of manganese in the genuine crusts. However, not every ancient marble develops or retains such a crust.

Obviously, in all of these tests the environment in which the marble lay or stood is a major factor. The samples taken from worked stone that was abandoned while still in the quarry, exposed for millennia and never cleaned, display much more convincing features of ageing than do the carved pieces that normally have been buried and then often extensively cleaned before appearing on the market. Very often no changes in the measured parameters could be observed through the surface layers on genuine ancient pieces that visually retained their ancient surfaces. Thus, overall, it should be concluded that the various tests may provide conclusive evidence via changes in the particular parameter they measure through the surface layers that would be almost impossible to fake, but that the absence of these various profiles could not be taken as evidence that the surface was not ancient.

Case study: The Getty *Kouros*

'*The Curious Spurious Kouros*'

Hoving (1996, p. 279)

Sources: General: True (1987); Kouros Colloquium (1993); Hoving (1996, pp. 279–310). Scientific examination: Margolis (1987, 1989); Margolis *et al.* (1988); Margolis and Showers (1988, 1990).

Although much discussed it is still the case that no firm conclusions have been drawn on this, by now, very famous statue (Figure 11.8). In 1986 the J. Paul Getty Museum of Malibu, California, announced the acquisition of a spectacular, virtually complete and over-life-size marble statue of a *kouros*, that is a standing youth, in the Archaic style of ancient Greece, dateable to the sixth century BC.

The statue caused a sensation, with the plaudits and brickbats in about equal proportions. The latter were understandable as the statue was not previously known, was in superb condition and came with a distinctly odd provenance that has since been shown to be false. Such was the furore that the Getty held a conference where the supporters and detractors could state their cases (Kouros Colloquium, 1993).

The history of the acquisition of the piece has been described prosaically by True (1987, 1993) and scurrilously by Hoving (1996, pp. 279–310). Inevitably the latter is the more interesting read, and is directed as much against Jiri Frel as against the *kouros*. Frel was the Getty curator, who had been instrumental in its acquisition. By the time of Hoving's book he had become the ex-curator, but during his short tenure he had acquired a host of other antiquities with equally plausible backgrounds (Norman and Hoving, 1987), and which are now slowly being scientifically investigated (Grossman and Maish, 2002).

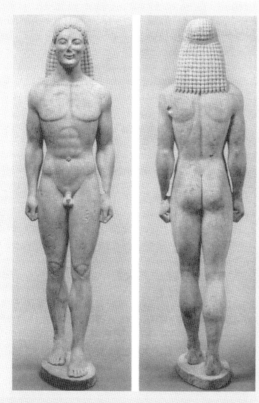

Figure 11.8   The Getty kouros (Courtesy the Kouros Colloquim)

The certain history of the *kouros* only really goes back to 1983 when it was imported into the USA from Switzerland in many fragments. Photocopies of documents purported to show that it had been acquired from a Dr Jean Lauffenberger, of Geneva, then recently deceased. The *kouros* was claimed to have been purchased in the 1930s. Photocopies of letters, supposedly of 1952, from Ernst Langlotz, the well-known German art historian, thanked Dr Lauffenberger for allowing him to view the 'marble youth'. This documentation was vital as, otherwise, the *kouros* had no history at all. Apparently after purchasing it, Dr Lauffenberger did not have it restored, but kept the fragments locked away in his apartment, where, despite claims to the contrary, none of his acquaintances who had visited him over the years recalls ever having seen it or hearing mention of it. It is particularly strange that Prof. José Doerig, the man charged with cataloguing the Lauffenberger collection, did not recall seeing what would have been its most important piece.

Scientific examination of the documents was pointless as these were photocopies. Even so, the signature of Langlotz was found to be spurious, and, more significantly, the 1952 letter was on notepaper with a printed address that included a post code that was only introduced in 1972. However, Norman and Hoving, in the course of their intensive sleuthing, did establish that in a letter to Frel written in 1984, Jacques Chamay of the Geneva Museum testified that he had seen the *kouros* in a photograph sent to him in the collection of a Geneva physician (Hoving, 1996, p. 303). This seems to show that Lauffenberger really did have a *kouros*, but the question then arose, was it the same one that the Getty bought? This is especially relevant, as in 1990 Jeffrey Spier (1990) discovered in Switzerland the torso of a smaller *kouros*, which was stylistically very similar to that in the Getty, but much inferior in quality and obviously a forgery. The Getty promptly acquired it, hoping it might yield information on the authenticity of their *kouros*. Rumours suggested that the two statues had been made from the same block of marble, by the same forger in Rome in the early 1980s. If this had indeed been the case then that would have been proof conclusive that the large Getty *kouros* was also a forgery. However, detailed analysis showed that the two were of totally different marbles and the patinas were also totally different. The patina on the torso had been achieved by acid dipping, followed by the application of iron salts to create its rather strange orange appearance.

Exhaustive scientific tests have been conducted over a number of years, mainly on the patina, but never seem to have resulted in a definitive scientific report, much less a conclusion. As in all such investigations the scientific examination had two objectives, to provenance the stone and to authenticate the patina. The former objective, based on trace element analysis, XRD, SIA (and of the radiogenic isotopes of strontium) and CL, suggest with some certainty that the marble is dolomite and came from Thasos. There is a slight problem here in that although the marble quarries on Thasos were certainly open from the Archaic period and producing stone for major sculptures of stone extracted from them, including *kouroi*, were fashioned for local use, it is much less certain when the quarries became a source of stone for the Greek world generally. Studies on sculpture by Herrmann Jr and Barbin (1993) and Tykot *et al.*

(2002), admittedly on a very small number of samples, suggested that sculptures of Thasos dolomitic marble are rare outside the island before the Hellenistic period. Notable exceptions include the Boston reliefs, which are themselves the subject of continuing debate (see below).

The studies on the patina have been less successful. The initial detailed study by Margolis and colleagues (Margolis, 1989) seemed to have assumed that the weathering crust was of calcite brought about by the process of de-dolomitisation (see p. 256) even though XRD was apparently carried out. Subsequent examination showed the patina to be largely composed of hydrated calcium oxalate, the mineral whewellite, with little or no calcium carbonate, calcite, present at all. As Bauer put in his rather critical summing up of the scientific work in the Kouros Colloquium (see p. 66), 'It is difficult to understand how x-ray diffraction identified calcium oxalate as calcium carbonate'.

It is interesting to reflect that if the oxalate crust really had been applied before 1983 as an artificial patination, then this would seem to pre-date the general realisation of the frequency of oxalate formation on exposed marble surfaces within the legitimate scientific community (see p. 254).

The studies of Doehne *et al.* (1992) suggest that oxalate patinas should form on marble that had been exposed not buried. Taken literally at face value, the implication for the *kouros* seems to be that for the patina to have formed naturally it would have had to have stood in the open for a considerable time, and was buried, if at all, in an environment where de-dolomitisation did not take place and no crusts formed. It is possible that a coherent oxalate layer could have protected the dolomite beneath from subsequent attack. It is also possible that, as with the front faces of the Boston relief, the crusts had been removed during cleaning and conservation, and an artificial patina applied, although as the *kouros* was acquired by the Getty as a pile of unrestored fragments, this seems unlikely. In this context it would be interesting to study some of the broken surfaces that might bear some evidence of calcite formation, if the pieces ever had been buried as fragments for any length of time. Also, there should have been some residual calcite penetrating down the grain boundaries of the dolomite.

The oxalate layer was reported as being between 10 and 50 microns thick, which is probably too thin for meaningful trace element or isotopic profiles to be built up from the unchanged stone to the surface such as was observed on some of the stone at the Thasos quarries (see Figure 11.7). AMS RC dates were obtained on the oxalate layer. These were of several thousand years, but as Preusser pointed out in the Kouros Colloquium (p. 64), similar dates were obtained from oxalates formed by modern lichens.

Heller and Herz (1995) found that it is reasonably easy to build up deposits of whewellite (see p. 267). However, the Getty team was unable to produce a whewellite layer that resembled the patina observed by SEM on the *kouros*.

Thus the scientific examination has not been able to find any evidence for a convincing natural patina, but neither has it found any conclusive evidence that the oxalate layer was artificially applied. Even if it was shown to be artificial, this would not automatically condemn the piece as it could have been cleaned.

Case study: The Boston Reliefs

The Boston Reliefs (Figure 11.9) are another controversial sculpture and have been the subject of detailed scientific study for many years first by Young and Ashmole (1968) and latterly by Newman and Herrmann (1995). Young's analyses by emission spectrometry (ES) and his petrographic work on the stone showed that it was dolomitic marble from the quarries on Thasos. Although the carved faces had been carefully cleaned and the encrustations removed, enough survived for a study to be made. The inner faces still had their original encrustation of calcite, identified by XRD, with the casts of the rootlets around which it had formed. Examination by UV proved somewhat

Figure 11.9   The Boston Reliefs (Courtesy Younge and Ashmole, 1968)

inconclusive as the carved surfaces gave a rather mottled fluorescence of amber (old) and purple (new). Young suggested that this was evidence of post-excavation cleaning. However, the more recent examination shows that the surfaces had been waxed, which would interfere with the fluorescence.

Despite Young and Ashmole's work doubts persisted, and another scientific survey was conducted. Newman and Herrmann (1995) examined thin sections taken from the rear faces of the reliefs petrographically and carried out inorganic analysis by electron microprobe analysis (EPMA), SIA and MS, and organic analysis by Fourier transform infra-red spectroscopy (FTIRS) and gas chromatography–mass spectrometry (GC–MS). Only stearic acid, which almost certainly derived from a wax, was positively identified by the latter. The especially detailed study of the crust on the rear faces showed that it was quite typical of long-term de-dolomitisation crusts, which form by the slow replacement of the dolomite by calcite. Furthermore, there was no trace of organic binders and the calcite really does seem to have formed around rootlets, presumably while buried in the ground for many years. Other tests could have been applied to the crusts but those already carried out do seem to have demonstrated beyond reasonable doubt that the crusts are the result of long-term burial. Furthermore, their use was unable to detect any trace of artificial patination on the front carved faces of the reliefs, contrary to what had been claimed by some of the detractors.

It had also been claimed that the reliefs had been made from a large but plain Roman sarcophagus, cut in half and with the end removed to create the three-sided shape. Both Ashmole and Young and Newman and Herrmann examined the ends of the reliefs very carefully and found that the patinated surfaces were continuous from both sides over the edges.

Despite these seemingly conclusive studies the debate still continues, with Hoving (1996, pp. 256–274) still adamant that they are a forgery.

The absolute dating of stone sculpture

The ability to date carved stone surfaces directly has long been the dream of art historians and the ambition of scientists. Recent developments are beginning to make these aspirations a reality, although so far mainly on surfaces that have always been exposed to light rather than on buried pieces (see Chapter 6 for the application of TL to marble).

The stone surface

The surface weathering of rock faces can sometimes be quantified and translated into relative and, possibly, absolute dates (Figure 11.10). Exposed surfaces

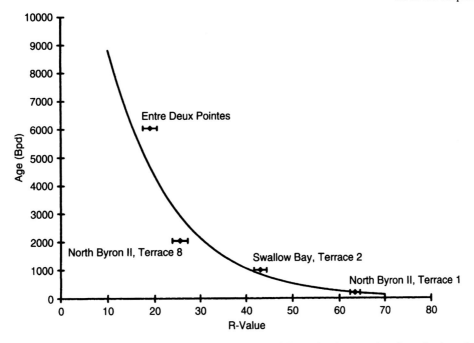

Figure 11.10 Age versus the R factor (related to the hardness of the rock) showing that the softening of exposed surfaces proceeds quite rapidly for the first few millennia. (Courtesy Betts and Latta, 2000)

of igneous rocks tend to become softer with age as more of the binding elements – sodium, potassium, calcium and magnesium – leach out and there are also associated changes in the mineralogy as well as the texture and grain size. These changes depend on the composition of the particular rock and its environment (even the direction the surface is facing can be locally very important). This having been said there is a correlation between the degree of softening and the age (McCarroll, 1994).

Betts and Latta (2000) have attempted to date some open pits dug into beaches on the north shores of Lake Superior in Canada. They did this by measuring the softening of the surfaces of granite cobbles in the sides of the pits and compared this to the degree of softening of the cobbles lying exposed on the successive geologically dated beach terraces. They measured the softening with a Schmidt hammer, which is quite widely used to test concrete surfaces, etc., but has also been used on natural rocks (McCarroll, 1994). The harder the stone the more the hammer rebounds (the R factor). Previous guesstimates of the age of the pits varied at between 300 and 4000 years, but the rock-softening suggests they were dug between 500 and 900 years ago. The technique is quick and

cheap, and it would seem applicable to granite and other non-sedimentary rocks at least to establish if their surfaces were of any great age, although surface treatment could affect the result.

Cosmogenic isotopes (Stuart, 2001)
Bombardment of the Earth's surface by cosmic rays generates new isotopes by interaction with the elements in the soil or rock. The increase in the new isotopes can give an indication of how long a rock surface has been exposed. The cosmic radiation can penetrate to about one or two metres in most rocks, and several elements can be changed (Table 11.2). These include ^{36}Cl, an isotope of chlorine (Phillips *et al.*, 1996, 1997) and ^{3}He, that is ordinary helium but also containing a neutron. ^{3}He is stable and can slowly accumulate in solid rocks, although, being gaseous, there are problems of diffusion. The method should be applicable to the dating of previously deep buried rock, such as good-quality marble from a mine or deep quarry that has been exposed or lightly buried. It may not be possible to give an absolute date, but it could show that the stone had been quarried in antiquity.

Hydration dating measures the penetration of hydration into glass (see Chapter 10, p. 208).

Table 11.2   Some elements investigated for dating by *in situ* cosmogenic isotope generation.

Isotope	Half-life (yr)	Production rate (atoms/g/yr)*	Target element	Minerals	Comments
^{3}He	Stable	115–121	All rock forming elements	Olivine, pyroxene, garnet	Highly diffusive in common minerals. Requires correction for thermal neutron capture ^{3}He.
^{10}Be	1.5×10^6	5–7	O (Mg, Al, Si)	Quartz, olivine	Absorbed 'meteoric' ^{10}Be must be chemically removed.
^{14}C	5730	~21	O	Quartz	Absorbed 'meteoric' ^{14}C must be chemically removed.
^{21}Ne	Stable	15–45	Na, Si, Mg, Al	Quartz, olivine, pyroxene	Requires correction for nucleogenic ^{21}Ne in old surfaces and atmospheric Ne.
^{26}Al	7.1×10^6	15–40	Al, Si	Quartz, olivine	Isobaric interference from ^{26}Mg restricts application to low Mg minerals.
^{36}Cl	3.0×10^5	7–30	K, Ca, Cl	Calcite, olivine, whole rock basalts	Isobaric interference from ^{36}S.

Source: Stuart, 2001
*Surface production scaled to sea level at >70°N or S, expressed per gramme of parent rock/mineral. With the exception of ^{3}He, isotope production rates are strongly dependent on the chemical composition of the target mineral.

It has been successfully applied to the volcanic glass, obsidian, to determine the age of artefacts made from it (see p. 269).

Ettinger and Frey (1980) suggested a dating method based on the slow absorption of nitrogen into the surfaces of materials, including marble and jade (see Chapter 16, p. 417).

The absolute dating of the patination on stone surfaces

Another potential method for the dating of stone artefacts is by measurement of the alpha recoil tracks in the surfaces (see Chapter 9, p. 188 and Wagner, 1998, pp. 212–217).

It is now potentially possible to date the formation of the calcite weathering crusts on ancient limestone or marble carved surfaces directly by the uranium series dating method (Aitken, 1990, pp. 124–130; Latham, 2001). This method has been widely applied to dating much older Pleistocene calcite concretions in cave deposits, etc., but it has now been successfully applied to much younger surfaces. Basically, all matter contains small amounts of uranium; the ^{238}U decays to ^{234}U which, in turn, decays to ^{230}Th, and thus in any rock etc. over geological time the ratio of these three radioactive species will stabilise. Uranium and thorium have very different solubilities, such that when the calcite (in this case) dissolves, the uranium enters the solution but the thorium does not. Thus, the calcite that re-deposits on the surface of the stone can be assumed to have a relatively high uranium/thorium ratio. Thereafter, the inexorable decay of the uranium will produce new thorium and thus the greater the thorium content relative to the uranium, the older the deposit.

Frank *et al.* (2002) have dated some rock-cut passages at Troy from the calcite deposits on their walls, obtaining dates such as 4350 ± 750 years old, which is archaeologically acceptable. The method has apparently not yet been applied to weathered stone artefacts, but it would seem to have considerable potential for authenticity studies. Frank *et al.* cut samples that were 0.3 cm^2 for their dating, which could easily have been done with a trepanning drill.

The absolute dating of rock varnish

Sources: Dorn (1989, 1993); Schneider and Bierman (1997); Watchman (2000).

Let it be stated at the outset that this is an area currently troubled with controversy, where many of the principal players seem to divide their communications between breathless papers announcing major breakthroughs for absolute dating methods, claiming them to be, for example, 'an obituary to the stylistic dating of Palaeolithic rock-art' (Schneider and Bierman, 1997; Bednarik, 1995), and more mature review papers drawing attention to the drawbacks, and pointing out the practical problems inherent in their own work and that of others (Bednarik, 2002). However, although reliable absolute dates may never be attainable, the various approaches do offer some possibilities for establishing probable antiquity. A serious drawback is that in order for any confidence to be placed on the interpretation of the data it is necessary to know something of the environment in which the surface deposits on the stone have formed, which is not possible with many high-profile sculptures on the market.

Two very different approaches have been taken, cation ratio dating and AMS RC dating.

Cation ratio (CR) dating

It is assumed that the cations in the initial rock varnish formation will reflect the composition of the rock itself. Thereafter, the more soluble cations, especially the Na, K, Mg, and Ca ions, will gradually be replaced by more insoluble cations such as Ti, Fe and Mn, and thus the ratio of the soluble cations to the Ti, etc. in the rock varnish relative to the corresponding ratio in the underlying rock should give an indication of age. A further development has been to measure the changes in concentration across profiles of the rock varnish itself. However, many scientists believed that such thin layers of forming varnish or patina were likely to be heavily contaminated from their immediate surroundings, and that it was not possible to establish a simple plot of time against the soluble cation: Ti ratio. Ronald Dorn, who did much to pioneer the absolute dating of rock varnish (1983), found no less than 23 different environmental variables (Dorn, 1989, p. 590). Other serious reservations based on geochemistry and practical sampling difficulties emerged (Schneider and Bierman, 1997; Watchman, 2000). On one rock carving it was found that the varnish covering the carving was apparently three times older that the varnish covering the adjacent original rock face into which the carving had been made (Watchman, 1992). Such discoveries do not inspire confidence.

Improvements in the AMS method over the years have meant that it is now possible to date exceedingly small samples of less than one milligram of carbon (Matteini and Moles, 1986; Watchman, 1993; Lambert, 1997, pp. 25–28). The problem for dating rock varnish is the origin of the carbon, especially if the rock substrate contains carbon in the form of carbonates or graphite, and/or the carving is buried in an environment rich in carbon in one form or another. Ideally, it is the oxalates that are being dated as they form from the decay of micro-organisms which fixed their carbon from the atmosphere.

Rock varnish builds up by layers, and, although it is probably never going to be feasible to produce meaningful absolute dates, it may be possible to produce age profiles across sections of varnish that are at least indicative of it having formed over a considerable period of time. A practical problem is that most stone antiquities tend to have very thin layers compared to the field samples taken from old quarries, etc.

AMS RC dating has been tried on the patinas covering prehistoric rock art in various parts of the world (Bednarik, 1995; Dorn, 1997), as well as stone artefacts (Whitely and Dorn, 1993), once again with not a little controversy (Schneider and Bierman, 1997; Dragovitch, 2000; Watchman, 2000; Bednarik, 2002; Zilhão 1995).

Case study: The omnipresent coal

Sources: Beck *et al.* (1998); Dorn (1998).

Ronald Dorn espoused the cause of CR and then AMS dating of rock art through the 1980s and 1990s. He scraped samples of the varnish from the rock surface and then submitted them for AMS dating at various institutions including the facility at Arizona University at Tucson.

Among the rock carvings sampled were a group from a remote canyon in the north-east of Arizona, which gave dates suggesting that they were carved into the rock surfaces around 5000 years ago, making them the earliest carvings ever encountered in that part of the world. However, concern was raised at Tucson over the unusual color of the sample and examination under the microscope revealed small black particles, later to be identified as charcoal and bituminous coal (Beck *et al.*, 1998). The latter being of geological age skewed the overall date, making it appear to be significantly older than it would otherwise have been. Examination of other samples submitted by Dorn to other institutions revealed similar fragments of charcoal and coal in eighty of them, including a fragment of coal 1 mm wide which purported to have come from a varnish layer that was only 0.2 mm thick (reported in *Nature* **394**, 21 July 1998, p. 6). How this coal and charcoal had got into the samples rapidly became a very contentious issue, with Beck suggesting that somehow it must have been introduced into the sample while in Dorn's laboratory, because when samples were taken independently from the self-same monuments no charcoal, much less coal, was found. Dorn (1998) attempted an explanation. Dorn claimed that other groups had reported find of charcoal and coal material mixed in rock varnish layers, that Beck *et al.* had not followed his sampling methods and did not take their replicate samples from the same locations as his originals. Specifically on the implications of deliberately adding ancient carbon to increase the radio carbon ages he pointed out that this would have been impossible for him to have known the ages of his material and the relatively large fragments of carbonaceous materials would have been very unlikely to have given consistent results. However, whatever the origin of the coal and charcoal all concerned, Dorn included, agree that this makes the radiocarbon dating of rock varnish very problematic.

The forging of Palaeolithic and prehistoric stone artefacts

Sources: Munro (1905, pp. 56–80, 110–117); Rieth (1970, pp. 34–35, 77–79).

From the middle of the nineteenth century a vogue for collecting both fossils and flint implements developed, with collectors and their agents avidly purchasing flints from gravel diggers. The trade became so well established that in some gravel quarries along the banks of the Thames in the outskirts of London for example, Palaeolithic flint hand axes were almost a second currency, accepted as payment in public houses, etc. It was thus inevitable that they were forged, apparently by more skilled tradesmen to sell through the less-skilled quarry men, who were supposed to have discovered them (Smith 1894, pp. 294–298; Evans, 1897, pp. 42, 659). Clarke, in his 1935 article on the knapping of gun flints in East Anglia, noted that forgeries of arrowheads, etc. were still being produced, and that the forgeries of polished flint axes were being made 'from cement, chalk and burnt umber, coated with soda and then with gumshellac'.

There has apparently been a revival of interest at the end of the twentieth century, with good specimens of Palaeolithic hand axes fetching between £500 and £1000 (*The Observer*, 9 April 2000), a price which may well promote a revival in forging. Apparently, specimens bearing nineteenth-century collectors' labels are especially sought.

Early man used hammers of stone, bone or antler, but the nineteenth-century forgers used steel hammers, following the contemporary practice of the craftsmen who knapped the gunflints. Steel hammers produce more pronounced bulbar swelling and sometimes left metallic traces. Modern forgeries could be more difficult to detect than the nineteenth-century forgeries as the techniques of flaking are now much better understood. There are publications explaining not only the basics of flake and blade production (Lord, 1993), but how the masterpieces of Egyptian predynastic pressure flaking were created (Kelterborn, 1984).

The ancient flint artefacts usually have some form of polish or patination which the forgers felt obliged to imitate (Smith, 1894, pp. 296–297; Munro, 1905, p. 118). In calcareous, slightly alkaline soils the flints often developed a milky white patina, and those in more acid sands and gravels often had some surface oxidisation of the iron minerals to give a rich orange–red coloration. The flints often display a glossy surface composed of silica deposited from the soil (Watchman, 1993). Rock varnishes, similar to those found on other rocks (see p. 256), and quite distinct from the silica skins, may

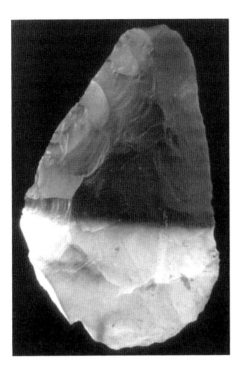

Figure 11.11 Hand axe of black flint from Brandon, Norfolk, flaked by Phil Harding. The lower half has been given a white patina by immersion in warm caustic soda solution. (Courtesy T. Milton)

also form. Both are very different from the polish that may have been acquired while in use.

The surfaces could be given a white patina by immersing the artefact in a hot and strong caustic

soda or potash solution for a few minutes (Hewitt, 1914, 1915) (Figure 11.11). If a brown or red patina was required, a handful of rusty nails in the caustic soda solution would do the trick. The false patinas now seem rather matt and powdery, but may originally have been waxed.

There has been extensive study of the distinctive wear marks on the edges and surfaces of flints and other stone artefacts to ascertain their functions (Keeley, 1980). These ephemeral marks would be very difficult to replicate short of going out and actually using the tool or weapon in the intended manner and suggest another method of detecting forgeries. Rots (2003) sought to characterise the distinctive wear due to the hafting of the stone, and this again could be difficult to replicate. Problems could arise recognising genuine wear if the surfaces of a stone tool had been scratched or otherwise damaged while it was in plough soil or even where it had been roughly handled since its discovery.

Artefacts of the natural volcanic glass obsidian are easier to authenticate. Many of the relatively limited number of exploited sources have been characterised by trace element analysis (Williams-Thorpe, 1995). In addition, the hydration of the surface can provide indications of age (see Chapter 10, p. 269). However, ancient obsidian tools have never been extensively forged, except in Mesoamerica, where superb flaked and polished artefacts of Pre-Hispanic times have been skilfully forged for nearly a century now (Ekholm, 1964; Jones (ed), 1990, pp. 230–231).

Case study: The painted pebbles of Mas d'Azil

Sources: Couraud and Bahn (1982); Jones (ed) (1990, pp. 92–93).

The very end of the Palaeolithic period in the south of France is represented by the Azilian culture, named after the type site of Mas d'Azil in the Department of Ariège in the French Pyrenees. One of the characteristic artefacts of this culture is pebbles engraved or painted with simple designs made up of dots and lines (Figure 11.12a). The meaning and significance of the designs have long been debated, and so, more prosaically, has their authenticity. Unfortunately, although genuine painted pebbles most certainly were excavated from Mas d'Azil in large numbers, many others are suspect. Edouard Piette, the excavator, was often away from the site and carried out the not uncommon practice of paying the workers extra for special finds, including the painted pebbles. They responded by forging painted pebbles in order to increase their rewards. Equally regrettably, the finds were disseminated from the site to collectors and museums all over Europe with no proper control. Thus, there is no real record of the genuine material from the type site, which also produced the vast

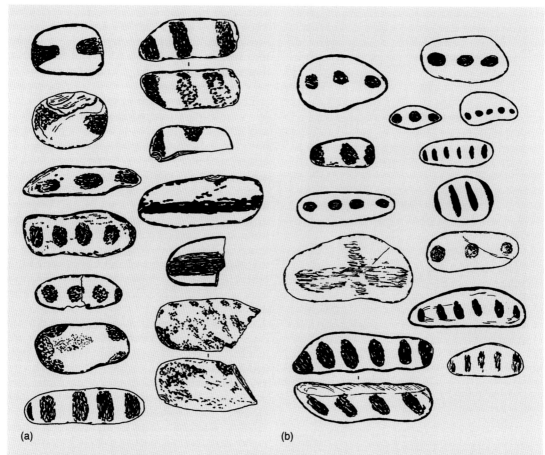

Figure 11.12   Spot the difference! (a) Azilian painted pebbles considered genuine. (b) Azilian painted pebbles considered to be fake. From the collections at the University Museum of Archaeology and Anthropology, Cambridge and the British Museum. (Courtesy Couraud and Bahn, 1982)

majority of the known pebbles. Latterly, Couraud attempted to clarify the situation and to identify the more obvious fakes by studying the pebbles in the various collections known to him and at the time of his 1982 publication with Paul Bahn, he had listed 1951 pebbles that purported to have come from a total of 37 sites, mainly in southern France, but no less than 1427 of these were said to have come from Mas d'Azil itself.

The criteria they established for distinguishing the forgeries were based on visual examination alone using a hand lens. Where the paint was covered by a calcite layer, it was judged as genuine. Unusual shades of red and sometimes the very obvious evidence of the use of a red crayon showed that the painting was spurious. The range of designs was also significantly different on the suspect pieces (Figure 11.12b). More recently, Pomiès *et al.* (1999) studied the paint on genuine pebbles excavated from the site of Troubat, also in the French Pyrenees, using a combination of XRD and transmission electron microscopy (TEM). They concluded that the pigment was of hematite, sometimes natural, but that some had been made by the controlled heating of the iron hydroxide mineral, goethite. Some Azilian engraved pebbles from the cave site at Rochedane, France-Compte, and experimental pieces made with a variety of flint tools, have been studied by d'Errico (1988).

12

Painting

I have written a practical manual to satisfy those people wanting to learn an art that seems to appeal to many people: the forging of paintings and drawings.

(Hebborn, 1997, p. xi)

This chapter deals with all aspects of painting and the techniques of their scientific study. This is followed by the examination of a picture from the frame through the painted layers to the varnish. The chapter concludes with a consideration of Han van Meegeren and his forged Vermeers.

Sources: Technique and Materials: Alexander (1969a, b; 1970); Hebblewhite (1986); Mayer (nd). Icons: Ramos-Poqui (1990); Skálová (1991). European painting: Bomford *et al.* (1988, 1989, 1990). Scientific Examination: Marijnissen (1985, with superb illustrations); van Schoute and Verougstraete-Marcq (eds) (1986); Mills and White (1994); Lomax (1997). Authenticity: Isnard (1955, 1959, 1960); Arnau (1961, pp. 51–84, 226–291); Fleming (1975, 1979a); Savage (1976, pp. 228–272); McCrone (1991); Hebborn (1997).

See also the *Technical Bulletin* of the National Gallery, London.

The usual classes of fraud are all here, turning the genuine but mundane into the exceptional, fraudulent restoration, together with outright forgery. Marijnissen (1985, pp. 20–34) listed fifteen 'categories of authenticity', ranging from the genuine autograph work solely by the artist to out-and-out forgeries using appropriate (old) materials and techniques in order to deceive.

Picture forgery has long history. From at least the time of Claude Lorrain in the seventeenth century, artists have sought to protect their output and reputation by producing lists, known as a *catalogue raisonée*, and even sketches of their paintings. However, even this is not foolproof as in at least one instance in London in the 1990s the forgers got access to an artist's manuscript *catalogue* held in a national institution and added the details of their own productions.

A favourite trick of Fernand Legros and Réal Lessard, the dealers who 'managed' the forger Elmyr de Hory, was to obtain old art books with folio photographs, remove one, get de Hory to paint a picture sufficiently close to the original to match the descriptive text, photograph it and stick it in where the original had been. Armed thus with de Hory's painting and the amended art book they had no problem in effecting a sale (Irving, 1970, p. 149). Some artists, such as Boucher and Corot, were not above signing copies of their paintings that they approved of (Tietze, 1948, p. 13).

The authentication of pictorial art, perhaps more than in any other medium covered by this book, is often concerned with confirming the association of the suspect piece with a specific artist. Perhaps the majority of serious scientific authentication of paintings is to separate the good copies, often done quite innocently, from the autograph work. In these investigations the scientist must work even more closely than usual with the art historian, using the methods of physical examination to reveal details of individual artistic technique.

Another problem related to authorship is trying to ascertain how much of a painting is the work of the named artist. In cases such as that of the American painter Albert Pinkham Ryder, this can be very difficult. Not only do straightforward forgeries of his paintings abound, but many of the works that he had at least begun were regularly finished, altered or restored by others (Homer, 1989).

A further problem is the workshop productions which are now thought to be much more prevalent than previously believed. Many famous and successful artists, such as El Greco, Rubens (Burroughs nd, pp. 123–152) and Veronese (Brown, 1989) ran large and prolific workshops in which much if not all of the actual execution of the painting might have been done by assistants. Trying to sort out how much of a particular painting might be by the named artist can be very difficult. Examination of the underpainting by radiography or IR reflectography can sometimes be very revealing (see pp. 287, 296). For example, radiographic studies of some paintings from Rubens' studio showed that the underpainting was unlike that on some other paintings attributed to Rubens (Burroughs nd, pp. 130–131). However, the very existence of workshops in which the master participated make it difficult to define an individual style.

Rubens and his workshop were also actively engaged in restoring, altering (Wood, 1995) and even copying paintings by other artists (Foucart, 1973). Rubens could be quite open about it. In 1618 he wrote to a customer, Sir Dudley Carlton, regarding a duplicate painting: 'As the reproduction is not yet quite completed, I am going to retouch it throughout myself. So it can pass for an original if necessary'. Moving on to other of his paintings that his workshop was copying for Sir Dudley, and trying to convince him that all was well, he wrote: 'I have retouched them to such effect that they can hardly be distinguished from the originals . . .' adding, disingenuously, that 'they are a perfect miracle at the price' (Schüller, 1960, p. 147).

Approaches to the technical and scientific studies of painting

The examination of paintings has advanced considerably in the past half century as scientific apparatus has become ever more sophisticated, and the palettes and techniques of individual artists are more fully known and published to the benefit of authenticator and forger alike. Conversely, it is also becoming clearer that with many earlier paintings which are the products of workshops led, perhaps, by a recognised master painter, it may not be possible to define technique too specifically.

In particular, the samples required for analysis are now much smaller, and, increasingly, completely non-destructive techniques such as Raman microscopy (RM) and non-invasive versions of standard techniques such as X-ray diffraction (XRD) are coming on stream. In addition, portable versions of some of the standard techniques are now available. These can be brought to the auction house or gallery rather than the painting having to be taken to the laboratory, although the performance of the portable instruments is often inferior to that of the standard versions. Despite these advances in micro-sampling and non-invasive techniques, samples often have to be physically removed or, ideally, sections cut through the painted layers and ground for a complete understanding of what has happened to a painting (Plesters, 1955/6; Khandekar, 2003). Even where sampling is allowed, selectivity is often conditioned by choosing least conspicuous areas rather than those areas that would yield the most information.

Thus, in order for a forgery to successfully outwit technical and scientific analysis, it is necessary that the correct materials and techniques are used. Many forgers and art critics mistakenly believe that this can be circumvented by copying 'modern' works, under the misapprehension that modern artists' materials are somehow uniform, still available and not subject to change (Johnson, 1973, for example). In reality, nothing could be further from the truth, the nineteenth and twentieth centuries seeing a succession of new pigments (Table 12.1), in a variety of natural and synthetic media. These often have very precisely known dates of introduction and withdrawal (it is, for example, almost impossible now to obtain a tube of cadmium yellow). These materials, particularly the synthetics, are also often assumed to be completely stable, yet all, particularly the organic materials, degrade quite as characteristically and inexorably as their natural analogues (see Chapter 18, p. 455).

Techniques of examination

The continuing advances in digital imaging have greatly facilitated all areas of examination, especially in the accurate recording of the images and with the facility to manipulate and enhance them (Saunders *et al.*, 2006). These improvements have been in visual imagery, including multispectral imaging and surface texture topographical imaging, radiographic imaging (see Chapter 2, p. 30), and IR reflectography (see p. 287).

The ability to accurately record and filter the topography has allowed distinctive features of an artist's style such as the brush strokes to be characterised and compared with those on suspect paintings, leading Berezhnoy *et al.* (2005) to conclude 'that the use of advanced digital analysis techniques will change the way in which authentication of visual art is currently performed'.

Multispectral imaging allows a much more accurate rendition of color than does the traditional three-color schemes (see Chapter 13, p. 332).

Table 12.1 Some of the principal modern synthetic pigments and the dates, where known, of their discovery, commercial production and first use.

White pigments	Discoveries and discoverers	Industrial introduction and production	Introduction and description as an artists' paint	Notable occurrences
Titanium as an element	1790 W. Gregor, England, Cornwall			
	1795 M.H. Klaproth, Germany			
	1821 H. Rose, Germany, titanic acid, intermediate product			
	1832 Elsner–Lampadius, dark-green pigment			
	1869 J.W. Ryland, England, black pigment			
	1892 J.W. Kidwell, USA, black pigment, U.S.Pat. 503.424			
	1893 J.W. Overton, USA, black pigment, British Pat. 9.825			
	1899 Barnes, red and yellow titanium tannate			
Titanium dioxide PW 6,77891	1908 A.J. Rossi, USA impure titanium dioxide	1916 Titanium Pigment Company, USA, start of production of composite pigments	1930 M. Fischer, USA, writes in book 'The permanent palette':	c. 1924 Arp, Shirt, Front and Fork
Anatase modification (composite pigments) (sulphate process)	1911 A.J. Rossi, USA, U.S. Pat 1.184.131, Method for Obtaining Titanic Oxide	1919 Titanium Pigment Company, USA, full-scale commercial production	F.J. Waugh uses Permalba	1928 O'Keeffe, Yellow Hickory Leaves with Daisy
USA development	1912 A.J. Rossi, USA, U.S. Pat. 1.205.267, Paint	1920 F. Weber & Company, USA, composite pigment, trade name: Permalba	after 1938 Danacolors Inc., USA	1929 Dove, Silver Sun
	1912 A.J. Rossi & L.E. Barton, USA, U.S.Pat. 1.106.406, Titanic Oxid Concentrate and Method for Producing the Same			1943 Picasso, Le Rocking Chair
	1912 A.J. Rossi & L.E. Barton, USA, U.S.Pat. 1.106.407, Method for Concentrating Titanic Oxide			1944 Dix, Winter in the Village
	1912 A.J. Rossi & L.E. Barton, USA, U.S. Pat. 1.106.408, Method for Concentrating Titanic Oxide from Substances Containing It and Iron Oxide			1945 Gorky, Table-paysage
	1913 A.J. Rossi & L. E. Barton, USA, U.S. Pat. 1.106.409, U.S.Pat 1.106.410, Method for Obtaining Titanic Oxide			1946– Mars, Mills' Panorama
	1914 L.E. Barton, USA, U.S.Pat. 1.155.462, Composite Titanic Oxide Pigment and Method of Producing Same			1947 Poliakoff, Composition Gris et Noir
	1916 L.E. Barton, USA, U.S.Pat. 1.205.144, British Pat. 105.645, Producing Composite Pigments			1951 Albers, Study for Homage to the Square
				1951 Davis, Visa
				1951 Newman, Cathedra
				1953 Pollock, The Deep
				1956 Picasso, Deux Femmes sur la Plage devant la Mer
				1956 Albers, Study for Homage to the Square
				1958 Francis, Towards Disappearance II
				1974 Miró, People, Birds in the Night

(Continued)

Table 12.1 (Continued)

White pigments	Discoveries and discoverers	Industrial introduction and production	Introduction and description as an artists' paint	Notable occurrences
Titanium dioxide PW 6,77891 **Anatase modification** (composite pigments) (sulphate process) *European development*	1909 P. Farup, Norway, Norwegian Pat. 19.978, German Pat. 242.271 1910 P. Farup, Norway, Norwegian Pat. 20.625, British Pat. 3.649, U.S. Pat. 966.185 1910 G. Jebsen, Norway, Norwegian Pat. 21.693 1912 P. Farup, Norway, German Pat. 260.906 1913 P. Farup, Norway, German Pat. 276.025 1916 P. Farup, Norway, U.S. Pat. 1.368.392, Manufacture of White Titanium–Oxid Products	1914 Production experiments on an industrial scale 1915 Test plant Lysaker, Norway 1916– Foundation and erection of the plant Titan Company A/S, Norway, Fredrikstad 1918 Regular production Kronos Titanvit	1925 Société Bourgeois, France, pure anatase 1927 Société Lefranc, France, pure anatase 1928– Winsor & Newton, England, 1934 H. Schmincke & Company, Germany early 1930s Talens N.V. Netherlands 1937– Sadolin & Holmblad A/S. Denmark 1938 G. Rowney & Company, England c.1938 after 1938	1948 De Kooning, Painting 1950 Kline, Chief 1955 Huszár, Composition 6 1956 Cohen, Black Trophy 1957– Motherwell, Elegy to the Spanish Republic 1961 Newman, Not there, here 1962 De St Pholle, La Mariée 1963 Baer, Primary Light 1964– Group: Red, Green, Blue 1965 Newman, Who's afraid of Red, Yellow and Blue III 1967 Bush, Color Field 1967 Dubuffet, Le Jardin d'Hiver 1968– Bill, Huit Groupes de 1969– 1970 Lignes autour du Blanc
Titanium dioxide PW 6,77891 **Anatase modification** (pure titanium dioxide) (sulphate process)	1920– J. Blumenfeld, Société de Produits Chimiques des Terres Rares, France, Serquigny 1923 1922 C. Weizmann & J. Blumenfeld, British Pat. 203.352, Improvements Relating to the Production of Titanic–Acid 1922 C. Weizmann & J. Blumenfeld, British Pat. 247.296, Improvements Relating to Titanium Pigments	1922 Blumenfeld process, some thousands of kilos pure titanium dioxide 1923 Fabriques de Produits Chimiques de Thann et de Muhlhouse, France, production of pure titanium dioxide, trade name: Blanc de Thann Or EB, Blanc de Thann Or P, Blanc de Thann (Cachet argent, blanc ou vert)		
Titanium dioxide PW 6,77891 **Rutile modification** (sulphate process)	1937 P.Tillmann. Titangesell – schaft, Germany, German Pat. 700.918 1937 Verein für chemische und metallurgische Produktion, Tsjechoslowakei, Czechoslovakian Pat. 7.502 1938 Titan Company, French Pat. 841.794	1937 Titangesellschaft, Germany, experimental production 1938 England, Billingham, semi-bulk scale, home decorated 1939 Production ceased due to World War II. 1940 National Lead Company, USA, Trade name: Titanox RC–HT, Titanox RC 1949 British Titan Products Comp. Ltd, England, Grimsby 1952 Titan Company A/S, West Germany, Leverkusen		

Titanium dioxide
PW 6, 77891
Rutile modification
(chlorine process)

Date	History / Manufacturer	Date	Artwork
1959	E.I. du Pont de Nemours & Comp. Inc., USA. Tennessee, New Johnson-ville	1970–1971	Hockney, Mr. and Mrs. Clark and Percy
1965	British Titan Products Comp. Ltd., England, Billingham	1971	Kelly, Two Panels: Black and White Bar II
1967	Titangesellschaft mbH., Germany	1972	Kelly, Red Curve II
		1972	Kelly, White Triangle with Black Curve
		1972	Bradford, Action at Schwebo
		1974	Miró, Personnages, Oiseaux dans la Nuit
		1976	Penck, TM 1976
		c.1980	Morrisseau, Animal Environment
		c.1980	Morrisseau, Poppy Tree

Red pigments

Cadmium red
PR 108, 77202
Cadmium orange
PO 20, 77202

Date	History / Manufacturer	Date	Reference / Artwork
1892	Welz, Germany, German Pat. 63558	1909	Eibner writes in book 'Malmateria-lienkunde' on cadmium red
1919	Farbenfabriken Bayer & Co., Germany, preparation of a more consistent cadmium red	1910	Toch writes in book 'Paints, Painting, Restoration': commercial production started not before 1910.
1924	Farbenfabriken Bayer & Co., Germany, German Pat. 388.535	1913	Blockx writes in book 'Compendium für Kunst-maler und Gemäldelieb-haber' on cadmium red
1961	Bayer AG./Siegle & Co. GmbH., West Germany, production of Cadmopur-rot-S-types	1914	Popova Liubov, Cubo-futurists
		1917	Léon Bakst, Boutique Fantasque: Woman in a Red Bonnet (Watercolor/Gouache)
		c. 1918	Matisse, Le Château Chenonceaux
		1921	Mondriaan, Composition with red, yellow and blue (Blok 273)
		1921	Mondriaan, Composition 1 with red, yellow and blue (Blok 275)
		1921–1925	Mondriaan, Diamond painting with Red, Yellow and Blue
		1925	Charles Demuth, Gladioli: Flower Study No. 4 (Watercolor/Gouache)
		1946–1947	Man, Mills' panorama
		1964	Kelly, Blue Green Red I
		1967	Newman, Who's afraid of Red, Yellow and Blue III
		1972	Kelly, Red Curve II

(*Continued*)

Table 12.1 (Continued)

Red pigments	Discoveries and discoverers	Industrial introduction and production	Introduction and description as an artists' paint	Notable occurrences
Cadmium red PR 108,77202 **Cadmium orange** PO 20,77202			1917 Bill for Willem Witsen for cadmium red of the firm Claus & Fritz, Amsterdam	
			1918 Talens N.V., Netherlands, catalogue: cadmium red extra, cadmium red ordinary	
			1919 Roelofs writes in book 'De Practyk van het schilderen' on cadmium red	
			1921 Doerner writes in book 'Malmaterial und seine Verwendung im Bilde' on cadmium red	
			1921 Pöschl writes in book 'Farbenwarenkunde' on cadmium red	
			1921 Paint tube cadmium red, firm Claus & Fritz, Amsterdam	
			1926 Wehlte buys his first cadmium red powder in Ivry sur Seine, France	
			1928 Pricelist firm A.J.van der Linde, Amsterdam: Extra fijne Olieverf voor Kunstschilders: cadmium red fijne Olieverf van de firm Claus & Fritz: cadmium red	
			1930 Fischer writes in book 'The permanent palette' on cadmium red	
Cadmium vermilion red PR 113,77201 **Cadmium vermilion orange** PO 23,77201	1955 Imperial Paper Color Corporation, USA	1955 Imperial Paper Color Corporation, USA, trade name: Mercadium		The Merkadiums are not produced anymore since c. 1980 because the price of selenium (for cadmium red) went down
	1955 U.S.Pat. 2.878.134 (submitted)	1956 Siegle & Co.GmbH., West Germany, trade name: Cadmiumzinnober, Merkadiumrot		
	1959 U.S.Pat. 2.878.134 (patented)			

Cadmopone red PR 108:1,77202:1 **Cadmopone orange** PO 20:1,77202:1 **Cadmopone yellow** PY 35:1,77205:1 **Cadmopone yellow** PY 37:1,77199:1	1921 Marston, USA	1926 USA 1933 Kalichemie, Germany, German Pat. 568.159 1935 L.G. Marquardt, Germany, German Pat. 613.644 1935 IG. Farbenindustrie AG., Germany, French Pat. 779.528 1939 J.Drucker, USA, U.S. Pat. 2.148.194 1940 V. Rizzini, Italy, Italian Pat. 366.372 1940 E.I. du Pont de Nemours & Comp.Inc., USA,U.S. Pat. 2.173.895	1953 Rooskens, Compositie 1, cadmopone yellow 1955 Huszár, Composition 6, cadmopone yellow
Cadmium barium-vermilion red PR 113:1,77201:1 **Cadmium barium-vermilion orange** PO 23:1,77201:1	After the discovery of the cadmium vermilion red and cadmium vermilion orange		
Molybdate red PR 104,77605 **Molybdate orange** PR 104,77605	1863 H. Schultze 1921 Jaeger & Germs 1930 E. Lederle, IG. Farben-industrie AG., Germany, German Pat. no 22F 1.52.30 1931 H.Wagner, Germany, German Pat. 630.660, 1932 E. Lederle, Germany, German Pat. 615.147 1933 Lederle & Grimm, IG. Farbenindustrie AG., Germany, German Pat. 574.379 1933 Lederle & Grimm, IG. Farbenindustrie AG., Germany, U.S. Pat. 1.926.447	1936 E. Lederle, Germany, U.S.Pat.2.030.009, U.S.Pat.2.157.712 1936 U.S.Pat 2.063.254 1937 Linz, Belgian Pat. 327.750, production patent 1937 IG. Farbenindustrie AG., Germany, British Pat. 483.765 1943 Huckle & Polzer, USA, U.S. Pat. 2.316.244 1944 Botti, E.I. du Pont de Nemours & Comp. Inc., USA, U.S. Pat. 2.365.171	

AZO PIGMENTS WITH ß-NAPHTHOL AS A COUPLING COMPONENT

Para red PR 1,12070	1880 Read Holliday & Sons Ltd., England, British Pat. 2.757 1885 R. Meldola	1889 Farbwerke Meister Lucius & Brüning, Germany

(*Continued*)

Table 12.1 (Continued)

Red pigments	Discoveries and discoverers	Industrial introduction and production	Introduction and description as an artists' paint	Notable occurrences
Toluidine red PR 3,12120	1904 Meister Lucius & Brüning, Germany 1905 BASF, Germany, German Pat. ap.F.20.265, British Pat. 19.100, French Pat. 357.858			1923–1924 Huszár, wall advertisement Miss Blanche, Culemborg, Netherlands 1964 Dubuffet, Chain de Mémoire III 1965 Dubuffet, LeTrain de Pendules
Chlorinated para red PR 4,12085	1906 W.Herzberg & O. Spengler, AGFA, Germany, German Pat. 180.301, French Pat. 368.259, US. Pat.865.587			1929 Missiemuseum, Steyl-Tegelen, Netherlands, pigment collection
Parachloro nitroaniline red PR 6,12090	1906 C. Schraube & E. Schleicher, AGFA, Germany, German Pat. 200.263, British Pat. 6227, U.S. Pat. 860.575			
Dinitro–aniline orange PO 5,12075	1907 R. Lauch, Germany	1908 AGFA, Germany, British Pat. 18.736 1909 AGFA, Germany, German Pat. 217.266, French Pat. 394.754 1909 R. Lauch, Germany, U.S.Pat. 912.138	1931 Talens N.V., Netherlands, list of artists' paints, Rembrandt series	

AZO PIGMENT LAKES WITH ß-NAPHTHOL AS A COUPLING COMPONENT

Red pigments	Discoveries and discoverers	Industrial introduction and production	Introduction and description as an artists' paint	Notable occurrences
Lithol red R PR 49,15630	1899 P.Julius, BASF, Germany, German Pat. 112.833, British Pat. 25.511 1900 P.Julius, BASF, Germany, U.S.Pat. 650.757, French Pat. 297.330			
Red lake C PR 53,15585	1902 K. Schirmacher, Germany 1903 Meister Lucius & Brüning, Germany, German Pat. 145.908, British Pat. 23.831, French Pat. 328.131, US.Pat.733.280			

AZO PIGMENT LAKES WITH β-OXYNAPHTHOIC ACID (BON/BONA/BONS) AS A COUPLING COMPONENT

Lithol rubine
PR 57,15850
- 1903 R.Gley & O.Siebert, Germany
- 1903 AGFA, Germany, German Pat. 151.205, British Pat. 11.004, French Pat. 332.145, U.S.Pat.743.071

Permanent red 2B
PR 48,15865
- 1928 Germany, trade name: Litholrubine A.Siegel, E.I.
- the Pont, USA, trade name:
- late
- 1920s Watchung Red

AZO PIGMENTS WITH β-OXYNAPHTHOIC ACID ARYLIDE (NAPHTHOL AS) AS A COUPLING COMPONENT

Permanent red FRR
PR 2,12310
- 1911 A.Winther, A. Laska & A.Zitscher, Griesheim-Elektron, Germany, German Pat. 256.999
- 1912 Griesheim-Elektron, Germany, British Pat. 6379, French Pat. 441.333, U.S.Pat. 1.034.853

Permanent red F4RH
PR 7,12420
- 1921 H.Wagner, Griesheim-Elektron, Germany
- 1921 IG. Farbenindustrie AG., Germany, German Pat. 421.205, British Pat. 199.771, French Pat. 549.020

Permanent red F4R
PR 8,12335
- 1911 A.Winther, A. Laska & A. Zitscher, Griesheim-Elektron, Germany, German Pat. 256.999
- 1912 Griesheim-Elektron, Germany, British Pat. 6379, French Pat. 441.333, U.S.Pat. 1.034.853

Permanent red FRLL
PR 9,12460
- 1922 A. Laska & A. Zitscher, Griesheim-Elektron, Germany, German Pat. 390.627, U.S.Pat. 1.457.114

Permanent bordeaux FRR
PR 12,12385
- 1921 H.Wagner, Griesheim-Elektron, Germany
- 1921 IG. Farbenindustrie AG., Germany, German Pat. 421.205, British Pat. 199.771, French Pat. 549.020

Permanent red FGR
PR 112,12370
- 1939 IG. Farbenindustrie AG., Germany

1970 Rancillac, La Suite Américaine

(Continued)

Table 12.1 (Continued)

Red pigments	Discoveries and discoverers	Industrial introduction and production	Introduction and description as an artists' paint	Notable occurrences
Permanent carmine FBB PR 146,12485	1953 Hoechst AG., West-Germany			
Permanent red F5RK PR 170,12475	1952 Harmon Colors, USA			1983 Dubuffet, Mire G 131 Kowloon
Perylenes		1955 Hoechst AG., West Germany, British Pat. 839.634 1956 Hoechst AG., West Germany, British Pat. 835.459, British Pat. 861.218, German Pat. 1.113.773 1960 BASF AG., West Germany, Belgian Pat. 589.209		
Perylene vermilion PR 123,71145	1952 Harmon Colors, USA			
Perylene scarlet PR 149,71137	1956 Hoechst AG., West Germany, German Pat. 1.067.157			
Perylene maroon PR 179,71130	1913 M. Kardos, Germany	BASF AG., West Germany, British Pat. 923.721		
Perylene red PR 190,71140	1919 P. Friedländer, Germany			
BENZIMIDAZOLONES				
Benzimidazolone PV Fast Maroon HFM PR 171,12512	1960 Hoechst AG., West Germany, U.S.Pat.3.124.565	1964 Hoechst AG., West Germany		
Benzimidazolone PV Fast Red HFT PR 175,12519	1960 Hoechst AG., West Germany, U.S.Pat. 3.124.565	1965 Hoechst AG., West Germany		
Benzimidazolone PV Carmine HF3C PR 176,12515	1960 Hoechst AG., West Germany, U.S.Pat. 3.124.565	1965 Hoechst AG., West Germany		

Benzimidazolone PV Carmine HF4C
PR 185,12516

1967 Hoechst AG., West Germany

Hoechst AG., West Germany, German Pat. 1.213.552, U.S.Pat.3.137.686

Benzimidazolone PV Red HF2B
PR 208,12514

1970 Hoechst AG., West Germany

Hoechst AG., West Germany, Belgian Pat. 733.711

Benzimidazolone orange HL
PO 36,11780

1964 Hoechst AG., West Germany

1960 Hoechst AG., West Germany, U.S.Pat. 3.109.842

PERINONES
Perinone orange
PO 43,71105

1953 Hoechst AG., West Germany, trade name: Indanthrenbrillant-orange GR

1924 Eckert & Gruene, Hoechst, Germany
1950 Hoechst AG., West Germany

1978 Royal Talens B.V., Netherlands, list of artists' paints, Rembrandt Oil Color

QUINACRIDONES
Quinacridone Magenta
PR 122,73915

1958 E.I. du Pont de Nemours & Comp. Inc., USA, U.S. Pat. 2.821.529, Struve, U.S.Pat.2.821.530, Struve, U.S.Pat. 2.821.541, Struve, U.S. Pat. 2.830.990, Struve, U.S.Pat.2.844.484, Reidinger, Struve, U.S. Pat. 2.844.485, Reidinger, Struve, U.S.Pat.2.844.581, Mager, Struve, trade name: Cinquasia, Monastral Red B

1935 H. Liebermann, Germany
1955 E.I. du Pont de Nemours & Comp. Inc., USA

1974 Royal Talens B.V., Netherlands, list of artists' paints, Rembrandt Oil Color

DIKETOPYRROLO-PYRROLE (DPP) PIGMENTS
Irgazin DPP Red BO PR 254,56110
Irgazin DPP Red 5G PR 255,-
Irgazin DPP Red 4013 PR 264,-
Irgazin DPP Orange 16A PO 73,-

1974 Discovery of the DPP group

1983 Ciba Geigy AG., Switzerland, U.S.Pat. 4.415.685

1996 Royal Talens B.V., Netherlands, list of artists' paints, Rembrandt Oil Color

(Continued)

Table 12.1 (Continued)

Yellow pigments	Discoveries and discoverers	Industrial introduction and production	Introduction and description as an artist' paint	Notable occurrences
Nickel titanium yellow PY 53,77788	1939 H.H. Schaumann, E.I. du Pont de Nemours & Comp. Inc., USA, U.S. Pat. 2.257.278	1954 Harshaw Chemical Comp., USA, trade name: Sun Yellow 1958 Siegle & Co. GmbH., West Germany, trade name: Nickeltitangelb AN 1958 Bayer AG., West Germany, trade name: Lichtgelb 100	1986 Royal Talens B.V., Netherlands, Rembrandt Soft Pastels	
Hansa yellows	1909 Meister Lucius & Brüning Germany, German Pat. 257.488			
Hansa yellow G PY 1,11680	1909 H. Wagner, Germany	1910 Meister Lucius & Brüning, Germany	1931 Talens N.V., Netherlands, list of artists' paints, Rembrandt series	
Hansa-yellow 10G PY 3,11710	1910 K. Desamari, Germany	1910 Meister Lucius & Brüning, Germany	1927 Talens N.V., Netherlands, list of artists' paints, Rembrandt Tempera paints (Talens green bright) 1931 Talens N.V., Netherlands, list of artists' paints, Rembrandt series	
Hansa-Brilliant yellow GX PY 73,11738	1957 Coating & Specialty Products Dep., Hercules Inc., USA, French Pat. 1.309.211, British. Pat. 938.047, DAS 1.231.367			
Hansa-Brilliant yellow 5GX PY 74,11741	1958 E.I. du Pont de Nemours & Comp. Inc., USA, U.S. Pat. 3.032.546, Canadian Pat. 612.395	1961 E.I. du Pont de Nemours & Comp. Inc, USA, trade name: Dalamar Yellow 1961 Sherwin Williams Comp, USA, trade name: Permansa Yellow GY 1961 Hoechst AG., West Germany, trade name: Hansa-Brillant 5GX		

Hansa yellow FGL PY 97,11767	1961	Hoechst AG., West Germany, U.S. Pat. 2.644.814	1961	Hoechst AG., West Germany
Hansa-Brilliant yellow 10GX PY 98,11727	1953 1961	Hoechst AG., West Germany U.S.Pat.3.165.507	1961	Hoechst AG., West Germany
Tartrazine yellow PY 100,19140	1884	H.J. Ziegler	1929	Missiemuseum, Steyl-Tegelen, Netherlands, trade name: Film GelbT, AGFA, Germany
Tetrachloro-isoindolinones	1956 1957	J.R.Geigy AG., Switzerland, Swiss Pat. 346.218 Ciba Geigy AG., Switzerland, Swiss Pat. 363.979,Swiss Pat. 363.980, Swiss Pat. 348.496	1961 1965	Ciba Geigy AG., Switzerland, U.S.Pat. 2.973.358, production patent, trade name: Irgazin Introduction USA
Isoindolinone Yellow G PY109		USA, trade name: Irgazin 2GLT	1980	Royal Talens B.V., Netherlands, list of artists' paints, Rembrandt Oil Color
Isoindolinone Yellow R PY 110,56280	1965	USA, trade name: Irgazin 3RLT	1978	RoyalTalens B.V, Netherlands, list of artists' paints, Rembrandt Oil Color

BENZIMIDAZOLONES

Benzimidazolone Yellow H4G PY 151,13980	1971	Hoechst AG., West Germany
Benzimidazolone Yellow H3G PY 154,11781	c. 1975	Hoechst AG., West Germany
Benzimidazolone Yellow H6G PY 175,11784	after 1980	Hoechst AG., West Germany

(Continued)

Table 12.1 (Continued)

Blue pigments	Discoveries and discoverers	Industrial introduction and production	Introduction and description as an artist's paint	Notable occurrences
Manganese blue PB 33, 77112	1907 Bong	1935 IG. Farbenindustrie AG., Germany, French Pat. 778.290 1936 W. Mühlberg, IG. Farben-industrie AG., Germany, French Pat. 802.687	1942 Talens N.V., Netherlands, list of artists' paints, World production 1988 ceased 1993 Royal Talens B.V., Netherlands, manganese blue replaced by copper phthalocyanineblue	
Copper phthalo cyanine blue PB 15, 74160	1907 Braun & Tcherniac, England 1927 de Diesbach & von der Weid, Switzerland 1928 Dandridge, Drescher & Thomas, Scottish Dyes Ltd., UK 1932–1934 Linstead, England, revelation of chemical structure, name given: phthalocyanine	1928 Scottish Dyes Ltd., UK, British Pat. 322.169 1929 Scottish Dyes Ltd., UK, German Pat. 586.906 1932 ICI Ltd., England, U.S.Pat. 2.000.051, U.S.Pat. 2.000.052 1934 ICI Ltd., England, British Pat. 410.814 1935 ICI Ltd., England, British Pat. 464.126 1935 ICI Ltd., England, trade name: Monastral Fast Blue BS 1935 IG. Farbenindustrie AG., Germany, German Pat. 603.552, German Pat. 717.164 1935–1936 IG. Farbenindustrie AG., Germany, trade name: Heliogenblau B Pulver 1936 E.I. du Pont de Nemours & Comp. Inc. USA, U.S.Pat.2.173.699 1953 BASF AG., West Germany, ß-modification phthalocyanine blue, trade name: Heliogenblau BG	1937 Winsor & Newton, England, artists' paints 1940 Talens N.V., Netherlands, list of artists' paints, Rembrandt blue	1967 Newman, Who's afraid of Red, Yellow and Blue III

Pigment	Year	Manufacturer / Event	Year	Reference
Metal-free phthalocyanine blue PB 16,74100	1939	ICI Ltd., England, trade name: Monastral Fast Blue G		
	1945–1955	Pigment is manufactured, later replaced by ß-modification copper phthalocyanine blue	1964	Kelly, Blue Green Red I
Indanthrene blue PB 60,69800	1901	R. Bohn, BASF, Germany German Pat. 129.845		
	1924	IG. Farbenindustrie AG., Germany, trade name: Indanthren	1996	Royal Talens B.V., Netherlands, list of water colors, Rembrandt Water Colors

Green pigments

Pigment	Year	Manufacturer / Event	Year	Reference
Polychloro copper-phthalocyanine green PG 7,74260	1935	Linstead & Dent, England	1939	Winsor & Newton, England,artists paints
	1935	Niemann, Schmidt, Mühlbauer & Wiest, Germany	1940	Talens N.V., Netherlands, list of artists' paints, Rembrandt green
	1936	ICI Ltd., England		
	1937	IG. Farbenindustrie AG., Germany		
	1940	E.I. du Pont de Nemours & Comp. Inc., USA		
Chloro bromo copper phthalocyanine green PG 36,74265	1957	Harmon Colors, USA, trade name: Viridine-green		
	1959	E.I. du Pont de Nemours & Comp. Inc., USA		
	1960	BASF AG., West Germany, trade name: Heliogrün 6G		
	1961	ICI Ltd., England, trade name: Monastral Fast Green 6YS	1964	Kelly, Blue Green Red I
	1967	BASF AG., West Germany, trade name: Heliogrün 8GA		
Pigment Green B PG 8,10006	1885	O. Hoffmann		
	1921	BASF AG., Germany, German Pat. 356,973, trade name: Pigmentgrün B		
Nickel azo-yellow PG 10,12775	1941	Woodward & Kvalnes, E.I. du Pont de Nemours & Comp. Inc., USA	1947	E.I. du Pont de Nemours & Comp. Inc., USA, trade name: Greengold-YT-562-D
	1946	E.I. du Pont de Nemours & Comp. Inc., USA, U.S. Pat. 2.396.327	1963	Siegle & Co. GmbH., West Germany, trade name: Grüngold Z
			1963	BASF AG., West Germany, trade name: Litholechtgelb 0830

(Continued)

Table 12.1 (Continued)

Violet pigments	Discoveries and discoverers	Industrial introduction and production	Introduction and description as an artists' paint	Notable occurrences
Quinacridone violet PV 19,46500	1935 H. Liebermann, Germany 1955 E.I. du Pont de Nemours & Comp. Inc., USA	1958 E.I. du Pont de Nemours & Comp. Inc., USA, U.S.Pat. 2.821.529, Struve, U.S. Pat. 2.821.530, Struve, U.S.Pat.2.821.541, Struve, U.S.Pat. 2.830.990, Struve, U.S. Pat. 2.844.484, Reidinger, Struve, U.S. Pat. 2.844.485, Reidinger, Struve, U.S.Pat.2.844.581, Mager, Struve	1974 Royal Talens B.V., Netherlands, list of artists' paints, Rembrandt Oil Color	
Carbazole dioxazine violet PV 23,51319	1928 Kränzlein, Gruene & Thiele, Farbwerke 1952 Hoechst, Germany Hoechst AG, West Germany German Pat. 946.560	1953 Hoechst AG, West Germany, trade name: PermanentViolett RL 1958 Cooper, E.I. du Pont de Nemours & Comp. Inc., USA, U.S.Pat. 2.857.400, production patent	1974 Royal Talens B.V., Netherlands, list of artists' paints, Rembrandt Oil Color	

Brown pigments

Chromium titanium yellow PBr 24,77310	1939 C.J. Harbert, Harshaw Chemical Comp., USA, U.S.Pat. 2.251.829	1967 Siegle & Co. GmbH., West Germany, trade name: Nickeltitangelb R, Lichtgelb 3R, Lichtgelb 5R, Lichtgelb 6R	1986 Royal Talens B.V., Netherlands, Rembrandt Soft Pastels	
Benzimidazolone PV Fast Brown HFR PBr 25,12510	1960 Hoechst AG, West Germany, U.S.Pat. 3.124.565	1966 Hoechst AG, West Germany, trade name: Hostaperm Brown HFR		

Source: de Keijzer, 2002

The spectral reflectance can be measured enabling non-destructive determination of the pigments to be made from their reflectance characteristics. As the spectral range recorded includes the near IR, multispectral imaging can 'see' much deeper into the painted layer than can the unaided eye, sometimes allowing the underpainting to be identified non-destructively (Casini *et al.*, 1999; Padfield *et al.*, 2002).

Optical microscopy has an important role to play (Eastaugh *et al.*, 2004a, b). This can often be important and related to specific production processes, as exemplified by the characterisation of the particles of chalk produced in the traditional manner (see p. 293) or in the preparation of lapis lazuli to form ultramarine (see p. 302). Skaug (1994) and Frinta (1978, 1982) have for many years studied the punches and punch marks made on the gilded decorative areas of some early Italian panel paintings. On some, Frinta found evidence that the same tool had been use on several otherwise unrelated paintings as well as on the supposedly antique frames of some totally different paintings. This suggested to Frinta that they were the result of either deceptive restoration or outright forgery in one particular workshop which, on other evidence, he believed to have been that of the prolific Italian art forger Icilio Federico Joni (Joni, 1936; Mazzoni, (ed), 2004), operating in Italy in the early twentieth century (but see the counterviews of Skaug, 1994).

Scanning electron microscopy (SEM) and electron microprobe analysis (EPMA) are widely used to observe and identify pigments in sample sections taken from the painting. Barba *et al.* (1995) described the use of transmission electron microscopy (TEM) on pigments in cut sections. The method is very sensitive and has the advantage that electron beam diffraction can be carried out, giving mineral identifications on individual observed particles, which can be very useful where there is a mixture of pigment minerals present.

UV, IR and Radiography

Examination of paintings by UV and IR is quick, relatively inexpensive, and non-destructive, covering the whole painting. The UV and IR radiations are nearly always reflected off the painting, whereas most X-ray techniques transmit the X-rays through the painting, revealing information at all levels from the support to the varnish. Details of a painting such as evidence of signatures can often be elucidated by a combination of these techniques (Martin *et al.*, 2001).

UV

Sources: Rorimer (1931, pp. 46–50); Savage (1976, pp. 294–304); Bell (1982a); de la Rie (1982a, b, c); Townsend (1992). (See de la Rie, 1982a for a more comprehensive bibliography.)

Most traditional paint media show a progressively greater tendency to fluoresce as they age and most of the synthetic materials do not fluoresce at all. The degree to which the paint media fluoresce depends on many factors, including age, exposure to sunlight, and the pigments that are in contact with them. Most varnishes fluoresce under UV, masking fluorescence from the paint layer beneath. Marijnissen (1985) regarded such coats with suspicion, suggesting that there was something to hide. Rorimer (1931, p. 48) recommended treating the surface of the varnish with turpentine to reduce the fluorescence.

IR

Sources: Bell (1982b); Marijnissen (1985, pp. 85–87, 178–181); van Asperen de Boer (1985); Townsend (1992); Le Chanu (1995); Sheldon and Eastaugh (1999); Bomford (ed) (2002).

IR has a far greater penetrating power than light (very approximately ×4 in most paint media). Black pigments absorb IR very well and thus appear particularly dark. This is useful for revealing preliminary charcoal sketches on white grounds that were subsequently covered by the main painting (see p. 296) but which are completely transparent to X-rays.

Pigments that contain black respond well, and thus a grey made up of black in white will appear dark, but a grey made up of blue and red pigments will not.

Two closely related techniques are usually employed for detecting and recording the images – IR photography and reflectography. Electronic detectors used in reflectography cover a wider wavelength range than does any one film, and are thus often able to record penetration to a greater depth. The reflected IR radiation can be picked up with purpose-made IR vidicon cameras to produce a video. Continued technical developments and the introduction of solid-state digital cameras have significantly improved performance, particularly in the acquiring and processing of signals (Bertani and Consolandi, 2006). Image spectroscopy mapping in the visible and near IR offer the prospect of non-destructive analysis of the entire surface (Casini *et al.*, 1999).

Radiography

If there was a frequent and extensive radiographic control, . . . , the market would undergo a considerable moral improvement and forgery would become extremely difficult.

Gilardoni *et al.* (1994, p. 118)

Sources: Burroughs (nd); de Wild (1929, pp. 92–104); Rawlins (1937, 1940); Fleming (1975, pp. 47–53); Marijnissen (1985); van Schoute and Verougstraete-Marcq (1986); Gilardoni *et al.* (1994); Martin and Ravaud (1995); Hassall (2005).

Radiography was one of the earliest physical scientific examination techniques to be employed, paintings being examined for evidence of restoration from the very inception of radiography in the late nineteenth century (Bridgman, 1964).

An obvious way to make a painting appear old is to reuse old supports of panel or canvas, contemporary with the purported age of the forged painting, or to modify an existing old painting. Radiography can reveal the history of the various components of the picture and their relation to the present painted layer (see Figures 12.2, 12.4 and 12.5).

Whilst on the subject of radiographic revelations beneath the painted layer, mention should be made of the ingenious method presently adopted by the painter Leo Stevens to foil future would-be dishonest dealers seeking to pass off his excellent copies of old masters as originals. On the primed surface, before commencing the main painting, he has painted some anachronism in white lead primer. Thus, in his copy of a painting of a seventeenth-century lady she can be seen on the radiograph to be wearing a Playtex brassiere. Similarly, his seventeenth-century harbour scene has a submarine lurking in the radiographic depths.

In a similar vein, Tom Keating, the well-known British art forger, claimed that he wrote swear words or 'ever been had' in white lead directly on the canvas before painting, specifically so that they could be detected radiographically (Keating *et al.*, 1977, p. 85). It would be interesting to X-ray some of his forged oil paintings to see if this was the case.

In fact this ploy is not as foolproof as it might at first seem. The dishonest dealer, knowing of the whereabouts of the chronological giveaway, has only to cut or scrape out the offending portion and then restore it. Many of the most famous apparently intact paintings have far more restoration that would be necessitated by this treatment. However, all is not lost because although Leo Stevens uses traditional techniques, many of the materials, the paints, etc., contain the standard modern pigments, and thus scientific examination would reveal the true nature of the whole painting.

The technique of autoradiography, more usually employed to examine works on paper (see Chapter 13, p. 320), has been used at the Hahn-Meitner-Institut in Germany for a number of years to examine paintings (Fischer *et al.*, 1999). Cotter *et al.* (1976) used the technique to investigate the authenticity and restoration history of a number of nineteenth-century North American paintings including works supposedly by Ralph Blakelock; they found that some paintings by Blakelock's daughter had been sold as his work after a suitable change of signature. An extensive programme of autoradiography was undertaken at the Metropolitan Museum, New York on its collection of seventeenth-century Dutch paintings (Ainsworth, 1982).

On a copper support the paint layers are rendered invisible to X-rays but Bridgman *et al.* (1965) successfully overcame this problem by using electron emission radiography (EMR) (see Chapter 13, p. 320).

Analysis

Physical analytical methods have largely taken over from traditional chemical methods. More recently, digital imaging techniques such as multispectral imaging have been used for the non-destructive identification of pigments (Saunders *et al.* 2006).

RS and RM

Sources: Guineau (1989); Coupry and Brissaud (1996); Majolino *et al.* (1996); Mathieson and Nugent (1996); Mairani *et al.* (1997); Clark (2002); Vandenabeele and Moens (2005).

Raman spectroscopy (RS) and Raman microscopy (RM) can be used to determine both organic and inorganic materials. This enables their respective interactions when in direct contact in the painting to be more easily studied. This promises to be invaluable for characterising the differential ageing of paints made up of organic media and inorganic pigments for example, with important implications for authenticity studies.

RM is versatile, in that either the painting can be analysed directly, or a tiny section removed so that each component analysed can be identified visually.

As the technique is based on light, it is capable of analysis through transparent materials, and thus it is possible to analyse a picture behind its glass if necessary (Derbyshire and Withnall, 1999), although the sensitivity and precision is reduced.

Although RS has gained rapid acceptance as an extremely versatile non-destructive technique for the analysis of pigments on manuscripts and watercolors, etc. (see Chapter 13, p. 324), some problems do arise. Compared with long-established techniques such as XRD there are relatively few published spectra, although libraries of pigment spectra are now being made available (Bell *et al.*, 1997; Burgio and Clark, 2001, for example; and details of important spectral libraries on the Internet are given in Vandenabeele and Moens, 2005, Table 4.2).

There are problems with fluorescence when the materials are in an oil medium. However, Clark *et al.* (1995) and Coupry (1992) have applied RM to the identification of pigments in oil media, and Mairani *et al.* (1997) have also analysed paint materials in oil media by using a near-IR source in place of the more usual visible or UV sources. Vandenabeele *et al.* (2000a) used a near-IR laser source to overcome fluorescence in the analysis of a wide range of proteinaceous and fatty acid media and varnishes.

Organic analysis

The most common techniques for the analysis of the organic components of painting are gas chromatography (GC) (Mills and White, 1994; Schilling and Khanijian, 1996a & b), high-performance liquid chromatography (HPLC) and Fourier transform infra-red (FTIR) (see Chapter 3, pp. 58–60). HPLC is especially useful for the analysis of more complex organics such as proteins in tempera media and organic dyes (Halpine, 1996; Lomax, 1997). Pyrolysis GC (Shedrinsky *et al.*, 1987/88, 1989; Learner, 1995; Sonoda, 1998) is proving useful for the determination of high molecular weight fractions in both natural and synthetic resins. The combination of GC with MS has been used to identify some complex organics (van der Doelen *et al.*, 1998) and natural resins used as varnishes on paintings (van der Doelen, nd; Chiavari *et al.*, 1995).

The other technique widely used technique is FTIR (see Chapter 3, p. 58; Mills and White, 1994; Doménech Carbó *et al.*, 1996; Lomax, 1997; Derrick *et al.*, 1999) and FTIR microscopy (Pilc and White, 1995). It is especially useful in the analysis of materials such as oil paint where RS suffers

from fluorescence. Langley and Burnstock (1999) developed a method of FTIR microscopy across sectioned paint layers on modern paintings. Bacci *et al.* (1992) have developed fibre optic reflectance IR that allows rapid non-destructive analysis at many points across a painting.

Inorganic analysis

In addition to RS the range of techniques used includes X-ray fluorescence (XRF), EPMA, particle (or proton)-induced X-ray emission (PIXE), mass spectrometry (MS) and XRD.

Open architecture XRF systems allow the whole picture to be presented to the X-ray beam without sampling (Lomax, 1997), and portable systems are available to enable pictures to be non-destructively analysed *in situ* (Gigante *et al.*, 1991; Glinsman, 2006).

PIXE is a quick, non-destructive technique, and as the beam can be employed in air a large number of analyses can rapidly be carried out over the surface of a painting merely by moving it in front of the beam (Griesser and Denker, 2000; Neelmeijer *et al.*, 2000b Tuurnala and Hautojärvi, 2000). By varying the energy of the beam it is possible to achieve controlled depth profiling over about 200 microns through the paint layer and beneath.

MS isotope determinations specifically for chronological and provenancing work on both the chalk and lead-white grounds as well as on pigments have been of great value in authenticity studies (Keisch, 1970, 1976; and see p. 295 & 303). Modern chromatography instruments now usually come equipped with MS and thus offer the potential of isotope identification on the individual components of the sample. Neutron activation analysis (NAA) has also been used for the trace element analysis of pigments to provide additional provenance and chronological information in authenticity studies (Kühn, 1966).

XRD has been used for many years and remains the most useful technique to identify crystalline minerals, especially those forming the pigments (Lahanier, 1986; Mantler *et al.*, 2000).

Daniels (1984) suggested the application of the Russell Effect to detect newly painted areas. Put very simply, some materials, notably freshly abraded metal surfaces and some organic materials, undergo autoxidation, releasing tiny quantities of hydrogen peroxide. These can produce an image on a photographic plate, and thus could be used to detect relatively recently applied drying oils or a new signature or alteration on a document.

Physical dating methods applied to painting

Physical dating techniques may be useful once it is ascertained that an old panel or canvas contemporary with the style of the forgery has not been reused (see p. 29). Dendrochronology has the potential to provide sometimes detailed chronological information on panel paintings (see Chapter 6, p. 131).

For the radiocarbon (RC) dating of paintings executed in the Post-Medieval period and later there exist the major problems of the fluctuations in the RC calibration curve (see Chapter 5, p. 13). Heart wood is likely to have been used for both the frame and for the stretchers, and thus unless some sapwood is present it will usually be impossible to judge the period of time that elapsed between when the wood of the sample was actually laid down and the felling of the tree-it could be in the order of centuries.

Media such as egg tempera and the drying oils from early paintings, where they can be separated from contaminants, should be ideal for accelerator mass spectrometry radiocarbon (AMS RC) dating. There are the possibilities of contamination from carbonate material of geological age from the pigments (Stulik *et al.*, 1992), or from synthetic materials made from mineral oil-based chemicals. The ^{14}C content of material such as linseed growing in the post-bomb era from the 1950s should be very distinctive (see Chapter 5, p. 96, Figure 5.10).

Finally, the forensic technique of fingerprinting has been applied to painting and even has a name, dactyloscopy (Holzheu, 1989). The technique seems unlikely, but is currently being applied on a painting purporting to be by Jackson Pollock (*Times of London*, 8 November 2006).

Examination

A painting comprises different components, the frame, support, ground, under sketch, paint, varnishes, etc. (Figure 12.1), to each of which a variety of examination techniques is appropriate. The surest guide to the true age of a painting is often hidden well beneath the current painted surface.

The frame and support, panel, canvas or copper

Frames (Mitchell and Roberts, 1996)

Radiography will often reveal details of the construction of the frame, and of the panel or the stretchers of a canvas (Burroughs, nd; Hassall, 2005). Elmyr de Hory had problems while in America obtaining stretchers with the distinctive joinings found only on the stretchers used in France (Irving, 1970, p. 73). This problem he neatly circumvented after the painting was complete, by cutting the canvas from its stretchers and remounting it onto another new canvas and attaching new stretchers. This is a routine restoration procedure for old, genuine paintings when the canvas has become damaged or weak. Remounting calmed doubts over the obviously new American-style stretchers as they appeared to be part of a restoration. Furthermore, the forged painting was now firmly attached to a new canvas, which prevented inspection of the back.

Panels

Sources: General: Dardes and Rothe (eds) (1998); and see Chapter 6, p. 131.

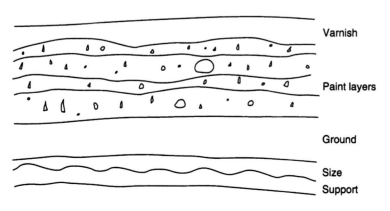

Figure 12.1 Schematic section through an oil painting. (Courtesy Conti and Glanville, 2007)

Varnish

Paint layers

Ground

Size

Support

Prior to the seventeenth century most European paintings were made on wooden panels, continuing the practice of antiquity. In central and northern Europe the use of oak predominated, although beech, spruce, lime, larch and some fir and pine species were also used (Klein, 1998a, b). In Italy poplar was the usual wood chosen. Ravaud (1999) identified the wood of painted panels using X-rays.

Verougstraete-Marcq and Van Schoute (1989) used radiography to study the methods used to join panels in the fifteenth and sixteenth centuries and anachronisms are often revealed by this method. For example a round-sectioned wire nail joining two panel sections was revealed by radiography in a nineteenth-century Madonna painted in the style of Botticelli (Hassall, 2005, Figure 5.7). The forger had paid attention to detail by driving an appropriate square-section hand-made nail into the edge of the panel in a prominent position where it could not be missed, but was unconcerned or unaware of the damning modern wire nail buried between the wood of the two panels! Note that additions to panels were regularly made in the sixteenth and seventeenth centuries even while the picture was being painted, and thus additions in themselves are not necessarily damning.

Forgers, such as Joni, often go to the trouble of using old wood of appropriate date for their panels. These can sometimes be revealed for what they are by radiography. A well-known example is provided by the painting of the Madonna and Child, attributed to Robert Camin, now in the National Gallery, London (Cat. 2069). The radiograph revealed that the panel beneath the right one third of the painting was full of worm holes and channels (Figure 12.2). Before it could be used it had been carefully primed with a lead-based white paint, which had filled the holes and showed up clearly on the radiograph. This demonstrated that the panel was old and in poor condition before use, such that no artist would have ordinarily chosen it (Rawlins, 1940, pp. 4–5; Fleming, 1975, p. 50).

A painting may not now be on its original support, or even ground. It is possible to transfer a painting onto a new support if the old is damaged. Thus in the eighteenth and nineteenth centuries old paintings on wooden panels were sometimes transferred onto new canvas supports (Marconi, 1967). This is now regarded as an over-drastic approach to restoration (Marijnissen, 1985, pp. 296–298; Mayer, nd, pp. 505–507). Current practice is to mount the complete picture, including the original canvas, onto a new canvas, thereby preserving

evidence of the picture's history and authenticity. Evidence of transferral can be detected by radiography (Ravaud and Martin, 2001).

Canvas

A variety of fabrics have been used, the most usual being linen and less frequently cotton (Mayer, nd, pp. 288–300). The manufacture and use of the cloth is likely to be close in time to the actual growth of the fibre and thus RC dating is appropriate. Unfortunately, painting on canvas only became popular in the sixteenth century but there are major problems translating the RC age into calendar years in the Post-Medieval period. The problems are well exemplified by the attempts of Van Styrdonck *et al.* (1998) to obtain meaningful dates from two late sixteenth to early seventeenth century paintings on canvas (see Chapter 5, p. 93).

Otherwise, it is rather difficult to date the canvas. Early hand loom canvases tend to be of a rather open square weave compared to the later much closer mechanical diagonal or twill weaves from the early nineteenth century, but this is a subject that

Figure 12.2 Radiograph of a panel painting of the Madonna and Child. Note the worm holes impregnated by the lead-white primer. (Reproduced with kind permission of the National Gallery, London)

has not yet been well researched. Thermally accelerated ageing experiments both on plain stretched canvases and those painted with a linseed oil-base paint showed progressive degradation of the polymers forming the cellulose chains in the linen fibres (Young and Hibberd, 1999; Seves *et al.*, 2000; and see Chapter 18, p. 465).

Forgers regularly circumvent the problems posed by obvious freshness of new materials by using old frames, panels and canvases (Hebborn, 1997, pp. 79–84). Fortunately, evidence that an old canvas has been reused frequently survives and can be revealed by radiography.

Usually the existing painted layer is removed, but another approach is to alter an existing old painting into something more valuable by overpainting (Savage, 1976, 266–268). This has long been a common practice among fakers, and as early as 1845 the British art journal, *The Art Union*, spoke out against the practice:

> *The way of proceeding is to find among worthless, old, unknown portraits, such as in period and costume bear some resemblance or arrangement of feature that may, by means of engravings of the above eminent persons, be readily altered into the generally received likeness of them. The cavaliers of Elizabeth's reign, with their frills and oval-shaped heads, make passable Shakesperes (sic); a priest of Charles I's reign will do for a Milton; any obscure general in armour with a tolerable nose, can be converted into an Oliver Cromwell; and a red-haired, long-faced lady with plenty of ruff, makes a Queen Elizabeth: but if it happens to be a pretty face, it is transformed into a Mary, Queen of Scots.*
>
> *The Art Union* **7**. p. 344.

This practice can often be revealed by UV, although paintings altered in 1845 might well have been revarnished by now and radiography might be necessary (Hassall, 2005, Figure 6.16 and Plate 6.7).

Having obtained a canvas of the appropriate age, the forger may well find that it is too large so that it has to be cut down. Evidence of this can often be seen unaided but is usually revealed more clearly by radiography (Hassall, 2005, p. 108) (Figure 12.16). The original fresh canvas, pulled tight over the stretcher, will have been held by tacks, around which the fabric would inevitably pull, distorting the weave for some centimetres into the canvas. The canvas will then be primed and, in time, will harden and stiffen. If an old stiff canvas is cut down and tacked to a new stretcher the stretch will no longer be there and the threads will not be

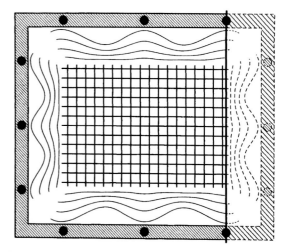

Figure 12.3 Sketch of the distortion in the weave of a canvas around the tacks at the edges, and how this can reveal where a canvas has been cut down. (Courtesy Coremans, 1949)

distorted (Figure 12.3). This difference in the distortion pattern should also be reflected in the crackle in the paint layer above (see p. 305). Note that the reuse of a canvas need not necessarily mean forgery.

A well-known example of overpainting is the painting of Edward VI of England as a child, now in the Victoria and Albert Museum, London (Forster Bequest, F.47) (Rawlins, 1937; Jones (ed), 1990, pp. 272–273) (Figures 12.4 and 12.5). It purports to be an original contemporary painting, but is overpainted onto an early seventeenth-century Dutch betrothal painting of a young girl.

Copper

In the sixteenth and seventeenth centuries there was a vogue in Europe for painting on copper (Horovitz, 1999; Scott, 2002, pp. 317–322). Some idea of the likely authenticity of the plate might be gained from the composition, with trace element patterns typical of Post-Medieval Europe (see Chapter 7. p. 141), or from evidence of how the sheet was made. Horovitz found evidence of combined hammering and rolling on some early seventeenth-century copper plates. This seems very early for rolled sheet and in general one would expect the sheets to have been hammered (see Chapter 8, pp. 157), evidence of which should be revealed by radiography.

Figure 12.4 Portrait of Edward VI of England (1537–53) © V & A F.47, Forster Bequest).

Painting grounds and the examination of white pigments

The support usually requires a priming or *ground* coat, and this would normally be white (although dark grounds were not uncommon in Post-Medieval Europe). The base of the primers was usually a size of animal glue or a resin–oil emulsion. This was stiffened and given density by addition of various, usually white, materials. Before the sixteenth century, painters in northern Europe favoured powdered chalk. In Italy, gypsum, $CaSO_4.H_2O$, was burnt to produce a mixture of gypsum and anhydride, $CaSO_4$, suggesting incomplete combustion (Gettens

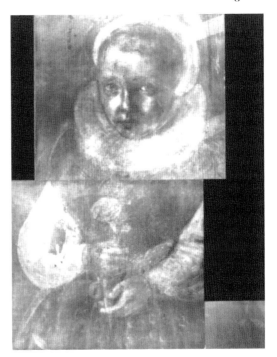

Figure 12.5 Radiograph of Figure 12.4 revealing another painting beneath. The overpainting follows the outlines of the original quite closely. Note, for example, the hands of the girl holding a carnation, and the King's hands holding a dagger.

and Mrose, 1954). After the sixteenth century, oil-based grounds containing lead white became common, although Rembrandt and his contemporaries in seventeenth-century Holland seem to have favoured kaolin and quartz (Bomford *et al.*, 1988). Chalk continued in use and natural chalk was used until the mid-nineteenth century, but thereafter synthetic chalk, known as precipitated chalk, was made by treating calcium chloride with sodium carbonate. This method was itself superseded in the late nineteenth century by precipitating calcium carbonate from solutions of calcium hydroxide with carbon dioxide gas from the burning of lime (Gettens *et al.*, 1993a, pp. 203–226). As the carbon dioxide came from decomposing chalk there will be no ^{14}C in either natural chalk and the synthetic product. Microscopic examination reveals the distinctive sharp edges of the ground natural chalk, and the rounded edges of the precipitated material. SEM examination can reveal remains of various marine micro-organisms, which abounded in the natural chalk. These are readily identifiable and can be quite specific to chalk from particular regions (Coremans *et al.*, 1952).

In the Far East, kaolin clay was common and in Japan, and crushed oyster shell was widely used as the white opacifier (Yamasaki and Emoto, 1979) and occasionally used in Europe. The characteristic fibrous structure can be recognised under the microscope.

In the West, lead white, hydrated lead carbonate, was widely used as a component of the ground and also of the paint (Gettens *et al.*, 1993b; Harley, 1982, pp. 166–172). In the Far East, basic lead chloride was the usual form of lead white (Winter, 1981; FitzHugh, 2003). XRD studies of Chinese and Japanese lead whites show that two minerals are usually present, laurionite, lead hydroxide chloride, and a form close to blixite, a lead oxide chloride. Zinc and titanium oxide whites are the usual whitening agents used now on prepared canvases.

Several approaches can be followed to determine the likely age of lead whites. These include the trace element composition, the isotope composition of the various components, the technique by which the lead white was prepared and even its degradation. This variety of approaches well exemplifies some of the investigational strategies that can be used in authenticity studies generally (Fleming, 1975, pp. 36–40).

Lead hydroxycarbonate occurs naturally as cerussite but was always prepared from lead metal to ensure purity and freedom from rock fragments. In the traditional process used from at least Roman times (Nriagu, 1983, pp. 294–299), strips of lead were exposed to a warm, damp atmosphere, laden with carbon dioxide and acetic acid fumes. The heat and carbon dioxide came from rotting horse manure and the acetic acid from vinegar, and after several months the forming lead white could be scraped off the metal strips.

The trace element composition of the lead white reflects that of the lead metal, which in turn is influenced by both the source of the ore and the smelting and refining processes, all of which can provide chronological indicators (Kossolapov and Sizov, 1984; Panczyk *et al.*, 1992).

The lead whites in Dutch and Flemish pictures of the sixteenth and seventeenth centuries contain little or no zinc, but from the mid-eighteenth century it is present in trace amounts in some lead whites (Houtman and Turkstra, 1965; Kühn, 1966). This probably reflects technological change. Instead of just manually scraping the lead white off the remaining metal, the Dutch began to pass it through brass rollers. Inevitably, the surface of the rolls in contact with the acidic residues from the lead would corrode and contaminate the lead white with a few ppm of zinc not found in the lead white previously.

After the mid-nineteenth century the zinc content fluctuates widely. The origin of this zinc is probably from the Parkes process introduced in the 1830s to de-silver the lead by adding zinc to it. The resulting de-silvered lead might still contain several per cent of zinc. After about 1850, zinc white began to be extensively used in competition with lead white, and small amounts of a few hundred ppm in the lead white are probably no more than unconscious contamination occurring when grinding or packing the two pigments in close proximity. Whatever the origin, more than a very few ppm of zinc in lead white should arouse suspicion if the painting is supposed to pre-date the eighteenth century.

The copper content in all the lead whites up to the early nineteenth century is variable from about 15 to about 100 ppm, but some contain several hundred ppm, possibly coming in part from the brass rollers as described above. Modern lead white has virtually none.

Similarly, the silver contents of the lead change through time. The usual silver content found in the lead white of Post-Medieval Dutch paintings varies between 8 and 100 ppm, but averages at around 20 ppm, which presumably represents the rather low intrinsic silver content found in the English lead that the Dutch used between the seventeenth and mid-nineteenth century, without any attempt to remove it. The lead whites in the contemporary Italian, Spanish and German paintings contain low levels, typically 2 to 6 ppm, of silver, showing that the continental lead had been cupelled to remove all but faint traces of the silver it contained. From the mid-nineteenth century, leads from other sources were used by the Dutch with silver contents as low as 4 ppm and clearly had been de-silvered (Houtman and Turkstra, 1965).

Chromium is another trace metal indicator found in Dutch lead white. In lead whites dating before the mid-seventeenth century, levels of 50 ppm or more are sometimes found, but thereafter these levels drop (Kühn, 1966; Fleming, 1975, p. 37). This presumably represents a change in English lead sources.

The ^{14}C content is potentially significant here. The traditional lead white used carbon ultimately derived from recent plant sources of one form or another and thus should have a detectable ^{14}C content. The carbon in modern lead white usually derives from fossil fuels and thus ^{14}C should not be present. There should also be a difference in the $^{12}C/^{13}C$ ratio between modern plant and fossil fuel carbon sources (see Chapter 3, p. 52, Figure 3.10).

The isotope ratios of the lead itself can provide information both on the provenance of the lead (see

Chapter 7, p. 139) and on the period of time that has elapsed since the lead was smelted. With increasing availability of lead isotope data from the principal European and Mediterranean lead sources there is a greater potential for the matching of lead isotope ratios of the lead whites with those from the mines. More pragmatically, the isotope ratios can be shown to be similar to those in contemporary genuine paintings. Preliminary studies performed by Keisch and Callahan (1976a) showed that the lead isotope ratios from most European paintings fall into a relatively narrow band and are coincident with the values found in the lead from most English lead sources (Rohl and Needham, 1998). After about 1800 the range expanded dramatically as lead began to be imported into northern Europe from Spain, etc. and latterly from all over the world (Figure 12.6).

Another approach makes use of lead isotopes to differentiate old from recently smelted lead. Lead ores contain small quantities of the isotope of radium, ^{226}Ra, which has a very long half-life but decays to produce the radioactive lead isotope ^{210}Pb, which has a much shorter half-life of 22 years. On smelting the lead ore the bulk of the radium goes into the slag, and thus the ^{210}Pb content rapidly decays to a much lower level in the metal and in the lead white made from it, until a new

equilibrium is reached after about 270 years based on the much-reduced radium content of the smelted lead (Figures 12.7 and 12.8) (Keisch, 1976). Thus, if the ^{210}Pb content in the lead white is

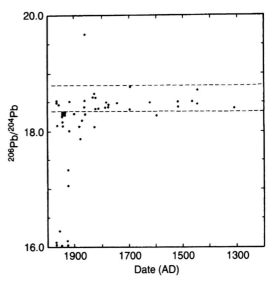

Figure 12.6 The lead isotope ratios $^{206}Pb/^{204}Pb$ from dated European pictures. (Courtesy Keisch, 1976)

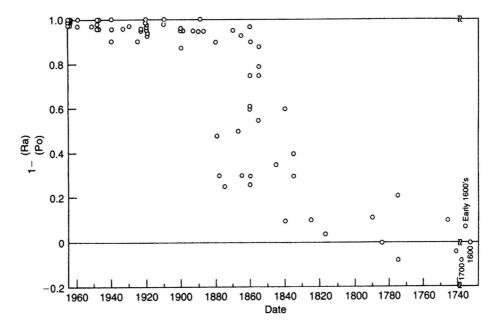

Figure 12.7 Polonium-210 and radium-226 contents of some lead white samples from paintings between the 1740s and 1960s. (Courtesy Keisch, 1976)

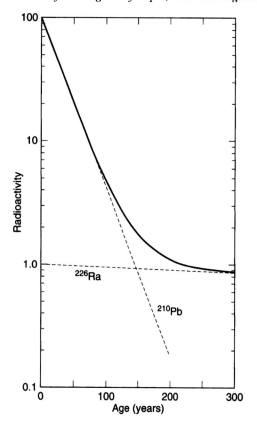

Figure 12.8 The return to radioactive equilibrium between the ^{226}Ra and ^{210}Pb in lead after smelting the lead ores. Initially there is a large contribution from the ^{210}Pb derived from the ^{226}Ra but, as the greater part of this was removed in the smelting, the ^{210}Pb decays sharply, while the remainder of the long-lived ^{226}Ra continues to give off small amounts of radioactivity. (Courtesy Keisch, 1976)

enhanced over that which could be predicted from the present radium content and the expected age of the painting, this would indicate that the lead had been smelted more recently (^{210}Pb is a β emitter, and since this is difficult to measure at low intensity against background cosmic radiation, in practice the next element in the decay series, polonium, ^{210}Po, which is an α emitter, is measured instead). This method was used to finally condemn van Meegeren's paintings (see p. 311).

Note that as the original activity of the lead immediately after smelting is not known, it impossible to extrapolate back from the present levels and give a date to the smelting. It has been suggested that this test may be circumvented by making one's own lead white using old lead and vinegar (Hoving, 1996, p. 248). However, although the lead is will now be isotopically old, the carbon will very likely be isotopically incorrect, the acetic acid containing 'bomb carbon' if organic and geological age carbon if industrial acetic acid was used.

Under sketches and *pentimento*

Sources: Fleming (1975, pp. 56–59); Van Schoute and Hollanders-Favart (eds) (1982); Marijnissen (1985, pp. 84–87, 178–181); Casini *et al.* (1999).

Artists often sketch out their intended work onto the prepared ground prior to painting. The under sketch will usually have been drawn with charcoal or painted with a dark pigment containing carbon and can be revealed by IR.

As the under sketch was part of the creative process of the original work there will usually be evidence of alteration and reworking as the picture developed (*pentimenti*). By contrast, most copies, whether legitimate or fraudulent, will have little need of extensive exploratory preliminary sketching. Ainsworth (1992) employed IR reflectography to establish by the simplicity of the under sketching that two paintings in the Metropolitan Museum of Art, New York, previously believed to be originals of Roger van der Weyden and Hieronymus Bosch, were in fact copies.

Some artists had very distinctive under sketch styles which a forger would either not know of or not bother to imitate as they could not be seen. For example, works attributed to Hieronymus Bosch have a particularly bold hatched under sketching, which the more prevalent eighteenth-century Spanish copies lack (Vandenbroeck, 1982), although as many of Bosch's paintings are products of his workshop the extent to which he may have been personally involved with every stage of a painting is uncertain.

The painted layer

Paint

The pigment may be applied directly to the ground, in the technique known as *pastel*; otherwise it is mixed in a *medium* to form a *paint*. The medium might be oil or *tempera* (an emulsion), joined in the twentieth century by synthetic polymers. These dry to give a permanent hard layer, and together with the pigment will form a colored, opaque paint. If the coloring material dissolves in the medium then it is a *dye*. In such cases the dye is precipitated onto an inert pigment, which is usually colorless or white, known as the *lake base* and this then becomes the pigment. Watercolor paints are transparent, relying on the color of the paper beneath for the whites and tints, and if opaque they are known as *gouache* (see Chapter 13, p. 325).

Media

Sources: Baer and Indictor (1972a, b; 1973; 1976; 1978); Mills and White (1994); Masschelein-Kleiner (1995); Trench (ed) (2000, pp. 341–343).

Tempera are miscible with water whilst liquid, but on drying and hardening become insoluble. A variety of tempera media have been used through the ages (Mayer, nd, pp. 264–287); natural emulsions such as egg-yolks were much favoured in the early Renaissance (Bomford *et al.*, 1989, pp. 27–29). Tempera emulsions may also be made with gums, such as *Gum arabica* in oil, casein in oil, or water in oil, and saponified beeswax (that is, wax that has been boiled with alkali to form the sodium or potassium salt). Note that wax tempera is not to be confused with *encaustic* painting, in which the medium is hot molten wax. Waxes are very stable over time and can be readily identified by GC (Mills and White, 1994, pp. 183–187). Drying oils have been used since at least the twelfth century and since about the sixteenth century they have been the favoured medium in Western pictorial art.

The drying or *siccative* oils in the paint are so called because they harden or dry to produce a tough, resilient and permanent material holding the pigment (Mills and White, 1994, pp. 35–40). They are composed mainly of the organic chemicals known as the triglycerides, which are esters of glycerol and fatty acids. The drying process is complex but mainly consists in the autoxidation and polymerisation of the unsaturated fatty acids of the triglycerides (Wexler, 1964). Linseed oil has always been the most popular. Walnut and poppy oils have also been used but not to the same extent. Lilac and lavender oils have been favoured by forgers because they dry quickly. Alternatively, various drying agents, (*siccatives*), can be added to accelerate the drying process. These are usually organometallic salts (Mayer, nd, pp. 244–247, 476).

Many synthetic paint media were developed during the twentieth century, the two principal classes being the alkyds and the acrylics, both introduced in the 1930s (de Keijzer, 1989; Learner, 2000). The alkyds are resins; as a paint media they are usually mixed with a natural drying oil, linseed oil being popular. Acrylics can form paint media by themselves when dissolved in a suitable solvent. More usually, acrylic paints are minute acrylic resin particles in water, often described as an emulsion, but more correctly a suspension. By itself this is a white liquid, and forms an excellent medium for almost the full range of artist's paint pigments. Acrylic paints are noted for their stability, but as yet little work has been published on their characteristic age-related degradation. The acrylic resins may be expected to undergo cross-linking with time, influenced by factors such as exposure to heat and light and the presence of other chemicals in the pigments, etc. (Jablonski *et al.*, 2003).

Newman (1996) has tabulated the principal media and the methods by which they can be analysed. The synthetic media present new problems to the analyst, and Klein *et al.* (1995) developed simple, non-instrumental tests that can distinguish between acrylic resins and emulsions, oil and alkyd media, which should be sufficient for many authenticity purposes. Learner (2001) used a combination of pyrolysis (Pyr) GC coupled with MS to analyse synthetic paints and Sonoda (1998) used Pyr GC to analyse alkyd-based paints. The ageing characteristics of acrylic paints have been studied by Learner *et al.* (2002) and Whitmore and Colaluca (1995).

Characteristic degradation as an indication of age

The main problem for the forger has always been the slow hardening of the drying oils of the paint, leaving the paint layer soft. Resort could be made to the relatively quick drying lavender or lilac natural oils. Careful heating can speed up the process to some degree, but the results are not fully satisfactory. Tom Keating (Keating *et al.*, 1977, p. 249) claimed to have resolved the problem by squeezing his oil colors from their tubes onto blotting paper to absorb the linseed oil, leaving them to dry overnight. He then mixed in some zinc white and egg tempera before use.

The traditional alcohol and needle tests are simple but often effective. The surface is moistened with a spot of alcohol, whereupon an old oil paint will remain unaffected but new paint will soften. A hot needle will penetrate into the softened surface of a relatively newly painted surface. However, these tests can be circumvented; for example Hebborn (1997,

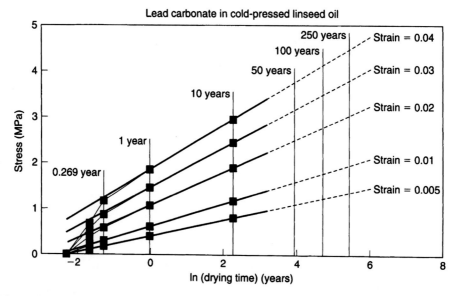

Figure 12.9 Plot of the increase in stress for a constant strain against the log of the drying time in years. The first 12 years or so were based on measurement; thereafter it is an extrapolation, but does suggest that the pigmented paint will not be fully dry even after centuries. (Courtesy Mecklenburg and Tumosa, 2001)

pp. 148–149) suggested the application of a coat of size over the oil to act as a barrier to the alcohol.

Egg tempera is perhaps the most enduring of media, suffering little from either the darkening or cracking associated with oil paint. There are some changes that seem to take place within a few years of the paint being applied, although some of the inorganic pigments in the immediate vicinity may have an inhibiting effect (Schilling *et al.*, 1996).

Most drying oils will have stabilised within a few years and after that there will be little perceptible change apart from the yellowing. However, some quite complex long-term degradation does occur, and can be affected by the presence of some pigments. Advanced GC analytical studies (Schilling *et al.*, 1997, 1999; Schilling and Khanjian, 1996a, b) are revealing the long-term degradation of the fatty acids, etc. in oil media. The gradual yellowing is the result of an oxidation and polymerisation reaction between contaminants and the oil (Mallégol *et al.*, 2001). This may be imitated by the addition of a yellow dye (van den Berg *et al.*, 1999), but its presence is often not really appreciated in media because of the yellowing of the varnish layer over it.

The hydrolysis of some of the glyceride esters in the oil produces carboxylic acids (Wexler, 1964; Erhardt *et al.*, 2005). These in turn can react with the metal ions in the pigments, producing carboxylates

(Meilunas *et al.*, 1990). In FTIR analysis there is a shifting and broadening of the carbonyl spectra owing to the formation of carboxylic acids and a decrease in ester content. These reactions may continue over many years long after the paint has apparently dried and is apparently chemically inactive. The degradation of linseed oil in the presence of a range of common pigments has been studied (Rasti and Scott, 1980). Mecklenberg and Tumosa's (2001) research over a decade or so has predicted changes in the stress in the paint layers under a constant applied strain for periods of up to 250 years (Figure 12.9). The mechanical stresses observed by them in some of the paint films may account for some of the observed crackle patterns (see p. 306). The related studies of Erhardt *et al.* (2005) suggest that the major chemical changes to the drying oils take place in the first 2 years with progressively slower changes over the following 10 years (Figure 12.10). This is measured by the amount of low molecular weight polymer remaining in the paint layer that can be removed by solvent extraction.

The comparison of the chemical and physical properties of the media in contact with various pigments may provide useful authenticity information. If the paint had been applied relatively recently there should not be appreciable differences between the media in contact with various pigments.

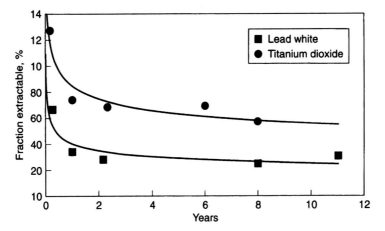

Figure 12.10 Plot of total extractable material (likely to result from the continuing polymerisation within the paint layer) in pigmented linseed against time. Changes are swift during the first 2 years but do continue. (Courtesy Erhardt *et al.*, 2005)

René de la Rie (1982a, b) measured the fluorescence under UV of pigments (not many show it), resins, and drying oils. In general the drying oils fluoresce more strongly with age, but the pigments within affect the fluorescent properties of the medium.

AMS RC dating of the actual media of the paint layer is possible provided that the sample is free of contaminants.

Pigments

Principal sources: Compilations: Mayer (nd, pp. 129–167); Alexander (1969a, b; 1970); Fleming (1975, pp. 27–47); Winter (1983); de Keijzer (1990, 2002); Guineau (ed) (1990). China: Winter (1984). Japan: Yamasaki and Emoto (1979); Eastaugh *et al.* (2004a, b).

The first books on the scientific investigation of paintings dealt almost exclusively with the pigments as exemplified by de Wild (1929) (Table 12.2). Von Sonnenburg (1993/4) made the important point that it was only with the publication of de Wild's book that technical and scientific examination of paintings, especially of the pigments, began to be regularly applied to the investigation of suspected restored or forged paintings. Forgers, notably van Meegeren (see p. 307), responded rapidly to this new challenge.

Investigations on the technical history of pigments continued, exemplified by Harley (1982).

These studies, based on exhaustive scientific examination, but also deeply grounded in the historical sources, both artistic and technical, have culminated in the magisterial volumes of *The Artists Pigments* series, surely one of the triumphs of historical technical documentation (Feller (ed), 1986; Roy (ed), 1993; FitzHugh (ed), 1997).

From the mid-nineteenth century a whole range of new synthetic organic dyes and pigments were introduced, starting off with the diazo dyes (Berrie and Lomax, 1997). Their history and the appropriate methods of analysis have been studied by de Keijzer (1990, 2002), Sonoda *et al.* (1993) and Rioux (1995). Hebblewhite (1986) describes the principal ingredients and properties of the main artist's colors for all the main manufacturers, giving a broad overview of the types of paint currently available (see also de Keijzer, 2002, Table 12.1).

A consequence of the existence and ready availability of this information is that the simple mineralogical identification of the pigments by itself is no longer sufficient for authentication purposes. Every serious forger now has a good knowledge not only of the appropriate pigments to use generally, but the specific palettes of many individual artists. For example, in a study carried out by Klockenkämper *et al.* (2000) on Modigliani paintings, the pigments Schweinfurter green and cerulean blue were never encountered. Thus, a putative Modigliani was rejected on the grounds that these pigments were present, although both pigments were in general use in the early twentieth century.

Table 12.2   de Wild's (1929) original chronological table showing the main pigments in use from about 1430 until 1900.

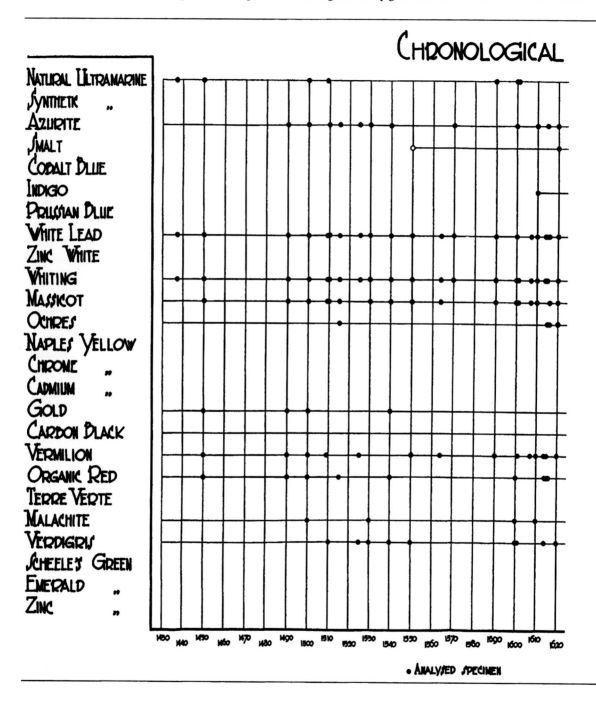

Most scientific studies are based on chemical analysis. For inorganic materials the standard techniques of XRF, EPMA, PIXE, RS and energy-dispersive X-ray analysis (EDX) in the scanning electron microscope are employed, with XRD indispensable for determining the minerals present, while GC, HPLC, FTIR and RM are used for organic materials. Bell *et al.* (1997) used RS

Chart of Pigments

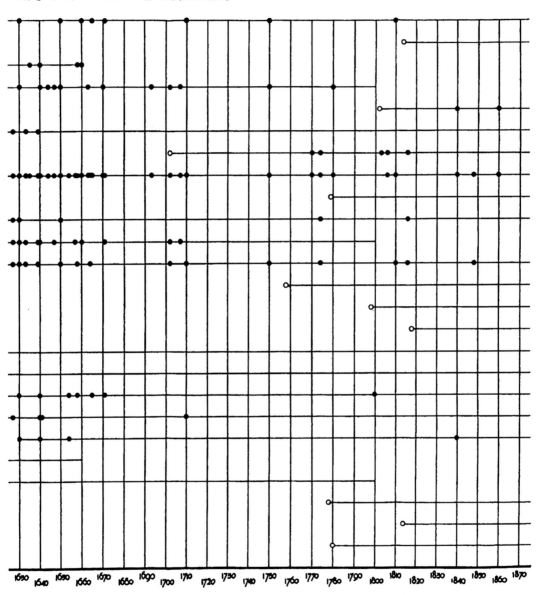

○ Date of Discovery

to analysis some of the natural and synthetic pigments in use up to about 1850, and Coupry *et al.* (1994) analysed some of the synthetic blues in use in France in the early nineteenth century by RS, while Vandenabeele *et al.* (2000b) used RS to analyse azo dyes found in painting.

At the simplest level the analyst can still look for anachronisms, i.e. a painting containing pigments whose introduction post-dates the supposed age of the picture. Zinc white for example, was apparently introduced as a paint opacifier only from the 1830s (Harley, 1982, pp. 176–180;

Kühn, 1986). If it were to be found in the paint of a picture purporting to be earlier than this, and not forming part of some repair or restoration work, this would suggest that the painting was not of the age ascribed to it. However, it is important not to totally exclude the unexpected or previously unknown. Zinc oxide has been reported as a constituent of some medieval pigments (Stós Fertner, 1980; Lehmann, 2000). It was prepared from classical antiquity for brass-making and medicinal purposes but there is no intrinsic reason why it could not also have been used as a pigment (Craddock *et al.*, 1998).

As noted above, most serious forgers since the late nineteenth century have used the appropriate pigment for the period imitated. Hebborn (1997, pp. 95–103), for example, provides an erudite and well-informed account of the pigments that should be used in the forgery of paintings from a variety of periods.

His recommended palette for the would-be forger of old masters comprised the following:

Lead (flake) white	Vermilion
Yellow ochre	Rome umber
Chrome yellow★	Burnt umber
Raw sienna	Terre verte
Red ochre	Genuine ultramarine
Burnt sienna	Ivory black

★for decorative forgeries only

All, with the exception of the chrome yellow, are mineralogically quite acceptable on an early painting. However, the examination of pigments is still an important part of authenticity studies of paintings, as the forger, even when aware of what the correct mineral should be, still has considerable problems.

For a start many traditional pigments are now almost unobtainable. Hebborn (1997, pp. 98-99) complained of some difficulty in obtaining certain pigments, notably natural madder and orpiment. The latter, along with other pigments containing toxic materials such as arsenic or cadmium, have become virtually unobtainable. Health and safety legislation, at least in Western countries, have brought about their withdrawal. However, there are many ways of overcoming the consequences of being unable to obtain the original pigment. For example, where a brilliant yellow was essential, the ever resourceful Hebborn suggested deliberately damaging that area, repairing it, and then painting

this with chrome yellow, or whatever was appropriate, giving the impression of its being a modern restoration.

Where a synthetic mineral has replaced the traditional natural mineral the morphology of the individual particles of pigment can appear very different under the microscope, as exemplified by ultramarine. Ultramarine was separated from naturally occurring lapis lazuli by careful hand picking and grinding (Harley, 1982, pp. 43–46; Kurella and Strauss, 1983), until largely replaced by synthetic ultramarine which was first prepared in the early nineteenth century (Plesters, 1993, pp. 37–65). This produced a pigment of the same chemical composition, but the mineralogical structure is somewhat different, resulting in a different XRD pattern. Furthermore, under the microscope the synthetic ultramarine appears as rounded particles, the natural as angular edged fragments (note that the mineralogical differences, based on the presence or absence of wollastonite, such as were used to differentiate the sources of the parent lapis lazuli (see Chapter 16, p. 411), would not be applicable here, as the wollastonite was largely removed during the separation process to make ultramarine).

In addition to the physical appearance, the changing sources of minerals can be detected by their different isotopic or trace element compositions, as again exemplified by lapis lazuli (see Chapter 16, p. 411, Figures 16.8 and 16.9). Thus it is necessary not only to use the correct mineral, but to have it in the appropriate form and from the right source, requirements which must at times become impossible to achieve, even if the forger was aware of the source of the material that should be used.

The trace element composition of the pigments, whether natural or synthetic, can sometimes be of great help in determining the likely period in which a given pigment was used, and thus whether or not it is commensurate with a particular artist. The changes, outlined above (see p. 294), in the trace element content of lead white through the years are a good example of this. Similarly, much work has been done on the distinctive patterns of trace elements associated with cobalt in glasses (see Chapter 10, p. 227), paper (see Chapter 13, p. 322), and ceramics (see Chapter 9, p. 192) that should be applicable to artists' pigments.

The isotopic ratios of some elements can be useful indicators, as exemplified by the changing sources of the carbon used in Prussian blue (Berrie, 1997). This synthetic pigment, iron or potassium ferrocyanate, was first synthesised in 1704 and soon became popular (Table 12.3), having been identified on Dutch paintings from 1715 (Groen *et al.*, 1996).

Table 12.3   Some of the principal blue pigments in use in Europe 1300 to 1900.

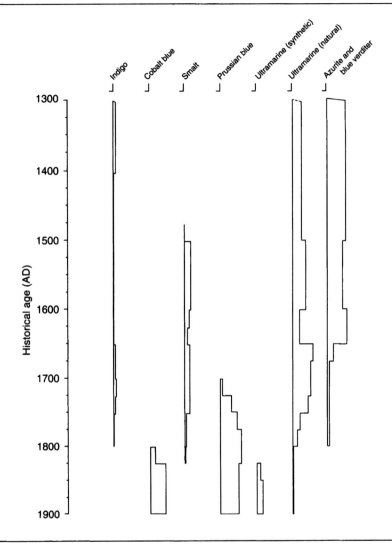

Source: Fleming, 1975, Plate 2

Animal blood and carcasses supplied the carbon and nitrogen content up to the mid-nineteenth century, and again in the late nineteenth century. Otherwise coal or coal distillates were the source, and in the modern process natural gas is used. The $^{12}C/^{13}C$ ratio of the carbon from these sources differs considerably and may be used to determine the likely date of a suspect Prussian blue.

Changes in the technology of pigment production hold an especial potential for the twentieth century, when the technology changed swiftly, and is well documented and precisely dated (see Table 12.1). For example, the ubiquitous titanium white, anatase (TiO_2), first used as a paint pigment in 1918 (Laver, 1997), went through many changes to produce ever better, ever whiter products. Braga *et al.* (1992) studied the changes in the morphology of the particles and of the trace elements associated with the different processes to establish a chronology of TiO_2 on twentieth-century paintings. This was for authentication purposes (see Chapter 13, p. 346).

Pigment degradation

Another approach is finding evidence of characteristic long-term chemical change of some of the pigment minerals on prolonged exposure to polluted atmospheres or light, or, in some cases, of interaction between the constituent components of the paint.

Among the most familiar types of degradation is the gradual darkening brought about by the conversion of the lead carbonate in lead white to black lead sulphide, caused by exposure to trace amounts of hydrogen sulphide in the atmosphere. The orange–red arsenic sulphide mineral, realgar, gradually changes on exposure to light to the more stable yellow polymorph para-realgar. Other chemicals such as lead white in the immediate vicinity can also affect the pigments. Thus, evidence of differential fading related to the lead white content might prove a good indicator of age (Spring *et al.*, 2001).

Oil and egg tempera media provide good protection against this type of degradation except where the pigments have been exposed in the vicinity of the cracks in the oil media. These cracks have often become filled with sulphur-laden soot, which seems to have been the fate of many pictures hung in rooms lit by gas and heated with coal for a century or more in the soot-laden atmosphere of our principal cities. Micro-examination of the pigments in a section taken through a crack might well prove very revealing. Artificially made or induced cracks are often emphasised with soot, and thus it would be suspicious if the lead white exposed by a soot-filled crack did not show signs of sulphur attack.

Some pigments are prone to change even when protected by the medium. For example, ultramarine can develop a mottled appearance with white spots, caused by local acidity. Copper resinate, a transparent green pigment of finely ground verdigris mixed in a resinous turpentine medium, has a tendency to turn brown (Scott, 2002, pp. 294–297), and Prussian blue can lose its coloration in alkaline conditions. Smalt, the blue cobalt frit, is prone to discoloration owing to the interaction of various other components, notably arsenious oxide, with the cobalt oxide.

It is possible that these characteristic degradations could be promoted by exposure to acid or alkaline environments, or simulated by mixing in or overpainting pigments of the desired color, although XRD or RM analysis should detect this. For example, the apparently brown discolored copper resinate in a painting of the *Madonna of the Veil*, now in

the Courtauld Gallery in London, supposedly of the fifteenth century, was found on examination to be ochre (Jones (ed), 1990, pp. 28, 34–35). In addition, Prussian blue was present. Kenneth Clark had already presciently pointed out the striking resemblance of the *Madonna* to Jean Harlow and other 1920s screen goddesses.

Painting technique revealed by microphotography, digital imaging and radiography

Some artists work up a painting from successive layers of paint, thickly applied (*impasto*), often with very characteristic brushwork, but obscured beneath the final surface layers. Laurie (1935, pp. 135–138) developed the forensic study of impasto using microphotography. This method worked particularly well with paintings by artists such as Rembrandt who had distinctive impasto techniques. These paintings were examined radiographically by the *Stichting Forschung* (1982–1989) in their comprehensive study of Rembrandt's work and painting methods.

Digital imaging allows a much more quantitative description of the physical characteristics of a painting to be made. For example Berezhnoy et al (2005) have built up a comprehensive record of Van Gogh's brush technique enabling them to recognise genuine paintings.

This approach can be exemplified by the case of the two Madonnas (Anon, 1955a, b). A London art dealer had the presumption to claim that he had the original of a painting by Francesco Francia of *The Madonna and Child with an Angel*, and that the 'original' in the National Gallery was but a copy. X-rays showed that his version had a carefully built-up underpainting, whereas the Gallery's version had but a single layer of paint. Furthermore, the crackle (see p. 305) on the painted layer did not extend into the ground beneath and had actually been accentuated by applied pigments.

Vincent van Gogh was another painter with a very distinctive impasto technique. In the 1920s a group of over 30 paintings purporting to be by van Gogh was foisted on the market by the dealer Otto Wacker. Van Gogh's work was then only just beginning to be appreciated, and as his works had never been sold during his lifetime, no one was at all sure how many van Goghs there should be (de la Faille, 1930). However, radiography revealed that the typical thick impasto was missing and thus the pictures were forgeries (Feilchenfeldt, 1989).

Varnishes

Sources: General: Mayer (nd, pp. 214–242); Carlyle and Bourdeau (eds) (1994); Wright and Townsend (eds) (1995); Harmssen (ed) (1999).

After painting, it has been the usual practise to apply a thin coat of clear varnish to the painting in order to give some protection against dirt and the elements. A thick varnish layer can also conceal a forgery or deceptive restoration from UV examination. Traditionally, tree resins have been used dissolved in turpentine. Mastic (from *Pistacia*) was the most common up until the end of the nineteenth century, superseded in popularity thereafter by dammar (from *Shorea* and *Hopea*) (White and Kirby, 2001). Amber and copal were also used in solution as a superior artist's varnish (Leonard *et al.*, 2001). Natural resins have been characterised and even provenanced by RS (good reference collections are kept at major international collections, such as The Royal Botanical Gardens at Kew in London). In the latter part of the twentieth century, synthetic varnishes became popular in North America, etc. (de la Rie, 1987). The properties of synthetic varnishes such as acrylics, nitrocellulose and the alkyds and their ageing characteristics have been studied by Cladbach (1999).

In most cases the varnish will have been replaced periodically, and thus its examination is not likely to be of much value in ascertaining the age of the painting beneath. Marijnissen (1985, p. 89) stated that he never examined a painting that had a varnish layer earlier than the nineteenth century. Occasionally, traces of earlier varnishes can survive beneath more recent coatings, as exemplified by the recent discovery of an old, if not contemporary, varnish of walnut oil and sandarac resin on a fifteenth-century painting (Dunkerton and White, 2000). Brammer (1999) studied a painting at the Picture Gallery in Kassel, where it had been the practice not to remove old varnish, but merely to add another coat, and found considerable survival of layers of old varnish.

Evidence of the removal and replacement of varnish, along with some overpainting and repair, can be an indicator that the painting has some 'history' (Lelekova, 1996), although that would be relatively easy to simulate.

Studies by van der Doelen *et al.* (1998), van der Doelen (nd) and Boon *et al.* (1999) showed that the age deterioration of the triturpenoid varnishes consists of autoxidation to produce radicals, which, in turn, can break up the polymer chains. In addition, some heavier more complex cross-linked molecules are formed, which seem to be implicated in the yellowing of the varnishes.

De la Rie (1988) carried out a series of accelerated ageing tests on films of dammar varnish in order to ascertain the degradation process, mainly by exposing the films to UV and strong light. Tests on artificially aged samples of natural varnishes have been conducted by Carlyle *et al.* (1999). The experiments of Van der Doelen *et al.* (1998) showed that the best and quickest method to produce an analytically convincing degraded varnish was to treat the fresh varnish in solution before application.

Forgers often apply a thick coat of varnish with a yellowish hue to give the verisimilitude of age to their productions. Keating used ordinary copal varnish mixed with varying amounts of vibert brown, depending on the age required, and kept in a series of jars such that, as Geraldine Norman put it, 'he could reach for 150 years or 250 at will' (Keating *et al.*, 1977, p. 249). There are varnishes specifically designed to create the appearance of age, if not the chemistry (Hebborn, 1997, pp. 150–152). These are *Vernis à vieillir* and *Vernis à craqueleur*. The former is very dark and, according to Hebborn, gives the picture a good golden hue. A few hours after its application, but while still slightly tacky, the *Vernis à craqueleur* is applied over it and after no more than about 20 minutes cracks begin to appear. These are filled with a special patina, also produced by the obliging varnish-makers. After this has dried out, a final coat of either the *Vernis à vieillir* or of a wax varnish is applied, depending on whether a shiny or matt surface is required. Hebborn recommended the former, preferably with a little dirt and black pigment rubbed in with petroleum jelly (Vaseline).

Crackle or craquelure, and the simulation of age

There is a certain kind of expert who gazes at the networks of fine cracks the way a fortune teller gazes at tea leaves.

Marijnissen (1985, p. 112)

General sources: Mayer (nd, pp. 209–214); Laurie (1928); Keck (1969); Marijnissen (1985, pp. 112–118); Hebborn (1997, pp. 141–151); Nicolaus (1999, pp. 165–187, 289).

The most obvious feature of age in a medium are the patterns of cracks, known as *crackle* or *craquelure*, and their imitation has long exercised the ingenuity of

Figure 12.11 Age crackle on the left of a sixteenth-century oil painting on panel. Viewed by raking light, highlighting the raised edges of the crackle islands. Compare with the false crackle pattern cut with a blade on the repaired section to the right. Note also the cracks run both parallel and at right angles to the grain of the panel. Compare with the parallel rolled crackle of Figure 12.14. (Courtesy Coremans, 1949)

forgers. Age cracking is caused primarily by the hardening and shrinkage of the paint layer such that it is no longer able to accommodate movement caused by fluctuating temperature and humidity in the support (Berger and Russell, 1986, 1994, 2000; Roche, 1993). Mechanical stresses on paint films may also be related (see p. 298). Bucklow (1997, 1999) sought to characterise the different forms of crackle and to relate them to the different schools of European painting. This has some potential application to authenticity studies.

The cracks commence in the surface and run down into the ground. The true age crack is thin, with a sharp edge, and is always visible on a radiograph. On panel paintings the crackle tends to run parallel to the wood grain, and also at right angles across it, leading to a distinctive pattern of rectangular islands (Figure 12.11). Where moisture has penetrated the crack the edges will have lifted (Figure 12.12). This in turn produces secondary cracks within the islands, which are particularly clear by raking light. The edges of induced crackle, by contrast, are usually quite flat (Figures 12.12, 12.14).

Simulated crackle can be used to disguise deceptive restoration but the crackle pattern on the restoration must match that of the surroundings. Wigfield (1998) found crackle painted and scratched onto the varnish covering a very badly damaged seventeenth-century oil painting that had been the subject of what amounted to a virtual remake sometime in the first half of the nineteenth century. Another celebrated case was the *Man of Sorrows*, which was exposed by its false crackle only months after its purchase by the Metropolitan Museum in 1974 (von Sonnenburg, 1993/4).

Figure 12.12 Schematic sketch of the raised edges of crackle islands on a painting, caused by the penetration of moisture.

Creation

No less an artist that Sir Joshua Reynolds attempted to give his pictures an instant crackle in imitation of that found on old masters. Unfortunately, these attempts were not successful and the pictures sometimes had to be extensively restored even in Reynold's lifetime (Talley, 1986). Age crackle can be imitated or induced in a number of ways. At the very simplest it can be painted onto the surface. A painting, *A Religious Procession*, purporting to be a sixteenth-century work by Pieter Breughel the Younger, now in the Courtauld Gallery, London, has a carefully painted crackle pattern. The picture was almost certainly painted in the 1920s, shortly before it first appeared on the market, at which time it had no genuine crackle. However, since then it has aged naturally and a real pattern has begun to appear in the paint layer and this now lies awkwardly alongside the forged crackle (Jones (ed), 1990, p. 227; item 303). Hebborn recommended drawing the crackle into the painted surface with a fine point while it was still wet. Nicolaus (1999) suggested applying to the painted surface the so-called crackle lacquer that will crack on drying. This is coated with a dark paint in an aqueous medium. Some of the paint will run into the varnish cracks onto the painted surface beneath. The varnish with its painted layer above is then removed, leaving a superficially convincing crackle pattern on the painted surface.

Simulated surface crackle patterns will not appear on a radiograph. Creating convincing age crackle penetrating from the paint layer down into the primed ground is more difficult. If the new painting is made on an old ground primed with crackled lead white, this will show clearly on a radiograph. As the primer crackle should have come from the painted layer, suspicions will be immediately roused if it does not appear on the surface of the present painted layer. Thus, the forger has to try to induce crackle from the old primer coat to enter the newly painted layer. Hebborn suggested relying on the expansion of damp sugars to effect the crackle. The cracks on the old surface were to be filled up with a stiff paste comprising three parts size (starch) to one part of sugar. Work then proceeded as normal, painting over the filled and dried cracks. When the paint layer was dry, the back was moistened causing the size and sugar to expand, splitting the paint layer above. Hebborn, and also Keating *et al.* (1977, p. 249), suggested painting size onto the surface of the dry painted layer, followed by heating, causing severe shrinkage of the size and cracks to appear in the painted layer beneath. It would be interesting to radiograph some of Hebborn's and Keating's paintings on old primed surfaces to see how successful they had really been.

With a new support, rapid cracking of the ground layer and of the painted surface above can be promoted by giving the canvas a thick coating of size followed by rapid drying. Within a relatively short time (Hebborn gave times variously between 2 weeks and 2 years) the crackle would begin to appear. This is in effect deliberately producing a defective ground, which, if left unchecked, would ruin the picture completely by causing the paint layer to flake. Thus, the process must be stopped by impregnating the size with wax or resins. Keating (p. 249) refined this method by applying unequal thicknesses of the underlying size to induce superficially convincing whorl crackle patterns.

Detection

Induced crackle is often quite distinct from true age crackle. In particular, it tends to follow the direction of the brush strokes far more than the age crackle; the fissures are often very wide, shrinking away from the ground layer beneath (Figure 12.13).

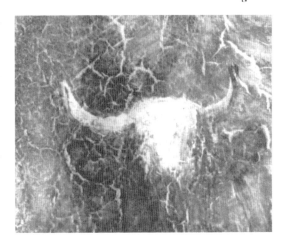

Figure 12.13 Young crackle; note the paint is shrinking away from the ground. Nineteenth-century oil painting on canvas. (Courtesy Coremans, 1949)

This is visible on van Meegeren's painting of the *Washing of the Feet*, which he believed had occurred because he had heated the picture too strongly or for too long.

Whorl crackle patterns can be created on the hardened medium via pressure applied from behind by the fingers or by judicious hammering, and linear patterns created by repeated rolling and unrolling of the canvas. This can be detected because the effect is too uniform and does not relate to differences in the paint layers in the way that a slowly forming crackle does. Rolling generates a series of long parallel cracks (Figure 12.14) (note that a genuine old painting may also have been rolled up at some time during its existence). When the crackle has been generated by hammering, it will have formed around a series of epicentres, often resulting in spirals of crackle.

Han van Meegeren and the birth of scientific picture forgery

Driven by the psychological effect of disappointment in not being acknowledged by my fellow artists and critics, on a fatal day in 1936 I decided upon proving to the world my value as a painter. The start of van Meegeren's confession

Sources: Coremans (1949); Schüller (1960, pp. 95–105); Arnau (1961, pp. 242–264); Kilbracken (1967); Mills (1972, pp. 14–19); Marijnissen (1974); Savage

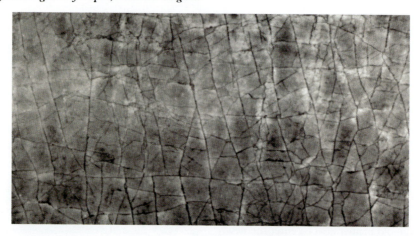

Figure 12.14   Simulated crackle on van Meegeren's *Christ and the Disciples at Emmaüs*, created by rolling the canvas. Note the network of parallel cracks, not otherwise encountered on canvas-supported paintings. Compare with the age crackle on the panel painting in Figure. 12.11. (Courtesy Coremans, 1949)

(1976, pp. 232–260); Beckett (1995, pp. 91–104); Hoving (1996, pp. 163–179).

Van Meegeren is perhaps the most famous forger of paintings of the twentieth century. It is possible that if he had stopped after his first major forgery, *Christ and the Disciples at Emmaüs* (Figure 12.15), the painting would still be accepted as a genuine work of Vermeer. He was probably the first major picture forger to seriously respond to the growing application of scientific methods to the authentication of pictures.

The story of Han van Meegeren's forgeries is generally believed to have started with the *Christ and the Disciples at Emmaüs*. However, Wheelock (1991) described some forged Vermeer paintings completed in the 1920s, and suggested that van Meegeren may well have known of them, and there has even been speculation that he painted them (van den Brandhof, 1979, p. 73). Another Vermeer forgery, *Lady and Gentleman at the Spinett*, which appeared on the market in 1932 (Bredius, 1932), and was condemned as a forgery in 1937, was later associated with van Meegeren but only after his death. Thus it was not mentioned at his trial and apparently has never been scientifically tested (van den Brandhof, 1979, p. 93).

Vermeer was a good choice, as there were no contemporary inventories of his work and it was generally believed that other paintings should exist. Here van Meegeren was following one of the best precepts in forgery, to provide the experts with works they had predicted should exist and

Figure 12.15   *Christ and the Disciples at Emmaüs*, painted by Han van Meegeren in 1936–37, now in the Museum Boymans-van Beuningen, Rotterdam.

which they would therefore want to be genuine. At the same time he was experimenting with a variety of materials and treatments to produce a paint medium that would deceive the technical experts. After long and careful trials with his new media, he produced a work, *Christ and the Disciples at Emmaüs* in the style of Vermeer, which by and large convinced the Dutch art establishment. After that a succession of works apparently by de Hooghs and Vermeer appeared, and notwithstanding that they were increasingly technically and artistically substandard, they nevertheless found purchasers in wartime Holland, including Reichsmarshall Hermann Goering.

After the war van Meegeren was charged with selling a national treasure to the Nazis, which amounted to collaboration. His defence, that they were all forgeries, was initially treated with some derision, but was rapidly accepted once he painted yet another 'Vermeer' in the same inimitable van Meegeren style. He was then charged with selling forged paintings, and for which he was eventually convicted. However, even after he had successfully demonstrated his technique, confirmed by Coreman's scientific study (1949), some still believed that the *Christ and the Disciples at Emmaüs*, at least, was genuine (Decoen, 1951). The controversy between Decoen and Coreman continued long after van Meegeren was dead and resulted in a bitter court case in 1955 (Kilbracken 1967, pp. 161–169; Marijnissen, 1974). As late as 1961 Arnau (1961, p. 264) could state that van Meegeren's confession should not be taken at face value, and held back from stating that all of van Meegeren's Vermeers were forgeries, concluding instead that 'thirteen years after the Amsterdam court's decision, the van Meegeren case is still shrouded in the same cloak of obscurity which characterised the life of the man himself'.

The serious scientific examination of paintings commenced in the 1920s and 1930s with the establishment of laboratories attached to museums and galleries and the publication of works dealing with scientific authentication studies.

Of the publications concerned with the scientific examination of paintings that would have been available to van Meegeren in the 1930s Martin de Wild's book, published in 1929, would probably have been the most influential. This work concentrated on Dutch paintings and the book's foreword stresses its value for differentiating between genuine old pictures from modern forgeries using scientific methods. Other works with which van Meegeren would have been familiar include Rorimer (1931), Laurie (1935), Rawlins (1937) and Burroughs (nd). Although the latter work was published in 1938, it is based on articles that Burroughs had been publishing since the 1920s, mainly on the radiography of paintings. It is instructive to study the methods that these works rely upon in relation to the steps that van Meegeren took to circumvent the unmasking of his forgeries. Overall, they concentrate on the identification of the inorganic pigments and on examination by radiography and UV. De Wild's

book devotes six of the eight chapters to pigments and one to radiography and UV. The first 10 pages of the book contain an in-depth study of ultramarine, showing the difference between the natural and the synthetic mineral; this is the pigment that van Meegeren was to take inordinate care in preparing.

In the radiography section crackle is not mentioned, but overpainting is, and van Meegeren went to great lengths to remove the original paint layers from his old canvases. What is very interesting is that de Wild actually illustrated the radiograph of a portion of a painting that had been cut from a larger picture and nailed to new stretchers (de Wild, 1929, Figures 38, 39). Although plainly visible, de Wild missed the significance that the new nails do not distort the old paint-stiffened canvas as they should if the canvas had been fresh when nailed to the stretcher (p. 292). Van Meegeren's cut-down canvases were to have the same telltale features (see Figure 12.3, 12.16). Laurie (1935) also concentrated on pigments, but where radiography is covered he mentioned overpainting and false crackle revealed by X-ray. Burroughs's work concentrates on radiography, and discussed the overpainting of canvases and underpainting revealed by X-ray, although crackle is not mentioned, mainly because the book does not deal with authenticity as such. Rorimer's book on examination of works of art by UV, including oil paintings, had recently appeared and van Meegeren's unique phenolic medium had the appearance of 'old paint' under UV.

These works make van Meegeren's strategy clear: they concentrate on the *composition* and microscopic form of the pigments and the *appearance* of the medium. This explains the apparent contradiction of his going to great trouble to use the correct pigments, but using a completely anachronistic medium that only *looked* right.

Van Meegeren used old stretchers and canvas of the appropriate age as the supports for his paintings but as the canvases were not of the dimensions he required they retained evidence of having been reused. He had cut down one side of the old canvas upon which he painted the *Christ and the Disciples at Emmaüs*. The 1946 radiograph (Coremans, 1949, pp. 7–9; and see Figure 12.16) showed distortion of the weave around the original edges, but an undistorted weave around the tacks on the new edges. If radiographs had been taken earlier this should have alerted investigators that the painting had been made on a canvas that was already very old, suggesting deception. As it was, this evidence was very nearly removed by H.G. Luitweiler, the picture restorer for the Boymans

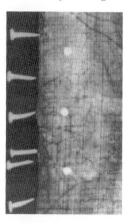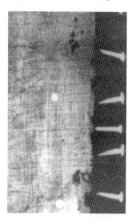

Figure 12.16   Details of radiographs of the stretched canvas from van Meegeren's *Christ and the Disciples at Emmaüs*. The threads in the weave on the right are stretched and distorted around the tacks as one would expect, but the threads in the canvas on the left are completely straight and undistorted even in the immediate vicinity of the nails. (Courtesy Coremans, 1949)

Gallery, which had purchased it. He removed the old canvas backing and replaced it with a new one, but fortunately he decided that the edges of the 'original' canvas could be preserved. Note that evidence of canvas reuse would not automatically have condemned the paintings; Vermeer himself is reported to have reused a canvas on at least one occasion (Kilbracken, 1967, p. 28).

Van Meegeren removed the old paint layers down to the priming layer, taking especial care to remove the lead whites of the old paint layer so that the original picture would not show up on a radiograph. However, in several instances where areas of the original canvas were weak or damaged, the painted layer was left and subsequently detected radiographically (Coremans, 1949, p. 9, Plates 53–56). For example, a head survived from the original *Resurrection of Lazarus*, which lay beneath van Meegeren's *Christ and the Disciples at Emmaüs*. This was of some importance to van Meegeren in substantiating his claim to have painted the picture, as he was able to tell his interrogators of the presence of an invisible head more or less exactly where it was subsequently located by radiography. As the years passed and it became obvious that the paintings were not being rigorously tested, van Meegeren became increasingly careless.

The problem of crackle was more serious, and van Meegeren thought he had resolved it by inducing the original pattern in the old primed

surface to enter the new painted layer via the thinly painted 'cellular' layer that was then baked prior to painting. He would then carefully roll up the canvas around a cylinder in a variety of directions. In general this was successful, a convincing crackle pattern being created in the painted layer which broadly matched that in the primer layer on the radiograph. However, in some areas of the radiographs of the paintings there was an additional hazy crackle pattern that did not always match the visible crackle. This was the crackle in the surviving lead-rich areas of the original priming layers from which crackle had not been imparted to the painted layer above.

Van Meegeren gave his crackle the appearance of ingrained dirt with Indian ink applied to a thin surface varnish layer above the paint layer, this being allowed to dry before removal of the inked varnish with alcohol or turpentine. The ink would have had time to penetrate the cracks in the varnish, and on down into those in the painted layer, so creating a superficially convincing appearance of dirty old crackle. When examined under the microscope, however, the 'dirt' appeared too homogeneous. Furthermore, it had somehow managed to seep through the painted medium in places into the white lead priming and stain it, showing that the dirt and dust must have been a liquid. Also, the correct paint medium of the drying oils should have been impervious to an aqueous medium. It was this which first aroused suspicions concerning the paint medium (Coremans, 1949, p. 7).

Van Meegeren was at pains to use the correct pigments, not just in terms of chemical makeup but also of physical appearance, obtaining the correct natural materials and then preparing them himself using traditional methods. However, this was not as simple as it might seem – natural ultramarine was always expensive and once the synthetic analogue was marketed, the natural material became increasingly difficult to obtain. Winsor and Newton in London held stocks until the 1940s, but sales were very limited. The four sales that they recorded in the early 1930s were almost certainly made to van Meegeren (Kilbracken, 1967, p. 25). Yet the blue of the robe of Christ in the *Woman taken in Adultery* and the lady's dress in *The Woman Reading Music* both contain cobalt blue (cobalt aluminium oxide) mixed in with the ultramarine. It is likely that some of the ultramarine sold to van Meegeren at this time was adulterated, or, at least, contaminated, with cobalt blue.

Note that the blue pigment smalt also contains cobalt. This was prepared by the controlled roasting of the naturally occurring cobalt mineral, and was in use as an artist's pigment from the mid-sixteenth century (Harley, 1982, pp. 53–56). Thus, the presence of cobalt in the pigment in this instance would not by itself have automatically condemned the picture as not being work by Vermeer – XRD identification of the mineral was necessary for that.

More recent isotopic analysis, described on p. 295, was able to show that the ^{210}Pb content was far too high for the lead to have been smelted in the seventeenth century and the alternative hypothesis that the lead was smelted in the recent past is much more likely. This finally condemned van Meegeren's *Christ and the Disciples at Emmaüs* and his other forgeries (Table 12.4) (Keisch, 1976).

Other isotopic studies on the carbon of the lead white and the sulphur in the ultramarine could potentially have shown that these pigments were not from the appropriate sources. There was no way that van Meegeren could have anticipated these future investigative approaches; all that he could do

was endeavour to ensure that his materials passed the current tests.

Van Meegeren's most original technical contribution to the science of painting forgery was to create a paint medium that not only looked convincing by light and UV but had the hard resilient surface of an authentic old paint layer. The story is told that a colleague of his, T. van Wijgaarden, with whom he had been experimenting on media for the restoration of paintings, had a heavily restored picture by or in the style of Frans Hals rejected by the art expert A. Bredius. This was principally on the grounds that the medium was too soft, thereby causing van Wijgaarden considerable loss of both credibility and money. This seems to have united two streams in van Meegeren's endeavours: he would produce a work that would fool Bredius, and, whatever other merit the painting might or might not possess, the medium would be hard.

His early experiments in heating the conventional drying oils to accelerate the ageing process were unsuccessful. He turned to lilac and

Table 12.4 ^{226}Ra and ^{210}Po contents of some of Van Meegeren's Vermeers in the 1970s; the ^{210}Po should since have perceptibly declined.

Description	Po-210 Concentration (dpm/g Pb)	Ra-226 Concentration (dpm/g Pb)	[I − (Ra)/(Po)]
Van Meegeren[a] – "Washing of Feet" – Vermeer Style	12.6 ± 0.7	0.26 ± 0.07	0.98 ± 0.01
Van Meegeren[a] – "Woman Reading Music" – Vermeer Style	10.3 ± 1.2	0.30 ± 0.08	0.97 ± 0.01
Van Meegeren[a] – "Woman Playing Mandolin" – Vermeer Style			
Pigment Sample	8.2 ± 0.9	0.17 ± 0.10	0.98 ± 0.02
Ground and Pigment Sample	7.4 ± 1.5	0.55 ± 0.17	0.93 ± 0.03
Van Meegeren[b] – "Woman Drinking" – Hals Style	8.3 ± 1.2	0.1 ± 0.1	0.99 ± 0.01
Van Meegeren[a] – "Disciples at Emmaus" – Vermeer Style	8.5 ± 1.4	0.8 ± 0.3	0.91 ± 0.04
Unknown[c] – "Boy Smoking" – Hals Style	4.8 ± 0.6	0.31 ± 0.14	0.94 ± 0.02
Vermeer[d] – "Lace-maker"	1.5 ± 0.3	1.4 ± 0.2	0.07 ± 0.23
Vermeer[d] – "Laughing Girl"	5.2 ± 0.8	6.0 ± 0.9	−0.15 ± 0.25

Source: Keisch, 1976

[a] Courtesy of the Rijksmuseum, Amsterdam, The Netherlands, Dr. A. van Schendel, Director–General.
[b] Courtesy of the Museum Boymans–van Beuningen, Rotterdam, The Netherlands, Dr. J.C. Ebbinge Wubben, Director.
[c] Courtesy of the Gröninger Museum, Gröningen, The Netherlands, Dr. A. Westers, Director.
[d] Courtesy of the National Gallery of Art, Washington, D.C., Dr. J. Walker, Director.

lavender oils mixed with synthetic thermosetting phenol-formaldehyde polymer resin (Bakelite), with which a convincingly hard surface could be rapidly created. The medium was prepared by mixing phenol and formaldehyde in benzene or turpentine. This he diluted with oils of lavender or lilac to make his paint medium into which he mixed his scrupulously prepared 'authentic' pigments. After painting, the finished work was kiln-dried at a temperature of about 100° to 120°C for a few hours. This brought about the polymerisation of the resin, producing a paint layer that passed all the usual tests of hot needle and alcohol, and, in addition, it developed a most convincing crackle pattern, based to some degree on the crackle pattern of the old primed surface beneath. This was clearly enough to disarm suspicion and prevent further investigation. If, for example, the needle had not just been warm but red hot, it would have

caused the decomposing phenolic resins to give off a very distinctive smell. But this simple test was not carried out because no one suspected that such an unlikely material was being used. Also, in the 1930s the chemical analysis of organic resins was difficult and van Meegeren's phenolic polymers were only fully analysed years later by Breek and Froentjes (1975) by pyrolysis GC, an early application of the method to paintings.

Bakelite was the new and fashionable material for a whole range of products (see Chapter 18, pp. 458) and phenolic paints had become commercially available in the 1920s (Kaufman, 1963, pp. 65–67). With hindsight this was the obvious synthetic resin for someone working in the 1920s or 1930s. In choosing it, van Meegeren was unconsciously dating his work, as surely as had the unknown forger who had used Jean Harlow as his model for the Madonna (see p. 304).

13

Paper, prints and documents

I have smelt them, I'm a minor historian and we know about the smell of old documents. They certainly smelt.
Charles Douglas-Home, editor of the *Sunday Times*, on the Hitler Diaries (see pp. 322, 338)

This chapter covers the following subject matter: Materials: papyrus, parchment, paper and ink. Art: watercolors and drawings. Reproductions: prints, photographic reproductions, photographs. Documents. Case study – the Vinland Map.

Papyrus

Sources: General: Ragab (1980); Wallert (1989); Leach and Tait (2000). Scientific Examination: Sturman (1987); de Bignicourt and Flieder (1996); Burgio and Clark (2000).

Papyrus was first used in Egypt around 3000 BC and continued to be produced until about AD 1000 when it was replaced by paper. Production was reintroduced into Egypt in 1962 by Dr Hassan Ragab (1980) and currently flourishes as a heritage cum tourist industry. Papyrus is made from the stalks of the papyrus plant, *Cyperus papyrus*. The ancient process of manufacture is uncertain but in the present process the fibrous sides and pithy core of the stalks are cut into thin strips, wetted and laid parallel and slightly overlapping onto a cotton cloth. A second layer is laid on top at right angles to the one beneath and these two layers form the sheet. Another piece of cloth is placed over the sheet and the process repeated until about 10 to 15 incipient sheets have been built up. These are then pressed for many hours to squeeze out the water, and the dried sheets are ready for use. Sturman (1987) showed that many of the modern Egyptian copies of ancient papyri were made from the related plant *Cyperus alopecuroides*, as the true papyrus plant was generally unavailable. On the modern copies the strips are often haphazardly laid, something never seen on the genuine article.

Radiocarbon (RC) dating is probably the best method of determining the age of a specimen. Papyrus tends to become brittle with age, but in general the cellulose of the pith is stable, heat or light tending to cause degradation by hydrolysis or oxidation. The processes are very dependent on the environment and thus not of much use as an age indicator. The inks used on papyrus in antiquity were carbon-based and thus there is no long-term interaction between papyrus and the ink such as could have been expected if iron gall ink had been used (see p. 323). Burgio and Clark (2000) used Raman microscopy (RM) to identify the pigments on genuine and forged illustrated papyri (Figure 13.1). The authenticity of the genuine papyrus was confirmed by the presence of para-realgar, a yellow photo-degradation product of the original red realgar pigment, detected through the glass of the mounted papyrus.

In antiquity the papyrus documents were stored as rolls and a common faking practice is to stick together worthless fragments into a complete roll (Leach and Tait, 2000).

Parchment

Sources: General: Reed (1972). Scientific analysis and degradation: Haines (1999); Edwards *et al.* (2001); Larsen (ed) (2002); Edwards and Pull Perez (2004).

Parchment is made from the skins of young sheep, goat, cows and deer. High-quality parchments that are whiter and smoother are often referred to as vellum, and are made from the skins of newborn calves or goats. Apart from a few Egyptian documents of the second millennium BC, parchment only really began to be regularly used in the Hellenistic period. Furthermore, it was only used in the Middle East and Europe, and was largely supplanted by paper in the Middle Ages. It is still used for some official or ceremonial documents, and more commonly as a high-quality book binding material.

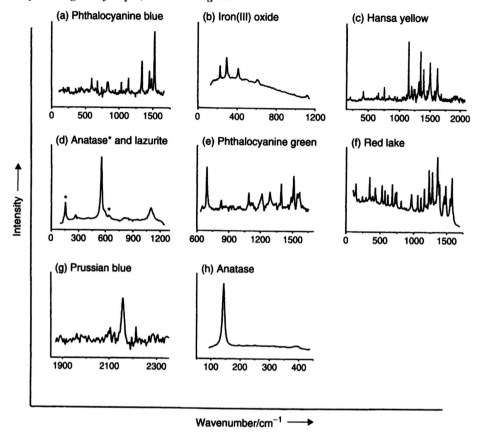

Figure 13.1   Raman spectra for the pigments found on six modern Egyptian papyri. (Courtesy Burgio and Clark, 2000)

The dehaired and lightly or untanned skins were usually bulked with chalk (nowadays done by steeping the skin in slaked lime) and stretched out on a frame to dry. The skins were scraped to make them thinner and more even and then degreased and treated with materials such as alum and with egg-yolks, brains, etc. to make them more supple. They were then polished to produce a uniform, smooth sheet.

The main material of parchment is the protein polymer collagen and the ageing processes are complex, involving the oxidation of the constituent amino acids and hydrolysis of the peptide chains (Larsen (ed), 2002). This can result in the unfolding of the collagen molecules and their degradation to form gelatin, coupled with the racemisation (change in molecular arrangement) of the aspartic acid, as observed for example in some of the Dead Sea Scrolls (Weiner et al., 1980). Parchment is also susceptible to microbiological attack and infestation, and, increasingly, attack from atmospheric sulphur and nitrogen oxides.

RC is the obvious dating method to employ. The skins themselves should have been new at the time of use but some of the materials used to treat them, such as chalk, contain carbon of geological age. Also, parchment was quite an expensive material and was often reused by washing and scraping off the original ink, etc. to create a new surface (known as *palimpsests*). IR examination may well reveal evidence of previous use no longer visible by ordinary light. More recent conservation and restoration treatments with modern chemicals can create serious problems, as exemplified by the Dead Sea Scrolls (see Chapter 5, p. 102). The presence of bomb carbon (see Chapter 5, p. 96) in the sample, as was the case with the Vinland Map (see p. 344), would establish at least that something had happened to the parchment since the mid-1950s.

Parchment can be usefully examined by means of UV irradiation. Recent treatment will make the surface fluoresce (as revealed on the Vinland Map, p. 345). Parchment has been analysed using Fourier transform infra-red (FTIR) and Raman spectroscopy (RS). Edwards *et al.* (2001) and Edwards and Pull Perez (2004) used Fourier transform Raman spectroscopy (FTRS) to study the characteristic deterioration of parchment. They found evidence of interaction between the parchment and the pigments placed upon it. The demonstration of long-term interaction between the parchment and the ink or paint upon it is clearly important for establishing whether the latter is an original or a recent addition.

The degradation of the collagen fibres as observed by scanning electron microscopy (SEM) should give some indication of age, although this is dependent on the environment in which the parchment has been kept. The weakening of the collagen fibres is reflected in the shrinkage behaviour. Reed (1972, p. 314, Figure 20) attempted to construct a shrinkage versus time relationship to date parchments. The edges of an old parchment will generally be in poorer condition than the interior. This can be partly due to the mechanical and chemical damage brought about by frequent handling with dirty fingers, and partly because the edges will have been more exposed to heat, light and short-term changes in humidity. This edge wear is frequently simulated but, as with forged wear generally, the result is often too coarse and even to be mistaken for the real thing.

Paper

Principal sources: General: Mayer (nd, pp. 329–332); Hunter (1957); Rudin (1990); Roberts (1996); Corrigan (1997b); Enshaian (1997); Trench (ed) (2000, pp. 343–351). Scientific examination: Art (1987); Browning (1977); James and Enshaian (1997). Forgery: Werthmann (1988, 1994); Colley (1990).

History and manufacture of paper

Paper is made of matted cellulose plant fibres. The first true paper seems to have been made by the Chinese rather over 2000 years ago using hemp fibres (Tsien Tsuen-Hsuin, 1985). Paper quickly became established in China followed by South-East Asia, and seems to have been in use in north India by the seventh century AD. Contact between ever-spreading Islam and China brought paper into the Islamic World in the last centuries of the first millennium AD where its use quickly became popular. From there it rapidly spread into Europe with local production established by the twelfth century AD.

In Asia paper has been made from a variety of plant fibres, hemp being soon joined by jute, ramie and flax as well as bamboo, rattan and the bark of some trees, notably the paper mulberry. In contrast, early Islamic and European papers were made from fibres derived from hemp, linen and cotton rags. These were beaten and stamped as well as partially rotted (*retted*) and boiled in water to separate the fibres. Stamps were replaced in Europe in the course of the eighteenth century by knife-mounted macerators, known as Hollanders (Hunter, 1957, p. 162). These cut the fibres and it is possible to tell stamped from macerated fibres by microscopic examination.

The fibrous pulp was mixed with fillers, white materials such as powdered chalk, gypsum, China clay, or latterly barytes (barium sulphate), together with dyes to control the color. Moulds were dipped into the resulting mixture, which had the consistency of thin gruel, to form the sheets (Figure 13.2).

The Chinese moulds had bottoms made from straight bamboo strips bound together by lines of threads at right angles. This regular rectangular mesh pattern was picked up by the forming paper. Western papermakers used brass wires instead. These wires are referred to as laid lines, held in place by a small number of thinner wires interwoven between them, known as the chain or warp lines, once again resulting in a rectangular mesh pattern on the paper (Figures 13.3 and 13.4). The pattern of lines is an obvious indication that the paper is hand made, although they can easily, if superficially, be imitated on machine-made paper. Up until the late eighteenth century the chain wires were attached directly to wooden ribs, which impeded the draining of the pulp, and consequently the paper tends to be thicker above them (Hunter, 1957, p. 120), giving early paper a slightly striped appearance (Figure 13.4). In the eighteenth century a woven wire mesh for hand moulds was introduced that did not leave such a prominent pattern, and thus hand-made paper does not always show laid lines.

To stop the pulp moving and slopping over the sides of the mould a frame known as the *deckle* was placed over the top (see Figure 13.3). Inevitably, some of the fibres were trapped between the underside of the deckle and the top of the mould, and when the deckle was removed they would create a distinctive frayed, 'deckled' edge. If the deckle did not fit over the mould perfectly, the sheet of paper can have quite uneven edges. Sheets of machine-made paper are cut from a roll and have a clean edge. The deckled

Figure 13.2 Making paper by hand. The vatman (left) dips the mould into warm pulp, which is swirled, and then removes the deckle and passes it to the coucher (right), who drains the liquor from the mould before depositing the new sheet of paper on to the felt. When sufficient numbers of sheets have built up, they will be pressed (far right) to squeeze out the bulk of the remaining liquid. (Diderot and d'Alembert, 1762, Papetterie; reproduced in Gillespie (ed), 1959)

edge has come to be appreciated as an indication of hand-made paper but is imitated by combing the edges. These tend to be more regular than the real thing.

The papermakers worked in twos, using a pair of moulds. After the *vatman* had swirled the pulp in the first mould to make the forming paper more uniform, the deckle would be removed and the mould passed to the *coucher*. He drained the paper and laid it onto a woollen felt to absorb more of the water, while the vatman filled the second (see Figure 13.2). After several hundred sheets and felts had been built up they would be pressed to squeeze out the bulk of the water before being hung out to dry.

Paper made only from matted fibres is very porous, and so, except for a few specialist uses such as blotting paper, the paper has to be sized. A variety of materials have been used through the centuries and their presence can provide useful dating and authentication evidence (Table 13.1). The paper can then be further pressed or burnished to create the texture and surface required for its particular function.

After the 1840s the use of wood pulp paper rapidly became predominant in Europe. The lignin has to be removed as its breakdown releases acids which attack the cellulose fibres, discoloring and ultimately destroying the paper altogether. Newsprint is the familiar example of this degradation in wood fibre paper that has only been mechanically treated. For other types of paper the wood is mechanically pulverised and the lignin chemically removed.

The problems faced by libraries with the preservation of huge masses of deteriorating newspapers has led to some, notably the British Library, to record them electronically and dispose of the originals (Baker, 2001). This destruction of information on its original verifiable material and its replacement by another secondary record that is much more susceptible to alteration is most dangerous, as is also the case with replacement of photographic negatives (see p. 337). This could ultimately lead to far more fundamentally dangerous frauds than any described in this book – amounting to the falsification of history itself.

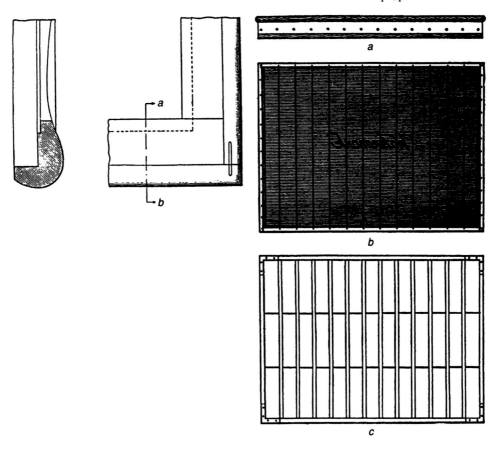

Figure 13.3   Section through the deckle (left) and the mould (right), showing the wooden slats (*c*) and the arrangement of wires forming the laid lines (*a* and *b*). (Courtesy Hunter, 1957)

Cloth fibre 'rag' paper is now used almost exclusively as artists' media and in the Far East paper continues to be made from the bark of the paper mulberry tree for artists' use.

From the beginning of the nineteenth century, mechanical paper-making came into use. In these processes pulp was introduced on to a continuous moving belt of woven wire which acted as the mould, before being fed through felt-lined rollers to remove the water and then onto a drying cylinder, so producing paper in a continuous roll rather than as separate sheets. The fibres in the machine-made paper tend to be orientated in the direction in which the belt was moving, whereas in hand-made paper they are more randomly orientated.

Watermarks and filigranology

Sources: Hunter (1957, pp. 238–308); Briquet (1968): Liljedhal (1990).

Almost from the inception of papermaking in Europe, watermarks were incorporated as a means of permanent identification. The laid and chain lines of the mould make a pattern on the paper and thus it was natural to incorporate a wire device into the mould wires (see Figure 13.4). Enormous numbers of designs have been recognised (estimated at over 150 000 before AD 1600 and well over a million by AD 1800). It is believed that a mould could produce approximately 250 000 sheets of paper over a life of about 2 years, but during this time the device forming the watermark will inevitably have slipped and become distorted. A watermark on a piece of paper that carries a date can be used to provide a date for papers with similar watermarks. As the sheets of paper were produced almost simultaneously in two moulds used alternately, the sheets of paper produced will have two different watermarks, and in books of paper these pairs of watermarks often still appear on alternate pages in the order in which the sheets

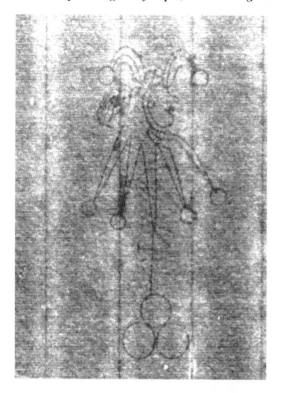

Figure 13.4 Radiograph of seventeenth-century paper with foolscap watermark. The laid lines are horizontal, the chain lines vertical. The paper is slightly thicker where the ribs were located underneath. Note the two small, dense white dots that are, very probably, metal particles. (Courtesy Lang and Middleton (eds), 2005)

were made. This is useful because even if only one watermark has been dated the other is dated by association. The identification of a watermark can often provide a date within a very few years as well as a provenance, as exemplified by Alan Stevenson's dating of the paper used in the volumes accompanying the Vinland Map (see p. 342). This study, known as filigranology, commenced in the nineteenth century and, by the beginning of the twentieth century, massive publications of identified watermarks began to appear, notably that of Charles-Moise Briquet in 1907, which has been expanded and re-issued several times (Briquet, 1968). These compilations have proved invaluable for document and print studies, including authenticity.

Watermarks can be made on the woven wire meshes used for machine-made paper, etc. by pressing the required image into the wire mesh. This method produces a very different image with gradations of light and shade giving a much more

sculptural or three-dimensional effect, as can be appreciated by holding any banknote to the light.

Alternatively, watermarks can be made on machine-made papers using what is known as a *dandy roll*. This is a drum carrying the device, manufacturer's name, etc., on its surface. It revolves between the belt on which the paper formed and the press, so impressing the paper. Papers that are destined to form the pages of receipt and account books or other important documents that it is advisable to be able to trace and verify will have identifications impressed by the dandy roll. Dates of the use of particular dandy rolls are carefully recorded in the appropriate trade directories of the papermakers. One watermark can be used for a long time, and even where the watermark incorporates a date, the actual use of that mark may extend well beyond.

False watermarks can be made either by impressing the dampened paper with a stamp or by drawing or stamping the design with grease. Both of these types of watermark should be easily revealed using radiography.

Examination of paper

To carry out a comprehensive examination of paper, reflected and transmitted light microscopy, SEM, UV, and radiography are necessary, preferably backed up by analytical facilities. Of the latter, Fourier transform infra-red (FTIR) spectroscopy (Sistach *et al.*, 1998) and RS are perhaps the most useful. The versatility and accuracy of digital imaging in all its forms render it of ever-increasing importance in all aspects of the examination of paper.

Microscopy and SEM examination are necessary to identify the types of fibre and the extent of pretreatment, retting, beating, etc. that has taken place on them as well as their chemical treatments (Browning, 1977; and see Table 13.1). They can be invaluable in dating the paper (Werthmann, 1994). Also, although synthetic fibres have traditionally not been used in papermaking, rags still are, and, as Harrison (1966, pp. 129–130) pointed out, some rags of cloth made of mixed fibres (see Chapter 18, p. 467) may well contain some synthetic fibres, the identification of which in a paper could provide vital dating evidence. Identification of any dyes remaining on the textile fibres can also be useful indicators.

Wood pulp and rag paper have very different responses to UV, and all types change with age, so insertions and repairs show up well Rorimer (1931, pp. 38–42). The fluorescent materials in recent paper also react to UV.

Table 13.1 The dating of paper: first use of various fibres, sizing and coating materials, fillers, dyes and adhesives in paper.

Material	Date	Material	Date
Fibrous raw materials		*Fillers and white pigments*	
Rags (cotton and linen)	From early times to present (all-rag book papers mostly before 1860)	Barium sulfate	1820
		Calcium sulfate (gypsum)	1823 (Europe)
		Clay	(1807), mostly after 1870
Rags with soda wood pulp	1845–1890	Satin white (coatings)	1879-1880 (England, Germany)
Straw	1800 to 1870–1890	Zinc sulfide	After 1932
Mechanical pulp (groundwood)	After 1869 (1875 in U.S.), with rag probably 1869–1880	Calcium carbonate	About 1925–1927
		Titanium oxide	(1906) 1930
Soda wood pulp	After 1853 (1860 in U.S.)	Zinc oxide	About 1933
Esparto	1857–1890 (England)	Diatomaceous earth	About 1938
Esparto with rags	Probably 1861–1890		
Esparto with wood pulps	After 1880–1883	*Dyes and colors*	
Sulfite wood pulp	After 1872 (1889 in U.S.)	Lead chromate	(1797) 1800 (Europe)
Sulfate (kraft) wood pulp	1884 (after 1907 in North America)	Ultramarine	1828
		Aniline dyes	(1856) 1870
Bagasse	After 1884	Synthetic organic pigments	About 1901
Cotton linters	After 1920	Luminescent pigments	About 1940
Semichemical wood pulps	After 1926	Optical whiteners	About 1950
Bleached sulfate wood pulps	After 1930		
Bamboo	After 1930 in India	*Adhesives (Ref. 16)*	
Alpha (wood) pulps	After 1933	Animal glue	From antiquity
Rayon fibers	1936–1945	Poly(vinyl acetate)	After 1940
Glass fibers	1950–1952	Starch	From antiquity
Organic synthetic fibers	1953–1954	Casein	
Sizing and coating materials		as sizing	From antiquity
Rosin	1807 (Germany), 1835 (Europe)	as adhesive	After about 1850
		Poly(vinyl alcohol)	In United States after 1939
Rosin and wax, no glue	After 1930		
Parchment paper	After 1857	Hot-melt adhesives	After 1930
Coated papers	After 1890	Latex-based adhesives	
Casein (coatings)	About 1900	Natural rubber	After 1930
Rubber latex (coatings)	1920	Synthetic latexes	In 1940s
Soya protein	1937	Remoistenable adhesives	In the 1830s the British Postal Service first put an adhesive on the back of postage stamps. In 1841 an envelope appeared which could be sealed without the use of sealing wax
Mannogalactan gums	About 1940		
Urea-formaldehyde resins	1940–1941		
Melamine-formaldehyde resins	1940–1941		
Polyethylimine resins	1946 (Germany)		
Styrene-butadiene latices	1947	Foil laminating adhesives (Neoprene latex, polyvinyl emulsions, casein-synthetic rubber, sodium silicate, thermoplastic and thermo-setting resins)	In early 1900s
Dialdehyde starch	(1947) 1959		

Source: Browning, 1977, Table 26.1

Radiography
Sources: Bridgman (1965); Lang *et al.* (1994); Daniels and Lang (2005).

Paper presents particular difficulties and opportunities for radiography, but a combination of β- and X-ray sources is very useful for revealing the paper's structure, the laid lines and the watermarks, as well as any inclusions (Ash, 1982).

Paper is one of the thinnest of materials and, being composed of light atoms – carbon, hydrogen and oxygen, it is very transparent to X-rays, necessitating the use of special techniques. The choice of these depends on whether it is the paper itself or the material it carries that is of the prime importance. There are four main techniques employed:

1. Simply to use standard radiography but at very low energy, typically between 5 and 10 kV (the X-rays so produced are sometimes referred to as Grenz rays). As the oxygen and nitrogen of the air are of higher atomic weight than that of the carbon of the paper, the X-ray tube must be as close as possible to the film (typically 10 to 30 cm). Van Aken (2003) replaced the air with helium, which has a very low atomic weight, and obtained much improved results.

   The X-ray tube from an XRD set may be used to produce the soft X-rays necessary for the examination of paper, attached to a suitable chamber. Rendle *et al.* (1990) described such a set-up used for forensic work.

2. Electron transmission radiography. In this process (Figure 13.5), high-energy X-rays are used to bombard a sheet of lead and generate electrons. The paper to be examined is sandwiched between the lead sheet and the film. The emitted electrons pick up and allow elucidation of the structure of the paper, but the pigments of the ink or paint upon it are unaffected.

3. Electron emission radiography, or autoradiography. This technique will enable detection of the heavy elements in and on the paper. The paper is bombarded with high-energy X-rays, which cause any heavy metal elements to emit electrons, some of which will be picked up by the film placed in close proximity (Bridgman *et al.*, 1957–8) (Figure 13.6). Sayre and Lechtmann (1968) developed the related technique of neutron activation autoradiography to examine manuscripts (Muether *et al.*, 1980) and paintings (see Chapter 12, p. 288).

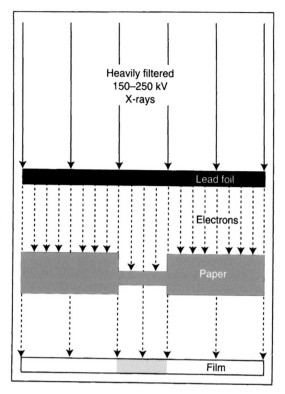

Figure 13.5 Electron transmission radiography. Electrons generated in the lead foil by the X-rays pass through the specimen and create an image on the film. (Courtesy Lang and Middleton (eds), 2005)

4. Beta radiography. This is radiography without use of a radiography set (Boutaine, 1976). High-energy electrons are generated by a radioactive source, the usual source being radioactive carbon, ^{14}C, incorporated into a sheet of Perspex. A sandwich is made of the Perspex sheet, the paper to be investigated and the film. The set-up has the great advantages of being cheap, eminently portable and easy to use on small papers such as postage stamps to examine the watermarks, evidence of repairs, etc. (Theimer, 1983). Note that although the radiation output is small, the health and safety regulations in operation in most countries mean that it would not be possible to operate such a device without prior registration and approval.

   There are other drawbacks. It is a slow technique, typical exposure times being between 5 and 20 hours, and the area examined is limited by the area of the Perspex sheet. A more

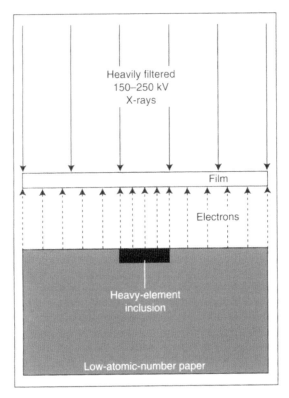

Figure 13.6 Autoradiography. Electrons generated by the X-rays from heavy elements in the specimen are recorded on the film. (Courtesy Lang and Middleton (eds), 2005)

fundamental drawback is that the electrons are emitted in all directions and this leads to the generation of a slightly fuzzy image (Figure 13.7). This is not a serious problem for major features, but it could lead to small features such as metallic particles in paper being missed altogether.

Ageing and analysis

Sources: Havermans and Dufour (1997); Daniels (1996).

The most important feature of the chemical degradation of paper is the breakdown of the cellulose fibres, causing embrittlement and discoloration (Daniels, 1988a: Strlič and Kolar (eds), 2005). This is a combination of hydrolysis leading to the breaking of the polymer chains and oxidation, the so-called slow fire effect. The degradation is dependent on factors such as temperature, light levels (Havermans and Dufour, 1997) and exposure to oxygen. Other factors are also important, such as the composition of the paper, including the acidity, some of the latter being caused locally by the ink, microbiological action, such as the familiar foxing, and the presence of metal particles (Daniels and Meeks, 1994).

Wood-pulp paper with its greater acidity caused by the breakdown of residual lignin tends to become discolored much more rapidly than

Figure 13.7 Image produced by beta radiography (Courtesy Lang and Middleton (eds), 2005)

traditional rag papers. Inaba and Sugisita (1988) demonstrated the correlation between the acidity and discoloration in Japanese paper. The degradation of the paper in different parts of a book or document can proceed at different rates owing to differences in the micro-environment. For example, the pages in the centre of a book decay more rapidly than those on the outside (Brandis and Lyall, 1997), presumably because of a build-up of acid. These differences should take some time to become established and thus could indicate whether the papers of a suspect piece had at least been together for some time.

Paper may be artificially aged by exposure to enhanced levels of light, heat, oxidising atmospheres and humidity (Stewart, 1982; Calvini *et al.*, 1996; Priest, 1992), although the artificial degradation may differ from the natural degradation (Duerr *et al.*, 1987; Havermans and Dufour, 1997).

Some of the fillers and binding agents also show characteristic decay, as exemplified by the degradation of the starch paste (*furu-nori*) used in Japanese paper (Daniels, 1988b).

Most surviving paper is too young to be meaningfully dated by RC (see Chapter 5, pp. 93, 96). The presence of bomb carbon would indicate that the paper must be post mid-1950s but, as the carbon would span the whole life of the tree, no accurate dating would be possible as is the case with some other single-year materials such as silk.

The various materials that have been added to paper over the past couple of centuries are reasonably well dated (see Table 13.1; and see Hagemeyer (ed), 1984, for pigments in paper). The first use of fillers and whiteners such as baryte, barium sulphate (in the 1820s; Hanley *et al.*, 1984), and anatase, titanium dioxide (in 1930; McGinnis, 1984), for example, provides the earliest possible date for paper containing them. The fluorescent materials added to papers since the 1950s, which were present in the paper of the cheap notebooks upon which the Hitler Diaries had been written, immediately showed that the paper could not have been contemporary with the Führer (Werthmann *et al.*, 1984).

Some traces and minor amounts of inorganic elements represent deliberate additions, as exemplified by the cobalt minerals added to paper in the eighteenth century as colorant. Barrandon and Irigoin (1979) carried out neutron activation analysis (NAA) on a series of Post-Medieval European papers and were able to establish a chronology of cobalt use (Figure 13.8). They could also distinguish between paper from Angoumois in the south-west of France and

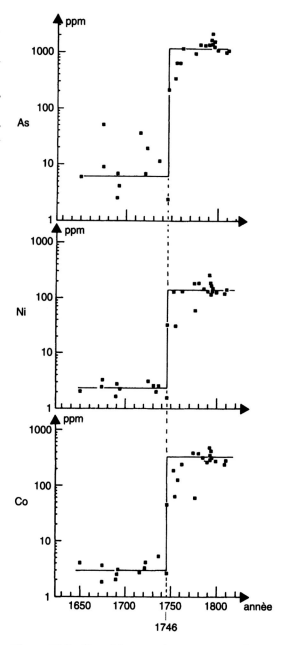

Figure 13.8   Plot of the trace element content of some Post-Medieval European papers against time. (Courtesy Barrandon and Irigoin, 1979)

contemporary Dutch copies on the basis of the trace elements associated with the cobalt (Figure 13.9). The Dutch used smalt from Schneeberg in Saxony, which contained relatively high quantities of arsenic, bismuth and nickel, whereas the sources used by the

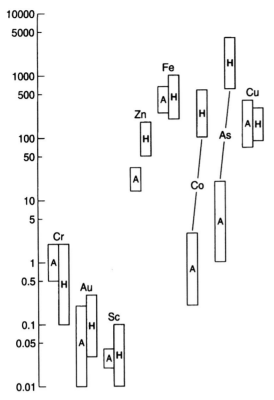

Figure 13.9 Trace element composition of Dutch paper (dark columns marked H) and French paper (light columns marked A). (Courtesy Barrandon and Irigoin, 1979)

French papermakers were more pure (Gratuze *et al.*, 1992, 1995, 1996; Soulier *et al.*, 1996) (see Chapter 9, p. 192 and Chapter 10, p. 227 for the identification of cobalt sources used in glazed ceramics and glass respectively).

Forgers often use old paper cut from blank pages in books, etc. Elmyr de Hory regularly used the end papers cut from big French art books of the 1920s for his Picassos (Irving, 1970, p. 95). When this was not available new paper of the appropriate quality was used, swabbed lightly with tea to give it the appearance of age, a simple technique but one used with great success by many other forgers.

Ink

Sources: General: Mayer (nd, pp. 550–552); Mitchell (1937); Harrison (1966, pp. 13–24); Trench (ed) (2000, pp. 235–236). Chinese ink: Tsien Tsuen-Hsuin (1985); Chia-jen Kecskes (1986). Printing inks: Wiborg (1926); Bloy (1967).

History and types

Ink has traditionally been of two main types, either elemental carbon in aqueous suspension or a metal salt, usually iron in aqueous solution. Note that whereas the particulate carbon sits *on* the surface of the medium, the solutions sink *into* the medium. The earliest inks were of carbon with an organic binder, now known as Indian or drawing inks. The carbon was usually soot, made by burning materials such as pine wood in early China; later on, lamp black, made by burning oil, came to be preferred. In Egypt, Greece and Rome, burnt bone and ivory was favoured. The binders could be animal-based gelatin glue or natural resins such as gum arabic. Sepia ink has been in use from classical antiquity. It is an aqueous suspension of the dark-brown pigment melanin, prepared from the black juice secreted by the cuttlefish.

The metal ion inks are known as writing inks. Iron gall ink was the most common writing ink in Europe between the eleventh and nineteenth centuries; however, its origins may go back to classical antiquity, as particle (or proton)-induced X-ray emission (PIXE) analysis of the inks on some demotic papyri used by the Greeks in Egypt showed that they had high iron content (Delange *et al.*, 1990). This suggested that the inks were of the iron gall type, although sulphur was not detected. It would have been more convincing if it had been possible to establish if elemental carbon was absent, but this element could not be detected by PIXE.

Iron gall ink was produced by the reaction of an aqueous solution of ferrous sulphate, known in Post-Medieval England as copperas, or ferrous acetate, with tannins traditionally obtained from oak-galls in Europe, to produce iron gallotannate. This only oxidises some time after application to give the familiar black. From 1836 other dyes were usually added to the ink so that it was more visible while being applied.

The reactions of iron gall inks with paper as they age are varied and complex. They can release acid ions causing hydrolysis and oxidation of the cellulose present (Banik, 1997; Neevel and Reißland, 1997), seriously weakening the paper, even locally producing holes (Reißland, 2002). Other forms of iron gall ink can be prepared with the ferric ions already formed as a precipitated pigment which sits on the surface reminiscent of carbon inks, sometimes referred to as Japan ink. Old iron gall ink often contains significant amounts of copper.

Ballpoint pen inks are of organic dyes in organic media such as polyethylene glycols (Harrison, 1966, pp. 22–24). Printing inks in Europe were traditionally of lamp black in an oily medium, olive oil and burnt linseed oil, known as plate oil, being favourites (Bloy, 1967).

Examination

Old iron gall inks tend to fluoresce more deeply brown or black than recent inks, which show up as a deep violet under UV (Rorimer, 1931, p. 39; Harrison, 1966, pp. 89–93). More specifically, near-UV produces a fluorescent halo around the inks, most clearly visible on the *verso* of the inked paper (Neevel and Reißland, 1997).

IR can be very useful for revealing obliterations or alterations on documents (see p. 338). Certain materials, notably iron-based inks and elemental carbon, are picked up by IR while more modern organic-based inks can be transparent (Harrison, 1966, pp. 93–94; Moss, 1954, pp. 12–15).

Analysis of ink

The traditional methods of analysing inks were reviewed by de Pas and Flieder (1976). The most commonly used techniques incorporate chromatography, but this has now been joined by Raman spectroscopy (RS) (Claybourn and Ansell, 2004; Kiefer (ed), 2004; Wise and Wise, 2004). The latter technique has the important advantage of being able to detect elemental carbon and is thus invaluable for the positive identification of modern carbon-based inks (Pagè-Camagna *et al.*, 2004; and see p. 339). Surface-enhanced resonance Raman scattering (SERRS), a sensitive variant of RS (see Chapter 3, p. 54) can, for example, detect differences in the composition of the ink from individual ballpoint pens (Seifar *et al.*, 2001; Smith *et al.*, 2001). Grim and Allison (2004) used laser desorption mass spectrometry (MS) to identify the pigments used on some seventeenth- and nineteenth-century manuscripts, including the blue and black of the inks. From the composition and characteristic degradation products on some of the lines they were able to establish that recent additions had been made to an original document. Cheng *et al.* (1997) employed Rutherford back-scatter spectrometry (RBS) (see Chapter 3, p. 50) to differentiate between modern and old Chinese ink. The potassium and calcium contents were found to be ×10 higher in the old ink. They also found compositional differences between the modern inks from Chinese production centres in different regions of Anhui and Shanghai.

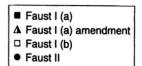

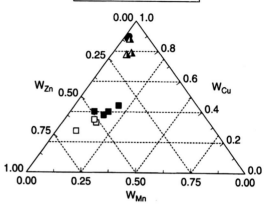

Figure 13.10 Ternary diagram of the Cu, Mn and Zn content of ink used by Goethe on the manuscripts of Faust. There is a link between the amendments made to Faust I and the later Faust II manuscript. (Courtesy Hahn *et al.*, 2005)

Hahn *et al.* (2004) used a combination of micro-XRF (X-ray fluorescence) on a portable system (for the inorganic components) and visual spectrophotometry (for the organic components) to characterise the colorants used on some early prints and in a variety of inks, pencils and colored crayons. Their (2005) study of the composition of the iron gall inks used on different manuscript versions of Goethe's Faust, for example (Figure 13.10), enabled these inks to be chronologically ordered, which is clearly relevant to authenticity studies. Duerr *et al.* (1987) examined the title page of a supposedly newly discovered symphony by Schubert. The microscopic examination and analysis of the ink by energy-dispersive X-ray (EDX) analysis and chromatography showed it to be modern. Havermans *et al.* (2003) used multi-spectral imaging over a wide spectral range from UV to near IR to identify iron gall inks.

Dating

RC dating of ink is not possible because of the tiny quantities involved. McNeil (1984) found that the migration of iron ions from iron gall ink into the paper is directly proportional to the time that has elapsed since application. He used scanning Auger microscopy to map the spread of iron ions from the ink on a test series of papers and parchments

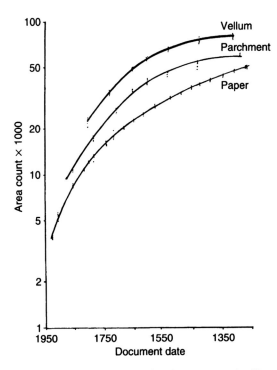

Figure 13.11 Regression plot showing spread of iron ions from the iron gall ink variously into paper, vellum and parchment over time. (Courtesy McNeil, 1984)

dated to between 1200 and 1972 (Figure 13.11). However, the depth of penetration depends on many other factors such as the amount and composition of the ink and how well the paper had been sized and finished, as well as on environmental factors (Reißland, 2002). Thus, although the penetration may not be able to give an absolute date, it could be an indicator of age. The method did not work easily on parchment owing to surface irregularities such as hair follicles, although with careful selection of sites the spread was still observed.

Watercolors and drawings: pastel, chalk, charcoal, pencil and ink

Sources: General: Mayer (nd, pp. 327–343); Cohn (ed) (1997). Scientific examination: Townsend (1992, 1998); Guineau (ed) (1990); Davis (1996); Corrigan (1997a).

UV, IR and radiography

Townsend (1992) claimed that, in general, there was little to be gained by UV or IR examination of watercolors, and furthermore that some organic pigments might well be damaged by prolonged exposure to UV. Only some pigments fluoresce under UV, although many modern papers fluoresce owing to the presence of whiteners, as described above. Fletcher (1984) found that IR reflectography (see Chapter 12, p. 287) revealed the underdrawing on watercolors. IR also revealed changes to the ink on the original work, indicating areas warranting more detailed investigation.

Radiography of watercolors is also not as productive as for oil paintings. The paper media is very transparent to X-rays, and radiographic information has to be obtained by using special techniques (p. 320). The color media are, by and large, transparent to light anyway, and thus there tend to be far fewer hidden changes and alterations to be revealed. Pigments based on heavy metals such as lead, cobalt, barium, chromium and zinc can be easily detected.

Townsend's (1998) work on chalk, pastel and watercolors suggested that a wide range of techniques could be used to identify pigments and to apply the knowledge that has been gained concerning their introduction to authentication studies.

RM is proving very useful as a non-invasive technique (Guineau (ed), 1990) and is becoming widely applied for the identification of pigments in watercolor media on paper (Burgio et al., 1999; Derbyshire and Withnall, 1999) and parchment (Best et al., 1992, 1993, 1995; Coupry et al., 1994; Clark, 1995, 1999; Clark and Huxley, 1996; Majolino et al., 1996; Burgio et al., 1997a, b; Mairani et al., 1997). Libraries of Raman spectra of natural and synthetic pigments have been published by Bell et al. (1997) and Burgio and Clark (2001).

Prints, photocopies, photographs and other copies

Sources: Boston (1892); Hayter (1962); Griffiths (1980); Gascoigne (1982); Ivins (1988); Rummonds (1998); Cohn (ed) (1997); James (1997a, b); Trench (ed) (2000, pp. 397–401).

States, restrikes and reproductions

There are two sorts of print, those produced individually under the artist's control from his or her own block, plate or screen, and the much more impersonal photomechanical reproductions.

Prints made by traditional methods vary individually, reflecting the condition of the block or plate from which they have been taken. Even before the appearance of a print has been finalised for the first official run, the artist may well run off a few near-complete prints to check quality and for record. These are known as *proofs* or *trial proofs*. Once the artist is satisfied, the first prints for publication can be run off, and these are known as the first *state*. The blocks or plates wear and have to be reworked; also, the artist may wish to rework them to obtain new effects – Rembrandt for example, reworked many of his plates to destruction. Each change represents a new state, and as print collecting (and dealing) became an established (and profitable) activity so the various states of the prints of the leading artists were researched and catalogued. The concept of limited editions of numbered prints arose in the eighteenth century, specifically to boost their value. Sometimes the block or plate was defaced after the edition was completed but this did not always end its productive life.

Identifying forged prints is, on occasion, made no easier by the actions of the artist. Forgeries of prints by the surrealist painter Salvador Dali are extremely common and it is possible that he connived in their creation. It is claimed that he signed thousands of blank sheets ready for photolithograph copies for nihilistic mischief, coupled, one suspects, with greed (Beckett, 1995, p. 133).

While the blocks or plates survive, further prints may be made, sometimes long after the artist's death, as exemplified by some of Goya's prints. These are known as *restrikes*. Eventually the blocks or plates become too worn for further prints to be taken from them without recutting and, once this is done, the prints can no longer be regarded as being by the original artist. Rembrandt's famous print *Christ Healing the Sick*, the 'Hundred Guilder print', provides a good example of what can happen to a popular image (Jones (ed), 1990, pp. 53–55; Cat.30). The plate continued to be used into the eighteenth century by which time it was badly worn, and the prints were often 'refreshed' by hand-penned lines before sale. The plate was then extensively but not very convincingly reworked by William Baillie, before being cut up and further prints taken from the pieces. Meanwhile those not fortunate enough to have the original plate made free copies on new plates. Finally, in the nineteenth century new processes such as photogravure enabled good copies to be made from original prints.

Prints were created as original works of art from the inception of printing, and thus were the target for illicit copying. Printers began commissioning exact copies of the more popular prints on new blocks or plates, and selling them as originals. Dürer became an early victim of this practice. Differentiating between an unrecorded state and a good contemporary copy can be difficult, and usually requires careful microscopic study of the lines, etc. to look for slight differences in areas where there should have been no change. A study of the watermarks on the paper can also prove illuminating.

The introduction of the electrotype and then photographic reproduction methods in the nineteenth century created a sea change in the scope and potential of printing generally. It became possible to mechanically produce copies endlessly without variation. In the nineteenth century the Arundel Society produced excellent color lithographs of famous works of art (see Chapter 4, p. 63). Although some of the processes, notably those relating to photogravure (see p. 332), required great technical skill, there was little or no input from the artist. These prints are known as *reproductions*.

More recently, color xerographic and inkjet printing (p. 333) have been used to produce reproductions of prints, watercolors and oil paintings. A big drawback with these processes, especially for reproducing painting, is that the image produced is essentially planar. Some firms such as Artagraph laser-scan the image to produce a good color print on an oil-base film. A copy is then overpainted by an artist to recreate the brush strokes and surface texture of the original. This is then silicone-moulded and a permanent negative mould produced. The flat color prints are then pressed and heated between the mould and a canvas backing; this causes the film to melt onto the canvas, giving the impression of the topography of an original painting (Beckett, 1995, p. 137).

Perhaps the ultimate process for verisimilitude is to mix pigments and photographic light-sensitive chemicals with egg. This twenty-first century egg tempera emulsion is spread on the canvas, dried, and exposed to light under a negative of the work to be copied. The print is then developed and fixed, before adding the next color. The finished color print can then be overpainted with clear tempera and varnish to give the correct three-dimensional appearance. As the web source (http://www. lavendera.com/Printingtech/PrintingTech.htm) for this recipe somewhat disingenuously puts it, 'Still not good enough for the museums? Put on some gold leaf'. Examination with a hand lens should reveal that the colors were made up from a matrix of dots (see p. 332) and analysis would certainly be revealing (see Chapter 12, p. 288).

An unfortunate practice has arisen of selling what are claimed to be original prints in limited editions (if an edition of up to 10 000 can be called limited). Here, at best, the artist has created an original image in whatever medium, which is then mechanically photo-reproduced. Sometimes the artist has been induced to sign and number the resulting prints, thereby 'joining in the jolly bullshit' as the London dealer Chris Beetles put it to Alice Beckett (1995, p. 135). Even so, the prints remain reproductions, not originals, as the artist played no part in their production, and, as such, they are of limited value.

Techniques of printing and their identification

Sources: Hayter (1962); Griffiths (1980); Gascoigne (1982).

Relief and intaglio prints were the first to be made and these need a soft, receptive and pliant surface, requirements which can only really be satisfied by paper. Thus it is no surprise that, almost everywhere, the art of printing followed on the availability of paper.

Traditional printing techniques can be considered under three broad headings, relief, intaglio and planar, depending on how the ink is held on the plate.

Relief printing
In relief printing, the face of the block or plate is carved away, leaving the design standing proud to be inked and transferred to the paper (Figure 13.12a). The earliest and most common example of relief printing is typography, practised in China by the eighth century AD on woodblocks, and as moveable type by the eleventh century (Tsien Tsuen-Hsuin, 1985). In the West, woodblock printing commenced in the late fourteenth century, and

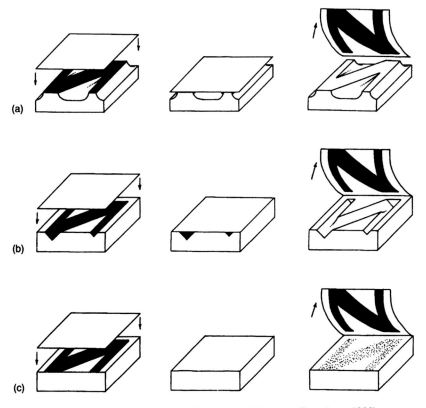

Figure 13.12   (a) Relief print; (b) Intaglio print; (c) Planar print. (Courtesy Gascoigne, 1982)

moveable type was introduced in the mid-fifteenth century.

To prepare the block for relief printing the greater part of the face must be carved away, and so a soft, easily carved material such as wood is eminently suitable. In the twentieth century, wood was joined by other synthetic materials, even linoleum (Chamberlain, 1978). The first woodblocks were carved running with the grain, as on the face of a plank for example. In the eighteenth century there was a revival of woodblock printing in Europe, but this time carved across the end grain of dense, fine-grained hardwoods, such as box. This created much finer prints, which became known as wood engravings to differentiate them from the ordinary woodcuts.

The raised design is then inked and impressed into the paper. Thus, the inked lines will be permanently depressed into the paper, and on the reverse the design may be apparent as a slightly raised or embossed feature. The ink is squeezed outwards, creating a rim around the edges of the printed line.

Prints made up of black lines could be colored by hand and a frequent source of controversy centres around whether the coloring is likely to have been contemporary or a subsequent add-ition. Identification of the pigments used can often resolve these disputes (Hahn *et al.*, 2004).

The earliest color prints were made by color woodblock printing, a technique known as *chiaroscuro* (literally, light and dark). This technique was popular in the sixteenth and again in the eighteenth century. The usual sixteenth-century practice was to leave the white areas completely uninked and standing proud, contrasting strongly with the various shades of the selected color, hence the name. Each color was printed from a separate block and so overlaps and gaps can occur. For more subtlety the colors were sometimes selectively overprinted.

Intaglio printing

Here the design is cut into the surface of the block or plate, creating depressions which hold the ink, some of which transfers to the paper during printing (Figure 13.12b). On the print the inked layer stands proud of the paper. Intaglio prints are thus the opposite of relief prints, and the whole area of the print will be depressed below the margins of the paper, known as the plate mark or *cuvette*. The paper is usually slightly dampened to ensure that the surface is pushed evenly into the inked areas of the plate, and dries unevenly. Thus, slight differences in dimensions can be found between intaglio prints that have been taken from the same block.

The design can be cut into the surface of the plate, which was traditionally of copper but latterly of steel, with a burin or graver (see Chapter 8, p. 172, Figure 8.18), to produce an *engraving* (Chamberlain, 1972). The graver is pushed into the surface of the metal, removing a sliver of metal and leaving a clean 'v' profiled line. Alternatively, a steel point may be drawn across the surface of the plate to produce a *dry point* (so called because no acid is involved in its preparation, unlike in etching). The point raises a burr of metal above the surface, and both the burr and the engraved depression will retain ink. When printed this leads to a very distinctive line, depending on how the point was held. As the burrs are standing proud they wear very quickly during a print run and thus the printed image will change relatively rapidly. Earlier and more expensive prints can be imitated by inking in the line on later prints taken from a worn plate.

Etching (Chamberlain, 1972)

Etching has been practised in Europe since the early sixteenth century. A copper plate is covered with a resist such as wax, and the design is drawn through this with a point or knife, exposing the metal beneath. Acid is then applied to the surface, attacking the exposed metal. The longer the acid is in contact with the metal, the deeper and broader will be the line or dot. The exposure of the metal can be controlled by stopping out areas to be less heavily attacked, or by adding lines at a later stage in the etching process. The acid-etched lines or dots have a much more irregular outline than an engraved or drawn line (Figure 13.13). Steel plates, introduced in the 1820s, have a much longer life, and initially were used to print banknotes.

From the eighteenth century the technique of soft ground etching has been used, particularly to imitate chalk or pencil drawing (Gascoigne, 1982, p. 15). Tallow is added to the wax resist to keep it soft. A piece of paper is laid over the stopped surface of the plate and the drawing made with a point, pushing the paper into the tacky resist. The paper is then lifted off and much of the resist in the line is pulled away, leaving a much more uneven line for etching. The effect is visually rather like lithography, but there should be no confusion as the printed line on the etching will stand proud, whereas that on the lithograph will be in the plane of the paper.

Stipple

In the techniques described so far, variation in the tonality of the printed area has been achieved

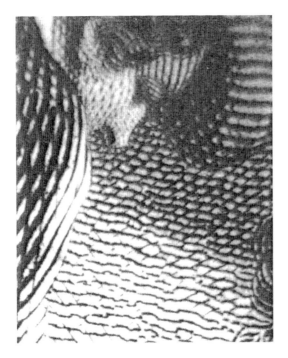

Figure 13.13 Comparison of engraved lines (left) and an etched lines (right) on the same print. (Courtesy Griffiths, 1980)

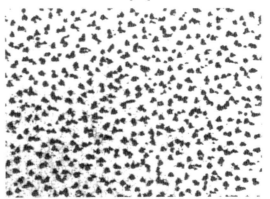

Figure 13.14 Stippled surface (×5). (Courtesy Gascoigne, 1982)

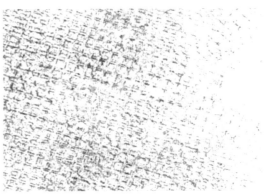

Figure 13.15 Mezzotint (×5). (Courtesy Gascoigne, 1982)

either by varying the density of lines or by differential inking. Some gradation in shade can be achieved by stippling the surface of the plate with a point or with a spiked roller (introduced in the sixteenth century). This creates a series of minor pits and burrs of raised metal on the plate, which can be modified or even polished out before inking depending on effect required (Figure 13.14). Stippling was done in conjunction with engraved lines from the early sixteenth century. In the eighteenth century, prints built up entirely from stippled areas became common in France in imitation of drawings done mainly with chalk, and also in England to copy popular paintings.

Mezzotint

In the seventeenth century in the Netherlands and in England, *mezzotint*, the much more sophisticated method of producing continuous gradation of shade or tone over the plate, was developed. The plate is prepared by rocking a curved serrated blade over the surface from a number of fixed angles, up to 40 being typical, until the whole surface is covered with a uniform array of lines of regularly spaced and angled incisions. The small, slightly burred incisions are clearly visible under low magnification, if not with the naked eye (Figure 13.15). Having prepared the plate, it can then be worked with scraper and burnisher, diminishing or even removing the incisions and burrs, which print black, thereby producing the lighter areas of the print. When inked, the print can have a continuous tonal range from black to white, the overall effect being reminiscent of charcoal drawing.

Aquatint

The plate is etched with a linear outline if required (Chamberlain, 1972, pp. 57–66). Resin or bitumen particles are then scattered over the surface of the plate, which is heated to fuse them to the surface.

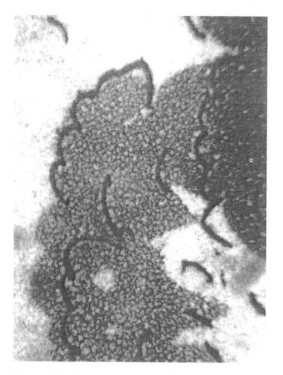

Figure 13.16   Aquatint. Note the irregular white dots typical of the process. (Courtesy Griffiths, 1980)

These act as a dappled resist to the acid etch. Alternatively, a solution of the resin may be poured onto the plate and evaporated in such a manner that it splits, so creating a maze of cracks. Areas that are not to be inked are varnished, and the acid is applied until the areas that are to be the lightest have been sufficiently etched. The acid is then washed off, and these areas are stopped off with more varnish. The process continues until the darkest areas have been etched. Variation of tone within areas can be achieved either by swabbing or swirling the acid, or by varying the density of the resin, and thus complete and continuous tonal range may be achieved, giving the print the appearance of a watercolor, hence the name.

Aquatints can be easily recognised at low magnification by the speckles of white in the printed surface, caused by the resin (Figure 13.16).

From the mid-nineteenth century it became usual practice to make electrotype copies of the original relief or intaglio plates when large editions were intended. Thus, for example, most woodcuts for magazine illustrations would have been printed from electrotypes of the original woodblock.

Planar processes

Lithography

In planar processes the ink lies directly on the flat surface of the plate (see Figure 13.12c) (Vicary, 1976; Croft, 2001). Lithography was invented in the late eighteenth century, and, as the name implies, the plates were originally of fine grained stone, but latterly were more usually of metal, such as zinc, and are now of plastic. The area to be printed is drawn with greasy wax or resin. After drawing, the surface of the plate is slightly dampened and further prepared. An oil-based ink is then rolled over the surface, but will only adhere to a greasy surface. Prints can then be taken from this.

Drawn lines are often done with a rough crayon to give an appearance similar to charcoal or chalk lines. For areas of more continuous tone or color a wax wash or stipple effect can be used.

For color lithography it was usual to use a separate stone for each color. The processes became more complex through the nineteenth century. First, just a single monotone, applied all over the print, was used. This was often fawn and was then joined by a blue tone, to be followed by the whole range of colors, with up to 20 separate stones used. These commercial prints became known as chromolithographs.

As the lithographic stone or plate is flat and only relatively light pressure is applied, there is not the evidence of pressure such as is observed on the relief and intaglio prints. Also, there is very little to wear, and thus long print runs are feasible with very little change through the series; consequently there are no states as such.

A color lithograph that has been manually printed from many separately inked stones or plates can sometimes be recognised by the holes in the paper for the locating pins. These pins pass through the paper and into precisely positioned holes in the stone for exact positioning of the paper, in order to print each color.

There are no permanent plates as such from which to make further copies, but some popular lithographs, such as those by Daumier or Lautrec, have been reprinted from existing prints. These can be superficially very convincing as they are also lithographs. However, they can be recognised because the grain pattern of the original interferes with that on the new. Wiedemann (2001) used thermogravimetry to distinguish between original oriental woodblock prints and modern copies and also between original twentieth-century European lithographs by masters such as Picasso and Dali, and the very numerous copies.

Instead of working directly on the stone, the artist could work on a specially prepared greasy paper which was then transferred to the stone. In the nineteenth century this technique was widely used to copy existing prints in large numbers. Another technique is offset lithography in which the image is picked up off the plate by a rubber roller and transferred to the paper. For the rapid printing of large numbers of prints by offset lithography, the image is printed photographically onto a cylinder which constitutes the plate. As this revolves it is continuously dampened and inked and transfers the image, now reversed, onto a second revolving rubber drum. This in turn transfers the image, once again the same way round as on the original plate, onto the paper on a third drum. The use of offset can often be detected because the color layer is much thinner than on an ordinary lithograph.

Screen printing
Perhaps the most effective and widely used method of making planar color prints is by screen printing (also known as *serigraphy* or *silk screen*), which is in effect a stencil technique (Mara, 1979). The technique originated in the Far East many centuries ago, but first appeared in the west in the late nineteenth century. Basically, the screen forms a permeable web with areas blocked out by applying stopping material to fill the spaces in the weave. If, for example, an oil-based ink were to be used then a water-based glue would make an effective block. The screen is stretched over a frame and the areas to be stopped out are treated and allowed to dry. The paper to be printed is placed beneath the screen and the color is applied to the other side and worked through the permeable areas of the screen onto the paper. Different screens can be used for each color until the print is complete. Screen printing is widely used for copying prints made by other techniques but can be distinguished from them because the weave of the silk is visible in the printed areas. Hayter (1962, p. 141, Plate 60) illustrates a silk screen forgery of a Miro lithograph.

Photographic processes

Following the development of photography there was considerable interest in the possibilities of printing photographs. This required a suitable light-sensitive and soluble medium as well as some method of representing tones, that is the shades of grey. Both problems were overcome and by the second half of the nineteenth century the photo-mechanical reproduction of prints became almost universal outside the world of art printing.

Relief processes
In these processes a plate is coated with a light-sensitive mixture such as potassium bichromate and gelatin. On exposure to the light the bichromate is reduced, hardening the gelatin and rendering it less soluble. A photographic negative of the image to be printed is placed over the coated plate and exposed to light. The plate is then washed, removing gelatin from the still-soluble areas that did not receive much light. Next, resin is dusted onto the plate, sticking onto the coated surfaces followed by heating to form a resist. The plate is then etched, eating away the unprotected surfaces but leaving the resin-coated areas. Thus, the plate now has the dark lines of the original image standing proud and they can be inked and prints made.

In order to produce tones, the original illustration is photographed through a fine cross-line screen. In the light areas, the light coming through the screen spreads, creating a large black dot on the negative; on darker areas less light would produce a smaller black dot (Figure 13.17). Most black and

Figure 13.17 Detail of a printed photograph that has been screened. (Courtesy Griffiths, 1980)

white illustrations were produced by this method during the twentieth century and are easy to recognise because of the regular array of dots.

Intaglio processes
Photogravure (also known as *heliogravure*)
Sources: Gamble (1910); Cartwright (1930).

A sheet of light-sensitive gelatin was exposed to light through a photographic negative. This was then transferred to a copper plate that had been given an aquatint ground, and the soft gelatin areas were washed away. The plate was then etched, and with careful control the acid penetrated the thinner areas of the remaining gelatin and thus selectively attacked the metal beneath. The aquatint ground created the tone and thus there is no regular array of dots as is found on the screened half-tone prints. The etched plate was then inked and printed in the usual manner for an intaglio print.

Photogravure makes very good reproductions and it was widely used in the late nineteenth century for the production of quality copies of etchings and engravings, replacing the traditional hand engraved or etched copies. However, it was itself a slow process requiring great skill on the part of the printer, frequently necessitating hand work on the plate before printing and thus the technique was little used after the introduction of photolithography in the early twentieth century. Some clues that a photographic process was involved might be given by the fine haloes around some of the original printed lines, which should be continuous but which are sometimes reproduced as a series of fine pits. The etching tends to be more even and overall much shallower than on the original, and this shows up clearly when the print is examined by raking polarised light.

Planar processes
Collotype
Collotype prints were produced by spreading light-sensitive gelatin onto a glass plate and exposing it to light through the negative. The surface was not then washed as with the other photomechanical processes, but merely moistened, the darker areas being damper. Thus, when lithographic ink was rolled over the gelatin, more was taken up on the drier areas (which had been the dark areas on the original photograph) than on the damper areas (which had been the light areas). This was the only way a good tonal print could be made before the introduction of screening in the late nineteenth century.

Photolithography
In this process the image is created on the light-sensitive gelatin spread on transfer paper. After washing, lithographic ink is rolled over the gelatine, which takes to the hardened drier areas but not to the wet paper. The transfer is then applied to the stone or plate and printed in the usual way. Copies of relief and intaglio prints can be easily detected, but copies of lithographs can be difficult to identify.

Color prints
Printing in more than one color has been done either by the *à la poupeé* method of dapping different colors onto one plate, or by building up the print color-by-color using separate plates. Since all colors are made up from the three primary colors, red, yellow and blue, if sufficient control can be gained over the colors then stippled or mezzotint plates made up of separate dots could produce all colors from just three plates. With the advent of half-tone screens this became possible. The image to be copied was screened and photographed three times with red, yellow and blue filters in place, and the photolithographic plates were produced as before. Color photolithographs rapidly replaced chromolithographs as the usual method of color printing. Although coincident dots of the three primary colors do produce black, it is usual to add a fourth plate with black ink to strengthen shadows. The regular array of dots generated by the screen differentiates color photolithographs from the dots produced by more recent computer-controlled processes (Figure 13.18a).

Figure 13.18a Magnified insert of the funnel of 13.18b clearly showing the dots in the three prime colors that constitute colors photolithographs. (Courtesy P. Craddock)

Figure 13.18b An apparently Victorian woven silk picture, depicting an early steam locomotive, set in an old frame with a small amount of lace to fool the unwary. (Courtesy P. Craddock)

Figure 13.19 Comparison of a woodcut line (left) and a Xerox of it (right). Note the dots of pigment around the Xerox line (×30). (Courtesy Gascoigne, 1982)

Photolithographs have been used to make copies of a wide range of two-dimensional images, including textiles. In the late nineteenth century, pictures woven from colored silks, known as Stevenographs, were made in Coventry, UK, and are now much collected. The author thought he had found one of the rarer and more expensive ones (Figure 13.18b) only to discover after purchase that it was a photolithograph copy (Figure 13.18a).

Photocopies and Inkjet printing

The images created in both of these processes are planar. Xerography creates an electrostatic charge on the paper where the image is required. The pigment in the form of a very fine powder is then dusted on, attracted to the charged areas and fixed by heat. Inevitably a few of the particles will stick outside the charged area, giving a somewhat speckled appearance near the edges of the image (Figure 13.19). This is likely to be more pronounced if old paper has been used. In computer-directed laser printing the computer indicates the areas to be charged on the paper by means of a laser. Laser-printed forgeries are now a major problem in philately (Bristow, 2004).

Inkjet printing is achieved by tiny jets of pigment being directed onto the paper by a computer. This can sometimes result in a slight splash effect around individual dots.

The ever-increasing sophistication and availability of inkjet printers makes color copies ever better and more easily accessible. It is now claimed to be easy to make passable images of banknotes on equipment costing less than £250. Previously the more expensive xerographic printers necessary for such work had anti-fraud software built in that could recognise a banknote's security marks and terminate the copying operation (although not with a Dali print!). The present generation of cheap copiers can produce copies of similar quality but are not so constrained. The world's biggest printer of banknotes, De La Rue, has warned that 'the world's central banks are having to deal with an increasing number of counterfeit banknotes generated by color inkjet printers' (Fox, 2003). There has been a spate of inkjet-printed joke sterling notes on sale in boot fairs and street markets in Britain with the heads of Margaret Thatcher, Princess Diana or well-known cartoon characters, etc. replacing that of the monarch (Figure 13.20).

The inkjet forgeries present new problems for forensic scientists trying to trace the source of forged prints. The printer itself is more or less anonymous, and unless there is a mechanical fault in the paper feed, etc., the actual font or layout is entirely determined by the program, not the printer. An apparent attempt to overcome this problem has consisted of building into some printers a device that prints a unique ID microdot onto every sheet (uncovered by the Electronic Frontier Foundation of San Francisco). However, many machines are

Figure 13.20   Bank of Bambi £50 note. Realistic joke Sterling banknote produced by a color inkjet copier with the head of the monarch digitally replaced by the head of Bambi. Other inkjet copies of banknotes may not be such innocent fun

so cheap that they are regarded as disposable once each job is completed.

Paper and inks are more distinctive than the process and, as they are rapidly changing, there is a good possibility that they can be traced to particular makers and times using techniques such as XRD, FTIR, RM and SERRS.

Fakes, forgeries and deceptive restoration

Sources: Gunn (1922, pp. 72–91); Kurz (1948, pp. 106–114); Hayter (1962, pp. 136–145); Griffiths (1980, p. 138); Ivins (1988, pp. 124–152); Jones (ed) (1990, p. 263–269); Beckett (1995, pp. 130–139). Maps: Dahl (1980).

Fakes and forgeries of prints include copies of existing prints, alteration of one state to resemble one of more value, and deceptive restoration of badly damaged prints.

The examination procedures set out for paper and ink are relevant here. Prints were copied almost from their inception in the late fifteenth century by free hand copying, great skill often being displayed (Jones (ed), 1990; Cat. 296, for example). From the late nineteenth century the various photomechanical processes described above made direct copying much easier.

A relief or intaglio print can be copied by making an electrotype directly from the print. This picks up the surface topography and in effect creates a new plate from the existing print. Prints made from

electroformed plates can be difficult to distinguish from the original. A very real difference is that the electrotype will have been taken from paper rather than from a plate, and thus in the unprinted areas of the print the topography of the paper surface can be reproduced. Electrotype techniques involve quite expensive and sophisticated equipment and thus they are more often used where it is intended to print very large numbers of copies. For example legitimate copies were made of some of the more famous Rembrandt and Dürer prints at the beginning of the twentieth century; they can be instantly recognised because they are not on the appropriate sixteenth- or seventeenth-century paper. The technique is also used to produce the plates for counterfeit banknotes.

Deceptive restoration can take the form of repairing badly damaged prints, or more subtly improving the quality of the printed line on a print taken from a worn plate by inking in faint lines or a lost burr on a drypoint. Evidence of distinctive past conservation or restoration treatments can also provide some evidence of the age of a print (Clarke, 2001).

Philately fraud

Philatelic forgeries are the weeds in the lawn of stamp collecting. Mercer Bristow, American Philatelic Society

Sources: Isnard (1960, pp. 319–335); Mills and Mansfield (1979, pp. 199–216); Bristow (2004); Vollmeir (2004).

Philatelic authenticity got off to a bad start when the genuine printing plates of obsolete issues were bought up by dealers who continued printing and selling the obviously convincing stamps as 'facsimiles'. Otherwise, forgeries may often be quickly uncovered by checking the method of printing, relief, intaglio or planar. Fakery usually involves adding some unusual but recorded error to a perfect genuine piece or adding a frank. Franked stamps, that is those that have been used, are often more valuable than unfranked examples. This is especially true of many colonial issues on whose behalf the stamps were often issued in Europe, with stamp collectors more in mind than the natives. The simple method was to make one's own franking stamp, but these are rarely convincing. Also, the ink should differ between fake and genuine. This would seem to be an area where non-destructive analysis by RM, etc. of the ink of both the frank on the questioned piece and on a genuine franked stamp would probably enable a fake to be detected, and also enable groups of suspected fakes to be linked.

The usual examination tools of light microscopy, UV and IR are all invaluable, and beta-radiography has proved useful (Theimer, 1983). The various printing processes and inks have particular UV reactions and specific printings of rare stamps, etc. can be recognised (Glazer and Dow, 1981). Gauges to measure the number of perforations and apparatus to measure paper thickness and to examine watermarks are more specific to philately (Bristow, 2004). The application of physical analytical techniques is discussed by Vollmeir (2004).

However, with enough perseverance and skills there are ways to circumvent science. Jean Sperati, doyen of stamp forgers, had an ingenious method of getting genuine franks onto genuine but different stamps. He photographed original, unused, valuable stamps and prepared printing blocks from them, and then took genuine but low-value franked stamps of the same period and press, with the correct watermark, etc. and bleached out the printed image leaving just the paper and frank. The forged stamp was then printed onto this, giving the right design on correct paper with an authentic frank. It is possible that some of the original printing survived under the frank.

Photographs

Sources: Jeffrey (1981); Coe and Haworth-Booth (1983); Martin (1988). Deterioration: Ware (1994).

Photographic prints are collected in their own right, either as art objects or historical records, or as examples of early photographic processes. Photographs play another role as they often form an important component in the documentation of artefacts and, as such, their authenticity can be crucial (see Chapter 12, p. 271, for example).

As with prints, there are problems with concepts of originality. Some photographic prints are issued in limited numbered and signed editions, but as long as the negative exists more prints can be made. While the original photographer still lives and makes the prints these are presumably all equal, although in practice early prints tend to be more valuable than later ones. The problems do not end there. Many famous photographers re-photographed some of their prints after the original negative became lost. What is the status of the prints from these negatives? Are they originals or copies?

The nineteenth century saw rapid developments in a variety of photographic processes, all ultimately relying on the effect of light on certain chemicals, notably silver salts (Jeffrey, 1981; Martin, 1988, pp. 32–113; Pols, 1993) (Figure 13.21). Some processes produced a positive image; that is, each photograph is a unique original. These include daguerreotypes, sensitised silver on a copper support, ambrotypes, an under-exposed collodion negative that appeared as a positive when mounted on a dark background on glass, and tintypes, mounted on a thin sheet of tinned iron. Note that daguerreotypes and ambrotypes were often mounted in protective cases made of early plastics such as bois durci (see Chapter 18, p. 449).

With the invention of permanent negatives the production of runs of prints became feasible. The first was the calotype (or talbotype) with sensitised silver salts on paper, with fixing carried out after exposure. The positive print would be made by exposing a fresh calotype to light through the negative and fixing with common salt, or latterly with sodium thiosulphate (the familiar hypo). Much finer negatives could be made by the wet collodion process, which used gun cotton (nitrocellulose) dissolved in ether, containing potassium iodide and silver nitrate, later supplanted by the gelatin dry process. From the 1850s prints were made on paper coated with egg-white albumen and salt to hold

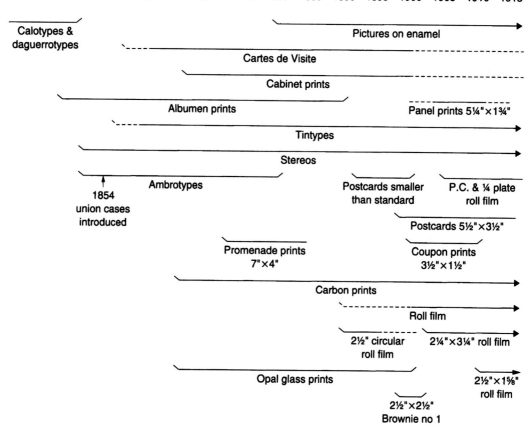

Figure 13.21 Principal forms of nineteenth and early twentieth century photographic images and their date (Courtesy Pols, 1993)

the silver salts, in turn supplanted by gelatin as the medium.

Other light-sensitive chemicals produced effects that were valued for art photographs; for example platinum salts gave more delicate tones than did silver salts. Carbon prints relied on a very different light-sensitive process. This was the hardening effect that potassium bichromate has on gelatin, which formed the basis of the photolithographic and photogravure processes described above (see p. 332). For photographic prints the gelatin bichromate emulsion contained the pigment, in this case carbon. On exposure to light through the negative, the more exposed areas preferentially hardened and after washing retained their carbon, which forms the image.

Clearly most of these processes could be identified by analysis, but usually examination with a lens

is sufficient, as exemplified by the distinctive surface structure of daguerreotypes (Lee, 1993). Martin (1988, p. 98) also observed that 'appreciating the different forms of degradation that can occur with each process is an important method of identifying the process of an image without the need to perform tests'. The different degradations can also be good indicators of age.

Degradation

The rate of decay depends on both the environment in which the print has been kept as well as the presence of residual chemicals in the emulsion after fixing and washing the print. The chemicals in most color prints will begin to decay quite rapidly and even in black and white prints the silver image degrades gradually with the conversion of the metallic silver to silver sulphide, specifically due to residual thiosulphate fixer (Kockaerts, 1992). A photographic print that is more than 20 years old and stored under the usual conditions should begin to show some signs of degradation in the emulsion. Prints tend to degrade preferentially at the edges. Albumen prints tend to crack on the surface over time as the image shrinks.

Alteration of photographs (Mitchell, 1992, 1994)

Since the advent of photography, images have been altered by tricks such as double exposure or photographing montages made from existing prints. Already in the 1850s, Oscar Rejlander was creating montages by printing from many negatives together and his successor Henry Peach Robinson made photographs from carefully arranged existing prints. These are usually visually easy to spot, the edges of the components of the montage or the double photography being apparent. The advent of digital imagery has greatly facilitated the ability to manipulate images. This extends beyond simple cut-and-paste to the creation of wholly new images together with the appropriate three-dimensional foreshortening and shadows. The facility with which this may done on digital images compared with the traditional chemical photographic negative makes it imperative that the latter should be preserved as the inviolate original records rather than being copied digitally and then discarded (see comment on preservation of newspapers, p. 316).

Documents and manuscripts: examination

Sources: Harrison (1964, 1966); Browning (1977, pp. 326–338); Flieder (1980); Art (1987); Ellen (1997); Giles (1998). Oriental forgeries: Whitfield (ed) (2002).

This section deals with the forensic examination of documents, and outlines some of the basic approaches to the detection of the fabrication or alteration of documentary evidence. Together with photographs, described above, this often forms an important part of the supporting evidence for the recent history of an object. This can be for the purpose of backing up the object's authenticity or to establish that the object is not a recent import and, therefore, not an illegal export from its supposed country of origin. The evidence can take the form of sale and exhibition catalogues, or invoices for sale or restoration, demonstrating ownership or establishing the existence of the artefact in a particular collection at a particular place and date.

Many of the analytical techniques used in the identification of paper and inks, etc. have been covered in previous sections, but there are often more practical approaches, requiring minimal equipment, that can provide useful information.

As usual a binocular microscope is a prerequisite, and an engraver's glass or a good magnifier are more portable aids. Examination under UV and IR

Case study: A fishy photo

The first coelacanth, the 'living fossil' fish, was caught off the coast of South Africa in 1938, and since then a very few others have also been caught off the south-east coast of Africa. In 1998 another was recognised by an American scientific team among the catch of a fisherman off Sulawesi, which forms part of Indonesia, some 10 000 km away (Erdmann *et al.*, 1998). Moreover, the Indonesian fishermen were familiar with the coelacanth, which they called 'the king of the sea', and, some months before the recorded discovery, Erdmann's wife had spotted another on a fisherman's trolley and managed to photograph it before it was sold. Shortly afterwards a French team claimed that they had recognised and obtained a coelacanth back in 1995 from the Bay of Pangandaran, off south-west Java. Unfortunately the fish itself had somehow disappeared, and the photograph had also been lost, but was then rediscovered. This was submitted to the journal *Nature* to support the French claim for the primacy of their discovery. However, the editor spotted that the photograph was that of the coelacanth found by the American team superimposed onto a photograph of a fishmonger's slab (McCabe and Wright, 2000;). As one of the French team remarked, 'This is very embarrassing'.

are especially useful for revealing alterations both to the surface of the paper and to the ink (Harrison, 1966, pp. 89–93, 94).

A good start with any document is to check the dimensions. For example, the present international paper sizes A1 to A5, etc. only came into being in the 1920s in Britain (and still have not been adopted in North America). Thus, a paper purporting to be of the early twentieth century with A4 dimensions would be suspicious. But note that the exact dimensions of a piece of paper are subject to variation in local moisture content, and thus very precise measurement can be rather meaningless.

The age of more recent papers and the inks used can often be revealed with some precision by their composition and treatments (see Table 13.1, p. 319), or by watermarks if present (see p. 317). Forgers seek to get round this by using old paper but even the most profligate of publishers rarely include more than about half a dozen blank end papers and thus if a long document has been forged, paper from a number of sources may have been used. Different responses to UV and to IR may well reveal this.

Records of changing typefaces used by various typewriter manufacturers through the years are available, and can be of considerable assistance in providing at least a *terminus post quem* for a typescript. Harrison (1964, pp. 51, 194) regarded the absence of odour on an old document as suspicious and Buchbauer *et al.* (1995) attempted to quantify this phenomena analytically. However, as Charles Douglas-Home and the *Sunday Times* discovered with the Hitler Diaries (Harris, 1986, p. 307), odours can be created (see the quote at the beginning of this Chapter, p. 313).

The detection of erasures and additions

Erasures and additions to documents can be detected (Harrison, 1966, pp. 89–138). An area of erasure can often be revealed by UV, the erasing process having exposed a new surface and thereby making it fluoresce more than its surroundings. IR can often pick up the original script that is no longer visible in light.

Physical erasure

Removal of the line with an ordinary eraser or with a scalpel blade usually causes some loss of paper and, almost inevitably, damage to the surface

glaze, leaving the paper in that area somewhat thinner and rougher. Such physical erasure can often be detected quite simply by transmitted light. The roughening can be emphasised by sprinkling graphite dust over the suspect paper, the particles sticking preferentially to the rubbed areas. There is an inherent danger that subsequently it may not be possible to remove all of the graphite, and special fluorescent powders are now available for this purpose. The damage to the surface of the paper is very clear when viewed by SEM, provided the paper sample is small enough to be inserted in the chamber of the microscope (Figures 13.22a and 13.22b). After erasure has taken place, the roughened surface can be burnished but the glaze cannot be locally replaced.

Lines leave impressions, and even when the graphite of a pencilled line, etc. has been totally removed the depressed line may still persist and can be emphasised by oblique illumination. The line is detected best when viewed at right angles and so the paper should be slowly rotated while observing closely.

Chemical erasure

The familiar hypochlorite- or permanganate-based ink removers in aqueous solution act by oxidising the colored metal ions in the inks and by dissolving them. The inks are usually dispersed in solution but can sometimes leave a faint yellow stain, best viewed under fluorescent light or daylight. Almost all chemical eradicators are water-based, and thus inevitably cause local wrinkling of the paper and the removal of the surface glaze. Bleaches of the hypochlorite–acid type are effective in quickly removing modern 'washable inks; but the old iron-based inks are better removed with iron-complexing agents such as EDTA. Ballpoint inks and crayons are oil- or wax-based and can be removed with organic solvents such as acetone, followed by aqueous-based eradicators to remove the metal ions. Chemical eradicators have no effect at all on the carbon-based inks or on pencil graphite.

Caverhill *et al.* (1996) investigated the use of lasers to remove ballpoint and fibre-tip pen inks from paper. The process caused unacceptable charring on wood-pulp papers but was reasonably successful on cotton-rag paper. Even so, some heat damage was done to the surface of the inked paper with attendant loss of glaze, which should enable

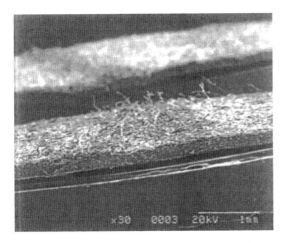

Figure 13.22a Side-view SEM micrograph of a cotton rag paper after removal of biro ink with a scalpel (field is 1.2 mm across).

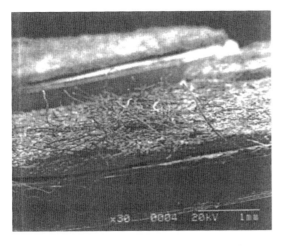

Figure 13.22b Side-view SEM micrograph of a cotton rag paper after removal of biro ink with a scalpel followed by smoothing with a solid eraser (field is 1.2 mm across).

such treatment to be recognised. Rather surprisingly there was some damage to the uninked regions of the paper where the fibres were raised (Figure 13.22c). This was superficially reminiscent of that caused by mechanical erasure (see Figures 13.22a and 13.22b), but in this instance was probably caused by the rapid generation of steam from the water entrapped in the paper's surface.

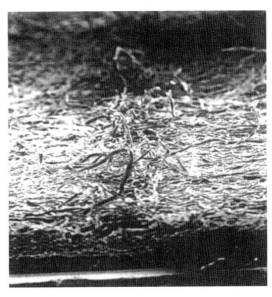

Figure 13.22c Side-view SEM micrograph of uninked cotton rag paper after laser removal treatment in the vicinity (field is 1.2 mm across). (Courtesy Caverhill *et al.*, 1996)

Additions

The investigation of possible additions concentrates on differences in the composition of the ink (see p. 324) and in the method of its application. Fakers encounter especial difficulties when additions have to be made to paper where erasures have been made. The glaze is very likely to have been lost, and water-based inks will tend to soak into the paper causing very obvious feathering. Oil-based inks may be used, but these could be incompatible with those used on the rest of the document. Another problem with a worn document is that creases, folds or the troughs of erased script will deform an inked line drawn across them.

The recognition that one line is superimposed over another, although potentially important and seemingly easy to demonstrate, is in practice often very difficult. To the unaided eye the heavier, darker line always appears to be on top. Where pencil and ink lines cross, the pencil line always appears on top because the ink sinks into the paper, whereas the graphite sits on it. Also, the ink does not adhere to the slightly greasy graphite particles. High magnification may well show the order of the channels in the paper created by the two lines at their crossing.

Case study: The Vinland Map

Sources: Skelton *et al.* (1965, revised edn 1995); Washburn (ed) (1971); Wallis *et al.* (1974); McCrone (1976, 1988); Cahill *et al.* (1987); Witten (1989); Towe (1990, 2004); Cahill and Kusko (1995); Saenger (1998); Olin (2003); Seaver (2004); Vinland Map Study Group (2004).

The continuing scientific investigations carried out on the Vinland Map are of interest because they show some of the difficulties of interpretation that can arise when different investigative strategies are adopted by two separate groups in an atmosphere of latent, if not active, hostility.

The Map

The Vinland Map depicts the world, drawn in ink on parchment and purports to date from the mid-fifteenth century. The map has been bound in recent times to a genuine fifteenth-century manuscript on parchment and paper of the *Tartar Relation*, a fairly free copy of a well-known description of the travels of two Franciscan monks to the Mongols in Central Asia in the thirteenth century.

The depiction of the bulk of the main land mass of the Old World would arouse little controversy. However, in the seas on either side of this land mass, islands are shown that are of great interest (Figure 13.23). On the left hand side of the map there is a reasonably accurate depiction of Iceland,

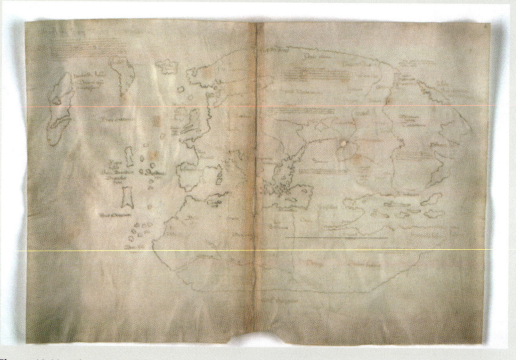

Figure 13.23 The Vinland Map with the island labelled Vinland Insula in the top left hand corner. The inked lines appear dense and black because of the special high-contrast film used by the photographers of the Yale Library. In ordinary light the lines are very pale, most of the ink having been worn or rubbed off. (© Beinecke Rare Book and Manuscript Library, Yale University)

and a remarkably prescient depiction of Greenland as an island, which, at the time the map purports to have been drawn, was believed to have been a peninsula. To the west of this another large island is depicted, prominently labelled Vinlanda Insula (possibly Vinalanda or Vimilanda), together with details of its discovery. The island has two large inlets on the east coast, one of which could be identified as the mouth of the St Lawrence river.

If genuine, this would be the earliest depiction of the mainland of America, and is seemingly more accurate than the hitherto earliest maps of the region, which are the late sixteenth to early seventeenth century maps of Stefánson and Resen, now in Copenhagen (Quin and Foote, 1966). Much has also been made of the accuracy of the north of Greenland, and, all in all, the Vinland Map would be the best depiction of the North Atlantic before the eighteenth century.

At least Europeans had travelled in the North Atlantic, but on the right hand side of the map are a group of major islands off the main land mass of Asia that resemble the Kamchatka Peninsula and the islands of Japan. It is unlikely that anyone in Medieval Europe had heard of the islands of Japan, much less be able to draw them on a world map (Cortazzi, 1983). Lopez, in the Vinland Map Conference (1971, p. 31) noted that the islands of Japan are drawn with 'somewhat disquieting carefulness'.

The discovery of the Map and the extraordinary reunion with its associated documents

The story, as given by Lawrence Witten (1971), the dealer from whom the map was purchased, is as follows. In 1957 the map, bound up with the *Tartar Relation*, together with a manuscript copy on parchment and paper of Vincent de Beauvais' *Speculum Historiale*, a well-known Medieval history source, was offered for sale by a dealer, Enzo Ferrajoli de Ry. They were purported to have come from an unknown, and never to be identified? Spanish? library. He supposedly took the items to London, including the British Museum, but only sold the *Speculum*, by itself of little value, to the London bookseller, J.I. Davis. Witten was shown the map and the *Tartar Relation*, bound together, in Geneva by Ferrajoli, shortly before they were returned, unsold, to their putative Spanish owner. Witten initially claimed (Witten, 1971, p. 5) that he had actually visited this library with Ferrajoli in September 1957 but subsequently had to admit that this was untrue (Witten, 1989, 1995). Even so, Witten acquired the map and its associated manuscript, and back in New York, in October 1957, showed them to Thomas Marston, curator of Medieval and Renaissance Literature at Yale University Library. However, the absence of any authenticating evidence apparently made Witten reluctant to offer the map for sale.

The only related material was the *Tartar Relation*, but here there was a problem. Both map and document had been attacked by bookworm, but the flight holes did not match, and the binding that joined the two was patently modern.

Then some fairly amazing things are supposed to have taken place.

In the spring of 1958 Marston spotted an early Italian manuscript which looked interesting in the latest catalogue of J.I. Davis, with whom Ferrajoli had supposedly dealt on his London visit. While placing his order Marston noticed another item, an incomplete and rather battered manuscript of the *Speculum Historiale*, in which Marston was interested for his own collection. The items arrived in May 1958 and Marston duly called up Witten to show him the Italian manuscript. Witten went round and spotted the *Speculum*, which he noted was in a script similar to that of the *Tartar Relation*. He asked to borrow it and immediately saw what the putative Spanish library, the British Museum, Ferrajoli de Ry and other book dealers across Europe had apparently missed, namely that they belonged together. Furthermore, the *Speculum* turned out to be the missing section between the Vinland Map and the *Tartar Relation*, because the wormholes on the latter exactly matched those on the front of the *Speculum*; those on the back matched, more or less, those on the map. Suddenly the authenticity of the map was established by its apparently unassailable association with the Medieval manuscripts.

This was a quite extraordinary coincidence and Marston's reaction was no less extraordinary. He then gave the *Speculum* to Witten's wife, who actually owned the map and the *Tartar Relation*, apparently to encourage them to sell the whole group to the Yale Library. Negotiations were entered into, and finally in 1959 Paul Mellon paid a very large sum, rumoured at a million dollars, for the map and manuscripts. Mellon then loaned them to the Yale Library until such time as they were fully authenticated. This inevitably introduced a bias to the subsequent study in that there was pressure to authenticate. It should be stated here that both the standard *Catalogue of Medieval and Renaissance Manuscripts II* (Shailor, 1984, 1987, 1992) and the reviewer (Saenger, 1998) of the revised edition of *The Vinland Map and the Tartar Relation* (Skelton *et al.*, 1995) cast considerable doubt on the veracity of the story of the discovery and reuniting of the manuscripts. Saenger and Shailor also set out in some detail the true position of Marston in the Yale Library and his collecting activities, including many other purchases made previously for the Yale Library, usually from Witten. Together they make the circumstances of the acquisition of the map more comprehensible.

The publication of and publicity for the Map

After detailed study a carefully selected group of scholars convinced themselves by 1964 of the map's authenticity. In the following year Mellon duly presented the Vinland Map to the Beinecke Library of Yale, and a major study, *The Vinland Map and the Tartar Relation* (Skelton *et al.* 1965) was published. The volume dealt exhaustively with all matters relating to the story of the acquisition, the cartography of the map, the related historical background, and the accompanying two manuscripts.

The eminent paper expert, Allan Stevenson, examined the watermarks of the paper from both the *Tartar Relation* and the *Speculum* manuscripts using beta-radiography (see letter in Skelton *et al.*, 1965, pp. 9–10). He showed that these manuscripts were made up of long runs of paper made in the same pair of moulds (p. 317). One of the watermarks had been found by Briquet (1968) on a piece of paper in the municipal accounts of Colmar dated 1441. To Stevenson's practised eye the watermark on the two documents seemed a little less damaged than the Colmar mark and thus he assigned a date of about 1440 for the manufacture of the paper. As both the *Tartar Relation* and *Speculum* were written on more or less continuous runs of paper as they had been made sheet by sheet, this further suggested to Stevenson that the manuscript was begun fairly soon after the paper was made. This dated the manuscripts fairly conclusively, but not the map, as was made plain.

Given the continuing uncertainty over the map's real provenance, there was precious little objective examination. In particular, there was little or no report of any scientific testing beyond a cursory examination by binocular microscope and some IR and UV photography. The unpublished results of the latter were apparently judged to be in order, even though when the same tests were conducted at the British Museum in 1967 (Wallis *et al.*, 1974; and see p. 344), the ink of the map was immediately shown to be suspect. Marston (Skelton *et al.*, 1965, p. 11) quite specifically sought to discourage scientific investigation, claiming that it could not achieve anything of interest.

The announcement attracted enormous attention both popular and scholarly. The former were attracted by this confirmation of the Norse discovery of America, but the reaction of the latter was very mixed with many claiming from the outset that the map was a fraud. Such was the clamour that only a year later a conference was called (Washburn (ed), 1971). It is clear from the published discussions following the contributions that there were many and varied areas of disquiet among the delegates on all aspects of the map, not least over the story of its discovery and acquisition. Witten (1971) was unforthcoming about the original owner and his library, which he again insisted he had visited and described in some detail, although subsequently had to admit that no such visit had taken place (Witten, 1989, 1995). Marston, although not a speaker, was questioned fairly rigorously in discussion, and seemed remarkably evasive on questions concerning his purchase of the *Speculum*.

Several speakers speculated on how the map could have been faked. Cortesão (1971, p. 18) suggested it might have been drawn on a blank sheet of parchment conveniently contained within the genuine *Tartar Relation*. It was pointed out that the wormholes penetrate through the ink-drawn lines of the map in several places; that is, the worm action apparently post-dated the inked lines. Lopez (1971, p. 31), claimed that the map could have been drawn on blank sheets of old parchment with ink made from old recipes, then aged, and the 'wormholes' introduced in the appropriate places with a hot wire, or even real worms. He claimed to know an Italian palaeographer who had 'heard from a reliable source of an English antiquarian who kept a stable of live worms'. One suspects that Mr Lopez was a little unfamiliar with the life-cycle of the bookworm, which is the larva of the *Anorbium* beetle. Even so, clearly the wormholes on the map itself should have been studied more carefully (see the comments of Baynes-Cope, p. 344).

Given this underswell of doubt over the authenticity of the map at the meeting, it was natural that enquiry was made over just what scientific tests had been conducted since the 1965 report. Marston replied (Washburn (ed), 1971, p. 34) that:

> the only tests that we have made – if you want to call them tests – are the examination of the inks with a low-power microscope. All the inks appear to be the same. I do not know that every one has been examined – I think there are five or six different batches of ink used in the manuscript – but the examination of the inks on the map and on the manuscript under a low-power microscope shows the same molecular constituents.

One envies Marston his low-power microscope that could differentiate the molecular constituents. Perhaps if Yale had availed themselves of the serious forensic and scientific advice offered to them at that time by the British Museum the subsequent story of the Vinland Map would have been very different. Dr Harold Plenderleith, head of the UNESCO Rome Center for the Study of Preservation of Cultural Property, was also consulted and suggested that the ink should be analysed and also examined by UV to determine how far the ink had migrated into the membrane of the parchment (Washburn (ed), 1971, pp. 34–35; and see p. 324 and Figure 13.11).

Following on from this meeting the map was studied by McCrone Associates, the well-known independent commercial laboratory specialising in forensic microscopic examination. McCrone's report to the Yale Library was typically unequivocal and damning: the ink contained anatase, the titanium dioxide mineral used in modern ink and paint only since the 1920s (see Chapter 12, p. 303). This prompted the Yale Library to announce rather forlornly that 'the famous Vinland Map may be a forgery'. Furthermore, by this time Yale must have known of the impending publication of the findings of the meeting held earlier at the Royal Geographic Society, London, containing the results of the British Museum's own scientific investigation of the map (see p. 344), together with a summary of the McCrone's work, which both concluded that the map was not ancient (Wallis *et al.*, 1974).

There the matter rested until the mid-1980s when the map was re-examined by scientists of the Crocker Historical and Archaeological Projects, of the University of California, Davis (Cahill *et al.*, 1987). They challenged McCrone's figures claiming that the titanium dioxide was much less prevalent, and that the ink on the map resembled that on many other Medieval manuscripts that they had investigated over the years. Predictably, this brought forth a spirited response from McCrone (1988) and also additional support for the modern origin of the anatase found in the ink, from scientists specialising in this field, notably Kenneth Towe (1990). Washburn convened another meeting in 1995 to coincide with the re-issue of the 1965 book. Although McCrone and Towe attended the meeting, they had declined to give presentations as they had been led to believe that no new material was to be included in the re-issue. On arriving at the meeting however, they were presented with a *fait accompli* in the form of the re-issued book (Skelton *et al.*, 1995) with no less than four new chapters summing up the work of the 30 years since the first issue, and each strongly partisan in favour of the map's authenticity (see Paul Saenger's 1998 thorough and trenchant review, pointing out the many palaeographic and historical shortcomings that remained unaddressed).

Without any critical scientific contributions, Painter and the new authors had a field day. Painter (1995, pp. ix–xix) clearly misunderstood the evidence, while Washburn (pp. xxi–xxvii) merely misrepresented it, chiding the British Museum (p. xxvii) for 'exhibiting a caution that went beyond a judicious and natural evaluation of the evidence', in failing to pronounce the map authentic.

The scientific study of the Vinland Map

The first detailed scientific examination of the map was carried out at the British Museum by A.D. Baynes-Cope in January 1967 (Wallis *et al.*, 1974). This was some 10 years after it had surfaced, during which time it was supposed to have been the subject of detailed scrutiny. The time available for examination at the British Museum was limited and there was a strict prohibition on sampling. The map and the manuscript were examined by optical microscopy, IR photography and UV.

The parchment

Baynes-Cope noted that the parchment fluoresced under UV and suggested that it had been chemically treated, although no specific chemicals could be detected. Cahill *et al.* (1987) and Cahill and Kusko (1995) noted anatase particles on the parchment in areas well away from the ink, which could also be evidence of some kind of treatment.

Baynes-Cope also noted differences in the wormholes in the map and in the manuscript. The characteristic lining found in the channels of the bookworm were missing from the holes on the map, suggesting that the parchment had subsequently been soaked. In addition, there had been attempts to patch the holes in the map, both of which occurrences made it difficult to establish that the holes really were the result of worm action.

Since the 1995 re-publication of the Vinland Map volume, the parchment of the map has been accelerator mass spectrometry–radio carbon (AMS RC) dated and this has provided confirmative evidence of extensive recent treatment (Gove, 1999, p. 116; Donahue *et al.*, 2002). The calibrated date of the parchment was reported at between AD 1423 and 1445 at 1 sigma and between AD 1411 and 1468 at 2 sigma. These dates would seem to support the authenticity of the map, but, as both Gove and Donahue point out, all that has been dated is the parchment, not the ink of the map itself. Fakers can obtain sheets of parchment of almost any age, and there is a strong possibility that the map was drawn on a sheet taken from the genuine *Tartar Relation* volume. Unfortunately there is not enough ink left for it to be dated. If the ink were modern, the carbon could well have derived from coal or oil.

Donahue and colleagues carried out a number of different pretreatments primarily designed to check that materials used for later cleaning and restoration had not contaminated the sample (see Chapter 5, p. 102). One sample was cleaned by the standard RC treatment of washing with dilute acid, followed by washing with caustic soda, and then neutralising with more acid, all in aqueous solution. The three other samples were washed in acetone. Overall there was a considerable weight loss, strongly suggesting that the parchment had undergone major treatment. On running the samples through the AMS spectrometer, the aqueous-only treated sample had an activity greater than modern; that is, there was bomb carbon present (see Chapter 5, p. 96). This could only mean that the parchment had undergone extensive treatment very shortly before its first appearance in 1958.

The extracts were not chemically identified, but organic material that is water soluble and that derives from living material suggests gelatin size, extracted from bones and hides, and McCrone (1999) found gelatin in some of the samples he examined. Ambers and Bowman (2003) suggested nitrocellulose as a possibility, but this would have dissolved in the acetone and not in the aqueous medium. Donahue and colleagues suggested this could be evidence of legitimate conservation. Another possibility was that a page taken from the *Tartar Relation* had had whatever writing, etc. it originally carried chemically removed, which necessitated resizing with gelatin before the map could be drawn.

This new result means that some of the previous hypotheses concerning the map's origins are unlikely. For example, Karen Seaver (1995, 2004) suggested that it was produced in Germany by the Jesuits before the Second World War, as part of an elaborate plan to discredit the Nazis.

The ink It has been known for many years that the components of iron gall ink gradually spread and separate over long periods of time (McNeil, 1984, and p. 324). The ink on the map comprised two layers, a light brown stain *in* the surface of the parchment, and very fragmentary remains of particulate crystalline material *on* the surface (Figures 13.24 and 13.25). Baynes-Cope, McCrone and latterly Brown and Clark (2002), stated that the two layers resulted from two separate applications, citing as evidence areas of the map depicting parts of the west of Britain, where the two lines diverge quite appreciably (although they never quite part company). This strange double inking could be an attempt to simulate the age-related separation of genuine iron gall ink.

Baynes-Cope also stated that the ink on the map had a peculiar structure unlike that on the accompanying manuscripts, or on any other Medieval manuscript that he had examined: 'It certainly does not have the appearance characteristic of a faded iron-gall ink'. IR photography showed that the ink was not typical of either iron gall or sepia inks. The behaviour of the ink under UV was of particular interest:

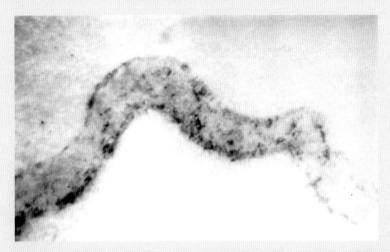

Figure 13.24 Line (0.6–0.8 mm wide) from the map showing the two components, a liquid and particles, which are often concentrated at the edges of the line. (Courtesy A.D. Baynes Cope/British Museum)

faded iron gallo-tannate ink, yellowish brown by daylight, will appear black against a black or yellowish fluorescent background....The inks used in both the Tartar Relation *and the* Speculum Historiale *showed this phenomenon whereas the ink used both for the outline of the map itself and for the text on the leaf did not show this phenomenon.*

More recently Brown and Clark (2002) studied the ink using RM. Their study reached much the same conclusions as those of Baynes-Cope and McCrone. They found evidence that the lines had two components, a faint wide line with particles detected at the edges (see Figure 13.24), overlain by a thinner black line. There was no evidence for iron gall ink but RM detected elemental carbon. Medieval European inks almost without exception were of iron gall (see p. 323), and carbon inks were very rare.

McCrone's work essentially consisted of microscopic examination, with selective sampling

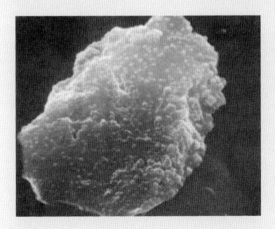

Figure 13.25 SEM micrograph of a yellow ink particle taken by McCrone from the map. The particle is approximately 10 microns across, and the small protuberances on the surface may be of anatase or calcite. (Courtesy McCrone, 1988)

viewed directly through the microscope, and analysis of these samples removed from the main matrices of the map (McCrone and McCrone in Wallis *et al.*, 1974; McCrone, 1987/8b; McCrone and Weiss, (eds), 1999). It is instructive to compare this approach to the very different, total analysis of the map surface, albeit using very the sensitive methods followed by Cahill *et al.* (1987). McCrone took 38 samples of particulate material from the lines, comprising 24 yellow crystals, 8 that were yellow-black, 2 that were black, and 4 fibres. They were examined by scanning and transmission electron microscopy respectively (SEM and TEM), coupled with elemental and X-ray diffraction (XRD) analysis. McCrone reported high concentrations of calcite and, more significantly, the mineral titanium dioxide, TiO_2, in the form known as anatase, in the particulate material, but found none in the surface of the parchment away from the ink (this is in contradiction to Cahill and Kusko, 1995, who did report particles of anatase in the parchment). Furthermore, the anatase was well crystallised with rounded rather than angular profiles and had a restricted size range (Figure 13.26). Crucially, there were no clay minerals associated with the anatase crystals. All of the above is commensurate with commercially treated anatase. It is important to emphasise the use of XRD which enabled the titanium dioxide to be identified as being in the form of anatase rather than the more common naturally occurring mineral of titanium dioxide, rutile. This has the same stoichiometry; that is, it has the same chemical composition, TiO_2, but in a different molecular configuration. In this context the work of Braga *et al.* (1992) characterising changes in the morphology and trace element composition of anatase through the twentieth century might be of some use in the precise dating of the anatase on the map.

The strategy of Cahill *et al.* (1987) was very different from that of McCrone. They eschewed sampling but relied instead on total non-destructive analysis over the whole surface, ink particles and parchment together. They used PIXE, which enabled a very sensitive analysis to be made of a wide range of elements (but not carbon). A total of 159 areas from all over the map were analysed, including both blank and inked areas, building up in effect a compositional map of the surface. Each area analysed by the beam was 0.3–1 mm $\times$ 2 mm; that is, even on the inked areas the greater part of the area analysed was the slightly stained surface of the parchment rather than the particulate constituents of the ink. In effect the vast bulk of the analysed area was background, but the strategy did at least remove any possible subjective selectivity, and was completely non-destructive. As can be appreciated, it is almost impossible to try to compare the analysis of a particle removed from the surface with that of the whole surface with the very scattered particles still in place.

Painter clearly did not understand these difficulties of equation at all, and merely trumpeted that McCrone's analyses were in error by factors of several hundreds of thousands. Cahill and Kusko of course did understand the problem and in the same publication tried to reconcile the two approaches, but still calculated that McCrone had overestimated the titanium content of the ink 500-fold. However, without direct consultation with McCrone Associates, or, more importantly, common samples, they had to make assumptions and guesses to arrive at their estimate. The actual titanium content of the particles clearly varied but as Towe (1990) pointed out, the mere fact that McCrone was able to obtain good XRD patterns from his particulate samples strongly suggests that the titanium dioxide must really have been there in quantities commensurate with his reported analyses. But in reality like was not being compared with like, and it is very possible that with a little more co-operation and less intransigence between the two laboratories, the apparent analytical differences could have been resolved.

The morphology of the anatase is of particular importance. On the map it is in the form in which it has been prepared commercially as the base for paints since the 1920s (Braga *et al.*, 1992; Laver, 1997) (see Figure 13.26). Responses to this varied from the uncomprehending to the dismissive. Painter (1995) claimed that titanium was a very common element in the Earth's surface and thus it should come as no surprise that it was found on the surface of the map. Rather more objectively, Cahill and Kusko (1995) pointed out that prepared anatase is in the paint on every wall and every ceiling of every room throughout the Western World and thus flecks of anatase are everywhere. This

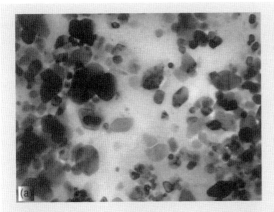

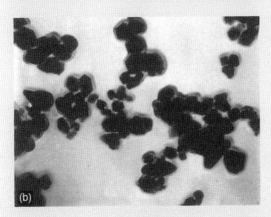

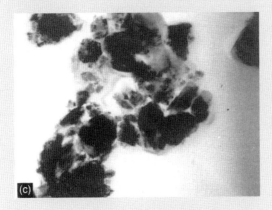

Figure 13.26 TEM images of anatase. (a) Anatase from the ink of the Map; (b) Modern commercially calcined and milled material; (c) Sample of ground mineral anatase. Note the regular size and rounded profile of the modern commercial sample and that from the Map, very different from the natural material. (Courtesy McCrone, 1988)

is where McCrone's strategy of analysing specific observed and identified samples was vindicated. The anatase was from the specific ink particles – it was not found in the general background of the surface of the parchment.

A different approach was to claim that the very well researched history of the use of anatase was completely wrong and that really it had been used in Medieval inks. Painter went to considerable lengths to demonstrate that temperatures of 700° to 900°C (temperatures reached in ordinary bonfires) were attainable by the Medieval craftsmen, and that somehow this meant that anatase was being prepared in Medieval Europe. Olin attempted to show that anatase could be inadvertently produced when attempting to make iron gall ink from the clay mineral illmenite. Washburn (1995, p.xxii) implied that these experiments were then an unpublished discovery. But in fact they had been described in the published preprints of a conference (Olin and Towe, 1976), and, more germanely, the products of these experiments had already been studied in some detail and the results published by Towe (1990) (see Figure 13.26). This showed that Olin's attempts had separated anatase, but that it was morphologically quite different from that produced commercially and found in the ink of the Vinland Map (Towe, 2004). The arguments over the morphology and XRD patterns of the various forms of anatase prepared by Olin as part of a putative process to make iron gall ink are rather arcane as the ink on the map is not an iron gall ink at all.

Washburn (1995, p. xxvi) discussed comments between Ardell Abrahamson, described as an independent researcher, and Towe in which the former drew attention to illustrations of samples of natural anatase that were free of clay, apparently similar to those observed by McCrone on the Vinland Map ink. These were published in a standard scientific text on clay minerals (Weaver, 1976). However, it was not made clear by Abrahamson or Washburn that the original caption to Weaver's illustration specifically stated that the illustrated samples had been magnetically separated from their clay matrix. The XRD pattern for the anatase produced in Olin's experiments was rather diffuse, as one would expect from a precipitated product, and very different from the sharp pattern obtained for modern commercial anatase and the anatase found in the ink particles on the map.

In more recent papers Olin (2000, 2003; with rebuttals by Towe, 2004) has defended her original claims and pointed out that Towe's remarks on the morphology of the anatase particles are invalid because no one has defined the shape of anatase particles in Medieval pigments. As no one has found any particles of Medieval anatase to define, this is likely to remain true forever.

And thus the acrimonious debate rolls on.

14

The patination of copper and its alloys

Decay demonstrates and secures antiquity.

Lowenthal (1988, p. 252)

This chapter deals with patination on copper alloy artefacts. The subject merits a whole chapter because not only is natural patination replicated on forgeries, but the patina has long been regarded as an embellishment in its own right. The chapter includes sections on natural patination, perceptions of surface treatments in antiquity, a history of patination treatments, and the scientific examination of patina.

First it is necessary to distinguish between the terms patination and corrosion. Both describe rather similar processes but there is the definite sense of patination being attractive but corrosion being destructive. Thus the Oxford Dictionary defines patina as the 'incrustation on the surface of old bronze, esteemed as ornament', whereas to corrode is to 'wear away, destroy gradually', and the results of this are the corrosion products. There is also the sense that the natural chemical processes taking place on the copper alloy over the years are corrosion, even though the more attractive results of this are termed the patina, but deliberate chemical treatments are almost invariably termed patination processes.

Natural patination

Sources: Lewin and Alexander (1967, 1968); Weil (1977); Cronyn (1990, pp. 166–237); Scott and Podany (1990); Drayman-Weisser (ed) (1992); Scott (1992, 2002); Sherwood (1992); McNeil and Selwyn (2001); Selwyn (2004, pp. 51–72).

In most naturally corroded metals there are two distinct layers (Figures 14.1 and 14.2): the actual mineralised surface, and above and, sometimes, below, the accumulations of minerals formed as the corrosion works ever deeper into the metal (Figure 14.3). In the long, slow natural corrosion process minor phase and structural differences in the metal assume great importance. The corrosion tends to penetrate into the metal along the boundaries between the grains of metal where the atoms are more disordered and thus more strained and energetically unstable. This creates an interdigitated boundary between the corrosion products and the metal as the chemical attack works deeper into the metal. Dissolved salts can be electrolytically transported to the surface, where they can be deposited, leading to a build-up of quite substantial deposits of copper minerals. These form the corrosion layer on top of the mineralised surface, and it is this layer which the conservator will endeavour to remove to reveal the surface beneath.

In an oxidising environment with some moisture present – the usual conditions prevailing over most of the planet – copper and its alloys oxidise at the surface. Usually, the first mineral to form is a layer of the deep red mineral cuprite, Cu_2O (Scott, 1997; 2002, pp. 85–88), and the presence of a firmly adhering cuprite layer (Figure 14.4) is the hallmark of a genuine, naturally developed patina that is difficult to replicate artificially. The black oxide of copper, tenorite (CuO) is not usually encountered unless the bronze has been strongly heated (Scott, 1997; 2002, pp. 95–96). Many of the chemical treatments that give attractive brown–black patinas comprise a mixture of cuprite and tenorite (see pp. 354, 359), and can thus be distinguished from a natural patina. The cuprite layer is liable to attack from such acidic ions as are in the vicinity, the most common of which include carbonates, chlorides and sulphates.

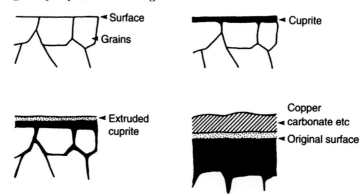

Figure 14.1   Idealised section through a corroding bronze. At the surface, cuprite forms and chemical reaction proceeds preferably down the more energetic grain boundaries, sometimes isolating the remaining metal in grains near to the surface as islands. The cuprite thus formed is susceptible to attack by acidic ions to form more stable corrosion products, typically hydroxycarbonates, -chlorides or, increasingly prevalent, -sulphates. The forming corrosion minerals occupy a larger volume than does the metal and thus extrude through the surface patination layer to build up as corrosion deposits. (Courtesy Cronyn, 1990)

Figure 14.2   Idealised taper section polished on the surface of a naturally patinated bronze exposing the metal in the centre with evidence of intergranular corrosion. There is an uneven annulus made up of cuprite on the inside with some islands of metal, surrounded by corrosion products. (Courtesy T. Simpson)

Figure 14.3   Metallographic section through the Sutton Hoo bronze cauldron. A green malachite layer lies on a thick layer of red cuprite, which penetrates the boundaries of the annealed and twinned grains (© British Museum)

The carbonates derive from carbon dioxide dissolved either in atmospheric moisture or in groundwater, causing the formation of a hydroxycarbonate, either the familiar green malachite, $Cu_2(OH)_2CO_3$, or more rarely the blue azurite, $Cu(OH)_2(CO_3)_2$. The hydroxycarbonates mainly form in buried environments and are only rarely encountered as

a component of recent above-ground copper alloy corrosion products (Meakin *et al.*, 1992; Selwyn *et al.*, 1996).

In saline conditions either in the ground or in the atmosphere near to the sea, chlorides are the principal agents, leading to the formation of hydroxychlorides, principally the basic copper chloride, which is a green mineral occurring in two forms, atacamite, alpha $Cu_2(OH)_3Cl$ and paratacamite, beta $Cu_2(OH)_3Cl$.

One particularly destructive form of chloride-based corrosion is the so-called bronze disease (Figure 14.5). Small quantities of nantokite, cuprous chloride (CuCl), can form beneath the hard coherent surface patina directly against the metal. Under reducing conditions the nantokite is only very slowly converted to cuprite, which builds up as a relatively thick layer protecting the remaining nantokite from oxygen and moisture. After excavation it often happens that the cuprite layer dries and cracks, exposing the nantokite to moisture and air, and so causing it to oxidise. The products are powdery masses of light-blue paratacamite and hydrochloric acid, which continue the attack on the copper. The paratacamite occupies a greater volume than the nantokite and

Figure 14.4 Base of a Medieval Islamic cast brass pot. Some of the green atacamite corrosion has become detached, revealing the cuprite of the original surface. (Courtesy John Heffron/British Museum)

the resultant expansion causes the protective layer to be further disrupted.

Doubts were once expressed whether paratacamite formed naturally, and thus its presence in the patina of a bronze cast doubt upon the latter's authenticity. Conversely, Lewin (1973) stated that copper alloys in a low-chloride environment should develop a patina comprised entirely of paratacamite. He believed that atacamite would only form under conditions of very high chloride concentration, and thus bronzes with an atacamite patina should also be heavily mineralised. He even stated that 'if the bulk of the patina contains detectable proportions of atacamite [with or without paratacamite], and if the object is not extensively and deeply corroded then the probability is great that the patina is false'. This initially caused confusion (see p. 167), but has been conclusively refuted by Scott (2002, pp. 131–133).

Years of X-ray diffraction (XRD) determination of corrosion products have shown that atacamite is the usual form of natural hydroxychloride to form on buried bronzes, but that paratacamite is also regularly encountered (Giangrande, 1987; Selwyn *et al.*, 1996). The theoretical work of Pollard *et al.* (1989, 1992) has demonstrated that the energy requirements for the formation of the two forms are very similar, and thus both would be expected to occur.

In modern polluted urban atmospheres the oxides of sulphur are the most active reagents, leading to the formation of hydroxysulphates, typically brochantite, $Cu_4(SO_4)(OH)_6$, or antlerite, $Cu_3(SO_4)(OH)_4$, and more rarely, posnjakite, $Cu_4(SO_4)(OH)_6.H_2O$. The sulphate minerals are indistinguishable from malachite by eye, and the usual green patina mineral on a bronze in an outdoor urban environment is in fact likely to be a hydroxysulphate (Scott, 2002, pp. 147–150).

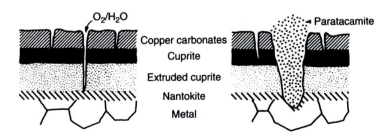

Figure 14.5 Idealised section through a corroding bronze suffering from 'bronze disease'. The nantokite remains passive while protected from oxidation. Once oxygen and moisture have penetrated the cuprite, the nantokite will oxidise to paratacamite causing it to expand, further breaking up the cuprite and in addition more hydrochloric acid is released to further attack the remaining copper. (Courtesy Cronyn, 1990)

The prevalence of hydroxysulphates in modern naturally forming patinas was first established by Vernon and Whitby (1929, 1930), with further work by Graedel (1987a, b), Graedel *et al.* (1987), Sherwood (1992), Lins and Power (1994), Selwyn *et al.* (1996) and Hayez *et al.* (2004). Strandberg *et al.* (1996) reported another copper hydroxysulphate, $Cu_{2.5}(OH)_3SO_4.2H_2O$, developing on the bronze statues in Gothenberg, in the south of Sweden.

Hydroxysulphates have usually been reported only on copper alloys standing exposed in the atmosphere, but the author has encountered brochantite on a Medieval brass recovered from the soil in a British urban environment (Craddock, 1981a). Based on the growing prevalence of reports of sulphates on recently excavated ancient bronzes, Fjaestad *et al.* (1997) have suggested that buried copper alloy antiquities with hitherto stable hydroxycarbonate or chloride patinas may be in the process of re-patination in the ground to hydroxysulphates. This is as a consequence of the pollution of the groundwater from an increasingly sulphur dioxide-laden atmosphere (see also Scott, 2002, p. 27). Examination of the huge Medieval bronze statue of the Buddha at Kamakura in Japan has shown that inside some of the grains of brochantite there is malachite, suggesting the patina has changed there also (Scott, 2002, p. 160).

There are also changes in patina as a result of restoration and/or conservation treatments involving a final lacquering or waxing to enhance and protect the bronze. All too often, especially on outdoor bronzes, interaction between the organic compounds and the copper results in fresh corrosion and an appearance at variance with the original or the intended restored appearance (Scott, 2002, pp. 299–305). Schrenk (1994) examined the recent corrosion products on some of the Benin bronzes in the National Museum of African Art in Washington, and found that the pieces, which had come to America via a variety of European private collections, now showed the presence of complex copper and zinc palmitic, stearic and oleic salts, which were the result of the various surface treatments. Thus Burmester and Koller (1987) recommended analysis for inorganic and organic compounds when investigating patinas, to pick up evidence both of natural corrosion and of subsequent treatment after conservation/restoration. The presence of some of the distinctive organometallic compounds in a suspect piece could provide some evidence concerning its history.

Occasionally the presence of basic hydroxynitrate, gerhardite ($Cu_2(NO_3)(OH)_3$), has been reported on free-standing copper alloys in urban environments (Hughes, 1993; Scott, 2002, pp. 250–251), most notably the Statue of Liberty, where the previously stable brochantite patina is being converted to gerhardite by the acidic environment of New York (Scott, 2002, p. 57). A related basic hydrated copper nitrate, $Cu_2(NO_3)_2(OH)_2$, was reported by Gettens (1970, p. 63) on bronze vessels excavated from one of the Royal Tombs at Gordion, in Anatolia. Brochantite was also found on the bronzes, Gettens considering that it probably originated from the food offerings that the bronze vessels would have originally contained.

These observations are of some significance as the presence of sulphates or nitrates in a copper patina is still usually taken as evidence of artificial patination. Long-term changes in the environment, both in the atmosphere and in the ground, may mean that a broader range of naturally occurring minerals will be encountered in the future.

Bronzes with a high tin content sometimes develop separate corrosion layers within the patina, composed almost entirely of the tin mineral cassiterite, SnO_2 (Gettens, 1949, 1970). (For the patination of tin and its alloys see Chapter 7, p. 153.)

Natural black patinas

Black oxide patinas

Sources: Collins (1934); Chase (1977); Chase and Franklin (1979); Meeks (1988b, 1993); Zhu Shoukang and He Tangkun (1993).

High-tin bronzes are sometimes found with a fine and hard coherent black patina. Such patinas have been particularly associated with ancient Chinese bronze mirrors, but they are a feature of ancient high-tin bronzes generally, and are regularly found on Roman mirrors for example (Meeks, 1988b, 1993). There has been much debate whether the black patinas found on the Chinese mirrors are natural or artificial (Collins, 1934; Chase, 1977). They seem to be comprised mainly of cassiterite with some silica. Zhu Shoukang and He Tangkun (1993) noted that the black patina was prevalent on mirrors from the south of China and suggested the formation of this patina was due to burial in oxidising conditions in the wet acidic soils that are prevalent there (they also informed the author that some black patinated belongs had actually been recovered from waterlogged tombs). On some high-tin bronze artefacts the black layer has formed continuously over broken areas, strongly suggesting that these patinas developed after the artefacts had been damaged and discarded, and are likely to be natural (Meeks, 1988b, 1993).

The two life-size Greek bronze statues found on the seabed off Riace in Sicily also have black patinas that have been the subject of detailed study and some debate as to whether they are natural or deliberate. There is a hard, black, coherent patina immediately against the metal surface and over this was a more diffuse layer of mixed hydroxy-copper salts containing some entrapped grains of sand (Garbassi and Mello, 1984; Mello *et al.*, 1984). The hard patina contains magnesium tin hydroxide, $MgSn(OH)_6$, the mineral $(Cu, Fe, Mn)Sn(OH)_6$, together with smaller amounts of alpha-quartz, cassiterite, cuprite and some black copper sulphide.

Patina on objects from maritime environments is often rich in magnesium salts, and this patina would seem to be the tin-rich magnesium analogy for the cassiterite patinas found on the Chinese mirrors associated with fresh water.

Black (and golden) sulphide patinas
Sources: MacLeod (1991); McNeil and Little (1992); Scott (2002, pp. 227–230).

In waterlogged anaerobic conditions copper sulphides can also form, due to the action of sulphur-fixing micro-organisms. Typically these take the form of hard, thin, coherent layers of cupric sulphide, Cu_2S. They may be black, or more rarely a golden copper–iron sulphide (Duncan and Ganiaris, 1987; Schweizer, 1994b; Scott 2002, p. 229). The golden patinas are frequently mistaken for the original bronze surface or even evidence of a deliberate 'pseudo gilding' technique (Oddy and Meeks, 1981).

It has also been claimed that the black sulphidic patinas are the result of deliberate patination, but it is striking that so many of the classical bronzes so patinated seem to have come from the sea. Eggert (1994) in his examination of the patinas occurring on many of the bronzes from a Roman wreck discovered off Tunisia in the early twentieth century, found it was almost impossible to tell whether they had been artificially created or due to the marine environment in which they had lain. If these black sulphidic patinas were indeed artificial then it is an extraordinary coincidence that so many and diverse bronzes so treated happened to be together on the vessel. In reality the only thing they had in common was their burial environment.

The thin sulphidic layer on the Riace bronzes (see above) was tentatively interpreted by Mello *et al.* (1984) and others as being an original artificial black patina overlain by a corrosion layer that had developed while the statues lay on the seabed. However, the authors also noted that sulphidic patinas were a feature of bronzes buried for long periods under water and admitted the possibility that the entire surface mineralisation was the result of natural corrosion (Scott 2002, pp. 328–329).

A history of patination techniques

Sources: Barnard (1961); Lewin and Alexander (1967, 1968); Hughes and Rowe (1982); Born (1990, 1993); Craddock (1992); Hughes (1992, 1993); Riederer (1992); Craddock and Giumlia Mair (1993a); Weil (1977, 1996); Scott (2002, pp. 322–351).

The deliberate patination of copper alloy artworks is intimately bound up with the changing aesthetics and perceptions of art historians and collectors. In the Renaissance it was commonly believed that classical bronzes were originally black or, at least, dark in color. Furthermore, some collectors in the Age of Enlightenment were not above giving their bronzes the surface appearance that they thought they would have had originally. Thus, for example, most of the classical bronzes from the collection of Richard Payne Knight have clearly been artificially darkened (Figure 14.6). His collection, numbering some hundreds of items, subsequently passed to the British Museum, where they can now be readily distinguished by their dark hues. Payne Knight never admitted to treating his bronzes, but examination of one of these, a small statuette of Herakles, BM GR Reg. 1824, 4–46, 13, showed that the surface had been lacquered. Beneath this was a thin layer of dark patina that did not give a recognisable XRD pattern. The lacquer was itself dark but with no evidence of inorganic pigments within it.

Similarly, the famous French collector, Jean-Jacques Compte de Caylus, was adamant that the hoard of Roman bronzes from Châlon-sur-Saone (now in the Bibliothèque Nationale in Paris) which he acquired in 1764 immediately after their discovery, came from the ground together with the thick black lacquer that still covers them (Hill, 1969; fn 25). In reality it is inconceivable that an organic lacquer could have survived over a thousand years of burial. If he was not directly responsible, someone else must have quickly embellished the bronzes after their discovery with the finish that would be acceptable to the great man!

Figure 14.6 Two genuine classical bronzes. The votive hand on the left, BM GR Reg. 1824, 4-1, 41, was given an artificial patination by Richard Payne Knight. The statuette of Athene on the right, BM GR Reg. 1920, 2-18, 1, retains its natural patina. (A. Milton/British Museum)

The well-known large bronze Hellenistic statue of the Praying Boy, now in the Berlin Museum, has been much restored and repaired through the centuries, acquiring a thick coat of black varnish in the eighteenth century (Rohnstock, 1998). The collection of over 700 ancient (and forged) bronzes formed in the late eighteenth century by Prince Christian zu Waldbeck (1744–98), now in the Württemberg Landes Museum, are all still covered by the dark-green lacquer the Prince thought appropriate. Cahn (1970) remarked 'the interest of the collection consists mainly in its date, there one could study how bronzes were treated before 1800; what an early forgery looks like; how a good bronze acquires a fake appearance through irreverent handling – adjusting, restoring, repatinating'.

Savage (1976, p. 81) noted that genuine Renaissance bronzes that had never been patinated were still being treated in the late nineteenth century for collectors who should have known better, and the Renaissance bronzes in the Capodimonte Museum, Naples have been coated with an opaque black layer for many years (Bewer, reported in Scott 2002, p. 330).

Note that some conservation treatments can result in surface mineralisation. For example, the sodium sesquicarbonate treatment of bronzes which was in use from the 1920s, has sometimes resulted in the deposition of light blue–green flaky deposits of copper hydroxycarbonates, as well as chalconatronite, $Na_2Cu(CO_3)_2.3H_2O$ (Horie, and Vint 1982). The latter mineral has very occasionally been identified as a corrosion product on some Egyptian bronzes (Gettens and Frondel, 1955) but does not develop on bronzes under normal burial conditions (Pollard et al., 1990). Bronzes that had been stripped of their original patination by electrochemical means were often repatinated (Organ, 1970, in Discussion, p. 96). Plenderleith (1956, p. 251) recommended that if the stripped bronzes had a silver inlay they should be boiled in distilled water to darken their surfaces, forming a thin layer of tenorite.

Evidence for the original appearance of classical bronzes

By the nineteenth century, opinion began to swing towards the idea that bronzes had originally just been polished, displaying only the color of the bronze itself (Reuterswärd, 1960). Thus Westmancott in 1854 in a wide-ranging paper on the coloring of statues, noted that there was considerable evidence for the taking of plaster casts of statues in antiquity (see Chapter 4, p. 64), which in turn would have necessitated releasing agents of oil or bitumen, thereby ruining a painted or patinated surface. He backed up this perfectly reasonable point with the unassailable moral argument that naked statuary was not originally naturalistically painted, for, 'Would any father of a family willingly take his wife and daughters into a gallery so peopled?'

In the twentieth century this view had become predominant (Pernice, 1910a, b; Richter, 1915; Kluge and Lehmann-Hartleben, 1927), and remains so (Hill, 1969; Weil, 1977; Craddock, 1992; Craddock and Giumlia Mair, 1993a), with Born (1985a, b; 1990; 1993) and Born et al., 1991) as the most prominent proponents of the opinion that ancient bronzes were often deliberately patinated and colored.

Many of the statuary bronzes have details inlaid with other metals. The eyes are often inlaid with silver and the lips and nipples with red copper. The inlays and body are now usually covered by a uniform green

Figure 14.7 Wall painting from Pompeii, showing street scene with bronze statuary. The latter are bronze colored, not patinated. (Courtesy Craddock and Giumlia-Mair, 1993a)

patina, but surely the metallic inlays were intended to contrast with the golden bronze of the face and body.

Surviving wall paintings that depict bronze statuary in outdoor locations show the metal as being gold or brown in color, never green (Figure 14.7).

The few ancient descriptions of copper and bronze used in architecture (capitals, columns, doors, etc.) all describe them as being ruddy, shining or golden, never dark or patinated. One could note here the discussion in Plutarch's *Moralia* (Richter, 1915, pp. xxix–xxx; Craddock and Giumlia Mair, 1993a; Babbitt, 1936, V 395) concerning the nature of metal corrosion. This was sparked off by a group of visitors to Delphi coming upon the bronze statues of the sea captains, which were collectively one of the best-known art works at the sanctuary. The statues apparently showed a blue–green patina and the visitors were unfamiliar with such a surface appearance on bronze statuary.

Finally, a number of surviving temple accounts, mainly from Egypt of the Graeco-Roman era, record payments made to workmen for the regular cleaning of the bronzes, usually with oil (Johnson,

1936), and inscriptions on statues to the effect that they were to be kept bright and rust-free (Pernice, 1910a). Similar accounts are recorded at least until the eleventh century for the annual cleaning and polishing of the bronze doors of some major churches (Craddock and Giumlia Mair, 1993a). As a counter to this, one of Born's strongest arguments against the general polishing of bronze statuary is the unabraded condition of the surfaces of so many of the surviving classical bronzes.

The consensus of this evidence is that the surfaces of the bronzes were kept clean and unpatinated. However, it is not quite as simple as that. Plutarch, in the story mentioned above, has his discussants say at one point that statues were usually treated with oil, and this produced some effect beyond just cleaning, suggesting that the oil spread the rust or patina. Pliny, in his *Natural History* (34.95; Rackham, 1952, p. 199), stated that the bronze alloy known as Capuan, which contained an addition of about 9% of lead, had the same color as that produced by oil and sun on an ordinary bronze (the English edition has the Latin *sel*, i.e. salt, rather than the *sol* that is found in the other versions, but 'sun' makes more sense). The leaded bronze would appear rather darker and greyer compared to ordinary bronze. Thus it would seem that the treatment with oil produced a perceptible effect beyond simply cleaning. It is common experience that oiled metalwork tends to hold dirt in the minute holes and scratches in the surface, and thus appears dark. Also, the oiled bronzes would begin to oxidise giving a dark red or brown patina, formed principally of cuprite but regular cleaning would prevent the formation of the various green copper hydroxy-salts.

Thus we may envisage, but probably never know, that originally much of the art bronzework produced in classical antiquity and beyond had a thin, dark patina over the surface which was still basically metallic and shiny. Born has argued for a more comprehensive dark chemical patination, with black minerals such as copper sulphide having been deliberately induced to cover much of the surface (see p. 353).

In other early cultures there is also little evidence for the deliberate chemical patination of metalwork. There is one exception, the specialised class of copper alloys, containing small amounts of precious metals, inlaid with precious metals and then patinated. The *Corinthium aes* of antiquity and the Japanese *shakudo* alloys of more recent times, are two familiar examples of this sophisticated technique (Craddock and Giumlia Mair, 1993b; Giumlia Mair and Craddock, 1993).

The later surface treatments of Chinese copper alloy artwork was mainly by lacquering (Kerr, 1990, p. 70; Cowell *et al.*, 2003) except where an antique effect was required, for which chemical patination was carried out.

Artificial patination

Historical

Patination in the East

The earliest attempts to imitate the natural green patination found on ancient bronzes by artificial patination occurred in China. There, the appreciation and collection of ancient bronzes, excavated from the graves of the Shang and subsequent dynasties, began as early as the Song dynasty at the end of the first millennium AD (Kerr, 1990, pp. 14–19; Jones (ed), 1990, pp. 258–259; Clunas, 1992).

Bronze patinas were much valued, as the Jesuit, Matteo Ricci, noted in the sixteenth century AD:

> In this kingdom they make much of antique things, and yet they have no statues nor medals, but rather many vases of bronze, which are highly valued, and they desire them with a certain particular corrosion, without which they are worth nothing. . . . they are greatly given to forging antique things, with great artifice and ingenuity, so that those who do not know enough can spend great sums of money on things which are then worth nothing.
>
> Quoted in Clunas (1992)

The appearance and formation of the various natural patinas was keenly debated. The Chinese scholar Zhao Xigu wrote in the thirteenth century AD that:

> bronze vessels that have been interred under the earth for a thousand years appear pure green the color of kingfisher feathers . . . those that have been immersed in water a thousand years are pure emerald in color with a jade-like lustre. Those that have not been immersed as long as a thousand years are emerald green but lack the lustre . . . those that have been transmitted down from antiquity, not under water or earth but through the hands of men, have the color of purple cloth and a red mottling like sand, which protrudes when excessive, and looks like first-quality cinnabar. When boiled in a pan of hot water the mottling becomes more pronounced.
>
> Kerr (1990, p. 70)

These patinas were imitated on the bronze copies that were already being produced in quantity. From the later Song and Ming dynasties there survive

many quite detailed recipes for the production of attractive and superficially convincing simulations of natural green patinas (Barnard, 1961, pp. 199–217; Kerr, 1990, p. 70–71).

A good later description is given from Gao Lian's *Zun sheng ba jian* published in 1591:

> After they [the bronze vessels] are cast they are scraped and polished until they are clean and shining; where the décor has not cast clearly it is engraved by tools. Then the vessel is soaked for a time in a mixture of morning-fresh well-water, clay, and alumina, it is taken out and baked, again immersed, and again baked. This is done three times and is termed 'making the basic color'. When the vessel is dry a solution of sal ammoniac, blue vitriol, halites [rock salt, salt evaporated from sea water], borax, and 'gold-thread- alumina' [these all being in the form of powder] in green brine [a concentrated solution] is applied by a clean brush two or three times and after one or two days is washed away; again dried and again washed. The whole process is in adjusting the surface color and the amount of washing may have to be done three or five times before it is settled. Next an oven is dug into the earth, red-hot charcoal is heaped in it and strong vinegar is sprinkled onto it; the bronze vessels are placed inside and still more vinegar is thrown over them and they are completely covered with earth and left buried for three days. When taken out and examined they are all found to have grown the colors of ancient patina mould; wax is rubbed over them. When the color is required to be deepened, they are smoked in burning bamboo leaves. There are two ways, by heat or by cold, in which other color details are added to the surface color; both employ clear gum resin which has exhausted its extreme astringent taste, compounded with melted white wax. For blue-green color, azurite is put in the wax; for green, his-chih-lu [malachite?] is used; for red, cinnabar is used [recalling the sleeve weight, Fig 14.8]. Wax is used most in the heat method; for the cold method equal quantities of wax and gum resin are used; with these blended as required they make the added color details. For colored protrusions from the surface they make small mounds of salt, metal filings, and cinnabar. The mercury color is made by an application of mercury and tin onto the sides and edges of the vessels, when covered with wax the color is hidden and dulled a little in order to dupe the collector. When rubbed in the hands a stench arises which cannot be got rid of even by washing. Sometimes after this process is completed they bury the vessel in the ground for a year or two; it seems then to have archaic characteristics.
>
> Barnard (1961, pp. 205–208)

Barnard (1968) also described some of the patination techniques used on present day forgeries of ancient Chinese bronzes.

A Song sleeve weight (Figure 14.8; NB the wrong illustration was used in Jones (ed), 1990, Figure 285, p. 258) provides a good example of the application of minerals to the surface. This is a leaded bronze in the style of the Han Dynasty, about 1000 years earlier. It has a very thin, brown patina of cuprite all over, with nodules of green and red minerals stuck to the surface. The green is crushed malachite mineral and the red is cinnabar, mercuric sulphide. Some defects in the casting have been plugged with this material, beneath which is a lead/mercury amalgam, recalling the more familiar tin/mercury amalgams widely used in Chinese patination processes. The lead/mercury amalgam is probably residual from a preliminary rubdown over the bronze surface. On the underside of the bronze there are eruptions of cerussite, hydrated lead carbonate

Figure 14.8 Chinese sleeve weight dating to the Late Song period, c. 1200 AD, BM OA Reg. 1894, 1-8, 8. The green patches are of malachite that have been stuck to the surface. (Courtesy A. Milton/British Museum)

$(Pb_3(CO_3)_2(OH)_2)$, which is almost certainly a relatively recent natural corrosion product.

Patination in the West

The Medieval craftsman-cleric, Theophilus, referred to the technique of *émail brun*, coating the bronze with linseed oil and then heating to give a deep brown or black patina (Hawthorne and Smith, 1963, pp. 147–148). Renaissance and Baroque bronzes were usually lacquered, the favoured colors being a dark red, brown or occasionally green. Some of these Renaissance finishes were analysed by Stone *et al.* (1990), who found evidence of drying oils and turpentine. Inevitably many of the pieces had been retreated, making it difficult to be sure of the original appearance (see p. 354, Savage, 1976, p. 81). At that time chemical patination was largely reserved for bronze forgeries. Stories of how freshly made bronze forgeries were to be buried in a dunghill or exposed for months on a workshop roof seem apocryphal and these techniques would be unlikely to work.

Pomponio Gaurico in 1504 (Chastel and Klein (eds), 1969) described how green patinas, imitating natural patinas, were produced with salted vinegar or by smoking the bronze above a fire of damp hay. Chemical techniques were sometimes used: a deep red patina could be made by oxidising the surface by heat to form a thin red layer of cuprite, coating with lacquer and rubbing it with beeswax or oil. Other polychrome effects simulating the patinated and worn surfaces of ancient bronzes could be painted on. Some of the eighteenth- and early nineteenth-century forgeries of ancient bronzes, coming from Italy, and now in the British Museum, have relatively simple patinas. For example, a bronze mirror, purporting to be South Italian Greek (BM GR Reg. 1814, 7-4, 966) from the Townley Collection, originally acquired in Italy in the eighteenth century, was found to have a coat of lacquer containing crushed malachite. Another mirror, purporting to be Etruscan, from the Townley collection (BM GR Reg. 1814, 7-4, 709), was found to have patches of malachite and azurite minerals beneath a coat of dark lacquer.

Thus in both Orient and Occident chemical patination was largely limited to the imitation of natural patinas until the early nineteenth century, when a much wider palette was developed.

Production of patinas in the nineteenth century

It is important to be aware of the standard commercial techniques of more recent times in order that their traces can be recognised when encountered on putative antiquities. Note that some of the recipes for chemical patination specifically warn that a particular treatment will not be immediately permanent, but will only 'take' after several months or even years, and should be protected by lacquer in the interim (CDA, 1966, p. 22, for example). This usually refers to treatments involving acidic salts where the deposition of the cation releases an acid, which can then slowly 'bite' into the surface down the grain boundaries. Such an active patina, probably with a pH well away from neutral, is at least potentially recognisable on a suspect bronze for some years after its application. Thereafter, the developing patina may well begin to resemble a fully natural patina, or the object may corrode in a manner similar to an excavated archaeological bronze (see p. 364).

Through the nineteenth century an ever-widening range of patination techniques were introduced. Although there were undoubtedly many processes, few were recorded or assessed at the time. Among the better contemporary accounts are those of Buchner (1891), Hiorns (1892) and Spon (1895). This was partly in response to the prevailing taste for color and ornamentation (Gage, 1993). The combination of existing and evolving craft skills with new materials and new methods produced an extraordinary range of colors and textures. Paris was in the forefront of these developments with its huge community of artist–craftsmen. It is estimated that by mid century in Paris over 6000 persons were employed in the art-bronze foundries alone (Savage, 1968, p. 227). However, it was in Berlin that the scientific study of natural and artificial corrosion and patination took place at institutions such as the then newly inaugurated Rathgen Labor, attached to the Staatliche Museum (Otto, 1979).

Hiorns (1892, p. 63) and Lacombe (1910) both ascribed the introduction of chemically induced patina on art metalwork to the Parisian bronze founder, Lafleur, who from about 1828 began to use brown patinations, produced by chemicals typically applied in a poultice. Later the vogue for Japanese metalwork, much of it patinated, encouraged the study and emulation of their patination methods (Roberts Austen, 1888; Gowland, 1894). Other techniques that were already practised on a small scale such as torching, smoking and lacquering continued and were expanded in their range and, to a degree, industrialised along with the new technique of electroplating.

As well as the semi-industrialised processes specially formulated to be reliable and give consistent patinas, there were also the myriad recipes of the small craftsmen. The chemicals could be applied by brush, sponge, swab or spray, or by soaking them in a poultice. Alternatively, the object could be immersed in a bath of the chemical solutions or merely exposed to their vapours. Each craftsman apparently had his own favoured and secret formulations; this was to some degree necessitated by the individual circumstances of each workshop, including things as mundane as the purity of the available water supply, which, no doubt, each smith fondly believed gave a distinctive and superior result. Most were not written down, and many of those that were published (see Hughes and Rowe, 1982, pp. 361–372 and Weil, 1977 for extensive bibliographies) are, in Weil's words, 'simple recipes . . . with ingredients often described in arcane or imprecise fashion-Explanations of the chemistry when given are usually incorrect!'. Fishlock (1962, p. 9) concurred, noting that 'whilst a great many formulae have been published, it is not unusual to find the technique practised with all the hocus pocus of a secret rite' and again, 'some contain ingredients whose only practical purpose can be to complicate the formula and bedevil the analysis'. The latter point is worth bearing in mind in the scientific examination of treated surfaces.

The most detailed and clearest nineteenth-century English account of chemical patination techniques is that of Arthur Hiorns (1892), in which very many recipes were tried and not a few found wanting.

In all serious descriptions of surface treatments of both the nineteenth and twentieth centuries, as well as those in the extant recipes from Japan, the importance of pre-treatment to obtain the required surface texture followed by careful cleaning is much stressed. The surfaces were first subjected to a variety of treatments – matting, sand blasting, acid etching and scratch-brushing through to fine polishing – depending on the texture required. They would then be carefully cleaned with an alkaline de-greasing chemical in aqueous solution followed by repeated washing in clean water to remove all traces of grease. It was common practice in many nineteenth-century surface treatments to electroplate the surface to be patinated, irrespective of the material; the surface of the fresh electroplate was clean and the texture was especially receptive to chemical treatment. In addition, the electroplated surface was uniform over the entirety of the object, whereas the original surface would have had many variations in degrees of strain from differential working, and heating from soldering operations, etc., as well as compositional differences. All of these factors could affect the response to the patination treatment. Conversely, if a variegated surface was required then this could be obtained by using techniques differentially, or by using a technique such as torching (Figure 14.9).

Chemical patination falls into two overall types, bronzing to produce a dark-brown 'antique' appearance, or treatments to produce the blue/green appearance of an excavated bronze (see Table 14.1).

Bronzing

The principal commercial publications on coloring refer to all chemical treatments aimed at producing a dark copper alloy finish as *bronzing*.

A wide range of methods were employed, including lacquering, heat treatment, dry and wet chemical treatments and metal deposition (see Table 14.1). The majority of the chemical bronzing treatments produced either oxides or sulphides on the underlying copper, both of which were dark. The nineteenth-century oxidation methods, using oxides, sulphates or nitrates, often produced rich brown or black mixtures of cuprite and tenorite. The latter is only rarely encountered in naturally formed patinas (see p. 349).

In the words of Hiorns (1892, p. 98):

Copper articles may be colored easily and safely by heating with certain compounds such as iron oxide. They may be bronzed quickly by immersion in certain acid, alkaline and neutral solutions such as copper sulphate, copper nitrate etc. The coloring will also in these cases depend on the temperature, strength of the solution, and time of exposure or immersion.

Figure 14.9 'Master Patineurs', Pierre and Jean Limet, in their Paris atelier in 1938, torching a bronze to give a variegated oxidation prior to chemical treatment. (Courtesy Hoffman, 1939)

Table 14.1 Traditional nineteenth-century copper-alloy patination techniques.

Technique	Black/Brown 'Bronzing'		Blue/Green	
Lacquer	Natural lacquers		Natural lacquers	
Heat	Baking/torching	then lacquered	Baking/torching	to create cuprite substrate
Metal Deposition	Finely divided metal + oxides	Pt, Ag, As, Sb		
Chemical: Dry	Oxides	Cu salts		
	Florentine	Fe oxides/graphite		
Chemical: Wet	Oxides	Soln. Cu salts	Carbonates	
	Sulphides	Soln. NH$_4$, Ba, K	Acetates	
			Chlorides	
Electrolytic Deposition	Metals	Cu, Au, Ag + Alloys		
	Substrate layer	For chemical treatment	Substrate layer	For chemical treatment

Typical 'dry' methods

The chemicals could be painted or swabbed onto the prepared surface and gently heated to temperatures in the region of 100° to 200°C. The rich brown color, known as Florentine brown, could be obtained by applying an aqueous paste of ferric oxide (Fe_2O_3) and graphite, and then heating. The copper or brass oxidised, and the deep red of the cuprite formed was tempered by the brown of the ferric oxide and the grey/black of the graphite. Good results could also be obtained by using an aqueous suspension of insoluble copper and iron salts followed by heating.

The freshly patinated surfaces would then be protected and enhanced by lacquering. Even this relatively simple technology became more elaborate through the nineteenth century. A good description of lacquering techniques in the 1870s is given by Field and Bonney (1925, p.xix). The lacquer was produced by grinding fine inorganic pigments in poppy oil and mixing with bronze powders and special varnishes, such as French mission (the natural oleo-resin from the *Pinnus maritina* tree, containing about 15% of essential oils and 70–80% of rosin). This was applied in five or six separate coats with polishing between coats, such that the finished work piece had the appearance of solid bronze.

Typical 'wet' methods

The article to be treated was brushed, sponged, swabbed or immersed in a solution of the oxidising chemicals and then left to dry. This resulted in a more rapid, uniform, but thinner deposit than that obtained with the dry methods, but the patina could be built up by repeated application. The solutions used were normally extremely dilute, and made acidic, if necessary, with acetic acid. Hiorns (1892, p. 116) instructed that commercial vinegar, sold for culinary use, was not to be used as it was frequently adulterated with hydrochloric and sulphuric acids! Ammonium and/or tartrate salts were commonly employed as buffering agents to control the pH, and copper and iron salts, especially the sulphates, were often part of the recipes. After immersion the patinated metal could be further treated by heating.

For bronzing brass, repeated immersion in warm aqueous solutions containing arsenic or antimony salts and ammonium sulphide was much favoured (the resulting sulphidic patina was sometimes referred to as Bronze Barbédienne). Note that the presence of arsenic in a copper alloy is often taken as an indicator of antiquity. Its presence in the patina could cause confusion if only the uncleaned surface were analysed. Alternatively, a thin paste containing red antimony sulphide, ferric oxide and ammonium sulphide could be applied to the surface and allowed to dry in a warm atmosphere.

More commonly, dark brown or black patinas were produced on art bronzes by treatment with aqueous solutions of soluble sulphides, such as ammonium polysulphide or potassium sulphide (*liver of sulphur*), resulting in the formation of copper sulphides.

Metallic deposition

An excellent, but expensive, dark patina could be produced by treatment with platinum chloride solutions. The platinum was precipitated on the metal surface as a thin amorphous layer, appearing black or deep brown. A nineteenth-century example of this treatment has been found on an eighteenth-century brass sculpture (Bewer and Scott, 1995), described as 'a subtle dark brown over steel-grey colored patina'. (See Smeaton, 1978 for a more general early history of platinum plating and deposition on metal.)

A more common, if not so beautiful effect, was produced using arsenious oxide or antimonous oxide precipitated from an acidic solution, often in conjunction with an iron salt. This gave a dark-grey or grey–brown antique bronzing and was used extensively on brass furniture, door and window fittings.

Heat

Another inexpensive method of bronzing items such as door and window furniture was by heat treatment to produce a finish known latterly in Britain as BMA (bronze metal antique) (Fishlock, 1962; CDA, 1966). The cleaned items were heated in an oven to about 200°C for brasses and up to 350°C for cast bronzes or gun metals, for between 1 and 2 hours, bringing about partial oxidation of the surface with the formation of cuprite. For best results it was recommended that brasses should contain some tin. The color was described by Fishlock as not being very stable and an occasional oiling was recommended as the best preservative, thereby unconsciously echoing the practice used in classical antiquity (see p. 354).

Smoke

The objects could be suspended for several days over a coal fire continually fed with wet straw or green twigs and leaves of evergreen trees such as laurel to produce copious smoke (Hiorns, 1892, p. 223). Fortnum (1877, p. 25) recommended old leather shoes. This was a finishing process for objects that had already been chemically treated. A very different smoking treatment was described by Field and Bonney (1925, pp. 181–182) on unpatinated surfaces. As a preliminary the surface was matted, sand blasted and then scratch-brushed or acid-etched. A coat of slow-drying varnish was applied, and while still tacky, the object was suspended over a smoky fire so that soot particles were retained in the varnish.

Blue/green 'natural' or 'antique' patinas
Hiorns devoted a whole chapter (1892, pp. 166–168) to the production of a green patina in imitation of natural patinas found on ancient bronzes. He stated, correctly, that the natural green patinas were mostly composed of carbonates or chlorides, and that in order to produce convincing patinas these minerals must be formed. The solutions should be very dilute and used cold so that the patinas could develop slowly, otherwise the resulting patina would flake. All of the above observations were quite correct and clearly based on long experience. The realisation that such well-informed instructions were current in the late nineteenth century should give pause to those concerned with authenticity studies.

To produce a natural patina the object was first carefully cleaned and immersed in vinegar. It was then suspended in a sealed earthenware vessel, in the bottom of which was a salt solution through which carbon dioxide gas had been bubbled. After several weeks the surface of the object had all the appearance of a natural patina. A somewhat quicker method was to place the object in a wooden box with a container of water on one side and another holding dilute hydrochloric acid on the other. Marble chips were periodically dropped into the acid, generating carbon dioxide.

This process may be compared with that of Smith (1978), who produced a malachite patina on copper as part of his studies on the carbon and oxygen isotope ratios of malachite patinas. He suspended copper foil in water saturated with a 1:1 air to carbon dioxide mixture at temperatures between 15° and 40°C, the temperatures being dictated by the isotope work which Smith was undertaking rather than the desire to produce a convincing patina. After a week a thin cuprite layer had formed, and thereafter the malachite slowly formed. This was clearly a very slow process, but even so the resulting minerals of the patination were still only very loosely attached

and tended to flake easily compared with the natural patinas formed on antiquities. Geneslay (1937) experimented with alkaline solutions of magnesium and potassium chlorides with sodium carbonate to produce both cuprite and malachite on copper surfaces.

Napier (1852, pp. 89–90) stated that green patinas took a little more time to form than ordinary black or brown patinas but might be produced by standing the object variously in strong solutions of salt or sal ammoniac, or in sugar solutions made acidic with oxalic or acetic acids. He also described a process for giving electroforms the appearance of ancient bronze by suspending them in a box containing bleaching powder.

Hiorns also noted that a better result could be obtained if the object had been pre-treated with potassium sulphide to produce a thin ground layer of copper sulphide. Thus, no matter how visually convincing the resulting patina may have been, some inappropriate minerals, acetates and sulphides may well have been present and these should be easy to detect using XRD or RS.

Fortnum (1877, p. 24) recommended treatment with a stronger solution containing 12 parts common salt with 6 parts potassium bitartrate and 2 parts ammonium chloride in 24 parts water, to which was then added 8 parts copper nitrate. The solution was to be repeatedly washed over the bronze, which was to be kept in a damp place, facilitating slow drying, until the 'true antique effect' was obtained.

The prolonged treatments just described were special procedures with the express purpose of imitating nature as closely as possible, at least visually. More practicable commercial chemical treatments to produce green patinations included lacquering, 'dry' treatments with vinegar, salt and ammonium solutions and wet treatments by immersion in aqueous solution. There were many variations of these treatments with the appropriate aqueous solutions to produce acetates, hydroxychlorides and possibly some hydroxysulphates or hydroxynitrates. The patinating solutions were often applied over a surface that had already received a sulphidic bronzing, thereby to some degree imitating at least the natural color order of green over dark red, if not the mineralogy. The solutions were applied by brush or dipping, and then typically the bronze was left to dry in a warm place for 24 hours or more. The treatment usually had to be repeated several times until an acceptable patina had developed. After the last application had dried, the surface could be finished, for example, by brushing in white wax.

Patination techniques in the twentieth century

The records of the nineteenth-century chemical treatments employed, together with those that were still commercially used in the twentieth century, are well summarised in Beutel (1925), Field and Bonney (1925), Hiscox (ed) (1927), DKI (1936), Krause (1937, [English trans. 1938]), Fishlock (1962), trade publications such as those issued by the CDA (1966), and in the various editions of Canning's invaluable handbook on electroplating and surface treatments (e.g. Canning, 1901, 1989). For the craftsman there are publications such as Maryon (1923, pp. 254–264) and Untracht (1968, pp. 415–419).

For most artistic metalwork, bronze sculpture, etc., the surface was merely lacquered. From the 1980s there was a revival in the use of chemical treatments on small art metalwork (Hughes and Rowe, 1982; Roberts (ed), 1993).

Techniques continued to evolve through the twentieth century, but the taste for ornate polychrome metals declined sharply, these being replaced by bright polished surfaces. This was the age of chrome plating, not of antique bronze. Whilst there was a proliferation of quick commercial surface treatments, the complex and often slow labour-intensive craft treatments declined. The skilled tasks of hand-brushing or swabbing liquids were largely replaced in the twentieth century by spray application or by immersion followed by spinning in a drum to remove the excess centrifugally.

Synthetic organic materials largely supplanted natural materials, and thus the traditional gum-based lacquers were replaced by cellulose-, epoxy- or vinyl-based lacquers such as Incralac. Such gum lacquers as are still commercially available usually contain synthetic materials.

Perhaps the most important innovations have been in the application of electrolytic treatments to the production of surface finishes, with both anodic and cathodic processes being developed. Anodising, which was introduced in the 1920s, notably for aluminium, produced an oxidised surface (Fishlock, 1962; Brace and Sheasby, 1979). It was soon appreciated that the anodised surfaces could be attractively and permanently dyed (reputedly the discovery was accidental, 'involving some freshly anodised panels, a bottle of red ink and a foot-loose cat' (Fishlock, 1962, p. 6). Since then, the process has been extended to other metals, notably copper alloys and titanium.

Bronzing

Heat bronzing to produce the BMA finish was still practised but only on actual alloys of bronze typically containing Cu (90%), Sn (8%) and Zn (2%). Many of the twentieth-century chemical oxidation treatments produce mixtures of cuprite and tenorite on the surface.

Typical 'dry methods'

The existing methods were augmented by techniques employing molten salts, notably mixtures of sodium nitrate and nitrite. The object is placed in the molten salt for about 5 minutes at temperatures of between 350° and 450°C to produce a red–brown patina composed mainly of cuprite.

Typical 'wet methods'

Black and brown patinas

(Note that the whole of the June 1982 issue of *Plating and Surface Finishing* **69,** 6, is devoted to black finishes on metals)

The existing reagents for the chemical blackening of copper alloys by the oxidation of the surface using copper salts were joined by many others. One technique uses a mixture of copper and silver nitrates to produce a fine black patina. A whole range of oxidising agents, including chlorates, chlorites, permanganates, persulphates and dichromates have been introduced as constituents of commercial patinating agents (see Table 14.2). These include alkaline solutions of ammonium persulphate, developed in Germany, as well as alkaline potassium chlorite solutions, which were the basis of the so-called Ebonal C treatment that was developed in America (Fishlock, 1962, p. 203). Other oxidising reagents include ammoniacal copper carbonate and mixed solutions of copper sulphate with either potassium permanganate or sodium dichromate as the oxidising agent (Fishlock, 1962, pp. 203–208).

For copper alloys generally, sulphidic treatments to produce a dark brown or black patina remain very common. The existing reagents were augmented by solutions of sodium thioantimoniate (Schlippe's salt), which reacts to form rich, glossy brown patinas.

Blue/green 'natural' or 'antique' patinas

The most significant change in the production of green patinas to simulate natural patinas has been the general appreciation that the patina forming naturally on most outdoor copper alloys in the modern polluted atmosphere is likely to be of hydroxysulphates (see p. 35). This, coupled with the acceptance that it is extremely difficult to reproduce

Table 14.2 Twentieth-century copper-alloy patination techniques.

Technique	Black/brown 'Bronzing'		Blue/green	
Lacquer	Mainly synthetic		Mainly synthetic	
Heat	BMA finish			
Metal Deposition	Finely divided metal + oxides	As, Sb, Ag		
Chemical: Dry	Oxides	Cu salts mixed Cu/Ag nitrates molten Na nitrate/nitrites		
	Florentine	Fe oxide + graphite		
Chemical: Wet	Oxides	Soln. Cu nitrate, sulphate, carbonate Soln. chlorites, chlorates, dichromates, permanganates	Hydroxycarbonate	
			Hydroxysulphate	
	Sulphides	Soln. K, NH$_4$, Ba, sulphides NH$_4$ polysulphide Na thioantimonate	acetate	
			chloride	
Electrolytic Deposition	Substrate layer	Anodising heat treatment	Substrate layer	Anodising
	Interference patterns Metallic layer	Electrolytic bronzing		

a convincing synthetic hydroxycarbonate patina on copper alloys, has led to a variety of chemical and electrolytic treatments to produce the hydroxysulphates, one of the most notable being brochantite, $Cu_4(SO_4)(OH)_6$.

Typical 'dry methods'

The existing methods continue to be used, together with previously unpublished formulations such as a paste of copper acetate and copper carbonate mixed with ammonium chloride, hydrochloric acid and arsenious oxide. This is applied evenly by brushing and left for 2 to 3 days. Alternatively, ammonium sulphate solution is repeatedly applied for at least a week, the solution drying on the surface between applications. This is followed by the application of alkaline copper sulphate solution, which also dries on the surface. Both of these are specialist treatments for art work, but should be readily distinguishable from natural patination.

CGF (1944) produced a green malachite patina by placing the cleaned bronze in a sealed chamber

exposed to acetic acid vapour for several days followed by ammonia vapour. After a blue–green patina had developed, the bronze was slowly heated to just above 100°C and finally sprayed with beeswax in benzol.

Typical 'wet methods'

The use of copper salts in buffered solutions continues with some treatments specifically designed for statuary work. For example a solution containing copper carbonate and acetate with ammonium and sodium chlorides in acetic acid and potassium bitartrate is brushed or sprayed on to the workpiece and then allowed to slowly dry in a warm place for 24 hours. This cycle of treatment is repeated several times, building up a thin green patina, presumably of atacamite. Finally, the object is polished with olive oil.

The modern copies of ancient Chinese bronzes produced at the Palace Museum, Taiwan (Liu Wann-Hong, 1976; and see Chapter 1, p. 10) were given a dark patina by repeated immersion of the

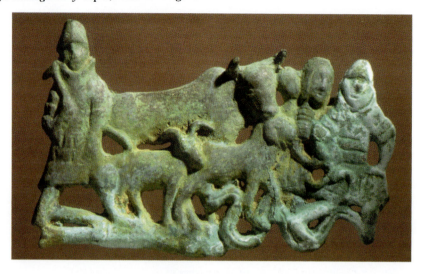

Figure 14.10   Patinated brass plaque, BM OA Reg. 1996, 1-15, 6, acquired in Kunming in western China in 1995. The artificial patina is now beginning to corrode because of residual original ferric chloride. (A. Milton/British Museum)

cleaned bronze in a hot solution of potassium sulphide. A green patina was produced by brushing on a solution containing one ounce of ammonia and one ounce of table salt in 50 ounces of vinegar and allowing this to dry for 4 or 5 hours. Four or five separate applications were recommended. Sometimes the green patina was developed on bronze that had already been blackened. Resin was sprayed on to the patina to protect it, followed by a final polish with beeswax or neutral shoe polish.

These patinas are composed principally of hydroxycarbonates and hydroxychlorides, but the cuprite layer is absent and thus the patinas should be easily recognised as being artificial. The presence of copper sulphide should also show that they are not natural.

More traditional methods involve the application of a dilute ammonium sulphate solution twice daily for a week, followed by the application of a weak copper sulphate solution, to oxidise the surface (Hemming, 1977).

It might be thought that such treatments would give protection to the bronzes by the production of a stable mineral on the surface, but research by Bastidas *et al.* (1997), exposing bronze which had been patinated with potassium sulphide to small amounts of sulphur dioxide in a humid environment, showed that a range of oxides, sulphates and sulphides was produced. This suggests that natural corrosion products might be expected to form on deliberately patinated bronzes.

An example of this is provided by a patinated brass plaque (approx. 95% copper, 5% zinc) purchased by the author from the Kunming Variegated Copper Factory, at Kunming, Yunnan in western China (Figure 14.10). This company produces a wide range of patinations on copper alloys, including imitations of antique naturally developed patinations. The plaque was selected because the patination was unusually variegated, with areas of light green and white patina interspersed with the more usual dark green patina. XRD of the patina detected atacamite and alumina. The Kunming Variegated Copper Factory had been very coy about revealing the chemical treatments, but outside the premises were stacked drums marked $FeCl_3$, and this, together with the XRD evidence, suggests the brass plaque had been treated with ferric chloride, probably applied in a poultice of alumina or, possibly, clay. Five years later, examination by XRD and SEM showed that nantokite (CuCl), the active agent in bronze disease, was present, together with the atacamite. This strongly suggests that natural corrosion had begun during those 5 years, induced by the residual chemicals in the artificial patina. Hereafter the patina on the plaque could begin to resemble a natural corrosion product.

In fact many patinas described as resulting from the chemical treatment of a natural corrosion could be the long-term development of an artificial chemical treatment.

Electrolysis

Anodic oxidation of copper and its alloys is now extensively used to produce dark patinas. Fine black patinas can be produced using electrolytes containing sodium hydroxide and sodium molybdate with chromic acid, alone or in mixed solutions, such as combinations of chrome and nickel chloride solutions.

A Florentine brown can be produced in one operation electrolytically, simultaneously depositing the copper and carrying out the surface treatment. This is very different from the traditional process as the electrolyte employs sulphur-containing proteins, such as gelatine or wheat gluten, to form sulphides on the surface of the workpiece.

Alternatively, the object to be treated is made the anode in an aqueous electrolyte of magnesium sulphate, manganese hydroxide and potassium bromide, producing a layer of brochantite. This patina slowly ages on the metal and is quite basic. The absence of the underlying cuprite layer would distinguish it from most natural patinas. A deep blue patina can be produced by making the object the cathode in an electrolyte containing copper acetate and gelatine.

Other more sophisticated electroplating techniques have been developed that produce oxide films with beautiful iridescence. These were pioneered by Leopoldo Nobili in nineteenth-century Italy (Pedeferri, 1994). The films are very thin and translucent and the iridescence colors are due to interference patterns forming as light passes through the oxide layer to be reflected back from the metal surface beneath. Very thin cathodic deposits on copper or nickel give a wide range of stable colors (Fishlock, 1962, p. 126).

Fake patinas: their examination and production

Sources: Brown *et al.* (eds) (1977, pp. 208–213); Fleming (1979a); Scott (1991a); Craddock (1997); Robbiola *et al.* (2004).

Examination

The patina should first be carefully examined through the binocular microscope and tested with a mounted needle. A natural patina should be firmly adherent to the surface; false patinas are much more loosely attached, flaking away and exposing shiny metal beneath. Shiny metal appearing on the edges and extremities of a patinated bronze is an indication of recent patination. Firmly adhering cuprite on the

bronze is a good sign of authenticity, being difficult to reproduce. This was already recognised back in 1877 by Fortnum (p.24) and in 1888 by the Egyptologist, Flinders Petrie, in a sometimes rather hair-raising account of the conservation of ancient metals. He did, however, recommend leaving the cuprite layer where possible 'not only as a guarantee of age, but also a proof that the bronze has not been over cleaned or tampered with'. (NB cerussite can also appear purple-red in color.)

In a natural patina the crystal structure will have built up slowly, developing large crystals with a regular crystal array, which in turn will produce a sharp XRD pattern, whereas the pattern from a rapidly developed patina will be much more diffuse (Riederer, 1975). The protective coats of lacquers, waxes or drying oils applied to patinas can give an insight into the history of an artefact (Burmester and Koller, 1987, and p. 352).

Even where an antiquity has been stripped of its natural patina, small areas often survive on the underside or in deep recesses. The removal of the patina from the surface may well expose the pattern of intergranular corrosion in the metal beneath (p. 350, Figure 14.2).

It might be thought that radiocarbon (RC) could be usefully employed to date patinas such as malachite that contain carbon. However, attempts have proved unreliable (see Chapter 5, p. 101), and attempts to date the crusts and patinas forming on stone have encountered similar problems (see Chapter 11, p. 287). Smith (1978; and see p. 361) has suggested that characteristic stable isotope ratios of the oxygen and carbon in the forming hydroxycarbonate corrosion might enable bronzes from different environments to be characterised, but this suggestion has not been taken further.

There are two approaches to the production of a convincing artificial patination: the formation of a patina can be induced on the surface by chemical attack (Figure 14.2), or the appropriate mineral(s) can be held to the surface with an organic binder (Figure 14.11).

Chemical attack produces a wide variety of surface colors and effects as described above, but those that are visually most convincing are unfortunately (for the forger, that is) of the wrong mineral, and they can be easily detected by XRD, Fourier transform infra-red (FTIR) (Scott, 2002, p. 9; fn5) or Raman spectroscopy (RS) (McCann *et al.* 1999; Hayez *et al.*, 2004). This is exemplified by the green mineral gerhardite, copper nitrate, which was found in the ear of the Getty Head (see Chapter 4, p. 72),

Figure 14.11 Detail of the patina applied to a copy of a Roman surgical instrument, BM GR 1920, 7-17, 8. As the organic binder has become old and brittle so it has begun to flake away, exposing the clean uncorroded golden metal surface of the brass beneath. (Courtesy S. La Niece/British Museum)

Figure 14.12 Base of a genuine Etruscan candelabra, BM GR Reg. 1873, 8-20, 211, with an artificial patina of malachite with some cerussite, which, although mineralogically correct, flakes easily revealing the shiny metal beneath. (see right hand dolphin) (© British Museum)

and on the piece 'The head of a youth', now in the Walker Gallery, Liverpool (see Chapter 8, p. 164), but which only rarely develops naturally (see p. 352).

The few cases discovered so far where there has been an attempt to induce the formation of naturally occurring minerals, notably malachite, on bronze have not proved very successful, the patina being very flaky. For example, the corrosion on a Late Etruscan candelabrum of heavily leaded bronze (see Figure 14.12) is very loosely attached to the metal beneath which retains a bright surface, and was almost certainly artificially induced. The piece was sold to the British Museum in the 1870s by the well-known dealer, restorer and jeweller, Alessandro Castellani (see Chapter 15, p. 384), and the false patina was probably applied in his workshops as part of the restoration of a genuine ancient bronze. This was suggested by the composition and confirmed using thermoluminescence (TL) on the remaining sandy clay core material surviving under the base (Jones, (ed), 1990, p. 259). Examination showed that the patina contains malachite and cerussite, reflecting the composition of the bronze. Although mineralogically correct, apart from the absence of cuprite, the XRD pattern for the minerals was rather diffuse, suggesting rapid crystal development.

Characteristic natural corrosion phenomena such as intergranular corrosion can only be incontrovertibly demonstrated by using a metallographic section cut from the metal, and this is rarely permissible on an antiquity (Figures 14.1 and 14.3). If it is possible to polish a taper section on the surface, intergranular corrosion between the grains may be evident

(Figure 14.2). Intergranular corrosion as an indicator of genuine ancient patinas is discussed in Brown *et al.* (1977, Structured Questions section), with Kruger (in Brown *et al.*, 1977, p. 213) claiming that he could produce intergranular corrosion 'on order for a number of different alloys'. He did not, however, specify which alloys or how the intergranular corrosion was to be achieved.

The absence of firmly anchored intergranular corrosion products is one of the reasons why artificial corrosion products tend to be loosely adhering. But as noted above (see p. 358), chemical processes in use from the nineteenth century were often described as taking a year or more to 'fix', and after a century intergranular corrosion may well have developed.

In leaded bronzes the lead is distributed throughout the bronze as disparate globules of almost pure lead. In areas where the metal has been corroding over many years the surface and near-surface globules will have corroded to white cerussite, which fluoresce under UV radiation (see Chapter 2, p. 34), or will have leached away completely, leaving voids (Bangs and Northover, 1999).

The alternative method of producing a patina is to apply the correct mineral, be it cuprite, malachite, atacamite, etc., ground up and mixed with an adhesive, to the surface. The problem for the forger is to disguise the presence of the adhesive.

Figure 14.13a Bronze figure of Buddha, supposedly Tang Dynasty.

Figure 14.13b Extensive damage disguised by false patina, revealed by UV radiation. The patina was found to contain lead chromate. (Courtesy A. Milton/British Museum)

There are two simple and non-destructive tests that can be applied to reveal the presence of some adhesives: the use of solvents and UV. These tests are certainly not infallible, but they are quick and easy and may enable detection of something suspicious that can be followed up by more rigorous examination and analysis; equally, they may reveal nothing at all.

In the former, an area of the suspect patina is carefully swabbed with a cotton bud soaked in a variety of solvents – acetone, toluene, ethyl and methyl alcohol, and 2-methoxy ethanol are suggested. One or other of these may well begin to dissolve the binder and the pigment appears on the swab.

Many common adhesives contain carbon double bonds and these fluoresce under UV (Figures 14.13a, 14.13b and 20.16). The effect is not always

very pronounced and thus the operation should be carried out in total darkness, allowing several minutes for the eyes to adjust. Note that cerussite fluoresces under UV, and thus the patina of a genuine lead or leaded object could well appear suspect.

Sometimes a totally inappropriate pigment has been applied that could never have developed naturally on the surface. Paris green, also known as emerald green, which is a mixed copper arsenate acetate, $Cu(CH_3OO)_4.3Cu(AsO_2)_4$, first synthesised in 1814, and Prussian blue, first synthesised in 1704 (see Chapter 12, p. 302), have both been found as the pigments in artificial patinations applied to bronzes. Some Luristan bronze forgeries (which were in fact brasses, see Chapter 7, p. 146, Figure 7.2) were found to have false patinas containing emerald green (Craddock, 1980). Another popular mineral found in artificial patinas is gerhardite (but, see p. 352).

Sometimes the applied patina does not even contain copper, as exemplified by the use of the grey–green clay mineral, glauconite, also known as terre verte, to cover a recent repair on an otherwise genuine bronze box brooch of the Migration period from the Carpathian Basin (BM MLA Reg. 1987, 1–1,1). Other false patinas sometimes contain modern paint media such as anatase (titanium oxide) or barytes (barium sulphate).

15

Gold and silver

Gold and silver have been the two leading prestige metals the world over since almost the inception of metallurgy. In this chapter, composition, metal-working techniques, evidence of age and authenticity are considered.

Gold

Sources: General: Grimwade (1985); Ogden (1982, 1992). Ancient Europe: Morteani and Northover (eds) (1995). Ancient Middle East: Maxwell-Hyslop (1971). Egypt: Wilkinson (1971). Greece and Rome: Higgins (1961); Williams and Ogden (1994); Williams (ed) (1998). India: Untracht (1997). Orient: Ogden (2003). Americas: Bray (1978); McEwan (ed) (2000). West Africa: Barbier (ed) (1989). Southern Africa: Oddy (1984, 1994). Materials: Rose (1915); Wise (ed) (1964).

Occurrence

Primary gold occurs as minute particles of metal in quartz veins. Upon erosion of the quartz deposits, the gold can be washed into streams where it can be concentrated by water action in beds known as placers. Such gold is known in English variously as placer, alluvial, stream, or secondary gold. This source of gold probably accounted for most of the gold produced in the ancient world. Water action can cause the particles of gold to join together to form larger pieces or nuggets, and can also pick up other metals.

Platinum group element (PGE) inclusions in gold
Sources: Ogden (1976, 1977, 1982, pp. 21, 31); Meeks and Tite (1980); Ramage and Craddock (2000, pp. 238–245).

Some gold antiquities have silvery white granules of PGEs visible in their surface layer. Primary gold is not directly associated with PGEs, but quite often the secondary gold can pick up PGE granules in stream beds, etc. Their presence was noted by the ancients and was known as *adamas*; they were very difficult to remove prior to the refining processes introduced in the mid-nineteenth century (Rose, 1915).

Thus their presence in gold should be taken as an indication that the metal was produced from placer deposits at a date prior to the late nineteenth century. Note that PGE inclusions are not found in all gold deposits; for example, they are very rare in gold originating from Europe north of the Alps and thus their absence is of no significance. Although their presence was noted in ancient Egyptian gold by Flinders Petrie and Quibell as long ago as 1896, their significance as potential indicators of antiquity did not really come into prominence until the publication of two major studies by Ogden (1976, 1977). Thus, antiquities of gold containing PGE inclusions that have been recorded as being in existence prior to Ogden's publications are likely to be authentic, and their presence has been used to authenticate antiquities that were under suspicion, such as the famous inscribed gold fibulae from Prenestina, now in the Museo Pigorini in Rome (Formigli, 1992, Tafel 94; 1, 2).

Sometimes PGE inclusions are clearly visible to the naked eye, even standing proud of the surface of gold, as exemplified by the gold chisels from Ur (La Niece, 1995). Examination with a low-power binocular microscope in most circumstances should reveal them as clearly distinct from their golden matrix, and equally clearly their angular profile shows that they have never been molten. Although apparently homogeneous, they are usually composed of a mixed natural alloy of several of the PGE metals, with osmium, iridium and ruthenium usually predominating. The composition of the inclusions can be determined by microanalysis in a scanning electron microscope (SEM); early hopes that variations in the proportions of the PGE metals could be used to provenance gold have proved to be illusory (Meeks and Tite, 1980) (NB the earlier analyses of PGE inclusions by Whitmore and

Young, 1973, erroneously identified them as being of platinum–iridium). Junk and Pernicka (2003) investigated the possibility of provenancing gold by means of the isotope ratios of the osmium in the inclusions but unfortunately there is considerable variation in the composition of the grains from any one gold source.

Platinum, palladium and rhodium are soluble in gold and any of these metals in the PGE inclusions should disperse in the gold on melting, although platinum inclusions have been found in the surface of gold artefacts as exemplified by the Braganza brooch of supposed western Mediterranean Iron Age origin (see Chapter 10, p. 240).

Composition: Silver and copper content

Almost all natural gold contains some silver, typically ranging from 5 to 35% (Wise 1964, p. 3). Copper is also sometimes present in gold as a sub-stantial trace, but rarely at a level of more than 1 or 2%. It seems that before the introduction of coin-age, around the mid first millennium BC, there was little effort to remove the silver; indeed, there was only a hazy concept then of what constituted pure gold (Ramage and Craddock, 2000, p. 31). Thus, artefacts that contain less than about 1% of silver should normally be regarded as being of refined gold and hence as post-dating 500 BC in the Old World (see example in Chapter 20, p. 503).

Gold refining by the salt-parting process became established, probably first at the Lydian capital of Sardis in western Anatolia (Ramage and Craddock, 2000) in the sixth century BC, but the gold used in artefacts as well as in some coinage continued to contain silver, representing either the intrinsic natural content or deliberate additions (contrary to the statement by Wakeling 1912, p. 21, that ancient Egyptian gold was pure 24 carat). Even after refin-ing, the gold would normally possess at least a few hundred ppm of silver, and much less than this should be regarded as suspicious in artefacts dating much before the mid-nineteenth century.

A good example of the latter case is provided by the so-called sword of Edward III, which was offered for sale to the Victoria and Albert Museum in the late nineteenth century by the well-known dealer and forger Louis Marcy, and which was almost cer-tainly made in his workshops in Paris (Blair, 1991, 1992), although it still has its supporters (Oakeshott, 1991). When the gold fittings on the hilt were ana-lysed, silver was not detected, but about 1% of platinum and several hundred ppm of palladium

were found to be present in solution, which, contra Oakeshott (1991, pp. 303–308) does not authenticate the metal, but suggests impure nineteenth-century gold, probably originating in Brazil (see p. 371).

In classical antiquity it was unusual for the gold to be alloyed with copper alone, so the copper content of most gold antiquities is rarely more than 5%, and is usually exceeded by the silver content. The forged Romano-Egyptian coiled wire bracelet (Figures 15.1 and 15.2; and see p. 376), for example, is made of gold alloyed with copper only. Some cultures, notably the Sumerians, Egyptians and the cultures of

Figure 15.1   Gold bangle of coiled wire with lion-head terminals (BM EA 1901, 3–9, 19), purporting to be Romano-Egyptian. (Courtesy A. Milton/British Museum)

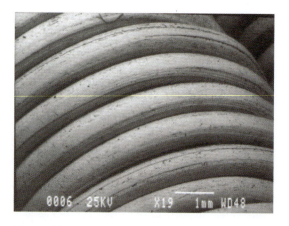

Figure 15.2   SEM photomicrograph of the wire of the bangle shown in Figure 15.1. The striations running paral-lel to the wire are characteristic of drawn wire, and show that it is unlikely to be Roman. (Courtesy N.D. Meeks)

South America, at certain periods added substantial quantities of copper to their gold (Ogden, 1982, pp. 18–19). Prehistoric British gold antiquities are of very varied composition and can sometimes be quite base (Hartmann, 1970, 1982 and Hook and Needham, 1989 for Bronze Age gold; Cowell, 1992 and Northover, 1992 for Iron Age gold).

The alloying of gold with copper only became usual practice in Europe from the Post-Medieval period. A more common practice in antiquity was to debase the gold with a mixture of two parts silver and one part copper, thereby preserving the golden color. This is well exemplified by the composition of Late Iron Age Celtic gold coins (Cowell, 1992). As the usual method of assay was by touchstone (Ramage and Craddock, 2000, pp. 245–250), the debasement would be difficult to detect.

During the last three centuries a vast number of gold simulants have been produced, often with colorful and suggestive names (Rudoe, 1989; Ogden, 1993). These were usually alloys of copper with zinc, notably *pinchbeck* (Becker, 1988, pp. 34–38, 57–60; and see Chapter 7, p. 148), but some contain metals only recently prepared such as the picturesquely named Abyssinian gold of the latter nineteenth century that is an alloy of copper and aluminium.

Gold has sometimes been fraudulently debased with tungsten, which has almost the same specific gravity (SG) as gold and thus will pass an SG determination, which is otherwise almost foolproof. Tungsten was not prepared commercially until the mid-nineteenth century, and thus its presence in the gold would show it was not only fraudulent but modern.

Platinum from South America and Russia was cheap in the nineteenth century and also used as a high-SG adulterant for gold. In the twentieth century it became fashionable as a setting for Art Deco jewellery. It is usually alloyed with a little iridium to harden it but in the 1920s the cheaper palladium was often used. As the price of platinum rose, so it became imitated by other white alloys, i.e. the white golds, gold alloyed with platinum, palladium, silver or nickel-silver, and completely base alloys such as platinin (Becker, 1988, pp. 119, 167).

Composition: Trace elements

Analytical studies endeavouring to provenance gold antiquities by their trace element composition have hitherto not met with great success (Hartmann, 1970, 1982; Ogden, 1982, pp. 19–21). Hartmann (1975), in a paper devoted to the detection of faked and forged antiquities of gold, suggested that the presence of certain trace elements, which he did not reveal, was indicative that the piece was likely to be modern. Using techniques such as emission spectrometry (ES), the range of trace elements that could be detected was not particularly diagnostic. New methods such as laser-ablated inductively coupled plasma mass spectrometry (LA-ICP-MS) have enabled elements to be determined down to parts per billion (see Chapter 3, p. 46). This is several orders of magnitude lower than with previous methods, and can include isotope separation and characterisation as well (Grigorova *et al.* 1998). It is claimed that at this level of concentration it should be possible to pick up characteristic traces that enable the gold to be traced to source.

The method was developed in Australia specifically to combat the theft of gold bars from mines. Using this technique the bars could be analysed and their trace element composition compared with that of the gold from the mines. As there are only a small number of producers and these are all known and analytically defined, it is quite feasible to obtain a unique fingerprint for each of the Australian producers. Studies are now in progress to ascertain whether this approach can be applied to ancient goldwork (Guerra *et al.* 1999; Watling *et al.* 1999; Guerra and Calligaro, 2004). At one level these studies seek to establish the compositional parameters for specific groups of goldwork, such as Byzantine *solidi*. This clearly has important implications for the ability to assign gold to specific groups and to exclude those that are alien, in much the same way as the lead isotope ratios are being used to provide compositional fingerprints for silver and copper alloy artefacts (see Chapter 7, p. 139).

The method is likely to prove most useful where large quantities of gold are being used on a regular basis, such as for minting coins, for which a sustained source of supply would have come from a limited number of known major mines, which is not the case with prehistoric gold antiquities.

Gondonneau *et al.* (1996) have already had some success in differentiating local Celtic gold in Gaul from the imported Greek gold. They were also able to recognise Brazilian gold in some eighteenth-century European gold coins. Barrandon *et al.* (1995, 2000) and Morrisson *et al.* (1999) have also identified Brazilian gold by the presence therein of several hundred ppm of palladium. Brazilian gold only appeared on the European market in quantity after 1700, and thus the presence of palladium is a good chronological indicator (see Oakeshott's so-called Sword of Edward III, p. 370).

Should it prove possible to establish trace element profiles or fingerprints for the gold used by specific cultures generally, this would prove a very potent authenticity method. Furthermore, the LA-ICP-MS method only requires a minimal sample, which can be ablated through the immediate surface layers that are likely to be most altered during burial.

Gold, in common with most natural materials, contains minute quantities of radioactive uranium and thorium, which produce helium on decay. The volumes of helium in native gold are tiny, typically of the order of $50–100 \, 10^{-8} \, cm^3$ and the gas is released by heating, which can be measured using mass spectrometry (MS). This has already been used to detect forgeries of natural gold nuggets (Eugster, 1996). During the 1990s, near-perfect gold octahedral crystals purporting to come from the St Elena mine in Venezuela came on to the market. The difference between the helium levels in the genuine natural crystals and those in the forgeries that had only very recently been molten was very noticeable. Eugster speculated on whether the method could be applied to antiquities, but calculated that the amount of helium likely to have been produced even over 3000 years was likely to be undetectable by present techniques and that there might be problems with very thin pieces or gold with intergranular corrosion (see also Kossolapov, 1999). Also, the method does require a sample to be taken.

Surface features, patina and texture

Elemental gold is extremely resistant to chemical change. It is, after all, this immutability that has been one of the metal's chief attractions through the ages.

Gold antiquities recovered from the ground can be expected to have some firmly adhering soil, or calcite deposits if from a calcareous soil. These materials are sometimes applied to gold forgeries with various degrees of sophistication (Meyers, 1997). Ogden (1982, pp. 168–170) described a variety of ageing techniques, including feeding the forged gold jewellery to camels and donkeys, 'the slow voyage through the beast apparently imparting a highly desirable old appearance'.

A very thin layer of pink material often adheres to gold surfaces. This has been identified as a gold silver sulphide (Frantz and Schorsch, 1990). Their study was mainly performed on Egyptian antiquities but the same distinctive pink layer is quite common on gold antiquities from around the world. It would seem to originate in the activities of sulphur-fixing micro-organisms on the surfaces

of the gold. The layers are usually very thin, firmly adhering such that it is difficult to remove sufficient material even for an X-ray diffraction (XRD) sample.

This natural pink patination is not to be confused with the visually similar deliberate pink–red iron-based patination that survives so well on certain Egyptian and Sumerian gold antiquities, exemplified by some of the gold work accompanying the burial of Tutankhamen (Ogden, 1982, p. 21). Pink patinas are still popular in China and South-East Asia (Ali and Kassim 1988).

The natural pink patina is sometimes imitated with lacquer (Wakeling, 1912, p. 213), and microscopic examination backed up by the application of solvents will normally reveal the true nature of the layer (see Chapter 14, p. 367). It can also be imitated by applying jeweller's rouge (iron oxide), or electroplating a very thin copper layer (see Chapter 14). Both should be detectable by X-ray fluorescence (XRF) and XRD.

The other metals – usually copper or silver – in the gold are prone to chemical attack (Scott, 1983), and small amounts of violet–white silver chloride are frequently present on the surface. Thus, there is typically some loss of the more base metals from the surface during burial, resulting in porosity which gives the surface of most gold antiquities their characteristic rather matt appearance (Ogden, 1982, p. 22). It is important to note that from the very inception of goldworking there is evidence of deliberate treatment to enhance the gold content of the surface (del Solar and Grimwade, 1982; La Niece, 1995; Ramage and Craddock, 2000, pp. 27–31). This would have been achieved by treating the surfaces with acid salts such as common salt, alum, saltpetre or iron sulphates.

It can be almost impossible to differentiate between enhancement that was deliberate and that which occurred during burial. It was the usual practice after treatment to burnish the gold to produce a bright compact surface. Of course, the surface of a genuine antiquity that had a developed a matt surface during burial could well have been burnished after recovery from the ground in order to improve its surface, thereby removing the evidence of its past and authenticity, as exemplified by an Egyptian gold headdress (see Chapter 20, p. 503). Conversely, forgeries of buried antiquities could be pickled in acid to produce a matt effect, but the forgers often seem to have used too strong a pickling solution and in fact dissolved some of the gold, producing an etched surface revealing the microstructure of the gold itself. For example, Castellani recorded that he used *aqua regia*, a mixture of hydrochloric and nitric acids, capable of dissolving gold. Examination of some of the pieces acquired from Castellani such as the half-and-half necklace discussed below (see p. 384), reveals that the nineteenth-century half had been pickled in a very acidic medium, presumably *aqua regia*, leaving the surface in a very different condition from that of the ancient half that had been subject only to the more benign effects of long burial. A later example from the same workshop, then under the direction of Mellilo, is provided by a bracelet also now in the British Museum (Rudoe, 1984; Cat. 959, pp. 149–151, Plate 45).

Electroplating is used both to disguise areas of heat treatment such as recent soldering, and to create an 'antique' surface, sometimes with additions of arsenic and lead to the electrolyte. Electroplated surfaces can sometimes be detected by the presence of minute bubbles or blisters on the gilded surface where the underlying metal had not been properly cleaned prior to plating (see Chapter 8, p. 175 and Figure 8.24b).

This was exemplified by many of the items in the notorious Greek Gold Exhibition (Hoffmann and Davidson, 1965). A major travelling exhibition, it included a selection of well-known and recently acquired material from both private collections and major museums in Europe and North America. Reviews of the catalogue, notably by Amandry (1967) and Greifenhangen (1968), suggested that many of the items were modern. This prompted Hoffmann (1969) to publish an article confirming the reviewer's fears, because the catalogue 'had come to be accepted as a criterion of authenticity'. Forgeries were sold on the strength of the book's authority and continued sale without any disclaimer (Ogden, 1982, p. 168). Hoffmann believed that about 20 of the 138 items were forgeries, but Ogden thought that the true figure was approximately 70. Regrettably this is not an isolated case; see Beckett (1995, pp. 105–117) for a discussion of the problems encountered with other rapidly acquired collections of ancient gold jewellery.

Technically, the forgeries from the Greek Gold Exhibition displayed evidence of modern processes, including drawn wire and rolled sheet gold. There were also similarities with technical features seen on modern imitations of ancient goldwork. Thus, the granulation work was flooded with solder, and many of the decorative and figurative components which should have been individually made from sheet, were mass produced by casting or electroforming, impressions having been taken from presumed genuine pieces.

After the pieces had been made and assembled they had been electroplated with gold, to disguise modern features and give an appearance of antiquity, although, as noted above, electroplated surfaces can be quite distinctive in themselves.

Conversely, Davidson (Hoffmann and Davidson, 1965 p. 36) in the technical introduction specifically stated that none of the wires he examined were drawn but instead had been made by strip twisting or by hammering and the compositions of 25 selected pieces were appropriate for ancient gold, containing between 4 and 25% of silver with not more than about 2% of copper.

Among the many items under suspicion were a group of early Greek enamelled gold rosettes (Amandry, 1967), mainly on the grounds that there were so many (50?) nearly identical pieces in various public and private collections. The British Museum had already published details of four of these (BM GR Reg. 1963, 5-24, 1a-d), which were subjected to rigorous scientific and technical study (Higgins, 1968/69). This showed that the wires were block-twisted (see p. 377) and that the surviving enamel was naturally weathered. Traces of chromium were detected in the enamel, which raised some doubts before similar traces were found in other glasses of undoubted antiquity, and in quantities well below those encountered where the chromium had been added intentionally as a colorant (see Chapter 10, p. 325). In addition, lead antimonate had been used to opacify the glass, which was appropriate for the period (see Chapter 10, p. 212, Table 10.2), although this was not noted in Higgin's paper.

Long-term structural changes within gold alloys

Scientists have speculated for many years on long-term changes in the structure of gold artefacts that could give information on their likely age or at least their authenticity (Ogden, 1982, p. 22; Scott, 1983). Seruya and Griffiths (1997) investigated the use of phase separation in ternary gold–silver–copper alloys as a dating method (see p. 388 for the related phenomenon in copper–silver alloys). As cast, the ternary alloy is in one phase but, very slowly, separation occurs into two phases, a silver-rich phase and a copper-rich phase. These phases can detected by XRD and the compositional differences confirmed by energy-dispersive X-ray (EDX) analysis in the scanning electron microscope and thus the sampling requirements should be minimal. There are potential problems in that the phase separation proceeds quite quickly at elevated temperature. Thus, if the gold had cooled only slowly from the initial casting, or more probably if the gold had been held at an elevated temperature during annealing or soldering, then appreciable separation could have occurred, equivalent to long periods at room temperature. Another problem is that the separation seems only to occur in alloys with at least about 2% of copper, which is high for the majority of early gold artefacts. It would also be easy to incorporate the appropriate phase into a forgery.

Grain boundary etching

Many gold surfaces appear etched with pronounced grain boundaries (Figure 15.21). This is likely to be mainly an effect of preferential corrosion at the grain boundaries, but it is possible that in part it may have been enhanced by long-term vacancy diffusion through the grains to the boundaries, thereby giving an indication of age, although this phenomenon is very slow at ambient temperatures.

Stress corrosion cracking

This occurs where mechanical or heat deformation of the grain structure has resulted in strain, such as at hammered or soldered joints (Scott, 1983; Ogden, 1985; Meeks 1998b; and see p. 380, 385). It is a well-known phenomenon in low-carat gold alloys (typically 9 to 14 carat, i.e. 37.5 to 58.0%), usually with a high silver or copper (Graf and Budke, 1955), or zinc or aluminium content, that have been subjected to stress, either thermal or mechanical, and vigorous pickling (Rapson and Groenewald, 1978; Dugmore and DesForges, 1979). It is especially common on low-carat gold solders, where differential cooling followed by pickling have created ideal conditions for such cracking to occur. It has been suggested that stress corrosion cracking may also take place in alloys of higher gold and silver content over long time periods, and thereby provide a useful authentication indicator.

Goldworking technology

Sources: General: Smith (1933); Edwards (1977); Kallenburg (1981); Untracht (1982). Europe and the Middle East: Ogden (1982, 1994, 1998; Formigli (1985); Nicolini (1990); Formigli and Heilmeyer, 1993. Egypt: Vernier (1907). India: Untracht (1997). Pre-Colombian America: Scott (1986a, b; 1995); La

Niece (1998); Meeks (1998a); La Niece and Meeks (2000). Southern Africa: Oddy (1984, 1994).

In the nineteenth century many reputable jewellery manufacturers were producing superb work in Classical, Medieval and Renaissance styles. Thus there was a body of highly trained goldsmiths and jewellers able to produce competent imitative work at relatively low cost. From this pool of talent there came many works of deceptive restoration, fakery and outright forgery. Many of their excellent productions were regarded as genuine until recently and have only been unmasked by scientific examination (see also Chapter 10, p. 239).

For over a century now, most of the minor jewellery fitments – the catches, clips, hinges, closers, joins, ear clips and collets (known collectively in the trade as 'findings') – have been supplied to the jewellery trade by specialised manufacturers (Abbey, 1968). As a consequence there is a general lack of experience with making them by hand, and where this attempted they are often demonstrable copies of the modern machine-made pieces, even to the extent of using anachronistic components such as screws.

Many gem or jewellery settings have a base or field of sheet metal; in antiquity this will have been hammered out, and from the more recent past it will have been rolled (see Chapter 8, pp. 157). Ancient and modern gold sheet can be very similar in thickness and uniformity, but surface striations indicative of rolling can sometimes be much more prominent on sheets of soft metals such as gold than on those of other metals. For example, Meyers (1997) observed such parallel lines on some sheet goldwork that purported to be ancient Chinese, and Ogden illustrated an acorn made of rolled sheet gold with prominent parallel striations on a forgery of a Greek wreath (1982, Plate 10.16).

Engraving

The history of engraving as a general metalworking technique is considered in Chapter 8, p. 173, but the special application to gold can be briefly considered here. Thus the technique was not generally applied until steel became available around the middle of the first millennium BC over most of the Old World. However, gold could be engraved with softer materials such as bronze, and Xenaki-Sakellariou (1989) has published details of some Mycenaean gold rings of the late second millennium BC that clearly have been engraved (Ogden, 1982, p. 167; 1998). The presence of the distinctive engraving technique on the superb Ring of Nestor, acquired by Arthur Evans in Greece, now in the Ashmolean Museum, helped its rehabilitation after it had been condemned as a forgery (Ogden, 1998, p. 18, Appendix 1; Pini, 1998). The designs on some Egyptian gold rings, examined by the author and dating from the end of the third millennium BC, show that they had been gouged out, using a tool shaped rather like a graver. Apparent bronze gravers with the distinctive diamond profile are known from Egypt (Vernier, 1907).

Cutting the gold
This is an area where there have been important changes since antiquity (Ogden, 1982, pp. 43–45). Most cutting of sheet or of wire was done with a knife or a chisel. Coarse metalworkers' shears had been in use since the Hellenistic period, and scissors were probably used in metalworking from Roman times on. The goldsmith's piercing saw was not used in antiquity.

Early wires were cut with a knife or chisel, giving a single-angled cut; modern wires are cut with snips or fine shears, only introduced in the Post-Medieval period, which give a 'v' profile cut (Figures 15.3 and 15.4a).

Sheet gold cut with scissors or fine shears very often has a characteristic curled edge with a ghost line running just inside and parallel to the real cut edge.

The cut out openwork (known as *opus intrasile*) was always cut with a chisel in antiquity, the goldsmith's piercing saw only being adopted much later (Ogden and Schmidt, 1990). Saw cuts in sheet metal are very distinctive, having parallel sides and, where they exist, square ends.

Figure 15.4a Two small gold rosettes, one ancient Greek (upper) and the other a recent creation (lower), note the 'v' cut at the end bottom left hand corner.

Figure 15.4b The ancient wire has signs of helical twists and is rather irregular in profile

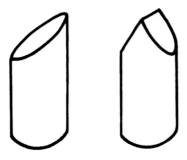

Figure 15.3 Wire end cut: left: with a knife; right: with snips. (Courtesy B. Craddock)

Figure 15.4c The more recent drawn wires have a much fuller, rounder and more regular profile than twisted wires. (Courtesy S. La Niece)

Wiremaking

Sources: Carroll (1970, 1972); Oddy (1977); Ogden (1982, pp. 46–58 and 1991, 1992, 2003); Whitfield (1990) and Nicolini (1995).

Wiremaking provides an excellent example of where the publication of the details of the ancient techniques has led to their adoption by forgers. No serious gold forgeries would now be made using drawn wire.

Wire is now universally made by drawing thin rods of metal through progressively narrower holes drilled in a steel plate (the *drawplate*) with periodic annealing (Untracht, 1968, pp. 244–245; Taimsalu, 1983). The wire is solid and of regular rounded section compared to that made by strip-twisting (see Figure 15.4b, c). If the drawplate hole is even slightly damaged, then a series of parallel scratches or striations will appear running longitudinally along the surface of the wire (see Figure 15.2). Note that the published examples of drawn wire tend, as here, to show where the striations are both numerous and deep. In practice if the drawplate used is in good condition there may be no striations and thus their absence does not necessarily preclude drawn wire.

The origins of wire-drawing are rather uncertain. Three enigmatic bronze plates pierced with irregular holes, from the Late Bronze Age hoard of metalwork found at Isleham in Cambridgeshire, UK, have been claimed as drawplates (Northover, 1995). However, the holes are rather large, with large differences in diameter between them, such that it would require considerable energy to pull even a gold wire through them, and it is generally believed that it is not possible to hand-draw a wire of greater than 2 mm thickness. Jacobi (1979) published details of several putative iron drawplates found on excavations of some Roman-period sites in Europe, but once again the holes appear rather large, typically between about 2 and 10 mm in diameter.

Epprecht and Mutz (1974–75) believed that some Roman copper alloy wires that they had examined were drawn because of the parallel striations running along the wire. Sim (1997) and Sim and Ridge (2002, pp. 102–103) have recently argued that several pierced plates of iron or steel, found on Roman military sites, should be regarded as drawplates for drawing iron wire specifically for use in the manufacture of chain mail. Thomsen and Thomsen (1974, 1976) published details of a convincing Roman iron drawplate from the Roman site of Altena, on the German *Limes*, near present-day Dusseldorf, and also suggested that iron wire was drawn from the mid first millennium BC in Iran.

It would seem that the drawplate was not used for the primary production of gold or other non-ferrous wires before the end of the Roman period, but thereafter it was quickly adopted (Whitfield, 1990; Ogden, 1991).

Chandra (1979, p. 100) stated drawplates were in use in India as early as the third millennium BC, but presented no convincing evidence. Riederer (1994) noted that drawn wire began to be used on gold in Java in the Protoclassic period, usually dated to AD 200–650.

Bunker (1997) suggested that strip-twisting was the prevalent technique in China from the inception of goldworking some time in the first millennium BC, with drawn wire appearing sometime in the first millennium AD, i.e. at approximately the same date as in the West. Ogden (1991, 2003) noted drawn wires on some Korean gold jewellery of the Silla period dated to between the fifth and seventh centuries AD. Ogden also pointed out that, in his long experience, strip-twisted wire in the West tends to have an 'S' twist whereas that in East tends to have a 'Z' twist, but stressed that this is not invariable.

Drawn wire was not used in Pre-Colombian America. Oddy (1994) studied some Medieval-period gold wires from the Iron Age cultures of southern Africa and found that in addition to hammered solid wires there were spiral-wound gold strip wires. However, drawn wires have been reported from the site of Great Zimbabwe, dating to the fourteenth century AD. Copper wire was also being drawn in southern Africa (Steel, 1975) and in central Africa from as early as the fourteenth century AD (Herbert, 1984, pp. 78–82).

The main methods by which non-ferrous wires were made in antiquity in Europe and the Middle East, are as follows:

1. Hammering: At its simplest a thin rod could be hammered until it was of the required thickness and with a more or less even thickness and section. The distinctive features are variations in diameter, hammer facets on the surface, and a solid cross-section. The hammered facets on the pin of the suspect inscribed gold fibula from Prenestina constituted one of the technical features which helped to rehabilitate the piece (Formigli, 1992, Figure 1). Most wires in prehistoric Europe would have been hammered (Nicolini, 1995). Hammered wire may have been finished by rolling or by passing the wire through a hole in a metal plate. Plates of pierced antler were used by the Indians in the

southern part of the United States for smoothing hammered wires of native copper (Cushing, 1894). This could remove some of the distinctive features such as faceting and even introduce striations. Some ancient wires have a flattened semicircular cross-section, suggesting that they were hammered into a semicircular groove on a swage block (Oddy, 1980), and this method was certainly used to produce decorative wire (Ogden, 1982, p. 56, Figure 4.45).

2. Block-twisting (Figures 15.5, 15.6 and 15.7): A thin rod was hammered out to the required thickness, and square in section. This was twisted as tightly as possible and then rolled. The resulting wire is solid and of relatively regular section, and has a series of helical grooves running around it. There should be one groove for each

of the four faces, if the section is truly square, but in practice this is not the case and instead there are only two, as Oddy (1979) pointed out in a correction to his 1977 paper. If the gold is very pure and soft, these grooves can be largely obliterated by the rolling process.

3. Strip-twisting (Figures 15.8–11): A narrow strip of gold was cut from a sheet, whereupon it began to curl. The strip was then wrapped around another wire, which was subsequently removed. Next, the twisted strip was gently tightened and extended, but always keeping the edges of the strip in contact. The wire so produced resembles an old-fashioned drinking straw. Strip-twisted wire is hollow with a single helical seam, and is of approximately round cross-section, although often appearing rather flattened (see Figure 15.4b). It has a reasonably regular cross-section,

Figure 15.5 Stages in block twisting. (Top) A thin rod of gold is hammered out; (Middle) The rod is twisted; (Bottom) The twisted rod is rolled, leaving the helical twists in the metal. (Courtesy Oddy, 1977)

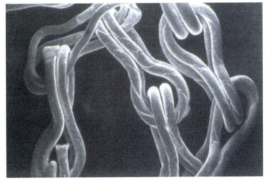

Figure 15.7 SEM photomicrograph of some of the links of Figure 15.6. The helical twists are very evident. (Courtesy N.D. Meeks/British Museum)

Figure 15.6 Roman chain from New Grange, Co. Meath, Ireland (BM PRB Reg. 1884, 5-20, 4). It is made of block-twisted wire. Some of the characteristic helical twists can be seen on this photograph. (Courtesy J. Heffron/British Museum)

Figure 15.8 Stages in strip twisting. (Top) The natural tendency to curl is encouraged by gently twisting; (Bottom) The tube is twisted more tightly and extended. (Courtesy J. Heffron/British Museum)

Figure 15.9 Swedish Iron Age bead, first century BC/AD (BM MLA Reg. 1921, 11-1, 46). This composite bead is made up of small lengths of strip-twisted wire and balls, soldered to gold sheet. (Courtesy J. Heffron/ British Museum)

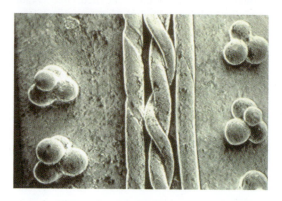

Figure 15.10 SEM photomicrograph of Figure 15.9 showing helical twists on the outside wires. Note the wire on the left seems not to have been twisted tightly enough and was unwinding before being held by the solder. (Courtesy N.D. Meeks/British Museum)

Figure 15.11 SEM photomicrograph of wire from the ancient Greek half of the 'half-and-half necklace' (Figure 15.19) with a broken strip-twisted wire showing that it is hollow (scale bar: 200 microns). (Courtesy N.D. Meeks/ British Museum)

Figure 15.12 Stages in strip drawing. (Top) Strip of gold drawn through one hole of the plate; note the hole where the two sides of the strip have not joined; (Middle) The same wire after drawing through further holes; (Bottom) The finished wire; note the straight seam. (Courtesy Oddy, 1977)

although there may be a progressive change in diameter if it had been twisted more tightly at one end than the other, for example. Occasionally the strip will have begun to unwind, as shown by the ancient example in Figure 15.10, or a break in the wire will reveal that it is hollow (Figure 15.11). Strip-twisted wire could be put through a drawplate in order to reduce the thickness still further and smooth out any irregularities of thickness, and some Roman strip-twisted wires do show parallel striations (Ogden, 1982, p. 50, Plate 4.33). Strip-twisting seems to have originated in the Middle East around the end of the third millennium BC.

4. Strip-drawing (Figures 15.12 and 15.13): It was pointed out by Carroll (1970, 1972) that some ancient wires had striations despite not being drawn in the modern sense. In this technique a metal strip was cut as before and the strip was drawn through a series of holes of varied diameter, forcing the strip to curve in on itself until the edges join. The wire so produced has a single longitudinal seam that runs more or less parallel along the seam of the wire and there may be parallel striations (Figures 15.12 and 15.13). The wire is round and of uniform thickness, and could be hollow in section.

Figure 15.13 Detail of a gold chain from a Parthian necklace of the first to second century AD (BM WAA 134628). Note the single seams on the gold wires, showing they were made by strip drawing. (Courtesy J. Heffron/British Museum)

Figure 15.14 SEM micrograph of cast gold false filigree work forming part of a gold earring; Pre-Hispanic Sinu culture from Colombia, (BM Ethno. Reg. 1955 AM 6.1). The dendrites show beyond doubt that these tiny wires are part of the casting and have not been separately added. (Courtesy N.D. Meeks/British Museum)

In Pre-Columbian South America, gold wire was made by hammering, and by block- and strip-twisting. However, many of the cultures, such as those in Mesoamerica, practised very fine casting, and often the wires, apparently attached to a piece of jewellery, are actually part of the original casting (Scott, 1991b; Meeks, 1998a) (Figure 15.14). This was one of the factors that condemned the famous gold statuette of Tizoc, ruler of the Aztecs. The piece appeared on the market early in the twentieth century and was eventually acquired by the Museum of the American Indian (Reg. No 16/5280). It was questioned on stylistic grounds in the 1930s, but was only condemned completely after full technical analysis (Easby and Dockstader, 1964). The figure has considerable quantities of wire decoration, but instead of being one with the casting of the body of the statuette, the wires have been soldered in place. Moreover, in the published photomicrographs the wires have the appearance of having been drawn although no comment was made on this very obvious feature, the authenticity study having taken place a decade before the significance of such features became widely understood (see right). In addition, one of the sheets of gold had been cut in places with a jeweller's saw, a tool that, like the drawplate, was not available to the Pre-Conquest Amerindian metalsmiths.

Interest in the early methods of wire-making began in the nineteenth century, and the criteria for distinguishing ancient wires were published as early as the 1920s by Williams (1924), and by Maryon (1937–38), who described the block-twisting method as observed on antiquities. Perhaps the first instance of the presence of drawn wire being used as evidence to condemn a supposed antiquity was on the famous eagle brooch from Königsberg (Lill, 1944/50; and see Chapter 1, p. 9). However, elsewhere the potential of these distinctive marks as authentication indicators was not generally realised. In the 1970s the results of many more examinations were published (Thouvenin, 1971 and Kratz, 1972, for example), and the various techniques were published in some detail by Oddy (1977) and Ogden (1982).

As a consequence of these publications from the 1970s, forged gold jewellery also began to be made using strip-twisted, block-twisted and swaged wires. The presence of such wires on pieces with a known provenance dating back before the 1970s may be a taken as supportive evidence of dating from antiquity. The presence of drawn wires on complex pieces of classical jewellery can reveal the extent of restoration, as exemplified by the half-and-half necklace (see p. 384). A study of Etruscan gold jewellery by Swaddling *et al.* (1991) revealed drawn wires in 4 out of 24 pieces examined, and in one piece they constituted the majority of the wires. Note that Ogden (1982, p. 158) found forged Etruscan gold earrings, dating from the 1940s, made of drawn wire on which a seam had been incised, the wire then having been twisted to give the superficial appearance of block-twisting. The real nature of the wire was indicated by the drawn striations which ran parallel to and twisted with the seam. This may be a very early attempt to copy ancient technology or it could be a completely unintentional similarity, caused by a damaged drawplate. As only short stretches of gold wire were produced by strip-twisting, etc., early gold chains tend to be made up of large numbers of separate links. After the introduction of drawing, extended lengths of wire could be produced, enabling chains to be made up from sections of wire 'knitted' together in a continuous fashion.

Joining

A variety of techniques were used to join gold in the past (Ogden, 1982, pp. 57–59; 1992; Duval *et al.*, 1989).

Owing to the ductility of gold and the lack of surface oxidation, it is possible to join the metal by hammering at room temperature to form a true metallurgical join. This technique was widely used in antiquity as exemplified by an earring from Susa, dating from the third millennium BC (Duval *et al.*, 1989) and by a set of four Late Bronze Age gold boxes found in Ireland at Mullingar (Ogden, 1982, p. 59).

In most cases, a metallic solder was used. Even small quantities of copper significantly depress the melting point of gold, with the added bonus of not unduly changing the color of the metal. Silver, in contrast, has relatively little effect on the melting point, but tends to be present in ancient solders probably to balance the copper and thereby preserve the golden color of the metal. Ogden (1982, p. 164) has noted that modern solders often appear lighter in color than ancient solders, owing to their higher silver content.

Granulation
Ancient gold joins often leave so little evidence of their presence that there is continuing debate over how some of them were achieved. The nineteenth-century goldsmith, Castellani, tried to replicate

the very fine soldering of the ancients but admitted that he could not match the quality of their work, despite continually experimenting and refining the techniques, using 'arsenite fluxes' etc. (Munn, 1984, pp. 131–143; Rudoe, 1991). The so-called invisible soldering is especially prevalent on the granulated goldwork of the Etruscans and their contemporaries (Wolters, 1981, 1983; Formigli and Heilmeyer, 1993), although in fact, as Wolters demonstrated, it was also used by goldsmiths before and afterwards. The successful methods devised by John Littledale (1936), and others, have been widely published (Edwards, 1977, pp. 209–212; Ogden, 1982, pp. 64–65; Untracht, 1982, pp. 388–425).

Overall, most students of ancient jewellery consider that it is likely that copper salts were usually employed (Duval *et al.*, 1989), as is the case for granulation work in present-day India; those involved are unaware that they are practising a 'lost' technology (Untracht, 1997, pp. 286–295).

Several ancient and Medieval authorities described gold solders based on copper salts used with alkaline materials such as ammonium chloride and an organic binder. Of the copper salts, copper acetate, verdigris, is the most successful as it dissolves in an aqueous glue and thus the resulting solder can be painted on as a thin, even coat. The join is then heated, whereupon the organic materials in the glue char and locally reduce the copper salts to metal, which in turn dissolves into the hot gold, lowering the local melting temperature and effectively forming a solder *in situ*. This is known as diffusion or colloidal bonding. Thus, it was possible to form an extremely neat join that was virtually invisible. If desired, the copper in the surface could be removed by heating to oxidise the copper, which could then be dissolved out with organic acids, rendering the join virtually undetectable.

It is also possible to fuse-join gold merely by heating at just below the melting point (Ogden, 1982, p. 65). However, such fusion can only be successful for pure gold as any copper or silver present would oxidise at the surface, rendering a metallurgical bond impossible.

Modern gold solders are predominantly alloys of gold, copper and silver (Untracht, 1982, pp. 391–393), but usually contain small amounts of tin and zinc, not found regularly in earlier solders. Note that after pickling the surface of the solder the tin and zinc may well be totally removed, and conversely an ancient solder could contain tin or zinc deriving from bronze or brass used as the source of copper. The presence of metals that were not used in antiquity is of more use in detecting modern work, cadmium being the most common and distinctive.

Solders containing cadmium and their supposed use in antiquity

For rather over 100 years, from the 1850s up until about the 1970s, gold solders often contained cadmium. Quite small quantities of cadmium can reduce the melting point significantly, but without unduly lightening the color. Cadmium-containing gold solders typically contained between 10 and 20% of silver, copper and cadmium, but there were exceptions; some contained as little as 2% (Untracht, 1982, pp. 388–424; Grimwade, 1985, p. 95). The well-documented history of cadmium and its widespread use as a component of gold solders should make it an ideal indicator of modern fabrication or at least repair; however, there have been claims for its use in antiquity.

Cadmium ores are usually found together with those of zinc, but the metal is even more volatile (MP 321°C; BP 768°C), and has to be condensed separately. Because of the difficulties in producing cadmium it was not separated and identified until 1817 (Budgen, 1924, p.xiii).

In a series of papers through the 1980s and beyond it was claimed that cadmium was used as a component of solder in antiquity, but that most analyses had previously failed to detect it (Demortier, 1984, 1987, 2004). The basis for this assertion was that the solders usually contained both silver and cadmium, and the cadmium was being missed by energy-dispersive X-ray (EDX) analysis because of the spectral overlap between the L-lines of silver and cadmium (Figure 15.15). It was also claimed that only techniques such as particle (or proton)-induced X-ray emission (PIXE) (see Chapter 3, p. 50) were capable of routinely detecting cadmium in the presence of silver. Moreover, using PIXE, cadmium had been detected on a range of gold antiquities. Finally, it was claimed that Pliny had specifically described the use of cadmium as a gold solder.

These claims were dealt with in detail in Meeks and Craddock (1991), but may be summarised here. The usual physical analytical techniques by which potential soldered areas on gold artefacts were analysed through the twentieth century were ES, succeeded by XRF and by EDX microanalysis via the scanning electron microscope. Using the first two methods there is no problem and there is no spectral overlap; by XRF the higher-energy K-lines, in which the cadmium and silver spectra

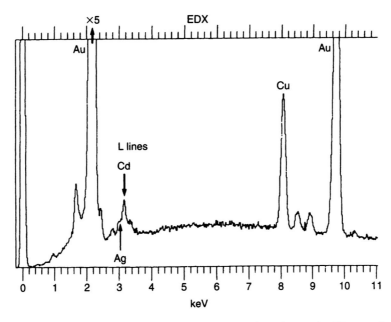

Figure 15.15 EDX spectra of soldered area on a gold mount forgery from the Lombard Treasure (see Figure 15.16b). Note the cadmium 'L' line is clearly displayed. (Courtesy British Museum)

are well separated, are excited. This leaves the EDX system on the SEM, where only the L-lines are excited at the usual operating voltages. Even here the reality is that, in the range of composition of the cadmium gold solders, there should be no problem in resolving the cadmium from the silver, with the standard deconvolution and correction routines. This was tested using compositions generated by mixing the spectra of real alloys to determine the detection limit of cadmium in silver-containing alloys. Cadmium could be detected down to 0.8% by weight in a solder containing 84.2% gold, 10% silver and 5% copper, and even in a matrix of silver alone the detection limit for cadmium was still 2%. In practice, cadmium is regularly detected in gold solders and quantified with ease by most EDX systems. For example, the soldered areas on forgeries from the well-known Lombard Treasure (Kidd, 1990), BM MLA Reg. 1989, 1-9, 1 and 2 (Figures 15.16a and 15.16b), were analysed in the SEM and gave the spectra shown in Figure 15.15 (see also Figure 2.3). The composition is 85.3% gold, 10.3% copper, 2.0% silver and 2.5% cadmium. For comparison, the soldered areas on a genuine Lombardic brooch, BM MLA Reg. 1989, 9-6, 1 (see Figure 15.16a), were analysed and found to contain gold with 5.6% of silver and a trace of copper, with no trace of a cadmium peak observable (Figure 15.17). It might be argued that the silver content was rather low in the example chosen and so to counteract this suggestion an alloy was made up containing gold with 3% of cadmium and 7% of silver, and the spectra is shown in Figure 15.18.

As noted above, large numbers of genuine gold antiquities from around the world have been analysed by ES (p. 45) and latterly by XRF (p. 47) and EDX (p. 49) without cadmium ever being reported in the solders, although it is regularly detected on forgeries. Surely, if it had ever been present in genuine antiquities, it would have been reported by now. The artefacts analysed by Demortier containing cadmium do not have archaeological provenances, most seeming to emanate from private collections in the Middle East, notably from the Lebanon.

The claims that cadmium solders were described in the ancient literature rest on equating the word *chrysocolla* with greenockite, the yellow cadmium sulphide (Demortier, 1987). However, this must be fallacious, as *chrysocolla* seems to have been a rather general term applied to a variety of materials, variously used as pigments and medications.

Where it was used as a gold solder (Pliny, *Natural History*, 33.29; Rackham, 1952, pp. 67–71) it is quite clear that it was made from Cypriot verdigris and soda, i.e. copper acetate and sodium carbonate. The description is clear, unambiguous and allows no other interpretation: copper is the only metal mentioned, there is certainly no reference to anything that could be interpreted as greenockite.

Figure 15.16 (a) Genuine Lombardic brooch (BM MLA 1989, 9-6, 1). (b) Forged mounts (BM MLA 1989, 1-9, 1 & 2) from the notorious Lombard Treasure. (Courtesy A. Milton/British Museum)

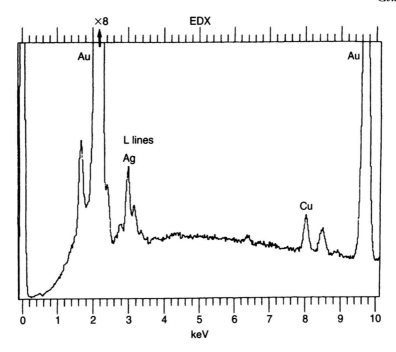

Figure 15.17 EDX spectra of soldered area on a genuine Lombardic disc brooch (see Figure 15.16a). No cadmium could be detected. (Courtesy British Museum)

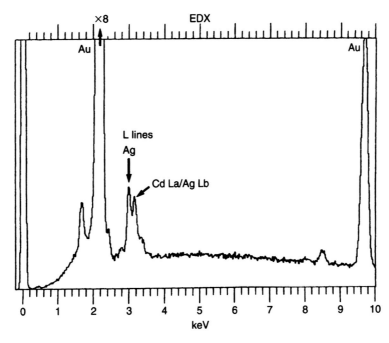

Figure 15.18 EDX spectra of a pseudo-alloy with twice as much silver as cadmium. Note the cadmium 'L' line is clearly differentiated from the adjacent silver 'L' line. (Courtesy British Museum)

Case study: The Greek 'half-and-half' necklace (Meeks, 1998b)

This is one of the more unusual and puzzling restorations: a gold necklace where approximately half is Greek of the late fourth or early third century BC, the other half being Italian of the nineteenth century (Figure 15.19). How the original came to be only half a necklace and the motives for restoring it to a complete necklace are the subject of speculation. It does, however, offer an almost unique opportunity for the comparative study of ancient and more recent goldworking practice.

The necklace was acquired by the British Museum in 1872 from Alessandro Castellani, whose eminent firm in Rome dealt in antiquities as well as making and restoring superb jewellery, often in the antique style, then much in vogue (Munn, 1984; Rudoe, 1991). The British Museum dealt extensively with the firm in the nineteenth century, and scholars and curators through the twentieth century have discovered Castellani's skills at, if not deliberate forgery, then at the least at comprehensive and deceptive restoration.

Figure 15.19 The 'half-and-half' gold strap-necklace (BM GR Reg. 1872, 6-4, 651). The left side is Hellenistic Greek, and the right, nineteenth-century Italian. (Courtesy A. Milton/British Museum)

Figure 15.20 SEM micrograph of the junction of the ancient and more modern wires forming the chains of Figure 15.19. The continuation of the ancient work has been very skilfully done. The ancient (right) wire is rather irregular in section and shows the characteristic helical groove of strip-twisted wire. The nineteenth-century wire is much more rounded and fuller with no helical grooves (scale bar: 1 mm). (Courtesy N.D. Meeks/British Museum)

The necklace was examined by binocular microscopy, backed up by SEM examination with EDX analysis.

It comprises a strap of six double loop-in-loop cross-linked chains. From the bottom a row of hollow seed or amphorae pendants are hung from decorated gold wires. At the junction of each pendant wire and the chain there is a rosette. There is a pear-shaped clasp at each end, terminating in the hook and loop.

The techniques employed include wiremaking and beading, granulation, hollow bead-making, soldering and surface treatment. Approximately half of the necklace is ancient, while the other half is nineteenth century (Figure 15.20). The original side shows a little damage (Figure 15.11) and repair but is quite worn (see Figure 2.15). The change from ancient to nineteenth-century chain links takes place at the same point in all the rows, as if a knife had cut through the intact necklace. The nineteenth-century section was not made and then simply joined to the ancient piece, but built up from it, a considerable technical achievement.

The many thousands of components of both sections, principally chain links, have quite consistent compositions, with a perceptible difference between the two sides. Surface EDX analysis on the heavily enriched surfaces gave compositions of about 3% of silver and about 0.5% of copper for the ancient goldwork, but on one scraped area where the interior metal was exposed the gold contained about 6% of silver and 1% of copper. The nineteenth-century section is of almost pure gold with approximately 0.5% each of silver and copper at the surface and the one scraped area had a composition of 100% gold. Artefacts of pure gold are also not uncommon in the ancient world after the introduction of gold refining in the sixth century BC. Thus, although the composition is not specific for either ancient or modern gold, it does group the various components enabling them to be unambiguously identified.

The most obvious difference in metalwork technique lies in the methods used to make the wires. The ancient wires are strip-twisted throughout, having rather irregular profiles and the characteristic helical twist, whereas the nineteenth-century drawn wires are fuller and more rounded, and, just occasionally, parallel drawing striations can be seen (see Figure 15.20).

The present condition of the surfaces of the two pieces is very different. The original half has pronounced surface enhancement and a matted etched surface. This may be due to the natural leaching of the copper and to a lesser extent of the silver during burial, a combination of deliberate ancient treatment to enhance the color and subsequent burial, or even of a combination of burial and post-excavation surface treatment in the nineteenth century. There is considerable grain

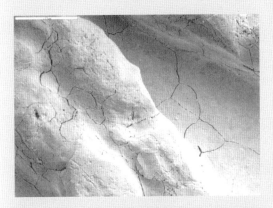

boundary etching that could be in part be due to long-term migration of vacancies in the crystal lattice to the grain boundaries during burial (Figure 15.21 and see p. 374). The nineteenth-century half has a very different, heavily etched surface. This suggests treatment with strong acid, recalling the aqua regia treatment recommended by Castellani, which alone would be capable of deep etching the almost pure gold. The nineteenth-century solders have suffered corrosion stress cracking. The ancient work was apparently not subjected to this treatment, either to preserve the ancient surface or because its rather more base composition was known and it was feared that the strong acid treatment could prove ruinous.

The solder work on the two halves is also very different (Figures 15.22a and 15.22b). On the nineteenth-century work the solder is clearly visible, especially on the wires defining

Figure 15.21 SEM micrograph of ancient soldered area on the 'half-and-half' necklace, showing extensive grain boundary etching, possibly enhanced by vacancy diffusion (scale bar: 100 microns). (Courtesy N.D. Meeks/British Museum)

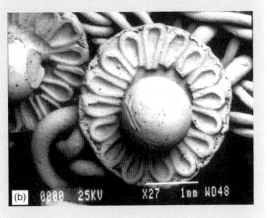

Figure 15.22 SEM micrograph of the rosettes of the 'half-and-half' necklace. The petals on the original rosette (a) are outlined with a continuous soldered wire, whereas the petals on the nineteenth-century copy (b) are of individual 'horseshoes' of wire, sunk in a copper-rich gold solder (scale bars: 1 mm). (Courtesy N.D. Meeks/British Museum)

the petals, yet on the ancient work virtually no solder can be seen. Indeed, this necklace exemplifies the problems that Castellani had, trying to match the cleanness of the ancient soldered joins. The analyses of the acid-treated surfaces of the nineteenth-century solders are very variable, but do reveal appreciable amounts of copper and silver leaving gold contents typically between 75 and 90%. By contrast, the apparently soldered areas on the ancient work have the same composition as the surrounding metal they are joining. As noted above (p. 380), this not unusual situation could have a number of explanations. Either a truly tiny amount of metallic solder was used, or a form of diffusion bonding was employed using copper salts; or, possibly, no solder was used at all, just heat.

Case study: The Festetic dinner service (the subject of an article by Keith Dovkants in the London *Evening Standard*, Monday, 13 March 1995)

In 1978 a British businessman, Leslie Mackie, was offered the chance to purchase a solid gold dinner service. The service purported to been the one made for the Austro-Hungarian aristocratic family, the Festetics von Tolna, in 1797 by the eminent goldsmith, Johann Keibel. The service had disappeared from the family's principal seat at the Keszthely Palace near Lake Balaton during the Second World War and was believed lost. After careful checks and authentication, Mr Mackie went ahead with the purchase and the service duly reappeared piece by piece, apparently smuggled from behind the Iron Curtain.

The 114-piece service of 18-carat gold, weighing over 100 kg, spent the next few years in a bank vault until 1994 when Mr Mackie decided to sell through the same dealers. They again had authenticity tests carried out, but in the intervening years the controversy over cadmium gold solders had arisen, as described above. This time the tests obviously included a careful examination of the joins, which revealed that the solders contained cadmium, not introduced until the mid-nineteenth century, and thus the service could not be the one made by Keibel.

When Keith Dovkants interviewed the present head of the family, Prince George Festetic (something that perhaps Mr Mackie should have done in the first place), he was able to vouchsafe that the real service was of gilt silver, not gold at all. Dovkants speculated that perhaps the whole scam was perpetrated by the Russians in order to very profitably move a very considerable quantity of gold at a time when sales of the metal were sluggish.

Silver

Sources: General: Grimwade (1985); Butts and Coxe (eds) (1967). Early and classical silver: Strong (1966); Kent and Painter (eds) (1977); Baratte and Painter (eds) (1989). British silver: Jackson (1911, 1921); Wardle (1963); Oman (1965); Pickford (1983); Glanville (1987). 18th- and 19th-century silver-plated wares: Bradbury (1912); Wardle (1963, pp. 29–49); Hughes (1970); Bury (1971). Marks: Bradbury (1959); Pickford (ed) (1989); Matheau-Raven (1997); Mappin (1999). Fakes and forgeries: Forbes (1971); Grimwade (1982); Waldron (1986); Marsh (1993, pp. 127–135); Harris (1999). Silversmithing, commercial: Selwyn (1948, 1954); Macfarlane (1967); Hallowell (1967); Abbey (1968); Blakemore (1983). Silversmithing, craft and traditional: Wilson (1951); Untracht (1968).

Silver production and its composition

The most common source of silver through the past several thousand years in the Old World has been argentiferous lead ores. Silver was also recovered from other ores that are not primarily lead ores (known as *dry ores*, such as the mixed sulphatic jarosites) by adding lead metal to the smelting charge to absorb the silver. Thus whatever the source of the silver, the first product was argentiferous lead. The silver was separated from the lead by *cupellation* (Craddock, 1995, pp. 221–231). In this process the lead is heated to about 1100°C and subjected to a strong air-blast, causing the molten lead and most of the other base metals to oxidise. Thus the melt separates into two phases, the molten oxides of lead and the base metals and the molten metallic silver floating upon it, 'like oil on water' in Pliny's apt phrase (*Natural History*, 33.95; Rackham, 1952, p. 75). Any gold contained in the ore runs off with the silver. Some base metals, notably bismuth, are also rather difficult to remove by cupellation (McKerrell and Stevenson, 1972); for example, spills of primary unrefined silver from Roman levels at the silver mine of Rio Tinto in the south of Spain had about 1% of gold and several per cent of bismuth (Craddock *et al.*, 1985) and some Islamic coins from the Hindu Kush have several hundred ppm of bismuth (Cowell and Lowick, 1988).

It is also very difficult to remove all traces of the lead, which is therefore normally present in trace amounts in early silver. Note that very early silver, originating from native silver or from very rich silver ores that could be smelted without recourse to lead to absorb the silver, may contain very little lead. For example, silver of the Bronze Age Argaric cultures from the south-east of Spain contains little or no detectable lead at the 0.01% analytical detection limit (Arribas *et al.*, 1989). Similarly, the presence of traces of volatile metals such as arsenic or zinc indicates that the metal had not been cupelled, as these metals would otherwise have been completely removed. However, there is always the possibility that the silver may subsequently have been alloyed with copper containing these two metals.

By far the most important trace metal for silver authenticity studies is gold (Plenderleith, 1933, 1935; Gordus and Gordus, 1974). Most, but not all, early silver metal contains some gold (Hughes and Hall, 1979; Gunter and Jett, 1992, pp. 241–250). Very broadly, the gold content decreases with time. Ancient silver regularly contains from several hundred ppm to a few per cent of gold, leading Meyers (2004) to suggest that the usual sources exploited in antiquity were oxidised ores such as cerussite, hydrated lead carbonate, or jarosite, a mixed sulphatic ore, both being ore types which have enhanced gold contents.

Gold contents found in silver antiquities are naturally variable, dependent on the deposits, but contents much below about 0.05% should be a cause for concern. For example, a series of forgeries of Roman silver ingots (Jones (ed), 1990, p. 283) (Figure 15.23) had gold contents below the XRF detection level of about 200 ppm, whereas a similar but genuine ingot contained 0.4% of gold (Painter, 1981). Gordus and Gordus (1974) were able to differentiate between genuine and forged Sasanian silver, the forgeries containing between about 0.002 and 0.2% of gold whereas the ancient silver contained between 0.3 and 1% of gold.

There is a widespread belief that forgeries of silver antiquities are often made from ancient silver. This is possible but the prevalence is uncertain. Poor-quality or badly damaged silver antiquities are not that common or cheap. Usually, such pieces are the subject of fraudulent restoration rather than forming a feedstock for 'new' antiquities. Silver coins are the obvious source of silver, but because of debasement policies, coinage is rarely of the same purity as the contemporary plate. A very few examples can be given where

Figure 15.23 This purports to be a late Roman silver ingot of the sort distributed to the army, etc. (BM GR 1979, 9-11,1). However, the gold content is very low, strongly suggesting it is not ancient (Courtesy J. Heffron/British Museum)

this practice may be the explanation for arte-facts which have the correct composition but which, on other evidence, are clearly forgeries. Three Sasanian silver forgeries from the Sackler Collection, acquired in the 1950s and 1960s, and now in the Freer Gallery of the Smithsonian Institution in Washington, each have about a half a per cent of gold, and trace elements, notably irid-ium, similar to those found in the genuine pieces, suggesting that genuine Sasanian silver may have been used to make these pieces (Gunter and Jett, 1992, pp. 224–239). Similarly, a Roman silver lamp, now in the British Museum (BM GR Reg. 1868, 1–10, 396), and declared by Bailey (1996, p. 124) to be 'probably not ancient', contains 0.5% of gold, in addition to 6.2% of copper and 0.5% of lead. Details of the lamp were first pub-lished in the 1840s, and if it is not ancient then it is probably another rare instance in which genu-ine ancient scrap silver has been reused to make a forgery. The Risley Lanx may be another example (see Chapter 20, p.508).

Medieval European silver has a gold content of the order of about 0.1%, typical of silver pro-duced from argentiferous galena. As the methods of removing gold from silver became more effective in the Post-Medieval period, so it became more viable to recover ever-smaller quantities of gold from the silver. Thus, the gold content dropped to about 0.05% in the Post-Medieval period, and to only about 0.01% in the nineteenth century (Forbes and Dalladay, 1958/59), and with the intro-duction of electrolytic refining at the end of the century, dropped still further to just a few parts per million.

Note, as with all metal compositions, that these are only very rough generalisations; individual artefacts can have very special histories and it is important to keep in mind that these overall trends mask much individual variation. Silver from the great Peruvian mine of Potosi, which entered the European market from the 1550s on, has a very low gold content (Gordus and Gordus, 1974), not due to any special processing but rather to the intrinsically low gold content of the ore. Thus the absence of gold does not automatically condemn an antiquity, but it should raise serious doubts.

In addition to its unusually low gold content, Potosi silver also has a distinctive indium content, as noted by Barrandon *et al.* (1991, 1995) and Guerra (2000). Gordus and Craig (1995) reported iridium contents above 0.002% in silver coins minted by the Bogota mint.

A variety of solders were used for joining silver in classical antiquity (Lang and Hughes, 1984). These included standard copper–silver hard solders and a silver–tin hard solder that seems never to have been used in recent times. There were also tin–lead and tin soft solders and silver–mercury amalgams used as a sol-der, which is also apparently not used in modern times.

Silver patina and ageing

The most common products of silver corrosion are silver chloride (*horn silver*), or silver sulphide (*sil-ver glance*), depending on the burial environment. The silver chloride forms a waxy deposit on the surface, the sulphide forming a dense black layer. Silver bromide is also often present together with the chloride (Hedges, 1976), and even sometimes the iodide, and their presence should be taken as an indication of authenticity. The patinas on genu-ine silver artefacts may have been reduced to silver metal electrolytically (see Chapter 20, p. 500).

Silver has frequently been alloyed with copper, and as the copper is more electronegative it will corrode preferentially, and thus a silver antiquity, with say, no more than 10% of copper, may have a firmly adhering green patina formed almost exclu-sively of copper salts. Even where silver chloride does form as well, its purple hue can be mistaken for cuprite (as exemplified by the corroded Roman silver mirror; see Chapter 20, p. 501, Figure 20.4).

The embrittlement of ancient silver
Sources: Schweizer and Meyers (1978a, b; 1979); Meyers (1981); Kallfass *et al.* (1985); Wanhill *et al.* (1998); Wanhill (2003).

Ancient silver is sometimes found to be in a very brittle condition, and permeated with cracks. On the other hand, recent silver of reasonable purity, i.e. 80% and above, is usually fairly ductile; thus brit-tleness is a good indicator of age. Brittleness can be alleviated in silver antiquities by careful annealing and quenching (see Chapter 20, p. 505, Figure 20.5). Even so, evidence of previous brittleness is often still present owing to the extensive remains of brittle fracture, which would be difficult to totally remove even by the most determined and drastic restoration.

The causes of age embrittlement in silver are not fully understood (Wanhill *et al.*, 1998), but it would seem that there are at least two, and perhaps three, separate processes involved. The most obvious expla-nation is the precipitation of copper from the alloy, but embrittlement also occurs in almost pure silver and therefore other mechanisms must play a part.

In equilibrium conditions copper only has a very low solubility in silver at room temperature (c.0.1%), but in practice the copper is only shed very slowly unless the silver is heated (Norbury, 1929; Cohen, 1937). At room temperature the copper is very slowly deposited along the grain boundaries, forming distinctive lamellae. If the silver is heated to between 300° and 400°C, the precipitation takes place over a few hours, such that repeated annealing operations during fabrication may have brought about significant precipitation. These copper-rich lamellae are more electronegative than the surrounding silver and thus more prone to corrosion. In addition, there is a volume change within the grains, causing stress and opening up the grains boundaries, all of which leads to the observed cracking. This phenomenon has been reported from the mid-twentieth century on antiquities, and clearly such preferential corrosion is a good indication of authenticity. Schweizer and Meyers (1978a, b) and Meyers (1981) suggested that the morphology of the precipitation along the grain boundaries differed with temperature and that the very slow, room-temperature precipitation could be distinguished from the accelerated precipitation brought about by heat treatment.

As noted above, this cannot be the only mechanism causing embrittlement. Research on an extremely embrittled and cracked Egyptian silver vase with 0.9% of copper and 0.3% of lead, suggested that lead precipitating along the grain boundaries was the cause of the brittle fracture (Wanhill *et al.*, 1998).

The phenomenon is only found in some silver, seeming to be more prevalent in hammered metalwork left in a work-hardened state. Schweizer and Meyers suggested that the process may not be noticeable, or even commence for centuries. Certainly, age embrittlement does not seem to be a problem encountered with Post-Medieval silver that has not been buried.

The faking and forging of antique silver plate, mainly British

Forged silver complete with hallmarks stamped with false dies (Figure 15.24) was very prevalent in the late nineteenth and early twentieth centuries (Cripps, 1914, pp. 197–211; Glanville 1987, pp. 293–301), sometimes appearing on the market in very considerable quantities as exemplified by the Lyon and Twinham forgeries (Johnson 1983; Tait, 1989; Jones (ed), 1990, pp. 261–263).

Figure 15.24 A set of false dies for the hallmarking of silver seized from the premises of Charles Twinham, the prolific silver forger. (Courtesy London Assay Office)

Until the nineteenth century, old plate was generally regarded as little more than bullion, and only latterly began, in quick succession, to be appreciated, collected and forged. In the late nineteenth century there were an enormous number of highly skilled and trained artisan craftsmen turning out good hand-made reproduction work for the well-known silver companies for sale to the rising middle classes. Any one of these craftsmen could turn out a competent piece of hollow ware and, what is more, only expect a few shillings for their trouble. Such a body of low-paid but skilled craftsmen has not existed in the West now for many years and consequently the production of hand-made silver forgeries of what one might call routine antiques, selling for under £1000, has all but ceased. However, the rising tide of sometimes quite proficient imitation or forged antiques coming from the Far East warns against complacency. Copies of occidental antiques are now appearing from the same sources and could one day include forgeries of European antique silver – if they don't already.

The usual indications of authenticity, composition, technique, patination, etc. applied to silver have been discussed above, but may be adumbrated here. European silver was regularly alloyed with small amounts of copper, necessary to give the metal some hardness and strength. Sterling silver is defined as containing 925 parts per thousand of silver, the remainder being copper, i.e. silver with 7.5% of copper.

The patina on antique silver is much discussed but poorly defined and understood, Pickford (1983, p. 71) being one of the very few to assign the patina to a specific cause. He believed it to be residual fire-staining, resulting from successive and prolonged heating of the piece on an open hearth to anneal the metal during the metalworking processes, causing the copper in the alloy to oxidise, which would impart to the surface a rather dull grey appearance that would be difficult to remove. Others have adopted more vague descriptions, based more on the cumulative effect of generations of wear and polishing. Rabinovitch (1990) attempted a scientific characterisation of patina on silver, but concluded that the characteristic 'mellow lambency', whatever that might be, was just the result of wear and polishing over the years.

Stamps and hallmarks

Sources: Bradbury (1959); Hare (ed) (1978); Pickford (ed) (1989).

From at least Byzantine times plate has often carried official control stamps guaranteeing the weight and purity of the metal, and from the end of the Medieval period most European plate carries some marks, known in English as hallmarks. The primary function of these marks was and is to show that the piece had been assayed and met the required standard of purity. As the marks, at least in Britain, usually indicate the place, year and maker of the piece, they also provide much information about the piece and thus guarantee its authenticity. Hence, much attention is paid to hallmarks by forgers and collectors alike, sometimes to the neglect of the other qualities of the piece. Certainly, much of the efforts of the forgers seem to have been expended in ensuring that a convincing hallmark appears on the forgery, and thus one of the most common ruses is to transpose the mark from a genuine piece to the forgery, as exemplified by forgeries of Viennese *Jugendstil* silverwares of the 1900s incorporating transposed marks (Neuwirth, 1980).

Perhaps at this point the legal situation, at least as it pertains to Britain, should be discussed. For centuries the Goldsmiths' Company of London have zealously guarded the purity of English silver, and this care over the last century has been extended to antique silver, with a specific body, the Antique Plate Committee, being established in 1939 (Tait, 1989).

Under the current 1973 Hallmarking Act of Parliament it is an offence to make a mark resembling a hallmark or to copy an existing mark. It is an offence to remove a mark or to transpose a hallmark from one piece to another. It is also an offence to substantially alter a hallmarked piece of plate without offering it for re-assay; even to knowingly own an illegally marked piece is an offence. The Goldsmiths' Company have the authority to seize pieces which it believes are suspect and to confiscate those that contravene the law. From 1939 to 1977 the Committee examined no less than 13 623 pieces and confiscated 7544.

Duty dodgers constitute a rather different form of hallmarking fraud. Between 1719 and 1757 a tax of sixpence per ounce was imposed on silverware, assessed and payable when the piece was sent for assay. The silversmiths protested vehemently and there was widespread avoidance, either by incorporating a hallmark taken from a piece of scrap silver, or by sending a small item for assay, paying the duty and then on its return cutting out the hallmark and incorporating it into a much heavier piece. The small item could be made to a specific shape such that the hallmarked piece could conveniently form an appropriate component, such as a base ring or rim, in the large piece. Such pieces can be very difficult to detect as they are genuinely contemporary with their mark. The superb wine fountain made for George Booth, 2nd Earl of Warrington in 1728 by Peter Archambo (Tait, 1989) is a good example. It is massively heavy weighing 575 ounces, on which the duty would have been a hefty 14 pounds and 15 shillings. When examined in the 1920s it was discovered that the hallmarks were on a small piece of silver inserted into the base, almost certainly taken from a small light piece of plate on which the duty had been paid. It should be stressed that such pieces are still technically illegal in Britain and liable to confiscation. Thus when the wine fountain was revealed as a duty-dodger it was seized, the old offending marks obliterated, and current ones substituted. Subsequent to the 1973 Hallmark Act, duty-dodging pieces are still assayed and if of acceptable quality, marked with current hallmarks. The original duty-dodging hallmarks are struck through but remain legible, and the maker's mark is left intact if deemed to be original.

There are three main categories of fakes and forgeries of antique plate, i.e. casts or electroforms of existing antique pieces that also reproduce the hallmarks, modern pieces that are struck with false dies to produce the hallmarks, and, most prevalent, fraudulently altered pieces, rendered so in particular by the insertion of a segment of silver bearing a hallmark from a less-valuable or badly damaged genuine piece into a more recent piece (Forbes, 1971; Grimwade, 1982).

The features which are characteristic of a casting are discussed in Chapter 4 (p. 69), and of an electroform in Chapter 4 (p. 84). Electroform forgeries of silver have been made almost since the inception of the method in the mid-nineteenth century, as exemplified by the presence of electroforms among the items of sixteenth- and seventeenth-century Baroque plate bequeathed to the British Museum as the Waddesdon Bequest (Tait, 1988 and see Chapter 1, p.15).

On both castings and electroforms there is an overall lack of crispness, especially in worked detail such as engraved or chased lines, and above all on the stamped hallmarks. Furthermore, punching or stamping should locally work-harden the silver and this could be detected using a microhardness tester, or techniques such as ultrasonics or acoustic microscopy (see Chapter 2, p. 36). Laue diffractometry may be able to distinguish between castings, electroforms and worked silver (see Chapters 3, p. 54 and 8, p. 183).

Pickford (1983, pp. 22–23) described a potentially disastrous method of determining whether a piece of flat ware is cast, stamped out or worked. The test depends on the differential bendability of the silver. Cast metalwork will not usually bend easily; pieces that have been stamped out on a press will tend to bend whereas true hand-hammered pieces will be springy and resilient. Thus, when trying to bend a piece at the stem, if it is found to resist (or, possibly break!) it is cast; if it bends it is stamped; and if it is springy then it is hammered. These distinctions are, at best, simplistic; if fully annealed then hammered, metalwork will bend as easily as stamped metal. There is potential for serious damage and thus it is not recommended that the test be carried out. Pickford instructed that if the piece does bend then one should 'remember to restore the slight bend you have made', without saying how this was to be done. In practice it is almost impossible, and one is left wondering whether Pickford ever actually tried out this test. Bending metal locally work-hardens it, such that trying to bend the stem back again would merely create another bend by the side of the first (try this with a thin metal rod or strip, but never with your antique flat ware!).

If the forgeries form a group taken from one genuine piece, such as a set of candlesticks or spoons, the hallmarks on cast or electroformed copies will have identical wear patterns and will all be in exactly the same position in relation to each other, whereas on genuine pieces the hallmarks will have been individually struck and appear in slightly different positions. From the end of the eighteenth century the assay marks denoting purity, assay office, date letter and, sometimes, duty paid, were often stamped on as one, and thus will appear in exactly the same order in relation to each other. However,

the maker's mark will still have been independently applied.

An alternative is to stamp the forgeries with false dies. The problems here are twofold, creating an acceptable piece and making a convincing hallmark. The latter necessitates the manufacture of dies. Die-cutting in steel is a highly skilled job and the die must make an impression that will pass scrutiny by the Antique Plate Committee (Figure 15.24). In practice, false dies are often made from copper or copper alloy, which are much easier to cut than steel, but which make a much less crisp impression in the silver.

Faking, i.e. converting a piece of plate into something more valuable, is also common. A variety of conversions are discussed and illustrated by Waldron (1986) and Harris (1999) (see also Figure 1.3). Plate may also have been repaired and embellished. Decoration by chasing, engraving or embossing of earlier plate considered too plain by the Victorians is very familiar, sometimes with subsequent attempts to remove their efforts. This was done either by grinding the surface or by filling with a silver solder. Richter (1971) described a method of infilling engravings with a silver amalgam. As this does not involve major removal or addition of silver, the pieces so altered did not need to be re-assayed and are thus technically legal.

The difficulty of forging hallmarks has meant that the usual fraudulent practice has been to insert genuine hallmarks into the forgery or to transform a common but genuine hallmarked piece into something more valuable. Frauds are particularly prevalent in flat ware, for example converting relatively common spoons of the late seventeenth or early eighteenth century into much rarer forks (Pickford, 1983, pp. 65–70). The easiest method is simply to cut off the bowl of a genuine spoon and solder on the new tines of a fork (Figures 15.25, 15.26a and 15.26b). Note that this method only works for flat ware up to the mid-eighteenth century when the ends of both spoons and forks turned up in the same way. The soldered joins are often disguised by electroplating with silver or gold. As flat ware was almost never gilded, its presence should arouse suspicions that there is something hidden underneath. Silver electroplate is pure silver and perceptibly whiter than sterling silver with its 7.5% copper content. The presence of a soldered line on unplated pieces can sometimes be revealed simply by breathing on the suspect area. Analysis in the region of the join might identify any solder present.

Figure 15.25   Fraudulent conversion. The tines of a fork have been soldered to the stem of a spoon bearing genuine early eighteenth-century hallmarks (the join has been marked). (Courtesy London Assay Office)

Figure 15.26   (a) Butter scoop where an electroplated nickel-silver blade has been soldered to the stem of an antique silver spoon, bearing the date letter for 1811. (b) Detail of soldered join of different color and with small air bubbles (illegal property of the author). (Courtesy A. Milton)

Figure 15.27   Stages in the conversion of a spoon into a fork. First, the bowl is hammered into a rectangular trough. Additional silver is then poured in. This is hammered into a rectangular tab. The tines are cut, worked and polished into a fork. (Courtesy London Assay Office)

A much more sophisticated conversion is outlined in Figure 15.27. Here the bowl is modified into a set of prongs and there is no join. If the added silver is from the same source as that for the spoon, the scientific detection of the fraud could be well-nigh impossible. If the added silver were modern, it may have a lower gold content than the genuine early piece (see p. 387). It might also be possible, if the problem was deemed sufficiently worthwhile, to carry out lead isotope analysis.

For hollow wares a piece of silver bearing the hallmarks taken from a genuine piece may be soldered in place onto the forged piece, but the possibility that this is a contemporary 'duty-dodger' must always be considered (see p. 390). The main source of genuine early hallmarks for reuse is, inevitably, the stems of old flat ware. In the heyday of the forging of plate in the late nineteenth and early twentieth centuries, it was common practice to turn the hallmarked stems of old spoons into the base rings of forged hollow wares. To turn the oval sectioned stems into thin sheet base rings without distorting the hallmarks was almost impossible. Also, the marks ran down the stem rather than side-by-side as one would expect if applied to a base ring.

Oman (1965, p. 217) stated that the only sure method of detecting a suspected solder was to heat the piece in an electric furnace whereupon any solder would melt and appear on the surface of the join. It is not certain if this was a serious suggestion, but it should never be attempted. Not only is there the danger of other solders melting and the object falling apart, but any lead in the solder could oxidise and react with the surrounding silver, ruining the whole piece. The silver experts of previous generations do seem to have been remarkably cavalier in their authenticity tests!

16

Gemstones and jade

'At what stage does a pink sapphire become a ruby?' 'When you want to sell it.'
Maggie Campbell Pedersen in *Gems & Jewellery* **15** 4, 2006; p. 95)

Gemstones: their imitation, improvement and forgery

Principal sources: Scarfe (1975); Newman (1981); Ogden (1982); O'Donoghue (1997, 2005); Trench (2000, pp. 186–193); O'Donoghue and Joyner (2003); Read (2005); O'Donoghue (ed) (2006). Authentication: Webster (1971); Ogden (1982, pp. 137–142).

See also the *Journal of Gemmological Studies, Gems and Jewellery* and *Revue du Gemmologie*.

The subjects addressed in this chapter reflect some very different motivations and include the following topics: 1. Gem-testing and scientific examination, 2. The imitation of natural gemstones, 3. The enhancement or treatment of gemstones and composites, 4. Dating indicators, including the type and source of natural gemstones and the methods used to work and facet them. (Beads are discussed in Chapter 10, p. 233.)

Introduction

The recognition of what are often closely dated techniques and materials, used to enhance, imitate, or even synthesise gemstones is clearly important in establishing the age of a piece. Ogden (1982, p. 156) noted that 'so far gemmological studies have not been used to their full potential in forgery detection, but have proved their worth in several cases' and goes on to list stones purporting to be Roman that gemmological tests revealed were variously synthetic, from a South American source, or made of plastic. Conversely simulants or synthetic stones can be set in an old piece of jewellery to help pass

them off as a genuine natural stone; the gemmological trade is full of such stories (Carbonin *et al.*, 2000 and Duroc-Danner, 2000, for example, from just one issue of *Gemmological Studies*).

Gem-testing and scientific examination

Gem-testing

Sources: Lewis (1977); Webster (1983, pp. 605–959); Liddicoat (1987); Anderson (1990); Karanth (2000, pp. 7–122); O'Donoghue and Joyner (2003); Read (2005). Organic jewellery materials: Campbell Pedersen (2004).

Gem-testing is a specialised business with dedicated laboratories (adverts are regularly placed in the standard journals dealing with gems). However, it is essential to have some idea of the approaches and techniques used and the potential information that scientific tests can reveal.

The forgery of gems, principally with glass, was rampant in Roman times. Pliny described how false gems were to be detected 'since it is only fitting that even luxury should be protected against deception' (*Natural History*, 37.198–200; Eichholz, 1962, (trans.) pp. 326–327). His tests included hardness, density, feel, inclusions on and in the material, and the reaction of the material to strong heat.

Hardness: Hard stones will scratch softer ones; for example, the ability of a diamond to scratch corundum (sapphire or ruby) is a quick and infallible test. There are standard sets of sticks or plates made of minerals of known hardness. Hardness tests are good for eliminating possibilities rather than for positive identification. However, if the stones fail the test, i.e. if they are softer than the material they are rubbed against, then they are liable to be damaged themselves, and thus the method is impracticable for the testing of gems which must be returned to their owner without visible damage.

Specific gravity (SG): Most gemstones tend to be of high density, at least relative to most glasses and resins (although the density of the latter can be adjusted with additives). Unfortunately, most ancient gemstones are firmly embedded in settings of other materials, which make specific gravity measurements impossible. Also, as a general principle, it is not advisable to wet antiquities, and even the immersion of a seemingly natural stone in an inert liquid should not be undertaken as there is the danger of dissolving or contaminating possible surface treatments or of the stone being a composite (see below) and the liquid penetrating the join, with potentially catastrophic consequences. Some gemstones are porous, such as turquoise and opal, and must never be immersed in any liquids.

Touch: Gemstones tend to be good conductors of heat and thus feel cold to the touch. Most simulants, notably glass and resins, are poor conductors and hence feel warm by comparison. The tongue is recommended by most authorities as the most sensitive organ for the touch test. The distinctive surface micro-topography of many gem simulants can be recognised by rubbing them against the teeth, and this is a standard method for detecting pearl simulants (see p. 404).

For the examination of gems, a quality binocular microscope with an adjustable white light source is a prerequisite. In addition, a standard compound microscope with transmitted light and facilities for polarised light is necessary for the detailed examination of the stones (Webster, 1983, pp. 774–828). There should be provision for dark field vision, in which, although the stone is viewed by transmitted light, the stage beneath is in darkness (Webster, 1983, p. 806). Through such instruments the major inclusions and other internal features in the material such as healed fractures, as well as surface blemishes can be viewed and recorded (Gübelin and Koivula, 1997, pp. 22–30). Note that the standard gem-testing texts recommend immersing the stone in a colorless liquid of similar refractive index (RI) to make inclusions and other internal features more visible. This should not be undertaken if the stone is in an ancient setting, and even if loose there are still dangers with ancient or porous stones.

On occasion, the use of such a liquid has led to the unmasking of a fraud. Many years ago a piece of gypsum containing the wing of an arachnid insect was reported in Australia, and duly deposited in the Geological Museum at Sydney (Cole, 1955, p. 54). There it received great attention, and learned papers and a new genetic name followed for this supposed ancestor of the common grasshopper. Years later photographs were required for yet another publication, and the stone was immersed in a liquid that promptly penetrated into the crystal along the plane in which the wing lay. From this it became obvious that the gypsum had been carefully sliced and hollowed, the wing then having been inserted and the two pieces cemented back together. In this instance, as the Museum was photographing its own object, there were no problems. However, if the object had been undergoing investigation by an outside party the consequences could have been very serious, with claims of negligence and damage. Collectors tend not to like their prize specimens returned to them as valueless pieces, and in this case it could have been difficult to prove that the cut had been made many years previously and was not a clumsy attempt to disguise an accident.

For quick preliminary examinations, and those conducted outside the laboratory, a good quality lens giving a ×10 magnification is essential. This can either be a pocket lens on a swivel fitting or a loupe that is held in the eye like a monocle.

As most gemstones are crystalline, their interactions with light are often highly characteristic. Since most ancient gems will be in settings which make it difficult to manoeuvre the stone into a light beam for transmission, techniques which utilise reflected radiation are preferable.

Refractive index (RI): The RI provides perhaps the simplest and most direct means of positive identification of gemstones, using a refractometer to measure the RI with either transmitted or reflected monochromatic light. It is also useful for the recognition of glasses. Glasses, which are singly reflective, have RIs in the range of 1.5 to 1.7, values which are not found in any singly refractive natural gemstones.

Single and double refractivity: Cubic crystalline gemstones, notably diamond, garnets and fluorspar, together with most non-crystalline materials such as glass and resins, are singly refractive (known as *isotropy*). However, most crystalline gemstones exhibit double refractivity (known as *anisotropy*); that is, they split a beam of white light into two separate polarised beams, which can be detected using a simple polariscope. However, the method only works for transmitted light, and thus might not be applicable where the gem is mounted in a closed setting.

Dichroism: In most of the double-refractive stones the emerging rays are of different colors (more usually different shades of the same color). Using a simple lenses arrangement in a tube, known as a dichroscope, the two colors are separated and can be viewed simultaneously.

Spectroscopy: White light, whether transmitted or reflected, is split by the crystalline gemstone into its constituent spectra, which can be observed and recorded with a spectroscope. Certain wavelengths are absorbed by the gemstone, leaving dark bands on the spectrum, and the positions of these are characteristic of specific minerals, and thus form a good means of identification. Note that in some spectroscopes the absorbency of components of the white light can generate a great deal of heat in the stone itself, which could be damaging.

A very simple but effective test can be made with colored dichromatic filters, such as Chelsea filters, which only allow through the deep red and yellow–green parts of the spectrum, and which are good for the testing of blue, green and some red gemstones (Webster, 1983, p. 912, Table 9). The suspect stone is illuminated by white light and observed through the filter. For example, natural and synthetic sapphires appear green, but most artificial stones and glass appear red. Blue stones, including synthetics that have been colored with cobalt appear deep red, although stones colored with copper salts are not affected. Natural and synthetic emeralds transmit a deep red light, whereas most of the simulants retain their green color when viewed through the filter.

UV: (Rorimer, 1931, p. 27; Read, 2005) Some gems show a characteristic fluorescence under UV radiation, which is different from that of their simulants, and glass only fluoresces weakly, with the exception of lead glass. UV can also reveal the presence of fillers in stones such as emeralds that often have impregnated fractures (see p. 409). Note that some gemstones that have had their color enhanced by heat treatment could have the color permanently changed by exposure to UV.

Scientific examination

Fourier transform infra-red (FTIR) spectroscopy is especially useful for gem identification (Fritsch and Stockton, 1987). The technique is also able to detect polymers impregnated into the stones and to easily pick up water absorption frequencies in natural emerald and other stones to distinguish them from simulants and synthetics (Stockton, 1987). Martin *et al.* (1989) used reflectance IR to identify the mineralogy of gemstones.

Many minerals display cathodoluminescence (CL), i.e. the fluorescence produced by exposure of the stone to an electron beam (see Chapter 11, p. 254). The method is quick and non-destructive, and was first used by Ponahlo (1992) to differentiate between synthetic and natural diamonds. Some minor inclusions containing minerals such as apatite, diopside and fluorite, that might otherwise be missed, fluoresce strongly (Ponahlo, 2002). More recently, Huang Fengming *et al.* (2003) have applied the method to the study of cultured pearls (see p. 404).

X-ray diffraction (XRD) is currently still the main technique for the precise identification of the mineral species present. Using the powder method this normally requires a very small sample (see Chapter 3, p. 53), but non-destructive methods on unprepared surfaces are now available (Chiari *et al.*, 1996).

Raman microscopy (RM) (p. 54) is a versatile and non-destructive technique (Pinet *et al.*, 1992; Hänni *et al.*, 1997; Smith and Robin, 1997; Kiefert *et al.*, 1999, 2001, 2005; Smith, 2005a). In conjunction with a petrological microscope, inclusions can be located and analysed, be they solid, liquid or even gaseous (Schubnel, 1992; Coupry and Brissaud, 1996; Gübelin and Koivula, 1997; Burke, 2001). A particular advantage of RM is the ability to analyse gems that are in their settings or are mounted beneath transparent materials. Hänni *et al.* (1997) gave the example of testing the diamonds set into the hands of a watch *through* the watch glass, although it must be stressed that the sensitivity is thereby compromised. Lightweight portable systems using fibre optics enable large and fragile gem-encrusted artefacts such as Medieval shrines to be comprehensively examined without being moved or even touched (Reiche *et al.*, 2004; Kieffert *et al.*, 2005; Smith, 2005a). RM is also useful for detecting evidence of some gem treatments, especially the fillers and pigments used.

Non-destructive analytical techniques such as X-ray fluorescence (XRF) (Chapter 3, p. 47) or energy-dispersive X-ray (EDX) analysis in the scanning electron microscope are useful for identifying the elements present. Particle (or proton)-induced X-ray or gamma-ray emission (PIXE or PIGE respectively) analysis are very sensitive techniques (see Chapter 3, p. 50). These techniques can be especially useful in the rapid detection of gem simulants, or by identifying the various inorganic coloring and opacifing elements of surface-enhancement (see p. 409).

Radiography can be useful for revealing a variety of internal features, from exposing the structure of a composite gem to the characteristics of drill holes in opaque gems. More specifically, radiography is the best method of revealing cultured pearls by their nuclei, and diamonds by their transparency, the imitations of the latter all being more opaque (Webster, 1983, pp. 548–551 [pearls], pp. 865–867 [diamonds]; La Niece, 2005; and see pp. 404, 400).

It should be noted that X- and radiation can permanently change the appearance of some gems (Nassau, 1974) – exposure to high-energy radiation is, after all one of the standard enhancement treatments (see p. 409).

Nuclear magnetic resonance (NMR) (p. 439) has also been used to quantify most of the major elements that constitute gemstones, such as hydrogen, aluminium, silicon, beryllium, lithium, sodium and phosphorus (Read, 2005). A full NMR printout can provide an analysis to check against that of standard known stones.

The trace element fingerprinting of gemstones has not been widely applied except for garnet (see p. 412). Harbottle and Weigand (1992) carried out neutron activation analysis (NAA) of some Mesoamerican turquoise to differentiate between the various potential sources used by the pre-Hispanic peoples of that region. NAA has also achieved some success in distinguishing between natural and synthetic stones, based on the presence of traces of gallium (see p. 407). This technique requires a sample measured in micrograms.

The imitation of natural gemstones

Imitations of gemstones fall into two quite distinct categories. There are copies that merely resemble the natural stone, known as *simulants*, and man-made stones that have the same structure and composition as the natural analogue, that alone are *synthetics*. The gemmological world, followed by the legal profession, differentiates them rigorously (Levy, 2003). Thus, a man-made synthesis of one natural stone used to imitate another would still be a classed as a simulant.

In the last half century there has been tremendous activity in the production of simulants and synthetics (Koivula *et al.*, 2000), and enhancement treatments (McClure and Smith, 2000). This activity has been matched only by the sophistication of the new methods used to distinguish them from the unaltered natural stone. Perusal of any of the gemmological journals reveals this contest between hi-tech deception and its scientific detection taking up a high percentage of the pages.

Natural and artificial simulants

Sources: Nassau (1980); Ogden (1982, pp. 137–139); Webster (1983, pp. 437–455); Anderson (1990, pp. 82–87); O'Donoghue (2005); Read (2005).

Much of man's interest in synthetic materials was developed in pursuit of substitutes for costly natural materials. Sophisticated imitation turquoise beads have been identified at the Neolithic site of Tell el-Kerkh in Syria, dated to about 5000 BC (Taniguchi *et al.*, 2002). These were apparently made by heating mineral apatite in the presence of iron and manganese minerals in a process that seems to have been a forerunner of glazing.

The long history of the imitation and falsification of gemstones is attested by the surviving ancient simulants (see Ogden, 1982, pp. 137–142 for examples), the comments of contemporary writers, and the rare survival of manuals on gem fakery. The Stockholm Papyrus is the most detailed early compilation of recipes for imitating precious metals, cheap substitutes for cloth dyed with Tyrian purple, and the largest section of all, some 74 recipes for making forgeries of pearls and other gemstones. It was probably compiled around AD 400 in Egypt (see Halleux (ed), 1981, for the text and commentary, Caley, 1927 for the English translation, and Nassau, 1984a, b, pp. 8–12; 1985 for the most informed gemmological comments).

Costume or decorative jewellery

Sources: Lewis (1970); Dinoto, 1985; Grasso, 1996; Kelley (1987); Becker (1988); Lane and Miller (1996). See also *Ornament* Magazine, especially for beads.

It must not be thought that imitation was always done out of necessity or for deception. Jewellers who produced the glass gemstones known as 'paste', from the late seventeenth century on (see p. 399), were accepted as leading and legitimate jewellers by their peers. Nowadays internationally respected firms either include or specialise in well-made imitation jewellery, such as Trifari of New York. Paste rapidly developed from mere imitation into a range of distinctively colored stones with styles of their own (see p. 399). Costume jewellery through the ages has conspicuously used the cheap and cheerful 'Junk Jewelry: A Flash Fad for Simple Styles', as *Life* Magazine headed a feature in its January 1938 issue. In the hands of extrovert artists such as Kenneth Jay Lane (Becker, 1988, pp. 192–196; Lane and Miller, 1996), for example, imitation gems are positively flouted in wonderfully outrageous and pretentious settings. His compositions are usually of glass or plastic, combined with clusters of much smaller, but genuine, natural stones. The use of plastics in jewellery was given respectability, and very soon chic, by designers such as Coco Chanel in France between the wars (Becker, 1988, pp. 127–131; Stancliffe, 1990; and see Chapter 18, p. 407).

Natural gem simulants

Less precious stones have been used to imitate more costly stones for millennia, as exemplified by the use of colorless varieties of quartz, topaz and corundum in imitation of diamond. They can be readily identified by the standard techniques outlined above, but being unchanged natural materials, there is nothing to indicate their age, except where a particular stone or source was not used before a particular date.

Alternatively, a natural gemstone could be treated, usually by dyeing, to imitate another. This practice has a long history, as exemplified by the recipes given in the Stockholm Papyrus (see p. 402). With only the gem-testing methods outlined by Pliny (see p. 394), which could at least distinguish between a gemstone and glass, using another natural stone as raw material would be sensible. Producing an acceptable color is all that would be necessary to achieve a convincing imitation. The stones used were predominantly quartz. Carefully controlled heating, variously described as opening or softening, to produce the necessary degree of cracking, was followed by soaking the stones in the appropriate solution as the coloring operation. The solutions could be aqueous or oil-based and included inorganic pigments such as copper salts to imitate emerald, or organic dyes such as cochineal or indigo.

Synthetic gem simulants

Sources: Elwell (1979, pp. 100–154); Nassau (1980); Webster (1983, pp. 372–456, etc.); Becker (1988); Anderson (1990, pp. 195–354); O'Donoghue (1997); Koivula *et al.* (2000).

This section includes minerals which have no counterpart in nature that are used to imitate a natural gemstone, as exemplified by the fused zircon oxide imitations of diamond. It also includes synthetic gems as used to imitate another stone, usually after appropriate color treatments, as exemplified by the synthetic spinels used to imitate diamond (see p. 399).

Owing to the technical and chemical problems involved, the production of artificial gemstones, in common with synthetic stones, is relatively recent,

and thus the identification of such stones should give a good indication of the recent age of at least the gems, if not the setting.

In the latter part of the twentieth century a series of basically colorless crystals, often subsequently colored, with good gemstone properties, were introduced as simulants. These include synthetic quartz, which has been synthesised for industrial purposes from the mid-twentieth century. In 1969 a quartz gem colored blue with cobalt was announced, and by the 1980s large quantities of colored quartz stones from the then USSR and Japan had become commercially available. The colors include green, blue, yellow and purple, using iron, cobalt, and manganese minerals respectively as colorants. The yellow varieties simulated citrines and the purple amethyst. Synthetic quartz is not easily distinguished by the standard gem-tests, or mineralogically by XRD and RM. The analytical detection of their inorganic colorants is often the best method of revealing them.

A range of artificial gemstones with the structure of garnet were introduced in the 1960s (Webster, 1983, pp. 419–4210, having the general formula $X_3Al_5O_{12}$, where X is usually a lanthanide metal or yttrium. They are produced by the Czochraslki method (see p. 406) of crystal-pulling from the melt and have a wide range of colors depending on the nature of 'X'. However, commercially the most common is yttrium aluminium garnet, $Yr_3Al_5O_{12}$ (YAG). This in its colorless form is a familiar diamond simulant (see p. 399), but it can be doped to produce a wide range of colors, such as yellow with chromium dioxide, to produce an artificial demantoid garnet, and also blue with cobalt, yellow with titanium, red with manganese, etc. Gadolinium–gallium garnet, $Gd_3Gl_5O_{12}$, (GGG), is a related synthetic gemstone. These synthetic garnets have lower hardness, higher SGs, and lower RIs than those of the natural stones, and can also be detected by the presence of their colorants.

Another series of artificial colored gemstones are based on lithium metaniobate ($LiNbO_3$), known commercially as linobate (Webster, 1983, p. 428). This is colorless, but can be doped with the usual metal salts to give a range of colors: chromium to give green, iron to give red, and cobalt blue and manganese or nickel to give yellow. The stones can be detected as described above. They are rather soft (hardness 4.5) and thus there is a potential for the facet edges to be damaged. The RI range is 2.2 to 2.3, indicating double refraction, the colored stones thus being dichromatic (see p. 396).

Diamond simulants

The vile man who fabricates false diamonds will sink into an awful hell, charged with a sin equal to murder. From the Indian classic, the Agastamta (Ogden, 1982, p. 142)

La production du diamond est un probleme pour les chimistes moderne le pendant de la pierre philosphe pour les alchemistes. H. Le Chatelier (1908) (quoted in Elwell, 1979, p. 73)

Sources: Lewis (1970); Lewis (1977, pp. 72–74); Bruton (1978, pp. 472–494); Elwell (1979, pp. 100–124); Nassau (1980, pp. 203–244); Hobbs (1981); Webster (1983, pp. 66–72); Liddicoat (1987, pp. 282–292); Becker (1988, pp. 13–32, 82–89); Sirakian (1997); Trench (ed) (2000, pp. 115–118); see also *Diamonds Treatments, Synthetic and Simulants: Integrity, Disclosure and Detection.* CD-ROM produced by Gem-A.

Ancient imitations of diamond are unusual, but not unknown. In antiquity, colored stones were more popular, the reds and greens being of garnet, ruby and emerald; colorless stones such as quartz or diamond were less favoured. Ogden (1982, p. 143, Plate 26) illustrated a Roman ring, set with a stone that is probably a rock crystal in imitation of diamond.

After the introduction of brilliant cutting in *c.*1700 (p. 416), which revealed diamonds' 'fire', their popularity increased enormously, and predictably imitation began in earnest. Rock crystal was used for centuries in Europe as a natural diamond simulant, faceted, foil-backed and set in the manner of the real thing. The quartz mined in England came from near Bristol, and the stones were known as bristows. In France the stones came from the Rhine and were called rhinestones, a name now more commonly applied to colored-glass costume jewellery.

The first acceptable synthetic imitations were the 'paste' diamonds made of flint glass (Lewis, 1970), following its seventeenth-century invention (see Chapter 10, p. 219), and it has remained the main diamond simulant ever since as it possesses good brilliance and fire. The glass now sometimes contains thorium compounds for increased brilliancy. An especially brilliant paste, known as 'Strass', after its Austrian inventor (Webster, 1983, p. 440), contains 35% of silica, 50% of lead oxide and 12% of potash, with traces of arsenic, boron and aluminium oxides, and this may be taken as typical of the composition of pastes.

Until the nineteenth century the making and cutting of paste gems was very much a craft industry until Daniel Swarovski (Becker, 1995) began developing ways of mechanising the cutting of the paste gems, ushering in mass-production methods.

Paste diamonds are very different from the real thing, being quite soft but much denser than diamond. They can be easily distinguished by radiography, the lead being very opaque to X-rays and the carbon of diamond being very transparent. This can be very useful on complex pieces of jewellery sometimes comprising hundreds of stones.

In the twentieth century a variety of artificial stones were produced as diamond simulants. The first synthetic stone to be used in imitation of diamond was the brilliant synthetic spinel (magnesium aluminate, $MgAl_2O_4$) introduced in the 1930s, causing a short-lived but considerable sensation and panic that an undetectable diamond substitute had been found. This is perhaps understandable, given that the search for a process to produce such a stone had been the subject of real endeavour as well as popular fiction for many years, and jewellers were unfamiliar with synthetic colorless stones. In fact, the properties of the so-called Jourado diamond are quite different from the real thing and the whole affair was quickly forgotten (Elwell, 1979, p. 47; Webster, 1983, p. 396).

The next imitation diamonds were made of crystals of rutile, TiO_2, which was first marketed as 'titania' in the late 1940s (Webster, 1983, pp. 403–404). The light dispersion of rutile is no less than six times that of diamond and even visually should not deceive. It is also quite soft and thus faceted edges may well show signs of wear.

Titania was soon challenged by crystals of strontium titanate ($SrTiO_3$), introduced in 1953, under the trade name of 'fabulite'. This is much closer to diamond in its optical properties, but is still rather soft and thus faceted edges may well be worn, and, once again, chemically and structurally, it is different from diamond.

The colorless synthetic garnet spinels (see p. 398) were introduced in the late 1960s under a variety of names such as Diamore, Diamonique, etc.

These imitations were largely displaced in 1976 by cubic zirconium oxide, zirconia (ZrO_3) (CZ), fused at temperatures in the region of 2750°C to produce the cubic structure. This is stabilised with the oxides of yttrium, magnesium and calcium. The CZ simulants have been marketed variously as Phainite, Djeuralite or Diamonique. It should be noted that a potential confusion between natural or synthetic zircon, zirconium silicate and fused zirconia, zirconium oxide, both used as diamond simulants. Despite their differences from diamond, suspected forgeries using zirconia have been reported, especially of the yellow stones (Duroc-Danner, 2000; and see Chapter 2, p. 37 and Figure 2.14).

The search for other, possibly more convincing diamond simulants continues. Even as this text is being written, a colorless gemstone of synthetic ortho silicon carbide, SiC, is causing a stir (*The Times* 1 September 1999, 'Fake takes sparkle out of diamond', although its use was first suggested by Webster (1983, p. 434) many years ago. The stone is known as Moissanite, and is a cubic variant of the more usual hexagonal silicon carbide known as carborundum.

Standard gemmological diagnostic tests for diamond include its very high RI (although note the RI of rutile is even higher). Another good practical test for a piece containing many stones is the reaction to UV. Diamonds usually fluoresce but the reaction from stone to stone is very variable, and some can be inert. If all the stones have the same reaction this would be very suspicious and warrant more rigorous testing. The simulants all have compositions very different from that of diamond, which consists of pure carbon, and hence compositional analysis by XRF or structural analysis by XRD or RM is applicable. Perhaps the most powerful technique is radiography (La Niece, 2005). Diamond, owing to the low atomic number (6) of carbon, is transparent to X-rays, whereas all of its simulants, with the exception of most plastics, are opaque. The resulting radiograph provides very direct and easily intelligible evidence.

Lapis lazuli simulants

Sources: Lewis (1977, p. 102); Webster (1983, pp. 250–254); Liddicoat (1987, pp. 108–109); Anderson (1990, pp. 321–323); Read (2005).

Lapis lazuli is rather unusual among gemstones in that it is a rock made up of a mixture of minerals, principally lazurite, haüyne, sodalite, calcite, diopside and pyrite, which occur in quite a wide range of proportions, making it difficult to give precise composition or properties. On the other hand, this can be used to advantage in provenancing sources, and makes it possible to distinguish modern from ancient lapis (see p. 412). Lapis was widely imitated in antiquity by blue glass, as exemplified

by the inlays on the gold mask of Tutankhamen (Bimson, 1974).

Perhaps one of the most famous, and in some ways mysterious, artefacts made of lapis simulant is the Bonus Eventus Plaque (Freestone and Tatton-Brown (Pers.com) (Figures 16.1, 16.2 and 16.3). For many years this was regarded as one of the treasures of the British Museum, a plaque of carved lapis lazuli dated to the first century BC. It had been acquired from the Townley collection in the early nineteenth century and was known from the late eighteenth century. Examination in the late nineteenth century showed that it was in fact of mould-pressed glass, but the authenticity was not questioned and it appeared in the British Museum's *Masterpieces of Glass* catalogue (Harden *et al.*, 1968, p. 47). Doubts were subsequently raised after analysis showed it to be most unlike Roman glass, with 13.2% of potassium oxide (see Chapter 10, p. 212, Table 10.1), and the piece was published as being questionable in the first edition of *Five Thousand Years of Glass* (Tait (ed), 1991, p. 18). By the time of the second edition in 1995, further work demonstrated that the composition was not Roman and the piece was accepted as being modern (Freestone and Tatton-Brown (Pers.com)). The blue derives from the cobalt, which has a long history as a

Figure 16.1 The Bonus Eventus Plaque, BM GR Reg. 1958, 2-11, 1. It is of blue glass, with the cobalt colorant almost certainly coming from a Post-Medieval German source. (Courtesy A. Milton/British Museum)

Figure 16.2 Detail of the back of the plaque (Figure 16.1) showing the pronounced cracks that came about during the moulding. (Courtesy A. Milton/British Museum)

Figure 16.3 Detail of the front of the plaque (Figure. 16.1) showing repaired damage. (Courtesy A. Milton/ British Museum)

colorant. However, this cobalt glass also contains substantial amounts of arsenic, nickel and bismuth, quite typical for the cobalt coming from sources in central Europe, such as Schneeberg in Germany, which were only mined between the sixteenth and nineteenth centuries, but which are unknown in such quantities in the ancient sources (Gratuze *et al.*, 1992, 1995, 1996; and see Chapter 10, p. 227).

The glass was pressed in a mould and then carved. The work was not very successful and the back of the plaque is severely cracked (see Figure 16.2),

which is likely to have happened during the moulding. The front has patches of fawn coloring at the surface, which were once mistaken for the golden pyrite particles that occur in lapis lazuli, and there is damage which probably dates from the time of manufacture (see Figure 16.3). Thus, the piece was apparently not especially well made, and raises the question as to whether this was poor but innocent workmanship that was subsequently mistaken for evidence of antiquity, or whether this was quite deliberate 'designer damage', similar to that found on the contemporary bronze 'Head of a youth', now in the Walker Art Gallery, Liverpool (see Chapter 8, p. 164).

Opaque colored glass continues to be used as a lapis simulant, sometimes with flakes of brass or even of gold to simulate the golden pyrite flakes of the original. In the second half of the twentieth century, fake ancient jewellery was found inlaid with imitation lapis lazuli made from a blue epoxy resin mixed with ground calcite and sprinkled with gold filings (Ogden, 1982, p. 156).

From the nineteenth century, lapis was simulated by treating natural jasper, an impure, often rather cloudy form of silica, with Prussian blue (see Chapter 12, p. 302) known as 'Swiss' or 'German' lapis. The color was good, although the simulant lacked the characteristic gold flakes of pyrites. In 1954 Degussa of Germany produced an imitation made from polycrystalline spinel, colored with cobalt salts, and speckled with brass or gold filings. Structural and chemical analysis reveals both of these simulants.

Coral simulants

Sources: Elwell (1979, pp. 147–150); Ogden (1982, pp. 117–118); Webster (1983, p. 566); Anderson (1990, p. 334); Campbell Pedersen (2004, pp. 192–218); Read (2005).

Coral has traditionally been imitated with colored glass formed by lampwork, and latterly plastics, but these lack the characteristic cellular structure of real coral. Stained calcined bone and the kernels of some hard nuts have also been used. In 1976 Gilson introduced a more convincing simulant known as 'created coral', which is made of compressed calcite with a coloring agent (Elwell, 1979, p. 150). This lacks the minor amounts of magnesium carbonate and the cellular structure found in natural coral and the SG is considerably lower, and thus it should be easily distinguishable. Created coral is extensively used for carvings in India (Karanth, 2000, p. 345), although Sreelatha Rao (1985) found no calcite in the local synthetic Indian corals; instead they seemed to be made of a magnesium aluminium silicate, colored with iron oxide.

Natural coral, being composed of calcium carbonate, is susceptible to chemical attack, especially in acid environments, and thus most coral from buried archaeological contexts has lost its lustre, and, in particular, its color (Rosen, 1990). Only in exceptional circumstances and conditions, such as occur in Egypt, can the color be preserved. Coral reflects the composition of the sea water in which it grew. For example, coral growing off the coast of the USA has shown a marked rise in cadmium and other heavy metals through the twentieth century resulting from industrial pollution (Shen *et al.*, 1987). This could form the basis of differentiating nineteenth- and twentieth-century coral from earlier material.

Opal simulants

Sources: Lewis (1977, pp. 104–108); Nassau (1980, pp. 257–261); Webster (1983, pp. 566–567); Liddicoat (1987, pp. 117–119, 328); Anderson (1990, p. 290); Read (2005).

Opal has traditionally been copied rather unsatisfactorily using glass, the iridescence being difficult to produce or to simulate. There has only been one commercially significant simulant and that is the so-called Slocum Opal, named after its discoverer, and introduced commercially in 1976 (Elwell, 1979, p. 139; Webster, 1983, p. 430). Opal simulants are made of alternate thin layers of alumina and silica, fused in a glass matrix to form multi-layer films. These give rise to the characteristic diffraction iridescence similar to that displayed by natural opal, but with a rather distinctive snake-skin surface and a honeycomb or chicken-wire internal structure. Typical inclusions are given in Gübelin and Koivula (1997, pp. 298–304 for real opals and pp. 459–460 for simulants).

Superficially convincing imitation opals have been produced by the controlled flocculation of polystyrene latex, which forms hexagonal crystallites when deionised (Webster 1983, pp. 451–455). This gives rise to diffraction iridescence very similar to that found on the natural opal. Compared with real opal the imitation is very soft, warm to the tongue, and the SG is low.

Ancient authors describe opals, and clearly valued them, but these stones would not be expected to survive prolonged burial, and thus examples purporting to be ancient should be regarded with suspicion, especially if still opalescent (Ogden, 1982, p. 104).

Natural pearl simulants: imitation and cultured

Sources: Lewis (1977, pp. 108–110); Ogden (1982, pp. 119–121; 1996); Webster (1983, pp. 501–561); Farn (1986); Liddicoat (1987, pp. 124–130); Becker (1988, pp. 5, 59, 95, 203); Anderson (1990, pp. 338–354); Kennedy (1996); Trench (ed) (2000, pp. 359–361); Landman *et al.* (2001); Campbell Pedersen (2004, pp. 142–168); Read (2005).

Natural pearl forms as a series of concentric layers laid down around a central point within a living oyster (Landman *et al.*, 2001) (Figure 16.4a). Each layer is a thin film of organic horny matter, conchiolin, infilled with aragonite (ortho-rhombic crystalline calcium carbonate). Even the smallest pearl will have been built up from tens of thousands of such films.

There is no evidence for the use of pearls in jewellery before the mid first millennium BC, but thereafter they became popular and very highly valued. In particular, the large, irregular, so-called baroque pearls were especially prized up to the Renaissance, and in the hands of imaginative jewellers formed parts of multi-component compositions (Ogden, 1982, pp. 49–51; 1996).

Imitation pearls

Because pearls were valuable there were many imitations in circulation, and manuals such as the

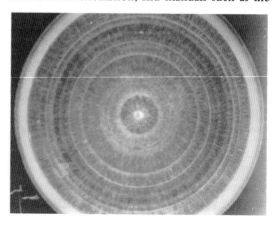

Figure 16.4a Section through a natural pearl, showing the concentric deposition of material around the original foreign body (Courtesy Anderson, 1990).

Stockholm Papyrus describe methods of making them (see p. 397). These simulants were usually of glass or of mother-of-pearl. Some Roman copies could be quite ingenious, with glass beads wrapped in silver foil that was then coated with more glass to create a resemblance to the silvery sheen of the real thing. Recipe 18 from the *Stockholm Papyrus*, describes the production of pearl simulants from a mixture of ground mica, wax, egg white and mercury held together with gum tragacanth.

A later treatise written in 1440, the *Segretti per Colori*, gave several recipes for making pearls, including some using fish scales (a similar method was already in use in China). In the seventeenth century, Venetian glassmakers produced imitation pearls which were of hollow beads of opalescent glass filled with white wax, whilst others used an unlikely sounding paste made up of crushed glass, egg white and snail slime.

In the late seventeenth century, Jaquin began making pearl simulants in Paris by applying fish scales to glass beads and these imitations are still being made in France. The vital lustrous component, known as *essence d'Orient*, is guarnine, secreted by the fish as tiny crystals on the surface of their scales. Historically, the scales of the small freshwater fish known as the bleak (*Albunus lucidus*) were used but now herring scales are more usually employed. The essence was applied in several coats in size or isinglass either to the inside of hollow glass beads that would then be filled with wax (known as Roman pearls), or, alternatively, onto the outside of solid beads (known as Paris pearls). Fish scales were applied to the surface of buttons made of casein in the early twentieth century to give them a pearly appearance (Mossman (ed), 1997, p. 48; and see Chapter 18, p. 458). Another French firm, Constant-Valvès, produced imitation pearls using opaline glass. Their speciality was pink pearls made by encasing a coral bead within the glass.

The characteristic surface could also be imitated using the hydrated lead carbonate mineral, cerussite, which occurs in the form of plates. These could be applied as a suspension in a lacquer to the bead (see Kennedy *et al.*, 1988). Another pearl simulant, also known as Roman pearl, was recorded by Reveley (1825, rep. by Ogden 2000). He stated that fine-grain 'alabaster' (more likely calcite) stone beads were threaded on to a sliver of bamboo and repeatedly dipped into a suspension of finely ground shell or mother-of-pearl in a suitable glue, followed by drying. Glass copies have been joined by copies in

vegetable ivory (see Chapter 17, p. 425) as well as in plastic. One imitation, known as 'Angelo Pearls', marketed in the 1980s had a mother-of-pearl core with three coats of plastic, the second being colored.

In common with other gems, prestigious and valuable pearls would sometimes be copied for wear while the original remained in the safe. De Meisner (Farn, 1986, p. 122), for example, made particularly convincing copies using matt glass around a mother-of-pearl core. This recalls the story, which may even be true, concerning the actress Gaby Deslys, who captivated the King of Portugal. He gave her a long rope of pearls, but during a splendidly histrionic lover's tiff on board the monarch's yacht, she tore off the enslaving baubles and threw them overboard. After a reconciliation, the remorseful King sent her another rope. Gratefully accepting them, Gaby felt it impolitic to tell his Majesty that the pearls so impulsively cast into the deep were in fact copies, and the originals were safe and dry in her bank vault.

Cultured pearls

The most significant imitations of natural pearls are cultured pearls (Landman *et al.*, 2001, pp. 153–184). Although the technology of introducing foreign matter into living oysters to promote growth had been known to the Chinese for centuries, the successful production of regular high-quality pearl-covered beads was only achieved by the Japanese in the early 1920s. They remain the principal suppliers of nucleated sea water pearls.

A nucleus of mother-of-pearl is introduced into the oyster, which proceeds to coat it with a skin of real pearl (Figure 16.4b). It takes 3 to 4 years for a cultured pearl to develop sufficient thickness. The nuclei are typically between 5 and 7 mm in diameter and become coated to a thickness of between 0.4 and 0.5 mm. The largest cultured Japanese pearls are around 10 mm in diameter, but some large South Sea oysters can accommodate pearls of up to 16 mm diameter; however, they are of rather poor quality.

From the 1950s the production of nucleated cultured pearls was joined by that of the non-nucleated cultured variety, which are usually grown in freshwater mussels rather than in oysters. The nucleus is formed of a piece of tissue, which soon rots and thus the forming cultured pearl is hollow, as revealed by radiography (Kennedy, 1996). Freshwater non-nucleated pearls have become very popular, currently accounting for 90% of the cultured pearl

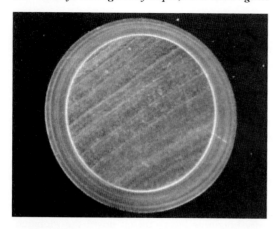

Figure 16.4b Section through a cultured pearl, showing the parallel straight bands of the mother-of-pearl nucleus surrounded by the thin outer layers of pearl deposition. (Courtesy Anderson, 1990)

market with enormous and growing production in the Far East (Huang Fengming *et al.*, 2003).

Dark pearls are very rare in nature and have always been very highly prized. Pearls can be darkened either by irradiation (see p. 409) or by treatment with silver nitrate solution, which penetrates the surface, and, on exposure to UV (or, more slowly, sunshine) silver precipitates, imparting a dark sheen to the pearl. The artificial darkening can usually be detected by UV, XRF, etc., and RM has also been successfully applied to some color-enhanced cultured pearls (Li Liping and Chen Zhonghui, 2001). As the silver concentrates in the growth gaps between the layers of the pearl, it often shows up as thin lines on radiographs (Kennedy, 1996).

The choice of testing strategy for pearls rests to a large extent on the particular problems involved and the age of the pearl as well as its true nature.

The survival rate of pearls from archaeological deposits is low. Pearl is basically made up of calcium carbonate and so will not survive at all when buried in an acid environment. Even in calcareous soils the aragonite tends to transform into calcite with a resultant loss of all lustre and coherence. Pearls that do survive burial are often badly stained by iron salts in the soil. Thus, one should be highly suspicious of a pearl in good condition that purports to be ancient.

A true pearl surface is very distinctive and even a hand lens reveals the serrated edges running across it. Rubbing a real pearl across one's teeth reveals the rough texture, whereas glass and other copies feel smooth.

Glass and plastic copies can also be revealed by the standard tests for these materials, and if the pearl has been drilled then inspection of the drill hole is often informative. True pearl tends to have neat, clean holes, whereas glass and plastic have much more ragged sides and edges. Also, in the immediate vicinity of the hole on a strung bead the surface is normally found to have rubbed against its neighbour revealing the material beneath a treated or coated surface.

To detect cultured pearls is much more difficult, because the surface layer is, after all, genuine pearl. Immediately after the introduction of cultured pearls in China and Japan a great many approaches to the problem of identifying them were tried with various degrees of success. The lucidoscope was the first genuinely successful apparatus (Webster, 1983, p. 540). Strong light is shone through the pearl revealing the distinctive straight parallel layers of the mother-of-pearl at the centre, surrounded by thin annuli of real pearl (see Figure 16.4b). Huang Fengming *et al.* (2003) used Raman spectroscopy (RS) and cathodoluminescence (CL) to differentiate between natural, nucleated seawater pearls and non-nucleated freshwater pearls, but problems arose if the pearls – of whatever origin – had been treated.

Radiography and XRD are the most widely used methods to detect cultured pearls. Radiographs of natural pearls often reveal a centre or inner ring of conchiolin. In a cultured pearl the conchiolin layer forms around the mother-of-pearl and the transparent ring is thus much closer to the edge of the pearl, and tends to be more irregular than the ring observed on a natural pearl. A greenish fluorescence is induced in most of the freshwater mother-of-pearl used in cultured pearls during exposure to X-rays, and short-lived phosphorescence persists when the source is turned off; this phenomenon can be observed through a lead glass safety window.

The drill holes are another distinctive feature revealed on the radiographs. Pearls, in common with all gems, are drilled from both sides, meeting in the middle (see p. 413), and in natural pearls the hole is straight and the two halves meet. The drill holes through the mother-of-pearl nucleus of the cultured pearls tend to be slightly off centre and often do not meet precisely, because the angled layered structure of the mother-of-pearl distorts the progress of the drill.

Natural pearl and the mother-of-pearl nucleus of cultured pearl have regular but very different structures and thus X-rays passing through are diffracted in

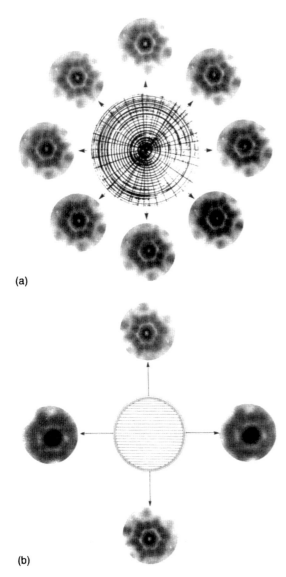

(a)

(b)

Figure 16.5 Lauegrams of a) a real pearl; b) a cultured pearl. The diffraction of a transmitted X-ray beam through natural pearl is the same for all paths through the radially concentric structure. For the cultured pearl the diffraction pattern varies as the pearl is rotated, depending on the orientation of the mother of pearl nucleus. (Courtesy Farn, 1986)

very different ways. Natural pearl is radially concentric around the centre and thus produces the same characteristic hexagonal pattern, or lauegram, no matter what position the pearl is moved to (Figure 16.5a). The X-ray diffraction lauegram of the cultured pearl

(Figure 16.5b) is mainly determined by the nucleus formed of a fragment of mother-of-pearl with a straight layered structure having no relation to the centre of the pearl, and thus the diffraction will not only be different from that for a natural pearl, but will vary from one position to another.

Artificial gemstones

Glass

Sources: Lewis (1977, pp. 92–93); Nassau (1980, pp. 268–274); Ogden (1982, pp. 138–139); Webster (1983, pp. 437–459); Liddicoat (1987, pp. 115–117); Andersen (1990, pp. 135–138); Liu (1995, pp. 220–227, 2001); O'Donoghue (2005).

Through the ages glass has been, and continues to be, the most common material used for imitation gems. In Roman times real emeralds and their glass imitations were often used indiscriminately as exemplified by the Thetford Treasure, now in the British Museum (Johns and Potter, 1983, pp. 60, 99–100; Plates 2 and 3), where the necklace (Cat. 31) contains one emerald and three glass beads, and the four loose green hexagonal-cut beads also comprise one emerald (Cat. 42) and three glass beads (Cats 43–46).

There are two main types of glass used in gem imitation, crown glass containing lime, which is much used in moulded stones for the cheaper costume jewellery, and the so-called flint glass (see p. 399 and Chapter 10, p. 219).

Colored-glass costume gems are often referred to as rhinestones, whereas their bright but colorless counterparts are known as diamanté, and the latter name is also used for costume jewellery generally (see p. 397).

Although visually convincing, glass is noticeably warmer to the touch than real crystalline stones, the tongue being the recommended gauge. If the glass is transparent, then examination under a microscope or even with the hand lens should reveal air bubbles, which clearly shows that the material has been molten, and thus is not a natural gemstone. Swirl marks, known as *striae*, where the molten material was imperfectly mixed as it set, may also be present and observed under low magnification. Other properties, especially the RI and the reaction to polarised light, are quite distinctive and diagnostic for glasses.

Surface analysis by XRF or by EDX in the SEM can be useful not just for determining that the material is a glass, but also for providing some idea of the likely age of the piece from the composition of the glass opacifiers and coloring agents, which changed through the past (see Chapter 10, pp. 212, 215).

Plastics

Sources: Nassau (1980, pp. 276–278); Webster (1983, pp. 449–455); Becker (1988); Liu (1995, pp. 220–227; 2001); Bakelite: Dinote, 1985; Grasso (1996).

Cheap imitation gems that were previously made exclusively of glass are now often made from synthetic organic polymers (Becker, 1988, pp. 127–130; and see Chapter 18, p. 458). The earliest such organic synthetic simulants were cellulose nitrate and casein plastics, used to imitate pearl and ivory from the late nineteenth century. The first transparent plastic simulants were probably the clear phenolic resins, made from the late 1920s (DiNoto, 1985; and see Chapter 18, p. 459). These were perhaps the most common plastic simulants through the 1930s and 1940s, but production ceased by about the mid-1950s. They were replaced by others, notably epoxy resins and Perspex.

Synthetic gemstones

Sources: Elwell (1979); Nassau (1980, 1997); Webster (1983, pp. 372–436); Miley (1984); Anderson (1990, pp. 82–97); Koivula *et al.* (2000); Read (2005).

Synthetic gemstones are man-made but are of the same composition and structure as their natural analogues. Synthetic gemstones, which would be indistinguishable from the natural stones, have been the subject of intense and continuing interest and experimentation from the nineteenth century. The first successful synthesis was of ruby in the late nineteenth century, but large-scale commercial production only really began in the second half of the twentieth century (see Nassau, 1997 for a succinct tabulated chronology of production of synthetic gemstones).

Inevitably the search for processes that could be used to produce synthetic stones indistinguishable from the natural analogues can also include introducing imperfections that would simulate those found in the natural stones, even though they compromise the perfection of the stone. For example, synthetic rubies are sometimes strongly heated and then plunged into cold water to induce internal cracking that simulates the fissures found in the natural stones. As Harry Levy mused in the September 2005 issue of *Gems and Jewellery* 'Are such crackled

stones made to thoughtfully provide customers reasonably priced alternatives to natural rubies, made to fool the public, or made to fool dealers?'.

Processes

The objective is to grow crystals of the relevant mineral with the same structure as found in the natural stone. The main approaches to the problem have been by using flame fusion, in which the material is fused, or flux-melting in which it is dissolved, but both involve very high temperatures.

Fusion can take place on the tip of a blowtorch burning oxygen and hydrogen, for example (flame fusion), or in a crucible heated by an induction coil. The growth of the crystals from the melt is controlled in a number of ways. In the Verneuil flame fusion process the growing crystal is attached to a ceramic pedestal, which is slowly moved away from the torch, the crystal being being built up from a succession of minute droplets. In the induction method, after the various constituents have been melted in a crucible, a small seed crystal is introduced into the surface of the melt and slowly withdrawn with the crystals growing beneath. This is known as crystal pulling or the Czochralski method, after its inventor. In both of these methods the material is being manipulated into and or out of the static heat source, and this movement can lead to the formation of inclusions and striae in the crystals.

To overcome this problem, the zone melting method was developed, in which the material is stationery, but the very localised high temperature zone moves, either by moving the container or the induction coil. This method is used for the production of Seiko synthetic rubies, sapphires, and alexandrites, and produces stone almost free of inclusions.

In the alternative approach, flux-melting, the material is dissolved in a solvent (the flux), and controlled crystallisation is carried out. Problems arise in controlling the number of nuclei and the rate of crystallisation. For gem-quality stones a relatively few, large perfect crystals are required. One solution to the problem is to only allow the constituents limited physical contact, as exemplified in the Espig process for synthesising emerald, I.G. Farben's 'igmerald' (Elwell, 1979, p. 59). Here, two of the constituent minerals, aluminium oxide and beryllium oxide, are melted in a flux on which floats silica glass, which forms the third constituent. The emeralds are formed very slowly around introduced seed crystals.

Hydrothermal processes, introduced in the 1960s, are really variants on the flux-melting methods, the flux in this case being the most universal solvent of all, water. At high temperature many gem-forming minerals will dissolve in water, and if water is heated under high pressure in an autoclave then it will remain liquid even at several hundred degrees centigrade. From these solutions the gemstones can be crystallised.

Detection of synthetic stones
Some stones such as sapphires or rubies made by flame fusion methods can form with curved growth lines and color bands owing to the intermittent nature of the deposition from a succession of minute droplets.

The inclusions in many synthetic stones are different from those encountered in the natural stone, as exemplified by the prevalence of water in some stones made by the hydrothermal method (Gübelin and Koivula, 1997, pp. 429–515; and see some examples for specific stones given below).

The light, UV and IR spectra of many synthetic stones are also quite distinct from their natural analogues, and thus analysis by spectrophotometer may well be useful, provided a suitable area can be exposed if the stone is in a setting.

Trace element analysis by techniques such as NAA can be informative. Natural stones contain traces of gallium, whereas synthetics usually did not. The past tense is used here quite deliberately as, since this diagnostic difference between synthetic and natural stones was published, synthetic gemstones that contain the element have started to be manufactured (in itself an interesting insight into the motivation and probity of some producers).

The CL of natural stones is largely independent of the beam energy, but for synthetics, especially emerald, ruby and sapphire the CL produced depends strongly on the electron beam energy.

Synthetic ruby, emerald and diamond
Synthetic rubies
The early experiments concentrated on synthesising stones based on alumina, aluminium oxide (Al_2O_3), known as corundum, in particular ruby and sapphire, and on mixed beryllium aluminium silicates, known as beryl, especially emerald. The first significant synthesis was that of the so-called Geneva rubies, marketed with some success as genuine stones in 1886. After suspicions concerning their origin were raised, they became easily detected (Kunz, 1886), because of the presence of microscopic

gas bubbles from the melt, which the natural stones do not have. Examination of the original Geneva rubies suggests that they were produced by a rather complex form of flame fusion.

Much superior synthetic rubies prepared by flame fusion were exhibited, and sold as synthetic stones, by Verneuil at the 1900 Paris World Fair. Thereafter synthetic ruby gemstones were sold either as natural or synthetic, many being sent from Europe to India from 1918 on for cutting and polishing by traditional processes (Untracht, 1997, p. 338). Trichy, in the southern state of Tamil Nadu, is the current centre for the cutting of synthetic stones (Karanth, 2000, p. 11). Shortly afterwards Verneuil produced synthetic sapphires, and in later life turned his attention to the imitation of the black glaze on the Greek red and black figure ceramic wares (see Chapter 9, p. 195).

Stones made via the Verneuil process often have curved growth layers that are visible under low magnification. This indicates where the individual drips of molten material have fallen, gradually building up the stone. Synthetic rubies are also made by the Czochralski 'pulling' process, and they have also been produced by the hydrothermal method since the 1960s, often commencing with a small seed of fusion ruby. More convincing synthetic rubies could be produced without the bubbles or layers of the Verneuil stones, by the flux-growth process at a lower temperature, as exemplified by the 'Kashan rubies' marketed in the 1970s.

Flux-grown rubies can be very similar to the natural stone, and are generally regarded as superior to synthetics made by other processes, although there are differences in the RI and in the inclusions, retaining distinctive particles of the flux in which they were grown. Synthetic rubies are quite common now and Ogden (1982, p. 156) reported a putative Roman ruby intaglio that turned out to be synthetic. Methods of differentiating synthetic rubies from natural are given in Liddicoat (1987, pp. 275–276), Anderson (1990, p. 116), Lewis (1977, pp. 114–122) and Read (2005). Differences in the inclusions are one of the main criteria; characteristic inclusions are illustrated in Gübelin and Koivula (1997, pp. 324–337 for natural rubies and pp. 475–500 for the synthetic and simulants). Duroc-Danner (2002) was able to identify a large ruby in an antique setting as being a flux-grown synthetic by identification of the inclusions.

Synthetic emeralds
Synthetic emeralds were first produced commercially in 1911 by I. G. Farben using the Espig process,

described above, although quantity production seems not to have begun until after the Second World War. Emeralds were also produced hydrothermally in the 1960s, and the inclusions of water can be easily detected by FTIR (Stockton 1984, 1987) or RM. The emerald was often overgrown on an inferior beryl, and the product, known variously as 'Ermerita' or 'Symerald', is thus strictly speaking a simulant, not a synthetic (Webster, 1983, p. 417). In the second part of the twentieth century nearly all synthetic emeralds were made by flux-growth methods.

Methods of differentiating synthetic emerald from natural are given in Lewis (1977, pp. 76–84), Webster (1983, pp. 410–417), Liddicoat (1987, pp. 245–248), Anderson (1990, pp. 124–129) and Read (2005). As with rubies, differences in the inclusions are important; characteristic inclusions are illustrated in Gübelin and Koivula (1997, pp. 244–268 for natural emeralds and pp. 461–474 for the synthetics and simulants).

Synthetic diamonds

The synthesis of diamond requires enormous pressure and very high temperatures. The first true synthesis was only attained in the 1950s, after almost a century of claims and counter-claims, involving mistaken identification and fraud to rival anything found in the rest of this work (Bruton, 1978, pp. 421–445; Elwell, 1979, pp. 75–80; Nassau, 1980, pp. 164–168; Webster, 1983, pp. 373–380; Sirakian, 1997; O'Donoghue, 2006, pp. 99–114). The first synthetic diamonds were small, industrial-grade stones; gem-quality diamonds were produced shortly afterwards but at a prohibitive cost. Only in the 1980s were gem-quality stones produced at a realistic price to compete with the natural stone, among the latest being the stones marketed by the GEC Company since 1999 under the name of GE POL, Pegasus Diamonds or Monarch Diamant. The newly formed Gemesis Company is producing what the company describe as 'cultured diamonds', yellow diamonds grown around a natural diamond, in a manner the company claims is analogous to that used for cultured pearls (*Times* of London, 27 October 2003; and Levy 2003). Other methods involve synthesis of diamonds in near-vacuum conditions from a carbon plasma by chemical vapour deposition, and these are known as CVD diamonds (O'Donoghue, 2006, pp. 106–108; Levy, 2003).

Methods of differentiating synthetic from natural diamonds are described in Ponahlo (1992), Sunagawa (1995), Chalain *et al.* (1999, 2000), and O'Donoghue (2006, pp. 108–116).

This section will conclude with the comments of Campbell (2000), who carried out an independent assessment of six De Beers synthetic diamonds, and concluded that at least one of the stones 'would create much consternation in the retail jewellery trade if it entered the supply pipeline. If stones with similar characteristics come into the trade in any numbers it would certainly underline the need for routine testing using high-tech means. Technology does not stand still-neither must defensive education'. The same remarks apply to authenticity studies generally!

The enhancement and treatment of gemstones and composites

Sources: Nassau (1980, pp. 281–290; 1984a, b; 1985); Webster (1983, pp. 455–470); Liddicoat (1987, pp. 157–165); Anderson (1990, pp. 98–104); O'Donoghue (1997); McClure and Smith (2000); Read (2005).

There is a subtle gradation between the use of the terms 'enhancement' and 'treatment' of gemstones (Levy, 2004). Enhancement is mainly concerned with waxing, mild heating and filling to improve the stones. The more drastic and irreversible operations for the removal or disguising of flaws, voids and inclusions are referred to as treatments. Like imitation, the enhancement and treatment of gemstones stretches back into antiquity, but many recent techniques are both distinctive and closely dated, and, once again, recognition of these more recent practices can be a good indicator of the age of a gemstone.

It must not be thought that treatments are necessarily fraudulent. Some stones such as blue aquamarine or yellow citrine, for example, are routinely heat-treated to produce or enhance their color. Details of the treatments carried out on new stones are now sometimes enclosed with the stone at time of sale together with the guarantee. In general, the more common treatments are not routinely listed, but instead it seems to be taken as understood that the stones will have been treated. The extent, nature and disclosure of the treatments remain a contentious issue in the gemmology world. The rapidly changing and ever-improving treatment technologies, coupled with the oft-near impossibility of detection without access to sophisticated analytical apparatus, is causing much debate and considerable unease throughout the trade (Nassau, 1984a, pp. 86–90; Cartier, 2001; Tay, 2001; Read, 2005).

New developments introduced either as commercially patented processes, or clandestinely, discovered as hitherto unrecorded treatments on fake gemstones, appear frequently in the trade journals.

There are fascinating historical surveys of the subject in Nassau (1984a, pp. 15–24; 1994), critically discussing the recipes given in works such as the Stockholm Papyrus (see p. 397).

The treatments include staining and waxing with dyes or polishes, coating, heating, filling of cracks and inclusions, irradiation to change the color, high pressure–high temperature (HPHT) used to treat diamonds, diffusion and deep diffusion where the colorant is actually melted into the surface of the stone, and lasering to burn out impurities.

The treatments can either affect the whole stone or just the surface. The main traditional techniques for treating the whole stone have been heating and impregnation, joined in the twentieth century by irradiation and latterly by laser treatments.

Impregnation

Impregnation covers a wide field of treatments, normally performed to fill in cracks and voids and/or to color the stone with a dye (Hänni, 1992; Kiefert *et al.*, 1999). The materials penetrate the stones along grain boundaries and fracture planes. Thus, cracks and voids can be successfully filled and rendered invisible with a variety of oils, waxes and resins, both natural such as Canada balsam, and synthetics such as an epoxy resin. A liquid that easily penetrates the stone will remain mobile and tend to bleed back onto the surface and to evaporate over time. This can be overcome by *in situ* polymerisation, using a slow-setting epoxy for example. A better result is obtained if the impregnating or doping material is appropriately colored. Emerald, for example, has been so treated for centuries, improving both clarity and color. Oils were traditionally used, before being largely replaced from the mid-1980s by epoxy resins.

A more radical and contentious treatment was introduced in the 1980s with the smoothing out of surface irregularities in stones such as rubies by glass-filling (Nelson, 1994), followed by a similar treatment to fill surface defects in diamonds.

Methods of detecting fillers have been summarised by Hänni (1992). Air bubbles can sometimes be seen in a filler, and some organic fillers fluoresce under UV. Application of a hot point – an electrically heated needle – to an inconspicuous part of the stone can reveal some organic impregnates by

localised melting or the smell. In transparent materials, doping agents can often be detected by departures from the expected RI for the stone, although this can sometimes be circumvented by using substances such as epoxy resins with a similar RI (Tennent and Townsend, 1984a), and they can be detected by long-wavelength UV, FTIR and RM (Hänni *et al.*, 1997: Kiefert *et al.*, 1999).

The color of stones can be changed by dyeing, traditionally with aqueous solutions containing iron salts, although many other types of dye are used nowadays. Most treatments are two-fold, i.e. moderate and carefully controlled heating to induce cracking, followed by dyeing, the stone being penetrated down the cracks.

Coloring has often been carried out in order to accentuate the color contrast of banded stones such as agates where the bands are of differing porosity and will absorb differing amounts of the solution. On removal and drying, the iron minerals remain in some bands, coloring them red, black or brown, but not penetrating other bands. Black bands can be produced by impregnation with carbon. This was traditionally achieved by boiling the stone in solutions of sugar, oil or honey for several weeks, allowing differential absorption of the solutions. This would be followed by heating to dry the stone and char the organic materials impregnating the stone. Rosenfeld *et al.* (2003) suggest that the Romans heated quartz stones with iron oxides and bone glue to produce a pleasing dark brown color; conversely, carnelian could be whitened by heating with calcium carbonate. In more recent times the charring of the organic material to darken the stone has been effected using concentrated sulphuric acid. Imitation sardonyx was created in this way. A variety of other chemicals containing metal ions such as copper, chromium or cobalt, or complex ions such as Prussian blue, have been used to produce a range of colors in agates. A whole range of costume jewellery, known as 'Craquelees', are made by heating colorless quartz to red heat, quenching to produce myriad small cracks in the surface and then dyeing to produce a wide range of colors.

Throughout the twentieth century the color of gemstones has been created, removed, changed or enhanced by irradiation. Early examples include the irradiation of diamond with α-particles to produce green colors. This rendered the diamond radioactive and some stones so treated may still retain activity (reported by K.M. Reese in *Chemical and Engineering News*, 11 October 1982).

At present the types of radiation used include γ-rays, UV or high-energy electron beams. Blue topaz, for example, can be produced by irradiating colorless stones with γ-rays or high-energy electrons. This turns the stone brown and the permanent blue color is produced by heating to about 250°C. Blue–green diamonds can be created by irradiation with high-energy electrons, and smokey quartz can be produced with a wide range of colors by means of γ-irradiation followed by heat treatment. Pearls darken on exposure to γ-radiation to produce the sought-after 'black pearls'. Natural zircons, used as a diamond simulant, can be rendered colorless by irradiation.

It can be very difficult to detect subsequent evidence of irradiation treatment in a stone, although characteristic thermoluminescence (TL) does develop in some stones such as topaz, and possibly in others.

Heat treatment

A wide range of gemstones react to heat to produce permanent change, normally in color or clarity. The corundum materials, sapphire and ruby, are regularly treated stones. A wide range of temperatures are employed from a few hundred degrees to well over a thousand. The stones can be heated in air or oxygen where oxidising conditions are required, or in hydrogen or under charcoal, where reducing conditions are required. The conditions are usually dictated by the required oxidation state of the iron colorant. Thus, the blue in a sapphire can be deepened by exposure to high temperatures in reducing conditions, or alternatively lightened by strong heat in oxidising conditions. Heat treatments can sometimes be detected in a stone by the pitting of the girdle (the circumference of a faceted stone), and by the effect on the inclusions, which will typically have whitened, and expanded causing localised stress cracking.

The value of gemstones can depend on their color, particularly so for diamonds, and hence artificial coloration is always a possibility (Collins, 2001). These practices are exemplified by the famous – or infamous – Deepdene diamond. Its auction price of £190 000 in 1971 was largely determined by its golden yellow color. Even before the sale, questions had been raised about the possibility of artificial coloration, suspicions that were subsequently proven well-founded at the London Gem-testing Centre (Bruton, 1978, p. 445).

Composites

Composites are made to create stones that are bigger or closer to perfection out of smaller components of the same stone, or to plate an inferior stone (Karanth, 2000, pp. 155–158; Rouse, 2006, pp. 531–545) (Figure 16.6). They have a long history;

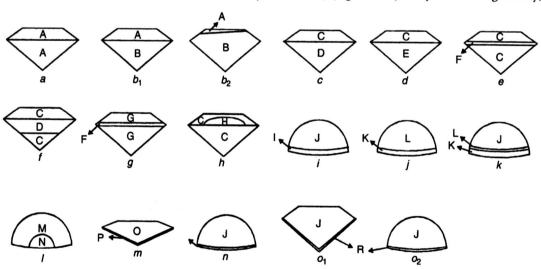

Figure 16.6   Some types of gemstone: A. Natural stone. B. Synthetic stone. C. Genuine pale/uncolored material that the stone imitates. D. Colored synthetic. E. Colored natural stone of same or different species of same value. F. Colored cement. G. Uncolored natural stone of lower value. H. Colored liquid. I. Chatoyant (changing, floating appearance, e.g. catseye and moonstone) stone. J. Transparent material. K. Black glass or onyx. L. Iridescent material. M. Pale or uncolored hollow cabochon. N. Dyed cabochon of same species or colored paste. O. Natural stone or glass. P. Foil reflective coating. Q. Foil scored with lines. R. Painted coating. (Courtesy Karanth, 2000)

banded beads have been reported from Mohenjo-Daro, in Pakistan, dating back to the third millennium BC. They were formed by sticking together slices of differently colored stone in imitation of banded onyx (Ogden, 1982, p. 140). Pliny described how sardonyx was fabricated from bands of red, black and white stones stuck together (*Natural History*, 37.197; Eichholz, 1962, pp. 324–325). They were then carved to form polychrome cameos.

In the early twentieth century when the use of synthetic corundum was becoming widespread, thin pieces of poor-quality but real sapphire were bonded to a synthetic sapphire or ruby, to create gems that passed all but the most stringent tests. A vogue also existed for fusing a thin slice of garnet on to appropriately colored glass, and passing the faceted and mounted composite as ruby or sapphire. Such creations are known as garnet-topped doublets (GTDs). Another ploy is to join poorly colored stones with a deeply colored transparent cement to create a single stone of apparent good color.

The union between stones is normally made with a colorless transparent cement, some of which can be surprisingly durable, as Ogden (1982, p. 149) related, a hitherto unsuspected Roman composite only being revealed as such when it finally came apart under examination on a hot microscope stage after two millennia of burial. Epoxy resins such as Araldite are much used now. Detection of a composite is not difficult if the stone is loose or if the join is on an exposed face (Karanth, 2000, pp. 157–158), as the line is sometimes visible and there is very often a perceptible difference in the surface texture between the two components. However, on fraudulent composites the joins will tend to occur at the facet edges, so being less obvious, and, of course, on forged antiquities the stone will be mounted in such a way that the union is covered by the setting. The appearance of a sudden discontinuity as the eyepiece of the microscope is focused through a transparent stone could raise suspicions of a composite, even if the surface edges were disguised. The presence of a cement could be revealed by microscopic bubbles or striae along the plane of the join. Also the transmitted spectra passing through the cement should be different from those from the gem itself, especially if the cement is dyed, and some cements will fluoresce under UV.

Ancient composites seem to have been simple joined slices, and more complex arrangements such as are shown in Figure 16.6 are likely to be much more recent. Sophisticated composites only

really began to develop in the 19th century, and the production of fraudulent composites seems to have peaked around the beginning of the 20th century, thereafter synthetic gems began to predominate.

The determination of the authenticity of ancient gemstones

This section covers two main approaches of authentication: provenancing a stone, and the technology by which it was worked.

Provenance

In common with other stones, precious and semiprecious stones often have distinctive features of composition, structure or inclusions specific to a particular source. The problems of determining the source of gemstones and the analytical techniques to be adopted have been discussed by Hänni (1994). Recognition of distinctive inclusions can be important. Clearly, for example, when a stone can be shown to have come from the Americas, Australasia, or southern Africa, it is unlikely to have been available to the Romans – although one certainly should not exclude sources in India, Sri Lanka or even South-East Asia. A good example is provided by the rubies set into the eyes of a Parthian statuette of the goddess Ishtar, of the second century AD, found at Babylon, and now in the Louvre. The trace element content as determined by particle (or proton)-induced X-ray emission (PIXE) suggested that the rubies came from Myanmar, several thousand kilometres away (Calligaro *et al.*, 2000a), thereby demonstrating the great distances over which small precious objects could be moved in antiquity.

Analytical studies by Moroz and Eliezri (1999) have shown that there are consistent differences in the composition of the inclusions in emeralds from various sources around the world. Modern forgeries of Roman emerald jewellery often use stones from South America, especially Colombia, the principal modern source since the seventeenth century. Note that much genuine Mughal jewellery also uses Colombian emeralds. These have the characteristic three-phase inclusions, with solid, liquid and gas all present, rather than the two-phase solid- and gas-phase inclusions found in Old World emeralds (Ogden, 1982, p. 156, Plate 10.5; Gübelin and Koivula, 1997). Giuliani *et al.* (2000) and Calligaro *et al.* (2000b) studied the oxygen isotopes in emerald and distinguished Pakistani from Egyptian stones, and Austrian from Colombian. However, Zwaan *et al.* (2004) carried out a more detailed study of emeralds from Zimbabwe and maintained that the values of the oxygen isotope ratios may be more variable from a single source than the previous studies suggested, and that oxygen isotope values by themselves may not be sufficient to unambiguously identify the sources.

Lapis lazuli has a very few, easily characterised sources. In antiquity just one source, the Sar-e-Sarang deposits in the Badakhshan Valley, in present-day Afghanistan, seems to have supplied the whole of the Middle East and the Mediterranean region (Herrmann, 1968; Wyart *et al.*, 1981). Lapis from other sources only came into use in the nineteenth century, notably from Lake Baikal in Central Asia, and from Cerro Tulahuén in Chile (Affonso, 1996). Lapis is made up of a mixture of minerals, and in the Badakhshan material the mineral wollastonite, calcium silicate, is absent, but it is present in the lapis from both the Central Asian and Chilean sources. For example, XRD analysis of a small head of a jackal made of lapis lazuli, purporting to an Egyptian antiquity (Figure 16.7) revealed the presence of wollastonite, strongly suggesting that the head is not ancient. Keisch (1970, 1976) and Keisch and Callahan (1976b) established that the isotope ratio of the sulphur in the pyrites of the lapis is totally different in the Badakhshan, Lake Baikal, South American and other natural sources (Figure 16.8) and different again in synthetic lapis simulants (Figure 16.9).

In contrast with lapis, gem-quality garnets are fairly widely distributed and thus potential sources are many. Garnets were probably the most widely used red gemstones in antiquity (Rouse, 1986, pp. 1–18). They have a wide range of mineralogy and composition, and analysis by a variety of techniques of the stones used in Dark-Age European jewellery has produced many interesting groupings (Bimson *et al.*, 1982; Farges, 1998; Greiff, 1998) and Arrhenius (1985) and Gübelin and Koivula (1997, pp. 287–297) have studied the associated inclusions. However, they failed to concur on likely sources but the specific groupings made by the individual methods could be useful for authenticity purposes.

Technology

For the study of worked surfaces, light microscopy has now been supplemented by SEM techniques,

Figure 16.7 Head of jackal of lapis lazuli, badly broken and restored and made up with beeswax (note the brown areas on the proper right ear) (BM EA 64075). (Courtesy A. Milton/British Museum)

especially the examination of silicone rubber moulds taken of the surfaces (see Chapter 2, p. 25).

Early technical developments have been comprehensively studied on Middle East cylinder seals dating from the fifth millennium BC onwards (Gorelick and Gwinnett, 1978, 1979; Sax and Meeks, 1994, 1995; Sax *et al.*, 1998, 2000a, b), and more recently on Chinese jade (see p. 418). The early seals were engraved by micro-flaking with a point, giving a distinctive jagged appearance to the grooves at high magnification. From the beginning of the second millennium BC the grooves were at least finished by filing with emery, probably embedded in a copper tool. At the beginning of the second millennium BC some seals have lines made up of drilled holes, the drill having been partly used as a milling tool, moving laterally. This was to be a short

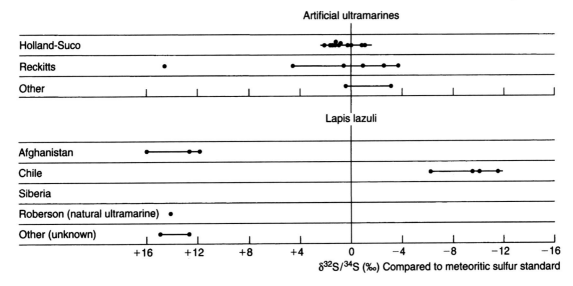

Figure 16.8 Sulphur isotope ratios ($^{34}S/^{32}S$) for lapis lazuli from natural sources around the world. The horizontal scale indicates the difference in parts per thousand between the sample and a standard. Note that the Badakhshan sources used in antiquity in the Old World are clearly distinguished from the Lake Baikal and Chile sources, which have been the principal sources used from about the mid-nineteenth century. (Courtesy Keisch, 1976)

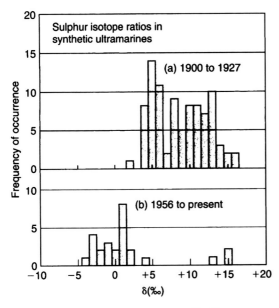

Figure 16.9 Sulphur isotope ratios ($^{34}S/^{32}S$) for samples of synthetic ultramarine made through the twentieth century. (Courtesy Keisch, 1976)

transition stage to the wheel, and after the mid second millennium BC wheel-engraved lines become common, at least in Mesopotamia. Thus, by the first millennium BC gem-carving was carried out with the drill and the wheel as well as with the point, all the techniques that were to be used up to the present day.

The methods used to drill beads in remote antiquity differed from those used more recently (Gwinnett and Gorelick, 1987, 1998/99). Based on their studies of Early Bronze Age Beads from Iran, Gwinnett and Gorlick (1981) suggested that beads of soft stone were drilled using drills mounted with tiny flint bits, and that hard stones were drilled by abrasion (see also Gwinnett and Gorlick (1993) on ancient Egyptian drilling methods). The introduction of the diamond-tipped drill into the Classical World from India was an important development and seems to have taken place in Roman times. Primitive diamond drills continue in use in India and Sri Lanka to this day (Karanth, 2000, p. 12). The marks left by such drills have been characterised by Gwinnett and Gorelick (1986 a & b) and Gorelick and Gwinnett (1988).

The abrasives used in antiquity for polishing may also prove important in differentiating between more modern work (Webster, 1983, pp. 484–494; Karanth, 2000, p. 153; Read, 2005). Emery was used in Mesopotamia from the second millennium BC (Heimpel *et al.*, 1988). Diamond pastes are currently believed only to have been used from Post-Medieval times and differences between gem surfaces polished with emery and diamond may provide a method of distinguishing between ancient and more modern work (see p. 419 for similar studies on jade polishing).

Studies on polishing techniques by Gwinnett and Gorlick (1989) on quartz beads revealed fine scratches on hand-polished beads and distinctive micro-pitting on beads that had been polished by tumbling in a drum with fine abrasives. The evidence for tumble-polishing is less certain but it seems to have been in use since at least the first millennium AD in Sri Lanka. Bellina and d'Errico (2000) have studied the characteristic polishing scratches on agate and cornelian beads from South-East Asia.

Some techniques such as wheel-cutting are distinctive, and, for antiquities purporting to come from certain regions of the world, such as the Americas, can provide the conclusive evidence for a more recent origin. The crystal skulls provide an excellent example of this.

Case study: The Crystal Skulls

The near life-size crystal skull on display in the British Museum was acquired in 1898 from Tiffanys in New York (Figure 16.10). Tiffanys, in turn, had acquired it from a collector who had been given it by Eugènne de Boban. The latter was a knowledgeable but rather shady collector and dealer of American antiquities, whose collections contained many forgeries. The Crystal Skull is perhaps the best known of a group of such artefacts of varying sizes and degrees of realism and that are popularly associated with the pre-Colombian civilisations of Mesoamerica.

However, although these cultures certainly carved rock crystal and crafted skulls in other materials, notably limestone and ceramic, no skulls of rock crystal have ever been found on a controlled archaeological excavation. Another large skull is claimed to have been found at the ancient Mayan city of

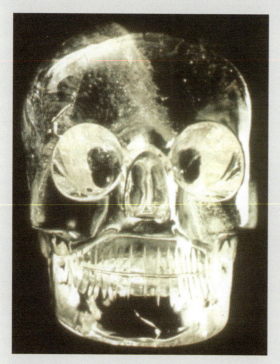

Lubaatun, now in Belize, in 1924 by Ann, the daughter of the excavator, Frederick Mitchell-Hedges. However, despite her graphic recall of the discovery as related to Morton and Thomas (1997, pp. 14–27), no mention was made of the skull in the account of the excavation in Mitchell-Hedge's 1954 autobiography. In fact, the first certain record of this skull was in the 1930s (Digby, 1936; Morant, 1936) at which time it apparently belonged to a Mr Sydney Burney, and was only purchased by Mitchell-Hedges in 1949.

The British Museum Skull is one of the most dramatic artefacts in the entire collection, whatever its age, and, as such, its true origins have been the source of speculation since its acquisition. Kunz, in his standard work on the precious stones of Mexico (1907, p. 121), believed that the ancient Mexicans had carved rock crystal into skulls and that the British Museum had the largest and best example. Morant (1936) and Digby (1936) stated (erroneously as it turned out) that the skull had not been shaped using modern tools, and others have noted a general stylistic similarity to some antiquities of the Mixtec culture which flourished in what is now central Mexico, many centuries ago.

Figure 16.10 The Crystal Skull, BM Ethno. Reg. 1898-1. (© British Museum)

Doubts were raised about the techniques used to carve the crystal. In particular, the teeth have been cut as lines into the face. Examination of the lines in 1967 suggested that they had been cut with an engraver's wheel, which was only introduced into the Americas at the time of the Spanish conquest. Comparison of the lines cut by a wheel into a test piece of crystal showed a strong similarity to those on the skull (Figure 16.11). However, in itself all that this demonstrated was that the depiction of the teeth was likely to have been post-conquest. The skull itself could still have been ancient, but with the teeth added later, or it could be that the skull was executed in the early years of the Spanish rule when the native inhabitants enthusiastically adopted Christianity, but managed to incorporate many elements of their earlier beliefs. Death, and, in particular, skulls, have always featured in ceremonies such as the Day of Dead, still celebrated in Mexico.

For several years, Jane Walsh of the Smithsonian Institution had been intrigued by these skulls ever since the donation of a large and rather crude example (Walsh, 1997). Over the years she had managed to track down several other skulls, both large and small. She had noted that some, especially the large examples, seemed to make their first appearance at the end of the nineteenth century, and furthermore there was a possible link, not with Central America, but to Germany and the small town of Idar-Oberstein in Bavaria. For centuries the craftsmen there had specialised in the carving of agate, jasper and quartz, but the local sources of stone had become exhausted by the mid-nineteenth century. New sources of excellent gem-quality quartz were discovered in Brazil and also in Madacasgar, and by the late nineteenth century the town was experiencing a renaissance carving Brazilian rock crystal. Was it possible that this was where the skulls had been made? If so then they would have been carved and polished with powered rotary tools using modern abrasives, and the quartz would be likely to have come from Brazil. Although Brazil and Mexico are on the same continent, there is no evidence of any contact prior to the arrival of the Europeans in the sixteenth century, and thus a Brazilian source would make a pre-conquest Mexican origin for the skulls highly unlikely.

Together with the documentary film-makers, Chris Morton and Ceri Louise Thomas, Walsh made arrangements for a group of the skulls to be brought together and examined at the Department of Scientific Research in the British Museum. They were compared with a small carved and polished rock-crystal goblet that had been excavated from a richly accoutered Mixtec burial at Mount Albán, near Oaxaca in central Mexico.

According to Morton and Thomas (1997, p. 219) 'a visual feast unfolded on the old wooden boards of the somewhat dilapidated laboratory'. The examination of the skulls adopted two approaches, the nature of the rock crystal and the manner in which in had been worked. Professor Andrew Rankin, of the University of Kingston, London, examined the inclusions within the crystal by light microscopy and the appearance of these, together with the unusual size of the piece of quartz, strongly suggested a source in Brazil.

Margaret Sax took silicone rubber moulds from the highly worked surfaces, especially around the teeth, eyes and ears of the skulls for examination in the scanning electron microscope (Sax et al., 2008). Many of the engraving and polishing lines on the British Museum's skull were parallel and quite deep, suggesting they had been cut with a wheel using an abrasive that was harder than the rock crystal. By contrast the Oaxaca cup had much shallower and randomly orientated polishing marks, typical of hand-polishing with an abrasive of similar hardness. Also traces of modern abrasives were found embedded in the surface.

Together, these findings reinforced the general feeling held before the examination on the technique and source of the crystal (Jones (ed), 1990, pp. 296–297; Cat. 328) and suggested that Jane Walsh's investigations had reached the correct conclusion.

Figure 16.11 Detail of the teeth of the Crystal Skull under low magnification that appears very similar to lines engraved in crystal with an engraver's wheel. (© British Museum)

More recently Ericson *et al.* (2004) have outlined a method of hydration-dating rock crystal, closely related to obsidian hydration-dating (see Chapter 10, p. 228). The technique relates the depth of water penetration to age, assuming that the artefacts have been buried through most of their existence. It is claimed that artefacts between 100 and 100 000 years old can be dated. As with obsidian dating, the hydration rate is temperature-dependent and thus the dating is not very accurate, but it does have potential for authenticity studies.

Cameos and intaglios

Sources: Ogden (1982, pp. 143–150); Rudoe (1992); Miller (1998); Roux (ed) (2000); Rosenfeld *et al.* (2003).

Forgeries of engraved intaglio and cameo gems purporting to date from classical antiquity have been a problem for collectors since the Renaissance (Miller, 1998, pp. 115–116). They have been produced in large quantities, especially in Italy, and differentiating good eighteenth- and nineteenth-century copies of antique gems can be very difficult as the same techniques and types of stone have been used (Ogden, 1982, p. 171). The English sculptor, Nollekens, recalled that in eighteenth-century Rome:

> *Jenkins [a notorious eighteenth-century dealer in antiquities, mainly over-restored or forged] followed the trade of supplying visitors with intaglios and cameos made by his own people, that he kept in a part of the ruins of the Coliseum, fitted up for 'em to work in slyly by themselves . . . Bless your heart! He sold 'em as fast as they made 'em.*
>
> Rudoe (1992)

There has been some study of the methods by which the stones were carved and polished (Younger, 1981). Ogden (1982, p. 172) suggested that on the more recent copies the edges of the lines are too sharp and the stones exhibit too little weathering for stones supposedly buried for millennia. Signed gems are especially sought after by collectors, and thus there is the additional problem of trying to establish whether the signature is ancient (Rudoe, 1992, pp. 24–25).

The most popular stones for cameos, intaglios and other carved gems have always been the various forms of quartz, cornelian, sard, jasper, and agate, especially the banded variety of the latter (see p. 411). Non-destructive PIXE analysis of some early beads of cornelian and agate excavated in Southeast Asia has had some success in differentiating local from Indian stones (Theunissen *et al.*, 2001).

The cutting of gemstones, the art of the lapidary

Sources: Scarfe (1975); Bruton (1978, pp. 195–234); Sinkankas (1984); Tillander (1995, 1998); Trench (ed) (2000, pp. 154–156); Read (2005).

In antiquity the regular symmetrical faceting of gemstones was rarely practised, most gemstones being cut and polished in their natural and irregular crystalline form. What mattered more was the preservation of the maximum amount of stone. The cutting and faceting of stones seems to have begun in Europe in the thirteenth century, and there are records of diamond faceting in Venice from the 1330s for example, but symmetrical faceting is, by and large, a Late- and Post-Medieval European phenomenon although the exact geographical and chronological limits are not at all well defined or agreed upon (Tillander, 1995; 1998). Thus, Untracht (1997, p. 318) noted that, 'if your Mughal setting contains a brilliant cut diamond, it will be a replacement'. In general however, it does seem that early gems were either abraded into a rounded form, known as a cabochon cut, or cut flat for use as inlays as exemplified by the familiar coral or garnet inlays. The objective of faceting is to achieve the maximum brilliance or light reflectance from the stone. If the stone has good light-dispersion properties, i.e. it disperses incident light into its spectral colors, then the faceting will also try and bring out this feature, known as the fire.

The table cut was among the earliest cuts, a flat being polished on one side of the stone, and, from this, various brilliant cuts evolved through the Post-Medieval period and later (Bruton, 1978, pp. 210–234; Tillander, 1995, 1998). The rose cut, which is also one of the earliest cuts, developed in Europe in the early seventeenth century, and its application spread rapidly to India for utilisation of the irregular flat-backed diamonds found there (Untracht, 1997, p. 317). Further developments led to a variety of new and distinctive cuts used on Art Deco jewellery in the 1930s.

The study of the cut of a stone can sometimes provide good indications of date and authenticity. The claim to fame of a small Roman bronze statuette of a female in the archaic style, now in the British Museum (BM GR Reg. 1873, 8–20, 4), was the eyes inlaid with diamonds. Examination in 1953 confirmed that the stones were indeed diamonds but as they were rose cuts, they could not be original, and were very likely nineteenth-century additions (Bruton, 1978, p. 13).

Jade

Sources: General: Markel (ed) (1992). China: Hansford (1950, 1968); Rawson (1995); Tang (ed) (1998). America: Lange (ed) (1993). New Zealand: Beck and Mason (2002). Mineralogical description: Middleton and Freestone (1995); Childs-Johnson (ed) (2002); Middleton (2006).

The familiar green translucent stone so much prized by the Chinese, and some other cultures, is almost impossible to succinctly define. The term greenstone is regularly applied to stones of a wide range of minerals that have been shaped and polished to reveal their attractive texture and variegated colors (Santallier *et al.*, 1998). The word jade is properly applied to two quite different minerals, nephrite and jadeite, both of which display considerable variability (Hauff, 1993). Because their structures, properties and histories are so different it is perhaps best to describe them separately.

Nephrite

Nephrite consists of calcium and magnesium silicate, with some iron, which, under pressure deep below the Earth's surface, formed an interlocking mass of crystals that were quite literally felted together to form a mineral that is quite hard (difficult to scratch) and exceptionally tough (difficult to break). The story is told of Alfred Krupp, the German steelmaker, being defeated by a lump of nephrite. He had heard of a large boulder of nephrite that needed breaking into smaller pieces. It was suggested that one of Krupp's great steam hammers at Essen could do the job in spectacular fashion, adding to the prestige of *Der Firma* and its products. However, the well-publicised event resulted in a still-intact piece of jade and a badly battered steel anvil.

This toughness has certain consequences for the working of jade. It is difficult to break or work by percussion, and cannot be flaked in the manner of flint for example; instead, it has to be worked by abrasion, drilling, grinding, etc.

The familiar and prized green color is largely due to ferrous iron, and this can become oxidised at the surface (see p. 420). If the iron content is low then the color is more creamy, such jade being referred to as 'mutton fat jade'. Many jades contain traces of chromium and this can also contribute to the color.

Nephrite occurs quite widely around the world, but is rarely of a suitable quality for working and thus has only been exploited in a relatively few instances. It was used from antiquity for tools and weapons by the Chinese, and by the Neolithic inhabitants of Switzerland, Central America (Bishop *et al.*, 1993; Lange (ed), 1993), and North America (Blackman and Nagle, 1983). In the more recent past nephrite was used by the inhabitants of Polynesia and the Maori of New Zealand (Beck and Neiche, 1992; Beck and Mason, 2002). Maori war clubs are quite widely copied. Sometimes, innocent copies such as those made at the beginning of the twentieth century by German lapidaries at Oberstein-Idar (see p. 415), have been passed off as genuine in the Antipodes, although the obvious use of wheel-carving makes them quite easy to spot (Jones (ed), 1990, p. 233). Much nephrite currently comes from British Colombia.

The principal sources of Chinese nephrite were traditionally in Central Asia well to the west of China proper, but in the Neolithic period sources in the north-east of China may well have been exploited (see p. 419).

Jadeite

Jadeite consists of crystals of sodium aluminium silicate. It is somewhat harder than nephrite, and the crystals are much more granular. It is less tough; Krupp's steam hammer would probably have been successful with a block of jadeite! Even so, jadeite has traditionally also been worked by abrasion rather than percussion. Jadeite displays a wide range of colors and, as with nephrite, this is mainly dependent on the ferrous iron content; some varieties have a bright green color owing to the presence of chromium.

Although deposits of reasonably attractive jadeite are found at many localities around the world, pure jadeite is much less common (Woolley, 1983, p. 265). The main deposits that have been commercially exploited in the recent past are in the northern part of Myanmar. These deposits furnished jade for the Chinese, but apparently only since about the eighteenth century, more or less replacing the nephrite that was used previously (Middleton and Freestone, 1995). This changeover from nephrite to jadeite by the Chinese can be an important indicator of the likely age of a suspect piece.

In Mesoamerica, jadeite was the most common stone used, together with nephrite and other similar stones such as chalcedony, opal and quartz. In New Zealand, nephrite was the stone most commonly found, along with some jadeite and other suitable stones.

Simulants
Sources: Anderson (1990, pp. 314–318); Middleton (2006, pp. 345–347).

A wide variety of other translucent semi-precious green stones have been used as simulants. For example, much Maori 'jade' is in fact serpentine stone, known as bowenite. Jade simulants are especially prevalent in China, where semi-precious stones such as pink rhodolite and serpentine rocks from Kashmir, Afghanistan and Korea, as well as from various localities within China itself, are sold under names such as 'Beijing jade' or 'New jade'. 'Korea jade' is a serpentine bowenite mineral. Elsewhere, stones such as green chalcedony and even green marble (Connemarra marble or Iona stone) have been used as jade simulants. Natural white translucent stones such as calcite, quartzite and marble are used as fake jades by dyeing them green. Both nephrite and jadeite are found to a greater or lesser degree in other rocks and some natural simulants are mineralogically similar, making it difficult to define precisely what constitutes a 'true' jade.

Enhancement or treatment
Sources: Nassau (1984a, pp. 139–141; 1985); Middleton (2006, pp. 347–348)

The most common jade enhancement treatment consists in dyeing white or pale jade stones green. This is more usually applied to jadeite, which is more porous than nephrite, and is also more frequently pale (Hansford, 1968, p. 79; Nassau, 1984a, pp. 139–141). To enhance jade simulants many recipes are used, but in most the warm stone is just dipped in an aqueous solution of a synthetic organic dye (Ehrmann, 1958, 1959). Surface irregularities can be filled with wax (Crowningfield, 1972), or with synthetic polymer resins (Fritsch et al., 1992). The latter seem prevalent in Hong Kong workshops; Tan et al. (1995) used photoelectron spectroscopy to detect these organic impregnations, Hodgkinson (1993) suggesting a simpler detection method using acid, but which unfortunately damages the surface. Examination under UV should also expose enhancement treatments.

In China the desired green color in pale 'mutton fat' jade has sometimes been achieved by means of a standard gemmological trick utilising composites (see p. 410) (Ehrmann, 1959; Anderson, 1990, p. 313). The white stone is hollowed out such that it can accommodate a second piece. The space between is filled with a green cement, making the whole piece appear green, this being sealed in place with a third plate of jade. The join with the outside piece is impossible to completely disguise and so it is contrived that the sealing strip is part of the base and, thus, covered by a plinth or base plate. Surface analysis would establish that the piece is indeed jade, and fail to detect the source of the color, buried, as it is, deep inside.

Jade working

Sources: General: Middleton (2006, pp. 351–352). China: Hildeburgh (1907); Hansford (1950, 1968); Aon (2002); Sax et al. (2004). Mesoamerica: Garza-Valdès (1991). New Zealand: Chapman (1891); Beck and Mason (2002).

As already stated, jade is too tough to be worked except by abrasion. Jade could be cut by a soft blade, such as thin slate, as attested in New Zealand, or a thin string of leather or of gut held taut in a bow, and fed with a variety of hard abrasive powders. The stones could be carved with a soft point, made of wood, bone or copper, for example, impregnated with a hard abrasive powder. In China, much work was done with a bow drill, mounted with either a solid bit or a tube of bamboo or of copper fed with abrasive powders (Lu Jianfang and Hang Tao, 2002). Wheels, both to cut and to carve, were introduced at some time. All of these methods were all either hand- or foot-powered operations, which have now been replaced by the use of rotary-action power tools that operate at much higher speeds. Consequently, these leave quite distinct abrasion patterns on the stones, although on serious forgeries after work using power tools has been completed, some superficial work is done with hand-tooling followed by careful polishing, the purpose of which is to obliterate the evidence of power tools.

Most earlier studies have been carried out by optical microscopy, but these have now been joined by SEM studies on silicone-rubber moulds of the surfaces (Sax et al., 2004). Most of the jades examined were in good condition, but problems were encountered on some of the earlier pieces that had been buried and which had weathered surfaces, obscuring detail. There are also likely to be problems, potentially even more confusing, when dealers or collectors have had weathered pieces re-polished after excavation (So and Douglas, 1998). The initial study of Sax and colleagues, based as it was on only a very few pieces, suggests that a range of techniques were used from the Neolithic period in China, including cutting with both stone and string saws, non-rotary carving and drilling. Evidence for rotary cutting with a wheel is now attested back to the Neolithic period, but the date of the introduction of wheel-carving in China is currently uncertain.

Garza-Validès (1991) has studied the techniques used to work Pre-Columbian jade from Mesoamerica, based partly on the evidence of the excavated jadeite workshop at Guaytan, in Guatemala, and on the contemporary artefacts, also using SEM. The techniques included shattering, sawing, grinding, both solid and tubular drilling and polishing. Some pieces carried evidence of having been re-polished in recent times, making their authentication very difficult.

Analysis and provenance studies

Elemental and XRD analysis can establish whether a particular stone should be classified as a true jade, and trace element analysis increasingly has the potential to establish the provenance of a piece or at least to provide an analytical fingerprint enabling its composition to be compared with that of other pieces of similar style (Woolley, 1983; Twilley, 1992; Eiland and Williams, 2001). These approaches are likely to be of increasing importance in the authentication of jade. Douglas (2003) has used XRF to carry out the non-destructive analysis of early Chinese nephrite jades.

Some of the standard gemmological tests can be applied to ascertain if a stone is a jade. These include hardness, SG, absorption of light, etc., but precision is difficult because neither nephrite nor jadeite is a pure mineral, but always contains various amounts of other minerals. Petrology is very useful and has been employed extensively to classify prehistoric axes for example, but does require a thin section to be cut (Woolley, 1983).

Wen Guang and Jing Zichuan (1992) used FTIR for their studies of Chinese Neolithic jades. Their method requires samples of a few milligrams to be taken, but both Curtiss (1993) and Gao Yan and Zhang Beili (1998) have developed non-destructive FTIR techniques. Xu *et al.* (1996) and Middleton and Ambers (2005) have explored the use of RM as a non-destructive analytical technique to characterise Chinese jade and its simulants (Figure 16.12).

Smith and Gendron (1997) used non-destructive RM to characterise two Mesoamerican greenstone axeheads, and demonstrated the value of this approach; further studies on Mesoamerican jadeite have been published by Gendron *et al.* (2002) and Smith (2005b). Garza-Validès (1991) used FTIR to characterise Mesoamerican jades, and also to pick up traces of modern abrasives embedded in the surfaces of some of the pieces examined. Mesoamerican sources have been extensively studied (Bishop *et al.*, 1993) by application of a combination of thin-section petrography, NAA and XRD to characterise some of the sources used by the Mayans.

It used to be thought that the sources of Chinese nephrite jades had always been to the west of

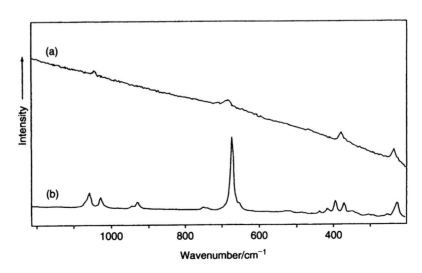

Figure 16.12 Raman spectra of (a) a Chinese Neolithic axe (BM Reg. OA +350). This is a jade simulant of serpentinite, probably antigorite and (b) a nephrite standard. (Courtesy Middleton and Ambers, 2005)

China, in Central Asia, but recent analytical studies utilising a combination of FTIR, XRD and SEM of Neolithic and other jade artefacts have suggested that the sources probably lay in the north-east of China, near in fact where the earliest jades are found (Wen Guang and Jing Zichuan, 1992; Middleton and Freestone, 1995). As jade working spread to the west of China, the traditional sources in Chinese Turkestan (now the province of Xinjiang), centred on the cities of Khotan and Yarkand, and in the region of Lake Baikal in Siberia, became important, and the putative sources in the east ceased significant production. The ability to assign jades to specific sources is complicated by the long-established practice of collecting cobbles or boulders of nephrite from Central Asian river beds that had been carried many kilometres from their primary sources by a combination of glaciation and water action.

Figure 16.13   Small plaque, simulating patinated 'burial' jade. The wheel-engraved stone is gypsum and the brown patina has been painted on. Acquired at Rochester market, the vendor insisting that it was an antique jade from a tomb. (Courtesy A. Milton)

Ageing and faking

Sources: Forgery: Garza-Valdès (1991, 1993); Douglas (2000); Eiland and Williams (2001); Aon (2002); Jiang Song (2002).

Jade forgery, both the forging of the material and the supposed age of the artefacts made from it, has a long history in China. There are also legitimate copies supplied by some museums of pieces in their collections as exemplified by the Liangzhu Culture Museum in Hangzhou. These are of soft rock, identified as serpentinite, chemically patinated to imitate the white patina of the genuine ancient jades.

Jade that has been buried, frequently undergoes some degree of surface alteration or patination, although formation of rock-varnish-type encrustation has not so far been reported (see Chapter 11, p. 256). The most common phenomenon is some degree of surface oxidisation which turns the ferrous greens of the iron minerals to ferric browns, often penetrating down between individual grains deep into the stone. Burial in the yellow–brown loess soils of much of central and north China can result in the formation of distinctive yellow–brown patina, the pieces being variously known as 'burial' or 'buried' jade (Figure 16.13).

Some jades, especially of the Shang period, have become very brittle and white. There seem to be two very different causes, alkalinity and heat. Experiments by Gaines and Handy (1975) and by Aert *et al.* (1995) suggested that some jades are degraded rapidly in a strongly alkaline environment.

In burials this could have come about owing to the presence of a decaying body.

The dark brown surfaces seen on some ancient jades can be simulated quite easily by placing the hot stone in a vat of boiling dye. Such pieces were referred to disparagingly in Beijing as 'fritters' (Hansford 1968, p. 39). Forgers are also supposed to try to induce similar surface effects by burial in horse dung for a few weeks (Preusser, 2002). Jades have been artificially aged since antiquity by heating to between about 600° and 800°C and then quenching in an acidic solution (Sinkankas, 1958; Nassau, 1984a, p. 140; Tsien and Ping, 1997), which results in a brittle white jade. Some ancient jades, known as chicken bone jade, have been strongly heated in the past, possibly in cremation fires (Douglas, 2001; Jiang Song, 2002).

A problem common to all examinations of antiquities is that the original weathering or patination may have been removed during ill-considered restoration, as noted by Douglas (2000) on Chinese jades, and by Garza-Validès (1991) on Mesoamerican pieces. Freshly cut jade fluoresces uniformly and brightly when exposed to UV whereas old carvings are more variable (Rorimer, 1931, p. 27), and thus the technique is a good preliminary to look for evidence of age and of recutting.

Relatively little work has been done on the real long-term surface alteration of jades, although Zacke and Zacken (1999) claimed to have authenticated a collection of jades based on the analysis of the patination present, but their conclusions were queried by Douglas (2001). Yang *et al.* (2004) used optical coherence tomography to study the subsurface morphology of patinated jades and were able to differentiate between the artificial patina induced by heating and naturally formed patina. Ettinger and Frey (1980) suggested a dating method based on the slow absorption of nitrogen into the surfaces of materials. A high-energy proton beam was used to produce depth-profiling of the nitrogen through the first 20 or so microns of the jade's surface. The method seems not to have been developed further, but even though it was found not to be able to give actual dates for the exposure of the surfaces, it might still prove useful as an authenticity method.

17

Organic materials: Mainly natural

Introduction

This chapter and that which follows deal with the whole range of natural and synthetic organic materials. This chapter concentrates on natural animal and vegetable products.

Natural organic materials derived from animals: ivory, bone, antler, horn, tortoiseshell and wax

Sources: MacGregor (1985); Starling and Watkinson (eds) (1987); O'Connor (1987); Trench (ed) (2000); Campbell Pedersen (2004).

Ivory

Sources: Bibliographic sources: Baer and Majewski (1970, 1971). General: Maskell (1905); Ritchie (1969); St Aubryn (ed) (1987); Penny (1993, pp. 153–163); Trench (ed) (2000, pp. 135, 243–245, 299–300, 365, 481, 524). Identification: Webster (1983, pp. 584–598); O'Connor (1987); Krzyszkowska (1990); Espinoza and Mann (1993, 2000); Krzyszkowska and Morkot (2000); Campbell Pedersen (2004, pp. 57–84).

True ivory originates from the mammalian dentine, i.e. the teeth and tusks (which are simply elongated teeth, usually the canines), of a variety of land and sea mammals. Ivory is easy to carve, has an attractive color, and is dense, resilient and takes an excellent polish. The structure is based on lamellae of collagen and clostin, which are strong and elastic, embedded in hydroxyapatite.

Recognition
Elephant ivory and teeth
The most familiar source of ivory in western parts of the Old World is the tusks of the African elephant (*Loxodonta africana*) and the smaller tusks of the Asian Elephant (*Elephas maximus*). Elephant ivory has quite distinct structures, which can sometimes be seen with the naked eye (Penniman, 1952). In longitudinal section they are lamellae which lie parallel to the pulp cavity of the tusk, and in transverse section they appear as a concentric oval ring pattern known as the 'lines of Owen'. There are also the patterns of intersecting lines of the dentinal tubules, creating 'engine turned' patterns, known as the Schreger patterns or, less usually now, as 'lines of Retzius' (Figure 17.1). Synthetic ivories have been made from chips and sawdust of ivory set in resin.

Occasionally the molar teeth of elephants are used, but these are very distinctive with bands of cement running through, and therefore should not be mistaken for tusk ivory.

Mammoth ivory
Another source is the enormous tusks of the Pleistocene mammoth (*Mammuthus primegnus*) which survive in large numbers in the permafrost of Siberia and to a lesser extent, Alaska. This is often referred to as fossil ivory, but strictly speaking this is incorrect; as the material is preserved chemically intact, there is no replacement by other mineral species such as occurs in real fossilisation, and mammoth ivory is a better term. Although references to ivory dug from the ground, made by some classical authors, notably Pliny (35.134; Eichholz, 1962, pp. 108–109) could be interpreted as referring to mammoth ivory, the first certain references to its use are Byzantine. There is little evidence for its systematic exploitation before the seventeenth century and not until Siberia was opened up in the nineteenth century was the potential of mammoth ivory properly realised. Thereafter it has been a significant source on international markets (Digby, 1926). Thus a radiocarbon (RC) date indicating an Upper Palaeolithic origin some 10000 to 20000 years ago would suggest that in fact the

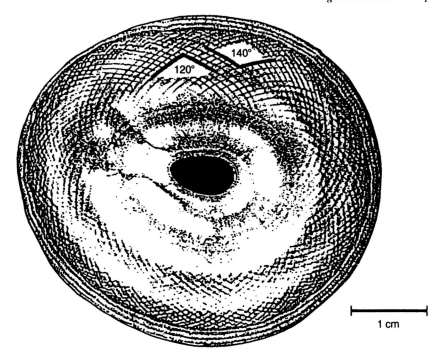

1 cm

Figure 17.1   Schreger patterns in mammoth ivory. (Courtesy Espinoza and Mann, 2000)

artefact made from it was unlikely to pre-date the nineteenth century. Mammoth ivory can be recognised by a rather yellow tinge and by the cracks which are often penetrated by a blue–black staining of vivianite, iron hydroxy phosphate. Also, the angle of intersection of the Schreger lines differs from that on modern elephant ivory (see Figure 17.1 and Table 17.1). Many copies of Medieval gothic ivories were made in the nineteenth century (Leewenberg, 1969; Jones (ed), 1990, pp. 180–182) and the recognition of mammoth ivory in supposedly Gothic pieces may lead to more of them being identified.

Rolandi (1999) suggested that recent and mammoth ivory could be distinguished by the amino acid content of their collagen. Edwards *et al.* (1997a, b; 1998a) have used Raman spectroscopy (RS) to differentiate between mammoth and modern ivory. Shimoyama *et al.* (1998) have developed non-destructive methods to differentiate between mammoth and modern ivory.

Hippopotamus
The teeth of the hippopotamus (*Hippopotamus amphibius*) are used as a source of ivory. Although now confined to Africa, in earlier times both elephant and hippopotamus were found in the Middle East, and it is becoming increasingly clear that hippo ivory

was quite prevalent (Krzyszkowska, 1990, pp. 38–47; Krzyszkowska and Morkot, 2000). Thus it is unlikely that a forger of early ivories would have used such an apparently unlikely material before the 1980s, and a piece known to have been extant before that date is likely to be genuine. This is one of the main reasons for believing that the 'first temple' pomegranate of hippo ivory which surfaced in 1979 may well be genuine even though the inscription it carries is not (Goren *et al.*, 2005 and Chapter 1, p. 13).

Boar's tusk or pig ivory
The tusks of wild pig and some domestic pigs have been used, necessarily for small items that are nearly always triangular in section. The ivory is covered with a dense enamel layer such that no grain is visible, even under moderate magnification.

Warthog
The tusks of the warthog (*Phacochoerus aethiopicus*) are also used and the ivory has a distinctive mottled appearance.

Walrus
Northern maritime cultures have often used ivory obtained from various marine mammals, notably the tusks of the walrus (*Odobenus rosmarus*) continuing

Table 17.1   Scheme for the investigation of ivory.

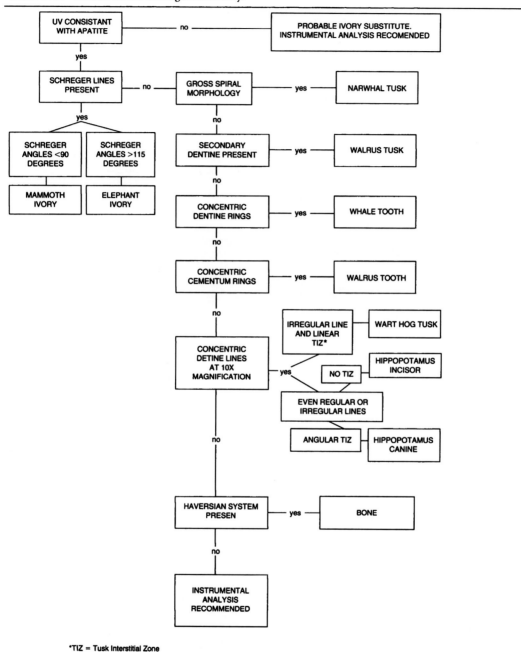

*TIZ = Tusk Interstitial Zone

Source: Espinoza and Mann, 2000, Table 1, p. 7

until the 19th century in Japan and the Far East. It is composed of a primary dentine which is very similar to elephant ivory but with a distinctive secondary dentine (*osteodentine*) which has a mottled oatmeal coloration.

Whale ivory and scrimshaw
The teeth of some whales, notably the sperm whale (*Physeter macrocephalus*), have been used as a source of ivory since antiquity, mainly by northern maritime cultures. Sperm whale ivory was carved into

artefacts by the whalers of the eighteenth and nineteenth centuries. Alternatively, the surface was engraved with scenes typically associated with ships and the sea. The lines were then filled in with black materials such as ink, charcoal, soot or tobacco juice. This work is known as scrimshaw, genuine pieces commanding a high price, and forgery is rife (Ridley, 1999, 2004). Distinguishing a modern copy made on whale dentine can be very difficult, the old teeth tend to become yellow with age, but this can be easily simulated on a modern tooth by the application of cold tea or apparently by burying it in manure (Peterson, 1975, pp. 137–141; Battie, 1986a, pp. 209–212). The surface of the whale ivory is prone to splitting and this would normally have occurred long after the scrimshaw decoration was made; the sequencing should be clear, the lines having become offset. From the 1960s the market has been flooded with forgeries made of injection-moulded synthetic resins (Tharp (ed), 1999, pp. 148–149). The most successful copies are made of the ubiquitous epoxy resins but even these tend to lack the distinctive polish of the dentine, and the imitation of the root cavity, although usually included, is rarely convincing.

In Japan from the seventeenth century, elephant ivory was obtained from Dutch merchants and it was the favoured material for items such as *netsuke* and *okimono*. Walrus ivory was used together with sperm whale teeth and narwhal tusk. Boars' tusk and the teeth of tiger and bear were also used in regional centres such as Iwami. Modern copies or cheap forgeries of *netsuke* and *okimono* are usually of moulded plastic (Battie, 1986b, pp. 143–150), epoxy and polyester resins being particularly popular.

The helmeted hornbill casque

The casque or horn of the Helmeted Hornbill (*Rhinoplax vigil*) was much favoured in its own right in China and South-East Asia, from where the bird originated (Cammann, 1950; Campbell Pedersen, 2004, pp. 226–227). The hollow casque has a bright red periphery which was usually incorporated into the carving.

Vegetable ivory

This type of ivory derives from the nut kernels of the ivory palm (*Phytelephas macrocarpa*). This tree is a native of the South American rain forests (Webster, 1983, pp. 595–598; Campbell Pedersen, 2004, pp. 232–234), where it is variously known as the Homeru, Anti or Tagua palm. The kernel is known as the Corozo nut and is of cellulose. Despite being

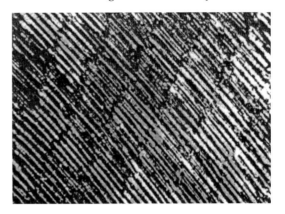

Figure 17.2 Cell pattern in vegetable ivory. (Courtesy Webster, 1983)

so chemically different, palm ivory does bear more than a passing resemblance to mammalian ivory, being very hard and white and with patterns of lines (Figure 17.2).

Another vegetable ivory is obtained from the nut kernel of the Doom or Doum palm (*Hyphaene thebaica*), which is native to northern and central Africa. This nut is also largely composed of cellulose, but is slightly less dense than the Corozo nut.

Bone and antler (Krzyszkowska, 1990, pp. 53–66)
Perhaps the most common imitations ivory are of bone or antler. They may be easily recognised at low-powered magnification by their characteristic structures (see p. 428).

Fictile ivory Maskell (1905, pp. 481–482; Webster (1983, p. 598).
As part of the nineteenth-century enthusiasm for taking casts of antiquities and art objects (see Chapter 4, p. 63), a large number of casts of ivories were made and issued by organisations such as the Arundel Society and commercial firms such as Elkington Brothers (see Chapter 4, p. 78). The Arundel Society alone issued casts of over 400 antique ivories taken from museums and collections around Europe (Oldfield, 1855). Institutions such as the South Kensington Museum (now the Victoria and Albert Museum) were quick to realise the educational and record potential of these copies (Westwood, 1876). Unfortunately, forgers also used them to produce more convincing forgeries, as pointed out by Cutler (2003) in his study of nineteenth-century copies and forgeries of the Vertouli Casket.

The procedure adopted by the Arundel Society for making casts of antique ivories was described by Maynard (1873, p. 35) as follows:

> Impressions have been taken in gutta-percha or gelatine from the ivories themselves; from these impressions matrices or models, technically termed types, are produced in copper by electro deposit; elastic moulds are then made from the types, from which casts are obtained in a superior kind of plaster, which, when saturated with a preparation employed for this purpose, acquires a hard smooth surface, in appearance like ivory, which improves with age.

The 'superior kind of plaster' referred to is likely to have had additions of ochre pigment to give the plaster a creamy antique appearance, and the preparation was probably wax, either stearine or spermaceti. Maskell (1905, p. 482) stated that the better casts were dipped in molten stearine to give an improved surface.

Synthetics

The desire to find an acceptable synthetic substitute for ivory was one of the driving forces behind the development of the plastics industry in the second half of the nineteenth century, as revealed in trade names for some of the early products such as Ivoride, Ivorine, Ivorite, French Ivory and even Genuine French Ivory (see Chapter 18, p. 476). Some of the first applications of the plastics based on nitrocellulose were used to make items such as piano keys and, more notoriously, billiard balls, which had an unfortunate propensity to combust explosively if struck too vigorously, thereby stimulating research for a more stable substitute.

Other synthetic ivories included casein (Ivorite), mixtures of casein and celluloid, early polyesters (Galolith) or phenolic resins (Dekorite). These date back to the first half of the twentieth century. Much superior ivory simulants are now made of polyesters (Vigopas) and epoxy resins (Jones (ed), 1990, pp. 251–252, item 274, Chapter 18, p. 459). To improve the color, opacity and density, etc. of these resins, fillers such as calcium carbonate are added, with trade names such as Alabrite.

Some synthetics have an artificial graining pattern in imitation of the Schreger patterns created by moulding together thin sheets of plastic, but do not accurately simulate the distinctive 'engine-turned' patterns (see Figure 17.1).

Identification by physical analytical techniques

The question is often two-fold, 'Is the material ivory?' and 'Is it ancient?'

The apatite constituent of the various true ivories and bone fluoresce under UV radiation (see Table 17.1). Vegetable ivory gives a similar response, but synthetic ivories tend to absorb UV and only to give a very faint fluorescence. If vivianite is present in mammoth ivory it will give a vivid purple fluorescence.

The various ivories based on real mammalian dentine have very distinctive structural patterns when viewed in transverse and longitudinal section (Penniman, 1952). However, there can be real problems trying to make a positive identification from the worn and irregular surface of an ivory antiquity, especially in trying to measure the angle of intersection of the Schreger lines necessary to differentiate between modern elephant and mammoth ivory.

The regular hydroxyapatite structures of the dentine of the true ivories produce characteristic X-ray diffraction (XRD) patterns (Sreelatha Rao and Subbaiah, 1983).

Characteristic spectra for elephant and the other ivories have been obtained by both Fourier-transform infra-red (FTIR) spectrometry (Banerjee and Schneider (1996) and Fourier-transform Raman spectroscopy (FTRS) (Edwards and Farwell, 1995; Edwards et al., 1997a, b; Edwards et al., 1998a; Edwards, 2005). The latter studies showed that the Raman techniques were able to distinguish between modern Asian and African ivory, and mammoth ivory, as well as to differentiate dentine from ancient and modern teeth. Edwards et al. (1997b) were able to differentiate between the dentine of the sperm whale, warthog, walrus and domestic pig. However, perhaps a note of caution should be made here: the reported differences in the spectra between the various ivories were often quite small and were all from modern materials in good condition. It remains to be seen how diagnostic the spectra from ancient degraded ivories would be. Withnall et al. (2000) identified tiny white crystals of magnesium hydrogen phosphate trihydrate (newberyite) on a small Medieval portrait miniature painted on ivory, using Raman microscopy (RM). Newberyite develops on the inner surface of ivory tusks.

The demand for genuine elephant ivory continues unabated such that at one time the very survival

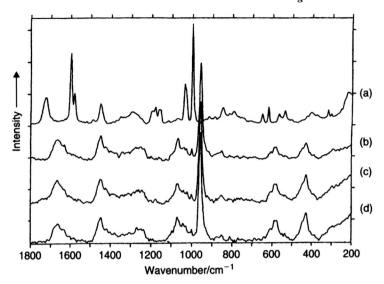

Figure 17.3   FTRM stack-plot of sperm whale teeth (b–d) and a synthetic copy (a). (Courtesy Edwards, 2005)

of the African elephant was threatened, leading to a ban on the trade in modern ivory. In order to effectively police the ban, analytical techniques have been evolved to distinguish between African, Asian and mammoth ivories (Espinoza and Mann, 1993; Edwards *et al.*, 1997a, b; 1998a; Rolandi, 1999).

The feasibility of provenancing ivories using isotope analysis has been tested on African ivory by Van der Merwe *et al.* (1990) and Vogel *et al.* (1990). They measured variations in the $^{13}C/^{12}C$ ratio, which reflects the proportions of C_3 (foliage) and C_4 (grass) photosynthesis pathways in the plants which formed the elephant's diet, the $^{15}N/^{14}N$ ratio, which is related to rainfall, and the $^{87}Sr/^{86}Sr$ ratio, which reflects the local geology of the environment in which the elephant lived. The isotope ratios so obtained to detect the geographic origin of modern poached ivory, illegally exported from Africa, could equally well be used to build up isotopic fingerprints of ivories used at particular places and times, or specific types of artefacts, although this was doubted by Krzyszkowska and Morkot (2000, p. 321).

Another approach has been by DNA profiling (*Times* report, April 2001). Initial work, based in Tanzania, sought to establish differences between forest- and savannah-dwelling elephants.

Synthetic simulants can be easily detected by techniques such as RS (Edwards *et al.*, 1995; Edwards and Farwell, 1995; Edwards, 2005). Edwards (2001) analysed a penholder purporting to

be scrimshaw work of the eighteenth century that turned out to be a synthetic resin of polystyrene and polymethyl methacrylate (Figure 17.3). In the wake of the international campaigns to ban whale-hunting, some dealers are now at pains to point out that the scrimshaw they offer for sale is not genuine.

The presence of synthetic consolidants used in conservation treatments is a cause of potential confusion. Even a knowledge of the recorded treatments may not always suffice. For example, Plenderleith and Werner (1971, pp. 158–159) described the consolidation treatments with methyl methacrylate performed at the British Museum on the ivories excavated from Nimrud by Sir Max Mallowan. They were probably unaware that his wife, Agatha Christie, had used her face lotion as a preliminary field treatment for the ivories when they first came out of the ground (Trümpler (ed), 2001, p. 152).

Age testing

New ivory has a bright lavender fluorescence when viewed by UV whereas old ivory has a yellow fluorescence (Rorimer, 1931, pp. 28–30). Hoving (1981, p. 228) listed some surface treatments that could be applied to produce the desired fluorescence. These included smoking the new ivory with burning pine needles, or wrapping the newly carved ivory in the skin of a freshly killed rabbit and burying it until the skin had rotted away.

Most ivory artefacts have been carved from ivory of relatively recent origin (with the exception of mammoth ivory), and thus RC dating is applicable. The usual caveats for the method (discussed in Chapter 5, p. 93) apply to ivory; in particular, in most circumstances meaningful calendar dates cannot be obtained for Post-Medieval material, although ivory from mammals that were alive in the second half of the twentieth century should be distinguishable by the presence of 'bomb carbon'. Ivories from creatures living a in marine environment have an age enhancement of several centuries (see Chapter 5, p. 96, Figure 5.11).

Ivory is remarkably stable over time if kept in a dry environment. However, the organic constituents are prone to decay in damp environments, and buried ivory can often be in a very parlous condition. Thus, antique ivory often has cracks and a tendency to delaminate. The latter are a good indicator that the ivory is likely to be of some age, but can also serve as a warning that the artefact is going to require specialist conservation and permanent storage thereafter in a carefully controlled environment. Savage (1976, p. 134) stated that cracks could be promoted by first putting the newly carved ivory into boiling water and then drying it quickly before a hot fire.

Freshly carved ivory is white and gradually becomes more creamy, yellow or even brown. This can be simulated by the usual stains of cold tea or tobacco juice. Savage (1976, p. 302) stated that:

> with what truth I do not know but it is likely, that forgeries of old ivory are sometimes given to young girls of more than average plumpness to wear between their breasts for a few months, the object being to give the surface a mellow patination from absorption of oily substances secreted by the skin.

Baer *et al.* (1978) determined the fluorine and nitrogen contents of some ancient Near Eastern ivories to study long-term chemical changes, and thus the authenticity of the items. Drillings of several milligrams were required for the analysis. As expected, there was a decrease in the nitrogen content but the predicted increase in fluorine content was more equivocal. The authors also demonstrated that it was possible, at least superficially, to introduce fluorine into modern ivory (see p. 428 for the corresponding fluorine dating of bone). They analysed a group of Assyrian ivories purchased by the Metropolitan Museum of Art that were without a firm provenance but were said to be from Khorsabad. Analysis of ivories actually excavated

from Khorsabad showed they had broadly similar compositions, but with rather different nitrogen contents. The overall impression was that the group was likely to be authentic, but perhaps not from Khorsabad itself.

Fiegenbaum (1996) examined toolmarks in an attempt to differentiate old from new ivory working. Cristoferi and Fiori (1992) looked for evidence of polishing, including traces of the original abrasives, identified by XRD and thermal analysis, etc. They found that powdered gypsum and marble 'soft' abrasives were the most common on the Medieval Italian ivories that they studied. They also found evidence of the subsequent use of much harder corundum and quartz abrasives, which had done serious damage to the original surfaces.

Forgeries

Ivory artworks have been widely imitated and forged (Kurz, 1948, pp. 162–174; Arnau, 1961, pp. 101–103; Savage, 1976, pp. 131–134), including Late Antique caskets and plaques, especially in nineteenth-century Italy (Maclagan, 1923; Cutler, 2003).

In the early years of the twentieth century, Arthur Evans, at his excavations at the Minoan Palace at Knossos on Crete, trained two local craftsmen to conserve and restore the excavated antiquities. They apparently went one better and began to make their own, including some quite spectacular gold and ivory *cryselephantine* statuettes of snake goddesses, aged by dipping the ivory in acid. These duped Evans and they were sold to the local museum at Heraklion, as well as to the Fitzwilliam Museum in Cambridge and the Museum of Fine Arts in Boston (Lapatin, 2001).

Bone and antler

Sources: MacGregor (1985); O'Connor (1987); Krzyszkowska (1990, pp. 52–66); Campbell Pedersen (2004, pp. 85–101).

Recognition

The presence of the channels which permeate the structure, known as the Haversian system, are diagnostic of bone and antler. Seen in cross-section the main channels are circular or oval and are surrounded by small cavities. In longitudinal section they appear as long cavities. Bone inlays, etc. will usually have been cut from long bones, exposing the longitudinal face; otherwise, the cut face of the artefact displays the obliquely cut canals and dots. These distinctive cavities in the bone surface are often filled with dirt, making them easy to see against the creamy-white background.

Wear patterns and toolmarks on bone and related material have been studied by d'Errico (1993) and Olsen (1988).

Age testing
UV testing can provide a good indication of age; bone reacts much like ivory, fluorescing brightly when first cut, with the fluorescence becoming yellower with age. This feature is used in forensic examinations as a rough guide to establish whether cuts or breaks on bones are likely to be recent; if the bone fluoresces then the cut or break is taken to be less than 100 years old. However, there are all sorts of caveats regarding treatments, burial conditions, etc. that could make a recent cut appear old.

Over the years other changes take place in the chemical composition of bone and antler which, before the advent of RC, formed the basis of dating methods. Bone is made up principally of an inorganic component, calcium phosphate (apatite), and an organic protein component (collagen), that contains both organic carbon and nitrogen. As with ivory, discussed above (see p. 428), the collagen content decreases as the proteins decay and this is measurable by noting the decline in the nitrogen content and moreover was used as a relative dating method for many years. The loss of collagen, or 'animal matter' as it was sometimes known in the nineteenth century, had been measured on the famous Moulin Quignon jawbone that fooled Boucher de Perthes back in 1863 (see Chapter 19, p. 471). The 'animal' content was estimated at 8% and thus the bone was unlikely to be ancient. This was probably the first time that a chemical test had been used in an authenticity study. However, the rate of loss is very dependant on the environment, and thus the method is not really of any use for dating.

The hydroxyapatite in buried bone absorbs fluorine from the fluorides in the groundwater, and the fluorine content has been used to determine the relative age of bone (Oakley, 1969). The method was applied in the investigation of the Moulin Quignon jaw (Oakley, 1948), the Sherborne bone and, most famously, the Piltdown forgeries (see Chapter 19, p. 488). As with the collagen content, the absorbency depends on the burial environment. Thus, the method has been almost entirely superseded by RC dating, which usually provides a more reliable date on a much smaller sample (see Chapter 5, p. 88). However, Tankersley *et al.* (1998) have continued to develop the method (see p. 428 for corresponding work on ivory).

Case study: The Sherborne Bone (d'Errico *et al.*, 1998) (Figure 17.4)

This seemingly trivial little piece, now housed in the Natural History Museum, London (Reg. E 5305), was the subject of considerable and often acrimonious debate through much of the twentieth century. Its authenticity or otherwise has had ramifications, not least for the Piltdown controversy, and has even called into question the one supposedly genuine piece of Palaeolithic parietal art from the British Isles.

In 1911 two schoolboys purportedly found the fragment of long bone in an old quarry near Sherborne in Dorset. It bore the scratched representation of a horse on the surviving original surface. The piece was shown to Arthur Smith Woodward, who was then very actively engaged in the excavation and evaluation of the material from Piltdown (see Chapter 19). He published it as a rare example of Palaeolithic parietal art (Woodward, 1914), comparable to the rather similar piece found some 30 years beforehand in Robin Hood's Cave in the Creswell Crags region of Derbyshire, now in the British Museum (Sieveking, Cat. 855) (Figure 17.4). Although the latter piece was excavated it had been under some suspicion, not least by the co-director of the excavation, as being a 'plant'. The new discovery supported its authenticity for Woodward, who seems not to have considered the possibility that the Sherborne piece could have been copied from the Creswell bone. However, some 10 years later, William Sollas in a revision of his popular 1915 book, *Ancient Hunters and their Modern*

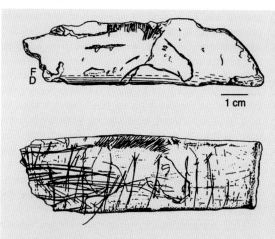

1 cm

Figure 17.4 (Upper) The Sherborne Horse; (Lower) The Creswell Horse. (Courtesy d'Errico *et al.*, 1998)

Representatives (1924, p. 536ff), added a footnote dismissive of both pieces. 'The horse figured here [the Creswell Horse] is, I am assured, a forgery introduced into the cave by a mischievous person. The horse described by Dr. Smith Woodward [the Sherborne Horse] is a forgery perpetrated by some school boys.' Thus began a long, and at time acrimonious dispute over the authenticity of the Sherborne Bone, ably summarised, and, hopefully, finalised, by d'Errico *et al.* (1998).

They carried out a detailed microscopy survey and accelerator mass spectrometry radiocarbon (AMS RC) dating. Even by relatively low powered light microscopy it was clear that the scratched lines of the horse were very clean compared with other scratches on the surface of the bone, but were similar in color to recent breaks on the bone. Examination by scanning electron microscopy (SEM) showed that the scratched figure did not have the characteristics of grooves cut into fresh bone, i.e. striae running parallel along the line of the groove. Instead there was flaking of the bone at the edge of the grooves, suggesting that they had been scratched into bone that was already old.

An attempt had been made previously to physically date the bone on the basis of its nitrogen, uranium and fluorine contents by Oakley (1979a), as an appendix to Farrar (1979), using the same methodology that he had used a quarter of a century earlier to expose the Piltdown forgery. The enhanced fluorine content of the Sherborne bone was comparable to that found in a control piece from the Upper Palaeolithic layers in the Cheddar Caves in Somerset, and suggested to Oakley that the bone was indeed of Pleistocene age.

However, the AMS RC date was (OxA 5239) 610 ± 45, showing that the bone came from an animal that had lived some time during the late thirteenth to early fifteenth centuries AD. Thus there is no possibility that the horse's head could be an example of Late Pleistocene art, but every possibility that it was a forgery. The question remained, who was the perpetrator?

There seems to have been little love lost between Sollas and Woodward, and the idea has been raised that Sollas set up the Sherborne bone as a hoax to trap the gullible Woodward. On the strength of this tenuous evidence it was even postulated that Sollas had also set up the entire Piltdown affair (Walsh, 1996, pp. 7–8, 99).

However, this still leaves the authenticity of the Creswell Crag horse unresolved.

Antler forgeries are uncommon but two sleeves of antler holding genuine Neolithic stone adze heads were found to be modern, not least because although supposedly found in Belgium, they were from *Cervus odocoileus*, an American species of deer (Otte and Hurt, 1982/3).

Keratinaceous materials: horn, tortoiseshell, baleen and leather

Sources: Hardwick (1981); Webster (1983, pp. 598–602); MacGregor (1985); O'Connor (1987); Trench (ed) (2000, p. 229 [horn], pp. 275–278 [leather], pp. 497–499 [tortoiseshell]) Campbell Pedersen (2004, pp. 102–141).

Horn

Recognition

Horn is related to hair and skin, being composed of keratin proteins (Hardwick, 1981; MacGregor, 1985; O'Connor 1987). It normally forms as a cone over a boney core, and traditionally in the West most horn comes from cattle. Horn has corrugations which are typically between about 100 and

400 microns across and are clearly discernible with only a hand lens. Horn ages by warping and cracking along the plane of the corrugations. It can be dated by RC (see Chapter 5, p. 93).

It is a thermoplastic material that can be softened and opened out into quite sizeable flat sheets (Ritchie, 1975; Hardwick, 1981 and see Chapter 18, p. 448). Horn has some translucence, which in the past was increased by treating with tallow to hot-press the sheets used to make *lanthorn*. Horn can be shaped by hot-pressing the sheets either singly or several sheets together between hot steel plates to obtain greater thickness. Horn has traditionally been used to make beakers and other containers. The small solid cones of the horn tips can be used as a more solid material suitable for carving in the round. Powdered horn can also be hot-pressed into a variety of shapes.

In China rhinoceros horn was highly valued, not only as an aphrodisiac, but as a medium for exquisite carving (Jenyns and Watson, 1965, pp. 189–232; Chapman, 1999; Campbell Pedersen, 2004, pp. 102–107). Being so expensive it has been copied in a variety of other materials from porcelain to synthetic plastics. It can be readily distinguished analytically by FTIR or FTRS (Akhtar and Edwards, 1997; Edwards *et al.*, 1998b).

Tortoiseshell

Sources: Vuilleumier (1979); O'Connor (1987); Trench (ed) (2000, pp. 497–499); Campbell Pedersen (2004, pp. 125–141).

Recognition
Natural tortoiseshell comes mainly from the carapace of the Hawksbill sea turtle (*Eretmochelys imbricata*), and to a lesser extent from the Green (*Chelonia mydas*) and the Loggerhead turtle (*Caretta caretta*). The mottled appearance is made up of myriad dots of color, which can be easily seen at low magnification, and is totally different from the continuous color of the dyed simulants.

Tortoiseshell has been used as a decorative material all over the world for millennia both for whole artefacts and as an inlay. It is a keratin-type proteinaceous material related to horn and to hair. It can be easily cut and carved, and as a thermoplastic (see Chapter 18, p. 448) it can be softened in boiling water and shaped by moulding while still hot. Chips and sawdust of tortoiseshell may be warmed and pressed together in a similar manner to horn and amber. Composites made up of sheets of tortoiseshell pressed around an inner sheet of horn

were produced in Europe in the Post-Medieval period until the nineteenth century.

Tortoiseshell was traditionally imitated using horn (known in English as *mockshell*) and was one of the very first materials to be successfully simulated by synthetic plastics. Celluloid was first used and a variety of plastics have been employed subsequently (see Chapter 18, p. 447).

Real tortoiseshell fluoresces yellow and brown under UV irradiation. The proteinaceous keratins of tortoiseshell are chemically very different from any of the stimulant materials, and can be easily detected by physical analytical techniques such as FTIR or FTRS (Akhtar and Edwards, 1997; Akhtar *et al.*, 1997; Edwards *et al.* 1998b). Scott Williams (1997) described a portable non-invasive probe FTIR system, specifically for museum work. Using it, a comb previously believed to be of tortoiseshell, was found to be made of celluloid.

Leather

Sources: General: Reed (1972); Trench (ed) (2000, pp. 275–278).

The chemical composition and analysis of the various leathers, together with their characteristic long-term degradation and identification, and the tanning and other associated processes, are covered in Calnan and Haines (eds) (1991) and Kite and Thomson (eds) (2005). The Leather Conservation Centre (1981) has published a useful atlas of micrographs of the skins of various animals used in leather after various tanning treatments and in various stages of decay. Parchment is discussed in Chapter 13, p. 313 and its RC dating in Chapter 5, p. 102.

Wax

Sources: Rich (1947, pp. 52–53); Murrell (1971); Penny (1993, pp. 215–218); Trench (2000, p. 525). Scientific: Mills and White (1994, pp. 49–55).

Waxes are not precisely defined chemical materials. They are classified as much by their physical properties as by their composition. They are materials that are translucent, of low melting point and with a 'waxy' feel. Organic waxes tend to be long-chain hydrocarbons – fatty acids and esters derived from a wide variety of plant, animal and synthetic sources – that are often mixtures of several chemicals. Waxes have a very long history of usage by man, and, as many of them are rather unreactive, they survive quite well (Mills and White, 1994, pp. 49–55). Regert *et al.* (2001) studied the chemical degradation of beeswax both on antiquities and from samples subjected to accelerated age degradation. Glastrup (1989) and Regert *et al.* (2005) used gas chromatography (GC) to analyse waxes and resins, and Edwards *et al.* (1996a) used FTRS.

Arnau (1961, pp. 103–104) noted that old wax frequently has dust firmly embedded in its surface and that this could be imitated by applying a very thin spray of turpentine, and then blowing on a little dust just before the turpentine had dried.

Case study: The Flora Bust (Figure 17.5)

Every director has a bust of Flora waiting for him at the end of the corridor.
1961 catalogue of the BM Exhibition of Forgeries and Deceptive Copies

Sources: Kurz (1948, p. 24); Schüller (1960, pp. 50–60); Arnau (1961, pp. 96–98); Ost (1984); Jones (ed) (1990, pp. 303–307).

The badly damaged painted wax bust of the goddess Flora has been the subject of embarrassment and acrimony almost since its acquisition for the Kaiser Friedrich Museum in Berlin 1909, by the redoubtable Wilhelm Bode, General Manager of the Prussian Art Collections. The bust had apparently been spotted in the window of a London antique shop and purchased for a trifling amount. Bode was convinced that the bust was by none other than Leonardo da Vinci, and this revelation created a sensation in Berlin, matched only by the consternation felt in London. *The Times* in particular was much vexed by the thought that Britain's rival had recognised and snatched a great art treasure from under their very noses. However, the situation changed quite dramatically just a few months later when *The Times* ran an article claiming that the bust had in fact been made by Richard Cockle Lucas, a well-known but far from exceptional sculptor, back in 1846. He had apparently been commissioned to produce it from a painting of a rather simpering Flora. Then Lucas's 81-year-old son came forward and swore on oath that the story was correct and moreover he had helped his father make it. He was able to give some significant information about the bust, describing how the layers of wax had been built up, and how his father collected old candle ends as a source of wax. He also described how his father stuffed bits of workshop debris, including old newspaper, etc., inside the bust. When the museum staff in Berlin removed the base, there was the debris just as Lucas's son had described it, including a letter bearing a 1840s date.

Things looked bleak not just for da Vinci's authorship of the bust, but also for Bode. Bode was the great authority on matters of attribution and authenticity in sculpture, and in attaining this position had made many enemies. *Schadenfreude*

Figure 17.5 The Flora bust. This bust stands 66 cm tall; the wax is badly decayed and there are now only traces of paint. (© Kaiser Friedrich Museum, Berlin)

seems to have been the general reaction of his colleagues, and in the Berlin museums, few would openly support his continued categorical insistence on his original attribution. The affair was used by his enemies in politics as well as art to attack him; polemic from the Left Wing press was met by unequivocal support from the Right Wing press.

Bode attempted to support his case by showing the Flora bust set among a selection of undoubted and rather insipid works by Lucas intended to show that the Flora was far superior to anything Lucas could have produced. However, this exhibition rather backfired, for what it also showed was that Lucas was in the habit of making wax sculptures inspired by the great works of previous ages.

Among the very voluminous archive on the bust is an album originally belonging to Lucas which contains a photograph showing the bust in the 1860s, but apparently with him disclaiming authorship. However, some link between the bust and Lucas seems certain. More recent arguments are between the figure being an out-and-out forgery (Schüller, 1960, pp. 59–60) and being a genuine sixteenth-century piece (although da Vinci seems to have dropped out of the running) that was heavily restored by Lucas (Johnson, 1973; Kratz and Bloch in Jones (ed), 1990, p. 307, where the piece is in the section devoted to mystery pieces). The latter hypothesis has big problems, not the least of which is that it completely discounts Lucas' son's sworn statement that it was a copy. Another problem is that it has absolutely no history prior to the 1840s.

Scientific examination was carried out almost from the moment the bust arrived in Berlin (Kissling, 1910 and Pinkus, 1910, who reported the presence of spermaceti wax). More recent GC analysis showed the wax principally to contain the constituents of beeswax, spermaceti and stearin, together with some pine resin (Mills and White, 1994, pp. 190–191). Beeswax has been used since antiquity; spermaceti, coming from the sperm whale, has been in use in Europe since the fifteenth century, and was a regular constituent of modelling and casting waxes, at least from the seventeenth century, because of its low melting point. Spermaceti was also used for quality candles from the nineteenth century in England. Stearin wax was obtained by the hydrolysis (saponification) of animal fats. This was the usual wax used for making cheap candles in the nineteenth century, but was not used as such in the sixteenth century. Lucas kept a supply of old candle ends as a supply of wax. After the mid-nineteenth century, stearin began to be synthesised from oil shales.

At one time it was even suggested that the Italian master forger, Giovanni Bastianini, might have been the author of Flora (Sox, 1987, p. 129). Sox interviewed Josef Riederer, head of the Rathgen Laboratory at the Staatliche Museum in Berlin, who told him that, as the wax contained a synthetic wax not made until 1833 (presumably stearin), the bust must have been made later. Rottländer (1988) also carried out GC analyses on samples taken from the surface layers and from the interior of the bust and found all the samples to contain spermaceti. Beeswax and spermaceti are mixtures of several organic compounds, and Rottländer challenged the previous interpretation, especially the identification of stearin wax, noting that stearic acid is, after all, a constituent of beeswax. Rottländer also noted that the wax was degraded, but speculated that the degradation had taken place inside the dead whale before it was processed. Thus the identification of the wax is still rather inconclusive.

In addition to the wax, the fragmentary paint has also been analysed and has revealed the presence of archil, an organic pigment based on mushrooms. This was claimed by one group to be unobtainable after the seventeenth century, and by another group to be freely available in nineteenth-century London (Kurz, 1948, p. 24; Arnau, 1961, pp. 96–97), typical of the contradiction and counterclaim concerning the studies on the Flora Bust in general.

RC dating was reported by Freundlich as an appendix to Ost's 1984 book. The date was 290 ± 40 BP (KN 3224), which after calibration gives a date of 94.4% probability of AD 1480–1780 and a 1% probability of AD 1780–1800 at 2σ (Figure 17.6).

This date has to be interpreted carefully. At face value it apparently supports a Renaissance origin, and comfortably accommodates Leonardo, but there are complications arising from the nature of the wax itself. By the time that synthetic stearin first began to be used for candles in the 1860s, photographs of the bust already existed and thus it is unlikely that the body of the bust contains synthetic waxes. However, there is a strong possibility that the bust was restored between the 1860s

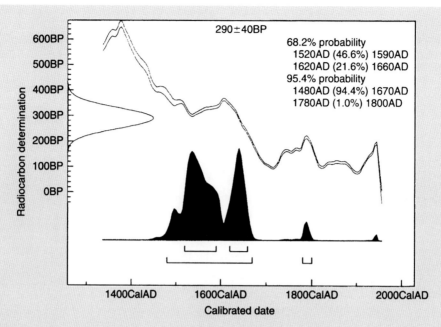

Figure 17.6   OxCal calibrated AMS date for the Flora Bust. (Courtesy J. Ambers and T. Simpson)

and 1907, which might have involved the use of synthetic materials, including stearin, made from chemicals based on coal or mineral oil. A mixture of nineteenth-century natural wax with a small amount of synthetic material derived from geological age carbon could easily result in an apparently earlier date.

An additional problem is that if spermaceti wax, extracted from whales, really is present then it would be subject to the marine effect (see Chapter 5, p. 98) adding several centuries to the real age of the sample.

It is apparently difficult to differentiate beeswax from spermaceti on the basis of their $^{13}C/^{12}C$ isotope ratios. If such an intermixture of waxes was suspected and was not macroscopically separable, then it should be possible to separate enough of the components that only occurred in natural non-marine waxes by gas–liquid chromatography mass spectrometry (GLC MS) to obtain the very small samples needed for AMS dating now.

Overall, despite much art historical and scientific work the true origins of the bust remains uncertain, and Flora retains her enigmatic, if somewhat cracked, smile.

Natural organic materials derived from plants: copal, amber, jet, lacquer and wood

Copal and amber

Sources: Bibliographies: Beck *et al.* (1966, 1967). General: Ogden (1982, pp. 116–119): Fraquet (1987); Beck and Bouzek (eds) (1993); Ganzelewski and Slotta (eds) (1996); Grimaldi (1996); Ross (1998); Trench (ed) (2000, pp. 8–11); Campbell Pedersen (2004, pp. 1–39).

Both copal and amber are fairly widely distributed around the world, although major deposits that have been worked on an industrial scale are relatively few (Fraquet, 1987, pp. 131–133; Grimaldi, 1996, pp. 16–19; Case *et al.*, 2003).

The appealing colors and tactile qualities of amber, coupled with the ease with which it may be carved and polished, have made it a prestigious material for jewellery and small carvings since the Palaeolithic period. An additional and quite separate interest lies in the wonderfully preserved insects, etc. entrapped for millions of years within the amber.

Amber contains natural thermoplastics. It is formed from the terpenoid resins exuded by certain pines, particularly those related to the modern *Agathis* and *Hymenaea* genus, and other conifers millions of years ago. These resins, when buried out of contact with the air, have polymerised over the ages, although the exact chemical composition remains uncertain (Mills *et al.*, 1984/5; Shedrinsky *et al.*, 1991; Mills and White 1994, Ch. 8). Most true amber dates from the Miocene and Eocene periods, approximately 30 million years ago.

Copal

Copal is normally found in the soil of old forests, just a few centimetres below the present ground surface, typically in the form of lumps weighing up to several kilograms, and is not to be confused with incense copal which is the freshly collected tree resin (Case *et al.*, 2003). Most copal is believed to have been formed in the Pleistocene period, but it should be noted that RC determinations carried out on selected samples from the Natural History Museum found they were all modern (Burleigh and Whalley, 1983), although possibly there was contamination from treatments.

The bulk of copal production was used for the manufacture of superior varnishes, before being largely supplanted by synthetic equivalents (Case *et al.*, 2003). Some is used as a substitute for amber, in China, East Africa and especially in the Dominican Republic. There the use of copal from the Cotui region, often coated with an epoxy resin in order to harden and consolidate the surface, to simulate true Dominican amber, has been on a sufficient scale to bring about a loss of confidence in the real material (Fraquet, 1987, p. 196). Copal is rather soft and the surface tends to craze after just a few years of exposure to the atmosphere, as a result of the evaporation of volatiles and oxidation. Crazing on an artefact is thus an indication both that it is copal and that it may have come from an old collection. However, in the past copal may have been coated with more durable resins to harden and protect it. For example, a process was patented in 1911 to treat copal with carbon disulphide or acetone to render the surface harder and more resilient, similar to amber (Fraquet, 1987, p. 67).

Copal can be easily distinguished from amber as it is readily soluble in acetone or ethanol. A drop of alcohol on the suspect surface will suffice to soften it, releasing an aromatic smell. However, this will leave a white mark on the surface if the sample is copal and may have an even more damaging effect on some synthetic amber simulants. Copal can be identified by some of the standard physical analytical techniques (Vandenabeele *et al.*, 2003).

Mills and White (1994, p. 185) carried out gas chromatography (GC) on a small head carved out of a resinous material that was initially expected to be of amber. The head was found on a Romano-British site and was thus of some interest. The analysis showed unambiguously that the resin had spectra corresponding to those of the copal-like kauri gum from New Zealand (Webster, 1983, p. 578). Thus, far from being carved by a native Romano-Celtic artisan, the head was probably made by a Maori craftsman in the nineteenth century.

Amber

The principal worked deposits of amber are in the Baltic, Sicily and Romania in Europe, Myanmar and Japan in East Asia, and the Dominican Republic and Mexico in the Americas. The unequivocal provenancing of individual pieces of amber is rarely possible because there are very many smaller deposits, and the amber from the main exploited deposits themselves has a wide range of appearance as well as physical and chemical properties. Thus, for example, it has been held that amber from the Baltic region, the principal European source, is distinguished chemically by the presence of about 3 to 8% of succinic acid, whereas Sicilian and Romanian amber have very little. Unfortunately, since then further ana-lyses have found that some sources of Baltic amber show a very low succinic acid content (Grimaldi, 1996, p. 53) and conversely that others have high succinic acid levels, although it is true to say that Baltic amber *generally* does have a high succinic acid content. Savkevich (1981) considered that succinic acid contents are too variable throughout the major European deposits to constitute a reliable provenancing criterion. This is especially true for single objects. Color and transparency are dependent on the environment in which the amber formed and also on the environment in which it has been since being formed into an artefact, be it a Bronze Age burial or a church sacristy. Beck and Hartnett (1993) showed that of 177 pieces supposedly of Sicilian amber, 4 were of copal and 28 were of Baltic amber that had been heat-treated to make them appear redder and thus more like the more valuable Sicilian amber.

Amber has been transported over very long distances since the inception of its use, and the carved piece found in Upper Palaeolithic deposits in the Cheddar Caves in Somerset, England, is several hundred kilometres from the nearest known source. In later times Baltic amber was distributed even further. There is even one instance of a piece of amber being found in a post-conquest Mayan tomb in central America, which was shown by nuclear magnetic resonance (NMR) analysis as likely to be from the Baltic, presumably brought to the Americas by the Conquistadors (Lambert *et al.*, 1994). The Baltic seems always to have been the major source of amber in Europe and the Middle East from prehistoric times as exemplified by the results of the IR analyses performed on material from the British Isles (Beck and Shennan, 1991, pp. 29–49, Figure 3.1, p. 30), and the Mycenaean world (Beck, 1986).

Baltic amber has been used for centuries by the Chinese. The other main Chinese source is Myanmar, and its distinctive amber, known as Burmite, is characterised by its deep, clear red color and inclusions of calcite (Webster, 1983, p. 337). It is rather hard and brittle, owing to its being substantially older than most other utilised amber, being formed 80 to 100 million years ago. The traditional Japanese source of amber is from the north-east coast of Honshu Island, and it has been studied by FTIR microscopy and fluorescence spectroscopy by Sato *et al.* (2003).

Baltic amber was traditionally gathered from the seashore, but in the nineteenth century dredging operations began, followed by deep mining, which continues at the Palanicken Mine on the Sammland Peninsular (Ganzelewski, 1996). These developments enabled production to soar to over a million pounds weight per annum by the end of the nineteenth century. These were colossal amounts compared to what had gone before, and dwarfed production figures from elsewhere in the world.

Properties and treatments

Amber is reasonably stable, but slowly oxidises, causing color changes and increased brittleness, crazing and the fragmentation of the surface.

Freshly carved pieces have always been treated by immersion in hot oil, etc. to fill in near-surface cracks and voids. Pliny recorded both the clarification of amber (by boiling it in pig fat) and dyeing treatments (*Natural History*, 37.46, 48; Eichholz, 1962, pp. 198–200). More recently, clarification with synthetic resins has become the usual practice (Nassau, 1984a).

Ambroid

The enormous number of small chips from the Baltic amber mining operations can be heated until soft and then pressed into shape as a thermosetting plastic. The material is known as *ambroid* and has been in use from the 1880s in Central Europe for making minor items such as beads and the mouthpieces of tobacco-pipes. During these processes dyes could be added to improve the color and oils (mainly colza, rapeseed oil) added for clarification. During the second half of the twentieth century it is estimated that about half of all Baltic amber was first clarified with deeply penetrating oils to fill the voids. This was then heated and pressed into uniform blanks convenient for bead production, etc.

A sure indication of ambroid is provided by the morphology of the tiny air bubbles that appear in most amber. In natural amber, these air bubbles are round, whereas in ambroid they are more elongated. The stressed amber in ambroid is often clearly revealed by polarised light.

Alternatively, amber chips could be set in molten copal. Since the mid-twentieth century in Eastern Europe they have been set in a polyester resin to form a simulant known as Polyburn, produced on a considerable scale. In both of these products the amber chips retain their identity such that they can sometimes be seen by natural light or UV. The amber substitute marketed as Amberdan is probably a similar material (Liddicoat, 1987, p. 260).

If the heat-treated amber of ambroid is cooled too quickly then very distinctive circular stress cracks appear (Figure 17.7). So far from detracting from the value of the ambroid, these so-called sun-spangles rapidly became a popular feature from the mid-twentieth century and should be an instantly

Figure 17.7 Circular sun-spangles in a bangle of heat-treated ambroid. Purchased on a street market in Rochester in 2001 as oriental amber. (Courtesy A. Milton)

recognisable characteristic of treated amber, although they are copied in plastic amber simulants.

Synthetic amber
Sources: Allen (1976a, b, c); Fraquet (1987, pp. 73–83); Shedrinsky *et al.* (1993); Campbell Pedersen (2004, pp. 26–27).

The hugely increased availability of amber in the second half of the nineteenth century, coupled with materials such as ambroid and copal, meant there was initially little call for a synthetic simulant. In the 1920s casein and celluloid were used to a limited extent to imitate amber, but they were cloudy, followed in the 1930s by the cast clear golden phenolic resins. These phenolic amber substitutes are visually quite convincing and were enormously popular. They have SGs of 1.25–2.0, which, as with most synthetic simulants, are appreciably higher than the SG of amber (1.05–1.12) (see below for distinguishing tests). In the 1930s amber simulants based on urea and thiourea formaldehyde polymers also became popular, followed in the second half of the twentieth century by polystyrene, which seem to come mainly from India, together with acrylic-based plastics such as polymethyl methacrylate (Perspex). Polyesters are very common simulants with trade names such as Bernit or Bernat (Germany), often treated to produce the much-appreciated sun-spangles (Fraquet, 1987, p. 83). Epoxy resins are now widely used as amber simulants, especially in Russia, and are also employed to strengthen the surfaces of copal and some heat-treated amber. The variously colored ambers – red, green, etc. – offered at low prices on stalls around the world, are often synthetic or ambroid (Campbell Pedersen, 2004; and see articles by her in various issues of *Gem & Jewellery News* for 2004).

Siewert (1984) employed IR to identify the range of amber substitutes used since the nineteenth century to imitate amber beads in North Africa and the Middle East. Nitrocellulose, Bakelite, polyesters, acrylamide and styrene were all regularly identified, showing that even traditional ethnic pieces can contain a wide range of modern materials.

Testing and analysis of amber

It can be appreciated from the previous sections that natural amber occurs with a wide range of colors and appearances, and that there is an almost continuous spectrum, from amber with minor surface adulteration through to entirely synthetic

simulants with no natural material present at all. It might be thought that at least the recent ambroids etc. could be unambiguously distinguished from the natural amber that would have been used in earlier times (allowing for the residues of natural oils used for clarification in the past). However, even the presence of synthetic chemicals does not necessarily provide an indication that the amber is of fairly recent production, as the chemicals used in conservation/restoration treatments of a genuine antiquity could cause confusion (Thickett *et al.*, 1995). The traditional consolidants included natural resins such as dammar etc., and, more insidiously for the analytical work, solutions of copal, kaura gum and amber itself. These have been joined by a wide range of synthetic materials such as celluloid, phenolic resins and, more recently, PVC, methacrylates and epoxy resins, the latter especially favoured by the Russians. In his survey of conservation workshops, Beck (1982) encountered a bewilderingly wide range of other materials. This must qualify any judgements made on surface analysis alone, where it is impossible to tell whether the other organic materials are present through the body of the artefact or just in the surface.

Gemmological tests
Sources: Lewis (1977, pp. 46–49); Webster (1983, pp. 574–580); Fraquet (1987, pp. 142–146); Liddicoat (1987, pp. 171–172, 259–260, 269); Anderson (1990, pp. 331–333); Read (1991, pp. 271–273); Campbell Pedersen (2004, pp. 27–33).

A range of standard gemmological tests are available, but these are often not suitable to the investigation of antiquities, because they are either destructive or not applicable to mounted pieces that cannot be removed from their setting (Table 17.2).

Hardness: Amber is quite soft, with a hardness of about 2–2.5 on the Moh scale, which can be determined with the appropriate scratch sticks (see Chapter 16, p. 394).

Fracture: Amber displays a distinctive conchoidal (shell-like) fracture, often visible on a damaged piece.

Density: Amber has a quite low SG of about 1.05–1.12 (some variation is inevitable because of air bubbles and inclusions, etc., and that of copal can be even lower, 1.03–1.08). This is significantly lower than the SGs of most of the common synthetic simulants such the phenolic resins (1.26), although polystyrene has a low SG of 1.05. Bearing these caveats in mind, amber can be identified by a

Table 17.2   Tests for distinguishing amber, copal and synthetic simulants.

Material	Specific gravity	Refractive index	On burning, shaving or similar	Under knife	Other useful data
Natural amber	1.08 (mean)	1.54 (mean)	Slightly aromatic. Subtle depending on when worked	Splinters except under newly sharpened blade	Learn to develop 'eye'; compare with actual example at all times
Copal	1.06	1.53	Very aromatic. Can stick in threads to needle	Splinters	Softens under ethyl alcohol. Leave drop on surface one minute; will then take imprint of finger, etc. Also releases aromatic smell when rubbed vigorously. Crazing is quite different from amber
Blond tortoiseshell	1.29	1.53	Smells like burnt hair	Sectile	
Cellulose nitrate	1.37–1.43*	1.49–1.52	Smells like camphor. May burn explosively	Sectile	Soluble in ether – amber not affected by short immersion
Cellulose acetate	1.29–1.35	1.49–1.51		Sectile	Thermoplastic
Casein	1.32–1.43	1.49–1.54	Smells like burnt milk	Sectile	Is *not* electrostatic
Phenol formaldehyde resin	1.26–1.28	1.64–1.66	Smells acrid	Sectile	Chars black, does not burn
Urea formaldehyde resin	1.48–1.55	1.55–1.62		Sectile	
Polymethyl methacrylate (Perspex or Diakon)	1.18–1.19	1.50	Smells like burnt fruit	Sectile	
Polystyrenes (Distrine or Trolutol)	1.05	1.58–1.67		Sectile	Soluble in benzene or toluene; softens at 70–90°C
Polyester	1.23	1.49–1.51		Sectile	

Source: Fraquet, 1987, Table 7.1
*Figures vary considerably depending on fillers used.

salt solution test. Ten level teaspoons of salt are dissolved in 250 ml water to give a salt solution with an SG of about 1.12 to 1.14, in which amber will float but most of the plastics will sink. The salt water test is probably the most reliable and safe 'simple' test, but even so, it is not recommended for amber with a crazed or fissured surface.

Heat: A small sliver will melt and give off a resinous, piney smell that in Baltic amber is often masked by the unpleasant smell of the burning succinic acid. (NB Heat is potentially extremely injurious to old

amber, causing it to split along incipient cracks, and thus must never be applied directly to an artefact. Even the heat generated by a microscope lamp can precipitate cracking; see p. 442.)

UV: Most ambers fluoresce when excited by UV. A range of colors from blue–white with long-wave UV radiation through to green by short-wave UV, are produced; Dominican amber is famously blue under UV, whereas most plastics do not fluoresce. The individual chips of amber set in synthetic resins in composites such as Polybern show up clearly under UV, and ambroid often fluoresces in a distinct-ive manner in which the pressed joints become clear. Freshly exposed amber surfaces fluoresce particularly strongly, and this can decay over a very few years, thus offering the possibility of recognising very recent working on a piece. Some amber, notably from the Dominican Republic and Sicily, has a natural fluo-rescence in light without UV excitation when first exposed, but this effect declines after only a few years of exposure, presumably due to the photo-oxidation of the chemicals responsible in the surface.

RI: Amber and copal have RIs in the range 1.5–1.65, which are different from those for most synthetic plastics and glass.

Polarised light: When the polarising lens is rotated, amber, copal and particularly ambroid dis-play a rainbow effect owing to the various inter-ference patterns caused by internal stresses etc., whereas most synthetic simulants do not. This is quite a good means of revealing composite pieces and where inserts of insects etc. have been made, as the interference patterns will be disrupted.

Physical analytical techniques
Sources: Mills *et al.* (1984/5); Fraquet (1987, pp. 146–154); Mills and White (1994, pp. 96–99).

A variety of techniques have been used, almost all of which give a characteristic 'fingerprint' rather than a true identification. Most analytical work has been carried out to establish the provenance of antiquities of amber and there has been a certain degree of success, although some of the diagnostic features are not as confidently cited now.

IR: (see Chapter 3, p. 58) This was the first physi-cal analytical technique to be seriously applied to amber and there is still far and away more analytical data on amber published for IRS, and latterly FTIR, than for any other technique. This is largely due to the lifetime research of Carl Beck (Beck, 1982, 1986; Beck and Bouzek (ed), 1993). This work has involved the analysis of amber sources and of arte-facts from the Upper Palaeolithic to the Belle Epoch. The spectrum obtained (Figure 17.8) is basically a fingerprint. The characteristic features can be estab-lished, as exemplified by the flat shoulder occurring at 1150–1300 cm^{-1}, often seen on the spectra of amber from the Baltic, and consequently known as the 'Baltic shoulder'. IRS seems to have been rea-sonably successful in characterising European amber, mainly differentiating Baltic amber from Sicilian (Beck and Hartnett, 1993) and Romanian (Banerjee *et al.*, 1999), but note the reservations of Savkevich

(1981) mentioned above. For the analysis a sample of a few milligrams is normally required. Scott Williams (1997) described a portable non-destructive FTIR probe system designed for museum use that, while it may not have the same sensitivity as the standard methods that require a sample, will easily distinguish between natural amber and synthetic simulants. The problems of surface treatments may be significant here (see p. 437).

There has been less success in characterising amber from other parts of the world by their IR spectra alone (Beck, 1986), and this was partially responsible for the investigation of other meth-ods, which could both provide additional prov-enancing data and more information on the actual composition of amber.

Nuclear magnetic resonance (NMR): This technique has been applied to the analysis of amber by Joseph Lambert (Lambert and Beck, 1993; Lambert, 1997, pp. 161–163; Lambert and Poinar, 2002), with work reported particularly on European (Lambert *et al.*, 1988) and American sources (Lambert *et al.*, 1985; Lambert *et al.*, 1989; Lambert *et al.*, 1994).

Put very briefly, certain atomic nuclei, e.g. hydrogen and carbon, can exist in two distinct spin states. When a strong magnetic field is applied, the nuclei can be elevated from the lower energy spin state to the higher energy state, thereby absorb-ing some energy. The energy difference between the two states depends on the environment of the nucleus, i.e. the other atoms with which it is com-bined, and thus the energy spectrum is characteris-tic of the particular molecule. The spectra obtained can be related to both the age and the hardness as well as to the provenance of the amber.

NMR has so far found only limited applica-tion to the study of antiquities and objects of art (Ghisalberti and Godfrey, 1998). This could, in part, be because a relatively large sample is required; for amber, Lambert uses about 30 mg.

Chromatography: Various refinements of GC have been applied, these including pyrolysis–gas chro-matography (Pyr GC) (Shedrinsky *et al.*, 1989, 1991) and Pyr–GC mass spectrometry (Pyr GC MS) (Boon *et al.*, 1993; Shedrinsky *et al.* 1993; Mills and White, 1994, pp. 185–186; Heck, 1999). Small samples in the microgram range are required (see Chapter 3, p. 58).

FTRS and RM: FTRS and RS have been applied to the analysis of amber antiquities and objects of art (Edwards and Farwell, 1996; Edwards 2001, 2005). A big advantage is that RM is non-destructive. Distinctive spectra have been obtained which clearly differentiate natural amber from

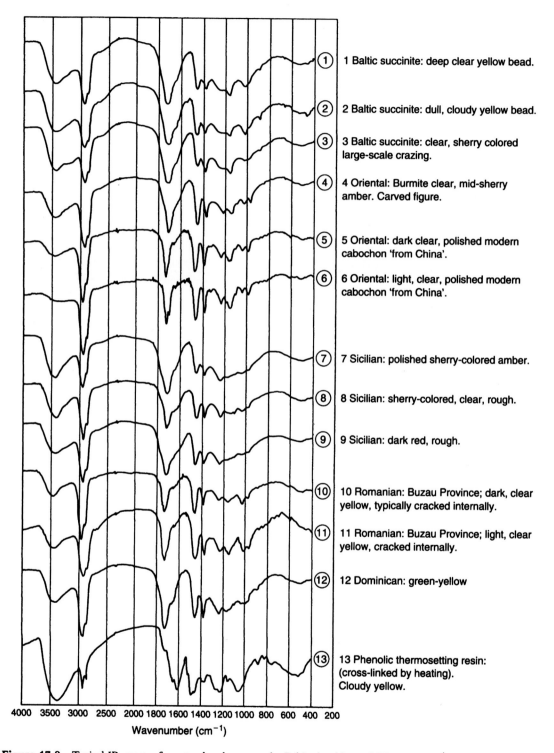

Figure 17.8   Typical IR spectra for natural amber; note the Baltic shoulder at 1150–1300 cm⁻¹ due to the presence of succinic acid. (Courtesy Fraquet, 1987)

synthetic simulants. RM spectra of amber do not suffer from the problems of fluorescence that are present with IR. Tay *et al.* (1998) analysed 173 specimens of amber and simulants by conventional gemmological methods and by RM using a near-IR laser source of excitation.

Inclusions

An ant beneath a poplar found,
An amber tear has covered round;
so she that was in life despised,
in death preserved is highly prized.
Martial *Epigrams* book VI. XV

Sources: Poinar and Poinar (1994); Grimaldi (1996); Gübelin and Koivula (1997, pp. 212–228).

One of the most interesting aspects of amber is the plant and insect inclusions that sometimes became entrapped within the resin as it dripped from the parent tree millions of years ago. However, some inclusions are not as old as they would seem, as the creation of forgeries by the insertion of insects, etc. into amber-like resins or into amber itself, has been an absorbing and profitable enterprise for many years. Because of the great rarity of genuine inclusions in natural amber, forgers have often chosen to make their own insertions, even small creatures such as frogs or lizards (Grimaldi *et al.*, 1994; Ross, 1998, pp. 6–9). Sometimes where these have decayed they have discolored the resin in the immediate vicinity in a way not observed on the genuine specimens. Similarly, large insects are often used which in nature would have been strong enough to struggle free from the amber's embrace. Fragments of plants are less easy to discredit, but sometimes the stem protrudes through to the edge

of the resin, and thus cannot be ancient, for unless there is total coverage by the amber the specimen could not have survived.

The simplest way to simulate genuine amber with inclusions is to place the dead insect in a solution of copal in alcohol and allow the copal to set. Although it is unusual, insects etc. have been found naturally entombed in copal, but the solution method of fake inclusions can be revealed by the presence of traces of the solvent, which can still be detected long after the copal forgeries were made. Synthetic resins have, by and large, replaced copal for inclusion forgeries, polyester being especially popular in the Dominican Republic and Mexico. These can be easily detected by IR.

A more sophisticated technique, although once again of many years standing, is to take a piece of Baltic amber – which often has natural cracks – split it open and carve or drill out a cavity. Into this the inclusion is inserted and covered with liquid copal, a mastic or a synthetic resin (Figure 17.9a).

If well done these fakes can be very difficult to detect. The two pieces of the original amber are then joined while the resin is still tacky. The cuts in the amber will usually have been flat, which itself is very rare in amber. Furthermore, the junction between the natural amber and the resin infilling will often be marked by concentrations of tiny air bubbles. The state of the ensnared creature can often give some hint (Grimaldi *et al.*, 1994). In genuine pieces the insect was usually alive, and quite literally kicking, causing swirls in the amber and often

Figure 17.9b Detail showing the insect was already dead when embalmed and thus unlikely to be authentic. Purchased 2003 in Malta, but said to come from Eastern Europe (probably correct). (Courtesy S. La Niece).

Figure 17.9a A droplet of copal (soluble in acetone) containing an insect.

contorting the insect's body, resulting in the loss of wings and legs, whereas in the forgeries it is usually obvious that the insect was already dead when immersed (Figure 17.9b). Also, although amber is probably the best natural preservative, some features such as the pigmentation of the eyes do decay.

Occasionally forgeries do slip through and remain undetected for many years. The Natural History Museum in London has a piece of amber (In. 22305) that is about 40 million years old, containing a specimen of the common sewer fly *Fannia scalaris*, identical to the modern sewer fly. This was acquired in 1922, and published as the classic example of evolutionary stasis, that is the passage of millions of years with no change in a species. However, in 1993 when it was once more being examined, the heat from a lamp caused the amber to split, revealing that the fly was an insertion (Grimaldi *et al.*, 1994; Ross, 1998, p. 5). It had been inserted into a carved hollow in a piece of genuine Baltic amber, and set in resin, probably a natural mastic. Re-examination of the fly, in the knowledge that it was a forgery, revealed the red pigment still persisting in the prominent eyes, which would not normally have been expected to survive. Also, the abdomen of the fly had broken in an unusual way suggestive of a very dead and dry fly being pushed into the mastic.

In a rueful reference to another forgery housed in the same institution, which also misled research into evolution for many years, the insect is now popularly known as the Piltdown Fly.

Lacquer

Sources: General: Trench (ed) (2000, pp. 266–267, 516–517); Webb (2000). China: Garner (1979). Myanmar: Isaacs and Blurton (2000). Scientific examination: Brommelle and Smith (eds) (1988); Mills and White (1994, pp. 118–122, 182).

Lacquer is formed from the polymerisation of the sap of trees of the genus *Rhus*, more correctly *Toxicodendron verniciflua*. This typically contains around 60 to 65% of pyrocatechols such as urushiol, laccol or thitsiol, which are themselves names for groups of catechols of varying composition. In the Orient, the liquid lacquer is applied to a solid former, usually of wood, but sometimes of cloth, and quite thick layers can be built up. Such lacquers are much copied with a variety of synthetic polymers, but analytically real lacquer is quite distinct.

The colors were traditionally produced from inorganic pigments, iron oxides for black and brown, arsenic sulphide (orpiment) for orange and yellow, and mercury sulphide (vermilion), for the reds. More recently, there has been a tendency for synthetic organic pigments and paints to be used in place of the traditional pigments (Isaacs and Blurton, 2000, p. 35).

European lacquers such as *Vernis Martin* (Mills and White, 1994, p. 182; Trench (ed), 2000, pp. 516–517) are composed of a variety of resins – copal, mastic, sandarac, etc. – dissolved in turpentine or in alcohol.

Burmester (1983) had some success analysing lacquers by Pyr-MS, enabling them to differentiate true lacquer from similar materials, and modern synthetic materials. Pyr-GC MS has also proved to be a successful method (Niimira *et al.*, 1999). Detecting the products of long-term lacquer degradation (Feller, 1994) could be a useful extension of this analytical work. Lacquer has also been analysed by FTIR to differentiate between the genuine urushi etc. lacquers used on antique oriental furniture and European imitations based on natural resins (Derrick, 1988; Derrick *et al.*, 1988). Jaeschke (1985) studied minute thin sections (typically less than a square millimetre and taken from damaged areas) of lacquer artefacts by transmission electron microscopy (TEM) followed by electron microprobe analysis (EPMA) to identify pigments such as vermilion although non-destructive XRF or PIXE analysis should be able to perform this task more simply. Lambert *et al.* (1991) used NMR to analyse lacquer using a solid sample. Hodgins *et al.* (2002) carried out AMS dating on a suspiciously well preserved lacquer coating on a Chinese ceramic pot of the Han dynasty. The date obtained on a sample of a few milligrams of the lacquer agreed well with the stylistic dating and with the thermoluminescence (TL) date on the ceramic itself, confirming the authenticity of the lacquer coating.

Wood

There is more English antique furniture exported to America in one year than could have been made in the entire 18th century.

Cescinsky (1931, p. 1)

Sources: General: Angst (1978); Trench (ed) (2000, pp. 531–553). Sculpture: Faillant-Dumas (1980); Penny (1993, pp. 123–152); Trench (ed) (2000, pp. 543–546). Furniture: Cescinsky (1931); Tietze (1948); Hayward (1970); Crawley (1971); Peterson (1975, pp. 17–55); Jenkins (1995); Rivers and Umney (2003). Plywood: Wood (1963).

The re-use of old materials, the conversion of old but inexpensive originals into expensive fakes and the fraudulent restoration of badly damaged pieces is very prevalent in the world of antique furniture, such that any scientific investigation would have to be very carefully directed. Authenticity studies of antique furniture encompass a wide range of specialist expertise, and the reader is recommended to the texts mentioned above that give an insight into the various stylistic and technical features of materials, and construction methods through the ages.

Scientific studies on chemical decay have generally led to the conclusion that there is little long-term degradation on wood that has been kept reasonably dry and free from infestation. Such decay as does take place has been summarised by Rivers and Umney (2003, pp. 285–315). Erhardt *et al.* (1996) found very little change in either the physical properties or the chemical make-up of pine over three centuries, certainly nothing that could be used to provide any indication of age. Thus, overall, there is relatively little scope for scientific authentication, with the exception of RC dating (see Chapter 5) and dendrochronology (see Chapter 6, and below, p. 445), in the relatively limited number of cases where these methods are applicable.

At a more practical level Cescinsky (1931, p. 9) noted that the interior of old wood is often similar to new wood and that if the old protective surface is removed then it is as prone to warping and splitting as new wood. Indeed the principal change to wood is the gradual drying out of the cellular structure, which some forgers were supposed to induce by heating their creations in special ovens (Arnau, 1961, p. 187).

To a large degree, degradation and dating studies on the wood itself would probably not be of much use anyway, as a practice is to re-use old timber. The inimitable André Mailfert (1935) ran a company which manufactured 'antique' furniture in France during the first part of the twentieth century on an industrial scale. He claimed that they took delivery of ten old oak beams from demolished buildings per day from 1908 until 1930, and converted them into 70 000 antiques (NB one should not necessarily believe all of his figures, any more than the dealers believed in the authenticity of the antiques they bought from him for their customers).

Evidence of woodworm infestation (Rivers and Umney, 2003, pp. 296–301) has long been popularly regarded as a sure indicator of age (Figure 17.10), and there must be more apocryphal stories of the various methods of simulating flight holes than in any other branch of fakery. In practice the very neat and regular flight holes made by the common furniture beetle (*Anobium punctatum*) are rather difficult to simulate, and it would be rather pointless to try to do so. If flight holes are required, Cescinsky suggested placing the piece – made from timbers that are especially susceptible to attack such as beech or walnut – in contact with an infected timber in a dark, slightly damp environment in February and by June the piece will have real worm holes. However, it is not really clear how the presence of flight holes, real or simulated, helps to establish the authenticity of a piece. It might show that a timber has been reused. Once the egg of the beetle has hatched the grub eats the cellulose, creating a passage beneath the surface, and after metamorphosis from grub to beetle the insect makes the circular flight hole perpendicular to and through the surface. Thus if the surface of infested wood is removed by planing etc., the passages created by the grubs are exposed, and, if cut, the passages will be cross-sectioned but usually at an angle, and so will appear oval. It is usually claimed, with some justification, that in ordinary circumstances a cabinet-maker would not use worm-infested wood (Figure 17.1). However, timber can become infested while still in the seasoning sheds.

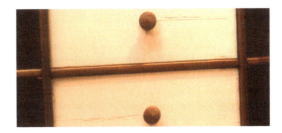

Figure 17.10 Fake woodworm flight holes in a dresser in the Grange Range of imitation Shaker furniture. The holes and channels were produced mechanically; note the identical pattern stamped into every panel. The horizontal exposed channel implies that the Shakers had been reusing old infested timber, which would have been quite useless. The accompanying promotional literature claims that Shaker furniture was made 'faithfully and well done'. Fake worm holes hardly seem in keeping with the Shaker ethos. (Photographed in Sanderson's shop in London by the author in 1992)

The consensus is that the only evidence for age and ageing is likely to be found in the condition of the surface of the wood. The cellulose is stable, but the lignin is rather more reactive and is prone to oxidation, generally leading to a darkening of the wood. Oxidation can be chemically induced by treatment with oxidising agents such as potassium permanganate or conversely the surface can be bleached with caustic soda. Cornec (2000) studied on the patinas acquired by African wooden ritual objects in the course of their use and anointment with various materials such as blood and grease. She suggested that a knowledge of these patinas and their chemical identification could be a powerful authentication method.

The finished wood surface is soft and must be sealed in some way to toughen and protect it, using paint, wax or varnish. The various resins employed in the past have been studied by Derrick (1988) using FTIR, obtaining spectra for shellac (the basis of French or button polish), sandarac, mastic, copal and rosin. On wooden surfaces that had once been painted, the original priming coats can penetrate quite deeply into the wood and are difficult to remove completely. The priming paints will often have been lead-based and thus the possibility of establishing the age from the ^{210}Pb content exists (see Chapter 12, p. 295). The survival of the priming in some areas may be responsible for differential darkening of the wood. Examination by UV can be informative (Rorimer, 1931, pp. 45–46). New wood does not fluoresce, but the surfaces of wooden artefacts can do so depending on the various surface treatments. As with other materials, areas of restoration can be distinguished.

Evidence of wear is an important consideration in the authentication of wooden furniture, which can be expected to have had a history of use, abuse and cleaning (Crawley, 1971). Thus the bases of items such as country long case clocks which will have stood on the damp stone flags of farmhouse entrance halls for generations, periodically wetted during floor washing, can be expected to show evidence of rot and cellular decay of the wood, or will have been replaced.

Draw runners can be expected to show traces of heavy wear. Mailfert (1935, p. 273) claimed that he employed men to repeatedly open and shut the draws on his fake antiques just to simulate generations of wear. The wear and abrasion of surfaces is quite subtle, and stories of attacking the piece with chains to simulate wear would seem apocryphal. The usual method resorted to is to work the surface with a wire brush, but which leaves tell-tale parallel scratches, visible beneath the varnish. Sometimes special scrapers have been used (Figure 17.11).

Determining the species of the timber and its place of origin is a potentially useful field of investigation. The sequence of oak, walnut and mahogany for English furniture in the Post-Medieval period is well known, but the situation is much more complex. There are at least thirty species of mahogany that have been used for furniture and the use of particular species can be very specific both in time and space. Thus in the eighteenth century, English furniture-makers used a limited range of mahogany from Cuba, Honduras and San Domingo, but a wider range of species from a much wider span of sources was used from the nineteenth century on.

The techniques by which the wood has been worked and the evidence of the types of tool used are clearly potentially important indicators of authenticity (Cescinsky, 1931, pp. 19–39; Crawley, 1971). For example, the straight saw-marks on hand-sawn wood are very different from the cuts made by a circular saw, and this is important for determining the likely age of veneered woodwork, etc. From the mid-nineteenth century, veneers tended to be cut by machine with blades, either rotary or straight (Cescinsky, 1931, p. 29). In straight cutting the blade swings in a pendulum fashion, cutting through the thickness of the wood, and thus through the rings, giving a figured pattern on the veneer, identical to that for wood cut by hand (albeit with no saw marks). In rotary cutting the blade cuts around the timber creating a continuous sheet of veneer, rather in the manner of

Figure 17.11 'The chipper', an old plane mounted and dragged across the wooden surfaces and edges to simulate wear. (Courtesy Cescinsky, 1931)

the sponge of a Swiss roll. On these veneers there are no figuring or saw marks.

The thickness of the various boards used in furniture can also be significant indicators of age and place. The boards were usually cut to standard thicknesses by the sawyers. For example, in Britain from the eighteenth century standard-cut one-inch boards were usually 13/16ths of an inch thick when planed, and these thicknesses can be diagnostic.

Developments in the manufacture of nails and screws in Post-Medieval Europe make them relatively easy to date (Savage, 1976, p. 58). However, as Cescinsky (1931, p. 36) pointed out, screws were and are regularly replaced in genuine pieces and the presence of a machine-made screw in an antique

certainly does not condemn it. Crawley (1971, p. 21) stated that one of the very few infallible signs of age was the discoloration of the wood around iron screws or nails, caused by the partial oxidation of the iron over the years.

For temperate timber species, dendrochronology presents the opportunity not just to date but to provenance the timber (Chapter 6, p. 131). For example, detailed studies made on Late Medieval–Renaissance panel paintings were able to show that much of the oak timber must have come from the east Baltic region (Figure 6.16). Tree-ring studies of most tropical species, including mahogany, however, are still very rudimentary.

Case study: The Courtrai Chest from New College, Oxford

Sources: ffoulkes (1914); Fletcher and Tapper (1984); Hall (1987).

In 1905, Dr E.A. Spooner (better known for his Spoonerisms), Warden of New College, Oxford, discovered the superb carved chest shown in Figure 17.12 at one of the college's tenanted farms at Stanton St John, near Oxford and purchased it for the college. Its importance was soon established and the busy scenes deeply carved on the front panel were recognised as depicting the Battle of Courtrai fought in 1302 (ffoulkes, 1914). The style of the carving suggested that the piece was carved in Flanders soon after the battle, very possibly in Courtrai itself, as one of the most prominent standards depicted is that of the city's guild of carpenters.

Some 60 years later the chest was exhibited at Courtrai as part of a commemoration of the battle, and New College considered selling it to the Belgians. However, first it was examined at the Institut Royal du Patrimoine artistique, in Brussels, where it was pronounced to be a nineteenth-century forgery, not least because of the freshness of the carving (Marijnissen and van der Voorde, 1978). Indeed, the carving is very crisp, suggesting that it may well have been sharpened up with a chisel before plaster casts were taken shortly after its discovery.

On its rather crestfallen return to Oxford the chest was examined at the Research Laboratory for Archaeology and the History of Art, and the age of the panel determined by dendrochronology backed up by AMS dating.

The chest in its present form appears to have been put together in the seventeenth century, incorporating the carved front panel. This had been shortened at some time as evidenced by the incomplete scenes on the ends. The panel is made up of two oak boards joined horizontally. The sequence of rings on both boards could be matched to the appropriate chronology with confidence. The upper panel had 274 rings, dated to between 970 and 1243 and the lower board had 234 rings dated to between 983 and 1216. Thus, one of the planks was part of a living tree in 1243, and the presence of sapwood would suggest the tree had been felled sometime in the second half of the thirteenth century. This is very close to the date of the battle and thus supports ffoulkes' view that the original carving was done immediately afterwards.

One has to sound a note of caution here. All that has been established is that the boards are likely to have been around to be carved in the early fourteenth century. Equally they could still have been around to be carved in the nineteenth century. However, the carving is crowded with incident, detail and heraldry, etc., all of which is correct in every particular. It would also be a considerable

Figure 17.12   The Courtrai Chest, depicting scenes from the Battle of the Golden Spurs fought at Courtrai in 1302 (wood) by Flemish School, (14th century). (© Courtesy of The Warden and Scholars of New College, Oxford/The Bridgeman Art Library)

coincidence if the putative nineteenth-century forger had selected anonymous 'old' plain boards that just happened to be of a very appropriate age to have been available as new just after the battle.

Thereby the Belgians missed the chance to possess an important icon of Flemish history and, as Professor Hall (1987), Director of the Oxford Laboratory, remarked, 'let us hope the relic stays in its present ownership for the foreseeable future'.

18

Organic materials: Mainly synthetic and cloth

This chapter continues the study of organic materials begun in Chapter 17, concentrating here on synthetic materials. The chapter also has a separate section on cloth, made from both natural and synthetic fibres. For synthetic organic materials used in fine art see Chapter 12, and for gems see Chapter 16, p. 405.

Plastics

A new material and manufacture now exhibited for the first time, has from its valuable properties induced the Inventor to . . . devote his attention for the last ten years to the development of the capabilities and application of this beautiful substance to the Arts.

It can be made Hard as Ivory, Transparent or Opaque, of any degree of Flexibility, and is Waterproof; may be of the most Brilliant Colors, can be used in the Solid, Plastic or Fluid State, may be worked in Dies and Pressure as Metals, may be Cast or used as a Coating to a great variety of substances; can be spread or worked in a similar manner to India Rubber, and has stood exposure to the atmosphere for years without change or decomposition. And may by the system of ornamentation Patented by Henry Parkes in 1861, the most perfect imitation of Tortoiseshell, Woods, and an endless variety of effects can be produced.

Alexander Parkes, from the Catalogue of the 1862 International Exhibition, London, describing Parkesine

Sources: Polymer chemistry: Brydson (1975); Mills and White (1994, pp. 129–140); Nicholson (1997). General: Katz (1984, 1986); Mossman and Morris (eds) (1994); Mossman (ed) (1997); Quye and Williamson (eds) (1999); Trench (ed) (2000); Campbell Pedersen (2004). See also *Plastiquarian*, the journal of the Plastics Historical Society.

The synthetic materials which are referred to as plastics are approached in three quite distinct ways in authenticity studies. They can be regarded as

materials used in imitation of other, usually natural materials, and their presence condemns the item, be it plastic ivory or an oil painting using acrylic paint. Determining the exact identity of the synthetic substitute is potentially useful as it not only denotes that the object is indeed a copy, but can date it. An epoxy resin substitute for ivory must post-date the mid-twentieth century; conversely, it is most unlikely that anyone would use nitrocellulose or even casein as a substitute in the latter part of the twentieth century.

Secondly, plastics are now the materials of objects that have become desirable items in their own right; many twentieth-century collectables, such as old radios or fountain pens are largely made of plastics. Plastics are now accepted as legitimate material for many art forms. Since the 1920s acrylic paints have become important for the artist (see Chapter 12, p. 297).Bakelite, casein, and Perspex were all much in vogue for Art Deco jewellery, latterly joined by epoxy resins, for example, and plastics have now become the material most commonly used for making costume jewellery (see Chapter 16, pp. 397).

Thirdly, synthetic organic materials play an important role in the conservation and restoration of antiquities and art objects and thus form an important part in establishing the life-history of a piece (Allen *et al.* (eds), 1992).

The approach to the examination of plastics is governed by their purpose. If there is concern that the supposed natural gemstone, marble, silk, or whatever, is of a synthetic analogue then this can usually be tested by what are now relatively simple and routine analytical techniques. If, however, the item is supposed to be of plastic, a 1930s vintage radio, for example, the process of authentication is more complex, and basically follows the lines of enquiry for all the other synthetic materials in this work. Is the material of the correct composition and method of manufacture for its period, and are there signs of characteristic age-related degradation? This is a new area of authenticity study, although well-established in forensic work, but there is considerable potential given the variety of materials and technologies available, their reasonably well documented histories, and, in many cases, their all-too-evident decay (see Tables 18.1, 18.2 and Figure 18.5).

Plastics are made up of polymer molecules, i.e. huge molecules consisting of large numbers of repeating units, often of quite simple organic molecules (the *monomers*) in long chains which may be conveniently visualised as cooked spaghetti; the chains are supple and can slip over each other with ease (Figure 18.1). The physical properties of the plastics depend very much on the length and shape of these chains, which can be made up of thousands of monomers. Thus polyethylene glycol, much used in conservation work, can exist at room temperature as grease or a hard wax, depending on the length of the chains.

There are two basic types of polymer. In the one type, the long chains remain free of each other and the properties of the polymer are very temperature dependent: they may be softened or even melted by heating. These are known as thermoplastics, and a familiar example is polyethylene (trade name Polythene).

In the second group of polymers the long chains cross-link with each other on heating, in effect creating permanent bonds in three dimensions. Obviously once this has taken place there is little or no flexibility. These plastics are shaped by heating the long-chain polymers in a mould whereupon the cross-linking takes place and they set

Table 18.1   Principal plastics and the dates of their introduction.

Type of Plastics	Name	Main Period of Use
Natural	Amber	c.2000BC–now
	Horn	c.2000BC–now
	Tortoiseshell	c.2000BC–now
	Bitumen	c.2000BC–now
	Rubber	AD 1736–now (in the Old World)
	Papier mâché	1772–now
	Gutta percha	1843–c.1945
	Shellac	1850–1950
	Bois Durci	1855–1880s
Semi-Synthetic	Vulcanite	1839–1970
	Cellulose nitrate (Celluloid, Parkesine)	1862–1980
	Viscose rayon	1892–now
	Casein (casein-formaldehyde)	1899–c.1970
	Cellulose acetate	1928–now
Synthetic	Phenol-formaldehyde (Bakelite)	1910–now
	Cast phenol-formaldehyde	1928–1960
	Thiourea-urea-formaldehyde	1928–1940
	Polyvinyl chloride (PVC)	c.1930–now
	Polystyrene	c.1930–now
	Urea-formaldehyde	c.1931–1940
	Ethyl cellulose	1935–now
	Melamine-formaldehyde (laminates)	1935–now
	Polymethyl Methacrylate (Acrylic, Perspex)	1935–now
	Polyamide (Nylon)	1938–now
	Polyethylene	c.1938–now
	Polyurethane	c.1939–now
	Polyester fibres (Polyethylene terephthalate, Terylene)	1941–now
	Glass-fibre-reinforced plastics (fibreglass)	1942–now

Source: Mossman, (ed), 1997, p. 3

Table 18.2 Additives to plastics.

Reinforcing fillers

- wood flour
- shredded cloth
- glass, as fibres or spheres
- carbon fibre
- carbon black

Non-reinforcing fillers

- talc
- calcium carbonate

Plasticisers and lubricants

- phthalate esters
- chlorinated paraffins
- organophosphates
- phosphate esters
- epoxidised oils
- metal stearates

Colors

- titanium .dioxide
- powdered metals
- cadmium sulphide
- zinc oxide
- ultramarines
- carbon
- phthalocyanines
- lead chromate
- azos
- iron oxides

Flame retardants

- aluminium tri-hydrate
- organo-bromines
- phosphates
- organo-chlorines
- antimony oxide

Heat and light stabilizers

- amines and phenol derivatives
- organotin
- carbon black
- lead salts
- stearates

Source: Quye and Williamson (eds), 1999, p. 28

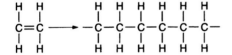

Figure 18.1 Polymer chains.

permanently. These are known as thermosetting plastics, Bakelite being a familiar example.

History

Sources: Kaufman (1963); Williamson (1999a, 1994); Mossman (ed) (1997).

Many of the constituents of living matter are polymers and man's involvement with the use and modification of polymers can be seen in some senses as a progression from carving materials such as wood or amber, through heating thermoplastic materials such as hoof and horn to soften them for shaping by pressing, chemically altering some natural polymers, such as rubber, and finally creating completely synthetic polymers (Figure 18.2).

In the nineteenth century chemical modification of natural materials began with the addition of sulphur to natural rubber to produce the hard thermoplastic known as Vulcanite or Ebonite in the 1840s (Mills and White, 1994, pp. 99–101; Connors, 1998). The next milestone was the production of nitrocellulose followed by cellulose acetate (see p. 457). Another modified natural product was bois durci, produced from a mixture of blood and albumen, which after mixing with wood flour was heated to produce a thermoplastic. The last of the modified natural product plastics was casein (see p. 458).

It should be borne in mind that these early plastics were not cast. Instead a wide variety of alternative shaping techniques were used (Newport, 1976; Morgan, 1991, pp. 45–48; Barker, 1999, pp. 28–33). They were sometimes cut and carved from a solid block, or, more usually, produced as a dough and shaped by pressing in hot moulds. Another common method was to cut sheets from a solid block and mould them in a press, very much continuing the traditional methods of shaping natural thermoplastic polymers such as horn or tortoiseshell, which the first plastics were often imitating. Techniques such as injection moulding (Figure 18.3), whereby the chemicals that were to form the plastic were injected as liquids into a hot mould in which polymerisation took place, although invented in the nineteenth century, did not see wide application until the large-scale production of thermosetting plastics began, notably with Bakelite (see p. 458).

Thus evidence of casting, such as mould flashes and the circular injection tabs, for example, can provide evidence of the earliest possible date for an artefact. Even so, the hot moulding of plastics while in a dough-like condition was still the usual method of shaping through the first half of the twentieth century, both for thermoplastics and even for thermosetting plastics, such as Bakelite. These were often produced as a sticky liquid that was mixed with dry, solid additives to render them mouldable.

In the twentieth century, plastics that were wholly of synthetic materials gradually replaced those that utilised natural products (see Table 18.1), the first of the synthetics being the thermosetting phenol formaldehyde, more usually known as Bakelite. It was also probably the first plastic which

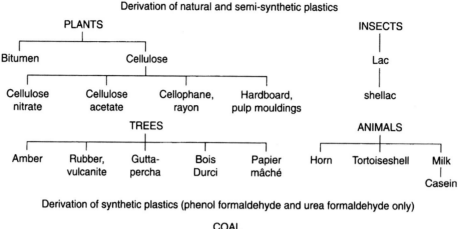

Figure 18.2   Some natural, semi-synthetic and synthetic plastics and their sources.

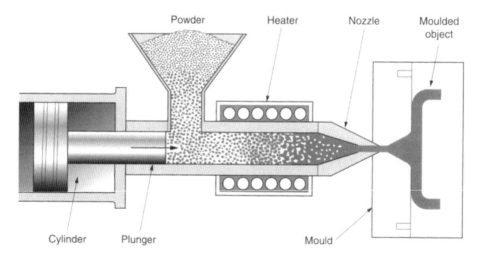

Figure 18.3   Injection moulding. (Courtesy Mossman (ed), 1997)

was used as a material in its own right rather than in imitation of a natural product. The familiar 1930s black Bakelite telephone handset was not intended to imitate any other material – it was of Bakelite and proud of it.

A drawback of the phenolic resins was that unless the reaction proceeded very slowly at low temperatures they had a dark color, and plastics based on urea and thiourea formaldehyde were developed to give a lighter range of plastics, under trade names such as Bandalasta and Beetle (see p. 459). Plastics came onto the market in ever-increasing numbers and wide-ranging properties from the late 1920s. Another rather important group of plastics introduced at about this time were based on methyl methacrylate, including materials as diverse as Perspex (Plexiglas), Orlon fibres and acrylic paints. Acrylic resins were widely used in conservation treatments as consolidants and surface strengthening coatings for a wide variety of materials from the second half of the twentieth century (Robson, 1992).

In the second half of the twentieth century, materials such as the epoxy resins (see p. 451) began to be widely used both as adhesive (Araldite) and for making casts of just about everything (see Chapter 4, p. 67 and Chapter 16, p. 397). Co-polymers, mixtures of polymers such as polyvinyl chloride (PVC) and polyvinyl acetate (PVA), developed through the 1930s and 1950s, further extending the range of plastics available (Kaufman, 1967).

From the 1920s, development came increasingly into the hands of the great chemical companies such as I.G. Farben (Wilson, 1994) (e.g. polystyrene, PS), ICI (e.g. polythene) and Dupont, with nylon as the first plastic to be deliberately and scientifically designed. Nylon was patented in 1935 and first marketed in 1938 (for hygienic toothbrush bristles), and the first nylon stockings appeared in 1939, albeit briefly before the entire production of nylon was commandeered for the war effort. These and other plastics were further developed during the Second World War, paving the way for the ever-increasing range of plastics used in the modern world. The 'Plastics Age' had arrived.

From the early days, the polymer resin was often just a component of the plastic, with a variety of other more inert materials mixed in. The additives were to serve a variety of purposes, to make the plastic easier to shape (usually by hot-moulding), to improve the mechanical properties, to make the plastic more closely resemble some natural material that it was intended to imitate, or simply to lower the cost. This range of motives resulted in an equally wide range of materials to be regularly added, such as wood flour, paper, cloth, various fibres, and minerals such as mica (Table 18.2). Thus, wood flour was added to Bakelite to stiffen the liquid resin before polymerisation had occurred, and camphor was added to nitrocellulose as a plasticiser to make it more pliable. A variety of other materials from plasticisers to fire-retarding agents were also added. A wide range of coloring agents have been developed specifically for plastics

and marketed over the years, with organic dyes tending to replace inorganic pigments from the latter half of the twentieth century (Kaul, 1993).

Examination and analysis of plastics for authentication purposes

Scientific examination and analysis should not just be confined to the identification of the polymer itself. Many of the additives or coloring agents may well be specific to particular periods or companies, and a thorough materials comparison of a suspect piece with a genuine piece will often prove decisive. This applies to the forming processes also. Although in theory it should be quite easy to make forgeries of early plastics, in practice it can prove very difficult. Even the early plastics were factory-made products that required complex forming processes involving skills and machinery that are no longer extant. For example, the production of jewellery from injection-moulded phenolic resins only began in the late 1920s, and had ceased by the mid-1950s, after which the specialist injection-moulding machinery and their highly trained operatives rapidly dispersed.

Identification tests and chemical analysis

Sources: Braun, D. (1982); Katz (1984, pp. 146–148; 1986, p. 29); Morgan (1991, pp. 35–44); Williamson (1995); Williamson (1999b).

Evidence of the forming process, appearance (Tables 18.3 and 18.4), color, density, hardness as adjudged by application of the fingernail to the surface, and even the smell can usually enable the expert to identify the material within the relatively small range of expected possibilities of plastics used for artefacts up to the mid-twentieth century, but for the rest of us it is maybe not so easy.

Note that the tests in the publications listed above are aimed at the quick, inexpensive identification of particular plastics where there is no element of deception. They are not intended, for example, for the testing of antiquities that could be made or restored with a modern plastic, or where there is a possibility that a modern plastic may have been deliberately disguised in order that it appeared to be a more traditional plastic. An appropriate addition to the plastic or the adoption of a particular treatment could ensure that it passed these simple identification tests based on smell, etc.

Table 18.3   Identification of plastics by their appearance.

Transparent moulded plastics

- poly(methyl methacrylate) eg Perspex
- cast phenolic
- polyester, both unsaturated and thermoplastic
- polystyrene
- polycarbonate
- cellulose acetate butyrate

Clear as sheet, opaque/translucent as moulded plastics

- cellulose nitrate
- cellulose acetate
- PVC
- polypropylene
- regenerated cellulose (cellophane)
- PET

Always opaque as moulded

- phenol-formaldehyde (compression-moulded)
- urea- and thiourea-formaldehyde
- melamine-formaldehyde
- gutta percha
- vulcanite
- Bois Durci and most other compositions
- shellac compositions
- bitumen and cold-moulded compounds
- vulcanised rubber
- vulcanised fibre
- composites including GRP

Source: Quye and Williamson (eds), 1999, p. 59

Table 18.4   Identification of plastics by smell.

ABS	like polystyrene + rubber
Acetal	formaldehyde, very strong
Bitumen	hot tar
Casein	burnt milk or hair
Cast phenolic	phenol or carbolic soap
Cellulose acetate	vinegar, burning paper
Cellulose acetate butyrate	rancid butter
Cellulose nitrate	camphor, then nitrogen oxides
Gutta percha	burning rubber
Melamine formaldehyde	Fishy
Nylon	burnt hair, celery
PET	burnt raspberry jam, sweet
Phenol-formaldehyde	phenol or carbolic soap
Poly(methyl methacrylate)	sweetish, fruity
Polyethylene	wax, candles, paraffin
Polypropylene	wax, candles, paraffin
Polystyrene	natural gas, marigolds
Polyurethanes	stinging
PVC rigid	hydrochloric acid, chlorine
PVC plasticised	hydrochloric acid + aromatic
Shellac	sealing wax
Urea-formaldehyde	formaldehyde, fishy, ammonia
Vulcanised fibre	burning hay
Vulcanite	burning sulphur/rubber

Sources: Quye and Williamson (eds), 1999, p. 67; Katz, 1994, p. 29

The drawback with specific identification tests is that they test for a specific characteristic in ignorance of the actual composition. Perhaps the most famous and glaring example of this concerns the phenolic resin used by Van Meegeren (see Chapter 12, p. 307). He added this to his paint medium to ensure that it passed the simple hot-needle test for old oil media, but its true nature could not possibly have remained undetected if chemical analysis had been carried out.

The hot needle will usually differentiate between thermoplastics which will melt and allow the needle to penetrate and thermosetting plastics, which will not. Thus, for example, a hot pin will penetrate amber, a natural thermoplastic, but would not penetrate a thermosetting synthetic phenolic imitation. The smell of the hot plastic can also be indicative. However, testing a putative amber antiquity with a hot needle to see if it is amber or Bakelite would

be completely inappropriate. Quite apart from the inherent danger of serious damage, such tests are rarely as simple in interpretation as they appear and they are relatively easy to circumvent. Thus, a thermoplastic that is loaded with an inert filler may well be resistant to a hot needle, and conversely a degraded thermosetting plastic may allow the needle to penetrate all too readily.

Table 18.5 Analytical techniques for plastics.

	DSC	FTIR	FT RAMAN	(py) GC-MS	GPC	IC	SEM-EDX	TGA	XRD	XRF
Organic compounds	✓	✓	✓	✓	✓	✓	✗	✓	✗	✗
Inorganic compounds	✗	●	✓	✗	✗	✓	✓	✗	✓	✓
Polymer identification	✗	✓	✓	✓	✗	✗	✗	✗	✗	✗
Laminate identification	●	●	●	✓	✗	✗	✗	✗	✗	✗
Plasticiser identification	✗	✓	✓	✓	✗	✗	✗	✗	✗	✗
Inorganic filler identification	✗	●	✓	✗	✗	✗	✓	✗	✓	✓
Organic filler identification	✗	●	●	✓	✗	✗	✗	✗	✗	✗
Other organic additives	✗	●	●	✓	✗	✓	✗	✗	✗	✗
Other inorganic additives	✗	●	●	✗	✗	✓	✓	✗	✓	✓
Organic degradation products	✗	✓	✓	✓	✗	✓	✗	✗	✗	✗
Inorganic degradation products	✗	●	✓	✗	✗	✓	✓	✗	✓	✓
Gaseous degradation products	✗	✗	✗	✓	✗	✗	✗	✓	✗	✗
Polymer degradation	✓	✓	✓	✓	✓	✗	✗	●	✗	✗
Plasticiser loss	✗	✓	●	✓	✗	✗	✗	✓	✗	✗
Filler degradation	✗	✗	✗	✗	✗	✓	✓	✗	●	✓

Source: Quye and Williamson (eds), 1999, p. 83 ✓ *suitable* ● *possible* ✗ *unsuitable*
DSC is differential scanning calorimetric; GPC is gel permeation chromatography; IC is ion chromatography; TGA is thermo gravimetric analysis. Other are as glossary.

Flame tests on a small sample taken from the plastic can be more informative, with distinctive burning characteristics also giving a range of characteristic odours (Table 18.4). Once again these would be relatively easy for a forger to circumvent, merely adding the appropriate chemicals to the plastic mixture. If, for example Celluloid was being imitated, camphor would be added to the mix to ensure the characteristic smell of mothballs was given off on heating; and similarly, if vulcanite, sulphur could be added to ensure that the characteristic smell of sulphur was given off on rubbing with the hands.

Plastics containing chlorine such as is found in PVC can be detected by the Beilstein test, although it is destructive. A copper wire is heated and held against the surface of the plastic, then being returned to the flame. If chlorine is present, a distinctive green flame is seen.

Chemical analysis (Table 18.5)
Sources: Braun, D. (1982); van Oosten (1999).

The analysis of plastics, which used to be very difficult and time consuming and required large samples, is now relatively easy to accomplish, owing to the advances made in instrumental organic analytical techniques over the last 20 years or so, as outlined in Chapter 3. Fourier transform infra-red (FTIR) analysis and Raman microscopy (RM)

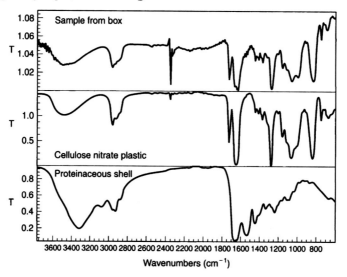

Figure 18.4   FTIR analysis special produced by an unknown plastic (top), compared to cellulose nitrate and natural shell. (Quye and Williamson (eds), 1999)

are perhaps the most useful techniques. FTIR is especially good for the identification of the polymers and other organic components (Figure 18.4), whereas RM is rather better suited to the identification of the inorganic fillers and pigments, etc. As with many other materials, the two techniques are complementary in their relative strengths and weaknesses for organic analysis. RM usually requires no sample at all, whereas FTIR usually requires a sample measured in milligrams. However, new non-invasive approaches utilising fibre optics are becoming more available (see Chapter 3). Scott Williams (1997), for example, describes a portable non-invasive probe FTIR system.

The main problems with FTIR and RM occur when dealing with mixed polymers where the spectra generated by the polymers overlie and interfere with one another. Gas chromatography (GC) and its variant, pyrolysis–gas chromatography (Pyr–GC), being basically separation techniques, are probably the best methods to deal with mixed polymers that are sufficiently volatile and their additives (see Chapter 3, p. 58). When linked to mass spectrometry (MS), Pyr–GC is a very powerful technique for the separation and identification of plastic materials. Samples of less than one milligram can be identified. Pyr–GC has been widely used in the analysis of natural and synthetic plastics such as

amber (see Chapter 17, p. 439), acrylic paints, etc. (see Chapter 12, p. 289).

The inorganic additives to plastics (see Table 18.2), fillers, pigments, etc., can also be identified, although not quantified, by the standard analytical techniques such as XRD X-ray fluorescence (XRF) (but with the attendant problems of detecting the lighter elements; see Chapter 3, p. 45), as well as by RM, already mentioned. If an open-architecture XRF system is used, then the technique is non-destructive.

Plastics can be examined by scanning electron microscopy (SEM) and the inorganic components analysed by energy-dispersive X-ray analysis (EDX), although sampling is usually necessary as the pieces have to be surface-coated to render them conducting. (NB any artefact with loose components or where there is evidence of flaking or severe cracking should not be put into a vacuum chamber.) SEM can graphically reveal the form and concentration of the various fillers, wood flour, shredded paper, cloth, etc., enabling comparison between fillers in genuine and suspect pieces. Its being able to record the various flow patterns and creases, etc. that developed while the piece was being formed could be useful in the recognition of particular fabrication processes used by specific firms at specific times. The characteristic physical features of long-term degradation can often be graphically revealed at high magnification by SEM. The EDX analytical systems associated with the scanning electron microscope could be useful for identifying some of the inorganic fillers used, but would, of course, be of no use at all in identifying the organic components.

Radiography

Radiography can reveal the distribution of inorganic fillers in the plastic, which, being organic, is relatively transparent to X-rays (see Figure 4.5b).

Overall, a combination of FTIR or RM and Pyr. GC for the identification of the polymer, along with SEM for information on the morphology and possible evidence of degradation of the polymer, and with EDX for information on the inorganic fillers, is likely to be of most value in authenticity studies on plastics.

Degradation

Sources: Selwitz (1988); Blank (1990); Morgan (1991, pp. 14–16); McNeill (1992); Williamson (1992); Feller (1994); Shashoua and Ward (1995); Nicholson (1997, pp. 144–150); Keneghan and Quye (1999); Quye and Keneghan (1999).
See also *Journal of Polymer Degradation Studies.*

The degradation of plastics, which is of concern to the collector, curator and conservator, can also provide some indication of age and thus of authenticity. Note that many of the most diagnostic forms of degradation will be taking place throughout the body of the plastic, and are both progressive and presently untreatable, leading ultimately to the total destruction of the object. Thus, while degradation provides reassuring evidence of authenticity, it may also be taken as an indication not to purchase (Figure 18.5).

Plastics age by the degradation of the polymer chains; these break down into smaller units, and if a plastic is a thermoplastic, they can also form a tendency to cross-link (McNeill, 1992). Typically, both natural and synthetic polymer chains often degrade with the creation of conjugated double bonds, i.e. ... —CH=CH—CH=CH—.... These are often yellow in color (carotene is probably the most familiar example), and are the origin of the characteristic yellowing of cellulose-based polymers from Celluloid to linen. These bonds can be easily detected by IR or Raman spectroscopy (RS). By and large, the polymers in most plastics are themselves fairly stable, although some such as PVA are susceptible to UV. The main problem is the various additives, residual chemicals from the original polymer-forming process, plasticisers, fire retardants, etc., which, on the whole, are much more reactive and can attack the polymer chains.

There are a variety of characteristic physical signs of such degradation, often visible to the naked eye or under binocular magnification (Williamson 1992) (Table 18.6).

Typical signs of degradation include the following:

Blistering: This is brought about by the localised decay of the polymer, resulting in physical distortion, and in some cases by the evolution of gas. It occurs in both cellulose nitrate and acetate.

Weeping or blooming: This is caused by additives or decay products coming to the surface. Sticky or oily deposits are likely to be the remnants of the plasticiser. Acids are generated

Figure 18.5 Extensive splitting and warping on a Celluloid clothes brush purchased new in 1935. (Courtesy A. Milton)

Table 18.6   Typical signs of degradation

	warping	crazing/cracking	brittle/crumbling	bloom	vinegar smell	sticky (weeping)	mothball smell	acid smell	'plastic' smell	discolouration
Cellulose nitrate		●	●	●			●	●		●
Cellulose acetate	●				●	●		●	●	
Flexible PVC	●		●	●		●			●	●
Poly(methyl methacrylate)		●								●
Polyurethane foam		●				●				●
Polystyrene		●								
Casein		●								
Phenol formaldehyde										●
Nylon			●							●

Source: Quye and Williamson (eds), 1999, p. 121

by the decay of some plastics such as nitrocellulose (nitric acid), cellulose acetate (acetic acid), or PVC (hydrochloric acid) (see Shashoua, 2002 for the deterioration of PVC). If the object has metal components then these can be attacked by the acids, causing staining of the surrounding plastics.

Crazing: This is quite common on casein, and is also found on nitrocellulose and on Perspex, as well as on some natural polymers such as copal and amber.

Warping and cracking: The internal strains brought about by the migration of plasticisers, etc., as well as the degradation of the polymer chains, can bring about considerable internal strain resulting in warping and cracking. Plastic foams such as polyurethane and some synthetic rubbers are prone to crumble as the polymer chains oxidise and break up.

Discoloration: Many plastics such as cellulose nitrate and acetates can tend to fog or go yellow on exposure to heat or to UV, as noted above. Sometimes the chemicals generated by the decay of the polymers can cause color changes.

The pigments and dyes in the plastics can also discolor.

The visible symptoms often go together. For example, a 70-year-old set-square made of celluloid and found among the effects of the author's father was barely recognisable; much of it had the consistency of wet sugar, with the remainder opaque and deep yellow in color. The latter was caused by the presence of the conjugated double bonds as described above, and also by the creation of deep brown nitrous compounds during the degradation of the nitrate polymer (Figure 18.6).

Many of these signs of age could be simulated (Feller, 1994), although as yet the signs of natural ageing and decay are not valued in their own right as is the case with other materials such as the copper alloys. Appreciative comments on the patina of a plastic are not yet being made by connoisseurs, but they will surely come. Obviously the forger would have to judge the degree of degradation carefully. It would be self-defeating to produce a plastic that was apparently well on the way to irredeemable destruction!

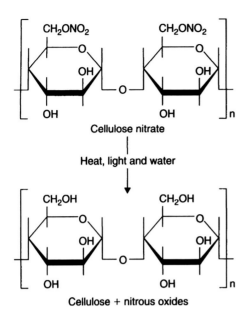

Figure 18.6 Degradation of nitrocellulose, releasing nitrous acid. (Courtesy Quye and Williamson (eds), 1999)

Some important synthetic plastics

Cellulose nitrate and acetate
Sources: Bersch (1904); Masselon *et al.* (1912); Böckmann (1921); Kaufman (1963); Brydson (1975, pp. 486–500); Friedel (1983); Blank (1990); Cardamone *et al.* (1992); Mossman (1994).
Some commercial names:

Nitrocellulose
USA and universal: Celluloid
UK: Parkesine, Bexoid, Cascelloid, Ivoride, Xylonite (for more ivory-deceived names, see Chapter 17, p. 422)
France: Naxoid, Pyroxylin, Rhodoid Sicoine
Germany: Cellolobrin, Cellunova, Celtid
USA: Amer-glo, Amerth, Biskoline Book Tex
Japan: Campholoid.

Cellulose acetate
Universal: Rayon
UK: Acetyloid, Bernit, Bexoid, Dorcasite, Doverite, Crayonne, Erinofort, Lanoplast, Lanzoid, Lensil, Lustrac, Novellon, Rhodialite, Rhodoid, Seracelle, Suprex, Tenite, Utex, Utilex, Vetroloid, Vitreo-Cellulose, Wireweld
France: Manusolite, Rhodoid, Sicoid

Germany: Cellidor, Cellon, Ercarit
Japan: Acetyloid
USA: Acele, Acelose, Amer-glo, Celastoid, Cellastine, Cellulate, Charmour, Clair de Lune, Clearsite, Vimlite, Vitapane, Vu-Lite, Vuepak.

Nitrocellulose is generally regarded as the earliest commercially viable plastic. The material was first exhibited at the 1862 London exhibition (see quote at the head of this chapter) as Parkesine by its inventor Alexander Parkes. It is often classed as semi-synthetic, and was first made by the treatment of cotton fibres with nitric and sulphuric acids. This converted a proportion of the cellulose into nitrocellulose and the whole mass became a thermoplastic dough. With oils and camphor being added as plasticisers the mixture was easily mouldable when hot. Very soon afterwards the process was taken up by the Hyatt brothers in the USA in the late 1860s, the product being marketed with considerable success as Celluloid, followed by production in the UK as Xylonite or Ivoride.

Nitrocellulose became very popular in the nineteenth century for a variety of artefacts previously made of expensive natural materials such as ivory, tortoiseshell or coral, and the nineteenth-century copies are probably more successful than any subsequent productions. This is because they were not regarded as cheap imitations, and a great deal of painstaking and skilled work often went into them. For example, craftsmen in the town of Oyonnax, in eastern France, which had long specialised in the production of hand-made combs of ivory, rapidly and quite openly changed over to using nitrocellulose as being a superior material (known locally as Naxoid). The teeth were not moulded but were still hand-cut as they had been previously, and even in the 1960s combs were still stamped 'genuine Celluloid'. However, most Celluloid was hot-moulded, and a significant proportion was cut into sheets that were then hot-pressed into shape, as exemplified by the familiar and now much-collected dolls (Fainges, 2000).

Another use was in dress accessories, where Celluloid rapidly replaced whalebone. Celluloid's biggest drawback was its flammability, especially in the form of fibres for clothes (see p. 467). A great deal of research went on for many years to replace the nitrate with something less flammable, and finally, in the early twentieth century, cellulose acetate was produced by treating the cotton fibres with acetic anhydride. This was initially used mainly for clear films and became the first successful synthetic fibre, known from the 1920s as Rayon (see p. 467). Horizontal injection-moulding, which was introduced in 1927, used cellulose acetate more or less exclusively until after World War II. It was also for a while the only light-colored thermoplastic in production until the arrival of polythene and polystyrene.

Celluloid was always a prestige material, for example being used by craftsmen in the workshops of René Lalique to make boxes etc., but increasingly it came under pressure from more modern plastics that were easier and less hazardous to produce and did not have a reputation for being dangerous. At the beginning of the third millennium Celluloid production still continues. It is the preferred material for designer spectacle frames and for table-tennis balls, the two hemispherical halves made in the traditional way by hot-moulding and then joined.

Casein

Sources: Kaufman (1963, pp. 55–57); Brydson (1975, pp. 697–704).

Some commercial names:

UK: Ameroid, Ambloid (NB not to be confused with Ambroid, pressed amber; see Chapter 17, p. 436), Catalin, CS, Defiance, Dorcasine, Ergolith, Erinoid, Fantasit, Gala, Ikilith, Keronyx, Lacrinith, Lactoid; Lupinit Papyrus

USA: Aralac, Alladite, Ameroid, Coronation, Gala, Gemstone, Styrolit, Lactoloid, Karolith, Kasolid, Kyloid, Marbelette, Maco, Opalon, Pearlith, Protflex, Prystal

France and Germany: Akalit, Baroliet, Galalith, Prystal

Holland: Beroliet, Casolite

Italy: Zoolite

Japan: Ambloid, Ambroid, Lactolid.

Casein polymer is made from the protein casein which occurs in milk, with formaldehyde as the usual polymerising agent. The discovery was apparently the result of the laboratory cat knocking over a bottle of formaldehyde into its saucer of milk. Casein plastics were first produced commercially by W. Krische and Adolf Spitteler in Bavaria in 1899 but only began to be made in America in 1919.

Solid casein was precipitated from skimmed milk by adding the enzyme rennet. The precipitate was then powdered and mixed with a little water to the consistency of dough, which was hot-pressed or extruded to form sheets or rods. These were submerged in aqueous formaldehyde to cure. The rods could be sliced to make buttons or drilled out to form the barrels of fountain pens, two very typical artefacts made from casein. Casein is naturally white but could be colored by the addition of pigments while still in a liquid form or subsequently dyed. Casein takes a high polish and was always popular for small decorative items and dress accessories. Most pearl buttons are in fact still made of casein, the pearly iridescence sometimes being produced by the addition of fish scales, analogous to the so-called Roman pearls (see Chapter 16, pp. 403, 406). Despite this, casein never seems to have been used as a simulant for pearl beads.

Casein absorbs water, causing it to swell slightly. Repeated cycles of wetting and drying, and swelling and shrinking, cause surface crazing and warping, a phenomenon often seen on shirt buttons that have been washed many times.

The main period of casein production was during the first half of the twentieth century, with very limited production continuing for some specialist items.

Phenol formaldehyde

Sources: Kimberley Mumford (1924); Kaufman (1963, pp. 61–67); Brydson (1975, pp. 509–41); Whitehouse et al (1967); DiNoto (1985); Grasso (1996).

Commercial names:

Solid:

USA and Universal: Bakelite

UK and USA: Abalack, Amalith, Amberdeen, Amberite, Ambrasite, Ambroin, Bakdura, Bakelaque, Buchneronium, Bosch-Catalin, Condensite, Dekorite, Durax, Elastolith, Elo, Estralite, Faturan, Formite, Gummon, Herolith, Invelith, Issolith, Juvelith, Kopan, Marbolith, Metakamanol, Resan, Ricolite, Sibolite, Sibilite, Tenacite, Tenalan, Trolon, Vigorite

France: Cérite, Laccain

Germany: Isolierstahl.

Liquid:

UK: Amberol, Dammard.

Commercially successful phenol-formaldehyde plastic was first produced by Leo Baekeland in 1907 and soon became very popular in a variety of forms both solid and liquid. As a solid it could be produced as a dark but clear thermosetting plastic or be mixed with various additives to produce an opaque, mouldable, thermosetting plastic. In liquid form it was used from the 1920s as a paint or varnish medium, thereby attracting the attention of van Meegeren as a promising medium for his forgeries of seventeenth-century oil paintings (see Chapter 12, p. 307). Phenol formaldehyde has also been recognised as the medium of some consolidants impregnated into stone during the 1920s (Ventikou, 1999; and see Chapter 20, p. 500).

Phenolic resins are made by reacting phenol with an aldehyde, usually formaldehyde. The reaction can take place either in the presence of an organic acid such as oxalic acid or of an alkali such as caustic soda, and it typically takes a number of hours for the polymer to form at room temperature.

The bulk of the solid production has always been in the form of a mouldable thermo-set. The reaction between the phenol and the formaldehyde was carefully controlled and stopped just before the polymerisation had gone to completion. The resulting solid resin was ground to a powder and mixed with a variety of fillers such as wood flour, cotton fibre, shredded paper or textile. The mixture was placed in a mould and compressed and heated, causing the previously interrupted cross-linking of the polymerisation to proceed to completion.

During the heating the plastic darkened and thus Bakelite tends to be both opaque and dark, although this was often turned to advantage by adding grains of different color density at the moulding stage to produce attractive wood-grain or mottled effects.

From the 1930s the pure phenolic resin (popularly known as Catalin) was produced. This was poured straight into a mould and heated at a moderate temperature for several days until it set, the lower the temperature the clearer and more colorless the resulting plastic. The castings could be in the form of rods and sheets that could then be cut to shape, machined and polished to produce costume jewellery (Becker, 1988, pp. 127–131; and see Chapter 16, p. 397). Alternatively, small decorative items could be cast directly, successfully imitating amber, jade, onyx or marble.

Phenolic formaldehyde plastics are very stable and apart from discoloration, there are as yet no obvious signs of age degradation. The cast phenol-formaldehyde resins ceased to be made in the 1950s but Bakelite itself is still in production.

Thiourea and urea formaldehyde

Sources: Brydson (1975, pp. 542–568).

Commercial names:

UK: Aerolite, Aminolac, Bandalasta, Beatl, Beckamine, Beetle, Beetel ware, Bonnyware, CIBA, Formica, Nestor, Nestorite, Pertinit, Pollopas, Prystalline, Rainbow ware, Retix, Roanoid, Scarab, Starpass, UF
France: Prystaline, Uralite, Urex, Urocristal
Germany: Ureit
Italy: Gabrite, Sibitle
USA: Arodure Beatl, Beetle, Formica, Rhonite.

These are produced by treating thiourea or urea with formaldehyde to produce a thermosetting resin. They were originally used as thermosetting powders and compression moulded. The main advantage of these plastics over the dark phenolic plastics was that, although opaque, they were white and thus could have a full range of shades and colors. In addition, they did not have the rather unpleasant aftertaste of the phenolic plastics. Under trade names such as Beetle or Bandalasta, a series of very attractive mottled or marbled items such as tea sets were produced in the 1930s that are now much collected. They were among the first plastics that did not set out to imitate any natural material, but instead produced quite distinctive effects utilising their own potentials as materials.

They are not as robust as the phenolics, being susceptible to heat and moisture, although there is little long-term degradation. They absorb water and this can lead to severe discoloration. This was clearly a big disadvantage for tea sets, etc. and they were soon replaced by heat- and water-resistant light plastics such as melamine formaldehyde.

Epoxy resins

Sources: Lee and Neville (1967); Brydson (1975, pp. 598–603); Nicholson (1997, pp. 15–16, 73–76).
Commercial names:

Solid

USA and UK: Epohen, Epolite, Epon, Eposir.

Liquid

USA and UK: Epolac.

Epoxy resins were first produced in Switzerland in the 1930s by Pierre Castan and others. They were first marketed in 1939 and the first cast epoxy resins were introduced in 1955. With suitable fillers and pigments a wide range of materials can be simulated (Chapter 4, p. 67). They are normally formed by injection-moulding. They harden at room temperature and have a very low shrinkage (c. 0.5%), which is very good compared with other organic casting materials.

Initially they were rather expensive compared with polyesters, but since the production costs have fallen, they have been produced as convincing simulants for an ever-widening range of natural and synthetic materials. They are synthesised by the reaction of epichlorhydrin and di-phenol propane or a hydroxy-containing phenol formaldehyde resin. This forms a thermosetting plastic, with reagents such as amines promoting crosslinking.

Epoxy resins now have a wide range of uses, for example as consolidants and protective coatings, and as the adhesive araldite, and, when mixed with glass fibre, epoxy resins form fibreglass. Keck and Feller (1964) found that an extensively repainted picture had been given an epoxy coating in imitation of aged varnish. The epoxy was easily identified by IR. The refractive index can be adjusted to match that of transparent materials, notably glass, when used in restoration work (Tennent and Townsend, 1984a).

Epoxy resins tend to yellow on ageing both by thermal reactions (Down, 1984) and by interaction with light (Tennent, 1979). Dyestuffs can also tend to discolor rather rapidly in an epoxy medium (Tennent and Townsend, 1984b). Thus, many of the numerous simulants now made of epoxy resins can be expected to discolor and fade over time.

Cloth

Sources: General history: Geijer (1979); Harris (ed) (1993); Frost (2000); Trench (ed) (2000). Degradation and conservation: Crighton (1992); Timar-Balazsy and Eastop (1998). Scientific investigation: Lambert (1997, pp. 139–147).

Cloth is one of the most familiar of materials and, as such, is collected in many and varied different forms from antique carpets, tapestries and quilts, through fine laces and embroideries to the *haute couture* and teddy bears of the more recent past. Many command high prices and are variously imitated, faked, forged and restored.

The principal approaches to authenticity examination are the determination of the nature of the fibre, and the means of producing the yarn and the cloth. These, together with the evidence for the various physical and chemical treatments of cleansing, bleaching, and conditioning the cloth prior to any dyeing treatments that may have been carried out, are likely to provide valuable dating clues. As with other materials, evidence for wear, repair and chemical degradation can also provide important indications of authenticity.

Fibres

Sources: Cook (1984); Textile Institute (1985); Needles and Zeronian (eds) (1986); Raheel (1994); Greaves and Saville (1995).

A very wide range of natural fibres have been spun to make thread or yarn, usually made up of short lengths known as the *staple*. These have been joined over the last 100 years by an ever-increasing range of synthetic fibres. Silk and synthetics are often spun or drawn as continuous fibres, known as *filament* threads. Natural or synthetic, the fibres all contain polymers with their chains orientated along the axis of the fibre.

The identification of natural fibres is usually carried out by light microscopy or SEM (de Castellar, 1987; Greaves and Saville, 1995). For synthetic fibres a polarising microscope is useful, the fibres producing a range of characteristic colors by transmitted light. Their reaction to heat can also be observed on a hot stage microscope. The standard works on identification are comprehensive but deal with situations in which large quantities of material in perfect condition are available. Robertson (ed) (1992) is a useful text for authenticity studies as it describes the identification of small samples of fibres from non-standard situations for forensic purposes. Goodway (1987) is also very useful, describing the particular problems encountered with the examination of degraded material from archaeological contexts, which often do not respond to the standard tests in the same manner as the perfect specimens.

Examination of textiles by UV is an essential prerequisite to further examination. This can often quickly reveal areas of restoration, which are likely to be present to a greater or lesser degree on most old textiles (Rorimer, 1931, pp. 35–38; Andrew and Eastop, 1994). The response to UV is primarily due to the chemistry of the fibres, many of which contain carbon double bonds which will fluoresce, and thus, other things being equal, old textile fibres tend to fluoresce less than the modern repairs. The response will also be affected by the nature of the weave, and by finishing and dyeing treatments.

IR can also be useful for detecting repairs, etc. Natural and matched synthetic dyes that appear similar in light can be very different by IR (Andrew and Eastop, 1994).

There are now a range of physical analytical techniques available that are either completely non-destructive or require only a few milligrams of sample to be removed.

Martoglio *et al.* (1990) and Greaves (1992) outlined sequences of tests, commencing with light microscopy, followed by SEM, with FTIR and RS to identify the fibres and additional analyses by EDX in the SEM or atomic absorption spectrometry (AAS), for example, to identify the mordants and inorganic pigments of the dyes (see p. 469).

FTIR and RS are being increasingly applied to the identification of natural fibres, especially those in degraded states (Michielsen, 2001; Edwards and Wyeth, 2005). Edwards *et al.* (1997c) were able to clearly differentiate between varieties of untreated animal fibres using FTRM. XRD can characterise a range of natural and synthetic fibres (French and Gardner, 1980).

Ageing

The principal cause of chemical degradation of all fibres is the breaking up of the polymer chains they contain into shorter lengths (Bresee, 1986; Slater, 1991; Crighton, 1992; and see below for specific tests for individual fibres). Artificial ageing tests on a range of fibres suggest that degradation is promoted by heat and UV radiation. The presence of mordants and dyes influence the rate of degradation of some fibres such as silk and wool (Needles *et al.*, 1986; Hersh *et al.*, 1989).

The typical sign of the ageing of cellulose fibres is their yellowing. Michielsen (2001) described the application of RS to study changes in fibre crystallinity as an indication of ageing.

Much research has been carried out on the degradation of cloth, principally directed towards its conservation rather than for authenticity testing (Slater, 1991; Feller, 1994). Uniquely, Kawanoba *et al.* (1996) recognised that the more sophisticated artificial ageing processes could be used in the forging of historical cloth (see Chapter 1, p. 9).

Dating

As all natural fibres were part of living organisms only a short time before being utilised, they are ideal candidates for radiocarbon (RC) dating (Jull and Donahue, 1990; Blair *et al.*, 1992;), most famously on the Turin Shroud (see Chapter 5, p. 102). The general problems and potentials of RC dating have been outlined in Chapter 5, but the more relevant can be outlined here. As most collectable textiles tend to be only a few centuries old, the problem of the Post-Medieval short-term variations (see Figure 5.6) is serious and precludes most pieces from meaningful RC dating. The 'bomb carbon' phenomenon (see Figures 5.9 and 5.10) is potentially very useful for establishing if some of the more recent collected fabrics such as embroidered samplers, lace or quilts, belong to the second half of the twentieth century or are earlier.

Some fibres such as Rayon produced from natural cotton waste and synthetic acetic acid could give a date that was apparently ancient but not of geological age. The same is true of textiles composed of mixtures of synthetic and natural fibres. There could also be problems with some organic conditioners and dyes, and even with residues of the detergents used to clean old textiles as exemplified by the Buyid Silks (see Case study on next page).

A potential sampling problem lies in the possibility of skilful repair (examination by UV can be invaluable here). For example, samples from two Coptic tapestry ornaments and the tunic to which they were sewn were RC dated (Jull and Donahue, 1990), and it was found that one of the pieces was contemporary with the seventh to ninth centuries AD date obtained for the tunic itself, but that the other piece was dated to the tenth to twelfth centuries AD, suggesting it was a later repair or addition.

Case study: The Buyid Silks

Sources: Wiet (1947); Day (1951); Shepherd (1967, 1974); Riggisberg Report (1973); Blair *et al.* (1992); Indictor (1998).

A number of silk textiles were dug up in 1924–25 at Bibi Shahr Banu, near the important Medieval settlement of Ravy just to the south of Teheran (Figure 18.7). Through a rather tangled succession of diggers, collectors and dealers they rapidly came on to the international market.

From their style and the woven inscriptions they were believed to date principally from the Buyid dynasty which reigned in Iran from AD 932 to 1035, and were found together with some earlier Sasanian pieces and some later Seljuq material.

Few early Islamic textiles were known to survive, and this, together with their claimed superb quality, technical sophistication and epigraphic interest, ensured that for two decades collectors and institutions around the world vied to obtain pieces, although there was some unease expressed concerning their authenticity even in the 1930s. Matters came to a head following the first substantive publication of a group of these 'Buyid' silks (Wiet, 1947). This brought forth a detailed, no-holds-barred, hostile review (Day, 1951), challenging their authenticity principally on the style and interpretation of the inscriptions. More technical problems were also raised: some of the cloth seemed never actually to have been made into anything; the damage, although extensive, was confined to just large tears and holes with no obvious traces of wear or decay. More significantly, the dyes had faded to a series of dull grey, brown and dead purple hues, contrasting with the vivid natural dyes on the very few surviving other early dyed silks.

Figure 18.7   An example of the 'Buyid silks'. Their AMS RC dates indicate that the silk cannot be more than a few centuries old. This piece Cat. 12, appears to have been produced on a Jacquard loom because of the very exact replication of the figure. (Courtesy Indictor, 1998)

The 'Buyid' silks were again discussed in detail, this time favourably, in the Proceedings of the Fourth Congress of the International Association of Iranian Art and Archaeology, with a major paper by the redoubtable Dorothy G. Shepherd (1967), who was to remain their most effective champion. She argued from the outset from a more technical standpoint, making the interesting and debatable comment that 'one can argue about matters of style, but one cannot argue about matters of technique'. The continuing vitriolic exchanges should have made plain the naivety of that statement (see Chapter 1, p. 2).

Soon after Shepherd's 1967 paper a major multi-authored report appeared in the *Bulletin* of the Centre International d'Étude des Textiles Ancien (hereafter CIETA), on a series of the 'Buyid' textiles that had been purchased by the Abegg-Stiftung at Riggisberg in Switzerland (Riggisberg Report, 1973). The authors variously concluded that the 39 pieces in the collection were not ancient. They noted the arbitrary nature of the damage coupled with the surprisingly good condition of the underlying fabric. Two specific discoveries were especially damning: the study of the weaves suggested the use of the Jacquard loom (introduced in the early nineteenth century) and analysis showed that aniline dyes (introduced from the mid-nineteenth century) were present.

The very next issue of the CIETA *Bulletin* (a double issue, **39** and **40**) contained a major rebuttal of the Riggisberg Report (Shepherd, 1974). This included a detailed and useful investigation into the origins of some of the pieces, following up some of the earlier descriptions of the first silks to be reported, which largely confirmed the reality of their discovery at Bibi Shahr. Shepherd also instigated a limited programme of RC dating on the silks. This was done by the old liquid scintillation method and required a sample of silk of between 0.5 and 2.0 gm. Although this was a very small amount for the procedure, explaining the large errors, it was still too large to permit sampling of most of the textiles.

The results which were obtained were puzzling to Shepherd, the RC ages being of the order of three centuries. This seemed to show that while the textiles could not belong to the Buyid dynasty, they were not modern either. What it did show to Shepherd was that there was quite clearly something wrong with the RC dating on silk, and in a sense she was correct. The problem was that in 1973 there was only the haziest notion of the need to calibrate RC years, and none at all of the problems of the Post-Medieval short-term variations (see Chapter 5, p. 93). The reality is, of course, that RC ages of a few centuries with the large errors, typically in the range of ± 85 years, when calibrated to 2σ (95% confidence), cover many centuries to the present. Thus, when the 1973 dates were calibrated by T. Jull of the accelerator mass spectrometry (AMS) dating laboratory at Tucson, Arizona for Blair *et al.* (1992), using the then current calibration curves, all of the 'Buyid' silks dates lay between the fifteenth century and 1955.

Examination under the microscope showed that one of the silks (No. 10 in Table 18.7) had sand grains and rootlets embedded in the weave, showing it had been buried. This was stated by Shepherd to be another indication of the authenticity of the Buyid silks. However, far from reassuring Shepherd, this should have given her pause for thought. It is true that the presence of attached soil and rootlets are commonly cited as evidence of authenticity on antiquities, but it is inconceivable that a proteinaceous material such as silk could have survived for centuries in a soil, replete with moisture and micro-organisms, in which plants were growing. Presumably the silk had been buried for a very few months or even just for weeks specifically to acquire its soil and roots.

Blair and colleagues' (1992) major study of the 'Buyid' Silks in the Cleveland Museum, and elsewhere, had two principal approaches, the epigraphy and, inspired by the then recent success of the dating of the Turin Shroud, AMS RC dating. The details of the epigraphic study are beyond the scope of this book, but suffice it to say that, on the majority of the inscriptions translated, the form of the address was usually appropriate for governors and rulers of some importance, yet none of the names could be found in any contemporary account or history. The exceptions were from the small group of silks associated with the original discovery, where identifiable historic figures were mentioned.

Table 18.7   AMS RC dates on a selection of the 'Buyid silks' calibrated to 68% confidence (1σ) and 95% confidence (2σ).

Catalogue No.		Accession No.	Radiocarbon Date (BP)	Calibrated Ages 1σ	Calibrated Ages 2σ
Group A	1	CMA 75.45	1000 ± 55	985–1149	899–1160
	2	CMA 68.246	1209 ± 59	692–890	670–980
			R) 911 ± 45	1029–1190	1002–1221
	3	TM 73.663	1233 ± 56	686–718	660–943
			R1) 963 ± 78		
			R2) 884 ± 48		
			Av) 906 ± 41	1037–1188	1023–1214
	4	CMA 39.506	886 ± 52	1036–1216	1004–1260
			R) 922 ± 48		
			Av) 905 ± 35	1038–1187	1027–1210
Group B	5	CMA 50.84	425 ± 85	1410–1630	1310–1650
			R1) 329 ± 49		
			R2) 299 ± 44		
			Av) 312 ± 33	1518–1640	1480–1649
	6	CMA 68.221	285 ± 50	1514–1657	1459–1669
Group C	7	CMA 88.98	240 ± 50	1639–1955	1516–1955
	8	CMA 82.281	225 ± 50	—	1521–1955
	9	CMA 66.134	201 ± 66	1645–1954	1517–1950
			R) 236 ± 47		
			Av) 224 ± 38	1645–1955	1526–1955
	10	CMA 53.331	195 ± 60	1650–1950	1530–1950
	11	CMA 54.780	185 ± 55	1650–1950	1640–1950
	12	CMA TR 15370/8	195 ± 45	1653–1955	1642–1955
	13	CMA 68.227	191 ± 45	1653–1954	1640–1954
			R) 181 ± 45		
			Av) 186 ± 32	1663–1955	1649–1955
	14	CMA 66.23	224 ± 45	1645–1954	1527–1954
			R) 125 ± 46		
			Av) 176 ± 32	1665–1955	1654–1955
	15	CMA 68.73	125 ± 50	1672–1955	1660–1955
Group D	16	CMA 85.59	101.7 ± 0.7	modern	modern
	17	CMA 82.23	modern	after 1950	after 1950

Source: Blair *et al.*, 1992

Seventeen silks were sampled for AMS dating, including three associated with the original discovery (1, 2 and 4), the rest being of less certain origin (see Table 18.7). Sample 12 was chosen because it was one of the pieces that had been claimed was made on a Jacquard loom and it had already been dated in the 1973 programme (see Figure 18.7).

The calibrated dates fall into four groups:

Group A, where the range of the calibrated dates coincides with the period of the Buyid dynasty in the tenth and eleventh centuries AD. Samples were taken from the three silks identified with the original discovery, and from just one of the pieces acquired later.

Group B samples were found to date from the Late Medieval period. So whilst they were genuine, they are not of the Buyid period, confirming the epigraphic and stylistic studies.

Group C constituted the nine where there are short-term variation problems, including No. 12, the previously dated Jacquard woven piece. There is a 95% chance that the silk was produced variously between the late fifteenth to mid-seventeenth centuries AD and the mid-twentieth century. However, by introducing other factors one can deduce rather more. Clearly the silks were not of the Buyid dynasty, yet equally clearly they purport to be Buyid pieces. None is known to have been in existence before the discovery of the original Bibi Shahr silks in the mid-1920s, and thus it seems likely that, inspired by these pieces, they date somewhere between the 1920s and 1950s.

Group D have the enhanced level of ^{14}C associated with bomb carbon showing that the mulberry leaves upon which the silkworms dined were growing after the mid-1950s. Thus, production of the forged Buyid silks continued even after Day's 1951 criticism of some of the pieces already in collections. The acquisition dates of the silks in groups C and D do not contradict these deductions.

In this exercise where the authentic material should have been about a thousand years old, the RC dating worked very well. Even though the majority of the dates had short-term variation problems, stylistic and other factors enabled them all to be placed to within a few decades. If the genuine silks had belonged to a later period, say in the seventeenth century or later, then it clearly would not have been possible to differentiate genuine from forgery except in those cases where the samples contained bomb carbon. Note also that the smaller error limits of the more recent AMS determinations allowed more precise dating. For example, Sample 6, which has an RC date of 285 ± 50 BP, calibrated to a 2σ date of AD 1459–1669, would have fallen into the 'Stradivarius Gap' at 2σ confidence had the error been ± 85. Finally, it is important to note that overall success of the exercise was due to the art historical and scientific approaches working together, not in conflict (cf. the remarks of Shepherd, 1967 and Indictor, 1998).

Vegetable fibres

Sources: Catling and Grayson (1982); Cook, J.G. (1984); Mills and White (1994; pp. 69–75).

Linen

Linen comes from the bast fibres of the flax plant (*Linum usitatissimum*) (Cook, J.G., 1984, pp. 4–12). Linen has been in use since antiquity to produce fine but strong fabrics. Its durability is evidenced by the condition of some of the most famous textiles of the past, such as Tutankhamen's burial cloth and the Turin Shroud. Linen has also been the artist's first choice for easel canvasses since their introduction in the sixteenth century (see Chapter 12, p. 290), and many survive in excellent condition.

Linen fibres are easily identifiable by optical microscopy or SEM. The main outward sign of linen degradation is a tendency to yellow, especially at the creases. Flax contains lignin, which has cellulose polymers with a chain-length typically of about 8000 to 10 000 polymer units when new, and on ageing this steadily decreases. Stoll and Fengel (1988) studied 50 ancient Egyptian linen textiles ranging over a timespan of more than 3000 years, from Pre-Dynastic to Coptic. They found extensive degradation of the polymer chains down to lengths typically of no more than 2500 to 3000 polymer units, with some as low as only 400 to 800 units. Attempts to relate the degree of degradation directly to age were not very convincing. Clearly, the degradation was the result of the particular use and burial environment for each individual piece. However, the ancient pieces were all clearly distinguishable from modern linen.

Edwards and Falk (1997) and Edwards *et al.* (1996b) studied the age-related degradation of linen. In their 1996 study they were able to show variations in the RS spectra obtained from modern and ancient linen, and in their 1997 paper they reported on the yellow–brown discoloration of ancient linen from Egyptian tombs.

Cotton

Cotton fibres grow attached to the seeds inside the forming fruit pods (*boll*) of plants of the *Gosspium* family and have been used since prehistory in many parts of the world (Cook, J.G., 1984, pp. 5–72).

The identification of the particular cotton-producing plants which produced the fibre can also provide dating evidence. For example, the familiar long staple 'Egyptian' cotton (*Gossypium barbadense*) is in reality a native of South America.

Cotton fibres are of cellulose and suffer the same discoloration and degradation of the polymer chains as do other cellulose-based fibres.

Animal fibres

There are two significant types of animal fibre used to make cloth: the hair or wool of a variety of mammals; and silk, the fibre from which the cocoon of the silkworm is made.

Fibres of animal hair/wool are comprised of polymers of the protein keratin, and those of silk, of polymers of the protein fibroin. The polymer chains are orientated along the axis of the fibre, but unlike cellulose polymer chains, there is a degree of cross-linking between them. Proteins are more chemically active than cellulose and thus animal fibres are more prone to degradation than plant fibres.

Wool

The use of wool from sheep and goats goes back deep into prehistory in the Old World, as does the use of alpaca, vicuna and llama in South America (Cook, J.G., 1984, pp. 79–144). The processing depends to a large degree on whether the wool is destined to be spun into a thick, loose *woollen* yarn, or into a thinner, stronger and more coherent *worsted* yarn.

The various wools from the variety of animals in regular use all have distinctive morphologies which can easily be discerned by both optical microscopy and SEM (Cook, J.G., 1984, pp. 132–141; Textile Institute, 1985; Appleyard, 2002).

Wool fibres degrade by the breakdown of the keratin polymer chains, producing amino acids whose presence is thus an indication of ageing. Kerr (1995) studied the degradation of wool artificially aged by damp heat and found there was an increase in the relative amino acid content of the aged samples as degradation progressed. Csapó *et al.* (1995) also studied the possibility of age determination based on the degradation of the keratin proteins as expressed in the changes in the cystine, cysteic acid, methionate and tyrosine amino acid contents. They took samples from old carpets and clothes, ranging from about 100 to 1750 years old, and compared them with samples of modern untreated wool and wool textiles taken from the pile of a new carpet. They found that the cysteic acid content increased 10-, 20- and 30-fold at 500 years, 1000 years and 1500 years respectively. Compared with the cystine content of modern control samples, the cystine content was 50% after 120–140 years, 35% after 500 years, and only 10% in the 1600–1700-year-old sample. It seems inevitable that treatments such as bleaching and dyeing, washing practices during use, and subsequent storage conditions must influence the extent of the protein degradation as well as the preservation of the decay products. Even so the method is potentially useful for authenticating material from the Post-Medieval period to which RC dating is not applicable. The method would also appear to be applicable to silk, or indeed other proteinaceous materials, such as horn or tortoiseshell.

The FTRM studies on human hair summarised by Edwards (2001) revealed characteristic degradation and breakdown of the proteins and the technique should be applicable to the hair and wool of other animals.

Silk

Silk is composed of filaments of the protein fibroin secreted by the silkworm, which is the caterpillar stage of the moth *Bombyx mori*, to build its cocoon (Scott, 1993). The liquid silk is secreted through a tube in the worm's head as two fine filaments, which harden and are cemented with another protein, sericin.

The thread is normally too thin for weaving and several threads are spun to produce a yarn of the required thickness. For the last 100 years or so in the West, after weaving, the textile has been boiled to remove the sericin, whereupon the silk attains its beautiful sheen. Early silks and those woven in the East tend to retain most of their sericin (Becker *et al.*, 1995).

Silk is very fine and light. In order to make a heavy fabric it has been the usual practice for centuries to increase the weight by soaking the fabric in a solution of relatively benign metallic salts, stannic chloride being the most common. Typically, between 25 and 50% of the cloth's weight could be contributed by the tin salt. The metallic salts promote chemical activity, resulting in long-term decay (Hersh *et al.*, 1989).

Identification and degradation
Silk fibres are rather featureless compared with most natural fibres. They are quite variable in thickness in contrast to synthetic fibres, but perhaps the most distinctive feature is their rather triangular cross-sections.

Silk ages by the action of heat and light, leading to the progressive degradation of the polymer chains. Hersh *et al.* (1989) studied the degradation of silks dating from the sixteenth to the nineteenth century and of some modern silks artificially aged by exposure to light and by heating to 150°C. Their historical textiles had been subjected to various treatments including a wide range of dyes, which had a pronounced local effect on the ageing processes and the tin-weighted silk fabrics were found to be much more prone to degradation. Marked local variation in degradation on a single piece of cloth may in itself be an indicator of age.

Becker *et al.* (1995, 1997) studied the degradation of the protein polymers in the silk by determining the amino acid content and composition by high-performance liquid chromatography (HPLC). The silks studied in the two papers form an interesting if eclectic comparison. The 1995 paper was on silks from the dresses of the wives of the Presidents of the United States over the last century or so, now displayed in the Smithsonian Institution, Washington, and the 1997 paper was on a selection of kimonos dating from the nineteenth century to the present, preserved in the Kyouritsu Women's University, Tokyo. The silk from the dresses of the First Ladies was generally in a poorer state than that from the kimonos. This was not necessarily solely due to the lower sericin levels in the occidental silks. They

had been on display, whereas the silks from Tokyo had been expertly stored in darkness and only very rarely exposed. Even so, in both groups there was evidence for progressive degradation as measured in terms of the amino acid content.

The overall picture presented by these studies is that the polymer chains degrade and this can be artificially reproduced by exposure to heat, light and UV, although some of the ageing may be rather superficial.

Synthetic fibres

Sources: Moncrieff (1975); Cook, J.G., (1984); Seymour and Porter (eds) (1993).

Almost from the introduction of plastics based on cellulose, attempts have been made to produce them as fibres (Morgan, 1981). A successful textile yarn based on cellulose xanthate was introduced in 1903, initially known as Stearn silk, but soon became famous across the world as artificial silk or Viscose (Hard 1933; Summers *et al.*, 1993; and see p. 457). After World War I, Viscose was joined in 1921 by Celanese, made from cellulose acetate (Foltzer, 1928). From about the 1920s, the trade name Rayon was adopted for synthetic fibres that had a cellulose base. The polyamide fibre, nylon, was introduced in the late 1930s but only became generally available after World War II. Through the second half of the twentieth century a succession of new synthetic fibres (Table 18.8) have become available.

Production
In a bulk plastic the polymer chains are randomly orientated and a filament thereof would not constitute a fibre. The polymers are oriented by a process known as *drawing*. The bulk polymer, either in solution or molten as a viscous liquid, is forced through a narrow aperture (the *spinneret*). As it emerges and the solvent evaporates, or the molten plastic begins to set, the forming fibre is pulled and stretched thereby imparting a degree of orientation to the polymer chains. Groups of fibres are usually drawn simultaneously through a circle of holes in a rotating disc to produce a twisted yarn ready for weaving, etc.

The fibres are continuous as produced and give what is termed a filament yarn. Until the 1930s all synthetic fibres were spun as filament yarns in imitation of silk. Thereafter it became increasingly common to cut the filaments into lengths similar to those of the natural fibres, making a staple,

Table 18.8   Some common synthetic fibres: their nomenclature, chemical composition and trade names.

Generic Name	Chemical Constitution	Examples of Trade Names
Acetate	Secondary cellulose acetate	Dicel
Acrylic	At least 85% by mass of acrylonitrile	Acrilan, Dralon, Courtelle, Orlon
Alginate	Metallic salts of alginic acid	Calcium alginate
Chlorofibre	At least 50% by mass of poly(vinyl chloride) or poly(vinylidene chloride)	Rhovyl, Leavil, Saran
Cupro	Regenerated cellulose produced by the cuprammonium process	Cuprama
Elastane	At least 85% by mass of polyurethane elastomer	Enkaswing, Lycra, Spanzelle
Elastodiene	Natural or synthetic polyisoprene	—
Fluorofibre	Polymer made from fluorocarbon monomer	Polifen, Teflon
Glass	Mixed silicates	Fibreglass, Marglass
Modacrylic	Polymer made from 50–85% by mass of acrylonitrile	Dynel, Teklan
Modal	Regenerated cellulose made by a high-wet-modulus process	Vincel
Nylon or polyamide	Polymer with the recurring functional group —CO—NH—	ICI Nylon, Enkalon, Perlon, Celon
Polycarbamide	Polymer with recurring functional group —NH—CO—NH—	—
Polyester	At least 85% by mass of an ester of a diol and terephthalic acid	Terylene, Dacron, Trevira
Polyethylene	Polyethylene polymer	Courlene, Drylene
Polypropylene	Polyethylene where one carbon in two carries a methyl side chain	Fibrite, Meraklon
Polyurethane	Polymer with the recurring functional group —O—CO—NH—	—
Triacetate	Cellulose with at least 92% by mass of hydroxyl groups acetylated	Tricel, Arnel
Trivinyl	Vinyl terpolymer of which no single component forms more than 50% by mass	—
Vinylal	Poly(vinyl alcohol)	Kuralon, Vinylon
Viscose	Regenerated cellulose obtained by the viscose process	Fibro, Sarille, Evlan

Source: Textile Institute, 1985, p. 23

spun and processed in exactly the same way as with the natural fibres. One big advantage of using synthetic fibres as a staple is that mixtures of different synthetic fibres or of synthetic and natural fibres can be made, giving a wide range of composite threads.

Cloth
Sources: Emery (1980); Hecht (1989).

The simplest technique to produce cloth is to heat and press the oiled fibres to form a *felt*. Otherwise the prepared fibres are twisted to form a thread or yarn. This may be interlocked in a variety of ways to produce the cloth, such as by interlooping (*knitting*), interlacing at right angles (*weaving*) to produce a *fabric* or *textile*, or knotting to produce some types of lace and also some carpets. The resultant cloth may be joined or decorated by stitching (*embroidering*) with needle and thread.

The best overall indication of a modern origin for a piece is that it is machine-made. As a general rule, machine-made cloth is more regular in its weave, etc. and the threads made for machine production are much more regular than those formerly made for the hand loom. However, the fineness of the fabric is not to be equated with the sophistication of the production apparatus. The seventeenth-century Dacca cotton muslins, which are among the finest (in every sense of the word) textiles ever produced, were made from hand-spun yarn on the simplest of looms.

Chemical treatments and dyeing

Sources: General: Brunello (1973); Geijer (1979, pp. 206–216); Trench (ed) (2000, pp. 124–129); Fereday (2003). Scientific analysis: Mills and White (1994, pp. 149–159); Koren (1996).

Cloth made from natural fibres requires chemical treatment to cleanse, consolidate, bleach and otherwise condition the fabric. Traditionally, the bleaching of cloth was accomplished by a combination of sunlight and mild alkalis. Prior to the introduction of synthetic alkalis, mild-acting ammoniacal alkalis were prepared from soured milk and urine.

Before the nineteenth century, all dyes were made from natural products, and they can be placed into one of two chemical categories. First there are the vat dyes applied as a solution, which then oxidise on the fibre as the insoluble colored form, for example woad and indigo (Clark *et al.*, 1993; Balfour-Paul, 1998). The second group are the mordant dyes, which remain soluble unless the textile to be dyed has already been soaked in a solution of a metal salt, known as the *mordant*, with which the mordant dye will form insoluble complexes. Aluminium, iron, copper, tin and chromium salts are common mordants; madder and the lac/kermes/cochineal insect-derived dyes are examples of mordant dyes.

A wide range of plant and animal materials have been used through the ages to produce dyes, and their presence can sometimes provide a *terminus ante quem* for the dyed fabric. For example, brilliant red dyes were made from the scales of the kermes and lac insects of the Old World. In the New World the cochineal beetle served the same role and from the mid-sixteenth century replaced kermes and lac in Europe. Three centuries later synthetic dyes rapidly became popular following the introduction of purple (*Mauveine*) and red (*Magenta*) aniline dyes in 1856 and blue types in 1860. Sustained development of new synthetic dyes followed through the last century and a half. Well-dated new commercial dyes have come on to the market at regular intervals, thus providing a succession of good *terminus ante quem* information for the dating of more recent fabrics, although the possibility of later re-dyeing must always be considered.

The first natural dye to be commercially synthesised was alizarin, the vital component of the red dye madder, in 1869, and indigo, perhaps the best-known dye of all, was synthesised at the end of the nineteenth century. Clearly there are going to be problems in differentiating natural dyes from their synthetic analogues, and equally clearly, where this is possible, the information provides valuable dating evidence.

The most obvious indication of age in a dye is fading (Padfield and Landi, 1966). The first aniline dyes faded quickly, but, in general, natural dyes fade faster than synthetic dyes. Mordants, especially tin and aluminium, tend to promote fading. The rate of fading is dependent on the environment and the nature of the cloth. Most natural yellow dyes, the red wood dyes and madder and cochineal fade, whilst indigo on wool, and some brown and black dyes are more permanent.

Analysis

Sources: Schweppe (1986); Mills and White (1994, pp. 155–156).

In authenticity investigations of ancient and art textiles the dyes are investigated on the fibre (Robertson (ed), 1992). This is where FTIR and RM (Michielsen, 2001; Smith and Clark, 2001) or EDX/SEM are so important, enabling the individual fibre being analysed to be viewed. There can be problems differentiating between the fibre and the dye in the overall spectra. Most FTIR and RM instrumentation allows for the reference spectra of the fibres, dyes and mordants, to be separately dealt with and subtracted from the overall spectra of the mordant-dyed fibre. Problems could be encountered as the reference spectra are on new material but the fibres, dyes, etc. are all variously chemically degraded. Gilliard *et al.* (1994) used FTIR microscopy to build up a library of spectra of fibres, dyes and mordants.

The mordants can be identified by use of the usual inorganic analytical techniques. The main organic analytical techniques are applicable to the analysis of dyes. In particular, these are FTIR, UV-visible, RM and SERS (Withnall *et al.*, 2005), and chromatography methods.

Martoglio *et al.* (1990) examined some early textiles using EDX to look for mordants and FTIR and visible spectroscopy to identify the organic dyes. They experienced some problems with interference of the spectra of the fibres. Chen *et al.* (1997) used non-destructive scanning near-IR spectroscopy to study a range of undyed fabrics and dyes and then dyed fabrics. Most of the spectra on the latter came from the fibre itself rather than from the dyes, but nonetheless the dyes were all correctly identified.

Coupry *et al.* (1997) have carried out a detailed RS survey of a variety of ancient and modern indigo dyes and their derivatives. They found that, in relation to recent textiles, top-quality makers of denim jeans used indigo dyes, whereas their cheaper rivals did not. Their analysis suggested ways of differentiating the genuine products of prestige producers from those of their rivals and imitators, or from subsequent forgeries. Such spectroscopic fingerprints would also be very difficult to replicate. The world-wide interest shown in what is believed to be the second-oldest surviving pair of jeans, and the enormous price paid for them in 2001, shows such research is both justified and necessary for authentication studies.

19

Scientific fraud and Charles Dawson

False facts are highly injurious to the progress of science, for they often endure long.

Charles Darwin, *The Ascent of Man*

Cases of academic and scientific fraud provide the opportunity to study something of the nature and motivation of the fraudster, normally rather anonymous in the majority of fake and forgery cases. Charles Dawson, the perpetrator of Piltdown and many other scientific frauds, is arguably the best-known forger of all time. Because so much is known of him and his career of forgery, and because he seems to have faked and forged just about everything including bird sightings, ceramics and metalwork, as well as the well-known palaeontological material, his career and forgeries are central to the study of academic fraud.

Sources: General: Broad and Wade (1985); Kohn (1986); Judson (2004). Palaeontological: Dance (1976).

Scientific fraud is graded. To some degree there can be bias even at the inception of an investigation when the scientist selectively designs the experiments, makes the data sets or collects the material that it is believed will provide the 'facts' to support a particular hypothesis. It is also common experience that the same data sets will often be differently interpreted by different individuals, based on their educational background, experience and associated beliefs. These factors are universal, and are in no way deceptive; if openly reported they are the stuff of the debate from which knowledge progresses. The problems begin when counter-data is known but deliberately suppressed or where the data as reported is flawed.

Scientific theories and statements are in general backed up by data or by experiments that are described and can be repeated to test their validity, thus making falsification difficult but not impossible. With archaeological or palaeontological material, the replication is not so easy, as to some degree each fossil or artefact and each excavation is unique, making verifiable recording essential. Similarly,

the palaeontological material should be recorded *in situ* and fossiliferous strata left for inspection and further sampling. The many finds of fossils claimed by V. J. Gupta in Himalayan strata, from where such fossils had never been previously reported, became suspect partly because their presence could not be verified in the field (Talent *et al.*, 1988; Talent, 1989, 1995; Webster *et al.*, 1993).

Archaeological sites can be salted by the digging labourer when the director is foolish enough to offer a reward for interesting finds, as exemplified by Boucher de Perthes, who claimed that the distinctive hand axes and other recently fashioned flints were definitely found in the Pleistocene gravels in association with the bones of creatures that were long extinct. He was the victim of a fraud after he had, somewhat naively, offered a reward of 200 francs to any quarryman who found human remains in contact with flint artefacts. Predictably, a jawbone was reported from a quarry at Moulin-Quignon, in Abbeville, on the Somme gravels (Vayson de Pradenne, 1932, pp. 65–101; Cole, 1955, pp. 121–127; Rieth, 1970, pp. 34–35).

Their appearance caused considerable debate, with the English experts immediately condemning them as forgeries, such that an international committee had to be set up to determine their authenticity. When scientifically tested, the jawbone was found to have collagen contents that were palpably modern (see Chapter 17, pp. 429, 430) and the flints had been knapped with steel tools.

Archaeological excavations can also be salted by the director and, where the material is unique, suspicions may be aroused. For example, the stone tools found on the excavations of the Japanese archaeologist, Shinichi Fujimura, apparently pushed back the earliest human occupation of Japan by hundreds of thousands of years, and thus gained considerable popular interest backed up by extensive media coverage. However, there was considerable disquiet over the finds for many years among fellow archaeologists, not least because the flint tools were found on his excavations only. The fraudulent nature of his excavations was only proved when he was secretly filmed salting stone tools on one of his sites by a journalist with a nose for a good story (Cyranoski, 2000). Glozel is probably an extreme example, where material was certainly planted on what was almost certainly a non-existent site, even though some of the material is apparently ancient (see Chapter 6, p. 119).

Material can be planted on excavations in order to validate similar material, as may be the case with the Clazomenae coin hoard (see Chapter 1, p. 17). The planting of spurious material by Charles Dawson at Pevensey (see p. 479) to give it and the related material credence must be one of the most successful 'plants' ever. It is instructive to consider the calculation of Dawson's efforts, the excavations at Piltdown. Recording at the site was almost non-existent and no proper excavation report was ever produced. Amidst all the furore and acrimonious discussion of the significance and association of the various fragments that made up the material from the site, the lack of this basic information seems never to have been considered important, yet its absence was crucial, and the contemporary scientific community was guilty of a neglect of duty in not seeking or requiring it.

Faked and forged fossils go back at least to the time of J.B.A. Beringer, professor of Medicine at Würzburg in the early eighteenth century (Jahn and Woolf, 1963; Rieth, 1970, pp. 22–24). He was fooled by forgeries of fossils that were crudely carved out of limestone (Figure 19.1), but nowadays synthetic resins, especially the epoxys (see Chapter 4, p. 67) doped with crushed limestone or other appropriate rock types, are used to make casts. The majority of these start off as innocent copies, eventually to become passed off as the real thing. More usually, fraud has been perpetrated by faking, taking genuine but fragmentary fossils of no value and creating more complete specimens, or carving additional features into the host rock. These frauds can sometimes be spotted because of gross anatomical contradictions in the various parts of the assembled fossil. The creation of new or mythical figures has a long history, as exemplified by the construction of mermaids by the joining of fish and mammal remains (Figures 19.2a and 19.2b), and of 'jenny hanivers', created from suitably manipulated dried skate (Dance, 1976). This type of fraud continues, as exemplified by the *archaeoraptor* case (see p. 474).

The usual defence against scientific fraud has been the system of peer review, whereby papers describing discoveries or researches are submitted to the appropriate journal to be independently read and assessed by other experts in the field, who might call for modification prior to publication, or even advise against publication altogether (Dixon, 1986). The primary intention is to examine the validity of the particular research and its reporting rather than the probity of the scientists conducting it, and in general it works well. One has only to try to make any sense of the acrimonious and confused statements on the authenticity or otherwise of the inscription on the ossuary of James, Brother of Jesus (see Chapter 1, p. 13) that have in the main been hastily published in non-refereed magazines and other outlets, often by partial authors, to appreciate the value of the peer-review system.

Peer review did not provide a defence against Gupta's frauds partly because the papers were usually co-authored in all innocence with respected scientists and the conclusions were quite acceptable in themselves, provided the material was what it was claimed to be. Another means by which fraud has been effectively exposed is the review of a publication dealing with ideas or artefacts that the reviewer believes to be wrong. Many of the cases discussed in this book have been exposed in this way, as exemplified by the review of Wace's 1927 book on the Cretan Goddess (Forsdyke, 1927, Chapter 11, p. 247), Day's 1951 review of Wiet's 1947 book on the

Figure 19.1   Plaster casts of two of the many hundreds of Beringer fossil forgeries. The 'originals' are now in the University Museum, Oxford. One appears to be of a slug with its young; the other appears to be a prototype of a boomerang! (Courtesy T. Springett)

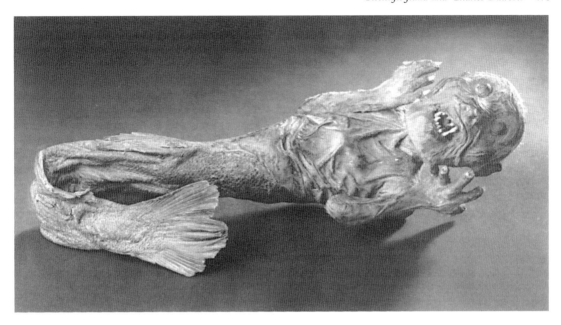

Figure 19.2a A Merman (BM ETH 1942. As.1.1). Such creations were not uncommon in the seventeenth, eighteenth and nineteenth centuries, often coming from the Far East, and graced the cabinet of many a scientific collector. (Courtesy Lang and Middleton (eds), 2005).

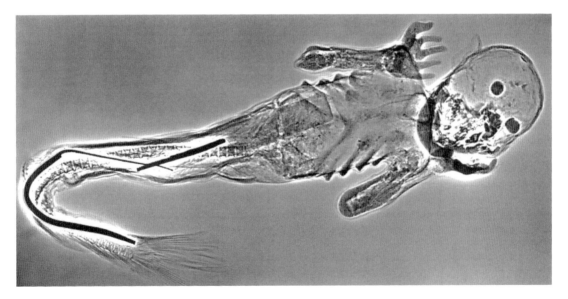

Figure 19.2b As revealed here by xero-radiography these creations usually took the form of the body of a monkey with the tail of a fish. Note the join running vertically in the pelvic region. (Courtesy Lang and Middleton (eds), 2005)

Buyid silks (see Chapter 18, p. 462), Amandry's 1967 and Greifenhangen's 1968 reviews of Hoffmann and Davidson's 1965 catalogue of the Greek Gold Exhibition (see Chapter 15, p. 373) and Saenger's 1998 review of the 1995 revision of Skelton *et al.*'s book on the Vinland Map (see Chapter 13, p. 340).

The consequences of ignoring peer-review are well exemplified by the *Archaeoraptor* fraud.

Case study: *Archaeoraptor*, 'the Piltdown bird'

Sources: Sloan (1999); Dalton (2000); Rowe *et al.* (2001); Chambers (2002, pp. 235–250); Zhou Zonge *et al.* (2002).

The story starts in the famous Liaoning fossil quarries in northern China where the palaeontological remains are often 'improved' by the local farmers and fossil hunters. One such improvement led to a major sensation and the apparent discovery of a flying dinosaur. It seems that a primitive bird was found lacking its lower region and legs. These were supplied by glueing-on fragments from a suitably sized small dinosaur, one leg, split down the middle to create two, and the dinosaur's tail. These fragments were probably found close together as the stone in which both the bird and the dinosaur are embedded seem identical.

Stephen Czerkas, who ran a small museum devoted to palaeontology at Blanding in Utah, spotted the fossil at an American fossil fair where the pastiche had wound up, together with many other Liaoning fossils illegally smuggled from China. He recognised its potential importance: 'I could see right away that it didn't belong on sale. It belonged in a museum'. More specifically. he wanted it to belong in *his* museum, and to this end he organised its purchase and study. The initial study by Czerkas together with professional palaeontologists Xu Xing and Phil Currie, was supported by *National Geographic* in order to maximise publicity. The latter wanted quick results which, in the event, did not leave sufficient time for a proper study. Consequently, the initial paper announcing the discovery was rejected by the two leading peer-reviewed journals, *Nature* and *Science*, to which it had been submitted. This left *National Geographic* magazine in the unhappy position of either publishing a major scientific discovery without the seal of approval of the scientific community or of pulling the story. Unfortunately they chose to publish, although apparently with strong reservations, and in the November 1999 issue the well-illustrated article, 'Feathers for *T. rex*' duly appeared (Sloan, 1999). The article was almost immediately questioned and subsequently a study of the remains using UV and CT showed that it was a composite glued together (Rowe *et al.*, 2001; Mees *et al.* (eds), 2003, pp. 17–18, Figure 15). Even more sadly it seems that some of the component pieces really were from new, otherwise unknown, species, but which would not have commanded such a high price as the flying dinosaur.

The above case is mirrored by the well-publicised claims of Hoyle and Wickramasinghe (1986) that the most famous fossil remains of an early bird, *Archaeopteryx*, were faked but in this instance the remains have been shown to be genuine (Chambers, 2002, pp. 198–209).

The harm done by these frauds is often very great, in misdirecting research and even in subverting the real evidence. For example British scientists, in the main, accepted the path of human development suggested by the fraudulent Piltdown remains, ultimately to the extent of not realising the significance of the material coming from Africa, thereby seriously undermining the standing of British palaeontology generally for almost half a century (Somerville, 1996). In particular, the work of Sir Arthur Keith, arguably the greatest expert on human palaeontology of the early twentieth century, was fatally compromised by his ultimate acceptance of the Piltdown skull.

Where suspect data or material has become intermixed with the legitimate, the effect can be doubly calamitous. Thus, the realisation that many of the sightings of rare birds made in Sussex must have been reported by Charles Dawson, has led to all the records made over many years having to be rejected (Nicholson and Ferguson-Lees, 1962; and see p. 489). Similar indiscriminate intermixing of information, this time of minerals claimed to have been found in Britain by A.W.G. Kingsbury has compromised the entire British collection in the Natural History Museum, after it was shown that many of his specimens were likely to have come from locations all over the world (Ryback *et al.*, 1998). Similarly, the prolific but now suspect publications of Gupta (see p. 471) greatly influenced the geological interpretation of northern Indian strata, such that the standard works on the geology of northern India, incorporating his suspect data, have had to be set aside.

Case study: The Dawson Forgeries and Piltdown – the evidence that was always there

Sources: Weiner *et al.* (1953, 1955); Cole (1955, pp. 136–162, 163–168); Weiner (1955); Rieth (1970, pp. 34–49); Millar (1972, 1998); Oakley (1976); Spencer (1990a, b); Somerville (1996); Walsh (1996); Russell (2003).

It had been the original intention to use the Piltdown hoax in this book to illustrate the improvements in scientific techniques made through the twentieth century that could have been applied to unmask the fraud. In fact not only were there a range of scientific approaches available by 1912 when the first Piltdown discoveries were announced, but some were actually applied. Even more surprising, suspicious contradictions were noted at the time but the obvious inferences were not drawn quite simply because fraud was not seriously considered as a possibility among the scientific community. In retrospect this is surprising as fraud was a valid explanation of the very major problems and contradictions inherent in the material from Piltdown, and also because there had been other well-publicised forgeries of palaeontological material, not least the Moulin-Quignon jaw that fooled Boucher de Perthes back in the 1860s (see p. 471). Furthermore, rumours of fraud were apparently abroad both in London and in Sussex.

It is now commonly believed that a single midnight revelation brought about the total exposure of the whole Piltdown fraud (see p. 488), whereas in fact official belief was tenaciously maintained and only slowly eroded in the face of mounting evidence over a number of years. A study of the interpretations put on the various analytical and dating evidence forms an interesting aspect of the case study. There does seem to have been a tendency always to try to fit the latest evidence into the established framework. Nowhere is this more apparent than in the continuing descriptions of the events at Piltdown which still follow Dawson's statements decades after their being discredited. Thus, for example, even in the definitive 1955 scientific report, Weiner commences:

> There are three sites on or near Piltdown Common, Sussex, to which attention was originally drawn by Charles Dawson and where in the years between 1908 to 1915 fossil and archaeological remains came to light.

A quarter of a century on, Hedges *et al.* (1989; and see p. 492) describe their specimen for radiocarbon (RC) dating as 'Piltdown 2, found 1915 by Dawson 2 miles from the original site' without comment.

They seemingly accept Dawson's version of events, whereas in reality most of the skull fragments had never been near Piltdown, and none of the material came from the site in the archaeological sense. As for the other two sites, they had no existence at all outside Dawson's imagination; his untimely death came before they could be created.

Rather more serious was the substitution of the correct geological description of the Piltdown gravel deposits by F.H. Edmunds with Dawson's fallacious description in the official Geological Survey Memoir, (White, 1926), thereby arguably delaying the exposure of the Piltdown Hoax for a further 20 years (see p. 487).

Setting the scene: Dawson the Man

An important aspect in the acceptance of Piltdown was the persona of Charles Dawson himself. His life and deeds are reasonably well known and offer an interesting insight into the mind and character of the academic fraudster (Russell, 2003). Dawson, the very public 'face' and almost certain instigator of the whole affair, seems to have impressed the scientific community; he was eminently plausible. Sir Arthur Keith's reaction on first meeting him is typical: 'His open, honest nature and his wide knowledge endeared him to me'. Keith wrote those lines in his biography (1950, p. 328), just 3 years before he was to learn that the open, honest-natured Dawson had duped him and thereby largely set his life's work at naught.

Charles Dawson was an established country solicitor, practising in Uckfield, and living in Lewes, both small Sussex towns only a few kilometres from Piltdown. It is possible that he felt the need to compete with his two younger, university-educated and highly successful brothers, and to prove that even without their formal education he was their equal. From his youth Dawson was interested in geology, archaeology, and above all in palaeontology. He was, moreover, anxious to demonstrate his knowledge and produced many academic publications on a wide range of subjects and recorded the sighting of all manner of unique phenomena from rare birds to sea monsters (see Walsh 1996, pp. 92–93 for a discussion of these attempts at academic research). His collecting activities brought more tangible success and through them he soon established regular contact not only with the local academic societies, but with the Geological Society in London and the British Museum (Natural History) (Now The National History Museum, but through much of the twentieth century it was often referred to just as the British Museum). The eclectic range of Dawson's finds is discussed in Walsh (1996, pp. 169–198) and Russell (2003, pp. 28–148). Some items are discussed below, including the supposed Roman cast-iron statuette (see p. 477) and inscribed Roman tiles (see p. 479). Indeed, because of the number and range of his finds, he was known locally in jest, but tinged with suspicion and contempt, as 'the Wizard of Lewes'.

Although apparently a model of probity and fair dealing in his professional legal duties, Dawson was also known for deceit and sharp practice amongst the local antiquarians, not least the Sussex Archaeological Society (Somerville, 1996). For many years they had their offices and small museum in Castle Lodge in Lewes, leased on the unwritten understanding that when the owner wished to sell they would have first refusal. To the Society's consternation, in 1903 Dawson suddenly appeared as the new owner, giving them notice to quit. It seems that the vendors had been led to believe by Dawson that he was acting for the Society, apparently even using their headed notepaper. Thereafter, the Society kept Dawson and his discoveries very much at arm's length.

Despite this local suspicion, Dawson was more successful in London, being made a fellow of the Geological Society and of the Society of Antiquaries of London, mainly on the strength of his discoveries, although he made seemingly erudite contributions on a wide range of subjects. As already noted, he made a number of donations of material from his collecting activities to the Natural History Museum (which apparently still have not been scientifically authenticated), where he met an assistant curator, Arthur Smith Woodward. The two built up a certain rapport and Dawson was a frequent correspondent. Thus, prior to the Piltdown discoveries he was known in London as an enthusiastic and intelligent amateur with wide-ranging interests and knowledge. This was quite genuine, but it was a *persona* that was to serve Dawson very well when he commenced on his greatest deceptions.

The development of Dawson's faking techniques

The pattern of Dawson's various forgeries in the years prior to the Piltdown affair illustrates the growing sophistication of his methods of creating a provenance for his 'antiquities' by introducing them onto archaeological excavations. Initially, he had only given verbal descriptions of where and under what circumstances his latest find was supposed to have been found, usually many years previously, such that the details of the discovery could not be checked. This had worked perfectly well until 1893 when he produced a cast-iron Roman statuette. To what must have been his great mortification, when it was presented at a meeting of a learned Society, without supporting evidence, its authenticity was publicly challenged. This was the only Dawson creation to be so condemned during his lifetime, and despite its importance it has only recently received full scientific examination.

Case study: The Beauport Park Figurine

Sources: Russell (2003, pp. 61–70); Craddock and Lang (2005a); Read (1893).

When Dawson showed the small iron figurine (Figure 19.3) to staff at the British Museum in 1893, he claimed that it had been found 16 years previously by a workman engaged in clearing away a large slag heap from the Roman iron-smelting site at Beauport Park, near Hastings in Sussex, and that he had purchased it from the man in 1883. This was eminently plausible, as the heap had been dug throughout the 1870s with many minor antiquities being reported (although no statuettes). By 1893 the heap had long since gone and after that passage of time there was little chance of being able to check his story.

Dawson claimed that the figurine was of cast iron, but before Charles Hercules Read, Deputy Keeper in the Department of Antiquities presented his paper (1893), he had it tested by the eminent metallurgist Sir William Roberts-Austen. He pronounced it to be of wrought iron, and so it was described at a meeting of the Society of Antiquaries of London. In the discussion that followed the paper, several eminent archaeologists suggested that it was a modern copy based on a life-size statue in the Quirinal Palace in Rome. This must have been a serious and extremely frustrating setback for Dawson. The statuette's importance lay in its being the only known example of a Roman figure of cast iron, and, as such, was intended to introduce him to the Society of Antiquaries, of which he hoped to become a Fellow. First Read described it as being of wrought iron (which was wrong) and then the Fellows challenged its authenticity (which was correct). As Dawson had in all probability obtained it in a reasonably sound condition before acid treatment to make it appear heavily corroded, he probably knew

Figure 19.3 Small cast iron figurine claimed by Charles Dawson to have been found at the Roman iron smelting site of Beauport Park (Hastings Museum Reg. 917.4.) (Courtesy T. Springett/Hastings Museum)

that it was cast iron and thus spoke with an authority that he could not disclose. Never one to give up easily he latterly sent it to Dr Kelner, metallurgist to the Royal Arsenal at Woolwich, near London, who duly reported that he had no doubt that it was of cast iron. Subsequently Dawson (1903) organised an exhibition of Sussex ironwork at the Sussex Archaeological Society's museum in Lewes and in the catalogue he was at pains to describe the piece as being the only known example of a Roman iron casting.

After the uncovering of the Piltdown fraud in 1953 the figure was examined metallographically at the behest of R.L. Downes, who was studying the Sussex iron industry and had become suspicious of the figure's authenticity. It was found to be of grey cast iron and to contain several per cent of silicon, between 0.5 and 1.0% of manganese and between 0.05 and 0.1% of sulphur. This suggested to the author of the report that the statuette was likely to be of coal- or coke-smelted iron and thus unlikely to be Roman. Unfortunately this report was never published, although it was mentioned

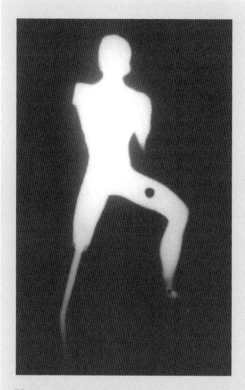

Figure 19.4 Radiograph of the cast iron figurine shown in Figure 19.3. Note the large hole in the left thigh, probably originally for holding an attachment peg. This had been partially filled up and disguised to make it resemble damage or corrosion. (Courtesy J. Ambers/British Museum).

by Russell's book (2003, p. 67). However, doubts remained; Russell had claimed, incorrectly, that it was impossible for the Romans to have produced cast iron in their small furnaces. In fact it is not difficult to produce cast iron in such furnaces and pieces have been found on ancient smelting sites, but apparently with no attempt to utilise them (Croddock and Larg, 2005a). If cast iron was being produced occasionally, what more natural than that the ironworkers should experiment with it to make small castings?

The statuette was examined more recently at the British Museum's laboratories initially by binocular microscope and by radiography. The radiography was carried out primarily to establish whether there was sound metal present beneath the corrosion before attempting to polish a taper section (see Chapter 2), but revealed other interesting features (Figure 19.4).

A taper section was ground on the right shoulder of the figure and showed the metal to be of grey cast iron (Figure 19.5). Grey cast iron is usually formed when several per cent of silicon is present in the iron, and which is indicative of a high smelting temperature, associated with the use of coal or coke rather than charcoal as fuel. As previously determined, the presence of sulphur in the figure also strongly suggests that it was smelted with fossil fuel, and thus most unlikely to have been smelted at the charcoal-fuelled furnaces of Beauport Park. The evidence

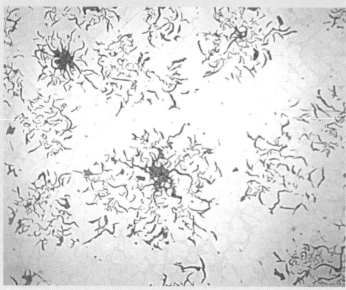

Figure 19.5 Micrograph of the unetched taper section on the figurine (see Figure 19.3) showing it to be of grey cast iron. The black strings are flakes of graphite. (Courtesy J. Lang/British Museum)

that it was of coal- or coke-smelted iron is much more problematical. At the Roman iron-smelting site at Widerspool in Cheshire, a few small lumps of coal-smelted iron have been found (Craddock and Lang, 2005a). These had sulphur contents of about 0.5%. These much higher levels are similar to those found in the early coke-smelted iron from eighteenth-century England before the processes improved, after which the levels sink to those found in the statuette (see Chapter 7, p. 154).

The figure also contains approximately 1% of manganese, which is likely to be a deliberate addition; manganese only began to be added to iron after 1840 (see Chapter 7, p. 154). Thus, overall the composition is quite typical of iron smelted with coal or coke in the second half of the nineteenth century.

Although the figure is much disfigured and apparently eaten away by corrosion there is relatively little deep intergranular penetration, and this suggests that the corrosion is not natural but has been induced. Analysis of the corrosion showed it to contain chromium. This is significant as Dawson was fond of treating his forged antiquities with potassium dichromate (see p. 482).

Thus, the metallographic structure shows that the iron was smelted by a sophisticated process using fossil fuel and the false patina was produced by Dawson's favoured method. Taken together the evidence suggests that the figure, far from being Roman, is likely to be Victorian, and to have been aged by Dawson himself.

The idea of using an archaeological excavation as the location for his forgeries was presented to Dawson shortly afterwards when he was invited to investigate a newly discovered flint mine known as the Lavant Caves on the South Downs above Chichester, in Sussex. Dawson obliged and duly produced a mass of Neolithic, Roman and Medieval artefacts, all supposedly excavated from the floor of the mine, but typically for Dawson, no plan or report was ever produced. The mines are now believed to be Post-Medieval chalk workings (Russell, 2000). However, at the time, both the excavation and the material were accepted, and Dawson was elected a fellow of the Society of Antiquaries in 1895. He must have judged the whole exercise a great success and thereafter, Dawson would ensure that his antiquities had impeccable archaeological credentials.

The next foray into archaeology was more audacious and cunning – the salting of someone else's excavation in order to give his material credence.

Case study: The Pevensey inscribed bricks (Peacock, 1973; Walsh 1996, pp. 190–192)

The first archaeological excavations at the great Roman shore fort at Pevensey on the coast of Sussex were conducted by L. Salzman in 1907. They produced brick fragments with the remains of a stamped inscription that was tantalising incomplete, reading . . . ON . . . AUG . . . NDR . . . (Salzman, 1908) (Figures 19.6 and 19.7). Then Dawson (1907) produced a brick bearing a complete stamp of HON AVG ANDRIA, which he claimed to have picked up on a visit to the fort in 1902. Salzman and generations of archaeologists afterwards took this to be a reference to the Roman Emperor Honorius and an abbreviated (and misspelled) form of the Roman name for the fort of Anderitum. The stamped bricks assumed great importance, as apparently the only tangible evidence ever found of the last concerted effort by the Romans to provide an effective defence of Britain. This was the repair of the forts by the Roman general Stilicho, which is recorded to have taken place in the reign of Honorius at the end of the fourth century AD.

There matters would have rested but for the unmasking of the Piltdown fraud in the 1950s which eventually led to the investigation of Dawson's other 'discoveries'. Thermoluminescence (TL) testing of the bricks, using the pre-dose technique, showed that the bricks were likely to be less than 100 years old (Peacock, 1973). That is, they were very probably fired only a short time before Dawson's announcement and publication, and were presumably made to his order.

Figure 19.6 The Pevensey brick (BM PRB Reg. 1908, 6-13, 1). Pre-dose TL dating established that it was fired much closer to the time of Charles Dawson than that of the Emperor Honorius. (© British Museum).

He must have planted the fragments bearing the tantalising incomplete inscription onto the excavation where they were duly found early in 1907. Then, later that year, Dawson announced that he previously had   picked up a tile fragment bearing the complete inscription. The excavated fragments had served first to excite curiosity and interest and then to validate Dawson's own otherwise unsupported find. The prestige of the discovery remained firmly with Dawson, who took all the credit.

It seems that his ultimate goal was to be made a Fellow of the Royal Society. Having perfected the method of introducing finds onto archaeological excavations to ensure that they were accepted without question, the next step was to create his own excavation. Clearly, to be made a Fellow of the Royal Society it would have to be geological or palaeontological rather than archaeological. The announcement of the discovery of the human jawbone at Heidelberg in 1907 must have provided the inspiration. He would trump this with a jawbone *and* a skull.

Figure 19.7   Drawing of the stamped inscription on the Pevensey tiles. (Left) That published by Dawson in 1907. (Right) Fragments excavated at Pevensey.

Setting the scene: Producing what was expected

From the mid-nineteenth century, the great antiquity of human origins as evidenced by flint tools found in the Pleistocene gravel deposits had been recognised. Collecting flint artefacts became a popular amateur and academic pursuit, with the attendant problems of forgeries (Chapter 1, p. 11) and eoliths (Spencer, 1988; O'Connor, 2003). The latter were broken flints that were believed by some to be artefacts shaped by man, and by others, correctly as we now believe, to be the result of natural fracture. The eoliths were found not only in the quaternary deposits of the

Pleistocene period, but also in the tertiary gravels of the preceding Pliocene period. If artefacts were abundant, then it was reasonable to expect that remains of their makers would also one day appear.

The material introduced onto the Piltdown site included several eoliths that had been stained in the same manner as the other introduced flints, and moreover most of them were found by Dawson himself, presumably only a short time after he had planted them on the site. This may seem surprising because Dawson was one of those who did not believe in the human authorship of eoliths and even gave lectures demonstrating that they were shaped naturally. Several of the local Sussex collectors and palaeontologists were very keen supporters of eoliths, such as Harry Morris, who not only disliked Dawson but harboured deep suspicions over the authenticity of the Piltdown material (Weiner, 1955; Spencer, 1990a, pp. 141–142). If Dawson had produced his 'Pliocene' skull without eoliths they might well have suggested that the whole exercise was a hoax carried out just to discredit them and their eoliths. As it was, the eoliths effectively spiked their guns, because here was the very evidence eolith supporters the world over had always hoped would one day appear. The reaction of Sir Ray Lankester, a very prominent supporter of eoliths, is typical: 'It seems quite possible that it is our Pliocene Man – the maker of rostro-carinate flints at any rate if they say to us . . . "You have no other evidence that such a man was there!" Now we can say "Here he is" ' (Moir, 1935, pp. 108–109, quoted in Spencer, 1990a, p. 28).

This aspect of the fraud also casts an interesting light on Dawson's motivation. Apologists sometimes try to excuse Dawson as an over-enthusiast who, when convinced of a particular idea, produced the evidence to support it. But Dawson was supplying evidence to fit a theory that he did not support – clearly, here the material was carefully chosen for expediency to ensure maximum acceptance.

Beginning in the late nineteenth century, a succession of finds of early man were made in western Europe, mainly of Neanderthals, but some were much earlier, such as the jawbone from Heidelberg. The few finds from Britain were demonstrably not that primitive in form (and subsequently have been found to be of no great age). Thus, when the Piltdown fragments were announced there was a palpable sense of expectation fulfilled and national prestige recovered (Somerville, 1996).

Furthermore the palaeontologists were confirmed in the then current theory of the likely manner of hominid development as expressed in the 1910 Anniversary Presidential address to the Geological Society by George Elliot-Smith:

> Given a strong ape-like animal with social instincts wresting his sustenance from the wild beasts of the plains and the evolutionary path to man lies open. The erect attitude, the dexterous hand and the enhanced intelligence are not inconsistent with the possession of brute force and brutal characteristics, but once acquired they render possible another acquisition, and this of tremendous import. A pointed stick, and the notion of using it to thrust, and we have the primitive spear. Once armed with this the necessity for natural weapons disappears. The massive jaws and fighting teeth

> can now be dispensed with, and may safely undergo a retrogressive development with adaptation to purely alimentary functions.

As Sollas (1915, p. 55) innocently remarked, 'in *Eoanthropus dawsoni* we seem to have realised precisely such a being as is here imagined, one, that is, which had already attained to human intelligence but had not yet wholly lost its ancestral jaws and fighting teeth'.

Preparing for Piltdown

Clearly Dawson did not possess a real Palaeolithic skull and so set himself to construct the plausible fragments of one. All there was for him to go on were the Neanderthal remains with their rather modern craniums and beetle brows, and the Heidelberg jawbone. However, there were obvious problems with the expected beetle brow and matching the lower ape jaw to the upper jaw on the skull. These were neatly circumvented by omitting almost all of the frontal bone, that is, the face of the skull (Figure 19.8).

It seems that Dawson had managed to acquire some unusually thick *Homo sapiens* skull fragments from several individuals which had the appearance of being of very great age, although subsequent ^{14}C dating has shown that they are of Medieval date (see p. 491, Table 19.10). Very significantly, John Clements (1997), a local archaeologist in Hastings, has pointed out that in the late nineteenth and early twentieth century some Anglo Saxon burials were excavated with skulls which were described as being very thickened. These bones were apparently stored in the Hastings Museum although they cannot now be traced, but Dawson would have had ready access to them.

The Heidelberg jawbone was to some extent not unlike that of a modern ape, and thus the jaw of a modern orang-utan was used. However, the dentition was very different and the teeth would have to be extensively modified. Similarly, the condyle where the jaw is attached to the skull is very different on ape and human jaws, this problem was sidestepped by removing it (Figure 19.8).

The American palaeontologist, G.S. Miller, who all along seems to have suspected fraud (see p. 486), actually wrote in 1915 that:

> deliberate malice could hardly have been more successful than the hazards of deposition in so breaking the

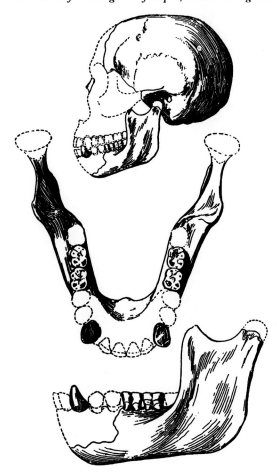

Figure 19.8 Reconstruction of the Piltdown I skull and mandible fragments, Eoanthropus Dawsoni, after Woodward. (Courtesy Sollas, 1915)

fossils as to give free scope to individual judgement in fitting them together.

quoted in Cole (1955, p. 143)

A motley collection of largely genuine Pliocene and Pleistocene mammalian teeth and bones was assembled to go with the human remains along some eoliths and struck flint artefacts. The purpose and significance of the eoliths has already been discussed (see p. 481), but as Dawson professed no confidence in them as antiquities he obviously felt it was necessary to add some real struck flakes. These do not seem to be genuine palaeoliths but rather forgeries struck with a steel hammer (see Chapter 11, p. 268 for more on the forgery of flint artefacts).

The sites Dawson chose for his discoveries were within a few kilometres of each other in the palaeo

gravels of the River Ouse. Part of Dawson's legal duties was to act as steward for several of the local manors, or agricultural estates, and these included Barcombe and Sheffield Park, as well as Barkham Manor in the village of Piltdown. As a regular visitor over a number of years and with his geological interests, it was entirely plausible that he would have become acquainted with them and be well placed to hear of any interesting finds. In fact, the gravels were not as suitable as Dawson imagined and even a cursory inspection of their situation should have revealed that they were not of the Pliocene period and could not have preserved bones or teeth of any age (see p. 487).

The Piltdown site was a clayey gravel bed exposed near the surface of a tiny gravel pit where the flint pebbles were dark brown or almost black. The various bones and flints, said to have been found therein, had to be treated to make it appear as though they had lain in the deposit for millennia. This was done with ferric sulphate to impart a deep brown coloration to the surfaces. Dawson also treated the bones with potassium dichromate, as he had done 20 years previously on the Beauport Park iron figurine (see p. 479), which was later seen as incriminating. In 1953 Weiner (1955, pp. 149–150) interviewed two men who, in 1915, had entered Dawson's office in Uckfield unannounced and found him busy treating bones. Weiner implied that this was evidence of Dawson's fraudulent activities, although Dawson was quite open about the treatment, stating it was done to harden them. Others, notably Sollas (Walsh, 1996, p. 98) and Martin Hinton (Gardiner, 2003), were later to be implicated in the Piltdown fraud on little more evidence than being in possession of potassium dichromate (see p. 494). However, as Oakley (1979b) had already pointed out, treating bones in this way with various concoctions was standard practice at that time, and thus Dawson was doing no more than most other palaeontologists. It was convenient for Dawson to have a plausible explanation as to why he was treating the material, but in itself it was not culpable. Thus the significance of the discovery of traces of sulphates and of chromium in and on the finds has been rather misplaced (Weiner *et al.*, 1955 and Table 19.1), and exemplifies how essential it is in authenticity studies to have a thorough knowledge of past treatments, both conservation and cosmetic, before condemning a practice as evidence of fraud.

It seems that the pieces of cranium selected for the Piltdown fraud were already chosen, treated and being shown around in Sussex by 1909 at the

Table 19.1 Analyses of bone and teeth said to be from Piltdown I and II and from Barcombe Mills.

Register No.	Description	Percentages											p.p.m.	
		N	C	H_2O	Ash	P_2O_5	F	F/P_2O_5 $(\times 100)$	$CaCO_3$	$CaSO_4$	Fe	Cr	U_3O_8	eU_3O_8
E.590a.	Piltdown I, left parietal	1.9	6.1	17.8	62.4	—	—	—	3.6	+	—	1.50	4	} 3
E.590b.	Piltdown I, left frontal	0.3	7.5	19.5	72.6	18.7	0.15	0.8	4.1	+	6	1.00	—	
E.591.	Piltdown I, left temporal	0.2	4.8	15.8	75.3	23.2	0.18	0.8	3.6	++	8	0.65	4	1
E.592.	Piltdown I, right parietal	1.4	5.3	19.0	68.7	19.8	0.15	0.8	3.0	++	5	nil	2	<1
E.593.	Piltdown I, occipital	0.3	6.8	16.7	76.1	—	—	—	4.5	14.4	—	0.15	8	2
	additional fragment	1.6	—	—	—	20.8	0.14	0.7	4.0	+	6	nil	—	—
E.594.	Piltdown I, mandible	3.9	14.5	25.0	60.5	20	<0.03	<0.2	6.5	0	3	0.30	nil	<1
E.610a.	Piltdown I, nasals	3.8	20.9	26.9	58.5	14.5	0.21	1.5	2.0	++	c.10	nil	—	<1
E.610b.	Piltdown I, "turbinal"	1.7	6.1	24.9	58.2	16.6	0.28	1.7	1.6	++	c.15	nil	—	—
E.644a.	Barcombe Mills, frontal	2.4	7.3	21.5	68.5	26.5	0.07	0.3	2.2	++	c.11	nil	—	1
E.644b.	Barcombe Mills, parietal	0.3	5.0	16.1	73.0	26.0	0.10	0.4	3.0	+	—	nil	—	2
E.644c.	Barcombe Mills, zygoma	1.81	6.9	22.0	62.9	13.4	0.04	0.3	1.1	++	—	nil	—	—
E.646.	Piltdown II, frontal	1.1	4.4	18.8	68.2	14.6	0.11	0.8	1.5	++	c.10	0.05	—	<1
E.647.	Piltdown II, occipital	0.6	3.9	18.6	67.2	13.6	0.03	0.2	2.0	++	c.9	0.04	—	0
E.594.	Piltdown I molars, dentine	4.3	10.0	21.0	67.1	26	<0.04	<0.2	5.5		trace	—	trace	—
E.611.	Piltdown I canine, dentine	5.1	12.1	25.4	61.7	22	<0.03	<0.2	5.0		trace	—	trace	—
E.645.	Barcombe Mills molar, dentine	2.1	7.3	16.1	73.1	26.2	0.10	0.4	6.7		0.6	nil		
E.648.	Piltdown II molar, dentine	4.2	10.7	22.6	56.8	25	<0.01	<0.1	8.0		trace	—	trace	

Source: Weiner et al., 1955

latest, at which time Teilhard de Chardin stated that he was shown some of them. Teilhard was then a young French Jesuit priest staying at a seminary in Hastings, who was latterly to become famous as a palaeontologist, and perhaps inevitably, fall under suspicion of involvement in the Piltdown hoax (see p. 494). Keenly interested in geology and palaeontology, he seems to have quite innocently made Dawson's acquaintance around 1909.

Having made his preparations, Dawson initiated the great scheme in February 1912 by mentioning in one of his frequent letters to Woodward that he had obtained a portion of an ancient skull 'that would rival Heidelberg' (Dawson, 1913). Woodward replied, but did not go down to Sussex and visit the site. After several weeks of waiting, the no doubt impatient Dawson came up to London, entered Woodward's office, unwrapped the pieces and proclaimed 'How's that for Heidelberg?' The fragments that Dawson brought up on this first visit were all of the skull itself, and were rather equivocal. Their condition and thickness suggested great age, but they were rounded and the contouring of the interior looked rather modern. There was no jawbone at this stage but the idea of an association with the Heidelberg jawbone had been effectively sown. Dawson was, as usual, vague about precise dates, but stated that he had been keeping an eye on the pit for a number of years. The bones had been given to him by a quarry worker several seasons previously, thus obviating the need to produce the man who had supposedly made the actual discovery. It should be pointed out here that because of the nature of the deposit it was the practice to dig the gravel out of the pit and leave it in heaps for rain to wash off the worst of the sticky clay. For the archaeological investigation, the heaps were often spread out and carefully scrutinised. Thus, many of the finds, although from a so-called archaeological excavation, were very often not *in situ* at all and it would have been very easy to introduce a bone or a flint into these spreads for someone to discover.

Woodward recognised the strong possibility that more of the skull might still be at the site and agreed to take part in the excavations. These commenced on the 2nd of June 1912 with a small team consisting of Dawson, Woodward and Teilhard. The first few weekend diggings produced a small fragment of the skull, and a few animal bones and teeth. Then at the end of a long hot day's digging, Dawson, making sure that Woodward was present and watching, attacked a portion of undug gravel in the pit with his geological hammer, causing the all-important

jawbone 'to fly out'. The piece was a substantial part of the proper right side of the mandible, but with much of the chin and condyle missing. Two molar teeth were in place. The digging continued through the rest of the summer with Dawson finding three fragments of the proper left parietal bone, and all three finding various flints, animal bones and teeth. The excavations, if such they can be called, were not properly recorded and in fact were never written up; Dawson (1913) is perhaps the most detailed account of the 1912 investigations.

The Piltdown discovery was formally announced at a meeting of the Geological Association on 18 December 1912, with Dawson recounting the circumstances of the discovery and Woodward describing the skull itself (Dawson and Woodward, 1913). Right from that first announcement the cranium fragments, their association with the jaw, and Woodward's reconstruction of them were the subject of intense debate, dissension, and apparently even the occasional suggestion of fraud (see p. 486). The anatomist David Waterston was adamant at the meeting and subsequently (Waterston, 1913), that the jaw was that of an ape. Woodward's first reconstruction of the cranium gave it a very primitive appearance and low brain capacity. This was quite correctly challenged by Arthur Keith, the leading expert in the field of human palaeontology, whose own reconstruction gave the creature a much more modern appearance, and, although never acknowledged, subsequent Woodward reconstructions seemed to approach Keith's interpretation of the cranium.

However, the main disagreement was over the reconstruction of the missing parts of the mandible and its relation to the skull. Woodward had given the creature large ape-like canine teeth that Keith claimed were impossible. Others were already claiming that the skull and jaw did not belong together. In the quite heated and sometimes angry debates it seemed that Keith was carrying the day. To Dawson it must have appeared that not only Woodward but the skull itself was being discredited, leading to a potentially disastrous re-evaluation and the possible unravelling of the whole deception. Something would have to be done. If the conjectural canine was not accepted then it would have to materialise.

But first Dawson had another opportunity to establish the site's credentials. Excavations recommenced in 1913, and on 9 August Woodward's wife, Maude, visited them at their diggings, and Dawson rose to the occasion by providing a find especially for her. He 'discovered' two small human nasal bones firmly stuck in the clay. It was agreed that a lady's fine fingers were more suitable for lifting these delicate finds and Maude was requested to help, and thereby another staunch and unimpeachable supporter was gained for the authenticity of the skull.

The discovery of the canine was recorded in some detail by Woodward (1948, pp. 11–12). On 30 August after a hard and unproductive day's digging, Teilhard was assigned by Dawson to the less-arduous task of inspecting the spread gravels, with Dawson apparently directing him to a specific pile. Almost immediately Teilhard called to his companions that he had found a tooth. Dawson appeared to dissemble, calling up that it was probably just a piece of ironstone. Teilhard persisted and so Dawson and Woodward clambered out of the trench, and, no doubt to former's relief, saw that he was indeed holding the missing canine.

As a codicil to the finds of the 1913 season, the American palaeontologist, H.F. Osborn (1921), later remarked on the difficulty of recognising material in the Piltdown gravels, and noted, perhaps not entirely disingenuously that:

> *Under these conditions . . . the finding of the canine or eye tooth by Teilhard de Chardin indicated an almost hawk-like vision; finally, the unearthing of the two minute black-colored nasal bones of the Dawn Man was almost a miracle . . .*
>
> Not such a miracle if they have only just been placed there . . .

The tooth completely vindicated Woodward's original reconstruction, as of course it was intended to do. Some palaeontologists, notably Elliot Smith, finding their ideas supported, backed Woodward, but Keith was still sceptical over the reconstruction and the association of the jaw and the skull. The exchanges between the two camps became quite heated and unpleasant at a personal level. Rather more seriously, dental experts such as Lyne (1916) pointed out the puzzling contradiction between the heavily worn surfaces of the canine, indicative of a mature creature, and the radiograph clearly revealing the immature pulp cavity indicating a juvenile. Also, Keith pointed out, perfectly correctly, the impossibility of accommodating the huge lower jaw with its equally large canine in anything like a modern skull, such as the Piltdown cranium seemed to be. He also noted that the heavy wear on the canine did not fit with the third molar in the jaw which was barely erupted, but in apes the canines and the third molars appear together. Keith speculated, ominously near to the truth for Dawson, whether or not the canine really came from the mandible at all,

pointing out that the color of the canine was much darker than that of the other teeth (see p. 489 for the banal explanation).

The continuing problem of doubts over the association of the jaw and skull was to be answered by Dawson not just with more material, but with two more sites. It seems that, already in 1913, Dawson had informed Woodward of another site yielding similar material to Piltdown's at Barcombe Mills several kilometres to the north-east. For some reason Woodward never revealed this and the material, supposedly from the site, having passed to him at the Natural History Museum after Dawson's death in 1916, did not surface until 1948 after his own death. In 1915 Dawson again wrote to Woodward, announcing yet another site, stating that 'we have been lucky again' because he had found material similar to that from Piltdown, at a site near Sheffield Park about 3 or 4 km to the west, in a similar gravel deposit.

Dawson was apparently reticent to show Woodward the new sites or the material supposedly from them, presumably biding his time, as was his wont, although Teilhard claimed many years later that he had been shown the site by Dawson back in 1913 (but see p. 494). Events were now moving out of Dawson's control: in the latter part of 1915 he became ill and, after many months, died on the 10th of August in the following year, and only then did Woodward receive the material from the new sites as part of Dawson's effects passed to him by Dawson's widow. Apparently Dawson had not divulged the location of the Sheffield Park site, but, announcing the finds at a meeting of the Geological Association on 28 February 1917, Woodward (1917) gave the impression that the location was known and, moreover, that he had visited the field with Dawson. In his rare subsequent mentions of the Piltdown II site (e.g. Woodward, 1933) he made no effort to dispel the impression that the location was known, even though he must have been aware that the general acceptance of the whole interpretation of the Piltdown skull largely depended on the existence of this site (although he did answer a private enquiry honestly stating that he did not know its exact location).

The apparent discovery at Piltdown II of two skull fragments together with a molar tooth identical to those already found, but in a similar gravel deposit some distance from the original site, dispelled doubts over the association of the original cranium fragments and jaw. It was felt they had to belong to the same creature; the coincidence would otherwise have been too great. Keith conceded, but seems to have felt that here was another strange coincidence, remarking ruefully, many years later to Weiner and Oakley, when asked if he had never suspected anything was amiss, 'I almost felt that they kept on finding things with which to confute me personally'. In this surmise he was, of course, correct.

Other opponents such as Osborn were allowed a detailed study of the all the material, and he too conceded, stating 'they agree precisely, there is not a shadow of difference' (Osborn, 1921, quoted in Walsh, 1996, p. 61). He also noted that 'If there is a providence hanging over the affairs of prehistoric men it certainly manifested itself in this case'. The three new fragments were 'exactly those we should have selected to confirm the comparison with the original type'. Perhaps not providence, just Charles Dawson.

It is usually stated that, with Dawson's death, the flow of material came to an abrupt halt. This is, strictly speaking, not true. Despite being referred to in Dawson's 1915 correspondence to Woodward, the Piltdown II material was only publicly described and displayed in 1917. Following Dawson's early and unexpected death, archaeologically the story rapidly winds down. Nothing more was found at Piltdown itself, and the chosen site for Piltdown II was never found despite Woodward's later attempts to locate it.

20 years of suspicion and doubts

In the 1920s the first discoveries of the *Australopithecines* began to be made in southern Africa, with their relatively advanced jaws, but small brains. Although they were initially doubted as significant links in human evolution just because they were so different from the Piltdown remains, it soon became clear that they were the real ancestors of mankind. The discovery of the Swanscombe skull in 1935, although lacking the face- and jaw-bones, also showed marked divergence from Piltdown. As well as doubts over the place of Piltdown in the evolutionary scheme and the association or not of the cranium and jaw, doubts were expressed over the age of the deposit from which they had come and it was the scientific resolution of this that finally led to the unravelling of the whole sorry business.

There do seem to have been some rumours of fraud as early as 1914 in London. The visiting American geologist, William Gregory (1914) wrote:

> It has been suspected by some that they [the Piltdown bones] are not old at all; and that they may even represent a deliberate hoax . . . artificially fossilized and 'planted' in the gravel bed to fool the scientists.

G.S. Miller, whose concerns in 1915 have already been noted (see p. 481), became increasingly suspicious and was apparently on the point of publishing his condemnations in the early 1930s, but was persuaded against it by colleagues (Oakley and Groves, 1970). Just occasionally however, suspicions of fraud did appear in print, such as those of the German anatomist, Herman Sicher (1937) who, whilst discussing the association of the skull and jaw wrote 'Einheitlichkeit oder – Fälschung', 'unity or forgery'.

The attitudes of some of those most closely involved with Piltdown are interesting. Woodward, in England where the skull for all its admitted contradictions was accepted, desperately continued the search for evidence that would vindicate the find and his commitment, whereas Teilhard, back in a sceptical France, soon distanced himself from the whole affair.

Walsh (1996, pp. 215–219) painted a convincing picture of Woodward post-Dawson, innocent, anxious to believe, yet frightened to instigate any investigation that might confirm his worst fears. Piltdown II was vital to the acceptance of his reconstruction of the Piltdown skull by the scientific community, but he did not know where it was, and, after failing to locate it in the months after Dawson's death, kept this disturbing fact very quiet. In the long years of desultory digging he must have sometimes wondered why he found nothing, and in the 1930s he was on the council of the Sussex Archaeological Society, where 15 years later Weiner was to find that a very active suspicion of Dawson still prevailed. It seems inconceivable that he cannot have had some doubts.

Days after his momentous discovery of the missing canine, Teilhard left Britain never to return to the excavations. Not only this, but in his long career as author and palaeontologist, closely involved with the excavations of the Choukentein caves of Peking Man, he rarely mentioned Piltdown, and never once mentioned his part in the discovery of the canine tooth, the key component of the Piltdown skull and what should have been the most important find he ever made.

In Teilhard's only two publications that mention Piltdown (1920 and 1943) he quite specifically stated that he did not believe the jaw and the skull were associated. More tellingly in the 1920 article he pointedly commented that the missing condyle of the jaw, was absent as if on purpose 'comme par exprès' (Walsh, 1996, p. 145). If the jaw was separate then this required the existence of a new species of the Pongoid family, but he must have known that ancient apes had never been found in Britain. This is where the Piltdown II site created real problems; the first Piltdown site could have been an incredible coincidence of almost unique human remains with totally unique Pongoid remains, but the same combination at Piltdown II was stretching credibility too far. Faced with these unhappy suspicions but with no way of proving them, he seems to have distanced himself from the project.

The scientific investigations

A variety of tests and examinations were made on both the Piltdown site and on the putative finds from this and the associated sites from their announcement. Although rather disparate, by the 1930s at the latest, they should have been sufficient to cast very grave doubts on the whole discovery. At the very least the site at Piltdown should have been questioned.

From the very first it should have been obvious that, as the Piltdown gravels are acidic, there was no way that bone or teeth could survive in them for long periods. The excavations continued by Woodward after Dawson's death and those by Oakley and Toombs (Toombs, 1952) failed to find anything other than a modern sheep's tooth. Secondly, there was a very obvious fault in the altitude of the gravels in relation to the river Ouse. Dawson claimed that they were about 80 feet above the present course of the Ouse, and thus represented the eroded surface of the 100-foot gravel terrace, which in southern England is believed to have been laid down in what is now termed the Anglian Ice Age and Hoxnian Interglacial, which is synonymous with the Lower Palaeolithic period of about 500 000 years ago (due to falling sea levels over the entire Pleistocene period gravel deposits were laid down at successively lower levels). In fact even a cursory glance at the Ordnance Survey maps available since the nineteenth century show that while the gravels are about 100 feet above Ordnance datum (sea level), they are only about 40 feet above the Ouse, and thus relate to a much later ice age–interglacial phase.

This discrepancy was noted by the geologist, F.H. Edmunds, working for the Geological Survey, but in the memoir *The Geology of the Lewes Area* (White, 1926) the text follows Dawson's erroneous claims, even though Edmunds' accompanying figure shows the true relationship as stressed by Edmunds (1950) and in Weiner *et al.* (1955).

The Pliocene mammal remains supposedly in the Piltdown gravel should have been associated with a much older and thus even higher deposit than the 100-foot terrace. This was realised from the start and Dawson and Woodward (1913) postulated that such gravel deposits must once have existed and material from them had slumped down to the 100-foot terrace during a glacial phase that had removed all other traces of it. This explanation puzzled Edmunds for many years before he published his doubts (1950), pointing out that there was absolutely no evidence for these putative higher gravels ever having existed, and that the only Pliocene deposits in the vicinity were maritime; if anything, Piltdown Man should have been accompanied by whale bones not elephants'!

Thus it was already known that the Piltdown gravels should not have preserved bone, were of a relatively recent geological age compared with the supposed age of the skull, and contained fauna that could not be accounted for.

Dawson had the bones of the Piltdown cranium analysed by the Sussex Public Analyst to determine the organic matter (see Chapter 17, for more on the analysis of bone). Dawson must have realised that the very obviously decayed cranium fragments that he intended to use for his deception would probably pass the test and would thus provide a convincing and appropriate scientific exercise (he may well have had preliminary tests carried out anonymously on other pieces before submitting the skull fragment as an identified Piltdown fragment). He would also have known that the modern jaw would certainly fail and thus the jaw was not submitted for testing. The tests on the cranium fragment duly recorded a low organic content consistent with a low collagen content and some age, as Dawson reported in his original 1912 presentation to the Geological Society (Dawson and Woodward, 1913). Thus, although right from the start there was a debate over the relation of the cranium to the jaw, no one thought to request a chemical analysis of the jaw for its organic content, which would have exposed the whole fraud as surely as the fluorine tests were to do 40 years later.

Examination of the teeth by optical microscopy failed to spot the filing marks that were so obvious to Oakley after only a cursory glance in 1953, once he had been apprised of the possibility that the Piltdown jaw was a fake. In fact, the dental expert, A.S. Underwood, specifically answering claims that the canine had been modified, stated that the wear was natural.

Radiography of the teeth was undertaken from the start (Underwood, 1913; Millar, 1998, pp. 33–34), and produced some disturbing facts. It was noted by Underwood, when comparing the canine to the 1912 reconstruction of the skull complete with the hypothetical, and very controversial canine, that the 'real' canine as found was 'absolutely as modelled at the British Museum'. More serious was the apparent discrepancy between the degree of wear on the teeth, indicating prolonged use, and the unerupted roots, indicating that the teeth were relatively recent and should not have been worn at all, as noted above, and this was pointed out bluntly by Lyne (1916). This was a very serious and real observation, which was not adequately followed up.

The final significant scientific investigations prior to the unmasking were the analyses performed to obtain some idea of the age of the skull. Kenneth Oakley, a geologist and anthropologist at the Natural History Museum, developed a method first proposed in 1844 for estimating the relative age of ancient buried bone and teeth by the amount of the element fluorine that they had absorbed from the soil (Oakley, 1948, 1963; and see Chapter 17, p. 429). Basically, the longer the bone or tooth had lain in the ground, the more fluorine it was likely to have absorbed. The process is very slow, typically taking tens if not hundreds of thousands of years to absorb 1% or so of the element. The method was applied to the Piltdown remains and both the jaw and the cranium, together with some of the animal teeth, all from the original Piltdown site were drilled (Oakley and Hoskins, 1950). Because of the unique importance of the material only tiny samples (5 mg) were permitted, which in retrospect were too small for the analytical methodology as it then existed. The results showed most of the animal teeth to contain about 2% of fluorine, which is quite typical of Pliocene/Pleistocene material, but the cranium, jaw and teeth had only 0.1, 0.4 and <0.1% respectively. However, the precision was poor (±0.2%), and with a detection limit of 0.1%, all three values fell within the same margin of error (see Chapter 3, p. 41, for more on precision, accuracy and detection limits). The results clearly showed that the skull and jaw were much more recent than had been previously believed, along with some of the animal teeth. The results were also interpreted as showing that the skull and jaw did indeed belong together. In fact, as the fluorine contents were so low and close to the detection limits of the method, it was not really possible to say anything about their association.

Still the obvious inferences were not drawn, but instead it was suggested that poor old Piltdown Man was some kind of late Pleistocene freak. It was known that Britain had been an island for long periods in the Pleistocene; perhaps in this isolation, some strange evolution had taken place. Oakley (1976) later claimed that his instinctive reaction 'was to believe that *Eoanthropus* was bogus' but in the published report he only stated: 'That the figures scarcely provide any differentiation between *Eoanthropus* and recent bone requires some explanation'. The problem was confounded as one of the undoubted ancient pieces tested also only had 0.1% of fluorine, and fluorine dating was after all, a relatively new technique.

The realisation of fraud and the subsequent scientific investigation

The Piltdown II material and the supposed existence of the site at Sheffield Park was still central to the acceptance of the association of the jaw and cranium. Another scientist, Joseph Weiner, then Reader in physical anthropology at Oxford University, pondered why the Natural History Museum had never investigated the site further and in 1953 asked Kenneth Oakley, only to be told that as far as could be ascertained Dawson had never divulged the exact whereabouts to anyone.

This was astonishing to Weiner; why, during Dawson's long illness, in the latter stages of which it must have become clear that he might well not survive, had he not divulged the location? Suddenly (apparently in the middle of the night) the solution came to Weiner: suppose that Piltdown II site did not exist? With Piltdown II removed, the original Piltdown material had to stand by itself. Consideration of the fluorine results did not exclude the possibility that the jaw could be modern; but that was completely impossible, an ape jaw with teeth showing human wear patterns. For that there was only one explanation – deliberate fraud. Weiner also noted a chance observation in Oakley and Hoskin's 1950 report that was now to take on great significance. Immediately below the dark brown surface of the sampled tooth from the jaw, the dentine was white, just as one would expect 'from a modern tooth taken from the soil' (p. 379).

So with the other evidence from the ends of the jawbone conveniently missing, all rested on the wear on the teeth that resembled that found on human dentition. Weiner obtained the jawbone of a chimpanzee and proceeded to carry out the necessary modification to the teeth with an ordinary file. It proved surprisingly easy to replicate the Piltdown jaw almost exactly. He took the jaw and his misgivings to his superior, Professor Le Gros Clark, who almost immediately accepted that the Piltdown jaw was likely to be a forgery. In turn Le Gros Clark phoned Oakley to apprise him of their suspicions and to request that he examine the teeth on the original jaw. Although Oakley later claimed to have been 'quite taken aback' (Spencer, 1990a, p. 137, en26), all it took was a cursory examination with a magnifying glass to reveal the blatant file marks, which he must surely have seen when he had taken his drillings, and to convince him that the teeth had been artificially modified. On the same day he had phoned back to agree that the teeth had been filed down and the jaw was thus a forgery. Can his conversion really have been that sudden? And if so, would he have admitted it openly and apparently without even consultation with his superiors in the Museum? His reaction strongly suggests that he and the Natural History Museum had long since realised that the Piltdown jawbone must be a forgery and had put off the opening of a particularly nasty can of worms until forced into action by renewed outside interest.

The major programme of scientific investigation which ensued included detailed microscopy, radiography, mineralogical and chemical analysis of the bone and teeth and detailed examination of the patina and surface treatment of all the finds, bone and flints, and was soon set in motion and reported (Weiner, *et al.*, 1953, 1955). This concluded that the jaw was a fake, but still seemed to accept the rest of the finds and the site of Piltdown itself as genuine (Figure 19.9). Thus, for example the Director of the Museum, replying to a very concerned E.M. Nicholson of the Nature Conservancy, which was responsible for maintaining the Piltdown site as a Site of Scientific Importance, stated that Piltdown 'as the source of portions of the authentic braincase, is in no way lessened by the recent discoveries'. E.M. Nicholson, an ornithologist, was already collecting evidence for a major article (Nicholson and Ferguson-Lees, 1962) exposing the Hastings Rarities, hundreds of unique bird sightings reported by Dawson in the decades around 1900. One wonders how reassured he really felt by the Director's letter that the jawbone was an isolated anomaly.

Optical microscopy revealed file marks on all the teeth associated with the Piltdown jaw with disquieting clarity. Improved radiography emphasised the already established discrepancy between the unerupted roots of the juvenile canine tooth and the heavy wear it bore, indicative of a mature tooth. In addition, radiography revealed angular particles of sand packing the hollow pulp cavity of that tooth, very different from the silts that should have filled it if it really had lain in the Piltdown clayey gravels. Improved apparatus revealed the discrepancies with more clarity than 40 years previously, but it was mainly the change in mindset in the scientists that brought about the changes in interpretation and the revelations of fraud.

Samples of the bone and teeth were analysed using X-ray diffraction (XRD) to determine the minerals present. This showed that in addition to calcium phosphate (apatite), calcium sulphate (gypsum) was also present in some of the material. The latter mineral could not have formed in the Piltdown gravels, but was indicative of chemical treatment, and much was made of this in the 1950s reports. However, Dawson had stated from the outset that he had treated the finds with concoctions containing potassium dichromate and ferric sulphate, ostensibly to harden them. Thus, the discovery that the acidic ferric sulphate had attacked the bone to form calcium sulphate was surely to be expected (the Natural History Museum ought to be concerned by the continued presence of acidic ferric sulphates within the bones if they wish them to survive).

The flints had also been stained with iron sulphate (and one with chromium), for which no hardening can have been necessary. This must have been a purely cosmetic treatment to make the flints introduced from elsewhere blend in with the darkly stained natural pebbles of the Piltdown gravel. These are stained throughout their thickness but the eoliths and the struck flakes were found to be quite white just below their surfaces, as one of their early local detractors, Harry Morris, had claimed many years previously.

Keith had noted that the coloration of the canine differed from that on the other bones and teeth (see p. 486). Following Piltdown's fall from grace, the staining on the canine was examined by scientists at the National Gallery, who found that it was a paint consisting of a natural bituminous pigment with a fairly high iron oxide content. Paints of this type are known as Vandyke Brown and would have been freely available from any colorman's store (Weiner et al., 1955).

Buried bone and teeth also pick up radioactive uranium and thorium from the soil and thus will become slightly radioactive themselves, the degree

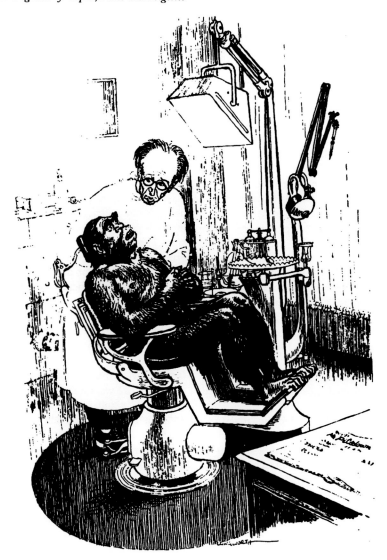

Figure 19.9 'I am afraid I am going to have to remove the whole jaw'. Note the cartoonist reflected the current belief that only the Piltdown I jaw was a forgery. (Courtesy Illingworth, Punch 29 December 1953)

of activity being very dependent on the locality. The β activity of the Piltdown teeth and bones was found to be unremarkable with the exception of some teeth of the Pliocene elephant *Elephas planiforms*, part of the fauna of the first Piltdown site. These had such a high level of radioactivity that not only could they not have originated from Piltdown, but they could not have come from anywhere in Britain at all. In the worldwide search for remains with comparable levels of radioactivity, apparently the only similar pieces were found in *planiforms* remains from the Pliocene site of Tchkeul

in Tunisia. This had some repercussions as Teilhard would have had access to the material from that site while he was staying in North Africa. Gould (1980) claimed this was the only site in the world where comparable levels existed (and thus Teilhard was the perpetrator). However, as with all such arguments based on provenance, the fact that the radioactivity levels were the same does not mean that the teeth could only have originated from that site, but simply that the teeth possibly came from there, but all the unknown and untested sites remain as potentials. In fact since the 1950s it has been found that similar levels exist in Pliocene elephant remains on Malta, and very recently, in bones in northern India (A. Currant at the Natural History Museum, 26/11/03) – the list grows.

In 1953 further determinations of the fluorine content were carried out on the bones and teeth (Table 19.1) and fully vindicated Weiner's suspicions. With much improved precision (±0.02%) and detection (0.03%) limits, the analyses showed that the skull and the jaw were clearly different. The various cranium fragments were of some age, but the fluorine content of the jaw was below the detection limits, and was relatively recent.

The analysis of bone had advanced considerably since the first tests in 1912 and as well as the organic content, decay of the proteins was measured by the nitrogen content (Oakley, 1963, 1969; and see Chapter 17). Oakley's new analyses (see Table 19.1) confirmed the previous low organic content of the skull fragments and showed that the nitrogen content was also low. However, the analysis of the jaw showed the levels of organic matter and of nitrogen to be much higher and consistent with those of modern bone.

Electron microscopy was becoming established in the 1950s and samples from the jaw showed that the collagen fibres were still intact, whereas the cranium fragments had no surviving fibres. Together,

the analyses and electron microscopy provided clear evidence not only that the skull and jaw were not associated, but that the jaw could not have been in the acidic Piltdown gravels for any length of time.

Scientific examination carried out after the Weiner *et al.* (1955) report

RC dating (de Vries and Oakley, 1959) produced dates of GrN-2204 500 ± 100 for the jaw (calibrated to 1290 AD – 1640 AD) and GrN-2203 620 ± 100 for the skull (calibrated to 1210 AD – 1490 AD) at the 2σ level of confidence (Figures 19.10 and 19.11). If these results had been available in the early 1950s at the time of the first fluorine tests they would have apparently confirmed the impression that the skull and jaw belonged together, although being nowhere near as old as Oakley had speculated from the fluorine determinations. However, by 1959 it was known that the jaw did not belong with the skull, but the RC dates still suggested it was of some age, which was puzzling. How could Dawson have obtained an antique orang-utan jaw? This reinforced the notion, prevalent ever since, that there must have been someone behind Dawson. De Vries and Oakley suggested that it could have come from a consignment that came to Britain in the 1870s, part of which went to

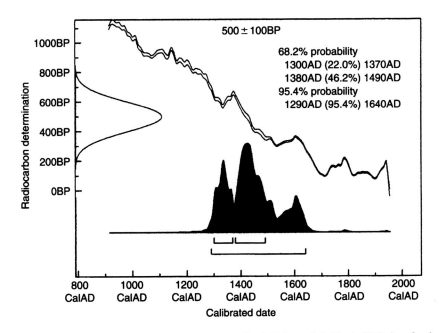

Figure 19.10 Plot of RC years and calibrated calendar years for de Vries and Oakley's, 1959 date for the Piltdown I jaw (date, using OxCal 3.5). (Courtesy J. Anbers and T. Simpson)

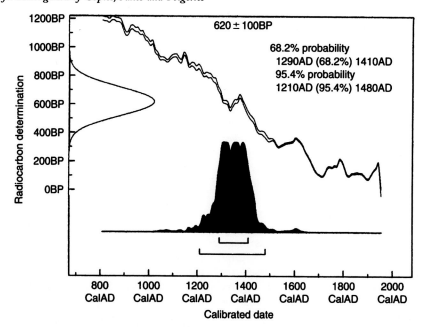

Figure 19.11   Plot of RC years and calibrated calendar years for de Vries and Oakley's 1959 date for the Piltdown I skull (date, using OxCal 3.5). (Courtesy J. Anbers and T. Simpson)

the Natural History Museum, and even though all of the documented specimens could be accounted for, it still raised speculation that someone from the Natural History Museum was involved.

Spencer (1990a, pp. 229–230; 1990b, pp. 197, 200) very disparately and briefly mentions the various RC dates in his massively documented survey but does not discuss their significance. Walsh (1996, pp. 79–80) in his otherwise generally informed account, makes some typical mistakes in his discussion of the RC dates. In particular he states that:

> *The cranium yielded an age reading of 620 years, with a plus/minus factor of one hundred years. The skull's owner, in other words, had died probably in the 14th century A.D., but no earlier than the 13th.*

In reality that error of ±100 was quoted at 1σ, which meant that there was a one in three chance that it lay outside the thirteenth/fourteenth century AD range (even though de Vries and Oakley, to their credit, were at pains to explain this). Even more seriously both Spencer and Walsh failed entirely to appreciate that the results were given in RC years, which are not equivalent to calendar years (see Figures 19.10 and 19.11; and see Chapter 5, p. 90). Finally, Walsh failed to note the significance

of the new RC determinations reported in 1989, although referencing them.

Hedges *et al.* (1989) carried out accelerator mass spectrometry radiocarbon (AMS RC) dating on the jaw and on a fragment of the Piltdown II skull. This gave dates of OxA 1395 90 ±120 at 1σ for the jaw, at variance with the previous date, and OxA 1394 970 ±140 for the skull fragment. When calibrated to calendar years at 2σ, these equate to 1524 AD – 1560 AD (2.2%) or 1630 AD to the present (93.2%) and 750 AD – 1300 AD respectively (Figures 19.12 and 19.13). Although at 2σ there is a slight overlap between the two dates on the jaw, it does seem that the later date is more likely to be accurate using the improved pretreatments possible with the AMS methods and that the jaw is recent. The general condition of the jaw also supports this interpretation. Thus, it is not necessary to invoke a collaborator to supply a centuries-old jaw – a recent specimen would have presented no great difficulty for Dawson to acquire. The differences in the two dates for the jaw rather dents confidence in the reliability of the Piltdown I skull date, but the very unusual condition of the bones does suggest that both skull fragments were from the same source, very possibly the

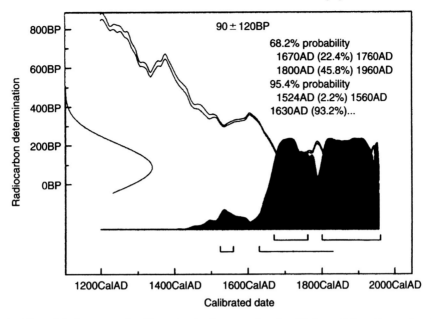

Figure 19.12 Plot of RC years and calibrated calendar years for the Piltdown I jaw (date, using OxCal 3.5). (Courtesy Hedges *et al.*, 1989)

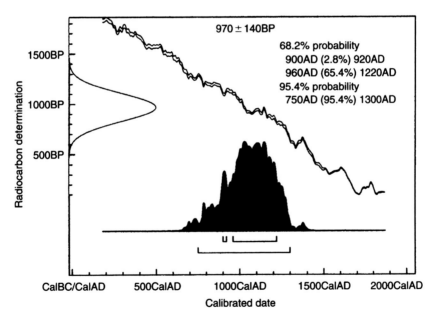

Figure 19.13 Plot of RC years and calibrated calendar years for the Piltdown II skull fragments (date, using OxCal 3.5) (Courtesy Hedges *et al.*, 1989)

Anglo-Saxon/Medieval burials from the Hastings area (see p. 481).

Shortly after the exposure of the Piltdown fraud, Sonia Cole, an employee of the Natural History Museum, wrote a book on fakes and forgeries (1955), in which very naturally Piltdown featured. Cole speculated on the role of scientific investigation in authentication studies as follows:

Is the forger of the future now doomed? It would seem that he has little chance of eluding the attacks of

Geiger counters, X-ray spectrography, and the electron-microscope photography capable of enlarging his crime 10,000 times. It was by modern scientific methods such as these that the Piltdown problem was finally solved. Sir Gavin de Beer, Director of the Natural History Museum, said 'These methods will not only make a successful repetition of a similar type of forgery impossible in the future, but will be of further value in palaeontological research. The exposure of the hoax is a gain to science.'

So, science will solve everything, and the Piltdown affair was really a benefit, which was surely the Director of the Natural History Museum attempting to make the best of a very bad job. Reality is very different from the simplistic optimism expressed above. The whole unfolding Piltdown affair demonstrated that scientific investigation by itself cannot uncover fraud, even when, in the case of Piltdown, science had actually already supplied the necessary information much earlier in the affair. It has to be the combination of previously formulated questions, encompassing all possibilities, including fraud, to direct the scientific investigation.

Who dunnit?

In Weiner (1955) the likely culprit(s) were reviewed. Weiner briefly considered the possibility that Dawson was the victim of a hoax (not entirely impossible, given the animosity towards him in Sussex; perhaps someone, realising that the Pevensey Tile was a plant, was giving Dawson a taste of his own medicine). Weiner concluded, quite properly, that the person responsible must have been present through the whole sequence of discoveries and excavations, and that person could only have been Dawson. But did he act alone or were other more knowledgeable members of the excavation team also involved in the fraud? Weiner briefly discussed the possibilities that either Woodward or Teilhard could have been involved, before concluding that this was very unlikely and that Dawson most likely acted alone. This is still about as far as it is possible to go with the question of involvement and should have been the end of the matter. Instead a veritable industry of suggestion, accusation and publication has sprung up, seeking other perpetrators or collaborators with Dawson. To some degree this was because of the unfortunate error in the first RC date of the jaw that suggested it was some centuries old and thus difficult for an amateur to have acquired. This often obsessive interest, in what is, after all, now a relatively minor question, has extended to wide range of

suspects - being famous, alive, and domiciled in Sussex at the time of the 'discovery' is usually all that is required for inclusion. The main suspects and their accusers are listed in Walsh (1996), where he systematically and quite logically disposes of them one by one. Unfortunately this did not end the flow of ever more painful speculations.

Some theories tend to seize on various real or imagined rivalries and personal dislikes or attempts to advance the suspect's own theories or career. Thus Spencer (1990a, pp. 188–208) suggested Sir Arthur Keith of being the perpetrator, done to advance his career, on the flimsiest of evidence. Currently interest seems to centre on poor Martin Hinton, a zoologist at the Museum, mainly on the grounds that some teeth stained with potassium dichromate were found among his possessions in the Natural History Museum attics, and more unforgivably, almost alone among his colleagues, he seems to have been reasonably human and enjoyed a joke (Gardiner, 2003).

The reasons for continuing to suspect that Dawson did not act alone are that the material evidence was too sophisticated for Dawson to have assembled by himself and that the whole fraud was too complex. However, considered examination of the material quickly showed that it had been crudely manipulated. Furthermore, the assemblage of stones and bones made no sense at all either as a group, or as being found in the late Pleistocene acidic gravels of the river Ouse in the vicinity of Piltdown.

The impression of the enthusiastic innocent, incapable of such a deceit so assiduously created in London, should be tempered by the recollections of those who had to deal with Dawson in Sussex and who were already deeply suspicious of the 'Wizard of Lewes', long before the reality of Piltdown was challenged internationally. His ability to conduct a campaign of fraudulent excavations over several seasons, and at the same time convincingly maintain a detailed academic debate at a high level for several years, is little short of astonishing, but we know that this was what he carried through at the Piltdown site.

In reality there is no substantive evidence that most of the suspects had any direct involvement with the site. The only two serious contenders who knew both Dawson and the Piltdown site before its verifiable public announcement were Teilhard de Chardin and Alfred Smith Woodward.

The evidence against Teilhard concerns his supposed visit to the Piltdown II site with Dawson and the source of the radioactive elephant tooth (Gould, 1980). With regard to the former, Lukas and Lukas (1983) and Walsh demonstrate (pp. 136–137) that there could easily be a confusion of dates or sites 40 years after the events. The accusation that he was the source of the ancient bones and teeth was based on the misuse of the analytical data (discussed above, p. 491). The other reasons for suspecting Teilhard were his lack of interest in the site after he left it in 1913. His rather aloof, embarrassed demeanour when informed of the fraud in 1953 surprised Weiner and led others to conclude that this signified guilt. In fact the news was probably no revelation, not because he was a perpetrator, but because he had long since worked it out for himself, as discussed above (see p. 486).

Of all those involved in the Piltdown story as it was unfolding, Arthur Woodward Smith seems to have escaped with little more than cursory examination. Yet he probably had a longer and deeper involvement with both Dawson and Piltdown than anyone else. Moreover, the developing series of 'discoveries' from 1912 to 1917 seems unerringly to have provided the evidence needed to support his ideas and always on cue, in a manner that caused comment at the time.

First it is necessary to try and establish how many other people knew of the Piltdown finds before the first recorded correspondence in February 1912 in which Dawson told Woodward of his discoveries. Dawson does seem to have shown pieces of the skull which he already claimed were from Piltdown to various people in Sussex from about 1908, but thereafter most things connected with Piltdown happen with Woodward somewhere in the picture. It is not difficult to build up a scenario for a conspiracy between the two with Woodward providing the expertise and materials and Dawson providing the site and excavations. On this basis, the 1912 correspondence between the two commencing with Dawson informing Woodward of the existence of the skull would be a necessary fabrication. Thereafter Woodward was at all the excavations, which *were* fabrications. Strangely Woodward, a trained palaeontologist, does not seem to have been particularly worried that the Piltdown gravels were patently unsuited to the preservation of bone, or that they were geologically misplaced (in fairness however, neither did anyone else). The real crisis for Woodward would have come with Dawson's illness and death.

His inability to get Dawson to disclose the location of the all-important Piltdown II and Barcombe Mills sites during the months when it must have been obvious that Dawson was seriously ill and likely not to recover, is perhaps the most inconsistent part of the whole Piltdown affair. This, coupled with his misleading statements in his 1917 address to the Geological Association, raises suspicion (see p. 485).

Woodward's strange behaviour would be explained if they were indeed partners in the fraud. Woodward knew that another site was necessary to convince an increasingly sceptical academic world that the jaw and cranium belonged together, and he also knew that, rather worryingly Dawson had apparently shown either the Piltdown II or the Barcombe Mills site to Teilhard, and quite possibly others. Thus, following Dawson's death he could not ignore them. His problem was that they didn't actually exist and without Dawson he could not create them. All he could do was to publish the material that was said to have come from the Piltdown II site, giving the impression that he knew the site's location, and keep quiet about the Barcombe Mills material.

Woodward moved down to Sussex specifically to be near Piltdown, and for a number of years after his retirement excavated there, finding neither bone nor flint artefact. If he had been in collusion with Dawson then this could be seen as a necessary exercise against the day when the fraud was discovered. Finding nothing after Dawson's death would ensure that the blame fell solely on Dawson. In this he was completely successful: one of the prime pieces of evidence for Dawson being the sole author has always been that nothing was discovered after his death (although as already noted this is not strictly true – the finds from Piltdown II were not publicly announced until many months after Dawson's death and the Barcombe Mills material was not announced until 1948).

The main reason for rejecting the hypothesis is the lack of any discernible motive. Woodward was near retirement and as a world authority on fossil fishes could not have expected Piltdown to further advance his career. His behaviour in the long years after Dawson's death also argues for his innocence. One or two seasons of fruitless excavations would have sufficed to distance himself from charge of involvement in the original hoax. He could have then quietly desisted and let the memory of his earlier involvement with Dawson and Piltdown fade away. Instead, he continued excavating for many years, and, when too old to excavate, was the prime mover in the scheme to raise a permanent monument to Dawson at Piltdown itself, unveiled by Keith in 1938. In the last year of his life Woodward completed *The Earliest Englishman* (1948) restating his belief in the central position of Piltdown Man in human evolution.

The various proposed Piltdown fraudsters/jokers were all given motivations that were variously attributed to revenge, rivalry, making colleagues look foolish, or just plain malice. Reading through the early reports and debates on Piltdown, there certainly was a great deal of professional rivalry and ill feeling. Dawson seems to have rather escaped these accusations of motive, beyond a desire for fame and recognition, although it is beyond doubt that he must have known that he was doing incalculable harm directly to the reputation and work of his supposed friend Alfred Smith Woodward, and only slightly more indirectly, the reputation of the Natural History Museum itself. No one seems to have tried to supply a plausible motive as to why he should have wanted to do this, but it is not too difficult to create such a scenario which is at least as convincing as the motives of most of the other so-called perpetrators, and, ultimately, it is no more believable or deniable.

There was a professional gentleman living in Lewes who had a lifelong interest in geology, archaeology and above all in palaeontology, coupled with a passion for collecting. His main finds came from the vicinity of Lewes. Naturally he was a member of the Sussex Archaeological Society, but the most important venue for announcing his discoveries was the Geological Society in London, of which he was a member; however, he long sought to be made a Fellow of the Royal Society. Is it Charles Dawson who is being described here? No, it is Gideon Mantell, the Lewes surgeon who in the first part of the nineteenth century made major and real discoveries all over east Sussex, but specifically at a quarry at Whiteman's Green, Cuckfield, in the Weald only

15 km west of Piltdown itself. Mantell's discoveries would have been very fresh in the minds of the local community and beyond. If Dawson was inspired it was surely by Mantell. For his achievements Mantell was finally and deservedly made a Fellow of the Royal Society, and thus it comes as no surprise that this was the distinction that Dawson most coveted.

But the identification with Mantell could be developed in an altogether more sinister direction. Gideon Mantell was thwarted and his theories challenged throughout his life by Richard Owen, whose own crowning achievement was the establishment of the Natural History Museum (Cadbury, 2001). It could be argued that Dawson's motivation was revenge against Owen by discrediting his creation.

This last section was prepared as an exercise to show how even after half a century of such theorising it is still easy to create new hypotheses and motives. As with all the other theories it is largely untestable, more suitable for after-dinner discussion than serious publication. Instead there is the extraordinary spectacle of the risible 'Wizard of Lewes', who saw sea monsters, directing the labours of two of the foremost palaeontologists of the twentieth century in his make-believe trenches. We can never be sure of Dawson's motivations, but it is likely that he acted alone, and his schemes were aided not by disgruntled scientists but rather by the stubbornness of the scientific community who, by and large, in Sherlock Holmes' famous expression, 'saw but did not observe'.

20

Conservation and concealment: The problems of restoration

The conscientious restorer has two aims — the first is to achieve an undetectable repair …

Parsons and Curl (1963)

Nowadays we may enjoy a restored ancient sculpture from an aesthetic point of view, archaeologically we regard such restoration as unethical.

Miller (1992)

This chapter deals with conservation and restoration and their relation to authenticity.

The aims of conservation are generally agreed but there are many differing concepts of what even legitimate restoration should constitute. It could be understood as recreating a perceived original appearance, replacing missing limbs on a marble statue for example. An alternative ideal could be the imparting of a more attractive appearance, albeit one that was still obviously antique, partially removing or replacing the patina on a bronze for example.

With the restoration of antiquities and works of art there is always the conflict over how visible or obvious a repair should be. It must be stressed straight away that there is no single general policy or philosophy on the subject; the attitude depends on the type of object, its material and its period. Also, attitudes to restoration themselves vary across the world and across cultures, and everywhere continually change. This lack of constancy has sometimes resulted in the cyclic restoration, de-restoration and even re-restoration of artefacts (p. 518). Current attitudes to restoration in the West for most fine art, paintings, etc. are that restorations should be invisible, but for art objects, and for antiquities, attitudes vary enormously. This is the dilemma between the desire for an 'invisible mend' and for it to be clear that the same mend is separate from the original. On major objects, conservators and curators sometimes adopt a policy of invisible at two metres viewing distance but visible at 20 cm close inspection.

Authentication investigations are necessary where the 'restoration' goes well beyond aesthetics and into the realms of deception. Here the motive is not to restore the original appearance but to disguise the true extent of damage and replacement, such that the artefacts concerned command a higher price.

If in the first chapter the concept of authenticity was shown to be fluid, how much more so is the concept of originality? This is the concept of the value of the material artefact both as the surviving witness of the reality of the past and as the very vulnerable exemplar or ambassador for the future. As Holtorf and Shadla-Hall (1999) demonstrate, in some cases the objects are so worn, damaged or restored there is literally nothing left of the 'original', yet in some senses they are still regarded as being 'real'. Perhaps all we can require of an object is that there is an unbroken continuity from the original to the present form. This also raises the question of the most suitable form of permanent record of an object. Usually this will be the object itself, but even this is not necessarily so; take for example badly corroded iron antiquities. The extreme case must be where a thick stable coat of iron oxide corrosion products forms over the iron artefact which itself has decayed completely leaving only a void. There is no original artefact as such but many of its original atoms now form the perfect negative mould of the original artefact, constituting an accurate record of the original and there is a continuity of material and process back to the original.

The Sutton Hoo sword provides a more subtle case in point. What was once a pattern-welded blade of metallic iron has become a few fragments of minerals largely made up of iron oxides and hydroxides (Figure 20.1), such that probably only about 50% of the atoms now present were in the original blade. In reality all the metallographic

Figure 20.1   Totally corroded fragments of the Sutton Hoo sword. (Courtesy L. Bell/British Museum)

structure with the nuances of the original pattern welding is lost – it is not actually the same material. However, a memory is preserved within the replacement material by slight differences in density that can now only be detected by radiography (Figure 20.2). Based on this, S.M. Lankton created a replica forged in a similar manner to the original (although using a combination of strips of mild steel and steel with 1.75% of nickel to accentuate the pattern) (Engstrom *et al.*, 1989). The replica blade has, we believe, a very similar appearance to the original (Figure 20.3). Which is more real, rust, radiograph or replication?

The rust is the perhaps closest to the material original, but the radiograph is the only means by which the original can be understood and the replication is far closer to the original state of the sword. Some archaeologists in Britain faced with large quantities of corroding iron recovered from major Post-Roman urban excavations have adopted the policy of radiographing everything and only treating and thereby preserving the more important pieces. For large numbers of ferrous artefacts the radiograph will be the permanent record.

Conservation

Sources: General: Croyn (1990). History: Daniels (ed) (1988); Gilberg and Vivian (2001); Oddy and Smith (eds) (2001). Responsibility: Ward (1994).

Conservation seeks to arrest decay and strengthen and protect the artefact, and as such should not compromise evidence of authenticity, but this may not always be the case. There can be a conflict between essential conservation to halt active corrosion and the desirability of retaining corroded surfaces that contain much of the artefact's history, and thereby its authenticity. Clearly, a record of the treatments is desirable, and major public collections usually now make and maintain such records. These are invaluable for understanding their

present condition as the case histories on a variety of silver antiquities given below demonstrate. Conversely, the absence of any record of earlier treatments on the large Etruscan bronze bowl (see Chapter 7, p. 137) led to its being briefly suspected of being a forgery. In the majority of cases where objects are from private collections no such records can be expected – the only record is likely to be the object itself. No one would advocate leaving a superb bronze, uncleaned and with active corrosion for example, but it should be possible and even aesthetically desirable to leave sufficient of the stable corrosion products, elevated to the status of patina, integrated with the surface (see Chapter 14, p. 365, Figure 14.3) to provide evidence of authenticity. Casts of other materials, textiles, etc. in the corrosion, as well as adhering soil, may also provide invaluable evidence of the provenance of the find spot for buried artefacts (see p. 502), and thus their history and authenticity. It may also be feasible to retain small areas, beneath the base for example, in a stable but untreated state for future study and as a guarantee of authenticity.

Conservation treatments can be considered under two heading, surface treatments that can be mechanical, chemical or electrolytic, and internal treatments of the whole body of the artefact, often involving heat, that can result in major structural changes.

Surface treatments

For most materials, where possible, conservation treatments seek to remove the corrosion products, artefacts of copper alloys being the main exception (see Chapter 14 and p. 501). Hand-controlled mechanical removal is likely to be the least damaging for future authenticity studies as it causes least change to the original surfaces beneath. Fine abrasion jets and other techniques such as the laser-cleaning of stone are also generally acceptable.

More drastic treatments involve the dissolution of the corrosion products chemically, or, on metal antiquities, by electrolysis. In the latter case

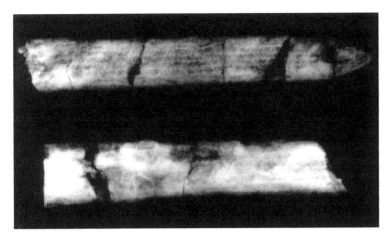

Figure 20.2 Radiograph showing ghost of the pattern-welded structure of the Sutton Hoo sword surviving in the corrosion products. (Courtesy J. Lang/British Museum)

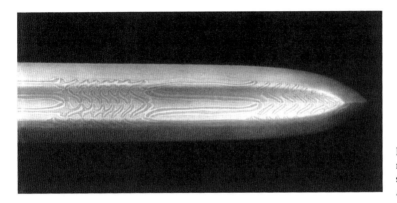

Figure 20.3 Detail of the reconstruction of the Sutton Hoo sword by S.M. Lankton. (Courtesy A. Milton/British Museum)

the artefact itself constitutes the cathode, causing the evolution of myriads of hydrogen bubbles at the surface. This partially loosens the corrosion mechanically; more dissolves in the electrolyte and some is reduced back to metal. A similar effect can be brought about electrochemically by wrapping the corroded artefact in electronegative metals such as zinc or aluminium in an electrolyte such as an aqueous solution of caustic soda, etc. (Gilberg, 1988). This can result in the almost total removal of all corroded material. Although there is less risk of physically damaging the exposed surface, in practice the treatments are often more damaging, removing the original surface if corroded along with the corrosion products sat upon it, together with any evidence for plating, etc. Furthermore, the chemicals can attack the newly exposed unchanged alloy, preferentially removing the more electronegative metals. Treated bronzes, for example, typically appear dark and coppery because of the preferential removal of the tin (Scott, 2002, pp. 363, 367–368).

It is still quite common for the patina on stone to be removed, or even for the sulphatic gypsum deposits that are formed on the surface of carbonate stones by the action of sulphur dioxide in the atmosphere, to be converted back to calcium carbonate (Skoulikidis and Beloyannis, 1984; Skoulikidis *et al.*, 1995). Removal or treatments such as these could compromise authentication (see Chapter 11, p. 257).

Another potential problem is the confusion of some ill-conceived past conservation treatments that could now be misidentified as treatments to create a false weathered appearance. A good example is provided by the famous outdoor marble pulpit at the Duomo of Prato in Florence by Donatello, which was conserved in the 1940s by a treatment involving the application of magnesium and zinc fluorosilicates (Spoto, 2002). Concern was raised over the deterioration of the pulpit in the 1990s and a detailed energy-dispersive X-ray (EDX) scanning electron microscopy (SEM) study showed deep cracking associated with the penetration of calcium fluoride. Although intended as a consolidation treatment, it had in fact had the opposite effect, and if the pulpit had appeared on the market with no history or provenance, the surface treatment would have appeared very suspicious.

Internal treatments

Treatments that alter the structure of the material are usually to be avoided wherever possible.

Some excavated pottery can be very soft and it is therefore baked in order to harden it. This was claimed for the forged ceramic figurines and anthropomorphic vessels from Haçilar (see Chapter 9, p. 193). Heating ceramics will inevitably preclude thermoluminescence (TL) testing, although it may at least be possible by judicious use of the pre-dose technique to establish that a ceramic body has been recently re-fired.

Where metal has become extensively mineralised there have been attempts to convert the minerals back to metal either by heating under strongly reducing conditions or by electrolysis.

The silver lyre excavated from the Royal Cemetery at Ur was the subject of rather drastic electrolytic treatments that were deemed to be necessary at the time (Organ, 1967). The silver had become completely mineralised to silver chloride, which, although stable, was very fragile such that pieces kept falling off, and it did not look like silver. The silver chloride was converted back to metallic silver by applying a current through a silver wire. The treatment changed the material completely, but as it is so different from ordinary metallic silver there should be no difficulty in recognising this, and it would also have a structure very different from that of an electroform (see Chapter 4, p. 81).

The treatment of corroding iron has long been one of the main problems in conservation. This is due to the presence of deep-seated minerals, mainly sulphides or chlorides, that are difficult to remove by mechanical means or by washing (Croyn, 1990, pp. 195–202). Consequently, a number of alternative methods have been developed. Back in 1888 the Egyptologist Flinders Petrie recommended baking corroded iron in an oven as part of the treatment, and Barker *et al.* (1982) developed a much more drastic technique to convert the iron corrosion salts back to metallic iron by heating at 800°–900°C in an atmosphere of hydrogen. After this treatment the corrosion as well as the internal structure would be lost (Tylecote and Black, 1980), making scientific authentication all but impossible. The new surface could be characteristic

of the treatment, but would be quite easy to replicate such that a forgery resembles a treated antiquity.

A less destructive but less effective alternative was developed using low-pressure plasmas operating at between 300° and 400°C for several hours (Veprek *et al.*, 1985). These temperatures have latterly been much reduced (Schmidt-Ott and Boissonnas, 2002), but even the newly recommended temperatures can still bring about changes in the metallographic structure, thereby compromising the record of the heat treatments (Craddock and Lang, 2005b). After the plasma treatment, the loosened iron salts are removed mechanically or by dissolution. This combination of internal and surface modification could make plasma-treated iron difficult to authenticate.

Conservation as part of the life history of an object can sometimes actually aid the authentication process. This situation obtains when the past treatments were carried out using methods and materials that are no longer used but which can be identified, although unfortunately not much has been written to document early treatments, especially with regard to the date range when they were used (but see Daniels (ed), 1988; Gilberg and Vivian, 2001; and Clarke, B., 2001, on prints and drawings). For example, traces of zinc on the surface of a bronze could be evidence that it had been treated electrochemically (see Chapter 7, p. 137 and see Chapter 14, p. 352). The consolidants used to impregnate weak materials have changed through the years, with the periods of their use being reasonably well documented. For example, phenolic resins of the Bakelite type (see Chapter 18, p. 459) were used as a consolidant between the 1920s and 1940s mainly on fossil bone and wood, although they have also been found in stone (Ventikou, 1999).

The value of knowing past restoration techniques is exemplified by a Seljuk lustre-glazed ewer examined by Koob (1999). This, when found, must have been no more than a very incomplete set of sherds. Ceramic replacements were made of the missing sherds and the pieces were reassembled, the vessel being presented as essentially complete. Koob (1998) had previously studied the fillers used for ceramic restorations over the years and was thus able to identify and approximately date the restoration, supportive that the sherds of the ewer at least, were likely to be genuine.

Restoration

Sources: General: Oddy (ed) (1994). Pictures: Nicolaus (1999, esp. pp. 285–289 on artificial ageing)

Berger (2000); Mayer (nd). Ceramics: Williams (2002); Parsons and Curl (1963).

Attitudes to restoration are extremely variable. They have changed in Europe considerably over the centuries, never more rapidly than during the twentieth century, resulting in the de-restoration of many restored pieces (Berducou, 2001) and some decidedly odd-looking antiquities. Attitudes to restoration are also very different from one culture to another, and there is a noticeable difference between East and West at the present time. In the East the aim is often to restore to original condition by replacement, whereas in the West some retention of age is usually required. There are even differences in approach between different types of artefact and material.

An example of the latter is provided by a Roman mirror in the British Museum (Craddock, 1983). This had long been regarded as being of bronze, and, as such, left in a patinated state (Figure 20.4a). But routine analysis showed that the disc was silver

with 8% of copper and 24% in the cast handle, and the quite attractive purple–brown patina was not copper oxide but silver chloride. Once it was established that the mirror was of silver, the corrosion products – for such they had now become – were immediately removed and the metal was polished (Figure 20.4b). It was fortunate that the discovery was made and published while the mirror was in the Museum's collections as it would now be impossible to establish its authenticity.

It is not the purpose of this section to review the various approaches to restoration, but only to discuss those aspects of the treatments that are likely to affect authenticity studies. As with conservation, these can be divided into surface and internal treatments.

Surface cleaning

Soil traces remaining on the surface can often provide useful indications not only of authenticity, but of

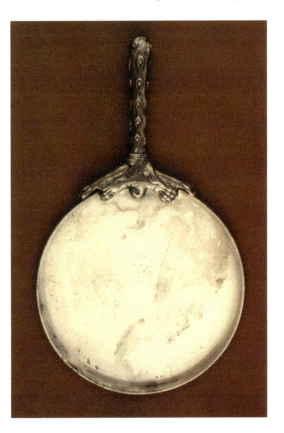

Figure 20.4a Changes in attitude: A Roman 'bronze' mirror with a preserved patina (BM GR Reg. 1856, 12–26, 808).

Figure 20.4b The same mirror after it was discovered that it was silver. The silver corrosion products have been removed and it has been vigorously polished. (Courtesy J. Heffron/British Museum)

provenance, and even identity (Elia, 1995; O'Keefe, 1995). For example, in the legal case between the Union of India and the Bunker Development Corporation Ltd, in the High Court in London (4 All ER 638) concerning the illegal export from India of a superb bronze Shiva Nataraja of the Chola period (Ghandi and James, 1992), much of the debate concerned the association or otherwise of the Nataraja with other bronzes that had been dug up from within the Visawanatha temple enclosure in the village of Pattur in the Cauvery Delta of Tamil Nadu in southern India. The Nataraja had been seized in London, where the treatment involved the removal of the adhering soil. Fortunately the job had not been completed (Figure 20.5a) and the very distinctive evidence of termite runs and brick fragments (Figure 20.5b) exactly matched the soil from the temple site and was the crucial evidence of association, as emphasised by O'Keefe at the 1993 UKIC conference 'Conservation and the Antiquities Trade' (reported by Ward, 1994 and subsequently by O'Keefe, 1995).

The sharpening or re-cutting of worn carved decoration in wood or stone can create problems, as exemplified by the Medieval Courtai Chest where some re-cutting of the design probably just after its discovery at the beginning of the twentieth century led to its being rejected as a nineteenth-century copy (see Chapter 17, p. 445).

Cleaning and re-polishing of surfaces can remove the evidence of authenticity. For example, the practice exists of grinding away the original surfaces of old Chinese porcelain and other glazed ceramics, resulting in the loss of the characteristic appearance of wear indicative of age and authenticity (Thompson, 1994). The surface is abraded away to remove all but the deepest scratches, and then polished with fine carborundum powder under water to produce an as-new appearance, which can further enhanced by waxing.

The temptation to over-polish artefacts of precious metal can result in their authenticity being called into question. The splendid Late Saxon silver brooch, known as the Fuller Brooch and now in the British Museum (BM PE Reg. 1952, 4–4, 1), was once regarded as a forgery because of over-cleaning (Bruce-Mitford, 1956).

Gold alloys that have been buried for considerable periods of time acquire a distinctive rather matt appearance where the more base metals, notably silver and copper, have been leached from the surface (see Chapter 15, p. 372). This is one of the few ways of authenticating ancient gold artefacts and the removal of such ageing features by polishing can have serious consequences. This is well exemplified by an ancient Egyptian gold headdress that was suspected of being a forgery because it was so heavily polished.

Figure 20.5a   Shiva's head with the locks on the proper left side cleaned and the soil still attached to the locks on the right side. (Reproduced with kind permission of the Government of India)

Figure 20.5b   Underside of the base of the Nataraja, revealing the remains of termite runs, brick fragments and a soil type identical to that found on the other bronzes and to the soil from the pit from which they are all believed to have been dug. (Reproduced with kind permission of the Government of India)

Case study: Egyptian statuette and headdress, antiquity re-established (Jones (ed), 1990, pp. 292–294)

In 1908 Sir William Budge of the British Museum, while travelling in the Nile Delta of Egypt, was shown the group of materials illustrated in Figure 20.6. It comprises a serpentine statuette, together with a chain, mask, fragmentary wig and a massive crown, all of gold (Budge 1914, pp. 19–20, pl. XLII). A factor cited in favour of authenticity was that this group of very valuable materials, with over half a kilogram of gold, was offered to Budge directly by the peasants who claimed to have found it, and who would not normally be expected to have access to the necessary resources for such a costly forgery, if such it is. However Wakeling (1912, pp. 11–19) recorded, at just this time, elaborate schemes between dealers and farmers to allay the suspicions of collectors, by which faked and forged antiquities were offered for sale by the poor, ignorant peasants who had supposedly found them. The specific case Wakeling described concerned forged gold antiquities in the Delta.

Figure 20.6 But do they belong? Egyptian bust of serpentine allegedly found together with the gold necklace, mask, wig and headdress, BM EA Reg. 48994-8. The gold headdress is at first glance very modern-looking. TL on the core material suggests that it is authentic, despite the impression given by ruinous over-cleaning and polishing. (© British Museum)

This group has been suspect for many years mainly because the various elements seem stylistically and iconographically at variance with one another. Also the crown, which with 350 grams of gold is by far the most costly item, has a very bright fresh polish – it looks new.

Scientific examination of the gold showed the metal of all of the items except the mask to contain about 80% of gold, the remainder being silver with a small amount of copper, consistent with ancient goldwork. The thin sheet metal of the mask is of almost pure gold, i.e. refined metal, which should post-date the mid first millennium BC when gold refining was introduced (see Chapter 15, p. 370). The wig is inlaid with lapis lazuli, which X-ray diffraction (XRD) showed was consistent with coming from the Afghan source used in antiquity (see Chapter 10, p. 411).

The gold items, with the exception of the mask, contain the small, distinctive, silvery-white PGE inclusions, which are typical of ancient goldwork obtained from stream or placer deposits (see Chapter 15, p. 369). It is conceivable that unrefined gold could have been obtained directly from placer deposits being mined at the beginning of the twentieth century in California or Australia, for example. Petrie (Petrie and Quibell, 1896) had already noted and presciently identified the PGE inclusions found in ancient Egyptian gold artefacts long before these antiquities were acquired; however, their potential significance in authenticity studies was not to be realised for at least another 60 years after the purchase of the group. Thus their presence is a strong indication that the gold metal at least is of some antiquity.

The face mask has the distinctive pinky-red deposit found on much ancient Egyptian gold, identified by XRD as being a gold sulphide (see Chapter 15, p. 372). This was often imitated by Egyptian forgers with a thin coat of a red lacquer (Wakeling, 1912, p. 23). As the mineral responsible for the red color was only identified long after this group was purchased, its presence is strong evidence of authenticity (Frantz and Schorsch, 1990).

There was still the problem of the crown, which does not belong stylistically with the group, or even fit properly on the head. It was possible, even though it was of ancient gold, as evidenced by the composition and the presence of a PGE inclusion, that it was not itself an antiquity. Old but badly damaged pieces of gold could have been bought at scrap metal prices and melted down to cast the crown, thereby hugely adding to the value of the whole group. Examination of the interior of the tall crown revealed small quantities of sandy core material surviving in the upper interstices, and this was removed for TL testing by the fine grain method. The results of this were somewhat anomalous, possibly suggesting some light bleaching, but did show that there had been a build-up of TL, suggesting that a considerable time had elapsed since the core was last very hot. Thus, although ill-advised over-cleaning had removed the evidence and even the appearance of age, sufficient core material survived to redeem the authenticity of the crown. Its association with the remaining items of the group is uncertain, but all are antiquities.

Heat treatments

Ancient artefacts of gold and silver alloys are characterised by an enhanced gold content at their surface owing either to deliberate treatment or to long burial (see Chapter 15, p. 372). Whether natural or deliberate, even quite gentle heat will remove this, as exemplified by some of the gold artefacts excavated by Woolley at Ur. Most were not heat-treated as part of their conservation treatment and retain their gold-enhanced surfaces, but one piece was recorded as being heated and now has a uniform composition throughout (La Niece, 1995). Here the records of the treatment were invaluable in understanding the present condition of the artefact.

Internal treatments

Where metal artefacts have been badly distorted it is usually necessary to anneal them before and during their restoration. This requires them to be heated to red heat (c. 600°C) and thus most of the original metallographic structure will be lost together with any patina the piece may have had. The internal structure of some metals such as silver can undergo quite pronounced changes over time, and these have been suggested as constituting evidence of age (see Chapter 15, p. 388). Such evidence will be removed by annealing treatments such as that applied by Organ (1967) during the restoration of a libation cup from Nuri in the Sudan, dating to about 500 BC (Figures 20.7a, 20.7b and 20.8).

This was an excavated piece and its treatment was fully recorded, but similarly treated pieces with no records, appearing on the market, would be difficult to authenticate. However, it might still be apparent that a piece had once had brittle fractures (Figure 20.7a) and that annealing had taken place.

Different approaches to restoration can be shown by the treatments applied to three Roman silver treasures found in Britain, varying from gentle surface cleaning with little invasive or chemical treatment, through full restoration of the original shape and surface polish, to a postulated re-creation of an individual piece by recasting the fragments. The role of such records as were made of the treatments in understanding the present condition of such a piece will become obvious, and, certainly, unrecorded treatments can be disastrous for future authentication.

Figure 20.7a Fragments of the silver libation cup from Nuri after annealing and cleaning (see Figure 20.8).

Figure 20.7b The reassembled fragments were moulded and casts taken of the missing areas; electroforms were taken and hard-soldered into place. (Courtesy L. Bell/British Museum)

Figure 20.8 Annealing treatment of the fragments of the libation cup (see Figure 20.7a). They were heated to about 900°C before quenching from red heat as shown here. (Courtesy L. Bell/British Museum)

Case study: The Water Newton Treasure

This group of items (BM Reg. P. 1975, 10-2, 1–27), currently the earliest group of Christian liturgical silver known, was found in a ploughed field in what had been the small Roman town of Durobrivae, which lies beneath present-day Water Newton, in Cambridgeshire (Painter, 1977; Kent and Painter (eds), 1977, pp. 29–33). The silver was not heavily corroded but had suffered some plough damage. The pieces were mechanically cleaned to remove adherent dirt and some of the silver chloride corrosion was removed electrolytically. This sometimes resulted in the deposition of silver metal on the surface, which was removed using ammonium thiosulphate.

Some of the pieces that had been badly damaged by the plough and were very brittle, were annealed with a gas-and-air torch prior to straightening and the missing parts were replaced with fibreglass, thus being clearly distinguishable from the original silver (Figures 20.9a and 20.9b). Fragments were soldered with easy-flo solder, locally heated with micro-welding equipment. The solder was silver-plated to match the rest of the silver, but which should be easily recognisable as being a modern repair.

The polishing was kept to an absolute minimum, using Duroglit. This was because some of the original setting-out lines and tool marks were still evident on the unfinished pieces.

(a)

(b)

Figure 20.9 Silver bowl from the Water Newton Treasure before (a) and after (b) conservation and restoration. (Courtesy J. Heffron/British Museum)

The conservation and restoration treatments carried out meant that there was considerable loss of metallographic structure in the pieces which had been annealed and/or soldered, but overall the original structure was preserved. The chemical removal of the corrosion products also compromised evidence that could be of value in authenticity studies, although every care was taken to preserve the physical appearance of the surfaces even when that meant the pieces could not be properly polished.

Case study: The Hockwold Treasure

This group of Roman silver cups was found at Hockwold, in Norfolk (BM PR Reg. 1962, 7–7, 1–14) (Johns, 1986, with appendices by R. Holmes and M.J. Hughes). The bowls of the cups had apparently been deliberately stove in before burial and the soldered handles and bases had become detached. The decision was taken to restore the cups to their undamaged state as far as possible, despite the obvious deliberate nature of the original damage. This in itself provides an interesting contrast with the more recent attitude to restoration taken when the equally damaged Bronze Age gold cup from Ringlemere, Kent, was acquired by the British Museum (BM PE Reg 2003, 5-1, 1).

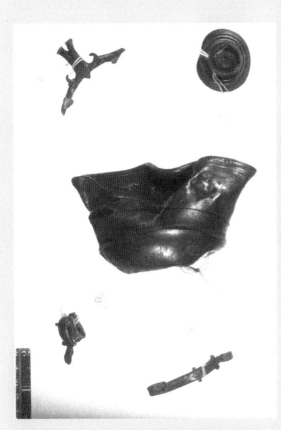

Figure 20.10 Electroform of one of the Hockwold cups – an extreme restoration? (Courtesy L. Bell/British Museum)

Despite the fact that the severe plough-damage must have been inflicted only a short time before the cup's discovery, the decision has been taken not to restore it to its original shape. This provides a further instance of how attitudes to restoration change very rapidly.

The restoration of the Hockwold cups is described in detail by Bob Holmes, who carried out the work (and see Oddy and Holmes, 1992). In order to preserve the form of one of the cups as it had been found, an electroform was made (Figure 20.10). The cups had a thin black patina, identified as silver sulphide, which was removed with acid. Some metallography was performed (but not published) before the restoration, primarily to establish that the thin silver of the bowls was sound enough to be reshaped. The metallography of the handles and bases suggested that they were cast and had then been lightly worked, but Holmes stated that the handles had been forged into shape from a billet.

During burial, the silver had become extremely brittle and all the pieces had to be annealed before any work could be attempted. The very thin silver of the bowls was manipulated, partly by hand and then by placing them over a wooden former and working with a mallet and wooden wedges. No metal tools were used, in order to avoid stretching the metal. The silver was regularly re-annealed throughout the procedure, and was pickled in dilute sulphuric acid after each operation to remove such oxides as had

Figure 20.11   The cup (see Figure 20.10) restored. (Courtesy L. Bell/British Museum)

formed on the surface. The fragmentary pieces and large cracks were joined with a silver solder with a melting point of 690° to 730°C, but the handles and base were reattached using an organic adhesive that could be easily removed (Figure 20.11).

The silver was analysed by X-ray fluorescence (XRF) both before (Hughes and Hall, 1979, Table 2.6, p. 329) and after the restoration and pickling. The metal was of high purity, with a little copper being the only deliberate addition, but the two sets of analyses differed significantly. The four analyses made prior to the restoration showed the metal to consist of between 93 and 95% of silver, 2.7 and 5.6% of copper and 0.9 and 1.5% of lead; those performed afterwards gave values of between 95.5 and 99% for silver, 0.5 and 3% for copper and 0.1 and 0.5% for lead. The preparation of the surface prior to analysis was the same in both instances and the differences are solely attributable to the pickling.

The annealing was performed at red heat, which would have compromised the metallographic evidence of the original metalworking and any evidence of age hardening, etc. that might have been present. In addition, the heating and oxidisation of the surface followed by acid treatment would have removed all surface evidence of age, and preferentially removed the non-precious metals, in this case the copper and lead, from the surface. Thus, in their present state the pieces are not able to be scientifically authenticated, although publication of the restoration procedure means that their authenticity could be inferred from their present condition. The electroform of one of the pieces in the state in which it was found, is an interesting record of the original but which would not really help the authentication process.

Case study: The Risley Lanx, a treasure at one remove?

In 1729 the fragments of a large silver tray or *lanx* were uncovered at Risley Park, midway between Derby and Nottingham in England, and almost immediately came to the notice of William Stukeley, the foremost British antiquarian of the day. He wrote an account of it and in 1730 visited the area, and it was probably at this time that he had the central panel of the lanx drawn. Nothing more was

Figure 20.12   The Risley Lanx. The dark areas were illustrated by Stukeley, and the shaded areas were described by him. The light areas are completely new. (Courtesy J. Heffron/British Museum)

Figure 20.13   Xeroradiograph of the Risley lanx, showing the extensive internal porosity defined by the borders of each fragment. (Courtesy J. Lang/British Museum)

done until 1736, when he was prompted by the discovery of an intact lanx, on the banks of the River Tyne at Corbridge near Newcastle in the north of England, to publish his account of the discovery of both pieces together with engravings of some of the surviving fragments of the Risley Lanx (Stukeley, 1736). Thereafter, all trace was seemingly lost (Johns, 1981).

According to Stukeley, the Risley lanx had been uncovered by the plough which broke off 'a bit'. The lanx was black and brittle, and was soon broken into pieces by those who had discovered it. He stated that 'nothing now remains intire, but the middle part. . . . As many of the fragments as could be got together, were reduc'd into form, and a model made of it in pasteboard, with a drawing upon it in the natural bigness, was sent to me'. This is what Stukeley had engraved.

It had always been assumed that the small number of fragments depicted on the engraving were all that had then survived. However, this is not necessarily the case. It would have been strange for him to have arranged the fragments so precisely if he knew nothing of their true positions. Stukeley actually described one of the corner fragments that is not illustrated. He also stated that 'there are at present seven pounds [3.2 kg] weight in silver', which suggests that considerably more had survived (the present lanx weighs 4.7 kg).

The lanx bore an inscription on its underside, *Exsvperivs episcopvs eclesiae bogiensi dedit*; that is, 'Dedicated to the Church of Bogiensi by Bishop Exsuperius', and most of the remainder of Stukeley's account was devoted to trying to place the location of Bogiensi. Thereafter, the few articles on the lanx concentrated on this aspect; the lanx itself was assumed to be completely lost. In discussing a puzzling aspect of the inscription as described by Stukeley, Johns in her 1981 article stated that 'the only thing we can now be sure of is that nobody will ever be able to establish what word was engraved on the lanx in the fourth century. This is a depressing conclusion, but the only permissable one in the circumstances'.

Circumstances have a habit of changing, especially where antiquities are concerned, and just 9 years after John's article, a large silver lanx made up of 26 fragments, crudely soldered together, was offered to Seaby's, the coin and antiquities dealers in London (Figure 20.12). Six of the fragments, including the central panel, were clearly the same as those depicted on the engraving made for Stukeley, but in addition there were now all the fragments that had apparently already been missing in 1736 (Johns and Painter, 1991).

The lanx was examined with a binocular microscope and by Xeroradiography (Figure 20.13). Analysis was carried out on each of the uncleaned surfaces of all of the fragments using XRF, and three tiny samples were drilled for atomic absorption spectrometry (AAS) analysis. XRD was carried out on some of the material that had become incorporated into the surface of the silver.

It was immediately apparent that the present fragments are individual castings. The metal is very clean and appears new with no signs of ever having been polished. The appearance of the upper side is rather strange: in many places the upstanding decorative features and scenes are very crisp and well delineated but the flat surfaces of the tray surrounding them are quite rough, with an orange-skin texture in places. It is as if the decorative features had been separately and more carefully moulded and then applied to a more coarsely moulded substrate. There are also numerous tiny nodules of silver, particularly in the grooves or channels of the design (Figure 20.14). They result from small air bubbles in the mould, which was filled with metal during the casting. These would usually have been filed or chiselled away unless an exact copy was required. Similarly, there are cold shots; that is, where droplets of metal adhering to the side of the mould in the first moments of the pouring of the metal had frozen and failed to melt in with the rest of the metal when they were enveloped. The surface of the lines of the inscription on the underside showed that although they had the appearance of being lightly chased or scorbed, they were actually casts of a worked surface.

Xeroradiography of the lanx revealed a great deal of intergranular porosity in the fragments, confirming that the metal is in an as-cast condition (see Figure 20.13). The pattern of the porosity was different in each fragment and never crossed breaks, showing that the fragments had been individually cast. The foot-ring had been attached on the original by quantities of solder that had been rather carelessly applied. Once again the small nodules on the present surface show that it is a cast of the original soldered join. Some of the fragments have cracks but closer examination show that these are now casts of cracks with nodules on their surfaces, and do not extend into the metal as the originals would have done.

In places, the nodules are present on casting faults, as if the present pieces are casts of casts, as was suggested by Johns and Painter (1991). However, this is indicative of the indirect lost wax process where there are two moulding stages, a negative cast being taken of the original with plaster and then a positive being made from that with the wax (see Chapter 4, p. 69).

In a very few places there are small, flat depressions in the surface, and one of them still contained rough, grey, ferruginous material. This was shown by XRD to contain aluminium magnesium silicate and the iron oxide magnetite, and almost certainly came from the clay of the mould. On pouring the metal into the mould, small scabs became detached and a few came to rest against the mould surface thereby creating a negative defect.

XRF analysis showed all but one of the fragments to have been cast from a very similar alloy, with approximately 95% of silver, 1% of gold, between 2 and 3% of copper and between about 0.05 and 0.2% of lead (NB because of the lavish and rather careless use of lead solder to join the fragments, the lead figures are unreliable). One fragment had a different composition with about 6.7% of copper and only 0.1% of gold. The analysis of the three drillings by AAS suggested that the XRF surface analyses are broadly representative of the body metal. The solders that presently join

Figure 20.14 Detail of the surface of the Risley lanx showing small nodules of silver sitting on the surface (circled lower) as well as in some of the lines of the incised design (circled upper right), showing that the piece is a cast not an original. (Courtesy S. La Niece/British Museum)

the fragments are soft solders containing lead, tin and antimony. However, a later repair has been made where the lanx broke in two, more or less along the line of the central breaks. The repair was effected using a soft solder containing cadmium, which was only used as a component of solders from the mid-nineteenth century onwards (see Chapter 15, p. 381).

The fragments are separate castings and therefore cannot be the original fragments of the lanx having apparently been broken up by the farm workers soon after its discovery. Clearly the original silver had become very brittle during burial. Stukeley recorded that the pieces had been reduced into form and a pasteboard model made, suggesting a rough mould had been made. Could it be that more of the fragments survived than was reported in Stukeley's article, and that when, some time later, the lanx was restored, it was decided that the fragments were too brittle to be used in their present state, and that rather than anneal them the silver would be used to make casts from the moulds? This is supported by the composition of the silver, which is very similar to the composition of Roman plate (Hughes and Hall, 1979) for all but one of the fragments. The one exception has a composition that approximates to that of sterling silver, having 7.5% of copper, and the 0.1% of gold is typical of silver used in Britain in the eighteenth century. The pieces would have been cast one at a time, with the sprues and risers also requiring to be filled with silver. When the last mould was ready, even if there had been no loss of silver in the re-melting and casting processes, there still would not have been enough to fill the mould and its sprue and risers and additional silver would inevitably have had to have been added, thus explaining the one different analysis.

After casting the pieces were probably not joined until much later because the present solder is very crude and seems totally out of character with the very careful moulding work.

If this is indeed the explanation for the features observed on the lanx, it calls into question the status of the restored piece or its connection with the original, and making formal authentication not only impossible, but probably meaningless, although the correct composition is an indicator.

Alternatively, the very clean and untarnished condition of the piece may suggest that it is of no age at all, but a very clever forgery, made in response to Johns' 1981 article, presenting the curator with the object she would most want to accept.

Through the 1990s the British Museum was offered, from the same source as the lanx (the Greenhalgh family based in a terraced council house in Bolton), a series of ever more bizarre, supposedly major, artefacts of Roman plate and jewellery. These often contained many kg of pure gold or silver, but were manifestly modern creations, very different in concept and execution from the very careful rendition of the Risley lanx castings, from whatever original they were taken.

Whilst this book was in proof stage events moved further on, and the vendors of the lanx were prosecuted and found guilty of the forgery and sale of what purported to be an ancient Egyptian alabaster statuette, and then admitted to a whole series of art forgeries, ranging from 19th century paintings, through 20th century studio ceramics to gold and silver antiquities including the Risley lanx.

This, at a stroke, would seem to answer the question posed in a previous paragraph, but doubts still linger, at least in the author's mind. Maybe this is nothing more than the syndrome, noted in some previous chapters (p. 309, for example), of the refusal to believe in the evidence regarding the authenticity or otherwise of an artefact, even when plainly stated and obvious to everyone else, but as Peter Pallister and Hilary Carter wrote in *The Guardian* for 29th January 2008:

> *Even today, after lengthy investigations the family remains an enigma. How did Shaun [Greenhalgh], who left school without qualifications, manage to acquire his dazzling talent, not only in copying such varied art forms but also in sourcing original materials and creating elaborate provenances?*

Bronze restorations

Gao Lian, the Chinese scholar of the Ming dynasty who wrote extensively on the forging of antique bronzes with false patinas (see Chapter 14, p. 356), also wrote about deceptive restoration. In his book

Zun sheng ba jian, published in 1591 (Kerr, 1990, p. 74) he stated that:

> *Now when objects of the Three Dynasties, and Han are minus a leg, have a lug broken, or the vessel body is damaged by a hole here, or a piece missing there,*

Figure 20.15 An apparently intact Chinese bronze fan ding (BM OA Reg. 1973. 7–26, 4). (Courtesy J. Heffron/ British Museum)

Figure 20.16 The fan ding examined by UV radiation, causing areas of artificial make-up to fluoresce. (Courtesy J. Heffron/British Museum)

these are not forged. Nowadays broken pieces can be fused by cold and hot methods. With the cold method of fusing bronze, the ancient color does not change; but with hot soldering the fused area is comparatively a little darker than other parts of the vessel. If lead has been used for repairs in conjunction with cold fusing [Plate 20.17], wax is used to fill up the décor, and within the vessel, yellow mountain clay is applied thickly to cover up the joins, appearing as the earth naturally found on excavated articles. Actually archaic vessels are seldom perfect [i.e. complete in all detail]; when compared with forged vessels they are greatly different.

Cited in Barnard (1961, p. 208)

Gao Lian also records the complete fabrication of vessels from ancient fragments:

Again there are cases of broken fragments of old vessels, each genuinely archaic, but the construction of the complete vessel only is new . . . When I was in the capital I saw two such vessels; one, known as the Tsu Fu Ting which was small and serviceable; they all liked the lay-out of its décor. It was forged by using the lid of an archaic Hu-vessel as the belly and fragments of broken vessels from ancient graves were fused together helter-skelter above it, the lugs of an ancient Ting-vessel were used for its own and it was finally made to appear as a Lu-vessel. It cannot be regarded as an authentic object. The other was a square vessel called the Ya Fu Ting, within and without it was covered with quicksilver and there was not a trace of decay on any part of it . . . I examined it carefully and saw that it was made from broken fragments of a mercury-covered square mirror which had been made into square pieces and fused together, by the cold process [i.e. by gluing], to form the four sides; fragmentary

lugs and the legs of a Lu-vessel completed the object; the workmanship was quite cleverly done . . .

Cited in Barnard (1961, p. 209)

This Chinese bronze *fan-ding* (Jones (ed), 1990; Cat. 308, p. 279) (Figure 20.15) is a genuine antiquity and apparently complete. UV showed that a false patina had been applied in some areas (Figure 20.16), which aroused suspicions, and radiography penetrated this disguise to reveal the major breaks and very crude repairs beneath the plaster make-up (Figure 20.17).

The restoration and improvement of stone sculpture

Sources: Howard (1990); Vaughan (1992); Bohlmann (1996); Grossman *et al.* (eds) (2003); Kunze and Rügler (eds) (2003).

Ancient stone sculpture is often fragmentary. Thus, from the Renaissance on when serious collecting of antiquities began in Europe, sculptures were often the subject of considerable restoration to enhance their value. Restoration ranged from the careful assembly of the conjoining fragments to the creation of completely spurious works from unrelated but often ancient fragments. For a variety of reasons this work reached its apogee in Italy in the eighteenth century, and the development of the restoration of sculpture there forms an interesting study in the often ambivalent and changing attitudes to restoration generally. After two centuries of restoration, de-restoration and even re-restoration, the subject is still contentious. This is of some importance, for how the present perceives the past is to some degree

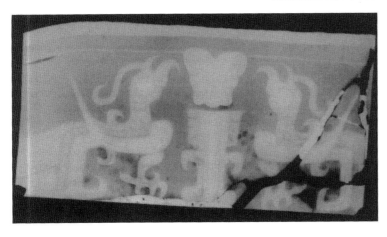

Figure 20.17 Radiograph revealing the major break hidden beneath. Note the dense white blobs of lead-based solder, effecting a very rough repair. (Courtesy J. Lang/British Museum)

conditioned by how the present currently chooses to view the surviving material culture generally.

In Medieval Europe fragments of classical antiquity were reset as curios or as conscious associations with the prestige of imperial wealth and power. Attitudes changed in the Renaissance and the abundant fragments of classical antiquity were valued as artistic creations in their own right. Restoration was often called for, and in Italy the restoration of statuary was seen as an integral part of the sculptor's work, which even the greatest of the Renaissance sculptors such Donatello and Verrocchio readily undertook. Already in the early sixteenth century, sculptors such as Lorenzetti di Ludvico were running large workshops devoted to the repair of antique sculpture. The familiarity with the antique that this engendered must in no small part explain the facility of the Italian sculptors to copy earlier styles and the seemingly never-ending flow of convincing sculpture forgeries from Italy.

These early attitudes to restoration were often very different from later concepts of restoration, with the original fragments often providing no more than an inspiration for what was otherwise, to all intents, an original work. Thus, Cellini described 'restoring' a torso into Ganymede teasing Zeus with an eagle (now in the Bagello, Florence). The Renaissance artist and writer Georgio Vasari believed that restoration should try to make the assembly of pieces appear as though they were but breaks in an original work, justifying this by stating that:

Antiquities, thus restored, have certainly a much more graceful effect than those mutilated trunks, those members without a head, or other figures defective and maimed in their various parts.

Milanesi (1878–85, III, p. 152)

Case study: Changing identities

A marble head, Cat. 614, now in the Ny Carlsberg Glyptotek, Copenhagen, once believed to be of Livia, the wife of Augustus Caesar, comprises three separate pieces, the head, the skull cap and the nose (Herz, 1990). Neutron activation analysis (NAA), petrography and stable isotope analysis (SIA) (see Chapter 11, p. 248), showed that the main bulk of the head was of Parian marble, from Greece, but that the skull cap was of marble from quarries near Ephesus in Turkey and the nose was Carrara marble from Italy. A likely scenario is that a damaged antique head of Parian marble was restored with a fragment from another ancient statue of approximately the same size, and that the nose was a replacement made from a piece of recently quarried Carrara marble.

Shorn of these alien pieces, the head is currently identified as being of Agrippina, the wife of Claudius.

The creation of sculptural groups with little or no relation to the original components, but posing as restorations, was already causing serious problems in the nascent study of ancient sculpture. By the eighteenth century the art historian Johann Joachim Winckelmann deplored the errors that scholars were led into by capricious restorations. The influence that these restorations sometimes had is well exemplified by the Discobolus of Myron.

Case study: Looking both ways – The Discobolus of Myron

Sources: Howard (1962; 1990, pp. 70–77); Jones (ed) (1990, Cat. 144, pp. 140–141); Vaughan (1992); Geominy (2003).

One of the most celebrated statues of antiquity was the bronze statue of a discus thrower made in the fifth century BC by the Greek sculptor Myron, described by Roman writers and widely copied in marble. Substantial fragments had been discovered from the sixteenth century but not recognised, and

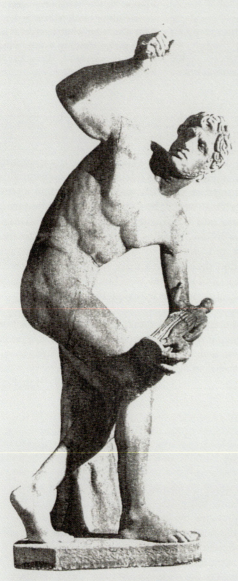

Figure 20.18 The Lansdowne Discobolus, Bowood House, heavily restored but at least with its replacement head facing in the correct direction.

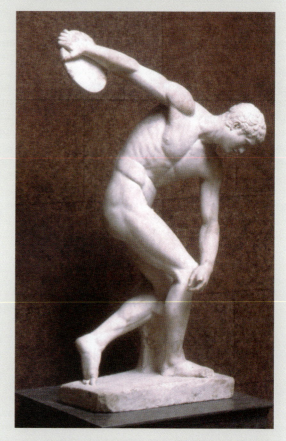

Figure 20.19 The Townley Discobolus (BM GR Reg. 1814, 7-4, 43). The head, which does not belong with the torso, faces forwards. (© British Museum)

currently there are about 20 known ancient marble copies, all in a more or less fragmentary state. One torso now in the Uffizi Gallery, Florence, found, possibly, in the sixteenth century, was originally restored as Endymion, later to be re-restored as one of the Niobid, in a group of Niobi and her children. Another torso became a fallen warrior and a third was restored by Cavaceppi (see p. 516) as Diomedes carrying off the Palladion, such are the vagaries of restoration (Picón, 1983, pp. 22–25). At last in the 1780s a torso was found that was sufficiently complete to be recognisable as being a copy of Myron's lost masterpiece (Geominy, 2003). Although inevitably damaged and restored by a student of Cavaceppi, it was clear that the discus-thrower's head was turned towards the discus. Other Discobolus torsos that were not initially recognised as such had the head turned in the same direction (Figure 20.18).

In 1791 another Discobolus torso was found at Hadrian's villa at Tivoli, near Rome. After restoration it was sold by the dealer Thomas Jenkins to the knowledgeable collector Charles Townley, and subsequently acquired by the British Museum. It was now complete with a head which faced forwards (Figure 20.19). Townley immediately pointed out this discrepancy. Jenkins assured Townley

that the head had been found with the other fragments of the statue, pointing out the similar veining in the marble, and thus it certainly belonged. In Jenkins' view, if the restoration was not totally accurate it was better, and the original was 'forced and certainly disgusting to the sight'.

In fact, as Jenkins had pointed out, the head is of identical Carrara marble and does have very similar veining, strongly suggesting that the marble for both torso and head were quarried at much the same time and thus it is likely that they formed part of a major consignment of statuary carved for Hadrian's villa, and in all probability were found together. However, it is certain that the head does not belong. Sufficient of the original neck remains on the torso to show that the original head did indeed turn. Some of the Adam's apple survives on the torso neck, and also on the head neck, such that the poor Discobolus now has two, as Howard (1990) observed (Figure 20.20).

When yet another torso was found at Hadrian's villa, a replacement head was carved also facing away from the discus. Although it seems to have been generally recognised from quite early in the nineteenth century that the head on the Townley Discobolus was not original and faced the wrong way, the incorrect version was usually preferred, an interesting example of fakery influencing art history and taste.

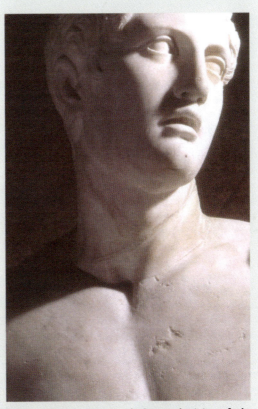

Figure 20.20 Detail of the neck join of the Discobolus showing that he apparently has two Adam's apples. (Courtesy T. Springett/British Museum)

Through the eighteenth century the demand grew for classical statuary to grace the stately homes of Europe, now built in a classical style; the statuary was generally required to be complete and, if that necessitated extensive restoration, then so be it. The collectors of

antique sculpture wanted entire pieces; for example, Thomas Jenkins remarked of one of his clients 'Lord Tavistock would not pay a guinea for the finest torso ever discovered' (Dallaway, quoted in Vaughan, 1992, p. 43). The particular torso that Jenkins wished to

516 Scientific Investigation of Copies, Fakes and Forgeries

acquire lacked a head, and, once Jenkins had obtained one and had had the statue 'restored' by Cavaceppi, the piece was sold on to another collector for considerably more than 21 shillings. Some such as Townley really were connoisseurs concerned above all for the preservation of the original form of the piece, but many others just wanted reasonably complete attractive statuary that incorporated at least some ancient pieces.

Thus a veritable industry arose assembling individual statues or whole groups from fragments that generally did belong together, to which were added heads and limbs from other figures. Care had to be taken with the selection of pieces and thus the major workshops kept large stocks of fragments. The most prolific and influential restorer of the eighteenth century was Bartolemo Cavaceppi.

Case study: Bartolemo Cavaceppi, 'doyen of the restorer–contrafactors'

Sources: Howard (1982, 1992); Jones (ed) (1990, pp. 140–144); Müller-Kaspar (1994, 1995); Barberini (2003); Ramage (2003).

Bartolemo Cavaceppi (1716[?]–1799) came from a family of sculptors based in Rome, and was a talented and industrious sculptor who specialised in restoring ancient work rather than creating new work (although some of his forgeries of classical sculpture should be classed as original work, and are actually rather good).

Through his long career his workshop dealt with several thousand pieces, often recorded in the three volumes of his *Raccolta d'antiche statue, busti …* (Cavaceppi, 1768–1772) (Figure 20.21), including some of the most famous and familiar pieces of classical sculpture. He always used white marble, usually Carrara, for the restored additions, attached to the main body of the sculpture with iron dowels. The subsequent corrosion of these in the damp halls of northern Europe has often led to splitting and discoloration of the marble. His stated aim was to make the restoration appear like a repair, i.e. a re-join of an original piece back to the body. Thus, it is often quite easy to detect the joins that Cavaceppi admitted existed. However, the restorations that he did not admit to can be much more difficult to detect. To make the original match with the new work, the surface of the original was often harshly cleaned with rasps and with acids before being given the same high polish as the restoration received. This sometimes led to evidence of original coloring being removed. Townley complained that Cavaceppi had taken off the original red paint from his statue of Jupiter Serapis. This gives some insight into Cavaceppi's priorities: the creation of a fine white surface outweighed preserving the original.

Cavaceppi's restored sculptures do have a distinctive style and appearance, which, owing to their number and importance, have come to influence our perception of antiquity to this day. He favoured a rather chaste style with smooth, highly polished white surfaces, which influenced the next generation of neo-classical sculptors, notably Canova.

Cavaceppi's restorations, in common with some others in the eighteenth century, were much more accurate and informed than those of previous centuries. He clearly possessed a deep knowledge and understanding of classical statuary, being familiar with the new discipline of art history then being expounded by Winckelmann, who in return knew of and generally approved of Cavceppi's restorations, even though he himself was on occasion deceived. In the *Raccolta* Cavaceppi made it clear that the objective should be to restore the damaged or incomplete piece to what was believed to be the original appearance. He insisted that he fully documented the true extent of the restorations made. Unfortunately, reality was rather different, with the stated high ideals of restoration often subsumed in the interests of the creation of the most saleable pastiche out of the random available fragments. As well as the total forgeries, many of the pieces were much more heavily restored than was admitted. Cavaceppi and his fellow restorers were not solely responsible for this deception as they were often instructed in their restoration by the dealers, such as Jenkins.

Studio di Bartolomeo Cavaceppi, ove sono state restaurate le Statue contenute nella presente Raccolta

Figure 20.21 Frontispiece to Cavaceppi's *Raccolta d'antiche statue* depicting his workshop in Rome with Cavaceppi himself sketching (lower left), and workmen variously cutting new inscriptions (lower right), repairing statuary (centre left) and cleaning (back). Several statues are standing in measuring frames, to be copied.

This attitude, already questioned in the eighteenth century, was to change in the nineteenth century. There arose a preference among collectors and curators for displaying sculpture unrestored. This change was most firmly and famously stated by Antonio Canova, the leading sculptor of the early nineteenth century when, in 1816, he refused to undertake the proposed restoration of the Elgin marbles, stating that no one should presume to recreate the work of Phidias.

This attitude was not universal, and, apart from deceptive restoration, some leading sculptors continued to carry out restoration, most famously Canova's Danish pupil, Bertel Thorvaldsen. His designs for the restoration of the sculptures from the west pediment of the Temple of Athena at Aigina, displayed in the Munich Glypothek Museum, were executed around 1816 by Finelli and set in a pediment in 1906 (Figure 20.22). This very complete painted restoration certainly gave a good impression of how such a sculptural group might have appeared in antiquity and their very thorough de-restoration in the late twentieth century is as famous as it was controversial (Figure 20.23).

De-restoration

Sources: Naud (1995); Restauration (1995); Berducou, 2001; Moltesen (2003); Ramage (2003).

As part of the general reaction against the restorations of the eighteenth century and later, many sculptures were de-restored in an attempt to return them as far as possible to their original surviving state as described in the previous sections.

De-restoration has often revealed both that the restoration had been far more extensive than previously believed, and the extent of further damage that had been inflicted on the originals during the restoration, with extremities sawn off in order to better accommodate the replacements. Some pieces looked so odd shorn of the additions that they been adapted to fit, that an active campaign of

Figure 20.22 The restored statuary set in a recreation of the west pediment of the Temple of Athena Aphai at Aigina. (Courtesy Howard, 1990)

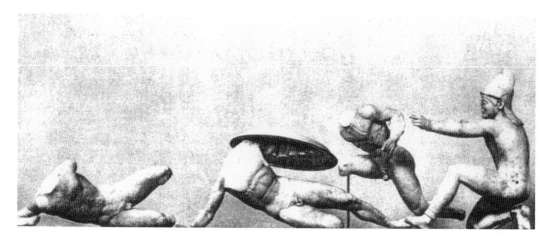

Figure 20.23 The left wing of the pediment at Aigina (see Figure 20.22) after de-restoration. (Courtesy Howard, 1990)

re-restoration began in some collections, with original work suffering once again from a change in taste. By and large, present opinion favours leaving things as they are now, the earlier restorations being appreciated as documents of earlier attitudes to antiquity, and also sometimes, as with Cavaceppi's work, the quality of the new composition is recognised. No one would presently de-restore the British Museum's Discobolus, even if the head does point the wrong way!

Attitudes change quickly, as exemplified by the Lansdowne *Herakles*. The statue had been heavily restored in Italy in the eighteenth century before coming to England, and was complete. After purchase by the J. Paul Getty Museum in 1976 it was comprehensively de-restored. In his 1994 article the Getty curator Jerry Podany seemingly distanced himself from the de-restoration performed but 14 years previously. He noted that, before de-restoration, the statue had been a good example of eighteenth-century taste and skill. Now it was nothing, not even a viable antiquity.

Case study: The Piranesi Vase

The famous Piranesi Vase (Figure 20.24) is a good example of a partial de-restoration revealing the full extent of deceptive restoration as well as the rapidly changing attitudes to restoration generally (Opper, 2005). The vase was described by its vendor, the engraver-turned-antiquarian, G.R. Piranesi,

Figure 20.24 The restored Piranesi Vase (GR Sculpture Cat. 2502). (© British Museum)

Figure 20.25 Detail of the Vase (see Figure 20.24), the few original bits (darker) now showing prominently against the restorations, certainly not Piranesi's intention! (Courtesy T. Springett/British Museum)

as being in wonderful condition. It would have been known at the time that there was some restoration involved, but there was no suggestion that this amounted to at least 70%, and that the base and stem might be from altogether different pieces. This only became fully apparent after extensive dismantling and cleaning in the 1980s prior to featuring in the British Museum's *Fake?* exhibition (Jones (ed), 1990, p. 133; Miller, 1992). Piranesi's original restoration set the various fragments in plaster, skilfully treated on the surface, to match the original ancient carved marble and the new Carrara marble. Miller's restoration involved replacing the plaster with a mixture of pulverised marble and paraloid B-72, an acrylic co-polymer. This was touched up with acrylic paints: 'Within the limitations of the materials, the intention was to make the joints and other repairs as unobtrusive as possible'. More recently the Vase was chosen as the centrepiece of the Enlightenment gallery, entirely appropriate as it was very much a creation of that period. However, the emphasis of the treatment this time round was on contrasting the variegated surface of the original stone with the more recent additions: 'The extent of the work [i.e. Piranesi's] can now be better appreciated than at the time when it was in Piranesi's workshop. There, it would have received a final coating that concealed all transitions between the ancient and modern parts' (Opper, 2005) (Figure 20.25).

Investigation
With large sculptures such as statuary, if the fragments to be attached to the torso were also large, such as the limbs or the head, then an iron pin or dowel would usually be used to hold the addition securely to the main body. The space between would be filled with a mason's mortar, for which there many recipes, from those given by Orfeo Boselli in the sixteenth century (Weil, 1967) to the nineteenth-century recipes recorded in Spon (1882, pp. 386–393). They often include a resinous material such as rosin, waxes, ground marble and appropriate pigments. Modern equivalents use synthetic materials such as polyesters and epoxy resins. (NB statuary was often assembled from pieces in antiquity; see Claridge, 1990, for the ancient methods of joining the components.)

Restorations are usually fairly easy to detect visually, especially if the passage of many years has caused the artificial patination to change color and some of the cements to discolor and decay.

The true extent of restoration can often be revealed by UV (see Chapter 11, p. 258, Figure 11.5) (Dubrana, 2001) and radiography (see Chapter 2, p. 28, Figures 2.6 and 2.7, and La Niece, 2005) or by CT (see Chapter 2, p. 32, Figure 2.11). Bourgeois *et al.* (1996) applied γ radiography to some large statuary which X-rays would not have penetrated.

Very often the original work was found in a number of pieces to which others were added, and the need exists to establish which are the original pieces. Here techniques such as SIA, electron spin resonance (ESR) and others used to characterise marble (see Chapter 11, p. 248) can be useful (Matthews, 1988). Pensabene *et al.* (2002) studied the surviving fragments of the colossal statue of Constantine the Great that lie in the Palazzo dei Conservatori in Rome, petrologically and by SIA. This established beyond doubt that the main statue was of a single piece of Parian marble, with additions of Carrara marble.

Case study: Relief with three (?) pairs of captive Amazons

Sources: Jones (1990, p. 283); Walker *et al.* (1993).

The relief originally ran around the lid of a sarcophagus and has been known since it was drawn in 1577 by Giovannantonio Dosio. His drawing omits the two figures on the right, and indeed there is a straight join in the marble separating them from the others to the left (Figure 20.26). This

Figure 20.26 Detail of the relief with captive Amazons (BM GR Reg. 1805, 7-3, 135), showing an apparent addition to the right. SIA measurements showed that the piece came from the same block of marble as did the remainder and hence the relief is all original. (Courtesy T. Springett/ British Museum)

suggested that the frieze could subsequently have been extended. However, SIA on samples taken from both ends of the current frieze show beyond reasonable doubt that all six Amazons had been carved on the same piece of Carrara marble.

Enamel restorations

The applied arts of Medieval and Renaissance Europe began to be seriously studied (along with collecting of the works themselves) in the nineteenth century, as were the techniques by which they were made. This is well exemplified by enamels which were frequently subjected to very extensive restoration, sometimes amounting more to re-creation (Philippon *et al.*, 1988; Richter, 1994; and see Chapter 10, p. 237). On occasion the nineteenth-century work could be so skilfully incorporated into the old work that not until detailed scientific examination was undertaken more recently was their true status revealed. The nineteenth-century restorers successfully re-learnt many of the Medieval techniques, but fortunately used many distinctive nineteenth-century materials.

Case study: *Basse taille* enamels

Richter (1994) studied four examples of *basse taille* enamels on silver (see Chapter 10, p. 237), now in the Cleveland Museum of Art, that purported to be French or Spanish work of the fourteenth century. He deployed a variety of techniques including optical microscopy, UV, SEM/EDX and electron microprobe analysis (EPMA).

Binocular microscope examination revealed that several of the pieces were in poor condition, not due to ageing or weathering but, rather, due to poor application of the enamel. Moreover, on one plaque, droplets of blue enamel had run from the ground onto and over the very worn gilded border, strongly suggesting that re-enamelling had taken place. On another plaque, traces of the original enamelling still survived in the corners. The removal of the original, presumably damaged, enamels would normally have been done by strong heat followed by rapid cooling, but on some plaques scratch marks suggested that the enamel had been removed mechanically. Examination by UV was very useful as it caused selective fluorescence where the re-enamelling had taken place, as, in general, Medieval enamels do not fluoresce. Radiography would have been a non-destructive method to detect and outline the areas of the later lead-rich enamel, although the restored enamels may be much thinner.

The smooth backs of the silver of several of the plaques suggested to Richter that they had been machine-made. This would presumably have been by rolling, although Richter does not mention any of the characteristic features of rolled metal (see Chapter 8, p. 157).

Analysis of the silver by EDX showed that two of the pieces had trace element patterns typical of fourteenth-century work, but that the gold content of the others was too low. Richter equated the remaining gold content of the silver to particular refining processes, and on these grounds dated two pieces to being pre-1850, one as post-1850 and one piece to being post-1870. In practice, it is not possible to link composition with the introduction of specific techniques of refining and purification with this degree of precision, and there is always the possibility that the silver may never have contained much gold in the first place (see Chapter 15, p. 388).

Enamel samples between 0.5 and 1 mm square were removed for EPMA and XRF analysis. They were all lead-alkali-silica glasses typical of nineteenth-century enamels, and thus not original. Genuine Medieval *basse taille* enamels were typically mixed potash soda alkali–lime–silica glasses, with no more than traces of lead and lime contents, usually in excess of 5%, whereas these enamels had only about 2% lime, typical of nineteenth-century glass. Similarly, the aluminium and magnesium contents were lower than in genuine Medieval enamels, but typical of more recent enamels made with purer materials. The elements sulphur, phosphorus and chlorine could not be detected, suggesting to Richter that the alkalis did not derive from plant ash, although it should be noted that the detection limit for the phosphorus by EDX was quite high (0.5%).

Richter ended his survey of the composition of the body of glasses rather lamely by stating that the presence of boron in the enamels would have been conclusive in establishing that the enamels were nineteenth century and not original, but that unfortunately the EDX system was unable to detect the boron (see Chapter 10, p. 239 for more on this serious problem). Analysis of the colorant elements was more helpful. All the enamels contained chromium – one had a uranium yellow and another, a nickel brown. One of the glasses had areas of opaque white, but none of the usual traditional opacifiers, tin, antimony or arsenic, could be detected. XRD gave weak patterns that were suggestive of fluorides.

Richter (1994, p. 247) concluded that 'although condemned in modern conservation views ... [they] can still be valued as a historical attempt to revive the beauty. Also they might be viewed in the future as documents meant to revive and surpass the work of their predecessors based on a strong belief in modern inventions and the improved manufacturing techniques in post-industrial times. Differentiating between genuine pieces of the historicism period and deliberate fakes made to please the collector's search for Medieval objects, however, is a difficult task because there is no definite borderline'.

Case study: The Court Casket

The enamels on a casket depicting the story of Abraham and Isaac (Figure 20.27) – the work of Susanna Court (c. 1570) – form part of the Waddesdon Bequest in the British Museum and provide another example of deceptive restoration (Tait and Freestone, 2004). The casket was found to have been heavily, but very competently restored, almost certainly in the late nineteenth century by Alfred André. Areas of repair and also of complete rearrangement of the original work

Figure 20.27 The heavily restored casket by Susanna Court (BM Cat. WB 51). Note the visibleges to the repairs where the masking material has decayed over the last century. (Courtesy A. Milton/British Museum)

were discovered. Radiographs showed the original sixteenth-century lock plate beneath the present enamel on one of the panels. However, it was not now in the position where one would expect a lock, and thus it likely that this panel was originally in the front of the casket.

Damaged areas would have been cut out and replaced with patches of newly fired enamels, which are likely to have been thinner than the original (Figure 20.28). The joins between the original and nineteenth-century 'hot' enamels were generally good, but minor gaps and cracks were filled with a 'cold' enamel. This was a colored material that over the past century had deteriorated sufficiently to have become visible. XRF analysis of the suspected 'hot' enamel repairs revealed chromium in the green areas, and other differences, especially higher lead oxide contents, so typical of nineteenth- and twentieth-century enamels generally. However, it is noticeable that the patch over the old lock plate is not opaque, suggesting that the opacity on the other patches may be mainly due to a lead-rich soft solder holding them in place, unless the lock plate repair had been done on a different occasion (Figure 20.29).

Figure 20.28 Sketch of the front panel of the Court casket (see Figures 20.27 and 20.29) with the restored areas delineated. (Courtesy Tait and Freestone, 2004)

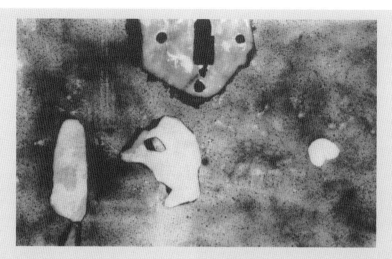

Figure 20.29   Radiograph of the front panel of the Court casket shown in Figures 20.27 and 20.28. Most of the nineteenth-century replacements are clearly visible, being opaque to the X-rays. (Courtesy J. Ambers/ British Museum).

Rehabilitation

Sometimes the scientific analysis of enamels has rehabilitated pieces that had been questioned on art historical grounds. Thus, Neil Stratford (1994) suggested that substantial parts of the enamels of two important twelfth-century Mosan triptychs from the Dutuit collection, now in the Museé de Petit Palais, in Paris were at best heavily restored in the nineteenth century, but more probably represented a pastiche made up of fragments. Stratford had to admit that the quality of some of the suspect pieces was superb, and as they had been known since about 1860, this would have meant that there must have been skilled forgers around at least a generation before the better-known forgers were at work.

Goaded by these accusations, the French team carried out detailed examination by radiography and analysis, using both particle-induced X-ray emission (PIXE) and XRF (Biron *et al.*, 1998).

A number of genuine enamels were also studied as comparison pieces, and thus their report forms a major study on the technique and composition of these enamels generally (see Chapter 10, pp. 222, 238). The green and blue enamels were soda–lime–silica glasses, whereas the red enamels were potash–lime–silica glasses. The Dutuit enamels were of similar composition, but totally different from the nineteenth-century enamels, which invariably contain lead. The minor quantities of aluminium, magnesium, manganese and chlorine, as well as the range of trace elements, were identical to those found in the Medieval enamels but different from the content in nineteenth-century enamels.

Examination by binocular microscope and by radiography showed that the enamelling technique was consistent with Medieval practice, and the surfaces of some of the Dutuit enamels showed characteristic natural weathering. All in all, Biron and colleagues concluded that the enamels were genuine.

Bibliography

Aarhus (1989) *Kunst og Kunstforfalskning*. Exhibition catalogue, Kunstmuseum, Aarhus.

Abbey, S. (1968) *The Goldsmith's and Silversmith's Handbook*. The Technical Press, London.

Abraham, M. (1999) Analysis of a collection of Egyptian tools and weapons at the Los Angeles County Museum of Art using typology, metallurgy and ICP. In: Young *et al.* (eds), 1999, pp. 172–178.

Accardo, G., Capannesi, G. and Seccaroni, C. (1988) Appilicazioni di nuove tecniche endoscopiche nell'esame delle opere d'arte. In: *Preprints of the 2nd International Conference on Non-Destructive Testing, Microanalytical Method and Environmental Evidence for the Study and Conservation of Works of Art*, Istitutio Centrale Per Il Restauro & Associazone Italiana Prove Non Distruttive, Rome and Bresica, 1988, pp. I/2.1–I/2.12.

Adam, S. (1966) *The Technique of Greek Sculpture*. The British School at Athens, London.

Adams, E. (2001) *Chelsea Porcelain*. British Museum Press, London.

Adan-Bayewitz, D., Asaro, F. and Giauque, R.D. (1999) Determining pottery provenance: Application of a new high-precision X-ray fluorescence method and comparison with instrumental neutron activation analysis. *Archaeometry* **41**, 1; pp. 1–24.

Adler, A.D. (1996) Updating recent studies on the Shroud of Turin. In: Orna (ed), 1996, pp. 223–228.

Adreeva, L.N. and Tcheremkhin, V.I. (1988) On the possibility of using burnt ceramic masses for making up for damaged ceramics. In: *Conservation–Restoration of Leather and Wood*, I. Éri and G. Sárközy (eds). National Centre of Museums, Budapest, pp. 437–442.

Aert, A., Janssens, K. and Adams, F. (1995) A chemical investigation of altered Chinese jade art objects. *Orientations* **26**, 11; pp. 79–80.

Affonso, M.T.C. (1996) Lapis Lazuli aus Afghanistan und Chile: Ein Einblick in die Geschicthe und Geologie. *Metalla* **3**, 2; pp. 71–82.

Ainsworth, M.W. (1982) *Art and Autoradiography: Insights into the Genesis of Paintings by Rembrandt, Van Dyck and Vermeer*. Metropolitan Museum of Art, New York.

Ainsworth, M.W. (1992) Implications of revised attributions in Netherlandish painting. *Metropolitan Museum Journal* **27**; pp. 59–76.

Aitken, M.J. (1976) Thermoluminescent age evaluation and assessment of error limits: revised system. *Archaeometry* **18**, 2; pp. 233–238.

Aitken, M.J. (1985) *Thermoluminescence Dating*. Academic Press, London.

Aitken, M.J. (1989) Luminescence dating: a guide for the non-specialist. *Archaeometry* **40**, 2; pp. 147–159.

Aitken, M.J. (1990) *Science-based Dating in Archaeology*. Longman, London.

Aitken, M.J. (1997) Luminescence dating. In: Taylor and Aitken (eds), 1997, pp. 183–216.

Aitken, M.J., Moorey, P.R.S. and Ucko, P.J. (1971) The authenticity of vessels and figurines in the Haçilar style. *Archaeometry* **13**, 1; pp. 89–141.

Aitken, M.J. and Alldred, J.C. (1972) The assessment of error limits in thermoluminescent dating. *Archaeometry* **14**, 2; pp. 257–267.

Aitken, M.J. and Huxtable, J. (1975) Thermoluminescence and Glozel: a plea for caution. *Antiquity* **49**, 195; pp. 223–226.

Aitken, M.J., Allsop, A.L., Bussell, G.D., Liritzis, Y. and Winter, M.B. (1989) Geomagnetic intensity measurements using bricks from Greek churches of the first and second millennia AD. *Archaeometry* **31**, 1; pp. 77–87.

Aitken, W.C. (1866) Cast and electro-deposit statuary in bronze and copper. In: *The Resources, Products, and Industrial History of Birmingham and the Midland Hardware District*, S. Timmins (ed). Robert Hardwicke, London, pp. 510–519.

Akhtar, W. and Edwards, H.G.M. (1997) Fourier-transform Raman spectroscopy of mammalian and avian keratotic biopolymers. *Spectrochimica Acta* **A53**; pp. 81–90.

Akhtar, W., Edwards, H.G.M., Tarwell, D.W. and Nutbrown, M. (1997) Fourier-transform Raman spectroscopic study of human hair. *Spectrochimica Acta* **A53**; pp. 1021–1031.

Alessandri, G. (ed) (1989) *Le Pellicole ad Ossalati: Originee Significato nella Conservazione delle Opere D'Arte*. Proceedings of the Symposium 25–26th October 1989. Centro CNR 'Gino Bozza', Politecnico di Milano, Milan.

Alexander, S.M. (1969a, b; 1970) Towards a history of art materials – a survey of published technical literature in the Arts. Part I: From Antiquity to 1599. *Art and Archaeology Technical Abstracts* **7**, 3; pp. 123–161. Part II: From 1600–1750 *Ibid.* **7**, 4; pp. 201–216. Part III: From 1751–late 19th century *Ibid.* **8**, 1; pp. 155–178.

Alföldy, G. (1974) *Noricum.* RKP, London.

Ali, Mohd and Kassim, bin Haji (1988) *Gold Jewelry and Ornaments of Malaysia.* Muzium Negara, Kuala Lumpur.

Allan, J. and Gilmour, B. (2000) *Persian Steel: The Tanavoli Collection.* Oxford University Press, Oxford.

Allen, A.J. (2000) *Allen's Authentication of Later Chinese Porcelain.* Allen's Enterprises Ltd, Takapuna, Auckland, New Zealand.

Allen, A.J. (2001) *Allen's Authentication of Ancient Chinese Bronzes.* Allen's Enterprises Ltd, Takapuna, Auckland, New Zealand.

Allen, J.D. (1976a) Amber and its substitutes, Pt. I: Historical aspects. *Bead Journal* **2**, 2; pp. 15–20.

Allen, J.D. (1976b) Amber and its substitutes, Pt. II: Mineral analyses. *Bead Journal* **2**, 4; pp. 11–21.

Allen, J.D. (1976c) Amber and its substitutes, Pt. III: Is it real? *Bead Journal* **3**, 1; pp. 20–31.

Allen, N.S., Edge, M. and Horie, C.V. (eds) (1992) *Polymers in Conservation.* Royal Society of Chemistry, Cambridge.

Allen, R.O. (ed) (1989) *Archaeological Chemistry IV.* American Chemical Society, Washington DC. Advances in Chemistry Series 220.

Allen, R., Hamroush, H., Nagle, C. and Fitzhugh, W. (1984) Use of rare earth element analysis to study the utilization and procurement of soapstone along the Labrador Coast. In: Lambert (ed), 1984, pp. 3–18.

Allison, A.H. and Pond, R.B., Sr. (1983) On copying bronze statuettes. *American Institute for Conservation Journal* **23**, 1; pp. 32–46.

Amandry, P. (1967) Review of: *Greek gold. Jewelry from the Age of Alexander.* In: *American Journal of Archaeology* **71**; pp. 202–205.

Ambers, J. and Bowman, S. (2003) Letter to the editor. *Radiocarbon* **44**, 2; p. 599.

Ambrose, W.R. (2001) Obsidian hydration dating. In: Brothwell and Pollard (eds), 2001, pp. 81–92.

Amico, L.N. (1996) *Bernard Palissy.* Flammarion, Paris.

Andersen, H.H. and Rehn, L.E. (eds) (2000) *Nuclear Instruments and Methods in Physics Research B: Beam Interactions with Materials and Atoms B161-3.* Elsevier, Amsterdam.

Anderson, B.W. (1990) *Gem Testing,* 10th edn revised. Butterworths, London. (E.A. Jobbing).

Andrasko, J., Kylsäter, P., Maehly, A.C. and Knuuttila, M. (1979) Analysis of counterfeit gold coins by scanning electron microscopy and X-ray diffraction. *Scanning Microscopy* **1**; pp. 455–458.

Andrén, A. (1986) *Deeds and Misdeeds in Classical Art and Antiquities.* Studies in Mediterranean Archaeology, Pocket Book 36. Paul Åström, Partille, Sweden.

Andrew, S.R. and Eastop, D. (1994) Using ultra-violet and infra-red techniques in the examination and documentation of historic textiles. *The Conservator* **18**; pp. 50–56.

Angst, W. (1978) Collector versus new antiques. *Curator* **21**, 4; pp. 265–282.

Anon, (1955a) Mystery of the Madonna. *Connoisseur* **136**; p. 118.

Anon, (1955b) The two Francais – The National Gallery forgery exposed by X-rays. *Illustrated London News* **226**; pp. 910–911.

Anon, (1973) *Birmingham Gold and Silver 1773–1973.* City Museum and Art Gallery, Birmingham.

Aon, F. (2002). Remarks on tool signatures relating to the question of authenticity. In: Childs-Johnson (ed), 2002, pp. 11–12.

A.P. (A. Piccirilli) (1944) Sculpture technique. In: *Encyclopaedia Britannica* **20**; pp. 219–221 Chicago.

Appleyard, H.M. (2002) *Guide to the Identification of Animal Fibres,* 2nd edn. Archetype Publications, London.

Archibald, M.M. and Cowell, M.R. (eds) (1993) *Metallurgy in Numismatics 3.* Royal Numismatic Society, Special Publication 24, London.

Arkell, A.J. (1950) Gold Coast copies of 5th–7th century bronze lamps. *Antiquity* **24**, 93; pp. 38–40.

Armiento, G., Attanasio, D. and Platania, R. (1997) Electron spin resonance study of white marbles from Tharros (Sardinia): A reappraisal of the technique, possibilities and limitations. *Archaeometry* **39**, 2; pp. 309–319.

Arribas, A., Craddock, P., Molina, F., Rothenberg, B. and Hoock (*sic*), D.R. (1989) Investigacion Arqueometalurgica en yacimientos de las Edades del Cobre y del Bronce en el Sudeste de Iberia. In: *Mineria y Metalurgia en las Antiguas Civilizaciones Mediterraneas y Europeas I,* C. Domergue (ed). Ministerio de Cultura, Madrid, pp. 71–80.

Arnau, F. (1961) *Three Thousand Years of Deception in Art and Antiques.* Jonathan Cape, London. [English trans. J. Maxwell Brownjohn of *Kunst der Fälscher der Kunst,* Econ, Düsseldorf, 1959].

Aronson, M. and Kingery, W.D. (1991) Patination of ceramic objects, modern and prehistoric: a case from West Mexico. In: Vandiver *et al.* (eds), 1991, pp. 571–589.

Arrhenius, B. (1985) *Merovingian Garnet Jewellery.* Kungl. Vitterhets Historie och Antikvitets Akademen Almqvist & Wiksell International, Stockholm.

Art, J. (1987) Objectifying the book: the impact of science on books and manuscripts. *Library Trends* **36**, 1; pp. 25–38.

Ash, N.E. (1982) Recording watermarks by beta-radiography and other means. In: *Post prints of the 10th Annual Meeting of the Book and Paper Group of the American Institute for Conservation of Historic and Artistic Works,* American Institute for Conservation of Historic and Artistic Works, Washington DC.

Ashe, G. (1966) *What Sort of Picture?* Sindon, London. pp. 15–19.

Ashmole, B. (1961) *Forgeries of Ancient Sculpture in Marble: Creation and Detection.* The First J.L. Myres Memorial Lecture, Blackwells, Oxford.

Ashmole, B. (1970) Aegean marble: Science and common sense. *The Annual of the British School at Athens* **65**; pp. 1–2.

Aston, B.G. (1994) *Ancient Egyptian Stone Vessels: Materials and Forms*. Studien zur Archäologie und Geschichte Altägyptiens **5**. Heidelberger Orientverlag, Heidelberg.

Aston, B.G., Harrell, J.A. and Shaw, I. (2000) Stone. In: Nicholson and Shaw (eds), 2000, pp. 5–77.

Atil, E., Chase, W.T. and Jett, P. (1985) *Islamic Metalwork in the Freer Gallery of Art*. Freer Gallery of Art, Smithsonian Institution, Washington DC.

Attanasio, D. (2003) *Ancient White Marbles: Analysis and Identification by Paramagnetic Resonance Spectroscopy*. "L' Erma" di Bretschneider, Rome.

Attanasio, D., Armiento, G., Brilli, M., Emanuele, M.C., Platania, R. and Turi, B. (2000) Multi-method marble provenance determinations: the Carrara marbles as a case study for the combined use of isotopic, electron spin resonance and petrographic data. *Archaeometry* **42**, 2; pp. 257–272.

Attanasio, D., Bultrini, G. and Ingo, G.M. (2001) The possibility of provenancing a series of bronze Punic coins found at Tharros (western Sardinia) using the literature lead isotope database. *Archaeometry* **43**, 4; pp. 529–548.

Attanasio, D., Armiento, G., Bruno, M., Emanuele, M.C., Pensabene, P. and Platania, R. (2002a) The re-establishment of an ESR database for provenancing white and grayish marbles: data for Italian and Greek quarries. In: Herrmann Jr, Herz and Newman (eds), 2002, pp. 97–102.

Attanasio, D., Armiento, G., Emanuele, M.C. and Platania, R. (2002b) The variability of the electron spin resonance parameters as a tool for identifying joining marble fragments. In: Herrmann, Jr., Herz and Newman (eds), 2002, pp. 91–96.

Atwood, R. (2001) Museum fails gold standard (Fake pre-Hispanic metal work collection at Peru's Gold Museum). *ARTNews* **100**, 10; p. 80. November.

Atzeni, C., Massidda, L. and Samna, U. (2004) Archaeometric data. In: *Archaeo Metallurgy In Sardina*, U. Sanna, R. Valera and F. Lo Schiavo (eds). Associazione Italiana di Metallurgia and Progetto Finalizza Beni Culturali del CNR.

Ayalon, A., Bar-Matthews, M. and Goren, Y. (2004) Authenticity examination of the inscription on the ossuary attributed to James, brother of Christ. *Journal of Archaeological Science* **31**, 8; pp. 1169–1185.

Babbitt, F.C. (1936) *Plutarch: The Moralia*, **5**, The Loeb edition. Heinemann, London. [Trans.].

Bacci, M. (2000) UV-VIS-NIR, FT-IR, and FORS spectroscopies. In: Ciliberto and Spoto (eds), 2000, pp. 321–361.

Bacci, M., Baronti, S., Casini, A., Lotti, F., Picollo, M. and Casazza, O. (1992) Non-destructive spectroscopic investigations on paintings using optical fibres. In: Vandiver *et al.* (eds), 1992, pp. 265–283.

Bachmann, H.-G. and Renner, H. (1984) Nineteenth century platinum coins. *Platinum Review* **28**, 3; pp. 126–131.

Baer, N.S. and Majewski, L.J. (1970 & 1971) Ivory and Related Materials in Art and Archaeology: An Annotated Bibliography, Section A (Conservation and Scientific Investigation & Section B (Working Techniques, Forgeries and History). *Supplements to Art and Archaeology Technical Abstracts* **8**, 2 & 3; pp. 229–275 & 189–225.

Baer, N.S. and Indictor, N. (1972a, b & 1973) Linseed oil and related materials: an annotated bibliography. Part I: From Antiquity to 1940. *Art and Archaeology Technical Abstracts* **9**, 1; pp. 153–240. (1972) Part II: From 1941–1960, *Ibid*. **9**, 2; pp. 159–241. Part III: From 1961–1972, *Ibid*. **10**, 1; pp. 155–256.

Baer, N.S. and Indictor, N. (1976) Linseed oil and related materials: an annotated bibliography. Part IV: From 1973–1975. In: *Lipids and Works of Art. Proceedings of the 13th International Society for Fat Research Congress, Marseille*, pp. 17–31.

Baer, N.S. and Indictor, N. (1978) Linseed oil and related materials: an annotated bibliography. Part V: From 1976–1977. In: *Lipids and Works of Art. Proceedings of the 14th International Society for Fat Research Congress, Brighton*, pp. 31–49.

Baer, N.S., Jochsberger, T. and Indictor, N. (1978) Chemical investigation on ancient Near Eastern archaeological ivory artifacts. Fluorine and nitrogen composition. In: Carter (ed), 1978, pp. 139–149.

Bailey, A.R. (1960) *A Text Book of Metallurgy*. Macmillan, London.

Bailey, D.M. (1960) Roman lamps – Reproductions and forgeries. *The Museums Journal* **60**, 2; pp. 39–46.

Bailey, D.M. (1972) *Greek and Roman Pottery Lamps*, 2nd edn. Trustees of the British Museum, London.

Bailey, D.M. (1988) *A Catalogue of the Lamps in the British Museum III. Roman Provincial Lamps*. British Museum Press, London.

Bailey, D.M. (1986) Charles Townley's *Cista Mystica*. In: *Italian Iron Age Artefacts in the British Museum*, J. Swaddling (ed). British Museum Publications, London, pp. 131–141.

Bailey, D.M. (1996) *A Catalogue of the Lamps in the British Museum IV. Lamps of Metal and Stone, and Lampstands*. British Museum Press, London.

Bailey, D.M. and Bowman, S.G.E. (1981) TL examination of five Samian poinçons of Central Gaulish type. *Antiquaries Journal* **61**, 2; pp. 352–356.

Baillie, M.G.L. (1982) *Tree-Ring Dating and Archaeology*. Croom Helm, London.

Baillie, M.G.L. (1984) Some thoughts on art-historical dendrochronology. *Journal of Archaeological Science* **11**, 5; pp. 371–393.

Baillie, M.G.L. (1995) *A Slice Through Time*. Batsford, London.

Baillie, M.G.L., Hillam, J., Briffa, K.R. and Brown, D.M. (1985) Re-dating the English art-historical tree-ring chronologies. *Nature* **315**, 6017; pp. 317–319.

Bakas, Th., Gangas, N.-H., Sigalas, I. and Aitken, M.J. (1980) Mössbauer study of Glozel tablet 198 b1. *Archaeometry* **22**, 1; pp. 69–80.

Baker, M. (1992) Terracotta and Plaster Multiples in 18th and 19th century France. In: *The Thyssen-Bornemisza*

Collection: *The Renaissance and Later Sculptures with Works of Art in Bronze*, A. Radcliffe, M. Baker and M. Maek-Gérard (eds). Sotheby, London, pp. 36–41.

Baker, N. (2001) *Double Fold: Libraries and the Assault on Paper*. Vintage, London.

Balfour-Paul, J. (1998) *Indigo*. British Museum Press, London.

Banerjee, A. and Schneider, B. (1996) Römisches Elfenbein-zerostörungsfreie Materialprüfung mit optischen und spekralphotometrischen Methoden. *Kölner Jahrbuch* **29**; pp. 331–342.

Banerjee, A., Ghiurca, V., Langer, B. and Wilheim, M. (1999) Determination of the provenance of two archaeological amber beads from Romania by FTIR and solid-state carbon-13 NMR spectroscopy. *Archäologisches Korrespondenzblatt* **294**; pp. 593–606.

Bangs, C. and Northover, P. (1999) Tales of two ewers, with a hint of a third; including some notes and observations. *Journal of the Antique Metalware Society* **7**, pp. 25–34. [And see vol. 9, 2001, *The Stratford and other ewers, an open discussion*, pp. 29–31, for a report on the discussion of the authenticity of this piece].

Banik, G. (1997) Decay caused by iron-gall-inks. In: *Iron-Gall Ink Corrosion*. Netherlands Institute for Cultural Heritage, Amsterdam, pp. 21–26.

Bannister, F.A. and Plenderleith, H.J. (1936) Physico-chemical examination of a scarab of Tuthmosis IV bearing the name of the God Aten. *Journal of Egyptian Archaeology* **22**, 1; pp. 3–6.

Bar-Adon, P. (1980) *The Cave of the Treasure: The Finds from the Caves in Nahal Mishmar*. Israel Exploration Society, Jerusalem.

Baratte, F. and Painter, K. (eds) (1989) *Tresors d'Orfevrerie Gallo-Romains*. Éditions de la Réunion des musées nationaux, Paris.

Barba, C., San Andrés, M., Peinado, J., Báez, M.I. and Baldonedo, J.L. (1995) A note on the characterization of paint layers by transmission electron microscopy. *Studies in Conservation* **40**, 3; pp. 194–200.

Barbaste, M., Robinson, K., Guilfoyle, S., Medina, B. and Lobinski, R. (2002) Precise determination of the strontium isotope ratios in wine by inductively coupled plasma sector field multicollector mass spectrometry. *Journal of Analytical Atomic Spectrometry* **17**, 2; pp. 135–137.

Barberini, M.G. (2003) Bartolomeo Cavaceppis Lehrjahre. In: Kunze and Rügler (eds), 2002, pp. 171–180.

Barbet, P. (1950) *La Passion de N-S Jésus-Christ selon de chirurgien*. Dillen et sie, Paris.

Barbet, P. (1953) *A Doctor at Calvary*. Clonmore & Reynolds, Dublin. [Trans. The Earl of Wicklow].

Barbetti, M. (1976) Archaeomagnetic analyses of six Glozelian ceramic artifacts. *Journal of Archaeological Science* **3**, 2; pp. 137–151.

Barbier, J.P. (ed) (1989) *Gold of Africa. Jewellery and Ornaments from Ghana, Côtes d'Ivorie, Mali and Senegal*. Prestel-Verlag, Munich.

Barbin, V., Ramseyer, K., Burns, S.J., Decrouez, D., Maier, J.L. and Chamay, J. (1991) Cathodoluminescence signature

of white marble artefacts. In: Vandiver *et al.* (eds), 1991, pp. 299–308.

Barbin, V., Ramseyer, K., Decrouez, D., Burns, S.J., Chamay, J. and Maier, J.L. (1992) Cathodoluminescence of white marbles: an overview. *Archaeometry* **34**, 2; pp. 175–184.

Barbour, D. and Glinsman, L.D. (1993) An investigation of Renaissance casting practices as a means for identifying forgeries. In: *Conservation Research*, R.M. Merrill (ed). Studies in the History of Art 41, Monograph Series II. National Gallery of Art, Washington DC, pp. 15–29.

Barker, B.D., Kendell. K., and O'Shea, C. (1982) *The Hydrogen Reduction Process for the Conservation of Ferrous Objects*. Maritime Museum Monographs and Reports No. 53.

Barker, H. and Rawson, J. (1971–72) A Chinese gilt bronze bear from the Oppenheimer Collection. *The British Museum Quarterly* **36**, 1–2; pp. 53–56.

Barker, M. (1999) Defining plastics. In: Quye and Williamson (eds), 1999, pp. 23–33.

Barkman, L. (1969) *Replica of Relics*. Wasastudier 7, Statens Sjöhistoriska Museum, Stockholm.

Barnard, N. (1961) *Bronze Casting and Bronze Alloys in Ancient China*. Mounumenta Serica Monograph XIV, Canberra.

Barnard, N. (1968) The incidence of forgery amongst archaic Chinese bronzes. *Monumenta Serica* **27**; pp. 91–168.

Barnard, N. (1996) *The Shan-fu Ch'I Kuei and Associated Inscribed Vessels*. SMC Publishing, Inc, Taipei.

Barnes, A. (1934) *The Holy Shroud*. Burns, Oates & Washbourne, London.

Barnes, I.L., Chase, W.T., Holmes, L.L., Joel, E.C., Meyers, P. and Sayre, E.V. (1988) The technical examination, lead isotope determination, and elemental analysis of some Shang and Zhou Dynasty bronze vessels. In: *The Beginning of the Use of Metals and Alloys*, R. Maddin (ed). MIT Press, Cambridge MA, pp. 296–306.

Barraclough, K.C. and Kerr, J.A. (1976) Steel from 100 years ago. *Journal of the Historical Metallurgy Society* **10**, 2; pp. 70–76.

Barrandon, J.N. and Irigoin, J. (1979) Papiers de hollande et papiers d'Angoumois de 1650 à 1810. Leur differenciation au moyen de l'analyse par activation neutronique. *Archaeometry* **21**, 1; pp. 101–106.

Barrandon, J-N., Guerra, M.F., Collins, B., Le Roy Ladurie, E. and Morrisson, C. (1991) The diffusion of silver from Potosi in the XVI century European coinage. In: Pernicka and Wagner (eds), 1991, pp. 11–18.

Barrandon, J.-N., Aubin, G., Benusiglio, J., Hiernard, J., Nony, D. and Scheers, S. (1994) *L'or Gaulois*. Cahiers Ernest-Babelon 6. CNRS editions, Paris.

Barrandon, J-N., Le Roy Ladurie, E., Morrison, C. and Morrisson, Ch. (1995) The true role of American precious metals transfers to Europe in the sixteenth to eighteenth centuries: new evidence from coin analyses.

In: D.R. Hook and D.R.M. Gaimster (eds), 1995, pp. 171–179.

Barrandon, J-N., Morrisson, Ch. and Morrisson, C. (2000) Brazilian gold, money and economic growth in Europe during the 18th century. In: Demortier and Adrians (eds), 2000, pp. 95–98.

Barrington Haynes, E. (1959) *Glass Through the Ages*. Pelican, Harmondsworth.

Bartman, E. (1992) *Ancient Sculpture Copies in Miniature*. E.J. Brill, Leiden.

Bassiakos, Y. and Doumas, C. (1998) *ESR Spectroscopy of Calcitic Encrustations on Archaeological Finds*. Preprints of the Archaeometry '98 meeting, Budapest, pp. 20–21.

Bastidas, J.M., López-Delgrado, A. and López, F.A. (1997) Characterization of artificially patinated layers on artistic bronze exposed to laboratory SO_2 contamination. *Journal of Materials Science* 32; pp. 129–133.

Bates, K.F. (1951) *Enameling: Principles and Practice*. The World Publishing Co.,, Cleveland.

Bates, J.K., Jardine, L.J. and Steindler, M.J. (1982) Hydration aging of nuclear waste glass. *Science* 218, 4567; pp. 51–54.

Battie, D. (1986a) Scrimshaw. In: Bly (ed), 1986, pp. 209–212.

Battie, D. (1986b) Netsuke and okimono. In: Bly (ed), 1986, pp. 143–150.

Battie, D. (1999) Pottery, porcelain and glass. In: Tharp (ed), 1999, pp. 16–55.

Bauch, J. (1978) Dendrochronology applied to the dating of Dutch, Flemish and German paintings. In: *Dendrochronology in Europe*, J. Fletcher (ed). British Archaeological Reports International Series 51, Oxford, pp. 307–314.

Bauch, J. and Eckstein, D. (1970) Dendrochronologcal dating of oak panels of Dutch seventeenth-century paintings. *Studies in Conservation* 15, 1; pp. 45–50.

Bauch, J. and Eckstein, D. (1978) Dendrochronological examination of oak panels from Rubens. *Jahrbuch Berliner Museen* 20; pp. 209–221.

Bauch, J. and Eckstein, D. (1981) Woodbiological investigations on panels of Rembrandt paintings. *Wood Science and Technology* 15; pp. 251–263.

Baumgartner, E. and Kreuger, I. (1988) *Phoenix aus Sand und Asche: Glas des Mittelalters*. Klinkhardt and Biermann, München.

Baumann, P. (1980) Bei Keramikfälschern in Ekuador. *Keramik Magazin* 2, 2; pp. 124–127.

Baxter, M.S. and Walton, A. (1971) Fluctuations of atmospheric carbon-14 concentrations. *Proceedings of the Royal Society* A321; pp. 105–127.

Bayley, J. and Butcher, S. (2004) *Roman Brooches in Britain*. Society of Antiquaries, London.

Beagrie, N. (1989) The Romano-British pewter industry. *Britannia* 20; pp. 169–181.

Beale, A. (1975) A technical view of nineteenth-century sculpture. In: *Metamorphoses in Nineteenth-Century Sculpture*, J.L. Wasserman (ed). Fogg Art Museum, Harvard University Press, Cambridge MA, pp. 25–55.

Beale, A. (1990) Scientific approaches to the question of authenticity. In: True and Podany (eds), 1990a, pp. 197–208.

Beck, C. (ed) (1994) *Dating in Exposed Surface Contexts*. University of New Mexico Press, Albuquerque NM.

Beck, C.W. (ed) (1974) *Archaeological Chemistry*. Advances in Chemistry Series 138, American Chemical Society, Washington DC.

Beck, C.W. (1982) Authentication and conservation of amber: conflict of interests. In: *Science and Technology in the Service of Conservation. Preprints of the Washington Congress, 3–9 Sept 1982*, N.S. Brommelle and G. Thomson (eds). IIC, London, pp. 104–107.

Beck, C.W. (1986) Spectroscopic studies of amber. *Applied Spectroscopy Review* 22, 1; pp. 57–110.

Beck, C.W., Gerving, M. and Wilbur, E. (1966 & 1967) The provenance of archaeological amber artefacts. Pt 1: 8th century BC to 1899, Pt 2: 1900–1966, *Art and Archaeology Technical Abstracts* 6, 2 & 3; pp. 215–302 & 203–273.

Beck, C. and Shennan, S. (1991) *Amber in Prehistoric Britain*. Oxbow Monograph 8, Oxford.

Beck, C.W. and Bouzek, J. (eds) (1993) Amber in Archaeology. *Proceedings of the Second International Conference on Amber in Archaeology, Liblice, 1990*. Czech Academy of Sciences, Prague.

Beck, C.W., and Hartnett, H. (1993) Sicilian amber. In: Beck and Bougek (eds), 1993, pp. 36–47.

Beck, R., and Neiche, R. (1992) Jades of the New Zealand Maori. In: Markel (ed), 1992, pp. 89–108.

Beck, R.J. and Mason, M. (2002) *Mana Pournamu, New Zealand Jade*, revised edn. Reed Books, Auckland.

Beck, W., Donahue, D.J., Jull, A.J.T., Burr, G., Broecker, W.S., Bonani, G., Hajdas, I. and Malotki, E. (1998) Ambiguities in direct dating of rock surfaces using radiocarbon measurements. *Science* 280; pp. 2132–2135.

Becker, K. and Moreno y Moreno, A. (1974) Applications of Thermoluminescence Measurements in Ancient Ceramics. *Proceedings of the Fourth International Conference on Luminescence and Dosimetry*, 3 pp. 1021–1041.

Becker, M.A., Willman, P. and Tuross, N.C. (1995) The U.S. First Ladies gowns: a biochemical study of silk preservation. *Journal of the American Institute for Conservation* 34, 2; pp. 141–152.

Becker, M.A., Magoshi, Y., Sakai, T. and Tuross, N.C. (1997) Chemical and physical properties of old silk fabrics. *Studies in Conservation* 42, 1; pp. 27–37.

Becker, V. (1988) *Fabulous Fakes*. Grafton Books, London.

Becker, V. (1995) *Swarovski*. Henry N. Abrams, New York.

Beckett, A. (1995) *Fakes: Forgery and the Art World*. Richard Cohen Books, London.

Bednarik, R.G. (1995) The Côa petroglyphs: an obituary to the stylistic dating of Palaeolithic rock-art. *Antiquity* 69, 266; pp. 877–883.

Bednarik, R.G. (2002) The dating of rock art: A critique. *Journal of Archaeological Science* 29, 11; pp. 1213–1233.

Begemann, F. and Schmitt-Strecker, S. (1987/88) Blei-Isotopendaten von Bronzeproben. In: 'Jüngling', 1987/88, p. 303.

Bell, I.M., Clark, R.J.H. and Gibbs, P.J. (1997) Raman spectroscopic library of natural and synthetic pigments (pre ~1850 AD). *Spectrochimica Acta* **A53**; pp. 2159–2179.

Bell, T.E. (1982a) Ultraviolet detection. *The Connoisseur* **210**, 843; pp. 140–143.

Bell, T.E. (1982b) Infrared reflectography reveals the hidden drawing behnd the painting. *The Connoisseur* **210**, 844; pp. 140–141.

Bellina, B. and d'Errico, F. (2000) Typology, morphometry and manufacturing techniques of agate and cornelian beads: Combining data to model acculturation processes. *Beads Study Trust Newsletter* **36**; pp. 12–13.

Bémont, C. and Gautier, J. (1985) Manipulations ou forgeries? A propos de quelques poinçons-matrices. *Notes et Documents* **9**; pp. 183–218.

Bémont C. and Gautier, J. (1987) Poinçons-matrices de Rheinabern et Blickweiler dans la collection Lafaye á Aix-en-Provence. *Melanges Lutz, Revue Archéologique de l'Est*, (ed). du C.N.R.S., **38**; pp. 13–22.

Bendall, S. (1971) The forgery of ancient coins. *The Year Book of the British Association of Numismatic Societies* **16**; pp. 10–14.

Benjamin, S. (1993) *English Enamel Boxes* (first published 1978, Macdonald Orbis, reissued Little Brown, London).

Benson, P.L. and Gilmore, R.S. (2003) Image recovery of worn-off hallmarks on silver and gold objects. In: *Conservation Science 2002*, J.H. Townsend, K. Eremin and A. Adriaens (eds). Archetype Books, London, pp. 215–221.

Berducou, M. (2001) La restauration: quells choix? Dérestauration, restauration-restitution. *Techne* **13–14**; pp. 211–218.

Berezhnoy, I.E., Postma, E.O. and van den Herik, J. (2005) Computerized Visual Analysis of Paintings. In: *Humanities, Computers and Cultural Heritage, Proceedings of the 16th International Conference of the Association for History and Computing*. Royal Netherlands Academy of Arts and Sciences, Amsterdam, pp. 28–32.

Berger, G.A. (2000) *Conservation of Paintings: Research and Innovations.* Archetype Publications, London.

Berger, G.A. and Russell, W.H. (1986) Investigations into the reactions of plastic materials to environmental changes. Part I: The mechanics of the decay of paint films. *Studies in Conservation* **31**, 1; pp. 49–64.

Berger, G.A. and Russell, W.H. (1994) Interaction between canvas and paint film in response to environmental changes. *Studies in Conservation* **39**, 2; pp. 73–86.

Berger, G.A. and Russell, W.H. (2000) Investigations into the causes of the deterioration of paintings and painted objects; Pt III of Berger, 2000. pp. 245–324.

Berrie, B.H. (1997) Prussian blue. In: FitzHugh (ed), 1997, pp. 191–217.

Berrie, B.H. and Lomax, S.Q. (1997) Azo Pigments: Their History, Synthesis, Properties and Use in Artists' Materials. *Conservation Research 1996/1997, Studies in the History of Art 57*. National Gallery of Art, Washington DC, pp. 9–33.

Bersch, J. (1904) *Cellulose, Cellulose Products and Artificial Rubber.* Bird, Philadelphia.

Bertani, D. and Consolandi, L. (2006) High resolution imaging in the near infrared. In: MacDonald (ed), 2006, pp. 211–238.

Bertoluzza, A., Cacciari, S., Cristini, G., Fagnano, C. and Tinti, A. (1995) Nondestructive 'in situ' Raman study of artistic glasses. *Journal of Raman Spectroscopy* **26**, 8/9; pp. 751–755.

Bessac, J.C. (1988) Problems of identification and interpretation of tool marks on ancient marbles and decorative stones. In: Herz and Waelkens (eds), 1988, pp. 41–53.

Best, S.P., Clark, R.J.H. and Withnall, R. (1992) Nondestructive pigment analysis of artefacts by Raman microscopy. *Endeavour* **16**, 2; pp. 66–73.

Best, S.P., Clark, R., Daniels, M. and Withnall, R. (1993) A Bible laid open. *Chemistry in Britain* **29**, 2; pp. 118–122.

Best, S.P., Clark, R.J.H., Daniels, M.A.M., Porter, C.A. and Withnall, R. (1995) Identification by Raman microscopy and visible reflectance spectroscopy of pigments on an Icelandic manuscript. *Studies in Conservation* **40**, 1; pp. 31–40.

Betts, M.W. and Latta, M.A. (2000) Rock surface hardness as an indication of exposure age. *Archaeometry* **42**, 2; pp. 209–223.

Beukens, R.P., Pavlish, L.A., Wilson, G.C. and Farquhar, R.M. (1999) Authenticity of a Korean Iron Warrior on Horseback. In: Young et al. (eds), 1999, pp. 297–300.

Beutel, E. (1925) *Bewährte Arbeitswesen der Metallfärbung*, 2nd edn. Universitäts Verlagsbuchhandlung, Vienna.

Bewer, F.G. (1995) Studying the technology of Renaissance bronzes. In: Vandiver et al. (eds), 1995, pp. 701–709.

Bewer, F.G. and Scott, D.A. (1995) A bronze sculpture attributed to Louis-Simon Boizot and platinum coating methods. *Archaeometry* **37**, 2; pp. 351–361.

Bhardwaj, H.C. (ed) (1987) *Archaeometry of Glass.* Indian Ceramic Society, Calcutta.

Biddle, M. (ed) (2000) *King Arthur's Round Table.* Boydell Press, Woodbridge, Suffolk.

Bieber, M. (1958) Review of Herbig, 1956. In: *American Journal of Archaeology* **62**; pp. 341–343.

Bieber, M. (1977) *Ancient Copies.* New York University Press, New York.

Bimson, M. (1956) Techniques of Greek black and *Terra Sigillata* red. *Antiquaries Journal* **36**, 3–4; pp. 200–204.

Bimson, M. (1974) Glass in the Tutankhman Treasure. In: *Annales du 6 Congrès International d'Étude Historique du Verre*, J. Philippe and J. Begun (eds). Association Internationale pour l'Histoire du Verr. pp. Liège, pp. 291–294.

Bimson, M. (1980) Ring 'pontil marks' and the empontiling of a group of seventh-century Anglo-Saxon glass. *Journal of Glass Studies* **22**; pp. 9–11.

Bimson, M., La Neice [sic], S. and Leese, M. (1982) The characterisation of mounted garnets. *Archaeometry* **24**, 1; pp. 51–58.

Bimson, M. and Freestone, I.C. (1983) An analtical study of the relationship between the Portland vase and other Roman cameo glasses. *Journal of Glass Studies* **25**; pp. 55–64.

Bimson, M. and Rose, M.J. (1983) A note on the analyses of occluded gases in ancient glass. *Archaeometry* **25**, 1; pp. 91–94.

Bimson, M. and Freestone, I.C. (1988) Some Egyptian glasses dated by royal inscriptions. *Journal of Glass Studies* **30**; pp. 1–15.

Biricotti, F. and Severi, M. (2004) A non-destructive methodology for the characterization of white marble of artistic and archaeological interest. *Journal of Cultural Heritage* **5**, 1; pp. 49–61.

Biron, I., Dandridge, P. and Wypyski, M. (1996) Techniques and materials in Limoges enamels. In: O'Neill (ed), 1996, pp. 48–62.

Biron, I., Morel, D. and Borel, T. (1998) Les triptyques reliquaries Dutuit: de l'oeil du connaisseur à l'examen en laboratoire, histoire d'une rehabilitation. *Techne* **8**; pp. 97–106.

Biron, I. and Pierrat-Bonnefois, G. (2002) La tête égyptienne en verre bleu du musée du Louvre: de la XVII dynastie au XX siècle. *Techne* **15**; pp. 30–38.

Birt, H., Jr. and Wagner, D. (1974) Die stress detection: Winning a battle in the war against cast copies. *The Numismatist* **87**, 6; pp. 1074–1077.

Birt, H., Jr. and Wagner, D. (1975) Defending genuine coins: The die stress controversy – evidence and numismatic scholarship. *The Numismatist* **88**, 6; pp. 1229–1238.

Bishop, R.L., Sayre, E.V. and Mishara, J. (1993) Compositional and structural characterization of Maya and Costa Rican jadeites. In: Lange (ed), 1993, pp. 30–60.

Bishop, R.L. and Blackman, M.J. (2002) Instrumental neutron activation analysis of archaeological ceramics: Scale and interpretation. *Accounts of Chemical Research* **35**, 8; pp. 603–610.

Black, J. (ed) (1987) *Recent Advances in the Conservation and Analysis of Artifacts.* Summer Schools Press, Institute of Archaeology, London.

Black, B. and Nadeau, H-W. (1990) *Michel Anguier's Pluto: The Marble of 1669 – New light on the French sculptor's career.* Athlone Press, London.

Blackman, M.J. and Nagle, C. (1983) Characterization of Dorset Paleo-Eskimo Nephrite Jade Artefacts. In: *Proceedings of the 22nd Symposium on Archaeometry, Bradford 1982*, A. Aspinall and S.E. Warren (eds). School of Physics and Arcaeological Sciences, University of Bradford, Bradford, Yorkshire, pp. 411–419.

Blair, C. (1991) Edward III's sword. *The Arms and Armour Society Newsletter* **1**; pp. 2–8. January.

Blair, C. (1992) Edward III's sword. *The Arms and Armour Society Newsletter*, **2**; pp. 4–9. April.

Blair, S.S., Bloom, J.M. and Wardwell, A.E. (1992) Reevaluating the date of the 'Buyid' silks by epigraphic and radiocarbon analysis. *Ars Orientalis* **22**; pp. 1–25.

Blakemore, K. (1983) *The Retail Jeweller's Guide*, 4th edn. Butterworths, London.

Blakemore, K. (1984) *The Retailer's Guide to Glass and Pottery.* Butterworths, London.

Blank, S. (1990) An introduction to plastics and rubbers in collections. *Studies in Conservation* **35**, 1; pp. 53–63.

Bloy, C.H. (1967) *A History of Printing Ink, Balls and Rollers.* Evelyn Adams and Mackay, London.

Bluemel, C. (1969) *Greek Sculptors at Work*, 2nd edn. Phaidon, London.

Bly, J. (ed) (1986) *Is it Genuine? How to Recognize an Authentic Antique.* Mitchell Beazley, London. Reissued 2002 as *Miller's Is it Genuine? How to Collect Antiques with Confidence.* Chancellor Press, London.

Boardman, J. (2001) *The History of Greek Vases: Potters, Painters and Pictures.* Thames and Hudson, London.

Böckmann, F. (1921) *Celluloid*, 2nd edn. Scott-Greenwood, London.

Boetzkes, M. and Stein, H. (eds) (1997) *Der Hildesheimer Silberfund.* Gerstenberg, Hildesheim.

Bohlmann, C. (1996) Zum Wandel der Antikenergänzungspaxis im Rom des ausgehenden 18. Jahrhunderts. *Arbeitsblätter für Restauratoren* **29**, 2; pp. 126–133.

Bomford, D. (ed) (2002) *Art in the Making: Underdrawings in Renaissance Paintings.* National Gallery Publications, London.

Bomford, D., Brown, C. and Roy, A. (1988) *Art in the Making: Rembrandt.* National Gallery Publications, London.

Bomford, D., Dunkerton, J., Gordon, D. and Roy, A. (1989) *Art in the Making: Italian Painting before 1400.* National Gallery Publications, London.

Bomford, D., Kirby, J., Leighton, J. and Roy, A. (1990) *Art in the Making: Impressionism.* National Gallery Publications, London.

Bonadies, S.D. (1994) Tomography of ancient bronzes. In: Scott *et al.* (eds), 1994, pp. 75–83.

Bonani, G., Ivy, S., Wölfli. W., Broshi, M., Carmi, I. and Strugnell, J. (1992) Radiocarbon Dating of Fourteen Dead Sea Scrolls. In: *Proceedings of the 14th International Radiocarbon Conference*, A. Long and R.S. Kra (eds). *Radiocarbon* **34**, 3; pp. 843–849.

Bonde, N., Tyers, I. and Wazny, T. (1997) Where does the timber come from? Dendrochronological evidence of the timber trade in Northern Europe 14th to 17th century AD. In: A. Sinclair, E. Slater and J. Gowlett (eds), 1997, pp. 201–204.

Boon, J.J., Tom, A. and Pureveen, J. (1993) Microgram scale pyrolysis mass spectrometry and pyrolysis gas chromatographic characterization of geological and archaeological amber and resin samples. In: Beck and Bouzek (eds), 1993, pp. 9–27.

Boon, J., van der Doelen, G., van der Horst, J., van den Berg, K.J. and Phenix, A. (1999) Advances in the current understanding of aged dammar and mastic triterpenoid varnishes on the molecular level. In: Harmssen (ed), 1999, pp. 92–104.

Boos, F.H. (1966) *The Ceramic Sculptures of Ancient Oaxaca.* A.S. Barnes, New York.

Bordenache Battaglia, G. and Emiliozzi, A. (1979 *et seq.*) *Le Ciste Prenestine.* Consiglio Nazionale della Ricerche, Firenze.

Borel, T. (1995) La radiographie des objets d'art. *Techne* 2; pp. 146–157.

Born, H. (ed) (1985) *Archäologische Bronzen antike Kunst moderne Technik.* Staatliche Museen Preussischer Kulturbesitz, Berlin.

Born, H. (1985a) Polychromie auf prähistorischen und antiken Kleinbronzen. In: Born (ed), 1985, pp. 71–84.

Born, H. (1985b) Korrosionsbilder auf ausgegrabenen Bronzen – Information für den Museumsbesucher. In: Born (ed), 1985, pp. 86–95.

Born, H. (1988) Die Bedeutung antiker Herstellungstechniken zur Beurteilung fälschungsverdächtiger Bronzen. In: *Vorträge des Symposiums-Zerstörungsfreie Prüfung von Kunstwerken.* Deutsche Gesellschaft für-Zerstörungsfreie Prüfung e V, Berlin, pp. 141–161.

Born, H. (1989) Antike Bohrung in Metall. *Acta Praehistorica et Archaeologica* 21; pp. 117–130.

Born, H. (1990) Patinated and painted bronzes: Exotic technique or ancient tradition? In: True and Podany (eds), 1990, pp. 179–196.

Born, H. (1993) Multi-colored antique bronze statues. In: La Niece and Craddock (eds), 1993, pp. 19–29.

Born, H., Metzen, H.A. and Ruthenberg, K. (1991) Antike Herstellungstechniken: Oberflächenuntersuchungen an enim süditalischen Muskelpanzer. *Acta praehistorica et archaeological* 22; pp. 157–168.

Borschneck, D., Schvoerer, M. and Bechtel, F. (2000) Étude Comparée de la cathodoluminescence de Marbres de Paros, Naxos et du Mont Pentélique. In: Schilardi and Katsonopoulou (eds), 2000, pp. 591–601.

Bortin, V. (1980) Science and the Shroud of Turin. *Biblical Archaeology* 43, 2; pp. 109–117.

Boston, N. (1892) *Exhibition Illustrating the Technical Methods of the Reproductive Arts from the Fifteenth Century to the Present Time, with Special Reference to the Photo-mechanical Processes.* Boston Museum of Fine Arts. A. Mudge & Son, Boston.

Bouquillon, A. and Gaborit, J.R. (1998) Chimie et authentification: les terres cuites des della Robbia. *Techne* 7; pp. 63–68.

Bourgarit, D., Mille, B., Borel, T., Baptiste, P. and Zéphir, T. (2003) A Millennium of Khmer Bronze Metallurgy: Analytical Studies of Bronze Artifacts from the Musée

Guimet and the Phnom Penh National Museum. In: Jett (ed), 2003, pp. 103–126.

Bourgeois, B., Boutaine, J-L. and Rattoni, B. (1996) Radiographie et restauration des marbes antiques: l'exemple du Musée du Louvre. In: Bridgland (ed), 1996, pp. 793–797.

Boutaine, J.L. (1976) Betagraphie et techniques connexes dans l'examen des documents graphiques. In: *Applicazione Deimethodi Nucleari nel Campo Opere Diarte,* R. Cesareo (ed). *Academia Nazionale dei Lincei,* Rome, pp. 459–477.

Bowman, H., Stross, F.H., Asaro, F., Hay, R.L., Heizer, R.F. and Michel, H.V. (1984) The northern colossus of Memnon: new slants. *Archaeometry* 26, 2; pp. 218–229.

Bowman, S.G.E. (1985) A study of the pre-dose characteristics of core material from a number of Benin and Lower Niger copper-alloy castings. *Nuclear Tracks* 10, 4–6; pp. 779–784.

Bowman, S.G.E. (1988) Observations of anomalous fading in maiolica. *Nuclear Tracks Radiation Measurement* 14, 1/2; pp. 131–137.

Bowman, S. (1990) *Radiocarbon Dating.* British Musuem Press, London.

Bowman, S. (1991a) Questions of chronology. In: Bowman (ed), 1991, pp. 117–140.

Bowman, S. (1991b) Authenticity testing using thermoluminescence analysis and its application to Italian maiolica. In: *Italian Renaissance Pottery,* T. Wilson (ed). British Museum Press, London, pp. 286–292.

Bowman, S. (ed) (1991) *Science and the Past.* British Musuem Press, London.

Bowman, S. (1994) Using radiocarbon: an update. *Antiquity* 68, 261; pp. 838–843.

Bowman, S.G.E., Cowell, M.R. and Cribb, J. (1989) Two thousand years of coinage in China: An analytical survey. *Journal of the Historical Metallurgy Society* 23, 1; pp. 25–30.

Brace, A.W. and Sheasby, P.G. (1979) *The Technology of Anodizing Aluminium,* 2nd edn. Technicopy, Stonehouse, Gloucsestershire.

Bradbury, F. (1912) *History of Old Sheffield Plate.* Macmillan, London.

Bradbury, F. (1959) *Collector's Guide to Marks of Origin on Silver Plate made in Great Britain and Ireland 1544–1959,* 10th edn. J.W. Northend, Sheffield.

Bradbury, S. and Bracegirdle, B. (1998) *Introduction to Light Microscopy.* BIOS Scientific in conjunction with the Royal Microscopical Society, Oxford.

Braga, M.G., Gallone, A., Samoggia, G. and Mazzetti, D. (1992) Cronologia di dipinti italiani contemporanei dalla caratterizzazione del bianco di titanio. In: *3a Conferenza Internazionale sulle prove non distruttive, metodi microanalitici e indagni ambientali per lo studio e la conservazione delle oprea d'arte,* M. Marabelli and P. Santopadre (eds). Associazone Italiana Prov. Non Distruttive, Rome, pp. 637–652.

Brammer, H. (1999) Firnisschichtungen: Beobachtungen an Farbfirnisquerschnitten vov vier Gemälden der

Kasseler Gemäldegalerie Alte Meister. In: Harmssen (ed), 1999, pp. 174–182.

Brandis, L. and Lyall, J. (1997) Properties of paper in naturally aged books. *Restaurator* **18**, 3; pp. 115–130.

Branigan, K. (1974) *Aegean Metalwork of the Early and Middle Bronze Age*. Oxford University Press, Oxford.

Braun, D. (1982) *Simple Methods for the Identification of Plastics*. Carl Hauser Verlag, Munich.

Braun, D.P. (1982) Radiographic analysis of temper in ceramic vessels: Goals and initial methods. *Journal of Field Archaeology* **9**, 3; pp. 183–192.

Bray, A. (1982) Mimbres black on white, melamine or Wedgwood? A ceramic wear-use analysis. *Kiva* **47**, 3; pp. 133–149.

Bray, W. (1978) *The Gold of Eldorado*. Times Newspapers, London.

Breas, O., Reniero, F. and Serrini, G. (1994) Isotope Mass Spectrometry: Analysis of wines from different countries. *Rapid Communications in Mass Spectrometry* **8**; pp. 967–970.

Bredius, A. (1932) An unpublished Vermeer. *The Burlington Magazine* **61**; pp. 145–147. October.

Breek, R. and Froentjes, W. (1975) Applications of pyrolysis gas chromatography on some of Van Meergeren's faked Vermeers and Pieter de Hooghs. *Studies in Conservation* **20**, 4; pp. 183–189.

Brent, M. (2001) Faking African art. *Archaeology* **54**, 1; pp. 27–32. Jan/Feb.

Bresee, R.R. (1986) General effects of ageing on textiles. *Journal of the American Institute for Conservation* **25**, 1; pp. 39–48.

Bridgland, J. (ed) (1996) *Preprints of the 11th Triennial ICOM Committee for Conservation Meeting*, Edinburgh 1–6 September 1996, ICOM. James and James, London.

Bridgman, C.F. (1964) The amazing patent on the radiography of paintings. *Studies in Conservation* **9**, 4; pp. 135–139.

Bridgman, C.F. (1965) Radiography of paper. *Studies in Conservation* **10**, 1; pp. 8–17.

Bridgman, C.F., Keck, S. and Sherwood, H.F. (1957–58) The radiography of panel paintngs by electron-emission. *Studies in Conservation* **3**, 4; pp. 175–182.

Bridgman, C.F., Michaels, P. and Sherwood, H.F. (1965) Radiography of a painting on copper by electron emission. *Studies in Conservation* **10**, 1; pp. 1–7.

Brill, R.H. (1969) The Scientific Investigation of Ancient Glasses. *Proceedings of the 8th International Congress on Glass,* London, July 1967. The Society of Glass Technology, Sheffield, pp. 47–68.

Brill, R.H., 1970 Lead and oxygen isotopes in ancient objects. In: *A Symposium on the Impact of the Natural Sciences on Archaeology, being Philosphical Transactions of the Royal Society of London* A. 269 i–iii; pp. 143–64.

Brill, R.H. (1987) Chemical analyses of some early Indian glasses. In: Bhardwaj (ed), 1987, pp. 1–25.

Brill, R.H. (1999) . *Chemical Analysis of Early Glasses*, 2 Vols. Corning Museum of Glass, Corning, New York.

Brill, R.H. (2001) Some thoughts on the chemistry and technology of Islamic glass. In: Carboni and Whitehouse, 2001, pp. 25–45.

Brill, R.H. and Hood, H.P. (1961) A new method of dating ancient glass. *Nature* **189**, 4758; pp. 12–14.

Brill, R.H., Fleischer, R.L., Buford Price, P. and Walker, R.M. (1964) The fission-track dating of man-made glasses: Preliminary results. *Journal of Glass Studies* **6**; pp. 151–156.

Brill, R.H., Yamasaki, K., Barnes, I.L., Rosman, K.J.R. and Diaz, M. (1979) Lead isotopes in some Japanese and Chinese glass. *Ars Orientalis* **11**; pp. 87–109.

Brill, R.H. and Martin, J.H. (eds) (1991) *Scientific Research in Early Chinese Glass*. Corning Museum of Glass, Corning, New York.

Brill, R.H., Shirahata, H., Lilyquist, C. and Vocke, R.D., Jr (1993) Lead isotope analysis of some objects from Egypt and the Near East: Pt 3. In: Lilyquist and Brill (eds), 1993, pp. 59–72.

Brill, R.H., Clayton, R.N., Mayeda, T.K. and Stapleton, C.P. (1999) Oxygen isotope analyses of early glasses. In: Brill, Vol. 1, 1999, pp. 303–322.

Brilli, M., Cavazzini, G. and Turi, B. (2005) New data of $^{87}Sr/^{86}Sr$ ratio in classical marble: an initial database for marble provenance determination. *Journal of Archaeological Science* **32**, 10; pp. 1543–1551.

Briquet, C-M. (1968) *Les Filigranes: Dictionaire historique des marques du papier dès leur apparition ver 1282 jusqu'en 1600*. Paper Publications Society, Amsterdam.

Bristow, M. (2004) Scientific detection of philatic forgeries. In: Weiss and Chartier (eds), 2004, pp. 55–65.

British Museum (1961) *An Exhibition of Forgeries and Deceptive Copies Held in the Department of Prints and Drawings*. Trustees of the British Museum, London.

Brittain, A., Wolpert, S. and Morton, P. (1958) *Engraving on Precious Metals*. N.A.G. Press, London.

Britton, D. and Richards, E.E. (1969) Optical emission spectroscopy and the study of metallurgy in the European Bronze Age. In: *Science in Archaeology,* D. Brothwell and E. Higgs (eds), 2nd edn. Thames and Hudson, London, pp. 603–613.

Broad, W. and Wade, N. (1985) *Betrayers of the Truth, Fraud and Deceit in the Halls of Science*. Oxford University Press, Oxford.

Brommelle, N. and Smith, P. (eds) (1988) *Urushi: Proceedings of the Urushi Study Group*. Getty Conservation Institute, Marina del Rey, CA. 1985, Tokyo.

Bronk, H., Adam, K., Müller, W. and Köcher, C.h. (1999) Electron probe microanalysis of a Jean II Pénicaud grisaille plaque from the Kunstgewerbemuseum Berlin – a first dating attempt of Limoges painted enamels by scientific investigations. *Berliner Beiträge zur Archäometrie* **16**; pp. 175–181.

Bronk, H., Schulze, G., Ritsema van Eck, P.C. and Bartel, H-G. (2000) Distinction of Venetian glass from façons de Venise glass on the basis of chemical analysis: an assessment of the chances and limitations. In: *Annales du 14th Congrès de l'Association Internationale pour l'Histoire du Verre.* J. Price (ed), Lochem, pp. 341–345.

Bronk, H. and Freestone, I.C. (2001) A quasi non-destructive microsampling technique for the analysis of intact glass objects by SEM/EDXA. *Archaeometry* **43**, 4; pp. 517–527.

Brothwell, D.R. and Pollard, A.M. (eds) (2001) *Handbook of Archaeological Sciences.* John Wiley & Sons, Chichester, Sussex.

Brown, B.F., Burnett, H.C., Chase, W.T., Goodway, M., Kruger, J. and Pourbaix, M. (eds) (1977) *Corrosion and Metal Artifacts.* National Bureau of Standards Special Publication 479, Washington DC.

Brown, B.L. (1989) Replication in the art of Veronese. *Studies in the History of Art* **20**; pp. 111–124.

Brown, K.L. and Clark, R.J.H. (2002) Analysis of pigmentary materials on the Vinland Map and Tartar Relation by Raman microprobe spectroscopy. *Analytical Chemistry* **74**, 15; pp. 3658–3661.

Brown, V.M. and Harrell, J.A. (1995) Topographical and petrological survey of ancient Roman quarries in the Eastern Desert of Egypt. In: Maniatis, Herz and Basiakos (eds), 1995, pp. 221–234.

Browning, B.L. (1977) *The Analysis of Paper*, 2nd edn. Marcel Dekker, New York.

Brownsword, R. (1988) A possible Romanesque object made from zinc. *Journal of the Historical Metallurgy Society* **22**, 2; pp. 102–103.

Brownsword, R. (2004) Medieval metalworking: an analytical study of copper-alloy objects. *Journal of the Historical Metallurgy Society* **28**, 2; pp. 88–105.

Brownsword, R. and Pitt, E.E.H. (1983) Alloy composition of some cast 'latten' objects of the 15/16th centuries. *Journal of the Historical Metallurgy Society* **17**, 1; pp. 44–49.

Brownsword, R. and Pitt, E.E.H. (1984) X-ray fluorescence analysis of English 13th–16th century pewter flatware. *Archaeometry* **26**, 2; pp. 237–244.

Brownsword, R. and Blackwell, R. (1984) Four bronze figures in the Ashmolean Museum: Reconsideration of their origins. *MASCA Journal* **3**, 3; pp. 82–86.

Brownsword, R. and MacGregor, A. (1986) False prophets? Four bronzes in the Ashmolean reconsidered. *Bruckmanns Pantheon* **44**; pp. 5–9.

Brownsword, R. and Pitt, E. (1996) Medieval phosphor-bronze not confirmed. *Journal of the Antique Metalware Society* **4**; pp. 14–15.

Bruce-Mitford, R.L.S. (1956) Late Saxon disc-brooches. In: *Dark-Age Britain*, D.B. Harden (ed). Methuen, London, pp. 171–201.

Brunello, F. (1973) *The Art of Dyeing in the History of Mankind.* Neri Poza, Vicenza. [Trans. B. Hickey].

Bruni, F. (1994) *La Fusione Artistica a Cera Persa.* Edizioni Arte in, Venezia-Marghera.

Bruton, E. (1978) *Diamonds*, 2nd edn. The Chilton Book Co, Radnor, Pa.

Brydson, J.A. (1975) *Plastic Materials.* Newnes-Butterworths, London.

Buchbauer, G., Jirovetz, L., Wasicky, M. and Nikiforov, A. (1995) On the odor of old books. *Journal of Pulp and Paper Science* **21**, 11; pp. J398–J400.

Buchner, G.J.A. (1891) *Die Metallfärbung und deren Ausführung, mit besonderer Berücksichtigung der chemischen Metallfärbung*, Revised editions 1907 and 1920. W.M. Krayn, Berlin.

Buck, C.E., Cavanagh, W.G. and Litton, C.D. (1996) *Bayesnian Approach to Interpreting Archaeological Data.* John Wiley & Sons, Chichester.

Bucklow, S. (1997) The description of craquelure patterns. *Studies in Conservation* **42**, 3; pp. 129–140.

Bucklow, S. (1999) The description and classification of craquelure. *Studies in Conservation* **44**, 3; pp. 233–244.

Buckton, D. (1988) Bogus Byzantine enamels in Baltimore and Washington DC. *Journal of the Walters Art Gallery* **46**; pp. 11–24.

Budd, P., Pollard, A.M., Scaife, B. and Thomas, R.G. (1995) The possible fractionation of lead isotopes in ancient metallurgical processes. *Archaeometry* **37**, 2; pp. 143–150.

Budde, L. and Nicholls, R. (1964) *A Catalogue of the Greek and Roman Sculpture in the Fitz William Museum, Cambridge.* Cambridge University Press, Cambridge.

Budge, E.A.W. (1914) *Catalogue of Egyptian Sculpture in the British Museum.* Trustees of the British Museum, London.

Budgen, N.F. (1924) *Cadmium.* Charles Griffin, London.

Bunker, E.C. (1994) A new dilemma: Recent technical studies and related forgeries. *Orientations* **25**, 3; p. 90.

Bunker, E.C. (1997) Gold wire in ancient China. *Orientations* **28**, 3; pp. 94–95.

Bunker, E.C., Chase, T., Northover, P. and Salter, C. (1993) Some early Chinese examples of mercury gilding and silvering. In: *Outils et ateliers d'orfèvres*, C. Eluère (ed). Antiquités nationales mémoire 2, Société des Amis du Musée des Antiquités Nationales et du château de Saint-Germain-en-Laye, Paris, pp. 55–66.

Burgio, L., Ciomartan, D.A. and Clark, R.J.H. (1997a) Raman microscopy study of the pigments on three illuminated Mediaeval Latin manuscripts. *Journal of Raman Spectroscopy* **28**; pp. 79–83.

Burgio, L., Ciomartan, D.A. and Clark, R.J.H. (1997b) Pigment identification on medieval manuscripts, paintings, and other artefacts by Raman microscopy: applications to the study of three German manuscripts. *Journal of Molecular Structure* **405**; pp. 1–11.

Burgio, L., Clark, R.J.H. and Gibbs, P.J. (1999) Pigment identification studies *in situ* of Javanese, Thai, Korean, Chinese and Uighur manuscripts by Raman microscopy. *Journal of Raman Spectroscopy* **30**; pp. 181–184.

Burgio, L. and Clark, R.J.H. (2000) Comparative pigment analysis of six modern Egyptian papyri and an authentic one of the 13th century BC by Raman microscopy and other techniques. *Journal of Raman Spectroscopy* **31**; pp. 395–401.

Burgio, L. and Clark, R.J.H. (2001) Library of FT- Raman spectra of pigments, minerals, pigment media and varnishes, and supplement to library of Raman spectra of pigments with visible excitation. *Spectrochimica Acta* **A57**; pp. 1491–1521.

Burkart, W. (1960) *Mechanical Polishing.* Robert Draper, Teddington, Middx. [Trans. H. Silman with addition material by R. Draper].

Burke, E.A.J. (2001) Raman microspectrometry of fluid inclusions. *Lithos* **55**, 1–4; pp. 139–158.

Burleigh, R. and Whalley, P. (1983) On the relative geological ages of amber and copal. *Journal of Natural History* **17**; pp. 121–919.

Burlington, Fine Arts Club (1924) *Catalogue of a Collection of Counterfeits, Imitations and Copies of Works of Art.* Burlington Fine Arts Club, London.

Burmester, A. (1983) Far eastern Lacquers: classification by pyrolysis mass spectrometry. *Archaeometry* **25**, 1; pp. 45–58.

Burmester, A. and Koller, J. (1987) Known and New Corrosion Products on Bronzes: Their identification and assessment, particularly in relation to organic protective coatings. In: Black (ed), 1987, pp. 97–104.

Burnett, A. (1992) Coin faking in the Renaissance. In: Jones (ed), pp. 15–22.

Burnett, A. (1998) Coin copying: forgery or reproduction. *CCNB Newsletter* **19**; pp. 1–2.

Burnett, A.M., Craddock, P.T. and Preston, K. (1982) New light on the origins of *orichalcum.* In: *Proceedings of the 9th International Congress of Numismatics*, T. Hackens and R. Weiller (eds). *Louvain-la-Neuve, Luxembourg*, pp. 263–268. Association Internationale des Numismates Professionnels, Publication **6**.

Burnham, R.J.P. and Tarling, D.H. (1975) Magnetization of shards as an assistance to the reconstruction of pottery vessels. *Studies in Conservation* **20**, 3; pp. 153–157.

Burroughs, A. (nd) *Art Criticism from a Laboratory.* George Allen and Unwin, London.

Bury, S. (1971) *Victorian Electroplate.* Country Life Books, London.

Butcher, K., and Ponting, M. (1998) Atomic absorption spectrometry and Roman silver coins. In: Oddy and Cowell (eds), 1998, pp. 308–334.

Butcher, K. and Gill, D.W.J. (1993) The Director, the Dealer, the Goddess, and Her Champions – The acquisition of the Fitzwilliam Goddess. *American Journal of Archaeology* **97**, 3; pp. 383–401.

Butcher, S.A. (1976) Enamelling. In: Strong and Brown (eds), 1976, pp. 43–51.

Button, V. (1997) The Arundel Society – techniques in the art of copying. *V & A Conservation Journal* **43**; pp. 16–19. April.

Butts, A. and Coxe, C.D. (eds) (1967) *Silver: Economics, Metallurgy, and Use.* D. Van Nostrand, Princeton, New Jersey.

Cadbury, D. (2001) *The Dinosaur Hunters.* Fourth Estate, London.

Cahill, T.A., Schwab, R.N., Kusko, B.H., Eldred, R.A., Möller, G., Dutschke, D., Wick, D.L. and Pooley, A.S. (1987) The Vinland Map, revisited: New compositional evidence on its inks and parchment. *Analytical Chemistry* **59**; pp. 829–833.

Cahill, T.A. and Kusko, B.H. (1995) Compositional and structural studies of the Vinland Map and Tartar Relation. In: Skelton, Marston and Painter, 1995, pp. xxix–xl.

Cahn, H.A. (1970) Some thoughts on the collecting of bronzes. In: Doeringer, Mitten and Steinberg (eds), 1970, pp. 271–278.

Caldararo, N. (1995) Storage conditions and physical treatments relating to the dating of the Dead Sea Scrolls. *Radiocarbon* **37**, 1; pp. 21–32.

Caldararo, N. (1997) The status of research into the authenticity of the Shroud. In: *Approfondimento Sidone* **1**, 1; pp. 51–66.

Caldararo, N. and Kahle, T.B. (1989) An analysis of the present state of research into the authenticity of the Shroud of Turin. *Maltechnik-Restauro* **95**, 4; pp. 297–305.

Caley, E.R. (1927) The Stockholm Papyrus. *Journal of Chemical Education* **4**; pp. 979–1002.

Caley, E.R. (1964) *Orichalcum and Related Ancient Alloys.* The American Numismatic Society, Monograph 151, New York.

Calliari, I., Magrini, M. and Martini, R. (1998) Characterization of Republican and Imperial Roman coins. *Science and Technology for Cultural Heritage* **7**, 2; pp. 81–89.

Calligaro, T., Dran, J.C. and Salomon, J. (2000a) PIXE analysis of gemstones as a tool for the determination of their provenance: The example of the Ishtar's Statuette rubies. In: Demortier and Adriaens (eds), 2000, pp. 60–62.

Calligaro, T., Dran, J-C., Poirot, J-P., Querré, G., Salomon, J.C. and Zwaan, J.C. (2000b) PIXE/PIGE characterisation of emeralds using an external micro-beam. In: Andersen and Rehn (eds), 2000, pp. 769–774.

Calnan, C. and Haines, B. (eds) (1991) *Leather: Its Composition and Changes with Time.* The Leather Conservation Centre, Northampton, Northants.

Calvini, P., Franceschi, E. and Palazzi, D. (1996) Artificially induced slow-fire in sized papers: FTIR, TG, DTA and SEM analyses. *Science and Technology for Cultural Heritage* **5**, 1; pp. 1–11.

Cameron, H.K. (1974) Technical aspects of monumental brasses. *The Archaeological Journal* **131**; pp. 215–237.

Cammann, S.V.R. (1950) The story of Hornbill ivory. *University Museum Bulletin* **15**, 4; pp. 19–47.

Campbell, I.C.C. (2000) An independent gemmological examination of six De Beers synthetic diamonds. *The Journal of Gemmology* **27**, 1; pp. 32–44.

Campbell, W. (1933) *Greek and Roman Plated Coins.* Numismatic Notes and Monographs 57. The American Numismatic Society, New York.

Campbell Pedersen, M. (2004) *Gem and Ornamental Materials of Organic Origin.* Elsevier Butterworth-Heinemann, Oxford.

Canning, (1901) *The Canning Handbook.* [Frequent new editions and reprints; later editions include a wide range of surface treatments; latest used here is the 1989 reprint of the 23rd edn], 1st edn. Canning and E. & F.N. Spon, Birmingham and London.

Caple, C. (1995) Factors in the production of Medieval and Post Medieval brass pins. In: D.R. Hook and D.R.M. Gaimster (eds), 1995, pp. 221–234.

Carboni, S., Pilosi, L. and Wypyski, M.T. (1998) A gilded and enamelled glass plate in the Metropolitan Museum of Art. In: McCray (ed), 1998, pp. 79–102.

Carboni, S. and Whitehouse, D. (2001) *Glass of the Sultans.* Metropolitan Museum of Art, New York.

Carbonin, S., Ajò, D., Rizzo, I. and De Zuane, F. (2000) Identification of synthetic spinels by means of photo-luminescence spectroscopy. *The Journal of Gemmology* **27**, 1; pp. 30–31.

Cardamone, J.M., Keister, K.M. and Osareh, A.H. (1992) Degradation and Conservation of Cellulosics and their Esters. In: Allen *et al.* (eds), 1992, pp. 108–124.

Cariati, F. and Bruni, S. (2000) Raman spectroscopy. In: Ciliberto and Spoto (eds), 2000, pp. 255–278.

Cariati, F., Rampazzi, L., Toniolo, L. and Pozzi, A. (2000) Calcium oxalate films on stone surfaces: Experimental assessment of the chemical formation. *Studies in Conservation* **45**, 3; pp. 180–188.

Carlson, J.H. (1977) X-ray fluorescence analysis of pewter: English and Scottish measures. *Archaeometry* **19**, 2; pp. 147–156.

Carlyle, L., Binnie, N., van der Doelen, G., Boon, J., McLean, B. and Ruggles, A. (1999) Traditional painting varnishes project: Preliminary report on natural and artificial aging and a note on the preparation of cross-sections. In: Harmssen (ed), 1999, pp. 110–127.

Carlyle, L. and Bourdeau, J. (eds) (1994) *Varnishes: Authenticity and Permanence. Workshop Handbook.* Canadian Conservation Institute, Extension Services, Ottawa.

Caron, B. (1997) Roman figure-engraved glass in the Metropolitan Museum of Art. *Metropolitan Museum Journal* **32**; pp. 19–50.

Carr, C. and Riddick, E.B., Jr. (1990) Advances in ceramic radiography and analysis: Laboratory methods. *Journal of Archaeological Science* **17**, 1; pp. 13–66.

Carradice, I. (1998) Museums and reproductions. *CCNB Newsletter* **19**; p. 3.

Carroll, D.L. (1970) Drawn wire and the identification of forgeries in ancient jewelry. *American Journal of Archaeology* **74**; p. 401.

Carroll, D.L. (1972) Wire drawing in antiquity. *American Journal of Archaeology* **76**; pp. 321–323.

Carswell, J. (2000) *Blue and White: Chinese Porcelain around the World.* British Museum Press, London.

Carter, G.F. (ed) (1978) *Archaeological Chemistry II, Advances in Chemistry Series 171.* American Chemical Society, Washington D.C.

Carter, G.F. (1984) Formation of the image on the Shroud of Turin by X-rays: A new hypothesis. In: Lambert (ed), 1984, pp. 425–446.

Carter, G.F. (1998) Coin analysis by wavelength dispersive X-ray fluorescence (WDXRF). In: Oddy and Cowell (eds), 1988, pp. 425–442.

Carter, G.F., Caley, E.R., Carlson, J.H., Carriveau, G.W., Hughes, M.J., Rengan, K. and Segebade, C. (1983) Comparison of analyses of eight Roman orichalcum coin fragments by seven methods. *Archaeometry* **25**, 2; pp. 201–213.

Cartier, R.H. (2001) Disclose, describe, dress-up, disguise, deceive …credibility and gem descriptions. *The Journal of Gemmology* **27**, 7; pp. 426–431.

Cartwright, H.M. (1930) *Photogravure.* American Photographic Publishing Co., Boston.

Case, R.J., Tucker, A.O., Maciarello, M.J. and Wheeler, K.A. (2003) Chemistry and ethnobotany of commercial incense copals, copal blanco, copal oro, and copal negro, of North America. *Economic Botany* **57**, 2; pp. 189–202.

Casini, A., Lotti, F., Picollo, M., Stefani, L. and Buzzegoli, E. (1999) Image spectroscopy mapping technique for non-invasive analysis of paintings. *Studies in Conservation* **44**, 1; pp. 39–48.

Casson, S. (1927) Review of *The Cambridge Ancient History: Vol 1 of Plates. Journal of Hellenic Studies* **47**; pp. 298–299.

Casson, S. (1933) *The Technique of Early Greek Sculpture.* Oxford University Press, Oxford.

Castorina, F., Preite Martinez, M. and Turi, B. (1997) Provenance determination of classical marbles by the combined use of oxygen, carbon and strontium isotopes: a preliminary study. *Science and Technology for Cultural Heritage* **6**, 2; pp. 145–150.

Catling, D. and Grayson, J. (1982) *Identification of Vegetable Fibres.* Chapman & Hall with Methuen, New York. (reissued 1998, Archeotype Books).

Cavaceppi, B. (1768, 1769 & 1772) *Raccolta d'Antiche Statue, Busti, Bassirilievi (ed) Altre Sculture Ristaurate I.* Salomoni, Roma.

Cavanagh, P.K. (1990) Practical Considerations and Problems of Bronze Casting. In: True and Podany (eds), 1990a, pp. 145–160.

Caverhill, J., Latimer, I. and Singer, B. (1996) An investigation into the use of a laser for the removal of modern ink marks from paper. *The Conservator* **20**; pp. 65–76.

CDA (1964a) *Copper Data.* Copper Development Association Publication 12, London.

CDA (1964b) *Copper and Copper Alloys: Compositions and Mechanical Properties.* Copper Development Association Publication 36, London.

CDA (1966) *Surface Treatments for Copper and Copper Alloys.* Copper Development Association Publication 67, London.

Cellini, P. (1955) Ne sutor ultra crepidam. *Paragone* **65**; pp. 44–47.

Cescinsky, H. (1931) *The Gentle Art of Faking Furniture.* Chapman & Hall, London. (reprinted 1967; Dover, New York).

C.G.F. (C.G. Fink) (1944) Patina. In: *Encyclopaedia Britannica* **20**; Chicago, pp. 230–231.

Chalain, J-P., Fritsch, E. and Hänni, H.A. (1999–2000) Identification des diamants GE POL (parts 1 & 2). *Revue de Gemmologie a.f.g.* **138/139–140**; pp. 32–33, 44–46.

Chamberlain, W. (1972) *Etching and Engraving*. Thames and Hudson, London.

Chamberlain, W. (1978) *Woodcut Printing*. Thames and Hudson, London.

Chambers, P. (2002) *Bones of Contention The Archaeopteryx Scandal*. John Murray, London.

Chandra, R.G. (1979) *Indo-Greek Jewellery*. Abhinav Publications, New Delhi.

Chapman, F.R. (1891) On the working of greenstone. *Transactions of the New Zealand Institute* **24**; pp. 279–538.

Chapman, I. (1999) *The Art of Rhinoceros Horn Carving in China*. Christies' Books, London.

Charleston, R.J. (1964) Wheel-engraving and -cutting: Some early equipment. I: Engraving. *Journal of Glass Studies,* **6**; pp. 83–100.

Charleston, R.J. (1965) Wheel-engraving and -cutting: Some early equipment. II: Water-power and cutting. *Journal of Glass Studies* **7**; pp. 41–54.

Charleston, R.J. (1972) Enamelling and gilding on glass. In: Glass Circle I, R.J. Charleston, W. Evans and A. Polak (eds). Newcastle, pp. 18–32.

Chase, W.T. (1974) Comparative analysis of archaeological bronzes. In: Beck (ed), 1974, pp. 148–185.

Chase, W.T. (1977) What is the smooth lustrous black surface on ancient bronze mirrors? In: the Structured Questions Section of Brown *et al.* (eds), 1977, pp. 191–203.

Chase, W.T. and Franklin, U.M. (1979) Early Chinese black mirrors and pattern-etched weapons. *Ars Orientalis* **11**; pp. 215–258.

Chastel, A. and Klein, R. [trans. and (eds)] (1969) *Gauricius Pomponius: De Sculpturo, 1504*. Hautes études médiévales et modernes, **5**. Dorz, Geneva.

Chen, C.-S., Brown, C.W. and Bide, M.J. (1997) Nondestructive near-infra-red analysis for the identification of dyes on textiles. *Journal of the Society of Dyers and Colorists* **113**, 2; pp. 51–57.

Cheng, C.F. and Schwitter, C.M. (1957) Nickel in ancient bronzes. *American Journal of Archaeology* **61**; pp. 351–365.

Cheng, H., He, W., Yao, H., Tang, J., Yang, F., Ma, C., Shan, G., Zhong, Y. and Wang, W. (1997) A study on the elemental compositions of ancient and modern Chinese inks. *Wenwu baohu yu kaogu kexue* **9**, 1; pp. 16–19. [Chinese with English summary].

Chevalier, U. (1899) *Le Saint Suaire de Turin, est-il l'original ou une copie?* Menard, Chambéry.

Chia-Jen Kecskes, L. (1986) Chinese ink and ink-making. *Printing History* **8**, 1; pp. 3–12.

Chiari, G., Giordano, A. and Menges, G. (1996) Non destructive X-ray diffraction analyses of unprepared samples. *Science and Technology for Cultural Heritage* **5**, 1; pp. 21–36.

Chiavari, G., Fabbri, D., Mazzeo, R., Bocchini, P. and Galletti, G.C. (1995) Pyrolysis gas chromatography-mass spectrometry of natural resins used for artistic objects. *Chromatographia* **41**, 5/6; pp. 273–281.

Child, R. (1993) Modern electroplating and elecroforming techniques. In: La Niece and Craddock (eds), 1993, pp. 291–300.

Childs-Johnson, E. (ed) (2002) *Enduring Art of Jade Age China: Vol. II. Chinese Jades of Late Neolithic Through Han Periods*. Throckmorton Fine Art, New York.

Chittenden, J. and Seltman, C. (1947) *Greek Art. A Commemorative Catalogue of the Royal Academy Exhibition 1946*. Faber and Faber, London.

Ciliberto, E. and Spoto, G. (eds) (2000) *Modern Analytical Methods in Art and Archaeology*. John Wiley, New York.

Cladbach, J. (1999) Modern varnishes: Ageing and possibility of stabilization. In: Harmssen (ed), 1999, pp. 105–109.

Claridge, A. (1990) Ancient techniques of making joins in marble statuary. In: True and Podany (eds), 1990b, pp. 135–62.

Clark, R.J.H. (1995) Raman microscopy: application to the identification of pigments on medieval manuscripts. *Chemical Society Review* **24**; pp. 187–196.

Clark, R.J.H. (1999) Raman microscopy: sensitive probe of pigments on manuscripts, paintings and other artefacts. *Journal of Molecular Structure* **480–1**; pp. 15–20.

Clark, R.J.H. (2002) Applications of Raman spectroscopy to the identification and composition of pigments and art objects. In: *Handbook of Vibrational Spectroscopy* 4, J.M. Chalmers and P.R. Griffiths (eds). John Wiley, London and New York, pp. 2977–2992.

Clark, R.J.H., Cooksey, C.J., Daniels, M.A.M. and Withnall, R. (1993) Indigo, woad and Tyrian purple: Important vat dyes from antiquity to the present. *Endeavour* **17**, 4; pp. 191–199.

Clark, R.J.H., Cridland, L., Kariuki, B.M., Harris, K.D.M. and Withnall, R. (1995) Synthesis, structural characterisation and Raman spectroscopy of the inorganic pigments lead tin yellow types I and II and lead antimonate yellow: their identification on medieval paintings and manuscripts. *Journal of the Chemical Society, Dalton Transactions* **16**; pp. 2577–2582.

Clark, R.J.H. and Huxley, K. (1996) Raman spectroscopic study of the pigments on a large illuminated Qur'an circa thirteenth century. *Science and Technology for Cultural Heritage* **5**, 2; pp. 95–101.

Clarke, B. (2001) Searching for evidence of 19th century print restoration. In: Oddy and Smith (eds), 2001, pp. 49–56.

Clarke, R. (1935) The flint-knapping industry at Brandon. *Antiquity* **9**, 33; pp. 38–56.

Claybourn, M. and Ansell, M. (2004) Using Raman spectroscopy to solve crimes: Inks, questioned documents and fraud. In: Weiss and Chartier (eds), 2004, pp. 275–297.

Clements, J. (1997) Piltdown Man again. *Current Archaeology* **13**, 7 (151); p. 279.

Clunas, C. (1992) Connoisseurs and aficionados: the real and the fake in Ming China (1368–1644). In: Jones (ed), 1992, pp. 151–156.

Coe, B. and Haworth-Booth, M. (1983) *A Guide to Early Photographic Processes*. Victoria and Albert Museum, London.

Cohen, M. (1937) Aging phenomena in a silver-rich copper alloy. *Transactions of AIME* **124**; pp. 138–157.

Cohn, M.B. [trans. and (ed).]. (1997) *Old Master Prints and Drawings*. Amsterdam University Press, Amsterdam.

Cohon, R. (1996) *Discovery and Deceit: Archaeology and the Forger's Craft*. Exhibition catalogue, Nelson-Atkins Museum, Kansas.

Cole, H., Sieber, R., Stevens, P., Jr. *et al.* (1975) Fakes, fakers and fakery: Authenticity in African art. *African Arts* **8**, 3; pp. 20–31, 48–74.

Cole, S. (1955) *Counterfeit*. John Murray, London.

Cole, S. (1961) Forgeries and the British Museum. *Antiquity* **35**, 138; pp. 103–106.

Coles, J. and Taylor, J. (1971) The Wessex culture: a minimal view. *Antiquity* **45**, 177; pp. 6–14.

Colley, J. (1990) Examination and identification of counterfeit paper. *AICCM Bulletin* **16**, 4; pp. 53–58.

Collins, A.T. (2001) The color of diamond and how it may be changed. *The Journal of Gemmology* **27**, 6; pp. 341–359.

Collins, W.F. (1934) The mirror-black and 'quick-silver' patinas of certain Chinese bronzes. *Journal of the Royal Anthropological Institute* **64**; pp. 69–79.

Colomban, Ph. (2003) Analysis of ancient European, Islamic and Asian ceramics by non-destructive Raman (micro)spectrometry. In: *Ceramics in the Society*, S. Di Perro, V. Serneels and M. Maggetti (eds). Dept. of Geosciences Universitas Friburgensis, Fribourg, pp. 87–97.

Colomban, Ph. (2005) Case study: Glasses, glazes and ceramics-recognition of ancient technology from the Raman spectra. In: Edwards and Chalmers (eds), 2005, pp. 192–206.

Colomban, Ph. and Treppoz, F. (2001) Identification and differentiation of ancient and modern European porcelains by Raman macro- and micro-spectroscopy. *Journal of Raman Spectroscopy* **32**; pp. 93–102.

Colomban, Ph., Sagon, G., Louhichi, A., Binous, H. and Ayed, N. (2001a) Identification par microscopie Raman des tessons et pigments de glaçures de céramiques de L'Ifriqiya (Dougga, XI–XVIIIèmes siècles). *Revue d'Archéométrie* **25**; pp. 101–112.

Colomban, Ph., Sagon, G. and Faurel, X. (2001b) Differentiation of antique ceramics from the Raman spectra of their colored glazes and paintings. *Journal of Raman Spectroscopy* **32**; pp. 351–360.

La Commission Internationale (1928) Fouilles de Glozel: Rapport de la Commission Internationale. *Revue Anthropologique* **27**; pp. 389–416.

Condamin, J. and Picon, M. (1972) Changes suffered by coins in the course of time and the influence of these on the results of different methods of analysis. In: Hall and Metcalf (eds), 1972, pp. 49–66.

Connors, S.A. (1998) *Chemical and Physical Characterization of the Degradation of Vulcanized Natural Rubber in the Museum Environment*. Queen's University at Kingston Press, Kingston, Ontario.

Conti, A. and Glanville, H. (2007) *History of the Restoration and Conservation of Work of Art*. Butterworth-Heinemann, Oxford.

Cook, J.G. (1984) *Handbook of Textile Fibres: Pt. 1 Natural Fibres, Pt 2 Man-made Fibres*, 5th edn. Merrow Technical Library, Shildon, Co, Durham.

Cook, A.C., Wadsworth, J. and Southon, J.R. (2001) AMS Radiocarbon Dating of Ancient Iron Artifacts: A New Carbon Extraction Method in Use at LLNL. In: *Proceedings of the 17th International Radiocarbon Conference*, I, Carmi and E. Boaretto (eds). *Radiocarbon* **43**, 2A; pp. 221–227.

Cook, A.C., Wadsworth, J., Southon, J.R. and van der Merwe, N.J. (2003) AMS radiocarbon dating of rusty iron. *Journal of Archaeological Science* **30**, 1; pp. 95–101.

Cook, B. (1984) A fake porphyry head. *Burlington Magazine* **126**, 970; pp. 19–20.

Cooney, J.D. (1960) Glass sculpture in Ancient Egypt. *Journal of Glass Studies* **2**; pp. 11–43.

Cooper, D.R. (1988) *The Art and Craft of Coinmaking*. Spink, London.

Cooper, E. (2000) *Ten Thousand Years of Pottery*, 4th edn. British Museum Press, London.

Corazza, M., Pratesi, G., Cipriani, C., Lo Giudice, A., Rossi, P., Vittone, E., Manfredotti, C., Pecchioni, E., Manganelli, D. and Fratini, F. (2001) Ionoluminescence and cathodoluminescence in marbles of historic and architectural interest. *Archaeometry* **43**, 4; pp. 439–446.

Coremans, P.B. (1949) *Van Meegeren's Faked Vermeers and Pieter de Hooghs*. J.M. Meulenhoff, Amsterdam.

Coremans, P., Gettens, R.J. and Thissen, J. (1952) La technique des 'Primitifs Flamands'. *Studies in Conservation* **1**, 1; pp. 1–29.

Cornec, S. (2000) Approche des patines sur bois d'Afrique. *Techne* **11**; pp. 40–45.

Corona, E. (1980) Richerche dendrochronologiche su due violini del XVIII secolo. *Italia For. E. Mont* **35**; pp. 112–115.

Corona, E. (1990) Note dendrochronologiche sugli strumenti dell'Istituto del Pieta di Venezia. In: *Collana di Studi Organologici*, M. Tiella and L. Primon (eds). Marco Tiella-Luca Primon, Trento, pp. 83–87.

Corrigan, C. (1997a). Drawing techniques. In: Cohn (ed), 1997, pp. 61–85.

Corrigan, C. (1997b). The constituent materials of paper. In: Cohn (ed), 1997, pp. 225–230.

Cortazzi, H. (1983) *Isles of Gold: Antique Maps of Japan*. Weatherhill, New York & Tokyo.

Cortesão, A. (1971). Is the Vinland Map genuine? In: Washburn (ed), 1971, pp. 15–18.

Cotter, M.J., Meyers, P., van Zelst, L., Olin, J. and Sayre, E.V. (1976) A study of the materials and techniques used by some XIX century American oil paint-ers by means of neutron activation autoradiography. In: *Applicazione Deimethodi Nucleari nel Campo Opere Diarte, Academia Nazionale dei Lincei*, Cesareo, R. (ed), Rome, pp. 163–203.

Coulston, J.C. and Phillips, E.J. (1988) *Corpus of Sculpture of the Roman World: Great Britain* **1**, *fasc. 6: Hadrian's Wall West of the North Tyne and Carlisle.* The British Academy, London.

Coupry, C. (1992) Les oeuvres d'art et les artisans à l'épreuve du laser. *Revue du Palais de la Découverte* **20**, 196; pp. 15–36.

Coupry, C., Lautié, A. and Revault, M. (1994) Contribution of Raman spectroscopy to art and his-tory. *Journal of Raman Spectroscopy* **25**; pp. 80–94.

Coupry, C. and Brissaud, D. (1996). Applications in art, jewelry and forensic science. In: Turrell and Corset (eds), 1996, pp. 421–454.

Coupry, C., Sagon, G. and Gorguet-Ballesteros, P. (1997) Raman spectroscopic investigation of blue contempo-rary textiles. *Journal of Raman Spectroscopy* **28**; pp. 85–89.

Couraud, C. and Bahn, P.G. (1982) Azilian Pebbles in British Collections: a Re-examination. *Proceedings of the Prehistoric Society* **48**; pp. 45–52.

Courty, M.A. and Roux, V. (1995) Identification of wheel throwing on the basis of ceramic surface features and microfabrics. *Journal of Archaeological Science* **22**, 1; pp. 17–50.

Cowell, M.R. (1988) A note on an early application of aluminium bronze. *Journal of the Historical Metallurgy Society* **22**, 2; pp. 93–95.

Cowell. M.R. (1992) An analytical survey of the British Celtic gold coinage. In: *Celtic Coinage: Britain and Beyond*, M. Mays (ed). British Archaeological Reports British Series 222, Oxford. pp. 207–233.

Cowell, M.R. (1998) Coin analysis by energy dispersive X-ray fluorescence spectrometry. In: Oddy and Cowell (eds), 1998, pp. 448–460.

Cowell, M.R. and Lowick, N.M. (1988) Silver from the Panjhir mines. In: Oddy (ed), 1998, pp. 65–74.

Cowell, M.R., Cribb, J., Bowman, S.G.E. and Shashoua, Y. (1993) The Chinese cash: Composition and produc-tion. In: Archibald and Cowell (eds), 1993, pp. 185–198.

Cowell, M.R. and Ponting, M. (2000). British Museum analyses. In: Hollstein (ed), 2000, pp. 49–54.

Cowell, M.R., Craddock, P.T., Pike, A.W.G. and Burnett, A.M. (2000) An analytical survey of Roman provincial copper-alloy coins and the continuity of brass production in Asia Minor. In: *XII. Intrnationaler Numismatischer Kongress Berlin 1997*, B. Kluge and B. Weisser (eds). Association Internationale des Numismates Professionnels, Berlin, pp. 70–77.

Cowell, M.R., La Niece, S. and Rawson, J. (2003). A Study of Later Chinese Metalwork. In: Jett (ed), 2003, pp. 80–89.

Cox, G.A. and Pollard, A.M. (1977) X-ray fluorescence analysis of ancient glass: the importance of sample preparation. *Archaeometry* **19**, 1; pp. 45–54.

Craddock, P.T. (1976) The composition of the cop-per alloys used by the Greek, Etruscan and Roman civilisations. 1: The Greeks before the Archaic Period. *Journal of Archaeological Science* **3**, 2; pp. 93–113.

Craddock, P.T. (1977) The composition of the copper alloys used by the Greek, Etruscan and Roman civili-sations. 2: The Archaic, Classical and Hellenistic Greeks. *Journal of Archaeological Science* **4**, 2; pp. 103–123.

Craddock, P.T. (1978) The composition of copper alloys used by the Greek, Etruscan and Roman civilisa-tions. 3: The origins and early use of brass. *Journal of Archaeological Science* **5**, 1; pp. 1–16.

Craddock, P.T. (1980) The first brass: Some early claims reconsidered. *MASCA Journal* **1**, 5; pp. 131–133.

Craddock, P.T. (1981a) A medieval Islamic brass trap-ping found in Rochester. *Archæologia Cantiana* **97**; pp. 296–297.

Craddock, P.T. (1981b) The copper alloys of Tibet and their background. In: *Aspects of Tibetan Metallurgy*, W.A. Oddy and W. Zwalf (eds). British Museum Occasional Paper 15, London, pp. 1–32.

Craddock, P.T. (1983) A Roman silver mirror 'discovered' in the British Museum: a note on its composition. *The Antiquaries Journal* **63**, 1; pp. 131–133.

Craddock, P.T. (1985a). Three thousand years of cop-per alloys: From the Bronze Age to the Industrial Revolution. In: England and van Zelst (eds), 1985, pp. 59–67 + micrcofiche.

Craddock, P.T. (1985b) Medieval copper alloy pro-duction and West African bronze Analyses – Part 1. *Archaeometry* **17**, 1; pp. 17–41.

Craddock, P.T. (1986) The metallurgy and composition of Etruscan bronze. *Studi Etruschi* **52**; pp. 211–271.

Craddock, P.T. (1992) A short history of the patination of bronze. In: Jones (ed), 1992, pp. 63–70.

Craddock, P.T. (1995) *Early Mining and Metal Production.* Edinburgh University Press, Edinburgh.

Craddock, P.T. (1996) Metals III: Shaping. In: Turner (ed), 1996, Vol. 21. pp. 320–324.

Craddock, P.T. (1997) The detection of fake and forged antiquities. *Chemistry and Industry* **13**; pp. 515–519. July.

Craddock, P.T. (1998) Zinc in Classical antiquity. In: Craddock (ed), 1998, pp. 1–6.

Craddock, P.T. (ed) (1998) *2,000 Years of Zinc and Brass.* British Museum Occasional Paper 50, 2nd edn, London.

Craddock, P.T. (2000/01) Some analyses of medieval monumental brasses. *Transactions of the Monumental Brass Society* **16**, 4; pp. 315–326.

Craddock, P.T. (2001) Conservative metal alloying tra-ditions in the Migration Period. In: *Archaeometallurgy in the Central Europe III, Acta Metallurgica Slovaca* **7**; pp. 175–181.

Craddock, P.T. (2003). Cast iron, crucible steel, fined iron: Liquid iron in the Ancient World. In: Craddock and Lang (eds), 2003, pp. 216–230.

Craddock, P.T, Burnett, A.M. and Preston, K. (1980) Hellenistic copper-base coinage and the origins of brass.

In: *Scientific Studies in Numismatics*, W.A. Oddy (ed). British Museum Occasional Paper 18, London, pp. 53–64.

Craddock, P.T. and Lang, J. (1983) Spinning, turning, polishing. *Journal of the Historical Metallurgy Society* **17**, 2; pp. 79–81.

Craddock, P.T., Freestone, I.C., Gale, N.H, Meeks, N.D., Rothenberg, B. and Tite, M.S. (1985) The investigation of a small heap of silver smelting debris from Rio Tinto, Huelva, Spain. In: *Furnaces and Smelting Technology in Antiquity*, P.T. Craddock and M.J. Hughes (eds). British Museum Occasional Paper 48, London. pp. 199–217.

Craddock, P.T., Pichler, B. and Riederer, J. (1987/88). Naturwissenschaftliche Untersuchungen. In: 'Jüngling' 1987/88, pp. 262–295.

Craddock, P.T. and Hook, D.R. (1990) Cornish copper and naval sheathing: New evidence for an old story. In: *Metals and the Sea*, J. Lang (ed). Historical Metallurgy Society, London, pp. 49–50.

Craddock, P.T. and Bowman, S. (1991) Spotting the fakes. In: Bowman (ed), 1991, pp. 141–157.

Craddock, P.T. and Giumlia-Mair, A.R. (1993a) Beauty is skin deep: evidence for the original appearance of classical statuary. In: La Niece and Craddock (eds), 1993, pp. 30–38.

Craddock, P.T. and Giumlia-Mair, A. R. (1993b) *Hśmn-km*: Corinthian bronze, *shakudo*: black-patinated bronze in the ancient world. In: La Niece and Craddock (eds), 1993, pp. 101–127.

Craddock, P.T. and Hook, D.R. (1997) The British Museum collection of metal ingots from dated wrecks. In: *Artefacts from Wrecks*, M. Redknap (ed). Oxbow Monongraph 84, Oxford, pp. 143–154.

Craddock, P.T., La Niece, S.C. and Hook, D.R. (1998) Brass in the Medieval Islamic world. In: Craddock (ed), 1998, pp. 73–114.

Craddock, P.T., Wayman, M.L. and Jull, A.J.T. (2002) The radiocarbon dating and authentication of iron artefacts. *Radiocarbon* **44**, 3; pp. 717–732.

Craddock, P.T. and Eckstein, K. (2003) Production of brass in Antiquity. In: Craddock and Lang (eds), 2003, pp. 216–230.

Craddock, P.T. and Zhou, Weirong (2003) Traditional zinc production in modern China: Survival and evolution. In: Craddock and Lang (eds), 2003, pp. 267–292.

Craddock, P.T., Wayman, M.L., Wang, H. and Michaelson, C., (2003) Chinese Cast Iron Through Twenty Five Hundred Years, in Jett (ed) 2003 pp. 36–46.

Craddock, P.T. and Lang, J. (eds) (2003) *Mining and Metal Production Through The Ages*. British Museum Press, London.

Craddock, P.T. and Lang, J. (2005a) Charles Dawson's cast-iron statuette: the authentication of iron antiquities and possible coal-smelting of iron in Roman Britain. *Journal of the Historical Metallurgical Society* **39**, 1; pp. 32–44.

Craddock, P.T. and Lang, J. (2005b) The effects of plasma treatment on the microstructure of metals. *Journal of the Historical Metallurgical Society* **39**, 2; pp. 106–119.

Craig, E.A. and Bresee, R.R. (1994) Image formation and the Shroud of Turin. *Journal of Imaging Science and Technology* **38**, 1; pp. 59–67.

Crane, A. (1994) Thermoluminescence will play its part in restoring pottery market confidence. *Antiques Trade Gazette*; p. 3. April.

Crawford, O.G.S. (1927a) L'Affaire Glozel. *Antiquity* **1**, 1; pp. 100–101.

Crawford, O.G.S. (1927b) L'Affaire Glozel. *Antiquity* **1**, 2; pp. 181–188.

Crawley, W. (1971) *Is it Genuine?* Eyre and Spottiswoode, London.

Cresswell, R.G. (1991) The radiocarbon dating of iron artefacts using accelerator mass spectrometry. *Journal of the Historical Metallurgy Society* **25**, 2; pp. 78–85.

Cresswell, R.G. (1992) Radiocarbon dating of iron artefacts. In: *Proceedings of the 14th International Radiocarbon Conference*, A. Long and R.S. Kra (eds). *Radiocarbon* **34**, 3; pp. 898–905.

Crighton, J.S. (1992) Textile conservation. In: Allen *et al.* (eds), 1992, pp. 82–107.

Cripps, W.J. (1914) *Old English Plate*, 10th edn. John Murray, London.

Cristoferi, E. and Fiori, C. (1992) Polishing techniques on ivory materials in the National Museum in Ravenna. *Studies in Conservation* **37**, 4; pp. 257–266.

Croft, P. (2001) *Stone Lithography*. A & C Black, London.

Crowningfield, R. (1972) Paraffin … its pros and cons. *Gems and Gemology* **14**; pp. 84–86.

Croyn, J.M. (1990) *The Elements of Archaeological Conservation*. Routledge, London.

Csapó, J., Csapó-Kiss, Z., Martin, T.G., Folestad, S., Orwar, O., Tivesten, A. and Nemethy, S. (1995) Age estimation of old carpets based on cystine and cysteic acid content. *Analytica chimica acta* **300**, 1–3; pp. 313–320.

Cuardo-Ruiz, J. and Vayson de Pradenne, A. (1931) Un Glozel Espagnol: Les falsifications d'objets préhistorique. *Bulletin des Societé Préhistorique Français* **28**; p. 371.

Cummings, K. (2002) *A History of Glassforming*. A & C Black, London.

Cunynghame, H.H. (1906) *European Enamels*. Methuen, London.

Cuomo di Caprio, N. (1993) *La galleria dei Falsi: dal vasaio al mercato di antiquariato*. L'Erma di Bretschneider, Rome.

Curtiss, B. (1993) Visible and near-infrared spectroscopy for jade artifact analysis. In: Lange (ed), 1993, pp. 73–81.

Cushing, F.H. (1894) Primitive copperworking: An experimental study. *American Anthropology* **7**, old series; pp. 93–117.

Cutler, A. (2003) Nineteenth century versions of the Veroli Casket. In: *Through a Glass Brightly*, C. Entwhistle (ed). Oxbow, Oxford, pp. 199–209.

Cyranoski, D. (2000) Fake finds reveal critical deficiency. *Nature* **408**, 6810; p. 280. November.

Czestochowski, J. and Pingeot, A. (2002) *Degas Sculptures Catalogue Raisonné of the Bronzes*. Torch Press and Internatioanl Arts, Memphis.

D.K.I. (1936) *Chemische Färbungen von Küpfer und Küpferlegierungen*. Deutsches Küpfer Institut, Berlin.

Dahl, E.H. (1980) Facsimile maps and forgeries. *Archivaria* 10; pp. 261–263.

Dai, Zhiqiang and Zhou, Weirong (1992) Studies in the alloy composition of more than two thousand years of Chinese coins (5th century BC–20th century AD). *Journal of the Historical Metallurgy Society* 26; pp. 45–55.

Dalton, O.M. (1927) *The Waddesdon Bequest*, 2nd edn. Trustees of the British Museum, London.

Dalton, R. (2000) Feathers fly over Chinese fossil bird's legality and authenticity. *Nature* 403, 6771; pp. 689–690. February.

Damon, P., Donahue, D.J., Gore, B.H., Hathaway, A.L., Jull, A.J.T., Linick, T.W., Sercel, P.J., Toolin, L.J., Bronk, C.R., Hall, E.T., Hedges, R.E.M., Housley, R., Law, I.A., Perry, C., Bonani, G., Trumbore, S., Woelfi, W., Ambers, J.C., Bowman, S.G.E., Leese, M.N. and Tite, M.S. (1989) Radiocarbon dating of the Shroud of Turin. *Nature* 337, 6208; pp. 611–615. February.

Dance, P. (1976) *Animal Fakes & Frauds*. Sampson Low, London.

Daniel, G. (1974) Editorial. *Antiquity* 48, 192; pp. 261–264.

Daniel, G. (1977) Editorial. *Antiquity* 51, 202; pp. 89–91.

Daniel, G. (1986) *Some Small Harvest*. Thames and Hudson, London.

Daniels, V. (1981) Manganese-containing stains on excavated pottery sherds. *MASCA Journal* 1, 8; pp. 230–231.

Daniels, V. (1984) The Russell Effect – A review of its possible uses in conservation and the scientific examination of materials. *Studies in Conservation* 29, 2; pp. 57–62.

Daniels, V. (ed) (1988) *Early Advances in Conservation*. British Museum Occasional Paper 65, London.

Daniels, V. (1988a) The discoloration of paper on ageing. *The Paper Conservator* 12; pp. 93–100.

Daniels, V.D. (1988b) A study of the properties of aged starch paste (*furu-nori*). Preprints of the 1988 Kyoto Congress. In: *The Conservation of Far Eastern Art*, J.S. Mills, P. Smith and K. Yamasaki (eds). IIC, London, pp. 5–10.

Daniels, V.D. (1996) The chemistry of paper conservation. *Chemical Society Reviews* 25, 3; pp. 179–186.

Daniels, V. and Lang, J. (2005) X-rays and paper. In: Lang and Middleton (eds), 2005, pp. 96–111.

Daniels, V.D. and Meeks, N.D. (1994) Foxing caused by copper alloy inclusions in paper. In: *Conservation of Historic and Artistic Works on Paper*, H.D. Burgess (ed). Canadian Conservation Institute, Ottawa, pp. 229–233.

Dardes, K. and Rothe (eds). (1998) The Structural Conservation of Panel Paintings. *Proceedings of a Symposium at the J. Paul Getty Museum*, 24–28th April, 1995. Getty Museum, Malibu.

Davis, M.J. (1996) A study of visual techniques for the identification of watercolor pigments. *The Book and Paper Group Annual* 15; pp. 45–52.

Davison, S. (2003) *Conservation of Glass*, 2nd edn. Butterworths, London.

Dawson, C. (1903) Sussex iron work and pottery. *Sussex Archaeological Collections* 46; pp. 1–62.

Dawson, C. (1907) Some inscribed bricks and tiles from the Roman *Castra* at Pevensey (*Anderira?*), Sussex. *Proceedings of the Society of Antiquaries of London* 21, 2; pp. 410–413.

Dawson, C. (1913) The Piltdown Skull. *The Hastings and East Sussex Naturalist* 2; pp. 73–82.

Dawson, C. and Woodward, A.S. (1913) On the discovery of a Palaeolithic human skull and mandible in a flint bearing gravel overlying the Wealden (Hastings Beds) at Piltdown, Fletching (Sussex). *Quarterly Journal of the Geological Society of London* 69; pp. 117–151.

Day, F. (1951) Review of *Soieries Persanes* by Gaston Wiet. *Ars Islamica* 15–16; pp. 231–251.

Dean, J.S. (1997) Dendrochronology. In: Taylor and Aitken (eds), 1997, pp. 31–64.

de Bignicourt, M.-C. and Flieder, F. (1996) L'Analyse des papyrus. In: Bridgland (ed), 1996, pp. 488–493.

de Castellar, M.D. (1987) Scanning electron microscope: effective instrument for textile research. *Investigacion e Informacion Textil y de Tensioactivos* 30, 4; pp. 177–186.

Decoen, J. (1951) *Back to the Truth: Two Genuine Vermeers*. Donker, Rotterdam. [Trans. E.J. Labarre].

de Froment, D. (ed) (1984) *Preprints for ICOM: Committee for Conservation, Seventh Triennial Meeting*, Copenhagen, 10–14 September 1984. ICOM, Paris.

de Grummond, N. (1982) Forgeries. In: *A Guide to Etruscan Mirrors*, N.T. de Grummond (ed). Archaeological News, Inc., Tallahassee, Florida. pp. 61–68.

de Keijzer, M. (1989) The colorful twentieth century. In: *Modern Art: The Restoration and Techniques of Modern Paper and Paints*, S. Fairbrass and J. Hermans (eds). UKIC, London, pp. 13–20.

de Keijzer, M. (1990) Microchemical analysis on synthetic organic artists' pigments discovered in the twentieth century. In: *Preprints of the 9th Triennial Meeting of the ICOM Committee for Conservation*, Dresden, 26–31 August, 1990, K. Grimstad (ed). ICOM, Los Angeles, pp. 220–225.

de Keijzer, M. (2002) The history of modern synthetic inorganic and organic artists' pigments. In: *Contributions to Conservation: Research in Conservation at the Netherlands Institute for Cultural Heritage (ICN)*, J.A. Mosk and N.H. Tennent (eds). James and James, London, pp. 42–54.

de la Faille, J.B. (1930) *Les Faux Van Gogh*. G. van Oest, Paris.

Delage, Y. (1902) Le linceul de Turin. *Révue Scientifique* 17, 22; pp. 683–687. May.

Delange, E., Grange, M., Kusko, B. and Mènei, E. (1990) Apparation de l'encre métallogallique en Égypte à partir de la Collection de Papyrus du Louvre. *Revue d'Egyptologie* 41; pp. 213–217.

de la Rie, E.R. (1982a, b & c) Fluorescence of paint and varnish layers I–III. *Studies in Conservation* 27. I: pp. 1–8. II: pp. 65–69. III: pp. 102–109.

de la Rie, E.R. (1987) The influence of varnishes on the appearance of paintings. *Studies in Conservation* **32**, 1; pp. 1–13.

de la Rie, E.R. (1988) Photochemical and thermal degradation of films of dammar resin. *Studies in Conservation* **33**, 1; pp. 53–70.

Delbrück, R. (1932) *Antike Porhyrwerke*. W. de Gruyter, Berlin.

Del Monte, M. and Sabbioni, C. (1987) A study of the patina called *scialbatura* on imperial Roman marbles. *Studies in Conservation* **32**, 3; pp. 114–121.

Del Monte, M., Sabbioni, C. and Zappa, G. (1987) The origin of calcium oxalates on historical buildings, monuments and natural outcrops. *The Science of the Total Environment* **67**; pp. 17–39.

Del Solar, T. and Grimwade, M. (1982) The art of depletion gilding. *Aurum* 12; pp. 37–45.

Demirci, í., Özer, A.M. and Summers, G.D. (1996) *Archaeometry, 94*. Tübitak, Ankara.

Dembélé, M. and van der Waals, J.D. (1991) Looting the antiquities of Mali. *Antiquity* **65**, 249; pp. 904–905.

Demortier, G. (1984) Analysis of gold jewellery artefacts: Characterization of ancient gold solders by PIXE. *Gold Bulletin* **17**, 1; pp. 27–38.

Demortier, G. (1987) La chrysocolle des orfèvres est-elle jaune? *Archaeometry* **29**, 2; pp. 275–288.

Demortier, G. (2000) Essentials of PIXE and RBS for archaeological purposes. In: Demortier and Adriaens (eds), 2000, pp. 125–136.

Demortier, G. (2004) Ion beam studies of ancient gold-solders. In: *Tecnología del Oro Antiguo: Europa y América*, A. Perea, I. Montero and Ó. García-Vuelta (eds). *Anejos de AEspa* **32**, Madrid, pp. 27–40.

Demortier, G. and Adriaens, A. (eds) (2000) *Ion Beam Study of Art and Archaeological Objects, COST*. European Communities, Luxembourg.

Denker, A. and Maier, K.H. (2000a) Investigation of objects d'art by PIXE with 68 MeV protons. In: Andersen and Rehn (eds), 2000, pp. 704–708.

Denker, A. and Maier, K.H. (2000b) Looking deep into the object. In: Demortier and Adriaens (eds), 2000, pp. 81–83.

De Pas, M. and Flieder, F. (1976) History and prospects for analysis of black manuscript inks. In: *Conservation and Restoration of Pictorial Art*, N. Brommelle and P. Smith (eds). Butterworths, London, for IIC. pp. 193–201.

De Raedt, I., Janssens, K., Veeckman, J. and Adams, F. (2000) Composition of *façon-de-venise* and Venetian glass from Antwerp and the Southern Netherlands. *Annales du 14e Congrès de l'Association Internationale pour l'Histoire du Verre*, J. Price (ed). AIHV, Lochem, pp. 346–350.

Derbyshire, A. and Withnall, R. (1999) Pigment analysis of portrait miniatures using Raman microscopy. *Journal of Raman Spectroscopy* **30**; pp. 185–188.

Derrick, M.R. (1988) Fourier Transform Infrared Spectral Analysis of Natural Resins used in Furniture Finishes. In: *Papers presented at the Wooden Artifacts Group Speciality Sessions:* June 5 1988 AIC Annual Meeting, New Orleans, Louisiana. American Institute of Conservation, Washington DC, pp. 1–12.

Derrick, M., Druzik, C. and Preusser, E. (1988) FTIR analysis of authentic and simulated black lacquer on 18th century furniture. In: Bromelle and Smith (eds), 1988, pp. 227–234.

Derrick, M.R., Stulik, D. and Landry, J.M. (1999) *Infrared Spectroscopy in Conservation Science*. The Getty Conservation Institute, Los Angeles.

d'Errico, F. (1988) A study of Upper Paleolithic and Epipaleolithic engraved pebbles. In: Olsen (ed), 1988, pp. 169–184.

d'Errico, F. (1993) La vie sociale de l'art mobilier paléolithique. Manipulation, transport, suspension des objets on os, bois de cervidés, ivoire. *Oxford Journal of Archaeology* **12**, 2; pp. 145–174.

d'Errico, F., Williams, C.T. and Stringer, C.B. (1998) AMS dating and microscopic analysis of the Sherborne Bone. *Journal of Archaeological Science* **25**, 8; pp. 777–787.

De Ryck, I., Van Biezen, E., Leyssens, K., Adriaens, A., Storme, P. and Adams, F. (2004) Study of tin corrosion: The influence of alloying elements. *Journal of Cultural Heritage* **5**, 2; pp. 189–195.

Deschler-Erb, E., Lehmann, E.H., Pernel, L., Vontobel, P. and Hartmann, S. (2004) The complimentary use of neutrons and X-rays for the non-destructive investigation of archaeological objects from Swiss collections. *Archaeometry* **46**, 4; pp. 647–662.

Destrée, J. (1927) The reliquary of the Holy Thorn in the Waddesdon Bequest at the British Museum. *The Connoiseur* **79**; pp. 138–143. [Trans. O.M. Dalton].

Desthomas, G. (1983) Electroforming of carat gold alloys. I: General principles & II : Jewellery production by electroforming. *Aurum* 14; pp. 17–21. 19–26.

de Vries, H. and Oakley, K.P. (1959) Radiocarbon dating of the Piltdown skull and jaw. *Nature* **184**, 4682; pp. 224–226.

de Wild, A.M. (1929) *The Scientific Examination of Pictures*. G. Bell and Sons, London.

Didier, R. (1996) Fälschungen und Repliken der Statuetten des Schreins. In: *Schutz aus den Trümmern der Silberschrein von Nivelles und die europäische Hochgothik*, H. Westermann-Angerhausen (ed). Exhibition Catalogue, Schnütgen Museum, Cologne, pp. 188–190.

Digby, A. (1936) Comments on the morphological comparison of two crystal skulls. *Man* **36**; pp. 142–178.

Digby, G.B. (1926) *The Mammoth and Mammoth Hunting in North-east Siberia*. Witherby, London.

Dimitrov, D., Prokopov, I. and Kolev, B. (1997) *Modern Forgeries of Greek and Roman Coins*. Vessela, Sofia.

DiNoto, A. (1985) Bakelite envy, Jazz Age plastic jewellery. *Connoisseur* **215**, 7; pp. 43–46. July.

Dixon, B. (1986) Peer review – In the best interests of science. *New Scientist* **145**, 1506; p. 58. March.

Doehne, E., Podany, J. and Showers, W. (1992) Analysis of weathered dolomitic marble from Thasos, Greece. In: Waelkens, Herz and Moens (eds), 1992, pp. 179–190.

Doeringer, S., Mitten, D.G. and Steinberg, A. (eds) (1970) *Art and Technology: A Symposium on Classical Bronzes.* MIT Press, Cambridge, MA.

Doktor, A., Mach, M. and Meissner, B. (2001) Neues zur Galvanoplastik 1: Geschichte und Analyse einer revolutionären Technik aus dem 19. Jahrhundert. *Restauro* **1**; pp. 48–53.

Doménech Carbó, M.T., Bosch Reig, R.F., Gimeno Adelantado, J.V. and Periz Martínez, V. (1996) Fourier transform imfrared spectroscopy and the analytical study of works of art for purposes of diagnosis and conservation. *Analytica Chimica Acta* **330**; pp. 207–213.

Donahue, D. J. and Jull, A.J.T. (1999) Acclerator radiocarbon dating of artistic artifacts. In: McCrone and Weiss (eds), 1999, pp. 92–100.

Donahue, D.J., Olin, J.S. and Harbottle, G. (2002) Determination of the radiocarbon age of the parchment of the Vinland Map. *Radiocarbon* **44**, 1; pp. 45–52.

Dorn, R.I. (1983) Cation-ratio dating: A new rock varnish age-determination technique. *Quaternary Research* **20**; pp. 49–73.

Dorn, R.I. (1989) Cation-ratio dating of rock varnish: A geographic assessment. *Journal of Physical Geography* **13**; pp. 559–596.

Dorn, R.I. (1991) Rock Varnish. *American Scientist* **79**, 6; pp. 542–553.

Dorn, R.I. (1993) Dating petrogylphs with a three-tier rock-varnish approach. In: *New Light on Old Art: Advances in Hunter-Gatherer Rock Art Research*, D.S. Whitley and L. Loendorf (eds). Institute of Archaeology, UCLA, Los Angeles, pp. 13–36.

Dorn, R.I. (1997) Constraining the age of the Côa valley (Portugal). engravings with radiocarbon dating. *Antiquity* **71**, 271; pp. 105–115.

Dorn, R.I. (1998) Response to Beck *et al. Science* **280**; pp. 2136–2139. June.

Douglas, J.G. (2000) On the authentication of Ancient Chinese jades using scientific methods. *Orientations* **31**, 2; p. 86.

Douglas, J.G. (2001) The Effect of Heat on Nephrite and the Detection of Heated Chinese Jades by X-ray Diffraction (XRD) and by Fourier-Transform Infra Red (FTIR). *Proceedings of the Conference on Archaic Jades across the Taiwan Strait.* Taipei, pp. 543–554.

Douglas, J.G. (2003) Exploring issues of geological sources for jade worked by Ancient Chinese cultures with the aid of X-ray fluorescence spectroscopy. In: Jett (ed), 2003, pp. 192–199.

Douglas, R.W. and Frank, S. (1972) *A History of Glassmaking.* G.T. Foulis & Co., Henley-on Thames, Oxfordshire.

Douglass, A.E. (1921) Dating our prehistoric ruins. *Natural History* **21**; pp. 27–30.

Down, J.L. (1984) The yellowing of epoxy resins adhesives: Report on natural dark aging. *Studies in Conservation* **29**, 2; pp. 63–76.

Doyle, L.R., Lorre, J.J. and Doyle, E.B. (1986) The application of computer image processing techniques to artifact analysis as applied to the Shroud of Turin study. *Studies in Conservation* **31**, 1; pp. 1–6.

Dragovitch, D. (2000) Rock engraving chronologies and accelerator mass spectrometry radiocarbon age of desert varnish. *Journal of Archaeological Science* **27**, 10; pp. 871–876.

Dran, J-C., Calligaro, T. and Salomon, J. (2000) Particle-induced X-ray emission. In: Ciliberto and Spoto (eds), 2000, pp. 135–166.

Drayman-Weisser, T. (ed) (1992) *Dialogue/89: The Conservation of Bronze Sculpture in the Outdoor Environment.* National Association of Corrosion Engineers, Houston, Texas.

Drayman-Weisser, T. (ed) (2000) *Gilded Metals.* Archetype Publications, London.

Dubin, L.S. (1987) *The History of Beads from 30,000 BC to the Present.* Thames and Hudson, London.

Dubrana, D. (2001) *Histoire secréte des chefs-d'œuvre.* Éditions SPE-BARTHÉLÉMY, Paris.

Duncan, S.J. and Ganiaris, H. (1987) Some sulphide corrosion products on copper alloys and lead alloys from London waterfront sites. In: Black (ed), 1987, pp. 109–118.

Duerr, W., Griebenow, W., Werthmann, B. and Ziegler, M. (1987) Determination of paper age, illustrated by a counterfeit Schubert symphony in 'E major' – a musical fairytale. *Papier (Darmstadt).* **41**, 7; pp. 321–331.

Dugmore, J.M.M. and DesForges, C.D. (1979) Stress corrosion in gold alloys. *Gold Bulletin* **12**, 4; pp. 140–144.

Dunkerton, J. and White, R. (2000) The Discovery and Identification of an Original Varnish on a Panel by Carlo Crivelli. *National Gallery Technical Bulletin* **21**; pp. 70–76.

Dunkle, S.E., Craig, J-R., Rimstiot, J.D. and Lusardi, W.R. (2003) Romarchite, hydromarchite and abhurite formed during the corrosion of pewter artifacts from the *Queen Anne's Revenge* (1718). *The Canadian Mineralogist* **41**; pp. 659–669.

Duroc-Danner, J.M. (2000) A very convincing forgery. *The Journal of Gemmology* **27**, 1; pp. 8–10.

Duroc-Danner, J.M. (2002) A comparison between a flux grown synthetic ruby and an untreated natural ruby. *The Journal of Gemmology* **28**, 3; pp. 137–142.

Duval, A.R., Eluère, C. and Hurtel, L.P. (1989) Joining techniques in ancient gold jewellery. *Jewellery Studies* **3**; pp. 5–14.

Easby, D.T., Jr. and Dockstader, F.J. (1964) Requiem for Tizoc. *Archaeology* **17**, 2; pp. 85–90.

Easby, D.T., Jr. and Collin, R.F. (1968) Legal aspects of forgery and protection of the experts. *Bulletin of the Metropolitan Museum of Art* **26**; pp. 258–261.

Eastaugh, N., Walsh, V., Chaplin, T. and Siddall, R. (2004a) *The Pigment Compendium: Optical Microscopy.* Elsevier, Amsterdam.

Eastaugh, N., Walsh, V., Chaplin, T. and Siddall, R. (2004b) *The Pigment Compendium: Dictionary.* Elsevier, Amsterdam.

Eckstein, D. (1984) *Handbooks for Archaeologists 2: Dendrochronological Dating.* European Science Foundation, Strasbourg.

Eckstein, D., Wazny, T., Bauch, J. and Klein, P. (1986) New evidence for the dendrochronological dating of Netherlandish paintings. *Nature* **320**, 6061; pp. 465–466. 19 April.

Edmunds, F.H. (1950) Note on the Gravel Deposit from which the Piltdown Skull was Obtained. *Proceedings of the Geological Society of London* **106**; pp. 133–134.

Edwards, H.G.M. (2001) Raman spectroscopy in the characterisation of archaeological material. In: Lewis and Edwards (eds), 2001, pp. 1011–1044.

Edwards, H.G.M. (2005) Overview: Biological materials and degradation. In: Edwards and Chalmers (eds), 2005, pp. 230–279.

Edwards, H.G.M., Farwell, D.W., Seddon, T. and Tait, J.K.F. (1995) Scrimshaw: real or fake? A Fourier-transform Raman diagnostic study. *Journal of Raman Spectroscopy* **26**, 8–9; pp. 623–628.

Edwards, H.G.M. and Farwell, D.W. (1995) Ivory and simulated ivory artefacts: A Fourier-transform Raman diagnostic study. *Spectrochimica Acta* **A51**; pp. 2073–2081.

Edwards, H.G.M. and Farwell, D.W. (1996) Fourier transform-Raman spectroscopy of amber. *Spectrochimica Acta* **A52**; pp. 1119–1125.

Edwards, H.G.M., Farwell, D.W. and Daffner, L. (1996a) Fourier transform-Raman spectroscopic study of natural waxes and resins. I. *Spectrochimica Acta* **A52**; pp. 1639–1648.

Edwards, H.G.M., Ellis, E., Farwell, D.W. and Janaway, R.C. (1996b) Preliminary study of the application of Fourier transform Raman spectroscopy to the analysis of degraded archaeological linen textiles. *Journal of Raman Spectroscopy* **27**; pp. 663–669.

Edwards, H.G.M. and Falk, M.J. (1997) Investigation of the degradation products of archaeological linens by Raman spectroscopy. *Applied Spectroscopy* **51**, 8; pp. 1134–1138.

Edwards, H.G.M., Farwell, D.W., Holder, E.E. and Lawson, E.E. (1997a) Fourier-transform Raman spectroscopy of ivory. II: Spectroscopic analysis and assignments. *Journal of Molecular Structure* **435**; pp. 49–58.

Edwards, H.G.M., Farwell, D.W., Holder, J.M. and Lawson, E.E. (1997b) Fourier-transform Raman spectra of ivory. III: Identification of mammalian specimens. *Spectrochimica Acta* **A53**; pp. 2403–2409.

Edwards, H.G.M., Farwell, D.W. and Webster, D. (1997c) FT Raman microscopy of untreated natural plant fibres. *Spectrochimica Acta* **A53**; pp. 2383–2392.

Edwards, H.G.M., Farwell, D.W., Holder, J.M. and Lawson, E.E. (1998a) Fourier transform Raman spectroscopy of ivory: A non-destructive diagnostic technique. *Studies in Conservation* **43**, 1; pp. 9–16.

Edwards, H.G.M., Hunt, D.E. and Sibley, M.G. (1998b) FT-Raman spectroscopic study of keratotic materials: Horn, hoof and tortoiseshell. *Spectrochimica Acta* **A54**; pp. 745–757.

Edwards, H.G.M., Farwell, D.W., Newton, E.M., Pull Perez, F. and Jorge Villar, S. (2001) Application of FT Raman spectroscopy in the characterisation of parchment and vellum I: Novel information for palaeographic and historiated manuscript studies. *Spectrochimica Acta* **A57**; pp. 1223–1234.

Edwards, H.G.M. and Pull Perez, F. (2004) Application of Fourier transform Raman spectroscopy to the characterization of parchment and vellum II: Effect of biodeterioration and chemical deterioration on spectral interpretation. In: Kiefer (ed), 2004, pp. 754–760.

Edwards, H.G.M. and Chalmers, J.M. (eds) (2005) *Raman Spectroscopy in Archaeology and Art History.* Royal Society of Chemistry, Cambridge.

Edwards, H.G.M. and Wyeth, P. (2005) Case study: Ancient textile fibres. In: Edwards and Chalmers (eds), 2005, pp. 304–323.

Edwards, R. (1977) *The Technique of Jewellery.* Batsford, London.

Edwards, R.P. and Charles, J.A. (1982) A preliminary report on the trace element content of Cornish copper ores with particular reference to archaeological provenance studies. *Cambourne School of Mines Journal* **82**; pp. 49–55.

Eggert, G. (1994) Schwarzfärbung oder Korrosion? Das Rätsel der schwarzen Bronzen aus chemischer Sicht. In: *Das Wrack*, G. Hellenkemper-Salies, H.-H. von Prittwitz and G. Bauchhenss (eds). Rheinisches Landesmuseum, Bonn, pp. 1033–1039.

Eggert, G. (2006) To whom the cracks tell. *Studies in Conservation* **51**, 1; pp. 69–75.

Ehrmann, M.L. (1958) How to color jadeite. *Lapidaries Journal* **12**; pp. 646–648.

Ehrmann, M.L. (1959) A secret and expensive process. *Gemmologist* **28**; pp. 38–41.

Eichholz, D.E. (trans.) (1962) *Pliny: The Natural History* **10**. The Loeb Classical Library, Heinemann, London.

Eiland, M. (2003) Beyond the straight and narrow: Faking Phoenician glass in Damascus. *Minerva* **14**, 2; pp. 20–21.

Eiland, M. (2005) Fake blown glass from Syria. *Minerva* **16**, 1; pp. 44–47.

Eiland, M. and Williams, Q. (2001) All that is green is not jade. *Minerva* **12**, 6; pp. 43–46.

Eisenberg, J.M. (1992) The aesthetics of the forger: stylistic criteria in ancient art forgery. *Minerva* **3**, 3; pp. 10–15.

Eisenberg, J.M. (1998) Recent forgeries of Egyptian Shabtis. *Minerva* **9**, 5; pp. 34–37.

Eisenberg, M. (2003) The Portland Vase: a glass masterwork of the late Renaissance? *Minerva* **14**, 5; pp. 37–41.

Eisenberg, M. (2004) The Portland Vase: further observations. *Minerva* **15**, 1; p. 18.

Ekholm, G.F. (1964) The problems of fakes in pre-Columbian Art. *Curator* **7**, 1; pp. 19–32.

Elbern, V.H. (1968) A group of pseudo-ancient glass vessels from Italy. *Journal of Glass Studies* **10**; pp. 171–175.

Elia, R.J. (1993) A seductive and troubling work; review of C. Renfrew's *The Cycladic Spirit*, 1991. *Archaeology* **46**, 1; pp. 64–69. Jan/Feb.

Elia, R.J. (1995) Conservation and unprovenanced objects: Preserving the cultural heritage or servicing the antiquities trade. In: Tubb (ed), 1995, pp. 244–255.

Ellen, D. (1997) *The Scientific Examination of Documents.* Taylor and Francis, London.

Elliot, W. (1939) Reproductions, and fakes of English eighteenth-century ceramics. *Transactions of the English Ceramic Circle* **2**, 7; pp. 67–82.

Elvidge, C.D. and Moore, C.B. (1980) Restoration of petroglyphs with artificial desert varnish. *Studies in Conservation* **25**, 3; pp. 108–117.

Elwell, D. (1979) *Man-Made Gemstones.* Ellis Horwood, Chichester.

Emery, I. (1980) *The Primary Structures of Fabrics: An Illustrated Classification*, 2nd edn. The Textile Museum, Washington DC.

England, P.A. and van Zelst, L. (eds) (1985) *Application of Science in Examination of Works of Art.* The Research Laboratory, Museum of Fine Arts, Boston.

Engstrom, R., Lankton, S.M. and Lesher-Engstrom, A. (1989) *Sword of Sutton Hoo.* Medieval Institute Publications, Western Michigan University, Kalamazoo.

Enshaian, M.C. (1997) Paper. In: Cohn (ed), 1997, pp. 36–60.

Epprecht, W. and Mutz, A. (1974–75) Gezongener römischer Draht. *Jahrbuch der Schweitzerischen Gesellschaft für Ur- und Frühgeschichte* **58**; pp. 157–161.

Erdmann, M.V., Caldwell, R.L. and Kasim Mousa, M. (1998) Indonesian 'king of the sea' discovered. *Nature* **395**, 6700; p. 335. 24 September.

Eretz, (1989) *Fakes and Forgeries from Collections in Israel.* Eretz Israel Museum, Tel Aviv.

Erhardt, D., Mecklenburg, M.F., Tumosa, C.S. and Olstad, T.M. (1996) New versus old wood: Differences and similarities in physical, mechanical and chemical properties. In: Bridgland (ed), 1996, pp. 903–910.

Erhardt, D., Tumosa, C.S. and Mecklenburg, M.F. (2005) Long-term chemical and physical processes in oil paint films. *Studies in Conservation* **50**, 2; pp. 143–150.

Erlach, R. (1987/88) Thermolumineszenz-Messungen am Gußkernmaterial. In: 'Jüngling', 1987/88, pp. 347–353.

Ericson, J.E., Dersch, O. and Rauch, F. (2004) Quartz hydration dating. *Journal of Archaeological Science* **31**, 7; pp. 883–902.

Ertz, K. (1976) *Fälschung und Forschung.* Catalogue of exhibitions at Museum Folkwang, Oct 1976–Jan 1977 and Staatliche Museum, Berlin, January–March 1977. Museum Folkwang, Essen.

Eshel, H., Broshi, M., Freund, R. and Schultz, B. (2002) New data on the cemetery east of Khirbet Qumran. *Dead Sea Discoveries* **9**; pp. 135–163.

Espinoza, E.O. and Mann, M.-J. (1993) The history and significance of the Schreger Patterns in proboscidean ivory characteristics. *Journal of the American Institute for Conservation* **32**, 3; pp. 241–248.

Espinoza, E.O. and Mann, M.-J. (2000) *Identification Guide for Ivory and Ivory Substitutes*, 3rd edn. Ivory Identification Inc., Richmond, VA.

Ettinger, K.V. and Frey, R.L. (1980) Nitrogen profiling: A proposed dating technique for difficult artefacts. In: Slater and Tate (eds), 1980, pp. 295–311.

Ettmayer, P. (1984) Versuch einer metallographischen Authentizitätabewertung einer Schallern. *Wiener Berichte über Naturwissenschaft in der Kunst* **1**; pp. 166–174.

Ettmayer, P. and Simon, M. (1987/88) Metallkundliche Untersuchungen am Eisen-Stützgerüst aus dem Gußkern. In: 'Jüngling', 1987/88, pp. 341–346.

Eugster, O. (1996) Dating gold artifacts: Applications for noble gas analyses of gold. *Gold Bulletin* **29**, 3; pp. 101–104.

Evans, J. (1897) *The Ancient Stone Implements, Weapons and Ornaments of Great Britain.* Longmans Green & Co, London.

Evershed, R.P. (2000) Biomolecular analyses by organic mass spectrometry. In: Ciliberto and Spoto (eds), 2000, pp. 177–239.

Eylon, D. (2002) On the Radiocarbon Dating of Charcoal-Reduced Iron and Steel. In: *BUMA-V Proceedings of the Fifth International Conference on The Beginnings of the Use of Metals and Alloys*, Gyu-Ho Kim, Kyung-Woo Yi and Hyung-Tai Kang (eds). Korea Institute of Metals and Materials, Seoul, pp. 161–168.

Failing, P. (1988) Cast in bronze: The Degas dilemma. *Art News* **87**, 1; pp. 136–141. January.

Faillant-Dumas, L. (1980) Bois. In: Hours (ed), 1980, pp. 173–200.

Fainges, M. (2000) *Celluloid Dolls of the World.* Kangaroo Press, East Roseville, New South Wales.

Farges, F. (1998) Mineralogy of the Louvre's Merovingian garnet cloisonné jewelry: Origins of the gems of the first kings of France. *American Mineralogist* **83**; pp. 323–330.

Farn, A.E. (1986) *Pearls: Natural, Cultured and Imitation.* Butterworths, London.

Farnsworth, M., Smith, C.S. and Rodda, J.L. (1949) Metallographic examination of a sample of metallic zinc from ancient Athens. *Hesperia*, Suppl. **8**; pp. 126–129.

Farquhar, R.M., Hancock, R.G.V. and Pavlish, L.A. (eds) (1988) *Proceedings of the 26th International Archaeometry Symposium.* Archaeometry Laboratory, Dept. of Physics, University of Toronto, Toronto.

Farrar, R.A.H. (1979) The Sherborne controversy. *Antiquity* **53**, 209; pp. 211–216.

Farrell, E. (1987) Non-destructive instrumental analysis of medals. In: *Italian Medals*, J.G. Pollard (ed). National Gallery of Art, Washington, pp. 35–43.

Feest, Ch.F., Erlach, R., Pichler, B., Vendl, A. and Vana, N. (1984) TL-Untersuchungen an südamerikanischen Keramiken 1. Figuralkeramik der Zapoteken. *Wiener Berichte über Naturwissenschaft in der Kunst* **1**; pp. 40–42.

Feilchenfeldt, W. (1989) Van Gogh fakes: The Wacker Affair, with an illustrated catalogue of the forgeries. *Simiolus* **19**, 4; pp. 289–316.

Feller, R.L. (ed) (1986) *Artists' Pigments* I. Cambridge University Press, Cambridge.

Feller, R.L. (1994) *Accelerated Aging: Photochemical and Thermal Aspects*. Getty Conservation Institute, Los Angeles.

Fereday, G. (2003) *Natural Dyes*. British Museum Press, London.

Ferretti, M. (1993) *Scientific Investigations of Works of Art*. ICCROM, Rome.

Ferretti, M. and Moioli, P. (1998) The use of portable XRF systems for preliminary compositional studies on large bronze objects. In: *Metal 98* (eds), W. Mourey and L. Robbiola (eds). James and James, London, pp. 39–44.

Festag, J.G., Gentner, W. and Müller, O. (1976) Search for uranium and chemical constituents in ancient Roman glass mosaics. In: *Applications of Nuclear Methods in the Field of Works of Art*, R. Cesareo (ed). Accademia Nazionale dei Lincei, Rome, pp. 493–503.

Feucht, G., Piehl, M. and Stuzinger, D. (1999) Der Sessel: der eine Kline war: der Geschichte eines Bronzesessels mit Röntgenstrahlen auf den Grund gegangen. *Antike Welt* **30**, 1; pp. 31–37.

ffoulkes, C. (1914) A carved Flemish chest at New College, Oxford. *Archaeologia* **65**; pp. 113–128.

Fiegenbaum, L. (1996) Towards a machine-based visual analysis of tool marks. In: *Imaging the Past*, T. Higgins, P. Main and J. Lang (eds). British Museum Occasional Paper 114, London, pp. 189–197.

Field, S. and Bonney, S.R. (1925) *The Chemical Coloring of Metals and Allied Processes*. Chapman & Hall, London.

Fink, C.G. and Polushkin, E.P. (1938) Drakes's plate of brass authenticated. *California Historical Society Quarterly* **17**, 4 Pt 2; pp. 7–28. (Special Publication 14).

Fischer, C.-O., Laurenze-Landsberg, C., Schmidt, C. and Slusallek, K. (1999) Neues zur Neutronen-Aktivierungs-Autoradiographie. Tizians 'Mädchen mit Fruchtschale' und die Verwendung von Neapelgelb. *Restauro* **105**, 6; pp. 426–431.

Fishlock, D. (1962) *Metal Coloring*. Robert Draper, Teddington, Middx.

FitzHugh, E.W. (ed) (1997) *Artists' Pigments* III. National Gallery of Art, Washington.

FitzHugh, E.W. (2003) Pigments on Japanese ukiyo-e paintings in the Freer Gallery of Art. In: Jett (ed), 2003, pp. 150–156.

Fjaestad, M., Nord, A.G. and Tronner, K. (1997) The decay of archaeological copper-alloy artefacts in soil. In: *Metal 95*, I.D. MacLeod, S.L. Pennec and L. Robbiola (eds). James and James, London, pp. 32–35.

Flamini, A. and de Lorenzo Flamini, P. (1985) Discrimination between Etruscan pottery and recent imitations by means of thermal analyses. *Archaeometry* **27**, 2; pp. 218–224.

Fleming, S.J. (1971) Thermoluminescent authenticity testing of ancient ceramics: The effects of sampling by drilling. *Archaeometry* **13**, 1; pp. 59–70.

Fleming, S.J. (1973a) The pre-dose technique: A new thermoluminescent dating technique. *Archaeometry* **15**, 1; pp. 13–30.

Fleming, S.J. (1973b) Authenticity testing of art ceramics by the thermoluminescence method: Some important examples. In: Young (ed), 1973, pp. 206–212.

Fleming, S.J. (1974) Thermoluminescent authenticity studies of unglazed T'ang dynasty ceramic tomb goods. *Archaeometry* **16**, 1; pp. 91–115.

Fleming, S.J. (1975) *Authenticity in Art: The Scientific Detection of Forgery*. Institute of Physics, London.

Fleming, S. (1976) *Dating in Archaeology*. J.M. Dent, London.

Fleming, S.J. (1979a) An evaluation of physico-chemical approaches to authentication. In: *Authentication in the Visual Arts*, H.L.C. Jaffe, J. Storm van Leeuwen and L.H. van der Tweel (eds). B.M. Israël BV, Amsterdam, pp. 103–139.

Fleming, S.J. (1979b) Revival of Pollajuolo's Combat of Nude Men. *MASCA Journal* **1**, 2; pp. 35–36.

Fleming, S.J. (1979c) *Thermoluminescence Techniques in Archaeology*. Clarendon Press, Oxford.

Fleming, S.J. (1981) Four figures from a retable by Nicholas of Verdun: A misattribution. *MASCA Journal* **1**, 8; pp. 227–229.

Fleming, S.J. (1993) Art forgeries: Scientific detection. In: *Concise Encyclopedia of Materials Characterization*, R.W. Cahn and E. Lifshin (eds). Pergamon Press, Oxford, pp. 16–23.

Fleming, S.J. (1999) *Roman Glass*. University of Pennsylvania Museum, Philadelphia.

Fleming, S.J., Moss, H.H. and Joseph, A. (1970) Thermoluminescence authenticity testing of some 'Six Dynasties' figures. *Archaeometry* **12**, 1; pp. 57–65.

Fleming, S.J. and Stoneham, D. (1971) Re-firing tests using `pre-dose' studies. Appendix A to Aitken *et al.* 1971, pp. 127–131.

Fleming, S.J., Jucker, H. and Riederer, J. (1971) Etruscan wall-paintings on terracotta: a study in authenticity. *Archaeometry* **13**, 2; pp. 143–167.

Fleming, S.J. and Sampson, E.H. (1972) The authenticity of figurines, animals and pottery facsimiles of bronzes in the Hui Hsien style. *Archaeometry* **14**, 2; pp. 237–244.

Fleming, S.J. and Stoneham, D. (1973) Thermoluminescent authenticity study and dating of Renaissance terracottas. *Archaeometry* **15**, 2; pp. 239–247.

Fletcher, J.M. (1974) Tree ring dates for some panel paintings in England. *The Burlington Magazine* **141**; pp. 250–258.

Fletcher, J.M. (1976) A group of English royal portraits painted soon after 1513: A dendrochronological study. *Studies in Conservation* **21**, 4; pp. 171–178.

Fletcher, J.M. (1978) Tree-ring analysis of panel paintings. In: *Dendrochronology in Europe*, J. Fletcher (ed). British Archaeological Reports International Series 51, Oxford, pp. 303–306.

Fletcher, J. (1980) Tree-ring Dating of Tudor Portraits. *Proceedings of the Royal Institution of Great Britain* **52**; pp. 81–104.

Fletcher, J.M. (1982) Panel examination and dendrochronology. *The J. Getty Museum Journal* **10**; pp. 39–44.

Fletcher, J.M. (1986) Dating of art-historical artefacts. *Nature* **320**, 6061; p. 466. 19 April.

Fletcher, J.M., Tapper, M.C. and Walker, F.S. (1974) Dendrochronology – a reference curve for slow grown oaks. *Archaeometry* **16**, 1; pp. 31–40.

Fletcher, J.M. and Tapper, M.C. (1984) Medieval artifacts and structures dated by dendrochronology. *Medieval Archaeology* **28**; pp. 112–132.

Fletcher, S. (1984) A preliminary study of the use of infrared reflectography in the examination of works of art. In: de Froment (ed), 1984, pp. 24–28.

Flieder, F. (1980) Documents graphiques. In: Hours (ed), 1980, pp. 217–244.

Flury-Lemberg, M. (2003) *Sindone 2002, L'intervento Conservative, Preservation, Konservierung.* Editrice ODPF, Torino.

Follo, L., Furlan, C., Gerbasi, C. and Marigo, A. (1981) Estami di Laboratorio. In: *Corpus Speculorum Etruscorum: Italia I Bologna Musem Civica I & II, G,* Vol. I. Sassatelli. Bretschneider, Rome, pp. 207–211. Vol. II: p. 102.

Foltzer, J. (1928) *Artificial Silk and its Manufacture,* 3rd edn. Pitman and Sons, London. [Trans. T. Woodhouse].

Forbes, J.S. (1971) Fakes and forgeries of Bristish antique silver ware. In: Morland, N. (ed), 1971, Papers from *The Criminologist,* Wolfe, London, pp. 217–230.

Forbes, J.S. and Dalladay, D.B. (1958–59) Metallic impurities in the silver coinage trial plates (1279–1900). *Journal of the Institute of Metals* **87**; pp. 55–58.

Formigli, E. (1985) *Techniche Dell' Oreficeria Etrusca e Romana: Originali e Falsificazoni.* Sansori, Florence.

Formigli, E. (1988) Zur Form- und Gußtechnik des Jünglings vom Magdalensberg. In: Gschwantler and Bernhard-Walcher (eds), 1988, pp. 35–38.

Formigli, E. (1992) Indagini archeometriche sull'autenticità della fibula Prenestina. *Mitteilungen des Deutschen Archaeologischen Instituts Roemische Abteilung* **99**; pp. 329–343.

Formigli, E. (ed) (1999) *I Grandi Bronzi Antichi.* Nuova Immagine Editrice, Siena.

Formigli, E. and Heilmeyer, W.-D. (1993) Einige Fälschungen antiken Goldschmucks im 19. Jahrhundert. *Archäologischer Anzeiger* **3**; pp. 299–332.

Formiglli, E. and Schneider, G. (1993) Antiche terre di fusione Indagini archeometriche sulle terre di fusione di bronzi greci, romani e rinascimentali. In: *Atti di studi (ed) espermenti, Murlo, 26–31 Juglio 1991,* E. Formigli (ed). Nuova Immagine Editrice, Siena, pp. 69–102.

Fortnum, C.D.E. (1877) *Bronzes.* South Kensington Museum Art Handbooks, London.

Forsdyke, E.J. (1927) Review of A.J.B. Wace: *A Cretan Statuette in the Fitzwilliam Museum. Journal of Hellenic Studies* **47**; pp. 299–300.

Foucart, J. (1973) Rubens: copies, répliques, pastiches. *Revue de l'Art* **21**; pp. 48–55.

Fox, B. (2003) Alert over inkjet printers. *New Scientist* **178**, 2396; pp. 10–24. May.

Francaviglia, V., Minardi, M.E. and Palmieri, A. (1975) Comparative study of various samples of Etruscan bucchero by X-ray diffraction, X-ray spectrometry, and thermoanalysis. *Archaeometry* **17**, 2; pp. 223–231.

Frank, N., Mangini, A. and Korfmann, M. (2002) 230Th/U dating of the Trojan 'water quarries'. *Archaeometry* **44**, 2; pp. 305–314.

Franklin, P. (1990) Deception and detection: The work of Doreen Stoneham in the field of 'TL' testing. *Apollo* **132**, 345; pp. 327–330.

Franks, A.W. (1858) Frauds and Forgeries of 'Antiques'. *Proceedings of the Society of Antiquaries* **5**; pp. 5 233.

Frantz, J.H. and Schorsch, D. (1990) Egyptian red gold. *Archeomaterials* **4**, 2; pp. 133–152.

Fraquet, H. (1987) *Amber.* Butterworths, London.

Freestone, I.C. (1982) Applications and potential of electron probe micro-analysis in technological and provenance investigations of ancient ceramics. *Archaeometry* **24**, 2; pp. 99–116.

Freestone, I.C. (1987) Composition and microstructure of early opaque red glass. In: *Early Vitreous Materials,* M. Bimson and I.C. Freestone (eds). British Museum Occasional Paper 56, London, pp. 173–191.

Freestone, I. (1991) Looking into glass. In: Bowman (ed), 1997, pp. 37–56.

Freestone, I.C. (1999a) The mineralogy and chemistry of early British porcelain. *Mineralogical Society Bulletin;* pp. 3–7. July.

Freestone, I.C. (1999b) The Science of Early British Porcelain. *British Ceramic Proceedings* **60**; pp. 11–17. Republished (2000) in *The International Ceramic Fair and Seminar,* London, pp. 19–27.

Freestone, I.C. (2001) Post-depositional changes in archaeological ceramics and glasses. In: Brothwell and Pollard (eds), 2001, pp. 615–625.

Freestone, I.C. (2002) The relationship between enamelling on ceramics and on glass in the Islamic world. *Archaeometry* **44**, 2; pp. 251–255.

Freestone, I.C. (2003) The Portland Vase: Roman or Renaissance? *Glass News* **14**; pp. 7–8.

Freestone, I.C., La Niece, S.C. and Meeks, N.D. (1984) A bronze statuette of *Minerva*: A study in mineralogical provenancing. *MASCA Journal* **3**, 1; pp. 10–12.

Freestone, I.C., Meeks, N.D. and Middleton, A.P. (1985) Retention of phosphate in buried ceramics: an electron microbeam approach. *Archaeometry* **27**, 2; pp. 161–177.

Freestone and Bimson, M. (1995) Early Venetian enamelling on glass: technology and origins. In: Vandiver *et al.* (eds), 1995, pp. 415–431.

Freestone, I.C. and Gaimster, D. (eds) (1997) *Pottery in the Making: World Ceramic Traditions.* British Museum Press, London.

Freestone, I.C. and Stapleton, C.P. (1998) Composition and technology of Islamic enamelled glass of the thirteenth and fourteenth centuries. In: Ward (ed), 1998, pp. 122–127.

Freestone, I.C., Leslie, K.A., Thirlwall, M. and Gorin-Rosen, Y. (2003a) Strontium isotopes in the investigation of early glass production: Byzantine and early

Islamic glass from the Near East. *Archaeometry* **45**, 1; pp. 19–32.

Freestone, I.C., Stapleton, C.P. and Rigby, V. (2003b) The production of red glass and enamel in the Late Iron Age, Roman and Byzantine periods. In: *Through a Glass Brightly*, C. Entwhistle (ed). Oxbow, Oxford, pp. 142–154.

Freiberger, V., Gschwantler, K. and Pacher, A. (1988) Beobachtungen zur Oberfläche des Jünglings vom Magdalensberg. In: Gschwantler and Bernard-Walcher (eds), 1998, pp. 28–34.

Frel, J. (1982) *The Getty Bronze.* The J. Paul Getty Museum, Malibu, California.

French, A.D. and Gardner, K.H. (1980) *Fiber Diffraction Methods.* American Chemical Society, Washington DC.

Friedel, R.D. (1983) *Pioneer Plastic.* Wisconsin University Press, Madison, Wisconsin.

Friedman, F.D. (1998) *Gifts of the Nile: Ancient Egyptian Faience.* Thames and Hudson, London.

Frinta, M.S. (1978) The quest for a restorer's shop of beguiling invention: Restorations and forgeries in Italian panel painting. *The Art Bulletin* **58**, 1; pp. 7–23.

Frinta, M.S. (1982) Drawing the net closer: The case of Ilicio Frederico Joni, painter of antique pictures. *Pantheon* **40**, 3; pp. 217–223.

Fritsch, E. and Stockton, C.M. (1987) Infrared spectroscopy in gem identification. *Gems and Gemmology* **23**, 1; pp. 18–26.

Fritsch, E., Wu, S.T.T., Moses, T., McLure, S.F. and Moon, M. (1992) Identification of bleached and polymer impregnated jadeite. *Gems and Gemmology* **28**, 3; pp. 176–189.

Frost, P. (2000) *Miller's Collecting Textiles.* Millers, London.

Furtwängler, A. (1893) *Meisterwerke der grieschischen Plastik,* Leipzig [English edition translated and edited by E. Sellers, as *Masterpieces of Greek Sculpture.* Heinemann, London, 1895].

Gage, J. (1993) *Color and Culture.* Thames and Hudson, London.

Gaimster, D.R.M. (1992) Renaissance stoneware from the Rhineland: continuing problems of authentication. In: Jones (ed), 1992, pp. 108–115.

Gaimster, D. (1997) *German Stoneware 1200–1900.* British Museum Press, London.

Gaines, A.M. and Handy, J.L. (1975) Mineralogical alteration of Chinese tomb jades. *Nature* **253**, 5491; pp. 433–434.

Gale, N.H., Einfalt, H.C., Hubberten, H.W. and Jones, R.E. (1988) The sources of Mycenaean gypsum. *Journal of Archaeological Science* **15**, 1; pp. 57–72.

Gale, N. H. and Stos-Gale, Z.A. (1996) Lead-isotope methodology: the possible fractionation of lead isotope compositions during metallurgical processes. In: Demirci *et al.* (eds), 1996, pp. 287–299.

Gale, N.H. and Stos-Gale, Z. (2000) Lead isotope analyses applied to provenance studies. In: Ciliberto and Spoto (eds), 2000, pp. 503–584.

Galetti, C., Lazzarini, L. and Maggetti, M. (1992) A first characterization of the most important granites used in antiquity. In: Waelkens, Herz and Moens (eds), 1992, pp. 167–177.

Gamble, W. (1910) *Line-Photo Engraving.* Percy Lund Humphries, London.

Ganzelewski, M.G. (1996) Berstein in Weichelmündungsgebiet und im Samland. In: Ganzelewski and Slotta (eds), 1996, pp. 161–298.

Ganzelewski, M.G. and Slotta, R. (eds) (1996) *Berstein: Tränen der Götter.* Deutsches Bergbau Museum, Bochum.

Gao Yan, and Zhang, Beili (1998) Identification of B jade by FTIR spectrometer with near-IR fibre-optic probe accessory. *The Journal of Gemmology* **26**, 5; pp. 302–307.

Garbassi, F. and Mello, E. (1984) Surface spectroscopic studies on patinas of ancient metal objects. *Studies in Conservation* **29**, 4; pp. 172–180.

Gardiner, B.G. (2003) The Piltdown forgery: A re-statement of the case against Hinton. *Zoological Journal of the Linnean Society* **139**, 3; pp. 315–335.

Gardiner, E.A. (1890) The processes of Greek sculpture as shown by some unfinished statues in Athens. *Journal of Hellenic Studies* **11**; pp. 129–142.

Garner, H. (1962) *Chinese and Japanese Cloisonné.* Faber and Faber, London.

Garner, H. (1979) *Chinese Lacquer.* Faber and Faber, London.

Garrod, D. (1968) Recollections of Glozel. *Antiquity* **42**, 167; pp. 172–177.

Garza-Valdès, L.A. (1990) *The DNA of God.* Doubleday, New York.

Garza-Valdès, L.A. (1991) Technology and weathering of Mesoamerican jades as guides to authenticity. In: Vandiver *et al.* (eds), 1991, pp. 321–357.

Garza-Valdès, L.A. (1993) Mesoamerican jades: Surface changes caused by natural weathering. In: Lange (ed), 1993, pp. 104–124.

Gascoigne, B. (1982) *How to Identify Prints.* Thames and Hudson, London.

Gebel, A. and Schmidt, K. (2000) Analyse der Pb-isotope römischer Silbermünzen mit Hilfe der Laserablation-ICP-MS. In: Hollstein (ed), 2000, pp. 55–70.

Gegus, E. (1998) Investigating coins by laser-microspectral analysis method. In: Oddy and Cowell (eds), 1998, pp. 335–347.

Geijer, A. (1979) *A History of Textile Art.* Philip Wilson, London.

Gendron, F., Smith, D.C. and Gendron-Badou, A. (2002) Discovery of jadeite-jade in Guatemala confirmed by non-destructive Raman microscopy. *Journal of Archaeological Science* **29**, 8; pp. 837–851.

Geneslay, G. (1937) Corrosive action of alkaline carbonates and of ammonium carbonate on copper. *Bulletin-Societé Chimique de France* **4**, 5; pp. 120–122.

Geominy, W. (2003) Der Diskobli Lancellotti und seine ergänzungen mit einem Beitrage von Antonella Basile. In: Kunze and Rügler (eds), 2003, pp. 229–242.

Germann, K., Holzmann, G. and Winkler, F.J. (1980) Determination of marble provenance: Limits of isotopic analysis. *Archaeometry* **22**, 1; pp. 99–106.

Gervasio, R. (1986) La struttura tessile della Sindone. Documentazioni tecnologiche, fotografiche e storiche.

La Sindone: nuovi Studi e Riceriche. Atti III Congresso Nazionale di studi sulla Sindone. Library Paolino Lugano, pp. 261–279.

Gettens, R.J. (1949) Tin-oxide patina of ancient high-tin bronze. *Bulletin of the Fogg Museum of Fine Art* **11**, 1; pp. 16–26.

Gettens, R.J. (1969) *The Freer Chinese Bronzes 2: Technical Studies*. Freer Gallery of Art Oriental Studies 7, Washington.

Gettens, R.J. (1970) Patina: Noble and Vile. In: Doeringer, Mittens and Steinberg (eds), 1970, pp. 57–72.

Gettens, R.J. and Mooradian, V.G. (1937) Appendix III. Report on the metallographic and microchemical investigations of gilded objects from Coclé. In: Lothrop, S.K., Memoirs of the Peabody Museum VII. Harvard University, Cambridge, MA.

Gettens, R.J. and Mrose, M.E. (1954) Calcium sulphate minerals in the grounds of Italian paintings. *Studies in Conservation* **1**, 4; pp. 174–189.

Gettens, R.J. and Frondel, C. (1955) Chalconatronite: An alteration product on some Ancient Egyptian bronzes. *Studies in Conservation* **2**, 1; pp. 64–75.

Gettens, R.J., Clarke, R.S., Jr. and Chase, W.T. (1973) *Two Early Chinese Bronze Weapons with Meteoritic Iron Blades*. Freer Gallery of Art Occasional Papers **4**, 1; Washington DC.

Gettens, R.J., FitzHugh, E.W. and Feller, R.L. (1993a) Calcium Carbonate Whites. In: Roy (ed), 1993, pp. 203–226.

Gettens, R.J., Kühn, H. and Chase, W.T. (1993b) Lead white. In: Roy (ed), 1993, pp. 67–82.

Ghandi, S. and James, J. (1992) The God that won. *International Journal of Cultural Property* **2**; p. 369.

Ghisalberti, E.L. and Godfrey, I.M. (1998) Application of nuclear magnetic resonance spectroscopy to the analysis of organic archaeological materials. *Studies in Conservation* **43**, 4; pp. 215–230.

Ghysels, M. (2003) CT scans in art work appraisal. *Art Tribal* **4**; pp. 116–131.

Giangrande, C. (1987) Identification of bronze corrosion products by infrared absorption spectroscopy. In: Black (ed), 1987, pp. 135–148.

Gigante, G.E., Maltese, C., Rinaldi, S. and Sciuti, S. (1991) In situ analyses of XVI and XVII centuries Italian paintings. In: Pernicka and Wagner (eds), 1991, pp. 255–264.

Gigante, G.E., Ridolfi, S., Visco, G. and Guida, G. (2003) Appraisal of the new approach to the archaeometric study of ancient metal artifacts by the use of movable EDXRF equipments. In: *Archaeometallurgy in Europe II*, A. Giumlia Mair (ed). Associazione Italiana di Metallurgia, Milano, pp. 293–302.

Gilardoni, A., Orsini, R.A. and Taccani, S. (1994) *X-Rays in Art*, 2nd edn. Gilardoni S.p.a, Mandello Lario, Como.

Gilberg, M. (1988) History of bronze disease and its treatment. In: Daniels (ed), 1988, pp. 59–70.

Gilberg, M. and Vivian, D. (2001) The rise of conservation science in archaeology (1830–1930). In: Oddy and Smith (eds), 2001, pp. 87–93.

Giles, A.G. (1998) *The Forensic Examination of Documents*. Royal Society of Chemistry, London.

Gill, D.W.J. and Chippindale, C. (1993) Material and intellectual consequences of esteem, for cycladic figurines. *American Journal of Archaeology* **97**; pp. 601–659.

Gillard, R.D., Hardman, S.M., Thomas, R.G. and Watkinson, D.E. (1994) The detection of dyes by FTIR microscopy. *Studies in Conservation* **39**, 3; pp. 187–192.

Gillespie, C.C. (ed) (1959) *A Diderot Pictorial Encyclopedia of Trades and Industry*. [Reprint and trans. from 2nd edn, 1763]. Dover, New York.

Gilmore, G.R. (1991) Sources of uncertainty in the neutron activation of pottery. In: Hughes *et al.* (eds), 1991, pp. 1–28.

Gilmore, G.R. (1998) Neutron activation using a reactor. In: Oddy and Cowell (eds), 1998, pp. 1–14.

Gilmore, R. (1999) Industrial ultrasonic imaging/microscopy. In: *Physical Acoustics*, E. Papadakis (ed), Academic Press, New York, **34**, pp. 275–346.

Giuliani, G., Chaussidon, M., Schubnel, H-J., Piat, D.H., Rollion-Bard, C., France-Lanord, C., Giard, D., de Narvaez, D. and Rondeau, B. (2000) Oxygen isotopes and emerald trade routes since antiquity. *Science* **287**, 5453; pp. 631–633.

Giumlia Mair, A.R. and Craddock, P.T. (1993) *Corinthium Aes – Das schwarze Gold der Alchimisten*. Philipp von Zaben, Mainz.

Glanville, P. (1987) *Silver in England*. Unwin Hyam, London.

Glascock, M.D. and Neff, H. (2003) Neutron activation analysis and provenance research in archaeology. *Measurement Science and Technology* **14**, 9; pp. 1516–1527.

Glastrup, J. (1989) An easy identification method of waxes and resins. In: Maniatis (ed), 1989, pp. 245–252.

Glazer, M. and Dow, J. (1981) Ultraviolet identification of Bermuda stamps. *The American Philatelist* **95**, 9; pp. 805–813.

Gleeson, J. (1998) *The Arcanum*. Bantam Press, London.

Glinsman, L.D. (2006) The practical application of air-path X-ray fluorescence spectrometry in the analysis of museum objects. *Reviews in Conservation* **6**; pp. 3–18.

Gnoli, R. (1988) *Marmora Romana*, 2nd edn. Edizoni dell'Elefante, Rome.

Goebbels, J. (2003) Herakles-Untersuchungen der Bronzestatue mittels Radiographie und Röntgen-Computertomographie 2001. In: *Herakles-Ein Held auf dem Prüfstand*, P. Gercke (ed). Staatliche Museen, Kassel, pp. 33–39.

Goedicke, C. (1994) Echtheitsprüfung an Tanagrafiguren nach der Thermoluminiszensmethode. In: *Bürgerwelten Hellenistische Tonfiguren und Nachtschöpfungen im 19Jh*, I. Kriseleit and G. Zimmer (eds). Philipp von Zaben, Mainz, pp. 77–81.

Goffer, Z. (1980) *Archaeological Chemistry*. John Wiley, New York.

Goldstein, S.M. (1977) Forgeries and reproductions of ancient glass in Corning. *Journal of Glass Studies* **19**; pp. 40–62.

Goldstein, J.I., Newbury, D.E., Echlin, P., Joy, D.C., Romig, A.D., Jr., Lyman, C.E., Fioroi, C. and Lifshin, E. (1992) *Scanning Electron Microscopy and X-Ray Microanalysis*, 2nd edn. Plenum, New York.

Gondonneau, A., Guerra, M.F. and Barrandon, J.-N. (1996) Sur les traces de l'or monnayé: recherche de provenances par LA-ICP-MS. *Révue d'Archéométrie* **20**; pp. 23–32.

Goodway, M. (1987) Fiber identification in practice. *Journal of the American Institute for Conservation* **26**, 1; pp. 27–44.

Gordus, A.A. (1972) Neutron activation analysis of coins and coin-streaks. In: Hall and Metcalf (eds), 1972, pp. 127–148.

Gordus, A.D. and Gordus, J.P. (1974) Neutron Activation Analysis of Gold Impurity Levels in Silver Coins and Art Objects. In: Beck (ed), 1974, pp. 124–147.

Gordus, A.A. and Craig, A.K. (1995) Metal contents of silver and gold ingots and coins from 16th–18th century Spanish shipwrecks. In: Vandiver *et al.* (eds), 1995, pp. 605–611.

Gorelick, L. and Gwinnett, A.J. (1978) Ancient seals and modern science –Using the scanning electron microscope as an aid in the study of ancient seals. *Expedition* **20**; pp. 18–47. Winter.

Gorelick, L. and Gwinnett, A.J. (1979) Ancient lapidary – A study using the scanning electron microscope and functional analysis. *Expedition* **21**; pp. 17–32.

Gorelick, L. and Gwinnett, A.J. (1986) Further authenticity analysis of statuettes similar to those in the Mildenberg Collection. In: Olin and Blackman (eds), 1986, pp. 63–72.

Gorelick, L. and Gwinnett, A.J. (1988) Diamonds from India to Rome and beyond. *American Journal of Archaeology* **92**; pp. 547–552.

Goren, Y., Ahituv, S., Ayalon, A.., Bar-Matthews, M., Dahari, U., Dayagi-Mendels, M., Demsky, A. and Levin, N. (2005) A Re-examination of the inscribed pomegranate from the Israel Museum. *Israel Exploration Journal* **55**; pp. 3–20.

Gorgoni, C., Lazzarini, L., Pallante, P. and Turi, B. (2002) An updated and detailed mineropetrographic and C–O stable isotopic reference database for the main Mediterranean marbles used in antiquity. In: Herrmann Jr. *et al.*, (eds), 2002, pp. 115–131.

Gould, S.J. (1980) The Piltdown Conspiracy. *Natural History* **89**, 8; pp. 8–28. August.

Gove, H.E. (1989) Letter to the Editor – The Turin Shroud. *Archaeometry* **31**, 2; pp. 235–237.

Gove, H.E. (1996) *Relic, Icon or Hoax? Carbon Dating the Turin Shroud*. Institute of Physics, Bristol.

Gove, H.E. (1999) *From Hiroshima to the Iceman: The Development and Application of Accelerator Mass Spectrometry*. Institute of Physics, Bristol and Philadelphia.

Gove, H.E., Mattingly, S.J., David, A.R. and Garza-Valdès, L.A. (1997) A problematic source of organic contamination of linen. *Nuclear Instruments and Methods in Physics Research* **B123**; pp. 504–507.

Gowland, W. (1894) A Japanese pseudo-speise (Shirome). *Journal of the Society of Chemical Industry* **13**, 5; pp. 1–26.

Graedel, T.E. (1987a) Copper patinas formed in the atmosphere 2: A qualitative assessment of mechanisms. *Corrosion Science* **27**, 7; pp. 721–740.

Graedel, T.E. (1987b) Copper patinas formed in the atmosphere 3: A semi-quantitative assessment of rates and constraints in the greater New York metropolitan area. *Corrosion Science* **27**, 7; pp. 741–770.

Graedel, T.E., Nassau, K. and Franey, J.P. (1987) Copper patinas formed in the atmosphere 1: an introduction. *Corrosion Science* **27**, 7; pp. 685–694.

Graf, L. and Budke, J. (1955) Zum Problem der Spannungskorrosion homogener Mischkristalle III: Abhängigheit der Spannungskorrosionsempfindlichke it von Kupfer-Gold und Silber-Gold Mischkristallen von Goldgehalt und Zusammenhang mit dem 'Mischkristall-Effect'. *Zeitschrift f ür Metallkunde* **46**; pp. 378–385.

Grant, M.E. (1992) Dendrochronology in South Asia, an Update. *South Asia Studies* **8**; pp. 115–123.

Grasso, T. (1996) *Bakelite Jewelry*. Quintet Publishing, New York.

Gratuze, B. and Barrandon, J.-N. (1990) Islamic glass weights and stamps: analysis using nuclear techniques. *Archaeometry* **32**, 2; pp. 155–162.

Gratuze, B., Soulier, I., Barrandon, J.-N. and Foy, D. (1992) De l'origine du cobalt dans les verres. *Revue d'Archéometrie* **16**; pp. 97–108.

Gratuze, B., Soulier, I., Barrandon, J.-N. and Foy, D. (1995) The origin of cobalt blue pigments in French glass from the thirteenth to the eighteenth centuries. In: Hook and Gaimster (eds), 1995, pp. 123–134.

Gratuze, B., Soulier, I., Blet, M. and Vallauri, L. (1996) De l'origine du cobalt: du verre à la céramique. *Revue d'Archéometrie* **20**; pp. 77–94.

Gratuze, B., Soulier, I. and Barrandon, J.N. (1997) L'analyse chimique, un outil au service de l'histoire du verre. *Verre* **3**; pp. 31–43.

Gratuze, B., Uzonyi, I., Elekes, Z., Kiss, Á.Z. and Mester, E. (2000) Cobalt-blue glass pigment in Europe during medieval times. In: Demortier and Adriaens (eds), 2000, pp. 50–53.

Graydon-Stannus, E. (1931) *Old Irish Glass*, revised edn. The Connoisseur, London.

Greaves, P.H. (1992) Microscopy, imaging and analysis. In: *Advances in Fibre Science*, S.K. Mukhopadhyay (ed). Textile Institute, Manchester, pp. 47–66.

Greaves, P.H. and Saville, B.P. (1995) *Microscopy of Textile Fibres*. RMS handbook 32. Royal Microscopy Society/ BOIS, Oxford.

Green, W.A., Young, S.M.M., van der Merwe, N.J. and Herrmann J.J. Jr (2002) Source tracing marble: trace element analysis with inductively coupled plasma-mass spectrometry. In: Herrmann Jr. *et al.* (eds), 2002, pp. 132–142.

Greenhalgh, D. (1998) Reproductions: A manufacturer's viewpoint. *CCNB Newsletter* **19**; pp. 2–3.

Gregory, W.K. (1914) The Dawn Man of Piltdown, England. *American Museums Journal* **14**; pp. 189–200.

Greifenhagen, A. (1968) Review of *'Greek Gold'* by H. Hoffmann and P.F. Davidson. In: *Gnomon* **40**; pp. 695–697.

Greiff, S. (1998) Naturwissenschaftliche Untersuchungen zur Frage der Rohsteinquellen für frümittelalterlichen Almandingranatschmuck rheinfränkischer Provenienz. *Jahrbuch des Römisch-Germanisches Zentralmuseum, Mainz* **45**, 2; pp. 599–646.

Greilich, S., Glassmacher, U.A. and Wagner, G.A. (2005) Optical dating of granitic stone surfaces. *Archaeometry* **47**, 3; pp. 645–665.

Griesser, M. and Denker, A. (2000) A 'new' non-destructive analysing technique for paintings? In: Demortier and Adriaens (eds), 2000, pp. 28–30.

Griffiths, A. (1980) *Prints and Printmaking.* British Museum Press, London.

Grigorova, B., Anderson, S., de Bruyn, J., Smith, W., Stülpner, K. and Barzev, A. (1998) The AARL gold fingerprinting technology. *Gold Bulletin* **31**, 1; pp. 26–29.

Grim, D.M. and Allison, J. (2004) Laser desorption mass spectrometry as a tool for the analysis of colorants: the identification of pigments used in illuminated manuscripts. In: *Archaeometry* **46**, 2; pp. 283–299.

Grimaldi, D.A. (1996) *Amber in Nature.* H.N. Abrams/American Museum of Natural History, New York.

Grimaldi, D.A., Shedrinsky, A., Ross, A. and Baer, N.S. (1994) Forgeries of fossils in 'amber': history, identification, and case studies. *Curator* **37**, 4; pp. 251–274.

Grimwade, A,G. (1982) A study of English silver fakes. *Apollo* **116**, 247; pp. 181–184. September.

Grimwade, M. (1985) *Introduction to Precious Metals.* Newnes Technical Books, Butterworth & Co, London.

Grissino-Mayer, H.D., Sheppard, P.R. and Cleaveland, M.K. (2004) A dendrochronological re-examination of the 'Messiah' violin and other instruments attributed to Antonio Stradivari. *Journal of Archaeological Science* **31**, 2; pp. 167–174.

Groen, K. de Keijzer, M. and Baadsgaard, E. (1996) Examination of the painting technique of nine Dutch pictures of the first half of the 18th century. In: Bridgland (ed), 1996, pp. 360–366.

Grose, D.F. (1989) *The Toledo Museum of Art: Early Ancient Glass.* Hudson Hills Press, New York.

Grossman, J.B. and Maish, J.P. (2002) An investigation of the authenticity of a Classical Attic funerary monument in the J. Paul Getty Museum. In: Herrmann Jr. *et al.*, (eds), 2002, pp. 274–281.

Grossman, J.B., Podany, J. and True, M. (2003) *History of Restoration of Ancient Stone Sculptures.* J. Paul Getty Museum, Los Angeles.

Grün, R. (2001) Trapped charge dating (ESR, TL, OSL). In: Brothwell and Pollard (eds), 2001, pp. 47–62.

Gschwantler, K. (1987/88) Naturwssenschaftliche untersuchungen an der bronzestatue *'Der Jüngling vom Magdalensberg'*. In: Jüngling, 1987/88, pp. 256–61.

Gschwantler, K. (1988) Der Jüngling vom Magdalensberg: Ein Forschungeprojekt der Antikensammulung des Kunsthistorische Museum. In: Gschwantler and Bernhard-Walcher (eds), 1988, pp. 16–27.

Gschwantler, K. and Bernhard-Walcher, A. (eds) (1988) *Griechishe und römische Statuetten und Großbronzen: Akten der 9. Internationalen Tagung über antike Bronzen: Wien 21-5 April 1986.* Kunsthistorisches Muesum, Wien.

Gschwantler, K. and Bernhard-Walcher, A. (1984) Zur Echteitsfrage eines etruskischen Terrakottapfes. *Wiener Berichte über Naturwissenschaft in der Kunst* **1**; pp. 26–29.

Gübelin, E.J. and Koivula, J.I. (1997) *Photoatlas of Inclusions in Gemstones,* 3rd edn. ABC, Zurich.

Gudenrath, W. (1991) Techniques of Glassmaking and Decoration. In: Tait (ed), 1991, pp. 213–241.

Gudenrath, W. (2001) A Survey of Islamic Glassworking and Glass-Decorating Techniques. In: Carboni and Whitehouse, 2001, pp. 46–70.

Guerra, M.F. (2000) The mines of Potosi: A silver Eldorado for the European economy. In: Demortier and Adriaens (eds), 2000, pp. 88–94.

Guerra, M.F., Sarthe, C-O., Gondonneau, A. and Barrandon, J.-N. (1999) Precious Metals and Provenance Enquiries using LA-ICP-MS. In: *Proceedings of the International Symposium on Archaeometry,* University of Illinois at Urbana, 20–24th May 1996, J. Henderson, H. Neff and Th. Rehren (eds). A special issue of *Journal of Archaeological Science* **26**; pp. 1101–1110.

Guerra, M.F. and Calligaro, T. (2004) Gold traces to trace gold. *Proceedings of the Newcastle Archaeometry Conference,* J. Henderson (ed). A special issue of *Journal of Archaeological Science* **31**; pp. 1199–1208.

Guineau, B. (1989) Non-destructive analysis of organic pigments and dyes using Raman microprobe, microfluorometer or absorption microspectrophotometer. *Studies in Conservation* **34**, 1; pp. 38–44.

Guineau, B. (ed) (1990) *Pigments et Colorants.* Colloque International du CNRS, Paris.

Guo, Y. (1987) Raw materials for making porcelain and the characteristics of porcelain wares in north and south China in ancient times. *Archaeometry* **29**, 1; pp. 3–19.

Gunn, M.J. (1922) *Print Restoration and Picture Cleaning.* The Bazaar, Exchange and Mart, London.

Gunter, A.C. and Jett, P. (1992) *Ancient Iranian Metalwork.* Freer Gallery of Art, Smithsonian Institution, Washington DC.

Gwinnett, A.J. and Gorelick, L. (1981) Beadmaking in Iran in the Early Bronze Age. *Expedition* **23**, 4; pp. 10–23. Autumn.

Gwinnett, A.J. and Gorelick, L. (1982) Authenticity analysis of two stone statuettes in the Mildenberg Collection. *MASCA Journal* **2**, 3; pp. 88–90.

Gwinnett, A.J. and Gorelick, L. (1983) An ancient repair on a cycladic statuette analyzed using scanning electron microscopy. *Journal of Field Archaeology* **10**; pp. 378–384.

Gwinnett, A.J. and Gorelick, L. (1986a) Experimenal evidence for the use of a diamond drill in Sri-Lanka ca. AD 700–1000. *Archeometerials* **1**, 2; pp. 149–152.

Gwinnett, A.J. and Gorelick, L. (1986b) Evidence for the use of a diamond drill for bead making in Sri-Lanka c.700–1000 A.D. *Scanning Electron Microscopy* **11**; pp. 473–477.

Gwinnett, A.J. and Gorelick, L. (1987) The change from stone drills to copper drills in Bronze Age Mesopotamia: an experimental perspective. *Expedition* **29**, 1; pp. 15–24.

Gwinnett, A.J. and Gorelick, L. (1989) Evidence for mass production polishing in ancient bead manufacture. *Archeomaterials* 3, 2; pp. 163–168.

Gwinnett, A.J. and Gorelick, L. (1993) Beads, scarabs, and amulets: Methods of manufacture in Ancient Egypt. *Journal of the American Research Center in Egypt* 30; pp. 125–131.

Gwinnett, A.J. and Gorelick, L. (1998–99) A brief history of drills and drilling. *Beads* **10–11**; pp. 49–56.

Haber, G.J. and Heimler, M. (1994) Kupfergalvanoplastik: Geschichte, Herstellungstechniken und Restaurier ungsproblematik kunstindustrieller Katalogware. In: *Metallrestaurierung: Beiträge zur Analyse, Konzeption und Technologie*, P. Heinrich (ed). Georg D.W. Callwey, Munich, pp. 160–181.

Hagemeyer, R.W. (ed) (1984) *Pigments for Paper*. TAPPI Press, Atlanta, Georgia.

Hahn, O., Oltrogge, D. and Bevers, H. (2004) Colored prints of the 16th century: non-destructive analyses on colored engravings from Albrecht Dürer and contemporary artists. *Archaeometry* 46, 2; pp. 273–282.

Hahn, O., Kanngießer, B. and Malzer, W. (2005) X-ray Fluorescence Analysis of Iron Gall Inks, Pencils and Colored Crayons. *Studies in Conservation* 50, 1; pp. 23–32.

Haines, B.M. (1999) *Parchment*. The Leather Conservation Centre, Northampton, Northants.

Hajdamach, C. (1986) Glass. In: Bly (ed), 1986, pp. 80–103.

Hall, E.T. (1975) The Glozel Affair. *Nature* 257, 5525; pp. 355–356.

Hall, E.T. (1987) The Courtrai chest from New College, Oxford, re-examined. *Antiquity* 61, 231; pp. 104–107.

Hall, E.T. (1989) The Turin Shroud: an editorial postscript. *Archaeometry* 31, 1; pp. 92–95.

Hall, E.T. and Metcalf, D.M. (eds) (1972) *Methods of Chemical and Metallurgical Investigation of Ancient Coinage*. Royal Numismatic Society, Special Publication 8, London.

Hall, E.T., Fletcher, J.M. and Barbetti, M.F. (1978) Recent work on dendrochronology and archaeomagnetism dating at Oxford. In: Young. (ed), 1978, pp. 68–76.

Halleux, R. [trans. and (ed).] (1981) *Les Alchemistes Grecs I: Papyrus de Leyde, Papyrus de Stockholm, Fragments de Recettes*. Société d'édition. Les Belles Lettres, Paris.

Hallowell, R.H. (1967) Manufacture of sterling silver hollow ware. In: Butts and Coxe (eds), 1967, pp. 331–342.

Hally, D.J. (1983) Use alteration of pottery vessel surfaces: An important source of evidence in the identification of vessel function. *North American Archaeologist* **4**, 1; pp. 3–24.

Halpine, S.M. (1996) An improved dye and lake pigment analysis method for high-performance liquid chromatography and diode-array detector. *Studies in Conservation* 41, 2; pp. 76–94.

Hamer, F. (1975) *The Potter's Dictionary of Materials and Techniques*. Pitman, London and Watson-Guptill, New York.

Hancock, V. (1974) Featuring fakes. *The Numismatist* **87**, 8 & 10; pp. 1552–1553. 2000–2001 August & October.

Hanley, T., Weisler, L., and Edgett, N. (1984) Barium sulphate. In: Hagemeyer (ed). pp. 39–52.

Handberry, A. (1997) Thermoluminescence revisited: a new look at the ceramics dating method. *Minerva* **8**, 3; pp. 43–46.

Hänni, H.A. (1992) Identification of fissure-treated gemstones. *The Journal of Gemmology* **23**, 4; pp. 201–205.

Hänni, H.A. (1994) Origin determination for gemstones: possibilities, restrictions and reliability. *The Journal of Gemmology* **24**, 3; pp. 139–148.

Hänni, H.A., Kiefert, L. and Chalain, J-P. (1997) A Raman microscope in the gemmological laboratory: first experiences of application. *The Journal of Gemmology* **25**, 6; pp. 394–406.

Hansford, S.H. (1950) *Chinese Jade Carving*. Lund Humphries, London.

Hansford, S.H. (1968) *Chinese Carved Jades*. Faber and Faber, London.

Hanson, V.F. (1973) The curator's dream instrument. In: Young (ed), 1973, pp. 18–30.

Harbottle, G. and Weigand, P.C. (1992) Turquoise in Pre-Columbian America. *Scientific American* **226**, 2; pp. 78–85.

Harbottle, G., Cresswell, R.G. and Stoenner, R.W. (1993) Carbon-14 dating of iron blooms from Kodlunarn Island. In: *Archaeology of the Frobisher Voyages*, W.W. Fitzhugh and J.S. Olin (eds). Smithsonian Institution, Washington DC, pp. 173–180.

Hard, A.H. (1933) *The Romance of Rayon*. Whittaker & Robinson, Manchester.

Harden, D.B. (1968) Ancient glass, I: Pre-Roman. *The Archaeological Journal* 125; pp. 46–72.

Harden, D.B. (1969) Ancient glass, II: Roman. *The Archaeological Journal* 126; pp. 44–77.

Harden, D.B. (1971) Ancient glass, III: Post-Roman. *The Archaeological Journal* 128; pp. 78–117.

Harden, D.B. (1987) *Glass of the Caesars*. Olivetti, Milan.

Harden, D.B., Painter, K.S., Pinder-Wilson, R.H. and Tait, H. (1968) *Masterpieces of Glass*. Trustees of the British Museum, London.

Hardwick, P. (1981) *Discovering Horn*. Lutterworth Press, Guildford, Surrey.

Hare, S. (ed) (1978) *Touching Gold and Silver: 400 Years of Hallmarks*. Goldsmiths' Hall, London.

Harley, R.D. (1982) *Artists' Pigments, c. 1600–1835*, 2nd edn. Butterworth, London.

Harmon, A.M. [trans.] (1925) (II) and 1936 (V) *The Works of Lucian*, The Loeb Edition. Heinemann, London.

Harmssen, A. (ed) (1999) Varnish: Material, Aesthetics, History. International Congress Braunschweig, 15–17 June 1998, AdR-Schriftenreihe zur Restaurierung und Grabungstechnik **3**. Braunschweig, Herzog-Anton-Ulrich Museum.

Harrell, J.A. (1992) Ancient Egyptian limestone quarries: a petrological study. *Archaeometry* **34**, 2; pp. 195–212.

Harris, I. (1999) Silver. In: Tharp (ed), 1999, pp. 104–125.

Harris, J. (ed) (1993) *5,000 Years of Textiles*. British Museum Press, London.

Harris, R. (1986) *Selling Hitler*. Faber & Faber, London.

Harris, V. (1994) *Japanese Imperial Craftsmen*. British Museum Press, London.

Harrison, W.R. (1964) *Forgery Detection*. Sweet and Maxwell, London.

Harrison, W.R. (1966) *Suspect Documents: Their Scientific Examination*. Sweet and Maxwell, London.

Harrison-Hall, J. (1997) Chinese porcelain from Jingsdezhen. In: Freestone and Gaimster (eds), 1997, pp. 194–199.

Harrison-Hall, J. (2001) *A Catalogue of Late Yuan and Ming Ceramics in the British Museum*. British Museum Press, London.

Hartmann, A. (1970) Prähistorische Goldfunde aus Europa. I. *Studien zu den Anfängen der Metallurgie* **3**. Gebr. Mann Verlag, Berlin.

Hartmann, A. (1975) Zur Erkennung von fälchungen antiken Goldschmucks. *Archäologischer Anzeiger* **2**; pp. 300–304.

Hartmann, A. (1982) *Prähistorisches Goldfunde aus Europa. II*. Studien zu den Anfängen der Metallurgie **5**. Gebr. Mann Verlag, Berlin.

Harvey, B.W. (1992) *Violin Fraud: Deception, Forgery Theft and the Law*. Clarendon Press, Oxford.

Harvey, B. (1995) *The Violin and its Makers in the British Isles*. Clarendon Press, Oxford.

Hassall, C. (2005) Paintings. In: Lang and Middleton (eds), 2005, pp. 112–129.

Hatcher, H., Tite, M.S. and Walsh, J.N. (1995) A comparison of inductively-coupled plasma emission spectrometry and atomic absorption analysis on standard refererence silicate materials and ceramics. *Archaeometry* **37**, 1; pp. 83–94.

Hauff, P.L. (1993) The enigma of jade, with mineralogical reference to Central American source materials. In: Lange (ed), 1993, pp. 82–103.

Havermans, J.B.G.A. and Dufour, J. (1997) Photo oxidation of paper documents. A literature review. *Restaurator* **18**, 3; pp. 103–114.

Havermans, J., Aziz, H.A. and Scholten, H. (2003) Non destructive detection of iron gall inks by means of multispectral imaging. *Restaurator* **24**; pp. 55–60.

Hawthorne J.G. and Smith, C.S. [eds and trans.] (1963) *On Divers Arts: The Treatise of Theophilus*. University of Chicago Press, Chicago.

Hayez, V., Guillame, J., Hubin, A. and Terryn, H. (2004) Micro-Raman spectroscopy for the study of corrosion products on copper alloys: setting up of a reference data base and studying works of art. In: Kiefer (ed), 2004, pp. 732–738.

Haynes, D.E.L. (1975) *The Portland Vase*, 2nd edn. British Museum Publications, London.

Haynes, D. (1992) *The Technique of Greek Bronze Statuary*. Philipp von Zabern, Mainz.

Hayter, S.W. (1962) *About Prints*. Oxford University Press, London.

Hayward, C.H. (1970) *Antique or Fake?* Evans Bros., London.

Hayward, J.F. (1974) Salomon Weiniger: Master faker. *The Connoisseur* **187**, 753; pp. 170–179.

Hebblewhite, I. (1986) *Artist's Materials*. Phaidon, Oxford.

Hebborn, E. (1997) *The Art Forger's Handbook*. Cassell, London.

Hecht, A. (1989) *The Art of the Loom*. British Museum Press, London.

Heck, G. (1999) Py-GC-Analysen zur Unterscheidung von Bernstein. *Berliner Beiträge zur Archäometrie* **16**; pp. 211–240.

Hedges, E.S. (ed) (1960) *Tin and its Alloys*. Edward Arnold, London.

Hedges, R.E.M. (1976) On the occurrence of bromine in corroded silver. *Studies in Conservation* **21**, 1; pp. 44–46.

Hedges, R.E.M. (1979) Analysis of the 'Drake Plate': Comparison with the composition of Elizabethan brass. *Archaeometry* **21**, 1; pp. 21–26.

Hedges, R.E.M. (1989) Reply to T.J. Phillips. *Nature* **337** 6208; p. 594. 16 February.

Hedges, R.E.M. (1997) A note concerning the application of radiocarbon dating to the Turin Shroud. *Approfondimento Sidone* **1**, 1; pp. 1–6.

Hedges, R.E.M., (2000) Radiocarbon dating. In: Ciliberto and Spoto (eds), 2000, pp. 465–502.

Hedges, R.E.M., Housley, R.A., Law, I.A. and Bronk, C.R. (1989) Radiocarbon dates from the Oxford AMS system. *Archaeometry datelist 9, Archaeometry* **31**, 2; pp. 207–234.

Hedges, R.E.M., Bronk, C.R. and van Klinken, G.J. (1998) An experiment to refute the likelihood of cellulose carboxylation. In: *Proceedings of the 16th International Radiocarbon Conference*, W.G. Monk and J. van der Pilcht (eds). *Radiocarbon* **40**, 1; pp. 59–61.

Heidsiek, H. and Clasing, M. (1983) The abrasive wear of gold jewellery alloys. *Gold Bulletin* **16**, 3; pp. 76–81.

Heilmeyer, W.-D. (1989) Fälsche Liebe, Rekonstruktionen von Arretiner Formschüsseln um 1900. *Archäologischer Anzeiger*, pp. 261–270.

Heimpel, W., Gorelick, L. and Gwinnett, A.J. (1988) Philological and archaeological evidence for the use of emery in the Bronze Age Near East. *Journal of Cuneiform Studies* **40**; pp. 195–210.

Heizer, R.F., Stross, F., Hester, T.R., Albee, A., Perlman, I., Asaro, F. and Bowman, H. (1973) The Colossi of Memnon revisited. *Science* **182**, 4118; pp. 1219–1225.

Heller, D. and Herz, N. (1995) Weathering of dolomitic marble and the role of oxalates. In: Maniatis, Herz and Basiakos (eds), 1995, pp. 267–276.

Heller, J.H. (1983) *Report on the Shroud of Turin.* Houghton Mifflin, Boston & New York.

Heller, J.H. and Adler, A.D. (1981) A chemical investigation of the Shroud of Turin. *Canadian Society of Forensic Science Journal* 14, 3; pp. 81–103.

Hemming, D.C. (1977) The production of artificial patination on copper. In: Brown *et al.* (eds), 1977, pp. 93–102.

Henderson, J. (1988) Electron probe micro analysis of mixed-alkali glasses. *Archaeometry* 30, 1; pp. 77–91.

Henderson, J. (1991) Technological characteristics of Roman enamels. *Jewellery Studies* 5; pp. 65–76.

Henderson, J. (1992) A scientific analysis of the enamel decorating a gold medallion in the Walker Art Gallery. *Journal of the Walters Art Gallery* 49/50; pp. 27–31.

Henderson, J. (1998a) Post-medieval glass production, characterisation and value. In: McCray (ed), 1998, pp. 33–59.

Henderson, J. (1998b) Blue and other colored translucent glass decorated with enamels: Possible evidence for trade in cobalt-blue colorants. In: Ward (ed), 1998, pp. 116–121.

Henderson, J. (2000) *The Science and Archaeology of Materials: An Investigation into Inorganic Materials.* Routledge, London.

Henderson, J. (2001) Glass and Glazes. In: Brothwell and Pollard (eds), 2001, pp. 471–482.

Henderson, J. (2002) Tradition and experiment in first millennium A.D. glass production – The emergence of Early Islamic glass technology in Late Antiquity. *Accounts of Chemical Research* 35, 8; pp. 594–602.

Henderson, J., Tregear, M. and Wood, N. (1989) The technology of sixteenth- and seventeenth-century Chinese *cloisonné* enamels. *Archaeometry* 31, 2; pp. 133–146.

Herb, C.O. (1936) *Die-Casting.* The Industrial Press, New York.

Herbert, E.W. (1984) *Red Gold of Africa.* The University of Wisconsin Press, Madison, Wisconsin.

Herbig, R. (1956) *Die Terracottagruppe einer Diana mit dem Hirschkalb,* Abhandlungen der Heidelberger Akademie der Wissenschaften, Philosophisch-historische Klasse 3. Carl Winter, Universitätsverlag, Heidelberg.

Herrmann, J., Jr. and Barbin, V. (1993) The exportation of marble from the Aliki quarries on Thasos: Cathodoluminescence of samples from Turkey and Italy. *American Journal of Archaeology* 97, 1; pp. 91–103.

Herrmann, J., Moens, L. and De Paepe, P. (2000) Some identifications of sculpture in Parian Marble in Boston. In: Schilardi and Katsonopoulou (eds), 2000, pp. 253–266.

Herrmann, J.J., Jr., Herz, N. and Newman, R. (eds) (2002) *Interdisciplinary Studies on Ancient Stone.* Archetype Publications, London. ASMOSIA 5.

Herrmann, G. (1968) Lapis lazuli: The early phases of its trade. *Iraq* 30, 1; pp. 21–54.

Hersh, S.P., Tucker, P.A. and Becker, M.A. (1989) Characterization of historical and artificially aged silk fabrics. In: Allen (ed), 1999, pp. 429–449.

Herscher, E. (1998) Tarnished reputations. *Archaeology* 51, 5; pp. 66–78. Sept/Oct.

Herz, N. (1987) Carbon and oxygen isotopic ratios: A data base for classical Greek and Roman marble. *Archaeometry* 29, 1; pp. 35–43.

Herz, N. (1990) Stable isotope analysis of Greek and Roman marble: Provenance, association and authenticity. In: True and Podany (eds), 1990b, pp. 101–110.

Herz, N. (1992) Provenance determination of Neolithic to Classical Mediterranean marbles by stable isotopes. *Archaeometry* 34, 2; pp. 185–194.

Herz, N. (2001) Sourcing lithic artifacts by instrumental analysis. In: *Earth Sciences and Archaeology,* P. Goldberg, V.T. Holliday and C. Reid Ferring (eds). Kluwer Academic/ Plenum Publishers, New York, pp. 449–469.

Herz, N., Kane, S.E. and Hayes, W.B. (1985) Isotopic analysis of sculpture from the Cyrene Demeter Sanctuary. In: England and van Zelst (eds), 1985, pp. 142–50.

Herz, N. and Waelkens, M. (eds) (1988) *Classical Marble: Geochemistry, Technology, Trade.* NATO ASI Series, 153. Kluwer Academic, Dordrecht.

Herz, N., Grimanis, A.P., Robinson, H.S., Wenner, D.B. and Vassilaki-Grimani, M. (1989) Science *versus* art history: The Cleveland Museum head of Pan and the Miltiades Marathon victory monument. *Archaeometry* 31, 2; pp. 161–168.

Herz, N. and Doumas, C. (1991) Marble sources in the Aegean Early Bronze Age. In: Pernicka and Wagner (eds), 1991, pp. 425–444.

Herz, N., Barker, W.W. and Showers, W.J. (1992) Detection of artificially induced weathering patina in sculptural marble. In: *La Conservation des Monuments dans le Bassin Méditerranéen: Actes du 2ème Symposium International,* D. Decrouez, J. Chamay and F. Zezza (eds). Ville de Genève, pp. 477–482.

Hewitt, H.D. (1914/15) Some Experiments on Patination. *Proceedings of the Prehistoric Society of East Anglia* 2, 1; pp. 45–51.

Hickman, W.L. (1989) The attribution of two Frederic Remington bronzes in the Metropolitan Museum of Art. In: *Papers Presented at the 14th Annual Art Conservation Training Programs Conference:* May 4–5 1988. Art Conservation Dept, Buffalo State College, pp. 11–16.

Higgins, R.A. (1961) *Greek and Roman Jewellery.* Methuen, London.

Higgins, R.A. (1968–69) Four Greek rosettes again. *British Museum Quarterly* 33, 3–4; pp. 110–113.

Higgins, R.A. (1976) Terracottas. In: Strong and Brown (eds), 1976, pp. 105–110.

Higgins, R.A. (nd) *Tanagra and the Figurines.* Trefoil Press, London.

Hildeburgh, W.L. (1907) Chinese methods of cutting hard stones. *Journal of the Royal Anthropological Institute* 37; pp. 189–195.

Hill, G.F. (1924–25) *Becker, the Counterfeiter.* Spink, London.

Hill, D.K. (1969) Bronze working. In: *The Muses at Work*, C. Roebuck (ed). MIT Press, Cambridge, MA, pp. 60–95.

Hill, W.E. (1891) *The Salabue Stradivarius: A History and Critical Description of the Famous Violin Commonly Known as 'Le Messie'*. W.E. Hill and Sons, London.

Hillam, J. and Tyers, I. (1995) The reliability and repeatability in dendrochronological analysis: Tests using the Fletcher archive of panel-dating data. *Archaeometry* **37**, 2; pp. 395–405.

Hillmann, M.-Ch. (1988) *Vrai ou Faux? Copier, Imiter, Falsifier*. Catalogue of exhibition 6th May–24th October 1988. Cabinet des Médalles et Antiques des Bibliothèques Nationale, Paris.

Hinman, C.W. (1941) *Pressworking of Metals*. McGraw Hill, New York. [Reprinted 1995 by Lindsay Publications, Bradley Iln.].

Hipkiss, E.J., Young, W.J. and Edgell, G.H. (1937) A modified tomb monument of the Italian Renaissance. *Bulletin of The Museum of Fine Arts, Boston* **35**, 82; pp. 83–90.

Hiorns, A.H. (1892) *Metal Coloring and Patination*. Macmillan, London.

Hiscox, G.D. (ed) (1907) *Henley's Twentieth Century Book of Formulas, Processes and Trade Secrets*. Norman W. Henley Publishing Co., New York. [Reissued 1927, and in 1979 by Avenel Books].

Hoare, R. (1994) *The Turin Shroud is Genuine*. Souvenir Press, London.

Hobbs, J. (1981) A simple approach to detecting diamond simulants. *Gems and Gemmology* **17**, 1; pp. 20–33.

Hochfield, S. (1989) Cast in doubt. *ARTnews* **88**, 2; pp. 108–115.

Hodges, H. (1964) *Artifacts*. John Baker, London.

Hodges, H. (1970) *Technology in the Ancient World*. Allen Lane, London.

Hodgins. G.W.L., Farrell, E. and Mowry, R.D. (2002) AMS radiocarbon dating of a Western Han Period (3rd–1st century BC) lacquer-coated earthenware jar. In: Vandiver *et al.* (eds), 2002, pp. 235–240.

Hodgkinson, A. (1993) Gemstone enhancement – detection of polymer-treated jadeite. *The Journal of Gemmology* **23**, 7; pp. 415–417.

Hoffman, M. (1939) *Sculpture Inside and Out*. George Allen & Unwin, London.

Hoffmann, H. (1969) 'Greek Gold' reconsidered. *American Journal of Archaeology* **73**; pp. 447–451.

Hoffmann, H. and Davidson, P.F. (1965) *Greek Gold. Jewelry from the Age of Alexander*. Philip von Zabern, Mainz.

Hollinshead, M.B. (2002) From two to three dimensions in unfinished Roman sculpture. In: Herrmann Jr, Herz and Newman (eds). (2002), pp. 225–230.

Hollister, P. (1983) Muranese millefiori revival of the nineteenth-century. *Journal of Glass Studies* **25**; pp. 201–206.

Hollstein, W. (ed) (2000) *Metallanalytische Untersuchungen an Münzen der Römischen Republik*. Berliner Numismatische Forschungen **6**. Mann Verlag, Berlin.

Holmes, L.L., Little, C..T. and Sayre, E.V. (1986) Elemental characterization of medieval limestone sculpture from Parisian and Burgundian sources. *Journal of Field Archaeology* **13**, 4; pp. 419–438.

Holmes, L.L. and Harbottle, G. (1991) Provenance study of cores from Chinese bronze vessels. *Archeomaterials* **5**, 2; pp. 165–184.

Holmes, L.L. and Harbottle, G. (1994) Compositional fingerprinting: new directions in the study of the provenance of limestone. *Gesta* **33**, 1; pp. 10–18.

Holmes, L.L., Harbottle, G. and Blanc, A. (1994) Compositional characterization of French limestone: a new tool for art historians. *Archaeometry* **36**, 1; pp. 25–39.

Holmes, L.L. and Harbottle, G. (2003) In the steps of William the Conqueror: neutron activation analysis of Caen stone. *Archaeometry* **45**, 2; pp. 199–220.

Holmes, W.H. (1886) On some spurious Mexican antiquities and their relation to ancient art. *Annual Report of the Board of Regents of the Smithsonian Institution*, p. 319.

Holtorf, C. and Schadla-Hall, T. (1999) Age as artefact: on archaeological authenticity. *European Journal of Archaeology* **2**, 2; pp. 229–247.

Holzheu, G. (1989) Die daktyloscopie als Mittel Identifizierungvon von Kunstwerken. *Maltechnik-Restauro* **95**, 1; pp. 40–42.

Homer, R.F. (1994) Silver'd wares and gilded tynne. *Journal of the Pewter Society* **9**, 3; pp. 99–101.

Homer, W.I. (1989) The Ryder cover-up. *ARTnews* **88**, 8; pp. 158–161.

Hook, D.R. (1998) Inductively-coupled plasma atomic emission spectrometry and its rôle in numismatic studies. In: Oddy and Cowell (eds), 1998, pp. 237–252.

Hook, D.R. and Craddock, P.T. (1988) Appendix II: The composition of Bristol brass. In: J. Day: Bristol Brass. *Journal of the Historical Metallurgy Society* **22**, 1; pp. 38–40.

Hook, D.R. and Needham, S.P. (1989) A comparison of recent analyses of British Late Bronze Age goldwork with Irish parallels. *Jewellery Studies* **3**; pp. 15–24.

Hook, D.R., and Gaimster, D.R.M. (eds) (1995) *Trade and Discovery: The Scientific Study of Artefacts from Post-Medieval Europe and Beyond*. British Museum Occasional Paper 109, London.

Hook, D.R. and Craddock, P.T. (1996) The scientific analysis of the copper-alloy lamps: Aspects of classical alloying practices. In: Bailey, 1996, pp. 144–163.

Horie, C.V. and Vint, J.A. (1982) Chalconatronite: A by-product of conservation? *Studies in Conservation* **27**, 4; pp. 185–186.

Horn, P., Schaaf, P., Holbach, B., Holzl, S. and Eschnauer, H. (1993) Sr-87/Sr-86 from rock and soil into vine and wine. *Zeitschrift für Lebensmittel Untersuchung und Forschung* **196**, 5; pp. 407–409.

Horn, P., Holzl, S., Todt, W. and Matthies, D. (1998) Isotope abundance ratios of Sr in wine provenance determinations, in a tree-root activity study, and of Pb in a pollution study of tree-rings.

Isotopes in Environmental and Health Studies **34**, 1–2; pp. 31–42.

Horovitz, I. (1999) The materials and techniques of European painting on copper supports. In: *Copper as Canvas: Two Centuries of Masterpiece Paintings on Copper, 1575–1775*, M.E. Komanecky (ed). Organised by the Phoenix Art Museum. Oxford University Press, New York, pp. 63–92.

Hours, M. (ed) (1980) *La vie mystérieuse des chef-d'œuvre La science au service de l'art*. Editions de la Réunion des musées nationaux, Paris.

Houtman, J.P.W. and Turkstra, J. (1965) Neutron activation analysis and its possible application for age determination of paintings. In: *Radiochemical Methods of Analysis*, I. International Atomic Energy Agency, Vienna, pp. 85–193.

Hoving, T. (1981) *King of the Confessors: The Quest for the Bury St. Edmund's Cross*. Hamish Hamilton, London.

Hoving, T. (1996) *False Impressions: the hunt for big time art fakes*. Andre Deutsch, London.

Howard, S. (1962) Some Eighteenth-Century Restorations of Myron's 'Discobolus'. *Journal of the Warburg and Courtauld Institutes* **25**; pp. 330–334.

Howard, S. (1982) *Bartolomeo Cavaceppi*. Garland Publications Inc., New York.

Howard, S. (1990) *Antiquity Restored*. IRSA, Vienna.

Howard, S. (1992) Fakes, intention, proofs and impulsion to know: The case for Cavaceppi and clones. In: Jones (ed), 1992, pp. 51–62.

Hoye, G.S. (1983) Magnetic properties of ancient coins. *Journal of Archaeological Science* **10**, 1; pp. 43–49.

Hoyle, F. and Wickramasinghe, C. (1986) *Archaeopteryx: The Primordial Bird*. Christopher Davies, Swansea.

Hua, Q. and Barbetti, M. (2004) Review of tropospheric bomb 14C data for carbon cycle modeling and age calibration purposes. *Radiocarbon* **46**, 3; pp. 1273–1298.

Huang, Fengming, Yun, X., Yang, M. and Zhonghui, C. (2003) Pearl cultivation in Donggou, Ezhou, Hubei, and cathodoluminescence of cultured pearls. *The Journal of Gemmology* **28**, 8; pp. 449–462.

Huang, W.H. and Walker, R.M. (1967) Fossil alpha-particle recoil tracks: A new method of age determination. *Science* **155**; pp. 1103–1106.

Hughes, A. and Ranfft, E. (eds) (1997) *Sculpture and its Reproduction*. Reaktion Books, London.

Hughes, G.B. (1970) *Antique Sheffield Plate*. B.T. Batsford, London.

Hughes, M. (1991) Tracing to source. In: Bowman (ed), 1991, pp. 99–117.

Hughes, M.J. (1998) Atomic absorption spectrometry in numismatics. In Oddy and Cowell (eds), 1998, pp. 223–236.

Hughes, M.J., Cowell, M.R. and Craddock, P.T. (1976) Atomic absorption techniques in archaeology. *Archaeometry* **18**, 1; pp. 19–37.

Hughes, M.J. and Hall, J.A. (1979) X-ray fluorescence analysis of late Roman and Sassanian (sic) Silver Plate. *Journal of Archaeological Science* **6**, 4; pp. 321–344.

Hughes, M.J., Northover, J.P. and Staniaszek, B.E.P. (1982) Problems in the analysis of leaded bronze alloys in ancient artefacts. *Oxford Journal of Archaeology* **1**, 3; pp. 359–363.

Hughes, M.J., Cowell, M.R., and Hook, D.R., (eds) (1991) *Neutron Activation and Plasma Emission Spectrometric Analyses in Archaeology: Techniques and Applications*. British Museum Occasional Paper 82, London.

Hughes, M.J., Cowell, M.R. and Hook, D.R. (1991) Neutron activation analysis procedure at the British Museum Research Laboratory. In: Hughes *et al.* (eds), 1991, pp. 29–46.

Hughes, M.K., Milsom, S.J. and Leggett, P.A. (1981) Sapwood estimates in the interpretation of tree-ring dates. *Journal of Archaeological Science* **8**, 4; pp. 381–390.

Hughes, R. (1992) Artificial patination. In: Drayman-Weisser (ed), 1992, pp. 231–256.

Hughes, R. (1993) Artificial patination. In: La Niece and Craddock (eds), 1993, 1–18.

Hughes, R. and Rowe, M. (1982) *The Coloring, Bronzing and Patination of Metals: A Manual for the Fine Metalworker and Sculptor*. Crafts Council, London.

Hume, I.N. (1974) *All the Best Rubbish*. Victor Gollancz, London.

Hunt, L.B. (1980) The long history of lost wax casting. *Gold Bulletin* **13**, 2; pp. 63–79.

Hunter, D. (1957) *Papermaking*. The Cresset Press, London.

Hurter, S. (1993) Review of *Elektronstatere aux Klazomenai: Der Schatzfund von 1989* by E Işik. *Schweizerische Numismatische Rundschau* **7**; pp. 201–207.

Ilani, S., Rosenfeld, A. and Dvoracheck, M. (2003) A stone tablet with an ancient Hebrew inscription attributed to Yehoash, King of Judea – archaeometry and epigraphy. *GSI Current Research* **13**; pp. 109–116.

Illerhaus, B., Goebbels, J., Reimers, P. and Riesemeier, H. (1994) The principle of computerized tomography and its application in the reconstruction of hidden surfaces in objects of art. In: NDTWA 1994; pp. 41–49.

Inaba, M. and Sugisita, R. (1988) Permanence of washi (Japanese paper). Preprints of the 1988 Kyoto Congress. *The Conservation of Far Eastern Art*, J.S. Mills, P. Smith and K. Yamasaki (eds). IIC, London, pp. 1–4.

Indictor, N. (1998) 14C-Datierungen durch Massenbeschleunigungs-Spektrometrie Sind die Buyiden-Seiden authentisch? *Restauro* **104**, 5; pp. 338–342.

Inglis, A. (1998) Taste for collecting. *The Strad* **109**; pp. 722–725.

Inskeep, R.R. (1992) Making an honest man of Oxford: Good news for Mali. *Antiquity* **66**, 250; p. 114.

Ioannis, L. (2006) The dating of ancient metals: review and a possible application of the 226Ra/230Th method. *Mediterranean Archaeology and Archaeometry* **6**, 2; pp. 81–95.

Irving, C. (1970) *Fake! The story of Elmyr de Hory*. Heinemann, London.

Ivins, W.M., Jr. (1988) *How Prints Look*, revised edn. John Murray, London.

Isçik, E. (1992) *Elektronstatere aux Klazomenai: der Schatzfund von 1989.* Saarbrücker Studien zur Archäologie und alten Geschichte **5**, Saarbrücken.

Isnard, G. (1955) *Les Pirates de la Peinture.* Flammarion, Paris.

Isnard, G. (1959) & 1960) *Faux et Imitations dans l'Art,* 2 vols. Librarie Arthème Fayard, Paris.

Issacs, R. and Blurton, T.R. (2000) *Visions from the Golden land: Burma and the Art of Lacquer.* British Museum Press, London.

Jablonski, E., Learner, T., Hayes, J. and Golden, M. (2003) Conservation concerns for acrylic emulsion paints. *Reviews in Conservation* 2003, 4; pp. 3–12.

Jackson, C.J. (1911) *An Illustrated History of English Plate, Ecclesiastical and Secular,* 2 vols. Country Life Publications and B.T. Batsford, London. [Reprinted 1969, Dover Books, New York].

Jackson, C.J. (1921) *English Goldsmiths and their Marks,* 2nd edn. Macmillan, London.

Jackson, R.P.J. and Craddock, P.T. (1995) The Ribchester Hoard: A descriptive and technical study. In: *Sites and Sights of the Iron Age,* B. Raftery (ed). Oxbow Monograph 56, Oxford.

Jacob, H. (1962) The New British Museum Replicas. *Museums Journal* **62**, 3; pp. 173–178.

Jacobi, G. (1979) Drahtzieheisen der Latènzeit. *Germania* **57**; pp. 11–15.

Jacobovci, S. and Pelleggrino, C. (2007) *The Jesus Family Tomb.* Harper Element, New York.

Jacoby, D. (1993) Raw materials for the glass industry of Venice and the Terraferma, about 1370 – about 1460. *Journal of Glass Studies* **35**; pp. 65–90.

Jaeschke, H.F. (1985) Oriental lacquer analysis: Thin-section and electron microprobe. In: England and van Zelst (eds), 1985, pp. 217–220.

Jahn, M.E. and Woolf, D.J. (1963) *The Lying Stones of Dr. Johann Bartholemew Adam Beringer.* University of California Press, Berkeley and Los Angeles.

James, C. (1997a) Print techniques. In: Cohn (ed), 1997, pp. 86–115.

James, C. (1997b) Visual identification of graphic techniques and their supports. In: Cohn (ed), 1997, pp. 116–135.

James, C. and Enshaian, M.C. (1997) Analytical methods. In: Cohn (ed), 1997, pp. 231–235.

Jeffrey, I. (1981) *Photography – A Concise History.* Thames and Hudson, London.

Jembrih-Simbürger, D., Neelmeijer, C., Schreiner, M., Mäder, M., Peev, M., Clausen, C. and Krejsa, P. (2003) Iridescent Art Nouveau Glass of Tiffany and Loetz: Scientific Investigations Concerning Authenticity and Technology. *Annales du 15e Congres de l'Association Internationale pour l'Histoire du Verre,* pp. 262–266.

Jenkins, E. (1995) *Reproduction Furniture.* Crown, New York.

Jenyns, S. (1974) *Japanese Porcelain.* Faber and Faber, London.

Jenyns, S. and Watson, W. (1965) *Chinese Art: The Minor Arts.* Faber and Faber, London.

Jeppson, L. (1971) *Fabulous Frauds.* Arlington Books, London.

Jett, P. (ed) (2003) Scientific Research in the Field of Asian Art. *Proceedings of the First Forbes Symposium at the Freer Galler of Art,* Archetype Publications, London.

Jiang Song (2002) Distinguishing modern copies of Ancient Liagzhu Period jades. In: Childs-Johnson (ed), 2002, pp. 25–30.

Johansen, F. (1990) The decline and fall of a Greek portrait: A fake portrait tells its story. In: True and Podany (eds), 1990b, pp. 223–227.

John, S.G., Park, J.G., Zhang, Z. and Boyle, E.A. (2007) The isotopic composition of some common forms of anthropogenic zinc. *Chemical Geology* **245**, 1–2; pp. 61–69.

Johns, C. (1971) *Arretine and Samian Pottery.* Trustees of the British Museum, London.

Johns, C. (1981) The Risley Park silver lanx: A lost antiquity from Roman Britain. *The Antiquaries Journal* **61**, 1; pp. 53–72.

Johns, C. (1986) The Roman silver cups from Hockwold. *Archaeologia* **108**; pp. 2–13.

Johns, C. and Painter, K. (1991) The Risley Park lanx 'rediscovered'. *Minerva* **2**, 6; pp. 6–13.

Johns, C. and Potter, T. (1983) *The Thetford Treasure.* British Museum Press, London.

Johnson, A.C. (1936) *Roman Egypt II.* Johns Hopkins Press, Baltimore.

Johnson, K.C. (1973) *Fakes and Forgeries.* Catalog of the exhibition held at the Minneapolis Institute of Arts, Minneapolis. July 11–Sept. 29, 1973.

Johnson, P.V.A. (1983) The Lyon and Twinham forgeries. *Proceedings of the Silver Society* **3**, 1–2; pp. 25–35.

Jones, M. (ed) (1990) *Fake?* British Museum Press, London.

Jones, M. (ed) (1992) *Why Fakes Matter.* British Museum Press, London.

Jones, R.E. (1986) *Greek and Cypriot Pottery: A Review of Scientific Studies.* British School at Athens, Athens.

Joni, I.F. (1936) *Affairs of a Painter.* Faber and Faber, London. [Trans. J.B. Shaw].

José-Yacamán, M. and Ascencio, J.A. (2000) Electron microscopy and its application to the study of archaeological material and art preservation. In: Ciliberto and Spoto (eds), 2000, pp. 405–443.

Judson, H.F. (2004) *The Great Betrayal: Fraud in Science.* Harcourt, New York.

Jull, A.J.T. and Donahue, D.J. (1990) Radiocarbon dating with accelerators: Methods and application to textiles. *Orientations* **21**, 6; pp. 75–79.

Jull, A.J.T., Donahue, D.J., Broshi, M. and Tov., E. (1995) Radiocarbon dating of scrolls and linen fragments from the Judean Desert. *Radiocarbon* **37**, 1; pp. 11–19.

Jull, A.J.T., Donahue, D.J. and Damon, P.E. (1996a) Factors affecting the apparent radiocarbon age of textiles: A comment on 'effects of fires and biofractionation of carbon isotopes on results of radiocarbon dating of old textiles: The Turin Shroud', D.A. Kouznetsov *et al. Journal of Archaeological Science* **23**, 2; pp. 157–160.

Jull, A.J.T., Donahue, D.J. and Damon, P.E. (1996b) factors that affect the apparent radiocarbon age of textiles. In: Orna (ed), 1996, pp. 248–253.

Jumper, E.J., Adler, A.D., Jackson, J.P., Pellicori, S.F., Heller, J.H. and Drusik, J.R. (1984) A comprehensive examination of the various stains and images on the Shroud of Turin. In: Lambert (ed), 1984, pp. 447–476.

Junge, E. (1992) *The Seaby World Coin Encyclopaedia*, revised edn. Seabys, London.

'Jüngling' (1987/88) Naturwissenschaftliche Untersuchungen an der Bronzstatue 'Der Jüngling vom Magdalensberg'. *Wiener Berichte über Naturwissenschaft in der Kunst* **4/5**; pp. 257–355.

Junk, S.A. and Pernicka, E. (2003) An assessment of osmium isotope ratios as a new tool to determine the provenance of gold with platinum-group metal inclusions. *Archaeometry* **45**, 2; pp. 313–332.

Kaczmarczyk. A. (1986) The source of cobalt in Ancient Egyptian pigments. In: Olin and Blackman (eds), 1986, pp. 369–376.

Kaczmarczyk, A. and Hedges, R.E.M. (1983) *Ancient Egyptian Faience.* Aris and Phillips, Warminster, Wiltshire.

Kallenburg, L. (1981) *Modeling in Wax for Jewelry and Sculpture.* Chilton Books, Radnor, Penns.

Kallfass, M., Juergen, P. and Jehn, H. (1985) Investigation on the embrittlement of an antique Roman silver bowl. *Praktische Metallographie* **22**, 7; pp. 317–323.

Kallithrakas-Kontos, N. and Katsanos, A.A. (1988) PIXE Analysis of ancient coins. In: Oddy and Cowell (eds), 1998, pp. 461–471.

Karanth, R.V. (2000) *Gems and Gem Industry in India.* Geological Society of India, Bangalore. Memoir 45.

Karlbeck, O. (1957) *Treasure Seeker in China.* The Cresset Press, London. [Trans. N. Walford].

Karlen, P.H. (1986) Fakes, forgeries and expert opinion. *Arts Management and the Law* **16**; pp. 5–23.

Karras, R.M. (1988) Analyses of silver content in a hoard of twelfth century Bohemian pennies. In: Oddy (ed), 1988, pp. 81–86.

Katz, M.P. (1999) *Portugese Palissy Wares.* Hudson Hills Press, New York.

Katz, M.P. and Lehr, R. (1996) *Palissy Ware.* Athlone Press, London.

Katz, S. (1984) *Classic Plastics.* Thames and Hudson, London.

Katz, S. (1986) *Early Plastics.* Shire Publications, Aylesbury, Bucks.

Kaufman, M. (1963) *The First Century of Plastics: Celluloid and its Sequel.* The Plastics Institute, London.

Kaufman, M. (1967) *History of PVC.* McClaren & Sons, London.

Kaul, B.L. (1993) Coloration of plastics using organic pigments. *Review of Progress in Coloration and Related Topics* **23**; pp. 19–35.

Kawanoba, W., Sano, C., Yoneyama, M., Miura, S., Taguro, T. and Oka, I. (1996) Possibility of application of an artificially deteriorated silk for restoration by ultraviolet rays. *Hozon Kagaku* **35**; pp. 40–48. [In Japanese; English summary].

Keall, E.J. (2003) New tests bolster case for authenticity. *Biblical Archaeology Review* **29**, 4; pp. 52–55, 70.

Keating, T., Norman, G. and Norman, F. (1977) *The Fake's Progress: Tom Keating's Story.* Hutchinson, London.

Keck, S. (1969) Mechanical alteration of the paint film. *Studies in Conservation* **14**, 1; pp. 9–30.

Keck, S. and Feller, R.L. (1964) Detection of an epoxy-resin coating on a seventeenth-century painting. *Studies in Conservation* **9**, 1; pp. 1–8.

Keeley, L.H. (1980) *Experimental Determination of Stone Tool Uses: A Microwear Analysis.* University of Chicago Press, Chicago and London.

Keisch, B. (1970) On the use of isotope mass spectrometry in the identification of artists' pigments. *Studies in Conservation* **15**, 1; pp. 1–11.

Keisch, B. (1976) Nuclear Applications at the National Gallery of Art Research Project. In: *Applicazione dei metodi nucleari nel campo delle opere d'arte*, R. Cesareo (ed). Academia Nazionale dei Lincei, Rome, 1976, pp. 359–379.

Keisch, B. and Callahan, C. (1976a) Lead isotope ratios in artists' lead white: a progress report. *Archaeometry* **18**, 2; pp. 181–194.

Keisch, B. and Callahan, C. (1976b) Sulfur isotope ratios in ultramarine blue: application to art forgery detection. *Journal of Applied Spectroscopy* **30**, 5; p. 515.

Keisch, B. and Miller, H.M. (1972) Recent art forgeries: Detection by carbon-14 measurements. *Nature* **240**, 5382; pp. 491–492.

Keith, A. (1950) *An Autobiography.* Watts, London.

Kelley, L. (1987) *Plastic Jewelry.* Schiffer, West Chester PA.

Kelterborn, P. (1984) Towards replicating Egyptian predynastic flint knives. *Journal of Archaeological Science* **11**, 6; pp. 433–454.

Kempe, D.R.C. and Harvey, A.P. (eds) (1983) *The Petrology of Archaeological Artefacts.* Clarendon Press, Oxford.

Keneghan, B. and Quye, A. (1999) Degradation causes. In: Quye and Williamson (eds), 1999, pp. 122–135.

Kennedy, S.J. (1996) Pearl identification. *The Australian Gemmologist* **20**, 1; pp. 2–19.

Kennedy, S.J., Francis, J.G. and Jones, G.C. (1988) Imitation pearl coatings. *The Journal of Gemmology* **21**, 4; pp. 211–214.

Kenoyer, J.M. (1996) Bead replicas. An alternative to antique bead collecting. *Ornament* **20**, 2; pp. 68–71.

Kent, J.P.C. and Painter, K.S. (eds) (1977) *Wealth of the Roman World Gold and Silver AD 300–700.* British Museum Publications, London.

Kerr, N. (1995) Advantages and limitations of the ninhydrin test for analysis of historic wool fibers. In: Vandiver *et al.* (eds), 1995, pp. 233–244.

Kerr, R. (1986) *Chinese Ceramics: Porcelain of the Qing Dynasty 1644–1911.* Victoria and Albert Museum, London.

Kerr, R. (1990) *Later Chinese Bronzes.* Victoria and Albert Museum, London.

Kersten, H. and Gruber, E.R. (1994) *The Jesus Conspiracy: The Turin Shroud and the Truth about the Resurrection.* Element, Shaftesbury, Dorset.

Khandekar, N. (2003) Preparation of cross-sections from easel paintings. *Reviews in Conservation* 4; pp. 52–64.

Kidd, D. (1990) The 'Lombard Treasure' 1930–1990. *Jewellery Studies* 4; pp. 59–72.

Kiefer, W. (ed) (2004) Special issue: Raman spectroscopy in art and archaeology. *Journal of Raman Spectroscopy* **35**, 8/9.

Kiefert, L., Hänni, H.A., Chalain, J-P. and Weber, W. (1999) Identification of filler substances in emerald by infrared and Raman spectroscopy. *The Journal of Gemmology* **26**, 8; pp. 501–510.

Kiefert, L., Hänni, H.A. and Ostertag, T. (2001) Raman spectroscopic applications to gemmology. In: Lewis and Edwards (eds), 2001, pp. 469–490.

Kiefert, L., Chalain, J-P. and Häberli, S. (2005) Case study: Diamonds, gemstones and pearls: From the past to the present. In: Edwards and Chalmers (eds), 2005, pp. 379–402.

Kilbracken, Lord (1967) *Van Meegeren*. Nelson, London. (previously J.A. Godley).

Kimberley Mumford, J. (1924) *The Story of Bakelite*. Robert L. Stillson, New York.

Kingery, W.D. (1986) The development of European porcelain. In: *High-Technology Ceramics Past, Present and Future: Ceramics and Civilisation III*, W.D. Kingery (ed). The American Ceramic Society, Westerville OH, pp. 153–180.

Kingery, W.D. (1991) Attic pottery gloss technology. *Archeomaterials* **5**, 1; pp. 47–54.

Kingery, W.D. and Vandiver, P.B. (1985) The technology of Tiffany art glass. In: England and van Zelst (eds), 1985, pp. 100–116.

Kingsley, S. (2007) *The Tomb of the Ten Ossuaries*. Minerva **18**, 3; pp. 27–31.

Kissling, R. (1910) Zum Streite um die Echtheit der Floraüte. *Chemiker-Zeitung* **34**, 56; p. 493.

Kite, M. and Thomson, R. (2005) *Conservation of Leather*. Butterworth-Heinemann, Oxford.

Klein, E., Tsang, J. and Baker, M. (1995) Non-instrumental methods for the identification and characterization of artists' acrylic paints. *Postprints: American Institute for Conservation of Historic and Artistic Works. Paintings Speciality Group*; pp. 49–60.

Klein, P. (1982) Grundlagen Dendrochronologie und ihre Anwendung für kunstgeschichtliche Fragestellungen. *Berliner Beiträge zur Archäometrie* 7; pp. 253–271.

Klein, P. (1985) Dendrochronologische Untersuchungen an gemaldetafeln und Musikinstrumenten. *Dendrochronologia* 3; pp. 25–44.

Klein, P. (1987) Dendrochronological analysis of European string instruments. *CIMCIM Newsletter*, pp. 37–94.

Klein, P. (1989) Dendrochronological studies on oak panels of Roger Van Der Weyden and his circle. *Le dessin sous-jacent dans la peinture: Colloque* **VII**. University of Louvain-la Neuve, Louvain, pp. 25–36.

Klein, P. (1994) Dendrochronologische Untersuchungen an Streichinstrumenten. In: NDTWA, 1994, pp. 469–471.

Klein, P. (1998a) Some aspects of the utilization of different wood species in certain European workshops. In: *Painting Techniques: History, Materials and Studio Practice*, A. Roy and P. Smith (eds). IIC, London, pp. 112–114.

Klein, P. (1998b) Dendrochronological analyses of panel paintings. In: Dardes and Rothe (eds), 1998, pp. 39–54.

Klein, P., (1999). Dendrochronological analyses of art-objects. In: McCrone and Weiss (eds), 1999, pp. 122–134.

Klein, P. and Baulch, J. (1983) Aufbau eine Jahrringchronologie für Buchenholz und ihre Anwendung für die Datierung. *Holzforschung* **37**, 1; pp. 35–39.

Klein, P., Mehringer, H. and Bauch, J. (1984) Tree-ring chronology of spruce wood and its application in the dating of stringed instruments. In: de Froment (ed), 1984, pp. 84.1.69–72.

Klein, P., Mehringer, H. and Baulch, J. (1986) Dendrochronological and wood biological investigations on stringed instruments. *Holzforschung* **40**, 4; pp. 197–203.

Klein, P. and Baulch, J. (1990) Analysis of wood used in Italian painting with especial reference to Raphael. In: *The Princeton Raphael Symposium*, J. Shearman and M.B. Hall (eds). Princeton University Press, Princeton, New Jersey, pp. 85–91.

Klein, P. and Pollens, S. (1998) The technique of dendrochronology as applied to violins made by Guiseppe Guarneri del Gesu. In: *Guiseppe Guarneri del Gesu*, P. Biddulph (ed). Biddulph, London.

Klemm, D.D., Klemm, R. and Steclaci, L. (1984) Die pharaonischen Steinbrüche des Silifizierten Sandsteins Ägypten und die Herkunft der Memnon-Kolosse. *Mitteilungen des Deutschen Archäologischen Instituts Kairo* **40**; pp. 207–220.

Klemm, R. and Klemm, D.D. (1993) *Steine und Steinbrüche im Alten-Ägypten*. Springer-Verlag, Berlin.

Klockenkämper, R., Bubert, H. and Hasler, K. (1999) Detection of near-surface silver enrichment on Roman imperial silver coins by X-ray spectral analysis. *Archaeometry* **41**, 2; pp. 311–320.

Klockenkämper, R., von Bohlen, A. and Moens, L. (2000) Analysis of pigments and inks on oil paintings and historical documents using 'total reflectance X-ray fluorescence spectrometry. *X-Ray Spectrometry* **29**, 1; pp. 119–129.

Kluge, K. and Lehmann-Hartleben, K. (1927) *Die antiken Grossbronzen I–III*. Walter de Gruyter, Berlin.

Knowles, J.A. (1923) Forgeries of ancient stained glass. *Journal of the Royal Society of Arts* **72**, 3707; pp. 38–56. 23 December.

Knowles, J.A. (1924) The detection of forgeries of old glass. *Connoisseur* **69**; pp. 201–208. August.

Knowles, J.A. (1928) Forgeries in stained glass. *Connoisseur* **81**; p. 207. August.

Kockaerts, R. (1992) Conservatie van moderne fotografische emulsies. In: *Conservatie en Restauratie van Moderne en Actuele Kunst*, C. van Damme (ed). Snoek-Ducaju-Zoon, Gent, pp. 147–155.

Kodak (1987) *Applied Infrared Photography*. Kodak, London.

Koeberl, C. (1987/88a) Aktivierungsanalytische Untersuchungen an Bronzeproben. In: 'Jüngling', 1987/88, pp. 296–302.

Koeberl, C. (1987/88b) Spurenelementanalytik von silikatischen Proben des Gußkerns. In: 'Jüngling', 1987/88, pp. 332–340.

Koh Choo, C.K. (1995) A scientific study of traditional Korean celadons and their modern developments. *Archaeometry* 37, 1; pp. 53–81.

Kohler, E.L. (1967) Ultimatum to terracotta-forgers. *Expedition* 9; pp. 16–21.

Kohn, A. (1986) *False Prophets: Fraud and Error in Science and Medicine*. Basil Blackwell, Oxford.

Koivula, J.I., Tannous, M. and Schmetzer, K. (2000) Synthetic gem materials and simulants in the 1990s. *Gems and Gemmology* 36, 4; pp. 360–379.

Koob, S. (1998) Obsolete fill materials found on ceramics. *Journal of the American Institute for Conservation* 37, 1; pp. 49–67.

Koob, S.P. (1999) Restoration skill or deceit: Manufactured replacement fragments on a Seljuk lustre-glazed ewer. In: *The Conservation of Glass and Ceramics*, N.H. Tennent (ed). James and James, London, pp. 156–166.

Koobatian, J. (1997) *Faking it: An International Bibliography of Art and Literary Forgeries 1949–1986*. SLA, New York.

Koren, Z.C. (1996) Historico-Chemical Analysis of Plant Dyestuffs Used in Textiles from Ancient Israel. In: Orna (ed), 1996, pp. 269–310.

Korte, E.H. and Staat, H. (1993) Infrared reflection studies on historical varnishes. *Fresenius' Journal of Analytical Chemistry* 347, 10/11; pp. 454–457.

Kossolapov, A.J. (1999) Helium radiogenic clock for dating of archaeological gold. In: McCrone and Weiss (eds), 1999, pp. 113–120.

Kossolapov, A.I. and Sizov, A.V. (1984) Impurities in white lead and the metallurgy of lead. In: de Froment (ed), 1984, pp. 84.1.27–28.

'Kouros Colloquium' (1993) *The Getty Kouros Colloquium*, Kapon Editions. Nicholas P. Goulandris Foundation, Museum of Cycladic Art, Athens.

Kouznetsov, D.A., Ivanov, A.A. and Veletsky, P.R. (1996a) Effects of fires and biofractionation of carbon isotopes on results of radiocarbon dating of old textiles: The Shroud of Turin. *Journal of Archaeological Science* 23, 1; pp. 109–121.

Kouznetsov, D.A., Ivanov, A.A. and Veletsky, P.R. (1996b) A re-evaluation of the radiocarbon date of the Shroud of Turin based on biofractionation of carbon isotopes and a fire-simulating model. In: Orna (ed), 1996, pp. 229–247.

Krämer, O.P. (1959) *Die Geschichte der Galvanotechnik*. Eug. G. Leuze, Saulgau, Württemberg.

Kratz, A. (1972) Goldschmiedetechnische Untersuchungen vor Goldarbeiten im Staatlichen Museum, Berlin. *Aachener Kunstblätter* 43; pp. 156–189.

Krause, H. (1937) *Metallfärbung*, 2nd edn. Julius Springer, Berlin. *Metal Coloring and Finishing* [English trans. 1938]. Chemical Publishing Co., New York and E. & F.H. Spon, London.

Kretschner, W., von Grundherr, K., Kritzler, K., Morgenroth, G., Scharf, A. and Uhl, T. (2004) The mystery of the Persian mummy: original or fake? *Nuclear Instruments and methods in Physics Research Section B: Beam Interactions with Materials and Atoms* 223/4; pp. 672–675.

Krzyszkowska, O. (1990) *Ivory and Related Materials*. Institute of Classical Studies, Bulletin Supplement 59, Classical Handbook 3, London.

Krzyszkowska, O. and Morkot, R. (2000) Ivory and related materials. In: Nicholson and Shaw (eds), 2000, pp. 320–331.

Küçükerman, Ö. (1988) *Glass Beads: Anatolian Glass Bead Making*. Turkish Touring and Automobile Association, Istanbul.

Kühn, H. (1966) Trace elements in white lead and their determination by emission spectrum and neutron activation analysis. *Studies in Conservation* 11, 4; pp. 163–169.

Kühn, H. (1986) Zinc white. In: Feller (ed), 1986, pp. 169–186.

Kühnemann, U. (1969) *Elasticglas*. M. Frech, Stuttgart-Botnang. [English translation, *Cold Enamelling*, 1972, Mills and Boon, London].

Kuniholm, P.I. (2001) Dendrochronology and other applications of tree-ring studies in archaeology. In: Brothwell and Pollard (eds), 2001, pp. 35–46.

Kunsthistorische Museum (1923) *Austellung gefälschte kunstwerk*. Kunsthistorische Museum, Vienna.

Kunz, G.F. (1886) On the new artificial rubies. *Transactions of the New York Academy of Sciences*; pp. 3–10. Oct. 4th 1886.

Kunz, G.F. (1907) *The Precious Stones of Mexico*. Imprenta y Fototipia de la Secretaría de Fomento, Mexico City.

Kunze, M. and Rügler, A. (eds) (2003) *'Wiedererstandene Antike' Ergänzungen antiker Kunstwerke seit der Renaissance*. Biering and Brinkmann, München.

Kurella, A. and Strauß, I. (1983) Lapislazuli und natürliches Ultramarin. *Maltechnik-Restauro* 89, 1; pp. 34–54.

Kurz, O. (1948) *Fakes: A Handbook for Collectors and Students*. Faber and Faber, London. [Revised edition 1967, Dover, New York].

Lacombe, M.S. (1910) *Nouveau Manuel Complet de Bronzage des Métaux et du Plâtre par G. Debonliez et F. Malepeyre*. Encyclopedie Roret, Paris.

Lahanier, C. (1986) The powder diffraction pattern applied to knowledge of works of art. *Chemica Scripta* 26A; pp. 47–55.

Lambert, J.B. (ed) (1984) *Archaeological Chemistry–III*. American Chemical Society, Washington DC. Advances in Chemistry Series 205.

Lambert, J.B. (1997) *Traces of the Past*. Addison-Wesley, Reading, MA.

Lambert, J.B., Frye, J.S. and Poinar, G.O., Jr. (1985) Amber from the Dominican Republic: Analysis by nuclear magnetic resonance spectroscopy. *Archaeometry* **27**, 1; pp. 43–51.

Lambert, J.B., Beck, C.W. and Frye, J.S. (1988) Analysis of European amber by carbon-13 nuclear magnetic resonance spectroscopy. *Archaeometry* **30**, 2; pp. 248–263.

Lambert J.B., Frye, J.S., Lee, T.A. Jr., Welch, C.J. and Poinar, G.O. Jr. (1989) Analysis of Mexican amber by carbon-13 NMR spectroscopy. In: Allen (ed), 1989, pp. 381–388.

Lambert, J.B., Frye, J.S. and Carriveau, G.W. (1991) The structure of oriental lacquer by solid state nuclear magnetic resonance spectroscopy. *Archaeometry* **33**, 1; pp. 87–94.

Lambert, J.B. and Beck, C. (1993) The structure of amber by carbon-13 nuclear resonance spectroscopy. In: Beck and Bouzek (eds), 1993, pp. 28–35.

Lambert, J.B., Graham, E., Smith, M.T. and Frye, J.S. (1994) Amber and Jet from Tipu, Belize. *Ancient Mesoamaerica* **5**; pp. 55–60.

Lambert, J.B. and Poinar, G.O., Jr. (2002) Amber: The organic gemstone. *Accounts of Chemical Research* **35**, 8; pp. 628–636.

Lamprecht, I., Reller, A. and Wiedemann, H.G. (1997) Ca-oxalate films and microbiological investigations of the influence of ancient pigments on the growth of lichen. *Journal of Thermal Analysis* **49**; pp. 1601–1607.

Lampropoulos, V., Kaliagri, A. and Valsamis, L. (2002) An attempt to face the problem of iridiscence on archaeological glass. In: *Proceedings of the First International Conference 'Hyalos-Vitrium-Glass: History, Technology and Conservation of Glass and Vitreous Materials in the Ancient World'*, G. Kordas (ed). 'Glasnet' Publications, Athens, pp. 311–316.

Landman, N.H., Mikkelsen, P.M., Bieger, R. and Bronson, B. (2001) *Pearls: A Natural History*. Harry N. Abrams, New York.

Landwehr, C. (1985) *Die Antiken Gipsabgüsse aus Baiae: Griechische Bronzestatuen in Abgüssen römischer Zeit*. DAI Forschungen **14**, Berlin.

Lane, K.J. and Miller, H.S. (1996) *Faking it*. Harry N. Abrahms, New York.

Lanford, W.A. (1977) Glass hydration: A method of dating glass objects. *Science* **196**, 4293; pp. 975–976.

Lanford, W.A. (1986) Ion-beam analysis of glass surfaces: Dating, authentication and conservation. *Nuclear Instrument and Methods in Physics Research, Section B* **B14**, 1; pp. 123–126.

Lang, G. (1986) Pottery and porcelain. In: Bly (ed), 1986, pp. 151–192.

Lang, J. and Hughes, M.J. (1984) Soldering Roman silver plate. *Oxford Journal of Archaeology* **3**, 3; pp. 77–107.

Lang, J., Middleton, A.P., La Niece, S. and Higgins, T. (1994) Radiography of cultural objects: Materials and methods. In: NDTWA, 1994, pp. 1–10.

Lang, J., Middleton, A., Ambers, J. and Higgins, T. (2005) Radiographic Images. In: Lang and Middleton (eds), 2005, pp. 20–48.

Lang, J. and Middleton, A. (eds) (2005) *Radiography of Cultural Material*, 2nd edn. Butterworth-Heinemann, Oxford.

Lange, F.W. (ed) (1993) *Precolumbian Jade: New Geological and Cultural Interpretations*. University of Utah Press, Salt Lake City.

Langbein, G. (1891) *A Complete Treatise on the Electro-Deposition of Metals*. Henry Carey Baird & Co, Philadelphia. [English trans. with additions by W.T. Brannt.].

Langley, A. and Burnstock, A. (1999) The analysis of layered paint samples from modern paintings using FTIR microscopy. In: *Preprints of the 12th ICOM Committee for Conservation Triennial Meeting*, Lyons, 29th August–3rd September, 1999. J. Bridgland (ed). James and James, London, pp. 234–241.

La Niece, S. (1991) Japanese polychrome metalwork. In: Pernicka and Wagner (eds), 1991, pp. 87–94.

La Niece, S. (1993) Silvering. In: La Niece and Craddock (eds), 1993, pp. 201–210.

La Niece, S. (1995) Depletion gilding from third millennium BC Ur. *Iraq* **57**; pp. 41–47.

La Niece, S. (1998) Metallurgical case studies from the British Museum's collections of pre-Hispanic gold. *Boletin Museo del Oro* **44/5**; pp. 139–157.

La Niece, S. (2003) Medieval Islamic metal technology. In: Jett (ed), 2003, pp. 90–96.

La Niece, S. (2005) Restoration, pastiche and fakes. In: Lang and Middleton (eds), 2005, pp. 175–188.

La Niece, S. and Carradice, I. (1989) White copper: The arsenical coinage of the Libyan revolt 241–238 BC. *Journal of the Historical Metallurgy Society* **23**, 1; pp. 9–15.

La Niece, S. and Craddock, P. (eds) (1993) *Metal Plating and Patination*. Butterworth-Heinemann, Oxford.

La Niece, S. and Meeks, N. (2000) Diversity of goldsmithing traditions in the Americas and the Old World. In: McEwan (ed), 2000, pp. 220–239.

Lankton, J.W. (2003) *A Bead Timeline I: Prehistory to 1200 CE*. The Bead Museum, Washington DC.

Lanmon, D.P., Brill, R.H. and Reilly, G.J. (1973) Some blown 'three-mold' suspicions confirmed. *Journal of Glass Studies* **15**; pp. 143–173.

Lanteri, E.D. (1904–11) *Modelling: A Guide for Teachers and Students*, 3 vols. Chapman & Hall, London.

Lapatin, K.D.S. (2001) Snake goddesses, fake goddesses. *Archaeology* **54**, 1; pp. 33–36. Jan/Feb.

Lapuente, P. and Turi, B. (1995) Marbles from Portugal: Petrographic and isotopic characterization. *Science and Technology for Cultural Heritage* **4**, 2; pp. 33–42.

Larsen, E.Benner. (1981) *Moulding and Casting of Museum Objects*. Konservatorskolen, The Royal Art Academy, Copenhagen.

Larsen, E.Benner. (1984) *Electrotyping*. Konservatorskolen, Royal Art Academy, Copenhagen.

Larsen, R. (ed) (2002) *Microanalysis of Parchment*. Archetype Publications, London.

Larson, C.M. (2004) *Numismatic Forgery: An Illustrated, Annotated Guide to the Practical Prniciples, Methods and Techniques Employed in the Private Manufacture of Rare Coins*. Zyrus Press, Irvine CA.

Latham, A.G. (2001) Uranium-series dating. In: Brothwell and Pollard (eds), 2001, pp. 63–72.

Lattimore, C.R. (1979) *English Nineteenth Century Press-Moulded Glass*. Barrie and Jenkins, London.

Laurie, A.P. (1928) Crackle and forgeries of primitives. *The Connoisseur* 81; pp. 157–161.

Laurie, A.P. (1935) *New Light on Old Masters*. The Sheldon Press, London.

Laver, M. (1997) Titanium dioxide whites. In: FitzHugh (ed), 1997, pp. 295–355.

Lavier, C. and Lambert, G. (1996) Dendrochronology and works of art. In: *Tree Rings, Environment and Humanity*, J.S. Dean, D.M. Meko and T.W. Swetman (eds). Radiocarbon, Dept. of Geosciences, University of Arizona, Tucson, pp. 543–556.

Lazzarini, L. and Salvadori, O. (1989) A reassessment of the formation of the patina called *scialbatura*. *Studies in Conservation* 34, 1; pp. 20–26.

Leach, B. and Tait, J. (2000) Papyrus. In: Nicholson and Shaw (eds), 2000, pp. 227–253.

Learner, T. (1995) The analysis of synthetic resins found in 20th century paint media. In: Wright and Townsend (eds), 1995, pp. 76–84.

Learner, T. (2000) A review of synthetic binding media in twentieth-century paints. *The Conservator* 24; pp. 96–103.

Learner, T. (2001) The analysis of synthetic paints by pyrolysis–gas chromatography–mass spectrometry (PyGCMS). *Studies in Conservation* 46, 4; pp. 225–241.

Learner, T., Chiantore, O. and Scalarone, D. (2002) Ageing studies of acrylic emulsion paints. In: *ICOM Committee for Conservation 13th Triennial Meeting*, Rio de Janeiro, 22–27 September 2002, R. Vontobel (ed). James and James, London, pp. 911–919.

Leather Conservation Centre (1981) *The Fibre Structure of Leather*. The Leather Conservation Centre, Northampton, Northants.

Le Chanu, P. (1995) Dessin sous-jacent et histoire de l'art. *Techne* 2; pp. 165–177.

Lee, H. and Neville, K. (1967) *Handbook of Epoxy Resins*. McGraw-Hill, New York.

Lee, R.H. (1993) Evaluating daguerreotypes. *The Microscope* 41, 1; pp. 7–11.

Leewenberg, J. (1969) Early nineteenth century Gothic ivories. *Aachener Kunstblätter* 39; pp. 111–148.

Lefferts, K.C., Majewski, L.J., Sayre, E.V. and Meyers, P. (1981) Technical examination of the classical bronze horse from the Metropolitan Museum of Art. *Journal of the American Institute for Conservation* 21, 1; pp. 1–42.

Lehmann, J. (2000) Seit wann wird mit zincweiß gemalt? Chemische Untersuchungen, mittelalterliche Quellenschriften. *Restauro* 106, 5; pp. 356–360.

Leichty, E. (1970) A remarkable forger. *Expedition* 12, 3; pp. 17–21.

Leigh, D. (1985) Differential abrasion and brooch usage. *Science and Archaeology* 27; pp. 8–12.

Lelekova, O., (1996) Expert examination of icons. In: Bridgland (ed), 1996, pp. 367–370.

Lemaire, A. (2002) Burial box of James the Brother of Jesus: Earliest archaeological evidence of Jesus found in Jerusalem. *Biblical Archaeology Review* 26, 6; pp. 25–33.

Lemoine, C. and Picon, M. (1982) La fixation du phosphore par les céramiques lors de leur enfouissement et ses incidences analytiques. *Revue d'Archéométrie* 6; pp. 101–112.

Leonard, M., Khandekar, N. and Carr, D.W. (2001) 'Amber varnish' and Orazio Gentileschi's *Lot and His Daughters*. *The Burlington Magazine* 143, 1174; pp. 4–10.

Lepsius, G.R. (1890) *Griechische Marmorstudien Abhandlugen der Konliglichen Preuss*. Akademie der Wissenschaften zu Berlin, Berlin.

Leslie, K.A. (2003) Identification of porcelain type using Raman spectroscopy. In: *Ceramics in the Society*, S. Di Perro, V. Serneels and M. Maggetti (eds). Dept. of Geosciences, Universitas Friburgensis, Fribourg, pp. 189–196.

Leung, P.L., Stokes, M.J. and Wang, W. (1995) Thermoluminiscent authentication of ancient Chinese pottery. *Hejishu* 6, 1; pp. 1–8.

Leung, P.L. and Luo, Hongjie (2000) A study of provenance and dating of ancient Chinese porcelain by X-ray fluorescence spectrometry. *X-Ray Spectrometry* 29; pp. 34–38.

Leung, P.L., Stokes, M.J., Tiemei, Chen and Dashu, Qin (2000) A study of ancient Chinese porcelain wares of the Song-Yuan dynasties from Cizhou and Ding kilns with energy dispersive X-ray fluorescence. *Archaeometry* 42, 1; pp. 129–140.

Levy, H. (2003) Artificial diamonds. *Gem & Jewellery News* 12, 5; pp. 83–85.

Levy, H. (2004) Gem and diamond terminology. *Gem & Jewellery News* 13, 5; pp. 75–76.

Lewin, S.Z. (1973) A new approach to establishing the authenticity of patinas on copper-base artifacts. In: Young (ed), 1973, pp. 62–66.

Lewin, S. and Alexander, S.M. (1967/68) The composition and structure of natural patinas I. Copper and copper alloys, Section A, Antiquity to 1929; Section B, 1937 to 1967. *Supplements in Art and Archaeology Technical Abstracts* 6, 4; pp. 199–283. Ibid. 7, 1; pp. 277–367.

Lewis, D. (1977) *Practical Gem Testing*. N.A.G. Press, London.

Lewis, I.R. and Edwards, H.G.M. (eds) (2001) *Handbook of Raman Spectroscopy*. Marcel Dekker, New York & Basel.

Lewis, M.D.S. (1970) *Antique Paste Jewellery*. Faber, London.

Li, Liping and Chen, Zhonghui (2001) Cultured pearls and color-changed cultured pearls: Raman spectra. *The Journal of Gemmology* 27, 8; pp. 449–455.

Libby, W.F. (1967) History of radiocarbon dating. In: *Radiocarbon Dating and Methods of Low Level Counting*, E.M. Counsell (ed). International Atomic Energy Agency, Vienna, pp. 3–25.

Liddicoat, R.T., Jr. (1987) *Handbook of Gem Identification*, 12th edn. Gemological Institute of America, Santa Monica CA.

Lierke, R. (2002) The 'grinding marks' of ancient glass – a critical assessment. *Glass Science and Technology* **75**, 4; pp. 201–208.

Lierke, R. (2004) Letter on Portland Vase debate. *Minerva* **15**, 1; pp. 21–22.

Lierkes, R. (ed) (1997) *Glass*. V & A Publications, London.

Li Hu Hou (1985) Characteristic elements of Longquan greenware. *Archaeometry* **27**, 1; pp. 53–60.

Liljedahl, G. (1990) Watermarks and filigranology. In: Rudins, 1990, pp. 211–237.

Lill, G. (1944/50) Die Adlerfibel von 1936 und andere Fälschungen aus einer Münchener Goldschmiedewerkstatt. *Germania* **28**; pp. 54–60.

Lilyquist, C. and Brill, R.H. (eds) (1993) *Studies in Early Egyptian Glass*. Metropolitan Museum of Art, New York.

Lins, A. and Power, T. (1994) The corrosion of bronze monuments in polluted urban sites: A report on the stability of copper mineral species at different pH levels. In: Scott *et al.* (eds), 1994, pp. 119–152.

Lins, A. and Malenka, S. (2000) The use of mercury salts in gold electroplating. In: Drayman-Weisser (ed), 2000, pp. 267–282.

Liritzis, I. and Galloway, R.B. (2000) Solar bleaching of thermoluminescence of ancient marble and limestone dating and provenance implications. In: Schilardi and Katsonopoulou (eds), 2000, pp. 603–608.

Littledale, H.A.P. (1936) *A New Process of Hard Soldering*. Lecture to the Worshipful Company of Goldsmiths, London.

Litton, C.D. and Buck, C.E. (1995) The Bayesian approach to the interpretation of archaeological data. *Archaeometry* **37**, 1; pp. 1–24.

Liu, R.K. (1974) Factory-made copies of native beads. *Bead Journal* **1**, 1; pp. 6–18.

Liu, R.K. (1980) Simulated materials in jewelry. *Ornament* **4**, 4; pp. 18–26.

Liu, R.K. (1987) India, Idar-Oberstein and Czechoslovakia: Imitations and competitors. *Ornament* **10**, 4; pp. 56–61.

Liu, R.K. (1995) *Collectible Beads: A Universal Aesthetic*. Ornament, Vista CA.

Liu, R.K. (2001) Fakes . . . Deducing attitudes from artefacts. *Ornament* **24**, 4; pp. 24–31.

Liu Wann-Hong (1976) Casting reproductions of Chinese bronze vessels by the lost-wax process. In: *Ancient Chinese Bronzes and Southeast Asian Metal and other Archaeological Artifacts*, N. Barnard (ed). National Gallery of Victoria, Melbourne, pp. 1–16.

Lloyd, R.V., Smith, P.W. and Haskell, H.W. (1985) Evaluation of the manganese ESR method of marble characterization. *Archaeometry* **27**, 1; pp. 108–116.

Lobanov-Rostovsky, N. (1990) Stop-press: Fakes in supremacist porcelain. *Apollo* **131**, 337; pp. 205–206.

Lomax, S.Q. (1997) Chemistry as applied to the study of works of art. *The Chemical Intelligencer* **4**, 1; pp. 47–53. January.

Lombardi, G. and Vidale, M. (1998) From the shell to its content: The casting cores of the two bronze statues from Riace (Calabria, Italy). *Journal of Archaeological Science* **25**; pp. 1055–1066.

Long, A. (1998) Attempt to affect the apparent 14C age of cotton by scorching in a CO_2 environment. In: *Proceedings of the 16th International Radiocarbon Conference*, W.G. Mook and J. van der Plicht (eds). *Radiocarbon* **40**, 1; pp. 57–58.

Lopez, R.S. (1971) The case is not settled. In: Washburn (ed), 1971, pp. 31–43.

Lord, J.W. (1993) *The Nature and Subsequent Uses of Flint*. John Lord.

Lowenthal, D. (1987) 'Limited edition' museum replicas from Beijing. *IFAR* **1**. Jan/Feb.

Lowenthal, D. (1988) *The Past is a Foreign Country*. Cambridge University Press, Cambridge.

Lowenthal, D. (1999) Authenticity: Rock of faith or quicksand and quagmire? *Getty Conservation Institute Newsletter* **14**, 3; pp. 5–8.

Lowery, P.R., Savage, R.D.A. and Wilkins, R.L. (1971) Scriber, graver, scorper, tracer: Notes on experiments in bronzeworking technique. *Proceedings of the Prehistoric Society* **37**, 1; pp. 167–182.

Lu Jianfang and Hang Tao (2002) Prehistoric jade working based on remains at the site of Dinshadi. In: Childs-Johnson (ed), 2002, pp. 31–42.

Lukas, M. and Lukas, E. (1983) The haunting. *Antiquity* **57**, 228; pp. 7–11.

Lusetti, W. (1955) *Alceo Dossena Scultore*. De Luca, Rome.

Lutz, J. and Pernicka, E. (1996) Energy dispersive X-ray fluorescence analysis of ancient copper alloys: Empirical values for precision and accuracy. *Archaeometry* **38**, 2; pp. 313–323.

Lyne, C.W. (1916) The significance of the radiographs of the Piltdown teeth. *Proceedings of the Royal Society of Medicine* **9**, 3; pp. 33–62. (odontology section).

McCabe, H. and Wright, J. (2000) Tangled tale of a lost, stolen and disputed coelacanth. *Nature* **406**, 6792; p. 114.

McCann, L.I., Trentelman, K., Possley, T. and Golding, B. (1999) Corrosion of ancient Chinese bronze money trees studied by Raman microscopy. *Journal of Raman Spectroscopy* **30**; pp. 121–132.

McCarroll, D. (1994) The Schmidt Hammer as a measure of degree of rock surface weathering and terrain age. In: Beck (ed), 1994, pp. 29–46.

McClure, S.P. and Smith, C.P. (2000) Gemstone enhancement and detection in the 1990s. *Gems and Gemmology* **36**, 4; pp. 336–359.

McConnell, A. (2004) The not so clear-cut story of Irish glass. *Country Life* **198**, 3; pp. 62–63. 15 January.

McCray, P. (ed) (1998) *The Prehistory and History of Glassmaking Technology*. American Ceramics Society, Westerville, Ohio. Ceramics and Civilisation **8**.

McCrone, W.C. (1976) Authenticity of medieval document tested by small-particle analysis. *Analytical Chemistry* **48**, 8; pp. 676A–679A.

McCrone, W.C. (1981) Light-microscopical study of the Turin Shroud III. *The Microscope* **29**; pp. 19–38.

McCrone, W.C. (1986) Microscopical study of the Turin 'Shroud'. In: *The American Institute for Conservation of Historic and Artistic Works – Preprints of Papers Presented at the Fourteenth Annual Meeting*, Chicago, Illinois. 21–25 May 1986, A.G. Brown (ed). The American Institute for Conservation of Historic and Artistic Works, Washington DC, pp. 77–96.

McCrone, W.C. (1987/88a) Microscopical study of the Turin 'Shroud'. *Wiener Berichte über Naturwissenschaft in der Kunst 4/5*; pp. 50–61.

McCrone, W.C. (1987/88b) The microscopical identification of artists' pigments. *Journal of IIC-CG* **7**, 1,2; p. 11.

McCrone, W.C. (1988) The Vinland Map. *Analytical Chemistry* **60**, 10; pp. 1009–1018.

McCrone, W.C. (1991) Authentication of paintings. *Wiener Berichte über Naturwissenschaft in der Kunst* **6/7/8**; pp. 94–120.

McCrone, W.C. (1997) *Judgement Day for the Turin Shroud.* Microscope Publications, McCrone Research Institute, Chicago.

McCrone, W.C. (1999) *The Microscope* **47**; pp. 271–274.

McCrone, W. and Weiss, R.J. (eds) (1999) *Fakebusters: Scientific Detection of Fakery in Art.* SPIE & The McCrone Institute, Chicago.

McCrone, W.C., McCrone, L.B. and Delly, J.G. (1999) *Polarised Light Microscopy.* McCrone Research Institute, Chicago.

McCrone, W.C. and Skirius, C. (1980) Light-microscopical study of the Turin Shroud I & II. *The Microscope* **28**; pp. 1–13.

McEwan, C. (ed) (2000) *Precolumbian Gold: Technology, Style and Iconography.* British Museum Press, London.

McGinnis, W.J. (1984) Titanium dioxide pigments. In: Hagemeyer (ed), 1984, pp. 241–281.

McKerrell, H. and Stevenson, R.B.K. (1972). Some analyses of Anglo-Saxon and associated oriental silver coinage. In: Hall and Metcalf (eds), 1972, pp. 195–209.

McKerrell, H., Mejdahl, V., François, H. and Portal, G. (1974) Thermoluminescence and Glozel. *Antiquity* **48**, 192; pp. 265–272.

McKerrell, H., Mejdahl, V., François, H. and Portal, G. (1975) Thermoluminescence and Glozel: a plea for patience. *Antiquity* **49**, 196; pp. 267–272.

McKerrell, H. and Mejdahl, V. (1978) Authenticity and thermoluminescence dating procedures. In: Young (ed), 1978, pp. 88–100.

McNeil, M. and Selwyn, L.S. (2001) Electrochemical processes in metallic corrosion. In: Brothwell and Pollard (eds), 2001, pp. 605–614.

McNeill, I.C. (1992) Fundamental aspects of polymer degradation. In: Allen *et al.* (eds), 1992, pp. 14–31.

McNeil, M.B. and Little, B.J. (1992) Corrosion mechanisms for copper and silver in near-surface environments. *Journal of the American Institute for Conservation* **31**; pp. 355–366.

McNeil, R.J. (1984) Scanning Auger microscopy for dating of manuscript inks. In: Lambert (ed), 1984, pp. 255–269.

MacDonald, L. (ed) (2006) *Digital Heritage.* Butterworth-Heinemann, Oxford.

MacFarlane, M.W. (1967) Manufacture of sterling silver flatware. In: Butts and Coxe (eds), 1967, pp. 322–330.

MacGregor, A. (1985) *Bone, Antler, Ivory and Horn.* Barnes & Noble, New Jersey.

Maclagan, E. (1923) Ivoires-faux fabriqués à Milan au début du XIXe Siècle. *Aréthuse* **1**; pp. 41–43.

MacLeod, I.D. (1991) Identification of corrosion products on non-ferrous metal artifacts recovered from shipwrecks. *Studies in Conservation* **36**, 4; pp. 222–234.

Magnusson, M. (2006) *Fakes, Forgers and Phoneys.* Mainstream, London.

Mailfert, A. (1935) *Au Pays des Antiquaries.* Flammarion, Paris.

Mairani, A., Matthaes, P., Pedemonte, E., Franceschi, E. and Piaggio, P. (1997) The use of FT-Raman spectroscopy for the characterisation of painting materials. *Science and Technology for Cultural Heritage* **6**, 2; pp. 217–226.

Majolino, D., Migliardo, P., Ponterio, R. and Rodriquez, M.T. (1996) *Ars illuminandi*, and FTIR microspectroscopy: an advanced way to disclose ancient secrets. *Science and Technology for Cultural Heritage* **5**, 2; pp. 57–74.

Malaro, M.C. (1998) *A Legal Primer on Managing Museum Collections.* Smithsonian Institution Press, Washington.

Mallégol, J., Lemaire, J. and Gardette, J.-L. (2001) Yellowing of oil-based paints. *Studies in Conservation* **46**, 2; pp. 121–131.

Mallory-Greenough, L.M., Greenough, J.D., Dobosi, G. and Owen, J.V. (1999a) Fingerprinting ancient Egyptian quarries: Preliminary results using laser ablation microprobe-inductively coupled plasma-mass spectrometry. *Archaeometry* **41**, 2; pp. 227–238.

Mallory-Greenough, L.M., Greenough, J.D., Greenough, J.D. and Owen, J.V. (1999b) The stone source of predynastic basalt vessels: Mineralogical evidence for quarries in northern Egypt. *Journal of Archaeological Science* **26**, 10; pp. 1261–1272.

Mallory-Greenough, L.M., Greenough, J.D. and Owen, J.V. (2000) The origin and use of basalt in Old Kingdom funerary temples. *Geoarchaeology* **15**, 4; pp. 315–330.

Mancini, C. 1984 Silver evaluation in Roma Republican Victoriatus, Revue d'Archéomerie. pp. 30–32.

Mandi, V., Maniatis, Y., Bassiakos, Y. and Kilikoglou, V. (1992) Provenance investigation of marbles with ESR spectroscopy: Further developments. In: Waelkens, Herz and Moens (eds), 1992, pp. 213–222.

Maniatis, Y. (ed). (1989) *Archaeometry: Proceedings of the 25th International Symposium.* Elsevier, Amsterdam.

Maniatis, Y. and Mandi, V. (1992) Electron-paramagnetic-resonance signals and effects in marble induced by working. *Journal of Applied Physics* **71**; pp. 4859–4867.

Maniatis, Y., Aloupi, E. and Stalios, A.D. (1993) New evidence for the nature of the Attic black gloss. *Archaeometry* **35**, 1; pp. 23–35.

Maniatis, Y., Herz, N. and Basiakos, Y. (eds) (1995) *The Study of Marble and Other Stones Used in Antiquity.* ASMOSIA III. Archetype Publications, London.

Maniatis, Y. and Polikreti, P. (2000) The characterization and discrimination of Parian marble in the Aegean region. In: Schilardi and Katsonopoulou (eds), 2000, pp. 575–584.

Manley, J.J. (1912) Analysis of green and blue glass from the Posipilan mosaic. *Archaeologia* 63; pp. 106–108.

Mannoni, L. and Mannoni, T. (1989) *Marble: The History of a Culture.* Facts on File Publications, New York.

Mantler, M., Schreiner, M. and Schweizer, F. (2000) Museum: Art and archaeology. In: *Industrial Applications of X-Ray Diffraction*, F.H. Chung and D.K. Smith (eds). Marcel Dekker, New York, pp. 621–658.

Mao, Y. (2000) Lead-alkaline glazed Egyptian faience: Preliminary technical investigation of Ptolemaic period faience vessels in the collection of the Walters Art Gallery. *Journal of the American Institute for Conservation* 39, 2; pp. 185–204.

Mappin, G. (1999) *Electroplated Nickel Silver Old Sheffield Plate and Close Plate Makers' Marks from 1784.* Foulsham, London.

Mara, T. (1979) *Screen Printing.* Thames and Hudson, London.

Marconi, B. (1967) The transfer of panel paintings on linen by Sidorov (Hermitage Museum, St Petersburg) in the nineteenth century. In: Young (ed), 1967, pp. 246–254.

Margolis, S.V. (1987) Evidence for dedolomitization in an archaic Greek (6th century BC) Kouros statue. *Geological Society of America Bulletin* 19, 7; p. 760.

Margolis, S.V. (1989) Authenticating ancient marble sculpture. *Scientific American* 260, 6; pp. 104–110.

Margolis, S.V., Preusser, F. and Showers, W.J. (1988) Ancient marble sculpture: Geochemical characterization of surficial weathering products. In: Sayre *et al.* (eds), 1988, pp. 53–58.

Margolis, S.V. and Showers, W. (1988) Weathering characteristics, age, and provenance determinations on ancient Greek and Roman marble artefacts. In: Herz and Waelkens (eds), 1988, pp. 233–242.

Margolis, S.V. and Showers, W. (1990) Ancient Greek and Roman marble sculpture: Authentication, weathering, and provenance determinations. In: True and Podany (eds), 1990b, pp. 283–299.

Marijnissen, R.H. (1974) De Van Meergeren-affaire of de gevolgen van een niet bedwongen ontroering. In: *Snoecks 74.* Snoeck-Ducaju, Ghent, pp. 196–209.

Marijnissen, R.H. (1985) *Paintings: Genuine, Fraud, Fake.* Elsevier, Brussels.

Marijnissen, R.H. and van der Voorde, G. (1978) De 'Chest de Courtrai'. Een vervalsing van het pasticcio-type. *Meddelingen van de Koninklijke Academie voor Wetenschappen, Letteren en Schone Kunsten van België* 11, 3; pp. 3–24.

Marinescu, C.A. (1998) Modern imitations of ancient coins from Bulgaria. *Minerva* 9, 5; pp. 46–48.

Markel, S. (ed) (1992) *The World of Jade.* Marg Publications, Bombay.

Marlowe, G. (1980) W.F. Libby and the archaeologists, 1946–1948. *Radiocarbon* 22, 3; pp. 1005–1014.

Marsh, M. (1993) *Art Detective.* Pelham Books, London.

Marshall, D.J. (1988) *Cathodoluminescence of Geological Materials.* Unwin Hyman, Boston.

Martin, E. (1988) *Collecting and Preserving Old Photographs.* Collins, London.

Martin, E. and Ravaud, E. (1995) La radiographie des peintures de chevalet. *Techne* 2; pp. 158–164.

Martin, F., Mérigoux, H. and Zecchin, P. (1989) Reflectance infrared spectroscopy in gemmology. *Gems and Gemmology* 25, 4; pp. 226–231.

Martin, E., Marsac, J., Belcourt, M.-A., Mallet, R. and Maurier, F. (2001) À la découverte de la signature du peintre. *Techne* 13–14; pp. 101–111.

Martini, M., Sibilia, E., Spinolo, G. and Zelaschi, C. (1995) Indirect dating of bronze artifacts using their thermoluminescent clay-cores. In: *The Ceramic Heritage, Proceedings of the 8th CIMTEC-World Ceramics Congress*, P. Vincenzini (ed), 2. Materials and Society, Techna, Faenza, pp. 387–391.

Martini, M. and Sibilia, E. (2003) Dating the cast of bronze statues by thermoluminescence. In: *Archaeometallurgy in Europe II*, A. Giumlia Mair (ed). Associazione Italiana di Metallurgia, Milano, pp. 331–336.

Martinot, L., Strivay, D., Guillaume, J. and Weber, G. (2000) PIXE analysis of brass alloys. In: Demortier and Adriaens (eds), 2000, pp. 76–80.

Martoglio, P.A., Bouffard, S.P., Sommer, A.J., Katon, J.E. and Jakes, K.A. (1990) Unlocking the secrets of the past: The analysis of archaeological textiles and dyes. *Analytical Chemistry* 62, 21; pp. 1123A–1128A.

Maryon, H. (1923) *Metalwork and Enamelling*, 2nd edn. Chapman & Hall, London. [4th and last edition published 1959, Chapman & Hall; reissued by Dover as 5th edn. New York, 1971].

Maryon, H. (1933) *Modern Sculpture, its Methods and Ideals.* Sir Isaac Pitman, London.

Maryon, H. (1937–38) The technical methods of the Irish Smith in the Bronze and Early Iron Age. *Proceedings of the Royal Irish Academy* 44; pp. 181–228. (Section C, no. 7) esp. p. 186.

Maskell, A. (1905) *Ivories.* The Connoisseur's Library, Methuen, London. [Reprinted 1966, Charles Tuttle, Rutland, Vermont and Tokyo].

Mason, R.B. and Tite, M.S. (1997) The beginnings of tin-opacification of pottery glazes. *Archaeometry* 39, 1; pp. 41–58.

Mason, R.B., Tite, M.S., Paynter, S. and Salter, C. (2001) Advances in polychrome ceramics in the Islamic world of the 12th century AD. *Archaeometry* 43, 2; pp. 191–216.

Masschelein-Kleiner, L., [trans.], J. Bridgland, S. Walston and A.E.A. Werner, (1995) *Ancient Binding Media, Varnishes and Adhesives*, 2nd edn. ICCROM, Rome.

Massé, H.J.L.J. (1911) *Chats on Old Pewter*. T. Fisher Unwin, London.

Masselon, Roberts and Cilliard, trans. H.H. Hodgson, (1912) *Celluloid, its Manufacture, Applications and Substitutes*. Charles Griffin, London.

Matcham, J. and Dreiser, P. (1982) *The Techniques of Glass Engraving*. B.T. Batsford, London.

Matheau-Raven, E.R. (1997) *The Identification and Dating of Sheffield Electroplated Wares 1843–1943*. Foulsham, London.

Mathieson, L. and Nugent, K.W. (1996) Raman laser microprobe spectroscopy and the analysis of materials from oil paintings. *AICCM Bulletin* **21**, 2; pp. 3–11.

Matteini, M. and Moles, A. (1986) Le patine d'ossalato di calico sui manufatti in marmot. In: *Restauro del Marmo: Opere e Problemi*. Opus Libri, Rome, pp. 65–73.

Matthews, K.J. (1997) The establishment of a data base of neutron activation analyses of white marble. *Archaeometry* **39**, 2; pp. 321–332.

Matthews, K.J. (1988) Variability in stable isotope analysis: Implications for joining fragments. In: Herz and Waelkens (eds), 1988, pp. 339–346.

Matthews, K.J., Leese, M.N., Hughes, M.J., Herz, N. and Bowman, S.G.E. (1995) Establishing the provenance of marble using statistical combinations of stable isotope and neutron activation analysis data. In: Maniatas, Herz and Basiakos (eds), 1995, pp. 171–180.

Mattusch, C.C. (1990) The casting of Greek bronzes: Variations and Repetition. In: True and Podany (eds), 1990a, pp. 125–144.

Mattusch, C.C. (1999) Lost-wax casting and the question of originals and copies. In: Formigli (ed), 1999, pp. 75–82.

Maxwell-Hyslop, K.R. (1971) *Western Asiatic Jewellery, c.3000 BC–612 BC*. Methuen, London.

Mayer, R. (nd) *The Artist's Handbook of Materials and Techniques*, 5th edn. Faber and Faber, London.

Maynard, F.W. (1873) *Five years of the Arundel Society, 1869–1673*. Nichols and Sons, London.

Mazzoni, G. (ed) (2004) *False d'Autore: Icilo Federico Jonie la Cultura del Falso tra Otto e Novecento*. Protagon, Siena.

Meacham, W. (1983) The Authentication of the Turin Shroud: An issue in archaeological epistemology. *Current Anthropology* **24**, 3; pp. 283–309.

Meacham, W. (2007) The amazing Dr. Kouznetsov. *Antiquity* **81**, 313; pp. 779–783.

Meakin, J.D., Ames, D.L. and Dolske, D.A. (1992) Degradation of monumental bronze. *Atmospheric Environment* **26B**; pp. 207–215.

Mecklenburg, M.F. and Tumosa, C.S. (2001) Traditional oil paints: The effects of long term chemical and mechanical properties on restoration efforts. *MRS Bulletin* **26**, 1; pp. 51–54. January.

Medley, M. (1980) *The Chinese Potter: A Practical History of Chinese Ceramics*, 2nd edn. Phaidon, Oxford.

Meeks, N.D. (1987) Artefacts, surfaces and the SEM. In: Black (ed), 1987, pp. 409–410.

Meeks, N.D. (1988a) Backscattered electron imaging of archaeological material. In: Olsen (ed). pp. 23–43.

Meeks, N.D. (1988b) Surface studies of Roman bronze mirrors: Comparative high-tin bronze Dark Age material and black Chinese mirrors. In: Farquhar *et al.* (eds), 1988, pp. 24–27.

Meeks, N.D. (1990) Report on the examination of silicone rubber moulds taken from the two Basse-Yutz flagons. Appendix 1. In: Megaw and Megaw, 1990, pp. 71–73.

Meeks, N. (1993) Patination phenomena on Roman and Chinese high-tin bronze mirrors and other artefacts. In: La Niece and Craddock (eds), 1993, pp. 63–84.

Meeks, N.D. (1998a) Pre-Hispanic goldwork in the British Museum: Some recent technological studies. *Boletin del Oro* **44/5**; pp. 107–137.

Meeks, N. (1998b) A Greek gold necklace: A case of dual identity. In: Williams (ed), 1998, pp. 127–138.

Meeks, N.D. and Tite, M.S. (1980) The analysis of platinum-group element inclusions in gold antiquities. *Journal of Archaeological Science* **7**, 3; pp. 267–275.

Meeks, N.D. and Craddock, P.T. (1991) The detection of cadmium in gold/silver alloys and its alleged occurrence in ancient gold solders. *Archaeometry* **33**, 1; pp. 95–107.

Meeks, N.D., Craddock, P.T. and Needham, S.P. (1992) Bronze age penannular gold rings from the British Isles. *Jewellery Studies* **11**; pp. 13–30.

Mees, F., Swennen, R., van Geet, M. and Jacobs, P. (eds) (2003) *Applications of X-ray Computed Tomography in the Geosciences*. The Geological Society, London.

Megaw, J.V.S. and Megaw, M.R. (1990) *The Basse-Yutz Find: Masterpieces of Celtic Art*. Society of Antiquaries of London Research Report 46, London.

Meilunas, R.J., Bentsen, J.G. and Steinberg, A. (1990) Analysis of aged paint binders by FTIR spectroscopy. *Studies in Conservation* **35**, 1; pp. 33–51.

Mejdahl, V. (1980) Further work on ceramic objects from Glozel. *Archaeometry* **22**, 2; pp. 197–203.

Mellaart, J. (1970) *Excavations at Hacilar*, 2 vols. Edinburgh University Press, Edinburgh.

Mello, E., Parrini, P. and Formigli, E. (1984) Alterazioni superficiali dei Bronzo dei Bronzi di Riace: le aree con patina nera della statua 'A'. In: *Due bronzi da Riace*. Bolletino d'Arte, Serie Speciale, Istituto Poligrafico dello Stato, Rome.

Merryman, J.H. and Elsen, A.E. (1987) *Law, Ethics and the Visual Arts*, 2nd edn. University of Pennsylvania Press, Philadelphia. esp. pp. 569–575.

Metcalf, D.M. and Oddy, W.A. (eds) (1980) *Metallurgy in Numismatics 1*. Royal Numismatic Society, London. Special Publication 13.

Meyer, K. (1973) *The Plundered Past*. Athenaeum Press, New York.

Meyers, P. (1978) Applications of X-ray radiography in the study of archaeological objects. In: Carter (ed), 1978, pp. 79–96.

Meyers, P. (1981) Technical study of Sasanian silver. *MASCA Journal* **1**, 8; pp. 242–244.

Meyers, P. (1990) The use of scientific techniques in provenance studies of ancient bronzes. In: True and Podany (eds), 1990a, pp. 237–252.

Meyers, P. (1997) Ancient Chinese gold: Is it really old? *Orientations* **28**, 3; pp. 117–118.

Meyers, P. (2004) Production of silver in antiquity: Ore types identified based upon elemental composition of ancient silver artefacts. In: *Patterns and Process*, L. van Zelst (ed). Smithsonian Center for Materials Research and Education, Suitland, Maryland, pp. 271–288.

Michael, C.T., Zacharias, N., Maniatis, Y. and Dimotikali, D. (1997) A new technique (foil technique) for measuring the natural dose in TL dating and its application in the dating of a mortar containing ceramic fragments. *Ancient TL* **15**, 2/3; pp. 36–42.

Michel, H.V. and Asaro, F. (1979) Chemical study of the Plate of Brass. *Archaeometry* **21**, 1; pp. 3–20.

Michielsen, S. (2001) Application of Raman spectroscopy to organic fibers and films. In: Lewis and Edwards (eds), 2001, pp. 749–798.

Middleton, A. (1991) Ceramics: Materials for all reasons. In: Bowman (ed), 1991, pp. 16–36.

Middleton, A. (1997) Ceramic petrography. *Revue do Museu de Arqueologia e Etnologia*, Suplemento 2; pp. 73–79. São Paulo.

Middleton, A. (2005) Ceramics. In: Lang and Middleton (eds), 2005, pp. 76–95.

Middleton, A. (2006) Jade. In: O'Donoghue (ed), 2006, pp. 332–555.

Middleton, A. and Lang, J. (2005) Radiography: Theory. In: Lang and Middleton (eds), 2005, pp. 1–29.

Middleton, A. and Freestone, I. (1995) The mineralogy and occurrence of jade. In: Rawson, 1995, pp. 413–423.

Middleton, A. and Ambers, J. (2005) Case study: Analysis of nephrite jade using Raman microscopy and X-ray fluorescence. In: Edwards and Chalmers (eds), 2005, pp. 403–411.

Milanesi, G. (1878–1885) *Le Opere di Georgio Vasari*. G.C. Sansoni, Firenze.

Milazzo, M. and Cicardi, C. (1997) Simple methods for quantitative X-ray fluorescence analysis of ancient metals of archaeological interest. *X-ray Spectrometry* **26**; pp. 211–216.

Milazzo, M. and Cicardi, C. (1998) X-ray fluorescence characterization of the *Corona Ferrea*. *Archaeometry* **40**, 2; pp. 351–360.

Miles, J.W. (1884) *The Russian Reproductions at the Metropolitan Museum of Art*. The Jeweller's Circular Publishing Co., New York.

Miley, F. (1984) Facts about synthetic and imitation gemstones. *Lapidary Journal* **38**, 7; pp. 954–958.

Millar, R. (1972) *The Piltdown Men*. Gollancz, London.

Millar, R. (1998) *The Piltdown Mystery*. S.B. Publications, Seaford, East Sussex.

Miller, A. (1948) *Stone and Marble Carving*. Tiranti, London.

Miller, A.M. (1998) *Cameos Old and New*. GemStone Press, Woodstock, Vermont.

Miller, E. (1992) The Piranesi Vase. In: Oddy (ed), 1992, pp. 122–136.

Miller, G.S. (1915) The Jaw of Piltdown Man. *Smithsonian Miscellaneous Collections* **65**; pp. 1–31.

Miller, J.C. and Miller, J.N. (1993) *Statistics for Analytical Chemistry*, 3rd edn. Ellis Horwood, New York.

Mills, A.A. (1995) Image formation on the Shroud of Turin. *Interdisciplinary Science Reviews* **20**, 4; pp. 319–324.

Mills, J.F. (1972) *How to Detect Fake Antiques*. Arlington, London.

Mills, J.F. and Mansfield, J.M. (1979) *The Genuine Article*. BBC, London.

Mills, J.S., White, R. and Gough, L.J. (1984/85) The chemical composition of Baltic amber. *Chemical Geology* **47**; pp. 15–39.

Mills, J.S. and White, R. (1994) *The Organic Chemistry of Museum Objects*, 2nd edn. Butterworths-Heinemann, London.

Mills, J.W. and Gillespie, M. (1969) *Studio bronze casting – lost wax*. Maclaren and Sons, London.

Mitchell, C.A. (1937) *Inks: Their Composition and Manufacture*, 4th edn. Charles Griffin & Co, London.

Mitchell, H.P. (1921) Two bronzes by Nicholas of Verdun. *The Burlington Magazine* **38**; pp. 157–166.

Mitchell, P. and Roberts, L. (1996) *A History of European Picture Frames*. Paul Mitchell with Merrell Holberton, London.

Mitchell, W.J. (1992) *The Reconfigured Eye: Visual Truth in the Post-Photographic Era*. MIT Press, Cambridge MA.

Mitchell, W.J. (1994) When is seeing believing? *Scientific American* **270**, 2; pp. 44–49. February.

Mitchiner, M.B. and Pollard, M. (1990) *Early South-East Asian Currency Systems*. Supplement 65 to *Annali* **50**, fascicle 4 of the Istituto Universitario Orientale, Napoli.

Moens, L., Roos, P., de Rudder, J., Hoste, J., de Paepe, P., van Hende, J., Marechal, R. and Waelkens, M. (1988a) White marble from Italy and Turkey: An archaeometric study based on minor- and trace-element analysis. *Journal of Radioanalytical and Nuclear Chemistry* **123**, 1; pp. 333–348.

Moens, L., Roos, P., de Rudder, J., de Paepe, P., van Hende, J. and Waelkens, M. (1988b) A multi-method approach to the identification of white marbles used in antique artefacts. In: Herz and Waelkens (eds), 1988, pp. 243–250.

Moens, L., de Paepe, P. and Waelkens, M. (1992) Multidisciplinary research and cooperation: Keys to a successful provenance determination of white marble. In: Waelkens, Herz and Moens (eds), 1992, pp. 247–254.

Moens, L., de Paepe, P. and Waelkens, M. (1995) A multidisciplinary contribution to the provenance determination of ancient Greek and Roman marbles artefacts. *Israel Journal of Chemistry* **35**; pp. 167–174.

Moens, L., von Bohlen, A. and Vandenabeele, P. (2000) X-ray fluorescence. In: Ciliberto and Spoto (eds), 2000, pp. 55–79.

Moir, J.R. (1935) *Prehistoric Archaeology and Sir Ray Lankester*. Norman Adlard, Ipswich.

Moltesen, M. (2003) De-restoring and re-restoring. In: Grossman, Podany and Trues (eds), 2003, pp. 207–224.

Moltesen, M., Herz, N. and Moon, J. (1992) The Lepsius Marbles. In: Waelkens, Herz and Moens (eds), 1992, pp. 277–281.

Moncrieff, R.W. (1975) *Man-Made Fibres*, 6th edn. Newnes-Butterworths, London.

Mongne, P. (1988) Les urnes funéraires zapotèques: Collectionisme et contrefaçon. *Journal de la Société des Américanistes* **73**, 1; pp. 7–50.

Mongne, P. (1992) Muséologie et contrefaçon, les urnes zapotè ques du Museum für Völkerkunde de Berlin. *Journal de la Société des Américanistes* **78**, 1; pp. 88–93.

Mongne, P. (2000) Le faux zapotèque et la collection Gustave Bellon. *La Techne* **11**; pp. 53–64.

Moorey, P.R.S. (1994) *Ancient Mesopotamian Materials and Industries*. Clarendon Press, Oxford.

Morant, G.M. (1936) A morphological comparison of two crystal skulls. *Man* **36**; pp. 142–178.

Morgan, J. (1991) *Conservation of Plastics*. The Plastics Historical Society/Museums and Galleries Commission, London.

Morgan, P.W. (1981) Brief history of fibres from synthetic polymers. *Journal of Macromolecular Science* **A15**, 6; pp. 1113–1131.

Morgenstein, M.E., Wicket, C.L. and Barkatt, A. (1999) Considerations of hydration-rind dating of glass artefacts: Alteration morphologies and experimental evidence of hydrogeochemical soil-zone pore water control. *Journal of Archaeological Science* **26**, 9; pp. 1193–1210.

Morlet, A. (1929) *Glozel*. G. Desgrandchamps, Paris.

Morlet, A. (1932) *Petit historique de l'affaire Glozel*. G. Desgrandchamps, Paris.

Moroney, M.J. (1956) *Facts from Figures*. Penguin Books, Harmondsworth, Middx.

Moroz, I.I. and Eliezri, I.Z. (1999) Mineral inclusions in emeralds from different sources. *The Journal of Gemmology* **26**, 6; pp. 357–363.

Morris, R.A., Schwalbe, L.A. and London, J.R. (1980) X-ray fluorescence investigation of the Shroud of Turin. *X-ray Spectrometry* **9**, 2; pp. 40–47.

Morrisson, Ch., Barrandon, J.-N. and Morrisson, C. (1999) *Or du Brésil, monnaie et croissance en France au XVIIIe siècle*. Cahiers Ernest-Babelon, CNRS editions, Paris.

Morteani, G. and Northover, J.P. (eds) (1995) *Prehistoric Gold in Europe*. NATO ASI Series **E280**. Kluwer, Dordrecht.

Mortimer, C. (1989) X-ray fluorescence analysis of early scientific instruments. In: Maniatis (ed), 1989, pp. 311–318.

Mortimer, C. (1995) Analysis of Post-Medieval glass from Old Broad Street, London, with reference to other contemporary glasses from London and Italy. In: Hook and Gaimster (eds), 1995, pp. 135–144.

Mortimer, C. and Stoney, M. (1997) A methodology for punchmark analysis using electron microscopy. In: Sinclair, Slater and Gowlett (eds), 1997, pp. 119–122.

Morton, C. and Thomas, C.L. (1997) *The Mystery of the Crystal Skulls*. Thorsons, London.

Moss, A.A. (1954) *The Application of X-Rays, Gamma Rays, Ultra-Violet and Infra-Red Rays to the Study of Antiquities*. Handbook for Museum Curators, Part **B**, Museum Techniques, Section 4. The Museums Association, London.

Moss, A.A. (1956) *Electrotyping*. Handbook for Museum Curators, Part **B**, Section 5. The Museums Association, London.

Mossman, S. (ed) (1997) *Early Plastics: Perspectives 1850–1950*. Leicester University Press, London.

Mossman, S.T.I. (1994) Parkesine and Celluloid. In: Mossman and Morris (eds), 1994, pp. 10–25.

Mossman, S.T.I. and Morris, P.J.T. (eds) (1994) *The Development of Plastics*. Royal Society of Chemistry, Cambridge University Press.

Muether, H.E., Balazs, N.L., Voelke, W. and Cotter, M.J. (1980) Neutron autoradiography and the Spanish Forger. *MASCA Journal* **1**, 4; pp. 112–113.

Muldroon, S. and Brownsword, R. (nd) *Pewter Spoons and other Related Material of the 14th–17th Centuries in the Collection of the Herbert Art Gallery & Museum, Coventry*. Leisure Services, Coventry.

Müller, P. and Schvoerer, M. (1993) Factors affecting the viability of thermoluminescence dating of glass. *Archaeometry* **35**, 2; pp. 299–304.

Müller-Kaspar, U. (1994) Cavaceppi zwischen Theorie und Praxix: Techniken und Methoden der Antikenergänzung im 18. Jahrhundert. *Jahreshefte des Österreichischen Archäologischen Institutes in Wien* **63**; pp. 98–152.

Müller-Kaspar, U. (1995) Der Cavaceppi-Sockel. Zur Struktur antiker versus moderner Büstenaufbauten. *Jahreshefte des Österreichischen Archäologischen Institutes in Wien* **64**; pp. pp113–pp123.

Mundt, B. (1980) Galvanos in Kunstgewerbe. *Reihe Kunst und Fälschung II. Gefälschte Blankwaffen*. Kunst und Antiquitäten Verlag, Hannover.

Munn, G.C. (1984) *Castellani and Giuliano. Revivalist Jewellers of the Nineteenth Century*. Trefoil, London.

Munro, R. (1905) *Archæology and False Antiquities*. The Antiquary's Books, Methuen, London.

Murrell, V.J. (1971) Some aspects of the conservation of wax models. *Studies in Conservation* **16**, 3; pp. 95–109.

Muscarella, O.W. (2000) *The Lie Became Great: The Forgery of Ancient Near Eastern Cultures*. Styx Publications, Groningen, Holland.

Mutz, A. (1972) *Die Kunst des Metalldrehens bei den Römern*. Birkhäuser, Basel.

Nadeau, H.-W. (1992) An unprecedented test on white marble. *Apollo* **135**, 360; pp. 108–111. February.

Napier, J. (1852) *A Manual of Electro-Metallurgy*, 2nd edn. John Joseph Griffin, London.

Nassau, K. (1974) The effect of gamma rays on tourmaline, greenish-yellow quartz, pearls, kunzite and jade. *Lapidaries Journal* **28**; pp. 104–109.

Nassau, K. (1980) *Gems Made by Man*. Chilton Book Co, Radnor PA.

Nassau, K. (1984a) *Gemstone Enhancement*. Butterworths, Oxford.

Nassau, K. (1984b) The early history of gemstone treatments. *Gems and Gemmology* 20; pp. 22–33.

Nassau, K. (1985) The early history of gemstone enhancement, Pts. 1 and 2. *Lapidary Journal* 38, 11 & 12; pp. 406–412. 1632–1641. February & March.

Nassau, K. (1994) More on the antiquity of emerald oiling. *The Journal of Gemmology* 24, 2; pp. 109–110.

Nassau, K. (1997) The chronology of synthetic gemstones. *The Journal of Gemmology* 25, 7; pp. 483–490.

Naud, C. (1995) Considération sur la dé-restauration: Le cas des tableaux de Saint-Henri-de-Lévis. In: *Restauration*, 1995, pp. 331–336.

NDTWA (1994) *Proceedings of the 4th International Conference on Non-Destructive Testing of Works of Art*, Berlin 1994. Deutsche Gesellschaft für Zerostörungsfreie Prüfung e V, 45, 1 & 2; Berlin.

Needham, J. (1958) *The Development of Iron and Steel Technology in China*. The Newcomen Society, London.

Needles, H.L., Cassman, V. and Collins, M..J. (1986) Mordanted, natural-dyed wool and silk fabrics. Light and burial-induced changes in the color and tensile properties. In: Needles and Zeronian (eds), 1986, pp. 199–210.

Needles, H.L. and Zeronian, S.H. (eds). (1986) *Historic Textile and Paper Materials: Conservation and Characterization*. American Chemical Society, Washington DC. Advances in Chemistry Series 212.

Neelmeijer, C., Mäder, M., Pietsch, U., Ulbricht, H. and Wacha, H.-M. (2000a) Johann Gregorius Höroldt fecit? In: Demortier and Adriaens (eds), 2000, pp. 54–59.

Neelmeijer, C., Mäder, M. and Schramm, H.-P. (2000b) Paint layers – Depth resolved analysis at the particle accelerator. In: Demortier and Adriaens (eds), 2000, pp. 15–20.

Neevel, J.G. and Reißland, B. (1997) The Ink Corrosion Project at the Netherlands Institute for Cultural Heritage. In: *Iron-gall Ink Corrosion*. Netherlands Institute for Cultural Heritage, Amsterdam, pp. 37–46.

Neff, H. (ed) (1992) *Chemical Characterization of Ceramic Pastes in Archaeology*. Monographs in World Archaeology 7. Prehistory Press, Madison, Wisconsin.

Neff, H. (2000) Neutron activation analysis for provenance determination in archaeology. In: Ciliberto and Spoto (eds), 2000, pp. 81–134.

Nelson, J.B. (1994) The glass filling of diamonds Part 2: A possible filling process. *The Journal of Gemmology* 24, 2; pp. 94–103.

Netzer, N. and England, P. (1989) Medieval enamels of questionable authenticity in the Museum of Fine Arts, Boston. *Jewellery Studies* 3; p. 85.

Neuwirth, W. (1980) *Wiener Jugendstilsilber Original, Fälschung, Pasticcion*. W. Neuwirth-verlag, Wien.

Newbury, B., Stephenson, B., Almer, J., Notis, M., Haeffner, D., Stephenson, B. and Cargill, G.S., III (2003) Synchroton analysis of high zinc brass astrolabes. *Archaeometallurgy in Europe*. Associazone Italiana di Metallurgia, Milano, pp. 359–368.

Newby, M.S. (1998) The Cavour Vase and gilt and enamelled Mamluk colored glass. In: Ward (ed), 1998, pp. 35–40.

Newman, E.P. (1974) Differences of opinion as to the 'Stress Detection' article in *The Numismatist*, June 1974. *The Numismatist* 87, 9; pp. 1808–1809.

Newman, H. (1977) *An Illustrated Dictionary of Glass*. Thames and Hudson, London.

Newman, H. (1981) *An Illustrated Dictionary of Jewellery*. Thames and Hudson, London.

Newman, R. (1984) *The Stone Sculpture of India: A Study of the Materials used by Indian Sculptors from ca. 2nd century BC to the 16th century*. Harvard University Art Museums, Cambridge MA.

Newman, R. (1988) The materials of Hoysala temples and sculpture: A petrographic characterization. *Archaeomtry* 30, 1; pp. 120–131.

Newman, R. (1990) Weathering layers and the authentication of marble objects. In: True and Podany (eds), 1990b, pp. 263–282.

Newman, R. (1992a) Authenticating your collection. *Caring for your Collections*. Harry N. Abrahms, New York, pp. 172–179.

Newman, R. (1992b) Applications of petrography and electron microprobe analysis to the study of Indian stone sculpture. *Archaeometry* 34, 2; pp. 163–174.

Newman, R. (1996) Binders in paintings. *MRS Bulletin* 21, 12; pp. 24–31.

Newman, R. and Herrmann J.J., Jr (1995) Further research on the Boston three-sided relief. In: Maniatis, Herz and Basiakos (eds), 1995, pp. 103–112.

Newport, R. (1976) *Plastic Antiques*. British Industrial Plastics, Oldbury, Warley, Staffordshire.

Newton, R.G. (1971) The enigma of the layered crusts on some weathered glasses: A chronological account of the investigation. *Archaeometry* 13, 1; pp. 1–9.

Newton, R.G. (1985) The durability of glass – A review. *Glass Technology* 26, 1; pp. 21–38.

Newton, R. and Brill, R.H. (1985) A 'weeping' glass bowl at the Ashmolean Museum. *Journal of Glass Studies* 27; pp. 93–96.

Neyses, M. (1996) Zur dendrochronologischen Untersuchungen mittelalterlicher Handscriften. *Funde und Ausgrabungen im Bezirk Trier* 28; pp. 63–70.

Nicholson, E.M. and Ferguson-Lees, I.J. (1962) The Hastings Rarities. *British Birds* 55, 8; pp. 299–345. August.

Nicholson, J.W. (1997) *The Chemistry of Polymers*, 2nd edn. Royal Society of Chemistry, London.

Nicholson, P.T. and Henderson, J. (2000) Glass. In: Nicholson and Shaw (eds), 2000, pp. 195–224.

Nicholson, P.T. and Peltenburg, E. (2000) Egyptian faience. In: Nicholson and Shaw (eds), 2000, pp. 177–194.

Nicholson, P.T. and Shaw, I. (eds) (2000) *Ancient Egyptian Materials and Technology*. Cambridge University Press, Cambridge.

Nicolaus, K. (1999) *The Restoration of Paintings*. Könemann, Cologne.

Nicolini, G. (1990) *Techniques des Ors Antiques: La Bijouterie Ibérique du VIIe au IVe Siècle*. Picard, Paris.

Nicolini, G. (1995) Gold wire techniques of Europe and the Mediterranean around 300 B.C. In: Morteani and Northover (eds), 1995, pp. 453–470.

Nicosia, F. and Ferretti, M. (eds) (1992) *La Chimera D'Arezzo*. Ministero per I Beni Culturali e Ambientali Soprintendenza Archeologica della Toscana & ENEA, Firenze.

Niimira, N., Miyakoshi, T., Onodera, J. and Higuchi, T. (1999) Identification of ancient lacquer film using two-stage pyrolysis-gas chromatography/mass spectrometry. *Archaeometry* 41, 1; pp. 137–150.

Nikolaus-Have, F. (1986) Der Herkules von Birdoswald-Unikum oder Fälschung? *Archäologischer Anzeiger* 3; pp. 571–581.

Nimmo, B.A.F. and Prescott, A.G. (1968) Moulding, casting and electrotyping. *The Conservation of Cultural Property*. The Unesco Press, Paris, pp. 95–109.

Noble, J.V. (1968) The forgery of our Greek bronze horse. *The Metropolitan Bulletin of Art Bulletin* 26; pp. 253–256.

Noble, J.V. (1988) *The Techniques of Painted Attic Pottery*, 2nd edn. Thames and Hudson, London.

Noll, W. (1979) Anorganische Pigmente in der Vorgeschichte und Antike. *Fortschritt Mineralogie* 57, 2; pp. 203–263.

Noll, W., Holm, R. and Born, L. (1973) Manganschwarz – Malerei – eine Technik der Ornamentierung antiker Keramik. *Berichte der Deutschen Keramischen Gesellschaft* 50, 10; pp. 328–333.

Norbury, A.L. (1929) The effect of quenching and tempering on standard silver. *Transactions of the Institute of Metals* 39; pp. 145–161.

Norman, G. and Hoving, T. (1987) It was bigger than they knew. *Connoisseur*. In: Hoving, 1996, pp. 302–303.

North, A. (1999) *Pewter at the Victoria and Albert Museum*. V & A Publications, London.

Northover, J.P. (1992) Materials issues in the Celtic coinage. In: *Celtic Coinage: Britain and Beyond*, M. Mays (ed). British Archaeological Reports British Series 222, Oxford, pp. 235–299.

Northover, P. (1995) Late Bronze Age drawplates in the Isleham Hoard. In: *Trans Europam: Beiträge zur Bronze- und Eisenzeit zwischen Atlantik und Altai: Festschrift für Margarita Primas*, B. Schmid-Sikimic and P. dela Casa (eds). Antiquitas 3 34; Rudolf Habelt, Bonn, pp. 15–22.

Northover, J.P. (1998) Analysis in the electron microprobe and scanning electron microscope. In: Oddy and Cowell (eds), 1998, pp. 94–113.

Nriagu, J.O. (1983) *Lead and Lead Poisoning in Antiquity*. John Wiley & Sons, New York.

Oakeshott, E. (1991) *Records of the Medieval Sword*. Boydell, Woodbridge, Suffolk.

Oakley, K.P. (1948) Fluorine and the relative dating of bone. *Advancement of Science* 16; pp. 336–337.

Oakley, K.P. (1963) Fluorine, uranium, and nitrogen dating of bone. In: *The Scientist and Archaeology*, E. Pydoke (ed). J.M. Dent & Sons, London, pp. 111–119.

Oakley, K.P. (1969) Analytical methods of dating bone. In: *Science and Archaeology*, 2nd edn. D. Brothwell and E. Higgs (eds), Thames and Hudson, London, pp. 35–45.

Oakley, K.P. (1976) The Piltdown problem reconsidered. *Antiquity* 50, 197; pp. 9–13.

Oakley, K.P. (1979a) Note on the antiquity of the Sherborne bone; Appendix to Farrar (1979). *Antiquity* 53, 209; pp. 215–216.

Oakley, K.P. (1979b) Piltdown stains. *Nature* 278; p. 302.

Oakley, K.P. and Hoskins, C.R. (1950) New evidence on the antiquity of Piltdown Man. *Nature* 165, 4193; pp. 379–382.

Oakley, K.P. and Groves, C.P. (1970) Piltdown Man: The realization of fraudulence. *Science* 169, 3947; p. 789.

O'Connor, A. (2003) Geology, Archaeology and 'the Raging Vortex of the "Eolith" Controversy'. *Proceedings of the Geologists' Association* 114; pp. 255–262.

O'Connor, S. (1987) The identification of osseous and keratinaceous materials from York. In: Starling and Watkinson (eds), 1987, pp. 9–21.

O'Connor, S., Maher, J. and Janaway, R. (2002) Towards a replacement for xeroradiography. *The Conservator* 26; pp. 100–113.

Oddy, W.A. (1977) The production of gold wire in antiquity. *Gold Bulletin* 10, 3; pp. 79–87.

Oddy, W.A. (1979) Hand-made wire in antiquity: A correction. *MASCA Journal* 1, 2; pp. 44–45.

Oddy, W.A. (1980) Swaged wire from the Bronze Age? *MASCA Journal* 1, 4; pp. 110–111.

Oddy, W.A. (1984) Gold in the Southern African Iron Age. *Gold Bulletin* 17, 2; pp. 70–78.

Oddy, W.A. (ed). (1988) *Metallurgy in Numismatics* II. Royal Numismatic Society, Special Publication 19, London.

Oddy, W.A. (ed) (1992) *The Art of the Conservator*. British Museum Press, London.

Oddy, A. (ed). (1994) *Restoration: Is It Acceptable?* British Museum Occasional Paper 99, London.

Oddy, W.A. (1994) Gold foil, strip, and wire in the Iron Age of southern Africa. In: Scott *et al.* (eds), 1994, pp. 183–196.

Oddy, A. (1998) The analysis of coins by the specific gravity method. In: Oddy and Cowell (eds), 1998, pp. 147–157.

Oddy, W.A. and Meeks, N.D. (1981) Pseudo-gilding: An example from the Roman period. *MASCA Journal* 1, 7; pp. 211–213.

Oddy, W.A., Cowell, M.R., Craddock P.T. and Hook, D.R. (1990) The gilding of bronze sculpture in the classical world. In: True and Podany (eds), 1990a, pp. 103–124.

Oddy, W.A. and Holmes, R. (1992) The Hockwold Treasure. In: Oddy (ed), 1992, pp. 137–150.

Oddy, A. and Cowell, M. (eds) (1998) *Metallurgy in Numismatics* IV. Royal Numismatic Society, Special Publication 30, London.

Oddy, A. and Smith, S. (eds) (2001) *Past Practice – Future Prospects.* British Museum Occasional Paper 145, London.

Odegaard, N., Carroll, S. and Zimmt, W.S. (2000) *Material Characterization Tests for Objects of Art and Archaeology.* Archetype Publications, London.

O'Donoghue, M. (1997) *Synthetic, Imitation and Treated Gemstones.* Butterworth-Heinemann, Oxford.

O'Donoghue, M. (2005) *Artificial Gemstones.* NAG Press, London.

O'Donoghue, M. (ed) (2006) *Gems.* Butterworth-Heinemann, Oxford.

O'Donoghue, M. and Joyner, L. (2003) *The Identification of Gemstones.* Butterworth-Heinemann, Oxford.

Offmann, B., Juranek, H. and Zamarchi Grassi, P. (1995) Some observations on the manufacturing techniques of Arretine terra sigillata with relief colors. In: *The Ceramics Cultural Heritage: Proceedings of the 8th International CIMTEC-World Ceramics Congress,* P. Vincenzini (ed). Monographs in Materials and Society 2. Techna, Faenza, pp. 229–239.

Ogden, J.M. (1976) The so-called 'platinum' inclusions in Egyptian goldwork. *The Journal of Egyptian Archaeology* **62**; pp. 138–144.

Ogden, J.M. (1977) Platinum Group metal inclusions in Ancient Gold Antiquities. *Journal of the Historical Metallurgy Society* **11**, 2; pp. 53–72.

Ogden, J.M. (1982) *Jewellery of the Ancient World.* Trefoil Books, London.

Ogden, J. (1985) Potentials and problems in the scientific study of ancient gold artefacts. In: England and van Zelst (eds), 1985, pp. 72–75.

Ogden, J.M. (1991) Classical gold wire: Some aspects of its manufacture and use. *Jewellery Studies* **5**; pp. 95–106.

Ogden, J.M. (1992) *Ancient Jewellery.* British Museum Press, London.

Ogden, J. (1993) Some eighteenth and nineteenth century jewellery alloys. *Jewellery Studies* **6**; pp. 77–79.

Ogden, J. (1994) The technology of medieval jewelry. In: Scott *et al.* (eds), 1994, pp. 153–182.

Ogden, J. (1996) The pearl in classical jewellery. *Jewellery Studies* **7**; pp. 37–42.

Ogden, J. (1998) The jewellery of Dark Age Greece: Construction and cultural connections. In: Williams (ed), 1998, pp. 14–21; esp. p. 18, Appendix 1.

Ogden, J. (2000) Early pearly. *Gem and Jewellery News* **9**, 4; p. 62. September.

Ogden, J. (2003) Connections between Islam, Europe, and the Far East in the Medieval Period: The evidence of jewelry technology. In: Jett (ed), 2003, pp. 2–7.

Ogden, J.M. and Schmidt, S. (1990) Late antique jewellery: Pierced work and hollow beaded wire. *Jewellery Studies* **4**; pp. 5–12.

O'Grady, C. (2006) The occurrence of rock varnish on stone and ceramic artefacts. *Reviews in Conservation* **6**; pp. 31–37.

O'Keefe, P.J. (1995) Conservation and actions for recovery of stolen or unlawfully exported cultural heritage. In: Tubb (ed), 1995, pp. 73–82.

O'Keefe, P.J. (1997) *Trade in Antiquities: Reducing Destruction and Theft.* UNESCO & Archetype Publications, London.

Okil, E.N. (2004) How appraisers deal with authenticity. In: Weiss and Chartier (eds), 2004, pp. 219–234.

Oldfield, E. (1855) *A Catalogue of Select Examples of Ivory Castings from the Second to the 16th Centuries.* The Arundel Society, London.

Olin, J.S. (2000) Without comparative studies of inks, what do we know about the Vinland Map? *Pre-Columbiana* **2**, 1; pp. 27–36.

Olin, J.S. (2003) Evidence that the Vinland Map is medieval. *Analytical Chemistry* **75**, 23; pp. 6745–6747.

Olin, J.S. and Sayre, E.V. (1974) Neutron activation analytical survey of some intact medieval glass panels and related specimens. In: Beck (ed), 1974, pp. 100–123.

Olin, J.S. and Towe, K.M. (1976) Abstracts for the International Congress for the History of Cartography, Washington DC, p. 25.

Olin, J.S., Harbottle, G. and Sayre, E.V. (1978) Elemental compositions of Spanish and Spanish-colonial majolica ceramics in the identification of provenience. In: Carter (ed), 1978, pp. 200–229.

Olin, J.S. and Franklin, A.D. (eds) (1982) *Archaeological Ceramics.* Smithsonian Institution Press, Washington DC.

Olin, J.S. and Blackman, M.J. (eds) (1986) *Proceedings of the 24th International Archaeometry Symposium,* Smithsonian Institution Press, Washington DC.

Olsen, S.L. (1988) The identification of stone and metal tools on some bone artifacts in: Olsen (ed), 1988, pp. 337–360.

Olsen, S.L. (ed). (1988) *Scanning Electron Microscopy in Archaeology.* British Archaeological Reports International Series 452, Oxford.

Oman, C. (1965) *English Domestic Silver.* A. and C. Black, London.

O'Neill, J.P. (ed) (1996) *Enamels of Limoges 1100–1350.* Metropolitan Museum of Art, New York.

Opper, T. (2005) Glory of Rome restored. *British Museum Magazine* **51**; pp. 38–40.

Organ, R.M. (1961) A new treatment for 'bronze disease'. *Museums Journal* **63**, 1; pp. 54–56.

Organ, R.M. (1967) The reclamation of the wholly-mineralized silver in the Ur Lyre. In: Young (ed), 1967, pp. 126–144, esp. pp. 131–132.

Organ, R.M. (1970) The conservation of bronze objects. In: Doeringer, Mitten and Steinberg (eds), 1970, pp. 73–83.

Organ, R.M. and Mandarino, J.A. (1971) Romarchite and hydroromarchite, two new stannous minerals. *The Canadian Mineralogist* **10**; p. 916.

Orna, M.V. (ed). (1996) *Archaeological Chemistry.* American Chemical Society Symposium Series 625, Washington DC.

Ortiz, G. (1990) Connoisseurship and Antiquity. In: True and Podany (eds), 1990, pp. 253–280.

Osborn, H.F. (1921) The Dawn man of Piltdown, Sussex. *Natural History* **21**; pp. 577–590.

Ost, H. (1984) *Falsche Frauen.* König, Cologne.

Otte, M. and Hurt, V. (1982–83) Les gaines d'herminettes découvertes à Gendron et à Boom: Un example de décèlement de faux. *Bulletin de Institut Royal du Patrimoine Artistique* 19; pp. 115–119.

Otto, H. (1957) Die chemische Untersuchungen von gefälschten Bronzen aus mitteldeutschen Mussen. *Wissenschaftlich Zeitschrift der Martin-Luther Universität Halle-Wittenberg* 7, 1; pp. 203–230.

Otto, H. (1979) *Das chemische Laboratorium der Königlichen Museen in Berlin, Berliner Beiträge zur Archäometrie* 4; pp. 1–304.

Padfield, J., Saunders, D., Cupitt, J. and Atkinson, R. (2002) Recent improvements in the acquisition and processing of X-ray images of paintings. *National Gallery Technical Bulletin* 23; pp. 62–75.

Padfield, T. and Landi, S. (1966) The light-fastness of natural dyes. *Studies in Conservation* 11, 4; pp. 181–196.

Pagan, H.E. (1971) Mr. Emery's Mint. *The British Numismatic Journal* 40; pp. 139–170.

Page, A. (1992) The Avar Treasure: Hot art, cold cash. *Art and Auction*; pp. 92–99, 130, 136 March.

Page, J-A., Pilosi, L. and Wypyski, M.T. (2001) Ancient mosaic glass or modern reproductions? *Journal of Glass Studies* 43; pp. 115–139.

Pagè-Camagna, Duval, A. and Guicharnaud, H. (2004) Study of Gustave Moreau's black drawings: Identification of the graphic materials by Raman microspectrometry and PIXE. In: Kiefer (ed), 2004, pp. 628–632.

Painter, G.D. (1995) Introduction to the New Edition. In: Skelton *et al.*, 1995,. pp.ix–xx.

Painter, K.S. (1977) *The Water Newton Early Christian Silver.* British Museum Publications, London.

Painter, K.S. (1981) A Roman silver ingot from Reculver, Kent. *The Antiquaries Journal* 61, 2; pp. 340–341.

Panczyk, E., Ligeza, M. and Walis, L. (1992) Trace elements in lead white from sacral paintings of the 15th century determined by instrumental neutron activation analysis. *Nukleonika* 37, 4; pp. 29–41.

Papachristou, O. (1996) Armour of a warrior from the Amir Temur citadel. *Obshchestvennye nauki y Uzbekistane* 7-10; pp. 148–153. [In Russian.].

Pappalardo, L., Romano, F.P. and Garraffo, S. (2003) The improved LNS PIXE-alpha portable system: Archaeometric applications. *Archaeometry* 45, 2; pp. 333–339.

Parsons, C.S.M. and Curl, F.H. (1963) *China Mending and Restoration.* Faber and Faber, London.

Parsons, H.W. (1962) The art of fake Etruscan art. *Art News* pp. 34–37, 68. February.

Paul, E. (1981) *Gefälschte: Antike von der Renaissance bis zur Gegenwart.* Koehler and Amelang, Leipzig.

Paulitsch, P. and Wittmer, S. (1987) Tin corrosion products on objects of art. In: Black (ed), 1987, pp. 163–164.

Pavlova, O.I. (1963) *Electrodeposition of metals, a historical survey*, S.A. Pogodin, Moscow (ed). Springfield, Washington. [English translation 1968, US Department of Commerce, Israel Program of Scientific Translations, Jerusalem].

Peacock, D.P.S. (1970) The scientific analysis of ancient ceramics: a review. *World Archaeology* 1; pp. 375–389.

Peacock, D.P.S. (1973) Forged brick-stamps from Pevensey. *Antiquity* 47, 186; pp. 138–140.

Peacock, D.P.S. (1976) The petrography of certain Glozelian sherds. *Journal of Archaeological Science* 3, 3; pp. 271–274.

Peacock, D. and Williams, D. (1997) A little bit of dirt. *Journal of Archaeological Science* 24, 12; pp. 1089–1091.

Peacock, D.P.S., Williams-Thorpe, O., Thorpe, R.S. and Tindle, A.G. (1994) Mons Claudianus and the problem of the 'granito del foro': A geological and geochemical approach. *Antiquity* 68, 259; pp. 209–230.

Pearce, M. (1982) 4000 years of sheet metal forming. In: *Formability of Metallic Materials – 2000 AD.* Proceedings of Chicago Conference June 24th–25th 1980, ASTM, Philadelphia, pp. 3–18.

Pearson, G.W. and Stuiver, M. (1986) High-precision calibration of the radiocarbon time scale 500–2500 BC. *Radiocarbon* 28, 2B; pp. 839–862.

Pearson, K. and Connor, P. (1967) *The Dorak Affair.* Michael Joseph, London.

Peck, C.W. (1964) *English Copper, Tin and Bronze Coins in the British Museum, 1558–1958*, 2nd edn. Trustees of the British Museum, London.

Pedeferri, P. (1994) La decorazione elettrochimica del titanio e l'arte della metallocromia de Leopoldo Nobili. *Ceramica informazione: periodico technico specializzato* 340; pp. 395–406.

Pellicori, S. and Evans, M.S. (1981) The Shroud of Turin through the microscope. *Archaeology* 34, 1; pp. 34–43.

Penniman, T.K. (1952) *Pictures of Ivory and other Animal Teeth, Bone and Antler*, Occasional Papers on Technology 5. Pitt Rivers Museum, Oxford.

Penny, N. (1993) *The Materials of Sculpture.* Yale University Press, Newhaven and London.

Pensabene, P., Lazzarini, L. and Turi, B. (2002) New archaeometric investigations on the fragments of the colossal statue of Constantine in the Palazzo dei Conservatori. In: Herrmann Jr, Herz and Newman (eds), 2002, pp. 250–255.

Percy, H.M. (1965) *New Materials in Sculpture*, 2nd edn. Alec Tiranti, London.

Percy, J. (1861) *Metallurgy Fuel; Fire-clays; Copper; Zinc; Brass.* John Murray, London.

Perez-y-Jorba, M., Rommeluere, M. and Mazerolles, L. (1993) Etude de la deterioration d'une plaque d'email peint de Limoges. *Studies in Conservation* 38, 3; pp. 206–212.

Perlman, I. and Asaro, F. (1969) Pottery analysis by neutron activation. *Archaeometry* 11, 1; pp. 21–52.

Pernice, E. (1910a) Untersuchungen zur antiken Toreutik, V. Natürliche und künstliche Patina im Altertum. *Jahreshefte des Österreichischen Archäologischn Institutes in Wien* 13; pp. 102–107.

Pernice, E. (1910b) Bronze Patina und Bronzetechnik in Altertum. *Zeitschrift für Bildende Kunst* **21**; pp. 219–224.

Pernicka, E. (1993) Evaluating lead isotope data: further observations: Comments... III. *Archaeometry* **35**, 2; pp. 259–262.

Pernicka, E. (1999) Trace element fingerprinting of ancient copper: A guide to technology or provenance? In: Young *et al.* (eds), 1999, pp. 163–171.

Pernicka, E. and Wagner, G.A. (eds) (1991) *Archaeometry '90*. Birkhäuser Verlag, Basel.

Peterson, A.G. (1963) Glass reproductions. *Hobbies Magazine* **68**, 3; pp. 64–65.

Peterson, H.L. (1975) *How Do You Know it's OLD?* Charles Scribner's Sons, New York.

Peterson, S. (1995) *The Craft and Art of Clay: A Complete Potter's Handbook*, 2nd edn. King, Laurens London.

Petrie, W.M.Flinders. (1888) The treatment of small antiquities. *The Archaeological Journal* **45**; pp. 85–89.

Petrie, W.M.Flinders. and Quibell, J.E. (1896) *Naqada and Ballas*. Egypt Exploration Society, London.

Pfanner, M. (1989) Über das Herstellen von Porträts. Ein Beitrag zu Rationalisierungmassnahmen und Produktionmechanismen von Massenware im späten Hellenismus und in der römischen Kaiserzeit. *JDAI* **104**; pp. 157–257.

Philippon, J., Bossiere, G. and Beillard, B. (1988) Examen par microscopie électonique à balayage des altérations d'emaux peints du XVIème siècle. In: Istituto.Centrale Per Il Restauro & Associazione Italiana Prove Non Distruttive (eds), pp. V/8.1–V/8.11.

Phillips, F.M., Zreda, M.G., Elmore, D. and Sharma, P. (1996) A reevaluation of cosmogenic 36Cl production rates in terrestrial rocks. *Geophysical Research Letters* **23**, 9; pp. 949–952.

Phillips, F.M., Flinsch, M., Elmore, D. and Sharma, P. (1997) Maximum ages of the Côa valley (Portugal) engravings measured with Chlorine-36. *Antiquity* **71**, 271; pp. 100–104.

Phillips, T.J. (1989) *Shroud Irradiated with Neutrons? Letter to Nature* **337**, 6208; p. 594. 16 February.

Pichler, B. and Erlach, R. (1987/88) Metallographische Befundungen am Bronzguß. In: 'Jüngling', 1987/88, pp. 304–317.

Pichler, B. and Vendl, A. (1987) Authentication of a Renaissance bronze statue. In: Black (ed), 1987, pp. 169–172.

Pickford, I. (1983) *Silver Flatware*. Antique Collectors' Club, Woodbridge, Suffolk.

Pickford, I. (ed) (1989) *Jackson's Silver and Gold Marks of England, Scotland and Ireland*. Antique Collectors' Club, Woodbridge, Suffolk.

Picón, C.A. (1983) *Cavaceppi: 18th Century Restoration of Ancient Marble Sculpture in English Private Collections*. Exhibition Catalogue, Clarendon Galleries, London.

Picon, M. (1976) Remarques preliminaries sur deux types d'altération de la composition chimiques des céramiques au cours du temps. *Figlina* **1**, Lyon; pp. 159–166.

Picon, M. (1991a) L'analyse par activation neurtonique est-elle la meilleure méthode que l'on puisse employer pour déterminer l'origine des céramiques? *Revue d'Archéométrie* **15**; pp. 95–102.

Picon, M. (1991b) Quelques observations complémentaires sur les altérations de composition des céramiques au cours du temps: Cas de quelques alcalins et alcalino-terreux. *Revue d'Archéométrie* **15**; pp. 117–122.

Picouet, P., Maggetti, M., Piponnier, D. and Schvoerer, M. (1999) Cathodoluminescence Spectroscopy of Quartz Grains as a Tool for Ceramic Provenance. In: *Proceedings of the International Symposium on Archaeometry*, University of Illinois at Urbana, 20-24th May 1996, J. Henderson, H. Neff and T. Rehren (eds). A special issue of *Journal of Archaeological Science* **26**, 8; pp. 943–950.

Pilc, J. and White, R. (1995) The application of FTIR-microscopy to the analysis of paint binders in easel paintings. *National Gallery Technical Bulletin* **16**; pp. 73–84.

Pilosi, L. and Wypyski, M.T. (2002a) Two Roman engraved glasses in the Metropolitan Museum of Art. *Journal of Glass Studies* **44**; pp. 25–34.

Pilosi, L. and Wypyski, M.T. (2002b) The Weathering of Ancient Cold Worked Glass Surfaces. In: *Proceedings of the First International Conference 'Hyalos-Vitrium-Glass: History, Technology and Conservation of Glass and Vitreous Materials in the Ancient World'*, G. Kordas (ed). 'Glasnet' Publications, Athens, pp. 101–107

Pinet, M., Smith, D.C. and Lasnier, B. (1992) Utilité de la microsonde Raman pour l'identification non destructive des gemmes. In: *La Microsonde Raman en Gemmologie*, special issue of *Revue de Gemmologie* Association Française de Gemmologie, Paris, pp. 11–60.

Pinkus, G. (1910) Das Wachs der Florabüste. *Chemiker-Zeitung* **34**, 38; p. 277.

Pini, I. (1998) The 'Ring of Nestor'. *Oxford Journal of Archaeology* **17**, 1; pp. 1–14.

Pinn, K. (1999) *Paktong: The Chinese Alloy in Europe*. The Antique Collectors Club, Woodbridge, Suffolk.

Plenderleith, H.J. (1935) The re-engraving of old silver. *Bulletin of the American Institute for Persian Art and Archaeology* **4**, 2; pp. 72–73.

Plenderleith, H.J. (1933) Scientific examination of an 11th century Persian silver salver. *The Museums Journal* **33**, 3; pp. 280–284.

Plenderleith, H.J. (1952) Fakes and Forgeries in Museums. *The Museums Journal* **52**, 6; pp. 143–148.

Plenderleith, H.J. (1956) *The Conservation of Antiquities and Works of Art*. Oxford University Press, London.

Plenderleith, H.J. and Organ, R. (1953) The decay and corrosion of museum objects of tin. *Studies in Conservation* **1**, 2; pp. 63–72.

Plenderleith, H.J. and Werner, A.E.A. (1971) *The Conservation of Antiquities and Works of Art*, 2nd edn. Oxford University Press, London.

Plesters, J. (1955–56) Cross-section and chemical analysis of paint samples. *Studies in Conservation* **2**, 3; pp. 110–157.

Plesters, J. (1993) Ultramarine blue, natural and artificial. In: Roy (ed), 1993, pp. 37–65.

Podany, J. (1994) Restoring what wasn't there: Reconsideration of the eighteenth-century restoration to the Lansdowne *Herakles* in the collection of the J. Paul Getty Museum. In: Oddy (ed), 1994, pp. 9–18.

Poinar, G.O. and Poinar, R. (1994) *The Quest for Life in Amber.* Addison-Wesley, Reading MA.

Polikreti, K. (2007) Detection of ancient marble forgery: Techniques and limitations. *Archaeometry* 49, 4; pp. 603–619.

Polikreti, K., Michael, C. and Maniatis, Y. (2000) An approach to authentication and dating of marble artifacts and monuments with thermoluminescence. In: Schilardi and Katsonopoulou (eds), 2000, pp. 609–617.

Polikreti, K. and Maniatis, Y. (2002) A new methodology for the provenance of marble based on EPR spectroscopy. *Archaeometry* 44, 1; pp. 1–21.

Pollard, A.M. and Hatcher, H. (1986) The chemical analysis of oriental ceramic body compositions. Part 2: Greenwares. In: *Journal of Archaeological Science* 13, 3; pp. 261–287.

Pollard, A.M. and Wood, N.D. (1986) Development of Chinese porcelain technology at Jingdezhen. In: Olin and Blackman (eds). pp. 105–114.

Pollard, A.M., Thomas, R.G. and Williams, P.A. (1989) Synthesis and stabilities of the basic copper (II) chlorides, atacamite, paratacamite and botallackite. *Mineralogical Magazine* 53; pp. 557–563.

Pollard, A.M., Thomas, R.G. and Williams, P.A. (1990) Mineralogical changes arising from the use of aqueous sodium carbonate solutions for the treatment of archaeological copper objects. *Studies in Conservation* 35, 3; pp. 148–152.

Pollard, A.M., Thomas, R.G. and Williams, P.A. (1992) The copper chloride system and corrosion: A complex interplay of kinetic and thermodynamic factors. In: Drayman-Weisser (ed), 1992, pp. 123–133.

Pollard, A.M. and Hatcher, H. (1994) The chemical analysis of oriental ceramic body compositions. Part 1: Wares from north China. *Archaeometry* 36, 1; pp. 41–62.

Pollard, M. and Heron, C. (1996) *Archaeological Chemistry.* The Royal Society of Chemistry, Cambridge.

Pollens, S. (1999) Le Messie. *The Journal of the Violin Society of America* 16; pp. 77–101.

Pols, R. (1993) *Dating Old Photographs.* Countryside Books, Newbury, Berks.

Pomiès, M.-P., Menu, M. and Vignaud, C. (1999) Red Palaeolithic pigments: Natural hematite or heated goethite? *Archaeometry* 41, 2; pp. 275–286.

Ponahlo, J. (1992) Cathodoluminescence (CL) and CL spectra of De Beers experimental synthetic diamonds. *The Journal of Gemmology* 23, 1; pp. 3–17.

Ponahlo, J. (2002) Inclusions in gemstones: Their cathodoluminescence (CL) and CL spectra. *The Journal of Gemmology* 28, 2; pp. 85–100.

Ponting, M.J. (2003) From Damascus to Denia: The scientific analysis of three groups of Fatimid period metalwork. *Journal of the Historical Metallurgy Society* 37, 2; pp. 85–105.

Pope, A.U. (1939) The general problem of falsifications. *Mémoires de IIIrd Congrès International d'Art et d'Archéologie Iraniens,* Leningrad, Septembre 1935. Académie des Sciences de l'URSS, Moscow and Leningrad, pp. 177–195.

Porten Palange, F.P. (1990) Fälschungen aus Arezzo: Die gefälschten arretinischen Punzen und Formen und ihre Geschichte. *Jahrbuch des Römisch-Germanischen ZentralMuseums Mainz* 37; pp. 521–652.

Postma, H., Schillebeeckx, P. and Halbertsma, R.B. (2004) Neutron resonance capture analysis of some genuine and fake Etruscan copper alloy statuettes. *Archaeometry* 46, 4; pp. 635–646.

Potts, P.J. (1987) *A Handbook of Silicate Rock Analysis.* Blackie, Glasgow.

Potts, P.J., Webb, P.C. and Watson, J.S. (1985) Energy-dispersive X-ray fluorescence analysis of silicate rocks: Comparisons with wavelength-dispersive performance. *Analyst (London)* 110; pp. 507–513.

Pousset, D. (2000) La dendrochronologie appiliquée au mobilier. *Coré: Conservation et Restauration du Patriomoine* 8; pp. 19–24.

Pradell, T., Vendrell-Saz, M., Krumbein, W.E. and Picon, M. (1996) Altérations de céramiques en milieu marin: Les amphores de l'épave romaine de la Madrague de Giens (Var). *Revue d'Archéométrie* 20; pp. 47–56.

Prag, A.J.N.W. (1972) Athena Mancuniensis: Another copy of the Athena Parthenos. *Journal of Hellenic Studies* 92; pp. 96–114.

Prag, A.J.N.W. (1983) Athena Parthenos: A nineteenth-century forger's workshop. *Journal of Hellenic Studies* 103; pp. 151–154.

Preusser, F.D. (2002) Evaluating the authenticity of jade objects. In: Childs-Johnson (ed), 2002, pp. 13–14.

Priest, D.J. (1992) Paper conservation: Some polymeric aspects. In: Allen *et al.* (eds), 1992, pp. 159–183.

Prudêncio, M.I., Figueiredo, M.O., Waerenborgh, J.C., Pereira, L.C.J, Gouveia, M.A., Silva, T.P., Morgado, I., Costa, I.R. and Rodrigues, J.D. (1995) Alteration of granite stones of 'Anta Do Zambujerio'. In: Maniatis, Herz and Basiakos (eds), 1995, pp. 285–289.

de Puma, R.D. (2002) Forgeries of Etruscan engraved mirrors. In: *From the Parts to the Whole II: Acta of the 13th International Bronze Congress,* C.C. Mattusch, A. Brauer and S.E. Knudsen (eds). *Journal of Roman Archaeology Supplementary Series* 39; Portsmouth, Rhode Island, pp. 53–64.

Quang Liem, N., Sagon, G., Quang, V.X., Tan, H.V. and Colomban, P. (2000) Raman study of the microstructure, composition and processing of ancient Vietnamese (proto)porcelains and celadons (13th–16th centuries). *Journal of Raman Spectroscopy* 31; pp. 933–942.

Quin, D.B. and Foote, P.G. (1966) The Vinland Map. *Saga-Book of the Viking Society for Northern Research* 17, 1; pp. 63–89.

Quye, A. and Keneghan, B. (1999) Degradation. In: Quye and Williamson (eds), 199, pp. 111–120.

Quye, A. and Williamson, C. (eds) (1999) *Plastics: Collecting and Conserving*. NMS Publishing, Edinburgh.

Rabinovitch, B.S. (1990) The patina of antique silver: A scientific appraisal. *The Silver Society Journal* 1; pp. 13–22.

Rackham, H. (1952) *Pliny: The Natural History IX*. [trans.], The Loeb Edition. Heinemann, London.

Radcliffe, A. (1992a) The replication of sculpture in bronze. In: *The Thyssen-Bornemisza Collection: The Renaissance and Later Sculptures with Works of Art in Bronze*, A. Radcliffe, M. Baker and M. Maek-Gérard (eds). Sotheby's, London, pp. 32–35.

Radcliffe, A. (1992b) Multiple production in the fifteenth century: Florentine stucco maddonas and the Della Robbia Workshop. In: *The Thyssen-Bornemisza Collection: The Renaissance and Later Sculptures with Works of Art in Bronze*, A. Radcliffe, M. Baker and M. Maek-Gérard (eds). Sotheby's, London, pp. 16–23.

Radnóti, S. (1999) *The Fake: Forgery and Its Place in Art*. Rowman and Littlefield, Lanham, Maryland. [Trans. E. Dunai].

Ragab, H. (1980) *Le Papyrus*. Dr Ragab Papyrus Institute, Cairo.

Raheel, M. (1994) History, identification and characterization of Old World fibers and dyes. In: *Ancient Technologies and Archaeological Materials*, S.U. Wisseman and W.S. Williams (eds). Gordon and Breach Science Publishers, Langhorne PA, pp. 121–153.

Ramage, N.H. (2003) Cavaceppi and modern Minimalism: The derestoration of Roman sculpture. In: Kunze and Rügler (eds), 2003, pp. 167–170.

Ramage, A. and Craddock, P.T. (2000) *King Croesus' Gold*. British Museum Press, London.

Ramos-Poqui, G. (1990) *The Technique of Icon Painting*. Burns and Oates, Tunbridge Wells, Kent.

Rapson, W.S. and Groenewald, T. (1978) *Gold Usage*. Academic Press, London.

Rasmussen, K.L., van der Plicht, J., Cryer, F.H., Doudna, G., Cross, F.M. and Strugnell, J. (2001) The effects of possible contamination on the radiocarbon dating of the Dead Sea Scrolls. 1: Castor oil. *Radiocarbon* 43, 1; pp. 127–132.

Rasmussen, K.L. (2001) FOCUS: Provenance of ceramics revealed by magnetic susceptibility and thermoluminescence. *Journal of Archaeological Science* 28, 5; pp. 451–456.

Rasti, F. and Scott, G. (1980) The effects of some common pigments on the photo-oxidation of linseed oil-based paint media. *Studies in Conservation* 25, 4; pp. 145–156.

Raub, Ch. (1993) The history of electroplating. In: La Niece and Craddock (eds), 1993, pp. 284–290.

Ravaud, E. (1999) Evaluation de la méthode radiographique dans l'identification des essences de bois des panneaux peints. In: *Preprints of the 12th ICOM Triennial Meeting*, Lyons, 29th August–3rd September, 1999. J. Bridgland (ed). James and James, London, pp. 391–397.

Ravaud, E. and Martin, E. (2001) Diagnostic radiologique des transpositions. *Techne* 13–14; pp. 112–119.

Rawlins, F.I.G. (1937) *The Physics and Chemistry of Painting*. Cantor Lectures, Royal Society of Arts, London.

Rawlins, I. (1940) *From the National Gallery Laboratory*. Trustees of the National Gallery, London.

Rawson, J. (1995) *Chinese Jade From the Neolithic to the Qing*. British Museum Press, London.

Read, C.H. (1893) Comments on Charles Dawson's iron statuette. *Proceedings of the Society of Antiquaries* 14; pp. 359–361.

Read, P.G. (2005) *Gemmology*, 3rd edn. Butterworth-Heinemann, Oxford.

Realini, M. and Toniolo, L. (eds) (1996) *The Oxalate Films in the Conservation of Works of Art*. Editeam, Bologna.

Redknap, M. and Freetone, I.C. (1995) Eighteenth century glass ingots from England and the Post-Medieval glass trade. In: Hook and Gaimster (eds), 1995, pp. 145–158.

Reed, R. (1972) *Ancient Skins Parchments and Leathers*. Seminar Press, London.

Reedy, C.L. (1991) Petrographic analysis of casting core materials for provenance studies of copper alloy sculptures. *Archeomaterials* 5, 2; pp. 121–163.

Reedy, C.L. (1997) *Himalayan Bronzes: Technology, Style and Choices*. University of Delaware Press, Newark and Associated University Presses, London.

Reedy, C. and Meyers, P. (1987) An interdisciplinary method for employing iechnical data to determine regional provenance of copper alloy statues. In: Black (ed), 1987, pp. 173–178.

Reeves, R. (1962) *Cire Perdue Casting in India*. Crafts Museum, New Delhi.

Regert, M., Colinart, S., Degrand, L. and Decavallas, O. (2001) Chemical alteration and use of beeswax through time: accelerated ageing tests and analysis of archaeological samples from various environmental contexts. *Archaeometry* 43, 4; pp. 549–569.

Regert, M., Langlois, J. and Colinart, S. (2005) Characterisation of wax works of art by gas chromographic procedures. *Journal of Chromatography* A, 1091; pp. 124–136.

Rehder, J.E. (1991) The decorated iron swords from Luristan: Their material and manufacture. *Iran* 29; pp. 13–19.

Rehren, Th. (1996) A Roman zinc tablet from Bern, Switzerland, reconstruction of the manufacture. In: Demirci *et al.* (eds), 1996, pp. 35–45.

Reiche, I., Pages-Camagna, S. and Lambacher, L. (2004) *In situ* Raman spectroscopic investigations of the adorning gemstones on the reliquary *Heinrich's Cross* from the treasury of Basil cathedral. In: Kiefer (ed), 2004, pp. 719–725.

Reimers, P., Riederer, J., Goebbels, J. and Kettschnau, A. (1989) Dendrochronology by means of X-ray computed tomography (CT). In: Maniatis (ed) 1989, pp. 121–125.

Reinach, S. (1927) Discoveries at Glozel, Allier. *Antiquaries Journal* 7, 1; pp. 1–5.

Reinach, S. (1928) *Ephémerides de Glozel*. KRA, Paris.

Reisner, R.G. (1950) *Fakes and Forgeries in the Fine Arts: A Bibliography*. Special Libraries Association, New York.

Reißland, B. (2002) Iron-gall ink corrosion – Progress in visible degradation. In: *Contributions to Conservation*, J.A. Mosk and N.H. Tennent (eds). James and James, London, pp. 113–118.

Rendle, D.F., Cain, P.M. and Smale, S.J.R. (1990) An inexpensive device for the examination of light objects using soft X-rays. *Measuring Science Technology* 1; pp. 986–988.

Renfrew, C. (1975) Glozel and the two cultures. *Antiquity* 49, 195; pp. 219–222.

Renfrew, C. (2000) *Loot, Legitimacy and Ownership*. Duckworth, London.

Renfrew, C. and Peacey, J.S. (1968) Aegean marble: A petrological study. *Annual of the British School at Athens* 63; pp. 45–66.

Renfrew, C. and Bahn, P. (1999) Garrod and Glozel: The end of a fiasco. In: *Dorothy Garrod and the Progress of the Paleolithic*, W. Davies and R. Charles (eds). Oxbow, Oxford. Ch. 7.

Reser, P.K. (1981) Precision casting of small fossils: An update. *Curator* 24, 3; pp. 157–180.

'*Restauratio*'(1995) *Restauration, dé-restauration, re-restauration: Colloque sur la conservation, restauration des biens culturels*. Associationdes restaurers d'art et d'archeologie de formation univsitaire, Paris.

Reuterswärd, P. (1960) *Studien zur Polychromie der Plastik (Griechenland und Rom)*. Svenska Bokforlaget, Stockholm.

Reveley, H.W. (1825) On the process of manufacturing Roman artificial pearls. *The Technical Repository* 17; pp. 235–236.

Reyntiens, P. (1977) *The Technique of Stained Glass*, 2nd edn. Batsford, London.

Rhodes, D. (1969) *Kilns: Design, Construction and Operation*. Pitman, London.

Rhodes, D. (1977) *Clay and Glazes for the Potter*. Pitman, London.

Rice, P.M. (1987) *Pottery Analysis: A Sourcebook*. University of Chicago Press, Chicago.

Rich, J.C. (1947) *The Methods and Materials of Sculpture*. Oxford University Press, New York.

Richter, E.-L. (1971) Note on the non-destructive removal of later engraving on silver. *Studies in Conservation* 16, 3; pp. 118–119.

Richter, G.M.A. (1915) *The Metropolitan Museum of Art: Greek, Etruscan and Roman Bronzes*. Metropolitan Museum of Art, New York.

Richter, G.M.A. (1929) Forgeries of Greek sculpture. *Bulletin of the Metropolitan Museum of Art* 24, 1; pp. 3–5.

Richter, G.M.A. (1937) *Etruscan Terracotta Warriors in the Metropolitan Museum of Art*, Paper no. 6. Metropolitan Museum of Art, New York.

Richter, G.M.A. (1951) *Three Critical Periods in Greek Sculpture*. Oxford University Press, Oxford.

Richter, G.M.A. (1955) *Ancient Italy*. University of Michigan Press, Ann Arbor.

Richter, G.M.A. (1962) How were the Roman Copies of Greek Portraits Made? *Römische Mitteilungen des Deutschen Archaeologischen Instituts: Abteilungen* 69; pp. 52–58.

Richter, G.M.A. (1970a) An aristogeiton from Baiae. *American Journal of Archaeology* 74; pp. 296–297.

Richter, G.M.A. (1970b) *The Sculpture and Sculptors of the Greeks*, 4th edn. Yale University Press, New Haven.

Richter, R. (1994) Between original and imitation: Four technical studies in basse-taille enameling and re-enameling of the historicism period. *Bulletin of the Cleveland Museum of Art* 81, 7; pp. 223–251.

Ridgway, B.S. (1969) Stone carving: Sculpture. In: *The Muses at Work*, C. Roebuck (ed). MIT Press, Cambridge MA, pp. 96–117.

Ridley, D.E. (1999) Scrimshaw forensics at the Kendall Whaling Museum. In: McCrone and Weiss (eds), 1999, pp. 387–396.

Ridley, D.E. (2004) Determination of authenticity of engraved scrimshaw. In: Weiss and Chartier (eds), 2004, pp. 33–54.

Riederer, J. (1975) Die Untersuchungen von Sinter und Patina zur Echteitspruefung antiker Bodenfunde. *Archäologischer Anzeiger* 2; pp. 295–299.

Riederer, J. (1976) Fälschungen von Marmor-Idolen und -Gafässen der Kykladenkultur. *Kunst der Kykladen* 94; pp. 94–96.

Riederer, J. (1977) Die Erkennung von Fälschungen kunst- und kulturgeschichtlicher Objekte aus Kupfer, Bronze und Messing durch naturwissenschaftliche Untersuchungen. *Berliner-Beiträge zur Archäometrie* 2; pp. 85–95.

Riederer, J. (1980) Metallanalysen von Statuetten der Wurzelbauer-Werkstatt in Nürnberg. *Berliner-Beiträge zur Archäometrie* 5; pp. 43–58.

Riederer, J. (1981) Naturwissenschaftliche Altersbestimmungen von Bronzen. *Kunstchronik* 1; p. 55.

Riederer, J. (1982a) Die Zusammensetzung deutscher Renaissance statuetten aus Kupferlegierungen. *Zeitschrift Deutscher Verein für Kunstwissenschaft* 36, 1–4; pp. 42–48.

Riederer, J. (1982b) Metallanalysen Nürnberger Statuetten aus der Zeit der Labenwolf-Werkstatt. *Berliner-Beiträge zur Archäometrie* 7; pp. 175–202.

Riederer, J. (1983) Metallanalysen an Erzeugnissen der Vischer-Werkstatt. *Berliner-Beiträge zur Archäometrie* 8; pp. 89–99.

Riederer, J. (1987/88) Die Nickelgehalte kulturgeschichtlicher Objekte aus Kupferlegierungen. *Wiener Berichte Über Naturwissenschaft in der Kunst* 4/5; pp. 246–255.

Riederer, J. (1988) Metallanalysen Augsburger Bronze- und Messingskulpturen des 16. Jahrhunderts. *Berliner Beiträge zur Archäometrie* 10; pp. 85–95.

Riederer, J. (1992) Zur historischen Entwicklung der Kenntnis von Korrosionprodukten auf kulturgeschichtlichen Objekten aus Kupferlegierungen. *Berliner Beiträge zur Archäometrie* 11; pp. 93–111.

Riederer, J. (1994) The goldsmithing techniques. In: *Old Javanese Gold (4th–15th century)*, W.H. Kal (ed).

Bulletin of the Royal Tropical Institute 334, KIT-Tropenmuseum Press, Amsterdam, pp. 46–57.

Riederer, J. (1995) Die Metallanalyse der Platten der mittelalterlichen Bronzetür des Augsburger Domes. *Berlin Beiträge zur Archäometrie* **13**; pp. 99–108.

Riederer, J. (1999a) Die Aussagekraft der Spurenelementkonzentrationen in mittelalterlichen Kupferlegierungen. *Berliner Beiträge zur Archäometrie* **16**; pp. 21–41.

Riederer, J. (1999b) Die Berliner Datenbank von Metallanalysen kulturgeschichtlicher Objekte. I: Objekte aus Kupferlegierungen des 19./20. Jahrhunderts. *Berliner Beiträge zur Archäometrie* **16**; pp. 251–264.

Riederer, J. (2000) Die Berliner Datenbank von Metallanalysen kulturgeschichtlicher Objekte. II: Objekte aus Kupferlegierungen des 17./18. Jahrhunderts der Renaissance und der Mittelalters. *Berliner Beiträge zur Archäometrie* **17**; pp. 143–216.

Rieth, A. (1967) *Vorzeit Gefälscht*. Ernst Wasmuth, Tübingen. [English edition, trans. D. Imber, 1970: *Archaeological Fakes*, Barrie and Jenkins, London.].

Rigby, V., Swaddling, J., Cowell, M. (1995) The Blandford Forum Group: Are any Etruscan figures true finds from Great Britain and Eire? In: *Italy in Europe: Economic Relations 700 BC – AD 50*, J. Swaddling, S. Walker and P. Roberts (eds). British Museum Occasional Paper 97, London, pp. 107–130.

'Riggisberg Report' (1973) Reports by several authors in *Bulletin de Liasion du Centre International d'Études des Textiles Anciens* **38**.

Rinaldi, P.M. (1972) *The Man in the Shroud*. Vantage Press, New York.

Rinne, D. and Frel, J. (1975) *An account of the recreation of an ancient statue*. The J. Paul Getty Museum, Malibu, California.

Rinuy, A. and Schweizer, F. (eds) (1994) *L'Oeuvre d'art sous le regard des sciences*. Musée d'art et d'histoire, Editions Slatkine, Genève.

Rioux, J.-P. (1995) Pigments organiques, liants et vernis du xxe siècle. *Techne* **2**; pp. 80–86.

Rising, B.A. (1999) Analysis of small glass samples by inductively coupled plasma (ICP) and optical emission spectroscopy (OES), Appendix A. In: Brill, Vol. 1, 1999, pp. 529–538.

Ritchie, C.I.A. (1969) *Ivory Carving*. Barker, London.

Ritchie, C.I.A. (1975) *Bone and Horn Carving: A Pictorial History*. Barnes, New Jersey.

Rivers, S. and Umney, N. (2003) *Conservation of Furniture*. Butterworth-Heinemann, Oxford.

Robbiola, L., Plowright, A. and Portier, R. (2004) A new data for improving authentication of bronze artefacts. In: *Metalla 2001*, I.D. MacLeod, J.M. Theile and C. Designy (eds). West Australia Museum, Perth, pp. 117–122.

Roberts, J.C. (1996) *The Chemistry of Paper*. Royal Society of Chemistry, Cambridge.

Roberts, P. (1997) Mass-production of Roman finewares. In: Freestone and Gaimster (eds). 1997, pp. 188–193.

Roberts, S. (ed) (1993) *The Chemistry Set*. Crafts Council, London.

Roberts Austen, W.C. (1888) Cantor lectures on alloys: Colors of metals and alloys considered in relation to their application to art. *Journal of the Society of Arts* **36**; pp. 1137–1146.

Robertson, J. (ed) (1992) *Forensic Examination of Fibres*. Ellis Horwood, London.

Robinson, P. (2003) Etruscan and other figurines from Avebury and nearby. *Wiltshire Studies* **96**; pp. 33–39.

Robson, M. (1992) Early advances in the use of acrylic resins for the conservation of antiquities. In: Allen *et al.* (eds), 1992, pp. 184–192.

Roche, A. (1993) Influence du type de chassis sur le viellissement mechanique d'une peinture sur toile. *Studies in Conservation* **38**, 1; pp. 17–24.

Rockwell, P. (1990) Some reflections on tools and faking. In: True and Podany (eds), 1990b, pp. 207–222.

Rockwell, P. (1993) *The Art of Stoneworking: A Reference Guide*. Cambridge University Press, Cambridge.

Rohl, B. and Needham, S.P. (1998) *The Circulation of Metal in the British Bronze Age: The Application of Lead Isotope Analysis*. British Museum Occasional Paper 102, London.

Rohnstock, U. (1998) Die Odyssee des 'Betenden Knaben'. Altrestaurierungen bei einer antiken Großbronze auf Wanderschaft. *Restauro*, **104**, 3; pp. 172–179.

Rolandi, V. (1999) Characterisation of recent and fossil ivory. *Australian Gemmologist* **20**, 7; pp. 266–276.

Romey, K.M. and Rose, M. (2001) Saga of the Persian Princess. *Archaeology* **54**, 1; pp. 24–25. Jan/Feb.

Rorimer, J.J. (1931) *Ultra-Violet Rays and their Use in the Examination of Works of Art*. Metropolitan Museum of Art, New York.

Rose, T.K. (1915) *The Metallurgy of Gold*, 6th edn. Charles Griffin, London.

Rosen, B.R. (1990). Appendix on the precious coral inlays. In: *The Basse-Yutz Find: Masterpieces of Celtic Art*, J.V.S. and M. Ruth Megaw. The Society of Antiquaries, London, pp. 78–81.

Rosenfeld, A., Dvorachek, M. and Amorai-Stark, S. (2003) Roman wheel-cut engraving, dyeing and painting microquartz gemstones. *Journal of Archaeological Science* **30**, 2; pp. 227–238.

Ross, A. (1998) *Amber*. The Natural History Museum, London.

Rostoker, W. and Bronson, B. (1990) *Pre-industrial Iron*. Archaeomaterials, Philadelphia.

Rots, V. (2003) Towards an understanding of hafting: The macro- and microscopic evidence. *Antiquity* **77**, 298; pp. 805–815.

Rottländer, R. (1988) Untersuchungen zur Echtheitsfrage der Flora-Büste. *Berliner Beiträge zur Archäometrie* **10**; pp. 139–149.

Rouse, J.D. (1986) *Garnet*. Butterworths, London.

Rouse, J. (2006) Composite Gemstones. In: O'Donoghue, 2006, pp. 531–544.

Roux, V. (ed) (2000) *Cornaline de l'Inde*. Éditions de la Maison des sciences de l'homme, Paris.

Roux, V. and Courty, M.-A. (1998) Identification of wheel-fashioning methods: Technological analysis of 4th–3rd millennium BC oriental ceramics. *Journal of Archaeological Science* **25**, 8; pp. 747–763.

Rowe, T., Ketcham, R.A., Denison, C., Colbert, M., Xing Xu. and Currie, P.J. (2001) The Archaeoraptor forgery. *Nature* **410**, 6828; pp. 539–540. 29 March.

Rowlett, R.M. (1975) Hazards of radiography and high energy light exposure for thermoluminescence analysis. *Current Anthropology* **16**; p. 263.

Rowlett, R.M. (1993) Authenticity test of the golden Celtic warrior fibula. In: *Studies in Mediterranean Archaeolgy* **101**; pp. 199–226.

Rowlett, R.M., Mandeville, M.D. and Zeller, E.J. (1974) The interpretation and dating of humanly worked siliceous materials by thermoluminescent analysis. *Proceedings of the Prehistoric Society* **40**; pp. 37–44.

Roy, A. (ed) (1993) *Artists' Pigments*, II. National Gallery of Art, Washington.

Roy, M.A. (2006) Scientific methods used in the authentication of metal artefacts. *Arts of Asia* **36**, 3; pp. 138–147.

Rudin, B. (1990) *Making Paper*. Rudin, Välingby.

Rudoe, J. (1984) *A Catalogue of the Hull Grundy Gift to the British Museum: Jewellery, Engraved Gems and Goldsmiths' Work*, H. Tait (ed). British Museum Press, London.

Rudoe, J. (1989) From Oroide to Platinageld: Imitation jewellery in the late nineteenth century. *Jewellery Studies* **3**; pp. 49–72.

Rudoe, J. (1991) Alessandro Castellani's letters to Henry Layard: Extracts concerning the 1862 International Exhibition in London and the revival of granulation. *Jewellery Studies* **5**; pp. 107–119.

Rudoe, J. (1992) The faking of gems in the eighteenth century. In: Jones (ed), 1992, pp. 23–31.

Rummonds, R.-G. (1998) *Printing on the Iron Handpress*. Oak Knoll Press, New Castle. Delaware and the British Library, London.

Russell, M. (2000) Of flint mines and fossil men: The Lavant Caves deception. *Oxford Journal of Archaeology* **19**, 1; pp. 105–108.

Russell, M. (2003) *Piltdown Man: The Secret Life of Charles Dawson and the World's Greatest Archaeological Hoax*. Tempus Publications, Stroud, Gloucestershire.

Ryback, G., Clark, A.M. and Stanley, C.J. (1998) Re-examination of the A.W.G. Kingsbury collection of British Minerals at the Natural History Museum, London. *The Geological Curator* **6**, 9; pp. 317–322.

Rye, O.S. (1977) Pottery manufacturing techniques: X-ray studies. *Archaeometry* **19**, 2; pp. 205–211.

Rye, O.S. (1981) *Pottery technology: Principles and Reconstruction*. Taraxacum, Washington DC.

Saenger, P. (1998) Vinland re-read. *Imago Mundi* **50**; pp. 199–202.

Saltron, F., Bouquillon, A. and Querré, G. (1992) Terracottas around Clodion: Chemical and mineralogical studies and thermoluminescence analysis. In: Vandiver et al. (eds), 1992, pp. 621–626.

Salzman, L.F. (1908) Excavations at Pevensey, 1906–7. *Sussex Archaeological Collections* **51**; pp. 99–114.

Sandon, J. (1997) *Starting to Collect Antique Porcelain*. The Antique Collectors Club, Woodbridge, Suffolk.

Santallier, D., Fillion, J.-P. and Mignot, A. (1998) A propos de ce que l'on appelle les 'roches vertes' en archéologie. *Revue d'Archéométrie* **22**; pp. 45–55.

Sato, M., Mmura, M. and Yamasaki, K. (2003) Studies on archaeological ambers in Japan. In: Jett (ed), 2003, pp. 8–14.

Sauer, R., Pichler, B. and Weber, J. (1987/88) Untersuchungen am Kernmaterial. In: 'Jüngling', 11987/88, pp. 318–331.

Saunders, D., Cupitt, J. and Padfield, J. (2006) Digital imaging for easel painting. In: MacDonald (ed), 2006, pp. 521–548.

Savage, L.G.G. (1954) *Porcelain through the Ages*. Pelican Books, Harmondsworth, Middx.

Savage, L.G.G. (1968) *A Concise History of Bronzes*. Thames and Hudson, London.

Savage, G. (1976) *Forgeries, Fakes and Reproductions: A Handbook for the Collector*. White Lion Publishers, London.

Savkevich, S.S. (1981) Physical methods used to determine the geological origin of amber and other fossil resin: Some critical remarks. *Physics and Chemistry of Minerals* **7**, 1; pp. 7–23.

Sax, M. and Meeks, N.D. (1994) The introduction of wheel cutting as a technique for engraving cylinder seals: Its distinction from filing. *Iraq* **56**; pp. 153–166.

Sax, M. and Meeks, N.D. (1995) Methods of engraving Mesopotamian quartz cylinder seals. *Archaeometry* **37**, 1; pp. 25–36.

Sax, M., McNabb, J. and Meeks, N.D. (1998) Methods of engraving Mesopotamian cylinder seals: Experimental confirmations. *Archaeometry* **40**, 1; pp. 1–21.

Sax, M., Meeks, N.D. and Collon, D. (2000a) The introduction of the lapidary engraving wheel in Mesopotamia. *Antiquity* **74**, 284; pp. 380–387.

Sax, M., Meeks, N.D. and Collon, D. (2000b) The early development of the lapidary engraving wheel in Mesopotamia. *Iraq* **62**; pp. 157–176.

Sax, M., Meeks, N.D., Michaelson, C. and Middleton, A.P. (2004) The identification of carving techniques on Chinese jade. *Journal of Archaeological Science* **51**, 10; pp. 1413–1428.

Sax, M., Walsh, J.M., Freestore, I.C., Rankin, A.H. and Mecks, N.D. (2008) The origins of two purportedly pre-Columbian crystal skulls, *Journal of Archaeological Science* **35**, pp. 2751–2760.

Sayre, E.V. and Lechtmann, H.N. (1968) Neutron activation autoradiography of oil paintings. *Studies in Conservation* **13**, 4; pp. 161–185.

Sayre, E.V., Vandiver, P.B., Drusik, J. and Stevenson, C. (eds) (1988) *Materials Issues in Art and Archaeology*. Materials Research Society, Pittsburgh.

Scarfe, H. (1975) *The Lapidary Manual*. B.T. Batsford, London.

Scharf, A., Kretschmer, W., Morgenroth, G., Uhl, T., Kritzler, K., Hunger, K. and Pernicka, E. (2004)

Radiocarbon Dating of Iron Artifacts at the Erlangen AMS Facility. *Proceedings of the 18th International Radiocarbon Conference*, N. Beavan Athfield and R.J. Sparks (eds). *Radiocarbon* **46**, 1; pp. 175–180.

Schilardi, D.U. and Katsonopoulou, D. (eds) (2000) π PIA ΑΙΘΟΣ *Paria Lithos: Parian Quarries, Marble and Workshops of Sculpture*. Paros and Cyclades Institute of Archaeology, Athens.

Schilling, M.R., Khanjian, H.P. and Souza, L.A.C. (1996) Gas chromatographic analysis of amino acids as ethyl chloroformate derivatives. Part 1: Composition of proteins associated with art objects and monuments. *Journal of the American Institute for Conservation* **35**, 1; pp. 45–59.

Schilling, M.R. and Khanjian, H.P. (1996a) Gas chromatographic analysis of amino acids as ethyl chloroformate derivatives. Part 2: Effects of pigments and accelerated aging on the identification of proteinaceous binding material. *Journal of the American Institute for Conservation* **35**, 2; pp. 123–144.

Schilling, M.R. and Khanjian H.P. (1996b) Gas chromatographic determination of the fatty acid and glycerol content of lipids. I. The effects of pigments and aging on the composition of oil paints. In: Bridgland (ed), 1996, pp. 220–227.

Schilling, M.R., Khanjian, H.P. and Carson, D.M. (1997) Fatty acid and glycerol content of lipids: Effects of ageing and solvent extraction on the composition of oil paints. *Techne* **5**; pp. 71–78.

Schilling, M.R., Carson, D.M. and Khanjian, H.P. (1999) Gas chromatographic determination of the fatty acid and glycerol content of lipids. IV. Evaporation of fatty acids and the formation of ghost images by framed oil paintings. In: *Preprints of the 12th ICOM Committee for Conservation Triennial Meeting*, Lyons, 29th August–3rd September, 1999, J. Bridgland (ed). James and James, London, pp. 242–247.

Schmid, J., Ambühl, M., Decrouez, D., Müller, S. and Ramseyer, K. (1999) A quantitative fabric analysis approach to the discrimination of white marbles. *Archaeometry* **41**, 2; pp. 239–252.

Schmidt-Ott, K. and Boissonnas, V. (2002) Low-pressure hydrogen plasma: An assessment of its application on archaeological iron. *Studies in Conservation* **47**, 2; pp. 81–87.

Schmitt-Korte, K. and Cowell, M. (1989) Nabataean coinage. Part 1. The silver content measured by X-Ray fluorescence analysis. *The Numismatic Chronicle* **149**; pp. 33–58.

Schnarr, H. (1998) Charakterisierung der Bearbeitung und der Verwendung archäologischer Werkstoffe mittels atmosphärischer Rasterelektronmikroskopie. *Berlin Beiträge zur Archäometrie* **15**; pp. 5–90.

Schneider, G. (1989) Investigation of crucibles and moulds from bronze founderies in Olympia and Athens and the determination of provenances of bronze statues. In: Manniatis (ed), 1989, pp. 305–310.

Schneider, G. and Zimmer, G. (1984) Technische Keramik aus antiken Bronzegußwerksttäten in Olympia und Athen. *Berliner Beiträge zur Archäometrie* **9**; pp. 17–60.

Schneider, J.S. and Bierman, P.R. (1997). Surface dating using rock varnish. In: Taylor and Aitken (eds), 1997, pp. 357–388.

Schreiber, T. (1999) *Athenian Vase Construction. A Potter's Analysis*. The J. Paul Getty Museum, Malibu CA.

Schrenk, J.L. (1994) The royal art of Benin: Surfaces, past and present. In: Scott *et al*. (eds), 1994, pp. 51–62.

Schubnel, H.-J. (1992) Une méthode moderne d'identification et d'authentification des gemmes. In: *La microsonde Raman en gemmology*. Association Française de Gemmologie, Paris, pp. 5–10.

Schuler, F. (1959a) Ancient glassmaking techniques: The molding process. *Archaeology* **12**, 1; pp. 47–52.

Schuler, F. (1959b) Ancient glassmaking techniques: The blowing process. *Archaeology* **12**, 2; pp. 116–122.

Schuler, F. (1962) Ancient glassmaking techniques: The Egyptian core vessel process. *Archaeology* **15**, 1; pp. 32–37.

Schuler, F. (1970) *Flameworking: Glassmaking for the Craftsman*. Pitman, London.

Schüller, S. (1960) *Forgers, Dealers, Experts*. Arthur Baker, London. [Trans. J. Cleugh from the original *Fälscher, Händler und Experten*, 1959, Franz Erenwirth, München].

Schvoerer, M., Muller, P., Bechtel, F., Ney, C. and Guibert, P. (1993) Est-il possible d'utiliser la thermoluminescence pour la datation des verres anciens? In: *Annales du 12e congrès de l'association internationale pour l'histoire du verre*, A. van Wiechen (ed). International Association for the History of Glass, Amsterdam, pp. 153–162.

Schvoerer, M. (ed) (1999) *Archéomatériaux. Marbres et autres roches, ASHMOSIA 4*. Centre de Recherche en Physique Appliquée à l'Archéologie-Presse Universitaires de Bordeaux, Bordeaux.

Schwalbe, L.A. and Rogers, R.N. (1982) Physics and chemistry of the Shroud of Turin: A summary of the 1978 investigation. *Analytica Chimica Acta* **135**, 1; pp. 3–49.

Schweizer, F. (1985) Röntgenfluoreszenzanalytise Untersuchung eines Glasgemäldes: Kopie oder Original? *Arbeitsblätter für Restauratoren* **18**, 1; pp. 126–135.

Schweizer, F. (1994a) Etudes techniques de laitons byzantins. In: Rinuy and Schwiezer (eds), 1994, pp. 175–186.

Schweizer, F. (1994b) Bronze objects from lake sides: From patina to 'biography'. In: Scott *et al*. (eds), 1994, pp. 33–50.

Schweizer, F. (1994c) De l'authenticité de deux émaux médiévaux. In: Rinuy and Schweizer (eds), 1994, pp. 103–119.

Schweizer, F. and Meyers, P. (1978a) Structural changes in ancient silver alloys: The discontinuous precipitation of copper. Preprints of the ICOM 5th Triennial Meeting of the ICOM Committee for Conservation, Zagreb, 1978, 78/23/5, pp. 1–16.

Schweizer, F. and Meyers, P. (1978b) Authenticity of ancient silver objects: A new approach. *MASCA Journal* **1**, 1; pp. 9–10.

Schweizer, F. and Meyers, P. (1979) A new approach to the authenticity of ancient silver objects: The discontinuous precipitation of copper from a silver-copper alloy. In: Scollar (ed), 1979, pp. 287–298.

Schweizer, F. and Rinuy, A. (1981) De l'authenticite d'une tete Etrusque. *Revue d'Archeometrie* **5**, Supplement: Actes du XX Symposium International d'Archéométrie III; pp. 273–283.

Schweizer, F. and Rinuy, A. (1982) Manganese black as an Etruscan pigment. *Studies in Conservation* **27**, 3; pp. 118–123.

Schweizer, F. and Bujard, J. (1994) Aspect metallurgie de quelques objets byzantins et omeyyades decouverts recemment en Jordanie. In: Rinuy and Schwiezer (eds), 1994, pp. 191–203.

Schweppe, H. (1986) Identification of dyes in historic textile materials. In: Needles and Zeronian (eds), 1986, pp. 153–174.

Scollar, I. (ed) (1979) *Proceedings of the 18th International Symposium on Archaeometry and Archaeological Prospection. Archaeo-Physika* **10**; Rheinland-Verlag, Bonn.

Scott, A. (1926) *The Cleaning and Restoration of Museum Exhibits.* Dept. of Science and Industrial Research, HMSO, London.

Scott, D.A. (1983) The deterioration of gold alloys and some aspects of their conservation. *Studies in Conservation* **28**, 4; pp. 194–203.

Scott, D.A. (1986a) Fusion gilding and and foil gilding in pre-Hispanic Columbia and Ecuador. In: *Metalurgia de América Precolumbina*, C. Plaza de Nieto (ed). Banco de la República, Bogotá, pp. 281–325.

Scott, D.A. (1986b) Gold and silver alloy coatings over copper: An examination of some artifacts from Ecuador and Columbia. *Archaeometry* **28**, 1; pp. 33–50.

Scott, D.A. (1991a) *Metallography and Microstructure of Ancient and Historic Metals.* The Getty Conservation Institute, J. Paul Getty Museum, Los Angeles.

Scott, D.A. (1991b) Technical examination of some gold wire from pre-Hispanic South America. *Studies in Conservation* **36**, 2; pp. 65–75.

Scott, D.A. (1992) An annotated bibliography for outdoor bronzes and their corrosion products. In: Drayman-Weisser (ed), 1992, pp. 187–208.

Scott, D.A. (1995) Goldwork of pre-Columbian Costa Rica and Panama: A technical study. In: Vandiver *et al.* (eds), 1995, pp. 499–526.

Scott, D.A. (1997) Copper Compounds in metals and colorants: Oxides and hydroxides. *Studies in Conservation* **42**, 2; pp. 93–100.

Scott, D.A. (2001) The application of scanning X-ray fluorescence microanalysis in the examination of cultural materials. *Archaeometry* **43**, 4; pp. 475–482.

Scott, D.A. (2002) *Copper and Bronze in Art: Corrosion, Colorants, Conservation.* The Getty Conservation Institute, Los Angeles.

Scott, D.A. and Podany, J. (1990) Ancient copper alloys: Some metallurgical and technical studies of Greek and Roman bronzes. In: True and Podany (eds), 1990a, pp. 31–60.

Scott, D.A., Podany, J. and Considine, B.B. (eds) (1994) *Ancient and Historic Metals – Conservation and Scientific Research.* Getty Conservation Institute, Los Angeles.

Scott, P. (1993) *The Book of Silk.* Thames and Hudson, London.

Scott Williams, R. (1997) On-site non-destructive mid-IR spectroscopy of plastics in museum objects using a portable FTIR spectrometer with fibre optic probe. In: *Materials Issues in Art and Archaeology V*, P.B. Vandiver, J.R. Druzik, J.F. Merkel and J. Stewart (eds). MRS (Materials Research Society), Pittsburgh PA, pp. 25–30.

Seaver, K.A. (1995) The 'Vinland Map': Who made it, and why? New light on an old controversy. *The Map Collector* **70**; pp. 32–40.

Seaver, K.A. (2004) *Maps, Myth, and Men: The Story of the Vinland Map.* Stanford University Press, Stanford CA.

Seddon, G.B. (1995) *The Jacobites and their Drinking Glasses.* The Antique Collectors Club, Woodbridge, Suffolk.

Segebade, C. and Wessel, H. (1996) Investigation of European medieval weapons – two swords and two helmets. In *Spectrometric Examination in Conservation.* National Research Institute of Cultural Properties, Tokyo, pp. 52–69.

Seifar, R.M., Verheul, J.M., Ariese, F., Brinkman, U.A.Th. and Gooijer, C. (2001) Applicability of surface-enhanced resonance Raman scattering for the direct discrimination of ballpoint pen inks. *The Analyst* **126**; pp. 1418–1422.

Sellwood, D.G. (1963) Some experiments in Greek minting technique. *Numismatic Chronicle* **123**; pp. 217–231.

Sellwood, D. (1976) Minting. In: Strong and Brown (eds), 1976, pp. 63–74.

Selwitz, C.M. (1988) *Cellulose Nitrate in Conservation.* Research in Conservation 2, Getty Conservation Insitute, Marina del Rey.

Selwyn, A. (1948) *The Retail Jeweller's Handbook.* Heywood and Co, London.

Selwyn, A. (1954) *The Retail Silversmith's Handbook.* Heywood and Co, London.

Selwyn, L. (2004) *Metals and Conservation.* Canadian Institute of Conservation, Ottawa.

Selwyn, L.S., Binnie, N.E., Poitras, J., Laver, M.E. and Downham, D.A. (1996) Outdoor bronze statues: Analysis of metal and surface samples. *Studies in Conservation* **41**, 4; pp. 205–228.

Sen Mamata Chaudhuri, S.N. (1985) *Ancient Glass and India.* Indian National Science Academy, New Delhi.

Sentimenti, E., Guerriero, R. and Tricherini, P.R. (1990) Physicochemical and microstructural studies. In: *The*

Lion of Venice, B.M. Scarfi (ed). Albrizzi editore, Venice, pp. 149–186.

Seruya, A.I. and Griffiths, D.R. (1997) Ageing processes in gold-copper-silver alloys. In: Sinclair, Slater and Gowlett (eds), 1997, pp. 132–143.

Seves, A.M., Sora, S., Scicolone, G., Testa, G., Bonfatti, A.M., Rossi, E. and Seves, A. (2000) Effect of thermal accelerated ageing on the properties of model canvas paintings. *Journal of Cultural Heritage* 1, 3; pp. 315–322.

Seymour, R.B. and Porter, R.S. (eds) (1993) *Manmade Fibers: Their Origin and Development*. Elsevier, London.

Shailor, B. (1984, 1987 & 1992), *Catalogue of Medieval and Renaissance Manuscripts in the Beinecke Rare Book and Manuscript Library*, Yale University Press, Binghamton, New York NY.

Shanks, H. (2003a) Assessing the Jehoash inscription. *Biblical Archaeology Review* 29, 3; pp. 27–29.

Shanks, H. (2003b) The storm over the bone box. *Biblical Archaeology Review* 29, 5; pp. 27–38, 83.

Shanks, H. and Witherington, B., III (2003) *James, The Brother of Jesus*. Continuum, London.

Shapiro, M.E. (1981a) *Cast and Recast: The Sculptures of Frederic Remington*. Exhibition Catalogue, Smithsonian Institution Press, Washington DC.

Shapiro, M.E. (1981b) The casting history of a Remington bronze. *National Sculpture Review* 30; pp. 221–226.

Shaplin, P.D. (1978) Thermoluminescence and style in the authentication of ceramic sculpture from Oaxaca, Mexico. *Archaeometry* 20, 1; pp. 47–54.

Sharma, V.C., Shankar Lal, U. and Nair, M.V. (1995) Zinc dust treatment – an effective method for the control of bronze disease on excavated objects. *Studies in Conservation* 40, 2; pp. 110–119.

Sharpe, M. (1997) *Plaster Waste-moulding, Casting and Life Casting*. Tiranti, Reading, Berks.

Shashoua, Y. (2002) Deterioration and conservation of plasticized poly (vinyl chloride) objects. In: *ICOM Committee for Conservation 13th Triennial Meeting*, Rio de Janeiro, 22–27 September 2002, R. Vontobel (ed). James and James, London, pp. 927–934.

Shashoua, Y. and Ward, C. (1995) Plastics: Modern resins with ageing problems. In: Wright and Townsend (eds), 1995, pp. 33–37.

Shaw, J. (1979) Rapid changes in the magnitude of the archaeomagnetic field. *Geophysical Journal of the Royal Astronomical Society* 58; pp. 107–116.

Shaw, T. and Craddock, P.T. (1984) Ghanian and Coptic brass lamps. *Antiquity* 58, 223; pp. 126–128.

Shearer, G.L. (1987) Use of diffuse reflectance Fourier transform infrared spectroscopy in art and archaeological conservation. In: Black (ed), 1987, pp. 253–256.

Shedrinsky, A.M., Wampler, T.P. and Baer, N.S. (1987/88) The identification of dammar, mastic, sandarac and copals by pyrolysis gas chromatography. *Wiener Berichte über Naturwissenschaft in der Kunst* 4/5; pp. 12–25.

Shedrinsky, A.M., Wampler, T.P., Indictor, N. and Baer, N.S. (1989) Application of analytical pyrolysis to problems in art and archaeology: A review. *Journal of Analytical and Applied Pyrolysis* 15; pp. 393–412.

Shedrinsky, A.M., Grimaldi, D.A., Wampler, T.P. and Baer, N.S. (1991) Amber and copal: Pyrolysis gas chromatographic (PyGC) studies of provenance. *Wiener Berichte über Naturwissenschaft in der Kunst* 6/7/8; pp. 37–65.

Shedrinsky, A.M., Grimaldi, D.A., Boon, J.J. and Baer, N.S. (1993) Application of pyrolysis–gas chromatography and pyrolysis–gas chromatography/mass spectrometry to the unmasking of amber forgeries. *Journal of Analytical and Applied Pyrolysis* 25; pp. 77–95.

Sheldon, L. and Eastaugh, N. (1999) Science illuminating art. *The Picture Restorer* 15; pp. 21–24.

Shen, G.T., Boyle, E.A. and Lea, D.W. (1987) Cadmium in corals as a tracer of historical upwelling and industrial fallout. *Nature* 238, 6133; pp. 794–796.

Shepherd, D.G. (1967) Technical aspects of the Buyid Silks. In: *A Survey of Persian Art*, A.U. Pope and P. Ackerman (eds). Oxford University Press, London, 14; pp. 3090–3100.

Shepherd, D.G. (1974) Medieval Persian silks in fact and fancy (a refuation of the Riggisberg Report). *Bulletin de Liasion du Centre International d'Études des Textiles Anciens* 39–40; pp. 1232–1239.

Sherwood, S.I. (1992) The greening of American monuments: The role of atmospheric chemistry in the corrosion of outdoor bronzes. In: Drayman-Weisser (ed), 1992, pp. 33–85.

Shi Meiguang, He Ouli, and Zhou Fuzheng (1987) Investigation of some Chinese potash glasses excavated in Han Dynasty tombs. In: Bhardwaj (ed), 1987, pp. 15–20.

Shimoyama, M., Ninomiya, T. and Ozaki, Y. (1998) Nondestructive discrimination of ivories and prediction of specific gravity by Fourier-transform Raman spectroscopy and chemometrics. *The Analyst* 128; pp. 950–953.

Sicher, H. (1937) Zur Phylogenese des menschlichen Kiefergelenke. *Zeitschrift für Stomatologie* 35, 4; p. 247.

Siewert, R. (1984) Untersuchungen an Bernsteinobjekten aus dem Museum für Völkerkunde der Staatlichen Museen Preußischer Kulturbesitz. *Berlin Beiträge zur Archäometrie* 9; pp. 139–145.

Sikes, E.L., Samson, C.R., Guilderson, T.P. and Howard, W.R. (2000) Old radiocarbon ages in the southwest Pacific Ocean during the last glacial period and deglaciation. *Nature* 405, 6786; pp. 555–559.

Silberman, N.A. and Goren, Y. (2003) Faking biblical history. *Archaeology* 56; pp. 20–29.

Sim, D. (1997) Roman chain-mail: Experiments to reproduce the techniques of manufacture. *Britannia* 28; pp. 359–371.

Sim, D. and Ridge, I. (2002) *Iron for the Eagles*. Tempus, Stroud, Gloucestershire.

Sinclair, A., Slater, E. and Gowlett, J. (eds) (1997) *Archaeological Sciences 1995*. Oxbow Monograph 64, Oxford.

Singh, R.N. (1989) *Ancient Indian Glass*. Pariaml, New Delhi.

Sinkankas, J. (1958) Some comments on the artificial alteration of jade by heating. *Lapidary Journal* **12**; pp. 676–678.

Sinkankas, J. (1984) *Gem Cutting*. Van Nostrand Rheinhold, New York NY.

Sirakian, D. (1997) Diamants: La synthèse a une histoire. *Revue de Gemmologie a.f.g.* **131**; pp. 6–10.

Sistach, M.C., Ferrer, N. and Romero, M.T. (1998) Fourier transform infrared spectroscopy applied to the analysis of ancient manuscripts. *Restaurator* **19**, 4; pp. 173–186.

Skálová, Z. (1991) Die Semiotik mittelalterlicher russischer ikonen, ihre Beschädigung, Restaurierung, Nachahmung und Fälschung. In: *Russische Ikonen*, E. Haustein-Bartsch (ed). Beiträge zur Kunst des Christlichen Ostens, **10**, pp. 170–180.

Skaug, E.S. (1994) *Punch marks from Giotto to Fra Angelico*. IIC-Nordic Group, Oslo.

Skelton, R.A., Marston, T.E. and Painter, G.D. (1965) *The Vinland Map and the Tartar Relation*. Yale University Press, New Haven. [Second edition with introductory essays, 1995].

Skoulikidis, T. and Beloyannis, N. (1984) Inversion of marble sulfation- reconversion of gypsum films into calcite on the surfaces of monuments and statues. *Studies in Conservation* **29**, 4; pp. 197–204.

Skoulikidis, T., Papakonstantinou, E., Kritou, E. and Tsangaldis, G. (1993) Production of artificial patinas on the surface of new marbles used for the restoration of ancient monuments and on the surface of white cement copies of statues. In: *Conservation of Stone and other Materials: Proceedings of the International RILEM/ UNESCO Congress*, M.-J. Thiel (ed), UNESCO, Paris, pp. 644–651.

Skoulikidis, Th., Georgopoulou, E. and Adamopoulou, P. (1995) Oriented inversion of gypsum on the surface of ancient monuments back into calcium carbonate. In: Maniatis, Herz and Basiakos (eds), 1995, pp. 291–294.

Slater, E.A. and Tate, J.O. (eds) (1980) *Proceedings of the 16th International Symposium on Archaeometry and Archaeological Prospection*, Edinburgh 1976. National Museum of Antiquities of Scotland, Edinburgh.

Slater, K. (1991) *Textile Degradation*. Textile Progress **21**. The Textile Institute, Manchester.

Slitine, F. (2002) *Samson: Génie de l'Imitation*. Massin, Paris.

Sloan, C. (1999) Feathers for T. rex? *National Geographic* **196**, 11; pp. 98–107. November.

Smeaton, W.A. (1978) Early methods of cladding base metals with platinum. *Platinum Metals Review* **22**; pp. 61–67.

Smith, A.W. (1978) Stable carbon and oxygen isotope ratios of malachite from the patinas of ancient bronze objects. *Archaeometry* **20**; pp. 123–134.

Smith, C.S. and Gnudi, M.T. [trans. and (eds)] (1942) *The Pirotechnia of Vannoccio Biringuccio*. Chicago: Basic Books.

Smith, D.C. (2005a) Overview: Jewellery and precious stones. In: Edwards and Chalmers (eds), 2005, pp. 335–378.

Smith, D.C. (2005b) Case study: Mesoamerican jade. In: Edwards and Chalmers (eds), 2005, pp. 412–426.

Smith, D.C. and Gendron, F. (1997) Archaeometric application of the Raman microprobe to the non-destructive identification of two Pre-Colombian ceremonial polished 'greenstone' axe-heads from Mesoamerica. *Journal of Raman Spectroscopy* **28**; pp. 731–738.

Smith, D.C. and Robin, S. (1997) Early Roman Empire intaglios from 'rescue excavations' in Paris: An application of the Raman microprobe to the non-destructive characterization of archaeological objects. *Journal of Raman Spectroscopy* **28**; pp. 189–193.

Smith, E.A. (1933) *Working in Precious Metals*. N.A.G. Press, London. [Reissued 1978].

Smith, G.D. and Clark, R.J.H. (2001) Raman microscopy in art history and conservation science. *Reviews in Conservation* **2**; pp. 92–106.

Smith, R., Carlson, J.H. and Newman, R.M. (1987) An investigation into the deterioration of painted Limoges enamel plaques *c.*1470–1530. *Studies in Conservation* **32**, 3; pp. 102–113.

Smith, W.E., White, P.C., Rodger, C. and Dent, G. (2001) Raman and surface enhanced resonance scattering: Applications in forensic science. In: Lewis and Edwards (eds), 2001, pp. 733–748.

Smith, W.G. (1894) *Man the Primeval Savage*. Edward Stanford, London.

So, J.F. and Douglas, J.G. (1998) Understanding and identifying jades from the Hongshan Culture. In: *East Asian Jades: Symbols of Excellence*, T. Chung (ed), Chinese University of Hong Kong Press, Hong Kong, I; pp. 148–163.

Sode, T. (1996) *Anatolske glasperler*. Forlaget Thot, København.

Sode, T. and Kock, J. (2001) Traditional raw glass production in northern India: The final stage of an ancient technology. *Journal of Glass Studies* **43**; pp. 155–169.

Sollas, W.J. (1915) *Ancient Hunters and their Modern Representatives*, 2nd edn. Macmillan, London.

Somerville, E.M. (1996) Piltdown reflections: A mirror for prehistory. *Sussex Archaeological Collections* **134**; pp. 7–20.

Sonoda, N. (1998) Application des méthodes chromatographiques pour la caractérisation des peintures alkydes pour artistes. *Techne* **8**; pp. 33–43.

Sonoda, N., Rioux, J.-P. and Duval, A.R. (1993) Identification des matériaux synthétiques dans les peintures modernes. II. Pigments organiques et matière picturale. *Studies in Conervation* **38**, 2; pp. 99–127.

Sotheby's (1981) *The Avar Treasure*. Sotheby's Catalogue, London.

Soulier, L., Gratuze, B. and Barrandon, J.N. (1996) The origin of cobalt blue pigments in French glass from the Bronze Age to the eighteenth century. In: Demirci *et al.* (eds), 1996, pp. 133–140.

Sox, H.D. (1981) *The Image on the Shroud: Is the Turin Shroud a Forgery?* Unwin Paperbacks, London.

Sox, D. (1987) *Unmasking the Forger: The Dossena Deception*. Unwin Hyman, London.

Sox, H.D. (1988) *The Shroud Unmasked: Uncovering the Greatest Fraud of All Time.* The Lamp Press, Basingstoke, Hants.

Speel, E. (1998) *Dictionary of Enamelling.* Ashgate, Aldershot, Hampshire.

Speel, E. and Bronk, H. (2001) Enamel painting: Materials and recipes in Europe from c.1500 to c.1920. *Berliner Beiträge zur Archäometrie* **18**; pp. 43–100.

Spencer, F. (1988) Prologue to a scientific forgery: The British Eolithic Movement from Abbeville to Piltdown. In: *Bones, Bodies, Behavior. Essays on Biological Anthropology,* G.W. Stocking (ed). University of Winsconsin Press, Wisconsin, pp. 84–116.

Spencer, F. (1990a) *Piltdown, a Scientific Forgery.* Natural History Museum, London.

Spencer, F. (1990b) *The Piltdown Papers.* Natural History Museum, London.

Spencer, L.F. (1973) Modern electroforming. *Metal Finish.* Over three issues **71**; pp. 64–72. (Feb), pp. 54–57 (March) and pp. 53–59 (April).

Spencer, R.D. (2004) The Expert versus the Object: Judging Facts and False Attributions in the Visual Arts. Oxford University Press, New York.

Sperl, G. (1988) Der Jüngling vom Magdalensberg – Untersuchung der Kernarmierung. In: Gschwantler and Bernhard-Walcher (eds), 1988, pp. 42–44.

Spier, J. (1990) Blinded with science: The abuse of science in the detection of false antiquities. *The Burlington Magazine* **132**, 1050; pp. 623–631. September.

Spier, J. (1994) Review of *Elektronstatere aus Klazomenai: der Schatzfund von 1989* by E. Isik. *Numismatic Chronicle* **154**; pp. 220–222.

Spiro, P. (1968) *Electroforming.* Robert Draper, Teddington, Middx.

Spon, E. (1882–1892) *Workshop Receipts,* 1st–5th series. E. & F.N. Spon, London (and 1895 2nd edn of 1st series).

Spon, E. (1932–1936). *Workshop Receipts,* **II** & **III**. E. & F.N. Spon, London.

Spoto, G. (2002) Detecting past attempts to restore two important works of art. *Accounts of Chemical Research* **35**, 8; pp. 652–659.

Spring, M., Penny, N., White, R. and Wyld, M. (2001) Color changes. In: *The Conversion of the Magdalen* attributed to Pedro Campăna. *National Gallery Technical Bulletin* **22**; pp. 54–63.

Sreelatha, Rao (1985) Studies on corals. *Journal of Archaeological Chemistry* **3**; pp. 73–76.

Sreelatha, Rao and Subbaiah, K.V. (1983) India ivory. *Journal of Archaeological Chemistry* **11**; pp. 1–10.

St. Aubryn, F. (ed) (1987) *Ivory: A History and Collector's Guide.* Thames and Hudson, London.

Stancliffe, J. (1990) Fantasy, fashion or pure style? Plastic jewellery of the twentieth century. In: *The International Silver and Jewellery Fair and Seminar 1990.* pp. 31–39.

Starkey, S. (1985) Seeing the wood for the trees. *History Today* **35**; pp. 4–5.

Starling, K. and Watkinson, D. (eds) (1987) *Archaeological Bone, Antler and Ivory,* Occasional Paper 5. United Kingdom Institute for Conservation, London.

Stead, I.M. and Meeks, N.D. (1996) The Celtic warrior fibula. *The Antiquaries Journal* **76**; pp. 1–16.

Steel, R.H. (1975) Ingot casting and wire drawing in Iron Age Southern Africa. *Journal of the South Africa Institute of Mining and Metallurgy* **75**; pp. 244–248.

Steinberg, A. (1973) Joining methods on large bronze statues: Some experiments in ancient technology. In: Young (ed), 1973, pp. 103–138.

Stephenson, G.B., Stephenson, B. and Haeffner, D.R. (2001) Investigations of astrolabe metallurgy using synchrotron radiation. *MRS Bulletin* **26**, 1; pp. 19–23.

Stern, E.M. (2001) *Roman, Byzantine and Early Medieval Glass.* Gerd Hatje and Cantz, Ostfildern.

Stern, E.M. and Schlick-Nolte, B. (1994) *Early Glass of the Ancient World.* Gerd Hatje, Ostfildern.

Stewart, L.F. (1982) Artificial aging of documents. *Journal of Forensic Science* **27**, 2; pp. 540–543.

Stichting Foundation (1982, 1986 & 1989) *A Corpus of Rembrandt Paintings.* M. Nijhoff, The Hague.

Stocks, D.A. (1993) Making stone vessels in ancient Mesopotamia and Egypt. *Antiquity* **67**, 256; pp. 596–602.

Stocks, D.A. (2003) *Experiments in Egyptian Archaeolgy: Stoneworking Technology in Ancient Egypt.* Routledge, London.

Stockton, C.M. (1984) The chemical distinction of natural from synthetic emeralds. *Gems and Gemmology* **20**, 3; pp. 141–145.

Stockton, C.M. (1987) The separation of natural from synthetic emeralds by infra red spectroscopy. *Gems and Gemmology* **23**, 2; pp. 96–99.

Stoll, M. and Fengel, D. (1988) Chemical and structural studies on Ancient Egyptian linen. *Berliner Beiträge zur Archäometrie* **10**; pp. 151–172.

Stone, J.F.S. and Thomas, L.C. (1956) The use and distribution of faience in the Ancient East and Prehistoric Europe. *Proceedings of the Prehistoric Society* **22**; pp. 37–84.

Stone, R.E. (1997) A noble imposture: The Fonthill Ewer and early nineteenth century fakery. *Metropolitan Museum Journal* **32**; pp. 175–202.

Stone, R.E., White, R. and Indictor, N. (1990) Surface composition of some Italian Renaissance bronzes. In: *Preprints of the ICOM Committee for Conservation 9th Triennial Meeting,* Dresden, 20–31 August 1990. K. Grimstad (ed). ICOM, Los Angeles, pp. 568–573.

Stoneham, D. (1983) Porcelain dating. In: *Third Specialist Seminar on TL and ESR Dating,* V. Medjdahl, S.G.E. Bowman, A.G. Wintle and M.J. Aitken (eds). Council of Europe, Strasbourg, PACT **9**, 1; pp. 227–239.

Stoneham, D. (1990a) Thermoluminescence testing of ceramic works of art. *Orientations* **21**, 6; pp. 70–74.

Stoneham, D. (1990b) Thermoluminescence testing of ceramic cores of bronzes. Appendix 5. In: *Western Zhou Ritual Bronzes from the Arthur M. Sackler Collections,* J. Rawson (ed). The Arthur M. Sackler Foundation and The Arthur M. Sackler Museum, Washington DC, pp. 166–167.

Stoneham, D. (1995a) Thermoluminescence testing of ceramic cores of bronzes. Appendix 5. In: *Eastern Zhou Ritual Bronzes from the Arthur M. Sackler Collections*, J. Rawson (ed). The Arthur M. Sackler Foundation and The Arthur M. Sackler Museum, Washington DC, p. 492.

Stoneham, D. (1995b) The eye of the beholder: Objectivity in authentication. *Orientations* **26**, 11; p. 82.

Stoneham, D. (1998) An update of forgery detection. *Orientations* **29**, 2; p. 94.

Stoneham, D. and Winter, M. (1988) The removal of anomalous fading from authenticity samples. *Nuclear Tracks Radiation Measurement* **14**, 1/2; pp. 127–130.

Stós-Fertner, Z. (1980) Application of X-ray fluorescence analysis to the determination of pigments from illuminations and miniatures in medieval incunabula. In: Slater and Tate (eds), 1980, pp. 126–138.

Stos-Gale, Z.A. (1998) Lead isotope analysis of coins – a review. In: Oddy and Cowell (eds), 1998, pp. 348–366.

Strahan, D. (2001) Uranium in glass, glazes and enamel: History, identification and handling. *Studies in Conservation* **46**, 3; pp. 181–195.

Strandberg, H., Johansson, L.-G. and Rosvall, J. (1996) Outdoor bronze sculpture – a conservation view on the examination of the state of preservation. In: Bridgland (ed), 1996, pp. 894–900.

Stratford, N. (1994) Some 'Mosan' enamels fakes in Paris. *Aachener Kunstblätter* **60**; pp. 199–216.

Strauss, J. (1962) Late nineteenth century German and Austrian enamelled glasses. *Journal of Glass Studies* **4**; pp. 109–116.

Striegel, M.F. (1998) X-ray diffraction in numismatics: A review. In: Oddy and Cowell (eds), 1998, pp. 405–424.

Strlič, M. and Kolar, J. (eds) (2005) *Ageing and Stabilisation of Paper*. National and University Library, Ljubljana.

Stromberg, C. (1988) A technical study of three cloisoinné enamels from the Botkin Collection. *Journal of the Walters Art Gallery* **46**; pp. 25–36.

Strong, D.E. (1966) *Greek and Roman Gold and Silver Plate*. Methuen, London.

Strong, D. and Brown, D. (eds) (1976) *Roman Crafts*. Duckworth, London.

Strong, D. and Claridge, A. (1976) Marble sculpture. In: Strong and Brown (eds), 1976, pp. 195–207.

Stross, F.H. and Eisenlord, W.J. (1965) *A Report on a Group of Limestone carvings Owned by M.A. Mansoor and Sons*. Alfred Mansoor. Privately circulated.

Stross, F.H., Hay, R.L., Asaro, F., Bowman, H.R. and Michel, H.V. (1988) Sources of the quartzite for some ancient Egyptian sculptures. *Archaeometry* **30**, 1; pp. 109–119.

Stuart, F.M. (2001) *In situ* cosmogenic isotopes: Principles and potential for archaeology. In: Brothwell and Higgs (eds), 2001 pp. 93–100.

Stuiver, M. and Pearson, G.W. (1986) High-precision calibration of the radiocarbon time scale AD 1950-500 BC. *Radiocarbon* **28**, 2b; pp. 805–838.

Stuiver, M. and Polach, H.A. (1977) Discussion and reporting of 14C data. *Radiocarbon* **19**; pp. 355–363.

Stukeley, W. (1736) *An Account of a Large Silver Plate of Antique Basso-Relievo, Roman Workmanship, found in Derbyshire, 1729*. G. Vander Gucht, London.

Stulik, D.C., Parker, A.E., Donahue, D.J. and Toolin, L.J. (1992) The ultimate challenge for radiocarbon dating: The paint layer. *Postprints (American Institute for Conservation of Historic and Artistic Works: Paintings Speciality Group)*. American Institute for Conservation, Washington DC, pp. 65–89.

Sturman, S. (1987) Investigations into the manufacture and identification of papyrus. In: Black (ed), 1987, pp. 263–265.

Suess, H.E. (1970) Bristlecone-pine calibration of the radiocarbon time-scale 5200 B.C. to the present. In: *Radiocarbon Variations and Absolute Chronology*, I.U. Olsson (ed). Nobel Symposium 12, John Wiley, New York and Almqvist and Wiksell, Stockholm, pp. 303–312

Summers, T.A., Collier, B.J., Collier, J.R. and Haynes, J.L. (1993) History of viscose rayon. In: Seymour and Porter (eds), 1993, pp. 72–90.

Sunagawa, I. (1995) The distinction of natural from synthetic diamonds. *The Journal of Gemmology* **24**, 7; pp. 485–499.

Sutton, S.R. and Zimmerman, D.W. (1976) Thermoluminescent dating using zircon grains from archaeological ceramics. *Archaeometry* **18**, 2; pp. 125–134.

Svoronos, J.N. (1922) *Synopsis de mille coins faux du faussaire C. Christodoulos*. M.M. Eleuthéroudakis & Barth, Athens.

Swaddling, J., Oddy, A. and Meeks, N. (1991) Etruscan and other early gold wire from Italy. *Jewellery Studies* **5**; pp. 7–22.

Swann, C.P. and Nelson, C.H. (2000) Böttger stoneware from North America and Europe: Are they authentic? In: Andersen and Rehn (eds), 2000, pp. 694–698.

Taimsalu, P. (1983) The production of carat gold chain wire. *Aurum* **14**; pp. 49–55.

Tait, H. (1979) *The Golden Age of Venetian Glass*. Trustees of the British Museum, London.

Tait, H. (1981) *The Waddesdon Bequest*. British Museum Press, London.

Tait, H. (1986) *Catalogue of the Waddesdon Bequest in the British Museum I. The Jewels*. British Museum Press, London.

Tait, H. (1988) *Catalogue of the Waddesdon Bequest in the British Museum II. The Silver Plate*. British Museum Press, London.

Tait, H. (1989) Old silver and the law. *The Antique Collector*, pp. 9–16. April.

Tait, H. (1991a) *Catalogue of the Waddesdon Bequest in the British Museum III. The 'Curiosities'*. British Museum Press, London.

Tait, H. (1991b) Europe from the Middle Ages to the Industrial Revolution. In: Tait (ed), 1991, pp. 145–187.

Tait, H. (ed) (1991) *Five Thousand Years of Glass*. British Museum Press, London.

Tait, H. (1999) Limoges enamels – Some 'signatures' and 'dates': Problems for the scientist? *Berliner Beiträge zur Archäometrie* **16**; pp. 137–144.

Tait, H. (2003) Felix Slade's forgotten version of the so-called Early Christain 'Amiens Chalice'. In: *Through a Glass Brightly*, C. Entwhistle (ed). Oxbow, Oxford, pp. 220–225.

Tait, H. and Freestone, I.C. (2004) Painted enamel 'patches': A 19th century virtuoso restorer's technique. In: *New research on Limoges painted enamels*, I. Müsch and H. Stege (eds). Herzog Anton Ulrich-Musuem, Braunsweig, pp. 117–122.

Talent, J.A. (1989) The case of the peripatetic fossils. *Nature* **338**, 6217; pp. 613–615. 20 April.

Talent, J.A. (1995) Chaos with conodonts and other fossil biota: V.J. Gupta's carreer in academic fraud: Bibliographies and a short biography. *Courier Forschung-Institut Senckenberg* **182**; pp. 523–551.

Talent, J.A., Goel, R.K., Jain, A.K. and Pickett, J.W. (1988) Silurian and Devonian of India, Nepal and Bhutan: Biostratigraphic and palaeobigeographic anomalies. *Courier Forschung-Institut Senckenberg* **106**; pp. 1–57.

Talley, M.K., Jr. (1986) All good pictures crack. In: *Reynolds*, N. Penny (ed). Royal Academy of Arts, London, pp. 55–69.

Tan, T.L., Tay, T.S., Loh, F.C., Tan, K.L. and Tang, S.M. (1995) Identification of bleached wax- and polymer-impregnated jadeite by X-ray photoelectron spectroscopy. *The Journal of Gemmology* **24**, 7; pp. 475–483.

Tang, C. (ed) (1998) *East Asian Jade: Symbol of Excellence*, **3**. Centre for Chinese Archaeology and Art, The Chinese University of Hong Kong, Hong Kong.

Taniguchi, Y., Hirao, Y., Shimadzu, Y. and Tsuneki, A. (2002) The first fake? Imitation turquoise beads recovered from a Syrian Neolithic tell site, Tell El-Kerkh. *Studies in Conservation* **47**, 3; pp. 175–183.

Tankersley, K.B., Schlecht, K.D. and Laub, R.S. (1998) Fluoride dating of mastodon bone from an Early Paleoindian spring site. *Journal of Archaeological Science* **25**, 8; pp. 805–811.

Tarbell, F.B. (1909) *Catalogue of Bronzes in the Field Museum of Natural History, reproduced from Originals in the National Museum of Naples*. Field Museum of Natural History Publication 130, Chicago.

Tauber, H. (1979) 14C activity of arctic marine mammals. In: *Radiocarbon Dating*, R. Berger and H.E. Suess (eds). University of California Press, Berkeley, pp. 447–452.

Tay, T.S. (2001) Disclosure-gemstones & synthetics: Does the jewellery industry care? *The Australian Gemmologist* **21**, 2; pp. 67–75.

Tay, T.S., Shen, Z.X. and Yee, S.L. (1998) On the identification of amber and its imitations using Raman spectroscopy – preliminary results. *Australian Gemmologist* **20**, 3; pp. 114–123.

Taylor, J., Craddock, P.T. and Shearman, F. (1998) Egyptian hollow-cast bronze statues of the early first millennium BC: The development of a new technology. *Apollo* **148**, 437; pp. 9–14.

Taylor, R.E. (1987) *Radiocarbon Dating: An Archaeological Perspective*. Academic Press, Orlando, Florida.

Taylor, R.E. (1997) Radiocarbon dating. In: Taylor and Aitken (eds), 1997, pp. 65–96.

Taylor, R.E. (2001) Radiocarbon dating. In: Brothwell and Pollard (eds), 2001, pp. 23–34.

Taylor, R.E. and Aitken, M.J. (eds) (1997) *Chronometric Dating in Archaeology*. Plenum Press, New York.

Teegen, W.-R. (2002) Late 19th–early 20th c. replicas, imitations and falsifications (?) of brooches from the Pyrmont spring: A light and scanning electron microscopic approach. *From the Parts to the Whole II: Acta of the 13th International Bronze Congress*, C.C. Mattusch, A. Brauer and S.E. Knudsen (eds). *Journal of Roman Archaeology Supplementary Series* 39, Portsmouth, Rhode Island, pp. 287–289.

Teilhard de Chardin, P. (1920) Le cas de l'homme de Piltdown. *Revue des questions scientifiques* **77**; pp. 149–155.

Teilhard de Chardin, P. (1943) *Fossil Men: Recent Discoveries and Present Problems*. Vetch, Peking.

Tennent, N.H. (1979) Clear and pigmented epoxy resins for stained glass conservation. *Studies in Conservation* **24**, 3; pp. 153–164.

Tennent, N.H. and Townsend, J.H. (1984a) Factors affecting the refractive index of epoxy resins. In: de Froment (ed), 1984, pp. 84.20.26–29.

Tennent, N.H. and Townsend, J.H. (1984b) The photo-fading of dyestuffs in epoxy, polyester and acrylic resins. In: de Froment (ed), 1984, pp. 84.16.8–11.

Terry, K.W. and de Laeter, J.R. (1974) X-ray diffraction analysis of grain size as a method of detection of reproduction among seventeenth-century Spanish silver reales. *Numismatic Chronicle* **134**; pp. 198–202.

Textile Institute, The (1985) *Identification of Textile Materials*, 7th edn. The Textile Institute, Manchester.

Tharp, L. (ed) (1999) *Antiques Roadshow: How to Spot a Fake*. Boxtree, Macmillan, London.

Theimer, E.T. (1983) Beta emission radiography, a new philatelic tool. *The American Philatelist* **97**, 7; pp. 620–622.

Theocaris, P.S., Liritzis, I. and Galloway, R.B. (1997) Dating of two Hellenic pyramids by a novel application of thermoluminescence. *Journal of Archaeological Science* **24**, 2; pp. 399–405.

Theunissen, R., Grave, P. and Bailey, G. (2001) Doubts on diffusion: Challenging the assumed Indian origin of Iron Age agate and carnelian beads in Southeast Asia. *World Archaeology* **32**, 1; pp. 84–105.

Thickett, D., Cruickshank, P. and Ward, C. (1995) The conservation of amber. *Studies in Conservation* **40**, 4; pp. 217–226.

Thomas, G. (1995) *Bronze Casting.* Crowood Press, Ramsbury, Marlborough, Wilts.

Thompson, J. (1994) The polishing of Chinese ceramics. *Orientations* **25**, 10; p. 102.

Thomsen, E.G. and Thomsen, H.H. (1974) Early wire drawing through dies. *Transactions of the ASME. Journal of Engineering for Industry* Series B **96**, 1; pp. 1216–1221. November.

Thomsen, E.G. and Thomsen, H.H. (1976) Drawing solid wires through soft dies in Antiquity. *Transactions of the ASME Journal of Engineering for Industry.* Paper 75WA-Prod.-6, **98**, 1; pp. 1–5.

Thornton, C.P., Lamberg-Karlovsky, C.C., Liezers, M. and Young, S.S.M. (2002) On pins and needles: Tracing the evolution of copper-base alloying at Tepe Yahya, Iran, via ICP-MS analysis of common-place items. *Journal of Archaeological Science* **29**, 12; pp. 1451–1460.

Thouvenin, A. (1971) La fabrication des fils et des filagranes de mètaux prècieux chez des anciens. *Revues de Histoire des Mines et de la Mètallurgie* **3**; pp. 89–108.

Tietze, H. (1948) *Genuine and False: Copies Imitations Forgeries.* Max Parrish & Co, London.

Tillander, H. (1995) *Diamond Cuts in Historic Jewellery, 1381–1910.* Art Books International, London.

Tillander, H. (1998) Further aspects of the history of rose-cut diamonds. *The Journal of Gemmology* **26**, 4; pp. 219–221.

Timar-Balazsy, A. and Eastop, D. (1998) *Chemical Principles of Textile Conservation.* Butterworth-Heinemann, Oxford.

Tiranti (1997) *The Polyester Resin Booklet.* Tiranti, Reading, Berks.

Tiranti (1998) *Flexible Moulds with Hot Melt re-usable Vinyl.* Tiranti, Reading, Berks.

Tiranti (1999) *The Silicone Rubber Booklet.* Tiranti, Reading, Berks.

Tite, M.S. (1972) *Methods of Physical Examination in Archaeology.* Seminar Press, London.

Tite, M.S. (1989) Iznik pottery: An investigation of the methods of production. *Archaeometry* **31**, 2; pp. 115–132.

Tite, M.S. (1992) The impact of electron microscopy on ceramic studies. In: *New Developments in Archaeological Science*, A.M. Pollard (ed). The British Academy, London, pp. 111–132.

Tite, M.S., Bimson, M. and Freestone, I.C. (1982a) An examination of the high gloss surface finishes on Greek Attic and Roman Samian wares. *Archaeometry* **24**, 2; pp. 117–126.

Tite, M.S., Freestone, I.C., Meeks, N.D. and Bimson, M. (1982b) The use of scanning electron microscopy in the technological examination of ancient ceramics. In: Olin and Franklin (eds), 1982, pp. 109–120.

Tite, M.S., Freestone, I.C. and Bimson, M. (1984) A technological study of Chinese porcelain of the Yuan dynasty. *Archaeometry* **26**, 2; pp. 139–154.

Tite, M.S. and Bimson, M. (1986) Faience: An investigation of the microstructures associated with the different methods of glazing. *Archaeometry* **28**, 1; pp. 69–78.

Tite, M.S. and Bimson, M. (1991) A technological study of English porcelain. *Archaeometry* **33**, 1; pp. 3–27.

Tite, M.S., Freestone, I., Mason, R., Molera, J., Vendrell-Saz, M. and Wood, N. (1998) Lead glazes in antiquity – methods of production and reasons for use. *Archaeometry* **40**, 2; pp. 241–260.

Tite, M.S., Shortland, A. and Paynter, S. (2002) The beginnings of vitreous materials in the Near East and Egypt. *Accounts of Chemical Research* **35**, 8; pp. 585–593.

Todd, M. (1996) *Pretia victoriae?* Roman lead and silver mining in the Mendip Hills, Somerset, England. *Munster Beiträge fur antiken Handelsgeschichte* **15**, 1; pp. 1–18.

Toombs, H.A. (1952) A new section in the Piltdown gravel. *South Eastern Naturalist* **57**; pp. 31–33.

Topham, J. and McCormick, D. (1998) A dendrochronological investigation of British stringed instruments of the violin family. *Journal of Archaeological Science* **25**, 11; pp. 1149–1157.

Topham, J. and McCormick, D. (2000) FOCUS: A dendrochronological investigation of stringed instruments of the Cremonese School (1666–1757) including 'The Messiah' violin attributed to Antonio Stradavari. *Journal of Archaeological Science* **27**, 3; pp. 183–192.

Touchette, L.-A. (2000) The mechanics of Roman copy production? In: *Periplous*, G.R. Tsetskhladze, A.J.N.W. Prag and A.M. Snodgrass (eds). Thames and Hudson, London, pp. 344–352.

Towe, K.M. (1990) The Vinland Map: Still a forgery. *Accounts of Chemical Research* **23**, 3; pp. 84–87.

Towe, K.M. (2004) Vinland Map ink is NOT medieval. *Analytical Chemistry* **76**, 3; pp. 863–865.

Townsend, J. (1992) Turner Research Project: Information on painting methods *via* standard imaging techniques. *Journal of Photographic Science* **40**, 2; pp. 58–65.

Townsend, J. (1998) Analysis of pastel and chalk materials. *The Paper Conservator: Journal of the Institute of Paper Conservation* **22**; pp. 21–28.

Treister, M.Y. (2001) *Hammering Techniques in Greek and Roman Jewellery and Toreutics.* Colloquia Pontica **8**, Brepols.

Trench, L. (ed) (2000) *Materials and Techniques in the Decorative Arts, An Illustrated Dictionary.* John Murray, London.

Troja, S.O. and Roberts, R.G. (2000) Luminescence dating. In: Ciliberto and Spoto (eds), 2000, pp. 585–640.

True, M. (1987) A Kouros at the Getty Museum. *The Burlington Magazine* **129**, 1006; pp. 3–11. January.

True, M. (1993) The Getty Kouros: Background on the problem. In: 'Kouros Colloquim', 1993, pp. 11–16.

True, M. and Podany, J. (eds) (1990a) *Small Bronze Sculpture from the Ancient World.* Depts of Antiquities and Conservation, the J. Paul Getty Museum, Malibu, California.

True, M. and Podany, J. (eds) (1990b) *Marble: Art Historical and Scientific Perspectives on Ancient Sculpture.* Depts of Antiquities and Conservation, the J. Paul Getty Museum, Malibu, Malibu, Calfornia.

Trümpler, C. (ed) (2001) *Agatha Christie and Archaeology.* British Museum Press, London.

Truncer, J., Glascock, M.D. and Neff, H. (1998) Steatite source characterization in eastern North America: New results using instrumental neutron activation analysis. *Archaeometry* **40**, 1; pp. 23–44.

Ho, Tsien.Hsien and Li, Ping.Tan (1997) Alteration of *Yu* artefacts. In: *Chinese Jades*, R.E. Scott (ed). Colloquies on Art and Archaeology in Asia no. 18. Percival David Foundation of Chinese Art, London, pp. 123–132.

Tsien Tsuen-Hsuin (1985) *Science and Civilisation in China* **V** *Chemistry and Chemical Technology Pt 1: Paper and Printing*. Cambridge University Press, Cambridge.

Tubb, K.W. (ed) (1995) *Antiquities: Trade or Betrayed*. Archetype Publications, London.

Tudor-Craig, P. (1973) *Richard III*. Exhibition Catalogue, National Portrait Gallery, London.

Turner, J. (ed) (1996) *The Dictionary of Art*. Macmillan, London.

Turner, W.E.S. and Rooksby, H.P. (1959) A study of the opalising agents in ancient glasses throughout three thousand four hundred years. *Glastechnische Berichte* **8**; pp. 17–28.

Turner, W.E.S. and Rooksby, H.P. (1961) Further historical studies based on X-ray diffraction methods of the reagents employed in making opal and opaque glasses. *Jahrbuch des Römisch-germanischen Zentralmuseums Mainz* **8**; pp. 1–6.

Türr, K. (1984) *Fälschungen antiker Plastik seit 1800*. Gebr. Mann verlag, Berlin.

Turrell, G. and Corset, J. (1996) *Raman Microscopy: Developments and Applications*. Academic Press, San Diego & London.

Tuurnala, T. and Hautojärvi, A. (2000) Original or forgery – pigment analysis of paintings using ion beams and ionizing radiation. In: Demortier and Adriaens (eds), 2000, pp. 21–27.

Twilley, J. (1992) Scientific description and technical analysis of jade. In: Markel (ed), 1992, pp. 109–124.

Twilley, J. (1999) Recognizing a smoking gun. *Orientations* **30**, 2; pp. 81–82.

Tykot, R.H. and Young, S.M.M. (1996) Archaeological applications of inductively coupled plasma-mass spectrometry. In: Orna (ed), 1996, pp. 116–130.

Tykot, R.H., Herrmann, J.J. Jr, van der Merwe, N.J., Newman, R. and Allegretto, K.O. (2002) Thasian marble sculptures in European and American collections: Isotopic and other analyses. In: Herrmann, Jr., Herz and Newman (eds), 2002, pp. 188–200.

Tylecote, R.F. and Black, J.W.B. (1980) The effect of hydrogen reduction on the properties of ferrous materials. *Studies in Conservation* **25**, 2; pp. 87–96.

Tyrer, J. (1981) Looking at the Turin Shroud as a textile. *Textile Horizons* **1**, 4; pp. 20–23.

Ucko, P.J. (1968) *Anthropomorphic Figurines*. Royal Anthropological Institute, Occasional Paper 24, London.

Ucko, P.J. and Hodges, H.W.M. (1963) Some predynastic Egyptian figurines: problems of authenticity. *Journal of the Warburg and Courtauld Institute* **26**; pp. 205–222.

Ulens, K., Moens, L., Dams, R. and De Paepe, P. (1994a) Study of the patina of ancient marble by stable isotope analysis. *The Science of the Total Environment* **158**; pp. 63–69.

Ulens, K., Moens, L., Dams, R., Van Winkel, S. and Vandevelde, L. (1994b) Study of element distributions in weathered marble crusts using laser ablation inductively coupled plasma mass spectrometry. *Journal of Analytical Atomic Spectrometry* **9**; pp. 1243–1248.

Ulens, K., Moens, L. and Dams, R. (1995) Analytical methods useful in authenticating ancient marble sculptures. In: Maniatis, Herz and Basiakos (eds), 1995, 1995. pp. 199–206.

Underwood, A.S. (1913) The Piltdown Skull. *British Journal of Dental Science* **56**; pp. 650–652.

Untracht, O. (1968) *Metal Techniques for Craftsmen*. Doubleday & Co., New York.

Untracht, O. (1982) *Jewelry: Concepts and Technology*. Robert Hale, London and Doubleday & Co., New York.

Untracht, O. (1997) *The Traditional Jewelry of India*. Thames and Hudson, London.

Vainker, S.J. (1991) *Chinese Pottery and Porcelain from Prehistory to the Present*. British Museum Press, London.

Van Aken, J. (2003) An improvement in Grenz radiography of paper to record watermarks, chain and laid lines. *Studies in Conservation* **48**, 2; pp. 103–110.

Van Arsdell, R.D. (1986) *The Forgery of the 'Haslemere Hoard'*. BNTA Special Publication 1.

van Asperen de Boer, J.R.J. (1985) Infrared reflectography of paintings: principles, development and application. In: *Conservation and Restoration of Mural Paintings II*, T. Suzuki and K. Masuda (eds). Tokyo National Research Institute of Cultural Properties, Tokyo, pp. 167–174.

Van Dantzig, M.M. (1953a) *Vincent? A New Method of Identifying the Artist and his Work and of Unmasking the Forger and his Products*. Keesing, Amsterdam.

Van Dantzig, M.M. (1953b) *True of False?* Exhibition catalogue, Corning Museum of Glass, New York.

van den Berg, J.D.J., van den Berg. K.J. and Boon, J.J. (1999) Chemical Changes in Curing and Ageing Oil Paints. In: *Preprints of the 12th ICOM Committee for Conservation Triennial meeting*, Lyons, 29th August–3rd September, 1999, J. Bridgland (ed). James and James, London, pp. 248–253.

Van den Brandhof, M. (1979) *Een vroege Vermeer iut 1937, Achtergronden van leven en werken van de schilder/vervalser Han van Meergeren*. Het Spectrum, Utrecht.

Vandenabeele, P., Wehling, B., Moens, L., Edwards, H., De Reu, M. and Van Hooydonk, G. (2000a) Analysis with micro-Raman spectroscopy of natural organic binding media and varnishes used in art. *Analytica Chimica Acta* **407**; pp. 261–274.

Vandenabeele, A., Moens, L., Edwards, H.G.M. and Dams, R. (2000b) Raman spectroscopic database of Azo pigments and application to modern art studies. *Journal of Raman Studies* **31**; pp. 50–517.

Vandenabeele, P., Grimaldi, D.M., Edwards, H.G.M. and Moens, L. (2003) Raman spectroscopy of different types of Mexican copal resins. *Spectrochimica Acta* **A59**, 10; pp. 2221–2229.

Vandenabeele, P. and Edwards, H.G.M. (2005) Overview: Raman spectroscopy of artefacts. In: Edwards and Chalmers (eds), 2005, pp. 169–178.

Vandenabeele, P. and Moens, L. (2005) Overview: Raman Spectroscopy of pigments and dyes. In: Edwards and Chalmers (eds), 2005, pp. 71–83.

Vandenbroeck, P. (1982) Problèmes concernant l'oeuvre de Jheronimus Bosch: Le dessin sous-jacent en relation avec l'authenticité et la chronologie. In: R. Van Schoute and D. Hollanders-Favart (eds), 1982, pp. 107–120.

Van der Doelen, G.A. (nd) *Molecular Studies of Fresh and Aged Triterpenoid Varnishes.* FOM, Amsterdam.

Van der Doelen, G.A., van den Berg, K.J. and Boon, J.J. (1998) Comparative chromatographic and mass-spectrometric studies of triterpenoid varnishes: fresh material and aged samples from paintings. *Studies in Conservation* **43**, 4; pp. 249–264.

Van der Merwe, N.J., Lee-Thorp, J.A., Thackeray, J.F., Hall-Martin, A., Kruger, F.J., Coetzee, H., Bell, R.H.V. and Lindeque, M. (1990) Source-area determination of elephant ivory by isotopic analysis. *Nature* **346**, 6286; pp. 744–746.

Van der Merwe, N., Herrmann, J. Jr, Newman, R., Tykot, R. and Herz, N. (1995) Stable carbon isotope and oxygen sourcing tracing of marble sculptures in the Museum of Fine Arts, Boston and the Sackler Museum, Harvard. In: Maniatis, Herz and Basiakos (eds), 1995, pp. 187–198.

Van der Sleen, W.G.N. (1967) *A Handbook on Beads.* 'Journées internationales du Verre', Liege.

Vandiver, P. (1982) Technological changes in Egyptian faience. In: Olin and Franklin (eds), 1982, pp. 167–180.

Vandiver, P. (1983) The manufacture of faience. Appendix A in: Kaczmarczyk and Hedges, 1983. pp.A1–A144.

Vandiver, P.B. (1990) Ancient Glazes. *Scientific American* **262**, 4; pp. 80–87. April.

Vandiver, P.B., Druzik, J. and Wheeler, G.S. (eds) (1991) *Materials Issues in Art and Archaeology II.* MRS (Materials Research Society), Pittsburgh PA.

Vandiver, P.B., Druzik, J.R., Wheeler, G.S. and Freestone, I.C. (eds) (1992) *Materials Issues in Art and Archaeology III.* MRS (Materials Research Society), Pittsburgh PA.

Vandiver, P.B., Druzik, J.R., Madrid, J.L.G., Freestone, I.C. and Wheeler, G.S. (eds) (1995) *Materials Issues in Art and Archaeology IV.* MRS (Materials Research Society), Pittsburgh PA.

Vandiver, P.B., Goodway, M., and Mass, J.L. (eds) (2002) *Materials Issues in Art and Archaeology VI.* MRS (Materials Research Society), Pittsburgh PA.

Van Mensch, P. (1985) Museums and authenticities: provocative thoughts. *ICOFOM Study Series* **8**, pp. 13–20.

Van Oosten, T. (1999) Analytical methods. In: Quye and Williamson (eds), 1999, pp. 70–83.

Van Rijn, M. (1993) *Hot Art, Cold Cash.* Little, Brown and Co., London.

Van Schoute, R. and Hollanders-Favart, D. (eds) (1982) *L'Attribution en Peinture. Apport du dessin sous-jacent.* Colloque IV, Université Catholique de Louvain. Institut Supérieur d'Archéologie et d'Histoire de l'Art, Louvain-la-Neuve.

Van Schoute, R. and Verougstraete-Marcq, H. (eds) (1986) *Art History and Laboratory: Scientific Examination Applied to Easel Paintings. PACT* **13**, Council of Europe, Strasbourg.

Van Schoute, R. and Verougstraete-Marcq, H. (1986) Radiography. In: R. Van Schoute and H. Verougstraete-Marcq (eds), 1986, pp. 131–153.

Van Strydonck, M.J.Y., Masschelein-Kleiner, L., Alderliesten, C. and de Jong, A.F.M. (1998) Radiocarbon dating of canvas paintings: Two case studies. *Studies in Conservation* **43**, 4; pp. 209–214.

Varndell, G. and Freestone, I.C. (1997) Early prehistoric pottery in Britain. In: Freestone and Gaimster (eds), 1997, pp. 32–37.

Vaughan, G. (1992) The restoration of classical sculpture in the eighteenth century and the problem of authenticity. In: Jones (ed), 1992, pp. 41–50.

Vayson de Pradenne, A. (1927) Chronologie de Glozel. *Bulletin de la Societé préhistorique français* **24**; pp. 293–319.

Vayson de Pradenne, A. (1930) The Glozel forgeries. *Antiquity* **4**, 14; pp. 201–222.

Vayson de Pradenne, A. (1932) *Les Fraudes en Archéologie Préhistorique.* Émile Nourry, Paris.

Vendl, A. and Pichler, B. (1988) Naturwissenschaftliche Untersuchungen zur Authentifizierung der Bronzestatue des Jünglings vom Magdalensberg. In: Gschwantler and Bernhard-Walcher (eds), 1988, pp. 39–41

Ventikou, M. (1999) Old treatment, new problem: Bakelite as a consolidant. *V & A Conservation Journal* **32**; pp. 5–7.

Vepřek, S., Patscheider, J. and Elmer, J. (1985) Restoration and conservation of ancient artifacts: A new area of application of plasma chemistry. *Plasma Chemistry and Plasma Processing* **5**, 2; pp. 203–209.

Verità, M., Basso, R., Wypyski, M.T. and Koestler, R.J. (1994) X-ray microanalysis of ancient glassy materials: A comparative study of wavelength dispersive and energy dispersive techniques. *Archaeometry* **36**, 2; pp. 241–251.

Vermeule, C. (1954) Some notes on ancient dies and coining methods. III: Coining methods as evidenced from ancient dies. *Numismatic Circular* **72**, 2; pp. 53–58.

Vernier, È. (1907) *La Bijouterie et la Joaillerie Égyptiennes.* Mémoires de L'Institut Français d'Archéologie Orientale **2**. L'Institut Français, Cairo.

Vernon, W.H.J. and Whitby, L. (1929 & 1930) The open air corrosion of copper 1: A chemical study of the surface patina; 2: The mineralogical relationships of corrosion products. *Journal of the Institute of Metals* **42**, 2; pp. 181–195. **44**, 2; pp. 389–408.

Verosub, K.L. and Moskowitz, B.M. (1988) Magneto-archaeometry: A new technique for ceramic analysis. In: Farquhar *et al.* (eds), 1988, pp. 252–255.

Verougstraete-Marcq, H. and Van Schoute, R. (1989) *Cardres et supports dans la peinture flamande aux 15e et 16e siecles.* Heure-le Roumain, Belgium.

Vicary, R. (1976) *Lithography*. Thames and Hudson, London.

Vignon, P. (1902) *The Shroud of Christ*. Archibald Constable, London.

Villard, F. (1977) Une tête romaine en porphyre. *La Revue du Louvre et des Museés de France* 4; pp. 235–236.

VMSG (Vinland Map Study Group) (2004) *The Vinland Map: A Short Summary*. PastPresented, Whitehaven, Cumbria.

Vogel, J.C., Eglington, B. and Auret, J.M. (1990) Isotope fingerprints in elephant bone and ivory. *Nature* 346, 6286; pp. 747–749.

Vollmeir, P. (2004) New methods to identify forgeries in philately. In: Weiss and Chartier (eds). pp. 151–156.

Von Bohlen, A. and Meyer, F. (1996) Arsen und Blei in Geigenlack. *Restauro* 102, 7; pp. 472–478.

von Bothmer, D. (1964) The head of an archaic Greek Kouros. *Archäologischer Anzeiger*, pp. 615–627.

von Bothmer, D. (1998) Forgeries of Greek vases. *Minerva* 9, 2; pp. 8–17.

von Bothmer, D. and Noble, J.V. (1961) *An Inquiry into the Forgery of the Etruscan Terracotta Warriors in the Metropolitan Museum of Art*, Paper 11. The Metropolitan Museum of Art, New York.

von Saldern, A. (1972) Originals–Reproductions–Fakes. *Annales du 5e Congrès de l'Association Internationale pour l'Histoire du Verre (Prague 6–11 Juilet 1970)*, L'Association Internationale pour l'Histoire du Verre, Liège, pp. 299–318.

Von Sonnenburg, H.F. (1993/4) A case of recurring deception. *Metropolitan Museum of Art Bulletin* 51, 3; pp. 8–19.

Vuilleumier, R. (1979) Schildpatt – Verarbeitungstech-niken und Imitationen. *Maltechnik-Restauro* 85, 1; pp. 40–47.

Wace, A.J.B. (1927) *A Cretan Statuette in the Fitzwilliam Museum*. Cambridge University Press, Cambridge.

Waddell, C. and Fountains, J.C. (1984) Calcium diffusion: A new dating method for archaeological ceramics. *Geology* 12; pp. 24–26.

Waelkens, M., Herz, N. and Moens, L. (eds) (1992) *Ancient Stones: Quarrying, Trade and Provenance*. Acta Archaeologica Lovaniensia Monographiae 4, Leuven University Press, Leuven.

Wager, V.H. (1938) *Plaster Casting for the Student Sculptor*. Tiranti, London.

Wagner, G.A. (1998) *Age Determination of Young Rocks and Artifacts*. Springer-Verlag, Berlin.

Wagner, G.A. and Van den Haute, P. (1992) *Fission-track Dating*. Kluwer Academic Publishers, Dordrecht.

Wainwright, C. (1971) Some objects from William Beckford's collection now in the Victoria Museum. *Burlington Magazine* 113; pp. 254–264.

Wakeling, T.G. (1912) *Forged Egyptian Antiquities*. Adam & Charles Black, London.

Waldron, P. (1986) English silver. In: Bly (ed), 1986, pp. 127–142.

Walker, D.R. (1976, 1977 & 1978) *The Metrology of the Roman Silver Coinage Pts I–III*. British Archaeological Reports: Supplementary Series 5, 22 & 40, Oxford.

Walker, S. (2004) The Portland Vase: History in the making. *Minerva* 15, 1; pp. 23–26.

Walker, S., Coleman, M.L. and Matthews, K.J. (1993) Roman sarcophagi from Lycia in the British Museum collections. In: *Akten des II. Internationalen Lykien-Symposions I*, J. Borchhardt and G. Dobesch (eds). Österreichischen Akademie der Wissenschaften, Wien, pp. 169–176.

Wallis, H., Maddison, F.R., Painter, G.D., Quinn, D. B., Perkins, R.M., Crone, G.R., Baynes-Cope, A.D., McCrone, W.C. and McCrone, L.B. (1974) The strange case of the Vinland Map. *The Geographical Journal* 140, 2; pp. 183–212.

Wallert, A. (1989) The reconstruction of papyrus manufacture: A preliminary investigation. *Studies in Conservation* 34, 1; pp. 1–8.

Walsh, J. (1964) *The Shroud*. Random House, New York.

Walsh, J.E. (1996) *Unravelling Piltdown*. Random House, New York.

Walsh, J.M. (1997) Crystal skulls and other problems: Or 'Don't look it in the eye'. In: *Exhibiting Dilemmas: Issues of Representation at the Smithsonian*, A. Henderson and A.L. Kaeppler (eds). Smithsonian Institution Press, Washington DC, pp. 116–139.

Wang, W. and Zhou, Z. (1983) Thermoluminescence dating of Chinese pottery. *Archaeometry* 25, 2; pp. 99–106.

Wanhill, R.J.H. (2003) Brittle archaeological silver: A fracture mechanism and mechanics assessment. *Archaeometry* 45, 4; pp. 625–636.

Wanhill, R.J.H., Leenheer, R., Steijaart, J.P.H.M. and Koens, J.F.W. (1998) Damage assessment and preservation of an Egyptian silver vase (300–200 BC). *Archaeometry* 40, 1; pp. 123–138.

Ward, B. (1994) Conservation and the Antiquities Trade, report on the meeting held 2nd – 3rd December 1993, London. *Journal of Cultural Property* 2, 3; pp. 358–363.

Ward, R. (ed) (1998) *Gilded and Enamelled Glass from the Middle East*. British Museum Press, London.

Wardle, P. (1963) *Victorian Silver and Silver-Plate*. Herbert Jenkins, London.

Ware, M. (1994) *Mechanisms of Image Deterioration in Early Photographs*. Science Museum, London.

Warren, P. (1970) *Irish Glass*. Faber, London.

Warren, P. (1977) Later Chinese glass 1650–1900. *Journal of Glass Studies* 19; pp. 84–126.

Washburn, W.E. (ed) (1971) *Proceedings of the Vinland Map Conference*. University of Chicago Press, Chicago.

Washburn, W.E. (1995) The case of the Vinland Map. In: Skelton, Marston and Painter, 1995. pp. xxi–xxviii.

Washington, H.S. (1898) The identification of marbles used in Greek sculpture. *American Journal of Archaeology* 13; pp. 1–18.

Watchman, A.L. (1991) Age and composition of oxalate-rich crusts in the Northern Territory, Australia. *Studies in Conservation* 36, 1; pp. 24–32.

Watchman, A. (1992) Investigating the cation-ratio calibration curve: evidence from South Australia. *Rock Art Research* 9; pp. 106–110.

Watchman, A. (1993) Perspectives and potentials for absolute dating of prehistoric rock paintings. *Antiquity* **67**, 254; pp. 58–65.

Watchman, A. (2000) A review of the history of dating rock varnishes. *Earth-Science Reviews* **49**, 1–4; pp. 261–277.

Waterston, D. (1913) Dissenting voice in discussion to Dawson and Woodward, 1913. p. 150.

Watling, R.J., Taylor, J.J., Shell, C.A., Chapman, R.J., Warner, R.B., Cahill, M. and Leake, R.C. (1999) The application of laser ablation inductively coupled plasma mass spectrometry (LA-ICP-MS) for establishing the provenance of gold ores and artefacts. In: Young *et al.* (eds), 1999, pp. 53–62.

Watt, A. and Philip, A. (1911) *The Electro-Plating and Electro-Refining of Metals.* Crosby, Lockwood & Son, London.

Watts, K.N. (1992) Samuel Pratt and armour faking. In: Jones (ed)., 1992, pp. 100–107.

Watts, L. and Leach, P. (1995) *Henley Wood Temples and Cemetery.* CBA, York.

Wayman, M.L. (2004) Metallography of archaeological alloys. In: *ASM Handbook* **9**: *Metallography and Microstructures*, G.F. Vander Voort (ed). ASM International, Materials Park, Ohio, pp. 468–477.

Wayman, M.L., King, J.C.H. and Craddock, P.T. (1992) *Aspects of Early North American Metallurgy.* British Museum Occasional Paper 79, London.

Weaver, C.E. (1976) The nature of titanium oxide in kaolinite. *Clay and Clay Minerals* **24**; pp. 215–218.

Weaver, K.F. (1980) The mystery of the Shroud. *National Geographic* **157**, 6; pp. 730–753.

Weaver, W. (1982) A seat for St. Peter. *The Connoisseur* **211**; pp. 112–113. September.

Webb, M. (2000) *Lacquer: Technology and Conservation.* Butterworth-Heinemann, Oxford.

Weber, G., Strivay, D., Martinot, L. and Garnir, H.P. (2002) Use of PIXE-PIGE under variable incident angle for ancient glass corrosion measurements. *Nuclear Instruments and Methods in Physics Research* **B** **189**; pp. 350–357.

Webster, G.D., Rexroad, C. and Talent, J.A. (1993) An evaluation of the V.J. Gupta conodont papers. *Journal of Paleontology* **67**; pp. 486–493.

Webster, R. (1971) Forensic problems in jewellery. In: *Papers from the Criminologist*, N. Morland (ed). Wolfe Publishing Ltd, London, pp. 193–204.

Webster, R. (1983) *Gems*, 4th edn. Butterworths, London.

Wedepohl, K.H. (2003) *Glas in Antike und Mittelalter: Geschichte eines Werkstoffes.* E. Schweizerbart'sche Verlagsbuchhandlung (Nägele u. Obermiller), Stuttgart.

Wedepohl, K.H., Krueger, I. and Hartmann, G. (1995) Medieval lead glass from northwestern Europe. *Journal of Glass Studies* **37**; pp. 65–82.

Weil, P.D. (1967) Contributions toward a history of sculpture techniques. I: Orfeo Boselli on the restoration of antique sculpture. *Studies in Conservation* **12**, 3; pp. 81–101.

Weil, P.D. (1977) A review of the history and practice of patination. In: Brown *et al.* (eds), 1977, pp. 77–92.

Weil, P.D. (1996) A review of the history and practice of patination. In: *Historical and Philosophical Issues in Conservation of Cultural Heritage*, N. Stanley-Price, M.K. Talley, Jr. and A.M. Vaccaro (eds). Getty Conservation Institute, Marina Del Rey CA, pp. 394–414. re-issued 2003.

Weiner, J.S. (1955) *The Piltdown Forgery.* Oxford University Press, London.

Weiner, J.S., Oakley, K.P. and Le Gros Clark, W.E. (1953) The solution of the Piltdown problem. *Bulletin of the British Museum (Natural History) Geology* **2**, 3; pp. 139–146.

Weiner, J.S., Le Gros Clark, W.E., Oakley, K.P., Fryd, C.F.M., Claringbull, G.F., Hey, M.H., Werner, A.E.A., Plesters, R.J., Edmunds, F.H., Bowie, S.H.U., Davidson, C.F. and Baynes-Cope, A.D. (1955) Further contributions to the solution of the Piltdown problem. *Bulletin of the British Museum (Natural History) Geology* **2**, 6; pp. 228–287.

Weiner, S., Kustanovich, Z., Gil-Av, E. and Traub, W. (1980) Dead Sea Scroll parchments: Unfolding of the collagen molecules and racemization of aspartic acid. *Nature* **280**; pp. 820–823. 30 October.

Weisman, B.M. and Reedy, C.L. (2002) Technical studies on Renaissance bronzes. In: Vandiver *et al.* (eds), 2002, pp. 483–495.

Weiss, R.J. and Chartier, D. (eds) (2004) *Fakebusters II: Scientific Detection of Fakery in Art and Philately.* World Scientific, Chicago.

Welter, J.-M. (2003) The zinc content of brass: A chronological indicator? *Techne* **18**; pp. 27–36.

Wen, Guang, and Jing, Zichuan, (1992) Chinese Neolithic jade, a preliminary geoarchaeological study. *Geoarchaeology* **7**, 3; pp. 251–275.

Werner, A.E.A. (1959). Problems in the conservation of glass. *Annales du 1er Congrès des 'Journées Internationales du Verre'* J. Philippe and J. Beguin (eds). Liège. pp. 189–197.

Werner, A.E. and Bimson, M. (1965). The Examination of Glass in the Museum Laboratory, *7th International Congress on Glass*, Brussels, 28th–3rd July 1965. Union Scientifique Continentale du Verre, Brussels, pp. 218, 1–2.

Werner, A.E., Bimson, M. and Meeks, N.D. (1975) The use of replica techniques and the scanning electron microscope in the study of ancient glass. *Journal of Glass Studies* **17**; pp. 158–160.

Werner, O. (1970) Über das Vorkommen von Zink und messing in Altertumund im Mittelalter. *Erzmetall* **23**; pp. 259–269.

Werner, O. (1972) *Spektralanalytische und Metallurgische Untersuchungen an Indischen Bronzen.* E.J. Brill, Leiden.

Werner, O. (1977) Analysen mittelalterlicher Bronzen und Messinge I. *Archäologie und Naturwissenschaften* **1**; pp. 144–220.

Werner, O. (1978) Metallurgische Untersuchungen der Benin-Bronzen des Museums für Völkerkunde, Berlin II. *Baessler Archiv* **26**, 2; pp. 333–439.

Werner, O. (1980) Zusammensetzung neuzeitlicher Nachgüsse und Fälschungen mittelalterlicher Messinge und Bronzen. *Berliner Beiträge zur Archäometrie* **5**; pp. 11–35.

Werner, O. (1981) Analysen mittelalterlicher Bronzen und Messinge II & III. *Archäologie und Naturwissenschaften* **2**; pp. 106–170.

Werner, O. (1982) Analysen mittelalterlicher Bronzen und Messing IV. *Berliner Beitrage zur Archäometrie* **7**; pp. 35–174.

Werthmann, B., Schiller, W. and Griebenow, W. (1984) Naturwissenschaftliche Aspekte der Echtheitspruefung der sogenannten 'Hitler-Tegenbuecher'. *Maltechnik-Restauro* **90**, 4; pp. 65–72.

Werthmann, B. (1988) Zur Altersbestimmung von Papieren. *Maltechnik-Restauro* **94**, 3; pp. 211–217.

Werthmann, B. (1994) Altersbestimmungen, Fälschungsnachweise, Materialanalysen an Papieren. In: NDTWA, 1994, pp. 521–526.

Wessel, K. (1969) *Byzantine Enamels from the 5th to th 13th Centuries*. Irish University Press, Shannon.

Westgate, J., Sandhu, A. and Shane, P. (1997) Fission-track dating. In: Taylor and Aitken (eds), 1997, pp. 127–158.

Westmancott, R. (1854) On coloring statues. *The Archaeological Journal* **44**; pp. 1–28.

Westphal, H. (1985) Galvanoplastische Nachbildungen aus Kupfer. In: Born (ed), 1985, pp. 181–185.

Westwood, J.O. (1876) *A Descriptive Catalogue of the Fictile Ivories in the South Kensington Museum*. HMSO, London.

Wexler, H. (1964) Polymerization of drying oils. *Chemical Reviews* **64**, 6; pp. 591–611.

Wharton, G. (1984) Technical examination of Renaissance medals: The use of Laue back reflection X-ray diffraction to identify electroformed reproductions. *Journal of the American Institute for Conservation* **23**; pp. 88–100.

White, H.J.O. (1926) The geology of the country near Lewes. *Memoir of the Geological Survey of England and Wales*. His Majesty's Stationary Office, London.

White, R. and Kirby, J. (2001) A survey of nineteenth- and early twentieth-century varnish compositions founded on a selection of paintings in the National Gallery Collection. *National Gallery Technical Bulletin* **22**; pp. 64–84.

Whitehouse, A.A.K., Pritchett, E.G.K. and Barnett, G. (1967) *Phenolic Resins*. Plastics Institute/Iliffe Books, London.

Whitehouse, D. (2001a) *Roman Glass in the Corning Museum of Glass*, 3 vols. Corning Museum of Glass, Corning NY.

Whitehouse, D. (2001b) Cut and engraved glass. In: Carboni and Whitehouse, 2001. pp. 155–198.

Whitehouse, D. (2001c) Imitations of Islamic Glass. In: Carboni and Whitehouse, 2001. pp. 227–311.

Whitehouse, D., Pilosi, L. and Wypyski, M.T. (2000) Byzantine silver stain. *Journal of Glass Studies* **42**; pp. 85–96.

Whiteley, D.S. and Dorn, R.I. (1993) New perspectives on the Clovis vs. Pre-Clovis controversy. *American Antiquity* **58**; pp. 626–647.

Whitfield, N. (1990) Round wire in the Early Middle Ages. *Jewellery Studies* **4**; pp. 13–28.

Whitfield, S. (ed) (2002) *Dunhuang Manuscript Forgeries*. British Library Studies in Conservation Science 3, British Library, London.

Whitmore, F.E. and Young, W.J. (1973) Application of laser microprobe and electron microprobe in the analysis of platiniridium inclusions in gold. In: Young (ed), 1973, pp. 88–95.

Whitmore, P.M. and Colaluca, V.G. (1995) The natural and accelerated aging of an acrylic artists' medium. *Studies in Conservation* **40**, 1; pp. 51–64.

Wiborg, F.B. (1926) *Printing Ink*. Harper, New York.

Wiedemann, M.C. (2001) Distinction of original and forged lithographs by means of thermogravimetry and Raman spectroscopy. *Journal of Thermal Analysis and Calorimetry* **64**, 3; pp. 987–1000.

Wiet, G. (1947). *Soieries persanes*. Institut d'Égypte, memoire 52, Cairo.

Wigfield, E.A. (1998) Examination of a painted craquelure on a 17th. century Dutch marine painting attributed to Willem van de Velde the Younger: A case study. *The Conservator* **22**; pp. 17–23.

Wilkinson, A. (1971) *Ancient Egyptian Jewellery*. Methuen, London.

Willett, F. and Fleming, S.J. (1976) A catalogue of important Nigerian copper-alloy castings dated by thermoluminescence. *Archaeometry* **18**, 2; pp. 135–146.

Williams, A. (2003) *The Knight and the Blast Furnace: A History of the Metallurgy of Armour in the Middle Ages and Early Modern Period*. Brill, Leiden.

Williams, C.R. (1924) *Catalogue of Egyptian Antiquities: Gold and Silver Jewelry and Related Objects*. New York Historical Society, New York. pp. 39–44.

Williams, D. (ed) (1998) *The Art of the Greek Goldsmith*. British Museum Press, London.

Williams, D. and Ogden, J. (1994) *Greek Gold Jewellery of the Classical World*. British Museum Press, London.

Williams, J. (ed) (1997) *Money: A History*. British Museum Press, London.

Williams, J.G. (1998) Inductively coupled plasma mass spectrometry: A new scientific method for investigating coins and coinage. In: Oddy and Cowell (eds), 1998, pp. 253–261.

Williams, N. (2002) *Porcelain: Repair and Restoration*, revised edn. British Museum Press, London.

Williamson, C.J. (1992) 150 Years of plastics degradation. In: Allen *et al.* (eds), 1992, pp. 1–13.

Williamson, C. (1994) Victorian plastics – foundations of an industry. In: Mossman and Morris (eds), 1994, pp. 1–9.

Williamson, C.J. (1995) Identification of plastics. In: *Kunst. . . . stof tot Nadenken: Problemen hij het behoud van Synthetische Materialen*, J.A. Mosk (ed). Cl Thermadag, Amsterdam, pp. 41–58.

Williamson, C. (1999a) Landmarks in the history of plastics. In: Quye and Williamson (eds), 1999, pp. 2–22.

Williamson, C. (1999b) Physical clues and simple analysis. In: Quye and Williamson (eds), 1999, pp. 55–69.

Williams-Thorpe, O. (1988) Provenancing and archaeology of Roman millstones from the Mediterranean area. *Journal of Archaeological Science* **15**, 3; pp. 253–305.

Williams-Thorpe, O. (1995) Obsidian in the Mediterranean and the Near East: a provenancing success story. *Archaeometry* **37**, 2; pp. 217–248.

Williams-Thorpe, O. and Thorpe, R.S. (1993) Magnetic susceptibility used in non-destructive provenancing of Roman granite columns. *Archaeometry* **35**, 2; pp. 185–195.

Williams-Thorpe, O., Jones, M.C., Tindle, A.G. and Thorpe, R.S. (1996) Magnetic susceptibility variations at Mons Claudianus and in Roman columns: a method of provenancing to within a single quarry. *Archaeometry* **38**, 1; pp. 15–41.

Williams-Thorpe, O., Potts, P.J. and Webb, P.C. (1999) Field-portable non-destructive analysis of lithic archaeological samples by X-ray fluorescence instrumentation using a mercury iodide detector: Comparison with wavelength-dispersive XRF and a case study in British stone axe provenancing. *Journal of Archaeological Science* **26**, 2; pp. 215–237.

Williams-Thorpe, O., Jones, P.C., Webb, P.C. and Rigby, I.J. (2000a) Magnetic susceptibility thickness corrections for small artefacts and comments of the effects of 'background' materials. *Archaeometry* **42**, 1; pp. 101–108.

Williams-Thorpe, O., Webb, P.C. and Thorpe, R.S. (2000b) Non-destructive portable gamma ray spectrometry used in provenancing Roman granitoid columns from Leptis Magna, North Africa. *Archaeometry* **42**, 1; pp. 77–100.

Williams-Thorpe, O., Webb, P.C. and Jones, M.C. (2003) Non-destructive geochemical and magnetic characterisation of Group XVIII dolerite stone axes and shafthole implements from England. *Journal of Archaeological Science* **30**, 10; pp. 1237–1267.

Wilson, G. (1994) Polythene: The early years. In: Mossman and Morris (eds), 1994, pp. 70–86.

Wilson, H. (1951) *Silverwork and Jewellery*, revised edn. Sir Isaac Pitman and Sons, London.

Wilson, I. (1998) *The Blood and the Shroud*. Weidenfeld and Nicholson, London.

Wilson, L. and Pollard, A.M. (2001) The Provenance Hypothesis. In: Brothwell and Pollard (eds), 2001, pp. 507–517.

Wiltzen, T.S. and Wayman, M.L. (1999) Steel files as chronological markers in North American fur trade sites. *Archaeometry* **41**, 2; pp. 117–135.

Winter, J. (1981) 'Lead White' in Japanese painting. *Studies in Conservation* **26**, 3; pp. 89–101.

Winter, J. (1983) The characterization of pigments based on carbon. *Studies in Conservation* **28**, 1; pp. 49–66.

Winter, J. (1984) Pigments in China – a preliminary bibliography. In: de Froment (ed), 1984, pp. 84.19. 11–12.

Wise, D. and Wise, A. (2004) Application of Raman microspectroscopy to problems in the conservation, authentication and display of fragile works of art on paper. In: Kiefer (ed), 2004, pp. 710–718.

Wise, E.M. (ed). (1964) *Gold: Recovery, Properties and Applications*. D. van Nostrand, Princeton NJ. In: Wise (ed), 1964.

Wise, E.M. (1964) Sources and Recovery of gold. In: Wise (ed). pp. 1–24.

Withnall, R., Derbyshire, A., Thiel, S. and Hughes, M.J. (2000) Raman microscopic analysis in museology. In: *Optical Devices and Diagnostics in Materials Science*, D.L. Andrews *et al.* (eds). *Proceedings of SPIE* **4098**; pp. 217–231.

Withnall, R., Shadi, I.T. and Chowdhry, B.Z. (2005) Case study: The analysis of dyes by SERRS. In: Edwards and Chalmers (eds), 2005, pp. 152–166.

Witten, L. (1971) Vinland's Saga recalled. In: Washburn (ed), 1971, pp. 3–14.

Witten, L.C., II (1989) Vinland's Saga recalled. *The Yale University Library Gazette* **64**, 1–2; pp. 10–36. October. [Reprinted in Skelton, Marston and Painter, 1995, pp. xli–lviii].

Wolfman, D. and Rolniak T.M. (1979) Alpha-recoil track dating: Problems and prospects. In: Scollar (ed), 1979, pp. 512–521.

Wolters, J. (1981) The ancient craft of granulation. *Gold Bulletin* **14**, 3; pp. 119–129.

Wolters, J. (1983) *Die Granulation Geschichte und Technik einer alten Goldschmiedekunst*. Callwey Verlag, Munchen.

Wood, D.A. (1963) *Plywoods of the World*. W. & A.K. Johnston and G.W. Bacon, London.

Wood, J. (1995) Damaged by time and Rubens: Ruben's restorations and retouchings. *Apollo* **142**, 406; pp. 16–23.

Woodward, A.S. (1914) On an apparently Palaeolithic engraving on a bone from Sherborne (Dorset). *Quarterly Journal of the Geological Society* **70**; pp. 100–102.

Woodward, A.S. (1917) Fourth note on the Piltdown gravel with evidence of a second skull of *Eoanthropus dawsoni*. *Quarterly Journal of the Geological Society* **73**; pp. 1–10.

Woodward, A.S. (1933) The second Piltdown skull. *Nature* **131**; p. 242.

Woodward, A.S. (1948) *The Earliest Englishman*. Watts and Co, London.

Woolley, A.R. (1983) Jade axes and other artefacts. In: Kempe and Harvey (eds), 1983, pp. 256–276.

Wright, M.M. and Townsend, J. (eds) (1995) *Resins Ancient and Modern*. Preprints of a Conference of the Scottish Society for Conservation. Edinburgh.

Wulff, H.E. (1966) *The Traditional Crafts of Persia*. M.I.T. Press, Cambridge MA.

Wulff, H.E., Wulff, H.S. and Koch, L. (1968) Egyptian faience: A possible survival in Iran. *Archaeology* **21**, 2; pp. 98–107. April.

Wyart, J., Bariand, P. and Filippi, J. (1981) Lapis-lazuli from Sar-e-Sang, Badakhshan, Afghanistan. *Gems and Gemmology* **17**, 4; pp. 184–190.

Wypyski, M.T. (2002) Renaissance enameled jewelry and 19th century Renaissance revival: Characterization of enamel composition. In: Vandiver *et al.* (eds), 2002, pp. 223–233.

Wypyski, M.T. and Richter, R.W. (1997) Preliminary compositional study of 14th and 15th C. European enamels. *Techne* 6; pp. 48–57.

Xenaki-Sakellariou, A. (1989) Techniques et evolution de la bague-cachet dans le art Crétomycénien. *CMS supplement* 3; pp. 323–338.

Xu, J-A., Huang, E., Chen, C-H., Tan, L-P. and Yu, B-S. (1996) A Raman spectroscopic study of Archaic jades. *Acta Geologica Taiwanica* 32; pp. 11–42.

Yamasaki, K. and Emoto, Y. (1979) Pigments used on Japanaese paintings from the protohistoric period through the 17th century. *Ars Orientalis* 11; pp. 1–14.

Yang Boda (1991) An account of Qing Dynasty glass-making. In: Brill and Martin (eds), 1991, pp. 131–150.

Yang, M.-L., Lu, C.-W., Hsu, I.J. and Yang, C.C. (2004) The use of optical coherence tomography for monitoring the subsurface morphologies archaic jades. *Archaeometry* 46, 2; pp. 171–182.

Yap, C.T. (1986a) Chinese porcelain: Genuine or fake? *Physics Bulletin* 37, 5; pp. 214–215.

Yap, C.T. (1986b) EDXRF analysis of Straits Chinese porcelains for zirconium and niobium using a cadmium-109 source. *Applied Spectroscopy* 40, 6; pp. 839–840.

Yap, C.T. (1986c) A non-destructive scientific technique of detecting modern fake reproduction porcelain. *Oriental Art* 32, 1; pp. 48–50.

Yap, C.T. (1986d) XRF analysis of Nonya wares using an annular americium source. *Archaeometry* 28, 2; pp. 197–201.

Yap, C.T. (1987a) Nondestructive spectrometric determination of trace element concentrations of rubidium, strontium, yttrium, zirconium and niobium in ceramics. *Zeitschrift für Naturforschung, Section C: Physical Sciences* 42, 11; pp. 1253–1256.

Yap, C.T. (1987b) X-ray fluorescence studies on low-Z elements of Straits Chinese porcelain using Fe-55 and Cd-109 annular sources. *X-ray Spectrometry* 16; pp. 55–56.

Yap, C.T. (1988) A quantitative spectrometric analysis of trace concentrations of manganese and cobalt in ceramics and the significance of As/Co and Mn/Co Ratios. *Journal of Archaeological Science* 15, 2; pp. 173–177.

Yap, C.T. and Tang, S.M. (1984) X-ray fluorescence analysis of modern and recent Chinese porcelains. *Archaeometry* 26, 1; pp. 78–81.

Yap, C.T. and Tang, S.M. (1985a) Energy-dispersive X-ray fluorescence analysis of Chinese porcelains using Am-241. *Archaeometry* 27, 1; pp. 61–63.

Yap, C.T. and Tang, S.M. (1985b) Quantitative XRF analysis of trace barium in porcelain by source excitation. *Applied Spectroscopy* 39, 6; pp. 1040–1042.

Yap, C.T. and Tang, S.M. (1985c) Zn K/Rb Kb ratio of Ch'ing, Republican and modern Chinese porcelain. *X-ray Spectrometry* 14, 4; pp. 157–158.

Young, C. and Hibberd, R. (1999) A comparison of the physical properties of 19th-century canvas linings with acid aged canvas. *Preprints of the 12th ICOM Committee for Conservation Triennial Meeting*, Lyons, 29 August–3rd September, 1999, J. Bridgland (ed). James and James, London, pp. 353–360.

Young, S.M.M., Pollard, A.M., Budd, P. and Ixer, R.A. (eds) (1999) *Metals in Antiquity*. Archaeopress, British Archaeological Reports: International Series 792, Oxford.

Young, S.M.M., Budd, P., Haggerty, R. and Pollard, A.M. (1997) Inductively coupled plasma-mass spectrometry for the analysis of ancient metals. *Archaeometry* 39, 2; pp. 379–392.

Young, S.M.M. and Pollard, A.M. (2000) Atomic spectroscopy and spectrometry. In: Ciliberto and Spoto (eds), 2000, pp. 21–53.

Young, W.J. (ed) (1967) *Application of Science in Examination of Works of Art*. Research Laboratory of the Museum of Fine Arts, Boston.

Young, W.J. (ed) (1973) *Application of Science in Examination of Works of Art*. Research Laboratory of the Museum of Fine Arts, Boston.

Young, W.J. (ed) (1978) *Application of Science to the Dating of Works of Art*. Research Laboratory of the Museum of Fine Arts, Boston.

Young, W.J. and Ashmole, B. (1968) The Boston Relief and the Ludovisi Throne. *Bulletin Museum of Fine Arts, Boston* 66, 346; pp. 124–166.

Younger, J.G. (1981) Creating a seal stone: A study of seals in the Greek Late Bronze Age. *Expedition* 23, 4; pp. 31–38.

Yu, K.N. and Miao, J.M. (1996) Non-destructive analysis of Jingdezhen blue and white porcelains. *Archaeometry* 38, 2; pp. 257–263.

Zacke, I.M. and Zacken, W. (1999) *Ancient Chinese Jades from a Private Collection*. Zacke, Vienna.

Zhou, Weirong (2001) The emergence and development of brass-smelting techniques in China. *Bulletin of the Metals Museum of the Japan Institute of Metals* 34; pp. 87–98.

Zhou, Weirong and Fan, Xiangxi, (1994) Application of zinc and cadmium for the dating and authenticating of metal relics in Ancient China. *Bulletin of the Metals Museum of the Japan Institute of Metals* 22, II; pp. 16–21.

Zhou, Zonge, Clarke, J.A. and Fucheng, Zhang (2002) Archaeoraptor's better half. *Nature* 420, 6913; p. 285. 21 November.

Zhu Shoukang and He Tangkun (1993) Studies of ancient Chinese mirrors and other bronze artefacts. In: La Niece and Craddock (eds), 1993, pp. 50–62.

Zilhaõ, J. (1995) The age of the Côa valley (Portugal) rock-art: Validation of archaeological dating to the Palaeolithic age and refutation of 'scientific'dating' to historic or proto-historic times. *Antiquity* 69, 2; pp. 883–901.

Zimmerman, D.W. (1971) Thermoluminescent dating using fine grains from pottery. *Archaeometry* 13, 1; pp. 29–52.

Zimmerman, D. (1978) Thermoluminescence dating using zircon grains. In: *A Specialist Session on Thermoluminescence Dating – Séminaire consacrées à la datation par thermoluminescence*, M.J. Aitken and V.Mejdhal (eds). *PACT* **2/3**. Council of Europe, Strasbourg, pp. 458–465.

Zimmerman, D.W., Yuhas, M.P. and Meyers, P. (1974) Thermoluminescence authenticity measurements on core material from the Bronze Horse of the New York Metropolitan Museum of Art. *Archaeometry* **16**, 1; pp. 19–30.

Zoppi, A., Lofrumento, C., Castellucci, E.M. and Migliorini, M.G. (2002) Micro-Raman technique for phase analysis on archaeological ceramics. *Spectroscopy Europe* **14**, 5; pp. 16–21.

Zwaan, J.C., Cheilletz, A. and Taylor, B.E. (2004) Tracing the emerald origin by oxygen isotope data: The case of Sandawana, Zimbabwe. *Comptes Rendus Geoscience* **336**; pp. 41–48.

Index

Figures in *Italic;* Tables in **Bold**